STATUTORY INSTRUMENTS 1970

PART I
(in two Sections)

SECTION 1

Published by Authority

LONDON
HER MAJESTY'S STATIONERY OFFICE
1970

© *Crown copyright* 1970

PRINTED AND PUBLISHED BY HER MAJESTY'S STATIONERY OFFICE

To be purchased from

49 High Holborn, LONDON, W.C.1

13a Castle Street, EDINBURGH, EH2 3AR   109 St. Mary Street, CARDIFF, CF1 1JW

Brazennose Street, MANCHESTER, M60 8AS   50 Fairfax Street, BRISTOL, BS1 3DE

258 Broad Street, BIRMINGHAM, 1   7 Linenhall Street, BELFAST, BT2 8AY

or through any Bookseller

1970

Price for the two Sections: £10 10s. 0d. [£10.50] net

PRINTED IN ENGLAND

SBN 11 840056 8*

Contents of the Volume

PART I, Section 1

PART I, Section 2

PART II

PART III

Preface

Scope and arrangement of the Volume

1. This volume gives the full text of the statutory instruments registered in the year 1970 which were classified as general, and gives particulars of those which were classified as local(a). Other instruments are contained in the Appendix (as to which see para. 3 below).

2. The general instruments are arranged according to their S.I. numbers(b), that is to say, in the order of their registration as statutory instruments. The volume is published in three Parts, containing the instruments registered between 1st January and 30th April, 1st May and 31st August, and 1st September and 31st December respectively.

Contents of the Volume

3. **Parts I and II.** At the beginning of each of these Parts is a list of the instruments whose text is contained in that Part, showing their S.I. numbers and titles. The list is followed by the text of the statutory instruments registered in the relevant period and an **Appendix of Instruments not registered as Statutory Instruments** issued in that period. This Appendix includes Orders in Council issued under the royal prerogative or otherwise outside the definition of a statutory instrument, Royal Proclamations which are of a legislative nature, and Letters Patent and Royal Instructions which relate to the constitutions, etc. of overseas territories.

At the end of each Part is a Table showing the modifications to legislation and an Index. Each Table is confined to the instruments in its own Part and gives particulars of those Acts and instruments which have been amended, extended, excluded, repealed or revoked by instruments in the Part. The Index to Part II will be cumulative to both Parts.

4. **Part III.** At the beginning is a list of the instruments in Part III similar to the lists in Parts I and II. It is followed by the text of the instruments comprising Part III, as in Parts I and II.

At the end of Part III are the features which are required by reg. 10 of the Statutory Instruments Regulations 1947 to be included in the Annual Volume of Statutory Instruments. They cover the instruments in all three Parts. In the order in which they occur in the Volume, they are as follows:—

The **Classified List of Local Instruments** gives particulars, including the dates of making, and the S.I. numbers, of all local statutory instruments registered in the S.I. series of the year to which the Annual Volume relates. They are grouped in classes according to their subject-matter.

(a) *See* Statutory Instruments Regulations 1947 (S.I. 1948/1 (Rev. XXI, p. 498: 1948 I. p. 4002)), reg. 4 of which provides that S.I. which are in the nature of public general Acts of Parliament shall be classified as general and those which are in the nature of local and personal or private Acts shall be classified as local.

(b) Reg. 3 of the Statutory Instruments Regulations 1947 provides for instruments to be numbered in a separate series for each calendar year. Certain instruments bear a subsidiary number—

   C. Commencement Orders (bringing an Act or part of an Act into operation).
   L. Instruments relating to fees or procedure in courts in England or Wales.
   S. Instruments made by a Scottish rule-making authority and applying to Scotland only.

The **Tables.** " Table A " gives particulars of the Acts of Parliament, and " Table B " particulars of statutory and other instruments, the operation of which was affected by the instruments appearing in the Volume. They include the information as to amendments, repeals, revocations, etc., already given in tables of " Modifications to Legislation " in Parts I and II and corresponding information with respect to the instruments in Part III, and also give particulars of Acts or instruments modified or restricted by general instruments throughout the Volume. In addition, Table B gives particulars of general instruments whose operation was affected expressly by Public General Acts of the year in question, or which ceased to operate through becoming spent during that year as a result of legislation of the year.

The **Numerical and Issue List** gives particulars of all statutory instruments which were printed and put on sale by the Queen's Printer of Acts of Parliament under the provisions of the Statutory Instruments Act 1946(**a**), during the year, with, in each case, the date of making and the date of first issue by Her Majesty's Stationery Office.

The **Index** will be cumulative to Parts I and II.

Definition of a statutory instrument

5. To determine whether or not any instrument is required to be a statutory instrument, reference must be made to s. 1 of the Statutory Instruments Act 1946, reg. 2 of the Statutory Instruments Regulations 1947, and arts. 1 and 2 of the Statutory Instruments (Confirmatory Powers) Order 1947(**b**).

The definition of what constitutes a statutory instrument, as respects instruments made under Acts passed before the commencement (1 Jan. 1948) of the 1946 Act, is governed by definitions contained in the Rules Publications Act 1893(**c**) (which was repealed and replaced by the 1946 Act); for those made under Acts passed after the commencement of the 1946 Act, the document is a statutory instrument if it is an Order in Council or if it is made by a Minister of the Crown and the Act provides that the power is to be exercisable by statutory instrument.

Citation

6. For the purposes of citation, statutory instruments are given a title. In addition, all statutory instruments may be identified by the year and number. The first instrument in Part I of this Volume would, by this method, be cited as " S.I. 1970/8 ". When a statutory instrument is referred to in another statutory instrument, a lettered footnote is provided in the latter, giving the identification of the first instrument as above, and also its Part and page reference in the Annual Volume The footnote reference for the same instrument would therefore be " S.I. 1970/8 (1970 I, p. 1) ".

If the text of the instrument is set out in the current edition of *S.R. & O. and S.I. Revised* (Third Edition, as at 31st Dec., 1948) the footnote references give the volume reference in that edition as well as the page reference in the Annual Volume (see, for example, footnote (**b**) below). If a footnote contains the references of a number of instruments, they may in certain circumstances be run together, so as to give all the instrument numbers together and all the volume references together, e.g. " S.R. & O. 1946/157; S.I. 1948/1073, 1961/ 1942 (1946 II, p. 26; 1948 II, p. 13; 1961 III, p. 2650) ".

(a) 1946 c. 36.
(c) 1893 c. 66.

(b) S.I. 1948/2 (Rev. XXI, p. 504: 1948 I, p. 4008).

Production in Court

7. Under section 2 of the Documentary Evidence Act 1868(**a**), read with section 2 of the Documentary Evidence Act 1882(**b**), *prima facie* evidence of any proclamation, order or regulation made by certain rule-making authorities may be given in courts of justice by production of a copy purporting to be printed by the Government Printer or under the superintendence or authority of Her Majesty's Stationery Office. The Act of 1868 has since been extended by numerous Acts(**c**) to rules, etc., made thereunder by other rule-making authorities. The copies of proclamations, orders, regulations, etc., made by the authorities referred to above as printed in these volumes may therefore be produced as *prima facie* evidence.

Up to date information on statutory instruments

8. The *Index to Government Orders* contains, under subject headings, summaries of all powers to make subordinate legislation conferred by statute on H.M. in Council, the Privy Council, government departments and certain other public bodies. Below each summary appear particulars of any general instruments made in exercise of it which were in force at the date of publication of the *Index*. Details are also given of certain instruments made under prerogative powers. The work contains also a Table of Statutes showing the subject headings under which references to particular sections of enabling Acts appear. (The *Index* is published every two years by H.M.S.O.).

9. Information as to whether any instrument is still in operation, or whether anything has happened to it since it was made, can be obtained from the *Table of Government Orders*. This Table lists general statutory rules and orders and statutory instruments in numerical order, and gives the history of those which have been affected (i.e. revoked, amended, etc.) by subsequent legislation, whether statute or subordinate legislation, identifying the Act or instrument in question. Where any instrument has been amended, the Table gives particulars of the article, section, rule, etc., affected. A user who is interested in one particular provision only of the earlier instrument can thus ascertain whether or not he need consult the text of the amending enactment at all. The *Table of Government Orders* is published annually by H.M.S.O. and is cumulative. A Noter-Up is issued twice yearly.

Authority for Publication

10. The Annual Volumes of Statutory Instruments are published in pursuance of reg. 10 of the Statutory Instruments Regulations 1947 and are prepared under the direction of the Statute Law Committee. Any suggestion or communication relating to their contents should be addressed to the Editor, Statutory Publications Office, Queen Anne's Chambers, 41, Tothill Street, S.W.1.

(**a**) 1868 c. 37.   (**b**) 1882 c. 9.
(**c**) *See* the entries relating to extensions of the 1868 Act in the *Chronological Table of the Statutes*.

Abbreviations

Addnl. Instructions	...	Additional Instructions.
A.S.	...	Act of Sederunt.
am., amdg., amdt.	...	amended, amending, amendment.
appx.	...	appendix.
art(s).	...	article(s).
bd(s).	...	board(s).
c.	...	chapter(s).
cl(s).	...	clause(s).
Cmd., Cmnd. ...	...	Command Paper.
Cont.	...	continued.
ct(s).	...	court(s).
E.	...	England.
exc.	...	except, excepted.
excl.	...	excluded.
expl.	...	explained.
ext.	...	extended.
G.B.	...	Great Britain.
gen.	...	generally.
govt.	...	government.
H.C.	...	House of Commons Paper.
H.M.	...	Her Majesty, Her Majesty's.
incl.	...	included, including.
instrt.	...	instrument.
L.P.	...	Letters Patent.
Min(s).	...	Minister(s).
mod., mod(s). ...	...	modified, modification(s).
N.	...	North.
N.I.	...	Northern Ireland.
No.	...	number.
O.	...	Order(s).
O. in C., O. of C.	...	Order(s) in Council, Order(s) of Council.
p., pp.	...	page(s).
para(s).	...	paragraph(s).
prerog.	...	prerogative.
prosp.	...	prospectively.
prov.	...	provisional, proviso.
pt.	...	part.
r.	...	revoked.
R.C.	...	Rules of the Court of Session.
R. Instructions ...	...	Royal Instructions.
R. Warrant ...	...	Royal Warrant.
reg(s).	...	regulation(s).
rep.	...	repealed.
restr.	...	restricted.
retrosp.	...	retrospectively.
Rev.	...	Statutory Rules and Orders and Statutory Instruments Revised (Third Edition, 1948).
Rev. 1903	...	Statutory Rules and Orders Revised (Second Edition, 1903).
revn.	...	revocation.
s., ...	...	Scotland.
s., ss.	...	section(s).
S.I.	...	Statutory Instrument(s).
S.R. & O.	...	Statutory Rule(s) and Order(s).

ABBREVIATIONS

sch(s).	...	...	...	schedule(s).
Secy.	...	...	...	Secretary.
susp.	...	...	...	suspended.
temp.	...	...	...	temporarily.
transfd.	...	...	...	transferred.
Treas.	...	...	...	Treasury.
U.K.	...	...	...	United Kingdom of Great Britain and Northern Ireland.
vol.	...	...	...	volume.
W. ...	...	...	...	Wales.

Statutory Instruments in Part I

OTHER INSTRUMENTS IN PART I

STATUTORY INSTRUMENTS

1970 No. 8

INDUSTRIAL TRAINING

The Industrial Training Levy (Iron and Steel) Order 1970

Made - - - -	*6th January* 1970
Laid before Parliament	*16th January* 1970
Coming into Operation	*28th January* 1970

The Secretary of State after approving proposals submitted by the Iron and
Steel Industry Training Board for the imposition of a further levy on employers in
the iron and steel industry and in exercise of her powers under section 4 of the
Industrial Training Act 1964(a) and of all other powers enabling her in that
behalf hereby makes the following Order:—

Title and commencement

1. This Order may be cited as the Industrial Training Levy (Iron and Steel)
Order 1970 and shall come into operation on 28th January 1970.

Interpretation

2.—(1) In this Order unless the context otherwise requires:—

(*a*) "an appeal tribunal" means an industrial tribunal established under
section 12 of the Industrial Training Act 1964;

(*b*) "assessment" means an assessment of an employer to the levy;

(*c*) "average number" in relation to the persons employed at or from an
establishment of an employer means the number that is equal to the
average (calculated to the lowest whole number) of the numbers of
the persons employed, or deemed under the provisions of paragraph (3)
of this Article to have been employed, at or from the establishment by the
employer on 4th April 1969 and on 3rd October 1969;

(*d*) "the Board" means the Iron and Steel Industry Training Board;

(*e*) "business" means any activities of industry or commerce;

(*f*) "employer" means a person who is an employer in the iron and steel
industry at any time in the fifth levy period;

(*g*) "the fifth levy period" means the period commencing with the day
upon which this Order comes into operation and ending on 31st August
1970;

(*h*) "the industrial training order" means the Industrial Training (Iron and
Steel Board) Order 1969(b);

(*i*) "iron and steel establishment" means an establishment in Great Britain
engaged wholly or mainly in the iron and steel industry for a total of
twenty-seven or more weeks in the period of twelve months that commenced on 4th October 1968 or, being an establishment that commenced
to carry on business in the said period, for a total number of weeks

---

(a) 1964 c. 16.   (b) S.I. 1969/884 (1969 II, p. 2517).

exceeding one half of the number of weeks in the part of the said period commencing with the day on which business was commenced and ending on the last day thereof;

(*j*) "the iron and steel industry" means any one or more of the activities which, subject to the provisions of paragraph 2 of the Schedule to the industrial training order, are specified in paragraph 1 of that Schedule as the activities of the iron and steel industry;

(*k*) "the levy" means the levy imposed by the Board in respect of the fifth levy period;

(*l*) "notice" means a notice in writing.

(2) For the purposes of this Order no regard shall be had to any person employed wholly in the supply of food or drink for immediate consumption.

(3) In the case where an iron and steel establishment is taken over (whether directly or indirectly) by an employer in succession to, or jointly with, another person, a person employed at or from the establishment on either or both of the days specified in paragraph (1)(*c*) of this Article by a person other than the employer carrying on the establishment on the day upon which this Order comes into operation shall be deemed for the purposes of this Order to have been employed by the last mentioned employer.

(4) Any reference in this Order to an establishment that commences to carry on business or that ceases to carry on business shall not be taken to apply where the location of the establishment is changed but its business is continued wholly or mainly at or from the new location, or where the suspension of activities is of a temporary or seasonal nature.

(5) The Interpretation Act 1889(**a**) shall apply to the interpretation of this Order as it applies to the interpretation of an Act of Parliament.

Imposition of the Levy

3.—(1) The levy to be imposed by the Board on employers in respect of the fifth levy period shall be assessed in accordance with the provisions of this Article.

(2) The levy shall be assessed by the Board separately in respect of each iron and steel establishment of an employer, but in agreement with the employer one assessment may be made in respect of any number of such establishments, in which case those establishments shall be deemed for the purposes of that assessment to constitute one establishment.

(3) Subject to the provisions of this Article, the levy in respect of an iron and steel establishment of an employer shall be assessed by reference to the average number of the persons employed at or from the establishment by the employer as follows—

(*a*) where the said average number of persons did not exceed twenty, by multiplying the sum of £12. 5s. 0d. by that average number; or

(*b*) in any other case, by multiplying the sum of £24. 10s. 0d. by the said average number of persons less twenty and by adding to the amount so obtained the sum of £245.

(4) The amount of the levy imposed in respect of an iron and steel establishment that ceases to carry on business in the fifth levy period shall be in the same proportion to the amount that would otherwise be due under paragraph (3)

(**a**) 1889 c. 63.

of this Article as the number of days between the commencement of the said levy period and the date of cessation of business (both dates inclusive) bears to the number of days in the said levy period.

Assessment Notices

4.—(1) The Board shall serve an assessment notice on every employer assessed to the levy, but one notice may comprise two or more assessments.

(2) An assessment notice shall state the Board's address for the service of a notice of appeal or of an application for an extension of time for appealing.

(3) An assessment notice may be served on the person assessed to the levy either by delivering it to him personally or by leaving it, or sending it to him by post, at his last known address or place of business in the United Kingdom or, if that person is a corporation, by leaving it, or sending it by post to the corporation, at such address or place of business or at its registered or principal office.

Payment of the Levy

5.—(1) Subject to the provisions of this Article and of Articles 6 and 7, the amount of each assessment appearing in an assessment notice served by the Board shall be payable to the Board in two equal instalments, and the said instalments shall be due respectively one month and seven months after the date of the notice.

(2) An instalment of an assessment shall not be recoverable by the Board until there has expired the time allowed for appealing against the assessment by Article 7(1) of this Order and any further period or periods of time that the Board or an appeal tribunal may have allowed for appealing under paragraph (2) or (3) of that Article or, where an appeal is brought, until the appeal is decided or withdrawn.

Withdrawal of Assessment

6.—(1) The Board may, by a notice served on the person assessed to the levy in the same manner as an assessment notice, withdraw an assessment if that person has appealed against that assessment under the provisions of Article 7 of this Order and the appeal has not been entered in the Register of Appeals kept under the appropriate Regulations specified in paragraph (5) of that Article.

(2) The withdrawal of an assessment shall be without prejudice to the power of the Board to serve a further assessment notice in respect of any establishment to which that assessment related and, where the withdrawal is made by reason of the fact that an establishment has ceased to carry on business in the fifth levy period, the said notice may provide that the whole amount payable thereunder in respect of the establishment shall be due one month after the date of the notice.

Appeals

7.—(1) A person assessed to the levy may appeal to an appeal tribunal against the assessment within one month from the date of the service of the assessment notice or within any further period or periods of time that may be allowed by the Board or an appeal tribunal under the following provisions of this Article.

(2) The Board by notice may for good cause allow a person assessed to the levy to appeal to an appeal tribunal against the assessment at any time within the period of four months from the date of the service of the assessment notice or within such further period or periods as the Board may allow before such time as may then be limited for appealing has expired.

(3) If the Board shall not allow an application for extension of time for appealing, an appeal tribunal shall upon application made to the tribunal by the person assessed to the levy have the like powers as the Board under the last foregoing paragraph.

(4) In the case of an establishment that ceases to carry on business in the fifth levy period on any day after the date of the service of the relevant assessment notice, the foregoing provisions of this Article shall have effect as if for the period of four months from the date of the service of the assessment notice mentioned in paragraph (2) of this Article there were substituted the period of six months from the date of the cessation of business.

(5) An appeal or an application to an appeal tribunal under this Article shall be made in accordance with the Industrial Tribunals (England and Wales) Regulations 1965(a) as amended by the Industrial Tribunals (England and Wales) (Amendment) Regulations 1967(b) except where the establishment to which the relevant assessment relates is wholly in Scotland in which case the appeal or application shall be made in accordance with the Industrial Tribunals (Scotland) Regulations 1965(c) as amended by the Industrial Tribunals (Scotland) (Amendment) Regulations 1967(d).

(6) The powers of an appeal tribunal under paragraph (3) of this Article may be exercised by the President of the Industrial Tribunals (England and Wales) or by the President of the Industrial Tribunals (Scotland) as the case may be.

Evidence

8.—(1) Upon the discharge by a person assessed to the levy of his liability under an assessment the Board shall if so requested issue to him a certificate to that effect.

(2) The production in any proceedings of a document purporting to be certified by the Director of the Board to be a true copy of an assessment or other notice issued by the Board or purporting to be a certificate such as is mentioned in the foregoing paragraph of this Article shall, unless the contrary is proved, be sufficient evidence of the document and of the facts stated therein.

6th January 1970.

Barbara Castle,
First Secretary of State and Secretary of State
for Employment and Productivity.

(a) S.I. 1965/1101 (1965 II, p. 2805).   (b) S.I. 1967/301 (1967 I, p. 1040).
(c) S.I. 1965/1157 (1965 II, p. 3266).   (d) S.I. 1967/302 (1967 I, p. 1050).

EXPLANATORY NOTE

(This Note is not part of the Order.)

This Order gives effect to proposals submitted by the Iron and Steel Industry Training Board to the Secretary of State for Employment and Productivity for the imposition of a further levy on employers in the iron and steel industry for the purpose of raising money towards the expenses of the Board.

The levy is to be imposed in respect of the fifth levy period commencing with the day upon which this Order comes into operation and ending on 31st August 1970. The levy will be assessed by the Board and there will be a right of appeal against an assessment to an industrial tribunal.

STATUTORY INSTRUMENTS

1970 No. 9

INDUSTRIAL TRAINING

The Industrial Training Levy (Knitting, Lace and Net) Order 1970

Made - - - -	6th January 1970
Laid before Parliament	16th January 1970
Coming into Operation	28th January 1970

The Secretary of State after approving proposals submitted by the Knitting, Lace and Net Industry Training Board for the imposition of a further levy on employers in the knitting, lace and net industry and in exercise of her powers under section 4 of the Industrial Training Act 1964(a) and of all other powers enabling her in that behalf hereby makes the following Order:—

Title and commencement

1. This Order may be cited as the Industrial Training Levy (Knitting, Lace and Net) Order 1970 and shall come into operation on 28th January 1970.

Interpretation

2.—(1) In this Order unless the context otherwise requires:—

(*a*) "an appeal tribunal" means an industrial tribunal established under section 12 of the Industrial Training Act 1964;

(*b*) "assessment" means an assessment of an employer to the levy;

(*c*) "the board" means the Knitting, Lace and Net Industry Training Board;

(*d*) "business" means any activities of industry or commerce;

(*e*) "emoluments" means all emoluments assessable to income tax under Schedule E (other than pensions), being emoluments from which tax under that Schedule is deductible, whether or not tax in fact falls to be deducted from any particular payment thereof;

(*f*) "employer" means a person who is an employer in the knitting, lace and net industry at any time in the fourth levy period;

(*g*) "the fourth base period" means the period of twelve months that commenced on 6th April 1968;

(*h*) "the fourth levy period" means the period commencing with the day upon which this Order comes into operation and ending on 31st December 1970;

(a) 1964 c. 16.

(*i*) "the industrial training order" means the Industrial Training (Knitting, Lace and Net Industry Board) Order 1966(**a**);

(*j*) "knitting, lace and net establishment" means an establishment in Great Britain engaged in the fourth base period wholly or mainly in the knitting, lace and net industry for a total of twenty-seven or more weeks or, being an establishment that commenced to carry on business in the fourth base period, for a total number of weeks exceeding one half of the number of weeks in the part of the said period commencing with the day on which business was commenced and ending on the last day thereof;

(*k*) "the knitting, lace and net industry" means any one or more of the activities which, subject to the provisions of paragraph 2 of Schedule 1 to the industrial training order, are specified in paragraph 1 of that Schedule as the activities of the knitting, lace and net industry;

(*l*) "the levy" means the levy imposed by the Board in respect of the fourth levy period;

(*m*) "notice" means a notice in writing.

(2) In the case where a knitting, lace and net establishment is taken over (whether directly or indirectly) by an employer in succession to, or jointly with, another person, a person employed at any time in the fourth base period at or from the establishment shall be deemed, for the purposes of this Order, to have been so employed by the employer carrying on the said establishment on the day upon which this Order comes into operation, and any reference in this Order to persons employed by an employer in the fourth base period at or from a knitting, lace and net establishment shall be construed accordingly.

(3) In reckoning the amount of emoluments for the purposes of this Order no regard shall be had to the emoluments of any person engaged wholly in the supply of food or drink for immediate consumption.

(4) Any reference in this Order to an establishment that commences to carry on business or that ceases to carry on business shall not be taken to apply where the location of the establishment is changed but its business is continued wholly or mainly at or from the new location, or where the suspension of activities is of a temporary or seasonal nature.

(5) The Interpretation Act 1889(**b**) shall apply to the interpretation of this Order as it applies to the interpretation of an Act of Parliament.

Imposition of the Levy

3.—(1) The levy to be imposed by the Board on employers in respect of the fourth levy period shall be assessed in accordance with the provisions of this Article.

(2) The levy shall be assessed by the Board separately in respect of each knitting, lace and net establishment of an employer (not being an employer who is exempt from the levy by virtue of paragraph (5) of this Article), but in agreement with the employer one assessment may be made in respect of any number of such establishments, in which case those establishments shall be deemed for the purposes of that assessment to constitute one establishment.

(3) Subject to the provisions of this Article, the levy assessed in respect of a knitting, lace and net establishment of an employer shall be an amount equal to one per cent. of the sum of the emoluments of all the persons employed in the fourth base period by the employer at or from that establishment.

(**a**) S.I. 1966/246 (1966 I, p. 506).   (**b**) 1889 c. 63.

(4) The amount of the levy imposed in respect of a knitting, lace and net establishment that ceases to carry on business in the fourth levy period shall be in the same proportion to the amount that would otherwise be due under paragraph (3) of this Article as the number of days between the commencement of the said levy period and the date of cessation of business (both dates inclusive) bears to the number of days in the said levy period.

(5) There shall be exempt from the levy an employer in whose case the sum of the emoluments of all the persons employed by him in the fourth base period at or from the knitting, lace and net establishment or establishments of the employer was less than £5000.

Assessment Notices

4.—(1) The Board shall serve an assessment notice on every employer assessed to the levy, but one notice may comprise two or more assessments.

(2) The amount of any assessment payable under an assessment notice shall be rounded down to the nearest £1.

(3) An assessment notice shall state the Board's address for the service of a notice of appeal or of an application for an extension of time for appealing.

(4) An assessment notice may be served on the person assessed to the levy either by delivering it to him personally or by leaving it, or sending it to him by post, at his last known address or place of business in the United Kingdom or, if that person is a corporation, by leaving it, or sending it by post to the corporation, at such address or place of business or at its registered or principal office.

Payment of the Levy

5.—(1) Subject to the provisions of this Article and of Articles 6 and 7, the amount of each assessment appearing in an assessment notice served by the Board shall be payable to the Board in two equal instalments, and the said instalments shall be due respectively one month and seven months after the date of the notice.

(2) An instalment of an assessment shall not be recoverable by the Board until there has expired the time allowed for appealing against the assessment by Article 7(1) of this Order and any further period or periods of time that the Board or an appeal tribunal may have allowed for appealing under paragraph (2) or (3) of that Article or, where an appeal is brought, until the appeal is decided or withdrawn.

Withdrawal of Assessment

6.—(1) The Board may, by a notice served on the person assessed to the levy in the same manner as an assessment notice, withdraw an assessment if that person has appealed against that assessment under the provisions of Article 7 of this Order and the appeal has not been entered in the Register of Appeals kept under the appropriate Regulations specified in paragraph (5) of that Article.

(2) The withdrawal of an assessment shall be without prejudice to the power of the Board to serve a further assessment notice in respect of any establishment to which that assessment related and, where the withdrawal is made by reason of the fact that an establishment has ceased to carry on business in the fourth levy period, the said notice may provide that the whole amount payable thereunder in respect of the establishment shall be due one month after the date of the notice.

Appeals

7.—(1) A person assessed to the levy may appeal to an appeal tribunal against the assessment within one month from the date of the service of the assessment notice or within any further period or periods of time that may be allowed by the Board or an appeal tribunal under the following provisions of this Article.

(2) The Board by notice may for good cause allow a person assessed to the levy to appeal to an appeal tribunal against the assessment at any time within the period of four months from the date of the service of the assessment notice or within such further period or periods as the Board may allow before such time as may then be limited for appealing has expired.

(3) If the Board shall not allow an application for extension of time for appealing, an appeal tribunal shall upon application made to the tribunal by the person assessed to the levy have the like powers as the Board under the foregoing paragraph.

(4) In the case of an establishment that ceases to carry on business in the fourth levy period on any day after the date of the service of the relevant assessment notice the foregoing provisions of this Article shall have effect as if for the period of four months from the date of the service of the assessment notice mentioned in paragraph (2) of this Article there were substituted the period of six months from the date of the cessation of business.

(5) An appeal or an application to an appeal tribunal under this Article shall be made in accordance with the Industrial Tribunals (England and Wales) Regulations 1965(a) as amended by the Industrial Tribunals (England and Wales) (Amendment) Regulations 1967(b) except where the establishment to which the relevant assessment relates is wholly in Scotland in which case the appeal or application shall be made in accordance with the Industrial Tribunals (Scotland) Regulations 1965(c) as amended by the Industrial Tribunals (Scotland) (Amendment) Regulations 1967(d).

(6) The powers of an appeal tribunal under paragraph (3) of this Article may be exercised by the President of the Industrial Tribunals (England and Wales) or by the President of the Industrial Tribunals (Scotland) as the case may be.

Evidence

8.—(1) Upon the discharge by a person assessed to the levy of his liability under an assessment the Board shall if so requested issue to him a certificate to that effect.

(a) S.I. 1965/1101 (1965 II, p. 2805).   (b) S.I. 1967/301 (1967 I, p. 1040).
(c) S.I. 1965/1157 (1965 II, p. 3266).   (d) S.I. 1967/302 (1967 I, p. 1050).

(2) The production in any proceedings of a document purporting to be certified by the Secretary of the Board to be a true copy of an assessment or other notice issued by the Board or purporting to be a certificate such as is mentioned in the foregoing paragraph of this Article shall, unless the contrary is proved, be sufficient evidence of the document and of the facts stated therein.

6th January 1970.

Barbara Castle,
First Secretary of State and Secretary of State
for Employment and Productivity.

EXPLANATORY NOTE

(This Note is not part of the Order.)

This Order gives effect to proposals submitted to the Secretary of State for Employment and Productivity by the Knitting, Lace and Net Industry Training Board for the imposition of a further levy upon employers in the knitting, lace and net industry for the purpose of raising money towards the expenses of the Board.

The levy is to be imposed in respect of the fourth levy period commencing with the day upon which this Order comes into operation and ending on 31st December 1970. The levy will be assessed by the Board and there will be a right of appeal against an assessment to an industrial tribunal.

STATUTORY INSTRUMENTS

1970 No. 10

EDUCATION, ENGLAND AND WALES

The Teachers' Superannuation (Amendment) Regulations 1970

Made - - -	*7th January* 1970
Laid before Parliament	*16th January* 1970
Coming into Operation—	
Regulations 1 *to* 17	*1st February* 1970
Regulations 18, 19, 20	*1st May* 1970

The Secretary of State for Education and Science, with the consent of the Minister for the Civil Service and after consultation with representatives of local education authorities and of teachers appearing to him to be likely to be affected, in exercise of the powers conferred upon him by section 1 of the Teachers' Superannuation Act 1967(a) as amended by the Minister for the Civil Service Order 1968(b), hereby makes the following Regulations :—

1.—(1) These Regulations may be cited as the Teachers' Superannuation (Amendment) Regulations 1970 and the Teachers' Superannuation Regulations 1967 to 1969(c) and these Regulations may be cited together as the Teachers' Superannuation Regulations 1967 to 1970.

(2) Regulations 1 to 17 of these Regulations shall come into operation on 1st February 1970 ; and regulations 18, 19 and 20 of these Regulations shall come into operation on 1st May 1970.

2. In these Regulations—

"the principal Regulations" means the Teachers' Superannuation Regulations 1967(d) ; and

"the Part-time Regulations" means the Teachers' (Part-time) Superannuation Regulations 1967(e).

3. In regulation 16 of the principal Regulations (which relates to exclusion from reckonable service) at the end of paragraph (1) there shall be added the following sub-paragraph :—

"(f) immediately before the appointed day he was employed in the same service and was not treated as in contributory service by virtue of the proviso to rule 3 of the Teachers Superannuation Amending Rules 1961(f)."

4. For regulation 17 of the principal Regulations there shall be substituted the following regulation :—

(a) 1967 c. 12. (b) S.I. 1968/1656 (1968 III, p. 4485).
(c) S.I. 1967/489, 948, 1286, 1968/1353, 1969/80, (1967 I, p. 1562; II, p. 2904; II, p. 3721, 1968 II, p. 3753; 1969 I, p. 241). (d) S.I. 1967/489 (1967 I, p. 1562).
(e) S.I. 1967/1286 (1967 II, p. 3721). (f) S.I. 1961/158 (1961 I, p. 268).

"Non-payment of Contributions

17. Without prejudice to the power of the Secretary of State to recover any contributions payable under the Acts of 1918 to 1956, the Act of 1967 or these Regulations, any period of service (other than service to which Part III of Schedule 1 applies) in respect of which the contributions have not been paid in full to the Secretary of State shall not, unless he consents, be reckonable service."

5. In regulation 20 of the principal Regulations (which relates to the payment of teachers' contributions by deduction from salary) for paragraph (3) there shall be substituted the following paragraph :—

"(3) The sums deducted under this regulation from the salary of a teacher shall be paid by the employer to the Secretary of State and shall be attributable to the financial year in which such payment is made."

6. In regulation 21 of the principal Regulations (which relates to the payment of teachers' contributions direct to the Secretary of State) for paragraph (2) there shall be substituted the following paragraph :—

"(2) Any sums paid to the Secretary of State under this regulation shall be attributable to the financial year in which such payment is made."

7. Regulation 23 of the principal Regulations (which relates to the payment of contributions by employers to the Secretary of State) is hereby revoked.

8. For regulation 27 of the principal Regulations there shall be substituted the following regulation :—

"Interest on Overdue Contributions

27. If any contributions payable by a teacher or by an employer under section 3 of the Act of 1967 or under any provision of these Regulations are not paid before 1st October in the financial year next after that in which the period to which they relate fell compound interest thereon from the said date, calculated at four per cent. per annum with yearly rests, shall be paid."

9. In regulation 28 of the principal Regulations (which relates to the repayment of repaid contributions) after the word "under" in paragraph (1) there shall be inserted the words "section 2 of the Act of 1922,".

10. In regulation 31 of the principal Regulations (which relates to the payment of contributions in respect of a period of absence from reckonable service) for paragraph (4) there shall be substituted the following paragraph :—

"(4) Contributions paid by a teacher under this regulation and any interest thereon shall be attributable to the financial year in which payment thereof is made to the Secretary of State."

11. In regulation 32 of the principal Regulations (which relates to the payment of contributions in respect of a period of previous employment) for paragraph (7) there shall be substituted the following paragraph :—

"(7) Additional contributions payable by a teacher by Method I and any interest thereon shall be attributable to the financial year in which payment thereof is made to the Secretary of State."

12. In regulation 49 of the principal Regulations (which relates to supplementary death gratuities) at the end of paragraph (2) there shall be added the words "or any like allocation or surrender made under provisions relating to class A external service."

13. For regulation 50 of the principal Regulations there shall be substituted the following regulation :—

"Re-employed Teachers

50.—(1) In this regulation—

"re-employed teacher" means a teacher who, after superannuation allowances have become payable to him under these Regulations, becomes employed—

(a) in reckonable service, class A external service, class B external service or service which would, if he had not attained the age of seventy, be such service ; or

(b) in other employment which is either—

(i) employment of which the remuneration is paid out of the Consolidated Fund or out of moneys provided by Parliament ; or

(ii) employment by a body, including a local authority, in respect of whose expenditure for the purpose for which he is employed grants are made out of moneys provided by Parliament ;

"last salary", in relation to a re-employed teacher, means the highest salary at which, before superannuation allowances last became payable to him, he was employed in reckonable service, external service or service which would have been such service if he had not attained the age of seventy, reduced by the amount of any allocation made by him under section 1 of the Act of 1937 or Part VI or under any provisions corresponding thereto relating to class A external service ;

"notional salary", in relation to a re-employed teacher, means the highest salary payable at the material time in respect of employment in the same service as, or in service similar to, that in which he was at any time employed in reckonable service, external service or service which would have been such service if he had not attained the age of seventy, reduced by the amount of any allocation made by him under section 1 of the Act of 1937 or Part VI or under any provisions corresponding thereto relating to class A external service ; and

"pension quarter" means—

(a) in relation to a re-employed teacher whose annual superannuation allowance is payable on the last day of a month otherwise than by reason of the anniversary of his birth falling on the first day of a month, a period of three months beginning on 1st January, 1st April, 1st July or 1st October ; and

(b) in relation to any other re-employed teacher, a period of three months beginning on the anniversary of his birth or on the day three, six or nine months thereafter."

(2) Subject as in paragraph (4) below provided, the annual superannuation allowance payable to a re-employed teacher employed in service of the kind specified in paragraph (1)(a) above shall—

(a) be suspended in respect of any period for which he is entitled to a salary at a rate not less than his last salary ; or

(b) be reduced in respect of any period for which he is entitled to a salary at a rate less than his last salary by such an amount as will result in the aggregate of the allowance and the salary to which he is entitled being equal in respect of that period to his last salary.

(3) The annual superannuation allowance payable to a re-employed teacher employed in employment of the kind specified in paragraph (1)(*b*) above shall—

(*a*) be suspended in respect of any pension quarter for which his remuneration is not less than his notional salary for that quarter; or

(*b*) be reduced in respect of any pension quarter for which his remuneration is less than his notional salary by such an amount as will, in respect of that pension quarter, result in the aggregate of the allowance, any increase thereof under the Pensions (Increase) Acts 1920 to 1969 and the remuneration being equal to his notional salary.

(4) No suspension or reduction of an annual superannuation allowance payable to a re-employed teacher employed in service of the kind specified in paragraph (1)(*a*) above shall be made under this regulation which would result in the aggregate amount received by him in respect of any period by way of—

(*a*) annual superannuation allowance,

(*b*) increase of such allowance under the Pensions (Increase) Acts 1920 to 1969, and

(*c*) salary

being less than the aggregate amount for that period of—

(*d*) his last salary, and

(*e*) any increase of his annual superannuation allowance which would be payable under the Pensions (Increase) Acts 1920 to 1969 apart from any suspension or reduction of that allowance under this regulation.

(5) For the purpose of determining the salary or remuneration to which a re-employed teacher is entitled the following payments to him shall be disregarded:—

(*a*) any payments in respect of employment in connexion with education which, while employed in reckonable service or external service, he undertook in addition to such service and which he continues after ceasing such service, not exceeding, when expressed as an annual rate, the annual average rate of such payments for the last three years of his employment in reckonable service or external service;

(*b*) any payments in respect of employment in connexion with education outside the British Isles, being employment in which, in the opinion of the Secretary of State, it is expedient to facilitate the employment of teachers from England and Wales;

(*c*) any payments in respect of employment as an examiner for the purposes of the General Certificate of Education; and

(*d*) any additional payments made to teachers employed in schools recognised by the Secretary of State as schools of exceptional difficulty under the provisions of an order made under the Remuneration of Teachers Act 1965(a) or of a document referred to in such an order.

(6) Any question arising under this regulation as to the amount of the notional salary of a re-employed teacher shall be decided by the Secretary of State and his decision thereon shall be final."

_____

(a) 1965 c. 3.

14. For regulation 89 of the principal Regulations there shall be substituted the following regulation :—

"Payment of Benefits

89.—(1) Every allowance, pension, annuity and other sum payable under these Regulations which does not consist of a single payment—

> (*a*) shall be paid at intervals of three months ; but

> (*b*) may, on the application of the person entitled thereto, be paid at intervals of one month.

(2) No apportionment of any such sum as aforesaid shall take place and accordingly the provisions of the Apportionment Act 1870(a) shall not extend thereto.

(3) Where payment of any such sum as aforesaid is due in respect of a period of less than the intervals at which it is payable—

> (*a*) the amount thereof in respect of each complete month of the period shall be one-twelfth of the annual rate of the sum ; and

> (*b*) the amount thereof in respect of a period of less than one complete month shall bear the same proportion to one-twelfth of the annual rate of the sum as the number of days in respect of which it is payable bears to the total number of days in the month in which those days occur."

15. In regulation 93 of the principal Regulations (which amends certain enactments) the following paragraph shall be added at the end :—

"(4) In each of the Pensions (Increase) Acts 1944 to 1965 any reference to a pension payable under the Teachers (Superannuation) Acts 1918 to 1956, or any of those Acts, shall be extended so as to include a reference to a pension payable under these Regulations."

16. In regulation 3 of the Part-time Regulations (which specifies the service which is to be part-time teaching service for the purposes of those Regulations) at the end of paragraph (2) there shall be added the following sub-paragraph :—

"(*d*) teachers of a kind specified in paragraph 8 of Schedule 1 to the principal Regulations."

17. In regulation 6 of the Part-time Regulations (which relates to the reckoning of service of part-time teachers) at the end of paragraph (3) there shall be added the following sub-paragraph :—

"(*d*) there shall be disregarded—

> (i) any period of part-time teaching service in respect of which the contributions have, under the provisions of Part IV of the principal Regulations, been repaid by the Secretary of State and not again paid to him in accordance with regulation 28 of those Regulations ; and

> (ii) unless the Secretary of State otherwise consents, any period of part-time teaching service in respect of which the contributions have not been paid in full to him."

(a) 1870 c. 35.

18. For regulation 72 of the principal Regulations there shall be substituted the following regulation:—

"*Admitted Schools*

72. For the purposes of this Part an admitted school shall, subject as in regulation 73 provided, be a school, establishment of further education or college of education to which this Part applied immediately before 1st May 1970."

19. In regulation 73 of the principal Regulations (which provides for the admission of admitted schools) paragraphs (1) and (2) are hereby revoked.

20. Regulation 79 of the principal Regulations (which relates to accounts and actuarial inquiries with respect to admitted schools) is hereby revoked.

Given under the Official Seal of the Secretary of State for Education and Science on 6th January 1970.

(L.S.)
Edward Short,
Secretary of State for Education
and Science.

Consent of the Minister for the Civil Service given under his Official Seal on 7th January 1970.

(L.S.)
K. H. McNeill,
Authorised by the Minister for
the Civil Service.

EXPLANATORY NOTE

(This Note is not part of the Regulations.)

These Regulations amend the Teachers' Superannuation Regulations 1967 to 1969. They extend to part-time teachers in colleges of education the optional superannuation arrangements already in operation for part-time teachers in primary and secondary schools; they make changes of procedure with respect to the collection of contributions; they provide that further schools shall not be admitted to the special superannuation arrangements established in 1926 which still apply to a limited number of independent schools; and they correct minor defects.

STATUTORY INSTRUMENTS

1970 No. 16 (L.1)

COUNTY COURTS

The County Court Districts Order 1970

Made - - -	*8th January* 1970	
Coming into Operation	*16th February* 1970	

The Lord Chancellor, in exercise of the powers conferred on him by section 2 of the County Courts Act 1959(**a**) and, so far as is required by sub-section (2) of that section, with the consent of the Chancellor of the Duchy of Lancaster, hereby makes the following Order :—

1.—(1) This Order may be cited as the County Court Districts Order 1970 and shall come into operation on 16th February 1970.

(2) The Interpretation Act 1889(**b**) shall apply to the interpretation of this Order as it applies to the interpretation of an Act of Parliament.

2.—(1) The district of each county court mentioned in column 1 of schedule 1 to this Order shall consist of those parts of the local authority areas mentioned in column 2 which are specified opposite thereto in column 3.

(2) Where the local authority mentioned in column 2 is a rural district, the names in column 3 are (unless the contrary appears) the names of civil parishes or rural boroughs.

(3) A reference in schedule 1 to any borough, urban district, rural district or civil parish is a reference to that borough, district or parish as constituted on the date of the making of this Order.

3.—(1) The county court for each district shall be held under the name mentioned in column 1 of schedule 1 to this Order and, (subject to paragraph (2) of this article) where more than one place is mentioned in the name, the court shall be held at each of those places.

(2) In the case of the county courts mentioned in column 1 of schedule 2 to this Order, courts shall be held at the place or places mentioned in column 2 opposite to the name of the court.

4. The Orders specified in schedule 3 to this Order, being the County Court Districts Order 1949(**c**) and all amending Orders, are hereby revoked.

Dated 5th January 1970.

Gardiner, C.

This Order, so far as it relates to any county court held for a Duchy of Lancaster district, is made with my consent.

Dated 8th January 1970.

G. M. Thomson,
Chancellor of the Duchy of Lancaster.

(**a**) 1959 c. 22.   (**b**) 1889 c. 63.
(**c**) S.I. 1949/2058 (1949 I, p. 955).

SCHEDULE 1

Column 1 Name of court	Column 2 Local authority areas	Column 3 Parts comprising court districts
ABERDARE	Aberdare Urban District	Aberdare.
	Merthyr Tydfil County Borough (part) *Other part* in Merthyr Tydfil County Court District.	Fair View, Incline Top, Nos. 1–42, Jenkin St. King Street, Nos. 80–82, Locke St. Parry's Houses.
	Mountain Ash Urban District (part). *Other part* in Pontypridd and Ystradyfodwg County Court District.	The Urban District with the exception of Ynysybwl.
	Neath Rural District (part). *Other part* in Neath and Port Talbot County Court District.	Rhigos.
	Vaynor and Penderyn Rural District (part). *Other parts* in Merthyr Tydfil and Neath and Port Talbot County Court Districts.	Penderyn.
ABER-YSTWYTH	Aberaeron Urban District	Aberaeron.
	Aberaeron Rural District (part). *Other parts* in Cardigan and Lampeter County Court Districts.	Cilcennin, Ciliau Aeron, Dihewid, Henfynyw Llanina, Llanllwchaiarn, Llansantffraid, Upper Llanarth, Llanbadarn Trefeglwys, Upper, Llanddewi Aberarth.
	Aberystwyth Municipal Borough.	Aberystwyth.
	Aberystwyth Rural District (part). *Other part* in Machynlleth County Court District.	Borth, Ceulany-measmawr, Cwmrheidol, Geneu'rglyn, Llanafan, Llanba-darnfawr, Llancynfelyn, Llanddeiniol, Llangorwen, Llangwyryfon, Llanilar, Llanrhystyd Haminiog, Llanrhystyd Mefenydd, Llanychaiarn, Lower Llanbadarn y Creuddyn, Lower Llanfihangel y Creuddyn, Melindwr, Parcel Canol, Tirymynach, Trefeirig, Upper Llanbadarn y Creuddyn, Upper Llanfihangel y Creuddyn, Upper Vaenor.
	New Quay Urban District.	New Quay.
	Teifiside Rural District (part) *Other parts* in Cardigan and Lampeter County Court Districts.	Llangranog.

Column 1	Column 2	Column 3
Name of court	Local authority areas	Parts comprising court districts
ABER-YSTWYTH—cont.	Tregaron Rural District (part) . *Other part* in Lampeter County Court District.	Gwnnws Issa, Upper Lledrod, Lower Lledrod, Yspytty Ystwyth. Upper Gwnnws,
ACCRING-TON	Accrington Municipal Borough.	Accrington.
	Burnley Rural District (part). *Other parts* in Burnley and Nelson County Court Districts.	Altham.
	Church Urban District.	Church.
	Clayton le Moors Urban District.	Clayton le Moors.
	Oswaldtwistle Urban District.	Oswaldtwistle.
ALDER-SHOT AND FARNHAM	Aldershot Municipal Borough.	Aldershot.
	Alton Urban District.	Alton.
	Alton Rural District (part). *Other parts* in Basingstoke and Winchester County Court Districts.	Bentley, Headley, Binsted, Kingsley, Chawton, Newton Valance, East Tisted, Selborne, Farringdon, Shalden, Froyle, Whitehill, Grayshott, Worldham.
	Bagshot Rural District (part). *Other part* in Guildford County Court District.	West End, Windlesham.
	Farnborough Urban District.	Farnborough.
	Farnham Urban District.	Farnham.
	Fleet Urban District.	Fleet.
	Frimley and Camberley Urban District.	Frimley and Camberley.
	Guildford Rural District (part). *Other parts* in Dorking and Guildford County Court Districts.	Ash, Puttenham, Normandy, Seale and Tongham.
	Hambledon Rural District (part). *Other part* in Guildford County Court District.	Dockenfield, Tilford. Frensham,
	Hartley Wintney Rural District (part). *Other part* in Basingstoke County Court District.	Crondall, Long Sutton, Crookham Village, Yateley. Hawley,
ALFRETON	Alfreton Urban District	Alfreton.

Column 1	Column 2	Column 3
Name of court	Local authority areas	Parts comprising court districts
ALFRETON —cont.	Basford Rural District (part). *Other parts* in Ilkeston, Loughborough, Mansfield and Nottingham County Court Districts.	Felley, Selston.
	Belper Rural District (part). *Other parts* in Derby, Ilkeston and Matlock County Court Districts.	Crich, South Pentrich, Wingfield.
	Blackwell Rural District (part). *Other parts* in Chesterfield and Mansfield County Court Districts.	Blackwell, Tibshelf. Pinxton, South Normanton,
	Chesterfield Rural District (part). *Other part* in Chesterfield County Court District.	Brackenfield, Stretton, Morton, Wessington. Pilsley, Shirland and Higham,
	Ripley Urban District	Ripley.
ALNWICK	Alnwick Urban District.	Alnwick.
	Alnwick Rural District.	Acklington, Lesbury, Alnmouth, Longhoughton, Craster, Newton Denwick, by the Sea, Edlingham, Newton Eglingham, on the Moor Embleton, Rennington, Felton, Shilbottle, Glanton, Togston, Hauxley, Warkworth. Hedgeley,
	Amble Urban District.	Amble.
	Belford Rural District (part). *Other part* in Berwick upon Tweed County Court District.	Beadnell, North Sunderland. Ellingham, Farne Islands,
	Glendale Rural District (part). *Other part* in Berwick upon Tweed County Court District.	Bewick, Chatton (part), viz:—So much of the civil parish as is south of a line running along the middle of the road from Belford Moor to the River Till and thence along the River to the boundary of the civil parish of Wooler. Chillingham, Lilburn, Earle, Roddam, Ilderton, Wooler. Ingram,
	Rothbury Rural District (part). *Other part* in Morpeth County Court District.	Alnham, Whittingham. Callaly,

Column 1	*Column 2*	*Column 3*
Name of court	Local authority areas	Parts comprising court districts
ALTRIN-CHAM	Altrincham Municipal Borough.	Altrincham.
	Bowdon Urban District.	Bowdon.
	Bucklow Rural District (part). *Other part* in Northwich County Court District.	Agden, Ashley, Bexton, Bollington, Carrington, Dunham Massey, High Legh, Little Warford, Marthall, — Mere, Millington, Mobberley, Ollerton, Partington, Ringway, Rostherne, Tabley Superior, Tatton, Warburton.
	Hale Urban District.	Hale.
	Knutsford Urban District.	Knutsford.
	Lymm Urban District.	Lymm.
	Sale Municipal Borough.	Sale.
AMER-SHAM	Amersham Rural District (part). *Other part* in High Wycombe County Court District.	Amersham, Ashley Green, Chalfont St. Giles, Chalfont St. Peter, Chartridge, Chenies, — Chesham Bois, Cholesbury cum St. Leonard's, Coleshill, Great Missenden, Latimer, Little Missenden, The Lee.
	Chesham Urban District.	Chesham.
	Hemel Hempstead Rural District (part). *Other parts* in Hemel Hempstead, Luton and St. Albans County Court Districts.	Flaunden.
AMMAN-FORD	Ammanford Urban District.	Ammanford.
	Cwmamman Urban District.	Cwmamman.
	Llandeilo Urban District.	Llandeilo.
	Landeilo Rural District (part). *Other parts* in Carmarthen, Lampeter and Llandovery County Court Districts.	Bettws, Llandeilo Rural, Llandybie, Llandyfeisant, Llanfihangel Aberbythych, — Llansawel, Quarter Bach, Talley.
	Llanelli Rural District (part). *Other part* in Llanelli County Court District.	Llanedy (part), viz.:—That part of the civil parish bounded on the west by a line drawn from a point on the northern boundary of the civil parish by the middle of the road leading from Capel Hendre to the main road at Coopers' House, along the main road northeastwards to a house named Gors, thence by the road leading southwards passing

Column 1	Column 2	Column 3
Name of court	Local authority areas	Parts comprising court districts
AMMAN-FORD —cont.	Llanelli Rural District (part). —cont.	Llwyn-y-fedwen and Clawdd-du to a point where this road crosses a stream north of Dyffryn; then in a south-easterly direction along this stream, passing Erw-wastad-fawr to its confluence with the River Loughor.
	Pontardawe Rural District (part). *Other part* in Neath and Port Talbot County Court District.	Llangiwg (part) The Caergurwen and Cwmllynfell Wards.
ANDOVER	Andover Municipal Borough.	Andover.
	Andover Rural District.	Abbot's Ann, Linkenholt, Amport, Longparish, Appleshaw, Monxton, Barton Stacey, Penton Grafton, Bullington, Penton Mewsey, Chilbolton, Quarley, Faccombe, Shipton Bellinger, Fyfield, Smannell, Goodworth Clatford, South Tedworth, Tangley, Grateley, Thruxton, Hurstbourne Upper Clatford, Tarrant, Vernham's Dean, Kimpton, Wherwell.
	Kingsclere and Whitchurch Rural District (part). *Other parts* in Basingstoke and Newbury County Court Districts.	Hurstborne Priors, St. Mary Bourne, Whitchurch. Laverstoke,
	Marlborough and Ramsbury Rural District (part). *Other parts* in Marlborough, Newbury and Swindon County Court Districts.	Tidcombe with Fosbury.
	Pewsey Rural District (part). *Other parts* in Devizes, Marlborough and Salisbury County Court Districts.	Chute, North Chute Forest, Tidworth. Ludgershall,
	Romsey and Stockbridge Rural District (part). *Other parts* in Salisbury, Southampton and Winchester County Court Districts.	Broughton, Nether Wallop, Buckholt, Over Wallop, Leckford, Stockbridge. Longstock,
ASHBY DE LA ZOUCH	Ashby de la Zouch Urban District.	Ashby de la Zouch.
	Ashby de la Zouch Rural District.	Appleby Magna, Oakthorpe and Bardon, Donisthorpe, Chilcote, Osgathorpe, Coleorton, Packington, Heather, Ravenstone with Measham, Snibston, Normanton le Heath, Snarestone, Staunton Harold,

Column 1	Column 2	Column 3
Name of court	Local authority areas	Parts comprising court districts
ASHBY DE LA ZOUCH —cont.	Ashby de la Zouch Rural District. —cont.	Stretton en le Field, Swepstone, Swannington, Worthington.
	Ashby Woulds Urban District.	Ashby Woulds.
	Castle Donington Rural District (part). *Other parts* in Derby and Loughborough County Court Districts.	Breedon on the Hill.
	Coalville Urban District.	Coalville.
	Market Bosworth Rural District (part). *Other parts* in Hinkley, Leicester and Nuneaton County Court Districts.	Bagworth, Nailstone, Barlestone, Shackerstone, Carlton, Twycross. Ibstock,
	Repton Rural District (part). *Other parts* in Burton upon Trent and Derby County Court Districts.	Calke, Smisby, Hartshorne, Ticknall, Netherseal, Woodville. Overseal,
ASHFORD	Ashford Urban District.	Ashford.
	East Ashford Rural District (part). *Other part* in Canterbury County Court District.	Aldington, Hastingleigh, Bilsington, Hinxhill, Bonnington, Mersham, Boughton Aluph, Molash, Brabourne, Orlestone, Brook, Ruckinge, Challock, Sevington, Crundale, Smeeth, Eastwell, Warehorne, Godmersham, Wye.
	Lydd Municipal Borough.	Lydd.
	New Romney Municipal Borough.	New Romney.
	Romney Marsh Rural District.	Brenzett, Newchurch, Brookland, Old Romney, Burmarsh, St. Mary in the Dymchurch Marsh, Ivychurch, Snargate.
	West Ashford Rural District.	Bethersden, Little Chart, Charing, Pluckley, Egerton, Shadoxhurst, Great Chart, Smarden, Hothfield, Westwell. Kingsnorth,
ASHTON UNDER LYNE AND STALY- BRIDGE	Ashton under Lyne Municipal Borough.	Ashton under Lyne.
	Audenshaw Urban District.	Audenshaw.
	Droylsden Urban District.	Droylsden.

Column 1	*Column 2*	*Column 3*
Name of court	Local authority areas	Parts comprising court districts
ASHTON UNDER LYNE AND STALY-BRIDGE *—cont.*	Dukinfield Municipal Borough.	Dukinfield.
	Mossley Municipal Borough.	Mossley
	Stalybridge Municipal Borough.	Stalybridge.
AXMINSTER AND CHARD	Axminster Rural District.	Axminster, Membury, Axmouth, Musbury, Beer, Shute, Chardstock, Stockland, Colyton, Uplyme, Combpyne Lands Rousdon, Common to Dalwood, Axminster and Hawkchurch, Kilmington civil Kilmington, parishes.
	Beaminster Rural District (part). *Other parts* in Bridport, Dorchester and Yeovil County Court Districts.	Thorncombe.
	Bridport Rural District (part), *Other part* in Bridport County County Court District.	Catherston Wooton Leweston, Fitzpaine. Charmouth,
	Chard Municipal Borough.	Chard.
	Chard Rural District (part). *Other part* in Yeovil County Court District.	Ashill, Donyatt, Broadway, Dowlish Wake, Buckland Ilminster Without, St. Mary, Ilton, Chaffcombe, Knowle St. Giles, Chard, Wambrook, Combe Whitelackington, St. Nicholas, Whitestaunton, Cricket Winsham. St. Thomas,
	Ilminster Urban District.	Ilminster.
	Langport Rural District (part). *Other parts* in Bridgwater, Taunton, Wells and Yeovil County Court Districts.	Barrington, Puckington.
	Lyme Regis Municipal Borough.	Lyme Regis.
	Seaton Urban District.	Seaton.
AYLES-BURY	Aylesbury Municipal Borough.	Aylesbury.
	Aylesbury Rural District (part). *Other part* in Thame County Court District.	Ashendon, Dinton with Aston Clinton, Ford, Bierton with Drayton Broughton, Beauchamp, Buckland, Fleet Marston, Creslow, Grendon Cuddington, Underwood,

Column 1	Column 2	Column 3
Name of court	Local authority areas	Parts comprising court districts
AYLES-BURY —cont.	Aylesbury Rural District —cont.	Halton, Hardwick, Hartwell and Stone with Bishopstone, Hulcott, Kingswood, Lower Winchendon, Oving, Pitchcott, Quainton, Quarrendon, / Stoke Manderville, Stone, Upper Winchendon, Upton, Waddesdon, Weedon, Wendover, Westcott, Weston Turville, Whitchurch, Woodham, Wotton Underwood.
	Berkhamstead Rural District (part). Other part in Hemel Hempstead County Court District.	Tring Rural.
	Buckingham Municipal Borough.	Buckingham.
	Buckingham Rural District (part). Other parts in Banbury, Bletchley and Leighton Buzzard, Northampton and Oxford County Court Districts.	Addington, Adstock, Akeley, Charndon, Edgcott, Hillesden, Maids Morton, Marsh Gibbon, / Middle Claydon, Padbury, Poundon, Radclive, Steeple Claydon, Stowe, Tingewick, Twyford.
	Tring Urban District.	Tring Urban.
	Wing Rural District (part). Other part in Bletchley and Leighton Buzzard County Court District.	Aston Abbots, Cublington, Marsworth, / Pitstone, Wingrave.
	Winslow Rural District (part). Other part in Bletchley and Leighton Buzzard County Court District.	Dunton, East Claydon, Granborough, Hoggeston, / Hogshaw, North Marston, Swanbourne, Winslow.
	Wycombe Rural District (part). Other parts in High Wycombe and Reading County Court Districts.	Ellesborough, Great and Little Kimble.
BANBURY	Banbury Municipal Borough.	Banbury.
	Banbury Rural District.	Alkerton, Barford St. John, and St. Michael, Bloxham, Bodicote, Bourton, Broughton, Claydon with Clattercote, Cropredy, Deddington, / Drayton, Duns Tew, East Adderbury, Epwell, Hanwell, Hook Norton. Horley, Hornton, Middle Aston, Milcombe, Milton,

Column 1	*Column* 2	*Column* 3
Name of court	Local authority areas	Parts comprising court districts
BANBURY —*cont.*	Banbury Rural District —*cont.*	Mollington, South Newington, North Aston, Steeple Aston, North Newington, Swalcliffe, Prescote, Tadmarton, Shenington, Wardington, Shutford, West Adderbury, Sibford Ferris, Wigginton, Sibford Gower, Wroxton,
	Brackley Municipal Borough.	Brackley.
	Brackley Rural District.	Aston le Walls, King's Sutton, Aynho, Marston Boddington, St. Lawrence, Chacombe, Middleton Cheney, Chipping Warden, Moreton Pinkney, Croughton, Newbottle, Culworth, Radstone, Edgcote, Sulgrave, Evenley, Syresham, Eydon, Thenford, Farthinghoe, Thorpe Greatworth, Mandeville, Helmdon, Warkworth, Hinton in the Whitfield. Hedges,
	Buckingham Rural District (part). *Other parts* in Aylesbury, Bletchley and Leighton Buzzard, Northampton and Oxford County Court Districts.	Biddlesden, Water Stratford, Shalstone, Westbury. Turweston,
	Chipping Norton Municipal Borough.	Chipping Norton.
	Chipping Norton Rural District (part). *Other part* in Oxford County Court District.	Ascott under Over Norton, Wychwood, Rollright, Bruern, Rousham, Chadlington, Salford, Charlbury, Sandford Chastleton, St. Martins, Chilson, Sarsden, Churchill, Shipton under Cornwell, Wychwood, Enstone, Shorthampton Fifield, or Chilson, Great Tew, Spelsbury, Heythrop, Steeple Barton, Idbury, Swerford Kingham, Wescot Barton, Little Tew, Worton. Lyneham, Milton under Wychwood,
	Daventry Rural District (part). *Other parts* in Northampton and Rugby County Court Districts.	Byfield, Woodford cum Canons Ashby, Membris.

Column 1	Column 2	Column 3
Name of court	Local authority areas	Parts comprising court districts
BANBURY —cont.	Ploughley Rural District (part). Other parts in Oxford and Thame County Court Districts.	Ardley, Bucknell, Cottisford, Finmere, Fritwell, Hardwick with Tusmore, Hethe, / Lower Heyford, Mixbury, Newton Purcell with Shelswell, Somerton, Souldern, Stoke Lyne, Upper Heyford.
	Shipston-on-Stour Rural District (part). Other part in Stratford-on-Avon County Court District.	Barton on the Heath, Bra, Compton Wynyates, / Little Compton, Tysoe.
	Southam Rural District (part). Other parts in Rugby and Warwick County Court Districts.	Avon Dassett, Burton Dassett, Farnborough, Fenny Compton, Radway, Ratley and Upton, / Shotteswell, Stoneton, Warmington, Wormleighton.
BANGOR	Bangor Municipal Borough.	Bangor.
	Bethesda Urban District.	Bethesda.
	Llanfairfechan Urban District.	Llanfairfechan.
	Menai Bridge Urban District.	Menai Bridge.
	Ogwen Rural District.	Aber, Llandegai, / Llanllechid, Pentir.
BARGOED	Gelligaer Urban District.	Gelligaer.
BARNET	Elstree Rural District.	Elstree, Ridge, / Shenley.
	Hatfield Rural District (part). Other parts in Hertford and St. Albans County Court Districts.	Northaw.
	London Borough of Barnet (part). Other part in Willesden County Court District.	That part of the Borough to the north and east of a line drawn from the point on the Borough boundary south of Barnet Lane and west of Hyver Hill, across Barnet Way to the north of Hyver Hill, south of Barnet Road to the point east of Hendon Wood Lane, thence along the east side of Hendon Wood Lane across Totteridge Lane, southwards to Folley Brook, eastwards along Folley Brook to a point north of the eastern end of Burton Hole Lane along the east side of Burton Hole Lane to the junction of Frith Road and Lullington Garth along the north side of Nether Court Golf

Column 1	Column 2	Column 3
Name of court	Local authority areas	Parts comprising court districts
BARNET —cont.	London Borough of Barnet (part). —cont.	Course to the Dollis Brook, southwards along the Dollis Brook to its junction with Mutton Brook, along Mutton Brook eastwards to its junction with Falloden Way across the end of Falloden Way along the middle of the North Circular Road to a point north of Connaught Drive, thence north of Brookland Rise and Hill Top to the west of Ossulton Way then southwards along the west side of Ossulton Way and Kingsley Way across the end of Kingsley Way to the point on Hampstead Golf Course at the end of Green Close and eastwards across the Golf Course to the west of Winnington Road, along the west of Winnington Road and Kenwood Close to the Borough Boundary.
	London Borough of Enfield (part). *Other part* in Edmonton County Court District.	That part of the Borough to the west of a line drawn from the point where the Borough boundary crosses Cockfosters Road along the east side of Cockfosters Road and Chase Side, then across the end of Chase Side to the Borough boundary at the end of Crown Lane.
BARNSLEY	Barnsley County Borough.	Barnsley.
	Cudworth Urban District.	Cudworth.
	Darfield Urban District.	Darfield.
	Darton Urban District.	Darton.
	Dodworth Urban District.	Dodworth.
	Hemsworth Rural District (part). *Other part* in Pontefract County Court District.	Billingley, Brierley, Great Houghton, Havercroft with Cold Hiendley, Little Houghton, Ryhill, Shafton, South Hiendley.
	Hoyland Nether Urban District.	Hoyland Nether.
	Penistone Urban District.	Penistone.
	Penistone Rural District.	Cawthorne, Dunford, High Hoyland, Hunshelf, Gunthwaite and Ingbirchworth, Langsett, Oxspring, Silkstone, Stainborough, Thurgoland.
	Royston Urban District.	Royston.
	Wakefield Rural District (part). *Other part* in Wakefield County Court District.	Notton, Woolley.

Column 1	Column 2	Column 3
Name of court	Local authority areas	Parts comprising court districts
BARNSLEY —cont.	Wombwell Urban District.	Wombwell.
	Worsbrough Urban District.	Worsbrough.
	Wortley Rural District (part). *Other part* in Sheffield County Court District.	Tankersley, Wortley.
BARN-STAPLE	Barnstaple Municipal Borough.	Barnstaple.
	Barnstaple Rural District (part). *Other part* in Bideford County Court District.	Arlington, Heanton Ashford, Punchardon, Atherington, High Bray, Berrynarbor, Kentisbury, Bishop's Landkey, Tawton, Loxhore, Bittadon, Martinhoe, Bratton Marwood, Fleming, Mortehoe, Braunton, Newton Tracey, Brendon, Parracombe, Challacombe, Shirwell, Combe Martin, Stoke Rivers, Countisbury, Swimbridge, East Down, Tawstock, Fremington, Trentishoe, Georgeham, West Down, Goodleigh, West Pilton.
	Crediton Rural District (part). *Other parts* in Exeter, Oke-hampton and Tiverton County Court Districts.	Chawleigh, Wembworthy. Eggesford,
	Ilfracombe Urban District.	Ilfracombe.
	Lynton Urban District.	Lynton.
	South Molton Rural District (part). *Other part* in Tiverton County Court District.	Bishop's Mariansleigh, Nympton, Meshaw, Burrington, Molland, Charles, North Molton, Cheldon, Queen's Nympton, Chittlehamholt, Romansleigh, Chittlehampton, Rose Ash, Chumleigh, Satterleigh and East Buckland, Warkleigh, Filleigh, South Molton George Rural Borough Nympton, Twitchen, King's Nympton, West Buckland.
	Torrington Rural District (part). *Other parts* in Bideford and Holsworthy County Court Districts.	Ashreigney, Roborough, Dowland, Winkleigh, High Bickington, Yarnscombe.

Column 1	*Column* 2	*Column* 3
Name of court	Local authority areas	Parts comprising court districts
BARROW IN FURNESS AND ULVER-STON	Barrow in Furness County Borough.	Barrow in Furness.
	Dalton in Furness Urban District.	Dalton in Furness.
	Grange Urban District.	Grange.
	Ulverston Urban District.	Ulverston.
	North Lonsdale Rural District (part). *Other part* in Kendal County Court District.	Aldingham, Kirkby Ireleth, Angerton, Lower Allithwaite, Blawith, Lower Holker, Broughton East, Lowick, Broughton West, Mansriggs, Cartmel Fell, Osmotherley, Colton, Pennington, Dunnerdale with Stavely, Seathwaite, Subberthwaite, Egton with Upper Allithwaite, Newland, Urswick, Haverthwaite,
		Birkrigg Common, land common to Aldingham and Urswick civil parishes. Lands common to Lowick and Subberthwaite civil parishes.
BARRY	Barry Municipal Borough.	Barry.
	Cardiff Rural District (part). *Other parts* in Cardiff, Caerphilly and Newport (Mon.) County Court Districts.	Bonvilston, Porthkerry, Lavernock, St. Andrew's Major, Llancarfan, St. Lythans, Llantrithyd, St. Nicholas, Llanvithyn, Sully, Penmark, Wenvoe.
BASING-STOKE	Alton Rural District (part). *Other parts* in Aldershot and Farnham and Winchester County Court Districts.	Bentworth, Lasham.
	Basingstoke Municipal Borough.	Basingstoke.
	Basingstoke Rural District (part). *Other part* in Winchester County Court District.	Basing, Oakley, Bradley, Pamber, Bramley, Popham, Cliddesden, Preston Candover, Deane, Sherborne St. John, Dummer with Sherfield on Kempshott, Loddon, Ellisfield, Silchester, Farleigh Wallop, Steventon, Hartley Wespall, Stratfield Saye, Herriard, Stratfield Turgis, Mapledurwell, Tunworth, and Up Nately, Upton Grey, Monk Sherborne, Weston Corbett, Mortimer West Weston Patrick, End, Winslade, Newnham, Woodmancott, North Waltham, Wootton St. Nutley, Lawrence.

Column 1	Column 2	Column 3
Name of court	Local authority areas	Parts comprising court districts
BASING-STOKE —*cont.*	Hartley Wintney Rural District (part). *Other part* in Aldershot and Farnham County Court District.	Bramshill, Dogmersfield, Eversley, Greywell, Hartley Witney, Heckfield, — Hook. Mattingley, Odiham, Rotherwick, South Warnborough, Winchfield,
	Kingsclere and Whitchurch Rural District (part). *Other parts* in Andover and Newbury County Court Districts.	Baughurst, Overton. — Tadley.
BATH	Bath County Borough.	Bath.
	Bathavon Rural District (part). *Other part* in Bristol County Court District.	Bathampton, Batheaston, Bathford Charlcombe, Claverton, Combe Hay, Compton Dando, Corston, Dunkerton, English Combe, Freshford, Hinton Charterhouse, — Kelston, Marksbury, Monkton Combe, Newton St. Loe, North Stoke, Peasedown St. John, Priston, St. Catherine, Shoscombe, South Stoke, Swainswick, Wellow.
	Bradford and Melksham Rural District (part). *Other parts* in Chippenham and Trowbridge County Court Districts.	Monkton Farleigh.
	Calne and Chippenham Rural District (part). *Other parts* in Devizes, Swindon, and Chippenham County Court Districts.	Box, Colerne,
	Sodbury Rural District (part). *Other part* in Bristol County Court District.	Cold Ashton, Marshfield.
BEDFORD	Ampthill Urban District.	Ampthill.
	Ampthill Rural District (part). *Other parts* in Bletchley and Leighton Buzzard, Hitchin and Luton County Court Districts.	Clophill, Cranfield, Eversholt, Flitton, Flitwick, Haynes, Houghton Conquest, Lidlington, — Marston Moretaine, Maulden, Millbrook, Pulloxhill, Ridgmont, Silsoe, Steppingley.
	Bedford Municipal Borough.	Bedford.

Column 1	*Column* 2	*Column* 3
Name of court	Local authority areas	Parts comprising court districts
BEDFORD —*cont.*	Bedford Rural District (part). *Other parts* in Biggleswade and Wellingborough County Court Districts.	Biddenham, Bletsoe, Bolnhurst and Keysoe, Bromham, Cardington, Carlton and Chellington, Clapham, Colmworth, Cople, Dean and Shelton, Eastcotts, Elstow, Felmersham, Great Barford, Harrold, Kempston Rural, Knotting and Souldrop, Little Staughton, Milton Ernest, Oakley, Odell, Pavenham, Pertenhall, Ravensden, Renhold, Riseley, Sharnbrook, Stagsden, Stevington, Stewartby, Swineshead, Thurleigh, Turvey, Wilden, Willington, Wilshamstead, Wootton.
	Kempston Urban District.	Kempston.
	Newport Pagnell Rural District (part). *Other parts* in Bletchley and Leighton Buzzard and Northampton County Court Districts.	Astwood, Hardmead.
BERWICK UPON TWEED	Belford Rural District (part). *Other part* in Alnwick County Court District.	Adderstone with Lucker, Bamburgh, Belford Easington, Middleton.
	Berwick upon Tweed Municipal Borough.	Berwick upon Tweed.
	Glendale Rural District (part). *Other part* in Alnwick County Court District.	Akeld, Bowsden, Chatton (part), viz:—So much of the civil parish as is north of a line running along the middle of the road from Belford Moor to the River Till, and thence along the River Till to the boundary of the civil parish of Wooler. Doddington, Ewart, Ford, Kilham, Branxton, Carham, Kirknewton, Lowick, Milfield.
	Norham and Islandshires Rural District.	Ancroft, Cornhill on Tweed, Duddo, Holy Island, Horncliffe, Kyloe, Norham, Ord, Shoreswood.

Column 1	Column 2	Column 3
Name of court	Local authority areas	Parts comprising court districts
BEVERLEY	Beverley Municipal Borough.	Beverley.
	Beverley Rural District (part). *Other part* in Kingston upon Hull County Court District.	Beswick, Bishop Burton, Brantingham, Cherry Burton, Dalton Holme, Ellerker, Elloughton, Etton, Leconfield, Leven, Lockington, Lund, Molescroft, Newbald, Routh, Rowley, South Cave, Tickton, Walkington, Wawne, Woodmansey.
	Driffield Urban District.	Driffield.
	Driffield Rural District (part). *Other part* in Bridlington County Court District.	Bainton, Cottam, Fimber, Fridaythorpe, Garton, Hutton Cranswick, Kirkburn, Langtoft, Middleton, North Dalton, Skerne, Sledmere, Tibthorpe, Watton, Wetwang.
	Holderness Rural District (part). *Other parts* in Gt. Grimsby and Kingston-upon-Hull County Court Districts.	Atwick, Bewholme, Brandesburton, Catwick, Hatfield, Rise, Riston, Seaton, Sigglesthorne.
	Hornsea Urban District.	Hornsea.
	Howden Rural District (part). *Other parts* in Goole and York County Court Districts.	Hotham, North Cave.
	Norton Rural District (part). *Other parts* in Bridlington, Malton and Scarborough County Court Districts.	Luttons, Weaverthorpe.
	Pocklington Rural District (part). *Other part* in York County Court District.	Goodmanham, Londesborough, Market Weighton, Sancton, South Cliffe.
BIDEFORD	Barnstaple Rural District (part). *Other part* in Barnstaple County Court District.	Horwood, Instow, Westleigh.
	Bideford Municipal Borough.	Bideford.
	Bideford Rural District (part). *Other part* in Holsworthy County Court District.	Abbotsham, Alwington, Buckland Brewer, Bulkworthy, Clovelly, East Putford, Hartland, Landcross, Littleham, Lundy Island (Extra Parochial), Monkleigh, Newton St. Petrock, Parkham, Woolsery.

Column 1	*Column* 2	*Column* 3
Name of court	Local authority areas	Parts comprising court districts
BIDEFORD —*cont.*	Great Torrington Municipal Borough.	Great Torrington.
	Holsworthy Rural District (part). *Other parts* in Holsworthy and Launceston County Court Districts.	West Putford.
	Northam Urban District.	Northam.
	Torrington Rural District (part). *Other parts* in Barnstaple and Holsworthy County Court Districts.	Alverdiscott, Beaford, Dolton, Frithelstock, Huish, Huntshaw, Langtree, Little Torrington, Merton, Peters Marland, Petrockstow, St. Giles, Weare Giffard.
BIGGLES-WADE	Bedford Rural District (part). *Other parts* in Bedford and Wellingborough County Court Districts.	Little Barford, Roxton, Staploe.
	Biggleswade Urban District.	Biggleswade.
	Biggleswade Rural District.	Arlesey, Astwick, Blunham, Campton, Chicksands, Clifton, Cockayne Hatley, Dunton, Edworth, Everton, Eyeworth, Henlow, Langford, Meppershall, Mogerhanger, Northill, Old Warden, Potton, Shefford, Southill, Stotfold, Sutton, Tempsford, Upper Stondon, Wrestlingworth.
	Hitchin Rural District (part). *Other part* in Hitchin County Court District.	Hinxworth.
	St. Neots Rural District (part). *Other part* in Huntingdon County Court District.	Abbotsley, Great Gransden, Tetworth, Waresley.
	Sandy Urban District.	Sandy.
	South Cambridgeshire Rural District (part). *Other parts* in Cambridge, Hitchin and Newmarket County Court Districts.	Gamlingay, Hatley, Little Gransden, Tadlow.
BIRKEN-HEAD	Bebington Municipal Borough.	Bebington.
	Birkenhead County Borough.	Birkenhead.
	Hoylake Urban District.	Hoylake.

Column 1	Column 2	Column 3
Name of court	Local authority areas	Parts comprising court districts
BIRKEN-HEAD —*cont.*	Neston Urban District.	Neston.
	Wallasey County Borough.	Wallasey.
	Wirral Urban District.	Wirral.
BIRMING-HAM	Birmingham County Borough.	Birmingham.
	Bromsgrove Rural District (part). *Other parts* in Bromsgrove, Redditch and Stourbridge County Court Districts.	Wythall.
	Meriden Rural District (part). *Other parts* in Coventry, Nuneaton and Tamworth County Court Districts.	Barston, Bickenhill, Castle Bromwich, Coleshill, Curdworth, Hampton in Arden, Kingshurst, Lea Marston, Maxstoke, Nether Whitacre, Over Whitacre, Shustoke, Water Orton, Wishaw.
	Solihull County Borough.	Solihull.
	Stratford on Avon Rural District (part). *Other parts* in Stratford-on-Avon and Warwick County Court Districts.	Hockley Heath, Tanworth.
	Sutton Coldfield Municipal Borough.	Sutton Coldfield.
BISHOP AUCK-LAND	Barnard Castle Rural District (part). *Other part* in Darlington County Court District.	Bolam, Cockfield, Eggleston, Etherley, Evenwood and Barony, Forest and Frith, Hamsterley, Hilton, Langleydale and Shotton, Lynesack and Softley, Marwood, Middleton in Teesdale, Morton Tinmouth, Newbiggin, Raby with Keverstone, Staindrop, Streatlam and Stainton, South Bedburn, Wackerfield, Woodland, Undivided Moor Common to Hamsterley, Lynesack and Softley and South Bedburn Civil Parishes.
	Barnard Castle Urban District.	Barnard Castle.
	Bishop Auckland Urban District.	Bishop Auckland.
	Crook and Willington Urban District.	Crook and Willington.

Column 1	*Column 2*	*Column 3*
Name of court	Local authority areas	Parts comprising court districts
BISHOP AUCK-LAND —*cont.*	Sedgefield Rural District (part). *Other parts* in Darlington, Durham and Stockton on Tees County Court Districts.	Windlestone, Woodham.
	Shildon Urban District.	Shildon.
	Spennymoor Urban District.	Spennymoor.
	Startforth Rural District (part). *Other part* in Darlington County Court District.	Boldron, Bowes, Cotherstone, Egglestone Abbey, Holwick, / Hunderthwaite, Lartington, Lunedale, Mickleton, Romaldkirk, Startforth.
	Tow Law Urban District.	Tow Law.
	Weardale Rural District (part). *Other part* in Consett County Court District.	Stanhope, Wolsingham, Wolsingham Park Moor, common to parts of Stanhope and Wolsingham civil parishes and to Tow Law Urban District.
BISHOP'S STORT-FORD	Bishop's Stortford Urban District.	Bishop's Stortford.
	Braughing Rural District (part). *Other parts* in Hitchin and Hertford County Court Dis-Districts.	Albury, Anstey, Braughing, Brent Pelham, Furneux Pelham, / High Wych, Little Hadham, Meesden, Much Hadham, Stocking Pelham, Thorley.
	Dunmow Rural District (part). *Other parts* in Braintree, Chelmsford and Harlow County Court Districts.	Great Hallingbury, Hatfield Broad Oak, / Little Hallingbury, Takeley.
	Saffron Walden Municipal Borough.	Saffron Walden.
	Saffron Walden Rural District (part). *Other part* in Cambridge County Court District.	Arkesden, Berden, Birchanger, Chrishall, Clavering, Debden, Elmdon, Elsenham, Farnham, Great Sampford, Hempstead, Henham, Langley, Littlebury, Little Sampford, / Manuden, Newport, Quendon and Rickling, Radwinter, Stansted Mountfichet, Strethall, Ugley, Wenden Lofts, Wendens Ambo, Wicken Bonhunt, Widdington, Wimbish.
	Sawbridgeworth Urban District.	Sawbridgeworth.

Column 1	Column 2	Column 3
Name of court	Local authority areas	Parts comprising court districts
BLACK-BURN	Blackburn County Borough.	Blackburn.
	Blackburn Rural District.	Balderstone, Pleasington, Billington, Ramsgreave, Clayton le Dale, Salesbury, Dinckley, Tockholes, Eccleshill, Wilpshire, Livesey, Yate and Mellor, Pickup Bank. Osbaldeston,
	Bowland Rural District (part). *Other part* in Preston County Court District.	Bashall Eaves, Horton, Bolton by Middop, Bowland, Newsholme, Bowland Newton, Forest Low, Paythorne, Easington, Rimington, Gisburn, Sawley, Gisburn Forest, Slaidburn, Great Mitton, Waddington, Grindleton, West Bradford.
	Clitheroe Municipal Borough.	Clitheroe.
	Clitheroe Rural District (part). *Other part* in Preston County Court District.	Aighton, Mearley, Bailey and Pendleton, Chaigley, Twiston, Chatburn, Whalley, Downham, Wiswell, Little Mitton, Worston.
	Darwen Municipal Borough	Darwen.
	Great Harwood Urban District.	Great Harwood.
	Rishton Urban District.	Rishton.
BLACK-POOL	Blackpool County Borough.	Blackpool.
	Fleetwood Municipal Borough.	Fleetwood.
	Fylde Rural District (part). *Other part* in Preston County Court District.	Little Eccleston Weeton with Larbreck, with Preese, Singleton, Westby with Staining, Plumptons.
	Garstang Rural District (part). *Other parts* in Lancaster and Preston County Court Districts.	Hambleton, Stalmine with Out Rawcliffe, Staynall. Pilling.
	Lytham St. Anne's Municipal Borough.	Lytham St. Anne's.
	Poulton le Fylde Urban District.	Poulton le Fylde.
	Preesall Urban District.	Preesall.
	Thornton Cleveleys Urban District.	Thornton Cleveleys.

Column 1	*Column* 2	*Column* 3
Name of court	Local authority areas	Parts comprising court districts
BLACK-WOOD, TREDEGAR AND ABER-TILLERY	Abercarn Urban District.	Abercarn
	Abertillery Urban District.	Abertillery.
	Bedwas and Machen Urban District (part). *Other part* in Newport (Mon.) County Court District.	That part which lies to the north of a line drawn from the junction of the civil parishes of Mynyddislwn, Machen Upper and Bedwas to the point on the River Rhymney where it was crossed by the Llanbradach Viaduct.
	Bedwellty Urban District.	Bedwellty.
	Brynmawr Urban District.	Brynmawr.
	Ebbw Vale Urban District.	Ebbw Vale.
	Mynyddislwyn Urban District.	Mynyddislwyn.
	Nantyglo and Blaina Urban District.	Nantyglo and Blaina.
	Rhymney Urban District.	Rhymney.
	Tredegar Urban District.	Tredegar.
BLETCH-LEY AND LEIGHTON BUZZARD	Ampthill Rural District (part). *Other parts* in Bedford, Hitchin and Luton County Court Districts.	Aspley Guise, Husborne Aspley Heath, Crawley, Battlesden, Milton Bryan, Hulcote and Potsgrove, Salford, Woburn.
	Bletchley Urban District.	Bletchley.
	Buckingham Rural District (part). *Other parts* in Aylesbury, Banbury, Northampton and Oxford County Court Districts.	Beachampton, Thornborough, Foscott, Thornton. Leckhampstead,
	Leighton-Linslade Urban District.	Leighton-Linslade.
	Luton Rural District (part). *Other part* in Luton County Court District.	Billington, Hockliffe, Eaton Bray, Stanbridge, Egginton, Tilsworth. Heath and Reach,
	Newport Pagnell Urban District.	Newport Pagnell.
	Newport Pagnell Rural District (part). *Other parts* in Bedford and Northampton County Court Districts.	Bow Brickhill, Moulsoe, Bradwell, North Crawley, Bradwell Abbey, Shenley Broughton, Church End, Castlethorpe, Sherington, Chicheley, Stantonbury, Gayhurst, Tyringham and Great Linford, Filgrave, Haversham cum Walton, Little Linford, Wavendon, Lathbury, Woburn Sands, Little Brickhill, Woolstone cum Loughton, Willen, Milton Keynes, Woughton.

Column 1	Column 2	Column 3
Name of court	Local authority areas	Parts comprising court districts
BLETCH-LEY AND LEIGHTON BUZZARD —cont.	Wing Rural District (part). *Other part* in Aylesbury County Court District.	Cheddington, Edlesborough, Great Brickhill, Grove, Ivinghoe and Ivinghoe Aston, Mentmore, Slapton, Soulbury, Stoke Hammond, Wing.
	Winslow Rural District (part). *Other part* in Aylesbury County Court District.	Drayton Parslow, Great Horwood, Little Horwood, Mursley, Nash, Newton Longville, Shenley Brook End, Stewkley, Tattenhoe, Whaddon.
	Wolverton Urban District.	Wolverton.
BLOOMS-BURY AND MARYLE-BONE	London Borough of Camden (part). *Other parts* in Clerkenwell and Westminster County Court Districts.	The whole of the Borough except that part south and east of a line drawn from the point where the Borough boundary crosses the junction of Tottenham Court Road and New Oxford Street, eastwards along the middle of New Oxford Street, north-wards along the middle of Southampton Row, Woburn Place and Upper Woburn Place to Euston Road and eastwards along the middle of Euston Road to the Borough boundary at King's Cross.
	London Borough of Kensington and Chelsea (part). *Other part* in West London County Court District.	That part of the Borough north of a line drawn from the point where the Borough boundary crosses the eastern end of the Uxbridge Road along the middle of Holland Park Avenue and Notting Hill to the point where the Borough boundary crosses the middle of Bayswater Road.
	London Borough of the City of Westminster (part). *Other parts* in West London and Westminster County Court Districts.	That part of the Borough to the north of a line drawn from the point where the Borough boundary crosses Bayswater Road eastward along the middle of Bayswater Road and Oxford Street to the Borough boundary.
BLYTH	Bedlingtonshire Urban District.	Bedlington.
	Blyth Municipal Borough.	Blyth.
BODMIN	Bodmin Municipal Borough.	Bodmin.
	Liskeard Rural District (part). *Other part* in Liskeard County Court District.	St. Winnow, Warleggan.

Column 1	Column 2	Column 3
Name of court	Local authority areas	Parts comprising court districts
BODMIN —cont.	St. Austell Rural District (part). *Other parts* in Newquay and St. Austell County Court Districts.	Lanlivery, Luxulyan, Lostwithiel Rural St. Wenn. Borough,
	Wadebridge and Padstow Rural District (part). *Other parts* in Camelford and Newquay County Court Districts.	Blisland, St. Mabyn, Cardinham, St. Merryn, Egloshayle, St. Minver Helland, Highlands, Lanhydrock, St. Minver Lanivet, Lowlands, Padstow, Wadebridge, St. Breock, Withiel. St. Issey,
BOLTON	Bolton County Borough.	Bolton.
	Farnworth Municipal Borough.	Farnworth.
	Horwich Urban District.	Horwich.
	Kearsley Urban District.	Kearsley.
	Little Lever Urban District.	Little Lever.
	Turton Urban District.	Turton
	Westhoughton Urban District.	Westhoughton.
BOSTON	Boston Municipal Borough.	Boston.
	Boston Rural District.	Algarkirk, Kirton Amber Hill, Leverton, Benington, Old Leake, Bicker, Pelham's Brothertoft, Lands, Butterwick, Sutterton, Fishtoft, Swineshead, Fosdyke, Wigtoft, Frampton, Wrangle, Freiston, Wyberton. Hart's Grounds,
	Horncastle Rural District (part). *Other parts* in Lincoln, Louth and Skegness and Spilsby County Court Districts.	Claxby Scrivelsby, Pluckacre, Tattershall, Coningsby, Tattershall Haltham, Thorpe, Mareham le Fen, Tumby, Miningsby, Wildmore, Moorby, Wood Enderby. Revesby,
	Spilsby Rural District (part). *Other part* in Skegness and Spilsby County Court District.	Carrington, Sibsey, Eastville, Stickford, Frithville, Stickney, Langriville, Thornton le Fen, Midville, West Fen, New Leake, Westville.

Column 1	Column 2	Column 3
Name of court	Local authority areas	Parts comprising court districts
BOURNE-MOUTH	Bournemouth County Borough.	Bournemouth.
	Christchurch Municipal Borough.	Christchurch.
	Ringwood and Fordingbridge Rural District (part). *Other part* in Salisbury County Court District.	Burley, Ringwood, Christchurch St. Leonards and East, St. Ives, Ellingham, Sopley. Hurn,
BOW	Chigwell Urban District (part). *Other parts* in Ilford and Edmonton County Court Districts.	The Buckhurst Hill Ward.
	London Borough of Newham.	Newham.
	London Borough of Redbridge (part). *Other part* in Ilford County Court District.	That part of the Borough west of a line commencing where Manor Road crosses the northern boundary, thence south-westwards to the east of Dr. Barnado's Homes and Roding Lane North to Southend Road, thence south-westwards to the River Roding and southwards along the River to the Borough boundary.
	London Borough of Tower Hamlets (part). *Other part* in Shoreditch County Court District.	That part of the Borough east of a line commencing in the River Thames approximately ¼ mile west of the entrance to the Regents Canal, running northwards along and including the west side of Butcher Row, eastwards and northwards along the south side of Cable Street and the east side of White Horse Road to its junction with Ben Jonson Road, thence eastwards along the south side of Ben Jonson Road, to the Regents Canal, northwards along the centre of the Regents Canal to the southernmost point of Victoria Park, north-eastwards along the north side of Old Ford Road until it rejoins the Canal and continuing in a north-easterly direction along the centre of the Canal to the River Lea, thence northwards along the River to the Borough boundary.
	London Borough of Waltham Forest (part). *Other part* in Edmonton County Court District.	That part of the Borough to the south of a line drawn from the point where the boundaries of the London Boroughs of Enfield, Haringey and Waltham Forest meet eastwards to the North Circular Road, along the south side of the North Circular Road across Chingford Road thence along the north side of Wadham Road, taking in the whole of Wadham Avenue, to Hale End

Column 1	*Column 2*	*Column 3*
Name of court	Local authority areas	Parts comprising court districts
BOW —*cont.*	London Borough of Waltham Forest (part). —*cont.*	Road, along the west side of Hale End Road to the River Ching thence northwards along the River to the Avenue, along the south side of The Avenue and the west side of Chingford Lane to the Borough boundary.
BRADFORD	Baildon Urban District.	Baildon.
	Bradford County Borough.	Bradford.
	Denholme Urban District.	Denholme.
	Pudsey Municipal Borough.	Pudsey.
	Shipley Urban District.	Shipley.
BRAIN- TREE	Braintree Rural District (part). *Other part* in Chelmsford County Court District.	Bardfield Saling, Black Notley, Bradwell, Coggeshall, Cressing, Fairstead, Faulkbourne, Feering, Finchingfield, Great Bardfield, Great Saling, Kelvedon, Panfield, Rayne, Shalford, Stisted, Wethersfield, White Notley.
	Braintree and Bocking Urban District.	Braintree and Bocking.
	Chelmsford Rural District (part). *Other parts* in Brentwood, Chelmsford and Maldon County Court Districts.	Great and Little Leighs.
	Dunmow Rural District (part). *Other parts* in Bishop Stortford, Chelmsford and Harlow County Court Districts.	Barnston, Broxted, Chickney, Felstead, Great Canfield, Great Dunmow, Great Easton, High Easter, Lindsell, Little Bardfield, Little Canfield, Little Dunmow, Little Easton, Stebbing, Thaxted, Tilty.
	Halstead Urban District.	Halstead Urban
	Halstead Rural District (part). *Other parts* in Cambridge, Colchester and Clacton and Sudbury County Court Districts.	Castle Hedingham, Gosfield, Great Maplestead, Greenstead Green and Halstead Rural, Little Maplestead, Pebmarsh, Sible Hedingham Stambourne, Toppesfield.
	Witham Urban District.	Witham.

Column 1	*Column* 2	*Column* 3
Name of court	Local authority areas	Parts comprising court districts
BRECK-NOCK	Brecon Municipal Borough.	Brecon.
	Brecknock Rural District.	Aberyscir, Llanfrynach, Battle, Llangasty Cantref, Tallyllyn, Cathedine, Llangorse, Cray, Llanhamlach, Garthbrengy, Llansantffraed, Glyn, Llanspyddid, Glyntawe, Llanywern, Llandetty, Maescar, Llanddew, Merthyr Cynog, Llandefaelog-fâch, Modrydd, Penpont, Llandefalle, St. David Llandeilo'r Fan, Without, Llanfigan, Senny, Llanfihangel-fechan, Talachddu, Traianglâs, Llanfihangel Traianmawr, Nant Brân, Trallong, Llanfihangel Vennyfâch, Talyllyn, Ysclydach. Llanfillo,
	Hay Urban District.	Hay Urban.
	Hay Rural District.	Aberllynfi, Llyswen, Bronllys, Pipton, Glynfâch, Talgarth, Hay Rural, Tregoyd and Llanelieu, Velindre. Llanigon,
	Painscastle Rural District (part). *Other part* in Builth County Court District.	Boughrood, Glasbury, Clyro, Llowes.
BRENT-FORD	London Borough of Ealing (part). *Other parts* in Uxbridge and Willesden County Court Districts.	The whole of the Borough except that part north of a line drawn from the point where the main line of British Railways, Western Region crosses the Borough boundary, westward along the middle of the railway to the junction with the North Acton and High Wycombe branch line thence along the middle of the branch line to the point where it meets the Boundary Borough south of Coronation Road and except that part south and west of a line drawn from the point where the Borough boundary crosses the Grand Union Canal near Balmoral Drive, northwards along the east bank of the Canal then eastwards along the south of Ruislip Road and southwards along the east of Allenby Road to Kings Avenue thence eastwards along the south of Kings Avenue across Greenford Road

Column 1	Column 2	Column 3
Name of court	Local authority areas	Parts comprising court districts
BRENT-FORD —*cont.*	London Borough of Ealing (part). —*cont.*	to the River Brent, southwards along the River to its confluence with the Grand Union Canal and southwards along the Canal to the Borough boundary.
	London Borough of Hounslow (part). *Other part* in Uxbridge County Court District.	That part of the Borough east of a line drawn from the point where the River Crane crosses the Bath Road, southwards along the River to the middle of the Great South West Road then westwards along the middle of that Road to the Borough boundary.
	London Borough of Richmond-upon-Thames (part). *Other parts* in Kingston-upon-Thames and Wandsworth County Court Districts.	The Central Twickenham, East Twickenham, Heathfield, South Twickenham, West Twickenham and Whitton Wards.
BRENT-WOOD	Basildon Urban District.	Basildon.
	Brentwood Urban District.	Brentwood.
	Chelmsford Rural District (part). *Other parts* in Braintree, Chelmsford and Maldon County Court Districts.	Mountnessing,
	Epping and Ongar Rural District (part). *Other parts* Chelmsford, Harlow and Ilford County Court Districts.	Blackmore, Navestock, Doddinghurst, Ongar, Fyfield, Stamford Rivers, Kelvedon Hatch, Stondon Massey.
	London Borough of Havering (part). *Other parts* in Grays Thurrock and Ilford County Court Districts.	That part of the borough east of a line drawn from where Nags Head Lane crosses the north eastern boundary, south along the west side of Nags Head Lane and Hall Lane to the Southend Arterial Road (A127), then east along the south side of the A127 to Warley Street, south along the west side of Warley Street to the Upminster-West Horndon Railway Line, then east along the north side of the Railway Line to the borough boundary.
BRIDGEND	Bridgend Urban District	Bridgend.
	Cowbridge Municipal Borough.	Cowbridge.
	Cowbridge Rural District (part). *Other part* in Pontypridd and Ystradfodwg County Court District.	Colwinston, Llanblethian, Eglwys Brewis, Llandow, Flemingston, Llanfair, Gileston, Llangan, Llanharan (except Pembroke Street, Thomastown and Ynysmardy Houses, near Llantrisant.

Column 1	Column 2	Column 3
Name of court	Local authority areas	Parts comprising court districts
BRIDGEND —cont.	Cowbridge Rural District (part). —cont.	Llanharry, Llanilid, Llanmaes, Llanmihangel, Llansannor, Llantwit Major, Llysworney, Marcross, Monknash, Nash, Penllyn, Peterston super Montem, St. Andrew's Minor, St. Athan, St. Donat's, St. Hilary, St. Mary Hill, Stembridge, Ystradowen.
	Maesteg Urban District.	Maesteg.
	Ogmore and Garw Urban District.	Ogmore and Garw.
	Penybont Rural District.	Coity Higher, Coychurch Higher, Coychurch Lower, Ewenny, Kenfig, Laleston, Llangynwyd Lower, Llangynwyd Middle, Merthyr Mawr Newcastle Higher, Pencoed, Pyle, St. Bride's Major, St. Bride's Minor, Sker, Tythegston Higher, Tythegston Lower, Wick, Ynysawdre.
	Porthcawl Urban District.	Porthcawl.
BRIDG- NORTH	Bridgnorth Rural District (part). Other parts in Kidderminster, Ludlow, Shrewsbury and Wellington County Court Districts.	Acton Round, Alveley, Astley Abbots, Aston Botterell, Aston Eyre, Barrow, Billingsley, Bridgnorth Rural Borough, Burwarton, Chelmarsh, Chetton, Claverley, Cleobury North, Deuxhill, Ditton Priors, Eardington, Glazeley, Middleton Scriven, Monkhopton, Morville, Much Wenlock Rural Borough, Neenton, Quatt Malvern, Romsley, Rudge, Shipton, Sidbury, Stanton Long, Stockton, Stottesdon, Sutton Maddock, Tasley, Upton Cressett, Worfield.
	Shifnal Rural District (part). Other parts in Wellington and Wolverhampton County Court Districts.	Badger, Beckbury, Ryton,

Column 1	Column 2	Column 3
Name of court	Local authority areas	Parts comprising court districts
BRIDG-WATER	Bridgwater Municipal Borough.	Bridgwater.
	Bridgwater Rural District.	Ashcott, Lyng, Bawdrip, Middlezoy, Bridgwater Moorlinch, Without, Nether Stowey, Broomfield, North Petherton, Cannington, Othery, Catcott, Otterhampton, Charlynch, Over Stowey, Chedzoy, Pawlett, Chilton Trinity, Puriton, Chilton Shapwick, Polden, Spaxton, Cossington, Stawell, Durleigh, Stockland East Huntspill, Bristol, Edington, Thurloxton, Enmore, West Huntspill, Fiddington, Wembdon, Goathurst, Westonzoyland, Greinton, Woolavington.
	Langport Rural District (part). *Other parts* in Axminster and Chard, Taunton, Wells and Yeovil County Court Districts.	Aller, High Ham.
	Williton Rural District (part). *Other part* in Minehead County Court District.	Stogursey.
BRIDLING-TON	Bridlington Municipal Borough.	Bridlington.
	Bridlington Rural District (part). *Other part* in Scarborough County Court District.	Barmston, Hunmanby, Bempton, Reighton, Boynton, Rudston, Burton Agnes, Skipsea, Burton Fleming, Thwing, Carnaby, Ulrome, Flamborough, Wold Newton. Grindale,
	Driffield Rural District (part). *Other part* in Beverley County Court District.	Beeford, Kilham, Foston, Nafferton, Harpham, North Kelk, Frodingham.
	Norton Rural District (part). *Other parts* in Beverley, Malton and Scarborough County Court Districts.	Foxholes.
BRIDPORT	Beaminster Rural District (part). *Other parts* in Axminster and Chard, Dorchester and Yeovil County Court Districts.	Beaminster, Netherbury, Bettiscombe, North Poorton, Broadwindsor, Pilsdon, Burstock, Powerstock, Hooke, Rampisham, Mapperton, Stoke Abbott. Marshwood,

Column 1	Column 2	Column 3
Name of court	Local authority areas	Parts comprising court districts
BRIDPORT —cont.	Bridport Municipal Borough.	Bridport.
	Bridport Rural District (part). *Other part* in Axminster and Chard County Court District.	Allington, Askerswell, Bothen- hampton, Bradpole, Burton Bradstock, Chideock, Chilcombe, Litton Cheney. Loders, Puncknowle, Shipton Gorge, Stanton St. Gabriel, Swyre, Symondsbury, Whitchurch Canonicorum.
BRIGHTON	Brighton County Borough.	Brighton.
	Chailey Rural District (part). *Other parts* in Haywards Heath and Lewes County Court Districts.	Falmer, Peacehaven.
	Chanctonbury Rural District (part) *Other parts* in Chichester and Worthing County Court Districts.	Ashurst, Bramber, Henfield, Shermanbury, Steyning, Upper Beeding, Woodmancote.
	Cuckfield Rural District (part). *Other parts* in East Grinstead and Haywards Heath County Court Districts.	Fulking, Newtimber, Poynings, Pyecombe.
	Hove Municipal Borough.	Hove.
	Portslade by Sea Urban District.	Portslade by Sea.
	Shoreham by Sea Urban District.	Shoreham by Sea.
	Southwick Urban District.	Southwick.
BRISTOL	Axbridge Rural District (part). *Other parts* in Wells and Weston super Mare County Court Districts.	Butcombe.
	Bathavon Rural District (part). *Other part* in Bath County Court District.	Camerton, Whitchurch.
	Bristol County Borough.	Bristol.
	Clutton Rural District (part). *Other part* in Wells County Court District.	Cameley, Chelwood, Chew Magna, Chew Stoke, Clutton, Compton Martin, Farmborough, High Littleton, Hinton Blewett, Nempnett Thrubwell, Norton Malreward, Paulton, Publow, Stanton Drew, Stowey-Sutton, Timsbury.

Column 1	*Column* 2	*Column* 3
Name of court	Local authority areas	Parts comprising court districts
BRISTOL —*cont.*	Keynsham Urban District.	Keynsham.
	Kingswood Urban District.	Kingswood.
	Long Ashton Rural District (part). *Other part* in Weston super Mare County Court District.	Abbots Leigh, Backwell, Barrow Gurney, Brockley, Clapton in Gordano, Dundry, Easton in Gordano, Flax Bourton, Long Ashton, Nailsea, North Weston, Portbury, Tickenham, Winford, Wraxall.
	Mangotsfield Urban District.	Mangotsfield.
	Portishead Urban District.	Portishead.
	Sodbury Rural District (part). *Other part* in Bath County Court District.	Acton Turville, Alderley, Badminton, Dodington, Doynton, Dyrham and Hinton, Filton, Frampton Cotterell, Hawkesbury, Horton, Iron Acton, Little Sodbury, Pucklechurch, Sodbury, Stoke Gifford, Tormarton, Westerleigh, Wick and Abson, Wickwar, Winterbourne, Yate.
	Warmley Rural District.	Bitton, Hanham Abbots, Mangotsfield Rural, Oldland, Siston.
BROMLEY	London Borough of Bexley (part). *Other part* in Dartford County Court District.	That part of the Borough which lies south and west of a line drawn from the point where the Dartford Loop line of the Southern Region crosses the Borough boundary east of New Eltham station, along the railway line to a point east of Albany Park station in line with the east side of Betterton Drive thence south-eastwards along the east side of Betterton Drive and Water Lane across North Cray Road to the north of Bunker's Hill then east of Cocksure Lane and Parsonage Lane to the Borough boundary.
	London Borough of Bromley (part). *Other part* in Croydon County Court District.	That part of the Borough east of a line drawn from the point where the Borough boundary crosses the Southern Region railway line between Sydenham station and Crystal Palace station, southward along the railway line to Trinity Road then along the middle of Trinity Road, Lennard Road, Parish

Column 1	Column 2	Column 3
Name of court	Local authority areas	Parts comprising court districts
BROMLEY —*cont*.	London Borough of Bromley (part). —*cont*.	Lane, Kent House Road, Beckenham Road, Ravenscourt Road, Elmers End Road and Marlow Road to the Borough boundary.
	London Borough of Lewisham (part). *Other parts* in Lambeth and Southwark County Court Districts.	The whole of the Borough except that part lying to the west of the Southern Region railway line running through Honor Oak, Forest Hill and Sydenham stations and except that part to the north of a line drawn from the point where the Borough boundary crosses Old Kent Road eastwards along the middle of New Cross Road to the point where the Borough boundary crosses the middle of Deptford Bridge.
BROMS- GROVE	Bromsgrove Urban District.	Bromsgrove.
	Bromsgrove Rural District (part). *Other parts* in Birmingham, Redditch and Stourbridge County Court Districts.	Belbroughton, Cofton Hackett, Dodford with Grafton, Franklev, Hunnington, Romsley, Stoke Prior.
	Droitwich Rural District (part). *Other parts* in Kidderminster, Redditch and Worcester County Court Districts.	Dodderhill, Elmbridge, Hampton Lovett, Hanbury, Upton Warren.
BUILTH	Builth Rural District (part). *Other part* in Llandrindod Wells County Court District.	Alltmawr, Crickadarn, Gwarafog, Gwenddwr, Llanafanfawr, Llanafanfechan, Llanddewi Abergwesyn, Llanddewi'r Cwm, Llandulas, Llanfihangel Abergwesyn, Llanfihangel Bryn Pabuan, Llanganten, Llangynog, Llanlleonfel, Llanwrtyd Without, Llanynis, Llysdinam, Maesmynis, Penbuallt, Rhosferig, Treflis.
	Builth Wells Urban District.	Builth Wells.
	Colwyn Rural District (part). *Other part* in Llandrindod Wells County Court District.	Aberedw, Bettws Disserth, Cregrina, Disserth and Trecoed, Llanbadarn y Garreg, Llanelwedd, Llanfaredd, Llansaintfraed in Elvel, Rhulen.
	Llanwrtyd Wells Urban District.	Llanwrtyd Wells.
	New Radnor Rural District (part). *Other parts* in Kington and Llandrindod Wells County Court Districts.	Glascwm.

Column 1	Column 2	Column 3
Name of court	Local authority areas	Parts comprising court districts
BUILTH —cont.	Painscastle Rural District (part). *Other part* in Brecknock County Court District.	Bryngwyn, Llandeilo Llanbedr Graban, Painscastle, Llanstephan. Llandde- wifâch,
BURNLEY	Burnley County Borough.	Burnley.
	Burnley Rural District (part). *Other parts* in Accrington and Nelson County Court Districts.	Briercliffe, Northtown, Cliviger, Read, Dunnockshaw, Reedley Habergham Hallows, Eaves, Sabden, Hapton, Simonstone, Higham Worsthorne with West with Close Booth, Hurstwood. Ightenhill,
	Padiham Urban District.	Padiham.
BURTON UPON TRENT	Burton upon Trent County Borough.	Burton upon Trent.
	Repton Rural District (part). *Other parts* in Ashby de la Zouch and Derby County Court Districts	Barton Blount, Hatton, Bretby, Hilton, Caldwell, Hoon, Castle Gresley, Linton, Catton, Lullington, Church Marston Broughton, on Dove, Coton in the Newton Elms, Solney, Drakelow, Repton, Egginton, Rosliston, Foston and Walton Scropton, upon Trent.
	Swadlincote Urban District.	Swadlincote.
	Tutbury Rural District (part). *Other part* in Lichfield County Court District.	Anslow, Outwards, Barton under Rolleston, Needwood, Stretton, Branston, Tatenhill, Dunstall, Tutbury, Hanbury, Wychnor.
BURY	Bury County Borough.	Bury.
	Heywood Municipal Borough.	Heywood.
	Radcliffe Municipal Borough.	Radcliffe.
	Ramsbottom Urban District.	Ramsbottom.
	Tottington Urban District.	Tottington.
	Whitefield Urban District.	Whitefield.

Column 1	Column 2	Column 3
Name of court	Local authority areas	Parts comprising court districts
BURY ST. EDMUNDS	Bury St. Edmunds Municipal Borough.	Bury St. Edmunds.
	Clare Rural District (part). *Other parts* in Cambridge, Newmarket and Sudbury County Court Districts.	Barnardiston, Denston, Depden, Hawkedon, Hundon, — Monks Risbridge, Stansfield, Wickhambrook.
	Cosford Rural District (part). *Other parts* in Ipswich, Stowmarket and Sudbury County Court Districts.	Cockfield, Thorpe Morieux.
	Melford Rural District (part). *Other parts* in Colchester and Clacton and Sudbury County Court Districts.	Lawshall.
	Mildenhall Rural District (part). *Other parts* in Newmarket and Thetford County Court Districts.	Barton Mills, Cavenham, Eriswell, Icklingham, — Lakenheath, Mildenhall, Tuddenham.
	Thedwastre Rural District (part). *Other part* in Stowmarket County Court District.	Badwell Ash, Beyton, Great Ashfield, Hessett, Hinderclay, Hunston, Langham, — Norton, Rickinghall Inferior, Stowlangtoft, Thurston, Walsham le Willows, Wattisfield.
	Thingoe Rural District (part). *Other part* in Thetford County Court District.	Ampton, Bardwell, Barrow, Bradfield Combust, Bradfield St. Clare, Bradfield St. George, Brockley, Chedburgh, Chevington, Culford, Denham, Flempton, Fornham All Saints, Fornham St. Genevieve, Fornham St. Martin, Great Barton, Great Livermere, Great Saxham, Great Welnetham, Hardwick, — Hargrave, Hawstead, Hengrave, Horringer, Ickworth, Ingham, Ixworth, Ixworth Thorpe, Lackford, Little Livermere, Little Saxham, Little Welnetham, Nowton, Pakenham, Rede, Risby, Rougham, Rushbrooke, Stanningfield, Stanton, Timworth, Troston, Westley, West Stow, Whepstead, Wordwell.

Column 1	Column 2	Column 3
Name of court	Local authority areas	Parts comprising court districts
BUXTON	Ashbourne Rural District (part). *Other parts* in Derby, Matlock and Uttoxeter County Court Districts.	Hartington Nether Quarter, Hartington Town Quarter.
	Bakewell Rural District (part). *Other parts* in Chesterfield, Matlock and Sheffield County County Court Districts.	Abney and Abney Grange, Ashford, Blackwell, Bradwell, Brushfield, Chelmorton, Eyam, Flagg, Foolow, Great Hucklow, Great Longstone, Grindlow, Hartington Middle Quarter, — Hazlebadge, Highlow, Little Blackwell Hucklow, Little Longstone, Litton, Monyash, Offerton, Rowland, Sheldon, Stony Middleton, Taddington, Tideswell, Wardlow, Wheston.
	Buxton Municipal Borough.	Buxton.
	Chapel en le Frith Rural District (part). *Other parts* in Hyde and Sheffield County Court Districts.	Aston, Bamford, Brough and Shatton, Castleton, Chapel en le Frith, Chinley, Buxworth and Brownside, — Edale, Green Fairfield, Hartington Upper Quarter, Hayfield, Hope, King Sterndale, Peak Forest, Thornhill, Wormhill.
	Leek Rural District (part). *Other parts* in Stoke on Trent and Leek County Court Districts.	Alstonefield, Quarnford.
	Macclesfield Rural District (part). *Other parts* in Congleton and Macclesfield County Court Districts.	Kettleshulme.
	New Mills Urban District.	New Mills.
	Whaley Bridge Urban District.	Whaley Bridge.
CAERNAR- VON	Caernarvon Municipal Borough.	Caernarvon.
	Gwyrfai Rural District (part). *Other part* in Portmadoc County Court District.	Bettws Garmon, Clynnog, Llanberis, Llanddeniolen, Llandwrog, Llanfaglan, Llanfair is Gaer, Llanllyfni, Llanrûg, Llanwnda, Waenfawr.

Column 1	Column 2	Column 3	
Name of court	Local authority areas	Parts comprising court districts	
CAER-PHILLY	Caerphilly Urban District.	Caerphilly.	
	Cardiff Rural District (part). *Other parts* in Barry, Cardiff and Newport (Mon.) County Court Districts.	Rudry,	Van.
CAM-BRIDGE	Cambridge Municipal Borough.	Cambridge.	
	Chesterton Rural District (part). *Other part* in Huntingdon County Court District.	Bar Hill, Barton, Bourn, Boxworth, Caldecote, Caxton, Childerley, Comberton, Coton, Cottenham, Dry Drayton, Elsworth, Fen Ditton, Fulbourn, Girton, Grantchester, Great Shelford, Great Wilbraham, Hardwick, Harlton, Harston, Haslingfield,	Hauxton, Histon, Horningsea, Impington, Knapwell, Landbeach, Little Shelford, Little Wilbraham, Lolworth, Longstanton, Madingley, Milton, Newton, Oakington, Rampton, Stapleford, Stow cum Quy, Teversham, Toft, Waterbeach, Westwick, Willingham.
	Clare Rural District (part). *Other parts* in Bury St. Edmunds Newmarket and Sudbury County Court Districts.	Withersfield.	
	Haverhill Urban District.	Haverhill.	
	Halstead Rural District (part). *Other parts* in Braintree, Colchester and Clacton and Sudbury County Court Districts.	Helions Bumpstead,	Steeple Bumpstead.
	Newmarket Rural District (part). *Other parts* in Ely and Newmarket County Court Districts.	Bottisham,	Lode.
	Saffron Walden Rural District (part). *Other part* in Bishops Stortford County Court District.	Ashdon, Great Chesterford,	Hadstock, Little Chesterford.
	South Cambridgeshire Rural District (part). *Other parts* in Biggleswade, Hitchin and Newmarket County Court Districts.	Arrington, Babraham, Balsham, Barrington, Bartlow,	Bassingbourne cum Kneesworth, Castle Camps, Croydon, Duxford,

Column 1	*Column* 2	*Column* 3
Name of court	Local authority areas	Parts comprising court districts
CAM-BRIDGE —*cont.*	South Cambridgeshire Rural District (part). —*cont.*	Fowlmere, Foxton, Great Abington, Great and Little Chishill, Great Eversden, Heydon, Hildersham, Hinxton, Horseheath, Ickleton, Kingston, Linton, Little Abington, Little Eversden, / Longstowe, Melbourn, Meldreth, Orwell, Pampisford, Sawston, Shepreth, Shingay cum Wendy, Shudy Camps, Thriplow, West Wickham, Whaddon, Whittlesford, Wimpole.
CAMEL-FORD	Camelford Rural District.	Advent, Camelford, Davidstow, Forrabury and Minster, Lesnewth, Michaelstow, / Otterham, St. Breward, St. Clether, St. Juliot, St. Teath, Tintagel, Travalga.
	Stratton Rural District (part). *Other part* in Holsworthy County Court District.	Jacobstow, / St. Genny's.
	Wadebridge and Padstow Rural District (part). *Other parts* in Bodmin and Newquay County Court Districts.	St. Endellion, St. Kew, / St. Tudy.
CANTER-BURY	Bridge Blean Rural District.	Adisham, Barham, Bekesbourne, Bishopsbourne, Bridge, Chartham, Chislet, Fordwich, Hackington, Harbledown, Hoath, Ickham and Well, Kingston, Littlebourne, / Lower Hardres, Patrixbourne, Petham, St. Cosmus and St. Damian in the Blean, Sturry, Thanington Without, Upper Hardres, Waltham, Westbere, Wickhambreaux, Womenswold.
	Canterbury County Borough.	Canterbury.
	East Ashford Rural District (part). *Other part* in Ashford County Court District.	Chilham.
	Eastry Rural District (part). *Other parts* in Deal, Dover, Margate and Ramsgate County Court Districts.	Aylesham, Goodnestone, Nonington, / Preston, Stourmouth, Wingham.

Column 1	Column 2	Column 3
Name of court	Local authority areas	Parts comprising court districts
CANTER-BURY —*cont.*	Faversham Municipal Borough.	Faversham.
	Herne Bay Urban District.	Herne Bay.
	Swale Rural District (part). *Other part* in Sittingbourne County Court District.	Badlesmere, Boughton under Blean, Dunkirk, Faversham Without, Goodnestone, Graveney, Hernhill, Leaveland, Oare, Ospringe, Selling, Sheldwich.
	Whitstable Urban District.	Whitstable.
CARDIFF	Cardiff County Borough.	Cardiff.
	Cardiff Rural District (part). *Other parts* in Barry, Caerphilly and Newport (Mon.) County Court Districts.	Leckwith, Lisvane, Llanedeyrn, Llanilterne, Llanvedw, Michaelston le Pit, Pendoylan, Pentyrch, Peterston super Ely, Radyr, St. Bride's super Ely, St. Fagans, St. George's, Tongwynlais, Welsh St. Donats.
	Magor and St. Mellons Rural District (part). *Other part* in Newport (Mon.) County Court District.	St. Mellons.
	Penarth Urban District.	Penarth.
CARDIGAN	Aberaeon Rural District (part). *Other parts* in Aberystwyth and Lampeter County Court Districts.	Llandisiliogogo.
	Cardigan Municipal Borough.	Cardigan.
	Cemaes Rural District.	Bayvil, Bridell, Capel Colman, Castellan, Cilgerran, Clydey, Dinas, Eglwyswrw, Llanfair, Nant Gwyn, Llanfihangel Penbedw, Llanfyrnach, Llantood, Llanychlwydog, Manordeifi, Meline, Monington, Moylgrove, Nevern, Newport, Penrydd, St. Dogmaels Rural, West Cilrdedyn, Whitechurch.
	Newcastle Emlyn Urban District.	Newcastle Emlyn.
	Newcastle Emlyn Rural District (part). *Other parts* in Carmarthen and Lampeter County Court Districts.	Cenarth.

Column 1	Column 2	Column 3
Name of court	Local authority areas	Parts comprising court districts
CARDIGAN —cont.	Teifiside Rural District (part). *Other parts* in Aberystwyth and Lampeter County Court Districts.	Aberporth, Llangoedmore, Bettws Evan, Llangynllo, Brongwyn, Orllwyn Teifi, Cardigan Island Penbryn, (Extra Parochial), Troedyraur, Llandyfriog, Verwig. Llandygwydd,
CARLISLE	Alston with Garrigill Rural District.	Alston with Garrigill.
	Border Rural District.	Arthuret, Kingwater, Askerton, Kirkandrews, Beaumont, Kirklinton, Bewcastle, Midgeholme, Brampton, Nether Denton, Burgh by Sands, Nicholforest, Burtholme, Orton, Carlatton, Rockcliffe, Castle Carrock, St. Cuthbert Cummersdale, Without, Cumrew, Scaleby, Cumwhitton, Solport, Dalston, Stanwix Rural, Farlam, Stapleton, Geltsdale, Upper Denton, Hayton, Walton, Hethersgill, Waterhead, Irthington, Westlinton, Kingmoor, Wetheral.
	Carlisle County Borough.	Carlisle.
	Haltwhistle Rural District. (part). *Other part* in Hexham County Court District.	Hartleyburn, Knaresdale with Kirkhaigh.
	Wigton Rural District,	Aikton, Ireby, Allhallows, Kirkbampton, Allonby, Kirkbride, Aspatria, Sebergham, Blennerhasset Silloth, and Thursby, Torpenhow, Waverton, Boltons, Westnewton, Bowness, Westward, Bromfield, Wigton, Caldbeck, Woodside, Dundraw, Skinburness Hayton and Marsh Mealo, (common to Holme Abbey, Holme Low, Holme Holme St. East Waver, Cuthbert and Holme Low, Holme Abbey Holme civil parishes). St. Cuthbert,

Column 1	Column 2	Column 3
Name of court	Local authority areas	Parts comprising court districts
CARMAR-THEN	Carmarthen Municipal Borough	Carmarthen.
	Carmarthen Rural District (part). *Other parts* in Haverfordwest, and Llanelli County Court Districts.	Abergwili, Abernant, Conwil Elvet, Laugharne Town, Llanarthney, Llanddarog, Llanddowror, Llandefeilog, Llangain, Llangendeirne (part)—the part of the civil parish to the north of the River Gwen-draethfawr, / Llangunnor, Llangynin, Llangynog, Llanllawddog, Llanpumsaint, Llanstephan, Llanwinio, Mydrim, Newchurch, St. Clears, St. Ishmael, Trelech a'r Bettws.
	Llandeilo Rural District (part). *Other parts* in Ammanford, Lampeter and Llandovery County Court Districts.	Llanegwad, Llanfynydd, / Llangathen.
	Newcastle Emlyn Rural District (part). *Other parts* in Lampeter and Cardigan County Court Districts.	Llanfihangel Rhosycorn (part)—the part of the civil parish west of the Afon Marlais from its junction with the civil parish boundary south of the Allt Lawr to its junction with the southern boundary of the civil parish, / Llanfihangel ar Arth, Llangeler.
CHELMS-FORD	Braintree Rural District (part). *Other part* in Braintree County Court District.	Hatfield Peverel, Terling.
	Chelmsford Municipal Borough.	Chelmsford.
	Chelmsford Rural District (part). *Other parts* in Braintree, Brentwood and Maldon County Court Districts.	Boreham, Broomfield, Chignall, Danbury, East Hanningfield, Good Easter, Great Baddow, Great Waltham, Highwood, Ingatestone and Fryerning, Little Baddow, / Little Waltham, Margaretting, Mashbury, Pleshey, Rettendon, Roxwell, Runwell, Sandon, South Hanningfield, Springfield, Stock, West Hanningfield, Writtle.
	Dunmow Rural District (part). *Other parts* in Bishop's Stortford, Braintree and Harlow County Court Districts.	Aythorpe Roding, High Roding, / Leaden Roding, Margaret Roding.

Column 1	Column 2	Column 3
Name of court	Local authority areas	Parts comprising court districts
CHELMS-FORD —cont.	Epping and Ongar Rural District (part). *Other parts* in Harlow, Brentwood and Ilford County Court Districts.	Abbess, Beauchamp and Berners Roding, High Ongar, Willingale.
CHELTEN-HAM	Charlton Kings Urban District.	Charlton Kings.
	Cheltenham Municipal Borough.	Cheltenham.
	Cheltenham Rural District.	Alderton, Ashchurch, Badgeworth, Bishop's Cleeve, Boddington, Buckland, Coberley, Cowley, Deerhurst, Dumbleton, Elmstone Hardwicke, Gotherington, Great Witcombe, Hawling, Leckhampton, Leigh, Oxenton, Prescott, — Prestbury, Shurdington, Snowshill, Southam, Stanton, Stanway, Staverton, Stoke Orchard, Sudeley, Swindon, Teddington, Toddington, Twyning, Uckington, Up Hatherley, Walton Cardiff, Winchcombe, Woodmancote.
	Evesham Rural District (part). *Other parts* in Eversham and Redditch County Court Districts.	Beckford.
	Gloucester Rural District (part). *Other parts* in Dursley, Gloucester and Stroud County Districts.	Forthampton.
	North Cotswold Rural District (part). *Other part* in Evesham County Court District.	Adlestrop, Bledington, Bourton on The Water, Broadwell, Clapton, Condicote and Longborough, Cutsdean, Donnington, Evenlode, Great Rissington, Guiting Power, — Icombe and Westcote, Little Rissington, Lower Slaughter Maugersbury, Naunton, Oddington, Stow on the Wold, Swell, Temple Guiting, Upper Slaughter, Wyck Rissington.
	Northleach Rural District (part). *Other part* in Cirencester County Court District.	Aldsworth, Andoversford Aston Blank, Barrington, Compton Abdale, — Dowdeswell, Farmington, Hampnett, Hazleton, Northleach with Eastington,

Column 1 Name of court	Column 2 Local authority areas	Column 3 Parts comprising court districts	
CHELTEN-HAM —cont.	Northleach Rural District (part). —cont.	Notgrove, Sevenhampton, Sherborne, Shipton, Turkdean,	Whittington, Windrush, Withington, Yanworth.
	Pershore Rural District (part). Other parts in Evesham, Redditch and Worcester County Court Districts.	Bredon, Bredon's Norton,	Strensham.
	Tewkesbury Municipal Borough.	Tewkesbury.	
	Upton-upon-Severn Rural District (part). Other parts in Great Malvern and Worcester County Court Districts.	Bushley, Eldersfield, Holdfast, Longdon,	Pendock, Queenhill, Ripple.
CHEPSTOW	Chepstow Urban District.	Chepstow.	
	Chepstow Rural District.	Caerwent, Caldicot, Devauden, Kilgwrrwg, Llangwm, Llanvihangel (near Rogiet),	Mathern, Portskewett, Rogiet, St. Arvans, Shirenewton, Tintern, Undy.
	Lydney Rural District.	Alvington, Aylburton, Hewelsfield, Lydney,	St. Briavels, Tidenham, Woolaston.
CHESTER	Chester County Borough.	Chester.	
	Chester Rural District (part). Other part in Ellesmere Port County Court District.	Aldford, Bache, Backford, Barrow, Bridge Trafford, Buerton, Capenhurst, Caughall, Chester Castle, Chorlton by Backford, Christleton, Churton Heath, Claverton, Croughton, Dodleston, Dunham on the Hill, Eaton, Eccleston, Elton, Great Boughton,	Guilden Sutton, Hapsford, Hoole Village, Huntington, Lea by Backford, Lea Newbold, Ledsham, Littleton, Lower Kinnerton, Marlston cum Lache, Mickle Trafford, Mollington, Moston, Picton, Poulton, Puddington, Pulford, Rowton, Saighton, Saughall, Shotwick,

Column 1	*Column 2*	*Column 3*	
Name of court	Local authority areas	Parts comprising court districts	
CHESTER —*cont.*	Chester Rural District (part). —*cont.*	Shotwick Park, Stoak, Thornton le Moors,	Upton by Chester, Wervin, Wimbolds Trafford, Woodbank.
	Hawarden Rural District (part). *Other parts* in Mold and Wrexham County Court Districts.	East Saltney, Hawarden, Higher Kinnerton,	Sealand, West Saltney.
	Northwich Rural District (part). *Other parts* in Crewe and Northwich County Court Districts.	Utkinton.	
	Tarvin Rural District (part). *Other parts* in Crewe and Whitchurch County Court Districts.	Aldersey, Ashton, Barton, Broxton, Bruen Stapleford, Burton, Burwardsley, Caldecott, Carden, Chowley, Churton by Aldford, Churton by Farndon, Clotton Hoofield, Clutton, Coddington, Cotton Abbotts, Cotton Edmunds, Crewe by Farndon, Duddon, Edgerley,	Farndon, Foulk Stapleford, Goldborn Bellow, Goldborn David, Handley, Harthill, Hatton, Hockenhull, Horton cum Peel, Huxley, Iddinshall, Kelsall, Kingsmarsh, Mouldsworth, Newton by Tattenhall, Pryors Hayes, Stretton, Tarvin, Tattenhall, Waverton, Willington.
CHESTER-FIELD	Bakewell Rural District (part). *Other parts* in Buxton, Matlock and Sheffield County Court Districts.	Baslow and Bubnell, Calver, Curbar,	Froggatt, Nether Padley, Stoke.
	Blackwell Rural District (part). *Other parts* in Alfreton and Mansfield County Court Districts.	Ault Hucknall, Glapwell,	Scarcliffe.
	Bolsover Urban District.	Bolsover.	
	Chesterfield Municipal Borough.	Chesterfield.	
	Chesterfield Rural District (part). *Other part* in Alfreton County Court District.	Ashover, Barlow, Brampton, Brimington, Calow, Eckington, Hasland, Heath, Holmesfield,	Killamarsh, North Wingfield, Sutton cum Duckmanton, Temple Normanton, Tupton, Unstone, Walton, Wingerworth.

Column 1	Column 2	Column 3	
Name of court	Local authority areas	Parts comprising court districts	
CHESTER-FIELD —cont.	Clay Cross Urban District.	Clay Cross.	
	Dronfield Urban District.	Dronfield.	
	Staveley Urban District.	Staveley.	
CHICHES-TER	Arundel Municipal Borough.	Arundel.	
	Bognor Regis Urban District.	Bognor Regis.	
	Chanctonbury Rural District (part). Other parts in Brighton and Worthing County Court Districts.	Amberley, Coldwaltham, Parham,	Pulborough, Thakeham, West Chiltington.
	Chichester Municipal Borough.	Chichester.	
	Chichester Rural District.	Aldingbourne, Appledram, Barnham, Bersted, Birdham, Bosham, Boxgrove, Chidham, Climping, Compton, Donnington, Earnley, Eartham, East Dean, Eastergate, East Wittering, Ford, Funtington, Hunston, Lavant, Madehurst, Marden,	Middleton on Sea, North Mundham, Oving, Pagham, Selsey, Sidlesham, Singleton, Slindon, Southbourne, Stoughton, Tangmere, Tortington, Up Waltham, Walberton, Westbourne, West Dean, Westhampnett, West Itchenor, West Thorney, West Wittering, Yapton.
	Littlehampton Urban District.	Littlehampton.	
	Midhurst Rural District (part). Other part in Petersfield County Court District.	Bepton, Cocking, Easebourne. East Lavington, Graffham, Heyshott,	Lodsworth, Lurgashall, Midhurst, South Ambersham. Tillington, West Lavington.
	Petworth Rural District.	Barlavington, Bignor, Bury, Duncton, Fittleworth, Kirdford, Loxwood,	North Chapel, Petworth, Plaistow, Stopham, Sutton, Wisborough Green.

Column 1	Column 2	Column 3
Name of court	Local authority areas	Parts comprising court districts
CHICHES-TER —cont.	Worthing Rural District (part). *Other part* in Worthing County Court District.	Burpham Houghton, Lyminster, Poling.	Rustington, South Stoke, Warningcamp.
CHIPPEN-HAM	Bradford and Melksham Rural District (part). *Other parts* in Bath and Trow-bridge County Court Districts.	Melksham Without. Land common to Melksham Without and Broughton Gifford civil parishes.
	Calne and Chippenham Rural District (part). *Other parts* in Bath, Devizes and Swindon County Court Dist-ricts.	Biddestone, Bremhill, Calne Without, Castle Combe, Cherhill, Chippenham, Without, Christian Malford, Corsham, Grittleton, Kington, Langley.	Kington St. Michael, Lacock, Langley Burrell Without, Nettleton, North Wraxall, Pewsham, Stanton St. Quintin, Sutton Benger, Yatton Keynell.
	Calne Municipal Borough.	Calne.
	Chippenham Municipal Borough.	Chippenham.
	Melksham Urban District.	Melksham.
CHORLEY	Adlington Urban District.	Adlington.
	Chorley Municipal Borough.	Chorley.
	Chorley Rural District.	Anderton, Anglezarke, Bretherton, Brindle, Charnock Richard, Clayton le Woods, Coppull, Croston, Cuerden, Eccleston,	Euxton, Heapey, Heath Charnock, Heskin, Hoghton, Mawdesley, Rivington, Ulnes Walton, Wheelton, Whittle le Woods.
	Withnell Urban District.	Withnell.
CIREN-CESTER	Cirencester Urban District.	Cirencester.
	Cirencester Rural District.	Ampney Crucis, Ampney St. Mary, Ampney St. Peter, Bagendon, Barnsley, Baunton,	Brimpsfield, Coates, Colesborne, Daglingworth, Down Ampney, Driffield, Duntisbourne Abbots,

Column 1	Column 2	Column 3
Name of court	Local authority areas	Parts comprising court districts
CIREN-CESTER —*cont.*	Cirencester Rural District. —*cont.*	Duntisbourne Rouse, Edgeworth, Elkstone, Fairford, Hatherop, Kemble, Kempsford, Lechlade, Maiseyhampton, North Cerney, Poole Keynes, / Poulton, Preston, Quenington, Rendcomb, Rodmarton, Sapperton, Siddington, Somerford Keynes, South Cerney, Syde, Winstone.
	Cricklade and Wootton Bassett Rural District (part). *Other part* in Swindon County Court District.	Ashton Keynes, Latton, / Leigh, Marston Meysey.
	Northleach Rural District (part). *Other part* in Cheltenham County Court District.	Bibury, Chedworth, Coln St. Aldwyn, Coln St. Dennis, / Eastleach, Southrop, Winson.
CLERKEN-WELL	London Borough of Camden (part). *Other parts* in Bloomsbury and Marylebone and Westminster County Court Districts.	That part of the Borough east of a line drawn from the point where the Borough boundary crosses High Holborn thence westwards along the middle of High Holborn northwards along the middle of Southampton Row, Woburn Place and Upper Woburn Place to Euston Road, thence eastwards along the middle of Euston Road to the Borough boundary at King's Cross.
	London Borough of Haringey (part). *Other part* in Edmonton County Court District.	That part of the Borough south and west of a line drawn from the point on the Borough boundary at the junction of Green Lanes and Endymion Road along the south side of Endymion Road to the Eastern Region railway line thence northwards along the railway line through Harringay West and Hornsey stations to the Filter Beds, then westwards along the south of the Filter Beds and Alexandra Park around the perimeter of the Park to the east side of The Avenue, thence northwestwards along the east side of The Avenue and Grosvenor Road to the Borough boundary.
	London Borough of Islington (part). *Other part* in Shoreditch County Court District.	The whole of the Borough except that part east of a line drawn from the point where the Borough boundary crosses the eastern end of Beech Street northwards along the middle of Whitecross Street, thence eastwards along the middle of Old Street and northwards along the middle of Bath Street to the Borough boundary.

Column 1	Column 2	Column 3
Name of court	Local authority areas	Parts comprising court districts
COL-CHESTER AND CLACTON	Brightlingsea Urban District.	Brightlingsea.
	Clacton-on-Sea Urban District.	Clacton-on-Sea.
	Colchester Municipal Borough.	Colchester.
	Frinton and Walton Urban District.	Frinton and Walton.
	Halstead Rural District (part). *Other parts* in Braintree, Cambridge, and Sudbury County Court Districts.	Colne Engaine, White Colne. Earls Colne,
	Lexden and Winstree Rural District (part). *Other parts* in Maldon and Sudbury County Court Districts.	Abberton, Langenhoe, Aldham, Langham, Birch, Layer Breton, Boxted, Layer de la Haye, Chappel, Layer Marney, Copford, Little Horkesley, Dedham, Marks Tey, East Donyland, Messing cum East Mersea, Inworth, Eight Ash Green, Peldon, Fingringhoe, Salcott, Fordham, Stanway, Great Horkesley, Virley, Great Tey, Wakes Colne, Great and Little West Bergholt, Wigborough, Wormingford.
	Melford Rural District (part). *Other parts* in Bury St. Edmunds and Sudbury County Court Districts.	Nayland with Wissington.
	Tendring Rural District (part). *Other part* in Harwich County Court District.	Alresford, Little Bromley, Ardleigh, Little Clacton, Elmstead, Manningtree, Frating, St. Osyth, Great Bentley, Thorpe le Soken Great Bromley, Thorrington. Lawford, Weeley. Little Bentley,
	West Mersea Urban District.	West Mersea.
	Wivenhoe Urban District.	Wivenhoe.
CONGLE-TON	Biddulph Urban District.	Biddulph.
	Congleton Municipal Borough.	Congleton.
	Congleton Rural District (part). *Other part* in Crewe County Court District.	Arclid, Newbold Astbury, Brereton, Odd Rode, Church Hulme, Smallwood, Church Lawton, Somerford, Cranage, Somerford Booths, Goostrey, Swettenham, Hulme Walfield, Twemlow. Moreton,

Column 1	Column 2	Column 3
Name of court	Local authority areas	Parts comprising court districts
CONGLE- TON —cont.	Macclesfield Rural District (part). Other parts in Buxton and Macclesfield County Court Districts.	Eaton, Marton.
CONSETT	Consett Urban District.	Consett.
	Hexham Rural District (part). Other parts in Hexham and Newcastle upon Tyne County Court Districts.	Blanchland, Shotley Low Quarter.
	Lanchester Rural District (part). Other part in Durham County Court District.	Greencroft, Muggleswick. Healeyfield,
	Stanley Urban District.	Stanley.
	Weardale Rural District (part). Other part in Bishop Auckland County Court District.	Edmondbyers, Hunstanworth.
CONWAY, LLAN- DUDNO AND COL- WYN BAY	Aled Rural District (part). Other parts in Denbigh and Ruthin and Rhyl County Court Districts.	Llanelian yr Rhos, Llansantffraid Glan Conway.
	Betws y Coed Urban District.	Betws y Coed.
	Colwyn Bay Municipal Borough.	Colwyn Bay.
	Conway Municipal Borough.	Conway.
	Hiraethog Rural District (part). Other part in Denbigh and Ruthin County Court District.	Eglwysbach, Llanrwst Rural, Gwytherin, Pentrevoelas, Llanddoget, Tir Ifan. Llangerniew,
	Llandudno Urban District.	Llandudno.
	Llanrwst Urban District.	Llanrwst.
	Nant Conway Rural District.	Capel Curig, Llanrhychwyn, Caerhun, Maenan, Dolgarrog, Penmachno, Dolwyddelan, The Abbey, Eidda, Trefriw. Henryd, Llanbedr y Cennim,
	Penmaenmawr Urban District.	Penmaenmawr.
COVENTRY	Coventry County Borough.	Coventry.
	Meriden Rural District (part). Other parts in Birmingham, Nuneaton and Tamworth County Court Districts.	Allesley, Great Packington, Balsall, Keresley, Berkswell, Little Packington, Corley, Meriden. Fillongley,

Column 1	Column 2	Column 3
Name of court	Local authority areas	Parts comprising court districts
COVENTRY —cont.	Rugby Rural District (part). *Other parts* in Hinckley, Nuneaton and Rugby County Court Districts.	Ansty, Binley Woods, Ryton on Dunsmore, — Shilton, Withybrook.
	Warwick Rural District (part). *Other part* in Warwick County Court District.	Baginton, Bubbenhall, — Stoneleigh.
CRANBROOK	Cranbrook Rural District.	Benenden, Cranbrook, Frittenden, — Goudhurst, Hawkhurst, Sandhurst.
	Tenterden Municipal Borough.	Tenterden.
	Tenterden Rural District.	Appledore, Biddenden, High Halden, Kenardington, Newenden, — Rolvenden, Stone cum Ebony, Wittersham, Woodchurch.
CREWE	Alsager Urban District.	Alsager.
	Congleton Rural District (part). *Other part* in Congleton County Court District.	Betchton, Bradwall, Elton and Tetton, — Hassall.
	Crewe Municipal Borough.	Crewe.
	Nantwich Urban District.	Nantwich.
	Nantwich Rural District (part). *Other part* in Whitchurch County Court District.	Acton, Alpraham, Aston juxta Mondrum, Audlem, Austerson, Baddiley, Baddington, Barthomley, Basford, Batherton, Bickerton, Blakenhall, Bridgemere, Brindley, Broomhall, Buerton, Bulkeley, Bunbury, Burland, Calveley, Checkley cum Wrinehill, Cholmondeley, Cholmondeston, Chorley, Chorlton, — Church Minshull, Coole Pilate, Crewe, Doddington, Edleston, Egerton, Faddiley, Hankelow, Haslington, Hatherton, Haughton, Henhull, Hough, Hunsterson, Hurleston, Lea, Leighton, Minshull Vernon, Newhall, Peckforton, Poole, Ridley, Rope, Shavington cum Gresty, Sound, Spurstow,

Column 1	Column 2	Column 3
Name of court	Local authority areas	Parts comprising court districts
CREWE —*cont.*	Nantwich Rural District (part). —*cont.*	Stapeley, Wistaston, Stoke, Woodcott, Walgherton, Woolstanwood, Wardle, Worleston, Warmingham, Wrenbury cum Weston, Frith, Wettenhall, Wybunbury. Willaston,
	Newcastle under Lyme Rural District (part). *Other parts* in Market Drayton and Newcastle under Lyme County Court Districts.	Balterley, Betley.
	Northwich Rural District (part). *Other parts* in Chester and Northwich County Court Districts.	Rushton, Tarporley.
	Sandbach Urban District.	Sandbach.
	Tarvin Rural District (part). *Other parts* in Chester and Whitchurch County Court Districts.	Beeston, Tiverton. Tilstone Fearnall,
CROYDON	Banstead Urban District (part). *Other parts* in Epsom and Reigate County Court Districts.	The Woodmansterne Ward.
	Caterham and Warlingham Urban District (part). *Other part* in Reigate County Court District.	The Caterham, Warlingham and Woldingham Wards.
	Godstone Rural District (part). *Other parts* in East Grinstead and Reigate County Court Districts.	Chelsham and Farleigh,
	London Borough of Croydon.	Croydon.
	London Borough of Merton (part). *Other part* in Kingston-upon-Thames County Court District.	That part of the Borough south of a line drawn from the point where the Borough boundary crosses the western end of Coombe Lane eastwards along the middle of Coombe Lane, Kingston Road, High Street Merton and High Street Colliers Wood to the Borough boundary.
	London Borough of Bromley (part). *Other part* in Bromley County Court District.	That part of the Borough west of a line drawn from the point where the Borough boundary crosses the Southern Region railway line between Sydenham and Crystal Palace stations southwards along the railway line to Trinity Road then along the middle of Trinity Road,

Column 1	Column 2	Column 3
Name of court	Local authority areas	Parts comprising court districts
CROYDON —*cont.*	London Borough of Bromley (part). —*cont.*	Lennard Road, Parish Lane, Kent House Road, Beckenham Road, Ravenscroft Road, Elmers End Road and Marlow Road to the Borough boundary.
	London Borough of Sutton (part). *Other part* in Epsom County Court District.	That part of the Borough east of a line drawn from the point on the Borough boundary at the junction of Love Lane and Green Lane, south-eastwards along the middle of Green Lane across the junction with Bishopsford Road to the middle of Wrythe Lane, along the middle of Wrythe Lane, West Street, Colston Avenue and Alma Road, across Carshalton Road along the middle of Harrow Road, Banstead Road and Banstead Road South to the Borough boundary.
DARLING-TON	Barnard Castle Rural District (part). *Other part* in Bishop Auckland County Court District.	Cleatlam, Langton, Gainford, Westwick, Headlam, Whorlton, Ingleton, Winston.
	Croft Rural District.	Barton, Eryholme, Cleasby, Girsby, Cliffe, Manfield, Croft, Newton Morrell, Dalton upon Over Dinsdale, Tees, Stapleton.
	Darlington County Borough.	Darlington.
	Darlington Rural District (part). *Other part* in Stockton on Tees County Court District.	Archdeacon Killerby, Newton, Low Coniscliffe, Barmpton, Low Dinsdale, Brafferton, Middleton Coatham St. George, Mundeville, Morton Palms, Denton, Neasham, Great Aycliffe, Piercebridge, Great Burdon, Sadberge, Heighington, Sockburn, High Coniscliffe, Summerhouse, Houghton le Walworth, Side, Whessoe. Hurworth,
	Sedgefield Rural District (part). *Other parts* in Bishop Auckland, Durham and Stockton on Tees County Court Districts.	Preston le Skerne.
	Startforth Rural District (part). *Other part* in Bishop Auckland County Court District.	Barforth, Ovington, Barningham, Rokeby, Brignall, Scargill, Gilmonby, Wycliffe with Hope, Thorpe. Hutton,

Column 1	Column 2	Column 3
Name of court	Local authority areas	Parts comprising court districts
DARTFORD	Dartford Municipal Borough.	Dartford.
	Dartford Rural District.	Ash cum Ridley, Longfield, Darenth, Southfleet, Eynsford, Stone, Farningham, Sutton at Hone, Fawkham, Swanley, Hartley, West Kingsdown, Horton Kirby, Wilmington.
	London Borough of Bexley (part). *Other part* in Bromley County Court District.	That part of the Borough which lies to the north and east of a line drawn from the point where the Dartford Loop Line of British Railways crosses the western Borough boundary, along the railway line eastwards to a point in line with the east side of Betterton Drive and thence south-eastwards along the east side of Betterton Drive and Water Lane across North Cray Road to the north side of Bunker's Hill, thence east of Cocksure Lane and Parsonage Lane to the Borough boundary.
DEAL	Deal Municipal Borough.	Deal.
	Dover Rural District (part). *Other part* in Dover County Court District.	Ringwould.
	Eastry Rural District (part). *Other parts* in Canterbury, Dover, Margate and Ramsgate County Court Districts.	Ash, Staple, Eastry, Sutton, Northbourne, Tilmanstone, Ripple, Woodnesborough, Sholden, Worth.
	Sandwich Municipal Borough.	Sandwich.
DENBIGH AND RUTHIN	Aled Rural District (part). *Other parts* in Conway, Llandudno and Colwyn Bay and Rhyl County Court Districts.	Bylchau, Llannefydd, Llanfair Llansannan, Talhaiarn, Trefnant.
	Denbigh Municipal Borough.	Denbigh.
	Hiraethog Rural District (part). *Other part* in Conway, Llandudno and Colwyn Bay County Court District.	Cerrigydruidion, Llangwm. Llanfihangel Glyn Myfyr,
	Ruthin Municipal Borough.	Ruthin.
	Ruthin Rural District.	Aberwheeler Gyffylliog, Rural, Llanarmon, Bryneglwys, yn Ial, Clocaenog, Llanbedr, Derwen, Llandegla, Efenechtyd, Llandyrnog,

Column 1	*Column 2*	*Column 3*
Name of court	Local authority areas	Parts comprising court districts
DENBIGH AND RUTHIN —cont.	Ruthin Rural District. —cont.	Llanelidan, Llangynhafal, Llanfair Duffryn Llanrhaiadr yn Clwyd, Cinmerch, Llanferres, Llanynys Rural, Llanfwrog, Nantglyn. Rural,
	St. Asaph Rural District (part). *Other part* in Rhyl County Court District.	Bodfari.
DERBY	Ashbourne Urban District.	Ashbourne.
	Ashbourne Rural District (part). *Other parts* in Buxton, Matlock and Uttoxeter County Court Districts.	Alkmonton, Kniverton, Atlow, Longford, Biggin, Mappleton, Bradley, Mercaston, Brailsford, Offcote and Clifton, Underwood, Edlaston and Osmaston, Wyaston, Rodsley, Fenny Bentley, Shirley, Hognaston, Snelston, Hollington, Thorpe, Hulland, Yeaveley, Hulland Ward, Yeldersley. Hungry Bentley,
	Belper Urban District.	Belper.
	Belper Rural District (part). *Other parts* in Alfreton, Ilkeston and Matlock County Court Districts.	Duffield, Quarndon, Hazelwood, Ravensdale Park, Holbrook, Shottle and Postern, Kedleston, Turnditch, Kirk Langley, Weston Underwood, Mackworth, Windley.
	Derby County Borough.	Derby.
	Repton Rural District (part). *Other parts* in Ashby de la Zouch and Burton upon Trent County Court Districts.	Ash, Osleston and Bearwardcote, Thurvaston, Burnaston, Radbourne, Dalbury Lees, Sutton on the Hill, Etwall, Trusley, Findern, Twyford and Foremark, Stenson, Ingleby, Willington.
	South East Derbyshire Rural District (part). *Other part* in Ilkeston County Court District.	Aston on Trent, Little Eaton, Barrow on Trent, Melbourne, Breadsall, Ockbrook, Breaston, Shardlow and Great Derby Hills, Wilne, Draycott and Stanton by Bridge, Church Wilne, Swarkestone, Elvaston, Weston upon Trent.
DEVIZES	Amesbury Rural District (part). *Other part* in Salisbury County Court District.	Tilshead.

Column 1	Column 2	Column 3
Name of court	Local authority areas	Parts comprising court districts
DEVIZES —cont.	Calne and Chippenham Rural District (part). *Other parts* in Bath, Chippenham and Swindon County Court Districts.	Heddington.
	Devizes Municipal Borough.	Devizes.
	Devizes Rural District.	Alleannings, Beechingstoke, Bishop's Cannings, Bromham, Chirton, Easterton, Erlestoke, Etchilhampton, Great Cheverell, Little Cheverell, Marden, Market Lavington, Marston, Patney, Potterne, Poulshot, Roundway, Rowde, Seend, Stanton St. Bernard, Stert, Urchfont, West Lavington, Worton.
	Pewsey Rural District (part). *Other parts* in Andover, Marlborough and Salisbury County Court Districts.	Charlton, Enford, North Newnton, Rushall, Upavon, Wilsford, Woodborough.
DEWSBURY	Batley Municipal Borough.	Batley.
	Dewsbury County Borough.	Dewsbury.
	Heckmondwike Urban District.	Heckmondwike.
	Mirfield Urban District.	Mirfield.
	Morley Municipal Borough.	Morley.
	Ossett Municipal Borough.	Ossett.
	Spenborough Municipal Borough.	Spenborough.
DIDCOT	Abingdon Rural District (part). *Other part* in Oxford County Court District.	Appleford, Drayton, Lyford, Milton, Steventon, Sutton Courtenay.
	Bradfield Rural District (part). *Other parts* in Newbury and Reading County Court Districts.	Streatley.
	Bullingdon Rural District (part). *Other parts* in Oxford and Thame County Court Districts.	Benson, Berinsfield, Berrick Salome, Brightwell Baldwin, Britwell, Clifton Hampden, Culham, Cuxham, Dorchester on Thames, Drayton St. Leonard, Ewelme, Newington, Warborough.

Column 1	Column 2	Column 3
Name of court	Local authority areas	Parts comprising court districts
DIDCOT —cont.	Faringdon Rural District (part). *Other parts* in Oxford and Swindon County Courts Districts.	Baulking, Charney Bassett, Kingston Lisle, / Littleworth, Uffington.
	Henley Rural District (part). *Other part* in Reading County Court District.	Checkendon, Crowmarsh, Goring, Ipsden, / Nuffield, South Stoke, Stoke Row, Woodcote.
	Wallingford Municipal Borough.	Wallingford.
	Wallingford Rural District.	Aston Tirrold, Aston Upthorpe, Brightwell-cum-Sotwell, Cholsey, Didcot, East Hagbourne, / Little Wittenham, Long Wittenham, Moulsford, North Moreton, South Moreton, West Hagbourne.
	Wantage Urban District.	Wantage.
	Wantage Rural District (part). *Other part* in Newbury County Court District.	Aldworth, Ardington, Blewbury, Brightwalton, Catmore, Chaddleworth, Childrey, Chilton, Compton, Denchworth, East Challow, East Hanney, East Hendred, East Ilsley, / Farnborough, Fawley, Goosey, Grove, Harwell, Letcombe Bassett, Letcombe Regis, Lockinge, Sparsholt, Upton, West Challow, West Hanney, West Hendred, West Ilsley.
DOLGELLAU	Bala Urban District.	Bala.
	Barmouth Urban District.	Barmouth.
	Dolgellau Urban District.	Dolgellau.
	Dolgellau Rural District (part). *Other part* in Machynlleth County Court District.	Brithdir and Islaw'rdref, Llanaber, Llanddwywe is y Graig, Llanddwywe Uwch y Graig, Llanegryn, Llanelltyd, / Llanenddwyn, Llanfachreth, Llanfihangel y Pennant, Llangelynin, Llanymawddwy. Mallwyd, Talyllyn.
	Penllyn Rural District.	Llandderfel, Llanfor, Llangower, / Llanuwchllyn, Llanycil.
DONCASTER	Adwick-le-Street Urban District.	Adwick-le-Street.
	Bentley with Arksey Urban District.	Bentley with Arksey.

Column 1	Column 2	Column 3	
Name of court	Local authority areas	Parts comprising court districts	
DON-CASTER—cont.	Conisbrough Urban District.	Conisbrough.	
	Dearne Urban District.	Dearne.	
	Doncaster County Borough.	Doncaster.	
	Doncaster Rural District.	Adwick on Dearne, Armthorpe, Askern, Austerfield, Awkley or Auckley, Barnburgh, Barnby Dun with Kirk Sandall, Bawtry, Blaxton, Braithwell, Brodsworth cum Pigburn and Scausby, Burghwallis, Cadeby, Cantley, Clayton with Frickley,	Conisbrough Parks, Denaby, Edenthorpe, Edlington, Fenwick, Hampole, Hickleton, Hooton Pagnell, Kirk Bramwith, Loversall, Marr, Melton (High), Moss, Norton, Owston, Rossington, Sprotborough, Stainton, Thorpe in Balne, Wadworth, Warmsworth.
	East Retford Rural District (part). Other parts in East Retford and Gainsborough County Court Districts.	Finningley, Misson.	
	Tickhill Urban District.	Tickhill.	
DOR-CHESTER	Beaminster Rural District (part). Other parts in Axminster and Chard, Bridport and Yeovil County Court Districts.	Wraxall.	
	Blandford Rural District (part). Other parts in Shaftesbury, Salisbury and Wimborne Minster County Court Districts.	Hilton, Milborne St. Andrew, Milton Abbas, Turnworth, Winterborne Clenston,	Winterborne Houghton, Winterborne Stickland, Winterborne Whitechurch.
	Dorchester Municipal Borough.	Dorchester.	
	Dorchester Rural District (part). Other part in Weymouth County Court District.	Alton Pancras, Athelhampton, Bradford Peverell, Broadmayne, Buckland Newton, Burleston, Cattistock, Cerne Abbas, Charminster,	Cheselbourne, Chilfrome, Compton Valence, Dewlish, Frampton, Frome St. Quintin, Frome Vauchurch, Godmanstone,

Column 1	*Column 2*	*Column 3*
Name of court	Local authority areas	Parts comprising court districts
DOR-CHESTER —cont.	Dorchester Rural District (part.) —cont.	Kingston Russell, Little Bredy, Long Bredy, Maiden Newton, Melcombe Horsey, Minterne, Nether Cerne, Piddlehinton, Piddletrenthide, Puddletown, Stinsford, Stratton, Sydling St. Nicholas, Tincleton, Toller Fratrum, Toller Porcorum, Tolpuddle, / Up Cerne, Warmwell, Watercombe, West Compton, West Knighton, West Stafford, Whitcombe, Winterborne Abbas, Winterborne Came, Winterborne Herringston, Winterborne Monkton, Winterborne St. Martin, Winterborne Steepleton, Woodsford, Wynford Eagle.
	Sherborne Rural District (part). *Other part* in Yeovil County Court District.	Batcombe, / Hilfield.
	Sturminster Rural District (part). *Other parts* in Shaftesbury and Yeovil County Court Districts.	Glanvilles Wooton, Hazelbury Bryan, Ibberton, / Mappowder, Pulham, Stoke Wake, Woolland.
	Wareham and Purbeck Rural District (part). *Other parts* in Poole, Swanage and Weymouth County Court Districts.	Affpuddle, Moreton, / Turners Puddle, Winfrith Newburgh.
DORKING	Dorking Urban District.	Dorking.
	Dorking and Horley Rural District (part). *Other parts* in Epsom and Reigate County Court Districts.	Abinger, Capel, Holmwood, / Newdigate, Ockley, Wotton.
	Guildford Rural District (part). *Other parts* in Aldershot and Farnham and Guildford County Court Districts.	Effingham.
DOVER	Dover Municipal Borough.	Dover.
	Dover Rural District (part). *Other part* in Deal County Court District.	Alkham, Capel le Ferne, Denton with Wootton, Guston, Hougham Without, Langdon, / Lydden, St. Margaret's at Cliffe, Shepherdswell with Coldred, Temple Ewell with River, Whitfield.

Column 1	Column 2	Column 3
Name of court	Local authority areas	Parts comprising court districts
DOVER —cont.	Eastry Rural District (part). *Other parts* in Canterbury, Deal, Margate and Ramsgate County Court Districts.	Eythorne.
DUDLEY	Dudley County Borough (part). *Other part* in Stourbridge County Court District.	The Castle, Coseley East, Coseley West, Gornal, Netherton & Woodside, . Priory, St. Andrew's, St. Jame's, St. Thomas's, and Sedgley Wards.
	Warley County Borough (part). *Other part* in West Bromwich County Court District.	The Cradley Heath, Old Hill and Blackheath, Rounds Green, Rowley and Tividale Wards.
	West Bromwich County Borough (part). *Other part* in West Bromwich County Court District.	The Horseley Heath, Market, Tibbington, Tipton Green and Wood Green Wards.
DURHAM	Brandon and Byshottles Urban District.	Brandon and Byshottles.
	Chester le Street Urban District.	Chester le Street.
	Chester le Street Rural District (part). *Other part* in Gateshead County Court District.	Bournmoor, Edmondsley, Great Lumley, Lambton, Little Lumley, Pelton, Plawsworth, Sacriston, South Biddick, Waldridge.
	Durham Municipal Borough.	Durham.
	Durham Rural District.	Bearpark, Belmont, Brancepeth, Cassop cum Quarrington, Coxhoe, Framwellgate Moor, Hett, Kelloe, Kimblesworth, Pittington, Shadforth, Sherburn, Sherburn House, Shincliffe, Sunderland Bridge, West Rainton, Whitwell House, Witton Gilbert, Lands common to Brandon and Byshottles civil parish (Brandon and Byshottles Urban District) and Brancepeth civil parish.
	Easington Rural District (part). *Other parts* in Sunderland and Hartlepool County Court Districts.	Haswell, Thornley, Wingate.
	Hetton Urban District.	Hetton.
	Houghton le Spring Urban District.	Houghton le Spring.

Column 1	Column 2	Column 3
Name of court	Local authority areas	Parts comprising court districts
DURHAM —cont.	Lanchester Rural District (part). *Other part* in Consett County Court District.	Cornsay, Esh, Hedleyhope, / Lanchester, Langley, Satley.
	Sedgefield Rural District (part). *Other parts* in Bishop Auckland, Darlington and Stockton on Tees County Court Districts.	Bishop Middleham, Chilton, Cornforth, / Ferryhill, Mainsforth, Trimdon.
DURSLEY	Dursley Rural District.	Cam, Coaley, Dursley, Kingswood, North Nibley, / Nympsfield, Slimbridge, Stinchcombe, Uley and Owlpen, Wotton under Edge.
	Gloucester Rural District (part). *Other parts* in Cheltenham, Gloucester and Stroud County Court Districts.	Frocester.
	Tetbury Rural District (part). *Other parts* in Malmesbury and Stroud County Court Districts.	Kingscote, / Ozleworth.
	Thornbury Rural District (part). *Other part* in Thornbury County Court District.	Alkington, Berkeley, Charfield, Cromhall, / Ham and Stone, Hamfallow, Hinton, Tortworth.
EAST-BOURNE	Eastbourne County Borough.	Eastbourne.
	Hailsham Rural District (part). *Other parts* in Hastings and Lewes County Court Districts.	Alfriston, Arlington, Chiddingly, Eastdean, Folkington, Friston, Hailsham, Heathfield, Hellingly, Herstmonceux, Horam, Jevington. / Litlington, Lullington, Pevensey, Polegate, Waldron, Warbleton, Wartling, Westdean, Westham, Willingdon, Wilmington.
EAST DEREHAM	East Dereham Urban District.	East Dereham.
	Mitford and Launditch Rural District (part). *Other parts* in Kings Lynn and Norwich County Court Districts.	Bawdeswell, Beeston with Bittering, Beetley, Billingford, Bintree, Brisley, Bylaugh, Cranworth, / East Tuddenham, Elsing, Foxley, Fransham, Garvestone, Gressenhall, Hockering, Hoe, Kempstone,

Column 1	Column 2	Column 3	
Name of court	Local authority areas	Parts comprising court districts	
EAST DEREHAM —cont.	Mitford and Launditch Rural District (part). —cont.	Litcham, Longham, Lyng, Mattishall, Mileham, North Elmham, North Tuddenham, Scarning,	Shipdham, Sparham, Stanfield, Swanton Morley, Tittleshall, Wendling, Whinburgh, Yaxham.
	Swaffham Rural District (part). *Other parts* in King's Lynn and Thetford County Court Districts.	Bradenham.	
EAST GRIN- STEAD	Cuckfield Rural District (part). *Other parts* in Brighton and Haywards Heath County Court Districts.	Crawley Down, Horstead Keynes, Turners Hill,	West Hoathly, Worth.
	East Grinstead Urban District.	East Grinstead.	
	Godstone Rural District (part). *Other parts* in Croydon and Reigate County Court Districts.	Felbridge,	Lingfield.
	Sevenoaks Rural District (part). *Other parts* in Sevenoaks and Tonbridge County Court District.	Cowden.	
	Uckfield Rural District (part). *Other parts* in Lewes and Tunbridge Wells County Court Districts.	Danehill, Forest Row,	Hartfield, Withyham.
EAST RETFORD	East Retford Municipal Borough	East Retford.	
	East Retford Rural District (part). *Other parts* in Doncaster and Gainsborough County Court Districts.	Askham, Babworth, Barnby Moor, Bevercotes, Bothamsall, Clarborough, Clayworth, Cottam, Darlton, Dunham, East Drayton, East Markham, Eaton, Elkesley, Everton, Fledborough, Gamston, Gringley on the Hill,	Grove, Haughton, Hayton, Headon cum Upton, Laneham, Lound, Markham Clinton or West Markham, Marnham, Mattersey, Normanton on Trent, North Leverton with Habblesthorpe, North Wheatley,

Column 1	Column 2	Column 3
Name of court	Local authority areas	Parts comprising court districts
EAST RETFORD —cont.	East Retford Rural District (part). —cont.	Ragnall, Sturton le Steeple, Rampton, Sutton, Ranskill, Torworth, Scaftworth, Treswell, Scrooby, Tuxford, South Leverton, West Drayton, South Wheatley, Wiseton. Stokeham,
	Southwell Rural District (part). *Other parts* in Mansfield, Newark, Nottingham and Worksop County Court Districts.	Kirton, Walesby.
EDMON- TON	Cheshunt Urban District.	Cheshunt.
	Chigwell Urban District (part). *Other parts* in Bow and Ilford County Court Districts.	The Loughton Ward.
	London Borough of Enfield (part). *Other part* in Barnet County Court District.	That part of the Borough east of a line drawn from the point where the Borough boundary crosses Cock-fosters Road along the east side of Cockfosters Road and Chase Side then across the end of Chase Side to the Borough boundary at the end of Crown Lane.
	London Borough of Haringey (part). *Other part* in Clerkenwell County Court District.	That part of the Borough north and east of a line drawn from the point on the Borough boundary at the junction of Green Lanes and Endymion Road along the south side of Endymion Road to the Eastern Region railway line thence northwards along the railway line through Harringay West and Hornsey stations to the Filter Beds, then westwards along the south of the Filter Beds and Alexandra Park around the perimeter of the Park to the east side of The Avenue, thence north-westwards along the east side of The Avenue and Grosvenor Road to the Borough boundary.
	Waltham Holy Cross Urban District.	Waltham Holy Cross.
	London Borough of Waltham Forest (part). *Other part* in Bow County Court District.	That part of the Borough to the north of a line drawn from the point where the boundaries of the London Boroughs of Enfield, Haringey and Waltham Forest meet eastwards to the North Circular Road, along the south side of the North Circular Road across Chingford Road thence along the north side of Wadham Road, taking in the whole of Wadham Avenue, to Hale End Road,

Column 1 Name of court	Column 2 Local authority areas	Column 3 Parts comprising court districts
EDMONTON —cont.	London Borough of Waltham Forest (part). —cont.	along the west side of Hale End Road to the River Ching thence northwards along the River to The Avenue, along the south side of The Avenue and the west side of Chingford Lane to the Borough boundary.
ELLES- MERE PORT	Chester Rural District (part). *Other part* in Chester County Court District.	Little Stanney.
	Ellesmere Port Municipal Borough.	Ellesmere Port.
ELY	Ely Urban District.	Ely.
	Ely Rural District.	Coveney, Sutton, Downham, Thetford, Haddenham, Wentworth, Littleport, Wilburton, Mepal, Witcham, Stretham, Witchford.
	Newmarket Rural District (part). *Other parts* in Cambridge and Newmarket County Court Dis- tricts.	Soham.
EPSOM	Banstead Urban District (part). *Other parts* in Croydon and Reigate County Court Districts.	The Banstead Village, Burgh Heath, Preston, Tadworth, Tattenhams, The Nork and Walton on the Hill Wards.
	Dorking and Horley Rural District (part). *Other parts* in Dorking and Reigate County Court Districts.	Headley.
	Epsom and Ewell Municipal Borough.	Epsom and Ewell.
	Leatherhead Urban District.	Leatherhead.
	London Borough of Sutton (part). *Other part* in Croydon County Court District	That part of the Borough west of a line drawn from the point on the Borough boundary at the junction of Love Lane and Green Lane south-eastwards along the middle of Green Lane across the junction with Bishopsford Road to the middle of Wrythe Lane along the middle of Wrythe Lane, West Street, Colston Avenue, and Alma Road across Carshalton Road along the middle of Harrow Road, Banstead Road and Banstead Road South to the Borough boundary.

Column 1	Column 2	Column 3
Name of court	Local authority areas	Parts comprising court districts
EVESHAM	Evesham Municipal Borough.	Evesham.
	Evesham Rural District (part). *Other parts* in Cheltenham and Redditch County Court Districts.	Aldington, Ashton under Hill, Aston Somerville, Badsey, Bickmarsh, Bretforton, Broadway, Childswickham, Church Lench, Cleeve Prior, Conderton, Harvington, Hinton on the Green, — Honeybourne, Kemerton, North and Middle Littleton, Norton and Lenchwick, Offenham, Overbury, Pebworth, Rous Lench, Sedgeberrow, South Littleton, Wickhamford.
	North Cotswold Rural District (part). *Other part* in Cheltenham County Court District.	Aston Subedge, Batsford, Blockley, Bourton on the Hill, Chipping Camden, Ebrington, — Mickleton, Moreton in Marsh, Saintbury and Willersey, Sezincote, Todenham, Weston Subedge.
	Pershore Rural District (part). *Other parts* in Redditch, Cheltenham and Worcester County Court Districts.	Abberton, Bishampton, Bricklehampton, Charlton, Cropthorne, Drakes Broughton and Wadborough, Elmley Castle, Fladbury, Great Comberton, — Hill and Moor, Little Comberton, Naunton Beauchamp, Netherton, Pershore, Pinvin, Throckmorton, Wick, Wyre Piddle.
EXETER	Budleigh Salterton Urban District.	Budleigh Salterton.
	Crediton Urban District.	Crediton.
	Crediton Rural District (part). *Other parts* in Barnstaple, Okehampton and Tiverton County Court Districts.	Bow, Cheriton Bishop, Clannaborough, Colebrook, Crediton Hamlets, Down St. Mary, Kennerleigh, — Lapford, Morchard Bishop, Newton St. Cyres, Nymet Rowland, Sandford, Shobrooke, Upton Hellions.
	Exeter County Borough.	Exeter.
	Exmouth Urban District.	Exmouth.

Column 1	Column 2	Column 3	
Name of court	Local authority areas	Parts comprising court districts	
EXETER —cont.	St. Thomas Rural District.	Alphington, Ashcombe, Ashton, Aylesbeare, Bicton, Brampford Speke, Bridford, Broad Clyst, Christow, Clyst Honiton, Clyst Hydon, Clyst St. George, Clyst St. Lawrence, Clyst St. Mary, Colaton Raleigh, Doddiscombsleigh, Dunchideock, Dunsford, East Budleigh, Exminster,	Farringdon, Harpford, Holcombe Burnell, Huxham, Ide, Kenn, Kenton, Lympstone, Mamhead, Nether Exe, Otterton, Poltimore, Powderham, Rewe, Rockbeare, Shillingford, Sowton, Stoke Canon, Tedburn St. Mary, Upton Pyne, Whimple, Whitestone, Woodbury.
FOLKE- STONE	Elham Rural District.	Acrise, Elham, Elmsted, Hawkinge, Lyminge, Lympne, Monks Horton, Newington, Paddlesworth,	Postling, Saltwood, Sellindge, Stanford, Stelling, Stelling Minnis, Stowting, Swingfield.
	Folkestone Municipal Borough.	Folkestone.	
	Hythe Municipal Borough.	Hythe.	
FROME	Frome Urban District.	Frome.	
	Frome Rural District.	Beckington, Berkley, Buckland Dinham, Coleford, Great Elm, Hemington, Kilmersdon, Leigh upon Mendip, Lullington,	Mells, Norton St. Philip, Nunney, Rode, Selwood, Tellisford, Trudoxhill, Upton Nobile, Wanstrow, Whatley, Witham Friary.
	Mere and Tisbury Rural District (part). *Other part* in Shaftesbury County Court District.	Kilmington, Maiden Bradley with Yarnfield.	
	Norton Radstock Urban District.	Norton Radstock.	

Column 1	Column 2	Column 3
Name of court	Local authority areas	Parts comprising court districts
FROME —cont.	Shepton Mallet Rural District (part). *Other part* in Wells County Court District.	Batcombe, Downhead, Stoke St. Michael.
GAINS- BOROUGH	East Retford Rural District (part). *Other parts* in Doncaster and East Retford County Court Districts·	Beckingham, Walkeringham, Bole, West Burton, Misterton, West Stockwith. Saundby,
	Gainsborough Urban District.	Gainsborough.
	Gainsborough Rural District (part). *Other part* in Lincoln County Court District.	Blyborough, Lea, Blyton, Marton, Brampton, Morton, Corringham, Newton on Trent, East Ferry, Northorpe, East Stockwith, Pilham, Fenton, Scotter, Fillingham, Scotton, Gate Burton, Springthorpe, Glentworth, Stow, Grayingham, Sturton by Stow, Harpswell, Thonock, Heapham, Torksey, Hemswell, Upton, Kettlethorpe, Walkerith, Kexby, Wildsworth, Knaith, Willingham, Laughton, Willoughton.
	Isle of Axholme Rural District (part). *Other parts* in Goole, Scunthorpe and Thorne County Court Districts.	Haxey, Owston Ferry.
GATES- HEAD	Chester le Street Rural District (part). *Other part* in Durham County Court District.	Birtley, Lamesley, Harraton and Ouston, North Biddick, Urpeth.
	Felling Urban District.	Felling.
	Gateshead County Borough.	Gateshead.
	Washington Urban District.	Washington.
	Whickham Urban District.	Whickham.
GLOU- CESTER	East Dean Rural District (part). *Other part* in Ross County Court District.	Awre, Huntley, Blaisdon, Littledean, Churcham, Longhope, Cinderford, Mitcheldean, Drybrook, Ruspidge.
	Gloucester County Borough.	Gloucester.

Column 1	Column 2	Column 3	
Name of court	Local authority areas	Parts comprising court districts	
GLOU-CESTER —cont.	Gloucester Rural District (part). *Other parts* in Cheltenham, Dursley and Stroud County Court Districts.	Arlingham, Ashleworth, Brockworth, Brookthorpe with Whaddon, Chaceley, Churchdown, Down Hatherley, Elmore, Frampton-on-Severn, Fretherne-with-Saul, Hardwicke, Harescombe, Haresfield, Hasfield, Highnam,	Hucclecote, Innsworth, Longford, Longney, Maisemore, Minsterworth, Moreton Valenze, Newnham, Norton, Quedgeley, Sandhurst, Standish, Tirley, Twigworth, Upton St. Leonards, Westbury-on-Severn, Whitminster.
	Newent Rural District.	Bromsberrow, Corse, Dymock, Hartpury, Kempley, Newent, Oxenhall, Pauntley,	Redmarley D'Abitôt, Rudford, Staunton, Taynton, Tibberton, Upleadon.
	West Dean Rural District (part). *Other part* in Monmouth County Court District.	Lydbrook.	
GOOLE	Goole Municipal Borough.	Goole.	
	Goole Rural District.	Adlingfleet, Airmyn, Eastoft, Fockerby, Goole Fields, Gowdall, Haldenby, Hook,	Ousefleet, Pollington, Rawcliffe, Reedness, Snaith and Cowick, Swinefleet, Whitgift.
	Howden Rural District (part). *Other parts* in Beverley and York County Court Districts.	Asselby, Barmby-on-the-Marsh, Blacktoft, Broomfleet, Eastrington, Gilberdyke,	Howden, Kilpin, Laxton, Newport, Spaldington, Wressle.
	Isle of Axholme Rural District (part). *Other parts* in Gainsborough, Scunthorpe and Thorne County Court Districts.	Garthorpe,	Luddington.
	Selby Rural District (part). *Other parts* in Pontefract and York County Court Districts.	Barlow, Camblesforth, Carlton,	Drax, Long Drax, Newland.

Column 1	*Column 2*	*Column 3*
Name of court	Local authority areas	Parts comprising court districts
GRANT-HAM	Grantham Municipal Borough.	Grantham.
	Melton and Belvoir Rural District (part). *Other parts* in Melton Mowbray and Oakham County Court Districts.	Belvoir, Bottesford.
	South Kesteven Rural District (part). *Other parts* in Sleaford, Stamford and Spalding County Court Districts.	Corby Glen, Swayfield, Irnham, Swinstead.
	West Kesteven Rural District (part). *Other part* in Newark County Court District.	Allington, Hougham, Ancaster, Hough on the Hill, Barkston, Ingoldsby, Barrowby, Lenton Keisby and Belton and Osgodby, Manthorpe, Little Ponton and Bitchfield and Stroxton, Bassingthorpe, Londonthorpe and Boothby Harrowby Without, Pagnell, Marston, Braceby and Normanton, Sapperton, North Witham, Burton Coggles, Old Somerby, Carlton Scroop, Pickworth, Colsterworth, Ropsley and Denton, Humby, Easton, Sedgebrook, Foston, Skillington, Great Gonerby, South Witham, Great Ponton, Stoke Rochford, Gunby and Syston, Stainby, Welby, Harlaxton, Woolsthorpe, Heydour, Wyville with Honington, Hungerton.
GRAVES-END	Gravesend Municipal Borough.	Gravesend.
	Northfleet Urban District.	Northfleet.
	Strood Rural District (part). *Other part* in Rochester County Court District.	Cobham, Meopham, Luddesdown, Shorne.
	Swanscombe Urban District.	Swanscombe.
GRAYS THUR-ROCK	London Borough of Havering (part). *Other parts* in Brentwood and Ilford County Court Districts.	That part of the borough south of a line drawn from where the West Horndon to Upminster Railway Line crosses the boundary, westwards along the north side of the Railway Line to Warley Street, northwards to the west of Warley Street to its junction with the Southend Arterial Road A127, along the south of that road to Front Lane, southwards on the west side of Front

Column 1	Column 2	Column 3
Name of court	Local authority areas	Parts comprising court districts
GRAYS THUR-ROCK —cont.	London Borough of Havering (part). —cont.	Lane to St. Mary's Lane, then west along the south side of St. Mary's Lane and south along the east side of Argyle Gardens to reach Ockendon Road, Corbets Tey east of the crematorium, then westwards on the south side of Ockendon Road, Harwood Hall Lane and Park Farm Road to the Ingrebourne River and southwards along the river to its confluence with the River Thames.
	Thurrock Urban District.	Thurrock.
GREAT GRIMSBY	Caistor Rural District (part). _Other parts_ in Lincoln, Louth and Scunthorpe County Court Districts.	Brocklesby, Cabourne, Caistor, Claxby, Great Limber, Keelby, Normanby le Wold, Riby, Rothwell, Swallow, Swinhope, Thoresway, Thorganby.
	Cleethorpes Municipal Borough.	Cleethorpes.
	Glanford Brigg Rural District (part). _Other part_ in Scunthorpe County Court District.	East Halton, Goxhill, North Killingholme, South Killingholme, Thornton Curtis, Ulceby, Wootton.
	Grimsby County Borough.	Grimsby.
	Grimsby Rural District.	Ashby cum Fenby, Aylesby, Barnoldby le Beck, Beelsby, Bradley, Brigsley, East Ravendale, Habrough, Hatcliffe, Hawerby cum Beesby, Healing, Humberston and Weelsby, Immingham, Irby, Laceby, New Waltham, Stallingborough, Waltham, West Ravendale, Wold Newton,
	Holderness Rural District (part). _Other parts_ in Beverley and Kingston upon Hull County Court Districts.	Bull Fort (Extra Parochial).
	Louth Rural District (part). _Other part_ in Louth County Court District.	Grainsby, Holton le Clay, Tetney, Waithe.
GREAT MALVERN	Ledbury Rural District (part). _Other part_ in Hereford County Court District.	Colwall, Mathon Rural.

Column 1	*Column* 2	*Column* 3
Name of court	Local authority areas	Parts comprising court districts
GREAT MALVERN —*cont.*	Malvern Urban District.	Malvern.
	Martley Rural District (part). *Other parts* in Kidderminster and Worcester County Court Districts.	Bransford,　　Leigh.
	Upton upon Severn Rural District (part). *Other parts* in Cheltenham and Worcester County Court Districts.	Berrow,　　Little Malvern, Birtsmorton,　Madresfield, Castlemorton,　Newland, Guarlford,　Upton upon Severn, Hanley Castle,　Welland.
GREAT YAR-MOUTH	Blofield and Flegg Rural District (part). *Other part* in Norwich County Court District.	Ashby with Oby,　Ormesby Caister on Sea,　　St. Michael, Filby,　Reedham, Fleggburgh,　Repps with Freethorpe,　　Bastwick, Halvergate,　Rollesby, Hemsby,　Somerton, Martham,　Stokesby with Mautby,　　Herringby, Ormesby　Thurne, St. Margaret　West Caister, 　with Scratby,　Winterton on Sea.
	Great Yarmouth County Borough.	Great Yarmouth.
	Loddon Rural District (part). *Other parts* in Lowestoft and Norwich County Court Districts.	Haddiscoe,　Thurlton, Norton Subcourse, Toft Monks.
	Lothingland Rural District (part). *Other parts* in Halesworth and Lowestoft County Court Districts.	Belton,　Fritton, Bradwell,　Hopton on Sea. Burgh Castle,
	Smallburgh Rural District (part). *Other part* in Norwich County Court District.	Brumstead,　Ludham, Catfield,　Sea Palling, Hickling,　Potter Heigham, Horsey,　Stalham, Ingham,　Sutton. Lessingham,
GUILD-FORD	Bagshot Rural District (part). *Other part* in Aldershot and Farnham County Court District.	Bisley,　Chobham.
	Godalming Municipal Borough.	Godalming.
	Guildford Municipal Borough.	Guildford.
	Guildford Rural District (part). *Other parts* in Aldershot and Farnham and Dorking County Court Districts.	Albury,　Ockham, Artington,　Pirbright, Compton,　Ripley, East Clandon,　St. Martha East Horsley,　　(Chilworth),

Column 1	Column 2	Column 3	
Name of court	Local authority areas	Parts comprising court districts	
GUILD-FORD —*cont.*	Guildford Rural District (part). —*cont.*	Send, Shackleford, Shalford, Shere, Wanborough,	West Clandon, West Horsley, Wisley, Worplesdon.
	Hambledon Rural District (part). *Other part* in Aldershot and Farnham County Court District.	Alford, Bramley, Busbridge, Chiddingfold, Cranleigh, Dunsfold, Elstead,	Ewhurst, Hambledon, Hascombe, Peper Harrow, Thursley, Witley, Wonersh.
	Haslemere Urban District.	Haslemere.	
	Woking Urban District.	Woking.	
HALES-WORTH	Blyth Rural District (part). *Other parts* in Ipswich and Woodbridge County Court Districts.	Blythburgh, Bramfield, Chediston, Cookley, Cratfield, Darsham, Dunwich, Heveningham, Huntingfield, Linstead Magna,	Linstead Parva, Middleton, Thorington, Ubbeston, Walberswick, Walpole, Wenhaston with Mells, Westleton.
	Halesworth Urban District.	Halesworth.	
	Hartismere Rural District (part). *Other parts* in Ipswich, Norwich and Stowmarket County Court Districts.	Athelington, Bedfield, Brundish, Fressingfield, Laxfield, Mendham, Metfield, Southolt,	Stradbroke, Syleham, Tannington, Weybread, Wilby, Wingfield, Worlingworth.
	Lothingland Rural District (part). *Other parts* in Gt. Yarmouth and Lowestoft County Court Districts.	Easton Bavents, Henham, Reydon,	Uggleshall, Wangford.
	Southwold Municipal Borough.	Southwold.	
	Wainford Rural District (part). *Other part* in Lowestoft County Court District.	Blyford, Brampton, Flixton, Holton, Homersfield or South Elmham St. Mary, Ilketshall St. Margaret, Rumburgh, Sotherton, South Elmham All Saints and St. Nicholas,	South Elmham St. Cross, South Elmham St. James, South Elmham St. Margaret, South Elmham St. Michael, South Elmham St. Peter, Spexhall, Stoven, Westhall, Wissett.

Column 1	*Column* 2	*Column* 3
Name of court	Local authority areas	Parts comprising court districts
HALIFAX	Brighouse Municipal Borough.	Brighouse.
	Elland Urban District.	Elland.
	Halifax County Borough.	Halifax.
	Queensbury and Shelf Urban District.	Queensbury and Shelf.
	Ripponden Urban District.	Ripponden.
	Sowerby Bridge Urban District.	Sowerby Bridge.
HARLOW	Dunmow Rural District (part). *Other parts* in Bishops Stortford, Braintree and Chelmsford County Court Districts.	White Roding.
	Epping Urban District.	Epping.
	Epping and Ongar Rural District (part). *Other parts* in Chelmsford and Ilford County Court Districts.	Bobbingworth, North Weald Bassett, Epping Upland, High Laver, Roydon, Little Laver, Sheering, Magdalen Laver, Stapleford Tawney, Matching, Theydon Bois, Moreton, Theydon Garnon, Nazeing, Theydon Mount.
	Harlow Urban District.	Harlow.
HARRO-GATE	Harrogate Municipal Borough.	Harrogate.
	Knaresborough Urban District.	Knaresborough.
	Nidderdale Rural District (part). *Other parts* in Ripon and York County Court Districts.	Allerton Killinghall, Mauleverer Kirby Hall, with Hopperton, Kirk Arkendale, Hammerton, Boroughbridge, Knaresborough Brearton, Outer, Cattal, Little Ouseburn, Coneythorpe Marton cum and Clareton, Grafton, Copgrove, Nidd, Dunsforths, Nun Monkton, Farnham, Pannal, Felliscliffe, Plompton, Ferrensby, Ripley, Flaxby, Roecliffe, Follifoot, Scotton, Goldsborough, Scriven, Great Ouseburn, Staveley, Great Ribston Thornville, with Walshford, Thorpe Green Underwoods, Hammerton, Walkingham Hill Hampsthwaite, with Occaney, Haverah Park, Whixley, Hunsingore, Widdington.

Column 1	Column 2	Column 3
Name of court	Local authority areas	Parts comprising court districts
HARRO-GATE—cont.	Ripon and Pateley Bridge Rural District (part). *Other part* in Ripon County Court District.	Bewerley, Birstwith, Bishop Thornton, Clint, Dacre, Down Stonebeck, Fountains Earth, Hartwith cum Winsley,	High and Low Bishopside, Menwith with Darley, Thornthwaite with Padside, Thruscross, Upper Stonebeck, Warsill.
	Thirsk Rural District (part). *Other parts* in Northallerton and Ripon County Court Districts.	Ellenthorpe.	
	Wetherby Rural District (part). *Other parts* in Leeds, Otley, and York County Court Districts.	Kearby with Netherby, Kirby Overblow, Kirk Deighton, North Deighton, North Rigton, Ribston Little,	Sicklinghall, Spofforth with Stockeld, Thorp Arch, Walton, Wetherby.
HARTLE-POOL	Easington Rural District (part). *Other parts* in Durham and Sunderland County Court Districts.	Castle Eden, Horden, Hutton Henry, Monk Hesleden, Nesbitt,	Peterlee, Sheraton with Hulam, Shotton.
	Hartlepool County Borough.	Hartlepool.	
	Stockton Rural District (part). *Other part* in Stockton on Tees County Court District.	Brierton with Dalton Piercy, Claxton with Greatham,	Elwick, Elwick Hall, Hart.
HARWICH	Harwich Municipal Borough.	Harwich.	
	Tendring Rural District (part). *Other part* in Colchester and Clacton County Court District.	Beaumont with Moze, Bradfield, Great Oakley, Little Oakley,	Mistley, Ramsey, Tendring, Wix, Wrabness.
HASTINGS	Battle Rural District (part). *Other part* in Tunbridge Wells County Court District.	Ashburnham, Battle, Beckley, Bodiam, Brede, Brightling, Camber, Catsfield, Crowhurst, Dallington, East Guldeford, Ewhurst, Fairlight, Guestling,	Icklesham, Iden, Mountfield, Northiam, Peasmarsh, Penhurst, Pett, Playden, Rye Foreign, Salehurst, Sedlescombe, Udimore, Westfield, Whatlington.

Column 1	*Column* 2	*Column* 3
Name of court	Local authority areas	Parts comprising court districts
HASTINGS —*cont.*	Bexhill Municipal Borough.	Bexhill.
	Hailsham Rural District (part). *Other parts* in Eastbourne and Lewes County Court Districts.	Hooe, Ninfield.
	Hastings County Borough.	Hastings.
	Rye Municipal Borough.	Rye.
HAVER- FORD- WEST	Carmarthen Rural District (part). *Other parts* in Carmarthen and Llanelli County Court Districts.	Cilymaenllwyd, Llandissilio East, Eglwyscummin, Pendine, Henllanfallteg, Whitland. Llanboidy.
	Fishguard and Goodwick Urban District.	Fishguard and Goodwick.
	Haverfordwest Municipal Borough.	Haverfordwest.
	Haverfordwest Rural District.	Ambleston, Llanreithan, Boulston, Llanrian, Brawdy, Llanstadwell, Burton, Llanstinan, Camrose, Llanwnda, Castlebythe, Llanychaer, Cathedral Manorowen, Close of Marloes, St. David's, Mathry, Dale, Morvil, Fishguard Nolton, South, North Prendergast, Freystrop, Pontfaen, Granston, Puncheston, Grassholm Robeston West, Island (Extra Roch, Parochial), Rosemarket, Hamlet of Rudbaxton, St. Martin, St. Bride's, Hamlet of St. David's, St. Thomas, St. Dogwells, Haroldston St. Edrens, St. Issells, St. Elvis, Haroldston St. Ishmael's, West, St. Lawrence, Hasguard, St. Nicholas, Hayscastle, Skokholm Island, Henry's Moat, Smalls Rock Herbrandston, (Lighthouse), Hubberston, South Bishop Ro k Johnston, (Lighthouse), Jordanston, Spittal, Lambston, Steynton, Letterston, Talbenny, Little Newcastle, Treffgarne, Llandeloy, Uzmaston, Llanfair Walton East, Nant y Gof, Walton West, Llangwm, Walwyn's Castle, Llanhowell, Whitchurch, Llanllawer, Wiston.

Column 1	Column 2	Column 3
Name of court	Local authority areas	Parts comprising court districts
HAVER-FORD-WEST —cont.	Milford Haven Urban District.	Milford Haven.
	Narberth Urban District.	Narberth.
	Narberth Rural District.	Amroth, Begelly, Bletherston, Clarbeston, Coedcanlas, Crinow, Crunwear, East Williamston, Grondre, Jeffreston, Lampeter Velfrey, Llanddewi Velfrey, Llandilo, Llandissilio West, Llanfellteg West, Llangan West, Llangolman, Llanycefn, Llawhaden, Llsysyfrân, Loveston, Ludchurch, Maenclochog, Martletwy, Minwear, Mounton, Mynachlogddu, Narberth North, Narberth South, New Moat, Newton North, Reynalton, Robeston Wathen, St. Issells, Slebech, Vorlan, Yerbeston.
	Neyland Urban District.	Neyland.
	Pembroke Municipal Borough.	Pembroke.
	Pembroke Rural District.	Angle, Bosherston, Caldy and St. Margaret's Islands, Carew, Castlemartin, Cosheston, Gumfreston, Hodgeston, Hundleton, Lamphey, Lawrenny, Manorbier, Nash, Penally, Pwllcrochan, Redberth, Rhoscrowther, St. Florence, St. Petrox, St. Twynnells, Stackpole Elidor, Tenby St. Mary out Liberty, Upton, Warran.
	Tenby Municipal Borough.	Tenby.
HAY-WARDS HEATH	Burgess Hill Urban District.	Burgess Hill.
	Chailey Rural District (part). *Other parts* in Brighton and Lewes County Court Districts.	Ditchling, Wivelsfield.
	Cuckfield Urban District.	Cuckfield.
	Cuckfield Rural District (part). *Other parts* in Brighton and East Grinstead County Court Districts.	Albourne, Ardingly, Balcombe, Bolney, Clayton, Cuckfield Rural, Hurstpierpoint, Keymer, Lindfield Rural, Slaugham, Twineham.

Column 1	Column 2	Column 3	
Name of court	Local authority areas	Parts comprising court districts	
HELSTON	Helston Municipal Borough.	Helston.	
	Kerrier Rural District (part). *Other parts* in Redruth and Truro and Falmouth County Court Districts.	Breage, Constantine, Crowan, Cury, Germoe, Grade Ruan, Gunwalloe, Landewednack, Manaccan, Mawgan in Meneage,	Mullion, St. Anthony in Meneage, St. Keverne, St. Martin in Meneage, Sithney, Wendron.
HEMEL HEMP- STEAD	Berkhamsted Urban District.	Berkhamsted.	
	Berkhamsted Rural District (part). *Other part* in Aylesbury County Court District.	Aldbury, Little Gaddesden, Nettleden with Pottens End,	Northchurch, Wigginton.
	Hemel Hempstead Municipal Borough.	Hemel Hempstead.	
	Hemel Hempstead Rural District (part). *Other parts* in Amersham, Luton and St. Albans County Court Districts.	Bovingdon, Chipperfield,	Great Gaddesden, Kings Langley.
HERE- FORD	Bromyard Rural District (part). *Other parts* in Leominster and Worcester County Court Districts.	Avenbury, Bishop's Frome, Bromyard, Felton, Little Cowarne, Morton Jeffries,	Much Cowarne, Ocle Pychard, Stoke Lacey, Ullingswick, Winslow.
	Dore and Bredwardine Rural District (part). *Other part* in Pontypool and Abergavenny County Court District.	Abbey Dore, Bacton, Bredwardine, Clifford, Craswall, Cusop, Dorstone, Dulas, Ewyas Harold, Kenderchurch, Kentchurch, Kilpeck, Kingstone, Llancillo, Madley,	Michaelchurch Escley, Newton, Orcop, Peterchurch, Rowlstone, St. Devereux, St. Margaret's, Thruxton, Treville, Turnastone, Tyberton, Vowchurch, Wormbridge.
	Hereford Municipal Borough.	Hereford.	

Column 1	Column 2	Column 3
Name of court	Local authority areas	Parts comprising court districts
HERE-FORD —*cont.*	Hereford Rural District.	Aconbury, Allensmore, Bartestree, Bolstone, Breinton, Burghill and Tillington, Callow, Clehonger, Credenhill, Dewsall, Dinedor, Dinmore, Dormington, Eaton Bishop, Fownhope, Grafton, Hampton Bishop, Haywood, Holme Lacy, Holmer and Shelwick, Kenchester, Little Birch, Little Dewchurch, Lower Bullingham, Lugwardine, Marden, Mordiford, Moreton on Lugg, Much Birch, Much Dewchurch, Pipe and Lyde, Preston Wynne, Stoke Edith, Stretton Sugwas, Sutton, Wellington, Westhide, Weston Beggard, Withington.
	Ledbury Rural District (part). *Other part* in Great Malvern County Court District.	Ashperton, Aylton, Bosbury, Canon Frome, Castle Frome, Coddington, Donnington, Eastnor, Eggleton, Ledbury Town, Ledbury Rural, Little Marcle, Much Marcle, Munsley, Pixley, Putley, Stretton Grandison, Tarrington, Wellington Heath, Woolhope, Yarkhill.
	Weobley Rural District (part). *Other parts* in Kington and Leominster County Court Districts.	Bishopstone, Blakemere, Bridge Sollers, Brinsop, Brobury, Byford, Canon Pyon, King's Pyon, Letton, Mansell Gamage, Mansell Lacy, Moccas, Monnington on Wye, Norton Canon, Preston on Wye, Staunton on Wye, Wormsley, Yazor.
HERT-FORD	Braughing Rural District (part). *Other parts* in Bishop's Stortford and Hitchin County Court Districts.	Aspenden, Westmill.
	Hatfield Rural District (part). *Other parts* in Barnet and St. Albans County Court Districts.	Essenden.
	Hertford Municipal Borough.	Hertford.
	Hertford Rural District (part). *Other part* in Hitchin County Court District.	Aston, Bayford, Bengeo Rural, Benington, Bramfield, Brickendon Liberty, Datchworth,

Column 1	Column 2	Column 3
Name of court	Local authority areas	Parts comprising court districts
HERT-FORD —cont.	Hertford Rural District (part). —cont.	Hertingfordbury, Little Amwell, Little Berkhampstead, Sacombe, Stapleford, Tewin, Watton at Stone.
	Hoddesdon Urban District.	Hoddesdon.
	Ware Urban District.	Ware.
	Ware Rural District.	Eastwick, Gilston, Great Amwell, Great Munden, Hunsdon, Little Munden, Standon, Stanstead Abbots, Stanstead St. Margarets, Thundridge, Ware Rural, Widford.
	Welwyn Garden City Urban District.	Welwyn Garden City.
	Welwyn Rural District.	Ayot St. Lawrence, Ayot St. Peter, Welwyn.
HEXHAM	Bellingham Rural District.	Bavington, Bellingham, Birtley, Corsenside, Falstone, Greystead, Kielder, Kirkwhelpington, Otterburn, Rochester, Tarset, Wark.
	Haltwhistle Rural District (part). Other part in Carlisle County Court District.	Bardon Mill, Coanwood, Featherstone, Greenhead, Haltwhistle, Henshaw, Melkridge, Plenmeller with Whitfield, Thirlwall.
	Hexham Urban District.	Hexham.
	Hexham Rural District (part). Other parts in Consett and Newcastle upon Tyne County Court Districts.	Acomb, Allendale, Broomhaughs and Riding, Broomley and Stocksfield, Bywell, Chollerton, Corbridge, Haydon, Healey, Hedley, Hexhamshire, Hexham Low Quarter, Horsley, Humshaugh, Newbrough, Ovingham, Ovington, Sandhoe, Simonburn, Slaley, Wall, Warden, West Allen, Whittington.
	Prudhoe Urban District.	Prudhoe.
HIGH WYCOMBE	Amersham Rural District (part). Other part in Amersham County Court District.	Penn, Seer Green.

Column 1	Column 2	Column 3
Name of court	Local authority areas	Parts comprising court districts
HIGH WYCOMBE —cont.	Beaconsfield Urban District.	Beaconsfield.
	High Wycombe Municipal Borough.	High Wycombe.
	Cookham Rural District (part). Other parts in Reading and Slough County Court Districts.	Bisham.
	Marlow Urban District.	Marlow Urban.
	Wycombe Rural District (part). Other parts in Aylesbury and Reading County Court Districts.	Bledlow cum Saunderton, Bradenham, Chepping Wycombe, Fingest, Great and Little Hampden, Great Marlow, Hedsor, Hughenden, Ibstone, Lacey Green, Little Marlow, Longwick cum Ilmer, Princes Risborough, Radnage, Stokenchurch, Turville, West Wycombe, Rural, Wooburn.
HINCKLEY	Blaby Rural District (part). Other part in Leicester County Court District.	Aston Flamville, Elmesthorpe, Sapcote, Sharnford, Stoney Stanton, Wigston Parva.
	Hinckley Urban District.	Hinckley.
	Lutterworth Rural District (part). Other parts in Leicester, Market Harborough and Rugby County Court Districts.	Broughton Astley, Claybrooke Magna, Claybrooke Parva, Frolesworth, Leire, Ullesthorpe.
	Market Bosworth Rural District (part). Other parts in Ashby de la Zouch, Leicester and Nuneaton County Court Districts.	Cadeby, Higham on the Hill, Market Bosworth, Osbaston, Peckleton, Sutton Cheney.
	Rugby Rural District (part). Other parts in Coventry, Nuneaton and Rugby County Court Districts.	Copston Magna, Wibtoft.
HITCHIN	Ampthill Rural District (part). Other parts in Bedford, Bletchley and Leighton Buzzard and Luton County Court Districts.	Gravenhurst, Higham Gobion, Shillington.
	Baldock Urban District.	Baldock.
	Braughing Rural District (part). Other parts in Bishop's Stortford and Hertford County Court Districts.	Ardeley, Buckland, Buntingford, Cottered, Hormead, Wyddial.

Column 1	Column 2	Column 3
Name of court	Local authority areas	Parts comprising court districts
HITCHIN —cont.	Hertford Rural District (part). *Other part* in Hertford County Court District.	Walkern.
	Hitchin Urban District.	Hitchin.
	Hitchin Rural District (part). *Other part* in Biggleswade County Court District.	Ashwell, Newnham, Barkway, Nuthampstead, Barley, Offley, Bygrave, Pirton, Caldecote, Preston, Clothall, Radwell, Codicote, Reed, Graveley, Rushden, Hexton, St. Ippollitts, Holwell, St. Paul's Walden, Ickleford, Sandon, Kelshall, Shephall, Kimpton, Therfield, King's Walden, Wallington, Knebworth, Weston, Langley, Wymondley. Lilley,
	Letchworth Urban District.	Letchworth.
	Royston Urban District.	Royston.
	South Cambridgeshire Rural District (part). *Other parts* in Biggleswade, Cambridge and Newmarket County Court Districts.	Abington Pigotts, Litlington, Guilden Morden, Steeple Morden.
	Stevenage Urban District.	Stevenage.
HOLS- WORTHY	Bideford Rural District (part). *Other part* in Bideford County Court District.	Welcombe.
	Bude-Stratton Urban District.	Bude-Stratton.
	Holsworthy Rural District (part). *Other parts* in Bideford and Launceston County Court Districts.	Abbots Holsworthy, Bickington, Holsworthy Ashwater, Hamlets, Black Torrington, Luffincott, Bradford, Milton Damerel, Bradworthy, Pancrasweek, Bridgerule, Pyworthy, Clawton, Sutcombe, Cookbury, Tetcott, Halwill, Thornbury. Hollacombe,
	Stratton Rural District (part). *Other part* in Camelford County Court District.	Kilkhampton, North Tamerton, Launcells, Poundstock, Marhamchurch, Week St. Mary, Morwenstow, Whitstone.

Column 1	Column 2	Column 3
Name of court	Local authority areas	Parts comprising court districts
HOLS-WORTHY —cont.	Torrington Rural District (part). *Other parts* in Barnstaple and Bideford County Court Districts.	Buckland Shebbear, Filleigh, Sheepwash.
HOLY-WELL	Connah's Quay Urban District.	Connah's Quay.
	Flint Municipal Borough.	Flint.
	Holywell Urban District.	Holywell.
	Holywell Rural District (part). *Other part* in Mold County Court District.	Brynford, Nannerch, Caerwys, Newmarket, Gwaenysgor, Trelawnyd, Halkyn, Whitford, Llanasa, Ysceifiog.
HONITON	Honiton Municipal Borough.	Honiton.
	Honiton Rural District.	Awliscombe, Monkton, Branscombe, Northleigh, Broadhembury, Offwell, Buckerell, Payhembury, Combe Raleigh, Plymtree, Cotleigh, Sheldon, Dunkeswell, Southleigh, Farway, Talaton, Feniton, Upottery, Gittisham, Widworthy, Luppitt, Yarcombe.
	Ottery St. Mary Urban District.	Ottery St. Mary.
	Sidmouth Urban District.	Sidmouth.
HORSHAM	Crawley Urban District.	Crawley.
	Horsham Urban District.	Horsham.
	Horsham Rural District.	Billingshurst, Rudgwick, Cowfold, Rusper, Horsham Rural, Shipley, Itchingfield, Slinfold, Lower Beeding, Warnham, Nuthurst, West Grinstead.
HUDDERS-FIELD	Colne Valley Urban District.	Colne Valley.
	Denby Dale Urban District.	Denby Dale.
	Holmfirth Urban District.	Holmfirth.
	Huddersfield County Borough.	Huddersfield.
	Kirkburton Urban District.	Kirkburton.
	Meltham Urban District.	Meltham.

Column 1	Column 2	Column 3
Name of court	Local authority areas	Parts comprising court districts
HUNTING-DON	Chesterton Rural District (part). *Other part* in Cambridge County Court District.	Conington, Croxton, Eltisley, Fen Drayton, Graveley,	Over, Papworth Everard, Papworth St .Agnes, Swavesey.
	Huntingdon and Godmanchester Municipal Borough.	Huntingdon and Godmanchester.	
	Huntingdon Rural District.	Abbots Ripton, Alconbury, Alconbury Weston, Barham and Woolley, Brampton, Brington and Molesworth, Buckworth, Bythorn and Keyston, Conington, Easton, Ellington, Great Gidding,	Hamerton, Kings Ripton, Leighton, Little Gidding, Old Weston, Sawtry, Spaldwick, Steeple Gidding, The Stukeleys, Upton and Coppingford, Upwood and the Raveleys, Winwick, Wood Walton.
	Oundle and Thrapston Rural District (part). *Other parts* in Kettering, Oakham, Peterborough, Stamford and Wellingborough County Court Districts.	Clopton, Luddington,	Thurning.
	Ramsey Urban District.	Ramsey.	
	St. Ives Municipal Borough.	St. Ives.	
	St. Ives Rural District.	Bluntisham, Broughton, Bury, Colne, Earith, Fenstanton, Hemingford Abbots, Hemingford Grey, Hilton,	Holywell cum Needingworth, Houghton and Wyton, Old Hurst, Pidley cum Fenton, Somersham, Warboys, Wistow, Woodhurst.
	St. Neots Urban District.	St. Neots.	
	St. Neots Rural District (part). *Other part* in Biggleswade County Court District.	Buckden, Catworth, Covington, Diddington, Eynesbury Hardwicke, Grafham, Great Paxton, Great Staughton, Hail Weston,	Kimbolton, Little Paxton, Offord Cluny, Offord D'Arcy, St. Neots Rural, Stow Longa, Southoe and Midloe, Tilbrook, Toseland, Yelling.

Column 1	Column 2	Column 3
Name of court	Local authority areas	Parts comprising court districts
HYDE	Chapel en le Frith Rural District (part). *Other parts* in Buxton and Sheffield County Court Districts.	Charlesworth, Chisworth.
	Denton Urban District.	Denton.
	Glossop Municipal Borough.	Glossop.
	Hyde Municipal Borough.	Hyde.
	Longdendale Urban District.	Longdendale.
	Tintwistle Rural District.	Tintwistle.
ILFORD	London Borough of Barking.	Barking.
	Chigwell Urban District (part). *Other parts* in Bow and Edmonton County Court Districts.	The Chigwell Ward.
	London Borough of Havering (part). *Other parts* in Brentwood and Grays Thurrock County Court Districts.	That part of the Borough northwest of a line drawn from where Nags Head Lane crosses the north-eastern boundary, south along the west side of Nags Head Lane and Hall Lane to the Southend Arterial Road (A127), then east along the south side of A127 to Front Lane, thence south along the west side of Front Lane to St. Mary's Lane, then west along the south side of St. Mary's Lane and south along the east side of Argyle Gardens to reach Ockendon Road, Corbets Tey, east of the Crematorium; then turning west and running to the south of Ockendon Road, Harwood Hall Lane and Park Farm Road to the Ingrebourne River and southwards along the River to its confluence with the River Thames.
	London Borough of Redbridge (part). *Other part* in Bow County Court District.	That part of the Borough east of a line commencing at the point where Manor Road crosses the northern boundary, thence south-westwards to the east of Dr. Barnado's Homes and Roding Lane North to Southend Road, thence south-west to the River Roding, thence southwards along the River to the Borough boundary.
	Epping and Ongar Rural District (part). *Other parts* in Brentwood, Harlow and Chelmsford County Court Districts.	Lambourne, Stapleford Abbots.

Column 1	*Column* 2	*Column* 3
Name of court	Local authority areas	Parts comprising court districts
ILKESTON	Basford Rural District (part). *Other parts* in Alfreton, Loughborough, Mansfield and Nottingham County Court Districts.	Awsworth, Cossall.
	Belper Rural District (part). *Other parts* in Alfreton, Derby and Matlock County Court Districts.	Denby, Kilburn, Horsley, Mapperley, Horsley Shipley, Woodhouse, Smalley.
	Eastwood Urban District.	Eastwood.
	Heanor Urban District.	Heanor.
	Ilkeston Municipal Borough.	Ilkeston.
	South East Derbyshire Rural District (part). *Other part* in Derby County Court District.	Dale Abbey, Sandiacre, Hopwell, Stanley, Morley, Stanton by Dale, Risley, West Hallam.
IPSWICH	Blyth Rural District (part). *Other parts* in Halesworth and Woodbridge County Court Districts.	Earl Soham.
	Cosford Rural District (part). *Other parts* in Bury St. Edmunds, Stowmarket and Sudbury County Court Districts.	Aldham, Layham, Elmsett, Semer, Kersey, Whatfield.
	Deben Rural District (part). *Other part* in Woodbridge County Court District.	Cretingham, Purdis Farm Culpho, Playford, Falkenham, Rushmere Foxhall, St. Andrew, Great Bealings, Stratton Hall, Grundisburgh, Swilland, Hemley, Trimley St. Martin, Kesgrave, Trimley St. Mary, Kirton, Tuddenham, Levington, Waldringfield, Little Bealings, Westerfield, Nacton, Witnesham. Newbourn,
	Felixstowe Urban District.	Felixstowe.
	Gipping Rural District (part). *Other part* in Stowmarket County Court District.	Akenham, Gosbeck, Ashbocking, Great Blakenham, Ashfield with Helmingham, Thorpe, Hemingstone, Barham, Henley, Baylham, Little Blakenham, Bramford, Nettlestead, Claydon, Offton, Coddenham, Pettaught, Crowfield, Somersham, Debenham, Whitton, Flowton, Willisham, Framsden, Winston.

Column 1	Column 2	Column 3
Name of court	Local authority areas	Parts comprising court districts
IPSWICH —cont.	Hadleigh Urban District.	Hadleigh.
	Hartismere Rural District (part). *Other parts* in Halesworth, Norwich and Stowmarket County Court Districts.	Kenton, Monk Soham.
	Ipswich County Borough.	Ipswich.
	Samford Rural District.	Arwarton, Hintlesham, Belstead, Holbrook, Bentley, Holton St. Mary, Brantham, Little Wenham, Burstall, Raydon, Capel St. Mary, Shelley, Chattisham, Shotley, Chelmondiston, Sproughton, Copdock, Stratford St. Mary, East Bergholt, Stutton, Freston, Tattingstone, Great Wenham, Washbrook, Harkstead, Wherstead, Higham, Woolverstone.
KEIGHLEY	Bingley Urban District.	Bingley.
	Keighley Municipal Borough.	Keighley.
	Skipton Rural District (part). *Other part* in Skipton County Court District.	Steeton with Sutton. Eastburn,
KENDAL	Kendal Municipal Borough.	Kendal.
	Lakes Urban District (part). *Other part* in Penrith County Court District.	The Ambleside, Rydal and Grasmere, Loughrigg and Langdales, Troutbeck Wards.
	Sedburgh Rural District.	Dent, Sedbergh. Garsdale,
	South Westmorland Rural District.	Arnside, Hugill, Barbon, Hutton Roof, Beetham, Kentmere, Burton, Killington, Casterton, Kirkby Crook, Lonsdale, Crosthwaite and Lambrigg, Lyth, Levens, Dalton, Longsleddale, Dillicar, Lupton, Docker, Mansergh, Fawcett Forest, Meathop, Firbank, and Ulpha, Grayrigg, Middleton, Helsington, Milnthorpe, Heversham, Natland, Hincaster, Nether Staveley, Holme, New Hutton,

Column 1	*Column 2*	*Column 3*
Name of court	Local authority areas	Parts comprising court districts
KENDAL —*cont.*	South Westmorland Rural District. —*cont.*	Old Hutton, and Holmescales, Over Staveley, Patton, Preston Patrick, Preston Richard, Scalthwaiterigg, Sedgewick, Skelsmergh, / Stainton, Strickland Ketel, Strickland Roger, Underbarrow and Bradleyfield, Whinfell, Whitwell and Selside, Witherslack.
	North Lonsdale Rural District (part). *Other part* in Barrow in Furness and Ulverston County Court District.	Claife, Coniston, Hawkshead, / Satterthwaite, Skelwith, Torver.
	Windermere Urban District.	Windermere.
KETTER-ING	Burton Latimer Urban District.	Burton Latimer.
	Corby Urban District.	Corby.
	Desborough Urban District.	Desborough.
	Kettering Municipal Borough.	Kettering.
	Kettering Rural District (part). *Other part* in Market Harborough County Court District.	Broughton, Cottingham, Cranford, Cransley, East Carlton, Geddington, Grafton Underwood, Gretton, Harrington, Loddington, / Middleton, Newton, Orton, Pytchley, Rushton, Stanion, Thorpe Malsor, Warkton, Weekley, Weldon.
	Oundle and Thrapston Rural District (part). *Other parts* in Huntingdon, Oakham, Peterborough, Stamford and Wellingborough County Court Districts.	Aldwincle, Benefield, Brigstock, Deene, Deenethorpe, Denford, Islip, Lilford cum Wigsthorpe, / Lowick, Pilton, Sudborough, Thorpe Achurch, Thrapston, Titchmarsh, Twywell, Wadenhoe, Woodford.
	Rothwell Urban District.	Rothwell.
KIDDER-MINSTER	Bewdley Municipal Borough.	Bewdley.
	Bridgnorth Rural District (part). *Other parts* in Bridgnorth, Ludlow, Shrewsbury, Wellington and Wolverhampton County Court Districts.	Highley, Kinlet, / Neen Savage.

Column 1	Column 2	Column 3
Name of court	Local authority areas	Parts comprising court districts
KIDDER-MINSTER —cont.	Droitwich Rural District (part). *Other parts* in Bromsgove, Redditch and Worcester County Court Districts.	Doverdale, Elmley Lovett, Hartlebury.
	Kidderminster Municipal Borough.	Kidderminster.
	Kidderminster Rural District (part). *Other part* in Stourbridge County Court District.	Chaddesley Corbett, Churchill and Blakedown, Kidderminster Foreign, / Ribbesford, Rock, Rushock, Stone, Upper Arley, Wolverley.
	Ludlow Rural District (part). *Other parts* in Ludlow and Shrewsbury County Court Districts.	Cleobury Mortimer, Hopton Wafers, / Neen Sollars, Woodhouse.
	Martley Rural District (part). *Other parts* in Great Malvern and Worcester County Court Districts.	Abberley, Astley.
	Stourport on Severn Urban District.	Stourport on Severn.
	Tenbury Rural District (part). *Other parts* in Leominster and Ludlow County Court Districts.	Bayton, Eastham, Hanley, Knighton on Teme, Lindridge, / Mamble, Pensax. Stanford with Orleton, Stockton on Teme.
KINGS-BRIDGE	Kingsbridge Urban District.	Kingsbridge.
	Kingsbridge Rural District.	Aveton Gifford, Bigbury, Blackawton, Buckland Tout Saints, Charleton, Chivelstone, Churchstow, East Allington, East Portlemouth, Kingston, Loddiswell, Malborough, / Modbury, Ringmore, Sherford, Slapton, South Huish, South Milton, South Pool, Stoke Fleming, Stokenham, Strete, Thurlestone, West Alvington, Woodleigh.
	Salcombe Urban District.	Salcombe.
KINGS LYNN	Docking Rural District.	Anmer, Bagthorpe with Barmer, Barwick, Bircham, Brancaster, Burnham Market, / Burnham Norton, Burnham Overy, Burnham Thorpe, Choseley, Dersingham, Docking, East Rudham,

Column 1	*Column* 2	*Column* 3
Name of court	Local authority areas	Parts comprising court districts
KINGS LYNN —*cont.*	Docking Rural District. —*cont.*	Fring, Sedgeford, Heacham, Shernborne, Holme Snettisham, next the Sea, South Creake, Houghton, Stanhoe, Ingoldisthorpe, Syderstone, North Creake, Thornham, Old Hunstanton, Titchwell, Ringstead, West Rudham.
	Downham Market Urban District.	Downham Market.
	Downham Rural District (part). *Other part* in Thetford County Court District.	Barton Bandish, Stow Bardolph, Boughton, Stradsett, Crimplesham, Tottenhill, Denver, Watlington, Downham West, Welney, Fincham, Wereham, Fordham, West Dereham, Hilgay, Wiggenhall St. Marham, German, Nordelph, Wiggenhall St. Runcton Holme, Mary Magdalen, Ryston, Wiggenhall St. Shouldham, Mary the Virgin, Shouldham Wimbotsham, Thorpe, Wormegay, Southery, Wretton. Stoke Ferry,
	Freebridge Lynn Rural District.	Bawsey, Hillington, Castle Acre, Leziate, Castle Rising, Little Massingham, Congham, Middleton, East Walton, North Runcton, East Winch, North Wootton, Flitcham with Pentney, Appleton, Roydon, Gayton, Sandringham, Great South Wootton, Massingham, West Acre, Grimston, West Winch. Harpley,
	Kings Lynn Municipal Borough.	Kings Lynn.
	Marshland Rural District (part). *Other part* in Wisbech County Court District.	Clenchwarton, Tilney All Saints, Terrington Tilney St. Lawrence. St. Clement, Terrington St. John,
	Mitford and Launditch Rural District (part). *Other parts* in East Dereham and Norwich County Court Districts.	Colkirk, Twyford, Gateley, Weasenham All Great Dunham, Saints, Guist, Weasenham Horningtoft, St. Peter, Lexham, Wellingham, Little Dunham, Whissonsett. Rougham,

Column 1	Column 2	Column 3
Name of court	Local authority areas	Parts comprising court districts
KINGS LYNN —*cont.*	Hunstanton Urban District.	Hunstanton.
	St. Faith's and Aylsham Rural District (part). *Other part* in Norwich County Court District.	Foulsham, Themelthorpe.
	Swaffham Urban District.	Swaffham.
	Swaffham Rural District (part). *Other parts* in East Dereham and Thetford County Court Districts.	Ashill, Narborough, Beachamwell, Narford, Cockley Cley, Necton, Didlington, Newton by Foulden, Castle Acre, Gooderstone, North Pickenham, Great Oxborough, Cressingham, Saham Toney, Hilborough, South Acre, Holme Hale, South Pickenham, Ickburgh, Sporle with Little Palgrave. Cressingham,
	Walsingham Rural District (part). *Other part* in Norwich County Court District.	Barsham, Kettlestone, Binham, Little Ryburgh, Briningham, Little Snoring, Brinton, Little Walsingham, Briston, Melton Constable, Dunton, Pudding Norton, Fakenham, Raynham, Fulmodeston, Sculthorpe, Great Ryburgh, Stibbard, Great Snoring, Stiffkey, Great Swanton Novers, Walsingham, Tattersett, Gunthorpe, Thurning, Helhoughton, Thursford, Hempton, Warham, Hindolveston, Wighton, Hindringham, Wood Norton. Holkham,
	Wayland Rural District (part). *Other parts* in Norwich and Thetford County Court Districts.	Carbrooke, Ovington, Griston, Watton. Merton,
	Wells next the Sea Urban District.	Wells next the Sea.
KINGSTON UPON HULL	Beverley Rural District (part). *Other part* in Beverley County Court District.	North Ferriby, Swanland, Skidby, Welton.
	Haltemprice Urban District.	Haltemprice.
	Hedon Municipal Borough.	Hedon.

Column 1	*Column* 2	*Column* 3
Name of court	Local authority areas	Parts comprising court districts
KINGSTON UPON HULL —*cont.*	Holderness Rural District (part). *Other parts* in Beverley and Great Grimsby County Court Districts.	Aldbrough, Bilton, Burstwick, Burton Constable, Burton Pidsea, Coniston, Easington, East Garton, Ellerby, Elstronwick, Halsham, Hollym, Holmpton, Humbleton, Keyingham, Mappleton, Ottringham, Patrington, Paull, Preston, Rimswell, Roos, Skeffling, Skirlaugh, Sproatley, Sunk Island, Swine, Thorngumbald, Welwick, Withernwick.
	Kingston-upon-Hull County Borough.	Kingston-upon-Hull.
	Withernsea Urban District.	Withernsea.
KINGSTON-UPON-THAMES	Chertsey Urban District.	Chertsey.
	Esher Urban District.	Esher.
	London Borough of Kingston-upon-Thames.	Kingston-upon-Thames.
	London Borough of Merton (part). *Other part* in Croydon County Court District.	That part of the Borough north of a line drawn from the point where the Borough boundary crosses the western end of Coombe Lane eastwards along the middle of Coombe Lane, Kingston Road, High Street Merton and High Street Collier's Wood to the Borough boundary.
	London Borough of Richmond-upon-Thames (part). *Other parts* in Brentford and Wandsworth County Court Districts.	The Hampton, Hampton Hill, Hampton Wick, Lower Teddington and Upper Teddington Wards.
	Sunbury on Thames Urban District.	Sunbury-on-Thames.
	Walton and Weybridge Urban District.	Walton and Weybridge.
KINGTON	Kington Urban District.	Kington.
	Kington Rural District.	Brilley, Byton, Combe, Eardisley, Huntington, Kington Rural, Kinsham, Knill, Lower Harpton, Lyonshall, Pembridge, Rodd, Nash and Little Brampton, Stapleton, Staunton on Arrow, Titley, Whitney, Winforton with Willersley.

Column 1	Column 2	Column 3
Name of court	Local authority areas	Parts comprising court districts
KINGTON —cont.	New Radnor Rural District (part). *Other parts* in Builth and Llandrindod Wells County Court Districts.	Colva, Ednol, Evenjobb, Gladestry, Harpton and Wolfpits, Kinnerton Salford and Badland, Llanfihangel Nant Melan,	Michaelchurch on Arrow, Newchurch, New Radnor, Old Radnor and Burlingjobb, Trewern and Gwaithla, Walton and Womaston.
	Weobley Rural District (part). *Other parts* in Hereford and Leominster County Court Districts.	Almeley, Kinnersley,	Sarnesfield.
KNIGHTON	Clun and Bishop's Castle Rural District (part). *Other parts* in Ludlow, Shrewsbury and Welshpool County Court Districts.	Bedstone, Bettws y Crwyn, Bucknell,	Hopton Castle, Llanfair Waterdine, Stowe.
	Knighton Urban District.	Knighton.
	Knighton Rural District (part). *Other parts* in Llandrindod Wells and Newtown County Court Districts.	Beguildy, Bleddfa, Cascob, Discoed, Heyope, Litton and Cascob,	Llanfihangel Rhydithon, Llangunllo, Norton, Pilleth, Stanage, Whitton.
	Leominster and Wigmore Rural District (part). *Other parts* in Leominster and Ludlow County Court Districts.	Adforton, Brampton Bryan, Buckton and Coxall,	Lingen, Walford, Letton and Newton Willey.
	Presteigne Urban District.	Presteigne.
LAMBETH	London Borough of Lambeth (part). *Other parts* in Southwark and Wandsworth County Court Districts.	That part of the Borough to the east and south of a line drawn from the point where the Borough boundary crosses Hermitage Bridge thence northwards along the middle of Streatham High Road, Streatham Hill, Brixton Hill, Acre Lane, Bedford Road, Clapham Road, Jeffreys Road, Southville Road and Wandsworth Road to the point on the north side of Nine Elms Lane where it is crossed by the Borough boundary.
	London Borough of Lewisham (part). *Other parts* in Bromley and Southwark County Court Districts.	That part of the Borough bounded in the east by the Southern Region railway line from the Borough boundary at Honour Oak Station to the point where the railway line crosses the Borough boundary south of Sydenham Station.

Column 1	Column 2	Column 3
Name of court	Local authority areas	Parts comprising court districts
LAMBETH —cont.	London Borough of Southwark (part). *Other part* in Southwark County Court District.	That part of the Borough south of a line drawn from the point where the Borough boundary crosses the junction of Lambeth Road with Kennington Road eastwards along the middle of Lambeth Road, St. George's Road, New Kent Road and Old Kent Road to the point where the Borough boundary crosses New Cross Road.
LAMPETER	Aberaeron Rural District (part). *Other parts* in Aberystwyth and Cardigan County Court Districts.	Cellan, Llangybi, Lampeter Rural, Llanwenog, Llanfair Llanwnen, Clydogau, Silian, Llanfihangel Trefilan. Ystrad,
	Lampeter Municipal Borough.	Lampeter.
	Llandeilo Rural District (part). *Other parts* in Ammamford, Carmarthen and Llandovery County Court Districts.	Conwil Gaio (part), viz:— That part of the civil parish lying west of the Afon Cothi from its junction with the civil parish boundary to its junction with the Afon Twrch, and thence west of the Afon Twrch to its junction with the civil parish boundary.
	Newcastle Emlyn Rural District (part). *Other parts* in Carmarthen and Cardigan County Court Districts.	Llanfihangel Rhosycorn (part), viz:— That part of the civil parish bounded on the north, east and south by the civil parish boundary, on the west by the Afon Marlais from the southern civil parish boundary to its junction with the civil parish boundary south of Allt Lawr, and thence by the civil parish boundary. Llanllwni, Llanycrwys, Llanybyther, Pencarreg.
	Teifiside Rural District (part). *Other parts* in Aberystwyth and Cardigan County Court Districts.	Llandyssul.
	Tregaron Rural District (part). *Other part* in Aberystwyth County Court District.	Bettws Lleucu, Gwynfil, Blaenpenal, Llanbadarn Odwyn, Caron is Clawdd, Llanddewi Brefi, Caron Uwch Llangeitho, Clawdd, Nantcwnlle. Gartheli,
LAN- CASTER	Carnforth Urban District.	Carnforth.
	Garstang Rural District (part). *Other parts* in Blackpool and Preston County Court Districts.	Bleasdale, Nether Wyresdale, Cabus, Winmarleigh. Forton,
	Lancaster Municipal Borough.	Lancaster.

Column 1	Column 2	Column 3	
Name of court	Local authority areas	Parts comprising court districts	
LAN-CASTER —cont.	Lancaster Rural District.	Ashton with Stodday, Bolton le Sands, Cockerham, Ellel, Heaton with Oxcliffe, Middleton, Overton,	Over Wyresdale, Priest Hutton, Scotforth, Silverdale, Slyne with Hest, Thurnham, Warton, Yealand Conyers, Yealand Redmayne.
	Lunesdale Rural District.	Arkholme with Cawood, Borwick, Burrow with Burrow, Cantsfield, Caton with Littledale, Claughton, Gressingham, Halton with Aughton, Hornby with Farleton,	Ireby, Leck, Melling with Wrayton, Nether Kellet, Over Kellet, Quernmore, Roeburndale, Tatham, Tunstall, Wennington, Whittington, Wray with Botton.
	Morecambe and Heysham Municipal Borough.	Morecambe and Heysham.	
	Settle Rural District (part). *Other part* in Skipton County Court District.	Bentham, Burton in Lonsdale,	Ingleton, Thornton in Lonsdale.
LAUNCES-TON	Holsworthy Rural District (part). *Other parts* in Bideford and Holsworthy County Court Districts.	Broadwood-widger, Northcott,	St. Giles on the Heath, Virginstow.
	Launceston Municipal Borough.	Launceston.	
	Launceston Rural District.	Altarnun, Boyton, Egloskerry, Laneast, Lawhitton Rural, Lewannick, Lezant, North Hill, North Petherwin, St. Stephen's by Launceston Rural,	St. Thomas the Apostle Rural, South Petherwin, Stoke Climsland, Tremaine, Treneglos, Tresmeer, Trewen, Warbstow, Werrington.
	Tavistock Rural District (part). *Other part* in Tavistock County Court District.	Bradstone, Dunterton,	Kelly, Lifton.
LEEDS	Horsforth Urban District.	Horsforth.	
	Leeds County Borough.	Leeds.	

Column 1	Column 2	Column 3
Name of court	Local authority areas	Parts comprising court districts
LEEDS —cont.	Rothwell Urban District.	Rothwell.
	Tadcaster Rural District (part). *Other parts* in Pontefract and York County Court Districts.	Aberford, Austhorpe, Barkston, Barwick in Elmet, Lead, Lotherton cum Aberford, Parlington, Saxton-with-Scarthingwell, Sherburn in Elmet, Sturton Grange, Stutton with Hazlewood, Swillington.
	Wetherby Rural District (part). *Other parts* in Harrogate, Otley, and York County Court Districts.	Bardsey with Rigton, Boston Spa, Bramham with Oglethorpe, Clifford, Collingham, East Keswick, Scarcroft, Thorner, Wothersome.
LEEK	Cheadle Rural District (part). *Other parts* in Stoke on Trent and Uttoxeter County Court Districts.	Blore with Swinscoe, Cheddleton, Consall, Cotton, Ipstones, Kingsley, Oakamoor, Waterhouses.
	Leek Urban District.	Leek.
	Leek Rural District (part). *Other parts* in Buxton and Stoke on Trent County Court Districts.	Bradnop, Butterton, Endon and Stanley, Fawfieldhead, Grindon, Heathylee, Heaton, Hollinsclough, Horton, Ilam, Leekfrith, Longnor, Longsdon, Onecote, Rushton, Sheen, Tittesworth, Warslow and Elkstones, Wetton.
LEICESTER	Barrow upon Soar Rural District (part). *Other part* in Loughborough County Court District.	Anstey, Barkby, Barkby Thorpe, Beeby, Birstall, Cossington, East Goscote, Newtown Linford, Queniborough, Ratcliffe on the Wreake, Rearsby, Rothley, South Croxton, Swithland, Syston, Thrussington, Thurcaston, Thurmaston, Ulverscroft, Warnlip.
	Billesdon Rural District (part). *Other part* in Oakham County Court District.	Allexton, Billesdon, Burton Overy, Carlton Curlieu, Cold Newton, East Norton, Frisby, Gaulby, Goadby, Great Glen, Great Stretton, Houghton on the Hill, Hungarton, Illston on the Hill, Keyham, Kings Norton, Launde, Little Stretton,

Column 1	Column 2	Column 3
Name of court	Local authority areas	Parts comprising court districts
LEICESTER —cont.	Billesdon Rural District (part). —cont.	Loddington, Lowesby, Marefield, Noseley, Rolleston, Scraptoft, Skeffington, Stoughton, Thurnby, Tilton, Tugby and Keythorpe, Wistow.
	Blaby Rural District (part). *Other part* in Hinckley County Court District.	Blaby, Braunstone, Cosby, Countesthorpe, Croft, Enderby, Glenfields, Glen Parva, Huncote, Kilby, Kirby Muxloe, Leicester Forest West, Lubbesthorpe, Narborough, Potters Marston, Thurlaston, Whetstone.
	Leicester County Borough.	Leicester.
	Lutterworth Rural District (part). *Other parts* in Hinckley, Market Harborough and Rugby County Court Districts.	Arnesby, Ashby Magna, Ashby Parva, Bruntingthorpe, Dunton Bassett, Peatling Magna, Peatling Parva, Shearsby, Willoughby Waterleys.
	Market Bosworth Rural District (part). *Other parts* in Ashby de la Zouch, Hinckley and Nuneaton County Court Districts.	Desford, Groby, Markfield, Newbold Verdon, Ratby.
	Oadby Urban District.	Oadby.
	Wigston Urban District.	Wigston.
LEIGH	Atherton Urban District.	Atherton.
	Golborne Urban District.	Golborne.
	Leigh Municipal Borough.	Leigh.
	Tyldesley Urban District.	Tyldesley.
LEO- MINSTER	Bromyard Rural District (part). *Other parts* in Hereford and Worcester County Court Districts.	Bredenbury, Collington, Edvin Loach, Edwyn Ralph, Grendon Bishop, Hampton Charles, Pencombe with Grendon Warren, Thornbury, Wacton, Wolferlow.
	Leominster Municipal Borough.	Leominster.
	Leominster and Wigmore Rural District (part). *Other parts* in Knighton and Ludlow County Court Districts.	Aymestrey, Bodenham, Croft, Docklow, Eye, Moreton and Ashton, Eyton, Ford, Hampton Wafer, Hatfield, Hope under Dinmore,

Column 1	*Column* 2	*Column* 3
Name of court	Local authority areas	Parts comprising court districts
LEO-MINSTER —*cont.*	Leominster and Wigmore Rural District (part). —*cont.*	Humber, Kimbolton, Kingsland, Laysters, Lucton, Luston, Middleton on the Hill, Monkland, New Hampton, Newton, Orleton, Pudlestone, Shobdon, Stoke Prior, Yarpole.
	Tenbury Rural District (part). *Other parts* in Kidderminster and Ludlow County Court Districts.	Bockleton, Kyre, Stoke Bliss.
	Weobley Rural District (part). *Other parts* in Hereford and Kington County Court Districts.	Birley, Dilwyn, Eardisland, Stretford, Weobley.
LEWES	Chailey Rural District (part). *Other parts* in Brighton and Haywards Heath County Court Districts.	Barcombe, Beddingham, Chailey, East Chiltington, Glynde, Hamsey, Iford, Kingston near Lewes, Lewes St. Ann Without, Lewes St. John Without, Newick, Piddinghoe, Plumpton, Ringmer, Rodmell, Southease, South Heighton, South Malling Without, Streat, Tarring Neville, Telscombe, West Firle, Westmeston.
	Hailsham Rural District (part). *Other parts* in Eastbourne and Hastings County Court Districts.	Alciston, Berwick, Chalvington, East Hoathly, Laughton, Ripe, Selmeston.
	Lewes Municipal Borough.	Lewes.
	Newhaven Urban District.	Newhaven.
	Seaford Urban District.	Seaford.
	Uckfield Rural District (part). *Other parts* in East Grinstead and Tunbridge Wells County Court Districts.	Buxted, Fletching, Framfield, Hadlow Down, Isfield, Little Horsted, Maresfield, Uckfield.
LICHFIELD	Lichfield Municipal Borough.	Lichfield.
	Lichfield Rural District (part). *Other parts* in Stafford and Tamworth County Court Districts.	Alrewas, Armitage with Handsacre, Burntwood, Curborough and Elmhurst, Farewell and Chorley, Fisherwick, Hammerwich, Hamstall Ridware,

Column 1	Column 2	Column 3
Name of court	Local authority areas	Parts comprising court districts
LICHFIELD —*cont.*	Lichfield Rural District (part). —*cont.*	King's Bromley, Longdon, Mavesyn Ridware, Shenstone, Streethay, Swinfen and Packington, Wall, Weeford, Whittington.
	Tutbury Rural District (part). *Other part* in Burton upon Trent County Court District.	Yoxall.
LINCOLN	Caistor Rural District (part). *Other parts* in Great Grimsby, Louth and Scunthorpe County Court Districts.	Buslingthorpe, Glentham, Linwood, Lissington, Middle Rasen, Osgodby, Tealby, Toft Newton, Walesby, West Rasen.
	Gainsborough Rural District (part). *Other part* in Gainsborough County Court District.	Hardwick.
	Horncastle Urban District.	Horncastle.
	Horncastle Rural District (part). *Other parts* in Boston, Louth and Skegness and Spilsby County Court Districts.	Baumber, Bucknall, Edlington, Fulletby, Gautby, Great Sturton, Greetham, Hatton, Hemingby, High Toynton, Horsington, Kirkby on Bain, Kirkstead, Langton, Langton by Wragby, Low Toynton, Mareham on the Hill, Minting, Panton, Roughton, Sotby, Stixwould, Thimbleby, Thornton, Tupholme, Waddingworth, West Ashby, West Barkwith, West Torrington, Wispington, Woodhall, Wragby.
	Lincoln County Borough.	Lincoln.
	Market Rasen Urban District.	Market Rasen.
	Newark Rural District (part). *Other part* in Newark County Court District.	Broadholme, Harby, Thorney.
	North Kesteven Rural District (part). *Other parts* in Newark and Sleaford County Court Districts.	Aubourn, Haddington and South Hykeham, Boothby Graffoe, Bracebridge Heath, Branston and Mere, Canwick, Coleby, Doddington and Whisby, Dunston, Eagle and Swinethorpe, Harmston, Heighington, Metheringham, Navenby, Nocton, North Hykeham, Potter Hanworth, Skellingthorpe, Thorpe on the Hill, Waddington, Washingborough.

Column 1	Column 2	Column 3
Name of court	Local authority areas	Parts comprising court districts
LINCOLN —cont.	Welton Rural District.	Aisthorpe, Apley, Bardney, Barlings, Brattleby, Broxholme, Bullington, Burton, Caenby, Cammeringham, Cherry Willingham, Cold Hanworth, Dunholme, Faldingworth, Fiskerton, Friesthorpe, Fulnetby, Goltho, Grange de Lings, Greetwell, Hackthorn, Holton cum Beckering, Ingham, Nettleham, / Newball, Normanby by Spital, North Carlton, Owmby, Rand, Reepham, Riseholme, Saxby, Saxilby with Ingleby, Scampton, Scothern, Snarford, Snelland South Carlton, Spridlington, Stainfield, Stainton by Langworth, Sudbrooke, Thorpe in the Fallows, Welton, West Firsby, Wickenby.
	Woodhall Spa Urban District.	Woodhall Spa.
LISKEARD	Liskeard Municipal Borough.	Liskeard.
	Liskeard Rural District (part). *Other part* in Bodmin County Court District.	Boconnoc, Broadoak, Duloe, Lanreath, Lansallos, Lanteglos, Linkinhorne, Liskeard, Menheniot, Morval, / Pelynt, St. Cleer, St. Ive, St. Keyne, St. Martin, St. Neot, St. Pinnock, St. Veep, South Hill.
	Looe Urban District.	Looe.
	St. Germans Rural District (part). *Other parts* in Plymouth and Tavistock County Court Districts.	Callington, Quethiock, St. Dominick, / St. Germans, St. Mellion.
LIVERPOOL	Bootle County Borough.	Bootle.
	Crosby Municipal Borough.	Crosby.
	Kirkby Urban District.	Kirkby.
	Litherland Urban District.	Litherland.
	Liverpool County Borough.	Liverpool.

Column 1	Column 2	Column 3
Name of court	Local authority areas	Parts comprising court districts
LIVERPOOL —*cont.*	West Lancashire Rural District (part). *Other parts* in Southport and Wigan County Court Districts.	Aintree, Netherton, Ince Blundell, Sefton, Lydiate, Simonswood, Maghull, Thornton. Melling,
LLAN-DOVERY	Llandeilo Rural District (part). *Other parts* in Ammanford, Carmarthen and Lampeter County Court Districts.	Cilycwm, Conwil Gaio (part), viz:— That part of the civil parish lying east of the Afon Cothi from its junction with the civil parish boundary to its junction with the Afon Twrch, and thence east of the Afon Twrch to its junction with the civil parish boundary. Llanddeusant, Llangadock, Llandingat Llansadwrn, Without, Llanwrda, Llanfairarybryn, Myddfai.
	Llandovery Municipal Borough.	Llandovery.
LLAN-DRINDOD WELLS	Builth Rural District (part). *Other part* in Builth County Court District.	Llanwrthwl.
	Colwyn Rural District (part). *Other part* in Builth County Court District.	Llandrindod Rural.
	Knighton Rural District (part). *Other parts* in Knighton and Newtown County Court Districts.	Llanbister, Llanddewi Ystradenny.
	Llandrindod Wells Urban District.	Llandrindod Wells.
	New Radnor Rural District (part). *Other parts* in Builth and Kington County Court Districts.	Llandegley.
	Rhayader Rural District.	Abbey Cwmhir, Llanyre, Cefnllys Rural, Nantmel, Llanbadarnfawr, Rhayader, Llanfihangel St. Harmon. Helygen, Llansantffraid Cwmdeuddwr,
LLANELLI	Burry Port Urban District.	Burry Port.
	Carmarthen Rural District (part). *Other parts* in Carmarthen and Haverfordwest County Court Districts.	Llangendeirne (part):— The part of the civil parish lying to the south of the River Gwendraeth-fawr.
	Kidwelly Municipal Borough.	Kidwelly.
	Llanelli Municipal Borough.	Llanelli.

Column 1	*Column* 2	*Column* 3
Name of court	Local authority areas	Parts comprising court districts
LLANELLI —*cont.*	Llanelli Rural District (part). *Other part* in Ammanford County Court District.	Llanedy (part),:— The part of the civil parish bounded on the east by a line drawn from a point on the northern boundary of the civil parish by the middle of the road leading from Capel Hendre to the main road at Cooper's House, along the main road north-eastwards to a house named Gors, thence by the road leading southwards passing Llwyn-y-fedwen and Clawdd-du to a point where this road crosses a stream north of Dyffryn, then in a south-easterly direction along this stream, passing Erw-wastad-fawr, to its confluence with the River Loughor.
		Llanelli Rural, Pembrey,
		Llangennech, Pontyberem.
		Llannon,
LLAN- GEFNI, AND HOLY- HEAD	Aethwy Rural District.	Llanddaniel Fâb, Llangristiolus,
		Llanddona, Llanidan,
		Llandegfan, Llaniestyn Rural,
		Llanfairpwll- Llansadwrn,
		gwyngyll, Newborough,
		Llanfihangel Penmynydd,
		Esgeifiog, Pentraeth,
		Llangadwaladr, Puffin Island
		Llangaffo, (Extra Parochial),
		Llangeinwen, Trefdraeth.
		Llangoed,
	Amlwch Urban District.	Amlwch.
	Beaumaris Municipal Borough.	Beaumaris.
	Holyhead Urban District.	Holyhead Urban.
	Llangefni Urban District.	Llangefni.
	Twrcelyn Rural District.	Carreglefn, Llanfairyn-
		Coedana, ghornwy,
		Llanallgo, Llanfechell,
		Llanbabo, Llanfihangel,
		Llanbadrig, Tre'r Beirdd,
		Llanddyfnan, Llangwyllog,
		Llandyfrydog, Llechcyn farwydd,
		Llaneilian, Penrhôs Lligwy,
		Llanerchymedd, Rhodogeidio,
		Llaneugrad, Rhosybol,
		Llanfair Tregaian.
		Mathafarn
		Eithaf,
	Valley Rural District.	Aberffraw, Llanfaethlu,
		Bodedern, Llanfair yn
		Bodwrog, Neubwll,
		Cerrigceinwen, Llanrhyddlad,
		Heneglwys, Llantrisant,
		Holyhead Rural, Llanynghenedl,
		Llanddeusant, Llechylched,
		Llandrygarn, Rhoscolyn,
		Llanfachraeth, Trewalchmai.
		Llanfaelog,

Column 1	Column 2	Column 3
Name of court	Local authority areas	Parts comprising court districts
LLANID-LOES	Llanidloes Municipal Borough.	Llanidloes.
	Newtown and Llanidloes Rural District (part). *Other part* in Newtown County Court District.	Llangurig, Trefeglwys. Llanidloes Without.
LOUGH-BOROUGH	Barrow upon Soar Rural District (part). *Other part* in Leicester County Court District.	Barrow upon Quorndon, Soar, Seagrave, Burton on the Sileby, Wolds, Walton on the Cotes, Wolds, Hoton, Woodhouse, Mountsorrel, Wymeswold. Prestwold,
	Basford Rural District (part). *Other parts* in Alfreton, Ilkeston, Mansfield and Nottingham County Court Districts.	Costock, Sutton Bonington, East Leake, Thorpe in the Kingston upon Glebe, Soar, West Leake, Normanton Willoughby on the upon Soar, Wolds, Ratcliffe upon Wysall. Soar, Rempstone, Stanford upon Soar,
	Castle Donington Rural District (part). *Other part* in Ashby de la Zouch County Court District.	Belton, Kegworth, Castle Lockington-Donington, Hemington, Charley, Long Whatton. Isley cum Langley,
	Loughborough Municipal Borough.	Loughborough.
	Shepshed Urban District.	Shepshed.
LOUTH	Caistor Rural District (part). *Other parts* in Great Grimsby, Lincoln and Scunthorpe County Court Districts.	Kirmond le Mire, Sixhills, Legsby, Stainton le Vale. North Willingham,
	Horncastle Rural District (part). *Other parts* in Boston, Lincoln and Skegness and Spilsby County Court Districts.	Asterby, Goulceby, Belchford, Market Stainton, Benniworth, Ranby, Cawkwell, Scamblesby. East Barkwith,
	Louth Municipal Borough.	Louth.
	Louth Rural District (part). *Other part* in Great Grimsby County Court District.	Aby with Belleau, Greenfield, Binbrook, Alvingham, Brackenborough, Authorpe, Burgh on Bain, Beesby in the Burwell, Marsh, Calcethorpe,

Column 1	*Column* 2	*Column* 3
Name of court	Local authority areas	Parts comprising court districts
LOUTH —*cont.*	Louth Rural District (part). —*cont.*	Claythorpe, Little Cawthorpe, Conisholme, Little Grimsby, Covenham St. Ludborough, Bartholomew, Ludford, Covenham St. Maidenwell, Mary, Maltby le Marsh, Donington on Manby, Bain, Marsh Chapel, East Wykeham, Muckton, Fotherby, North Coates, Fulstow, North Cockerington, Gayton le North Elkington, Marsh, North Ormsby, Gayton le Wold, North Reston, Grainthorpe, North Somercotes, Great Carlton, North Thoresby, Grimoldby, Raithby cum Hainton, Maltby, Hallington, Saleby with Hannah cum Thoresthorpe, Hagnaby, Saltfleetby All Haugh, Saints, Haugham, Saltfleetby St. Keddington, Clement, Kelstern, Saltfleetby St. Peter, Legbourne, Skidbrooke with Little Carlton, Saltfleet Haven.
	Louth Rural District (part). *Other part* in Great Grimsby County Court District.	South Tathwell, Cockerinton, Theddlethorpe South Elkington, all Saints, South Reston, Theddlethorpe South St. Helen, Somercotes, Tothill, South Thoresby, Utterby, South Walmsgate, Willingham, Welton le Wold, Stenigot, Withcall, Stewton, Withern with Stain, Strubby with Wyham cum Woodthorpe, Cadeby, Swaby, Yarburgh.
	Mablethorpe and Sutton Urban District.	Mablethorpe and Sutton.
LOWE-STOFT	Beccles Municipal Borough.	Beccles.
	Loddon Rural District (part). *Other parts* in Great Yarmouth and Norwich County Court Districts.	Aldeby, Gillingham, Burgh St. Peter, Stockton, Geldeston, Wheatacre.
	Lothingland Rural District (part). *Other parts* in Great Yarmouth and Halesworth County Court Districts.	Ashby, Covehithe, Barnby, Flixton, Benacre, Frostenden, Blundeston, Gisleham, Carlton Colville, Henstead, Corton, Herringfleet,

Column 1	Column 2	Column 3
Name of court	Local authority areas	Parts comprising court districts
LOWE-STOFT —cont.	Lothingland Rural District (part). —cont.	Kessingland, Lound, Mutford, Oulton,	Rushmere, Somerleyton, South Cove, Wrentham.
	Lowestoft Municipal Borough.	Lowestoft.
	Wainford Rural District (part). *Other part* in Halesworth County Court District.	Barsham, Ellough, Ilketshall St. Andrew, Ilketshall St. John, Ilketshall St. Lawrence, Mettingham,	North Cove, Redisham, Ringsfield, Shadingfield, Shipmeadow, Sotterley, Weston, Willingham, Worlingham.
LUDLOW	Bridgnorth Rural District (part). *Other parts* in Bridgnorth, Kidderminster, Shrewsbury, Wellington and Wolverhampton County Court Districts.	Farlow.
	Clun and Bishop's Castle Rural District (part). *Other parts* in Knighton, Shrewsbury and Welshpool County Court Districts.	Clun, Clunbury, Clungunford,	Edgton, Hopesay, Mainstone.
	Leominster and Wigmore Rural District (part). *Other parts* in Knighton and Leominster County Court Districts.	Brimfield, Burrington, Downton, Elton, Leinthall Starkes,	Leintwardine, Little Hereford, Pipe Aston, Richards Castle, Wigmore.
	Ludlow Rural District (part). *Other parts* in Kidderminster and Shrewsbury County Court Districts.	Abdon, Acton Scott, Ashford Bowdler, Ashford Carbonel, Bitterley, Boraston, Bromfield, Burford, Caynham, Clee St. Margaret, Coreley, Culmington, Diddlebury, East Hamlet, Eaton under Heywood, Greete, Halford, Heath,	Hope Bagot, Hope Bowdler, Hopton Cangeford, Ludford, Ludlow Rural Borough, Milson, Munslow, Nash, Onibury, Rushbury, Sibdon Carwood, Stanton Lacey, Stoke St. Milborough, Stokesay, Tugford, Wheathill, Whitton, Winstanstow.
	Tenbury Rural District (part). *Other parts* in Kidderminster and Leominster County Court Districts.	Rochford,	Tenbury.

Column 1	Column 2	Column 3
Name of court	Local authority areas	Parts comprising court districts
LUTON	Ampthill Rural District (part). *Other parts* in Bedford, Bletchley and Leighton Buzzard and Hitchin County Court Districts.	Harlington, Westoning. Tingrith,
	Dunstable Municipal Borough.	Dunstable.
	Hemel Hempstead Rural District (part). *Other parts* in Amersham, Hemel Hempstead and St. Albans County Court Districts.	Markyate.
	Luton County Borough.	Luton.
	Luton Rural District (part). *Other part* in Bletchley and Leighton Buzzard County Court District.	Barton le Clay, Streatley, Caddington, Studham, Chalgrave, Sundon, Houghton Regis, Toddington, Hyde, Totternhoe, Kensworth, Whipsnade.
LYMING-TON	Lymington Municipal Borough.	Lymington.
	New Forest Rural District (part). *Other part* in Southampton County Court District.	Boldre, Rhinefield, Brockenhurst, Sway. East Boldre,
MACCLES-FIELD	Alderley Edge Urban District.	Alderley Edge.
	Bollington Urban District.	Bollington.
	Macclesfield Municipal Borough.	Macclesfield.
	Macclesfield Rural District (part). *Other parts* in Buxton and Congleton County Court Districts.	Adlington, North Rode, Bosley, Over Alderley, Chelford, Pott Shrigley, Chorley, Poynton with Gawsworth, Worth, Great Warford, Prestbury, Henbury, Rainow, Hurdsfield, Siddington, Lyme Handley, Snelson, Macclesfield Sutton, Forest, Wildboarclough, Mottram St. Wincle, Andrew, Withington. Nether Alderley,
	Wilmslow Urban District.	Wilmslow.
MACHYN-LLETH	Aberystwyth Rural District (part). *Other part* in Aberystwyth County Court District.	Scybor-y-coed.
	Dolgellau Rural District (part). *Other part* in Dolgellau County Court District.	Pennal.

Column 1	Column 2	Column 3
Name of court	Local authority areas	Parts comprising court districts
MACHYN-LLETH —*cont.*	Machynlleth Urban District.	Machynlleth.
	Machynlleth Rural District.	Caerinion Fechan, Llanbrynmair, Cemmaes, Llanwrin, Darowen, Penegoes, Isygarreg, Uwchygarreg.
	Tywyn Urban District.	Tywyn.

MAID-STONE	Hollingbourne Rural District (part).
	   Other part in Sittingbourne County Court District.
		Boughton Headcorn,
		   Malherbe, Hollingbourne,
		Boxley, Hucking,
		Bredhurst, Langley,
		Broomfield, Leeds,
		Chart Sutton, Lenham,
		Detling, Sutton Valence,
		East Sutton, Thurnham,
		Harrietsham, Ulcombe.

	Maidstone Municipal Borough.	Maidstone.
	Maidstone Rural District.	Barming, Loose, Bearsted, Marden, Boughton Nettlestead, Monchelsea, Otham, Coxheath, Staplehurst, East Farleigh, Teston, Hunton, West Farleigh, Linton, Yalding.
	Malling Rural District (part). *Other parts* in Rochester and Sevenoaks County Court Districts.	Addington, Offham, Aylesford, Ryarsh, Birling, Snodland, Ditton, Trottiscliffe, East Malling, Wateringbury, East Peckham, West Malling, Leybourne, West Peckham. Mereworth,
MALDON	Burnham on Crouch Urban District.	Burnham on Crouch.

	Chelmsford Rural District (part).
	   Other parts in Braintree, Brentwood and Chelmsford County Court Districts.
		Woodham
		   Ferrers.

	Lexden and Winstree Rural District (part). *Other parts* in Colchester and Clacton and Sudbury County Court Districts.	Tiptree.
	Maldon Municipal Borough.	Maldon.
	Maldon Rural District.	Althorne, Goldhanger, Asheldham, Great Braxted, Bradwell on Sea, Great Totham, Cold Norton, Hazeleigh, Dengie, Langford,

Column 1	Column 2	Column 3
Name of court	Local authority areas	Parts comprising court districts
MALDON —cont.	Maldon Rural District. —cont.	Latchingdon, Little Braxted, Little Totham, Mayland, Mundon, North Fambridge, Purleigh, St. Lawrence, Southminster, Steeple, — Stow Maries, Tillingham, Tollesbury, Tolleshunt D'Arcy, Tolleshunt Knights, Tolleshunt Major, Ulting, Wickham Bishops, Woodham Mortimer, Woodham Walter.
MALMES- BURY	Malmesbury Municipal Borough.	Malmesbury.
	Malmesbury Rural District.	Brinkworth, Brokenborough, Charlton, Crudwell, Dauntsey, Easton Grey, Great Somerford, Hankerton, Hullavington, Lea and Cleverton, — Little Somerford, Luckington, Malmesbury St. Paul Without, Minety, Norton, Oaksey, Sherston, Sopworth.
	Tetbury Rural District (part). *Other parts* in Dursley and Stroud County Court Districts.	Ashley, Beverston, Boxwell with Leighterton, Cherington, Didmarton, — Long Newnton, Shipton Moyne, Tetbury, Tetbury Upton, Westonbirt with Lasborough.
MALTON	Helmsley Rural District.	Ampleforth, Arden, Beadlam, Bilsdale West Side, Byland with Wass, Cawton, Cold Kirby, Coulton, Dale Town, East Newton and Laysthorpe, Gilling East, Grimstone, — Harome, Hawnby, Helmsley, Laskill Pasture, Murton, Old Byland, Oldstead, Oswaldkirk, Pockley, Rievaulx, Scawton, Snilesworth, Sproxton, Stonegrave, Thorpe le Willows.
	Kirkbymoorside Rural District.	Appleton le Moors, Bransdale, Fadmoor, Farndale East, Farndale West, Gillamoor, Great Edstone, Hutton le Hole, Kirkbymoorside, Lastingham, — Little Edstone, Muscoates, Nawton, Ness, North Holme, Nunnington, Salton, Skiplam, Spaunton, Welburn, Wombleton.

Column 1	Column 2	Column 3
Name of court	Local authority areas	Parts comprising court districts
MALTON —cont.	Malton Urban District.	Malton.
	Malton Rural District.	Airyholme with Howthorpe and Baxter Howe, Amotherby, Appleton le Street with Easthorpe, Barton le Street, Barton le Willows, Broughton, Bulmer, Butterwick, Coneysthorpe, Crambe, Foston, Fryton, Ganthorpe, Great Habton, Henderskelf, — Hildenley, Hovingham, Huttons Ambo, Little Habton, Newsham and Brawby, Ryton, Scackleton, Sheriff Hutton with Cornborough, Slingsby, South Holme, Stittenham, Swinton, Terrington with Wigganthorpe, Thornton le Clay, Wath, Welburn, Whitwell on the Hill.
	Norton Urban District.	Norton.
	Norton Rural District (part). *Other parts* in Beverley, Bridlington and Scarborough County Court Districts.	Acklam, Birdsall, Burythorpe, Firby, Heslerton, Howsham, Kirby Grindalythe, Langton, Leavening, Rillington, — Scagglethorpe, Scampston, Scrayingham, Settrington, Thixendale, Thorpe Bassett, Westow, Wharram, Wintringham, Yedingham.
	Pickering Urban District.	Pickering.
	Pickering Rural District.	Aislaby, Allerston, Barughs Ambo, Cawthorne, Cropton, Ebberston, Hartoft, Kingthorpe, Kirby Misperton, Levisham, Lockton, Marton, — Middleton, Newton, Normanby, Pickering Marishes, Rosedale East, Rosedale West, Sinnington, Thornton Dale, Thornton Riseborough, Wilton, Wrelton.
	Stokesley Rural District (part). *Other parts* in Middlesbrough, Northallerton and Stockton on Tees County Court Districts.	Bilsdale Midcable.
MAN-CHESTER	Manchester County Borough.	Manchester.

Column 1	*Column* 2	*Column* 3
Name of court	Local authority areas	Parts comprising court districts
MANS-FIELD	Basford Rural District (part). *Other parts* in Alfreton, Ilkeston, Loughborough and Nottingham County Court Districts.	Annesley, Newstead.
	Blackwell Rural District (part). *Other parts* in Alfreton and Chesterfield County Court Districts.	Pleasley, Shirebrook.
	Kirkby in Ashfield Urban District.	Kirkby in Ashfield.
	Mansfield Municipal Borough.	Mansfield.
	Mansfield Woodhouse Urban District.	Mansfield Woodhouse.
	Southwell Rural District (part). *Other parts* in East Retford, Newark, Nottingham and Worksop County Court Districts.	Bilsthorpe, Haywood Oaks, Blidworth, Lindhurst, Boughton, Ollerton, Clipstone, Rufford, Edwinstowe, Wellow. Farnsfield,
	Sutton in Ashfield Urban District.	Sutton in Ashfield.
	Warsop Urban District.	Warsop.
MARCH	Chatteris Urban District.	Chatteris.
	March Urban District.	March.
	North Witchford Rural District.	Benwick, Manea, Doddington, Wimblington.
MARGATE	Broadstairs and St. Peter's Urban District.	Broadstairs and St. Peter's.
	Eastry Rural District (part). *Other parts* in Canterbury, Deal, Dover and Ramsgate County Court Districts.	Acol, St. Nicholas at Wade.
	Margate Municipal Borough.	Margate.
MARKET DRAYTON	Market Drayton Rural District (part). *Other part* in Whitchurch County Court District.	Adderley, Moreton Say, Cheswardine, Norton in Hales, Child's Ercall, Stoke upon Tern, Hinstock, Sutton upon Tern, Hodnet, Woore. Market Drayton,

Column 1	*Column* 2	*Column* 3
Name of court	Local authority areas	Parts comprising court districts
MARKET DRAYTON —*cont.*	Newcastle under Lyme Rural District (part). *Other parts* in Crewe and Newcastle under Lyme County Court Districts.	Ashley, Mucklestone, Tyrley.
	Stafford Rural District (part). *Other parts* in Stafford and Wellington County Court Districts.	Adbaston.
MARKET HAR- BOROUGH	Brixworth Rural District (part). *Other part* in Northampton County Court District.	Arthingworth, Clipston, East Farndon, Great Oxendon, Haselbech, Kelmarsh, — Marston Trussell, Naseby, Sibbertoft, Sulby, Welford.
	Kettering Rural District (part). *Other part* in Kettering County Court District.	Ashley, Brampton Ash, Braybrooke, Dingley, Rockingham, — Stoke Albany, Sutton Basset, Weston by Welland, Wilbarston.
	Lutterworth Rural District (part). *Other parts* in Hinckley, Leicester and Rugby County Court Districts.	Knaptoft, North Kilworth.
	Market Harborough Urban District.	Market Harborough.
	Market Harborough Rural District.	Blaston, Bringhurst, Cranoe, Drayton, East Langton, Fleckney, Foxton, Glooston, Great Easton, Gumley, Hallaton, Horninghold, Husbands Bosworth, Kibworth Beauchamp, Kibworth Harcourt, — Laughton, Lubenham, Medbourne, Mowsley, Nevill Holt, Saddington, Shangton, Slawston, Smeeton Westerby, Stockerston, Stonton Wyville, Theddingworth, Thorpe Langton, Tur Langton, Welham, West Langton.
	Uppingham Rural District (part). *Other part* in Oakham County Court District.	Caldecott.
MARL- BOROUGH	Marlborough Municipal Borough.	Marlborough.

Column 1	*Column* 2	*Column* 3
Name of court	Local authority areas	Parts comprising court districts
MARL-BOROUGH —*cont.*	Marlborough and Ramsbury Rural District (part). *Other parts* in Andover, Newbury and Swindon County Court Districts.	Avebury, Berwick Bassett, Broad Hinton, Chilton Foliat, East Kennett, Froxfield, Fyfield, Grafton, Great Bedwyn, Little Bedwyn, Mildenhall, Ogbourne St. Andrew, — Ogbourne St. George, Preshute, Ramsbury, Savernake, Shalbourne, West Overton, Winterbourne Bassett, Winterbourne Monkton.
	Pewsey Rural District (part). *Other parts* in Andover, Devizes and Salisbury County Court Districts.	Alton, Burbage, Collingbourne Ducis, Collingbourne Kingston, Easton Royal, — Everleigh, Manningford, Milton Lilbourne, Pewsey, Wilcot and Huish, Wootton Rivers.
MATLOCK	Ashbourne Rural District (part). *Other parts* in Buxton, Derby and Uttoxeter County Court Districts.	Ballidon, Bradbourne, Brassington, Callow, Carsington, Eaton and Alsop, Hopton, — Ible, Kirk Ireton, Lea Hall, Newton Grange, Parwich, Tissington.
	Bakewell Rural District (part). *Other parts* in Buxton, Chesterfield and Sheffield County Court Districts.	Aldwark, Beeley, Birchover, Chatsworth, Edensor, Elton, Gratton, Harthill, Hassop, Ivonbrook Grange, — Middleton and Smerrill, Nether Haddon, Over Haddon, Pilsley, Rowsley, Stanton, Winster, Youlgreave.
	Bakewell Urban District.	Bakewell.
	Belper Rural District (part). *Other parts* in Alfreton, Derby and Ilkeston County Court Districts.	Alderwasley, Ashleyhay, Dethick, Lea and Holloway, — Idridgehay and Alton.
	Matlock Urban District.	Matlock.
	Wirksworth Urban District.	Wirksworth.
MELTON MOWBRAY	Bingham Rural District (part). *Other parts* in Newark and Nottingham County Court Districts.	Upper Broughton.

Column 1	Column 2	Column 3
Name of court	Local authority areas	Parts comprising court districts
MELTON MOWBRAY —*cont.*	Melton and Belvoir Rural District (part). *Other parts* in Grantham and Oakham County Court Districts.	Ab Kettleby, Gaddesby, Asfordby, Garthorpe, Broughton and Grimston, Old Dalby, Hoby with Buckminster, Rotherby, Burton and Redmile, Dalby, Scalford, Clawson and Somerby, Harby, Sproxton, Croxton Stathern, Kerrial, Twyford and Eaton, Thorpe, Freeby, Waltham, Frisby, Wymondham.
	Melton Mowbray Urban District.	Melton Mowbray.
MERTHYR TYDFIL	Merthyr Tydfil County Borough (part). *Other part* in Aberdare County Court District.	Merthyr Tydfil, except Fair View, Incline Top, Nos. 1-42 Jenkin Street, King Street, Nos. 80 and 82 Locke Street and Parry's Houses.
	Vaynor and Penderyn Rural District (part). *Other parts* in Aberdare and Neath and Port Talbot County Court Districts.	Vaynor.
MIDDLES-BROUGH	Guisborough Urban District.	Guisborough.
	Saltburn and Marske by the Sea Urban District.	Saltburn and Marske by the Sea.
	Skelton and Brotton Urban District.	Skelton and Brotton.
	Stokesley Rural District (part). *Other parts* in Malton, Northallerton and Stockton on Tees County Court Districts.	Carlton, Little Ayton, Crathorne, Little Busby, Easby, Maltby, Faceby, Middleton upon Great and Little Leven, Broughton, Newby, Great Ayton, Nunthorpe, Great Busby, Rudby in Hilton, Cleveland, Hutton Rudby, Seamer, Ingleby Sexhow, Greenhow, Skutterskelfe, Kildale, Stokesley. Kirkby in Cleveland,
	Teesside County Borough (part). *Other part* in Stockton on Tees County Court District.	That part of the Borough south of the River Tees and east of the old River Tees, the Fleet and Stainsby Beck.

Column 1	Column 2	Column 3
Name of court	Local authority areas	Parts comprising court districts
MINE-HEAD	Dulverton Rural District (part). *Other parts* in Taunton and Tiverton County Court Districts.	Exford, Exmoor,	Winsford, Withypool.
	Minehead Urban District.	Minehead.	
	Watchet Urban District.	Watchet.	
	Williton Rural District (part). *Other part* in Bridgwater County Court District.	Bicknoller, Brompton Ralph, Carhampton, Clatworthy, Crowcombe, Cutcombe, Dunster, East Quantoxhead, Elworthy, Holford, Kilve, Luccombe, Luxborough, Minehead Without,	Monksilver, Nettlecombe, Oare, Old Cleeve, Porlock, Sampford Brett, Selworthy, Stogumber, Stringston, Timberscombe, Treborough, West Quantoxhead, Williton, Withycombe, Wootton Courtney.
MOLD	Buckley Urban District.	Buckley.	
	Harwarden Rural District (part). *Other parts* in Chester and Wrexham County Court Districts.	Treuddyn.	
	Holywell Rural District (part). *Other part* in Holywell County Court District.	Cilcain, Leeswood, Mold Rural,	Nerquis, Northop.
	Mold Urban District.	Mold.	
MON-MOUTH	Monmouth Municipal Borough.	Monmouth.	
	Monmouth Rural District.	Llandeilo United, Llangattock Vibon Avel United,	Mitchell Troy United, Raglan United, Trelech United.
	Ross and Whitchurch Rural District (part). *Other part* in Ross County Court District.	Ganarew, Garway, Llanrothal,	Welsh Bicknor, Welsh Newton, Whitchurch.
	West Dean Rural District (part). *Other part* in Gloucester County Court District.	Coleford, English Bicknor, Newland,	Staunton, West Dean.

Column 1	Column 2	Column 3
Name of court	Local authority areas	Parts comprising court districts
MORPETH	Ashington Urban District.	Ashington.
	Castle Ward Rural District (part). *Other part* in Newcastle upon Tyne County Court District.	Stannington, Whalton.
	Morpeth Municipal Borough.	Morpeth.
	Morpeth Rural District.	Cresswell, Mitford, East Netherwitton, Chevington, Pegswood, Ellington, Thirston, Hartburn, Tritlington, Hebron, Ulgham, Hepscott, Wallington Longhirst, Demesne, Longhorsley, West Chevington, Lynemouth, Widdrington. Meldon,
	Newbiggin by the Sea Urban District.	Newbiggin by the Sea.
	Rothbury Rural District (part). *Other part* in Alnwick County Court District.	Alwinton, Longframlington, Biddlestone, Netherton, Brinkburn, Nunnykirk, Cartington, Rothbury, Elsdon, Rothley, Harbottle, Snitter, Hepple, Thropton, Hesleyhurst, Tosson. Hollinghill,
NEATH AND PORT TALBOT	Glyncorrwg Urban District.	Glyncorrwg.
	Neath Municipal Borough.	Neath.
	Neath Rural District (part). *Other part* in Aberdare County Court District.	Baglan Higher, Dylais Lower, Blaengwrach, Michaelston Blaenhonddan, Higher, Clyne, Neath Higher, Coedffranc, Neath Lower, Dyffryn Resolven, Clydach, Tonna. Dylais Higher,

	Pontardawe Rural District (part). *Other part* in Ammanford County Court District.	Cilybebyll,
		Llangiwg (part) The Blaenegel and
		   Mawr, Godre'rgraig and Alltygrug
		   Wards.
		Mawr,
		Rhyndwyclydach,
		Ynisymond.

	Port Talbot Municipal Borough.	Port Talbot.
	Vaynor and Penderyn Rural District (part). *Other parts* in Aberdare and Merthyr Tydfil County Court Districts.	Ystradfellte,
	Ystradgynlais Rural District.	Ystradgynlais Ystradgynlais Higher, Lower.

Column 1	*Column* 2	*Column* 3
Name of court	Local authority areas	Parts comprising court districts
NELSON	Barrowford Urban District.	Barrowford.
	Brierfield Urban District.	Brierfield.
	Burnley Rural District (part). *Other parts* in Accrington and Burnley County Court Districts.	Barley with Wheatley Booth, Blacko, Foulridge, Goldshaw Booth, Old Laund Booth, Roughlee Booth.
	Colne Municipal Borough.	Colne.
	Nelson Municipal Borough.	Nelson.
	Trawden Urban District.	Trawden.
NEWARK	Bingham Rural District (part). *Other parts* in Melton Mowbray and Nottingham County Court Districts.	Flawborough, Flintham, Shelton, Sibthorpe.
	Newark on Trent Municipal Borough.	Newark on Trent.
	Newark Rural District (part). *Other part* in Lincoln County Court District.	Alverton, Balderton, Barnby in the Willows, Besthorpe, Coddington, Cotham, East Stoke, Elston, Farndon, Girton, Hawton, Holme, Kilvington, Langford, Meering, North Clifton, North Collingham South Clifton, South Collingham, South Scarle, Spalford, Staunton, Syerston, Thorpe, Wigsley, Winthorpe.
	North Kesteven Rural District. (part). *Other parts* in Lincoln and Sleaford County Court Districts.	Bassingham, Beckingham, Brant Broughton and Straggle-thorpe, Carlton le Moorland, North Scarle, Norton Disney, Stapleford, Swinderby, Thurlby.
	Southwell Rural District (part). *Other parts* in East Retford, Mansfield, Nottingham and Worksop County Court Districts.	Averham, Bathley, Bleasby, Carlton on Trent, Caunton, Cromwell, Eakring, Edingley, Egmanton, Fiskerton cum Morton, Grassthorpe, Halam, Halloughton, Hockerton, Hoveringham, Kelham, Kersall, Kirklington, Kneesall, Laxton, Maplebeck, North Muskham, Norwell, Ompton, Ossington, Rolleston,

Column 1	Column 2	Column 3
Name of court	Local authority areas	Parts comprising court districts
NEWARK —cont.	Southwell Rural District (part). —cont.	South Muskham, Southwell, Staythorpe, Sutton on Trent, Thurgarton, Upton, Weston, Winkburn.
	West Kesteven Rural District (part). Other part in Grantham County Court District.	Caythorpe, Claypole, Fenton, Fulbeck, Long Bennington, Stubton, Westborough and Dry Doddington.
NEWBURY	Bradfield Rural District (part). Other parts in Didcot and Reading County Court Districts.	Aldermaston, Bucklebury, Frilsham, Stanford Dingley, Yattendon.
	Hungerford Rural District.	Combe, East Garston, East Shefford, Hungerford, Inkpen, Kintbury, Lambourn, West Shefford, West Woodhay.
	Kingsclere and Whitchurch Rural District (part). Other parts in Andover and Basingstoke County Court Districts.	Ashmansworth, Burghclere, East Woodhay, Ecchinswell and Sydmonton, Highclere, Kingsclere, Litchfield and Woodcott, Newtown.
	Marlborough and Ramsbury Rural District (part). Other parts in Andover, Marlborough and Swindon County Court Districts.	Buttermere, Ham.
	Newbury Municipal Borough.	Newbury.
	Newbury Rural District.	Boxford, Brimpton, Chieveley, Cold Ash, Enborne, Greenham, Hamstead Marshall, Leckhampstead, Midgham, Shaw cum Donnington, Speen, Thatcham, Wasing, Welford, Winterbourne, Woolhampton.
	Wantage Rural District (part). Other part in Didcot County Court District.	Beedon, Hampstead Norris, Hermitage, Peasemore.
NEW- CASTLE UNDER LYME	Newcastle under Lyme Municipal Borough.	Newcastle under Lyme.
	Newcastle under Lyme Rural District (part). Other parts in Crewe and Market Drayton County Court Districts.	Audley Rural, Chapel and Hill Chorlton, Keele, Madeley, Maer, Whitmore.

Column 1	*Column 2*	*Column 3*
Name of court	Local authority areas	Parts comprising court districts
NEW-CASTLE UNDER LYME —*cont.*	Stone Rural District (part). *Other parts* in Stoke on Trent and Stafford County Court Districts.	Standon, Swynnerton.
NEW-CASTLE UPON TYNE	Blaydon Urban District.	Blaydon.
	Castle Ward Rural District (part). *Other part* in Morpeth County Court District.	Belsay, Matfen, Brunswick, North Gosforth, Capheaton, Ponteland, Dinnington, Stamfordham, Hazlerigg, Woolsington. Heddon on the Wall,
	Gosforth Urban District.	Gosforth.
	Hexham Rural District (part). *Other parts* in Consett and Hexham County Court Districts.	Wylam.
	Longbenton Urban District.	Longbenton.
	Newburn Urban District.	Newburn.
	Newcastle upon Tyne County Borough.	Newcastle upon Tyne and Moot Hall and Precincts (extra parochial).
	Ryton Urban District.	Ryton.
NEW-MARKET	Clare Rural District (part). *Other parts* in Bury St. Edmunds, Cambridge and Sudbury County Court Districts.	Cowlinge, Little Bradley, Great Bradley, Little Thurlow, Great Thurlow, Ousden, Lidgate, Stradishall.
	Mildenhall Rural District (part). *Other parts* in Bury St. Edmunds and Thetford County Court Districts.	Dalham, Higham, Freckenham, Kentford, Gazeley, Moulton, Herringswell, Worlington.
	Newmarket Urban District.	Newmarket.

	Newmarket Rural District (part). *Other parts* in Cambridge and Ely County Court Districts.	Ashley cum Kennett,
		    Silverley, Kirtling,
		 Brinkley, Reach,
		 Burrough Snailwell,
		    Green, Stetchworth,
		 Burwell, Swaffham Bulbeck,
		 Cheveley, Swaffham Prior,
		 Chippenham, Westley Waterless,
		 Dullingham, Wicken,
		 Fordham, Woodditton.
		 Isleham,

	South Cambridgeshire Rural District (part). *Other parts* in Biggleswade, Cambridge and Hitchin County Court Districts.	Carlton cum Weston Colville, Willingham, West Wratting.

Column 1	Column 2	Column 3
Name of court	Local authority areas	Parts comprising court districts
NEWPORT ISLE OF WIGHT	Cowes Urban District.	Cowes.
	Isle of Wight Rural District.	Bembridge, Newchurch, Brading, Niton, Brighstone, Shalfleet, Calbourne, Shorwell, Chale, South Arreton, Freshwater, Totland, Gatcombe, Yarmouth. Godshill,
	Newport Municipal Borough.	Newport.
	Ryde Municipal Borough.	Ryde.
	Sandown-Shanklin Urban District.	Sandown-Shanklin.
	Ventnor Urban District.	Ventnor.
NEWPORT (MON.)	Bedwas and Machen Urban District (part). *Other part* in Blackwood, Tredegar and Abertillery County Court District.	That part which lies to the south of a line drawn from the junction of the civil parishes of Mynyddislwn, Machen Upper and Bedwas to the point on the river Rhymney where it was crossed by the Llanbradach Viaduct together with Machen Upper.
	Caerleon Urban District.	Caerleon.
	Cardiff Rural District (part). *Other parts* in Barry, Caerphilly and Cardiff County Court Districts.	Rhyd y Gwern.
	Cwmbran Urban District.	Cwmbran.
	Magor and St. Mellons Rural District (part). *Other part* in Cardiff County Court District.	Bettws, Magor, Bishton, Marshfield, Coedkernew, Michaelston y Duffryn, Vedw, Goldcliff, Nash, Graig, Penhow, Henllys, Peterstone Kemeys Wentlloog, Inferior, Redwick, Llandevenny, Rogerstone, Llangstone, St. Bride's Llanmartin, Wentlloog, Llanvaches, Whitson, Llanwern, Wilcrick. Machen Lower,
	Newport County Borough.	Newport.
	Pontypool Rural District (part). *Other part* in Pontypool and Abergavenny County Court District.	Llanfrechfa Llanhennock Lower, Fawr.
	Risca Urban District.	Risca.

Column 1	*Column 2*	*Column 3*
Name of court	Local authority areas	Parts comprising court districts
NEWQUAY	Newquay Urban District.	Newquay.
	St. Austell Rural District (part). *Other parts* in Bodmin and St. Austell County Court Districts.	Colan, St. Columb Major, Mawgan in St. Enoder. Pydor,
	Truro Rural District (part). *Other parts* in Redruth and Truro and Falmouth County Court Districts.	Cubert, Newlyn.
	Wadebridge and Padstow Rural District (part). *Other parts* in Bodmin and Camelford County Court Districts.	St. Ervan, St. Eval.
NEWTON ABBOT	Ashburton Urban District.	Ashburton.
	Dawlish Urban District.	Dawlish.
	Newton Abbot Urban District.	Newton Abbot.
	Newton Abbot Rural District (part). *Other part* in Torquay County County District	Bickington, Kerswells, Bishopsteignton, Kingsteignton, Bovey Tracy, Lustleigh, Broadhempston, Manaton, Buckland in the Moretonhampstead, Moor, North Bovey, Chudleigh, Ogwell, Coffinswell, Teigngrace, Haccombe with Torbryan, Combe, Trusham, Hennock, Widecombe, Ideford, in the Moor, Ilsington, Woodland. Ipplepen,
	Teignmouth Urban District.	Teignmouth.
NEWTOWN	Forden Rural District (part). *Other parts* in Shrewsbury and Welshpool County Court Districts.	Llandyssil, Llanmerewig.
	Knighton Rural District (part). *Other parts* in Knighton and Llandrindod Wells County Court Districts.	Llananno, Llanbadarn Fynydd.
	Newtown and Llanidloes Rural District (part). *Other part* in Llanidloes County Court District.	Aberhafesp, Llanwnog, Bettws, Llanwyddelan, Carno, Manafon, Kerry, Mochdre, Llandinam, Penstrowed, Llanllugan, Tregynon.
	Newtown and Llanllwchaiarn Urban District.	Newtown and Llanllwchaiarn.

Column 1	Column 2	Column 3
Name of court	Local authority areas	Parts comprising court districts

NORTH-ALLERTON	Aysgarth Rural District.	Askrigg, Hawes,
		 Aysgarth, High Abbotside,
		 Bainbridge, Low Abbotside,
		 Bishopdale, Newbiggin,
		 Burton cum Thoralby,
		     Walden, Thornton Rust.
		 Carperby cum
		     Thoresby,

	Bedale Rural District (part).
	 Other part in Ripon County Court District.
		Ainderby Miers Killerby,
		     with Holtby, Kirkby Fleetham
		 Aiskew, with Fencote,
		 Bedale, Langthorne,
		 Burrill with Rand Grange,
		     Cowling, Rookwith,
		 Clifton upon Ure, Scruton,
		 Crakehall, Swainby with
		 Exelby Leeming Allerthorpe,
		     and Newton, Theakston,
		 Firby, Thirn,
		 Gatenby, Thornton Watlass.
		 Hackforth,

	Leyburn Rural District.	Agglethorpe Finghall,
		     with Coverham, Garriston,
		 Akebar, Harmby,
		 Arrathorne, Hornby,
		 Barden, Hunton,
		 Bellerby, Hutton Hang,
		 Caldbergh with Leyburn,
		     East and West Melmerby,
		     Scrafton, Middleham,
		 Carlton Highdale, Newton le Willows,
		 Carlton Town, Patrick Brompton,
		 Castle Bolton, Preston,
		 Constable Redmire,
		     Burton, Spennithorne,
		 East Hauxwell, Thornton Steward,
		 East Witton Wensley,
		     Within, West Hauxwell,
		 East Witton West Witton.
		     Without,

	Northallerton Urban District.	Northallerton.

	Northallerton Rural District.	Ainderby Hutton Bonville,
		     Steeple, Kiplin,
		 Appleton Kirby Sigston,
		     Wiske, Landmoth cum
		 Birkby, Catto,
		 Borrowby, Lazenby,
		 Brompton, Leake,
		 Cotcliffe, Little Langton,
		 Crosby, Little Smeaton,
		 Danby Wiske, Morton upon
		 Deighton, Swale,
		 East Cowton, Nether Silton,
		 East Harlsey, North
		 Ellerbeck, Otterington,
		 Great Langton, Osmotherley,
		 Great Smeaton, Over Silton,
		 Hornby, Romanby,

Column 1	*Column* 2	*Column* 3
Name of court	Local authority areas	Parts comprising court districts
NORTH-ALLERTON —*cont.*	Northallerton Rural District. —*cont.*	South Cowton, Sowerby under Cotcliffe, Thimbleby, Thornton le Beans, Thrintoft, Warlaby, Welbury, West Harlsey, West Rounton, Whitwell, Winton, Stank and Hallikeld, Yafforth.
	Stokesley Rural District (part). *Other parts* in Malton, Middlesbrough and Stockton on Tees County Court Districts.	East Rounton, Ingleby Arncliffe, Potto, Whorlton.
	Thirsk Rural District (part). *Other parts* in Harrogate and Ripon County Court Districts.	Ainderby Quernhow, Bagby, Balk, Birdforth, Boltby, Carlton Miniott, Catton, Cowesby, Dalton, Eldmire with Crakehill, Fawdington, Felixkirk, Holme, Hood Grange, Howe, Hutton Sessay, Kepwick, Kilburn, Kirby Knowle, Kirby Wiske, Knayton with Brawith, Maunby, Newby Wiske, Newsham with Breckenbrough, North Kilvington, Pickhill with Roxby, Sand Hutton, Sessay, Sinderby, Skipton on Swale, South Kilvington, South Otterington, Sowerby, Sutton under Whitestone Cliffe, Thirkleby, Thirlby, Thirsk, Thornbrough, Thornton le Moor, Thornton le Street, Topcliffe, Upsall.
NORTH-AMPTON	Brixworth Rural District (part). *Other part* in Market Harborough County Court District.	Althorp, Boughton, Brington, Brixworth, Chapel Brampton, Church Brampton, Cold Ashby, Cottesbrooke, Draughton, East Haddon, Great Creaton, Guilsborough, Hannington, Harlestone, Holcot, Holdenby, Hollowell, Lamport, Maidwell, Moulton, Old, Overstone, Pitsford, Ravensthorpe, Scaldwell, Spratton, Thornby, Walgrave.
	Buckingham Rural District (part). *Other parts* in Aylesbury, Banbury, Bletchley and Leighton Buzzard and Oxford County Court Districts.	Lillingstone Dayrell, Lillingstone Lovell, Luffield Abbey.

Column 1	Column 2	Column 3
Name of court	Local authority areas	Parts comprising court districts
NORTH-AMPTON—*cont.*	Daventry Municipal Borough.	Daventry.
	Daventry Rural District (part). *Other parts* in Banbury and Rugby County Court Districts.	Badby,　　　　Newnham, Brockhall,　　　Norton, Charwelton,　　Preston Capes, Dodford,　　　　Staverton, Everdon,　　　　Stow Nine Farthingstone,　　　　Churches, Fawsley,　　　　Weedon Bec, Flore,　　　　　Welton, Long Buckby,　Whilton.
	Newport Pagnell Rural District (part). *Other parts* in Bedford and Bletchley and Leighton Buzzard County Court Districts.	Clifton Reynes,　Olney, Cold Brayfield,　Olney Park, Emberton,　　　Petsoe Manor, Hanslope,　　　Ravenstone, Lavendon,　　　Stoke Goldington, Newton　　　　Warrington, 　Blosomville,　Weston Underwood.
	Northampton County Borough.	Northampton.
	Northampton Rural District.	Ashton,　　　　Harpole, Billing,　　　　Hartwell, Brafield on the　Kislingbury, 　Green,　　　　Little Houghton, Bugbrooke,　　Milton Malsor, Castle Ashby,　Nether Heyford, Cogenhoe,　　Quinton, Collingtree,　　Roade, Courteenhall,　Rothersthorpe, Denton,　　　　Upper Heyford, Great Houghton,　Upton, Hackleton,　　Wootton, Hardingstone,　Yardley Hastings.
	Towcester Rural District.	Abthorpe,　　　Paulerspury, Adstone,　　　　Potterspury, Blakesley,　　　Shutlanger, Blisworth,　　　Silverstone, Bradden,　　　Slapton, Cold Higham,　Stoke Bruerne, Cosgrove,　　　Tiffield, Deanshanger,　Towcester, Easton Neston,　Wappenham, Gayton,　　　　Weston and Grafton Regis,　　　　Weedon, Green's Norton,　Whittlebury, Litchborough,　Wicken, Maidford,　　　Woodend, Old Stratford,　Yardley Gobion. Pattishall,
NORTH SHIELDS	Seaton Valley Urban District.	Seaton Valley.
	Tynemouth County Borough.	Tynemouth.
	Wallsend Municipal Borough.	Wallsend.
	Whitley Bay Municipal Borough.	Whitley Bay.

Column 1	*Column* 2	*Column* 3	
Name of court	Local authority areas	Parts comprising court districts	
NORTH-WICH	Bucklow Rural District (part). *Other part* in Altrincham County Court District.	Aston by Budworth, Peover Inferior, Peover Superior,	Pickmere, Plumley, Tabley Inferior, Toft.
	Middlewich Urban District.	Middlewich.	
	Northwich Urban District.	Northwich.	
	Northwich Rural District (part). *Other parts* in Chester and Crewe County Court Districts.	Acton Bridge, Allostock, Anderton, Barnton, Bostock, Byley, Comberbach, Crowton, Cuddington, Darnhall, Davenham, Delamere, Hartford, Lach Dennis, Little Budworth,	Little Leigh. Lostock Gralam, Marbury, Marston, Marton, Moulton, Nether Peover, Oakmere, Rudheath, Sproston, Stanthorne, Weaverham, Whatcroft, Wimboldsley, Wincham.
	Runcorn Rural District (part). *Other parts* in Runcorn and Warrington County Court Districts.	Antrobus, Dutton,	Great Budworth.
	Winsford Urban District.	Winsford.	
NORWICH	Blofield and Flegg Rural District (part). *Other part* in Gt. Yarmouth County Court District.	Acle, Beighton, Blofield, Brundall, Burlingham, Cantley, Great and Little Plumstead,	Hemblington, Postwick, South Walsham, Strumpshaw, Thorpe St. Andrew, Upton with Fishley, Woodbastwick.
	Bungay Urban District.	Bungay.	
	Cromer Urban District,	Cromer.	
	Depwade Rural District.	Alburgh, Ashwellthorpe, Aslacton, Bressingham, Brockdish, Bunwell, Burston, Carleton Rode Denton, Dickleburgh, Earsham, Forncett, Gissing,	Great Moulton, Hempnall, Long Stratton, Morning Thorpe, Needham, Pulham Market, Pulham St. Mary, Redenhall with Harleston, Roydon, Scole, Shefanger, Shelton,

Column 1	*Column* 2	*Column* 3	
Name of court	Local authority areas	Parts comprising court districts	
NORWICH —*cont.*	Depwade Rural District. —*cont.*	Starston, Tacolneston, Tarsburgh, Tharston, Tibenham, Tivetshall St. Margaret,	Tivetshall St. Mary, Wacton, Winfarthing, Wortwell.
	Diss Urban District.	Diss.	
	Eye Municipal Borough.	Eye.	
	Erpingham Rural District.	Alby with Thwaite, Aldborough, Antingham, Aylmerton, Baconsthorpe, Beeston Regis, Bodham, Cley next Sea, Colby, Corpusty, East Beckham, Edgefield, Erpingham, Felbrigg, Gimingham, Gresham, Hanworth, Hempstead, Holt, Ingworth, Itteringham, Kelling,	Letheringsett with Glandford, Little Barningham, Matlask, Mundesley, Northrepps, Overstrand, Plumstead, Roughton, Runton, Salthouse, Sidestrand, Southrepps, Stody, Suffield, Sustead, Thornage, Thorpe Market, Trimingham, Upper Sheringham. West Beckham, Weyborne, Wickmere.
	Forehoe and Henstead Rural District.	Barford, Barnham Broom, Bawburgh, Bixley, Bracon Ash, Bramerton, Caister St. Edmund, Colney, Costessey, Cringleford, Deopham, East Carleton, Easton, Flordon, Framingham Earl, Framingham Pigot, Great Melton, Hethersett, Hingham, Holverston, Keswick, Ketteringham,	Kimberley, Kirby Bedon, Little Melton, Marlingford, Morley, Mulbarton, Newton Flotman, Poringland, Rockland, St. Mary, Runhall, Saxlingham Nethergate, Shotesham, Stoke Holy Cross, Surlingham, Swainsthorpe, Swardeston, Trowse with Newton, Wicklewood, Wramplingham, Wreningham.

Column 1	Column 2	Column 3	
Name of court	Local authority areas	Parts comprising court districts	
NORWICH —cont.	Hartismere Rural District (part). *Other parts* in Halesworth, Ipswich and Stowmarket County Court Districts.	Bedingfield, Botesdale, Braiseworth, Brome, Burgate, Denham, Gislingham, Horham, Hoxne, Mellis, Oakley, Occold, Palgrave,	Redgrave, Redingfield, Ricklinghall Superior, Rishangles, Stoke Ash, Stuston, Thorndon, Thornham Magna, Thornham Parva, Thrandeston, Wortham, Yaxley.
	Loddon Rural District (part). *Other parts* in Lowestoft and Gt. Yarmouth County Court Districts.	Alpington, Ashby St. Mary, Bedingham, Bergh Apton, Brooke, Broome, Carlton St. Peter, Chedgrave, Claxton, Ditchingham, Ellingham, Hales, Heckingham, Hedenham, Hellington,	Howe, Kirby Cane, Kirstead, Langley with Hardley, Loddon, Mundham, Raveningham, Seething, Sisland, Thurton, Thwaite, Topcroft, Woodton, Yelverton.
	Mitford and Launditch Rural District (part). *Other parts* in East Dereham and Kings Lynn County Court Districts.	Hardingham.	
	North Walsham Urban District.	North Walsham.	
	Norwich County Borough.	Norwich.	
	Sheringham Urban District.	Sheringham.	
	Smallburgh Rural District (part). *Other part* in Gt. Yarmouth County Court District.	Ashmanhaugh, Bacton, Barton Turf, Dilham, East Ruston, Felmingham, Happisburgh, Honing, Horning, Hoveton, Knapton, Neatishead,	Paston, Scottow, Skeyton, Sloley, Smallburgh, Swafield, Swanton Abbott, Trunch, Tunstead, Westwick, Witton, Worstead.
	St. Faith's and Aylsham Rural District (part). *Other part* in Kings Lynn County Court District.	Aylsham, Alderford, Attlebridge, Beeston, St. Andrew, Belaugh,	Blickling, Booton, Brampton, Brandiston, Buxton with Lammas,

Column 1	*Column* 2	*Column* 3
Name of court	Local authority areas	Parts comprising court districts
NORWICH —*cont.*	St. Faith's and Aylsham Rural District (part). —*cont.*	Catton, Cawston, Coltishall, Crostwick, Drayton, Felthorpe, Frettenham, Gt. Witchingham, Guestwick, Hainford, Haveringland, Hellesden, Hevingham, Heydon, Horningham, Horsford, Horsham St. Faith, with Newton, St. Faith, Horstead with Stanninghall, Little Witchingham, Marsham, Morton on the Hill, Oulton, Rackheath, Reepham, Ringland, Salhouse, Sall, Spixworth, Sprowston, Stratton Strawless, Swannington, Taverham, Tuttington, Weston Longville, Wood Dalling, Wroxham.
	Walsingham Rural District (part). *Other part* in Kings Lynn County Court District.	Blakeney, Field Dalling, Langham. Morston, Wiveton,
	Wayland Rural District (part). *Other parts* in Kings Lynn and Thetford County Court Districts.	Attleborough, Banham, Besthorpe, Blo' Norton, Garboldisham, Gt. Ellingham, Little Ellingham, New Buckenham, North Lopham, Old Buckenham, Quidenham, Rocklands, Scoulton, Shropham, Snetterton, South Lopham.
	Wymondham Urban District.	Wymondham.
NOTTING-HAM	Arnold Urban District.	Arnold.
	Basford Rural District (part). *Other parts* in Alfreton, Ilkeston, Loughborough and Mansfield County Court Districts.	Barton in Fabis, Bestwood Park, Bradmore, Brinsley, Bunny, Burton Joyce, Calverton, Gotham, Greasley, Kimberley, Lambley, Linby, Nuthall, Papplewick, Ruddington, Stoke Bardolph, Strelley, Thrumpton, Trowell, Woodborough.
	Beeston and Stapleford Urban District.	Beeston and Stapleford.
	Bingham Rural District (part). *Other parts* in Melton Mowbray and Newark County Court Districts.	Aslockton, Bingham, Car Colston, Clipston, Colston Bassett, Cotgrave, Cropwell Bishop, Cropwell Butler, East Bridgford, Elton, Gamston, Granby, Hawksworth, Hickling,

Column 1	*Column* 2	*Column* 3
Name of court	Local authority areas	Parts comprising court districts
NOTTING-HAM —*cont.*	Bingham Rural District (part). —*cont.*	Holme Pierrepont, Keyworth, Kinoulton, Kneeton, Langar cum Barnstone, Normanton on the Wolds, Orston, Owthorpe, Plumtree, Radcliffe on Trent,	Saxondale, Scarrington, Screveton, Shelford, Stanton on the Wolds, Thoroton, Tithby, Tollerton, Whatton, Widmerpool, Wiverton Hall.
	Carlton Urban District.	Carlton.
	Hucknall Urban District.	Hucknall.
	Long Eaton Urban District.	Long Eaton.
	Nottingham County Borough.	Nottingham and Shire Hall (extra parochial).
	Southwell Rural District (part). *Other parts* in East Retford, Mansfield, Newark, and Worksop County Court Districts.	Bulcote, Caythorpe, Epperstone, Gonalston,	Gunthorpe, Lowdham, Oxton.
	West Bridgford Urban District.	West Bridgford.
NUN-EATON	Atherstone Rural District (part). *Other part* in Tamworth County Court District.	Ansley, Atherstone, Baddesley Ensor, Baxterley, Bentley,	Caldecote, Hartshill, Mancetter, Merevale, Oldbury.
	Bedworth Urban District.	Bedworth.
	Market Bosworth Rural District (part). *Other parts* in Ashby-de-la Zouch, Hinckley and Leicester County Court Districts.	Sheepy, Witherley.
	Meriden Rural District (part). *Other parts* in Birmingham, Coventry and Tamworth County Court Districts.	Arley, Astley.
	Nuneaton Municipal Borough.	Nuneaton.
	Rugby Rural District (part). *Other parts* in Coventry, Hinckley and Rugby County Court Districts.	Burton Hastings, Stretton Baskerville,	Wolvey.
OAKHAM	Billesdon Rural District (part). *Other part* in Leicester County Court District.	Owston, Newbold and Withcote,	Whatborough.

Column 1	Column 2	Column 3	
Name of court	Local authority areas	Parts comprising court districts	
OAKHAM —cont.	Ketton Rural District (part). *Other part* in Stamford County Court District.	Ketton.	
	Melton and Belvoir Rural District (part). *Other parts* in Grantham and Melton Mowbray County Court Districts.	Knossington.	
	Oakham Rural District (part). *Other part* in Stamford County Court District.	Ashwell, Barleythorpe, Barrow, Braunston, Brooke, Burley, Cottesmore, Edith Weston, Egleton, Empingham, Exton, Greetham, Gunthorpe, Hambleton,	Horn, Langham, Leighfield, Lyndon, Manton, Market Overton, Martinsthorpe, Normanton, Stretton, Teigh, Thistleton, Whissendine, Whitwell.
	Oakham Urban District.	Oakham.	
	Oundle and Thrapston Rural District (part). *Other parts* in Huntingdon, Kettering, Peterborough, Stamford and Wellingborough County Court Districts.	Harringworth,	Wakerley.
	Uppingham Rural District (part). *Other part* in Market Harborough County Court District.	Ayston, Barrowden, Beaumont Chase, Belton, Bisbrooke, Glaston, Liddington, Morcott, North Luffenham,	Pilton, Preston, Ridlington, Seaton, South Luffenham, Stoke Dry, Thorp by Water, Uppingham, Wardley, Wing.
OKE-HAMPTON	Crediton Rural District (part). *Other parts* in Barnstaple, Exeter, and Tiverton County Court Districts.	Brushford, Coldridge,	Hittisleigh, Zeal Monachorum.
	Okehampton Municipal Borough.	Okehampton.	
	Okehampton Rural District.	Ashbury, Beaworthy, Belstone, Bondleigh, Bratton Clovelly, Bridestowe, Broadwoodkelly, Chagford,	Drewsteignton, Exbourne, Germansweek, Gidleigh, Hatherleigh, Highampton, Iddesleigh, Inwardleigh,

Column 1	Column 2	Column 3
Name of court	Local authority areas	Parts comprising court districts
OKE-HAMPTON —cont.	Okehampton Rural District. —cont.	Jacobstowe, Meeth, Monk-okehampton, Northlew, North Tawton, Okehampton Hamlets, Sampford Courtenay, / Sourton, South Tawton, Spreyton, Throwleigh, Lands Common to Bridestowe and Sourton civil parishes.
OLDHAM	Chadderton Urban District.	Chadderton.
	Crompton Urban District.	Crompton.
	Failsworth Urban District.	Failsworth.
	Lees Urban District.	Lees.
	Middleton Municipal Borough.	Middleton.
	Oldham County Borough.	Oldham.
	Royton Urban District.	Royton.
	Saddleworth Urban District.	Saddleworth.
OSWESTRY	Ceiriog Rural District (part). *Other part* in Wrexham County Court District.	Llanarmon Dyffryn Ceiriog, Llanarmon Mynydd Mawr, / Llangadwaladr, Llangedwyn, Llanrhaiadr-ym-mochnant, Llansilin.
	Llanfyllin Municipal Borough.	Llanfyllin.
	Llanfyllin Rural District (part). *Other part* in Welshpool County Court District.	Careghofa, Hirnant, Llandrinio, Llandysillio, Llanfechain, Llanfihangel yng Ngwynfa, Llangynog, Llanrhaiadr-ym-mochnant, / Llansantffraid Deytheyr, Llansantffraid Pool, Llanwddyn, Meifod, Pennant.
	North Shropshire Rural District (part). *Other parts* in Shrewsbury and Whitchurch County Court District.	Cockshutt, Ellesmere Rural, Ellesmere Urban, / Hordley, Welshampton.
	Oswestry Rural District.	Kinnerley, Knockin, Llanyblodwel, Llanymynech and Pant, Melverley, Oswestry Rural Borough, Oswestry Rural, / Ruyton of the Eleven Towns, St. Martin's, Selattyn and Gobowen, West Felton, Weston Rhyn, Whittington.

Column 1	Column 2	Column 3
Name of court	Local authority areas	Parts comprising court districts
OTLEY	Aireborough Urban District.	Aireborough.
	Ilkley Urban District.	Ilkley.
	Otley Urban District.	Otley.
	Wetherby Rural District (part). *Other parts* in Harrogate, Leeds, and York County Court Districts.	Harewood, Weeton.
	Wharfedale Rural District.	Arthington, Leathley, Askwith, Lindley, Blubberhouses, Little Timble, Bramhope, Middleton, Carlton, Nesfield-with- Castley, Langbar, Clifton-with- Newall with Norwood, Clifton, Denton, Norwood, Farnley, Pool, Fewston, Stainburn, Great Timble, Weston.
OXFORD	Abingdon Municipal Borough.	Abingdon.
	Abingdon Rural District (part). *Other part* in Didcot County Court District.	Appleton with Kingston Eaton, Bagpuize, Besselsleigh, Marcham, Cumnor, North Hinksey, Draycott Moor, Radley, Frilford, St. Helen Without, Fyfield and South Hinksey, Tubney, Sunningwell, Garford, Wooton, Kennington, Wytham.
	Bicester Urban District.	Bicester.
	Buckingham Rural District (part). *Other parts* in Aylesbury, Banbury, Bletchley and Leighton Buzzard and Northampton County Court Districts.	Barton Hartshorn, Preston Bissett. Chetwode,
	Bullingdon Rural District (part). *Other parts* in Didcot and Thame County Court Districts.	Beckley and Marston, Stowood, Nuneham Cuddesdon and Courtenay, Denton, Risinghurst and Elsfield, Sandhills, Forest Hill with Sandford on Shotover, Thames, Garsington, Stadhampton, Holton, Stanton St. John, Horspath, Toot Baldon, Littlemore, Wheatley, Marsh Baldon, Woodeaton.
	Chipping Norton Rural District (part). *Other part* in Banbury County Court District.	Blenheim, Fawler, Cornbury and Finstock, Wychwood, Glympton, Combe, Hensington Without,

Column 1	*Column* 2	*Column* 3
Name of court	Local authority areas	Parts comprising court districts
OXFORD —*cont.*	Chipping Norton Rural District (part). —*cont.*	Kiddington with Asterleigh, Leafield,	Stonesfield, Tackley, Wootton.
	Faringdon Rural District (part). *Other parts* in Didcot and Swindon County Court Districts.	Buckland, Great Faringdon, Hatford, Hinton Waldrist, Longworth,	Pusey, Shellingford, Stanford in the Vale.
	Oxford County Borough.	Oxford.
	Ploughley Rural District (part). *Other parts* in Banbury and Thame County Court Districts.	Ambrosden, Arncott, Begbroke, Blackthorn, Bletchingdon, Caversfield, Charlton on Otmoor, Chesterton, Fencott and Murcott, Fringford, Godington, Gosford and Water Eaton, Hampton Gay and Poyle, Horton cum Studley,	Islip, Kidlington, Kirtlington, Launton, Merton, Middleton Stoney, Noke, Oddington, Shipton on Cherwell and Thrupp, Stratton Audley, Wendlebury, Weston on the Green, Yarnton.
	Witney Rural District (part). *Other part* in Witney County Court District.	Bladon,	Cassington.
	Woodstock Municipal Borough.	Woodstock.
PENRITH	Appleby Municipal Borough.	Appleby.
	Lakes Urban District (part). *Other part* in Kendal County Court District.	The Patterdale Ward.
	North Westmorland Rural District.	Asby, Askham, Bampton, Barton, Bolton, Brough, Brougham, Brough Sowerby, Cliburn, Clifton, Colby, Crackenthorpe, Crosby Garrett, Crosby Ravensworth, Dufton,	Great Strickland, Hartley, Hillbeck, Hoff, Kaber, King's Meaburn, Kirkby Stephen, Kirkby Thore, Little Strickland, Long Marton, Lowther, Mallerstang, Martindale, Milburn, Morland, Murton,

Column 1	Column 2	Column 3
Name of court	Local authority areas	Parts comprising court districts
PENRITH —cont.	North Westmorland Rural District. —cont.	Musgrave, Soulby, Nateby, Stainmore, Newbiggin, Tebay, Newby, Temple Sowerby, Ormside, Thrimby, Orton, Waitby, Ravenstonedale, Warcop, Shap, Wharton, Shap Rural, Winton, Sleagill, Yanwath and Sockbridge and Eamont Bridge. Tirril,
	Penrith Urban District.	Penrith.
	Penrith Rural District (part). *Other part* in Workington and Cockermouth County Court District.	Ainstable, Hunsonby, Castle Sowerby, Hutton, Catterlen, Kirkoswald, Culgaith, Langwathby, Dacre, Lazonby, Glassonby, Matterdale, Great Salkeld, Mungrisdale, Greystoke, Ousby, Hesket, Skelton.
PENZANCE	Penzance Municipal Borough.	Penzance.
	St. Ives Municipal Borough.	St. Ives.
	St. Just Urban District.	St. Just.
	Scilly Islands.	Bryher, St. Mary's, St. Agnes, Tresco. St. Martin's,
	West Penwith Rural District (part). *Other part* in Redruth County Court District.	Ludgvan, St. Michael's Madron, Mount, Marazion, Sancreed, Morvah, Sennen, Paul, Towednack, Perranuthnoe, Zennor, St. Buryan, Wolfe Rock St. Erth, Lighthouse St. Hilary, (Extra St. Levan, Parochial).

PETER-BOROUGH	Norman Cross Rural District.	Alwalton, Holme,
		Chesterton, Morborne,
		Denton and Orton Longueville,
		   Caldecote, Orton Waterville,
		Elton, Sibson cum
		Farcet, Stibbington,
		Folksworth and Stilton,
		   Washingley, Water Newton,
		Glatton, Yaxley.
		Haddon,

	Old Fletton Urban District.	Old Fletton.
	Oundle Urban District.	Oundle.

Column 1	*Column* 2	*Column* 3
Name of court	Local authority areas	Parts comprising court districts
PETER-BOROUGH —*cont.*	Oundle and Thrapston Rural District (part). *Other parts* in Huntingdon, Kettering, Oakham, Stamford and Wellingborough County Court Districts.	Ashton, Barnwell, Cotterstock, Fotheringhay, Glapthorn, Hemington, Lutton, Nassington, Polebrook, Southwick, Stoke Doyle, Tansor, Warmington, Woodnewton, Yarwell.
	Peterborough Municipal Borough.	Peterborough.
	Peterborough Rural District.	Ailsworth, Borough Fen, Castor, Deeping Gate, Etton, Eye, Glinton, Helpston, Marholm, Maxey, Newborough, Northborough, Peakirk, Sutton and Upton.
	Thorney Rural District.	Stanground North, Thorney.
	Whittlesey Urban District.	Whittlesey.
PETERS-FIELD	Droxford Rural District (part). *Other parts* in Portsmouth, Southampton and Winchester County Court Districts.	Corhampton and Meonstoke, Droxford, Exton and Warnford, West Meon.
	Midhurst Rural District (part). *Other part* in Chichester County Court District.	Chithurst, Elsted, Fernhurst, Harting, Iping, Linch, Linchmere, North Ambersham, Rogate, Stedham, Treyford, Trotton, Woolbeding.
	Petersfield Urban District.	Petersfield.
	Petersfield Rural District.	Bramshott, Buriton, Clanfield, Colemore and Priors Dean, East Meon, Froxfield, Greatham, Hawkley, Horndean, Langrish, Liss, Rowlands Castle, Steep.
PLY-MOUTH	Plymouth County Borough.	Plymouth.
	Plympton St. Mary Rural District.	Bickleigh, Brixton, Cornwood, Ermington, Harford and Ivybridge, Holbeton, Newton and Noss, Shaugh Prior, Sparkwell, Wembury, Yealmpton, Plymouth Breakwater, (Fort and Lighthouse) and Eddystone Lighthouse.

Column 1	Column 2	Column 3	
Name of court	Local authority areas	Parts comprising court districts	
PLY- MOUTH —cont.	St. Germans Rural District (part). *Other parts* in Liskeard and Tavistock County Court Districts.	Antony, Botusfleming, Landrake with St. Erney, Landulph,	Maker with Rame, Millbrook, Pillaton, St. John, Sheviock.
	Saltash Municipal Borough.	Saltash.	
	Torpoint Urban District.	Torpoint.	
PONTE- FRACT	Castleford Municipal Borough.	Castleford.	
	Featherstone Urban District.	Featherstone.	
	Garforth Urban District.	Garforth.	
	Hemsworth Urban District.	Hemsworth.	

	Hemsworth Rural District (part).
	Other part in Barnsley County Court District.
		Ackworth,
		Badsworth,
		Hessle and
		   Hill Top,
		Huntwick with
		   Foulby and
		     Nostell,
		Kirk Smeaton,
			Little Smeaton,
			North Elmsall,
			South Elmsall,
			South Kirkby,
			Thorp Audlin,
			Upton,
			Walden Stubbs,
			West Hardwick.

	Knottingley Urban District.	Knottingley.	

	Osgoldcross Rural District.	Balne,
		Beal otherwise
		   Beaghall,
		Birkin,
		Brotherton,
		Burton Salmon,
		Byram cum
		   Sutton,
		Cridling Stubbs,
		Darrington,
		East Hardwick,
			Eggborough,
			Fairburn,
			Heck,
			Gensall,
			Hillam,
			Kellington,
			Monk Fryston,
			Stapleton,
			Whitley,
			Womersley.

	Pontefract Municipal Borough.	Pontefract.	
	Selby Rural District (part). *Other parts* in Goole and York County Court Districts.	Burn, Chapel Haddlesey, Gateforth,	Hirst Courtney, Temple Hirst, West Haddlesey,

	Tadcaster Rural District (part).
	Other parts in Leeds and York County Court Districts.
		Great and
		   Little Preston,
		Huddleston with
		   Newthorpe,
			Ledsham,
			Ledston,
			Micklefield,
			South Milford.

PONTY- POOL AND ABER- GAVENNY	Abergavenny Municipal Borough.	Abergavenny.	

	Abergavenny Rural District.	Abergavenny
		   Rural,
		Crucorney
		   Fawr,
		Grosmont
		   Fawr,
			Llanarth Fawr,
			Llanddewi Sgyrrid,
			Llanfoist Fawr,
			Llanover Fawr,
			Llantilio
			     Pertholey.

Column 1	*Column* 2	*Column* 3
Name of court	Local authority areas	Parts comprising court districts
PONTY-POOL AND ABER-GAVENNY —*cont.*	Blaenavon Urban District.	Blaenavon.
	Crickhowell Rural District.	Crickhowell, Llangattock, Llanbedr Llangenny, Ystradwy, Llangynidr, Llanelly, Partrishow. Llanfihangel Cwmdû.
	Dore and Bredwardine Rural District (part). *Other part* in Hereford County Court District.	Llanveynoe, Walterstone. Longtown,
	Pontypool Urban District.	Pontypool.
	Pontypool Rural District (part). *Other part* in Newport (Mon.) County Court District.	Goetre Fawr, Llangybi Fawr, Gwehelog Fawr, Llantrisant Fawr. Llanbadoc Fawr,
	Usk Urban District.	Usk.
PONTY-PRIDD AND YSTRADY-FODWG	Cowbridge Rural District (part). *Other part* in Bridgend County Court District.	Llanharan (Pembroke Street, Thomastown and Yngsmardy Houses, near Llantrisant, only).
	Llantrisant and Llantwit Fardre Rural District.	Llantrisant, Llantwit Fardre.
	Mountain Ash Urban District (part). *Other part* in Aberdare County Court District.	Ynsybwl.
	Pontypridd Urban District.	Pontypridd.
	Rhondda Municipal Borough.	Rhondda.
POOLE	Poole Municipal Borough.	Poole.
	Wareham and Purbeck Rural District (part). *Other parts* in Dorchester, Swanage and Weymouth County Court Districts.	Corfe Castle (part), viz.: Furzey, Green, Long and Round Islands. Lytchett Matravers, Lytchett Minster, Studland (part), viz., Brownsea Island.
PORT-MADOC	Criccieth Urban District.	Criccieth.
	Deudraeth Rural District.	Llanbedr, Maentwrog, Llandanwg, Penrhyndeudraeth, Llandecwyn, Talsarnau, Llanfair, Trawsfynydd. Llanfrothen,
	Ffestiniog Urban District.	Ffestiniog.

Column 1	Column 2	Column 3
Name of court	Local authority areas	Parts comprising court districts
PORT-MADOC —cont.	Gwyrfai Rural District (part). *Other part* in Caernarvon County Court District.	Beddgelert.
	Lleyn Rural District.	Aberdaron, Llanbedrog, Bardsey Island Llanengan, (Extra Parochial), Llannor, Botwnnog, Llanystumdwy, Buan, Nefyn, Dolbenmaen, Pistyll, Llanaelhaidrn, Tudweiliog.
	Portmadoc Urban District.	Portmadoc.
	Pwllheli Municipal Borough.	Pwllheli.
PORTS-MOUTH	Droxford Rural District (part). *Other parts* in Petersfield, Southampton and Winchester County Court Districts.	Boarhunt, Soberton. Denmead, Southwick Hambledon, and Widley, Shedfield, Wickham.
	Fareham Urban District.	Fareham.
	Gosport Municipal Borough.	Gosport.
	Havant and Waterloo Urban District.	Havant and Waterloo.
	Portsmouth County Borough.	Portsmouth.
PRESTON	Bowland Rural District (part). *Other part* in Blackburn County Court District.	Bowland Forest High.
	Clitheroe Rural District (part). *Other part* in Blackburn County Court District.	Bowland with Thornley with Leagram, Wheatley. Chipping,
	Fulwood Urban District.	Fulwood.
	Fylde Rural District (part). *Other part* in Blackpool County Court District.	Bryning with Newton with Warton, Clifton, Elswick, Ribby with Freckleton, Wrea, Greenhalgh with Treales, Thistleton, Roseacre and Medlar with Wharles. Wesham,
	Garstang Rural District (part). *Other parts* in Blackpool and Lancaster County Court Districts.	Barnacre with Inskip with Bonds, Sowerby, Bilsborrow, Kirkland, Catterall, Myerscough, Claughton, Nateby, Garstang, Upper Rawcliffe Great with Tarnacre. Eccleston,
	Kirkham Urban District.	Kirkham.

Column 1	*Column* 2	*Column* 3
Name of court	Local authority areas	Parts comprising court districts
PRESTON —*cont.*	Leyland Urban District.	Leyland.
	Longridge Urban District.	Longridge,
	Preston County Borough.	Preston.
	Preston Rural District.	Barton, Lea, Broughton, Little Hoole, Cuerdale, Longton, Dutton, Much Hoole, Farington, Penwortham, Goosnargh, Ribchester, Grimsargh, Samlesbury, Haighton, Whittingham, Hothersall, Woodplumpton. Hutton,
	Walton le Dale Urban District.	Walton le Dale.
RAMS-GATE	Eastry Rural Disrict (part). *Other parts* in Canterbury, Deal, Dover and Margate County Court Districts.	Minster, Sarre. Monkton,
	Ramsgate Municipal Borough.	Ramsgate.
RAWTEN-STALL	Bacup Municipal Borough.	Bacup.
	Haslingden Municipal Borough.	Haslingden.
	Rawtenstall Municipal Borough.	Rawtenstall.
READING	Bradfield Rural District (part). *Other parts* in Didcot & New-bury County Court Districts.	Ashampstead, Sulhamstead, Basildon, Sulhamstead Beech Hill, Bannister, Beenham, Theale, Bradfield, Tidmarsh, Burghfield, Tilehurst, Englefield, Ufton Nervet, Grazeley, Wokefield, Padworth, Saltney Mead Pangbourne, (common to the Purley, civil parishes of Stratfield Purley and Sul- Mortimer, ham). Sulham,
	Cookham Rural District (part). *Other parts* in High Wycombe and Slough County Court Districts.	Hurley.
	Easthampstead Rural District (part). *Other part* in Slough County Court District.	Binfield, Easthampstead, Bracknell, Sandhurst, Crowthorne, Warfield.

Column 1	Column 2	Column 3	
Name of court	Local authority areas	Parts comprising court districts	
READING —cont.	Henley Rural District (part). *Other part* in Didcot County Court District.	Bix, Eye and Dunsden, Goring Heath, Harpsden, Highmoor, Kidmore End, Mapledurham, Nettlebed, Pishill with Stonor,	Rotherfield Greys, Rotherfield Peppard, Shiplake, Sonning Common, Swyncombe, Whitchurch.
	Henley on Thames Municipal Borough.	Henley on Thames.	
	Reading County Borough.	Reading.	
	Wokingham Municipal Borough.	Wokingham Within.	
	Wokingham Rural District.	Arborfield and Newland, Barkham, Earley, Finchampstead, Remenham, Ruscombe, St. Nicholas Hurst, Shinfield,	Sonning, Swallowfield, Twyford, Wargrave, Winnersh, Wokingham Without, Woodley and Sandford.
	Wycombe Rural District (part). *Other parts* in Aylesbury and High Wycombe County Court Districts.	Fawley, Hambleden,	Medmenham.
REDDITCH	Alcester Rural District (part). *Other part* in Stratford-on-Avon County Court District.	Alcester, Arrow, Coughton, Exhall, Great Alne, Haselor, Kinwarton, Morton Bagot,	Oldberrow, Salford Priors, Sambourne, Spernall, Studley, Weethley, Wixford,
	Bromsgrove Rural District (part). *Other parts* in Birmingham, Bromsgrove and Stourbridge County Court Districts.	Alvechurch, Bentley Pauncefoot,	Beoley, Tutnall and Cobley.
	Droitwich Rural District (part). *Other parts* in Bromsgrove, Kidderminster and Worcester County Court Districts.	Stock and Bradley.	
	Evesham Rural District (part). *Other parts* in Cheltenham and Evesham County Court Districts.	Abbots Morton,	Inkberrow.

Column 1	Column 2	Column 3
Name of court	Local authority areas	Parts comprising court districts
REDDITCH —cont.	Pershore Rural District (part). Other parts in Cheltenham, Evesham and Worcester County Court Districts.	Dormston, Kington.
	Redditch Urban District.	Redditch.
REDRUTH	Camborne—Redruth Urban District.	Camborne—Redruth.
	Kerrier Rural District (part). Other parts in Helston and Truro and Falmouth County Court Districts.	Stithians.
	Truro Rural District (part). Other parts in Newquay and Truro and Falmouth County Court Districts.	Gwennap.
	West Penwith Rural District (part). Other part in Penzance County Court District.	Gwinear-Gwithian, Hayle.
REIGATE	Banstead Urban District (part). Other parts in Croydon and Epsom County Court Districts.	The Chipstead and Kingswood Wards.
	Caterham and Warlingham Urban District (part). Other part in Croydon County Court District.	The Chaldon Ward.
	Dorking and Horley Rural District (part). Other parts in Dorking and Epsom County Court Districts.	Betchworth, Buckland, Charlwood, Horley, Leigh.
	Godstone Rural District (part). Other parts in Croydon and East Grinstead County Court Districts.	Bletchingley, Burstow, Crowhurst, Godstone, Horne, Limpsfield, Nutfield, Oxted, Tandridge, Tatsfield, Titsey.
	Reigate Municipal Borough.	Reigate.
RHYL	Abergele Urban District.	Abergele.
	Aled Rural District (part). Other parts in Conway, Llandudno and Colwyn Bay and Denbigh and Ruthin County Court Districts.	Abergele Rural, Bettws yn Rhos or Bettws Abergele, Cefn.
	Prestatyn Urban District.	Prestatyn.

Column 1	Column 2	Column 3
Name of court	Local authority areas	Parts comprising court districts
RHYL —cont.	Rhyl Urban District.	Rhyl.	
	St. Asaph Rural District (part). *Other part* in Denbigh and Ruthin County Court District.	Bodelwyddan, Cwm, Dyserth, Rhuddlan,	St. Asaph, Tremeirchion, Waen.
RICH- MOND	Reeth Rural District.	Arkengarthdale, Ellerton Abbey, Grinton, Marrick,	Melbecks, Muker, Reeth.
	Richmond Municipal Borough.	Richmond.	
	Richmond Rural District.	Aldbrough, Appleton, Aske, Bolton upon Swale, Brompton on Swale, Brough, Caldwell, Catterick, Colburn, Dalton, Downholme, Easby, East Layton, Ellerton upon Swale, Eppleby, Forcett with Carkin, Gayles, Gilling, Hipswell,	Hudswell, Kirby Hill, Marske, Melsonby, Middleton Tyas, Moulton, New Forest, Newsham, North Cowton, Ravensworth, St. Martin, Scorton, Scotton, Skeeby, Stainton, Stanwick St. John, Tunstall, Uckerby, Walburn, West Layton, Whashton.
RIPON	Bedale Rural District (part). *Other part* in Northallerton County Court District.	Burnston, Carthorpe, East Tanfield, Howgrave, Kirklington cum Upsland,	Snape with Thorpe, Sutton with Howgrave, Well, West Tanfield.
	Masham Rural District.	Burton upon Ure, Colsterdale, Ellingstring, Ellingtons, Fearby,	Healey, Ilton cum Pott, Masham, Swinton with Wathermarske.
	Nidderdale Rural District (part). *Other parts* in Harrogate and York County Court Districts.	Burton Leonard, South Stainley with Cayton,	Westwick.
	Ripon Municipal Borough.	Ripon.	

Column 1	*Column* 2	*Column* 3
Name of court	Local authority areas	Parts comprising court districts
RIPON —*cont.*	Ripon and Pately Bridge Rural District (part). *Other part* in Harrogate County Court District	Aldfield, Azerley, Bishop Monkton, Bridge Hewick, Clotherholme, Copt Hewick, Eavestone, Givendale, Grantley, Grewelthorpe, Kirby Malzeard, Laverton, Lindrick with Studley Royal and Fountains, Littlethorpe, Markingfield Hall, Markington with Wallerthwaite, Newby with Mulwith, North Stainley with Scenningford, Nunwick with Howgrave, Sawley, Sharow, Skelding, Skelton, Studley Roger, Sutton Grange, Winksley.
	Thirsk Rural District (part). *Other parts* in Harrogate and Northallerton County Court Districts.	Humberton, Kirby Hill, Lanthorpe, Milby, Norton le Clay, Thornton Bridge.
	Wath Rural District.	Asenby, Baldersby, Cundall with Leckby, Dishforth, Hutton Conyers, Marton le Moor, Melmerby, Middleton Quernhow, Norton Conyers, Rainton with Newby, Wath.
ROCHDALE	Littleborough Urban District.	Littleborough.
	Milnrow Urban District.	Milnrow.
	Rochdale County Borough.	Rochdale.
	Wardle Urban District.	Wardle.
	Whitworth Urban District.	Whitworth.
ROCHES-TER	Chatham Municipal Borough.	Chatham.
	Gillingham Municipal Borough.	Gillingham.
	Malling Rural District (part). *Other parts* in Maidstone and Sevenoaks County Court Districts.	Burham, Wouldham.
	Rochester Municipal Borough.	Rochester.
	Strood Rural District (part). *Other part* in Gravesend County Court District.	All Hallows, Cliffe, Cooling, Cuxton, Frindsbury Extra,

Column 1	Column 2	Column 3
Name of court	Local authority areas	Parts comprising court districts
ROCHES-TER —cont.	Strood Rural District (part). —cont.	Halling, Higham, High Halstow, Hoo St. Werburgh, Isle of Grain, St. Mary Hoo, Stoke.
ROSS	East Dean Rural District (part). Other part in Gloucester County Court District.	Ruardean.
	Ross and Whitchurch Rural District (part). Other part in Monmouth County Court District.	Aston Ingham, Ballingham, Brampton Abbots, Bridstow, Brockhampton, Foy, Goodrich, Harewood, Hentland, Hope Mansell, How Caple, King's Caple, Lea, Linton, Llandinabo, Llangarron, Llanwarne, Marstow, Pencoyd, Peterstow, Ross Rural, St. Weonards, Sellack, Sollors Hope, Tretire with Michaelchurch, Upton Bishop, Walford, Weston under Penyard, Yatton.
	Ross on Wye Urban District.	Ross on Wye.
ROTHER-HAM	Maltby Urban District.	Maltby.
	Mexborough Urban District.	Mexborough.
	Rawmarsh Urban District.	Rawmarsh.
	Rotherham County Borough.	Rotherham.
	Rotherham Rural District.	Ashton cum Aughton, Bramley, Brampton Bierlow, Brinsworth, Catcliffe, Dalton, Hooton Levitt, Hooton Roberts, Orgreave, Ravenfield, Thrybergh, Thurcroft, Treeton, Ulley, Wentworth, Whiston, Wickersley.
	Swinton Urban District.	Swinton.
	Wath upon Dearne Urban District.	Wath upon Dearne.
RUGBY	Daventry Rural District (part). Other parts in Banbury and Northampton County Court Court Districts.	Ashby St. Ledgers, Barby, Braunston, Catesby, Claycoton, Crick, Elkington, Hellidon,

Column 1	Column 2	Column 3
Name of court	Local authority areas	Parts comprising court districts
RUGBY —cont.	Daventry Rural District (part). —cont.	Kilsby, West Haddon, Lilbourne, Winwick, Stanford, Yelvertoft. Watford,
	Lutterworth Rural District (part). *Other parts* in Hinckley, Leicester and Market Harborough County Court Districts.	Bittesby, Lutterworth, Bitteswell, Misterton, Catthorpe, Shawell, Cotesbach, South Kilworth, Gilmorton, Swinford, Kimcote and Westril and 　　　　Walton, 　　　　Starmore.
	Rugby Municipal Borough.	Rugby.
	Rugby Rural District (part). *Other parts* in Coventry Hinckley and Nuneaton County Court Districts.	Binley, Kings Newnham, Birdingbury, Leamington Bourton on 　　　　Hastings, 　　　Dunsmore, Little Lawford Brandon Long Lawford, 　and Bretford, Marton, Brinklow, Monks Kirby, Church Newton and Biggin, 　　　Lawford, Pailton, Churchover, Princethorpe, Clifton upon Stretton on 　　　Dunsmore, 　　　Dunsmore, Combe Fields, Stretton under Cosford, 　　　　Fosse, Dunchurch, Thurlaston, Easenhall, Willey, Frankton, Willoughby, Grandborough, Wolfhampcote Harborough Wolston. 　　Magna,
	Southam Rural District (part). *Other parts* in Banbury and Warwick County Court Districts.	Lower Priors Marston, 　Shuckburgh, Upper Shuckburgh. Priors 　Hardwick,
RUNCORN	Runcorn Urban District.	Runcorn.
	Runcorn Rural District (part). *Other parts* in Northwich and Warrington County Court Districts.	Alvanley, Manley, Aston, Norley, Frodsham, Preston Brook, Helsby, Sutton. Kingsley,
St. ALBANS	Harpenden Urban District.	Harpenden.
	Hatfield Rural District (part). *Other parts* in Barnet and Hertford County Court Districts.	Hatfield, 　　North Mimms.

Column 1	Column 2	Column 3
Name of court	Local authority areas	Parts comprising court districts
St. ALBANS —cont.	Hemel Hempstead Rural District (part). _Other parts_ in Hemel Hempstead and Luton County Court Districts.	Flamstead.
	St. Albans Municipal Borough.	St. Albans.
	St. Albans Rural District.	Colney Heath, St. Michael Rural, Harpenden Rural, St. Stephen, London Colney, Sandridge, Redbourne, Wheathampstead.
ST. AUSTELL	St. Austell with Fowey Municipal Borough.	St. Austell with Fowey.
	St. Austell Rural District (part). _Other parts_ in Bodmin and Newquay County Court Districts.	Creed, St. Mewan, Grampound, St. Michael Roche, Caerhays. St. Dennis, St. Sampson, St. Ewe, St. Stephen St. Goran, in Brannel.
ST. HELENS AND WIDNES	Haydock Urban District.	Haydock.
	Huyton with Roby Urban District.	Huyton with Roby.
	Prescot Urban District.	Prescot.
	Rainford Urban District.	Rainford.
	St. Helens County Borough.	St. Helens.
	Whiston Rural District.	Bold, Knowsley, Cronton, Rainhill, Eccleston, Tarbock, Hale, Whiston, Halewood. Windle.
	Widnes Municipal Borough.	Widnes.
SALFORD	Eccles Municipal Borough.	Eccles.
	Irlam Urban District.	Irlam.
	Prestwich Municipal Borough.	Prestwich.
	Salford County Borough.	Salford.
	Stretford Municipal Borough.	Stretford.
	Swinton and Pendlebury Municipal Borough.	Swinton and Pendlebury.
	Urmston Urban District.	Urmston.
	Worsley Urban District.	Worsley.

Column 1	Column 2	Column 3
Name of court	Local authority areas	Parts comprising court districts
SALISBURY	Amesbury Rural District (part). *Other part* in Devizes County Court District.	Allington, Amesbury, Bulford, Cholderton, Durnford, Durrington, Figheldean, Idmiston, Milston,	Newton Toney, Orcheston, Shrewton, Wilsford cum Lake, Winterbourne, Winterbourne Stoke, Woodford.
	Blandford Rural District (part). *Other parts* in Dorchester, Shaftesbury and Wimborne Minster County Court Districts.	Chettle,	Farnham.
	Pewsey Rural District (part). *Other parts* in Andover, Devizes and Marlborough County Court Districts.	Fittleton,	Netheravon.
	Ringwood and Fordinbridge Rural District (part). *Other part* in Bournemouth County Court District.	Breamore, Damerham, Fordingbridge, Hale, Harbridge and Ibsley,	Martin, Rockbourne, Whitsbury, Woodgreen.
	Romsey and Stockbridge Rural District (part). *Other parts* in Andover, Southampton and Winchester County Court Districts.	East Dean, East Tytherley Frenchmoor,	Lockerley, West Tytherley.
	Salisbury (or New Sarum) Municipal Borough.	New Sarum.	
	Salisbury and Wilton Rural District.	Alderbury, Barford St. Martin, Berwick St. James, Bishopstone, Bower Chalke, Britford, Broad Chalke, Burcombe Without, Clarendon Park, Compton Chamberlayne, Coombe Bissett, Dinton, Downton, Ebbesborne Wake, Fovant,	Great Wishford, Grimstead, Landford, Laverstock, Netherhampton, Odstock, Pitton and Farley, Quidhampton, Redlynch, South Newton, Stapleford, Steeple Langford, Stratford Toney, West Dean, Whiteparish, Winterslow, Wylye.
	Wilton Municipal Borough.	Wilton.	

Column 1	Column 2	Column 3
Name of court	Local authority areas	Parts comprising court districts
SALISBURY —cont.	Wimborne and Cranborne Rural District (part). *Other part* in Wimborne Minster County Court District.	Pentridge, Sixpenny Handley.
SCARBOROUGH	Bridlington Rural District (part). *Other part* in Bridlington County Court District.	Folkton, Muston.
	Filey Urban District.	Filey.
	Norton Rural District (part). *Other parts* in Beverley, Bridlington and Malton County Court Districts.	Ganton, Willerby. Sherburn,
	Scalby Urban District.	Scalby.
	Scarborough Municipal Borough	Scarborough.
	Scarborough Rural District.	Brompton, Lebberston, Broxa, Seamer, Burniston, Silpho, Cayton, Snainton, Cloughton, Staintondale, East Ayton, Suffield cum Gristhorpe, Everley, Hackness, Troutsdale, Harwood Dale, West Ayton, Hutton Buscel, Wykeham. Irton,
SCUNTHORPE	Barton upon Humber Urban District.	Barton upon Humber.
	Brigg Urban District.	Brigg.
	Caistor Rural District (part). *Other parts* in Great Grimsby, Lincoln and Louth County Court Districts.	Bigby, Searby cum Bishop Norton, Owmby, Grasby, Snitterby, Holton-le-Moor, Somerby, Nettleton, South Kelsey, North Kelsey, Waddingham. Owersby,
	Glanford Brigg Rural District (part). *Other part* in Great Grimsby County Court District.	Alkborough, Croxton, Appleby, East Butterwick, Barnetby Elsham, le Wold, Flixborough, Barrow-upon- Gunness, Humber, Hibaldstow, Bonby, Holme, Bottesford, Horkstow, Broughton, Kirmington, Burringham, Kirton in Burton Lindsey, upon Stather, Manton, Cadney, Melton Ross,

Column 1	Column 2	Column 3
Name of court	Local authority areas	Parts comprising court districts
SCUN-THORPE —cont.	Glanford Brigg Rural District (part.) —cont.	Messingham, Redbourne, Roxby cum Risby, Saxby All Saints, Scawby, South Ferriby, West Halton, Whitton, Winteringham, Winterton, Worlaby, Wrawby.
	Isle of Axholme Rural District (part). *Other parts* in Gainsborough, Goole and Thorne County Court Districts.	Amcotts, Keadby with Althorpe, West Butterwick.
	Scunthorpe Municipal Borough.	Scunthorpe.
SEVEN-OAKS	Malling Rural District (part). *Other parts* in Maidstone and and Rochester County Court Districts.	Borough Green, Ightham, Platt, Plaxtol, Shipbourne, Stansted, Wrotham.
	Sevenoaks Urban District.	Sevenoaks.
	Sevenoaks Rural District (part). *Other parts* in East Grinstead and Tonbridge County Court Districts.	Brasted, Chevening, Dunton Green, Halstead, Kemsing, Otford, Riverhead, Seal, Sevenoaks Weald, Shoreham, Sundridge, Westerham.
SHAFTES-BURY	Blandford Rural District (part). *Other parts* in Dorchester, Salisbury and Wimborne Minster County Court Districts.	Durweston, Iwerne Courtney, otherwise Shorton, Iwerne Steepleton, Stourpaine.
	Mere and Tisbury Rural District (part). *Other part* in Frome County Court District.	Alvediston, Ansty, Berwick St. John, Berwick St. Leonard, Chicklade, Chilmark, Donhead St. Andrew, Donhead St. Mary, East Knoyle, Fonthill Bishop, Fonthill Gifford, Hindon, Mere, Sedgehill, Semley, Stourton with Gasper, Sutton Mandeville, Swallowcliffe, Teffont, Tisbury, Tollard Royal, West Knoyle, West Tisbury, Zeals.
	Shaftesbury Municipal Borough.	Shaftesbury.

Column 1	Column 2	Column 3
Name of court	Local authority areas	Parts comprising court districts
SHAFTES-BURY —cont.	Shaftesbury Rural District (part). *Other part* in Wincanton County Court District.	Ashmore, Cann, Compton Abbas, East Orchard, East Stour, Fontmell Magna, Gillingham, Iwerne Minster, Kington Magna, Margaret Marsh, Melbury Abbas, Motcombe, Silton, Stour Provost, Sutton Waldron, Todber, West Orchard, West Stour.
	Sturminster Rural District (part). *Other parts* in Dorchester and Yeovil County Court Districts.	Child Okeford, Fifehead Magdalen, Fifehead Neville, Hammoon, Hanford, Hinton St. Mary, Lydlinch, Manston, Marnhull, Okeford Fitzpaine, Shillingstone, Sturminster Newton.
SHEERNESS	Queenborough-in-Sheppey Municipal Borough.	Queenborough-in-Sheppey.
SHEFFIELD	Bakewell Rural District (part). *Other parts* in Buxton, Matlock and Chesterfield County Court Districts.	Eyam Woodlands, Hathersage, Outseats.
	Chapel en le Frith Rural District (part). *Other parts* in Buxton and Hyde County Court Districts.	Derwent, Hope Woodlands.
	Sheffield County Borough.	Sheffield.
	Stocksbridge Urban District.	Stocksbridge.
	Wortley Rural District (part). *Other part* in Barnsley County Court District.	Bradfield, Ecclesfield.
SHORE-DITCH	London Borough of Hackney.	Hackney.
	London Borough of Islington (part). *Other part* in Clerkenwell County Court District.	That part of the Borough east of a line drawn from the point where the Borough boundary crosses the eastern end of Beech Street northwards along the middle of Whitecross Street thence eastwards along the middle of Old Street and northwards along the middle of Bath Street to the Borough boundary.

Column 1	*Column* 2	*Column* 3
Name of court	Local authority areas	Parts comprising court districts
SHORE-DITCH —*cont*.	London Borough of Tower Hamlets (part). *Other part* in Bow County Court District.	That part of the Borough west of a line drawn from a point in the River Thames to the south of Butcher Row northwards along the west side of Butcher Row, eastwards and northwards along the south side of Cable Street and the east side of White Horse Road to its junction with Ben Jonson Road, thence eastwards along the south side of Ben Jonson Road to the Regent's Canal, northwards along the centre of the Canal to the southernmost point of Victoria Park, north-eastwards along the north side of Old Ford Road to the Canal thence north-eastwards along the centre of the Canal to its junction with the River Lea and along the centre of the River to the Borough boundary.
SHREWS-BURY	Atcham Rural District (part). *Other part* in Wellington County Court District.	Acton Burnell, Alberbury with Cardeston, All Stretton, Astley, Atcham, Bayston Hill, Berrington, Bicton, Buildwas, Cardington, Church Preen, Church Pulverbatch, Condover, Cound, Cressage, Ford, Frodesley, Great Hanwood, Great Ness, Harley, Hughley, Kenley, Leebotwood, Leighton, Little Ness, Longnor, Minsterley, Montford, Pimhill, Pitchford, Pontesbury, Ruckley and Langley, Sheinton, Smethcott, Uffington, Upton Magna, Westbury, Wollaston, Woolstaston, Wroxeter.
	Bridgnorth Rural District (part). *Other parts* in Bridgnorth, Kidderminster, Ludlow, Wellington and Wolverhampton County Court Districts.	Easthope.
	Clun and Bishop's Castle Rural District (part). *Other parts* in Knighton, Ludlow and Welshpool County Court Districts.	Bishop's Castle Rural Borough, Colebatch, Lydbury North, Lydham, More, Myndtown, Norbury, Ratlinghope Shelve, Wentnor, Worthen.
	Forden Rural District (part). *Other parts* in Newtown and Welshpool County Court Districts.	Bausley.

Column 1	Column 2	Column 3
Name of court	Local authority areas	Parts comprising court districts
SHREWS-BURY —cont.	Ludlow Rural District (part). *Other parts* in Kidderminster and Ludlow County Court Districts.	Church Stretton.
	Shrewsbury Municipal Borough	Shrewsbury.
	North Shropshire Rural District (part). *Other parts* in Oswestry and Whitchurch County Court Districts.	Baschurch, Broughton, Clive, Grinshill, Hadnall, Lee Brockhurst, Loppinton, Myddle, / Moreton Corbet, Petton, Shawbury, Stanton upon Hine Heath, Wem Rural, Wem Urban.
SITTING-BOURNE	Hollingbourne Rural District (part). *Other part* in Maidstone County Court District.	Bicknor, Frinsted, Otterden, / Stockbury, Wichling, Wormshill.
	Sittingbourne and Milton Urban District.	Sittingbourne and Milton.
	Swale Rural District (part). *Other part* in Canterbury County Court District.	Bapchild, Bobbing, Borden, Bredgar, Buckland, Doddington, Eastling, Hartlip, Iwade, Kingsdown, Lower Halstow, Luddenham, Lynsted, / Milstead, Newington, Newnham, Norton, Rodmersham, Stalisfield, Stone, Teynham, Throwley, Tonge, Tunstall, Upchurch.
SKEGNESS AND SPILSBY	Alford Urban District	Alford.
	Horncastle Rural District (part). *Other parts* in Boston, Lincoln & Louth County Court Districts.	Asgarby, Hagworthingham, Hameringham, Lusby, / Salmonby, Somersby, Tetford, Winceby.
	Skegness Urban District.	Skegness.
	Spilsby Rural District (part). *Other part* in Boston County Court District.	Addlethorpe, Anderby, Ashby with Scremby, Aswardby, Bilsby with Thirlby, Bratoft, Brinkhill, Burgh le Marsh, Calceby, Candlesby, Carrington, / Chapel St. Leonards, Claxby, Croft, Cumberworth, Dalby, Driby, East Keal, East Kirkby, Farlesthorpe, Firsby, Friskney, Great Steeping,

Column 1	*Column* 2	*Column* 3
Name of court	Local authority areas	Parts comprising court districts
SKEGNESS AND SPILSBY —*cont.*	Spilsby Rural District (part). —*cont.*	Gunby, Hagnaby, Halton Holegate, Hareby, Harrington, Hogsthorpe, Hundleby, Huttoft, Ingoldmells, Irby in the Marsh, Langton by Spilsby, Little Steeping, Markby, Mavis Enderby, Mumby, Old Bolingbroke, Orby, Partney, Raithby, Rigsby with Ailby, Sausthorpe, Skendleby, South Ormsby cum Ketsby, Spilsby, Thorpe St. Peter, Toynton All Saints, Toynton St. Peter, Ulceby with Fordington, Wainfleet All Saints, Wainfleet St. Mary, Well, Welton le Marsh, West Keal, Willoughby with Sloothby.
SKIPTON	Barnoldswick Urban District.	Barnoldswick.
	Earby Urban District.	Earby.
	Settle Rural District (part). *Other part* in Lancaster County Court District.	Airton, Arncliffe, Austwick, Clapham with Newby, Giggleswick, Halton Gill, Halton West, Hanlith, Hawkswick, Hellifield, Horton in Ribblesdale, Kirkby Malham, Langcliffe, Lawkland, Litton, Long Preston, Malham, Malham Moor, Nappa, Otterburn, Rathmell, Scosthrop, Settle, Stainforth, Swinden, Wigglesworth.
	Silsden Urban District.	Silsden.
	Skipton Urban District.	Skipton.
	Skipton Rural District (part). *Other part* in Keighley County Court District.	Addingham, Appletreewick, Bank Newton, Barden, Beamsley, Bolton Abbey, Bordley, Bracewell, Bradleys Both, Brogden, Broughton, Buckden, Burnsall, Calton, Carleton, Cold Coniston, Coniston with Kilnsey, Cononley, Cowling, Cracoe, Draughton, Elslack, Embsay with Eastby, Eshton,

Column 1	*Column* 2	*Column* 3
Name of court	Local authority areas	Parts comprising court districts
SKIPTON *—cont.*	Skipton Rural District (part). *—cont.*	Farnhill, Flasby with Winterburn, Gargrave, Glusburn, Grassington, Halton East, Hartlington, Hazlewood with Storiths, Hebden, Hetton, Kettlewell with Starbotton, Kildwick, Linton, Lothersdale, Martons Both, Rylstone, Salterforth, Stirton with Thorlby, Thornton in Craven, Thorpe, Threshfield.
SLEAFORD	East Kesteven Rural District	Anwick, Asgarby and Howell, Ashby de la Launde and Bloxholm, Aswarby and Swarby, Aunsby and Dembleby, Billinghay, Blankney, Brauncewell, Burton Pedwardine, Cranwell and Byard's Leap, Culverthorpe and Kelby, Digby, Dogdyke, Dorrington, Ewerby and Evedon, Great Hale, Heckington, Helpringham, Kirkby la Thorpe, Leasingham, Little Hale, Martin, Newton and Haceby, North Kyme, North Rauceby, Osbournby, Rowston, Roxholm, Ruskington, Scopwick, Scredington, Silk Willoughby, South Kyme, South Rauceby, Swaton, Temple Bruer with Temple, High Grange, Threekingham, Timberland Walcot (near Billinghay), Walcot (near Folkingham), Wilsford.
	North Kesteven Rural District (part). *Other parts* in Lincoln and Newark County Court Districts.	Leadenham, Welbourn, Wellingore.
	Sleaford Urban District.	Sleaford.
	South Kesteven Rural District (part). *Other parts* in Grantham, Spalding and Stamford County Court Districts.	Aslackby and Laughton, Billingborough, Folkingham, Horbling, Pointon and Sempringham.

Column 1	Column 2	Column 3
Name of court	Local authority areas	Parts comprising court districts
SLOUGH	Cookham Rural District (part). *Other parts* in High Wycombe and Reading County Court Districts.	Bray, Cookham, Shottesbrooke, Waltham St. Lawrence, White Waltham.
	Easthampstead Rural District (part). *Other part* in Reading County Court District.	Winkfield.
	Egham Urban District.	Egham,
	Eton Urban District.	Eton.
	Eton Rural District (part). *Other part* in Uxbridge County Court District.	Burnham, Datchet, Dorney, Farnham Royal, Horton, Stoke Poges, Taplow, Wraysbury.
	Maidenhead Municipal Borough.	Maidenhead.
	New Windsor Municipal Borough.	New Windsor.
	Slough Municipal Borough.	Slough.
	Staines Urban District.	Staines,
	Windsor Rural District.	Old Windsor, Sunningdale, Sunninghill,
SOUTH-AMPTON	Droxford Rural District (part). *Other parts* in Petersfield, Portsmouth and Winchester County Court Districts.	Curdridge, Durley.
	Eastleigh Municipal Borough.	Eastleigh.
	New Forest Rural District (part). *Other part* in Lymington County Court District.	Beaulieu, Bramshaw, Copythorne, Denny Lodge, Dibden, Eling, Exbury and Lepe, Fawley, Lyndhurst, Marchwood, Minstead, Netley Marsh.
	Romsey Municipal Borough.	Romsey.
	Romsey and Stockbridge Rural District (part). *Other parts* in Andover, Salisbury and Winchester County Court Districts.	Chilworth, Melchet Park and Plaitford, Mottisfont, North Baddesley, Nursling and Rownhams, Romsey Extra, Sherfield English, Wellow.
	Southampton County Borough.	Southampton.
	Winchester Rural District (part). *Other part* in Winchester County Court District.	Botley, Bursledon, Hamble, Hedge End, Hound, West End.

Column 1	Column 2	Column 3
Name of court	Local authority areas	Parts comprising court districts
SOUTH-END	Benfleet Urban District.	Benfleet.
	Canvey Island Urban District.	Canvey Island.
	Rayleigh Urban District.	Rayleigh.
	Rochford Rural District.	Ashingdon, Hockley, Barling Magna, Hullbridge, Canewdon, Paglesham, Foulness, Rochford, Great Stambridge, Wakering, Sutton. Hawkwell,
	Southend on Sea County Borough.	Southend on Sea.
SOUTH-PORT	Formby Urban District.	Formby.
	Ormskirk Urban District.	Ormskirk,
	Southport County Borough.	Southport.
	West Lancashire Rural District (part). *Other parts* in Liverpool and Wigan County Court Districts.	Altcar, North Meols, Aughton, Rufford, Bickerstaffe, Scarisbrick, Downholland, Tarleton. Halsall, Hesketh with Becconsall.
SOUTH SHIELDS	Boldon Urban District.	Boldon.
	Hebburn Urban District.	Hebburn.
	Jarrow Municipal Borough.	Jarrow.
	South Shields County Borough.	South Shields.
SOUTH-WARK	London Borough of Lambeth (part). *Other parts* in Lambeth and Wandsworth County Court Districts.	That part of the Borough north of a line drawn from the River Thames at Lambeth Bridge along the middle of Lambeth Road to the point where the Borough boundary crosses that road.
	London Borough of Lewisham (part). *Other parts* in Bromley and Lambeth County Court Districts.	That part of the Borough north of a line drawn from the point where the Borough boundary crosses Old Kent Road eastwards along the middle of New Cross Road to the point where the Borough boundary crosses the middle of Deptford Bridge.
	London Borough of Southwark (part). *Other part* in Lambeth County Court District.	That part of the Borough north of a line drawn from the point where the Borough boundary crosses Lambeth Road eastwards along the middle of Lambeth Road, St. George's Road, New Kent Road, Old Kent Road and New Cross Road to the Borough boundary.

Column 1	Column 2	Column 3
Name of court	Local authority areas	Parts comprising court districts
SPALDING	Bourne Urban District.	Bourne.
	East Elloe Rural District.	Fleet, Sutton Bridge, Gedney, Sutton Gedney Hill, St. Edmund, Holbeach, Sutton Little Sutton, St. James, Long Sutton, Tydd St. Mary. Lutton, Whaplode.
	South Kesteven Rural District (part). *Other parts* in Grantham, Sleaford and Stamford County Court Districts.	Baston, Market Deeping St. James, Deeping, Dowsby, Morton, Dunsby, Rippingale, Edenham, Thurlby, Haconby, Toft with Kirkby Lound and Underwood, Manthorpe, Langtoft, Witham on the Hill.
	Spalding Urban District.	Spalding.
	Spalding Rural District.	Cowbit, Moulton, Crowland, Pinchbeck, Deeping Quadring, St. Nicholas, Surfleet, Donington, Weston. Gosberton,
STAFFORD	Cannock Rural District (part). *Other parts* in Walsall, Wellington and Wolverhampton County Court Districts.	Acton Trussell Dunston, and Bednall, Penkridge, Blymhill, Teddesley Hay. Coppenhall,
	Lichfield Rural District (part). *Other parts* in Lichfield and Tamworth County Court Districts.	Brindley Heath, Colton.
	Rugeley Urban District.	Rugeley.
	Stafford Municipal Borough.	Stafford.
	Stafford Rural District (part). *Other parts* in Market Drayton and Wellington County Court Districts.	Baswich, Hopton and Bradley, Coton, Brocton, Ingestre, Castle Church, Marston, Church Eaton, Norbury, Colwich, Ranton, Creswell, Salt and Enson, Ellenhall, Seighford, Fradswell, Stowe by Chartley, Gayton, Tixall, Gnosall, Weston upon Haughton, Trent, High Offley, Whitgreave.
	Stone Urban District.	Stone.

Column 1	Column 2	Column 3
Name of court	Local authority areas	Parts comprising court districts
STAFFORD —cont.	Stone Rural District (part). *Other parts* in Stoke on Trent and Newcastle under Lyme County Court Districts.	Chebsey, Eccleshall, Milwich, Sandon, Stone Rural.
STAMFORD	Barnack Rural District.	Bainton, Barnack, St. Martin's Without, Southorpe, Thornhaugh, Ufford, Wansford, Wittering, Wothorpe,
	Ketton Rural District (part). *Other part* in Oakham County Court District.	Clipsham, Essendine, Great Casterton, Little Casterton, Pickworth, Ryhall, Tinwell, Tixover.
	Oakham Rural District (part). *Other part* in Oakham County Court District.	Tickencote.
	Oundle and Thrapston Rural District (part). *Other parts* in Huntingdon, Kettering, Oakham, Peterborough and Wellingborough County Court Districts.	Apethorpe, Blatherwycke, Bulwick, Collyweston, Duddington, Easton on the Hill, Fineshade, King's Cliffe, Laxton.
	South Kesteven Rural District (part). *Other parts* in Grantham, Sleaford and Spalding County Court Districts.	Barholm and Stowe, Braceborough and Wilsthorpe, Careby Aunby and Holywell, Carlby, Castle Bytham, Counthorpe and Creeton, Greatford, Little Bytham, Tallington, Uffington, West Deeping.
	Stamford Municipal Borough	Stamford.
STOCKPORT	Bredbury and Romiley Urban District.	Bredbury and Romiley.
	Cheadle and Gatley Urban District.	Cheadle and Gatley.
	Disley Rural District.	Disley.
	Hazel Grove and Bramhall Urban District.	Hazel Grove and Bramhall.
	Marple Urban District.	Marple.
	Stockport County Borough.	Stockport.
STOCKTON ON TEES	Darlington Rural District (part). *Other part* in Darlington County Court District.	Bishopton, East and West Newbiggin, Great Stainton, Little Stainton.

Column 1	*Column* 2	*Column* 3
Name of court	Local authority areas	Parts comprising court districts
STOCKTON ON TEES —*cont.*	Sedgefield Rural District (part). *Other parts* in Bishop Auckland, Darlington and Durham County Court Districts.	Bradbury and the Isle, Butterwick and Oldacres, Elstob, Embleton, — Fishburn, Foxton and Shotton, Mordon, Sedgefield, Stillington.
	Stockton Rural District (part). *Other part* in Hartlepool County Court District.	Aislaby with Newsham, Carlton, Egglescliffe, Elton, Grindon, — Longnewton. Newton Bewley, Preston on Tees, Redmarshall, Whitton, Wolviston.
	Stokesley Rural District (part). *Other parts* in Malton, Middlesbrough and Northallerton County Court Districts.	Castlelevington, High Worsall, Ingleby Barwick, Kirklevington, — Low Worsall, Picton, Yarm.
	Teesside County Borough (part). *Other part* in Middlesbrough County Court District.	That part of the Borough North of the River Tees and West of the old River Tees, the Fleet and Stainsby Beck.
STOKE ON TRENT	Cheadle Rural District (part). *Other parts* in Leek and Uttoxeter County Court Districts.	Caverswall, Cheadle, Dilhorne, — Draycott in the Moors, Forsbrook.
	Kidsgrove Urban District.	Kidsgrove.
	Leek Rural District (part). *Other parts* in Buxton and Leek County Court Districts.	Bagnall, Brown Edge, — Norton in the Moors.
	Stoke on Trent County Borough.	Stoke on Trent.
	Stone Rural District (part). *Other parts* in Newcastle under Lyme, and Stafford County Court Districts.	Barlaston, Fulford, — Hilderstone.
STOUR-BRIDGE	Bromsgrove Rural District (part). *Other parts* in Birmingham, Bromsgrove and Redditch County Court Districts.	Clent, Hagley.
	Dudley County Borough (part). *Other part* in Dudley County Court District.	The Brierley Hill, Brockmoor and Pensnett, Kingswinford and Wallheath, Quarry Bank and Wordsley Wards.
	Halesowen Municipal Borough.	Halesowen.
	Kidderminster Rural District (part). *Other part* in Kidderminster County Court District.	Broome.

Column 1	Column 2	Column 3	
Name of court	Local authority areas	Parts comprising court districts	
STOUR-BRIDGE—cont.	Seisdon Rural District (part). *Other part* in Wolverhampton County Court District.	Bobbington, Enville,	Kinver.
	Stourbridge Municipal Borough.	Stourbridge.	
STOW-MARKET	Cosford Rural District (part). *Other parts* in Bury St. Edmunds, Ipswich and Sudbury County Court Districts.	Bildston, Brettenham, Hitcham, Kettlebaston,	Nedging with Naughton, Wattisham.
	Gipping Rural District (part). *Other part* in Ipswich County Court District.	Badley, Barking, Battisford, Buxhall, Combs, Creeting St. Mary, Creeting St. Peter, Gipping, Great Bricett, Great Finborough, Harleston, Haughley.	Little Finborough, Little Stonham, Mickfield, Needham Market, Old Newton, Onehouse, Ringshall, Shelland, Stonham Aspell, Stonham Earl, Stowupland, Wetherden,
	Hartismere Rural District (part). *Other parts* in Halesworth, Ipswich and Norwich County Court Districts.	Aspall, Bacton, Cotton, Finningham, Mendlesham, Thwaite,	Westhorpe, Wetheringset cum Brockford, Wickham and Skeith, Wyverstone.
	Stowmarket Urban District.	Stowmarket.	
	Thedwastre Rural District (part). *Other part* in Bury St. Edmunds County Court District.	Drinkstone, Elmswell, Felsham, Gedding,	Rattlesden, Tostock, Woolpit.
STRAT-FORD ON AVON	Alcester Rural District (part). *Other part* in Redditch County Court District.	Aston Cantlow,	Bidford-on-Avon.
	Shipston on Stour Rural District (part). *Other part* in Banbury County Court District.	Barcheston, Burmington, Butlers Marston, Cherington, Great Wolford, Halford, Honington, Idlicote, Ilmington, Little Wolford, Long Compton, Oxhill,	Pillerton Hersey, Pillerton Priors, Shipston on Stour, Stourton, Stretton on Fosse, Sutton under Braibes, Tidmington, Tredington, Whatcote, Whichford.

Column 1	Column 2	Column 3
Name of court	Local authority areas	Parts comprising court districts
STRAT-FORD ON AVON —cont.	Stratford on Avon Rural District (part). *Other parts* in Birmingham, and Warwick County Court Districts.	Admington, Alderminster, Atherstone on Stour, Bearley, Beaudesert, Billesley, Binton, Charlecote, Clifford Chambers, Combrook, Compton Verney, Dorsington, Ettington, Fulbroke, Hampton Lucy, Henley-in-Arden, Kineton, Long Marston, Loxley, Luddington, Milcote, Moreton Morrell, Newbold Pacey and Ashorne, Old Stratford and Drayton, Preston on Stour, Quinton, Snitterfield, Temple Grafton, Ullenhall, Welford on Avon, Wellesbourne, Weston on Avon, Whitchurch, Wootton Wawen.
	Stratford upon Avon Municipal Borough.	Stratford upon Avon.
STROUD	Gloucester Rural District (part). *Other parts* in Cheltenham, Dursley and Gloucester County Court Districts.	Eastington.
	Nailsworth Urban District.	Nailsworth.
	Stroud Urban District.	Stroud.
	Stroud Rural District.	Bisley with Lypiatt, Chalford, Cranham, Horsley, King's Stanley, Leonard Stanley, Minchinhampton, Miserden, Painswick, Pitchcombe, Randwick, Rodborough, Stonehouse, Thrupp, Whiteshill, Woodchester.
	Tetbury Rural District (part). *Other parts* in Dursley and Malmesbury County Court Districts.	Avening.
SUDBURY	Clare Rural District (part). *Other parts* in Bury St. Edmunds, Cambridge and Newmarket County Court Districts.	Cavendish, Clare, Great Wratting, Kedington, Little Wratting, Roslingford, Stoke by Clare, Wixoe.
	Cosford Rural District (part). *Other parts* in Bury St. Edmunds, Ipswich and Stowmarket County Court Districts.	Boxford, Brent Eleigh, Chelsworth, Edwardstone, Groton, Lavenham, Lindsey, Milden, Monks Eleigh, Polstead, Preston St. Mary.

Column 1	Column 2	Column 3
Name of court	Local authority areas	Parts comprising court districts
SUDBURY —cont.	Halstead Rural District (part). *Other parts* in Braintree, Cambridge and Colchester and Clacton County Court Districts.	Alphamstone, Ashen, Belchamp Otten, Belchamp St. Paul, Belchamp Walter, Birdbrook, Borley, Bulmer, Bures Hamlet, Foxearth, Gestingthorpe, / Great Henny, Great Yeldham, Lamarsh, Liston, Little Henny, Little Yeldham, Middleton, Ovington, Pentlow, Ridgewell, Sturmer, Tilbury Juxta Clare, Twinstead, Wickham St. Paul.
	Lexden and Winstree Rural District (part). *Other parts* in Colchester and Clacton and Maldon County Court Districts.	Mount Bures.
	Melford Rural District (part). *Other parts* in Bury St. Edmunds and Colchester and Clacton County Court Districts.	Acton, Alpheton, Assington, Boxted, Bures St. Mary, Chilton, Glemsford, Great Cornard, Great Waldingfield, Hartest, / Leavenheath, Little Cornard, Little Waldingfield, Long Melford, Newton, Shimpling, Somerton, Stanstead, Stoke by Nayland.
	Sudbury Municipal Borough.	Sudbury.
SUNDER-LAND	Easington Rural District (part). *Other parts* in Durham and Hartlepool County Court Districts.	Burdon, Cold Hesledon, Dalton le Dale, Easington, East Murton, / Hawthorn, Seaton with Slingley, Warden Law.
	Seaham Urban District.	Seaham.
	Sunderland County Borough.	Sunderland.
SWANAGE	Swanage Urban District.	Swanage.
	Wareham Municipal Borough.	Wareham.
	Wareham and Purbeck Rural District (part). *Other parts* in Dorchester, Poole and Weymouth County Court Districts.	Arne, Bere Regis, Bloxworth, Church Knowle, Coombe Keynes, Corfe Castle (part), viz.: the entire civil parish except / Furzey, Green, Long and Round Islands. East Holme, East Lulworth, East Stoke, Kimmeridge, Langton Matravers, Morden, Steeple,

Column 1	Column 2	Column 3
Name of court	Local authority areas	Parts comprising court districts
SWANAGE —cont.	Wareham and Purbeck Rural District (part). —cont.	Studland (part), viz.: the entire civil parish except Brownsea Island, Tyneham, — Wareham St. Martin, West Lulworth, Wool, Worth Matravers.
SWANSEA	Gower Rural District.	Bishopston, Cheriton, Ilston, Knelston, Llanddewi, Llangennith, Llanmadoc, Llanrhidian Higher, Llanrhidian Lower, — Nicholaston, Oxwich, Pennard, Penmaen, Penrice, Port Eynon, Reynoldston, Rhossili, Cefn y bryn, land common to the civil parishes of Llanrhidian Higher, Llanrhidian Lower, Nicholaston, Penmaen, Penrice and Reynoldston.
	Llwchwr Urban District.	Llwchwr.
	Swansea County Borough.	Swansea.
SWINDON	Calne and Chippenham Rural District (part). Other parts in Bath, Chippenham and Devizes County Court Districts.	Compton Bassett, Hilmarton.
	Cricklade and Wootton Bassett Rural District (part). Other part in Cirencester County Court District.	Braydon, Broad Town, Clyffe Pypard, Cricklade, Lydiard Millicent, Lydiard Tregoze, — Lyneham, Purton, Tockenham, Wootton Bassett.
	Faringdon Rural District (part). Other parts in Didcot and Oxford County Court Districts.	Ashbury, Bourton, Buscot, Coleshill, Compton Beauchamp, Eaton Hastings, — Fernham, Great Coxwell, Little Coxwell, Longcot, Shrivenham, Watchfield, Woolstone.
	Highworth Rural District.	Bishopstone, Blunsdon St. Andrew, Castle Eaton, Chiseldon, Hannington, Haydon Wick, Highworth, Inglesham, — Liddington, South Marston, Stanton Fitzwarren, Stratton St. Margaret, Wanborough, Wroughton.

Column 1	Column 2	Column 3
Name of court	Local authority areas	Parts comprising court districts
SWINDON —cont.	Marlborough and Ramsbury Rural District (part). Other parts in Andover, Marlborough and Newbury County Court Districts.	Aldbourne, Baydon.
	Swindon Municipal Borough.	Swindon.
TAMWORTH	Atherstone Rural District (part). Other part in Nuneaton County Court District.	Austrey, Newton Regis, Dordon, Polesworth, Grendon, Seckington, Kingsbury, Shuttington.
	Lichfield Rural District (part). Other parts in Lichfield and Stafford County Court Districts.	Clifton, Fazeley, Campville Harleston, Drayton Hints, Bassett, Thorpe Edingale, Constantine, Elford, Wigginton.
	Meriden Rural District (part). Other parts in Birmingham, Coventry and Nuneaton County Court Districts.	Middleton.
	Tamworth Municipal Borough.	Tamworth.
TAUNTON	Dulverton Rural District (part). Other parts in Minehead and Tiverton County Court Districts.	Huish Champflower.
	Langport Rural District (part). Other parts in Axminster and Chard, Bridgwater, Wells and Yeovil County Court Districts.	Beer Crocombe, Huish Episcopi, Curry Mallet, Isle Abbotts, Curry Rival Isle Brewers, Drayton, Langport, Fivehead, Muchelney.
	Taunton Municipal Borough.	Taunton.
	Taunton Rural District.	Ash Priors, Lydeard St. Bickenhall, Lawrence, Bishop's Hull North Curry, Without, Norton Fitzwarren, Bishop's Orchard Lydeard, Portman, Cheddon Otterford, Fitzpaine, Pitminster, Churchstanton, Ruishton, Combe Florey, Staple Corfe, Fitzpaine, Cothelstone, Staplegrove, Creech Stoke St. Michael, St. Gregory, Curland, Stoke St. Mary, Durston, Thornfalcon, Halse, Tolland, Hatch Trull, Beauchamp, West Bagborough, Kingston West Hatch, St. Mary, West Monkton.

Column 1	Column 2	Column 3
Name of court	Local authority areas	Parts comprising court districts
TAUNTON —cont.	Tiverton Rural District (part). *Other parts* in Tiverton County Court District.	Clayhidon, Culmstock,	Hemyock.
	Wellington Rural District.	Ashbrittle, Bathealton, Bradford, Chipstable, Fitzhead, Langford Budville, Milverton, Nynehead, Oake,	Sampford Arundel, Stawley, Thorne St. Margaret, Wellington Without, West Buckland, Wiveliscombe, Wiveliscombe Without.
	Wellington Urban District.	Wellington.
TAVISTOCK	St. Germans Rural District (part). *Other parts* in Liskeard and Plymouth County Court Districts.	Calstock.
	Tavistock Rural District (part). *Other part* in Launceston County Court District.	Bere Ferrers, Brentor, Buckland Monachorum, Coryton, Horrabridge, Lamerton, Lewtrenchard, Lydford, Marystowe, Mary Tavy, Meavy, Milton Abbot,	Peter Tavy, Sampford Spiney, Sheepstor, Stowford, Sydenham Damerel, Tavistock, Tavistock Hamlets, Thrushelton, Walkhampton, Whitchurch.
THAME	Aylesbury Rural District (part). *Other part* in Aylesbury County Court District.	Aston Sandford, Boarstall, Brill, Chearsley, Chilton, Dorton, Haddenham,	Ickford, Kingsey, Long Crendon, Ludgershall, Oakley, Shabbington, Worminghall,
	Bullingdon Rural District (part). *Other parts* in Didcot and Oxford County Court Districts.	Adwell, Aston Rowant, Chalgrove, Chinnor, Crowell, Great Haseley, Great Milton, Lewknor, Little Milton, Pyrton, Shirburn,	Stoke Talmage, Sydenham, Tetsworth, Thomley, Tiddington with Albury, Towersey, Waterperry, Waterstock, Watlington, Wheatfield.

Column 1	Column 2	Column 3
Name of court	Local authority areas	Parts comprising court districts
THAME —cont.	Ploughley Rural District (part). *Other parts* in Banbury and Oxford County Court Districts.	Piddington.
	Thame Urban District.	Thame.
THETFORD	Downham Rural District (part). *Other part* in King's Lynn County Court District.	Feltwell, Methwold, Hockwold Northwold. cum Wilton.
	Mildenhall Rural District (part). *Other parts* in Bury St. Edmunds and Newmarket County Court Districts.	Brandon, Wangford. Elveden, Santon Downham,
	Swaffham Rural District (part). *Other parts* in East Dereham and King's Lynn County Court Districts.	Cranwich, Sturston, Lynford, Weeting with Mundford, Broomhill. Stanford,
	Thetford Municipal Borough.	Thetford.
	Thingoe Rural District (part). *Other part* in Bury St. Edmunds County Court District.	Barnham, Honington, Barningham, Hopton, Coney Weston, Knettishall, Euston, Market Weston, Fakenham Sapiston, Magna, Thelnetham. Hepworth,
	Wayland Rural District (part). *Other parts* in King's Lynn and Norwich County Court Districts.	Brettenham, Kilverstone, Bridgham, Riddlesworth, Caston, Roudham, Croxton, Stow Bedon, Harling, Thompson, Hockham, Tottington, Kenninghall, Wretham.
THORN-BURY	Thornbury Rural District (part). *Other part* in Dursley County Court District.	Almondsbury, Olveston, Alveston, Patchway, Aust, Pilning & Falfield, Severn Beach, Hill and Rangeworthy, Rockhampton, Thornbury, Oldbury Tytherington. on Severn,
THORNE	Isle of Axholme Rural District (part). *Other parts* in Gainsborough, Goole and Scunthorpe County Court Districts.	Belton, Epworth, Crowle, Wroot. Eastoft,
	Thorne Rural District.	Fishlake, Sykehouse, Hatfield, Thorne. Stainforth,

Column 1	*Column* 2	*Column* 3
Name of court	Local authority areas	Parts comprising court districts
TIVERTON	Crediton Rural District (part). *Other parts* in Barnstaple, Exeter and Okehampton County Court Districts.	Cheriton Fitzpaine, Poughill, Puddington, Stockleigh English, Stockleigh Pomeroy, Thelbridge, Washford Pyne, Woolfardisworthy.
	Dulverton Rural District (part). *Other parts* in Minehead and Taunton County Court Districts.	Brompton Regis, Brushford, Dulverton, Exton, Skilgate, Upton.
	South Molton Rural District (part). *Other part* in Barnstaple County Court District.	Creacombe, East Anstey, East Worlington, Knowstone, Rackenford, West Anstey, Witheridge.
	Tiverton Municipal Borough.	Tiverton.
	Tiverton Rural District (part). *Other part* in Taunton County Court District.	Bampton, Bickleigh, Bradninch, Burlescombe, Butterleigh, Cadbury, Cadeleigh, Clayhanger, Cruwys Morchard, Cullompton, Halberton, Hockworthy, Holcombe Rogus, Huntsham, Kentisbeare, Loxbeare, Morebath, Oakford, Sampford Peverell, Silverton, Stoodleigh, Templeton, Thorverton, Uffculme, Uplowman, Washfield, Willand.
TOD-MORDEN	Hebden Royd Urban District.	Hebden Royd.
	Hepton Rural District.	Blackshaw, Erringden, Heptonstall, Wadsworth.
	Todmorden Municipal Borough.	Todmorden.
TON-BRIDGE	Sevenoaks Rural District (part). *Other parts* in East Grinstead and Sevenoaks County Court Districts.	Chiddingstone, Edenbridge, Hever, Leigh, Penshurst.
	Tonbridge Urban District.	Tonbridge.
	Tonbridge Rural District (part). *Other part* in Tunbridge Wells County Court District.	Bidborough, Capel, Hadlow, Hildenborough.
TORQUAY	Buckfastleigh Urban District.	Buckfastleigh.
	Dartmouth Municipal Borough.	Dartmouth.

Column 1	Column 2	Column 3
Name of court	Local authority areas	Parts comprising court districts
TORQUAY —cont.	Newton Abbot Rural District (part). *Other part* in Newton Abbot County Court District.	Stokeinteignhead.
	Torbay County Borough.	Torbay.
	Totnes Municipal Borough.	Totnes.
	Totnes Rural District.	Ashprington, Littlehempston, Berry Pomeroy, Marldon, Cornworthy, Moreleigh, Dartington, North Huish, Dean Prior, Rattery, Diptford, South Brent, Dittisham, Staverton, Halwell, Stoke Gabriel Harberton, Ugborough, Holne, West Buck- Kingswear, fastleigh.
TROW- BRIDGE	Bradford and Melksham Rural District (part). *Other parts* in Chippenham and Bath County Court Districts.	Atworth, Semington, Broughton South Wraxhall, Gifford, Staverton, Hilperton, Westwood, Holt, Wingfield, Limpley Winsley. Stoke,
	Bradford on Avon Urban District.	Bradford on Avon.
	Trowbridge Urban District.	Trowbridge.
	Warminster and Westbury Rural District (part). *Other part* in Warminster County Court District.	Bratton, Heywood, Bulkington, Keevil, Dilton Marsh, North Bradley, East Coulston, Southwick, Edington, Steeple Ashton, Great Hinton, West Ashton.
	Westbury Urban District.	Westbury.
TRURO AND FAL- MOUTH	Falmouth Municipal Borough.	Falmouth.
	Kerrier Rural District (part). *Other parts* in Helston and Red- ruth County Court Districts.	Budock, Mawnan, Mabe, St. Gluvias.
	Penryn Municipal Borough.	Penryn.
	Truro Municipal Borough.	Truro.
	Truro Rural District (part). *Other parts* in Newquay and Redruth County Court Dis- tricts.	Chacewater, Probus, Cuby, Ruan Lanihorne, Feock, St. Agnes, Gerrans, St. Allen, Kea, St. Clement, Kenwyn, St. Erme, Ladock, St. Just in Roseland, Mylor, St. Michael Parranarworthal, Penkevil, Perranzabuloe, Tregoney, Philleigh, Veryan.

Column 1	*Column* 2	*Column* 3
Name of court	Local authority areas	Parts comprising court districts
TUN BRIDGE WELLS	Battle Rural District (part). *Other part* in Hastings County Court District.	Burwash, Etchingham, Hurst Green, Ticehurst.
	Southborough Urban District.	Southborough.
	Tonbridge Rural District (part). *Other part* in Tonbridge County Court District.	Brenchley, Horsmonden, Lamberhurst, Paddock Wood, Pembury, Speldhurst.
	Royal Tunbridge Wells Municipal Borough.	Tunbridge Wells.
	Uckfield Rural District (part). *Other parts* in East Grinstead and Lewes County Court Districts.	Crowborough, Frant, Mayfield, Rotherfield, Wadhurst,
UTTOX-ETER	Ashbourne Rural District (part). *Other parts* in Buxton, Derby and Matlock County Court Districts.	Boyleston, Cubley, Doveridge, Marston Montgomery, Norbury and Roston, Somersal Herbert, Subdury.
	Cheadle Rural District (part). *Other parts* in Stoke on Trent and Leek County Court Districts.	Alton, Checkley, Farley.
	Uttoxeter Urban District.	Uttoxeter.
	Uttoxeter Rural District.	Abbot's Bromley, Blithfield, Croxden, Denstone, Draycott in the Clay, Ellastone, Kingston, Leighe, Marchington, Mayfield, Newborough, Okeover, Ramshorn, Rocester, Stanton, Uttoxeter Rural, Wootton.
UXBRIDGE	Eton Rural District (part). *Other part* in Slough County Court District.	Denham, Fulmer, Gerrards Cross, Hedgerley, Iver, Wexham.
	London Borough of Hillingdon.	Hillingdon.
	London Borough of Ealing (part). *Other parts* in Brentford and Willesden County Court Districts.	That part of the Borough south and west of a line drawn from the point where the Borough boundary crosses the Grand Union Canal near Balmoral Drive, northwards along the east bank of the canal then eastwards along the south of Ruislip Road and southwards along the east of Allenby Road to Kings Avenue thence eastwards along the

Column 1 Name of court	Column 2 Local authority areas	Column 3 Parts comprising court districts
UXBRIDGE —cont.	London Borough of Ealing (part). —cont.	south of King's Avenue across Greenford Road to the River Brent, southwards along the River to its confluence with the Grand Union Canal and southwards along the Canal to the Borough boundary.
	London Borough of Hounslow (part). Other part in Brentford County Court District.	That part of the Borough west of a line drawn from the point where the River Crane crosses the Bath Road, southwards along the River to the middle of the Great South West Road then westwards along the middle of that road to the Borough boundary.
WAKE- FIELD	Horbury Urban District.	Horbury.
	Normanton Urban District.	Normanton.
	Stanley Urban District	Stanley.
	Wakefield County Borough.	Wakefield.

	Wakefield Rural District (part).
	    Other part in Barnsley County Court District.
		Bretton West, Sharlston,
		Chevet, Sitlington,
		Crigglestone, Walton,
		Crofton, Warmfield
		Newland with cum Heath,
		    Woodhouse Wintersalt.
		    Moor,

WALSALL	Aldridge Brownhills Urban District.	Aldridge Brownhills.
	Cannock Rural District (part). Other parts in Stafford, Wellington and Wolverhampton County Court Districts.	Cheslyn Hay, Hatherton, Great Wyrley, Huntington.
	Cannock Urban District.	Cannock.
	Walsall County Borough.	Walsall.
WANDS- WORTH	London Borough of Lambeth (part). Other parts in Lambeth and Southwark County Court Districts.	That part of the Borough to the west of a line drawn from the point where the Borough boundary crosses Nine Elms Lane eastwards along the north of Nine Elms Lane then generally southwards along the middle of Wandsworth Road, Southville Road, Jeffreys Road, Clapham Road, Bedford Road, Acre Lane, Brixton Hill, Streatham Hill and Streatham High Road to the Borough boundary at Hermitage Bridge.

Column 1	*Column* 2	*Column* 3
Name of court	Local authority areas	Parts comprising court districts
WANDS-WORTH —cont.	London Borough of Richmond upon Thames (part). *Other parts* in Brentford and Kingston upon Thames County Court Districts.	That part of the Borough to the east and south of a line drawn along the middle of the River Thames.
	London Borough of Wandsworth.	Wandsworth.
WAR-MINSTER	Warminster Urban District.	Warminster.
	Warminster and Westbury Rural District (part). *Other part* in Trowbridge County Court District.	Bishopstrow, Knook, Boyton, Longridge Brixton Deverill, Deverill, Norton Bavant, Chapmanslade, Sherrington, Chitterne, Stockton, Codford, Sutton Veny, Corsley, Upton Lovell, Heytesbury, Upton Horningsham, Scudamore. Imber, Kingston Deverill,
WARRINGTON	Newton le Willows Urban District.	Newton le Willows.
	Runcorn Rural District (part) *Other parts* in Northwich and Runcorn County Court Districts.	Appleton, Stockton Heath, Daresbury, Stretton, Grappenhall, Walton, Hatton, Whitley. Moore,
	Warrington County Borough.	Warrington.
	Warrington Rural District.	Burtonwood, Poulton with Croft, Fearnhead, Cuerdley, Rixton with Great Sankey, Glazebrook, Penketh, Winwick, Woolston.
WARWICK	Kenilworth Urban District.	Kenilworth.
	Royal Leamington Spa Municipal Borough.	Leamington Spa.
	Southam Rural District (part). *Other parts* in Banbury and Rugby County Court Districts.	Bishop's Lower Itchington, Radbourn, Chadshunt, Napton on Chapel Ascote, the Hill, Chesterton Southam, and Kingston, Stockton, Gaydon, Ufton, Harbury, Upper Hodnell, Radbourn, Ladbroke, Watergall, Lighthorne, Wills Pastures. Long Itchington,

Column 1	Column 2	Column 3
Name of court	Local authority areas	Parts comprising court districts
WARWICK —cont.	Stratford on Avon Rural District (part). *Other parts* in Birmingham and Stratford on Avon County Court Districts.	Claverdon, Preston Bagot, Langley, Wolverton.
	Warwick Municipal Borough.	Warwick.
	Warwick Rural District (part). *Other part* in Coventry County Court District.	Ashow, Lapworth, Baddesley Leek Wootton, Clinton, Norton Barford, Lindsey, Beausale, Offchurch, Bishops Old Milverton, Tachbrook, Radford Blackdown, Semele, Budbrooke, Rowington, Bushwood, Sherbourne, Cubbington, Shrewley, Eathorpe, Wappenbury, Guy's Cliffe, Wasperton, Haseley, Weston under Hatton, Wetherley Honiley, Whitnash, Hunningham, Wroxall.
WATFORD	Bushey Urban District.	Bushey.
	Chorleywood Urban District.	Chorleywood.
	London Borough of Harrow (part). *Other part* in Willesden County Court District.	The Harrow Weald, Headstone, Pinner North and Hatch End, Pinner South, Roxbourne and Stanmore North Wards.
	Rickmansworth Urban District.	Rickmansworth.
	Watford Municipal Borough.	Watford.
	Watford Rural District.	Abbots Langley, Sarratt, Aldenham, Watford Rural.
WELLING- BOROUGH	Bedford Rural District (part). *Other parts* in Bedford and Biggleswade County Court Districts.	Melchbourne Podington, and Yielden, Wymington.
	Higham Ferrers Municipal Borough.	Higham Ferrers.
	Irthlingborough Urban District.	Irthlingborough.
	Oundle and Thrapston Rural District (part). *Other parts* in Huntingdon, Oakham, Kettering, Peterborough and Stamford, County Court Districts.	Chelveston cum Hargrave, Caldecott, Little Addington, Great Addington, Ringstead.
	Raunds Urban District.	Raunds.

Column 1	Column 2	Column 3
Name of court	Local authority areas	Parts comprising court districts
WELLING-BOROUGH —cont.	Rushden Urban District.	Rushden.
	Wellingborough Urban District.	Wellingborough.
	Wellingborough Rural District.	Bozeat, Earls Barton, Easton Maudit, Ecton, Great Doddington, Great Harrowden, Grendon, Hardwick, Irchester, Isham, Little Harrowden, Mears Ashby, Newton Bromswold, Orlingbury, Strixton, Sywell, Wilby, Wollaston.
WELLING-TON	Atcham Rural District (part). Other part in Shrewsbury County Court District.	Uppington, Withington.
	Bridgnorth Rural District (part). Other parts in Bridgnorth, Kidderminster, Ludlow, Shrewsbury and Wolverhampton County Court Districts.	Broseley.
	Cannock Rural District (part). Other parts in Stafford, Walsall and Wolverhampton County Court Districts.	Weston under Lizard
	Dawley Urban District.	Dawley.
	Newport Urban District.	Newport.
	Oakengates Urban District.	Oakengates.
	Shifnal Rural District (part). Other parts in Bridgnorth and Wolverhampton County Court Districts.	Kemberton, Sheriff Hales, Shifnal, Tong.
	Stafford Rural District (part). Other parts in Market Drayton and Stafford County Court Districts.	Forton.
	Wellington Urban District.	Wellington.
	Wellington Rural District.	Bolas Magna, Cherrington, Chetwynd, Chetwynd Aston, Church Aston, Edgmond, Ercall Magna, Eyton upon the Weald Moors, Hadley, Kynnersley, Lilleshall, Little Wenlock, Longdon upon Tern, Longford, Preston upon the Weald Moors, Rodington, Tibberton, Waters Upton, Wellington Rural, Woodcote, Wrockwardine.

Column 1	Column 2	Column 3
Name of court	Local authority areas	Parts comprising court districts
WELLS	Axbridge Rural District (part). *Other parts* in Bristol and Weston-super-Mare County Court Districts.	Axbridge, Mark, Blagdon, Weare, Chapel Allerton, Wedmore. Cheddar,
	Clutton Rural District (part). *Other part* in Bristol County Court District.	Chilcompton, Litton, East Harptree, Ston Easton, Farrington Ubley, Gurney, West Harptree.
	Glastonbury Municipal Borough.	Glastonbury.
	Langport Rural District (part). *Other parts* in Axminster & Chard, Bridgewater, Taunton & Yeovil County Court Districts.	Compton Kingweston. Dundon,
	Shepton Mallet Urban District.	Shepton Mallet.
	Shepton Mallet Rural District (part). *Other part* in Frome County Court District.	Ashwick, Holcombe, Binegar, Lamyat, Cranmore, Lydford, Croscombe, Milton Clevedon, Ditcheat, Pilton, Doulting, Pylle, East Pennard, Stratton on Emborough, the Fosse, Evercreech, West Bradley.
	Street Urban District.	Street.
	Wells Municipal Borough.	Wells.

	Wells Rural District.	Baltons- Priddy,
		  borough, Rodney Stoke,
		Butleigh, St. Cuthbert Out,
		Chewton Sharpham,
		  Mendip, Walton,
		Dinder, Westbury,
		Godney, West Pennard,
		Meare, Wookey.
		North Wootton,

WELSH-POOL	Clun and Bishop's Castle Rural District (part). *Other parts* in Knighton, Ludlow and Shrewsbury County Court Districts.	Brompton and Chirbury. Rhiston,
	Forden Rural District (part). *Other parts* in Newtown and Shrewsbury County Court Districts.	Berriew, Churchstoke, Castle Forden, Caereinion Middletown, Rural, Trelystan.
	Llanfyllin Rural District (part). *Other part* in Oswestry County Court District.	Garthbeibio, Llanfair Guilsfield Caereinion, Without, Llangadfan, Llanerfyl, Llangyniew.

Column 1	*Column* 2	*Column* 3
Name of court	Local authority areas	Parts comprising court districts
WELSH-POOL —*cont.*	Montgomery Municipal Borough.	Montgomery.
	Welshpool Municipal Borough.	Welshpool.
WEST BROM-WICH	Warley County Borough (part). *Other part* in Dudley County Court District.	The Abbey, St. Paul's, Bearwood, Sandwell, Brandhall, Soho, Bristnall, Uplands, and Langley, Victoria Wards.
	West Bromwich County Borough (part). *Other part* in Dudley County Court District.	The Charlemont, Hill Top, Friar Park, Lyng, Great Barr, Newton, Greets Green, Sandwell and Hateley Heath, Tantany Wards.
WEST LONDON	London Borough of Hammersmith (part). *Other part* in Willesden County Court District.	That part of the Borough south of a line drawn along the middle of the Uxbridge Road.
	London Borough of Kensington and Chelsea (part). *Other part* in Bloomsbury and Marylebone County Court District.	That part of the Borough south of a line drawn from the point where the Borough boundary crosses the eastern end of the Uxbridge Road along the middle of Holland Park Avenue and Notting Hill to the point where the Borough boundary crosses the middle of Bayswater Road.
	London Borough of the City of Westminster (part). *Other parts* in Bloomsbury and Marylebone and Westminster County Court Districts.	That part of the Borough to the west of a line drawn from the point where the Borough boundary crosses Bayswater Road along the middle of Bayswater Road to the point where it is crossed by the Serpentine River thence along the Serpentine to Rotten Row and along the middle of the road through Albert Gate to Knightsbridge, thence eastwards along the middle of Knightsbridge to Grosvenor Place down the middle of Grosvenor Place and Grosvenor Gardens West to Buckingham Palace Road, southwards along the middle of Buckingham Palace Road to the middle of Eccleston Bridge thence along the middle of the Grosvenor Canal to the River Thames.
WEST-MINSTER	London Borough of Camden (part). *Other parts* in Bloomsbury and Marylebone and Clerkenwell County Court Districts.	That part of the Borough south of a line drawn from the Borough boundary at the juntion of Tottenham Court Road and New Oxford Street along the middle of New Oxford Street and High Holborn to the Borough boundary.

Column 1	Column 2	Column 3
Name of court	Local authority areas	Parts comprising court districts
WEST-MINSTER—cont.	London Borough of the City of Westminster (part). *Other parts* in Bloomsbury and Marylebone and West London Court Districts.	That part of the Borough south and east of a line drawn from the Borough boundary at the junction of Tottenham Court Road and Oxford Street westwards along the middle of Oxford Street and Bayswater Road to the point where it is crossed by the Serpentine River thence along the Serpentine to Rotten Row and along the middle of the road through Albert Gate to Knightsbridge thence eastwards along the middle of Knightsbridge to Grosvenor Place down the middle of Grosvenor Place and Grosvenor Gardens West to Buckingham Palace Road, southwards along the middle of Buckingham Palace Road to the middle of Eccleston Bridge thence along the middle of the Grosvenor Canal to the River Thames.
WESTON SUPER MARE	Axbridge Rural District (part). *Other parts* in Bristol and Wells County Court Districts.	Badgworth, Banwell, Berrow, Bleadon, Brean, Brent Knoll, Burnham Without, Burrington, Churchill, Compton Bishop, Congresbury, East Brent, Hutton, Kewstoke, Locking, Loxton, Lympsham, Puxton, Shipham, Steep Holme Island (Extra Parochial), Wick St. Lawrence, Winscombe, Wrington.
	Burnham on Sea Urban District.	Burnham on Sea.
	Clevedon Urban District.	Clevedon.
	Long Ashton Rural District (part). *Other part* in Bristol County Court District.	Cleeve, Kenn, Kingston Seymour, Walton in Gordano, Weston in Gordano, Yatton.
	Weston super Mare Municipal Borough.	Weston super Mare.
WEY-MOUTH	Dorchester Rural District (part). *Other part* in Dorchester County Court District.	Abbotsbury, Bincombe, Chickerell, Fleet, Langton Herring, Osmington, Owermoigne, Portesham, Poxwell.
	Portland Urban District.	Portland.

Column 1	*Column* 2	*Column* 3
Name of court	Local authority areas	Parts comprising court districts

WEY-
MOUTH
—*cont.*
	Wareham and Purbeck Rural District (part).
	    Other parts in Dorchester, Poole and Swanage County Court Districts.
		Chaldon
		        Herring.

	Weymouth and Melcombe Regis Municipal Borough.	Weymouth and Melcombe Regis.
WHITBY	Loftus Urban District.	Loftus.
	Whitby Urban District.	Whitby.

	Whitby Rural District.	Aislaby, Hinderwell,
		Barnby, Hutton,
		Borrowby, Mulgrave,
		Commondale, Lythe,
		Danby, Mickleby,
		Egton, Newholme,
		Ellerby, with Dunsley,
		Eskdaleside cum Newton
		    Ugglebarnby, Mulgrave,
		Fylingdales, Roxby,
		Glaisdale, Sneaton,
		Goathland, Ugthorpe,
		Hawsker with Westerdale,
		    Stainsacre,
		Fylingdales Moor, land common to the civil parishes of Hawsker with Stainsacre and Fylingdales.

WHIT- CHURCH	Market Drayton Rural District (part). *Other part* in Market Drayton County Court District.	Ightfield.

	Nantwich Rural District (part).
	    Other part in Crewe County Court District.
		Dodcott cum Norbury,
		    Wilkesley, Wirswall.
		Marbury with
		    Quoisley,

	Maelor Rural District (part). *Other part* in Wrexham County Court District.	Bettisfield, Iscoyd, Bronington, Tybroughton, Halghton, Willington, Hanmer,

	Tarvin Rural District (part).
	    Other parts in Chester and Crewe County Court Districts.
		Agden, Macefen,
		Bickley, Malpas,
		Bradley, Newton by
		Chidlow, Malpas,
		Chorlton, Oldcastle,
		Church Overton,
		    Shocklach, Shocklach
		Cuddington, Oviatt,
		Duckington, Stockton,
		Edge, Threapwood,
		Grafton, Tilston,
		Hampton, Tushingham with
		Horton by Grindley,
		Malpas, Wigland,
		Larkton, Wychough.

Column 1	Column 2	Column 3
Name of court	Local authority areas	Parts comprising court districts
WHIT-CHURCH —cont.	North Shropshire Rural District (part). *Other parts* in Oswestry and Shrewsbury County Court Districts.	Prees, Weston under Redcastle,	Whitchurch Rural, Whitchurch Urban, Whixhall.
WHITE-HAVEN	Ennerdale Rural District.	Arlecdon and Frizington, Cleator Moor, Distington, Egremont, Ennerdale and Kinniside, Gosforth, Haile, Lamplugh, Lowca,	Lowside Quarter, Moresby, Netherwasdale, Parton Ponsonby, Rottington, St. Bees, St. Bridget's, St. John's, Weddicar.
	Millom Rural District.	Bootle, Drigg and Carleton, Eskdale, Irton with Santon, Millom,	Millom Without, Muncaster, Seascale, Ulpha, Waberthwaite, Whicham.
	Whitehaven Municipal Borough.	Whitehaven.	
WIGAN	Abram Urban District.	Abram.	
	Ashton in Makerfield Urban District.	Ashton in Makerfield.	
	Aspull Urban District.	Aspull.	
	Billinge and Winstanley Urban District.	Billinge and Winstanley.	
	Blackrod Urban District.	Blackrod.	
	Hindley Urban District.	Hindley.	
	Ince in Makerfield Urban District.	Ince in Makerfield.	
	Orrell Urban District.	Orrell.	
	Standish with Langtree Urban District.	Standish with Langtree.	
	Skelmersdale and Holland Urban District.	Skelmersdale and Holland,	
	West Lancashire Rural District (part). *Other parts* in Liverpool and Southport County Court Districts.	Bispham.	

Column 1	Column 2	Column 3
Name of court	Local authority areas	Parts comprising court districts
WIGAN —cont.	Wigan County Borough.	Wigan.
	Wigan Rural District.	Dalton, Shevington, Haigh, Worthington, Parbold, Wrightington.
WILLESDEN	London Borough of Barnet (part). *Other part* in Barnet County Court District.	That part of the Borough to the south and west of a line drawn from the point on the Borough boundary south of Barnet Lane and west of Hyver Hill across Barnet Way to the north of Hyver Hill, south of Barnet Road to the point east of Hendon Wood Lane thence along the east side of Hendon Wood Lane across Totteridge Lane southwards to Folley Brook eastwards along Folley Brook to a point north of the eastern end of Burton Hole Lane along the east side of Burton Hole Lane to the junction of Frith Road and Lullington Garth along the north side of Nether Court Golf Course to the Dollis Brook, southwards along Dollis Brook to its junction with Mutton Brook eastwards along Mutton Brook to its junction with Falloden Way, across the end of Falloden Way along the middle of the North Circular Road to a point north of Connaught Drive thence north of Brookland Rise and Hill Top to the west of Ossulton Way thence southwards along the west side of Ossulton Way and Kingsley Way across the end of Kingsley Way to the point on Hampstead Golf Course at the end of Green Close and eastwards across the Golf Course to the west of Winnington Road along the west of Winnington Road and Kenwood Close to the Borough boundary.
	London Borough of Brent.	Brent.
	London Borough of Ealing (part). *Other parts* in Brentford and Uxbridge County Court Districts.	That part of the Borough to the north of a line drawn from the point where the main line of British Railways, Western Region crosses the Borough boundary westwards along the middle of the railway to the junction with the North Acton and High Wycombe branch line, thence along the middle of the branch line to the point where it meets the Borough boundary south of Coronation Road.
	London Borough of Hammersmith (part). *Other part* in West London County Court District.	That part of the Borough to the north of a line drawn along the middle of the Uxbridge Road.

Column 1	Column 2	Column 3
Name of court	*Local authority areas*	*Parts comprising court districts*
WILLESDEN —*cont.*	London Borough of Harrow (part). *Other part* in Watford County Court District.	The Belmont, Harrow on the Hill and Greenhill, Kenton, Queensbury, Roxeth, Stanmore South, Wealdstone North, Wealdstone South and West Harrow Wards.
WIMBORNE MINSTER	Blandford Rural District (part). *Other parts* in Dorchester, Shaftesbury and Salisbury County Court Districts.	Anderson, Blandford St. Mary, Bryanston, Charlton Marshall, Langton Long Blandford, Pimperne, Spetisbury, Tarrant Crawford, Tarrant Gunville, Tarrant Hinton, Tarrant Keynston, Tarrant Launceston, Tarrant Monkton, Tarrant Rawston, Tarrant Rushton, Winterborne Kingston, Winterborne Zelston.
	Blandford Forum Municipal Borough.	Blandford Forum.
	Wimborne and Cranborne Rural District (part). *Other part* in Salisbury County Court District.	Alderholt, Chalbury, Colehill, Corfe Mullen, Cranborne, Edmondsham, Gussage All Saints, Gussage St. Michael, Hampreston, Hinton Martell, Hinton Parva, Holt, Horton, Long Crichel, More Crichel, Pamphill, Shapwick, Sturminster Marshall, Verwood, West Moors, West Parley, Wimborne St. Giles, Witchampton Woodlands.
	Wimborne Minster Urban District.	Wimborne Minster.
WINCANTON	Shaftesbury Rural District (part). *Other part* in Shaftesbury County Court District.	Bourton, Buckhorn Weston.
	Wincanton Rural District.	Abbas and Templecombe, Alford, Ansford, Bratton Seymour, Brewham, Bruton, Castle Cary, Charton Horethorne, Charlton Musgrove, Compton Pauncefoot, Corton Denham, Cucklington, Henstridge, Holton, Horsington, Lovington, Maperton, Milborne Port, North Barrow, North Cadbury,

Column 1	Column 2	Column 3
Name of court	Local authority areas	Parts comprising court districts
WIN-CANTON —cont.	Wincanton Rural District. —cont.	North Cheriton, Penselwood, Pitcombe, Queen Camel, Shepton Montague, / South Barrow, South Cadbury, Sparkford, Stoke Trister, Wincanton, Yarlington.
WIN-CHESTER	Alton Rural District (part). *Other parts* in Aldershot and Farnham and Basingstoke County Court Districts.	Four Marks, Medstead, Ropley, / West Tisted, Wield.
	Basingstoke Rural District (part). *Other part* in Basingstoke County Court District.	Candovers.
	Droxford Rural District (part). *Other parts* in Petersfield, Portsmouth and Southampton County Court Districts.	Bishops Waltham, / Swanmore, Upham.
	Romsey and Stockbridge Rural District (part). *Other parts* in Andover, Salisbury and Southampton County Court Districts.	Ampfield, Ashley, Bossington, Braishfield, Houghton, / King's Somborne, Little Somborne, Michelmersh.
	Winchester Municipal Borough	Winchester.
	Winchester Rural District (part). *Other part* in Southampton County Court District.	Abbott's Barton, Beauworth, Bighton, Bishops Sutton, Bramdean, Cheriton, Chilcomb, Colden Common, Compton, Crawley, Fair Oak, Headbourne Worthy, Hursley, Itchen Stoke and Ovington, / Itchen Valley, Kilmeston, Kings Worthy, Littleton, Micheldever, New Alresford, Northington, Old Arlesford, Olivers Battery, Otterbourne, Owlslebury, Sparsholt, Tichbourne, Twyford, Wonston.
WISBECH	Marshland Rural District (part). *Other part* in King's Kynn County Court District.	Emneth, Marshland St. James, Outwell, (Norfolk), Upwell, (Norfolk), / Walpole St. Andrew, Walpole St. Peter Walsoken, West Walton.
	Wisbech Municipal Borough.	Wisbech.

Column 1	Column 2	Column 3
Name of court	Local authority areas	Parts comprising court districts
WISBECH —cont.	Wisbech Rural District.	Elm, Leverington, Newton, Outwell (Isle), Parson Drove, — Tydd St. Giles, Upwell, (Isle), Wisbech St. Mary.
WITNEY	Witney Urban District.	Witney.
	Witney Rural District (part). *Other part* in Oxford County Court District.	Alvescot, Asthal, Aston Bampton and Shifford, Bampton, Blackbourton, Brize Norton, Broadwell, Burford and Upton and Signet, Clanfield, Crawley, Curbridge, Ducklington, Eynsham, Filkins and Broughton Poggs, Freeland, Fulbrook, Grafton and Radcot, Hailey, — Hanborough, Hardwick with Yelford, Holwell, Kelmscott, Kencot, Langford, Lew, Little Faringdon, Minster Lovell, North Leigh, Northmoor, Ramsden, Shilton, South Leigh, Standlake, Stanton Harcourt, Swinbrook and Widford, Taynton, Westwell.
WOLVER-HAMPTON	Cannock Rural District (part). *Other parts* in Stafford, Walsall and Wellington County Court Districts.	Brewood, Essington, Featherstone, Hilton, — Lapley, Saredon, Shareshill, Stretton.
	Seisdon Rural District (part). *Other part* in Stourbridge County Court District.	Codsall, Himley, Lower Penn, Patshull, Pattingham, — Swindon, Trysall and Seisdon, Wombourn, Wrottesley.
	Shifnal Rural District (part). *Other parts* in Bridgnorth and Wellington County Court Districts.	Albrington, Boningale, — Boscobel, Donington.
	Wolverhampton County Borough.	Wolverhampton.
WOOD-BRIDGE	Aldeburgh Municipal Borough.	Aldeburgh.
	Blyth Rural District (part). *Other parts* in Halesworth and Ispwich County Court Districts.	Aldringham with Thorpe, Badingham, Benhall, · Brandeston, Bruisyard, Cransford, — Dennington, Easton, Farnham, Framlingham, Friston, Great Glemham, Hacheston,

Column 1	*Column 2*	*Column 3*
Name of court	Local authority areas	Parts comprising court districts
WOOD-BRIDGE —*cont.*	Blyth Rural District (part). —*cont.*	Kelsale with Carlton, Kettleburgh, Knodishall, Little Glemham, Marlesford, Parham, Peasenhall, Rendham, Saxtead, Sibton, Snape, Sternfield, Stratford St. Andrew, Swefling, Theberton, Yoxford.
	Deben Rural District (part). *Other part* in Ipswich County Court District.	Alderton, Bawdsey, Blaxhall, Boulge, Boyton, Bredfield, Brightwell, Bromeswell, Bucklesham, Burgh, Butley, Campsey Ash, Capel St. Andrew, Charsfield, Chillesford, Clopton, Dallinghoo, Dallinghoo Wield, Debach, Eyke, Gedgrave, Haskerton, Havergate Island, Hollesley, Hoo, Iken, Letheringham, Martlesham, Melton, Monewden, Orford, Otley, Pettistree, Ramsholt, Rendlesham, Shottisham, Sudbourne, Sutton, Tunstall, Ufford, Wantisden, Wickham Market.
	Leiston cum Sizewell Urban District.	Leiston cum Sizewell.
	Saxmundham Urban District.	Saxmundham.
	Woodbridge Urban District.	Woodbridge.
WOOLWICH	London Borough of Greenwich.	Greenwich.
WOR-CESTER	Droitwich Municipal Borough.	Droitwich.
	Droitwich Rural District (part). *Other parts* in Bromsgrove, Kidderminster and Redditch County Court Districts.	Crowle, Hadzor, Himbleton, Hindlip, Huddington, Martin Hussingtree, North Claines, Oddingley, Ombersley, St. Martin County, Salwarpe, Tibberton, Warndon, Westwood.
	Martley Rural District (part). *Other part* in Great Malvern and Kidderminster County Court Districts.	Alfrick, Broadheath, Broadwas, Clifton upon Teme, Cotheridge, Doddenham, Great Witley, Grimley, Hallow,

Column 1	Column 2	Column 3
Name of court	Local authority areas	Parts comprising court districts
WOR-CESTER cont.	Martley Rural District (part). —cont.	Hillhampton, Holt, Kenswick, Knightwick, Little Whitley, Lower Sapey, Lulsley, Martley, North Hallow, Rushwick, Shelsley Beauchamp, Shelsley Kings, Shelsley Walsh, Shrawley, Suckley, Wichenford.
	Pershore Rural District (part). Other parts in Cheltenham, Evesham and Redditch County Court Districts.	Besford, Birlingham, Bredicot, Broughton Hackett, Churchill, Defford, Eckington, Flyford Flavell, Grafton Flyford, North Piddle, Norton juxta Kempsey, Peopleton, Pirton, St. Peter the Great County, Spetchley, Stoulton, Upton Snodsbury, White Ladies Ashton, Whittington.
	Upton upon Severn Rural District (part). Other parts in Cheltenham and Great Malvern County Court Districts.	Croome D'Abitôt, Earls Croome, Hill Croome, Kempsey, Powick, Severn Stoke.
	Worcester County Borough.	Worcester.
	Bromyard Rural District (part). Other parts in Leominster and Hereford County Court Districts.	Acton Beauchamp, Brockhampton and Linton, Cradley, Evesbatch, Norton, Saltmarshe, Stanford Bishop, Tedstone Delamere, Tedstone Wafer, Upper Sapey, Whitbourne.
WORKING-TON AND COCKER-MOUTH	Cockermouth Urban District.	Cockermouth.
	Cockermouth Rural District.	Above Derwent, Bassenthwaite, Bewaldeth and Snittlegarth, Blindbothel, Blindcrake, Borrowdale, Bothel and Threapland, Bridekirk, Brigham, Broughton, Broughton Moor, Buttermere, Camerton, Crosscanonby, Dean, Dearham	Embleton, Gilcrux, Great Clifton, Greysouthern, Little Clifton, Lorton, Loweswater, Oughterside and Allerby, Papcastle, Plumbland, St. John's Castlerigg and Wythburn, Seaton, Setmurthy, Underskiddaw, Winscales, Wythop.

Column 1	Column 2	Column 3
Name of court	Local authority areas	Parts comprising court districts
WORKING-TON AND COCKER-MOUTH —cont.	Keswick Urban District.	Keswick.
	Maryport Urban District.	Maryport.
	Penrith Rural District (part). *Other part* in Penrith County Court District.	Threlkeld.
	Workington Municipal Borough.	Workington.
WORKSOP	Clowne Rural District.	Barlborough, Clowne, Cresswell, Whitwell.
	Kiveton Park Rural District.	Dinnington St. Johns, Firbeck, Gildingwells, Harthill with Woodall, Letwell, North and South Anston, Thorpe Salvin, Todwick, Wales, Woodsetts.
	Southwell Rural District (part). *Other parts* in East Retford, Mansfield, Newark and Nottingham County Court Districts.	Perlethorpe cum Budby.
	Worksop Municipal Borough.	Worksop.
	Worksop Rural District.	Blyth, Carburton, Carlton in Lindrick, Cuckney, Harworth, Hodsock, Holbeck, Nether Langwith, Norton, Styrrup with Oldcotes, Wallingwells, Welbeck.
WORTHING	Chanctonbury Rural District (part). *Other parts* in Brighton and Chichester County Court Districts.	Ashington, Storrington, Sullington, Washington, Wiston.
	Worthing Municipal Borough.	Worthing.
	Worthing Rural District (part). *Other part* in Chichester County Court District.	Angmering, Clapham, Coombes, East Lancing, East Preston, Ferring, Findon, Kingston, North Lancing, Patching, Sompting, West Lancing.
WREXHAM	Ceiriog Rural District (part). *Other part* in Oswestry County Court District.	Chirk, Glyn Traian, Llansantffraid Glyn Ceiroig.

Column 1	Column 2	Column 3
Name of court	Local authority areas	Parts comprising court districts
WREXHAM —*cont.*	Edeyrnion Rural District.	Betws a Gwerfil Goch, Corwen, Gwyddelwern, Llandrillo, Llangar, Llansantffraid Glyn Dyfrdwy.
	Hawarden Rural District (part). *Other parts* in Chester and Mold County Court Districts.	Hope, Llanfynydd, Marford and Hoseley.
	Llangollen Urban District	Llangollen Urban.
	Maelor Rural District (part). *Other part* in Whitchurch County Court District.	Bangor, Overton, Penley, Worthenbury.
	Wrexham Municipal Borough.	Wrexham.
	Wrexham Rural District.	Abenbury, Allington, Bersham, Bieston, Broughton, Brymbo, Burton, Cefn, Erbistock, Erthig, Esclusham Above, Esclusham Below, Gresford, Gwersyllt, Holt, Isycoed, Llangollen Rural, Llantysilio, Llay, Marchwiel, Minera, Penycae, Rhosllaner-chrugog, Ruabon, Sesswick.
YEOVIL	Beaminster Rural District (part) *Other parts* in Axminster and Chard, Bridport and Dorchester County Court Districts.	Chedington, Corscombe, East Chelborough, Evershot, Halstock, Melbury Osmond, Melbury Sampford, Mosterton, Seaborough, South Perrott, West Chelborough.
	Chard Rural District (part). *Other part* in Axminster and Chard County Court District.	Chillington, Cudworth, Dinnington, Hinton St. George, Kingstone, Lopen, Merriott, Misterton, Seavington St. Mary, Seavington St. Michael, Shepton Beauchamp, Stocklinch, Wayford, West Crewkerne.
	Crewkerne Urban District.	Crewkerne.
	Langport Rural District (part). *Other parts* in Axminster and Chard, Bridgwater, Taunton and Wells County Court Districts.	Babcary, Barton St. David, Charlton Mackrell, Keinton Mandeville, Kingsbury Episcopi, Kingsdon, Long Sutton, Pitney, Somerton.
	Sherborne Urban District.	Sherborne.

Column 1	Column 2	Column 3
Name of court	Local authority areas	Parts comprising court districts
YEOVIL —cont.	Sherborne Rural District (part). *Other part* in Dorchester County Court District.	Beer Hackett, Bishop's Caundle, Bradford Abbas, Castleton, Caundle Marsh, Chetnole, Clifton Maybank, Folke, Goathill, Haydon, Hermitage, Holnest, Holwell, Leigh,	Leweston, Lillington, Long Burton, Melbury Bubb, Nether Compton, North Wotton, Oborne, Over Compton, Poyntington, Purse Caundle, Ryme Intrinseca, Sandford Orcas, Stockwood, Thornford, Trent, Yetminster.
	Sturminster Rural District (part). *Other parts* in Dorchester and Shaftesbury County Court Districts.	Stalbridge,	Stourton Caundle.
	Yeovil Municipal Borough.	Yeovil.	
	Yeovil Rural District.	Ash, Barwick, Brympton, Chilthorne Domer, Chilton Cantelo, Chiselborough, Closworth, East Chinnock, East Coker, Hardington Mandeville, Haselbury Plucknett, Ilchester, Limington, Long Load,	Marston Magna, Martock, Montacute, Mudford, North Perrott, Norton sub Hamdon, Odcombe, Rimpton, South Petherton, Stoke sub Hamdon, Tintinhull, West Camel, West Chinnock, West Coker, Yeovilton, Yeovil Without.
YORK	Derwent Rural District.	Barlby, Cliffe, Deighton, Dunnington, Elvington, Escrick, Fulford, Hemingborough, Heslington,	Kelfield, Kexby, Naburn, North Duffield, Riccal, Skipwith, Stillingfleet, Thorganby, Wheldrake.
	Easingwold Rural District.	Aldwark, Alne, Angram Grange, Benningborough, Brafferton, Brandsby-cum-Stearsby,	Carlton Husthwaite, Coxwold, Crayke, Dalby-with Skewsby, Easingwold,

Column 1	Column 2	Column 3	
Name of court	Local authority areas	Parts comprising court districts	
YORK— —cont.	Easingwold Rural District. —cont.	Farlington, Flawith, Helperby, Huby, Husthwaite, Linton-upon-Ouse, Marton-with-Moxby, Myton-upon-Swale, Newburgh, Newton-upon-Ouse, Oulston,	Overton, Raskelf, Shipton, Stillington, Sutton-on-the-Forest, Tholthorpe, Thormanby, Thornton-on-the-Hill, Tollerton, Whenby, Wildon Grange, Yearsley, Youlton.
	Flaxton Rural District.	Buttercrambe with Bossall, Claxton, Clifton Without, Earswick, Flaxton, Gate Helmsley, Harton, Haxby, Heworth Without Holtby, Huntington, Lillings Ambo,	Murton, New Earswick, Osbaldwick, Rawcliffe, Sand Hutton, Skelton, Stockton-on-Forest, Strensall, Towthorpe, Upper Helmsley, Warthill, Wigginton.
	Howden Rural District (part). Other parts in Beverley and Goole County Court Districts.	Bubwith, Ellerton, Foggathorpe,	Holme-on-Spalding Moor.
	Nidderdale Rural District (part). Other parts in Harrogate and Ripon County Court Districts.	Hessay, Knapton, Moor Monkton,	Nether Poppleton, Rufforth, Upper Poppleton.
	Pocklington Rural District (part). Other part in Beverley County Court District.	Allerthorpe, Barmby Moor, Bielby, Bishop Wilton, Bugthorpe, Catton, Cottingwith, Everingham, Fangfoss, Full Sutton, Hayton, Huggate, Kirby under Dale, Melbourne,	Millington, Nunburnholme, Pocklington, Seaton-Ross, Shipton Thorpe, Skirpendbeck, Stamforth Bridge, Sutton-upon-Derwent, Thornton, Warter, Wilberfoss, Yapham.
	Selby Urban District.	Selby.	
	Selby Rural District (part). Other parts in Goole and Pontefract County Court Districts.	Brayton, Cawood, Hambleton,	Thorpe Willoughby, Wistow.

Column 1	*Column* 2	*Column* 3
Name of court	Local authority areas	Parts comprising court districts
YORK —*cont.*	Tadcaster Rural District (part). *Other part* in Leeds and Pont-fract County Court Districts.	Acaster Malbis, Acaster Selby, Appleton Roebuck, Askham Bryan, Askham Richard, Biggin, Bilbrough, Bishopthorpe, Bolton Percy, Catterton, Church Fenton, Colton, Copmanthorpe, East Tadcaster, Grimston, Healaugh, Kirkby Wharfe-with-North Milford, Little Fenton, Newton Kyme cum Toulston, Oxton, Ryther with Ossendyke, Steeton, Towton, Ulleskelf, West Tadcaster.
	Wetherby Rural District (part). *Other parts* in Harrogate, Leeds and Otley County Court Districts.	Angram, Bilton and Bickerton, Hutton Wandesley, Long Marston, Tockwith, Wighill, Wilstrop.
	York County Borough.	York.

SCHEDULE 2

Column 1 Name of court	Column 2 Place of sitting
Aldershot and Farnham	Aldershot
Ashton under Lyne and Stalybridge	Stalybridge
Axminster and Chard	Axminster
Bletchley and Leighton Buzzard	Leighton Buzzard
Bloomsbury and Marylebone	Bloomsbury
Chichester	Arundel, Chichester and Petworth
King's Lynn	Fakenham and King's Lynn
Norwich	Cromer, Diss and Norwich
Rhyl	Prestatyn

SCHEDULE 3

Column 1	Column 2
Orders Revoked	References
The County Court Districts Order 1949	S.I. 1949/2058 (1949 I, p. 955)
The County Court Districts Miscellaneous Order 1950	S.I. 1950/391 (1950 I, p. 455)
The County Court Districts (Miscellaneous) No. 2 Order 1950	S.I. 1950/1483 (1950 I, p. 448)
The County Court Districts (Miscellaneous) Order 1951	S.I. 1951/346 (1951 I, p. 350)
The County Court Districts (Miscellaneous) No. 2 Order 1951	S.I. 1951/1063 (1951 I, p. 352)
The County Court Districts (Miscellaneous) Order 1952	S.I. 1952/1380 (1952 I, p. 633)
The County Court Districts (Miscellaneous) Order 1953	S.I. 1953/433 (1953 I, p. 375)
The County Court Districts (Miscellaneous) No. 2 Order 1953	S.I. 1953/1275 (1953 I, p. 379)
The County Court Districts (Redhill and Reigate) Order 1953	S.I. 1953/1459 (1953 I, p. 381)
The County Court Districts (Miscellaneous) Order 1954	S.I. 1954/565 (1954 I, p. 520)
The County Court Districts (Shaftesbury) Order 1955	S.I. 1955/445
The County Court Districts (Miscellaneous) Order 1955	S.I. 1955/1342 (1955 I, p. 525)
The County Court Districts (Canterbury) No. 2 Order 1955	S.I. 1955/1470
The County Court Districts (Miscellaneous) No. 2 Order 1955	S.I. 1955/1916 (1955 I, p. 528)
The County Court Districts (Miscellaneous) Order 1956	S.I. 1956/1231 (1956 I, p. 533)
The County Court Districts (Haverfordwest) Order 1956	S.I. 1956/1674 (1956 I, p. 532)
The County Court Districts (Chesham and Amersham) Order 1956	S.I. 1956/1797 (1956 I, p. 532)
The County Court Districts (Calne) Order 1956	S.I. 1956/2000 (1956 I, p. 531)
The County Court Districts (Windsor and Slough) Order 1957	S.I. 1957/1045 (1957 I, p. 508)
The County Court Districts (Miscellaneous) Order 1957	S.I. 1957/2200 (1957 I, p. 506)
The County Court Districts (Miscellaneous) Order 1958	S.I. 1958/949 (1958 I, p. 366)
The County Court Districts (Miscellaneous No. 2) Order 1958	S.I. 1958/1506 (1958 I, p. 369)
The County Court Districts (Long Eaton and Parish of Lymm) Order 1959	S.I. 1959/1423 (1959 I, p. 791)
The County Court Districts (Wells) Order 1959	S.I. 1959/1424 (1959 I, p. 792)
The County Court Districts (Miscellaneous) Order 1959	S.I. 1959/1992 (1959 I, p. 793)
The County Court Districts (Stow on the Wold and Parish of Mickleton) Order 1960	S.I. 1960/361 (1960 I, p. 806)
The County Court Districts (Hay and Parish of Aston Sandford) Order 1960	S.I. 1960/882 (1960 I, p. 800)
The County Court Districts (Seaham and Parish of Norton Mandeville) Order 1960	S.I. 1960/1249 (1960 I, p. 804)

Column 1	*Column* 2
Orders Revoked	References
The County Court Districts (Harlow) Order 1960	S.I. 1960/2329 (1960 I, p. 798)
The County Court Districts (Nantwich and Tadcaster) Order 1960	S.I. 1960/2330 (1960 I, p. 802)
The County Court Districts (Wells) Order 1961	S.I. 1961/486 (1961 I, p. 1124)
The County Court Districts (Eye) Order 1961	S.I. 1961/2254 (1961 III, p. 3964)
The County Court Districts (Bletchley and Leighton Buzzard) Order 1962	S.I. 1962/1885 (1962 II, p. 2336)
The County Court Districts (Ellesmere Port) Order 1963	S.I. 1963/1932 (1963 III, p. 3786)
The County Court Districts (Ashton under Lyne) Order 1964	S.I. 1964/1104 (1964 II, p. 2436)
The County Court Districts (Haltwhistle) Order 1964	S.I. 1964/1215 (1964 II, p. 2835)
The County Court Districts (Miscellaneous) Order 1964	S.I. 1964/1977 (1964 III, p. 4486)
The County Court Districts (Chard) Order 1965	S.I. 1965/1252
The County Court Districts (Rhyl) Order 1965	S.I. 1965/2093
The County Court Districts (Bromyard) Order 1966	S.I. 1966/332
The County Court Districts (Wigton and Appleby) Order 1966	S.I. 1966/1056 (1966 II, p. 2591)
The County Court Districts (Bloomsbury, Marylebone and Ashbourne) Order 1966	S.I. 1966/1454 (1966 III, p. 3856)
The County Court Districts (Miscellaneous) Order 1967	S.I. 1967/381 (1967 I, p. 1288)
The County Court Districts (Miscellaneous) (No. 2) Order 1967	S.I. 1967/1832 (1967 III, p. 4878)
The County Court Districts (Aldershot and Farnham) Order 1968	S.I. 1968/404 (1968 I, p. 1085)
The County Court Districts (Hemel Hempstead) Order 1968	S.I. 1968/938 (1968 II, p. 2449)
The County Court Districts (Miscellaneous) Order 1968	S.I. 1968/1442 (1968 III, p. 4170)
The County Court Districts (Newport, Essex) Order 1968	S.I. 1968/1596 (1968 III, p. 3495)
The County Court Districts (Miscellaneous) Order 1969	S.I. 1969/295 (1969 I, p. 803)
The County Court Districts (Miscellaneous) (No. 2) Order 1969	S.I. 1969/1178 (1969 II, p. 5467)
The County Court Districts (Wisbech and March) Order 1969	S.I. 1969/1397 (1969 III, p. 4124)

EXPLANATORY NOTE

(This Note is not part of this Order.)

This Order replaces the County Court Districts Order 1949 and consolidates a large number of amending Orders. Court districts are defined by reference to local government areas and a number of minor changes are made in the districts of courts in London, the West Midlands and other areas to take account of altered local government boundaries. Changes are also made in the boundaries of the districts of the Epsom and Reigate County Courts and the Shaftesbury and Yeovil County Courts. The districts of the Wisbech and March County Courts, which were consolidated as a temporary measure, are restored as separate districts.

STATUTORY INSTRUMENTS

1970 No. 18 (C.1)

EVIDENCE

The Civil Evidence Act 1968 (Commencement No. 3) Order 1970

Made - - - - *9th January* 1970

The Lord Chancellor, in exercise of the powers conferred on him by section 20(4) of the Civil Evidence Act 1968(a), hereby makes the following order:—

1. This order may be cited as the Civil Evidence Act 1968 (Commencement No. 3) Order 1970.

2. Part I and section 20(2) of the Civil Evidence Act 1968 shall come into force on 16th February 1970 for the purposes of civil proceedings (other than proceedings in bankruptcy) in a county court or the Mayor's and City of London Court.

Gardiner, C.

Dated 9th January 1970.

EXPLANATORY NOTE
(This Note is not part of the Order.)

For the purposes of proceedings (except bankruptcy proceedings) in a county court or in the Mayor's and City of London Court, this order brings into force on 16th February 1970 those provisions of the Civil Evidence Act 1968 which make hearsay evidence admissible in civil proceedings.

(a) 1968 c. 64.

STATUTORY INSTRUMENTS

1970 No. 19

SUGAR

The Composite Sugar Products (Surcharge and Surcharge Repayments—Average Rates) Order 1970

Made - - - -	*8th January* 1970
Laid before Parliament	*13th January* 1970
Coming into Operation	*14th January* 1970

Whereas the Minister of Agriculture, Fisheries and Food (hereinafter called " the Minister ") has on the recommendation of the Commissioners of Customs and Excise (hereinafter called " the Commissioners ") made an order(a) pursuant to the powers conferred upon him by sections 9(1) and 9(4) of the Sugar Act 1956(b), having effect subject to the provisions of section 3 of, and Part II of Schedule 5 to, the Finance Act 1962(c), to the provisions of section 52(2) of the Finance Act 1966(d), and to the provisions of section 58 of the Finance Act 1968(e) providing that in the case of certain descriptions of composite sugar products surcharge shall be calculated on the basis of an average quantity of sugar or invert sugar taken to have been used in the manufacture of the products, and that certain other descriptions of composite sugar products shall be treated as not containing any sugar or invert sugar, and that in the case of certain descriptions of goods in the manufacture of which sugar or invert sugar is used, surcharge repayments shall be calculated on the basis of an average quantity of sugar or invert sugar taken to have been so used :

Now, therefore, the Minister, on the recommendation of the Commissioners and in exercise of the powers conferred upon him by sections 9(1), 9(4) and 33(4) of the Sugar Act 1956, having effect as aforesaid, and of all other powers enabling him in that behalf, hereby makes the following order : —

1.—(1) This order may be cited as the Composite Sugar Products (Surcharge and Surcharge Repayments—Average Rates) Order 1970, and shall come into operation on 14th January 1970.

(2) The Interpretation Act 1889(f) shall apply for the interpretation of this order as it applies for the interpretation of an Act of Parliament.

2. Surcharge payable on or after 14th January 1970 under and in accordance with the Sugar Act 1956, having effect as aforesaid, in respect of sugar and invert sugar used in the manufacture of the descriptions of imported composite sugar products specified in column 2 of Schedule 1 to this order shall, notwithstanding the provisions of the Sugar (Rates of Surcharge and Surcharge Repayments) (No. 13) Order 1969(g) and the Composite Sugar Products (Surcharge and Surcharge Repayments—Average Rates) (No. 13) Order 1969(a), be calculated by reference to the weight of the products at the rates specified in relation thereto in column 3 of the said Schedule.

(a) S.I. 1969/1665 (1969 III, p. 5213).	(b) 1956 c. 48.	(c) 1962 c. 44.
(d) 1966 c. 18.	(e) 1968 c. 44.	(f) 1889 c. 63.
(g) S.I. 1969/1664 (1969 III, p. 5210).		

3. Imported composite sugar products other than those of a description specified in Schedules 1 and 2 to this order shall be treated as not containing any sugar or invert sugar for the purposes of surcharge payable on or after 14th January 1970.

4. Surcharge repayments payable on and after 14th January 1970 under and in accordance with the provisions of section 8 of the Sugar Act 1956, having effect as aforesaid, in respect of sugar and invert sugar used in the manufacture of the descriptions of goods specified in column 1 of Schedule 3 to this order shall, notwithstanding the provisions of the Sugar (Rates of Surcharge and Surcharge Repayments) (No. 13) Order 1969(a) and the Composite Sugar Products (Surcharge and Surcharge Repayments—Average Rates) (No. 13) Order 1969(b), be calculated by reference to the quantity of the goods at the rates specified in relation thereto in column 2 of the said Schedule.

In Witness whereof the Official Seal of the Minister of Agriculture, Fisheries and Food is hereunto affixed on 8th January 1970.

R. P. Frazer,
Authorised by the Minister.

SCHEDULE 1

In this Schedule:—

" Tariff heading " means a heading or, where the context so requires, a subheading of the Customs Tariff 1959 (see paragraph (1) of Article 2 of the Import Duties (General) (No. 3) Order 1969(c)).

Tariff heading	Description of Imported Composite Sugar Products	Rate of Surcharge
		Per cwt. s. d.
04.02	Milk and cream, preserved, concentrated or sweetened, containing more than 10 per cent. by weight of added sugar	10 4
17.02 (B) (2) and 17.05 (B).	Syrups containing sucrose sugar, whether or not flavoured or coloured, but not including fruit juices containing added sugar in any proportion:—	
	Containing 70 per cent. or more by weight of sweetening matter	14 10
	Containing less than 70 per cent., and more than 50 per cent., by weight of sweetening matter	10 8
	Containing not more than 50 per cent. by weight of sweetening matter	5 2
17.02 (F) ...	Caramel:—	
	Solid	23 4
	Liquid	16 4
17.04	Sugar confectionery, not containing cocoa ...	19 0

(a) S.I. 1969/1664 (1969 III, p. 5210). (b) S.I. 1969/1665 (1969 III, p. 5213).
(c) S.I. 1969/1413 (1969 III, p. 4150).

Tariff heading	Description of Imported Composite Sugar Products	Rate of Surcharge
		Per cwt. s. d.
18.06	Chocolate and other food preparations containing cocoa and added sugar:—	
	Chocolate couverture not prepared for retail sale; chocolate milk crumb, liquid ...	10 4
	Chocolate milk crumb, solid	12 9
	Solid chocolate bars or blocks, milk or plain, with or without fruit or nuts; other chocolate confectionery consisting wholly of chocolate or of chocolate and other ingredients not containing added sugar, but not including such goods when packed together in retail packages with goods liable to surcharge at a higher rate	10 6
	Other	13 6
19.08	Pastry, biscuits, cakes and other fine bakers' wares containing added sugar:—	
	Biscuits, wafers and rusks containing more than 12½ per cent. by weight of added sugar, and other biscuits, wafers and rusks included in retail packages with such goods ...	5 10
	Cakes with covering or filling containing added sugar; meringues	7 9
	Other	2 11
20.01	Vegetables and fruit, prepared or preserved by vinegar or acetic acid, containing added sugar:—	
	Containing 10 per cent. or more by weight of added sugar	8 2
	Other	1 9
20.03	Fruit preserved by freezing, containing added sugar	2 11
20.04	Fruit, fruit-peel and parts of plants, preserved by sugar (drained, glacé or crystallised)	15 4
20.05	Jams, fruit jellies, marmalades, fruit purée and fruit pastes, being cooked preparations, containing added sugar	14 8
20.06	Fruit otherwise prepared or preserved, containing added sugar:—	
	Ginger	11 8
	Other	2 11

SCHEDULE 2

Tariff heading	Description of Imported Composite Sugar Products
17.05 (A) and (B)	Sugar and invert sugar, flavoured or coloured.

SCHEDULE 3

Description of goods	Rate of surcharge repayment per bulk barrel of 36 gallons
Lager	11·7d.
All beer other than lager	10·4d.

EXPLANATORY NOTE

(This Note is not part of the Order.)

This order provides for the substitution on and after 14th January 1970 of specific rates of surcharge per cwt. for ad valorem rates on the imported composite sugar products specified in Schedule 1 under tariff headings 19.08, 20.01, 20.03 and 20.06.

It re-enacts the provisions of the Composite Sugar Products (Surcharge and Surcharge Repayments—Average Rates) (No. 13) Order 1969 in respect of the surcharge on imported composite sugar products under the other tariff headings specified in that Schedule, with minor changes in the descriptions of the products under tariff headings 04.02, 18.06, 19.08, 20.01, 20.05 and 20.06. It also re-enacts unchanged Schedules 2 and 3 of that Order.

STATUTORY INSTRUMENTS

1970 No. 20

AGRICULTURE

The Price Stability of Imported Products (Rates of Levy No. 1) Order 1970

Made	- - - -	*9th January* 1970
Coming into Operation	-	*10th January* 1970

The Minister of Agriculture, Fisheries and Food, in exercise of the powers conferred upon him by section 1(2), (4), (5), (6) and (7) of the Agriculture and Horticulture Act 1964(a) and of all other powers enabling him in that behalf, hereby makes the following order:—

1. This order may be cited as the Price Stability of Imported Products (Rates of Levy No. 1) Order 1970, and shall come into operation on 10th January 1970.

2.—(1) In this order—

" the Principal Order " means the Price Stability of Imported Products (Levy Arrangements) Order 1966(b) as amended (c) and as amended by any subsequent order, and if any such order is replaced by any subsequent order the expression shall be construed as a reference to such subsequent order;

AND other expressions have the same meaning as in the Principal Order.

(2) The Interpretation Act 1889(d) shall apply to the interpretation of this order as it applies to the interpretation of an Act of Parliament and as if this order and the orders hereby revoked were Acts of Parliament.

3. In accordance with and subject to the provisions of Part II of the Principal Order (which provides for the charging of levies on imports of certain specified commodities)—

(a) the rate of general levy for such imports into the United Kingdom of any specified commodity as are described in column 2 of Part I of the Schedule to this order in relation to a tariff heading indicated in column 1 of that Part shall be the rate set forth in relation thereto in column 3 of that Part;

(b) the rate of country levy for such imports into the United Kingdom of any specified commodity as are described in column 2 of Part II of the Schedule to this order in relation to a tariff heading indicated in column 1 of that Part shall be the rate set forth in relation thereto in column 3 of that Part.

(a) 1964 c. 28.   (b) S.I. 1966/936 (1966 II, p. 2271).
(c) S.I. 1969/758, 1564 (1969 II, p. 2137; III, p. 5018).   (d) 1889 c. 63.

4. The Price Stability of Imported Products (Rates of Levy No. 24) Order 1969(**a**) and the Price Stability of Imported Products (Rates of Levy No. 25) Order 1969(**b**) are hereby revoked.

In Witness whereof the Official Seal of the Minister of Agriculture, Fisheries and Food is hereunto affixed on 9th January 1970.

(**L.S.**)   *R. J. E. Taylor,*
                                                    Assistant Secretary.

SCHEDULE

PART I

1. Tariff Heading	2. Description of Imports	3. Rate of General Levy
		per ton £ s. d.
10.03	Imports of:— Barley	2 10 0
11.01	Wheat flours	2 0 0
11.02	Cereal meal— of barley	7 5 0
11.02	Rolled, flaked, crushed or bruised cereals— barley	5 15 0

PART II

1. Tariff Heading	2. Description of Imports	3. Rate of Country Levy
		per ton £ s. d.
10.03	Imports of:— Barley which has been grown in and consigned to the United Kingdom from—	
	the Kingdom of the Netherlands	1 15 0
	the French Republic	1 15 0
	Canada	2 10 0

(**a**) S.I. 1969/1677 (1969 III, p, 5300).   (**b**) S.I. 1969/1889 ; (1969 III, p. 5830).

EXPLANATORY NOTE

(This Note is not part of the Order.)

This order, which comes into operation on 10th January 1970, supersedes the Price Stability of Imported Products (Rates of Levy No. 24) Order 1969 and the Price Stability of Imported Products (Rates of Levy No. 25) Order 1969. It—

(*a*) removes all levies, general and country, on imports of denatured wheat;

(*b*) reduces to 35*s*. per ton the country levies on imports of barley which has been grown in and consigned to the United Kingdom from France or the Netherlands; and

(*c*) reimposes unchanged the other rates of general and country levy in force immediately before the commencement of the order.

STATUTORY INSTRUMENTS

1970 No. 22

TRANSPORT

PENSIONS AND COMPENSATION

The British Transport (Southern Railway Superannuation Fund) Order 1970

Made - - -	*8th January* 1970
Laid before Parliament	*20th January* 1970
Coming into Operation	*21st January* 1970

The Minister of Transport makes this Order in exercise of his powers under section 74 of the Transport Act 1962(**a**), as read with section 136 of the Transport Act 1968(**b**), and of all other enabling powers :—

1.—(1) This Order shall come into operation on the 21st January 1970, and may be cited as the British Transport (Southern Railway Superannuation Fund) Order 1970.

(2) The Interpretation Act 1889(**c**) shall apply for the interpretation of this Order as it applies for the interpretation of an Act of Parliament.

2.—(1) Notwithstanding the limits imposed by section 3 of the Southern Railway (Superannuation Fund) Act 1927(**d**) (as amended by sections 4 and 5 of the Southern Railway (Superannuation Fund) Act 1941(**e**), on the alterations which can be made to the rules of the pension fund established by the said Act of 1927, it shall be lawful for the said rules to be altered from time to time in accordance with the relevant provisions thereof so as to enable provision to be made for the payment from the said pension fund, with the agreement of the member concerned and the consent of the British Railways Board, of annuities payable during the joint lives of any member of the said pension fund and his wife or other dependant relative of his and during the life of the survivor of them, in lieu of any annuity or any other benefit to which the said member would otherwise be entitled under the said rules.

(2) Nothing in this Order shall affect the application of Article 17 of the British Transport Reorganisation (Pensions of Employees) (No. 3) Order 1962(**f**) (which relates to the payment of pensions by the authorities referred to in that Order) to any such alteration of the rules of the said pension fund as is mentioned in paragraph (1) of this Article.

Sealed with the Official Seal of the Minister of Transport the 8th January 1970.

(L.S.)

Fred Mulley,
Minister of Transport.

(**a**) 1962 c. 46. (**b**) 1968 c. 73.
(**c**) 1889 c. 63. (**d**) 1927 c. xi.
(**e**) 1941 c. iii. (**f**) S.I. 1962/2758 (1962 III, p. 3866).

EXPLANATORY NOTE

(This Note is not part of the Order.)

This Order enables the rules of the pension fund established under the Southern Railway (Superannuation Fund) Act 1927 (as amended by the Southern Railway (Superannuation Fund) Act 1941) to be altered from time to time so as to permit payment from the fund, with the agreement of the member and the British Railways Board, of annuities payable during the joint lives of the member and his wife or other dependant relative and during the life of the survivor of them, in lieu of any annuity or other benefit to which the member would otherwise be entitled under the rules.

STATUTORY INSTRUMENTS

1970 No. 24

SOCIAL SECURITY

The Family Allowances (Qualifications) Amendment Regulations 1969

Made	- - -	*7th January* 1970
Laid before Parliament		19*th January* 1970
Coming into Operation		6*th April* 1970

The Secretary of State for Social Services, in conjunction with the Treasury, in exercise of his powers under sections 13 and 20 of the Family Allowances Act 1965(**a**), and of all other powers enabling him in that behalf, hereby makes the following regulations :—

Citation, interpretation and commencement

1. These regulations, which may be cited as the Family Allowances (Qualifications) Amendment Regulations 1969, shall be read as one with the Family Allowances (Qualifications) Regulations 1969(**b**) (hereinafter referred to as "the principal regulations") and shall come into operation on 6th April 1970.

Amendment of Part III of the principal regulations

2.—(1) Part III of the principal regulations (rules for determining whether presence in or absence from Great Britain is or is not to be treated as temporary) shall be amended in accordance with the following provisions of this regulation.

(2) In regulation 8(1) of the principal regulations, for the words "For the purposes of section 20(2) of the Act—", there shall be substituted the words "Subject to the provisions of this Part of these regulations, for the purposes of section 20(2) of the Act—".

(3) After regulation 10 of the principal regulations there shall be inserted the following regulation :—

"Persons receiving emoluments exempted from United Kingdom income tax

10A.—(1) Subject to paragraph (2) of this regulation, for the purposes of section 20(2) and (4) of the Act, the presence of a person and, unless he and his spouse are not living together and he is not wholly or mainly maintaining his spouse, of his spouse shall be treated as temporary during any period in respect of which he receives emoluments which are exempt from income tax under—

(*a*) section 73 of the Finance Act 1960(**c**) (exemptions from income tax etc. of visiting forces and staffs of allied headquarters) ;

(*b*) section 461 or section 462 of the Income Tax Act 1952(**d**), or section 24 of the Finance Act 1954(**e**) (exemptions from income tax etc. of Commonwealth Agents-General and their staffs, of certain foreign consular staffs and of other official agents of foreign countries) ;

(**a**) 1965 c. 53.   (**b**) S.I. 1969/212 (1969 I, p. 543).
(**c**) 1960 c. 44.   (**d**) 1952 c. 10.
(**e**) 1954. c. 44.

(c) Article 34 or Article 37 of Schedule 1 to the Diplomatic Privileges Act 1964(**a**), or, as from the day appointed under section 16(3) of the Consular Relations Act 1968(**b**), Article 49 or Article 66 of Schedule 1 to that Act (exemptions from income tax etc. of members of diplomatic missions and their staffs etc. and of certain consular officers etc.) ;

(d) section 6 of the Arbitration (International Investment Disputes) Act 1966(**c**) (status, immunities and privileges conferred by the convention on the settlement of investment disputes between States and nationals of other States) ;

(e) an Order in Council or statutory notice made or given under, or continuing to have effect by virtue of, any of the following enactments—

  (i) the Bretton Woods Agreements Act 1945(**d**), section 3 (status, immunities and privileges of the International Monetary Fund, the International Bank for Reconstruction and Development and governors, executive directors etc., of the Fund and Bank) ;

  (ii) the Income Tax Act 1952, section 347 (relief from double taxation) ;

  (iii) the Diplomatic Immunities (Commonwealth Countries and Republic of Ireland) Act 1952(**e**), section 1(2) as amended by section 12 of the Consular Relations Act 1968 (immunities and privileges of certain persons whose duties substantially correspond with those of consular officers and their staffs) ;

  (iv) the International Finance Corporation Act 1955(**f**), section 3 (status, immunities and privileges of the International Finance Corporation, its governors, directors etc.) ;

  (v) the International Development Association Act 1960(**g**), section 3 (status, immunities and privileges of the Association, its governors, directors etc.) ;

  (vi) the Diplomatic Immunities (Conferences with Commonwealth Countries and Republic of Ireland) Act 1961(**h**), section 1 (diplomatic immunities of Commonwealth representatives attending conferences) ;

  (vii) the Diplomatic Privileges Act 1964, section 2(6) (certain privileges and immunities admitted by, or certain additional privileges and immunities granted by, the receiving state) ;

  (viii) the International Organisations Act 1968(**i**), sections 1 to 6 and 12(5) (privileges and immunities of certain international organisations and their officers etc.).

(2) Paragraph (1) of this regulation shall not apply—

  (a) so as to disentitle a person to an allowance in respect of a child of a family, being an allowance which began to accrue before 6th April 1970 ; or

  (b) so as to disentitle a person to an allowance in respect of a child of a family if, on the date on which, but for the provisions of paragraph

---

(a) 1964 c. 81.
(c) 1966 c. 41.
(e) 1952 c. 18.
(g) 1960 c. 35.
(i) 1968 c. 48.

(b) 1968 c. 18.
(d) 9 & 10 Geo. c. 19.
(f) 4 & 5 Eliz. 2c. 5.
(h) 1961 c. 11.

(1) of this regulation, an allowance would first become payable in respect of that child, there is included in that family another child in respect of whom an allowance is payable ; or

(c) so as to disentitle a person to an allowance in respect of any period falling within an income tax year if, in relation to the immediately preceding income tax year, that person proves that the amount of his emoluments exempted from United Kingdom income tax under any of the provisions referred to in paragraph (1) of this regulation was less than his total income as defined in section 524 of the Income Tax Act 1952.

(3) For the purposes of this regulation any reference to the emoluments or income of a person shall include the emoluments or income of that person's spouse, unless that person is neither living with nor wholly or mainly maintaining his spouse ; and "income tax year" means the 12 months beginning with 6th April in any year."

Signed by authority of the Secretary of State for Social Services.

David Ennals,
Minister of State,
Department of Health and Social Security.
24th December 1969.

Joseph Harper,
Walter Harrison,
Two of the Lords Commissioners of
Her Majesty's Treasury.
7th January 1970.

EXPLANATORY NOTE

(This Note is not part of the Regulations.)

Under the Family Allowances Act 1965 it is a condition of eligibility for family allowances that the claimant or, if they are living together, the spouse of the claimant is in Great Britain ; temporary presence in Great Britain is disregarded. These Regulations, which amend the Family Allowances (Qualifications) Regulations 1969, provide, subject to certain exceptions, that where, under certain specified provisions, the emoluments of members of visiting forces, staffs of allied headquarters, diplomatic and consular personnel and other foreign government officials and persons connected with certain international organisations are exempted from income tax, their presence and, with a limited exception, the presence of their spouses in Great Britain is to be treated as temporary.

STATUTORY INSTRUMENTS

1970 No. 25

EXCHANGE CONTROL

The Exchange Control (Authorised Dealers and Depositaries) (Amendment) Order 1970

Made	-	-	-	*12th January* 1970
Coming into Operation				*21st January* 1970

The Treasury, in exercise of the powers conferred upon them by sections 36(5) and 42(1) of the Exchange Control Act 1947(**a**), hereby make the following Order :—

1.—(1) This Order may be cited as the Exchange Control (Authorised Dealers and Depositaries) (Amendment) Order 1970, and shall come into operation on 21st January 1970.

(2) The Interpretation Act 1889(**b**) shall apply for the interpretation of this Order as it applies for the interpretation of an Act of Parliament.

2. Schedule 2 to the Exchange Control (Authorised Dealers and Depositaries) Order 1969(**c**), as amended(**d**), shall be further amended as follows :—

(*a*) by inserting the words " Atlantic International Bank Ltd." after the words " Arbuthnot Latham & Co., Ltd." ;

(*b*) by inserting the words " Bankers Trust International Ltd." after the words " Bankers Trust Company." ;

(*c*) by substituting the words " Banque de Paris et des Pays-Bas." for the the words " Banque de Paris et des Pays-Bas Ltd." ;

(*d*) by inserting the words " Chase and Bank of .Ireland (International) Ltd." after the words " Charterhouse Japhet & Thomasson Ltd." ;

(*e*) by substituting the words " Fleming, Suez, Brown Brothers Ltd." for the words " Fleming-Suez Ltd." ;

(*f*) by inserting the words " Korea Exchange Bank." after the words " Kleinwort, Benson Ltd." ;

(*g*) by deleting the words " Martins Bank Ltd." ;

(*h*) by inserting the words " National Westminster Bank Ltd." after the words " National Provincial Bank Ltd." ;

(*i*) by deleting the words " Ralli Brothers (Bankers) Ltd." ;

(*j*) by deleting the words " Rodo International Ltd." ; and

(*k*) by inserting the words " Slater, Walker Ltd." after the words " Singer & Friedlander Ltd."

3. This Order shall extend to the Channel Islands, and any reference in this Order to the Exchange Control Act 1947 includes a reference to that Act as extended by the Exchange Control (Channel Islands) Order 1947(**e**).

Neil McBride,
Joseph Harper,

Two of the Lords Commissioners
of Her Majesty's Treasury.

12th January 1970.

(**a**) 1947 c. 14.   (**b**) 1889 c. 63.   (**c**) S.I. 1969/517 (1969 I, p. 1432).
(**d**) S.I. 1969/1414. 1624 (1969 III, pp. 4475, 5119).   (**e**) S.R. & O. 1947/2034 (Rev. VI, p. 1001: 1947 I, p. 660).

EXPLANATORY NOTE

(*This Note is not part of the Order.*)

This Order amends the list of persons authorised by the Treasury under the Exchange Control Act 1947 to act as dealers in gold and foreign currencies and as depositaries for the purpose of the deposit of securities.

STATUTORY INSTRUMENTS

1970 No. 28

EDUCATION, ENGLAND AND WALES

The Remuneration of Teachers (Primary and Secondary Schools) (Amendment) Order 1970

Made - - -	*12th January* 1970
Coming into Operation	*13th January* 1970

Whereas—

(1) in pursuance of section 2(2) of the Remuneration of Teachers Act 1965(a) (hereinafter referred to as "the Act") the Committee constituted under section 1 of the Act for the purpose of considering the remuneration payable to teachers in primary and secondary schools maintained by local education authorities (hereinafter referred to as "the Committee") have transmitted to the Secretary of State for Education and Science (hereinafter referred to as "the Secretary of State") certain recommendations agreed on by them with respect to the remuneration of such teachers;

(2) there is in force an order made under section 2(4) of the Act with respect to the remuneration of such teachers, namely, the Remuneration of Teachers (Primary and Secondary Schools) Order 1969(b);

(3) it appears to the Secretary of State that effect can more conveniently be given to the recommendations of the Committee by amending the scales and other provisions set out in the document referred to in the said Order, namely, the document published by Her Majesty's Stationery Office on 28th April 1969 under the title "SCALES OF SALARIES FOR TEACHERS IN PRIMARY AND SECONDARY SCHOOLS, ENGLAND AND WALES, 1969";

(4) in pursuance of section 2(5) of the Act the Secretary of State has prepared a draft Order setting out the amendments of the scales and other provisions contained in the said document which, in his opinion, are requisite for giving effect to the recommendations of the Committee; and

(5) the Secretary of State, as required by section 2(6) of the Act, has consulted the Committee with respect to the draft Order and the Committee have made no representations with respect thereto.

Now therefore the Secretary of State, in pursuance of section 2(6) of the Act, hereby orders as follows—

Citation and Commencement

1. This Order may be cited as the Remuneration of Teachers (Primary and Secondary Schools) (Amendment) Order 1970 and shall come into operation on 13th January 1970.

Interpretation

2. The Interpretation Act 1889(c) shall apply for the interpretation of this Order as it applies for the interpretation of an Act of Parliament.

(a) 1965 c. 3.   (b) S.I. 1969/618 (1969 I, p. 1725).   (c) 1889 c. 63.

Amendment of Document

3. The scales and other provisions set out in the document published by Her Majesty's Stationery Office as aforesaid are hereby amended—

(*a*) with effect from 1st April 1969, in the manner specified in Schedule 1 to this Order; and

(*b*) with effect from 1st January 1970, in the manner specified in Schedule 2 to this Order.

SCHEDULE 1

AMENDMENTS EFFECTIVE FROM 1ST APRIL 1969

1. In Section J of the document (which relates to additional payments for teachers holding graded posts) the following shall be substituted for paragraph 3(b):—

"(b) Special Schools

Review Average or Unit Total	361–600	601–900	901–1,260	1,261–1,620	1,621–1,980
Score	2	4	6	8	10

Where, however, the "score" for graded posts in a special school is increased as a result of the increase of the unit total calculated under Part A of Appendix VIII, the increased "score" shall not be applied before 1st January 1970, notwithstanding any other provision in this document."

2. In Section L of the document (which relates to allowances for deputy head teachers)—

(a) the following shall be substituted for paragraph 4(b):—

"(b) Special Schools

Group	3(S)	4(S)	5(S)	6(S)	7(S)	8(S)
Review Average or Unit Total	181– 360	361– 600	601– 900	901– 1,260	1,261– 1,620	1,621– 1,980
	£ 164	£ 249	£ 334	£ 450	£ 567	£ 684

"

(b) the following shall be substituted for paragraph 5:—

"5. Where the Unit Total (S) of a Special School exceeds 1,980 the Local Education Authority shall determine a Deputy Head Teacher Allowance, appropriately related to the allowance for Group 8(S)."

3. In Section O of the document (which relates to the salaries of qualified head teachers)—

(a) the following shall be substituted for paragraph 4(b):—

"(b) Special Schools

Incremental point	Group	1(S)	2(S)	3(S)	4(S)	5(S)	6(S)	7(S)	8(S)
	Review Average or Unit Total	*Up to* 60	61– 180	181– 360	361– 600	601– 900	901– 1,260	1,261– 1,620	1,621– 1,980
			£	£	£	£	£	£	£
0		(See	1,972	2,062	2,231	2,401	2,565	2,735	2,905
1		note	2,025	2,124	2,293	2,463	2,643	2,813	2,983
2		below)	2,078	2,186	2,355	2,525	2,723	2,893	3,063
3			2,131	2,251	2,420	2,590	2,803	2,973	3,143
4			2,184	2,316	2,485	2,655	2,883	3,053	3,223

NOTE.—The commencing salary of Qualified Head Teachers of schools in Group 1(S) is determined under the provisions of paragraph 8(a) of Appendix VI and Head Teachers of such schools shall proceed by increments of £53 to a maximum of £2,078."

(b) the following shall be substituted for paragraph 5:—
"5. In a case where the Unit Total (S) of a Special School exceeds 1,980 the Local Education Authority shall determine a Head Teacher Scale appropriately related to the Scale for Group 8(S)."

4. In Appendix I of the document (which specifies the qualifications entitling a qualified assistant teacher to be placed in Group II or Group III) the following first degree shall be added to Part D:—
"Warwick   Bachelor of Education (B.Ed.)"

5. In Appendix VIII of the document (which relates to unit totals and review averages)—

(a) the following shall be substituted for paragraph 3 of Part A:—
"3. In the case of Special Schools (including Hospital Schools), a procedure similar to that described in paragraph 1 above shall be followed. The further classification of the enrolled pupils shall be on the basis of the specific handicap of the individual pupil and not according to the age of the pupil. Where a pupil has multiple handicaps, the handicap from which he/she is suffering which attracts the highest unit value shall count for this purpose.

For the purposes of this document the unit total (S) for 1969 and subsequent years shall be calculated as follows:—

For each pupil count

Delicate or Educationally sub-normal children... ...	5½ units
Blind, Partially sighted, Epileptic or Physically Handicapped children	7 units
Deaf, Partially hearing, Maladjusted or children suffering from Speech defect	8 units

The unit total (S) for 1968 and earlier years shall be as calculated under the provisions of the Primary and Secondary Salaries Documents in operation before 1st April 1969."

(b) the following shall be substituted for paragraph 4 of Part A:—
"4. "Review average" of a school or department is the average of the unit totals for the year of the review and the previous two years except that the average of the unit totals for the years 1969 and 1970 shall, if greater, be deemed to be the review average for 1970 for the purposes of this Appendix. The last review average was calculated in 1967, the next shall be calculated in 1970, and thereafter every third year."

(c) the following shall be substituted for paragraph 1 of Part B:—
"1. Subject to the conditions of paragraph 2 immediately following, the Head Teacher Scale and the Deputy Head Teacher Allowance shall be determined as follows:
(a) for the year beginning 1st April 1969, on the review average for 1967 or the unit total for 1969, whichever is the greater;
(b) for the three years beginning 1st April 1970, on the review average for 1970 (see paragraph 4 of Part A of this Appendix);
(c) for the three years beginning 1st April 1973, on the review average for 1973;
(d) for every three years thereafter beginning 1st April the procedure in (c) above shall apply with appropriate adjustment of dates."

SCHEDULE 2
AMENDMENTS EFFECTIVE FROM 1ST JANUARY 1970

1. In Section K of the document (which relates to allowances for heads of departments) the following shall be substituted for paragraph 3:—

"3. In Special Schools, the Local Education Authority shall establish one or more posts of Head of Department in schools in Group 6(S) or above and may, in its discretion, establish such posts in schools below Group 6(S) (see paragraph 1 of Appendix IX)."

2. In Appendix VIII of the document (which relates to unit totals and review averages) the following shall be substituted for paragraph 1 of Part C:—

"1. Subject to the conditions of paragraph 2 immediately following, the "score" for graded posts for a school or department shall be calculated as follows:—
  (a) for the period from 1st January 1970 to 31st March 1970 on—
     (i) the review average for 1967 or the unit total for 1969, whichever is the greater, in the case of schools other than Special Schools,
     (ii) the unit total for 1969 in the case of Special Schools;
  (b) for the three years beginning 1st April 1970, on the review average for 1970 (see paragraph 4 of Part A of this Appendix);
  (c) for the three years beginning 1st April 1973, on the review average for 1973;
  (d) for every three years thereafter beginning 1st April, the procedure in (c) above shall apply with appropriate adjustment of dates."

3. In Appendix IX to the document (which relates to grading of posts of head of department) the following shall be substituted for paragraph 1:—

"1. It will not normally be appropriate for a Local Education Authority to grade Head of Department posts in primary schools or special schools above Grade B, or to establish Head of Department posts in such schools where the unit total or review average, on which the group of the school is determined, is below 451 units in the case of a primary school and 751 units in the case of a special school."

Given under the Official Seal of the Secretary of State for Education and Science on 12th January 1970.

(L.S.)

Edward Short,
Secretary of State for Education
and Science.

EXPLANATORY NOTE
(This Note is not part of the Order.)

This Order amends the scales and other provisions relating to the remuneration of teachers in primary and secondary schools maintained by local education authorities in accordance with recommendations agreed on by the Committee for the consideration of the remuneration of such teachers.

The amendments have retrospective effect by virtue of section 7(3) of the Remuneration of Teachers Act 1965.

STATUTORY INSTRUMENTS

1970 No. 29 (L.2)

MATRIMONIAL CAUSES
SUPREME COURT OF JUDICATURE, ENGLAND
COUNTY COURTS
The Matrimonial Causes (Amendment) Rules 1970

Made - - -	*12th January* 1970
Laid before Parliament	*20th January* 1970
Coming into Operation	*16th February* 1970

We, the authority having power to make rules of court for the purposes mentioned in section 7(1) of the Matrimonial Causes Act 1967(**a**), hereby exercise that power as follows :—

1.—(1) These Rules may be cited as the Matrimonial Causes (Amendment)‹ Rules 1970 and shall come into operation on 16th February 1970.

(2) In these Rules a rule referred to by number means the rule so numbered in the Matrimonial Causes Rules 1968(**b**), as amended (**c**).

(3) The Interpretation Act 1889(**d**) shall apply for the interpretation of these Rules as it applies for the interpretation of an Act of Parliament.

2. The following paragraph shall be added to rule 9 :—

"(8) A petitioner who, in reliance on section 11 or 12 of the Civil Evidence Act 1968(**e**), intends to adduce evidence that a person—

(*a*) was convicted of an offence by or before a court in the United Kingdom or by a court-martial there or elsewhere, or

(*b*) was found guilty of adultery in matrimonial proceedings or was adjudged to be the father of a child in affiliation proceedings before a court in the United Kingdom,

must include in his petition a statement of his intention with particulars of—

(i) the conviction, finding or adjudication and the date thereof,

(ii) the court or court-martial which made the conviction, finding or adjudication and, in the case of a finding or adjudication, the proceedings in which it was made, and

(iii) the issue in the proceedings to which the conviction, finding or adjudication is relevant.

3. Rule 21 shall be amended as follows :—

(1) The following paragraphs shall be inserted after paragraph (4) :—

"(5) Rule 9(8) shall apply with the necessary modifications to a pleading other than a petition as it applies to a petition.

(**a**) 1967 c. 56. (**b**) S.I. 1968/219 (1968 I, p. 665).
(**c**) There are no relevant amendments.
(**d**) 1889 c. 63. (**e**) 1968 c. 64.

(6) Where a party's pleading includes such a statement as is mentioned in rule 9(8), then if the opposite party—

(*a*) denies the conviction, finding or adjudication to which the statement relates, or

(*b*) alleges that the conviction, finding or adjudication was erroneous, or

(*c*) denies that the conviction, finding or adjudication is relevant to any issue in the proceedings,

he must make the denial or allegation in his pleading."

(2) Paragraph (5) shall stand as paragraph (7).

4. Paragraph (4) of rule 28 shall be omitted.

5. Paragraph (2) of rule 29 shall be omitted and paragraph (3) of that rule shall stand as paragraph (2).

6. In rule 38 for the words "Evidence Act 1938" there shall be substituted the words "Civil Evidence Act 1968".

7. After rule 42 there shall be inserted the following rule :—

"Hearsay evidence

42A.—(1) R.S.C. Order 38, rules 20 to 33, shall apply in relation to a defended cause as if in rule 21—

(*a*) for the reference in paragraph (4) to Order 38, rule 3, there were substituted a reference to rule 39 of these Rules ;

(*b*) paragraph (5) were omitted.

(2) Unless in any particular case the court otherwise directs—

(*a*) R.S.C. Order 38, rule 21(1), shall not apply in relation to an undefended cause pending in the High Court ;

(*b*) C.C.R. Order 20, rule 21(1), shall not apply in relation to an undefended cause pending in a divorce county court,

and where the court otherwise directs, then—

(i) if the cause is pending in the High Court, paragraph (1) shall apply as it applies in the case of a defended cause ;

(ii) if the cause is pending in a divorce county court, C.C.R. Order 20, rules 20 to 30, shall apply as if paragraph (2) of rule 21 were omitted".

> *Gardiner, C.,*
> *J. E. S. Simon, P.,*
> *John Latey, J.,*
> *Ifor Lloyd,*
> *Irvon Sunderland,*
> *W. D. S. Caird,*
> *J. L. Williams,*
> *Alan de Piro,*
> *Joseph Jackson,*
> *J. D. Clarke,*
> *David E. Morris,*

Dated 12th January 1970.

EXPLANATORY NOTE

(This Note is not part of the Rules.)

These Rules amend the Matrimonial Causes Rules 1968 for the purposes of the Civil Evidence Act 1968. Rules 2 and 3 specify the particulars to be included in a petition or other pleading where it is intended to put in evidence (by virtue of section 11 or 12 of the Act) a previous conviction, finding of adultery or adjudication of paternity. Rules 4 and 5 delete from the Rules of 1968 the restrictions on the making of an order against a party for the discovery or production of any document, or the service of any interrogatory, which may tend to show that he has been guilty of adultery. Rule 7 applies, with modifications, the provisions of the Rules of the Supreme Court and the County Court Rules with regard to the procedure to be followed where a party intends to adduce hearsay evidence under Part I of the Act. He will not have to give notice of his intention in an undefended cause, unless the court otherwise directs.

STATUTORY INSTRUMENTS

1970 No. 30 (L. 3)

COUNTY COURTS

PROCEDURE

The County Court (Amendment) Rules 1970

Made - - - -   9th January 1970
Coming into Operation   16th February 1970

1.—(1) These Rules may be cited as the County Court (Amendment) Rules 1970.

(2) In these Rules an Order and Rule referred to by number means the Order and Rule so numbered in the County Court Rules 1936(a), as amended(b).

(3) The Interpretation Act 1889(c) shall apply for the interpretation of these Rules as it applies for the interpretation of an Act of Parliament.

2. In Order 14, Rule 3(2), the words " that it relates only to his own title, he being the defendant in the proceedings, or " and the word " other " shall be omitted.

3. The following Rule shall be inserted in Order 20 after Rule 7 :—

" 7A.—(1) Any party to an action who intends in reliance on section 11 or 12 of the Civil Evidence Act 1968(d) to adduce evidence of a conviction, finding of adultery or adjudication of paternity shall include in his particulars of claim or defence, as the case may be, a statement of his intention with particulars of— *(Pleading of conviction, etc.)*

(a) the conviction, finding or adjudication and the date thereof,

(b) the court or court martial which made the conviction, finding or adjudication, and

(c) the issue in the action to which the conviction, finding or adjudication is relevant.

(2) Where a plaintiff's particulars of claim include such a statement as is mentioned in paragraph (1), then if the defendant—

(a) denies the conviction, finding or adjudication, or

(b) alleges that it was erroneous, or

(c) denies that it is relevant to any issue in the action,

he shall make the denial or allegation in his defence."

(a) S.R. & O. 1936/626 (1936 I, p. 282).
(b) The relevant amending instruments are S.I. 1950/1231, 1969/585 (1950 I, p. 400; 1969 I, p. 1551).   (c) 1889 c. 63.   (d) 1968 c. 64.

4. Order 20 shall be amended by inserting immediately before Rule 1 the words " Part I—GENERALLY " and by adding at the end of the following Part:—

" PART II

HEARSAY EVIDENCE

Interpretation and application.

20.—(1) In this Part of this Order " the Act " means the Civil Evidence Act 1968 and any expressions used in this Part of this Order and in Part I of the Act have the same meanings in this Part of this Order as they have in the said Part I.

(2) This Part of this Order shall apply in relation to the trial or hearing of an issue arising in an action or matter and to a reference under section 92 or 93 of the County Courts Act 1959 as it applies to the trial or hearing of an action or matter.

Notice of intention to give certain statements.

21.—(1) Subject to the provisions of this rule, a party to an action or matter who desires to give in evidence at the trial or hearing any statement which is admissible in evidence by virtue of section 2, 4 or 5 of the Act shall, not less than 14 clear days before the day fixed for the trial or hearing, give notice of his desire to do so to the registrar and to every other party.

(2) Unless in any particular case the court otherwise directs, paragraph (1) shall not apply to an action or matter in which no defence or answer has been filed ; and where a defence or answer is filed less than 14 clear days before the day fixed for the trial or hearing, any party required to give notice pursuant to paragraph (1) shall apply to the court for an adjournment of the trial or hearing or for such other directions as may be appropriate.

(3) Paragraph (1) shall not apply in relation to any statement which is admissible as evidence of any fact stated therein by virtue not only of the said section 2, 4 or 5 but by virtue also of any other statutory provision within the meaning of section 1 of the Act.

(4) Paragraph (1) shall not apply in relation to any statement which any party to a probate action desires to give in evidence at the trial of that action and which is alleged to have been made by the deceased person whose estate is the subject of the action.

(5) Where, by virtue of any provision of these rules or of any order or direction of the court, the evidence in any proceedings is to be given by affidavit then, without prejudice to paragraph (3), paragraph (1) shall not apply in relation to any statement which any party to the proceedings desires to have included in any affidavit to be used on his behalf in the proceedings.

Application of Rules of Supreme Court.

22. Order 38, Rules 22 to 25, of the Rules of the Supreme Court shall apply with the necessary modifications to a notice under the last foregoing rule as they apply to a notice under Rule 21 of the said Order 38.

Counter-notice requiring person to be called as a witness.

23.—(1) Subject to paragraphs (2) and (3), any party on whom a notice under Rule 21 is served may, within 7 clear days after service of the notice on him, give to the registrar and to the party who gave the notice a counter-notice requiring that party to call as a witness at the trial or hearing any person (naming him) particulars of whom are contained in the notice.

(2) Where any notice under Rule 21 contains a statement that any person particulars of whom are contained in the notice cannot or should not be called as a witness for the reason specified therein, a party shall not be entitled to serve a counter-notice under this rule requiring that person to be called as a witness at the trial or hearing unless he contends that that person can or, as the case may be, should be called, and in that case he must include in his counter-notice a statement to that effect.

(3) Where a statement to which a notice under Rule 21 relates is one to which Rule 25 applies, no party on whom the notice is served shall be entitled to serve a counter-notice under this rule in relation to that statement, but the foregoing provision is without prejudice to the right of any party to apply to the court under Rule 25 for directions with respect to the admissibility of that statement.

(4) If any party by whom a notice under Rule 21 is served fails to comply with a counter-notice duly served on him under this rule, then, unless any of the reasons specified in paragraph (5) applies in relation to the person named in the counter-notice, and without prejudice to the powers of the court under Rule 26, the statement to which the notice under Rule 21 relates shall not be admissible at the trial or hearing as evidence of any fact stated therein by virtue of section 2, 4 or 5 of the Act, as the case may be.

(5) The reasons referred to in paragraph (4) are that the person in question is dead, or beyond the seas, or unfit by reason of his bodily or mental condition to attend as a witness or that despite the exercise of reasonable diligence it has not been possible to identify or find him or that he cannot reasonably be expected to have any recollection of matters relevant to the accuracy or otherwise of the statement to which the notice relates.

24.—(1) Where a question arises whether any of the reasons specified in Rule 23(5) applies in relation to a person particulars of whom are contained in a notice under Rule 21, the court may, on the application of any party to the action or matter, determine that question before the trial or hearing or give directions for it to be determined before the trial or hearing and for the manner in which it is to be determined. *Determination of question whether person can or should be called as a witness.*

(2) Unless the court otherwise directs, notice of any application under paragraph (1) must be served on every other party to the action or matter.

(3) Where any such question as is referred to in paragraph (1) has been determined under or by virtue of that paragraph, no application to have it determined afresh at the trial or hearing may be made unless the evidence which it is sought to adduce in support of the application could not with reasonable diligence have been adduced at the hearing which resulted in the determination.

25. Where a party has given notice in accordance with Rule 21 that he desires to give in evidence at the trial or hearing— *Directions with respect to statement made in previous proceedings.*

(a) a statement falling within section 2(1) of the Act which was made by a person, whether orally or in a document, in the course of giving evidence in some other legal proceedings (whether civil or criminal), or (*b*) a statement falling within section 4(1) of the Act which is contained in a record of direct oral evidence given in some other legal proceedings (whether civil or criminal),

any party to the action or matter may apply to the court for directions as to whether, and if so on what conditions, the party desiring to give the statement in evidence will be permitted to do so and (where applicable) as to the manner in which that statement and any other evidence given in those other proceedings is to be proved.

Power of court to allow statement to be given in evidence.

26.—(1) Without prejudice to section 2(2)(*a*) and 4(2)(*a*) of the Act and Rule 25, the court may, if it thinks it just to do so, allow a statement falling within section 2(1), 4(1) or 5(1) of the Act to be given in evidence at the trial or hearing of an action or matter notwithstanding—

(*a*) that the statement is one in relation to which Rule 21(1) applies and that the party desiring to give the statement in evidence has failed to comply with that rule, or

(*b*) that that party has failed to comply with any requirement of a counter-notice relating to that statement which was served on him in accordance with Rule 23.

(2) Without prejudice to the generality of paragraph (1), the court may exercise its power under that paragraph to allow a statement to be given in evidence at the trial or hearing if a refusal to exercise that power might oblige the party desiring to give the statement in evidence to call as a witness at the trial or hearing an opposite party or a person who is or was at the material time the servant or agent of an opposite party.

Restriction on adducing evidence as to credibility of maker etc. of certain statements.

27. Where—

(*a*) a notice given under Rule 21 in an action or matter relates to a statement which is admissible by virtue of section 2 or 4 of the Act, and

(*b*) the person who made the statement, or, as the case may be, the person who originally supplied the information from which the record containing the statement was compiled, is not called as a witness at the trial or hearing of the action or matter, and

(*c*) none of the reasons mentioned in Rule 23(5) applies so as to prevent the party who gave the notice from calling that person as a witness,

no other party to the action or matter shall be entitled, except with the leave of the court, to adduce in relation to that person any evidence which could otherwise be adduced by him by virtue of section 7 of the Act unless he gave a counter-notice under Rule 23 in respect of that person or applied under Rule 25 for a direction that that person be called as a witness at the trial or hearing of the action or matter.

Notice required of intention to give evidence of certain inconsistent statements.

28.—(1) Where a person, particulars of whom were contained in a notice given under Rule 21, is not to be called as a witness at the trial or hearing, any party who is entitled and intends to adduce in relation to that person any evidence which is admissible for the purpose mentioned in section 7(1)(*b*) of the Act must, not more than 7 clear days after service of that notice on him, give notice of his intention to do so to the registrar and to the party who gave the notice under Rule 21.

(2) Order 38, Rule 22(1) and (2), of the Rules of the Supreme Court shall apply to a notice under this rule as if the notice were a notice under Rule 21 and the statement to which the notice relates were a statement admissible by virtue of section 2 of the Act.

(3) The court may, if it thinks it just to do so, allow a party to give in evidence at the trial or hearing of an action or matter any evidence which is admissible for the purpose mentioned in the said section 7(1)(b) notwithstanding that that party has failed to comply with the provisions of paragraph (1).

29. If—   Costs.

(a) a party to an action or matter serves a counter-notice under Rule 23 in respect of any person who is called as a witness at the trial of the action or matter in compliance with a requirement of the counter-notice, and

(b) it appears to the court that it was unreasonable to require that person to be called as a witness,

then, without prejudice to Order 47 and, in particular, to Rule 17 thereof, the court may direct that any costs to that party in respect of the preparation and service of the counter-notice shall not be allowed to him and that any costs occasioned by the counter-notice to any other party shall be paid by him to that other party.

30. Order 48, Rule 4, shall have effect in relation to the jurisdic- Exercise of tion of the court under sections 2(2)(a), 2(3), 4(2)(a) and 6(1) of jurisdiction. the Act as it has effect in relation to any jurisdiction conferred by these Rules."

We, the undersigned members of the Rule Committee appointed by the Lord Chancellor under section 102 of the County Courts Act 1959(a), having by virtue of the powers vested in us in this behalf made the foregoing Rules, do hereby certify the same under our hand and submit them to the Lord Chancellor accordingly.

> *D. O. McKee.*
> *Connolly H. Gage.*
> *Hugh Mais.*
> *H. S. Ruttle.*
> *David Pennant.*
> *W. Ralph Davies.*
> *E. A. Everett.*
> *Arthur Figgis.*
> *Brian D. Bush.*
> *A. F. Stapleton Cotton.*
> *D. A. Marshall.*

I allow these Rules, which shall come into operation on 16th February 1970.

Dated 9th January 1970.

> *Gardiner, C.*

(a) 1959 c. 22.

EXPLANATORY NOTE

(This Note is not part of the Rules.)

These Rules amend the County Court Rules for the purposes of the Civil Evidence Act 1968. Rule 2 deletes from Order 14, Rule 3(2), words enabling a defendant to resist a notice to produce a document on the ground that it relates only to his own title. Rule 3 inserts in Order 20 a new Rule 7A specifying the particulars to be included in a pleading where it is intended to put in evidence (by virtue of section 11 or 12 of the Act of 1968) a previous conviction, finding of adultery or adjudication of paternity. Rule 4 adds to Order 20 a new Part II prescribing the procedure to be followed where it is intended to adduce hearsay evidence under Part I of the Act. These provisions follow fairly closely the corresponding provisions made by the Rules of the Supreme Court (Amendment) 1969 (S.I., 1969/1105). Under the new Rule 21 of Order 20 a party intending to adduce hearsay evidence must give notice of his intention to do so not less than 14 clear days before the day fixed for the trial or hearing, but, unless the court otherwise directs, this requirement is not to apply unless a defence or answer has been filed ; and where a defence or answer is filed too late to enable notice to be given, the party required to give notice must apply for an adjournment.

STATUTORY INSTRUMENTS

1970 No. 39

SUGAR

The Sugar (Rates of Surcharge and Surcharge Repayments) Order 1970

Made - - - -	16*th January* 1970
Laid before Parliament	19*th January* 1970
Coming into Operation	20*th January* 1970

The Minister of Agriculture, Fisheries and Food, in exercise of the powers conferred on him by sections 7(4), 8(6) and 33(4) of the Sugar Act 1956(a) having effect subject to the provisions of section 3 of, and Part II of Schedule 5 to, the Finance Act 1962(b), and section 58 of the Finance Act 1968(c) and of all other powers enabling him in that behalf, with the concurrence of the Treasury, on the advice of the Sugar Board, hereby makes the following order:—

1.—(1) This order may be cited as the Sugar (Rates of Surcharge and Surcharge Repayments) Order 1970; and shall come into operation on 20th January 1970.

(2) The Interpretation Act 1889(d) shall apply for the interpretation of this order as it applies for the interpretation of an Act of Parliament.

2. Notwithstanding the provisions of Article 2 of the Sugar (Rates of Surcharge and Surcharge Repayments) (No. 13) Order 1969(e), the rates of surcharge payable under and in accordance with the provisions of section 7 of the Sugar Act 1956, having effect as aforesaid, in respect of sugar and invert sugar imported or home produced or used in the manufacture of imported composite sugar products shall on and after 20th January 1970 be those rates specified in Schedule 1 to this order.

3. For the purpose of section 8(3)(b) of the Sugar Act 1956, having effect as aforesaid, the rates of surcharge repayments in respect of invert sugar produced in the United Kingdom from materials on which on or after 20th January 1970 sugar duty has been paid or, by virtue of paragraph 1 of Part II of Schedule 5 to the Finance Act 1962, is treated as having been paid shall, notwithstanding the provisions of Article 3 of the Sugar (Rates of Surcharge and Surcharge Repayments) (No. 13) Order 1969 be those specified in Schedule 2 to this order.

(a) 1956 c. 48.   (b) 1962 c. 44.
(c) 1968 c. 44.   (d) 1889 c. 63.
(e) S.I. 1969/1664 (1969 III, p. 5210).

In Witness whereof the Official Seal of the Minister of Agriculture, Fisheries and Food is hereunto affixed on 14th January 1970.

(L.S.)

R. P. Fraser,

Authorised by the Minister.

We concur.

16th January 1970.

E. G. Perry,
Neil McBride,

Two of the Lords Commissioners of
Her Majesty's Treasury.

SCHEDULE 1

PART I

SURCHARGE RATES FOR SUGAR

Polarisation									Rate of Surcharge per cwt.	
									s.	d.
Exceeding—										
99° ...	...	...	...	...	...	...	...	...	21	0·0
98° but not exceeding 99° ...			...	...	...	...	...	...	19	9·6
97° ,, ,, ,, 98° ...			...	...	...	...	...	...	19	3·8
96° ,, ,, ,, 97° ...			...	...	...	...	...	...	18	9·7
95° ,, ,, ,, 96° ...			...	...	...	...	...	...	18	3·7
94° ,, ,, ,, 95° ...			...	...	...	...	...	...	17	9·6
93° ,, ,, ,, 94° ...			...	...	...	...	...	...	17	3·6
92° ,, ,, ,, 93° ...			...	...	...	...	...	...	16	9·6
91° ,, ,, ,, 92° ...			...	...	...	...	...	...	16	3·5
90° ,, ,, ,, 91° ...			...	...	...	...	...	...	15	9·5
89° ,, ,, ,, 90° ...			...	...	...	...	...	...	15	3·4
88° ,, ,, ,, 89° ...			...	...	...	...	...	...	14	9·4
87° ,, ,, ,, 88° ...			...	...	...	...	...	...	14	4·3
86° ,, ,, ,, 87° ...			...	...	...	...	...	...	13	11·3
85° ,, , ,, 86° ...			...	...	...	...	...	...	13	6·7
84° ,, ,, ,, 85° ...			...	...	...	...	...	...	13	2·2
83° ,, ,, ,, 84° ...			...	...	...	...	...	...	12	9·7
82° ,, ,, ,, 83° ...			...	...	...	...	...	...	12	5·1
81° ,, ,, ,, 82° ...			...	...	...	...	...	...	12	1·1
80° ,, ,, ,, 81° ...			...	...	...	...	...	...	11	9·1
79° ,, ,, ,, 80° ...			...	...	...	...	...	...	11	5·0
78° ,, ,, ,, 79° ...			...	...	...	...	...	...	11	1·0
77° ,, ,, ,, 78° ...			...	...	...	...	...	...	10	9·0
76° ,, ,, ,, 77° ...			...	...	...	...	...	...	10	4·9
Not exceeding 76° ...			...	...	...	...	...	...	10	0·9

PART II
SURCHARGE RATES FOR INVERT SUGAR

Sweetening matter content by weight	Rate of Surcharge per cwt.
	s. d.
70 per cent. or more	13 4
Less than 70 per cent. and more than 50 per cent.	9 7
Not more than 50 per cent.	4 8

SCHEDULE 2
SURCHARGE REPAYMENT RATES FOR INVERT SUGAR

Sweetening matter content by weight	Rate of Surcharge Repayment per cwt.
	s. d.
More than 80 per cent.	15 9
More than 70 per cent. but not more than 80 per cent.	13 4
More than 60 per cent. but not more than 70 per cent.	9 7
More than 50 per cent. but not more than 60 per cent.	7 7
Not more than 50 per cent. and the invert sugar not being less in weight than 14 lb. per gallon	4 8

EXPLANATORY NOTE
(This Note is not part of the Order.)

This order prescribes—

(a) reductions equivalent to 2s. 4d. per cwt. of refined sugar in the rates of surcharge payable on sugar and invert sugar which become chargeable with surcharge on or after 20th January 1970;

(b) correspondingly reduced rates of surcharge repayment in respect of invert sugar produced in the United Kingdom from materials on which surcharge has been paid.

STATUTORY INSTRUMENTS

1970 No. 40

SUGAR

The Composite Sugar Products (Surcharge and Surcharge Repayments—Average Rates) (No. 2) Order 1970

Made - - - -	16*th January* 1970
Laid before Parliament	19*th January* 1970
Coming into Operation	20*th January* 1970

Whereas the Minister of Agriculture, Fisheries and Food (hereinafter called " the Minister ") has on the recommendation of the Commissioners of Customs and Excise (hereinafter called " the Commissioners ") made an order(a) pursuant to the powers conferred upon him by sections 9(1) and 9(4) of the Sugar Act 1956(b), having effect subject to the provisions of section 3 of, and Part II of Schedule 5 to, the Finance Act 1962(c), to the provisions of section 52(2) of the Finance Act 1966(d), and to the provisions of section 58 of the Finance Act 1968(e), providing that in the case of certain descriptions of composite sugar products surcharge shall be calculated on the basis of an average quantity of sugar or invert sugar taken to have been used in the manufacture of the products, and that certain other descriptions of composite sugar products shall be treated as not containing any sugar or invert sugar, and that in the case of certain descriptions of goods in the manufacture of which sugar or invert sugar is used, surcharge repayments shall be calculated on the basis of an average quantity of sugar or invert sugar taken to have been so used:

Now, therefore, the Minister, on the recommendation of the Commissioners and in exercise of the powers conferred upon him by sections 9(1), 9(4) and 33(4) of the Sugar Act 1956, having effect as aforesaid, and of all other powers enabling him in that behalf, hereby makes the following order:—

1.—(1) This order may be cited as the Composite Sugar Products (Surcharge and Surcharge Repayments—Average Rates) (No. 2) Order 1970; and shall come into operation on 20th January 1970.

(2) The Interpretation Act 1889(f) shall apply for the interpretation of this order as it applies for the interpretation of an Act of Parliament.

2. Surcharge payable on or after 20th January 1970 under and in accordance with the Sugar Act 1956, having effect as aforesaid, in respect of sugar and invert sugar used in the manufacture of the descriptions of imported composite sugar products specified in column 2 of Schedule 1 to this order shall, notwithstanding the provisions of the Sugar (Rates of Surcharge and Surcharge Repayments) Order 1970(g) and the Composite Sugar Products (Surcharge and Surcharge Repayments—Average Rates) Order 1970(a), be calculated by reference to the weight of the products at the rates specified in relation thereto in column 3 of the said Schedule.

(a) S.I. 1970/19 (1970 I, p. 208).   (b) 1956 c. 48.   (c) 1962 c. 44.
(d) 1966 c. 18.   (e) 1968 c. 44.   (f) 1889 c. 63.
(g) S.I. 1970/39 (1970 I, p. 235).

3. Imported composite sugar products other than those of a description specified in Schedules 1 and 2 to this order shall be treated as not containing any sugar or invert sugar for the purposes of surcharge payable on or after 20th January 1970.

4. Surcharge repayments payable on and after 20th January 1970 under and in accordance with the provisions of section 8 of the Sugar Act 1956, having effect as aforesaid, in respect of sugar and invert sugar used in the manufacture of the descriptions of goods specified in column 1 of Schedule 3 to this order shall, notwithstanding the provisions of the Sugar (Rates of Surcharge and Surcharge Repayments) Order 1970(a) and the Composite Sugar Products (Surcharge and Surcharge Repayments—Average Rates) Order 1970(b), be calculated by reference to the quantity of the goods at the rates specified in relation thereto in column 2 of the said Schedule.

In Witness whereof the Official Seal of the Minister of Agriculture, Fisheries and Food is hereunto affixed on 16th January 1970.

(L.S.)

R. P. Fraser,

Authorised by the Minister.

SCHEDULE 1

In this Schedule:—

" Tariff heading " means a heading or, where the context so requires, a subheading of the Customs Tariff 1959 (see paragraph (1) of Article 2 of the Import Duties (General) (No. 3) Order 1969(c)).

Tariff heading	Description of Imported Composite Sugar Products	Rate of Surcharge
		per cwt. s. d.
04.02	Milk and cream, preserved, concentrated or sweetened, containing more than 10 per cent. by weight of added sugar	9 4
17.02 (B) (2) and 17.05 (B)	Syrups containing sucrose sugar, whether or not flavoured or coloured, but not including fruit juices containing added sugar in any proportion:—	
	Containing 70 per cent. or more by weight of sweetening matter	13 4
	Containing less than 70 per cent., and more than 50 per cent., by weight of sweetening matter...	9 7
	Containing not more than 50 per cent. by weight of sweetening matter	4 8

(a) S.I. 1970/39 (1970 I, p. 235).   (b) S.I. 1970/19 (1970 I, p. 208).
(c) S.I. 1969/1413 (1969 III, p. 4150).

Tariff heading	Description of Imported Composite Sugar Products	Rate of Surcharge
		per cwt. s. d.
17.02 (F) ...	Caramel:—	
	Solid	21 0
	Liquid	14 8
17.04	Sugar confectionery, not containing cocoa	17 1
18.06	Chocolate and other food preparations containing cocoa and added sugar:—	
	Chocolate couverture not prepared for retail sale; chocolate milk crumb, liquid	9 4
	Chocolate milk crumb, solid	11 6
	Solid chocolate bars or blocks, milk or plain, with or without fruit or nuts; other chocolate confectionery consisting wholly of chocolate or of chocolate and other ingredients not containing added sugar, but not including such goods when packed together in retail packages with goods liable to surcharge at a higher rate	9 5
	Other	12 2
19.08	Pastry, biscuits, cakes and other fine bakers' wares containing added sugar:—	
	Biscuits, wafers and rusks containing more than 12½ per cent. by weight of added sugar, and other biscuits, wafers and rusks included in retail packages with such goods	5 3
	Cakes with covering or filling containing added sugar; meringues	7 0
	Other	2 7
20.01	Vegetables and fruit, prepared or preserved by vinegar or acetic acid, containing added sugar:—	
	Containing 10 per cent. or more by weight of added sugar	7 4
	Other	1 7
20.03	Fruit preserved by freezing, containing added sugar	2 7
20.04	Fruit, fruit-peel and parts of plants, preserved by sugar (drained, glacé or crystallised)	13 10
20.05	Jams, fruit jellies, marmalades, fruit purée and fruit pastes, being cooked preparations, containing added sugar	13 2
20.06	Fruit otherwise prepared or preserved, containing added sugar:—	
	Ginger	10 6
	Other	2 7

SCHEDULE 2

Tariff heading	Description of Imported Composite Sugar Products
17.05 (A) and (B)	Sugar and invert sugar, flavoured or coloured.

SCHEDULE 3

Description of goods	Rate of surcharge repayment per bulk barrel of 36 gallons
Lager	10·5d.
All beer other than lager	9·4d.

EXPLANATORY NOTE

(*This Note is not part of the Order.*)

This order provides for reductions on and after 20th January 1970 in the average rates of surcharge payable on imported composite sugar products of the descriptions specified in Schedule 1 and in the average rates of surcharge repayment in respect of exported goods of the descriptions specified in Schedule 3. These correspond to the reductions in surcharge rates effected by the Sugar Rates of Surcharge and Surcharge Repayments) Order 1970 (S.I. 1970/39). Provision is also made for certain imported composite sugar products to be treated as not containing any sugar or invert sugar.

STATUTORY INSTRUMENTS

1970 No. 41 (C. 2)

TRANSPORT

The Transport Act 1968 (Commencement No. 4) Order 1970

Made - - - - - 16th January 1970

The Minister of Transport hereby makes this Order in exercise of his powers under section 166 of the Transport Act 1968(a) and of all other enabling powers :—

1. This Order may be cited as the Transport Act 1968 (Commencement No. 4) Order 1970.

2. Subsections (10) and (12) of section 96 of the Transport Act 1968 shall come into force on the 22nd January 1970.

Sealed with the Official Seal of the Minister of Transport the 16th January 1970.

(L.S.)

G. R. W. Brigstocke,
An Under Secretary of the
Ministry of Transport.

EXPLANATORY NOTE

(This Note is not part of the Order.)

This Order brings into operation on 22nd January 1970 subsections (10) and (12) of section 96 of the Transport Act 1968, which enable the Minister of Transport by subordinate legislation to modify the requirements of section 96 (which relates to the permitted driving time and periods of duty of drivers of passenger and goods vehicles) and also to empower the traffic commissioners or licensing authorities to dispense with the observance of those requirements in certain cases.

(a) 1968 c. 73.

STATUTORY INSTRUMENTS

1970 No. 46

SOCIAL SECURITY

The Family Allowances, National Insurance, Industrial Injuries and Miscellaneous Provisions (Decimalisation of the Currency) Regulations 1970

Made - - -	*1st January* 1970
Laid before Parliament	*28th January* 1970

Coming into Operation—

Regulations 1, 13(3)-(6), (8)-(10), 14, 17(1)-(3), 33(2)(5), 34(4)(5)	*6th April* 1970
Regulations 13(7), 17(4)	End of transitional period (see reg. 1(2))
Remainder	*15th February* 1971

ARRANGEMENT OF REGULATIONS

PART I

GENERAL

Part V

Miscellaneous Amendments

28. Amendments to sections 2 and 7 of the Industrial Injuries and Diseases (Old Cases) Act.

29. Amendments to Articles 2, 5 and 10 of, and Schedules 1 and 2 to, the Workmen's Compensation (Supplementation) Scheme.

30. Amendments to Article 4 of, and Schedule 3 to, the Pneumoconiosis, Byssinosis and Miscellaneous Diseases Benefit Scheme.

31. Amendment to the Schedule to the National Health Service Contributions Act.

32. Amendment to section 27 of the Redundancy Payments Act.

Part VI

Miscellaneous Transitional Provisions

33. Transitional provisions relating to benefit.

34. Transitional provisions relating to contributions.

35. Transitional provisions relating to equivalent pension benefits, a payment in lieu of contributions and a refund of graduated contributions in certain cases.

SCHEDULES

1. Schedule substituted for Schedule 1 to the National Insurance Act.

2. Schedule substituted for Schedule 3 to the National Insurance Act.

3. Schedule substituted for Schedule 4 to the National Insurance Act.

4. Schedule substituted for the Schedule to the National Insurance (Widow's Benefit and Retirement Pensions) Regulations.

5. Schedule substituted for Schedule 2 to the National Insurance (Unemployment and Sickness Benefit) Regulations.

6. Schedule substituted for the First Schedule to the National Insurance (Death Grant) Regulations.

7. Further Schedule inserted in the National Insurance (Mariners) Regulations as Schedule 4 thereto.

8. Further Schedule inserted in the National Insurance (Mariners) Regulations as Schedule 5 thereto.

9. Further Schedule inserted in the National Insurance (Mariners) Regulations as Schedule 6 thereto.

10. Schedule substituted for Schedule 3 to the National Insurance (Members of the Forces) Regulations.

11. Schedule substituted for Schedule 5 to the National Insurance (Members of the Forces) Regulations.

12. Schedule substituted for Schedule 5A to the National Insurance (Members of the Forces) Regulations.

13. Schedule substituted for Schedule 1 to the National Insurance (Pensions, Existing Beneficiaries and Other Persons) (Transitional) Regulations.

14. Schedule substituted for Schedule 2 to the National Insurance (Pensions, Existing Beneficiaries and Other Persons) (Transitional) Regulations.

15. Schedule substituted for Schedule 3 to the National Insurance (Pensions, Existing Beneficiaries and Other Persons) (Transitional) Regulations.
16. Schedule substituted for Schedule 2 to the National Insurance (Pensions, Existing Contributors) (Transitional) Regulations.
17. Tables to be substituted for the three Tables in Part III of the Fifth Schedule to the National Insurance (Pensions, Existing Contributors) (Transitional) Regulations.
18. Further Schedule inserted in the National Insurance (Assessment of Graduated Contributions) Regulations as Schedule 4 thereto.
19. Further Schedule inserted in the National Insurance (Assessment of Graduated Contributions) Regulations as Schedule 5 thereto.
20. Schedule substituted for the First Schedule to the National Insurance (Graduated Retirement Benefit and Consequential Provisions) Regulations.
21. Schedule substituted for Schedule 2 to the National Insurance (Non-Participation—Assurance of Equivalent Pension Benefits) Regulations.
22. Schedule substituted for the Schedule to the National Insurance (Earnings-related Benefit) Regulations.
23. Provisions to be substituted for Part I of Schedule 2 to the National Insurance (Industrial Injuries) Act.
24. Schedule substituted for Schedule 3 to the National Insurance (Industrial Injuries) Act.
25. Schedule substituted for Schedule 3 to the National Insurance (Industrial Injuries) (Benefit) Regulations.
26. Schedule substituted for Schedule 4 to the National Insurance (Industrial Injuries) (Benefit) Regulations.
27. Schedule substituted for Schedule 1 to the Workmen's Compensation (Supplementation) Scheme.
28. Schedule substituted for the Schedule to the National Health Service Contributions Act.
29. Method of calculating in certain cases the amount in new pence corresponding to an amount in shillings and pence.

The Secretary of State for Social Services, in conjunction with the Treasury, in exercise of his powers under section 8 of the National Insurance Act 1969(a), hereby makes the following regulations which, by virtue of the provisions of section 10(1)(b) of the said Act of 1969, are exempt from the requirements of section 108 of the National Insurance Act 1965(b) (preliminary draft of regulations under that Act to be submitted to the National Insurance Advisory Committee) and section 62(2) of the National Insurance (Industrial Injuries) Act 1965(c) (proposal to make regulations under that Act to be submitted to the Industrial Injuries Advisory Council):—

PART I

GENERAL

Citation, commencement and interpretation

1.—(1) These regulations may be cited as the Family Allowances, National Insurance, Industrial Injuries and Miscellaneous Provisions (Decimalisation of the Currency) Regulations 1970, and shall come into operation in the case of regulations 1, 13(3)-(6), (8)-(10), 14, 17(1)-(3), 33(2)(5), 34(4)(5) 6th April 1970; in the case of regulations 13(7) and 17(4) the end of the transitional period (see regulation 1(2); and in the case of the remainder of the regulations 15th February 1971.

(a) 1969 c. 44.   (b) 1965 c. 51.
(c) 1965 c. 52.

(2) In these regulations, unless the context otherwise requires—

"the Family Allowances Act" means the Family Allowances Act 1965**(a)**;

"the National Insurance Act" means the National Insurance Act 1965;

"the Industrial Injuries Act" means the National Insurance (Industrial Injuries) Act 1965;

"the 1969 Act" means the National Insurance Act 1969;

"the Old Cases Act" means the Industrial Injuries and Diseases (Old Cases) Act 1967**(b)**;

"the appointed day" means 15th February 1971 (the day appointed under section 1 of the Decimal Currency Act 1967)**(c)**;

"the new currency" means the new currency of the United Kingdom provided for by the Decimal Currency Act 1967;

"the old currency" means the currency of the United Kingdom in force before the appointed day;

"the transitional period" means the period beginning with the appointed day and ending with such day as the Treasury may appoint under section 16(1) of the Decimal Currency Act 1969**(d)**;

"the Secretary of State" means the Secretary of State for Social Services;

and other expressions have the same meaning as in whichever of the enactments referred to in the regulations is, in the context, appropriate.

(3) References in these regulations to any enactment shall, except in so far as the context otherwise requires, be construed as references to that enactment as amended or extended by or under any other enactment, order or regulation.

(4) The rules for construction of Acts of Parliament contained in the Interpretation Act 1889**(e)** shall apply for the purpose of the interpretation of these regulations as they apply for the purpose of the interpretation of an Act of Parliament.

General provision relating to payment of a sum payable by way of benefit

2.—(1) Where, notwithstanding the application of regulation 33(3) of these regulations, payment falls to be made of a sum payable by way of benefit and that sum is not a new penny or a multiple thereof, the sum payable shall be paid by rounding the payment to the nearest new penny, a new halfpenny being rounded to the next new penny above.

(2) In this regulation the expression "benefit" means benefit under the National Insurance Act, the Industrial Injuries Act or the Old Cases Act.

PART II

AMENDMENTS TO THE FAMILY ALLOWANCES ACT

Amendments to sections 1 and 3 of and the Schedule to the Family Allowances Act

3.—(1) In section 1 of the Family Allowances Act (payment and amount of allowances), as amended by section 1(1)(*a*) of the Family Allowances and

---

(a) 1965 c. 53. **(b)** 1967 c. 34.
(c) 1967 c. 47. **(d)** 1969 c. 19.
(e) 1889 c. 63.

National Insurance Act 1968**(a)**, for the reference to "eighteen shillings" there shall be substituted a reference to "90 new pence" and for the reference to "twenty shillings" there shall be substituted a reference to "£1.00".

(2) In section 3(2) of, and in the proviso to paragraph 1(1) of the Schedule to, the Family Allowances Act (minimum weekly contribution required from a person towards the maintenance of a child not living with him if the child is to be included in a family as being his issue or maintained by him), as amended by section 1(1)(*b*) of the said Act of 1968, for the references to "eighteen shillings" there shall be substituted references to "90 new pence".

PART III

AMENDMENTS TO THE NATIONAL INSURANCE ACT AND STATUTORY INSTRUMENTS

MADE THEREUNDER

Amendments to the National Insurance Act

4.—(1) In section 5 of the National Insurance Act (automatic increases in contributions) as amended by paragraph 4 of Schedule 1 to the National Insurance Act 1966**(b)** and section 1(3) of the 1969 Act, for references to "fivepence" and "tenpence" there shall respectively be substituted references to "2 new pence" and "4 new pence".

(2) In section 12 of the National Insurance Act (recovery by employer of insured person's flat-rate contributions), for the reference in proviso (*b*) to paragraph (3) to "a penny", there shall be substituted a reference to "a new penny".

(3) In section 30(7) of the National Insurance Act (reduction of retirement pension on account of earnings), as amended by section 3(1) of the 1969 Act, for the reference to "seven pounds ten shillings" there shall be substituted a reference to "£7.50" and in section 3(2) of the 1969 Act for the words "by a shilling for each complete two shillings of the excess or, if the excess is more than two pounds, then by one pound in respect of the first two pounds of the excess and by a shilling for each further complete shilling of the excess" there shall be substituted the words "by 5 new pence for each complete 10 new pence of the excess or, if the excess is more than £2.00, then by £1.00 in respect of the first £2.00 of the excess and by 5 new pence for each further complete 5 new pence of the excess".

(4) In section 31(1) of the National Insurance Act (increase of pension for contributions after pensionable age), as amended by section 1(1)(*e*) of the National Insurance Act 1967**(c)**, for the reference to "by one shilling" there shall be substituted a reference to "by 5 new pence".

(5) In section 34(1) of the National Insurance Act (increase of woman's retirement pension in certain cases), as amended by section 1(1)(*e*) of the National Insurance Act 1967, for the references in sub-paragraphs (*a*) and (*b*) to "sixpence" there shall be substituted references to "2½ new pence".

(6) In section 36 of the National Insurance Act (graduated retirement benefit), as amended by paragraph 5 of Schedule 1 to the National Insurance Act 1966, in subsection (1), for the reference to "sixpence" there shall be substituted a reference to "2½ new pence", in subsection (2)(*a*) for the reference to "seven pounds ten shillings" there shall be substituted a reference to "£7.50" and in subsection (2)(*b*) for the words "to the nearest shilling above, or to the nearest

shilling below" there shall be substituted the words "to the nearest 5 new pence above, or to the nearest 5 new pence below".

(7) In section 37 of the National Insurance Act (special provisions as to graduated retirement benefit for widows), for the words "plus sixpence for every shilling or part of a shilling" there shall be substituted the words "plus $2\frac{1}{2}$ new pence for every 5 new pence or part of 5 new pence".

(8) In section 57 of the National Insurance Act (equivalent pension benefits, etc.), in subsection (1)(*d*), for the words "in the case of a man, three pounds nine shillings and seven pence a year, and, in the case of a woman, two pounds eighteen shillings a year" there shall be substituted the words "in the case of a man, £3.47$^{11}/_{12}$ a year, and, in the case of a woman, £2.90 a year".

(9) In section 58 of the National Insurance Act (payments in lieu of contributions in certain circumstances), as amended by section 11(3)(*a*) of, and paragraph 8 of Schedule 1 to, the National Insurance Act 1966 and section 1(2) of the 1969 Act, for the words from "equal to the difference between—" to the end of the section there shall be substituted the words:—

"for each complete contribution week during that period for which contributions were payable at the non-participating employment rate of an amount, in the case of a man, of $52\frac{1}{2}$ new pence and of an amount, in the case of a woman, of $61\frac{2}{3}$ new pence, the total of any amounts due in respect of the insured person's said period of service, if not a multiple of a new penny, being rounded to the nearest new penny, a halfpenny being disregarded; and on the making of any payment required by this section the insured person shall be treated for the purposes of this Act as having paid in respect of the employment in question, in addition to any graduated contributions paid by him in respect of that employment as a non-participating employment, graduated contributions at a weekly rate of $38\frac{1}{3}$ new pence, or, if the payment is of an amount less than the full amount required, graduated contributions of the said weekly amount for each week in respect of which a payment in lieu of contributions has been made."

(10) In section 91 of the National Insurance Act (information as to proof of age, marriage or death), in subsection (2)(*b*), as amended**(a)**, for the references to "two shillings" there shall be substituted references to "10 new pence".

(11) For the provisions set out in Schedules 1 (rates of flat-rate contributions), 3 (rates of periodical benefits and of increases for dependants) and 4 (amounts of grants) to the National Insurance Act, as substituted respectively by the provisions set out in Schedules 1, 2 and 3 of the 1969 Act, there shall be substituted respectively the provisions set out in Schedules 1, 2 and 3 to these regulations.

(12) In Schedule 11 to the National Insurance Act (transitory provisions), in paragraphs 7 and 8 (increase of retirement pension for contributions after pensionable age), for references to "one shilling", "one shilling and sixpence" and "sixpence" there shall respectively be substituted references to "5 new pence", "$7\frac{1}{2}$ new pence" and "$2\frac{1}{2}$ new pence".

(13) In the said Schedule 11, in paragraph 15 (payments in lieu of contributions), for sub-paragraph (*a*) there shall be substituted the following sub-paragraph:—

"(*a*) as respects service before 6th January 1964, that section shall have effect as if for the references therein to "$52\frac{1}{2}$ new pence", "$61\frac{2}{3}$ new pence" and "$38\frac{1}{3}$ new pence" there were respectively substituted references to "$36\frac{2}{3}$ new pence", "$44^{7}/_{12}$ new pence" and "$25^{5}/_{12}$ new pence"."

(a) S.I. 1968/1177, 1242, 1309 (1968 II, pp. 3189, 3354, 3633).

Amendment to the National Insurance Contributions Regulations

5. In regulation 14 of the National Insurance (Contributions) Regulations 1969**(a)** (income for the purposes of certificates of exception), for the references in paragraph (1)(*f*) to "thirty shillings" and "fifteen shillings" there shall respectively be substituted references to "£1.50" and "75 new pence".

Amendments to the National Insurance Widow's Benefit and Retirement Pensions Regulations

6.—(1) In regulation 12(2) of the National Insurance (Widow's Benefit and Retirement Pensions) Regulations 1948**(b)** as amended**(c)** (contributions to be disregarded in computing increase of retirement pension), for the reference to "thirty shillings a week" there shall be substituted a reference to "£1.50 a week".

(2) For the provisions set out in the Schedule to the said regulations (reduced rates of widow's benefit and retirement pension and of increase of retirement pension in respect of an adult dependant), there shall be substituted the provisions set out in Schedule 4 to these regulations.

Amendments to the National Insurance Unemployment and Sickness Benefit Regulations

7.—(1) In regulation 7 of the National Insurance (Unemployment and Sickness Benefit) Regulations 1967**(d)** as amended**(e)** (days not to be treated as days of unemployment or incapacity for work), in paragraph (1)(*h*) for the reference to "40 shillings" there shall be substituted a reference to "£2.00" and in paragraph (1)(*i*) for the reference to "six shillings and eight pence" there shall be substituted a reference to "33½ new pence".

(2) For the provisions in Schedule 2 to the said regulations (reduced rates of unemployment and sickness benefit and of increase of benefit in respect of adult dependants), there shall be substituted the provisions set out in Schedule 5 to these regulations.

Amendment to the National Insurance Death Grant Regulations

8. For the provisions set out in the First Schedule to the National Insurance (Death Grant) Regulations 1949**(f)** as amended**(g)** (reduced amount of death grant payable if the contribution conditions are not fully satisfied), there shall be substituted the provisions set out in Schedule 6 to these regulations.

Amendment to the National Insurance Overlapping Benefits Regulations

9. In regulation 6(1) of the National Insurance (Overlapping Benefits) Regulations 1948**(h)** as amended**(i)** (adjustment of dependency benefit where personal benefit is payable), for the references in the proviso to "twenty-six shillings" there shall be substituted references to "£1.30".

Amendments to the National Insurance Hospital In-Patients Regulations

10. In the National Insurance (Hospital In-Patients) Regulations 1949**(j)** as amended**(k)** (adjustment of benefit), for references to "£1 0s. 0d.", "£1 5s. 0d.", "£2 0s. 0d.", "£2 5s. 0d.", "£2 18s. 0d.", "£3 0s. 0d.", "£3 5s. 0d." and "£7 0s. 0d." wherever they appear, there shall respectively be substituted references to "£1.00", "£1.25", "£2.00", "£2.25", "£2.90", "£3.00", "£3.25" and "£7.00".

(a) S.I. 1969/1696 (1969 III, p. 5323).
(b) S.I. 1948/1261 (Rev. XVI, p. 207: 1948 I, p. 2704).
(c) The relevant amending instruments are S.I. 1964/2001, 1969/1361 (1964 III, p. 5061; 1969 III, p. 4048).
(d) S.I. 1967/330 (1967 I, p. 1131).
(e) The relevant amending instrument is S.I. 1969/1361 (1969 III, p. 4048).
(f) S.I. 1949/1204 (1949 I, p. 2708).
(g) The relevant amending instrument is S.I. 1967/1265 (1967 II, p. 3673).
(h) S.I. 1948/2711 (Rev. XVI, p. 196: 1948 I, p. 2657).
(i) The relevant amending instrument is S.I. 1957/2077 (1957 I, p. 1556).
(j) S.I. 1949/1461 (1949 I, p. 2718).
(k) The relevant amending instrument is S.I. 1969/1361 (1969 III, p. 4048).

Amendments to the National Insurance Maternity Benefit and Miscellaneous Provisions Regulations

11.—(1) For the table set out in regulation 13(2) of the National Insurance (Maternity Benefit and Miscellaneous Provisions) Regulations 1954**(a)**, as amended**(b)** (reduced amount of maternity allowance payable and of increase in respect of an adult dependant where contribution conditions only partially satisfied) there shall be substituted the following table:—

Numbers including the number of contributions paid or credited in respect of the relevant period 1	Weekly rate	
	Of maternity allowance without increase 2	Of increase in respect of adult dependant 3
	£	£
48—49	4.80	3.00
46—47	4.60	2.90
43—45	4.40	2.75
40—42	4.05	2.55
37—39	3.65	2.35
34—36	3.30	2.10
30—33	2.90	1.85
26—29	2.50	1.55

(2) Regulation 15 of the said regulations (rounding of fractions of a penny) is hereby revoked.

Amendment to the National Insurance Child's Special Allowance Regulations

12. In regulation 2 of the National Insurance (Child's Special Allowance) Regulations 1957**(c)** (minimum weekly rate of contributions for child's special allowance), for the reference to "five shillings" there shall be substituted a reference to "25 new pence".

Amendments to the National Insurance Mariners Regulations

13.—(1) In regulation 2(2)(b) of the National Insurance (Mariners) Regulations 1967**(d)** as amended**(e)** (insurance of mariners), for the words "include a fraction of a penny" to "is a halfpenny or more", there shall be substituted the words "include a fraction of a new penny, that fraction shall be disregarded if it is less than a new halfpenny and shall be treated as a new penny if it is a new halfpenny or more."

(a) S.I. 1954/189 (1954 I, p. 1387).
(b) The relevant amending instrument is S.I. 1969/1361 (1969 III, p. 4048).
(c) S.I. 1957/1835 (1957 I, p. 1523).   (d) S.I. 1967/386 (1967 I, p. 1294).
(e) The relevant amending instruments are S.I. 1967/1573, 1969/1277 (1967 III, p. 4382; 1969 III, p. 3811).

(2) In regulation 5 of the said regulations (contributions of mariners employed as masters or members of the crews of any ships or vessels other than home-trade ships), in paragraph (1)(*a*) for the reference to "one shilling and eight-pence" there shall be substituted a reference to "£0.089", and in paragraph (1)(*b*) for the reference to "ninepence-halfpenny" there shall be substituted a reference to "£0.041".

(3) Regulation 18 of the said regulations (seamen's liability for graduated contributions and their assessment) shall be amended in accordance with the provisions of paragraphs (4), (6) and (7) of this regulation.

(4) With effect from 6th April 1970, for paragraph (6) of the said regulation 18 there shall be substituted the following paragraph:—

"(6) In this regulation 'the appropriate Schedule' means—

(*a*) where amounts are not expressed in decimal form—

(i) Schedule 1 to these regulations in the case of an employment which is not a non-participating employment; and

(ii) Schedule 2 to these regulations in the case of an employment which is a non-participating employment; and

(*b*) where amounts are expressed in decimal form—

(i) Schedule 4 to these regulations in the case of an employment which is not a non-participating employment; and

(ii) Schedule 5 to these regulations in the case of an employment which is a non-participating employment."

(5) With effect from 6th April 1970, after Schedule 4 to the said regulations there shall be inserted the Schedules set out in Schedules 7 and 8 to these regulations.

(6) With effect from 6th April 1970, for paragraph (7) of the said regulation 18, there shall be substituted the following paragraph:—

"(7) Where, in the case of any payments to which the provisions of paragraph (3) or paragraph (4) of this regulation or of regulation 20 apply, it would, having regard to the means by which the net sums payable are to be calculated, be unduly difficult or inconvenient to calculate the graduated contributions payable in respect of those payments in accordance with those provisions, the amounts of those contributions may be calculated as if those provisions did not apply; and in any case in which the amount of any graduated contribution payable is not calculated in accordance with those provisions, that amount shall be calculated to the nearest penny (any amount of a halfpenny being disregarded) or, where amounts are expressed in decimal form, to the nearest £0.01, any amount of £0.005 being disregarded and the provisions of regulation 2 of the National Insurance (Assessment of Graduated Contributions) Regulations 1967(a) as amended(b) (equivalent amounts) shall have effect subject to the necessary modifications:

Provided that 4¾ per cent., 4¼ per cent., 3¼ per cent., 2¾ per cent. and ½ per cent. of any amount (other than the amount of the graduated contribution) or of any equivalent amount referred to in section 4(1)(*c*) of the Act, as amended by section 1(2) of the National Insurance Act 1969, or of the total of more than any one such amount or equivalent amount, may be calculated to the nearest penny (any amount of a halfpenny being disregarded), or, where amounts are expressed in decimal form, to the nearest £0.01, any amount of £0.005 being disregarded."

(a) 1967/844 (1967 II, p. 2513).
(b) The relevant amending instrument is S.I. 1969/1133 (1969 II, p. 3363).

(7) With effect from the end of the transitional period, Schedules 1 and 2 to the said regulations shall be revoked and for paragraphs (6) and (7) of regulation 18 of the said regulations, as amended by these regulations, there shall be substituted the following paragraphs:—

"(6) In this regulation 'the appropriate Schedule' means Schedule 4 to these regulations in the case of an employment which is not a non-participating employment and means Schedule 5 to these regulations in the case of an employment which is a non-participating employment.

(7) Where, in the case of any payments to which the provisions of paragraph (3) or paragraph (4) of this regulation or of regulation 20 apply, it would, having regard to the means by which the net sums payable are to be calculated, be unduly difficult or inconvenient to calculate the graduated contributions payable in respect of those payments in accordance with those provisions, the amounts of those contributions may be calculated as if those provisions did not apply; and in any case in which the amount of any graduated contribution payable is not calculated in accordance with those provisions, that amount shall be calculated to the nearest £0.01, any amount of £0.005 being disregarded and the provisions of regulation 2 of the National Insurance (Assessment of Graduated Contributions) Regulations 1967**(a)** as amended **(b)** (equivalent amounts) shall have effect subject to the necessary modifications:

Provided that $4\frac{3}{4}$ per cent., $4\frac{1}{4}$ per cent., $3\frac{1}{4}$ per cent., $2\frac{3}{4}$ per cent. and $\frac{1}{2}$ per cent. of any amount (other than the amount of the graduated contribution), or of any equivalent amount referred to in section $4(1)(c)$ of the Act, as amended by section 1(2) of the National Insurance Act 1969, or of the total of more than any one such amount or equivalent amount, may be calculated to the nearest £0.01, any amount of £0.005 being disregarded."

(8) Regulation 20 of the said regulations (separate additional payments) shall be amended in accordance with paragraph (10) of this regulation.

(9) With effect from 6th April 1970, after Schedule 6 to the said regulation, there shall be inserted the Schedule set out in Schedule 9 to these regulations.

(10) With effect from 6th April 1970, for the references in the said regulation 20 to "Schedule 3", there shall be substituted references to "Schedule 3 or Schedule 7" and with effect from the end of the transitional period for references to "Schedule 3 or Schedule 7" there shall be substituted references to "Schedule 7" and Schedule 3 shall be revoked.

(11) In regulation 21 of the said regulations (annual maximum amount payable by way of graduated contributions), for the references in paragraph $(2)(a)$(vi) to "£43 15s. 8d" and "£43 5s. 8d" there shall respectively be substituted references to "£43.96" and "£43.46".

(12) There shall be inserted in Part III of the said regulations (miscellaneous provisions), after regulation 24, the following regulation:—

"Transitory decimalisation provision relating to flat-rate contributions

24A. The contributions (not being graduated contributions) payable in respect of a mariner for a voyage (including any period of leave on pay immediately following the voyage) commencing after 5th April 1970 and ending during the transitional period as defined in regulation 1(2) of the Family Allowances, National Insurance, Industrial Injuries and Miscellaneous

---

(a) 1967/844 (1967 II, p. 2513).
(b) The relevant amending instrument is S.I. 1969/1133 (1969 II, p. 3363).

Provisions (Decimalisation of the Currency) Regulations 1970**(a)** may be calculated either by reference to the appropriate old currency rate or by reference to the corresponding new currency rate."

Amendments to the National Insurance Members of the Forces Regulations

14.—(1) With effect from 6th April 1970, but subject to paragraph (2) of this regulation, in Schedule 4 to the National Insurance (Members of the Forces) Regulations 1968**(b)** as amended**(c)** (statutory provisions applying to graduated contributions which are modified in their application to employment as a serving member of the forces), for the words in column (3) "may be calculated to the nearest penny, any amount of a halfpenny being disregarded", there shall be substituted the words "may be calculated to the nearest £0.01, any amount of £0.005 being disregarded"; and for the provisions set out in Schedules 3 (reduction of weekly rates of contributions of members of the forces), 5 and 5A (calculation of graduated contributions of members of the forces) of the said regulations there shall be substituted the provisions set out in Schedules 10, 11 and 12 to these regulations.

(2) From and including 6th April 1970 to the end of the transitional period the provisions of the said regulations, as amended by paragraph (1) of this regulation, may in any case be applied either as so amended or as in force immediately before 6th April 1970, or partly on one basis and partly on the other basis.

Amendments to the National Insurance Pensions, Existing Beneficiaries and Other Persons Transitional Regulations

15.—(1) In regulation 6 of the National Insurance (Pensions, Existing Beneficiaries and Other Persons) (Transitional) Regulations 1948**(d)** as amended**(e)** (conversion of old age pension under or by virtue of the Contributory Pensions Acts into retirement pension or contributory old age pension), in paragraph (3), for the reference to "one shilling" there shall be substituted a reference to "5 new pence".

(2) In regulation 9 of the said regulations (rates of converted pensions) for the references to "30 shillings" "£3 2s. 0d." and "£5 0s. 0d." there shall respectively be substituted references to "£1.50", "£3.10" and "£5.00".

(3) For the provisions set out in Schedules 1, 2 and 3 to the said regulations (special rates of benefit payable to or in respect of certain persons to whom the regulations apply) there shall be substituted the provisions set out in Schedules 13, 14 and 15 to these regulations.

Amendments to the National Insurance Pensions, Existing Contributors Transitional Regulations

16.—(1) In regulation 5 of the National Insurance (Pensions, Existing Contributors) (Transitional) Regulations 1948**(f)** as amended**(g)** (modification of conditions for retirement pensions for existing pensions contributors and their wives and widows), in paragraph (2), for the reference to "one shilling" there shall be substituted a reference to "5 new pence".

(a) S.I. 1970/46.   (b) S.I. 1968/827 (1968 II, p. 2228).
(c) S.I. 1969/1508 (1969 III, p. 4898).
(d) S.I. 1948/55 (Rev. XVI, p. 36: 1948 I, p. 2822).
(e) The relevant amending instruments are S.I. 1949/1151, 1951/1232, 1965/35, 1969/1361.
    (1949 I, p. 2744; 1951 I, p. 1457; 1965 I, p. 34; 1969 III, p. 4048).
(f) S.I. 1948/612 (Rev. XVI, p. 18: 1948 I, p. 2834).
(g) The relevant amending instruments are S.I. 1949/1150, 1964/2001, 1965/35, 1969/1361
    (1949 I, p. 2746; 1964 III, p. 5061; 1965 I, p. 34; 1969 III, p. 4048).

(2) In regulation 6 of the said regulations (widow's basic pension, etc., for certain widows not entitled to widow's benefit), in paragraph (2), for the reference to "30 shillings a week" there shall be substituted a reference to "£1.50 a week".

(3) For the provisions set out in Schedule 2 (reduced rates of widow's basic pension and contributory old age pension) there shall be substituted the provisions set out in Schedule 16 to these regulations.

(4) In the Fifth Schedule to the said regulations (reduction of rates of retirement pension of certain existing pensions contributors who attain pensionable age within five years from 5th July 1948 and the wives of such contributors), for the provisions contained in Tables 1, 2 and 3 set out in Part III of the said Schedule, there shall be substituted the provisions contained in the three tables set out in Schedule 17 to these regulations.

Amendments to the National Insurance Assessment of Graduated Contributions Regulations

17.—(1) Regulation 3 of the National Insurance (Assessment of Graduated Contributions) Regulations 1967(a) as amended(b) (calculation of graduated contributions), shall be amended in accordance with the provisions of paragraphs (2)—(4) of this regulation.

(2) For paragraphs (3) and (4) of the said regulation 3 there shall, with effect from 6th April 1970, be substituted the following paragraphs:—

"(3) Where, in the case of any payments to which the provisions of paragraph (1) or paragraph (2) of this regulation apply, it would, having regard to the means by which the net sums payable are to be calculated, be unduly difficult or inconvenient to calculate the graduated contributions payable in respect of those payments in accordance with those provisions, the amounts of those contributions may be calculated as if those provisions did not apply; and in any case in which the amount of any graduated contribution payable is not calculated in accordance with those provisions, whether by virtue of the foregoing provisions of this paragraph or because the graduated contribution period is not a week or a month or a multiple of either a week or a month, that amount shall be calculated to the nearest penny (any amount of a halfpenny being disregarded), or, where amounts are expressed in decimal form, to the nearest £0.01, any amount of £0.005 being disregarded:

Provided that 4¾ per cent., 4¼ per cent., 3¼ per cent., 2¾ per cent. and ½ per cent. of any amount (other than the amount of the graduated contribution), or of any equivalent amount, referred to in section 4(1)(c) of the Act, as amended by section 1(2) of the National Insurance Act 1969, or of the total of more than any one such amount or equivalent amount, may be calculated to the nearest penny (any amount of a halfpenny being disregarded), or, where amounts are expressed in decimal form, to the nearest £0.01, any amount of £0.005 being disregarded.

(4) In this regulation "appropriate Schedule" means—

(a) where amounts are not expressed in decimal form—

(i) Schedule 1 to these regulations in the case of an employment which is not a non-participating employment; and

(ii) Schedule 2 to these regulations in the case of an employment which is a non-participating employment; and

---

(a) S.I. 1967/844 (1967 II, p. 2513).
(b) The relevant amending instrument is S.I. 1969/1133 (1969 II, p. 3363).

(*b*) where amounts are expressed in decimal form—
    (i) Schedule 4 to these regulations in the case of an employment which is not a non-participating employment; and
    (ii) Schedule 5 to these regulations in the case of an employment which is a non-participating employment."

(3) After Schedule 3 to the said regulations there shall, with effect from 6th April 1970, be inserted the Schedules set out in Schedules 18 and 19 to these regulations.

(4) With effect from the end of the transitional period, Schedules 1 and 2 of the said regulations shall be revoked and for paragraphs (3) and (4) of regulation 3 of the said regulations, as amended by these regulations, there shall be substituted the following paragraphs:—

"(3) Where, in the case of any payments to which the provisions of paragraph (1) or paragraph (2) of this regulation apply, it would, having regard to the means by which the net sums payable are to be calculated, be unduly difficult or inconvenient to calculate the graduated contributions payable in respect of those payments in accordance with those provisions, the amounts of those contributions may be calculated as if those provisions did not apply; and in any case in which the amount of any graduated contribution payable is not calculated in accordance with those provisions, whether by virtue of the foregoing provisions of this paragraph or because the graduated contribution period is not a week or a month or a multiple of either a week or a month, that amount shall be calculated to the nearest £0.01, any amount of £0.005 being disregarded:

Provided that $4\frac{3}{4}$ per cent., $4\frac{1}{4}$ per cent., $3\frac{1}{4}$ per cent., $2\frac{3}{4}$ per cent. and $\frac{1}{2}$ per cent. of any amount (other than the amount of the graduated contribution), or of any equivalent amount, referred to in section $4(1)(c)$ of the Act, as amended by section 1(2) of the National Insurance Act 1969, or of the total of more than any one such amount or equivalent amount, may be calculated to the nearest £0.01, any amount of £0.005 being disregarded.

(4) In this regulation "appropriate Schedule" means Schedule 4 to these regulations in the case of an employment which is not a non-participating employment and means Schedule 5 to these regulations in the case of an employment which is a non-participating employment."

(5) In regulation 9 of the said regulations (annual maximum amount payable by way of graduated contributions), in head (*f*), for the references to "£43 15s. 8d." and "£43 5s. 8d." there shall respectively be substituted references to "£43.96" and "£43.46".

Amendments to the National Insurance Graduated Retirement Benefit and Consequential Provisions Regulations

18.—(1) In regulation 2 of the National Insurance (Graduated Retirement Benefit and Consequential Provisions) Regulations 1961(a) as amended(b) (single payment in satisfaction of right to graduated retirement benefit), for the reference to "sixpence" and for the references to "three shillings" there shall respectively be substituted a reference to "$2\frac{1}{2}$ new pence" and references to "15 new pence".

(2) For the provisions set out in the First Schedule to the said regulations there shall be substituted the provisions set out in Schedule 20 to these regulations.

    (a) S.I. 1961/557 (1961, I, p. 1228).
    (b) There is no amendment which relates expressly to the subject matter of these regulations.

Amendments to the National Insurance Non-participation Assurance of Equivalent Pension Benefits Regulations

19.—(1) In regulation 6A of the National Insurance (Non-participation—Assurance of Equivalent Pension Benefits) Regulations 1960(a) as amended(b) (calculation of equivalent pension benefits), after paragraph (4) thereof, there shall be added the following paragraph:—

"(5) Where under the foregoing provisions of this regulation the total amount of equivalent pension benefits is not a multiple of a new penny, that amount shall be rounded to the next new penny above."

(2) Regulation 21 of the said regulations is hereby revoked.

(3) For the provisions set out in Schedule 2 to the said regulations (minimum annual rates of pension required to constitute equivalent pension benefits) there shall be substituted the provisions set out in Schedule 21 to these regulations.

Amendment to the National Insurance Graduated Contributions and Non-participating Employments Miscellaneous Provisions Regulations

20. In regulation 4 of the National Insurance (Graduated Contributions and Non-participating Employments—Miscellaneous Provisions) Regulations 1960 (c) as amended(d) (calculation of excess graduated contributions), in head (c), for the reference to "7s. 8d." there shall be substituted a reference to "£0.38".

Amendment to the National Insurance Earnings-related Benefit Regulations

21. For the provisions set out in the Schedule to the National Insurance (Earnings-related Benefit) Regulations 1966(e) (calculation of earnings-related benefit), there shall be substituted the provisions set out in Schedule 22 to these regulations.

Amendments to the National Insurance Computation of Earnings Regulations

22. In regulation 4 of the National Insurance (Computation of Earnings) Regulations 1967(f) (payments to be disregarded in calculating earnings), in paragraph (1)(*a*), for the reference to "three shillings" there shall be substituted a reference to "15 new pence", and in regulation 5 of the said regulations (deductions to be made in calculating earnings), in head (*f*), likewise.

PART IV

AMENDMENTS TO THE INDUSTRIAL INJURIES ACT
AND STATUTORY INSTRUMENTS MADE THEREUNDER

Amendments to the Industrial Injuries Act

23.—(1) In section 19 of the Industrial Injuries Act (death benefit for widows), in subsection (3), as amended by section 2(1)(*c*) of the National Insurance Act 1967, for the reference to "one pound ten shillings" there shall be substituted a reference to "£1.50".

(2) In section 22 of the Industrial Injuries Act (death benefit for parents of deceased persons), in subsection (5)(*a*), for the reference to "fifteen shillings" there shall be substituted a reference to "75 new pence".

(a) S.I. 1960/1103 (1960 II, p. 2244).
(b) The relevant amending instruments are S.I. 1963/676, 1966/1048 (1963 I, p. 815; 1966 II, p. 2567).   (c) S.I. 1960/1210 (1960 II, p. 2234).
(d) The relevant amending instrument is S.I. 1966/1048 (1966 II, p. 2567).
(e) S.I. 1966/959 (1966 II, p. 2306).   (f) S.I. 1967/760 (1967 II, p. 2266).

(3) In section 23 of the Industrial Injuries Act (death benefit for relatives of deceased persons), in subsection (4)(*b*), for the reference to "one pound sixteen shillings" there shall be substituted a reference to "£1.80".

(4) In section 27 of the Industrial Injuries Act (administration of benefit), subsection (4) shall cease to have effect.

(5) For the provisions set out in Part I of Schedule 2 to the Industrial Injuries Act, as substituted by Schedule 4 to the 1969 Act (weekly rates of contributions payable by insured persons and employers), there shall be substituted the provisions set out in Schedule 23 to these regulations.

(6) For the provisions set out in Schedule 3 to the Industrial Injuries Act, as amended by Schedule 5 to the 1969 Act (rate or amount of benefit, etc.), there shall be substituted the provisions set out in Schedule 24 to these regulations.

Amendments to the National Insurance Industrial Injuries Benefit Regulations

24.—(1) In regulation 3 of the National Insurance (Industrial Injuries) (Benefit) Regulations 1964**(a)** as amended**(b)** (amount of disablement gratuities), in head (*b*), for the references to "a shilling" there shall be substituted references to "5 new pence".

(2) In regulation 4 of the said regulations (injury benefit payable to children of school age), in paragraph (2), for the references to "£4 10s. 0d." and "£1 11s. 0d." there shall respectively be substituted references to "£4.50" and "£1.55".

(3) In regulation 7 of the said regulations (increase of disablement pension for constant attendance), for the references to "£3 6s. 0d.", "£4 19s. 0d.", and "£6 12s. 0d." there shall respectively be substituted references to "£3.30", "£4.95" and "£6.60".

(4) In regulation 18 of the said regulations (widow's pension), for the references to "5 shillings" and "one pound ten shillings", there shall respectively be substituted references to "25 new pence" and "£1.50".

(5) In regulation 28 of the said regulations (provisions as to maintenance for purposes of death benefit), in head (3), for the reference to "5 shillings" there shall be substituted a reference to "25 new pence".

(6) In regulation 39 of the said regulations (adjustment of dependency benefit under the Act where personal benefit is payable), in paragraph (1), for the references to "26 shillings", there shall be substituted references to "£1.30".

(7) For the provisions set out in Schedule 3 (scale of disablement gratuities) and in Schedule 4 (rate of disablement pension payable in lieu of disablement gratuity in certain circumstances) to the said regulations there shall respectively be substituted the provisions set out in Schedules 25 and 26 to these regulations.

Amendment to the National Insurance Industrial Injuries Determination of Claims and Questions Regulations

25. In regulation 23 of the National Insurance (Industrial Injuries) (Determination of Claims and Questions) (No. 2) Regulations 1967**(c)** (adjustment of benefits), in paragraph (2)(*a*)(i), for the words "fractions of a penny being disregarded" there shall be substituted the words "fractions of a new penny being disregarded" and, in paragraph (2)(*a*)(ii), for the words "fractions

---

(a) S.I. 1964/504 (1964 I, p. 833).
(b) The relevant amending instruments are S.I. 1966/338, 1969/1168 (1966 I, p. 788; 1969 II, p. 3432).
(c) S.I. 1967/1571 (1967 III, p. 4362).

of a shilling being disregarded" there shall be substituted the words "fractions of 5 new pence being disregarded".

Amendment to the National Insurance Industrial Injuries Mariners Regulations

26. In regulation 6 of the National Insurance (Industrial Injuries) (Mariners) Regulations 1948**(a)** as amended**(b)** (contributions in respect of masters or members of the crew of ships or vessels other than home trade ships), for the words "in the case of a person over the age of 18, by one penny, and, in the case of a person under the age of 18, by one half-penny" there shall be substituted the words "in the case of a person over the age of 18, by £0.004 and, in the case of a person under the age of 18, by £0.002."

Amendment to the National Insurance Industrial Injuries Prescribed Diseases Regulations

27. In regulation 47 of the National Insurance (Industrial Injuries) (Prescribed Diseases) Regulations 1959**(c)** as amended**(d)** (fees for initial and periodical examinations), for the references to "six shillings", "nineteen shillings" and "one pound eleven shillings and sixpence", there shall respectively be substituted references to "30 new pence", "95 new pence" and "£1.57".

PART V

MISCELLANEOUS AMENDMENTS

Amendments to the Old Cases Act

28.—(1) In section 2 of the Old Cases Act (schemes for supplementing workmen's compensation), in subsection (6)(c) as amended by section 6(2) of the 1969 Act, for the reference to "three pounds one shilling" there shall be substituted a reference to "£3.05".

(2) In section 7 of the Old Cases Act (nature and amount of benefit under section 5 of that Act), in subsection (2)(b), as amended by section 6(2) of the 1969 Act, for the reference to "three pounds one shilling" there shall be substituted a reference to "£3.05".

Amendments to the Workmen's Compensation Supplementation Scheme

29.—(1) In Article 2 of the Workmen's Compensation (Supplementation) Scheme 1966**(e)**, as amended**(f)** (basic allowances under Scheme), in paragraph (3), for the references to "40s." there shall be substituted references to "£2.00".

(2) In Article 5 of the said Scheme (lesser incapacity allowances under Scheme), for the references to "one shilling", "40s." and "sixpence" there shall respectively be substituted references to "5 new pence", "£2.00" and "2½ new pence".

(3) In Article 10 of the said Scheme (allowances in respect of two or more different injuries or diseases), for the references to "40s.", "61s." and "20s." there shall respectively be substituted references to "£2.00", "£3.05" and "£1.00".

(4) For the provisions set out in Schedule 1 to the said Scheme (calculation of amount of lesser incapacity allowances under Scheme), there shall be substituted the provisions set out in Schedule 27 to these regulations.

(a) S.I. 1948/1471 (Rev. XVI, p. 432: 1948 I, p. 2990).
(b) The relevant amending instrument is S.I. 1957/2244 (1957 II, p. 1739).
(c) S.I. 1959/467 (1959 II, p. 1943).
(d) The relevant amending instrument is S.I. 1969/1195 (1969 II, p. 3529).
(e) S.I. 1966/165 (1966 I, p. 325).
(f) The relevant amending instrument is S.I. 1969/1195 (1969 II, p. 3529).

(5) In Schedule 2 to the said Scheme (provisions of the Industrial Injuries Act and of regulations made thereunder applicable (with the necessary modifications) to claims for and payment of allowances), the first entry (section 27(4), fractions of a penny to be disregarded) is hereby revoked.

Amendments to the Pneumoconiosis, Byssinosis and Miscellaneous Diseases Benefit Scheme

30.—(1) In Article 4 of the Pneumoconiosis, Byssinosis and Miscellaneous Diseases Benefit Scheme 1966(a) as amended(b) (allowances payable under the Scheme), in paragraph (1), for the references to "61s." and "20s." there shall respectively be substituted references to "£3.05" and "£1.00".

(2) In Schedule 3 to the said Scheme (provisions of the Industrial Injuries Act and of regulations made thereunder applicable (with the necessary modifications) to claims for and payment of allowances), the first entry (section 27(4), fractions of a penny to be disregarded) is hereby revoked.

Amendment to the National Health Service Contributions Act

31. For the provisions set out in the Schedule to the National Health Service Contributions Act 1965(c), as substituted by Schedule 2 to the Public Expenditure and Receipts Act 1968(d) (rates of national health service contributions), there shall be substituted the provisions set out in Schedule 28 to these regulations.

Amendment to the Redundancy Payments Act

32. In section 27 of the Redundancy Payments Act 1965(e) as amended(f) (contributions to redundancy payments fund), in subsection (2), for the reference to "one shilling and three pence" and "sevenpence", there shall respectively be substituted references to "£0.063" and "£0.029".

Part VI

Miscellaneous Transitional Provisions

Transitional provisions relating to benefit

33.—(1) Payment of any amount by way of benefit made during the transitional period shall be in the new currency.

(2) Where, before the appointed day, payment of an amount by way of benefit is made in respect of a period which commences before, but which ends on or after, that day, then the amount of that payment, in so far as it relates to a period throughout which (apart from any modifications made by these regulations) the rate of the benefit in question is the rate current immediately before the appointed day, shall be calculated by reference to the rate of that benefit current immediately before the appointed day.

(3) Where, on or after the appointed day, payment of an amount by way of benefit falls to be made to a person and the total weekly rate of benefit that would be payable to that person in respect of any week (whether falling before or after the appointed day) and comprised in any such payment would be of an amount which would not be a new penny or a multiple thereof, then, unless, as respects any period during which the person entitled to the weekly rate of benefit which would not be a new penny or a multiple thereof is absent from Great

---

(a) S.I. 1966/164 (1966 I, p. 303).
(b) The relevant amending instrument is S.I. 1969/1196 (1969 II, p. 3531).
(c) 1965 c. 54.   (d) 1968 c. 14.
(e) 1965 c. 62.   (f) S.I. 1968/1264 (1968 II, p. 3568).

Britain and is paid benefit in a currency other than the currency of the United Kingdom, the Secretary of State otherwise directs, the said weekly rate shall be rounded to the next new penny above.

(4) Where, during the transitional period, it is determined that there has been an overpayment of benefit in respect of a period commencing before the appointed day, then the amount of the overpayment in respect of that period, in respect of so much of it as is in shillings or pence, shall be the corresponding amount in the new currency calculated in accordance with the provisions of Schedule 29 to these regulations, which Schedule reproduces the provisions of Schedule 1 to the Decimal Currency Act 1969; and where, before the appointed day, it has been determined that there has been an overpayment of benefit and that overpayment has not been repaid, or repaid in full, before the appointed day, then on the appointed day that overpayment, or so much of it as has not been repaid, shall, in respect of so much of it as is in shillings or pence, be converted into the new currency in accordance with the provisions of the said Schedule 29.

(5) In this regulation the expression "benefit" means benefit under the National Insurance Act, the Industrial Injuries Act, the Old Cases Act, or a family allowance under the Family Allowances Act.

Transitional provisions relating to contributions

34.—(1) Subject to the provisions of paragraph (4) of this regulation, where, during the transitional period, an amount falls to be paid in respect of contributions (not being graduated contributions) payable in respect of a period before the appointed day, then the amount which falls to be paid, in so far as it relates to a period throughout which (apart from any modifications made by these regulations) the rate of the contributions in question is the rate current immediately before the appointed day, shall be calculated by reference to the rate of the contributions current on the appointed day.

(2) Subject to the provisions of paragraph (4) of this regulation, where, during the transitional period, an amount falls to be paid in respect of contributions (including graduated contributions) payable in respect of a period before the appointed day, being a period in relation to which the provisions of paragraph (1) of this regulation do not apply, that amount, in respect of so much of it as is in shillings or pence, shall be the corresponding amount in the new currency calculated in accordance with the provisions of Schedule 29 to these regulations.

(3) Where, during the transitional period, an amount is refunded in respect of contributions (including graduated contributions) paid in respect of a period before the appointed day, that amount, in respect of so much of it as is in shillings or pence, shall be the corresponding amount in the new currency calculated in accordance with the provisions of Schedule 29 to these regulations.

(4) With the consent of the Secretary of State, an employer who pays contributions (not being graduated contributions) under arrangements made by virtue of regulation 6(5)(a) of the National Insurance and Industrial Injuries (Collection of Contributions) Regulations 1948**(a)** as amended**(b)** (special arrangements relating to the time and manner of payment of contributions), may, in respect of an accounting period beginning before the appointed day and ending on or after that day but not later than 28th February 1971, account and pay for contributions either by reference to the appropriate old currency rate or by reference to the corresponding new currency rate, or partly by reference to the one and partly by reference to the other.

(a) S.I. 1948/1274 (Rev. XVI, p. 148: 1948 I, p. 3037).
(b) The amending Regulations are not relevant to the subject matter of these Regulations.

(5) For the purposes only of section 12 of the National Insurance Act (recovery by employer of insured person's flat-rate contributions) as it applies in relation to contributions under that Act, the Industrial Injuries Act and the National Health Service Contributions Act 1965, the amount of any deduction to be made may, for any period during the period from 6th April 1970 to the end of the transitional period or, if earlier, to the date as from which any relevant contribution rates are changed (otherwise than in accordance with these regulations), be calculated either by reference to the appropriate old currency rate or by reference to the corresponding new currency rate.

Transitional provisions relating to equivalent pension benefits, a payment in lieu of contributions and a refund of graduated contributions in certain cases.

35.—(1) Where equivalent pension benefits are assured or a payment in lieu of contributions is made on or after the appointed day, all requisite calculations shall be in accordance with the provisions of sections 57 and 58 of, and Schedule 11 paragraph 15 to, the National Insurance Act as amended by regulation 4(8), (9) and (13) of these regulations.

(2) The amount of a refund of graduated contributions made on or after the appointed day in respect of a period falling within the income tax year beginning on 6th April 1970, shall be calculated by reference to head (*c*) of regulation 4 of the National Insurance (Graduated Contributions and Non-participating Employments—Miscellaneous Provisions) Regulations 1960 as amended by regulation 20 of these regulations.

Signed by authority of the Secretary of State for Social Services.

David Ennals,
Department of Health and
Social Security.

22nd December 1969.

Joseph Harper,
E. G. Perry,
Two of the Lords Commissioners of
Her Majesty's Treasury.

1st January 1970.

Regulation 4(11)

SCHEDULE 1

Schedule substituted for Schedule 1 to the National Insurance Act 1965

RATES OF FLAT-RATE CONTRIBUTIONS

PART I

Employed Persons

Description of employed person	Weekly Rate of Contribution	
	Unless by virtue of a non-participating employment	If by virtue of a non-participating employment
1	2	3
	£	£
Men between the ages of 18 and 70 (other than men over the age of 65 who have retired from regular employment)—		
Earning remuneration at a weekly rate exceeding £6	0·676	0·796
Earning remuneration at a weekly rate of £6 or less	0·406	0·466
Women between the ages of 18 and 65 (other than women over the age of 60 who have retired from regular employment)—		
Earning remuneration at a weekly rate exceeding £6	0·592	0·672
Earning remuneration at a weekly rate of £6 or less	0·342	0·392
Boys under the age of 18	0·470	—
Girls under the age of 18	0·389	—

For the purposes of this Part and Part II of this Schedule a person shall be deemed to be earning remuneration at a weekly rate of £6 or less if, but only if, his remuneration does not include the provision of board and lodging by the employer and the rate of the remuneration neither exceeds, nor is deemed in accordance with regulations made under section 114(5) of this Act to exceed, £6 a week, and to be earning remuneration at a weekly rate exceeding £6 in any other case.

Part II

Employers

Description of employed person	Weekly Rate of Contribution	
	Unless by virtue of a non-participating employment	If by virtue of a non-participating employment
1	2	3
	£	£
Men over the age of 18—		
Earning remuneration at a weekly rate exceeding £6 or not being liable to pay a contribution as an employed person	0·754	0·874
Earning remuneration at a weekly rate of £6 or less and being liable to pay a contribution as an employed person	1·024	1·204
Women over the age of 18—		
Earning remuneration at a weekly rate exceeding £6 or not being liable to pay a contribution as an employed person	0·650	0·730
Earning remuneration at a weekly rate of £6 or less and being liable to pay a contribution as an employed person	0·900	1·010
Boys under the age of 18	0·516	—
Girls under the age of 18	0·420	—

For the purposes of this Part of this Schedule a person over pensionable age, not being an insured person, shall be treated as an employed person if he would be an insured person were he under pensionable age and would be an employed person were he an insured person.

Part III

Self-Employed Persons

Description of self-employed person	Weekly Rate of Contribution
1	2
	£
Men between the ages of 18 and 70 (other than men over the age of 65 who have retired from regular employment)	1·073
Women between the ages of 18 and 65 (other than women over the age of 60 who have retired from regular employment)	0·897
Boys under the age of 18	0·612
Girls under the age of 18	0·512

PART IV

Non-Employed Persons

Description of non-employed person 1	Weekly Rate of Contribution 2
	£
Men between the ages of 18 and 65	0·823
Women between the ages of 18 and 60	0·647
Boys under the age of 18	0·472
Girls under the age of 18	0·372

SCHEDULE 2   Regulation 4(11)

Schedule substituted for Schedule 3 to the National Insurance Act 1965

Rates of Periodical Benefits and of Increases for Dependants

1 Description of Benefit	2 Weekly rate	3 Increase for only, elder or eldest qualifying child	4 Increase for second qualifying child	5 Increase for each additional qualifying child	6 Increase for adult dependant (where payable)
	£	£	£	£	£
1. Unemployment or sickness benefit under s.19(2)—					
(a) in the case of a person over the age of 18, not being a married woman...	5·00	1·55	0·65	0·55	3·10
(b) in the case of a person under the age of 18, not being a married woman—					
(i) during any period during which that person is entitled to an increase of benefit in respect of a child or adult dependant...	5·00	1·55	0·65	0·55	3·10
(ii) during any other period	2.75	—	—	—	—
(c) in the case of a married woman over the age of 18-					
(i) during any period during which she is entitled to an increase of benefit in respect of her husband, or during which she is not residing with her husband nor is he contributing to her maintenance at not less than the relevant rate	5·00	1·55	0·65	0·55	3·10
(ii) during any other period	3·50	1·55	0·65	0·55	3·10

1	2	3	4	5	6
Description of Benefit	Weekly rate	Increase for only, elder or eldest qualifying child	Increase for second qualifying child	Increase for each additional qualifying child	Increase for adult dependant (where payable)
	£	£	£	£	£
1. Unemployment or sickness benefit under s.19(2)—cont. (d) in the case of a married woman under the age of 18—					
(i) during any period during which she is entitled to an increase of benefit in respect of her husband, or during which she is entitled to an increase of benefit in respect of a child or an adult dependant other than her husband and she is not residing with her husband nor is he contributing to her maintenance at not less than the relevant rate	5·00	1·55	0·65	0·55	3·10
(ii) during any other period during which she is entitled to an increase of benefit in respect of a child or adult dependant ...	3·50	1·55	0·65	0·55	3·10
(iii) during any other period	2·75	—			
2. Unemployment or sickness benefit at a weekly rate determined under s.19(3)	—	1·55	0·65	0·55	3·10
3. Maternity allowance	5·00	1·55	0·65	0·55	3·10
4. Widow's allowance	7·00	2·45	1·55	1·45	—
5. Widowed mother's allowance	5·00	2·45	1·55	1·45	—
6. Widow's pension	5·00	—	—	—	—
7. Guardian's allowance ...	2·45	—	—	—	—
8. Retirement pension— (a) where the pension is payable to a woman by virtue of her husband's insurance and he is alive	3·10	1·55	0·65	0·55	—
(b) in any other case ...	5·00	1·55	0·65	0·55	3·10
9. Child's special allowance ...	2·45	—	1·55	1·45	—

1. In paragraphs 1(c)(i) and 1(d)(i) of this Schedule "the relevant rate" means a weekly rate equal to the difference under this Schedule between the rates of benefit applying if the husband is, and if he is not, contributing to the wife's maintenance at not less than the relevant rate.

2. In paragraph 2 of this Schedule, column 6 shall have effect subject to section 43(3)(b) of this Act.

SCHEDULE 3   Regulation 4(11)

Schedule substituted for Schedule 4 to National Insurance Act 1965

Amounts of Grants

Description of Grant	Amount
	£
1. Maternity grant	25·00
2. Death grant, where the person in respect of whose death the grant is paid was at his death:—	
(a) under the age of 3	9·00
(b) between the ages of 3 and 6	15·00
(c) between the ages of 6 and 18	22·50
(d) over the age of 18:—	
(i) if on 5th July 1948 that person had attained the age of 55 in the case of a man or 50 in the case of a woman ...	15·00
(ii) in any other case	30·00

SCHEDULE 4   Regulation 6(2)

Schedule substituted for the Schedule to the National Insurance (Widow's Benefit and Retirement Pensions) Regulations

SCHEDULE   Regulation 7(2)

Showing Reduced Rates of Widow's Benefit and Retirement Pensions and of Increase of Retirement Pensions in respect of an Adult Dependant

1	2	3	4
	Full weekly rate of benefit applicable under Schedule 3 of the National Insurance Act 1965		
Yearly average of contributions paid or credited	£ 7·00	£ 5·00	£ 3·10
	Reduced rate at which benefit is payable		
	£	£	£
48—49	6·70	4·80	3·00
46—47	6·45	4·60	2·90
43—45	6·05	4·40	2·75
40—42	5·65	4·05	2·55
37—39	5·15	3·65	2·35
34—36	4·60	3·30	2·10
30—33	4·05	2·90	1·85
26—29	3·50	2·50	1·55
22—25	2·95	2·15	1·30
18—21	2·45	1·75	1·05
13—17	1·85	1·40	0·90

Regulation 7(2)   SCHEDULE 5

Schedule substituted for Schedule 2 to the National Insurance (Unemployment and Sickness Benefit) Regulations

Regulation 13(2)   SCHEDULE 2

Showing reduced rates of unemployment and sickness benefit and of increase of benefit in respect of adult dependants

(1)	(2)	(3)	(4)	(5)
Number of contributions paid or credited in the relevant contribution year	Full weekly rate of benefit applicable under Schedule 3 to the Act			
	£ 5·00	£ 3·50	£ 3·10	£ 2·75
	Reduced rate at which benefit is payable			
	£	£	£	£
48—49	4·80	3·45	3·00	2·65
46—47	4·60	3·35	2·90	2·55
43—45	4·40	3·15	2·75	2·45
40—42	4·05	2·95	2·55	2·30
37—39	3·65	2·65	2·35	2·10
34—36	3·30	2·35	2·10	1·90
30—33	2·90	2·10	1·85	1·70
26—29	2·50	1·75	1·55	1·40

SCHEDULE 6   Regulation 8

Schedule substituted for the First Schedule to the National Insurance (Death Grant)
Regulations

FIRST SCHEDULE   Regulation 10(2)

Showing reduced amount of death grant payable if the contribution conditions are not
fully satisfied

(1)	(2)	(3)	(4)	(5)	(6)
	and the age of deceased at death was				
	over 18				
Yearly average of contributions paid or credited	and, if a man was under 55 on 4th July 1948, or, if a woman was under 50 at that date	and, if a man was over 55 and under 65 on 4th July 1948, or, if a woman was over 50 and under 60 at that date	between 6 and 18	between 3 and 6	under 3
	Full amount of death grant payable under Schedule 4 of the National Insurance Act 1965				
	£30·00	£15·00	£22·50	£15·00	£9·00
	Reduced amount of death grant payable:—				
30—44	£22·50	£11·25	£16·87	£11·25	£6·75
13—29	£15·00	£7·50	£11·25	£7·50	£4·50

Regulation 13(5)   SCHEDULE 7

The following Schedule is, by regulation 13(5) of these Regulations, inserted in the National Insurance (Mariners) Regulations as Schedule 5 thereto

Regulation 18   SCHEDULE 4

Employment which is not a non-participating employment

PART I

Scale for pay period of a week or for a voyage period for which no or one weekly employer's contribution is payable

Amount of payment (1)	Amount of contribution (2)
£	£
9·01	0·01
9·25	0·02
9·50	0·04
10·00	0·06
10·50	0·08
11·00	0·11
11·50	0·13
12·00	0·15
12·50	0·18
13·00	0·20
13·50	0·23
14·00	0·25
14·50	0·27
15·00	0·30
15·50	0·32
16·00	0·34
16·50	0·37
17·00	0·39
17·50	0·42
18·00	0·44
19·00	0·48
20·00	0·51
21·00	0·54
22·00	0·57
23·00	0·61
24·00	0·64
25·00	0·67
26·00	0·70
27·00	0·74
28·00	0·77
29·00	0·80
30·00 or more	0·82

PART II

Scale for pay period of one month

Amount of payment (1)	Amount of contribution (2)
£	£
39·02	0·02
40·00	0·09
42·00	0·19
44·00	0·28
46·00	0·38
48·00	0·47
50·00	0·57
52·00	0·66
54·00	0·76
56·00	0·85
58·00	0·95
60·00	1·04
62·00	1·14
64·00	1·23
66·00	1·33
68·00	1·42
70·00	1·52
72·00	1·61
74·00	1·71
76·00	1·80
78·00	1·92
82·00	2·05
86·00	2·18
90·00	2·31
94·00	2·44
98·00	2·57
102·00	2·70
106·00	2·83
110·00	2·96
114·00	3·09
118·00	3·22
122·00	3·35
126·00	3·48
130·00 or more	3·54

Regulation 13(5)   SCHEDULE 8

The following Schedule is, by regulation 13(5) of these Regulations, inserted in the
National Insurance (Mariners) Regulations as Schedule 6 thereto

Regulation 18   SCHEDULE 5

Non-participating employment

PART I

Scale for pay period of a week or for a voyage period for which no or one weekly
employer's contribution is payable

Amount of payment (1)	Amount of contribution (2)
£	£
9·01	0·01
12·00	0·02
15·00	0·04
18·00	0·06
19·00	0·09
20·00	0·13
21·00	0·16
22·00	0·19
23·00	0·22
24·00	0·26
25·00	0·29
26·00	0·32
27·00	0·35
28·00	0·39
29·00	0·42
30·00 or more	0·43

PART II

Scale for pay period of one month

Amount of payment (1)	Amount of contribution (2)
£	£
39·01	0·01
40·00	0·03
50·00	0·08
60·00	0·13
70·00	0·17
78·00	0·26
82·00	0·39
86·00	0·52
90·00	0·65
94·00	0·78
98·00	0·91
102·00	1·04
106·00	1·17
110·00	1·30
114·00	1·43
118·00	1·56
122·00	1·69
126·00	1·82
130·00 or more	1·88

SCHEDULE 9   Regulation 13(9)

The following Schedule is, by regulation 13(9) of these Regulations, inserted in the National Insurance (Mariners) Regulations as Schedule 7 thereto

SCHEDULE 6   Regulation 20

Scale for separate payment of overtime

Amount of payment (1)	Amount of contribution	
	Employment which is not a non-participating employment (2)	Non-participating employment (3)
£	£	£
1	0·05	0·00
2	0·09	0·01
3	0·14	0·01
4	0·19	0·02
5	0·24	0·02
6	0·28	0·03
7	0·33	0·03
8	0·38	0·04
9 or more	0·43	0·04

Regulation 14(1)   SCHEDULE 10

Schedule substituted for Schedule 3 to the National Insurance (Members of the Forces) Regulations

Regulation 4   SCHEDULE 3

Reduction of weekly rates of contributions

Contributions payable otherwise than by virtue of a non-participating employment

Description of employed persons who are serving members of the forces	Reduction of weekly rate of contribution	
	Employed person	Employer
1	2	3
	£	£
Men over the age of 18	0·094	0·117
Women over the age of 18	0·077	0·083
Boys under the age of 18	0·059	0·069
Girls under the age of 18	0·048	0·043

Contributions payable by virtue of a non-participating employment

Description of employed persons who are serving members of the forces	Reduction of weekly rate of contribution	
	Employed person	Employer
1	2	3
	£	£
Men over the age of 18	0·104	0·107
Women over the age of 18	0·087	0·083

SCHEDULE 11

Regulation 14(1)

The Schedule substituted for Schedule 5 to the National Insurance (Members of the Forces) Regulations

SCHEDULE 5

Regulation 5

Employment which is not a non-participating employment

PART I

WEEKLY SCALE

Amount of payment	Amount of contribution
£	£
9·01	0·01
9·25	0·02
9·50	0·03
10·00	0·05
10·50	0·07
11·00	0·10
11·50	0·12
12·00	0·14
12·50	0·16
13·00	0·18
13·50	0·20
14·00	0·22
14·50	0·24
15·00	0·27
15·50	0·29
16·00	0·31
16·50	0·33
17·00	0·35
17·50	0·37
18·00	0·39
19·00	0·42
20·00	0·44
21·00	0·47
22·00	0·49
23·00	0·52
24·00	0·54
25·00	0·57
26·00	0·59
27·00	0·62
28·00	0·64
29·00	0·67
30·00 or more	0·68

PART II

MONTHLY SCALE

Amount of payment	Amount of contribution
£	£
39·02	0·02
40·00	0·08
42·00	0·17
44·00	0·25
46·00	0·34
48·00	0·42
50·00	0·51
52·00	0·59
54·00	0·68
56·00	0·76
58·00	0·85
60·00	0·93
62·00	1·02
64·00	1·10
66·00	1·19
68·00	1·27
70·00	1·36
72·00	1·44
74·00	1·53
76·00	1·61
78·00	1·71
82·00	1·81
86·00	1·91
90·00	2·01
94·00	2·11
98·00	2·21
102·00	2·31
106·00	2·41
110·00	2·51
114·00	2·61
118·00	2·71
122·00	2·81
126·00	2·91
130·00 or more	2·96

SCHEDULE 12 Regulation 14(1)

The Schedule substituted for Schedule 5A to the National Insurance (Members of the Forces) Regulations

SCHEDULE 5A

Non-participating employment

PART I

WEEKLY SCALE

Amount of payment	Amount of contribution
£	£
18·01	0·01
19·00	0·04
20·00	0·06
21·00	0·09
22·00	0·11
23·00	0·14
24·00	0·16
25·00	0·19
26·00	0·21
27·00	0·24
28·00	0·26
29·00	0·29
30·00 or more	0·30

PART II

MONTHLY SCALE

Amount of payment	Amount of contribution
£	£
78·05	0·05
82·00	0·15
86·00	0·25
90·00	0·35
94·00	0·45
98·00	0·55
102·00	0·65
106·00	0·75
110·00	0·85
114·00	0·95
118·00	1·05
122·00	1·15
126·00	1·25
130·00 or more	1·30

Regulation 15(3)   **SCHEDULE 13**

Schedule substituted for Schedule 1 to the National Insurance (Pensions, Existing Beneficiaries and Other Persons) (Transitional) Regulations.

Regulations 8 and 9   **SCHEDULE 1**

Table showing increased rates of widowed mother's allowance, widow's pension or retirement pension for a widow by virtue of husband's insurance and increased rates of widow's basic pension and contributory old age pension by virtue of husband's insurance in cases where benefit is payable at less than full rate.

Rate of widow's basic pension or contributory old age pension by virtue of husband's insurance and rate (apart from additional allowance or increase) of widow's pension immediately before the appointed day	Corresponding rate of widowed mother's allowance, widow's pension or retirement pension for a widow by virtue of husband's insurance	Corresponding increased rate of widow's basic pension or of contributory old age pension by virtue of husband's insurance
1	2	3
s. d.	£	£
9 0	4·50	1·35
8 0	4·00	1·20
7 0	3·50	1·05
6 0	3·00	0·90
5 0	2·50	0·75
4 0	—	0·60
3 0	—	0·45
2 0	—	0·30

SCHEDULE 14   Regulation 15(3)

Schedule substituted for Schedule 2 to the National Insurance (Pensions, Existing Beneficiaries and Other Persons) (Transitional) Regulations.

SCHEDULE 2   Regulation 10(1)

Table showing:—

(1) in column (1) the rates of retirement pension payable to existing old age pensioners other than those to whom the provisions of section 14(3) of the Contributory Pensions Act of 1939 applied; and

(2) in column (2) the corresponding rates of an increase of retirement pension in respect of an adult dependant of such a pensioner, or of a retirement pension payable to a wife of such a pensioner, by virtue of her husband's insurance if she had not attained pensionable age at the appointed day.

Rate of Retirement Pension 1	Corresponding rate of increase in respect of an adult dependant or of retirement pension for a wife 2
£	£
4·50	2·80
4·13	2·55
4·00	2·50
3·65	2·23
3·50	2·18
3·30	2·05
3·00	1·85
2·90	1·80
2·73	1·75
2·50	1·55
2·25	1·48
2·15	1·33
2·00	1·30
1·88	1·23
1·75	1·13
1·68	0·98
1·50	0·95
1·40	0·90
1·25	0·80
1·18	0·70
1·00	0·60
0·90	0·60
0·75	0·53
0·68	0·38
0·55	0·38
0·45	0·35
0·43	0·30

Regulation 15(3)   SCHEDULE 15

Schedule substituted for Schedule 3 to the National Insurance (Pensions, Existing Beneficiaries and Other Persons) (Transitional) Regulations.

Regulation 9(3)   SCHEDULE 3

Table showing rates of retirement pension payable under regulation 9(3) and corresponding increased rates under paragraph (*b*) of the proviso thereto.

Rate at which old age or widow's pension would, apart from the Increase of Pensions Regulations and but for the repeal of the Contributory Pensions Acts, have been payable	Rate of retirement pension (except in a case where column 4 applies) being the rate at which an old age or widow's pension would, but for the repeal of the Contributory Pensions Acts, have been payable	Corresponding increased rate of retirement pension	Rate of retirement pension for wife by virtue of husband's insurance, where he is alive, being the rate at which an old age pension would, but for the repeal of the Contributory Pensions Acts, have been payable	Corresponding increased rate of retirement pension
1	2	3	4	5
s. d.	£ s. d.	£	s. d.	£
9 0	1 3 0	4·50	14 0	2·80
8 3	1 1 0	4·13	12 6	2·55
8 0	1 0 0	4·00	12 0	2·50
7 3	18 6	3·65	11 0	2·23
7 0	18 0	3·50	11 0	2·18
6 6	16 6	3·30	10 0	2·05
6 0	15 0	3·00	9 0	1·85
5 9	14 6	2·90	9 0	1·80
5 6	14 0	2·73	8 6	1·75
5 0	13 0	2·50	8 0	1·55
4 6	11 6	2·25	7 0	1·48
4 3	11 0	2·15	6 6	1·33
4 0	10 0	2·00	6 0	1·30
3 9	9 6	1·88	6 0	1·23
3 6	9 0	1·75	5 6	1·13
3 3	8 6	1·68	5 0	0·98
3 0	8 0	1·50	5 0	0·95
2 9	7 0	1·40	4 6	0·90
2 6	6 6	1·25	4 0	0·80
2 3	6 0	1·18	3 6	0·70
2 0	5 0	1·00	3 0	0·60
1 9	4 6	0·90	3 0	0·60
1 6	4 0	0·75	2 6	0·53
1 3	3 6	0·68	2 0	0·38
1 0	3 0	0·55	2 0	0·38
9	2 0	0·45	1 6	0·35
6	1 6	0·43	1 0	0·30

SCHEDULE 16   Regulation 16(3)

Schedule substituted for Schedule 2 to the National Insurance (Pensions, Existing Contributors) (Transitional) Regulations

SCHEDULE 2   Regulation 6(3)

Showing reduced rates of widow's basic pension and contributory old age pension

Yearly average of contributions paid or credited 1	Reduced rate at which pension is payable 2
	£
48—49	1·43
46—47	1·35
43—45	1·28
40—42	1·20
37—39	1·13
34—36	0·98
30—33	0·90
26—29	0·75
22—25	0·60
18—21	0·53
13—17	0·38

SCHEDULE 17   Regulation 16(4)

Tables to be substituted for the 3 Tables in Part III of the Fifth Schedule to the National Insurance (Pensions, Existing Contributors) (Transitional) Regulations

TABLE 1

Rate at which an old age pension would, but for the repeal of the Contributory Pensions Acts, have been payable	Corresponding rate of retirement pension where pensionable age attained during period				
	From 5th July 1948 to 4th July 1949	From 5th July 1949 to 4th July 1950	From 5th July 1950 to 4th July 1951	From 5th July 1951 to 4th July 1952	From 5th July 1952 to 4th July 1953
1	2	3	4	5	6
£ s. d.	£	£	£	£	£
1 3 0	4·60	4·60	4·80	4·80	4·80
1 0 0	4·13	4·28	4·50	4·60	4·80
18 0	3·70	4·00	4·28	4·60	4·80
15 0	3·10	3·50	4·13	4·50	4·80
13 0	2·73	3·33	4·00	4·28	4·80
10 0	2·43	3·00	3·50	4·13	4·60
8 0	2·00	2·50	3·33	4·13	4·60
5 0	1·40	2·15	3·10	4·00	4·60
3 0	1·00	2·00	3·00	3·70	4·60
—	0·55	1·50	2·50	3·50	4·50

Table 2 showing:—
(1) in column (1) the yearly average of contributions paid by or credited to persons mentioned in Part I, and
(2) in the remaining columns the corresponding rates of retirement pensions for such persons on attaining pensionable age within five years from the appointed day.

Rates at which retirement pensions would have been payable in accordance with the Table 1 if the yearly average had been fifty:—

TABLE 2

| Yearly average of contributions paid or credited | Corresponding rates of retirement pensions:— | | | | | | | | | | | | | | | | | | | |
1	2	3	4	5	6	7	8	9	10	11	12	13	14	15	16	17	18	19	20	21
	£	£	£	£	£	£	£	£	£	£	£	£	£	£	£	£	£	£	£	£
	0·55	1·00	1·40	1·50	2·00	2·15	2·43	2·50	2·73	3·00	3·10	3·33	3·50	3·70	4·00	4·13	4·28	4·50	4·60	4·80
	£	£	£	£	£	£	£	£	£	£	£	£	£	£	£	£	£	£	£	£
48—49	0·53	0·90	1·25	1·43	1·88	2·03	2·25	2·45	2·68	2·90	3·03	3·30	3·45	3·65	3·75	4·00	4·13	4·28	4·50	4·60
46—47	0·53	0·90	1·25	1·43	1·75	2·00	2·15	2·43	2·50	2·73	3·00	3·10	3·33	3·50	3·70	3·75	4·00	4·13	4·28	4·50
43—45	0·53	0·90	1·18	1·40	1·68	1·88	2·03	2·25	2·45	2·68	2·73	3·00	3·10	3·33	3·50	3·65	3·75	4·00	4·13	4·28
40—42	0·53	0·75	1·03	1·25	1·50	1·75	2·00	2·03	2·25	2·45	2·50	2·68	2·90	3·03	3·30	3·33	3·50	3·65	3·70	4·00
37—39	0·45	0·68	1·00	1·18	1·43	1·50	1·75	1·88	2·03	2·25	2·25	2·43	2·50	2·73	3·00	3·03	3·30	3·33	3·45	3·65
34—36	0·45	0·68	0·90	1·00	1·25	1·40	1·50	1·68	1·88	2·03	2·03	2·15	2·43	2·45	2·68	2·73	2·90	3·00	3·03	3·30
30—33	0·43	0·55	0·75	0·90	1·18	1·25	1·40	1·43	1·50	1·75	1·75	1·88	2·03	2·15	2·43	2·45	2·50	2·68	2·73	2·90
26—29	0·43	0·53	0·68	0·75	1·00	1·03	1·18	1·25	1·40	1·43	1·43	1·50	1·75	1·88	2·00	2·03	2·15	2·25	2·43	2·45
22—25	0·43	0·45	0·55	0·68	0·75	0·90	1·00	1·03	1·18	1·18	1·25	1·40	1·43	1·50	1·68	1·75	1·88	1·88	2·00	2·03
18—21	0·30	0·43	0·53	0·55	0·68	0·75	0·75	0·90	1·00	1·00	1·03	1·18	1·18	1·25	1·40	1·43	1·50	1·50	1·68	1·68
13—17	0·30	0·43	0·45	0·45	0·53	0·55	0·55	0·68	0·75	0·75	0·90	1·00	1·00	1·00	1·03	1·03	1·18	1·18	1·25	1·25

TABLE 3

Table 3 showing:—

(1) in columns (1) and (3) the rates of retirement pension, apart from any increase, payable to existing pensions contributors by virtue of regulation 14; and

(2) in columns (2) and (4) the corresponding rates of an increase of retirement pension in respect of an adult dependant or of a retirement pension payable to a wife by virtue of her husband's insurance.

Rate of retirement pension	Corresponding rate of increase in respect of an adult dependant or of retirement pension for a wife	Rate of retirement pension	Corresponding rate of increase in respect of an adult dependant or of retirement pension for a wife
1	2	3	4
£	£	£	£
4·80	3·00	2·25	1·48
4·60	2·85	2·15	1·33
4·50	2·80	2·03	1·33
4·28	2·70	2·00	1·30
4·13	2·55	1·88	1·23
4·00	2·50	1·75	1·13
3·75	2·35	1·68	0·98
3·70	2·30	1·50	0·95
3·65	2·23	1·43	0·90
3·50	2·18	1·40	0·90
3·45	2·10	1·25	0·80
3·33	2·05	1·18	0·70
3·30	2·05	1·03	0·70
3·10	1·88	1·00	0·60
3·03	1·88	0·90	0·60
3·00	1·85	0·75	0·53
2·90	1·80	0·68	0·38
2·73	1·75	0·55	0·38
2·68	1·60	0·53	0·35
2·50	1·55	0·45	0·35
2·45	1·50	0·43	0·30
2·43	1·50	0·30	0·25

Regulation 17(3)   SCHEDULE 18

The following Schedule is, by Regulation 17(3) of these regulations, inserted in the National Insurance (Assessment of Graduated Contributions) Regulations as Schedule 4 thereto.

Regulation 3   SCHEDULE 4

Employment which is not a non-participating employment

PART I

WEEKLY SCALE

Amount of payment	Amount of contribution
£	£
9·01	0·01
9·25	0·02
9·50	0·04
10·00	0·06
10·50	0·08
11·00	0·11
11·50	0·13
12·00	0·15
12·50	0·18
13·00	0·20
13·50	0·23
14·00	0·25
14·50	0·27
15·00	0·30
15·50	0·32
16·00	0·34
16·50	0·37
17·00	0·39
17·50	0·42
18·00	0·44
19·00	0·48
20·00	0·51
21·00	0·54
22·00	0·57
23·00	0·61
24·00	0·64
25·00	0·67
26·00	0·70
27·00	0·74
28·00	0·77
29·00	0·80
30·00 or more	0·82

PART II

MONTHLY SCALE

Amount of payment	Amount of contribution
£	£
39·02	0·02
40·00	0·09
42·00	0·19
44·00	0·28
46·00	0·38
48·00	0·47
50·00	0·57
52·00	0·66
54·00	0·76
56·00	0·85
58·00	0·95
60·00	1·04
62·00	1·14
64·00	1·23
66·00	1·33
68·00	1·42
70·00	1·52
72·00	1·61
74·00	1·71
76·00	1·80
78·00	1·92
82·00	2·05
86·00	2·18
90·00	2·31
94·00	2·44
98·00	2·57
102·00	2·70
106·00	2·83
110·00	2·96
114·00	3·09
118·00	3·22
122·00	3·35
126·00	3·48
130·00 or more	3·54

Regulation 17(3)   SCHEDULE 19

The following Schedule is, by Regulation 17(3) of these regulations, inserted in the National Insurance (Assessment of Graduated Contributions) Regulations as Schedule 5 thereto.

Regulation 3   SCHEDULE 5

Non-participating employment

PART I

WEEKLY SCALE

Amount of payment	Amount of contribution
£	£
9·01	0·01
12·00	0·02
15·00	0·04
18·00	0·06
19·00	0·09
20·00	0·13
21·00	0·16
22·00	0·19
23·00	0·22
24·00	0·26
25·00	0·29
26·00	0·32
27·00	0·35
28·00	0·39
29·00	0·42
30 00 or more	0·43

PART II

MONTHLY SCALE

Amount of payment	Amount of contribution
£	£
39·01	0·01
40·00	0·03
50·00	0·08
60·00	0·13
70·00	0·17
78·00	0·26
82·00	0·39
86·00	0·52
90·00	0·65
94·00	0·78
98·00	0·91
102·00	1·04
106·00	1·17
110·00	1·30
114·00	1·43
118·00	1·56
122·00	1·69
126·00	1·82
130·00 or more	1·88

SCHEDULE 20　　　　Regulation 18(2)

Schedule substituted for the First Schedule to the National Insurance (Graduated Retirement Benefit and Consequential Provisions) Regulations

FIRST SCHEDULE　　　　Regulation 2

AMOUNTS OF SINGLE PAYMENTS PAYABLE IN SATISFACTION OF RIGHTS TO GRADUATED BENEFIT OF 2½ NEW PENCE A WEEK

MEN		WOMEN	
Age at appropriate date	Amount	Age at appropriate date	Amount
	£		£
65 and under 66	12·00	60 and under 61	17·00
66 ,, ,, 67	11·50	61 ,, ,, 62	16·50
67 ,, ,, 68	11·00	62 ,, ,, 63	16·00
68 ,, ,, 69	10·50	63 ,, ,, 64	15·50
69 ,, ,, 70	10·00	64 ,, ,, 65	15·00
70 ,, ,, 71	9·50	65 ,, ,, 66	14·50
71 ,, ,, 76	8·50	66 ,, ,, 71	13·00
76 ,, ,, 81	6·50	71 ,, ,, 76	10·00
81 or above	4·50	76 ,, ,, 81	7·50
		81 or above	5·00

SCHEDULE 21　　　　Regulation 19(3)

Schedule substituted for Schedule 2 to the National Insurance (Non-Participation-Assurance of Equivalent Pension Benefits) Regulations

SCHEDULE 2　　　　Regulation 6A

Minimum Annual Rates of Pension Required to Constitute Equivalent Pension Benefits.

PART I

(Applying to service on or after the 3rd April 1961, and not later than the 5th January 1964)

Annual rate of pension in the case of a man 1	Number of weeks in period of service 2	Annual rate of pension in the case of a woman 3
£		£
0·04$7/_{12}$	1	0·03$9/_{12}$
0·09$2/_{12}$	2	0·07$6/_{12}$
0·13$4/_{12}$	3	0·11$3/_{12}$
0·17$11/_{12}$	4	0·15
0·22$6/_{12}$	5	0·18$9/_{12}$
0·26$8/_{12}$	6	0·22$6/_{12}$
0·31$3/_{12}$	7	0·25$10/_{12}$

Annual rate of pension in the case of a man 1	Number of weeks in period of service 2	Annual rate of pension in the case of a woman 3
£		£
$0.35^5/_{12}$	8	$0.29^7/_{12}$
0.40	9	$0.33^4/_{12}$
$0.44^7/_{12}$	10	$0.37^1/_{12}$
$0.48^9/_{12}$	11	$0.40^{10}/_{12}$
$0.53^4/_{12}$	12	$0.44^7/_{12}$
$0.57^6/_{12}$	13	$0.47^{11}/_{12}$
$0.62^1/_{12}$	14	$0.51^8/_{12}$
$0.66^8/_{12}$	15	$0.55^5/_{12}$
$0.70^{10}/_{12}$	16	$0.59^2/_{12}$
$0.75^5/_{12}$	17	$0.62^{11}/_{12}$
$0.79^7/_{12}$	18	$0.66^8/_{12}$
$0.84^2/_{12}$	19	0.70
$0.88^9/_{12}$	20	$0.73^9/_{12}$
$0.92^{11}/_{12}$	21	$0.77^6/_{12}$
$0.97^6/_{12}$	22	$0.81^3/_{12}$
$1.02^1/_{12}$	23	0.85
$1.06^3/_{12}$	24	$0.88^9/_{12}$
$1.10^{10}/_{12}$	25	$0.92^6/_{12}$
1.15	26	$0.95^{10}/_{12}$
$1.19^7/_{12}$	27	$0.99^7/_{12}$
$1.24^2/_{12}$	28	$1.03^4/_{12}$
$1.28^4/_{12}$	29	$1.07^1/_{12}$
$1.32^{11}/_{12}$	30	$1.10^{10}/_{12}$
$1.37^1/_{12}$	31	$1.14^7/_{12}$
$1.41^8/_{12}$	32	$1.17^{11}/_{12}$
$1.46^3/_{12}$	33	$1.21^8/_{12}$
$1.50^5/_{12}$	34	$1.25^5/_{12}$

Annual rate of pension in the case of a man 1	Number of weeks in period of service 2	Annual rate of pension in the case of a woman 3
£		£
1·55	35	1·29^2/$_{12}$
1·59^2/$_{12}$	36	1·32^{11}/$_{12}$
1·63^9/$_{12}$	37	1·36^8/$_{12}$
1·68^4/$_{12}$	38	1·40
1·72^6/$_{12}$	39	1·43^9/$_{12}$
1·77^1/$_{12}$	40	1·47^6/$_{12}$
1·81^8/$_{12}$	41	1·51^3/$_{12}$
1·85^{10}/$_{12}$	42	1·55
1·90^5/$_{12}$	43	1·58^9/$_{12}$
1·94^7/$_{12}$	44	1·62^6/$_{12}$
1·99^2/$_{12}$	45	1·65^{10}/$_{12}$
2·03^9/$_{12}$	46	1·69^7/$_{12}$
2·07^{11}/$_{12}$	47	1·73^4/$_{12}$
2·12^6/$_{12}$	48	1·77^1/$_{12}$
2·16^8/$_{12}$	49	1·80^{10}/$_{12}$
2·21^3/$_{12}$	50	1·84^7/$_{12}$
2·25^{10}/$_{12}$	51	1·87^{11}/$_{12}$
2·30	52	1·91^8/$_{12}$
2·34^7/$_{12}$	53	1·95^5/$_{12}$
2·38^9/$_{12}$	54	1·99^2/$_{12}$
2·43^4/$_{12}$	55	2·02^{11}/$_{12}$
2·47^{11}/$_{12}$	56	2·06^8/$_{12}$
2·52^1/$_{12}$	57	2·10
2·56^8/$_{12}$	58	2·13^9/$_{12}$
2·60^{10}/$_{12}$	59	2·17^6/$_{12}$
2·65^5/$_{12}$	60	2·21^3/$_{12}$
2·70	61	2·25

Annual rate of pension in the case of a man 1	Number of weeks in period of service 2	Annual rate of pension in the case of a woman 3
£		£
$2\cdot74^2/_{12}$	62	$2\cdot28^9/_{12}$
$2\cdot78^9/_{12}$	63	$2\cdot32^6/_{12}$
$2\cdot83^4/_{12}$	64	$2\cdot35^{10}/_{12}$
$2\cdot87^6/_{12}$	65	$2\cdot39^7/_{12}$
$2\cdot92^1/_{12}$	66	$2\cdot43^4/_{12}$
$2\cdot96^3/_{12}$	67	$2\cdot47^1/_{12}$
$3\cdot00^{10}/_{12}$	68	$2\cdot50^{10}/_{12}$
$3\cdot05^5/_{12}$	69	$2\cdot54^7/_{12}$
$3\cdot09^7/_{12}$	70	$2\cdot57^{11}/_{12}$
$3\cdot14^2/_{12}$	71	$2\cdot61^8/_{12}$
$3\cdot18^4/_{12}$	72	$2\cdot65^5/_{12}$
$3\cdot22^{11}/_{12}$	73	$2\cdot69^2/_{12}$
$3\cdot27^6/_{12}$	74	$2\cdot72^{11}/_{12}$
$3\cdot31^8/_{12}$	75	$2\cdot76^8/_{12}$
$3\cdot36^3/_{12}$	76	$2\cdot80$
$3\cdot40^5/_{12}$	77	$2\cdot83^9/_{12}$
$3\cdot45$	78	$2\cdot87^6/_{12}$
$3\cdot49^7/_{12}$	79	$2\cdot91^3/_{12}$
$3\cdot53^9/_{12}$	80	$2\cdot95$
$3\cdot58^4/_{12}$	81	$2\cdot98^9/_{12}$
$3\cdot62^{11}/_{12}$	82	$3\cdot02^6/_{12}$
$3\cdot67^1/_{12}$	83	$3\cdot05^{10}/_{12}$
$3\cdot71^8/_{12}$	84	$3\cdot09^7/_{12}$
$3\cdot75^{10}/_{12}$	85	$3\cdot13^4/_{12}$
$3\cdot80^5/_{12}$	86	$3\cdot17^1/_{12}$
$3\cdot85$	87	$3\cdot20^{10}/_{12}$
$3\cdot89^2/_{12}$	88	$3\cdot24^7/_{12}$

Annual rate of pension in the case of a man 1	Number of weeks in period of service 2	Annual rate of pension in the case of a woman 3
£		£
$3 \cdot 93^{9}/_{12}$	89	$3 \cdot 27^{11}/_{12}$
$3 \cdot 97^{11}/_{12}$	90	$3 \cdot 31^{8}/_{12}$
$4 \cdot 02^{6}/_{12}$	91	$3 \cdot 35^{5}/_{12}$
$4 \cdot 07^{1}/_{12}$	92	$3 \cdot 39^{2}/_{12}$
$4 \cdot 11^{3}/_{12}$	93	$3 \cdot 42^{11}/_{12}$
$4 \cdot 15^{10}/_{12}$	94	$3 \cdot 46^{8}/_{12}$
$4 \cdot 20$	95	$3 \cdot 50$
$4 \cdot 24^{7}/_{12}$	96	$3 \cdot 53^{9}/_{12}$
$4 \cdot 29^{2}/_{12}$	97	$3 \cdot 57^{6}/_{12}$
$4 \cdot 33^{4}/_{12}$	98	$3 \cdot 61^{3}/_{12}$
$4 \cdot 37^{11}/_{12}$	99	$3 \cdot 65$
$4 \cdot 42^{1}/_{12}$	100	$3 \cdot 68^{9}/_{12}$
$4 \cdot 46^{8}/_{12}$	101	$3 \cdot 72^{6}/_{12}$
$4 \cdot 51^{3}/_{12}$	102	$3 \cdot 75^{10}/_{12}$
$4 \cdot 55^{5}/_{12}$	103	$3 \cdot 79^{7}/_{12}$
$4 \cdot 60$	104	$3 \cdot 83^{4}/_{12}$
$4 \cdot 64^{7}/_{12}$	105	$3 \cdot 87^{1}/_{12}$
$4 \cdot 68^{9}/_{12}$	106	$3 \cdot 90^{10}/_{12}$
$4 \cdot 73^{4}/_{12}$	107	$3 \cdot 94^{7}/_{12}$
$4 \cdot 77^{6}/_{12}$	108	$3 \cdot 97^{11}/_{12}$
$4 \cdot 82^{1}/_{12}$	109	$4 \cdot 01^{8}/_{12}$
$4 \cdot 86^{8}/_{12}$	110	$4 \cdot 05^{5}/_{12}$
$4 \cdot 90^{10}/_{12}$	111	$4 \cdot 09^{2}/_{12}$
$4 \cdot 95^{5}/_{12}$	112	$4 \cdot 12^{11}/_{12}$
$4 \cdot 99^{7}/_{12}$	113	$4 \cdot 16^{8}/_{12}$
$5 \cdot 04^{2}/_{12}$	114	$4 \cdot 20$
$5 \cdot 08^{9}/_{12}$	115	$4 \cdot 23^{9}/_{12}$

Annual rate of pension in the case of a man 1	Number of weeks in period of service 2	Annual rate of pension in the case of a woman 3
£		£
$5 \cdot 12^{11}/_{12}$	116	$4 \cdot 27^{6}/_{12}$
$5 \cdot 17^{6}/_{12}$	117	$4 \cdot 31^{3}/_{12}$
$5 \cdot 21^{8}/_{12}$	118	$4 \cdot 35$
$5 \cdot 26^{3}/_{12}$	119	$4 \cdot 38^{9}/_{12}$
$5 \cdot 30^{10}/_{12}$	120	$4 \cdot 42^{1}/_{12}$
$5 \cdot 35$	121	$4 \cdot 45^{10}/_{12}$
$5 \cdot 39^{7}/_{12}$	122	$4 \cdot 49^{7}/_{12}$
$5 \cdot 44^{2}/_{12}$	123	$4 \cdot 53^{4}/_{12}$
$5 \cdot 48^{4}/_{12}$	124	$4 \cdot 57^{1}/_{12}$
$5 \cdot 52^{11}/_{12}$	125	$4 \cdot 60^{10}/_{12}$
$5 \cdot 57^{1}/_{12}$	126	$4 \cdot 64^{7}/_{12}$
$5 \cdot 61^{8}/_{12}$	127	$4 \cdot 67^{11}/_{12}$
$5 \cdot 66^{3}/_{12}$	128	$4 \cdot 71^{8}/_{12}$
$5 \cdot 70^{5}/_{12}$	129	$4 \cdot 75^{5}/_{12}$
$5 \cdot 75$	130	$4 \cdot 79^{2}/_{12}$
$5 \cdot 79^{2}/_{12}$	131	$4 \cdot 82^{11}/_{12}$
$5 \cdot 83^{9}/_{12}$	132	$4 \cdot 86^{8}/_{12}$
$5 \cdot 88^{4}/_{12}$	133	$4 \cdot 90$
$5 \cdot 92^{6}/_{12}$	134	$4 \cdot 93^{9}/_{12}$
$5 \cdot 97^{1}/_{12}$	135	$4 \cdot 97^{6}/_{12}$
$6 \cdot 01^{3}/_{12}$	136	$5 \cdot 01^{3}/_{12}$
$6 \cdot 05^{10}/_{12}$	137	$5 \cdot 05$
$6 \cdot 10^{5}/_{12}$	138	$5 \cdot 08^{9}/_{12}$
$6 \cdot 14^{7}/_{12}$	139	$5 \cdot 12^{1}/_{12}$
$6 \cdot 19^{2}/_{12}$	140	$5 \cdot 15^{10}/_{12}$
$6 \cdot 23^{4}/_{12}$	141	$5 \cdot 19^{7}/_{12}$
$6 \cdot 27^{11}/_{12}$	142	$5 \cdot 23^{4}/_{12}$

Annual rate of pension in the case of a man 1	Number of weeks in period of service 2	Annual rate of pension in the case of a woman 3
£		£
$6\cdot32^6/_{12}$	143	$5\cdot27^1/_{12}$
$6\cdot36^8/_{12}$	144	$5\cdot30^{10}/_{12}$

PART II

(Applying to service on or after the 6th January 1964)

Annual rate of pension in the case of a man 1	Number of weeks in period of service 2	Annual rate of pension in the case of a woman 3
£		£
$0\cdot07^1/_{12}$	1	$0\cdot05^{10}/_{12}$
$0\cdot13^9/_{12}$	2	$0\cdot11^3/_{12}$
$0\cdot20^5/_{12}$	3	$0\cdot17^1/_{12}$
$0\cdot27^1/_{12}$	4	$0\cdot22^6/_{12}$
$0\cdot33^9/_{12}$	5	$0\cdot27^{11}/_{12}$
$0\cdot40^5/_{12}$	6	$0\cdot33^9/_{12}$
$0\cdot47^1/_{12}$	7	$0\cdot39^2/_{12}$
$0\cdot53^9/_{12}$	8	$0\cdot44^7/_{12}$
$0\cdot60^5/_{12}$	9	$0\cdot50^5/_{12}$
$0\cdot67^1/_{12}$	10	$0\cdot55^{10}/_{12}$
$0\cdot73^9/_{12}$	11	$0\cdot61^3/_{12}$
$0\cdot80^5/_{12}$	12	$0\cdot67^1/_{12}$
$0\cdot87^1/_{12}$	13	$0\cdot72^6/_{12}$
$0\cdot93^9/_{12}$	14	$0\cdot77^{11}/_{12}$
$1\cdot00^5/_{12}$	15	$0\cdot83^9/_{12}$
$1\cdot07^1/_{12}$	16	$0\cdot89^2/_{12}$
$1\cdot13^9/_{12}$	17	$0\cdot94^7/_{12}$
$1\cdot20^5/_{12}$	18	$1\cdot00^5/_{12}$

Annual rate of pension in the case of a man 1	Number of weeks in period of service 2	Annual rate of pension in the case of a woman 3
£		£
$1 \cdot 27^{1}/_{12}$	19	$1 \cdot 05^{10}/_{12}$
$1 \cdot 33^{9}/_{12}$	20	$1 \cdot 11^{3}/_{12}$
$1 \cdot 40^{5}/_{12}$	21	$1 \cdot 17^{1}/_{12}$
$1 \cdot 47^{1}/_{12}$	22	$1 \cdot 22^{6}/_{12}$
$1 \cdot 53^{9}/_{12}$	23	$1 \cdot 27^{11}/_{12}$
$1 \cdot 60^{5}/_{12}$	24	$1 \cdot 33^{9}/_{12}$
$1 \cdot 67^{1}/_{12}$	25	$1 \cdot 39^{2}/_{12}$
$1 \cdot 73^{9}/_{12}$	26	$1 \cdot 44^{7}/_{12}$
$1 \cdot 80^{5}/_{12}$	27	$1 \cdot 50^{5}/_{12}$
$1 \cdot 87^{1}/_{12}$	28	$1 \cdot 55^{10}/_{12}$
$1 \cdot 93^{9}/_{12}$	29	$1 \cdot 61^{3}/_{12}$
$2 \cdot 00^{5}/_{12}$	30	$1 \cdot 67^{1}/_{12}$
$2 \cdot 07^{1}/_{12}$	31	$1 \cdot 72^{6}/_{12}$
$2 \cdot 13^{9}/_{12}$	32	$1 \cdot 77^{11}/_{12}$
$2 \cdot 20^{5}/_{12}$	33	$1 \cdot 83^{9}/_{12}$
$2 \cdot 27^{1}/_{12}$	34	$1 \cdot 89^{2}/_{12}$
$2 \cdot 33^{9}/_{12}$	35	$1 \cdot 94^{7}/_{12}$
$2 \cdot 40^{5}/_{12}$	36	$2 \cdot 00^{5}/_{12}$
$2 \cdot 47^{1}/_{12}$	37	$2 \cdot 05^{10}/_{12}$
$2 \cdot 53^{9}/_{12}$	38	$2 \cdot 11^{3}/_{12}$
$2 \cdot 60^{5}/_{12}$	39	$2 \cdot 17^{1}/_{12}$
$2 \cdot 67^{1}/_{12}$	40	$2 \cdot 22^{6}/_{12}$
$2 \cdot 73^{9}/_{12}$	41	$2 \cdot 27^{11}/_{12}$
$2 \cdot 80^{5}/_{12}$	42	$2 \cdot 33^{9}/_{12}$
$2 \cdot 87^{1}/_{12}$	43	$2 \cdot 39^{2}/_{12}$
$2 \cdot 93^{9}/_{12}$	44	$2 \cdot 44^{7}/_{12}$
$3 \cdot 00^{5}/_{12}$	45	$2 \cdot 50^{5}/_{12}$

Annual rate of pension in the case of a man 1	Number of weeks in period of service 2	Annual rate of pension in the case of a woman 3
£		£
$3·07^1/_{12}$	46	$2·55^{10}/_{12}$
$3·13^9/_{12}$	47	$2·61^3/_{12}$
$3·20^5/_{12}$	48	$2·67^1/_{12}$
$3·27^1/_{12}$	49	$2·72^6/_{12}$
$3·33^9/_{12}$	50	$2·77^{11}/_{12}$
$3·40^5/_{12}$	51	$2·83^9/_{12}$
$3·47^1/_{12}$	52	$2·89^2/_{12}$
$3·53^9/_{12}$	53	$2·94^7/_{12}$
$3·60^5/_{12}$	54	$3·00^5/_{12}$
$3·67^1/_{12}$	55	$3·05^{10}/_{12}$
$3·73^9/_{12}$	56	$3·11^3/_{12}$
$3·80^5/_{12}$	57	$3·17^1/_{12}$
$3·87^1/_{12}$	58	$3·22^6/_{12}$
$3·93^9/_{12}$	59	$3·27^{11}/_{12}$
$4·00^5/_{12}$	60	$3·33^9/_{12}$
$4·07^1/_{12}$	61	$3·39^2/_{12}$
$4·13^9/_{12}$	62	$3·44^7/_{12}$
$4·20^5/_{12}$	63	$3·50^5/_{12}$
$4·27^1/_{12}$	64	$3·55^{10}/_{12}$
$4·33^9/_{12}$	65	$3·61^3/_{12}$
$4·40^5/_{12}$	66	$3·67^1/_{12}$
$4·47^1/_{12}$	67	$3·72^6/_{12}$
$4·53^9/_{12}$	68	$3·78^4/_{12}$
$4·60^5/_{12}$	69	$3·83^9/_{12}$
$4·67^1/_{12}$	70	$3·89^2/_{12}$
$4·73^9/_{12}$	71	$3·95$
$4·80^5/_{12}$	72	$4·00^5/_{12}$

Annual rate of pension in the case of a man 1	Number of weeks in period of service 2	Annual rate of pension in the case of a woman 3
£		£
$4 \cdot 87^1/_{12}$	73	$4 \cdot 05^{10}/_{12}$
$4 \cdot 93^9/_{12}$	74	$4 \cdot 11^8/_{12}$
$5 \cdot 00^5/_{12}$	75	$4 \cdot 17^1/_{12}$
$5 \cdot 07^1/_{12}$	76	$4 \cdot 22^6/_{12}$
$5 \cdot 13^9/_{12}$	77	$4 \cdot 28^4/_{12}$
$5 \cdot 20^5/_{12}$	78	$4 \cdot 33^9/_{12}$
$5 \cdot 27^1/_{12}$	79	$4 \cdot 39^2/_{12}$
$5 \cdot 33^9/_{12}$	80	$4 \cdot 45$
$5 \cdot 40^5/_{12}$	81	$4 \cdot 50^5/_{12}$
$5 \cdot 47^1/_{12}$	82	$4 \cdot 55^{10}/_{12}$
$5 \cdot 53^9/_{12}$	83	$4 \cdot 61^8/_{12}$
$5 \cdot 60^5/_{12}$	84	$4 \cdot 67^1/_{12}$
$5 \cdot 67^1/_{12}$	85	$4 \cdot 72^6/_{12}$
$5 \cdot 73^9/_{12}$	86	$4 \cdot 78^4/_{12}$
$5 \cdot 80^5/_{12}$	87	$4 \cdot 83^9/_{12}$
$5 \cdot 87^1/_{12}$	88	$4 \cdot 89^2/_{12}$
$5 \cdot 93^9/_{12}$	89	$4 \cdot 95$
$6 \cdot 00^5/_{12}$	90	$5 \cdot 00^5/_{12}$
$6 \cdot 07^1/_{12}$	91	$5 \cdot 05^{10}/_{12}$
$6 \cdot 13^9/_{12}$	92	$5 \cdot 11^8/_{12}$
$6 \cdot 20^5/_{12}$	93	$5 \cdot 17^1/_{12}$
$6 \cdot 27^1/_{12}$	94	$5 \cdot 22^6/_{12}$
$6 \cdot 33^9/_{12}$	95	$5 \cdot 28^4/_{12}$
$6 \cdot 40^5/_{12}$	96	$5 \cdot 33^9/_{12}$
$6 \cdot 47^1/_{12}$	97	$5 \cdot 39^2/_{12}$
$6 \cdot 53^9/_{12}$	98	$5 \cdot 45$
$6 \cdot 60^5/_{12}$	99	$5 \cdot 50^5/_{12}$

Annual rate of pension in the case of a man 1	Number of weeks in period of service 2	Annual rate of pension in the case of a woman 3
£		£
$6.67^1/_{12}$	100	$5.55^{10}/_{12}$
$6.73^9/_{12}$	101	$5.61^8/_{12}$
$6.80^5/_{12}$	102	$5.67^1/_{12}$
$6.87^1/_{12}$	103	$5.72^6/_{12}$
$6.93^9/_{12}$	104	$5.78^4/_{12}$
$7.00^5/_{12}$	105	$5.83^9/_{12}$
$7.07^1/_{12}$	106	$5.89^2/_{12}$
$7.13^9/_{12}$	107	5.95
$7.20^5/_{12}$	108	$6.00^5/_{12}$
$7.27^1/_{12}$	109	$6.05^{10}/_{12}$
$7.33^9/_{12}$	110	$6.11^8/_{12}$
$7.40^5/_{12}$	111	$6.17^1/_{12}$
$7.47^1/_{12}$	112	$6.22^6/_{12}$
$7.53^9/_{12}$	113	$6.28^4/_{12}$
$7.60^5/_{12}$	114	$6.33^9/_{12}$
$7.67^1/_{12}$	115	$6.39^2/_{12}$
$7.73^9/_{12}$	116	6.45
$7.80^5/_{12}$	117	$6.50^5/_{12}$
$7.87^1/_{12}$	118	$6.55^{10}/_{12}$
$7.93^9/_{12}$	119	$6.61^8/_{12}$
$8.00^5/_{12}$	120	$6.67^1/_{12}$
$8.07^1/_{12}$	121	$6.72^6/_{12}$
$8.13^9/_{12}$	122	$6.78^4/_{12}$
$8.20^5/_{12}$	123	$6.83^9/_{12}$
$8.27^1/_{12}$	124	$6.89^2/_{12}$
$8.33^9/_{12}$	125	6.95
$8.40^5/_{12}$	126	$7.00^5/_{12}$

Annual rate of pension in the case of a man 1	Number of weeks in period of service 2	Annual rate of pension in the case of a woman 3
£		£
$8 \cdot 47^{1}/_{12}$	127	$7 \cdot 05^{10}/_{12}$
$8 \cdot 53^{9}/_{12}$	128	$7 \cdot 11^{8}/_{12}$
$8 \cdot 60^{5}/_{12}$	129	$7 \cdot 17^{1}/_{12}$
$8 \cdot 67^{1}/_{12}$	130	$7 \cdot 22^{6}/_{12}$
$8 \cdot 73^{9}/_{12}$	131	$7 \cdot 28^{4}/_{12}$
$8 \cdot 80^{5}/_{12}$	132	$7 \cdot 33^{9}/_{12}$
$8 \cdot 87^{1}/_{12}$	133	$7 \cdot 39^{7}/_{12}$
$8 \cdot 93^{9}/_{12}$	134	$7 \cdot 45$
$9 \cdot 00^{5}/_{12}$	135	$7 \cdot 50^{5}/_{12}$
$9 \cdot 07^{1}/_{12}$	136	$7 \cdot 56^{3}/_{12}$
$9 \cdot 13^{9}/_{12}$	137	$7 \cdot 61^{8}/_{12}$
$9 \cdot 20^{5}/_{12}$	138	$7 \cdot 67^{1}/_{12}$
$9 \cdot 27^{1}/_{12}$	139	$7 \cdot 72^{11}/_{12}$
$9 \cdot 33^{9}/_{12}$	140	$7 \cdot 78^{4}/_{12}$
$9 \cdot 40^{5}/_{12}$	141	$7 \cdot 83^{9}/_{12}$
$9 \cdot 47^{1}/_{12}$	142	$7 \cdot 89^{7}/_{12}$
$9 \cdot 53^{9}/_{12}$	143	$7 \cdot 95$
$9 \cdot 60^{5}/_{12}$	144	$8 \cdot 00^{5}/_{12}$
$9 \cdot 67^{1}/_{12}$	145	$8 \cdot 06^{3}/_{12}$
$9 \cdot 73^{9}/_{12}$	146	$8 \cdot 11^{8}/_{12}$
$9 \cdot 80^{5}/_{12}$	147	$8 \cdot 17^{1}/_{12}$
$9 \cdot 87^{1}/_{12}$	148	$8 \cdot 22^{11}/_{12}$
$9 \cdot 93^{9}/_{12}$	149	$8 \cdot 28^{4}/_{12}$
$10 \cdot 00^{5}/_{12}$	150	$8 \cdot 33^{9}/_{12}$
$10 \cdot 07^{1}/_{12}$	151	$8 \cdot 39^{7}/_{12}$
$10 \cdot 13^{9}/_{12}$	152	$8 \cdot 45$
$10 \cdot 20^{5}/_{12}$	153	$8 \cdot 50^{5}/_{12}$

Annual rate of pension in the case of a man 1	Number of weeks in period of service 2	Annual rate of pension in the case of a woman 3
£		£
10·27¹/₁₂	154	8·56³/₁₂
10·33⁹/₁₂	155	8·61⁸/₁₂
10·40⁵/₁₂	156	8·67¹/₁₂
10·47¹/₁₂	157	8·72¹¹/₁₂
10·53⁹/₁₂	158	8·78⁴/₁₂
10·60⁵/₁₂	159	8·83⁹/₁₂
10·67¹/₁₂	160	8·89⁷/₁₂
10·73⁹/₁₂	161	8·95
10·80⁵/₁₂	162	9·00⁵/₁₂
10·87¹/₁₂	163	9·06³/₁₂
10·93⁹/₁₂	164	9·11⁸/₁₂
11·00⁵/₁₂	165	9·17¹/₁₂
11·07¹/₁₂	166	9·22¹¹/₁₂
11·13⁹/₁₂	167	9·28⁴/₁₂
11·20⁵/₁₂	168	9·33⁹/₁₂
11·27¹/₁₂	169	9·39⁷/₁₂
11·33⁹/₁₂	170	9·45
11·40⁵/₁₂	171	9·50⁵/₁₂
11·47¹/₁₂	172	9·56³/₁₂
11·53⁹/₁₂	173	9·61⁸/₁₂
11·60⁵/₁₂	174	9·67¹/₁₂
11·67¹/₁₂	175	9·72¹¹/₁₂
11·73⁹/₁₂	176	9·78⁴/₁₂
11·80⁵/₁₂	177	9·83⁹/₁₂
11·87¹/₁₂	178	9·89⁷/₁₂
11·93⁹/₁₂	179	9·95
12·00⁵/₁₂	180	10·00⁵/₁₂

Annual rate of pension in the case of a man 1	Number of weeks in period of service 2	Annual rate of pension in the case of a woman 3
£		£
$12·07^{1}/_{12}$	181	$10·06^{3}/_{12}$
$12·13^{9}/_{12}$	182	$10·11^{8}/_{12}$
$12·20^{5}/_{12}$	183	$10·17^{1}/_{12}$
$12·27^{1}/_{12}$	184	$10·22^{11}/_{12}$
$12·33^{9}/_{12}$	185	$10·28^{4}/_{12}$
$12·40^{5}/_{12}$	186	$10·33^{9}/_{12}$
$12·47^{1}/_{12}$	187	$10·39^{7}/_{12}$
$12·53^{9}/_{12}$	188	$10·45$
$12·60^{5}/_{12}$	189	$10·50^{5}/_{12}$
$12·67^{1}/_{12}$	190	$10·56^{3}/_{12}$
$12·73^{9}/_{12}$	191	$10·61^{8}/_{12}$
$12·80^{5}/_{12}$	192	$10·67^{1}/_{12}$
$12·87^{1}/_{12}$	193	$10·72^{11}/_{12}$
$12·93^{9}/_{12}$	194	$10·78^{4}/_{12}$
$13·00^{5}/_{12}$	195	$10·83^{9}/_{12}$
$13·07^{1}/_{12}$	196	$10·89^{7}/_{12}$
$13·13^{9}/_{12}$	197	10.95
$13·20^{5}/_{12}$	198	$11·00^{10}/_{12}$
$13·27^{1}/_{12}$	199	$11·06^{3}/_{12}$
$13·33^{9}/_{12}$	200	$11·11^{8}/_{12}$
$13·40^{5}/_{12}$	201	$11·17^{6}/_{12}$
$13·47^{1}/_{12}$	202	$11·22^{11}/_{12}$
$13·53^{9}/_{12}$	203	$11·28^{4}/_{12}$
$13·60^{5}/_{12}$	204	$11·34^{2}/_{12}$
$13·67^{1}/_{12}$	205	$11·39^{7}/_{12}$
$13·73^{9}/_{12}$	206	$11·45$
$13·80^{5}/_{12}$	207	$11·50^{10}/_{12}$

Annual rate of pension in the case of a man 1	Number of weeks in period of service 2	Annual rate of pension in the case of a woman 3
£		£
$13 \cdot 87^1/_{12}$	208	$11 \cdot 56^3/_{12}$
$13 \cdot 93^9/_{12}$	209	$11 \cdot 61^8/_{12}$
$14 \cdot 00^5/_{12}$	210	$11 \cdot 67^6/_{12}$
$14 \cdot 07^1/_{12}$	211	$11 \cdot 72^{11}/_{12}$
$14 \cdot 13^9/_{12}$	212	$11 \cdot 78^4/_{12}$
$14 \cdot 20^5/_{12}$	213	$11 \cdot 84^2/_{12}$
$14 \cdot 27^1/_{12}$	214	$11 \cdot 89^7/_{12}$
$14 \cdot 33^9/_{12}$	215	$11 \cdot 95$
$14 \cdot 40^5/_{12}$	216	$12 \cdot 00^{10}/_{12}$
$14 \cdot 47^1/_{12}$	217	$12 \cdot 06^3/_{12}$
$14 \cdot 53^9/_{12}$	218	$12 \cdot 11^8/_{12}$
$14 \cdot 60^5/_{12}$	219	$12 \cdot 17^6/_{12}$
$14 \cdot 67^1/_{12}$	220	$12 \cdot 22^{11}/_{12}$
$14 \cdot 73^9/_{12}$	221	$12 \cdot 28^4/_{12}$
$14 \cdot 80^5/_{12}$	222	$12 \cdot 34^2/_{12}$
$14 \cdot 87^1/_{12}$	223	$12 \cdot 39^7/_{12}$
$14 \cdot 93^9/_{12}$	224	$12 \cdot 45$
$15 \cdot 00^5/_{12}$	225	$12 \cdot 50^{10}/_{12}$
$15 \cdot 07^1/_{12}$	226	$12 \cdot 56^3/_{12}$
$15 \cdot 13^9/_{12}$	227	$12 \cdot 61^8/_{12}$
$15 \cdot 20^5/_{12}$	228	$12 \cdot 67^6/_{12}$
$15 \cdot 27^1/_{12}$	229	$12 \cdot 72^{11}/_{12}$
$15 \cdot 33^9/_{12}$	230	$12 \cdot 78^4/_{12}$
$15 \cdot 40^5/_{12}$	231	$12 \cdot 84^2/_{12}$
$15 \cdot 47^1/_{12}$	232	$12 \cdot 89^7/_{12}$
$15 \cdot 53^9/_{12}$	233	$12 \cdot 95$
$15 \cdot 60^5/_{12}$	234	$13 \cdot 00^{10}/_{12}$

Annual rate of pension in the case of a man 1	Number of weeks in period of service 2	Annual rate of pension in the case of a woman 3
£		£
$15 \cdot 67^1/_{12}$	235	$13 \cdot 06^3/_{12}$
$15 \cdot 73^9/_{12}$	236	$13 \cdot 11^8/_{12}$
$15 \cdot 80^5/_{12}$	237	$13 \cdot 17^6/_{12}$
$15 \cdot 87^1/_{12}$	238	$13 \cdot 22^{11}/_{12}$
$15 \cdot 93^9/_{12}$	239	$13 \cdot 28^4/_{12}$
$16 \cdot 00^5/_{12}$	240	$13 \cdot 34^2/_{12}$
$16 \cdot 07^1/_{12}$	241	$13 \cdot 39^7/_{12}$
$16 \cdot 13^9/_{12}$	242	$13 \cdot 45$
$16 \cdot 20^5/_{12}$	243	$13 \cdot 50^{10}/_{12}$
$16 \cdot 27^1/_{12}$	244	$13 \cdot 56^3/_{12}$
$16 \cdot 33^9/_{12}$	245	$13 \cdot 61^8/_{12}$
$16 \cdot 40^5/_{12}$	246	$13 \cdot 67^6/_{12}$
$16 \cdot 47^1/_{12}$	247	$13 \cdot 72^{11}/_{12}$
$16 \cdot 53^9/_{12}$	248	$13 \cdot 78^4/_{12}$
$16 \cdot 60^5/_{12}$	249	$13 \cdot 84^2/_{12}$
$16 \cdot 67^1/_{12}$	250	$13 \cdot 89^7/_{12}$
$16 \cdot 73^9/_{12}$	251	$13 \cdot 95$
$16 \cdot 80^5/_{12}$	252	$14 \cdot 00^{10}/_{12}$
$16 \cdot 87^1/_{12}$	253	$14 \cdot 06^3/_{12}$
$16 \cdot 93^9/_{12}$	254	$14 \cdot 11^8/_{12}$
$17 \cdot 00^5/_{12}$	255	$14 \cdot 17^6/_{12}$
$17 \cdot 07^1/_{12}$	256	$14 \cdot 22^{11}/_{12}$
$17 \cdot 13^9/_{12}$	257	$14 \cdot 28^4/_{12}$
$17 \cdot 20^5/_{12}$	258	$14 \cdot 34^2/_{12}$
$17 \cdot 27^1/_{12}$	259	$14 \cdot 39^7/_{12}$
$17 \cdot 33^9/_{12}$	260	$14 \cdot 45$
$17 \cdot 40^5/_{12}$	261	$14 \cdot 50^{10}/_{12}$

Annual rate of pension in the case of a man 1	Number of weeks in period of service 2	Annual rate of pension in the case of a woman 3
£		£
$17{\cdot}47^{1}/_{12}$	262	$14{\cdot}56^{3}/_{12}$
$17{\cdot}53^{9}/_{12}$	263	$14{\cdot}62^{1}/_{12}$
$17{\cdot}60^{5}/_{12}$	264	$14{\cdot}67^{6}/_{12}$
$17{\cdot}67^{1}/_{12}$	265	$14{\cdot}72^{11}/_{12}$
$17{\cdot}73^{9}/_{12}$	266	$14{\cdot}78^{9}/_{12}$
$17{\cdot}80^{5}/_{12}$	267	$14{\cdot}84^{2}/_{12}$
$17{\cdot}87^{1}/_{12}$	268	$14{\cdot}89^{7}/_{12}$
$17{\cdot}93^{9}/_{12}$	269	$14{\cdot}95^{5}/_{12}$
$18{\cdot}00^{5}/_{12}$	270	$15{\cdot}00^{10}/_{12}$
$18{\cdot}07^{1}/_{12}$	271	$15{\cdot}06^{3}/_{12}$
$18{\cdot}13^{9}/_{12}$	272	$15{\cdot}12^{1}/_{12}$
$18{\cdot}20^{5}/_{12}$	273	$15{\cdot}17^{6}/_{12}$
$18{\cdot}27^{1}/_{12}$	274	$15{\cdot}22^{11}/_{12}$
$18{\cdot}33^{9}/_{12}$	275	$15{\cdot}28^{9}/_{12}$
$18{\cdot}40^{5}/_{12}$	276	$15{\cdot}34^{2}/_{12}$
$18{\cdot}47^{1}/_{12}$	277	$15{\cdot}39^{7}/_{12}$
$18{\cdot}53^{9}/_{12}$	278	$15{\cdot}45^{5}/_{12}$
$18{\cdot}60^{5}/_{12}$	279	$15{\cdot}50^{10}/_{12}$
$18{\cdot}67^{1}/_{12}$	280	$15{\cdot}56^{3}/_{12}$
$18{\cdot}73^{9}/_{12}$	281	$15{\cdot}62^{1}/_{12}$
$18{\cdot}80^{5}/_{12}$	282	$15{\cdot}67^{6}/_{12}$
$18{\cdot}87^{1}/_{12}$	283	$15{\cdot}72^{11}/_{12}$
$18{\cdot}93^{9}/_{12}$	284	$15{\cdot}78^{9}/_{12}$
$19{\cdot}00^{5}/_{12}$	285	$15{\cdot}84^{2}/_{12}$
$19{\cdot}07^{1}/_{12}$	286	$15{\cdot}89^{7}/_{12}$
$19{\cdot}13^{9}/_{12}$	287	$15{\cdot}95^{5}/_{12}$
$19{\cdot}20^{5}/_{12}$	288	$16{\cdot}00^{10}/_{12}$

Annual rate of pension in the case of a man 1	Number of weeks in period of service 2	Annual rate of pension in the case of a woman 3
£		£
$19 \cdot 27^1/_{12}$	289	$16 \cdot 06^3/_{12}$
$19 \cdot 33^9/_{12}$	290	$16 \cdot 12^1/_{12}$
$19 \cdot 40^5/_{12}$	291	$16 \cdot 17^6/_{12}$
$19 \cdot 47^1/_{12}$	292	$16 \cdot 22^{11}/_{12}$
$19 \cdot 53^9/_{12}$	293	$16 \cdot 28^9/_{12}$
$19 \cdot 60^5/_{12}$	294	$16 \cdot 34^2/_{12}$
$19 \cdot 67^1/_{12}$	295	$16 \cdot 39^7/_{12}$
$19 \cdot 73^9/_{12}$	296	$16 \cdot 45^5/_{12}$
$19 \cdot 80^5/_{12}$	297	$16 \cdot 50^{10}/_{12}$
$19 \cdot 87^1/_{12}$	298	$16 \cdot 56^3/_{12}$
$19 \cdot 93^9/_{12}$	299	$16 \cdot 62^1/_{12}$
$20 \cdot 00^5/_{12}$	300	$16 \cdot 67^6/_{12}$
£20·00$^5/_{12}$ for each 300 weeks plus the appropriate amount shown in this column in relation to any weeks in excess of 300 or a multiple thereof.	Any number exceeding 300.	£16·67$^6/_{12}$ for each 300 weeks plus the appropriate amount shown in this column in relation to any weeks in excess of 300 or a multiple thereof.

SCHEDULE 22

Regulation 21

Schedule substituted for the Schedule to the National Insurance (Earnings-related Benefit) Regulations

SCHEDULE

Regulation 5

Table of annual reckonable earnings with corresponding figures for one-third of the excess up to £21 of average weekly earnings over £9 and 85 per cent. of average weekly earnings.

Annual reckonable earnings (1)	One-third of the excess up to £21 of average weekly earnings over £9 (2)	85 per cent. of average weekly earnings (3)
£	£	£
450	0·05	7·90
465	0·15	8·15
480	0·25	8·43
495	0·35	8·68
510	0·45	8·93
525	0·55	9·18
540	0·65	9·43
555	0·75	9·70
570	0·85	9·95
585	0·95	10·20
600	1·05	10·45
615	1·15	10·70
630	1·25	10·98
645	1·35	11·23
660	1·45	11·48
675	1·55	11·73
690	1·65	11·98
705	1·75	12·25
720	1·85	12·50
735	1·95	12·75
750	2·05	13·00
765	2·15	13·25
780	2·25	13·53
795	2·35	13·78
810	2·45	14·03
825	2·55	14·28
840	2·65	14·53
855	2·75	14·80
870	2·85	15·05
885	2·95	15·30
900	3·05	15·55
915	3·15	15·80
930	3·25	16·08
945	3·35	16·33
960	3·45	16·58

Annual reckonable earnings	One-third of the excess up to £21 of average weekly earnings over £9	85 per cent. of average weekly earnings
(1)	(2)	(3)
£	£	£
975	3·55	16·83
990	3·65	17·08
1,005	3·75	17·35
1,020	3·85	17·60
1,035	3·95	17·85
1,050	4·05	18·10
1,065	4·15	18·35
1,080	4·25	18·63
1,095	4·35	18·88
1,110	4·45	19·13
1,125	4·55	19·38
1,140	4·65	19·63
1,155	4·75	19·90
1,170	4·85	20·15
1,185	4·95	20·40
1,200	5·05	20·65
1,215	5·15	20·90
1,230	5·25	21·18
1,245	5·35	21·43
1,260	5·45	21·68
1,275	5·55	21·93
1,290	5·65	22·18
1,305	5·75	22·45
1,320	5·85	22·70
1,335	5·95	22·95
1,350	6·05	23·20
1,365	6·15	23·45
1,380	6·25	23·73
1,395	6·35	23·98
1,410	6·45	24·23
1,425	6·55	24·48
1,440	6·65	24·73
1,455	6·75	25·00
1,470	6·85	25·25
1,485	6·95	25·50
1,500	7·00	25·50

SCHEDULE 23   Regulation 23(5)

Provisions to be substituted for Part I of Schedule 2 to the Industrial Injuries Act

SCHEDULE 2   Sections 2, 3.

PROVISIONS AS TO CONTRIBUTIONS

PART I

WEEKLY RATES OF CONTRIBUTIONS PAYABLE BY INSURED PERSONS AND EMPLOYERS

Weekly rates where contributions are paid otherwise than jointly with contributions under the Insurance Act

Class of insured person to which rate applies	Weekly rate of contribution	
1.	By the insured person 2.	By the employer 3.
	£	£
Men over the age of 18	0·04	0·05
Women over the age of 18	0·03	0·04
Boys under the age of 18	0.02	0·02
Girls under the age of 18	0·01	0·02

Weekly rates where contributions are paid jointly with contributions under the Insurance Act

Class of insured person to which rate applies	Weekly rate of contribution	
1.	By the insured person 2.	By the employer 3.
	£	£
Men over the age of 18	0·046	0·050
Women over the age of 18	0·033	0·038
Boys under the age of 18	0·021	0·021
Girls under the age of 18	0·012	0·017

Regulation 23(6)   SCHEDULE 24

Schedule substituted for Schedule 3 to the Industrial Injuries Act

SCHEDULE 3

RATE OR AMOUNT OF BENEFIT, ETC.

Description of benefit, etc.	Amount
1. Injury benefit under s.11 (weekly rate)	(a) for any period during which the beneficiary is over the age of 18 or is entitled to an increase of benefit in respect of a child or adult dependant ... £7·75
	(b) for any period during which the beneficiary is between the ages of 17 and 18 and not entitled as aforesaid ... £5·25
	(c) for any period during which the beneficiary is under the age of 17 and not entitled as aforesaid ... £4·50
2. Maximum disablement gratuity under s.12(3)	... ... £550
3. Disablement pension under s.12(5) (weekly rate).	For the several degrees of disablement set out in column 1 of the following Table, for the following periods respectively the respective amounts set out in the following columns respectively of that Table, namely—
	(a) for any period such as is mentioned in paragraph 1(a) of this Schedule, column 2;
	(b) for any period such as is mentioned in paragraph 1(b) of this Schedule, column 3;
	(c) for any period such as is mentioned in paragraph 1(c) of this Schedule, column 4.

TABLE

Degree of Disablement (1)	Weekly Rate		
	(2)	(3)	(4)
per cent	£	£	£
100	8·40	5·50	5·00
90	7·55	4·95	4·50
80	6·70	4·40	4·00
70	5·90	3·85	3·50
60	5·05	3·30	3·00
50	4·20	2·75	2·50
40	3·35	2·20	2·00
30	2·50	1·65	1·50
20	1·70	1·10	1·00

Description of benefit, etc.	Amount
4. Unemployability supplement under s.13 (increase of weekly rate of disablement pension).	(*a*) for any period such as is mentioned in paragraph 1(*a*) of this Schedule ... £5·00
	(*b*) for any period such as is mentioned in paragraph 1(*b*) or (*c*) of this Schedule ... £2·75
5. Maximum increase under s.14 of weekly rate of disablement pension in cases of special hardship.	£3.35, or the amount (if any) by which the weekly rate of the pension, apart from any increase under s.15, 17 or 18 of this Act or under section 6 of the National Insurance Act 1966, falls short of £8.40, whichever is the less.
6. Maximum increase under s.15 of weekly rate of disablement pension where constant attendance needed.	(*a*) except in cases of exceptionally severe disablement ... £3·30
	(*b*) in any case ... £6·60
7. Increase under s.17 of weekly rate of injury benefit or disablement pension in respect of children.	(*a*) in respect of only, elder or eldest child of beneficiary's family... £1·55
	(*b*) in respect of second child of beneficiary's family ... £0·65
	(*c*) in respect of each additional child of beneficiary's family ... £0·55
8. Increase under s.18 of weekly rate of injury benefit or disablement pension in respect of adult dependant.	... ... £3·10
9. Widow's pension under s.19— (*a*) weekly rate where payable by virtue of s.19(3)(*a*)-(*e*)	... ... £5·55
(*b*) maximum higher weekly rate for prescribed period after deceased's death.	... ... £7·00
10. Widower's pension under s.20 (weekly rate).	... ... £5·55
11. Allowance under s.21 in respect of children of deceased's family— (*a*) weekly rate of allowance under s.21(1)	(i) in respect of only, elder or eldest qualifying child ... £1·55
	(ii) in respect of second qualifying child ... £0·65
	(iii) in respect of each additional qualifying child ... £0·55
(*b*) increase under s.21(2)	... ... £0·90

Description of benefit, etc.	Amount
12. Maximum under s.29(1)(*a*) of aggregate of weekly benefits payable for successive accidents.	(*a*) for any period such as is mentioned in paragraph 1(*a*) of this Schedule ... £8.40
	(*b*) for any period such as is mentioned in paragraph 1(*b*) of this Schedule—
	(i) apart from any increase under s.14 ... £5.50
	(ii) including any such increase ... £8.40
	(*c*) for any period such as is mentioned in paragraph 1(*c*) of this Schedule ... £5.00

Regulation 24(7) **SCHEDULE 25**

Schedule substituted for Schedule 3 to the National Insurance (Industrial Injuries) (Benefit) Regulations

Regulation 3 **SCHEDULE 3**

SCALE OF DISABLEMENT GRATUITIES

Degree of disablement	Amount of gratuity
	£
1 per cent.	55·00
2 per cent.	82·50
3 per cent.	110·00
4 per cent.	137·50
5 per cent.	165·00
6 per cent.	192·50
7 per cent.	220·00
8 per cent.	247·50
9 per cent.	275·00
10 per cent.	302·50
11 per cent.	330·00
12 per cent.	357·50
13 per cent.	385·00
14 per cent.	412·50
15 per cent.	440·00
16 per cent.	467·50
17 per cent.	495·00
18 per cent.	522·50
19 per cent.	550·00

SCHEDULE 26   Regulation 24(7)

Schedule substituted for Schedule 4 to the National Insurance (Industrial Injuries) (Benefit) Regulations

SCHEDULE 4   Regulation 6

RATE OF DISABLEMENT PENSION PAYABLE IN LIEU OF DISABLEMENT GRATUITY IN ACCORDANCE WITH REGULATION 6

Where the degree of disablement is as specified in column 1 of the following table, the weekly rate of the pension shall be determined in accordance with column 2 of that table:—

Degree of disablement	Weekly rate of pension
	£
less than 20 per cent. but not less than 16 per cent. ...	1·70
less than 16 per cent. but not less than 11 per cent. ...	1·28
less than 11 per cent. but not less than 6 per cent. ...	0·85
less than 6 per cent.	0·43

SCHEDULE 27   Regulation 29(4)

Schedule substituted for Schedule 1 to the Workmen's Compensation (Supplementation) Scheme

SCHEDULE 1   Article 5

Loss of earnings	Rate of lesser incapacity allowance
£	£
0·49½	0·13
0·99½	0·25
1·74½	0·38
2·49½	0·50
3·24½	0·75
3·99½	1·00
4·74½	1·25
5·49½	1·63
6·24½	2·00
6·99½	2·38
7·74½	2·75
7·75	3·05

Regulation 31   SCHEDULE 28

The following Schedule is, by regulation 31 of these Regulations, substituted for the
Schedule to the National Health Service Contributions Act 1965

SCHEDULE

RATES OF NATIONAL HEALTH SERVICE CONTRIBUTIONS

Description of persons	Weekly Rate of Contribution
	£
1. Employed men between the ages of 18 and 70, other than men over the age of 65 who have retired from regular employment	0·158
2. Employed women between the ages of 18 and 65, other than women over the age of 60 who have retired from regular employment	0·125
3. Employed boys and girls under the age of 18	0·079
4. Employers	0·033
5. Self-employed men between the ages of 18 and 70, other than men over the age of 65 who have retired from regular employment...	0·167
6. Self-employed women between the ages of 18 and 65, other than women over the age of 60 who have retired from regular employment	0·133
7. Self-employed boys and girls under the age of 18	0·088
8. Non-employed men between the ages of 18 and 65 ...	0·167
9. Non-employed women between the ages of 18 and 60 ...	0·133
10. Non-employed boys and girls under the age of 18	0·088

SCHEDULE 29

Regulations 33(4) and
34(2) and (3)

METHOD OF CALCULATING IN CERTAIN CASES THE AMOUNT IN NEW
PENCE CORRESPONDING TO AN AMOUNT IN SHILLINGS AND PENCE

The amount in the new currency corresponding to an amount in shillings, shillings
and pence or pence shall be calculated as follows—

(a) for any whole two shillings or multiple thereof the corresponding amount in
the new currency shall be taken to be ten new pence or that multiple thereof;
and

(b) for any amount or remaining amount of less than two shillings shown in
column 1 of the following Table the corresponding amount in the new currency
shall be taken to be the amount (if any) in new pence shown opposite that
amount in column 2 of that Table (and accordingly an amount or remaining
amount of one penny shall be disregarded).

TABLE

Amount in old currency	Corresponding amount in new pence
1d.	—
2d.	1p
3d.	1p
4d.	2p
5d.	2p
6d.	3p
7d.	3p
8d.	3p
9d.	4p
10d.	4p
11d.	5p
1s. 0d.	5p
1s. 1d.	5p
1s. 2d.	6p
1s. 3d.	6p
1s. 4d.	7p
1s. 5d.	7p
1s. 6d.	7p
1s. 7d.	8p
1s. 8d.	8p
1s. 9d.	9p
1s. 10d.	9p
1s. 11d.	10p

EXPLANATORY NOTE
(This Note is not part of the Regulations.)

These Regulations are made under powers conferred by section 8 of the National Insurance Act 1969 and accordingly, by virtue of section 10(1)(*b*) of that Act, they have not been referred to the National Insurance Advisory Committee or the Industrial Injuries Advisory Council.

The Regulations amend various provisions which are contained in or have effect under the Family Allowances Act 1965, the National Insurance Act 1965, the National Insurance (Industrial Injuries) Act 1965, the Industrial Injuries and Diseases (Old Cases) Act 1967, section 1 of the National Health Service Contributions Act 1965 and section 27 of the Redundancy Payments Act 1965 so as to take account of the introduction of decimal currency on 15th February 1971, the date on which the bulk of the provisions contained in the Regulations take effect.

In the Regulations, the rates and amounts expressed in terms of the new decimal currency are based upon the rates and amounts in the old currency (£ s d) operative when the relevant provisions of the National Insurance Act 1969 and of regulations made in consequence of that Act took effect, in general, the total amount payable by way of a flat-rate contribution in the old currency by employer and employee, by a self-employed person, or by a non-employed person is converted into the new currency by reference to the whole new penny conversion table (see Schedule 29), while total weekly benefit rates which do not convert to a whole new penny amount are rounded up to the next new penny.

In certain cases, to secure equivalency or near equivalency between rates or amounts in the new currency and rates or amounts in the old currency, rates or amounts in the new currency are expressed in fractions of a pound or a new penny.

The Regulations contain provisions for rounding payable amounts to a whole new penny and various transitional provisions.

The "ARRANGEMENT of REGULATIONS" indicates the provisions of the various enactments and statutory instruments that have been amended.

STATUTORY INSTRUMENTS

1970 No. 47

MEDICAL PROFESSION

The General Medical Council (Registration Regulations) Order of Council 1970

Made - - - *19th January* 1970

At the Council Chamber, Whitehall, the 19th day of January 1970

By the Lords of Her Majesty's Most Honourable Privy Council

Whereas in pursuance of section 4 of the Medical Act 1969(a) the General Medical Council have made regulations entitled "The Medical Practitioners Registration (No. 2) Regulations 1969":

And whereas by subsection (8) of the said section such regulations shall not have effect until approved by Order of the Privy Council:

Now, therefore, Their Lordships, having taken the said regulations into consideration, are hereby pleased to approve the same as set out in the Schedule to this Order.

This Order may be cited as the General Medical Council (Registration Regulations) Order of Council 1970.

W. G. Agnew.

SCHEDULE

THE MEDICAL PRACTITIONERS REGISTRATION (NO. 2) REGULATIONS 1969

The General Medical Council in exercise of their powers under section 4(4), (5) and (6) of the Medical Act 1969 hereby make the following Regulations:—

PART I

PRELIMINARY

Citation and Commencement

1. These Regulations may be cited as the Medical Practitioners Registration (No. 2) Regulations 1969, and shall come into operation on 26th January 1970.

Interpretation

2.—(1) In these Regulations, unless the context otherwise requires:—

"the Act of 1969" means the Medical Act 1969;

"the Council" means the General Medical Council;

(a) 1969 c. 40.

"the Executive Committee" means the Committee of that name of the General Medical Council constituted by virtue of the Medical Act 1956, section 1(3) and Schedule 1, paragraph 6(1) ;

"the Overseas List" means the list of that name established in accordance with section 3(2) of the Medical Act 1969 ;

"the President" means the President of the General Medical Council ;

"the Principal List" means the list of that name established in accordance with section 3(2) of the Medical Act 1969 ;

"the register" means the register of medical practitioners ;

"the Registrar" means the Registrar of the General Medical Council ;

"the Registration Committee" means the Committee of that name of the General Medical Council constituted by virtue of the Medical Act 1956, section 1(3) and Schedule 1, paragraph 6(1).

(2) Any reference in these Regulations to a numbered Regulation shall be construed as a reference to the Regulation bearing that number in these Regulations, and any reference to a numbered paragraph shall be construed as a reference to the paragraph bearing that number in the Regulation in which it occurs.

3.The Interpretation Act 1889(a) shall apply to the interpretation of these Regulations as it applies to the interpretation of an Act of Parliament.

PART II

THE OVERSEAS LIST

4. A person shall be treated as residing overseas for the purposes of the Act of 1969 and of any Regulations made thereunder if he satisfies the Registrar that at the time of making application for inclusion in or for the restoration of his name to the Overseas List—

(a) he resides outside the United Kingdom, the Republic of Ireland, the Channel Islands, and the Isle of Man, and

(b) he intends to remain so resident for at least one year.

5. A fully or provisionally registered person shall not be entitled to be included in the Overseas List unless—

(a) he is to be treated as residing overseas under the provisions of Regulation 4 ; and

(b) he makes an application in the manner prescribed in Form A in the Schedule to these Regulations, and gives the undertaking prescribed in the said Form A that he will inform the Registrar if at any time he ceases to be entitled to be included in the Overseas List, as provided for in Regulation 6.

6. A person who is included in the Overseas List shall cease to be entitled to be included therein if at any time he enters the United Kingdom or the Republic of Ireland or the Channel Islands or the Isle of Man and either—

(a) remains there for a period of more than three months ; or

(b) renders while there any service as a medical practitioner for gain.

7. The Registrar shall transfer from the Overseas List to the Principal List the name of any person who applies to have his name so transferred, and who pays such fee (if any) as may be due from him, in connection with such transfer, under the provisions of Regulations made under section 5 of the Act of 1969.

8.—(1) Where it appears to the Registrar that a person who is included in the Overseas List has ceased to be entitled to be included therein, and where that

(a) 1889 c. 63,

person has not applied for his name to be transferred to the Principal List, and paid the fee, if any, which is due from him in connection with such transfer, the Registrar shall cause to be sent to that person at his registered address and at his last known address, if this is different from his registered address, a letter setting out the ground on which it appears to the Registrar that the person has ceased to be so entitled and stating that, unless the person can, within a period of 14 days from the date of issue of the letter, satisfy the Registrar that he continues to be entitled to be included in the Overseas List, his name may be erased from that List. The Registrar shall also, if appropriate, invite the person concerned to apply for the transfer of his name to the Principal List.

(2) Where within the period specified in paragraph (1) the Registrar has not been satisfied that the person continues to be entitled to be included in the Overseas List, the Registrar may then erase the name of the person from the Overseas List.

(3) On erasing the name of a person from the Overseas List under the provisions of paragraph (2), the Registrar shall notify the person in writing at his registered address and at his last known address, if this is different from his registered address, of such erasure, and of the ground on which the name has been erased, and shall inform him of his right of appeal under paragraph (4).

(4) A person whose name has been erased from the Overseas List under the provisions of paragraph (2) may appeal against such erasure, by letter addressed to the Registrar, within three months of the date of issue of the notification of such erasure referred to in paragraph (3). The statement of appeal shall contain a concise statement of the facts and contentions on which the appellant bases his appeal.

(5) The Registration Committee shall consider and determine such appeals. Before reaching such a determination the Committee may cause such investigation (if any) of the appellant's conduct to be made as they think fit and may invite the appellant or any other person to furnish them with information either in writing or orally and in person before the Committee. If the appellant shall request an oral hearing, the Committee shall accede to that request. The appellant may be legally represented at such a hearing.

(6) The Registrar shall notify the appellant in writing at his registered address and at his last known address, if this is different from his registered address, of the decision of the Committee.

(7) If the Registration Committee so direct, the Registrar shall immediately restore the name of the appellant to the Overseas List.

Part III

Restoration of Names to the Principal List or the Overseas List after Erasure Otherwise than by Direction or Order of the Disciplinary Committee

9.—(1) Any person whose name has been erased—

(a) from the register by virtue of section 3(5) of the Act of 1969, or

(b) from the register by virtue of Regulations made under section 5(2) of the Act of 1969, or

(c) from the Overseas List by virtue of Regulation 8(2)

may make application for his name to be restored to the Principal List.

(2) Unless the President or, if the President be unable to act, one of the Treasurers of the Council, shall otherwise direct, such an application—

(a) must be made in the form set out in Form B in the Schedule to these Regulations and (*b*) must be accompanied by such fee or fees, if any, as are prescribed in Regulations made under section 5(1)(*a*) of the Act of 1969 for such restoration.

(3) Where an application has been duly made in accordance with paragraph (2), and where the provisions of Regulation 11 do not apply, the Registrar shall forthwith restore the name of the applicant to the Principal List.

10.—(1) Any person whose name has been erased—

(*a*) from the register by virtue of section 3(5) of the Act of 1969, or

(*b*) from the register by virtue of Regulations made under section 5(2) of the Act of 1969, or

(*c*) from the Overseas List by virtue of Regulation 8(2)

and who is to be treated as residing overseas under the provisions of Regulation 4 may make application for his name to be restored to the Overseas List:

Provided that a person whose name has been erased under Regulation 8(2) and who has appealed against such erasure under Regulation 8(4) may not make application for restoration under this Regulation until his appeal has been determined under Regulation 8.

(2) Unless the President or, if the President be unable to act, one of the Treasurers of the Council, shall otherwise direct, such an application—

(*a*) must be made in the manner set out in Form C in the Schedule to these Regulations, and

(*b*) must be accompanied by such fee, if any, as is prescribed in Regulations made under section 5(1)(*a*) of the Act of 1969 for such restoration.

(3) Where an application has been duly made in accordance with paragraph (2), and where the provisions of Regulation 11 do not apply, the Registrar shall forthwith restore the name of the applicant to the Overseas List.

11.—(1) The Registrar shall submit to the President or, if the President be unable to act, to one of the Treasurers of the Council, any application made under Regulations 9 or 10 which, whether as the result of receipt of information as to the conduct of the applicant or for some other reason, appears to be of a questionable nature.

(2) If it appears to the President, or the Treasurer as the case may be, that a question arises whether the name of the applicant shall not be restored to the Principal List or to the Overseas List as the case may be or shall not be restored forthwith, he may direct the Registrar to write to the applicant,

(*a*) informing him of the ground on which it appears that such question arises and, if the ground relates to the alleged conduct of the applicant, giving particulars of the conduct in question ; and

(*b*) informing the applicant of the date of the next meeting of the Executive Committee, and inviting him to forward in writing any statement or evidence in support of his application.

(3) Subject to the foregoing provisions of this Regulation the President, or the Treasurer as the case may be, may refer the application to the Executive Committee, and the application shall then be considered and determined by that Committee. Before coming to a determination the Committee may adjourn the consideration to a future date, and cause such investigations of the conduct of the applicant to be made as they consider fit, and for this purpose the Committee may invite the applicant or any other person to furnish them with information, either in writing or orally and in person before the Committee. If the applicant requests to be heard on his application the Committee shall accede to such request. The applicant may be legally represented if he so desires.

(4) The Executive Committee may if they think fit direct the name of the applicant to be restored to the Principal List or the Overseas List as the case may be and if they so direct, the Registrar shall so restore it.

(5) The Registrar shall notify the applicant in writing at his last known address of the determination of the Committee in such terms as the Committee may direct.

SCHEDULE

Regulation 5

FORM A

APPLICATION FOR INCLUSION IN THE OVERSEAS LIST

I am the person now registered as a medical practitioner under the Medical Acts of the United Kingdom as follows:—

....

(FULL NAME)

....

(REGISTERED ADDRESS)

....

(REGISTERED QUALIFICATIONS)

I am at present resident at:—

....

....

(FULL ADDRESS)

I hereby declare that it is my intention to remain resident outside the United Kingdom, the Republic of Ireland, the Channel Islands and the Isle of Man for at least one year from the date of this application.

I hereby apply for inclusion in the Overseas List of the register of medical practitioners. I understand that entitlement to be included in the Overseas List ceases if at any time I enter the United Kingdom, the Republic of Ireland, the Channel Islands or the Isle of Man, and

(a) remain there for a period of more than three months, or

(b) render while there any service as a medical practitioner for gain.

I hereby undertake to inform the Registrar of the Council if at any time I cease to be entitled to be included in the Overseas List.

Signature of practitioner: ....

Date: ....

Regulation 9

Form B

Application for Restoration to the Principal List after Erasure otherwise than by Direction or Order of the Disciplinary Committee

I, the undersigned ....

of ....

now holding the qualification(s) of ....

....

hereby declare as follows:—

1. I am the person formerly registered as a medical practitioner with the name

....

and with the qualification(s) of ....

....

2. I desire that my name be restored to the Principal List of the register of medical practitioners.

(Signed)..

Date:................................

Regulation 10

Form C

Application for Restoration to the Overseas List after Erasure otherwise than by Direction or Order of the Disciplinary Committee

I, the undersigned ....

of ....

now holding the qualification(s) of ....

hereby declare as follows:—

1. I am the person formerly included in the register of medical practitioners with

the name ....

and with the qualification(s) of ....

2. I am at present resident at:—

....

....

(FULL ADDRESS)

3. It is my intention to remain resident outside the United Kingdom, the Republic of Ireland, the Channel Islands and the Isle of Man for at least one year from the date of this application.

4. I desire my name to be restored to the Overseas List of the register of medical practitioners. I understand that entitlement to be included in the Overseas List ceases if at any time I enter the United Kingdom, the Republic of Ireland, the Channel Islands or the Isle of Man, and

(*a*) remain there for a period of more than three months, or

(*b*) render while there any service as a medical practitioner for gain.

5. I hereby undertake to inform the Registrar of the Council if at any time I cease to be entitled to be included in the Overseas List.

(Signed)..

Date:................................

Given under the official seal of the General Medical Council, this twenty-fifth day of November, nineteen hundred and sixty-nine.

(L.S.)

COHEN OF BIRKENHEAD,
President.

EXPLANATORY NOTE

(This Note is not part of the Order.)

The regulations approved by this Order

(1) prescribe the conditions under which persons may be registered in the Overseas List of the register of medical practitioners maintained by the General Medical Council ;

(2) authorise the erasure from the Overseas List of the names of persons ceasing to fulfil such conditions, and provide for appeal against erasure;

(3) provide for the restoration to the appropriate List of the register of medical practitioners of names removed other than by the direction or order of the Disciplinary Committee of the General Medical Council.

STATUTORY INSTRUMENTS

1970 No. 48

ROAD TRAFFIC

The Road Vehicles Lighting (Amendment) Regulations 1970

Made - - -	*15th January* 1970
Laid before Parliament	*27th January* 1970
Coming into Operation	*1st March* 1970

The Minister of Transport, in exercise of his powers under sections 3, 5(2)(*a*) and 10(2)(*b*) of the Road Transport Lighting Act 1957(**a**) and of all other enabling powers, and after consultation with representative organisations in accordance with the provisions of section 13 of the said Act of 1957, as amended by section 264 of, and Schedule 17 to, the Road Traffic Act 1960(**b**), hereby makes the following Regulations :—

1.—(1) These Regulations shall come into operation on the 1st March 1970 and may be cited as the Road Vehicles Lighting (Amendment) Regulations 1970.

(2) The Interpretation Act 1889(**c**) shall apply for the interpretation of these Regulations as it applies for the interpretation of an Act of Parliament.

2. The Road Vehicles Lighting Regulations 1964(**d**), as amended (**e**), shall have effect as though—

(1) in Regulation 14(5), for the word and figures "Regulation 15(5)", there were substituted the word and figures "Regulation 15(10)" ; and

(2) for Regulation 15 there were substituted the following Regulation : —
    "**15.**—(1) In this Regulation "approval mark" means a marking designated as an approval mark by Regulation 2(2) of the Motor Vehicles (Designation of Approval Marks) Regulations 1968(**f**), and "motor bicycle" means a bicycle propelled by mechanical power with or without a sidecar attached thereto.

    (2) Save as provided in paragraphs (8) and (9) of this Regulation, every obligatory rear lamp fitted with an electric bulb and carried on—

        (*a*) every mechanically propelled vehicle registered on or after the 1st April 1959 but before the 1st September 1964,

        (*b*) every mechanically propelled vehicle not required to be registered under the Vehicles (Excise) Act 1962(**g**) and supplied by its manufacturer to the Crown or any person on or after the 1st April 1959 but before the 1st September 1964,

        (*c*) every trailer supplied as aforesaid,
    shall be marked—

        (i) with the specification number of the British Standard for Tail Lights for Vehicles, namely, B.S.2516,

---

(**a**) 1957 c. 51.   (**b**) 1960 c. 16.
(**c**) 1889 c. 63.   (**d**) S.I. 1964/205 (1964 I, p. 345).
(**e**) The relevant amending instruments are S.I. 1965/870, 1967/1640, 1934 (1965 I, p. 2367; 1967 III, p. 4492; III, p. 5387).   (**f**) S.I. 1968/171 (1968 I, p. 403).
(**g**) 1962 c. 13.

(ii) with the grade "Grade 1" or "Grade 2" ; and

(iii) with the name, trade mark or other means of identification of the manufacturer of the lamp.

(3) Every obligatory rear lamp fitted with an electric bulb and carried on a cycle or any other vehicle not mechanically propelled and not a trailer shall be marked—

(a) with the specification number of the British Standard for Cycle Rear Lamps, namely, B.S.3648, and

(b) with the name, trade mark or other means of identification of the manufacturer of the lamp.

(4) Save as provided in paragraphs (8) and (9) of this Regulation, every obligatory rear lamp fitted wth an electric bulb and carried on a vehicle to which this paragraph applies shall be marked—

(a) with the particulars specified in sub-paragraphs (i) and (iii) of paragraph (2) of this Regulation, and

(b) with the grade "Grade 1".

(5) The last preceding paragraph applies to the following vehicles—

(a) every motor bicycle registered on or after the 1st September 1964 ;

(b) every mechanically propelled vehicle (other than a motor bicycle) registered on or after the 1st September 1964 and before the 1st July 1973 ;

(c) every mechanically propelled vehicle (other than a motor bicycle) registered on or after the 1st July 1973, if manufactured before the 1st January 1973 ;

(d) every mechanically propelled vehicle not required to be registered under the Vehicles (Excise) Act 1962 and every trailer, in each case supplied by its manufacturer to the Crown or any person—

(i) on or after the 1st September 1964 and before the 1st July 1973, or

(ii) on or after the 1st July 1973, if manufactured before the 1st January 1973.

(6) Every obligatory rear lamp fitted with an electric bulb and carried on a vehicle to which this paragraph applies shall be marked with an approval mark and—

(a) in the case of a rear lamp not combined with a stop lamp, the symbol "R" enclosed in a square above such mark, or

(b) in the case of a rear lamp combined with a stop lamp the symbol "R-S2" enclosed in a rectangle above such mark.

(7) The last preceding paragraph applies to the following vehicles—

(a) every mechanically propelled vehicle (other than a motor bicycle) manufactured on or after the 1st January 1973 and registered on or after the 1st July 1973 ;

(b) every mechanically propelled vehicle (other than a motor bicycle) not required to be registered under the Vehicles (Excise) Act 1962, manufactured on or after the 1st January 1973 and supplied by its manufacturer to the Crown or any person on or after the 1st July 1973 ;

(c) every trailer manufactured on or after the 1st January 1973 and supplied as aforesaid.

(8) Nothing in paragraph (2) or (4) of this Regulation shall require an obligatory rear lamp to be marked as provided in that paragraph, if it is carried on such a mechanically propelled vehicle or trailer as is mentioned in Regulation 14(4) of these Regulations.

(9) Nothing in paragraph (2) or (4) of this Regulation shall require an obligatory rear lamp to be marked as provided in that paragraph if, in the case of a rear lamp carried on a vehicle other than a motor bicycle, it is marked with an approval mark and—

> (i) in the case of a rear lamp not combined with a stop lamp, the symbol "R" enclosed in a square above such mark, or
>
> (ii) in the case of a rear lamp combined with a stop lamp, the symbol "R-S1" or "R-S2" enclosed in a rectangle above such mark.

(10) The provisions of Regulation 14(5) of these Regulations shall not apply to any obligatory rear lamp to which paragraph (2), (3), (4) or (6) of this Regulation applies or to any such lamp marked as provided in paragraph (9) of this Regulation.

(11) Nothing in this Regulation shall be taken to authorise any person to apply the said specification number B.S.2516, the said specification number B.S.3648, an approval mark, the said symbol "R", the said symbol "R-S1" or the said symbol "R-S2" to any obligatory rear lamp in contravention of the Trade Descriptions Act 1968(a)." ;

(3) in Regulation 45, in sub-paragraph (1)(b)(iii), before the word "maintaining," there were inserted the word "testing,".

Given under the Official seal of the Minister of Transport the 15th January 1970.

(L.S.)

Fred Mulley,
Minister of Transport.

(a) 1968 c. 29.

EXPLANATORY NOTE

(This note is not part of the Regulations.)

These Regulations further amend the Road Vehicles Lighting Regulations 1964. The principal changes are :—

1. Certain motor vehicles (except motor bicycles) and trailers are permitted to be fitted with obligatory rear lamps marked with an approval mark designated by the Motor Vehicles (Designation of Approval Marks) Regulations 1968 instead of with, *inter alia*, the specification number of the British Standard for Tail Lights for Vehicles, namely, B.S.2516 (paragraph (9) of the new Regulation 15) ;

2. Motor vehicles (except motor bicycles) and trailers manufactured on or after 1st January 1973 and registered or supplied on or after 1st July 1973 are required to be fitted with obligatory rear lamps marked with an approval mark designated by the Motor Vehicles (Designation of Approval Marks) Regulations 1968 (paragraphs (6) and (7) of the new Regulation 15) ;

3. Vehicles testing roads are permitted to carry certain lamps showing an amber light to the rear (Regulation 2(3)).

STATUTORY INSTRUMENTS

1970 No. 49

ROAD TRAFFIC

The Motor Vehicles (Construction and Use) (Amendment) Regulations 1970

Made - - - -	*15th January* 1970
Laid before Parliament	*27th January* 1970
Coming into Operation	*1st March* 1970

The Minister of Transport, in exercise of his powers under section 64(1) of the Road Traffic Act 1960(a) as amended by section 51 of and Schedule 4 to the Road Traffic Act 1962(b) and of all other enabling powers, and after consultation with representative organisations in accordance with the provisions of section 260(2) of the said Act of 1960, hereby makes the following Regulations:—

1.—(1) These Regulations shall come into operation on the 1st March 1970 and may be cited as the Motor Vehicles (Construction and Use) (Amendment) Regulations 1970.

(2) The Interpretation Act 1889(c) shall apply for the interpretation of these Regulations as it applies for the interpretation of an Act of Parliament.

2. The Motor Vehicles (Construction and Use) Regulations 1969(d), as amended(e), shall be further amended in accordance with the following provisions of these Regulations.

3. Regulation 3(1) (*Interpretation*) shall have effect as though—

(a) after the definition of "indivisible load" there were inserted the following definition:—

" 'industrial tractor' means a tractor, not being a land tractor, which—

(a) has an unladen weight not exceeding 7¼ tons,

(b) is designed and used primarily for work off roads, or for work on roads in connection only with road construction or maintenance (including any such tractor when fitted with an implement or implements designed primarily for use in connection with such work, whether or not any such implement is of itself designed to carry a load), and

(c) is so constructed as to be incapable of exceeding a speed of 20 miles per hour on the level under its own power;";

(a) 1960 c. 16.
(b) 1962 c. 59.
(c) 1889 c. 63.
(d) S.I. 1969/321 (1969 I, p. 829).
(e) There is no relevant amending instrument.

(b) for the definition of "stop light", there were substituted the following definition:—

> " 'stop lamp' means a lamp fitted to a motor vehicle, or to a trailer drawn by a motor vehicle, for the purpose of warning other road users, when the lamp is lit, that the brakes of the motor vehicle or, in the case of a trailer, the brakes of the drawing vehicle or of the combination of vehicles, are being applied;".

4. Regulation 4 (*Application and Exemptions*) shall have effect as though—

(a) in paragraph (6), in sub-paragraph (a) for the words "Part I" there were substituted the words "Part I, Part II (so far as it relates to direction indicators and stop lights)"; and

(b) after paragraph (6) there were inserted the following paragraph:—

> "(6A) Part II of these Regulations, except Regulations 7, 33 to 35 inclusive, 39, 43, 48 and 57, shall not apply to any motor vehicle manufactured in Great Britain which has been purchased by a person who is temporarily in Great Britain and is or is about to be resident abroad and in respect of which—
>
>> (a) relief from purchase tax has been afforded by virtue of section 23 of the Purchase Tax Act 1963(a), or
>>
>> (b) there is no liability to pay purchase tax,
>
> for a period—
>
>> (i) in the case at (a), not exceeding one year during which relief from purchase tax continues to be afforded in respect of that vehicle, and
>>
>> (ii) in the case at (b), not exceeding one year from the date it was purchased by such a person as a new vehicle from a manufacturer of or dealer in mechanically propelled vehicles,
>
> provided the vehicle complies in every respect with the requirements specified in the last preceding paragraph of this Regulation and contained in the Conventions of 1949 and 1926 therein referred to as if the vehicle had been brought temporarily into Great Britain.".

5. For the heading above Regulation 31 (Direction indicators) and Regulation 32 (Stop lights), namely, "B.-Direction Indicators and Stop Lights" and for those Regulations there shall be substituted the following heading and Regulations:—

"B.-Direction Indicators and Stop Lamps

Provision as to direction indicators when fitted

31.—(1) Every motor vehicle (other than a two-wheeled motor cycle with or without a sidecar attached) first used on or after 1st January 1936 and before 1st September 1965 which is fitted with a direction indicator shall—

(a) if it is a vehicle fitted with electric lighting equipment, comply with the provisions relating to direction indicators contained in either Part I or Part II or Part III of Schedule 3; or

(b) if it is a vehicle not fitted with such equipment, comply with the provisions relating to direction indicators contained in Part V of the said Schedule.

(a) 1963 c. 9.

(2) Every two-wheeled motor cycle with or without a sidecar attached first used on or after 1st January 1936 which is fitted with a direction indicator shall comply with the provisions relating to direction indicators contained in either the said Part I or Part II or in Part V of the said Schedule.

(3) Save as provided in paragraph (4) of this Regulation, every trailer manufactured after 1st July 1955 and before 1st January 1971 which is fitted with a direction indicator shall comply with the provisions relating to direction indicators contained in either Part III or Part VI of Schedule 3.

(4) Every motor vehicle (other than a two-wheeled motor cycle with or without a sidecar attached) first used on or after 1st September 1965 and before 1st January 1971 which is fitted with a direction indicator shall comply with the provisions relating to direction indicators contained in Part III of Schedule 3, and any trailer drawn by such a motor vehicle, or by a motor vehicle first used before 1st September 1965 and fitted with direction indicators in accordance with those provisions, shall be fitted with direction indicators in accordance with those provisions.

Requirements for direction indicators to be fitted

31A.—(1) Save as provided in paragraph (2) of this Regulation, on and after 1st January 1971—

(a) every motor vehicle first used before 1st September 1965 shall be fitted with direction indicators in accordance with the provisions of either Part I, Part II or Part III of Schedule 3, and

(b) every motor vehicle first used on and after 1st September 1965 and before 1st July 1973 shall be fitted with direction indicators in accordance with the provisions of Part III of Schedule 3,

(c) every trailer manufactured after 1st July 1955 and before 1st July 1973 shall be fitted with direction indicators in accordance with the provisions of either Part III or Part VI of Schedule 3, except that if it is drawn by a motor vehicle fitted with direction indicators in accordance with Part III of the said Schedule it shall be fitted with direction indicators in accordance with that Part.

(2) Nothing in this Regulation shall apply to—

(a) a motor vehicle—

(i) which is a two-wheeled motor cycle with or without a sidecar attached;

(ii) which is an industrial tractor, a land locomotive, a land tractor, a works truck or a pedestrian controlled vehicle;

(iii) which carries lamps for the purposes of section 1 of the Road Transport Lighting Act 1957(a) which are not electrically operated or which carries no lamps for such purposes;

(iv) first used before 1st January 1936;

(v) which it is unlawful at all times to drive at a speed exceeding 15 miles per hour; or

(vi) which is incapable by reason of its construction of exceeding a speed of 15 miles per hour on the level under its own power; or

(b) to a trailer—

(i) which is a land implement, a works trailer or an agricultural trailer;

(a) 1957 c. 51.

(ii) which carries lamps for the purposes of section 1 of the Road Transport Lighting Act 1957 which are not electrically operated or which carries no lamps for such purposes;

(iii) which is drawn by a motor vehicle not fitted with direction indicators;

(iv) which forms part of an articulated vehicle and was manufactured before 1st September 1965;

(v) the dimensions of which are such that when the longitudinal axis of the trailer lies in the same vertical plane as the longitudinal axis of the drawing vehicle both rear or both side direction indicators on that vehicle are visible to an observer in that vertical plane, from a point 6 metres behind the rear of the trailer whether it is loaded or not; or

(vi) which is a broken-down motor vehicle or forms part of a broken-down articulated vehicle or which draws another trailer behind it.

31B.—(1) In this Regulation, "excepted motor vehicle" means a motor vehicle mentioned in Regulation 31A(2)(*a*) and "excepted trailer" means a trailer mentioned in Regulation 31A(2)(*b*).

(2) Except as provided in paragraph (3) of this Regulation, this Regulation applies to the following vehicles, namely,—

(*a*) every motor vehicle (other than an excepted motor vehicle) first used on or after 1st July 1973;

(*b*) every trailer (other than an excepted trailer) manufactured on or after the said date;

(*c*) every excepted motor vehicle (other than a two-wheeled motor cycle with or without a sidecar attached) first used on or after the said date which is fitted with a direction indicator;

(*d*) every excepted trailer manufactured on or after the said date which is fitted with a direction indicator.

(3) This Regulation does not apply to a motor vehicle manufactured before 1st January 1973.

(4) Every vehicle to which this Regulation applies shall be fitted with direction indicators in accordance with the provisions of Part III of Schedule 3.

(5) Every direction indicator fitted to a vehicle in accordance with the last preceding paragraph shall be marked with an approval mark and—

(*a*) in the case of a front indicator, the number "1" above such mark, or

(*b*) in the case of a rear indicator, the number "2b" above such mark, or

(*c*) in the case of a side indicator, the number "3" above such mark, or

(*d*) in the case of a shoulder indicator, the number "4" above such mark, or

(*e*) in the case of a flank indicator, the number "5" above such mark.

(6) Every rear direction indicator fitted to a vehicle in accordance with paragraph (4) of this Regulation shall be capable of being operated on either of two levels of illumination and be wired in such a way that, when the obligatory front and rear lamps of the motor vehicle on which the indicator is fitted, or of the motor vehicle which is drawing the trailer on which the indicator is fitted, are switched off, the indicator when operated is lit at the higher level

of illumination, and when the obligatory front and rear lamps of the motor vehicle are switched on, the indicator when operated is lit at the lower level of illumination, so, however, that the foregoing provisions shall not preclude each rear direction indicator and the obligatory front and rear lamps of the motor vehicle being wired in such a way that, when such lamps are switched on and any fog lamp on that motor vehicle is switched on, the indicator when operated is lit at the higher level of illumination, and when such obligatory lamps are switched on but no fog lamp is switched on, the indicator when operated is lit at the lower level of illumination:

Provided that nothing in this paragraph shall apply to a rear direction indicator fitted to a motor vehicle mentioned in Regulation 31A(2)(a)(iii) or to a trailer mentioned in Regulation 31A(2)(b)(ii) or (iii).

(7) Nothing in this Regulation shall be taken to authorise any person to apply an approval mark or the said numbers "1", "2b", "3", "4" or "5" to any direction indicator in contravention of the Trade Descriptions Act 1968(a).

(8) In this Regulation—

"obligatory front and rear lamps" means the lamps showing to the front a white light and to the rear a red light which are required to be carried under section 1 of the Road Transport Lighting Act 1957 and any regulations made thereunder;

"fog lamp" means a lamp on a motor vehicle which is designed primarily to be used only in conditions of fog or whilst snow is falling;

"approval mark" means a marking designated as an approval mark by Regulation 2(2) of the Motor Vehicles (Designation of Approval Marks) Regulations 1968(b).

Provision as to stop lamps when fitted

32.—(1) Every stop lamp fitted to a motor vehicle first used on or after 1st January 1936 and before 1st January 1971 or to a trailer manufactured before the last mentioned date shall be fitted at the rear of the vehicle and not to the left of the centre thereof and when in operation shall show a red or amber light, except that on and after 1st January 1971 no such lamp shall show an amber light:

Provided that nothing in this paragraph shall prevent the fitting of a duplicate stop lamp on the left or near side of the vehicle which (except when the stop lamp fitted on the right or offside of the vehicle is showing a flashing light as a direction indicator) comes into operation at the same time as the stop lamp fitted at the centre or on the right or offside of the vehicle.

(2) Every light shown by a stop lamp shall be diffused by means of frosted glass or other adequate means and shall be a steady light.

Requirements for stop lamps to be fitted

32A.—(1) Save as provided in paragraph (2) of this Regulation, on and after 1st January 1971, every motor vehicle first used before that date and every trailer manufactured before that date shall be fitted with a stop lamp and in relation to that lamp the provisions of the last preceding Regulation shall apply as they apply to a stop lamp mentioned in that Regulation.

(a) 1968 c. 29.   (b) S.I. 1968/171 (1968 I, p. 403).

(2) Nothing in paragraph (1) of this Regulation shall require any vehicle specified in Part I of Schedule 12 to be fitted with any stop lamp.

32B.—(1) Save as provided in paragraph (2) of this Regulation, every two-wheeled motor cycle with or without a sidecar attached and every invalid carriage first used on or after 1st January 1971 shall be fitted with one stop lamp, and every other motor vehicle first used on or after that date and every trailer manufactured on or after that date shall be fitted with two stop lamps.

(2) Nothing in paragraph (1) of this Regulation shall require any vehicle specified in Part I of Schedule 12 to be fitted with any stop lamp.

(3) On and after 1st January 1971, every stop lamp fitted to any motor vehicle or trailer mentioned in paragraph (1) of this Regulation (whether or not in pursuance of the said paragraph (1)) shall comply with the conditions set out in Part II of Schedule 12.

32C.—(1) Save as provided in paragraph (2) of this Regulation, every stop lamp fitted to a motor vehicle first used on or after 1st July 1973 or to a trailer manufactured on or after that date shall, in addition to complying with the conditions set out in Part II of Schedule 12, comply with the conditions set out in Part III of that Schedule.

(2) Nothing in paragraph (1) of this Regulation shall in so far as it requires compliance by a stop lamp with Part III of Schedule 12 apply to any stop lamp fitted—

(a) to any motor vehicle manufactured before 1st January 1973; or

(b) to any two-wheeled motor cycle with or without a sidecar attached thereto, or

(c) to any trailer which is being drawn by a motor vehicle first used before 1st July 1973 or manufactured before 1st January 1973; or

(d) to any vehicle mentioned in paragraph 5 of Part I of Schedule 12.".

6. After Regulation 81 (Maintenance of lighting equipment and reflectors), there shall be added the following Regulations:—

"Maintenance of direction indicators

81A. Every direction indicator fitted to a motor vehicle or trailer shall at all times while the vehicle is used on a road be maintained in a clean condition and in good and efficient working order.

Maintenance of stop lamps

81B. Every stop lamp fitted to a motor vehicle or trailer shall at all times while the vehicle is used on a road be maintained in a clean condition and in good and efficient working order.".

7. In Regulation 108, in paragraph (1), there shall be added at the end the following words:—

"or in the case of a broken down vehicle being drawn by a motor vehicle in consequence of the breakdown.".

8. In Schedule 3, in Part III—

(a) for paragraph 9 there shall be substituted the following paragraph:—

"9. Every direction indicator shall be so placed that the outermost part of its illuminated area furthest from the longitudinal axis of the vehicle is not more than 400 millimetres nearer to that longitudinal

axis than is the outermost part of the vehicle which is comprised in
the overall width of the vehicle on the side on which the indicator is
placed, except that in the case of a public service vehicle having combined rear and side entrances a nearside rear indicator may be so
placed that the outermost part of its illuminated area furthest from
the longitudinal axis of the vehicle is not more than 760 millimetres
nearer to that longitudinal axis than is the said outermost part of the
vehicle.";

(*b*) after paragraph 16, there shall be added the following paragraph:—

"17. The provisions of this Part of this Schedule and of Part IV
of this Schedule shall in relation to—

(*a*) a direction indicator marked with an approval mark and a
number as required by Regulation 31B(5), and

(*b*) a direction indicator marked with such a mark and number,
notwithstanding it is not required to be so marked by the said
Regulation,

have effect as though—

(i) paragraphs 6(2), 7 and 13 in this Part were omitted;

(ii) in paragraph 8, in this Part, for the words 'not exceeding
10 degrees' there were substituted the words 'not exceeding
5 degrees';

(iii) in each of the diagrams 2 and 4 set out in the said Part IV
for the words '10° Blind Angle' there were substituted the
words '5° Blind Angle'.".

9. As from 1st January 1971, in Schedule 3, in Part III, paragraph 4(2) shall
be omitted.

10. After Schedule 11, shall be added the following Schedule:—

"SCHEDULE 12 (See Regulations 32A, 32B and 32C)

STOP LAMPS

PART I

Vehicles not required to be fitted with stop lamps

1. Agricultural trailers, land implements, land locomotives, land tractors,
pedestrian controlled vehicles, works trailers and works trucks.

2. Motor cycles whereof the cylinder capacity of the engine does not
exceed 50 cubic centimetres, being cycles equipped with pedals by means
whereof they are capable of being propelled.

3. Motor vehicles first used before 1st January 1936.

4. Motor vehicles—

(*a*) which it is at all times unlawful to drive at a speed exceeding 15 miles
per hour; or

(*b*) which are incapable by reason of their construction of exceeding a
speed of 15 miles per hour on the level under their own power.

5. Motor vehicles and trailers the lamps of which carried for the purposes
of section 1 of the Road Transport Lighting Act 1957 are not electrically
operated and motor vehicles and trailers which carry no lamps for such
purposes.

6. Trailers whilst drawn by any motor vehicle not required to be fitted with stop lamps in accordance with Regulation 32A or 32B.

7. Trailers drawn by motor vehicles fitted with two stop lamps, the dimensions of the trailer being such that when the longitudinal axis of the trailer lies in the same vertical plane as the longitudinal axis of the drawing vehicle both such stop lamps are visible to an observer in that vertical plane from a point 6 metres behind the rear of the trailer whether it is loaded or not.

8. Every trailer which is a broken down motor vehicle or which forms part of a broken down articulated vehicle.

9. In the case of a combination of two or more vehicles, being a motor vehicle drawing a trailer or trailers, the vehicles in that combination other than the rearmost.

PART II

Conditions to be complied with by stop lamps fitted to motor vehicles first used on or after 1st January 1971 and to trailers manufactured on or after that date.

1. Every stop lamp shall show a steady red light, when the braking system which operates the lamp is applied, visible to the rear of the vehicle at any point between at least 15 degrees above and 15 degrees below the horizontal throughout an angle of at least 45 degrees in the horizontal plane on each side of a line parallel to the longitudinal axis of the vehicle and passing through the centre of the illuminated area of the lamp.

2. The total rating of the filament illuminated in a stop lamp shall not be less than 15 watts nor more than 36 watts and the rated wattage of that filament shall be durably marked upon the glass or the metal cap of the filament lamp in a readily legible manner:

Provided that this paragraph shall not apply in the case of a stop lamp fitted to any vehicle other than a two-wheeled motor cycle with or without a sidecar attached, if the stop lamp is marked with an approval mark and symbol as required by paragraph 1(1)(b) of Part III of this Schedule or with such a mark and symbol notwithstanding it is not required to be so marked by the said paragraph.

3. No part of the illuminated area of a stop lamp shall be less than 400 millimetres or more than 1500 millimetres above the level of the ground when the vehicle is unladen so, however, that the said measurement of 1500 millimetres may be increased to 2100 millimetres, if it is not practicable by reason of the structure of the vehicle at its rear for the said measurement of 1500 millimetres to be complied with.

4. Every stop lamp fitted to a motor vehicle shall be operated by the application of a braking system designed to be used to bring the motor vehicle when in motion to a halt and when fitted to a trailer drawn by a motor vehicle shall be operated by the application of such a system.

5. Where one stop lamp is fitted to a vehicle it shall be fitted at the rear of the vehicle and on or to the offside of the vertical plane passing through the longitudinal axis of the vehicle (disregarding, for the purpose of ascertaining such axis, any sidecar attached to a two wheeled motor cycle).

6. In any case where two or more stop lamps are fitted to a vehicle—

(a) they shall be fitted at the rear of the vehicle;

(b) at least two shall be so designed that the light emitted thereby is emitted at the same time and shall be fitted to the vehicle so that they are—

    (i) symmetrically positioned on each side of the vertical plane passing through the longitudinal axis of the vehicle;

    (ii) at the same height from the ground; and

    (iii) in such positions that no part of the illuminated area of one such lamp is nearer than 600 millimetres to any part of the illuminated area of the other such lamp;

(c) the wiring required for the illumination of the lamps shall be so arranged that in the event of any failure of a bulb in one of the lamps the other lamp or lamps shall not thereby be extinguished.

Part III

Conditions to be complied with by stop lamps fitted to motor vehicles first used on or after 1st July 1973 and trailers manufactured on or after that date.

1.—(1) Every stop lamp fitted to a motor vehicle or to a trailer shall—

(a) be capable of being operated on either of two levels of illumination and be wired in such a way that, when the obligatory front and rear lamps of the motor vehicle on which the stop lamp is fitted, or of the motor vehicle which is drawing the trailer on which the stop lamp is fitted, are switched off, the stop lamp when operated is lit at the higher level of illumination, and when the obligatory front and rear lamps of the motor vehicle are switched on, the stop lamp when operated is lit at the lower level of illumination, so, however, that the foregoing provisions shall not preclude each stop lamp and the obligatory front and rear lamps of the motor vehicle being wired in such a way that, when such obligatory lamps are switched on and any fog lamp on that motor vehicle is switched on, the stop lamp when operated is lit at the higher level of illumination, and when such obligatory lamps are switched on but no fog lamp is switched on, the stop lamp when operated is lit at the lower level of illumination;

(b) be marked with an approval mark and—

    (i) in the case of a stop lamp not combined with a rear lamp, the symbol "S2" enclosed in a square above such mark, or

    (ii) in the case of a stop lamp combined with a rear lamp the symbol "R—S2" enclosed in a rectangle above such mark.

(2) Nothing in this Part of this Schedule shall be taken to authorise any person to apply an approval mark, the said symbol "S2" or the said symbol "R—S2" to any stop lamp in contravention of the Trade Descriptions Act 1968.

(3) In this paragraph—

"obligatory front and rear lamps" means the lamps showing to the front a white light and to the rear a red light which are required to be carried under section 1 of the Road Transport Lighting Act 1957 and any regulations made thereunder;

"fog lamp" means a lamp on a motor vehicle which is designed primarily to be used only in conditions of fog or whilst snow is falling; and "approval mark" means a marking designated as an approval mark by Regulation 2(2) of the Motor Vehicles (Designation of Approval Marks) Regulations 1968.".

Given under the Official Seal of the Minister of Transport the 15th January 1970.

(L.S.)

Fred Mulley,
Minister of Transport.

EXPLANATORY NOTE

(This Note is not part of the Regulations.)

These Regulations further amend the Motor Vehicles (Construction and Use) Regulations 1969. The principal change is to introduce into the 1969 Regulations various Regulations, namely, Regulations 31 to 32C and Regulations 81A and 81B, imposing new requirements as respects the fitting of direction indicators and stop lamps to motor vehicles and trailers. The main new requirements are as follows:—

1. As from 1st January 1971, subject to certain exceptions, motor vehicles and trailers are required to be fitted with direction indicators and stop lamps complying with specified conditions (Regulations 31A, 32A and 32B).

2. As from 1st July 1973, subject to certain exceptions, motor vehicles first used and trailers manufactured on or after 1st July 1973 are required to be fitted with direction indicators complying with specified conditions and being marked with an approval mark designated by the Motor Vehicles (Designation of Approval Marks) Regulations 1968 (Regulation 31B).

3. As from 1st July 1973, subject to certain exceptions, motor vehicles first used and trailers manufactured on and after 1st July 1973 are required to be fitted with stop lamps complying with specified conditions and being marked with an approval mark designated by the Motor Vehicles (Designation of Approval Marks) Regulations 1968 (Regulation 32C).

4. All direction indicators and stop lamps fitted to vehicles, when in use on roads, must be properly maintained (Regulations 81A and 81B).

These Regulations also grant temporary exemption for motor vehicles from certain constructional requirements of the 1969 Regulations if purchased by persons only temporarily in Great Britain and who are or who are about to be resident abroad (Regulation 4), and provide that, where a broken down vehicle is being towed by a motor vehicle, the overall length of the combination may exceed 18 metres (Regulation 7).

STATUTORY INSTRUMENTS

1970 No. 50

ANIMALS

PREVENTION OF CRUELTY

The Spring Traps Approval (Amendment) Order 1970

Made	- - -	*19th January* 1970
Coming into Operation		*1st February* 1970

The Minister of Agriculture, Fisheries and Food, in exercise of the powers vested in him by section 8 of the Pests Act 1954(a) and of all other powers enabling him in that behalf, hereby makes the following order :—

Citation, commencement and interpretation

1.—(1) This order may be cited as the Spring Traps Approval (Amendment) Order 1970 and shall come into operation on 1st February 1970.

(2) The Interpretation Act 1889(b) shall apply to the interpretation of this order as it applies to the interpretation of an Act of Parliament.

Amendment of principal order

2. The Spring Traps Approval Order 1957(c), as amended by the Spring Traps Approval (Amendment) Order 1966(d) and the Spring Traps Approval (Amendment) Order 1968(e), is hereby further amended by adding at the end of the first column of the Schedule thereto (in which are set out the types and makes of trap approved for the purposes of section 8 of the Pests Act 1954) the following description—

"Fenn Vermin Trap Mark IV (Heavy Duty) manufactured by or under the authority of Mr. A. A. Fenn, of F.H.T. Works, High Street, Astwood Bank, Redditch, Worcestershire."

and by adding at the end of the second column of the said Schedule (in which are set out the conditions as to the animals for which or the circumstances in which approved traps may be used), opposite the aforesaid description, the following conditions—

"The trap shall be used only—

(*a*) for the purpose of killing or taking grey squirrels and stoats, weasels, rats, mice or other small ground vermin, and set in natural tunnels or in artificial tunnels constructed for the purpose, or

(*b*) for the purpose of killing or taking rats or mice and set in the open on their runs.".

(a) 1954 c. 68.
(c) S.I. 1957/2216 (1957 I, p. 146).
(e) S.I. 1968/645 (1968 I, p. 1482).

(b) 1889 c. 63.
(d) S.I. 1966/849 (1966 II, p. 1988).

In Witness whereof the official seal of the Minister of Agriculture, Fisheries and Food is hereunto affixed on 19th January 1970.

(L.S.)   *Cledwyn Hughes,*
Minister of Agriculture, Fisheries and Food.

EXPLANATORY NOTE

(This Note is not part of the Order.)

By virtue of section 8 of the Pests Act 1954 it is an offence to use for the killing or taking of animals a spring trap other than one approved by the Minister of Agriculture, Fisheries and Food. This order adds the Fenn Vermin Trap Mark IV (Heavy Duty) to those already approved by the Minister in the Spring Traps Approval Order 1957, in the Spring Traps Approval (Amendment) Order 1966 and in the Spring Traps Approval (Amendment) Order 1968, and specifies the animals for which and the circumstances in which it may be used.

STATUTORY INSTRUMENTS

1970 No. 54

SUGAR

The Sugar (Rates of Surcharge and Surcharge Repayments) (No. 2) Order 1970

Made - - - -	*20th January* 1970
Laid before Parliament	*21st January* 1970
Coming into Operation	*22nd January* 1970

The Minister of Agriculture, Fisheries and Food, in exercise of the powers conferred on him by sections 7(4), 8(6) and 33(4) of the Sugar Act 1956(a) having effect subject to the provisions of section 3 of, and Part II of Schedule 5 to, the Finance Act 1962(b), and section 58 of the Finance Act 1968(c) and of all other powers enabling him in that behalf, with the concurrence of the Treasury, on the advice of the Sugar Board, hereby makes the following order:—

1.—(1) This order may be cited as the Sugar (Rates of Surcharge and Surcharge Repayments) (No. 2) Order 1970; and shall come into operation on 22nd January 1970.

(2) The Interpretation Act 1889(d) shall apply for the interpretation of this order as it applies for the interpretation of an Act of Parliament.

2. Notwithstanding the provisions of Article 2 of the Sugar (Rates of Surcharge and Surcharge Repayments) Order 1970(e), the rates of surcharge payable under and in accordance with the provisions of section 7 of the Sugar Act 1956, having effect as aforesaid, in respect of sugar and invert sugar imported or home produced or used in the manufacture of imported composite sugar products shall on and after 22nd January 1970 be those rates specified in Schedule 1 to this order.

3. For the purpose of section 8(3)(b) of the Sugar Act 1956, having effect as aforesaid, the rates of surcharge repayments in respect of invert sugar produced in the United Kingdom from materials on which on or after 22nd January 1970 sugar duty has been paid or, by virtue of paragraph 1 of Part II of Schedule 5 to the Finance Act 1962, is treated as having been paid shall, notwithstanding the provisions of Article 3 of the Sugar (Rates of Surcharge and Surcharge Repayments) Order 1970 be those specified in Schedule 2 to this order.

(a) 1956 c. 48.   (b) 1962 c. 44.
(c) 1968 c. 44.   (d) 1889 c. 63.
(e) S.I. 1970/39.(1970 I, p. 235).

In Witness whereof the Official Seal of the Minister of Agriculture, Fisheries and Food is hereunto affixed on 20th January 1970.

(L.S.)   *R. P. Fraser,*

Authorised by the Minister.

We concur.

20th January 1970.

Neil McBride,

Walter Harrison,

Two of the Lords Commissioners of
Her Majesty's Treasury.

SCHEDULE 1

PART I

SURCHARGE RATES FOR SUGAR

Polarisation	Rate of Surcharge per cwt.	
	s.	d.
Exceeding—		
99°	18	8·0
98° but not exceeding 99°	17	7·2
97° ,, ,, ,, 98°	17	2·0
96° ,, ,, ,, 97°	16	8·7
95° ,, ,, ,, 96°	16	3·3
94° ,, ,, ,, 95°	15	9·9
93° ,, ,, ,, 94°	15	4·5
92° ,, ,, ,, 93°	14	11·2
91° ,, ,, ,, 92°	14	5·8
90° ,, ,, ,, 91°	14	0·4
89° ,, ,, ,, 90°	13	7·0
88° ,, ,, ,, 89°	13	1·6
87° ,, ,, ,, 88°	12	9·2
86° ,, ,, ,, 87°	12	4·7
85° ,, ,, ,, 86°	12	0·7
84° ,, ,, ,, 85°	11	8·6
83° ,, ,, ,, 84°	11	4·6
82° ,, ,, ,, 83°	11	0·6
81° ,, ,, ,, 82°	10	9·0
80° ,, ,, ,, 81°	10	5·4
79° ,, ,, ,, 80°	10	1·8
78° ,, ,, ,, 79°	9	10·2
77° ,, ,, ,, 78°	9	6·6
76° ,, ,, ,, 77°	9	3·1
Not exceeding 76°	9	0·0

PART II
SURCHARGE RATES FOR INVERT SUGAR

Sweetening matter content by weight	Rate of Surcharge per cwt.
	s. d.
70 per cent. or more	11 10
Less than 70 per cent. and more than 50 per cent.	8 6
Not more than 50 per cent.	4 2

SCHEDULE 2
SURCHARGE REPAYMENT RATES FOR INVERT SUGAR

Sweetening matter content by weight	Rate of Surcharge Repayment per cwt.
	s. d.
More than 80 per cent.	14 0
More than 70 per cent. but not more than 80 per cent.	11 10
More than 60 per cent. but not more than 70 per cent.	8 6
More than 50 per cent. but not more than 60 per cent.	6 9
Not more than 50 per cent. and the invert sugar not being less in weight than 14 lb. per gallon	4 2

EXPLANATORY NOTE
(*This Note is not part of the Order.*)

This order prescribes—

(*a*) reductions equivalent to 2s. 4d. per cwt. of refined sugar in the rates of surcharge payable on sugar and invert sugar which become chargeable with surcharge on or after 22nd January 1970;

(*b*) correspondingly reduced rates of surcharge repayment in respect of invert sugar produced in the United Kingdom from materials on which surcharge has been paid.

STATUTORY INSTRUMENTS

1970 No. 55

SUGAR

The Composite Sugar Products (Surcharge and Surcharge Repayments—Average Rates) (No. 3) Order 1970

Made	-	-	-	-	*20th January* 1970
Laid before Parliament					*21st January* 1970
Coming into Operation					*22nd January* 1970

Whereas the Minister of Agriculture, Fisheries and Food (hereinafter called " the Minister ") has on the recommendation of the Commissioners of Customs and Excise (hereinafter called " the Commissioners ") made an order(a) pursuant to the powers conferred upon him by sections 9(1) and 9(4) of the Sugar Act 1956(b), having effect subject to the provisions of section 3 of, and Part II of Schedule 5 to, the Finance Act 1962(c), to the provisions of section 52(2) of the Finance Act 1966(d), and to the provisions of Section 58 of the Finance Act 1968(e), providing that in the case of certain descriptions of composite sugar products surcharge shall be calculated on the basis of an average quantity of sugar or invert sugar taken to have been used in the manufacture of the products, and that certain other descriptions of composite sugar products shall be treated as not containing any sugar or invert sugar, and that in the case of certain descriptions of goods in the manufacture of which sugar or invert sugar is used, surcharge repayments shall be calculated on the basis of an average quantity of sugar or invert sugar taken to have been so used:

Now, therefore, the Minister, on the recommendation of the Commissioners and in exercise of the powers conferred upon him by sections 9(1), 9(4) and 33(4) of the Sugar Act 1956, having effect as aforesaid, and of all other powers enabling him in that behalf, hereby makes the following order:—

1.—(1) This order may be cited as the Composite Sugar Products (Surcharge and Surcharge Repayments—Average Rates) (No. 3) Order 1970, and shall come into operation on 22nd January 1970.

(2) The Interpretation Act 1889(f) shall apply for the interpretation of this order as it applies for the interpretation of an Act of Parliament.

2. Surcharge payable on or after 22nd January 1970 under and in accordance with the Sugar Act 1956, having effect as aforesaid, in respect of sugar and invert sugar used in the manufacture of the descriptions of imported composite sugar products specified in column 2 of Schedule 1 to this order shall, notwithstanding the provisions of the Sugar (Rates of Surcharge and Surcharge Repayments) (No. 2) Order 1970(g) and the Composite Sugar Products (Surcharge and Surcharge Repayments—Average Rates) (No. 2) Order 1970(a), be calculated by reference to the weight of the products at the rates specified in relation thereto in column 3 of the said Schedule.

(a) S.I. 1970/40 (1970 I, p. 238).   (b) 1956 c. 48.   (c) 1962 c. 44.
(d) 1966 c. 18.   (e) 1968 c. 44.   (f) 1889 c. 63.
(g) S.I. 1970/54 (1970 I, p. 338).

3. Imported composite sugar products other than those of a description specified in Schedules 1 and 2 to this order shall be treated as not containing any sugar or invert sugar for the purposes of surcharge payable on or after 22nd January 1970.

4. Surcharge repayments payable on and after 22nd January 1970 under and in accordance with the provisions of section 8 of the Sugar Act 1956, having effect as aforesaid, in respect of sugar and invert sugar used in the manufacture of the descriptions of goods specified in column 1 of Schedule 3 to this order shall, notwithstanding the provisions of the Sugar (Rates of Surcharge and Surcharge Repayments) (No. 2) Order 1970(a) and the Composite Sugar Products (Surcharge and Surcharge Repayments—Average Rates) (No. 2) Order 1970(b), be calculated by reference to the quantity of the goods at the rates specified in relation thereto in column 2 of the said Schedule.

In Witness whereof the Official Seal of the Minister of Agriculture, Fisheries and Food is hereunto affixed on 20th January 1970.

R. P. Fraser,
Authorised by the Minister.

SCHEDULE 1

In this Schedule:—

" Tariff heading " means a heading or, where the context so requires, a subheading of the Customs Tariff 1959 (see paragraph (1) of Article 2 of the Import Duties (General) (No. 3) Order 1969(c)).

Tariff heading	Description of Imported Composite Sugar Products	Rate of Surcharge
		per cwt. s. d.
04.02	Milk and cream, preserved, concentrated or sweetened, containing more than 10 per cent. by weight of added sugar	8 3
17.02 (B) (2) and 17.05 (B)	Syrups containing sucrose sugar, whether or not flavoured or coloured, but not including fruit juices containing added sugar in any proportion:— containing 70 per cent. or more by weight of sweetening matter	11 10
	containing less than 70 per cent., and more than 50 per cent., by weight of sweetening matter ..	8 6
	containing not more than 50 per cent. by weight of sweetening matter	4 2

(a) S.I. 1970/54(1970 I, p.338).   (b) S.I. 1970/40(1970 I, p.238).
(c) S.I. 1969/1413 (1969 III, p. 4150).

Tariff heading	Description of Imported Composite Sugar Products	Rate of Surcharge
		Per cwt. s. d.
17.02 (F) ..	Caramel:—	
	Solid	18 8
	Liquid	13 1
17.04	Sugar confectionery, not containing cocoa ..	15 2
18.06	Chocolate and other food preparations containing cocoa and added sugar:—	
	Chocolate couverture not prepared for retail sale; chocolate milk crumb, liquid ..	8 3
	Chocolate milk crumb, solid	10 3
	Solid chocolate bars or blocks, milk or plain, with or without fruit or nuts; other chocolate confectionery consisting wholly of chocolate or of chocolate and other ingredients not containing added sugar, but not including such goods when packed together in retail packages with goods liable to surcharge at a higher rate	8 5
	Other	10 10
19.08	Pastry, biscuits, cakes and other fine bakers' wares containing added sugar:—	
	Biscuits, wafers and rusks containing more than 12½ per cent. by weight of added sugar, and other biscuits, wafers and rusks included in retail packages with such goods.. ..	4 8
	Cakes with covering or filling containing added sugar; meringues	6 3
	Other	2 4
20.01	Vegetables and fruit, prepared or preserved by vinegar or acetic acid, containing added sugar:—	
	Containing 10 per cent. or more by weight of added sugar	6 6
	Other	1 5
20.03	Fruit preserved by freezing, containing added sugar	2 4
20.04	Fruit, fruit-peel and parts of plants, preserved by sugar (drained, glacé or crystallised)	12 3
20.05	Jams, fruit jellies, marmalades, fruit purée and fruit pastes, being cooked preparations, containing added sugar	11 9
20.06	Fruit otherwise prepared or preserved, containing added sugar:—	
	Ginger	9 4
	Other	2 4

SCHEDULE 2

Tariff heading	Description of Imported Composite Sugar Products
17.05 (A) and (B)	Sugar and invert sugar, flavoured or coloured.

SCHEDULE 3

Description of goods	Rate of surcharge repayment per bulk barrel of 36 gallons
Lager	9 · 3d.
All beer other than lager	8 · 3d.

EXPLANATORY NOTE

(This Note is not part of the Order.)

This order provides for reductions on and after 22nd January 1970 in the average rates of surcharge payable on imported composite sugar products of the descriptions specified in Schedule 1 and in the average rates of surcharge repayment in respect of exported goods of the descriptions specified in Schedule 3. These correspond to the reductions in surcharge rates effected by the Sugar (Rates of Surcharge and Surcharge Repayments) (No. 2) Order 1970 (S.I. 1970/54). Provision is also made for certain imported composite sugar products to be treated as not containing any sugar or invert sugar.

STATUTORY INSTRUMENTS

1970 No. 56

DEFENCE

The Naval Detention Quarters (Amendment) Rules 1970

Made - - -	20*th January* 1970
Laid before Parliament	27*th January* 1970
Coming into Operation	9*th February* 1970

The Secretary of State, in exercise of the powers conferred upon him by sections 81 and 82 of the Naval Discipline Act, 1957**(a)** and of all other powers enabling him in that behalf hereby makes the following Rules:—

1.—(1) These Rules may be cited as the Naval Detention Quarters (Amendment) Rules 1970 and shall come into operation on the 9th February 1970.

(2) The Interpretation Act 1889**(b)** shall apply to the interpretation of these Rules as it applies to the interpretation of an Act of Parliament.

2. Rule 57 of the Naval Detention Quarters Rules, 1959**(c)** shall be deleted and the following Rule substituted therefor:—

"The use of special clothing.

57(1) Where a man under sentence destroys, or attempts to destroy, his clothing or refuses to wear uniform, the Commanding Officer may order him to wear special clothing of a type approved by the Secretary of State.

(2) The Commanding Officer shall report to the monthly visitor, on the occasion of every visit, any subsisting orders made by him under paragraph (1) of this Rule and shall arrange for the monthly visitor to see every man who is wearing the clothing for which that paragraph provides.

(3) The Commanding Officer shall record every order made under this Rule and the periods during which, in pursuance of such order, the clothing provided for in paragraph (1) of this Rule is worn".

Dated this 20th day of January 1970.

Denis Healey,
One of Her Majesty's Principal
Secretaries of State.

(a) 1957 c. 53.   (b) 1889 c. 63.   (c) S.I. 1959/61 (1959 II, p. 2436).

EXPLANATORY NOTE

(This Note is not part of the Rules.)

These Rules amend the Naval Detention Quarters Rules 1959 to provide that sailors who destroy or refuse to wear uniform may be ordered to wear special clothing of a type approved by the Secretary of State. They replace a provision which required a canvas suit to be worn in such cases.

STATUTORY INSTRUMENTS

1970 No. 57

DEFENCE

The Imprisonment and Detention (Army) (Amendment) Rules 1970

Made - - -	*20th January* 1970
Laid before Parliament	*27th January* 1970
Coming into Operation	*9th February* 1970

The Secretary of State, in exercise of the powers conferred upon him by sections 119, 122, 123, 124, 126, 127 and 129 of the Army Act 1955(a) and of all other powers enabling him in that behalf hereby makes the following Rules:—

1.—(1) These Rules may be cited as the Imprisonment and Detention (Army) (Amendment) Rules 1970 and shall come into operation on the 9th February 1970.

(2) The Interpretation Act 1889(b) shall apply to the interpretation of these Rules as it applies to the interpretation of an Act of Parliament.

2. Rule 84 of the Imprisonment and Detention (Army) Rules 1956(c) shall be deleted and the following Rule substituted therefor:—

"The use of special clothing.

84 (1) Where a soldier under sentence destroys, or attempts to destroy, his clothing or refuses to wear uniform, the commandant of a military establishment may order him to wear special clothing of a type approved by the Secretary of State.

(2) The commandant shall report to the Visiting Officer, on the occasion of every visit, any subsisting orders made by him under paragraph (1) of this Rule and shall arrange for the Visiting Officer to see every soldier who is wearing the clothing for which that paragraph provides.

(3) The commandant shall record every order made under this Rule and the periods during which, in pursuance of such order, the clothing provided for in paragraph (1) of this Rule is worn".

Dated this 20th day of January 1970.

Denis Healey,
One of Her Majesty's Principal
Secretaries of State.

(a) 1955 c. 18.   (b) 1889 c. 63.   (c) S.I. 1956/1914 (1956 I, p. 310).

EXPLANATORY NOTE

(This Note is not part of the Rules.)

These Rules amend the Imprisonment and Detention (Army) Rules 1956 to provide that soldiers who destroy or refuse to wear uniform may be ordered to wear special clothing of a type approved by the Secretary of State. They replace a provision which required a canvas suit to be worn in such cases.

STATUTORY INSTRUMENTS

1970 No. 58

DEFENCE

The Imprisonment and Detention (Air Force) (Amendment) Rules 1970

Made - - -	*20th January* 1970
Laid before Parliament	*27th January* 1970
Coming into Operation	*9th February* 1970

The Secretary of State, in exercise of the powers conferred upon him by sections 119, 122, 123, 124, 126, 127 and 129 of the Air Force Act 1955 and of all other powers enabling him in that behalf hereby makes the following Rules:—

1.—(1) These Rules may be cited as the Imprisonment and Detention (Air Force) (Amendment) Rules 1970 and shall come into operation on the 9th February 1970.

(2) The Interpretation Act 1889**(b)** shall apply to the interpretation of these Rules as it applies to the interpretation of an Act of Parliament.

2. Rule 84 of the Imprisonment and Detention (Air Force) Rules 1956**(c)** shall be deleted and the following Rule substituted therefor:—

"The use of special clothing.

84(1) Where an airman under sentence destroys, or attempts to destroy, his clothing or refuses to wear uniform, the commandant of an air-force establishment may order him to wear special clothing of a type approved by the Secretary of State.

(2) The commandant shall report to the Visiting Officer, on the occasion of every visit, any subsisting orders made by him under paragraph (1) of this Rule and shall arrange for the Visiting Officer to see every airman who is wearing the clothing for which that paragraph provides.

(3) The commandant shall record every order made under this Rule and the periods during which, in pursuance of such order, the clothing provided for in paragraph (1) of this Rule is worn".

Dated this 20th day of January 1970.

Denis Healey,
One of Her Majesty's Principal
Secretaries of State.

(a) 1955 c. 19.　　(b) 1889 c. 63.　　(c) S.I. 1956/1981 (1956 II, p. 2118).

EXPLANATORY NOTE

(This Note is not part of the Rules.)

These Rules amend the Imprisonment and Detention (Air Force) Rules 1956 to provide that airmen who destroy or refuse to wear uniform may be ordered to wear special clothing of a type approved by the Secretary of State. They replace a provision which required a canvas suit to be worn in such cases.

STATUTORY INSTRUMENTS

1970 No. 60

WAGES COUNCILS

The Wages Regulation (Retail Drapery, Outfitting and Footwear) Order 1970

Made - - - -   20*th January* 1970

Coming into Operation   16*th March* 1970

Whereas the Secretary of State has received from the Retail Drapery, Outfitting and Footwear Trades Wages Council (Great Britain) the wages regulation proposals set out in the Schedule hereto ;

Now, therefore, the Secretary of State in exercise of her powers under section 11 of the Wages Councils Act 1959(a), and of all other powers enabling her in that behalf, hereby makes the following Order :—

1. This Order may be cited as the Wages Regulation (Retail Drapery, Outfitting and Footwear) Order 1970.

2.—(1) In this Order the expression " the specified date " means the 16th March 1970, provided that where, as respects any worker who is paid wages at intervals not exceeding seven days, that date does not correspond with the beginning of the period for which the wages are paid, the expression " the specified date " means, as respects that worker, the beginning of the next such period following that date.

(2) The Interpretation Act 1889(b) shall apply to the interpretation of this Order, as it applies to the interpretation of an Act of Parliament and as if this Order and the Orders hereby revoked were Acts of Parliament.

3. The wages regulation proposals set out in the Schedule hereto shall have effect as from the specified date and as from that date the Wages Regulation (Retail Drapery, Outfitting and Footwear) Order 1967(c) and the Wages Regulation (Retail Drapery, Outfitting and Footwear) (Amendment) Order 1968(d) shall cease to have effect.

Signed by order of the Secretary of State.

20th January 1970.

A. A. Jarratt,
Deputy Under Secretary of State,
Department of Employment and Productivity.

(a) 1959 c. 69.   (b) 1889 c. 63.   (c) S.I. 1967/618 (1967 I, p. 1830).
(d) S.I. 1968/1428 (1968 III, p. 4160).

ARRANGEMENT OF SCHEDULE

PART I

STATUTORY MINIMUM REMUNERATION

PART II

ANNUAL HOLIDAY AND HOLIDAY REMUNERATION

PART III

GENERAL

Article 3   SCHEDULE

The following minimum remuneration and provisions as to holidays and holiday remuneration shall be substituted for the statutory minimum remuneration and the provisions as to holidays and holiday remuneration fixed by the Wages Regulation (Retail Drapery, Outfitting and Footwear) Order 1967 (hereinafter referred to as " Order R.D.O. (50) ") as amended by the Wages Regulation (Retail Drapery, Outfitting and Footwear) (Amendment) Order 1968 (Order R.D.O. (52)).

PART I

STATUTORY MINIMUM REMUNERATION
APPLICATION

1. Subject to the provisions of paragraphs 5, 8 and 9, the minimum remuneration payable to workers to whom this Schedule applies shall be the remuneration set out in paragraphs 2, 3 and 4.

Any increase in remuneration payable under the provisions of paragraphs 2, 3 or 4 shall become effective on the first day of the first full pay week following the date upon which the increase would otherwise become payable under those provisions.

WORKERS OTHER THAN TEMPORARY SHOP MANAGERS, TEMPORARY SHOP MANAGERESSES AND TRANSPORT WORKERS

2.—(1) Subject to the provisions of paragraph 1, the minimum remuneration payable to male or female workers of the classes specified in Column 1 of the following table employed in the London Area, Provincial A Area or Provincial B Area, as the case may be, shall be the appropriate amount set out in Column 2.

Column 1	LONDON AREA Per week		PROVINCIAL A AREA Per week		PROVINCIAL B AREA Per week	
	Male	Female	Male	Female	Male	Female
	s. d.	s. d.	s. d.	s. d.	s. d.	s. d.
(a) SHOP MANAGERS, SHOP MANAGERESSES where the number of staff (computed in accordance with the provisions of sub-paragraph (2) of this paragraph) is:—						
1 or 2	290 0	252 6	284 0	246 6	273 0	237 6
3	296 0	258 6	290 0	252 6	279 0	243 6
4	302 6	265 0	296 6	259 0	285 6	250 0
5	309 0	271 6	303 0	265 6	292 0	256 6
6	315 6	278 0	309 6	272 0	298 6	263 0
(b) CLERKS GRADE I, aged 23 years or over	263 6	205 6	256 0	200 0	242 6	189 6
(c) CLERKS GRADE I, aged under 23 years, CLERKS GRADE II, SALES ASSISTANTS, CASHIERS, CENTRAL WAREHOUSE WORKERS, CREDIT TRAVELLERS, STOCK HANDS—						
Aged 22 years or over	257 6	201 0	250 0	195 6	236 6	185 0
„ 21 and under 22 years ...	240 0	187 6	234 0	182 0	220 0	172 0
„ 20 „ „ 21 „ ...	198 6	158 6	193 6	153 0	181 0	146 0
„ 19 „ „ 20 „ ...	188 0	152 6	183 0	147 0	170 6	140 0
„ 18 „ „ 19 „ ...	174 6	145 0	169 6	139 6	159 0	132 6
„ 17 „ „ 18 „ ...	146 0	123 6	141 0	118 0	132 6	111 6
„ 16 „ „ 17 „ ...	137 0	118 0	132 0	112 6	124 6	106 0
„ under 16 years	130 6	112 6	125 6	106 6	118 0	100 0
(d) ALL OTHER WORKERS (OTHER THAN THE WORKERS SPECIFIED IN PARAGRAPH 3 AND PARAGRAPH 4)—						
Aged 22 years or over	249 6	196 0	242 0	190 6	232 0	180 0
„ 21 and under 22 years ...	237 0	185 6	231 0	180 0	217 0	170 0
„ 20 „ „ 21 „ ...	197 6	156 6	192 6	151 0	180 0	144 0
„ 19 „ „ 20 „ ...	187 0	151 6	182 0	146 0	169 6	139 0
„ 18 „ „ 19 „ ...	173 6	144 0	168 6	138 6	158 0	131 6
„ 17 „ „ 18 „ ...	145 0	122 6	140 0	117 0	131 6	110 6
„ 16 „ „ 17 „ ...	136 0	117 0	131 0	111 6	123 6	105 0
„ under 16 years	129 6	111 6	124 6	105 6	117 0	99 0

Provided that where a sales assistant enters, or has entered, the retail drapery, outfitting and footwear trades for the first time at or over the age of 20 years, the minimum remuneration payable shall be—

(i) during the first three months of the employment, 10s. 0d. per week less, and

(ii) during the second three months of the employment, 5s. 0d. per week less

than the minimum remuneration otherwise applicable to the worker under (c) of this sub-paragraph.

(2) In the foregoing table " number of staff " means the number of persons (including the manager or manageress) normally employed by the employer, for whose control the manager or manageress is responsible to the employer, and in computing that number both full-time workers and workers other than full-time workers shall be included, except that in the case of workers other than full-time workers the number to be counted shall be the number of such workers or the number (treating any fraction as one) obtained by dividing by 30 the aggregate of the hours normally worked in the week by all such workers whichever is the less.

TEMPORARY SHOP MANAGERS AND TEMPORARY SHOP MANAGERESSES

3.—(1) Subject to the provisions of this paragraph, the minimum remuneration payable to temporary shop managers and temporary shop manageresses, for each continuous period of employment as temporary shop manager or temporary shop manageress (reckoned in accordance with the provisions of sub-paragraph (2) of this paragraph) shall be the appropriate minimum remuneration for a shop manager or shop manageress, as the case may be, under the provisions of paragraph 2(1)(a).

(2) In reckoning any continuous period of employment as temporary shop manager or temporary shop manageress for the purposes of sub-paragraph (1) of this paragraph, no account shall be taken of any period of employment—

(a) not exceeding two consecutive working days ; or

(b) not exceeding a total of two weeks in any year, being a period when the shop manager or shop manageress is absent on holiday:

Provided that for the purposes of this paragraph where in any year a worker is employed by the same employer as a temporary shop manager or temporary shop manageress at more than one shop during the absence on holiday of the shop manager or shop manageress, the first period of such employment and any subsequent periods of such employment in the same year shall be treated as a continuous period of employment.

(3) The minimum remuneration payable to temporary shop managers and temporary shop manageresses for any period of employment mentioned in (a) or (b) of sub-paragraph (2) of this paragraph, shall be not less than the appropriate minimum remuneration for a sales assistant under the provisions of this Schedule.

(4) For the purposes of this paragraph " year " means the 12 months commencing with 1st January and ending with 31st December.

TRANSPORT WORKERS

4. Subject to the provisions of paragraph 1, the minimum remuneration payable to Transport Workers employed in the London Area, Provincial A Area or Provincial B Area, as the case may be, shall be the appropriate amount set out in Column 3 of the following table:—

Column 1	Column 2		Column 3		
	Type of Vehicle		LONDON AREA	PROVIN- CIAL A AREA	PROVIN- CIAL B AREA
Age of transport worker	Mechanically propelled vehicle with carrying capacity of	Horse- drawn vehicle	Per week	Per week	Per week
			s. d.	s. d.	s. d.
21 years or over	⎫	⎧	257 6	250 0	236 0
20 and under 21 years ...	⎪	⎪	206 6	204 6	193 0
19 ,, ,, 20 ,, ...	1 ton or less	one-	196 6	194 6	183 0
18 ,, ,, 19 ,, ...	⎪	horse	183 6	181 6	172 0
under 18 years	⎭	⎩	156 0	154 0	145 6
All ages	Over 1 ton and up to 2 tons	two- horse	261 6	254 0	240 0
	Over 2 tons and up to 5 tons	—	265 6	258 0	244 0
	Over 5 tons ...	—	269 6	262 0	248 0

MINIMUM OVERTIME RATES

5.—(1) Subject to the provisions of this paragraph, overtime shall be payable to all workers at the following minimum rates :—

(a) For work on a Sunday or customary holiday,

    (i) where time worked does not exceed 4½ hours   double time for 4½ hours

    (ii) where time worked exceeds 4½ hours but does not exceed 8 hours ... ...   double time for 8 hours

    (iii) where time worked exceeds 8 hours ... ...   double time for all time worked

Provided that where it is or becomes the practice in a Jewish undertaking for the employer to require attendance on Sunday instead of Saturday, the provisions of this paragraph shall apply as if in such provisions the word " Saturday " were substituted for " Sunday ", except where such substitution is unlawful.

(b) On the weekly short day in any week during which, under sub-section (3) of section 40 of the Shops Act 1950(a), the employer is relieved of his obligation to allow the worker a weekly half day,

    for any time worked after 1.30 p.m. ...   ... double time

(c) On the weekly short day (not being a weekly short day to which (b) of this sub-paragraph applies),

    for any time worked after 1.30 p.m. ...   ... time-and-a-half

(d) In any week, exclusive of any time in respect of which a minimum overtime rate is payable under the foregoing provisions of this paragraph,

    for all time worked in excess of 42 hours   ... time-and-a-half

---

(a) 1950 c. 28.

Provided that in any week which includes one customary holiday " 35 hours " shall be substituted for " 42 hours ", and in any week which includes two customary holidays " 28 hours " shall be substituted for the said " 42 hours ".

(2) Overtime rates in accordance with provisions (*a*), (*c*) and (*d*) of sub-paragraph (1) of this paragraph shall be payable to a shop manager, temporary shop manager, shop manageress or temporary shop manageress only if the overtime worked is specifically authorised in writing by the employer or his representative.

WAITING TIME

6. A worker is entitled to payment of the minimum remuneration specified in this Schedule for all the time during which he is present on the premises of the employer, unless he is present thereon in any of the following circumstances, that is to say—

(1) without the employer's consent, express or implied ;

(2) for some purpose unconnected with his work, and other than that of waiting for work to be given to him to perform ;

(3) by reason only of the fact that he is resident thereon ; or

(4) during normal meal times and he is not waiting for work to be given to him to perform.

WORKERS WHO ARE NOT REQUIRED TO WORK ON A CUSTOMARY HOLIDAY

7.—(1) Subject to the provisions of sub-paragraph (2) of this paragraph, a worker who is not required to work on a customary holiday shall be paid for that holiday not less than the amount to which he would have been entitled under the foregoing provisions of this Schedule had the day not been a customary holiday and had he worked the number of hours ordinarily worked by him on that day of the week.

(2) A worker shall not be entitled to any payment under this paragraph unless he—

(*a*) worked for the employer throughout the last working day on which work was available for him preceding the holiday ; and

(*b*) presents himself for employment at the usual starting time on the first working day after the holiday :

Provided that (*a*) or (*b*), as the case may be, of this sub-paragraph shall be deemed to be complied with where the worker is excused by his employer or is prevented by his proved illness or injury from working or presenting himself for employment as aforesaid.

GUARANTEED WEEKLY REMUNERATION PAYABLE TO A FULL-TIME WORKER

8.—(1) Notwithstanding the other provisions of this Schedule, where in any week the total remuneration (including holiday remuneration but excluding the amount specified in sub-paragraph (2) of this paragraph) payable under those other provisions to a full-time worker is less than the guaranteed weekly remuneration provided under this paragraph, the minimum remuneration payable to that worker for that week shall be that guaranteed weekly remuneration with the addition of any amount excluded as aforesaid.

(2) The amount to be excluded from the total remuneration referred to in the foregoing sub-paragraph is the whole of the remuneration payable in respect of overtime.

(3) The guaranteed weekly remuneration is the remuneration to which the worker would be entitled under paragraph 2, 3 or 4 for 42 hours' work in his normal occupation:

Provided that—

(a) where the worker normally works for the employer on work to which this Schedule applies for less than 42 hours in the week by reason only of the fact that he does not hold himself out as normally available for work for more than the number of hours he normally works in the week, and the worker has informed his employer in writing that he does not so hold himself out, the guaranteed weekly remuneration shall be the remuneration to which the worker would be entitled (calculated as in paragraph 9) for the number of hours in the week normally worked by the worker for the employer on work to which this Schedules applies ;

(b) where in any week a worker at his request and with the written consent of his employer is absent from work during any part of his normal working hours on any day (other than a holiday allowed under Part II or a customary holiday or a holiday allowed to all persons employed in the undertaking or branch of an undertaking in which the worker is employed), the guaranteed weekly remuneration payable in respect of that week shall be reduced in respect of each day on which he is absent as aforesaid by one-sixth where the worker's normal working week is six days or by one-fifth where his normal working week is five days.

(4) Guaranteed weekly remuneration is not payable in respect of any week unless the worker throughout his normal working hours in that week (excluding any time allowed to him as a holiday or during which he is absent from work in accordance with proviso (b) to sub-paragraph (3) of this paragraph) is

(a) capable of and available for work ; and

(b) willing to perform such duties outside his normal occupation as the employer may reasonably require if his normal work is not available in the establishment in which he is employed.

(5) Guaranteed weekly remuneration is not payable in respect of any week if the worker's employment is terminated before the end of that week.

(6) If the employer is unable to provide the worker with work by reason of a strike or other circumstances beyond his control and gives the worker four clear days' notice to that effect, guaranteed weekly remuneration shall not be payable after the expiry of such notice in respect of any week during which or during part of which the employer continues to be unable to provide work as aforesaid:

Provided that in respect of the week in which the said notice expires there shall be paid to the worker in addition to any remuneration payable in respect of time worked in that week, any remuneration that would have been payable if the worker had worked his normal hours of work on every day in the week prior to the expiry of the notice.

HOURS ON WHICH REMUNERATION IS BASED

9.—(1) The minimum remuneration specified in paragraphs 2, 3 and 4 relates to a week of 42 hours exclusive of overtime and, except in the case of guaranteed weekly remuneration under paragraph 8, is subject to a proportionate reduction according as the number of hours worked is less than 42.

(2) In calculating the remuneration for the purpose of this Schedule recognised breaks for meal times shall, subject to the provisions of paragraph 6, be excluded.

BENEFITS OR ADVANTAGES

10.—(1) The benefits or advantages set out in (a), (b), (c) and (d) of this sub-paragraph, being benefits or advantages provided, in pursuance of the terms and conditions of the employment of a worker to whom this Schedule applies, by the employer or by some other person under arrangements with the employer, are authorised to be reckoned as payment of wages by the employer in lieu of payment in cash in the following manner:—

(*a*) Dinner of good and sufficient quality and quantity provided on each day on which the worker normally works in the week, other than the weekly short day, as an amount of *14s. 0d.* per week except in the circumstances provided for in (*d*) of this sub-paragraph.

(*b*) Tea of good and sufficient quality and quantity provided on each day on which the worker normally works in the week, other than the weekly short day, as an amount of *5s. 0d.* per week except in the circumstances provided for in (*d*) of this sub-paragraph.

(*c*) Full board on Sunday and customary holidays, part board only on the other days of the week and lodging for the full week, as the appropriate amount set out in the table below:—

In the case of a worker aged	LONDON AREA	PROVINCIAL A AREA	PROVINCIAL B AREA
	Per week	Per week	Per week
	s. d.	s. d.	s. d.
21 years or over	43 0	38 0	34 0
20 and under 21 years	40 0	36 0	31 0
19 ,, ,, 20 ,, ...	36 0	30 0	26 0
18 ,, ,, 19 ,, ...	33 0	28 0	24 0
17 ,, ,, 18 ,, ...	30 0	25 0	21 0
16 ,, ,, 17 ,, ...	25 0	20 0	16 0
under 16 years	23 0	18 0	13 0

(*d*) Full board and lodging for the full week, as the appropriate amount set out in the table below:—

In the case of a worker aged	LONDON AREA	PROVINCIAL A AREA	PROVINCIAL B AREA
	Per week	Per week	Per week
	s. d.	s. d.	s. d.
21 years or over	56 0	50 0	47 0
20 and under 21 years	54 0	48 0	44 0
19 ,, ,, 20 ,, ...	49 0	44 0	40 0
18 ,, ,, 19 ,, ...	46 0	40 0	37 0
17 ,, ,, 18 ,, ...	43 0	38 0	33 0
16 ,, ,, 17 ,, ...	38 0	33 0	29 0
under 16 years	36 0	30 0	26 0

Provided that where in any week the total amount which, in accordance with the foregoing provisions of this sub-paragraph, the employer would be entitled to reckon as payment of wages to a worker in lieu of payment in cash, exceeds the appropriate amount (according to the age of the worker and the area in which he is employed) set out in (*d*) of this sub-paragraph, then in the case of that worker the employer shall not be entitled in respect of that week, so to reckon as payment of wages as aforesaid, more than such appropriate amount set out in (*d*) of this sub-paragraph:

Provided also that where a worker is employed in a shop—

(i) which is registered under section 53 of the Shops Act 1950 (which relates to persons observing the Jewish Sabbath), this sub-paragraph in relation to such a worker shall have effect as if for the word "Sunday" in (*c*) thereof, there were substituted the word "Saturday";

(ii) situated in a district in which an order is in force under section 54 of the Shops Act 1950, authorising shops to be open for the serving of customers on Sunday and which it is the practice to keep open on Sunday, this sub-paragraph in relation to such a worker shall have effect as if for the word " Sunday " there were substituted the words " the week-day upon which the shop in which the worker is employed must be closed in pursuance of an order made under section 54 of the Shops Act 1950 ".

(2) In this paragraph—

" PART BOARD " means breakfast and supper, being meals of good and sufficient quality and quantity ;

" FULL BOARD " means breakfast, dinner, tea and supper, being meals of good and sufficient quality and quantity ; and

" LODGING " means clean and adequate accommodation and clean and adequate facilities for eating, sleeping, washing and leisure.

(3) Nothing in this paragraph shall be construed as authorising the making of any deduction or the giving of remuneration in any manner which is illegal by virtue of the Truck Acts 1831 to 1940(a), or of any other enactment.

Part II

ANNUAL HOLIDAY AND HOLIDAY REMUNERATION

ANNUAL HOLIDAY

11.—(1) Subject to the provisions of paragraph 12, an employer shall, between 1st April 1970 and 31st October 1970, and in each succeeding year between 1st April and 31st October, allow a holiday (hereinafter referred to as an " annual holiday ") to every worker (other than a worker who normally works for the employer for less than 9 hours in a week) in his employment to whom this Schedule applies who has been employed by him during the 12 months immediately preceding the commencement of the holiday season for any one of the periods of employment (calculated in accordance with the provisions of paragraph 18) set out in the table below and the duration of the annual holiday shall in the case of each such worker be related to that period as follows :—

Period of employment	Duration of annual holiday			
	Where the worker's normal working week is			
	Six days	Five days	Four days	Three days or less
12 months	12 days	10 days	8 days	6 days
Not less than 11 months but less than 12 months ...	11 ,,	9 ,,	7 ,,	5 ,,
,, ,, ,, 10 ,, ,, ,, ,, 11 ,, ...	10 ,,	8 ,,	7 ,,	5 ,,
,, ,, ,, 9 ,, ,, ,, ,, 10 ,, ...	9 ,,	7 ,,	6 ,,	4 ,,
,, ,, ,, 8 ,, ,, ,, ,, 9 ,, ...	8 ,,	7 ,,	5 ,,	4 ,,
,, ,, ,, 7 ,, ,, ,, ,, 8 ,, ...	7 ,,	6 ,,	5 ,,	3 ,,
,, ,, ,, 6 ,, ,, ,, ,, 7 ,, ...	6 ,,	5 ,,	4 ,,	3 ,,
,, ,, ,, 5 ,, ,, ,, ,, 6 ,, ...	5 ,,	4 ,,	3 ,,	2 ,,
,, ,, ,, 4 ,, ,, ,, ,, 5 ,, ...	4 ,,	3 ,,	3 ,,	2 ,,
,, ,, ,, 3 ,, ,, ,, ,, 4 ,, ...	3 ,,	2 ,,	2 ,,	1 day
,, ,, ,, 2 ,, ,, ,, ,, 3 ,, ...	2 ,,	2 ,,	1 day	1 ,,
,, ,, ,, 1 month ,, ,, ,, 2 ,, ...	1 day	1 day	1 ,,	nil

(a) 1831 c. 37; 1887 c. 46; 1896 c. 44; 1940 c. 38.

(2) Notwithstanding the provisions of the last foregoing sub-paragraph—

> (a) the number of days of annual holiday which an employer is required to allow to a worker in any holiday season shall not exceed in the aggregate twice the number of days constituting the worker's normal working week ;

> (b) where a worker does not wish to take his annual holiday or part thereof during the holiday season in any year and, before the expiration of such holiday season, enters into an agreement in writing with his employer that the annual holiday or part thereof shall be allowed, at a date or dates to be specified in that agreement, after the expiration of the holiday season but before the first day of January in the following year, then any day or days of annual holiday so allowed shall be treated as having been allowed during the holiday season ;

(3) In this Schedule the expression " holiday season " means in relation to the year 1970 the period commencing on 1st April 1970, and ending on 31st October 1970, and, in each succeeding year, the period commencing on 1st April and ending on 31st October of the same year.

12. Where at the written request of the worker at any time during the three months immediately preceding the commencement of the holiday season in any year, his employer allows him any day or days of holiday and pays him holiday remuneration in respect thereof calculated in accordance with the provisions of paragraphs 15 and 16, then—

> (1) the annual holiday to be allowed in accordance with paragraph 11 in the holiday season in that year shall be reduced by the day or days of holiday so allowed prior to the commencement of that holiday season ; and

> (2) for the purpose of calculating accrued holiday remuneration under paragraph 17 any day or days of holiday deducted in accordance with sub-paragraph (1) hereof shall be treated as if they had been allowed in the holiday season.

13.—(1) Subject to the provisions of this paragraph, an annual holiday shall be allowed on consecutive working days, being days on which the worker is normally called upon to work for the employer.

(2) Where the number of days of annual holiday for which a worker has qualified exceeds the number of days constituting his normal working week, the holiday may by agreement between the employer and the worker be allowed in two periods of consecutive working days ; so however that when a holiday is so allowed, one of the periods shall consist of a number of such days not less than the number of days constituting the worker's normal working week.

(3) For the purposes of this paragraph, days of annual holiday shall be treated as consecutive notwithstanding that a customary holiday on which the worker is not required to work for the employer or a day on which he does not normally work for the employer intervenes.

(4) Where a customary holiday on which the worker is not required to work for the employer immediately precedes a period of annual holiday or occurs during such a period and the total number of days of annual holiday required to be allowed in the period under the foregoing provisions of this paragraph, together with any customary holiday, exceeds the number of days constituting the worker's normal working week then, notwithstanding the foregoing provisions of this paragraph, the duration of that period of annual holiday may be reduced by one day and in such a case one day of annual holiday may be allowed on a day on which the worker normally works for the employer (not being the worker's weekly short day) in the holiday season or after the holiday season in the circumstances specified in sub-paragraph (2)(b) of paragraph 11.

(5) No day of annual holiday shall be allowed on a customary holiday.

(6) A day of annual holiday under this Schedule may be allowed on a day on which the worker is entitled to a day of holiday (not being a customary holiday) or to a half-holiday under any enactment other than the Wages Councils Act 1959 :

Provided that where the total number of days of annual holiday allowed to a worker under this Schedule is less than the number of days in his normal working week, the said annual holiday shall be in addition to the said day of holiday or the said half-holiday.

14. An employer shall give to a worker reasonable notice of the commencing date or dates and of the duration of his annual holiday. Such notice may be given individually to the worker or by the posting of a notice in the place where the worker is employed.

REMUNERATION FOR ANNUAL HOLIDAY

15.—(1) Subject to the provisions of paragraph 16, a worker qualified to be allowed an annual holiday under this Schedule shall be paid by his employer, on the last pay day preceding such holiday, one day's holiday pay (as defined in paragraph 19) in respect of each day thereof.

(2) Where an annual holiday is taken in more than one period the holiday remuneration shall be apportioned accordingly.

16. Where any accrued holiday remuneration has been paid by the employer to the worker (in accordance with paragraph 17 of this Schedule or with Order R.D.O. (50) as amended), in respect of employment during any of the periods referred to in that paragraph, or that Order, the amount of holiday remuneration payable by the employer in respect of any annual holiday for which the worker has qualified by reason of employment during the said period shall be reduced by the amount of the said accrued holiday remuneration unless that remuneration has been deducted from a previous payment of holiday remuneration made under the provisions of this Schedule or of Order R.D.O. (50) as amended.

ACCRUED HOLIDAY REMUNERATION PAYABLE ON TERMINATION OF EMPLOYMENT

17. Where a worker (other than a worker who normally works for the employer for less than 9 hours in a week) ceases to be employed by an employer after the provisions of this Schedule become effective the employer shall, immediately on the termination of the employment (hereinafter referred to as the " termination date "), pay to the worker as accrued holiday remuneration—

(1) in respect of employment in the 12 months up to 1st April immediately preceding the termination date, a sum equal to the holiday remuneration for any days of annual holiday for which he has qualified except days of annual holiday which he has been allowed or has become entitled to be allowed before leaving the employment ; and

(2) in respect of any employment since 1st April immediately preceding the termination date, a sum equal to the holiday remuneration which would have been payable to him if he could have been allowed an annual holiday in respect of that employment at the time of leaving it :

Provided that—

(a) no worker shall be entitled to the payment by his employer of accrued holiday remuneration if he is dismissed on the grounds of misconduct and is so informed by the employer at the time of dismissal ;

(b) where during the period or periods in respect of which the said accrued holiday remuneration is payable the worker has at his written request been allowed any day or days of holiday (other than days of holiday allowed by the employer under paragraph 12) for which he had not qualified under the provisions of this Schedule, any accrued holiday remuneration payable as aforesaid may be reduced by the amount of any sum paid by the employer to the worker in respect of such day or days of holiday ;

(c) where a worker is employed under a contract of service under which he is required to give not less than one week's notice before terminating his employment and the worker, without the consent of his employer, terminates his employment without having given not less than one week's notice or before one week has expired from the beginning of such notice, the amount of accrued holiday remuneration payable to the worker shall be the amount payable under the foregoing provisions of this paragraph less an amount equal to the statutory minimum remuneration which would be payable to him at the termination date for one week's work if working his normal working week and the normal number of daily hours worked by him.

CALCULATION OF EMPLOYMENT

18. For the purpose of calculating any period of employment qualifying a worker for an annual holiday or for any accrued holiday remuneration, the worker shall be treated as if he were employed for a month in respect of any month (as defined in paragraph 19) throughout which he has been in the employment of the employer.

Part III

GENERAL

DEFINITIONS

19. For the purposes of this Schedule—

" CARRYING CAPACITY " means the weight of the maximum load normally carried by the vehicle, and such carrying capacity when so established shall not be affected either by variations in the weight of the load resulting from collections or deliveries or emptying of containers during the course of the journey, or by the fact that on any particular journey a load greater or less than the established carrying capacity is carried.

" CASHIER " means a worker employed in a shop and engaged wholly or mainly in receiving cash or giving change.

" CENTRAL WAREHOUSE WORKER " means a worker wholly or mainly employed in a central warehouse, that is to say, a warehouse from which an undertaking in the retail drapery, outfitting and footwear trades supplies its branch shops.

" CLERK GRADE I " means a worker engaged wholly or mainly on clerical work which includes responsibility for maintaining ledgers or wages books or for preparing financial accounts of the undertaking or of a branch or department thereof.

" CLERK GRADE II " means a worker, other than a Clerk Grade I, engaged wholly or mainly on clerical work.

" CREDIT TRAVELLER " means a worker employed in an undertaking engaged in credit trading and wholly or mainly engaged in calling upon customers or prospective customers for the purpose of opening accounts, collecting payments or selling goods.

" CUSTOMARY HOLIDAY " means

(1) (a) In England and Wales—

Christmas Day (or, if Christmas Day falls on a Sunday, such weekday as may be appointed by national proclamation, or, if none is so appointed, the next following Tuesday), Boxing Day, Good Friday, Easter Monday, Whit Monday (or where another day is substituted therefor by national proclamation, that day), August Bank Holiday, *one other day (being a day on which the worker would normally work) between 24th December and the following 2nd January inclusive, to be fixed by the employer and notified to the worker not less than three weeks before the holiday,* and any day proclaimed as a public holiday throughout England and Wales ;

(*b*) In Scotland—

New Year's Day (or, if New Year's Day falls on a Sunday, the following Monday) ;

the local Spring holiday ;

the local Autumn holiday ;

Christmas Day (or, if Christmas Day falls on a Sunday, the following Monday) ;

two other days *in the course of a calendar year and one other day between 24th December and the following 3rd January inclusive* (being days on which the worker would normally work) to be fixed by the employer and notified to the worker not less than three weeks before the holiday, and any day proclaimed as a public holiday throughout Scotland ;

or (2) where in any undertaking it is not the custom or practice to observe such days as are specified in (1)(*a*) or (1)(*b*) above as holidays, such other days, not fewer in number, as may by agreement between the employer or his representative and the worker or his representative be substituted for the specified days.

" FULL-TIME WORKER " means a worker who normally works for the employer for at least 34 hours in the week on work to which this Schedule applies.

" MONTH " means the period commencing on a date of any number in one month and ending on the day before the date of the same number in the next month, or if the commencing date is the 29th, 30th or 31st day of a month, and there is no date of the same number in the next month, then on the last day of that month.

" NORMAL WORKING WEEK " means the number of days on which it has been usual for the worker to work in a week while in the employment of the employer during the 12 months immediately preceding the commencement of the holiday season, or, where accrued holiday remuneration is payable under (2) of paragraph 17, on the termination of the employment, during the 12 months immediately preceding the termination date :

Provided that—

(1) part of a day shall count as a day ;

(2) no account shall be taken of any week in which the worker did not perform any work for which statutory minimum remuneration has been fixed.

" ONE DAY'S HOLIDAY PAY " means the appropriate proportion of the remuneration which the worker would be entitled to receive from his employer at the date of the annual holiday (or where the holiday is taken in more than one period at the date of the first period) or at the termination date, as the case may be, for one week's work—

(1) if working his normal working week and the number of daily hours normally worked by him (exclusive of overtime),

(2) if the employer were not providing him with meals or board and lodging, and

(3) if paid at the appropriate rate of statutory minimum remuneration for work for which statutory minimum remuneration is payable and at the same rate for any work for the same employer for which such remuneration is not payable,

and in this definition " appropriate proportion " means—

where the worker's normal working week is six days					...	one-sixth
,,	,,	,,	,,	,,	five ,, ...	one-fifth
,,	,,	,,	,,	,,	four ,, ...	one-quarter
,,	,,	,,	,,	,,	three ,, ...	one-third
,,	,,	,,	,,	,,	two ,, ...	one-half
,,	,,	,,	,,	,,	one day ...	the whole.

" SALES ASSISTANT " means a worker who is wholly or mainly engaged in the serving of customers.

" SHOP MANAGER ", " SHOP MANAGERESS " means a worker who is employed at, and is normally immediately in charge of the operation of, an undertaking or branch (but not of a department of an undertaking or branch), who has the custody of cash and stock, and who has immediate control of other workers (if any) employed at that undertaking or branch ; and for the purposes of this definition a worker shall not be deemed not to be immediately in charge of the operation of an undertaking or branch by reason only of being subject to the supervision of the employer or some person acting on his behalf, being in either case a person who is not normally, during the hours when the undertaking or branch is open to the public, wholly or mainly engaged in work at that undertaking or branch.

" STOCK HAND " means a worker employed in a shop, or in a warehouse operated in connection with a shop, and wholly or mainly engaged in the custody of goods or the receiving and checking of stock or the assembly of orders.

" TEMPORARY SHOP MANAGER ", " TEMPORARY SHOP MANAGERESS " means a worker who during the absence of the shop manager or shop manageress performs all the duties of the shop manager or the shop manageress, whilst he is performing the said duties.

" TIME-AND-A-HALF " and " DOUBLE TIME " mean, respectively, one and a half times and twice the hourly rate obtained by dividing by 42 the minimum weekly remuneration to which the worker is entitled under the provisions of paragraph 2, 3 or 4.

" TRANSPORT WORKER " means a worker engaged wholly or mainly in driving a mechanically propelled or horse drawn road vehicle for the transport of goods and on work in connection with the vehicle and its load (if any) while on the road.

" WATCHMAN " means a worker wholly or mainly engaged in guarding the employer's premises for the prevention of theft, fire, damage or trespass.

" WEEK " means pay week.

" WEEKLY SHORT DAY " means :—

    (1) that day in any week on which the worker is, in accordance with the provisions of section 17 of the Shops Act 1950, required not to be employed about the business of a shop after half-past one o'clock in the afternoon, or,

    (2) where there is no such day, or where the day falls on a customary holiday, a working day in the week not being a customary holiday, fixed by the employer and notified to the worker not later than the Saturday preceding the week during which it is to have effect ; or, failing such notification, the last working day in the week which is not a customary holiday:

    Provided that where the day specified in (1) of this definition falls on Christmas Day or Boxing Day in England and Wales or Christmas Day or New Year's Day in Scotland the employer may fix as the weekly short day for that week a working day in the following week not being either a customary holiday or the weekly short day for that following week.

AREAS

20. In this Schedule:—

(1) "LONDON AREA" means the Metropolitan Police District, as defined in the London Government Act 1963(a), the City of London, the Inner Temple and the Middle Temple.

(2) "PROVINCIAL A AREA" means

(a) In Scotland,

(i) the following burghs:—

ABERDEEN COUNTY
 Aberdeen (including part in Kincardine County)
 Fraserburgh
 Peterhead

ANGUS COUNTY
 Arbroath
 Brechin
 Dundee
 Forfar
 Montrose

ARGYLL COUNTY
 Dunoon

AYR COUNTY
 Ardrossan
 Ayr
 Irvine
 Kilmarnock
 Largs
 Prestwick
 Saltcoats
 Stevenston
 Troon

BANFF COUNTY
 Buckie

BUTE COUNTY
 Rothesay

CLACKMANNAN COUNTY
 Alloa

DUMFRIES COUNTY
 Dumfries

DUNBARTON COUNTY
 Bearsden
 Clydebank
 Dumbarton
 Helensburgh
 Kirkintilloch
 Milngavie

EAST LOTHIAN COUNTY
 North Berwick

FIFE COUNTY
 Buckhaven and Methil
 Burntisland
 Cowdenbeath
 Dunfermline
 Kirkcaldy
 Leven
 Lochgelly
 St. Andrews

INVERNESS COUNTY
 Inverness

KINCARDINE COUNTY
 Stonehaven

LANARK COUNTY
 Airdrie
 Coatbridge
 Glasgow
 Hamilton
 Lanark
 Motherwell and Wishaw
 Rutherglen

MIDLOTHIAN COUNTY
 Dalkeith
 Edinburgh
 Musselburgh

MORAY COUNTY
 Elgin

ORKNEY COUNTY
 Kirkwall

PERTH COUNTY
 Perth

RENFREW COUNTY
 Barrhead
 Gourock
 Greenock
 Johnstone
 Paisley
 Port Glasgow
 Renfrew

ROSS AND CROMARTY COUNTY
 Stornoway

ROXBURGH COUNTY
 Hawick

SELKIRK COUNTY
 Galashiels

STIRLING COUNTY
 Denny and Dunipace
 Falkirk
 Grangemouth
 Kilsyth
 Stirling

WEST LOTHIAN COUNTY
 Armadale
 Bathgate
 Bo'ness

WIGTOWN COUNTY
 Stranraer

ZETLAND COUNTY
 Lerwick

(a) 1963 c. 33.

(ii) The following Special Lighting Districts, the boundaries of which have been defined, namely:—Vale of Leven and Renton in the County of Dunbarton ; and Larbert and Airth in the County of Stirling ; and

(iii) The following areas, the boundaries of which were defined as Special Lighting Districts prior to 10th March 1943, namely:— Bellshill and Mossend, Blantyre, Cambuslang, Larkhall and Holytown, New Stevenston and Carfin, all in the County of Lanark.

(b) In England and Wales, the areas administered by County Borough, Municipal Borough or Urban District Councils, except where they are included in the London area or are listed in (3)(b) of this paragraph.

(3) " PROVINCIAL B AREA " means

(a) in Scotland, all areas other than those listed in (2)(a) of this paragraph ;

(b) in England and Wales, all areas not included in the London area administered by Rural District Councils, and the areas administered by the following Municipal Borough and Urban District Councils:—

ENGLAND (excluding Monmouthshire)

BEDFORDSHIRE
Ampthill
Sandy

BERKSHIRE
Wallingford
Wantage

BUCKINGHAMSHIRE
Buckingham
Linslade
Marlow
Newport Pagnell

CHESHIRE
Alsager
Longdendale

CORNWALL
Bodmin
Bude Stratton
Fowey
Helston
Launceston
Liskeard
Looe
Lostwithiel
Padstow
Penryn
St. Just
Torpoint

DERBYSHIRE
Bakewell
Whaley Bridge
Wirksworth

DEVON
Ashburton
Buckfastleigh
Budleigh Salterton
Crediton
Dartmouth
Great Torrington
Holsworthy
Honiton
Kingsbridge
Lynton
Northam
Okehampton
Ottery St. Mary
Salcombe
Seaton
South Molton
Tavistock
Totnes

DORSET
Blandford Forum
Lyme Regis
Shaftesbury
Sherborne
Wareham
Wimborne Minster

DURHAM
Barnard Castle
Tow Law

ELY, ISLE OF
Chatteris

ESSEX
Brightlingsea
Burnham-on-Crouch
Saffron Walden
West Mersea
Wivenhoe

GLOUCESTERSHIRE
Nailsworth
Tewkesbury

HEREFORDSHIRE
Bromyard
Kington
Ledbury

HERTFORDSHIRE
Baldock
Chorleywood
Royston
Sawbridgeworth

HUNTINGDONSHIRE
Huntingdon and
   Godmanchester
Ramsey
St. Ives
St. Neots

KENT
Lydd
New Romney
Queenborough
Sandwich
Tenterden

ENGLAND (excluding Monmouthshire)—*contd.*

LANCASHIRE
Carnforth
Grange

LINCOLNSHIRE
Alford
Barton-upon-Humber
Bourne
Brigg
Horncastle
Mablethorpe and Sutton
Market Rasen
Woodhall Spa

NORFOLK
Cromer
Diss
Downham Market
Hunstanton
North Walsham
Sheringham
Swaffham
Thetford
Wells-next-the-Sea
Wymondham

**NORTHAMPTON-
       SHIRE**
Brackley
Burton Latimer
Higham Ferrers
Oundle

NORTHUMBERLAND
Alnwick
Amble

OXFORDSHIRE
Bicester
Chipping Norton
Thame
Woodstock

RUTLAND
Oakham

SHROPSHIRE
Bishop's Castle
Church Stretton
Ellesmere
Market Drayton
Newport
Wem

SOMERSET
Chard
Crewkerne
Glastonbury
Ilminster
Portishead
Shepton Mallet
Street
Watchet
Wellington

SUFFOLK
Aldeburgh
Beccles
Bungay
Eye
Hadleigh
Halesworth
Haverhill
Leiston-cum-Sizewell
Saxmundham
Southwold
Sudbury

SUFFOLK—*contd.*
Stowmarket
Woodbridge

SUSSEX
Arundel
Rye

WESTMORLAND
Appleby
Lakes

WILTSHIRE
Bradford-on-Avon
Calne
Malmesbury
Marlborough
Melksham
Westbury
Wilton

WORCESTERSHIRE
Bewdley
Droitwich

YORKSHIRE
Hedon
Hornsea
Malton
Norton
Pickering
Richmond
Tickhill
Withernsea

WALES AND MONMOUTHSHIRE

ANGLESEY
Amlwch
Beaumaris
Llangefni
Menai Bridge

BRECONSHIRE
Builth Wells
Hay
Llanwrtyd Wells

CAERNARVONSHIRE
Bethesda
Betws-y-Coed
Criccieth
Llanfairfechan
Penmaenmawr
Portmadoc
Pwllheli

CARDIGANSHIRE
Aberayron
Cardigan
Lampeter
New Quay

CARMARTHENSHIRE
Cwmamman
Kidwelly
Llandeilo
Llandovery
Newcastle Emlyn

DENBIGHSHIRE
Llangollen
Llanrwst
Ruthin

FLINTSHIRE
Buckley
Mold

GLAMORGAN
Cowbridge

MERIONETHSHIRE
Bala
Barmouth
Dolgellau
Towyn

MONMOUTHSHIRE
Caerleon
Chepstow
Usk

WALES AND MONMOUTHSHIRE—*contd.*

MONTGOMERYSHIRE	PEMBROKESHIRE	RADNORSHIRE
Llanfyllin	Fishguard and	Knighton
Llanidloes	Goodwick	Llandrindod Wells
Machynlleth	Narberth	Presteigne
Montgomery	Neyland	
Newtown and	Tenby	
Llanllwchaiarn		
Welshpool		

(4) Any reference to a local government area shall be construed as a reference to that area as it was on 23rd April 1961, unless otherwise stated.

WORKERS TO WHOM THIS SCHEDULE APPLIES

21.—(1)—(i) Subject to the provisions of sub-paragraph (2) of this paragraph, the workers to whom this Schedule applies are all workers employed in Great Britain in any undertaking or any branch or department of an undertaking, being an undertaking, branch or department engaged—

(a) wholly or mainly in the retail drapery, outfitting and footwear trades ; or

(b) wholly or mainly in those trades and one or more of the groups of retail distributive trades set out in the Appendix to this paragraph, and to a greater extent in the retail drapery, outfitting and footwear trades than in any one of those groups:

Provided that if a branch or department of an undertaking is not so engaged this Schedule shall not apply to workers employed in that branch or department (notwithstanding that the undertaking as a whole is so engaged), except in the case of workers as respects their employment in a department of that branch if that department is so engaged.

(ii) For the purposes of this sub-paragraph

(a) in determining the extent to which an undertaking or branch or department of an undertaking is engaged in a group of trades, regard shall be had to the time spent in the undertaking, branch or department on work in that group of trades ;

(b) an undertaking or branch or department of an undertaking which is engaged in any operation in a group of trades shall be treated as engaged in that group of trades.

(2) This Schedule does not apply to any of the following workers in respect of their employment in any of the following circumstances, that is to say—

(i) workers employed on the making, trimming, fitting, alteration or repair of wearing apparel ;

(ii) workers in relation to whom the Road Haulage Wages Council operates in respect of any employment which is within the field of operation of that Council ;

(iii) workers employed on post office business ;

(iv) workers employed on the maintenance or repair of buildings, plant, equipment or vehicles (but not including workers employed as cleaners) ;

(v) workers employed on the cutting, sewing, making up and fixing of blinds, curtains, pelmets and loose covers ;

(vi) workers employed as watchmen.

(3) For the purpose of this Schedule the retail drapery, outfitting and footwear trades consist of

(i) the sale by retail of

(a) wearing apparel of all kinds (including footwear, headwear and hand-wear) and accessories, trimmings and adornments for wearing apparel (excluding jewellery and imitation jewellery);

(b) haberdashery;

(c) textile fabrics in the piece, leather cloth, plastic cloth and oil cloth (but not including carpets, linoleum and other kinds of floor covering);

(d) knitting, rug, embroidery, crochet and similar wools or yarns;

(e) made-up household textiles (but excluding mattresses and floor coverings);

(f) umbrellas, sunshades, walking sticks, canes and similar articles;

(ii) operations in or about the shop or other place where any of the articles included in (i) of this sub-paragraph are sold by retail, being operations carried on for the purpose of such sale or otherwise in connection with such sale;

(iii) operations in connection with the warehousing or storing of any of the articles included in (i) of this sub-paragraph for the purpose of the sale thereof by retail, or otherwise in connection with such sale, where the warehousing or storing takes place at a warehouse or store carried on in conjunction with one or more shops or other places where the said articles are sold by retail;

(iv) operations in connection with the transport of any of the articles included in (i) of this sub-paragraph when carried on in conjunction with their sale by retail or with the warehousing or storing operations specified in (iii) of this sub-paragraph; and

(v) clerical or other office work carried on in conjunction with the sale by retail of any of the articles included in (i) of this sub-paragraph and relating to such sale or to any of the operations specified in (ii) to (iv) of this sub-paragraph;

and for the purpose of this definition the sale by retail of any of the articles in (i) of this sub-paragraph includes the sale of that article to a person for use in connection with a trade or business carried on by him if such sale takes place at or in connection with a shop engaged in the retail sale to the general public of any of the articles included in (i) of this sub-paragraph.

APPENDIX TO PARAGRAPH 21

GROUPS OF RETAIL DISTRIBUTIVE TRADES

Group 1.—The Retail Food Trades, that is to say, the sale by retail of food or drink for human consumption and operations connected therewith including:—

(i) operations in or about the shop or other place where the food or drink aforesaid is sold, being operations carried on for the purpose of such sale or otherwise in connection with such sale;

(ii) operations in connection with the warehousing or storing of such food or drink for the purpose of sale by retail, or otherwise in connection with such sale, where the warehousing or storing takes place at a warehouse or store carried on in conjunction with one or more shops or other places where such food or drink is sold by retail;

(iii) operations in connection with the transport of such food or drink when carried on in conjunction with its sale by retail or with the warehousing or storing operations specified in (ii) above ; and

(iv) clerical or other office work carried on in conjunction with the sale by retail aforesaid and relating to such sale or to any of the operations in (i) to (iii) above ;

but not including

the sale by retail of bread, pastry or flour confectionery (other than biscuits or meat pastries) or the sale by retail of meat (other than bacon, ham, pressed beef, sausages or meat so treated as to be fit for human consumption without further preparation or cooking) or the sale by retail of milk (other than dried or condensed milk) or the sale by retail of ice-cream, aerated waters, chocolate confectionery or sugar confectionery, or the sale of food or drink for immediate consumption.

For the purpose of this definition " sale by retail " includes any sale of food or drink to a person for use in connection with a catering business carried on by him, when such sale takes place at or in connection with a shop engaged in the retail sale of food or drink to the general public.

Group 2.—The Retail Furnishing and Allied Trades, that is to say—

(1) the sale by retail of the following articles:—

(a) household and office furniture, including garden furniture, mattresses, floor coverings and mirrors, but excluding billiard tables, clocks, pianos, gramophones and pictures ;

(b) ironmongery, turnery and hardware, of kinds commonly used for household purposes, including gardening implements ;

(c) hand tools ;

(d) woodware, basketware, glassware, potteryware, chinaware, brassware, plasticware and ceramic goods, being articles or goods of kinds commonly used for household purposes or as household ornaments ;

(e) electrical and gas appliances and apparatus, of kinds commonly used for household purposes (excluding clocks), and accessories and component parts thereof ;

(f) heating, lighting and cooking appliances and apparatus, of kinds commonly used for household purposes, and accessories and component parts thereof ;

(g) radio and television sets and their accessories and component parts ;

(h) pedal cycles and their accessories and component parts ;

(i) perambulators, push chairs and invalid carriages ;

(j) toys, indoor games, requisites for outdoor games, gymnastics and athletics, but excluding billiard tables and sports clothing ;

(k) saddlery, leather goods (other than articles of wearing apparel), travel goods and ladies' handbags ;

(l) paint, distemper and wallpaper, and oils of kinds commonly used for household purposes (excluding petrol and lubricating oils) ;

(m) brushes, mops and brooms, used for household purposes, and similar articles ;

(n) disinfectants, chemicals, candles, soaps and polishes, of kinds commonly used for household purposes ;

(2) operations in or about the shop or other place where any of the articles specified in (1) above are sold by retail, being operations carried on for the purpose of such sale or otherwise in connection with such sale ;

(3) operations in connection with the warehousing or storing of any of the articles specified in (1) above for the purpose of the sale thereof by retail, or otherwise in connection with such sale, where the warehousing or storing takes place at a warehouse or store carried on in conjunction with one or more shops or other places where the said articles are sold by retail ;

(4) operations in connection with the transport of any of the articles specified in (1) above when carried on in conjunction with their sale by retail or with the warehousing or storing operations specified in (3) above ; and

(5) clerical or other office work carried on in conjunction with the sale by retail of any of the articles specified in (1) above and relating to such sale or to any of the operations specified in (2) to (4) above ;

and for the purpose of this definition the sale by retail of any of the articles specified in (1) above does not include sale by auction (except where the auctioneer sells articles by retail which are his property or the property of his master) but includes the sale of any of the articles therein specified to a person for use in connection with a trade or business carried on by him if such sale takes place at or in connection with a shop engaged in the retail sale to the general public of any of the said articles.

Group 3.—The Retail Bookselling and Stationery Trades, that is to say—

(1) the sale by retail of the following articles :—

   (*a*) books (excluding printed music and periodicals) ;

   (*b*) all kinds of stationery including printed forms, note books, diaries and similar articles, and books of kinds used in an office or business for the purpose of record ;

   (*c*) pens, pencils, ink, blotting paper and similar articles ;

   (*d*) maps and charts ;

   (*e*) wrapping and adhesive paper, string, paste and similar articles ;

(2) operations in or about the shop or other place where any of the articles specified in (1) above are sold by retail, being operations carried on for the purpose of such sale or otherwise in connection with such sale ;

(3) operations in connection with the warehousing or storing of any of the articles specified in (1) above for the purpose of the sale thereof by retail, or otherwise in connection with such sale, where the warehousing or storing takes place at a warehouse or store carried on in conjunction with one or more shops or other places where the said articles are sold by retail ;

(4) operations in connection with the transport of any of the articles specified in (1) above when carried on in conjunction with their sale by retail or with the warehousing or storing operations specified in (3) above ; and

(5) clerical or other office work carried on in conjunction with the sale by retail of any of the articles specified in (1) above and relating to such sale or to any of the operations specified in (2) to (4) above.

Group 4.—The Retail Newsagency, Tobacco and Confectionery Trades, that is to say—

(1) the sale by retail of the following articles :—

   (*a*) newspapers, magazines and other periodicals ;

   (*b*) tobacco, cigars, cigarettes, snuff and smokers' requisites ;

   (*c*) articles of sugar confectionery and chocolate confectionery and ice-cream ;

(2) operations in or about the shop or other place where any of the articles specified in (1) above are sold by retail, being operations carried on for the purpose of such sale or otherwise in connection with such sale ;

(3) operations in connection with the warehousing or storing of any of the articles specified in (1) above for the purpose of the sale thereof by retail, or otherwise in connection with such sale, where the warehousing or storing takes place at a warehouse or store carried on in conjunction with one or more shops or other places where the said articles are sold by retail ;

(4) operations in connection with the transport of any of the articles specified in (1) above when carried on in conjunction with their sale by retail or with the warehousing or storing operations specified in (3) above ; and

(5) clerical or other office work carried on in conjunction with the sale by retail of any of the articles specified in (1) above and relating to such sale or to any of the operations specified in (2) to (4) above.

EXPLANATORY NOTE

(This Note is not part of the Order.)

This Order, which has effect from 16th March 1970, sets out the statutory minimum remuneration payable and the holidays to be allowed in substitution for the statutory minimum remuneration and holidays set out in the Wages Regulation (Retail Drapery, Outfitting and Footwear) Order 1967 (Order R.D.O. (50)), as amended by the Wages Regulation (Retail Drapery, Outfitting and Footwear) (Amendment) Order 1968 (Order R.D.O. (52)), which Orders are revoked.

New provisions are printed in italics.

STATUTORY INSTRUMENTS

1970 No. 65
AGRICULTURE

CEREALS MARKETING
The Home-Grown Cereals Authority (Additional Functions) Order 1970

Made - - -	*20th January* 1970
Laid before Parliament	*28th January* 1970
Coming into Operation	*29th January* 1970

The Minister of Agriculture, Fisheries and Food, the Secretaries of State respectively concerned with agriculture in Scotland and Northern Ireland and the Secretary of State for Wales, acting jointly in exercise of the powers conferred on them by section 7 of the Cereals Marketing Act 1965(a) as read with the Transfer of Functions (Wales) Order 1969(b) and of all other powers enabling them in that behalf, it appearing to them after consultation with the Home-Grown Cereals Authority (hereinafter referred to as "the Authority") that for the purposes of improving the marketing of home-grown cereals it is expedient for the Authority to perform the additional non-trading functions which are specified in this order and which the said Ministers certify to be in their opinion similar in character to those conferred on the Authority by section 6 of the said Act, hereby make the following order :—

Citation, commencement and interpretation

1.—(1) This order may be cited as the Home-Grown Cereals Authority (Additional Functions) Order 1970, and shall come into operation on 29th January 1970.

(2) The Interpretation Act 1889(c) shall apply to the interpretation of this order as it applies to the interpretation of an Act of Parliament.

Additional non-trading functions

2. The Authority may conduct research or other experimental work in connection with the assessment and development of home-grown cereals for the purpose of improving the marketing thereof for new or existing uses or for new or existing processes and may carry out demonstrations of the results of any such work ; and any power conferred on the Authority by this article to carry on any activity shall be construed as including a power—

(*a*) to carry on that activity in co-operation with any other person, or

(*b*) to do anything (including the provision of financial assistance) calculated to procure, promote or facilitate the carrying on of that activity by any other person.

In Witness whereof the Official Seal of the Minister of Agriculture, Fisheries and Food is hereunto affixed on 5th January 1970.

(L.S.)   *Cledwyn Hughes,*

Minister of Agriculture, Fisheries and Food.

(a) 1965 c. 14.   (b) S.I. 1969/388 (1969 I, p. 1070).
(c) 1889 c. 63.

Given under the Seal of the Secretary of State for Scotland on 7th January 1970.

(L.S.) *William Ross,*
Secretary of State for Scotland.

Given under the hand of the Secretary of State for the Home Department on 20th January 1970.

James Callaghan,
Secretary of State for the Home Department.

Given under my hand on 10th January 1970.

George Thomas,
Secretary of State for Wales.

EXPLANATORY NOTE

(This Note is not part of the Order.)

This order, which comes into operation on 29th January 1970, confers on the Home-Grown Cereals Authority additional non-trading functions similar in character to functions already conferred on the Authority by the Cereals Marketing Act 1965. The additional functions enable the Authority to extend their research and experimental work to include the assessment and development of home-grown cereals for new or existing uses or processes.

STATUTORY INSTRUMENTS

1970 No. 66

POLICE

The Police (Amendment) Regulations 1970

Made - - - -		*19th January* 1970
Laid before Parliament		*29th January* 1970
Coming into Operation		*30th January* 1970

In exercise of the powers conferred on me by section 33 of the Police Act 1964(a), and after consulting the Police Council for Great Britain in accordance with section 45(4) of that Act, I hereby make the following Regulations:—

PART I

CITATION, OPERATION ETC.

1. These Regulations may be cited as the Police (Amendment) Regulations 1970.

2. These Regulations shall come into operation on 30th January 1970 but, for the purposes of authorising any increase in pay or allowances, they shall have effect as from 1st September 1969 except that—

(*a*) for the purposes of Regulation 4 thereof, they shall have effect as from 1st February 1968, and

(*b*) for the purposes of Regulation 5 thereof, they shall have effect as from 12th November 1965.

3. In these Regulations any references to the principal Regulations is a reference to the Police Regulations 1968(b), as amended(c).

PART II

RECKONING OF SERVICE IN BRITISH SOUTH AFRICA POLICE

4.—(1) For paragraph (1) of Regulation 28 of the principal Regulations (which provides for the reckoning by constables of certain overseas police service) there shall be substituted the following paragraph:—

"(1) A member of a police force of the rank of constable shall be entitled to reckon for the purposes of the scale of pay for that rank the following periods of service, that is to say, any period of—

(*a*) service in the Palestine Police Force;

(*b*) service in the Royal Ulster Constabulary;

(*c*) certified overseas police service such as is mentioned in paragraph (2);

(*d*) certified service in the British South Africa Police such as is mentioned in paragraph (4),

---

(a) 1964 c. 48.　　　　　　　　　　(b) S.I. 1968/26 (1968 I, p. 38).
(c) The relevant amending instruments are S.I. 1968/766, 1761; 1969/137 (1968 II, p. 2142; III, p. 4774; 1969 I, p. 369).

notwithstanding that such service is not service in the rank of constable in a police force in Great Britain.".

(2) At the end of the said Regulation 28 there shall be added the following paragraph:—

"(4) The reference in paragraph (1) to certified service in the British South Africa Police is a reference to continuous service as a member thereof, for a period which included 11th November 1965, up to such time, on or after that date, as the person concerned ceased to perform duties therein, subject to it having been certified by or on behalf of the Secretary of State that in his opinion the person concerned so ceased to perform duties in circumstances which rendered him eligible for assistance as a loyal Rhodesian public servant under the scheme announced in the House of Commons on 22nd December 1965.".

5. Where for any period beginning after 11th November 1965 and ending before the revocation of the Police Regulations 1965(a), as amended(b), by the principal Regulations, that is to say, before 1st February 1968, the pay of a member of a police force holding the rank of constable was less than it would have been if—

(a) the amendments made by the preceding Regulation to Regulation 28 of the principal Regulations had been made to Regulation 31 of the said Regulations of 1965, and

(b) any certificate given by or on behalf of the Secretary of State for the purposes of the said Regulation 28, as so amended, had been given for the purposes of the said Regulation 31,

then, the member in question shall be entitled to the difference by way of an increase in pay for that period.

PART III

SUBSISTENCE, REFRESHMENT AND LODGING ALLOWANCES

6. In Schedule 5 to the principal Regulations (which relates to subsistence, refreshment and lodging allowances) for the Table in paragraph 1 there shall be substituted the following Table:—

"TABLE

Description of Allowance	Superin-tendents		Inspectors, Sergeants and Constables	
	s.	d.	s.	d.
Refreshment Allowance:				
(i) for one meal	8	3	7	6
(ii) for two meals	12	0	10	9
Subsistence Allowance:				
Period of retention or engagement on duty—				
(i) over 5 hours and not exceeding 8 hours	12	0	10	9
(ii) over 8 hours and not exceeding 12 hours	17	6	15	9
(iii) over 12 hours and not exceeding 24 hours	30	0	26	0
(iv) over 24 hours—at the rate under (iii) above for each complete period of 24 hours' retention or engagement, together with whichever is the appropriate amount under the preceding provisions of this Table for any excess over the aggregate of such complete periods.				
Lodging Allowance—for each night	54	0	42	0"

(a) S.I. 1965/538 (1965 I, p. 1555).
(b) The amending Regulations are not relevant to the subject matter of this Regulation.

PART IV

Persons Nominated for University Courses

7. At the end of Part II of the principal Regulations (which relates to duty, overtime and leave) there shall be added the following Regulation:—

"University scholars

24A. This Part of these Regulations shall have effect in relation to a university scholar within the meaning of Schedule 11 subject to the provisions of paragraph 2 thereof.".

8. At the end of Regulation 25 of the principal Regulations (which relates to pay) there shall be added the following paragraph:—

"(5) Paragraph (1) and Schedule 3 shall have effect in relation to a university scholar within the meaning of Schedule 11 subject to the provisions of paragraph 3 thereof.".

9. In Regulation 35(1)(*b*) of the principal Regulations (which relates to supplementary rent allowance) the words "or in Regulation 37(1)" shall be omitted.

10. Regulation 37 of the principal Regulations (which relates to the application of Regulation 34 to persons nominated by the Secretary of State for university courses) shall be omitted.

11. At the end of Part IV of the principal Regulations (which relates to allowances and other emoluments) there shall be added the following Regulation:—

"University scholars

57A. This Part of these Regulations shall have effect in relation to a university scholar within the meaning of Schedule 11 subject to the provisions of paragraph 4 thereof.".

12. After Schedule 10 to the principal Regulations there shall be added the following Schedule:—

"SCHEDULE 11

University Scholars

1. In this Schedule a reference to a university scholar is a reference to a member of a police force nominated for a course of university study by the Secretary of State or by the police authority maintaining the force of which he is a member in pursuance of arrangements in that behalf approved by the Secretary of State and, in relation to such a member, the expression "course" means the course for which he has been nominated and which he has undertaken and "study" means study for the purposes of that course.

2. Regulations 18, 19 and 20 shall not apply to a university scholar for the duration of his course except for such period or periods, if any, as he is engaged otherwise than in study.

3.—(1) This paragraph shall apply to a university scholar, not being a member of the City of London or of the metropolitan police force, who has undertaken a course of study given wholly or mainly at an institution within the City of London or the metropolitan police district.

(2) Where such a university scholar takes up residence within the City of London or the metropolitan police district and the taking up of such residence is, in the opinion of the police authority, due to his having undertaken his course, then, for the duration of the course (whether or not he is so resident throughout that period), he shall be entitled to supplementary pay at the rate of £50 a year and his rate of pay, determined in accordance with Regulation 25(1) and Schedule 3, shall be increased accordingly.

4.—(1) Where a university scholar moves his home and the removal is in the opinion of the police authority due to his having undertaken his course, then, notwithstanding the provisions of Regulation 34, the rent allowance to be paid to him shall be that which would be payable to him under that Regulation if he was a member of the force of the police area in which his home is for the time being situate.

(2) Where a university scholar does not move his home, then, Regulation 35 shall have effect in relation to him for the duration of his course—

(a) as if for paragraph (1)(a)(iii) there were substituted the following provision:—

'(iii) satisfies the police authority that the only reason why he is not so living is that he could not, without detriment to his studies, return daily to the family home;';

(b) as if for paragraph (1)(b) there were substituted the following provision:—

'(b) a member of a police force, other than such a member as is mentioned in sub-paragraph (a), who satisfies the police authority that the only reason why he is not living in his former accommodation is that he could not, without detriment to his studies, return daily thereto,';

(c) as if for paragraph (2)(a) and (b) there were substituted the following provision:—

'if he were living with his family or, as the case may be, in his former accommodation.';

(d) where he is a widower with a child or children or a married man and, if he were a member of the force of the police area in which he is for the time being living and entitled to a flat-rate rent allowance under Regulation 34, that allowance would be payable at a higher rate than 50s. 0d. a week, as if for the reference in paragraph (3)(b) to the rate of 50s. 0d. a week there were substituted a reference to that higher rate.

(3) Where a university scholar moves his home and the removal is, in the opinion of the police authority, due to his having undertaken or completed

his course of study and is, in their opinion, reasonable in all the circumstances of his case, Regulation 40 shall have effect in his case as if the removal were such as is mentioned in paragraph (1) thereof.".

James Callaghan,

One of Her Majesty's Principal
Secretaries of State.

Home Office,
Whitehall.

19th January1970.

EXPLANATORY NOTE

(This Note is not part of the Regulations.)

These Regulations (with the exception of Regulation 5) amend the Police Regulations 1968. Except as mentioned in the following paragraph, for the purposes of authorising any increase in pay or allowances the present Regulations have effect from 1st September 1969 (Regulation 2—made in exercise of the power conferred by section 33(4) of the Police Act 1964).

Part II of the present Regulations provides that a member of a police force of the rank of constable shall be entitled to reckon for the purposes of his scale of pay previous service in the British South Africa Police (the Southern Rhodesian police force) where he was serving in that force on 11th November 1965 (the date of the illegal declaration of independence) and ceased to do duty therein in circumstances which, in the opinion of the Secretary of State, rendered him eligible for assistance as a loyal Rhodesian public servant. The provision made by the two Regulations contained in Part II, taken together, has effect from 12th November 1965 (Regulation 2).

Part III of the present Regulations increases the rate of subsistence, refreshment and lodging allowances.

Part IV of the present Regulations relates to a member of a police force nominated for a university course either by the Secretary of State or by his police authority in pursuance of arrangements approved by the Secretary of State. Regulation 12 inserts a new Schedule 11 in the Regulations of 1968; it modifies those Regulations in their application to such a member. Paragraph 2 of the new Schedule states expressly that the provisions of the 1968 Regulations relating to the normal daily period of duty, overtime and public holidays and rest days shall not apply to a member engaged in university study. Paragraph 3 provides that a member of a police force (other than the City of London or metropolitan police force) who resides in the City of London or the metropolitan police district for the purpose of study at an institution therein shall be entitled to supplementary pay at the rate of £50 p.a. Paragraph 4 modifies the provisions of the 1968 Regulations relating to rent allowances, supplementary rent allowances and removal allowances.

STATUTORY INSTRUMENTS

1970 No. 71

REPRESENTATION OF THE PEOPLE

The County and Borough Election Forms Regulations 1970

Made - - - -	*19th January* 1970
Coming into Operation	*16th February* 1970

In pursuance of the powers conferred upon me by rules 4, 5 and 10 of the local elections rules in Schedule 2 to the Representation of the People Act 1949(a), and by section 61 of the Local Government Act 1933(b), I hereby make the following Regulations prescribing forms for use at elections of county councillors, councillors of a borough and elective auditors and the form of declaration of acceptance of office to be made by the chairman of a county council, a county alderman or a county councillor, or by the mayor, an alderman or a councillor of a borough, or by an elective auditor.

1.—(1) These Regulations may be cited as the County and Borough Election Forms Regulations 1970 and shall come into operation on 16th February 1970.

(2) The Interpretation Act 1889(c) shall apply to the interpretation of these Regulations as it applies to the interpretation of an Act of Parliament.

2. The County and Borough Election Forms Regulations 1951(d) are hereby revoked.

3. At an election of a county councillor the forms in Schedule 1 hereto, or forms to the like effect, shall be used, with such modifications as circumstances require.

4. At an election of a councillor of a borough and at an election of elective auditors, the forms in Schedule 2 hereto, or forms to the like effect, shall be used, with such modifications as circumstances require.

5. The declaration of acceptance of office by the chairman of a county council, a county alderman or a county councillor or by the mayor, an alderman or a councillor of a borough or by an elective auditor shall be in the form in Schedule 3 hereto, or in a form to the like effect.

6. Any reference in these Regulations to a borough shall be construed as excluding a reference to a London borough.

James Callaghan,
One of Her Majesty's Principal
Secretaries of State.

Home Office,
   Whitehall.
19th January 1970.

(a) 1949 c. 68.	(b) 1933 c. 51.
(c) 1889 c. 63.	(d) S.I. 1951/264 (1951 II, p. 350).

SCHEDULE 1

Regulation 3.

Forms for use at an election of a county councillor

FORM A

NOTICE OF ELECTION

COUNTY OF

ELECTION OF A COUNTY COUNCILLOR for the
Electoral Division.

1. An election is to be held of a County Councillor for the said electoral division.

2. Nomination papers must be delivered at   on any day after the date of this notice, but not later than noon on the day of   .

If the notice relates to more than one election, adapt form accordingly.

3. Forms of nomination paper may be obtained at
from the undersigned, who will, at the request of any elector for the said electoral division, prepare for signature a nomination paper.

4. If the election is contested, the poll will take place on the day of   .

(Signed).......................................
Returning Officer/Town Clerk.

day of   , 19 .

NOTE 1.—The attention of candidates and electors is drawn to the rules for filling up nomination papers and other provisions relating to nomination contained in the local elections rules in Schedule 2 to the Representation of the People Act 1949 as amended by the Representation of the People Act 1969.

NOTE 2.—Every person guilty of a corrupt or illegal practice will, on conviction, be liable to the penalties imposed by the Representation of the People Act 1949.

NOTE 3.—Electors and their proxies should take note that applications to be treated as an absent voter and other applications and notices about postal or proxy voting must reach the electoral registration officer at (*insert address*) by the   day of next if they are to be effective for this election.

Form B

Nomination Paper

ELECTION OF A COUNTY COUNCILLOR for the
Electoral Division of the County of .

Date of publication of notice of election..

We, the undersigned, being local government electors for the said electoral division do hereby nominate the undermentioned person as a candidate at the said election.

Candidate's surname	Other names in full	Description (if any)	Home address in full

Signatures	Electoral Number (*see* note 3)	
	Distinctive Letter(s)	Number
Proposer..	....	....
Seconder..	....	....
We, the undersigned, being local government electors for the said electoral division, do hereby assent to the foregoing nomination.		
1.	....	....
2.	....	....
3.	....	....
4.	....	....
5.	....	....
6.	....	....
7.	....	....
8.	....	....

Note 1.—The attention of candidates and electors is drawn to the rules for filling up nomination papers and other provisions relating to nomination contained in the local elections rules in Schedule 2 to the Representation of the People Act 1949 as amended by the Representation of the People Act 1969.

Note 2.—Where a candidate is commonly known by some title he may be described by his title as if it were his surname.

Note 3.—A person's electoral number consists of the distinctive letter or letters of the parliamentary polling district in which he is registered together with his number in the register to be used at the election except that before publication of the register the distinctive letter or letters of the parliamentary polling district in which he is entitled to be registered together with his number (if any) in the electors lists for that register shall be used instead.

Note 4.—An elector may not subscribe more than one nomination paper in respect of the same electoral division.

Note 5.—A person whose name is entered in the register or electors lists may not subscribe a nomination paper if the entry gives as the date on which he will become of voting age a date later than the day fixed for the poll.

FORM C

STATEMENT AS TO PERSONS NOMINATED

COUNTY OF

The following is a statement as to the persons nominated for election as County Councillor for the Electoral Division.

Persons nominated					Decision of returning officer that nomination paper is invalid, or other reason why a person nominated no longer stands nominated
Surname	Other names in full	Home address in full	Description (if any)	Proposer's name	
1.	2.	3.	4.	5.	6.

The persons opposite whose names no entry is made in column 6 have been and stand validly nominated.

Dated this   day of   , 19   .

....
Returning Officer.

Regulation 4.   SCHEDULE 2

Forms for use at an election of a councillor
of a borough or of elective auditors

FORM A

NOTICE OF ELECTION

BOROUGH OF

ELECTION OF [A COUNCILLOR] [COUNCILLORS] [ELECTIVE AUDITORS] for the [Ward of the] [Wards of the] Borough.

If the
notice relates
to two or
more wards,
indicate the
number of
councillors
to be elected
for each
ward.

1. An election is to be held of   [Councillor(s)] [Elective Auditors] for the said [ward] [wards] [borough].

2. Nomination papers must be delivered at   on any day after the date of this notice, but not later than noon on the day of   .

3. Forms of nomination paper may be obtained at
from the undersigned, who will, at the request of any elector for the electoral area, prepare for signature a nomination paper.

4. If the election is contested, the poll will take place on the day of   .

(Signed).....................................

Town Clerk.

day of   , 19   .

NOTE 1.—The attention of candidates and electors is drawn to the rules for filling up nomination papers and other provisions relating to nomination contained in the local elections rules▪in Schedule 2 to the Representation of the People Act 1949 as amended by the Representation of the People Act 1969.

NOTE 2.—Every person guilty of a corrupt or illegal practice will, on conviction, be liable to the penalties imposed by the Representation of the People Act 1949.

NOTE 3.—Electors and their proxies should take note that applications to be treated as an absent voter and other applications and notices about postal or proxy voting must reach the electoral registration officer at (*insert address*) by the
day of   next if they are to be effective for this election.

Form B

Nomination Paper

ELECTION OF [A COUNCILLOR] [COUNCILLORS] [ELECTIVE AUDITORS] for the [**Ward of the] Borough of**

Date of publication of notice of election...

We, the undersigned, being local government electors for the said [ward] [borough] do hereby nominate the undermentioned person as a candidate at the said election.

Candidate's surname	Other names in full	Description (if any)	Home address in full

Signatures	Electoral Number (*see* note 3)	
	Distinctive Letter(s)	Number
Proposer...	....	....
Seconder...	....	....
We, the undersigned, being local government electors for the said [ward] [borough], do hereby assent to the foregoing nomination.		
1.	....	....
2.	....	....
3.	....	....
4.	....	....
5.	....	....
6.	....	....
7.	....	....
8.	....	....

Note 1.—The attention of candidates and electors is drawn to the rules for filling up nomination papers and other provisions relating to nomination contained in the local elections rules in Schedule 2 to the Representation of the People Act 1949 as amended by the Representation of the People Act 1969.

Note 2.—Where a candidate is commonly known by some title he may be described by his title as if it were his surname.

Note 3.—A person's electoral number consists of the distinctive letter or letters of the parliamentary polling district in which he is registered together with his number in the register to be used at the election except that before publication of the register the distinctive letter or letters of the parliamentary polling district in which he is entitled to be registered together with his number (if any) in the electors lists for that register shall be used instead.

Note 4.—An elector may not—

(*a*) subscribe more nomination papers than there are vacancies to be filled in the electoral area; or

(*b*) subscribe a nomination paper for more than one ward of a borough divided into wards; or

(*c*) subscribe more than one nomination paper in respect of the same candidate.

Note 5.—A person whose name is entered in the register or electors lists may not subscribe a nomination paper if the entry gives as the date on which he will become of voting age a date later than the day fixed for the poll.

FORM C

STATEMENT AS TO PERSONS NOMINATED

BOROUGH OF

The following is a statement as to the persons nominated for election as [a Councillor] [Councillors] [Elective Auditors] for the [Ward of the] [Wards of the] Borough.

[Ward] [Wards] [Borough]	Persons nominated					Decision of mayor that nomination paper is invalid, or other reason why a person nominated no longer stands nominated
	Surname	Other names in full	Home address in full	Description (if any)	Proposer's name	
1.	2.	3.	4.	5.	6.	7.

The persons opposite whose names no entry is made in column 7 have been and stand validly nominated.

Dated this   day of   , 19 .

....

                                   Mayor.

SCHEDULE 3

Declaration of Acceptance of Office

I, A.B., having been elected to the office of *   hereby ***Insert** declare that I take the said office upon myself, and will duly and faithfully fulfil **description** the duties thereof according to the best of my judgment and ability.   **of office.**

Dated this   day of   , 19 .

                      Signature...

This declaration was made and subscribed before us

Members of the [County]...

[Borough] Council†... **†If the declaration is made and subscribed before the clerk of the county council or the town clerk, or a justice of the peace or magistrate, or a commissioner for oaths, or a British consul, adapt form accordingly.**

EXPLANATORY NOTE

(This Note is not part of the Regulations.)

These Regulations revoke and replace the County and Borough Election Forms Regulations 1951, with amendments consequential on the provisions of the Representation of the People Act 1969 (c. 15).

STATUTORY INSTRUMENTS

1970 No. 73

RATING AND VALUATION
The Rate Product (Passenger Transport Authorities) Rules 1970

Made - - -	*21st January* 1970
Laid before Parliament	*29th January* 1970
Coming into Operation	*5th February* 1970

The Minister of Housing and Local Government, after consultation with the local authority and the associations of local authorities with whom consultation appeared to him desirable, in exercise of his powers under section 113 of the General Rate Act 1967(**a**), as extended by section 13(5) of the Transport Act 1968(**b**), and of all other powers enabling him in that behalf, hereby makes the following rules :—

Title and commencement

1. These rules may be cited as the Rate Product (Passenger Transport Authorities) Rules and shall come into operation on 5th February 1970.

Interpretation

2.—(1) In these rules—

"appropriate factor" has the meaning ascribed by rule 4 of these rules ;

"authority" means the council of a constituent area ;

"constituent area" means a constituent area of a designated area within the meaning of section 9(1) of the Transport Act 1968 ;

"Minister" means the Minister of Housing and Local Government ;

"relevant year" means a year in respect of which a rate product is being ascertained ;

"year" means a period of twelve months beginning with 1st April ;

"year following" means the year immediately following a relevant year.

(2) The Interpretation Act 1889(**c**) shall apply for the interpretation of these rules as it applies for the interpretation of an Act of Parliament.

Precepts under section 13 of Transport Act 1968

3. For the purposes of section 13(2) of the Transport Act 1968 (which section empowers Passenger Transport Authorities constituted under that Act to issue precepts) the product of a rate of one penny in the pound for any constituent area shall be determined by—

(*a*) ascertaining the product of a rate of one penny in the pound for that area in the manner provided in the Schedule to the Rate Product Rules 1968(**d**) ; and

(*b*) multiplying the resulting product by the appropriate factor.

(**a**) 1967 c. 9.　　　　　　　　　　(**b**) 1968 c. 73.
(**c**) 1889 c. 63.　　　　　　　　　　(**d**) S.I. 1968/491 (1968 I, p. 1202).

Definition of the appropriate factor

4. For the purposes of these rules the appropriate factor for a relevant year shall be the number as last notified to the authority by the Minister in the year following with his notification of the amount (or estimated amount) of the resources element of rate support grant payable for the relevant year, the said number being—

(*a*) in the case of an authority not qualifying for a payment of the resources element for the relevant year (or not appearing to the Minister so to qualify when he estimates and notifies to the authority the amount of that element payable for the relevant year), one ; and

(*b*) in the case of an authority qualifying for such a payment (or appearing to the Minister so to qualify when he estimates and notifies as aforesaid) the number produced by dividing the amount (or estimated amount) of the expenditure of the authority for the relevant year for the purposes of Part II of Schedule 1 to the Local Government Act 1966(**a**) by the difference between that amount (or estimated amount) and the amount (or estimated amount) of the resources element payable to the authority for the relevant year.

Given under the official seal of the Minister of Housing and Local Government on 21st January 1970.

(L.S.)   *Anthony Greenwood,*
Minister of Housing and Local Government.

EXPLANATORY NOTE
(*This Note is not part of the Rules.*)

These Rules prescribe the manner in which the product of a rate of one penny in the pound is to be determined for purposes of precepts issued by Passenger Transport Authorities upon their constituent authorities. This product is determined by (i) taking the product of a rate of one penny in the pound for the area of the authority as ascertained by the standard method prescribed in the Rate Product Rules 1968 and (ii) multiplying the result by the appropriate factor. This factor is a ratio which reflects any increase in the authority's rate resources arising from their entitlement to a payment of the resources element of rate support grant.

(**a**) 1966 c. 42.

STATUTORY INSTRUMENTS

1970 No. 79

NATIONAL HEALTH SERVICE, ENGLAND AND WALES

HOSPITAL AND SPECIALIST SERVICES

The National Health Service (Functions of Regional Hospital Boards, etc.) Amendment Regulations 1970

Made - - - -	*22nd January* 1970
Laid before Parliament	*29th January* 1970
Coming into Operation	*1st February* 1970

The Secretary of State for Social Services, in exercise of his powers under section 12 of the National Health Service Act 1946(**a**) and of all other powers enabling him in that behalf, hereby makes the following regulations:—

1.—(1) These regulations may be cited as the National Health Service (Functions of Regional Hospital Boards, etc.) Amendment Regulations 1970, and shall come into operation on 1st February 1970.

(2) The Interpretation Act 1889(**b**) applies to the interpretation of these regulations as it applies to the interpretation of an Act of Parliament.

2. The National Health Service (Functions of Regional Hospital Boards, etc.) Regulations 1969(**c**) shall be amended by the substitution for regulation 5(1) (Powers of a Hospital Management Committee of a university hospital to carry out building or civil engineering works) of the following paragraph :—

" (1) If the Hospital Management Committee manages and controls a university hospital, designated under section 5 of the Act of 1968, the functions of the Board under section 3(1)(a) of the Act with respect to the undertaking of building or civil engineering works, the estimated total cost of which does not exceed £120,000."

R. H. S. Crossman,
Secretary of State for Social Services.

22nd January 1970.

EXPLANATORY NOTE

(This Note is not part of the Regulations.)

These Regulations amend the National Health Service (Functions of Regional Hospital Boards, etc.) Regulations 1969 by providing that (subject to any direction by the Regional Hospital Board or the Secretary of State) a Hospital Management Committee which manages and controls a university hospital shall have power to undertake building or civil engineering works, the estimated total cost of which does not exceed £120,000.

(**a**) 1946 c. 81.　　(**b**) 1889 c. 63.　　(**c**) S.I. 1969/297 (1969 I, p. 809).

STATUTORY INSTRUMENTS

1970 No. 87

LOCAL GOVERNMENT, ENGLAND AND WALES

The Local Government (Allowances to Members) Regulations 1970

Made - - -	*22nd January* 1970
Laid before Parliament	*30th January* 1970
Coming into Operation	*6th February* 1970

The Minister of Housing and Local Government, in exercise of his powers under sections 113 and 117 of the Local Government Act 1948(a) and of all other powers enabling him in that behalf, hereby makes the following regulations :—

Citation and commencement

1. These regulations may be cited as the Local Government (Allowances to Members) Regulations 1970, and shall come into operation on 6th February 1970.

Interpretation

2.—(1) The Interpretation Act 1889(b) applies for the interpretation of these regulations as it applies for the interpretation of an Act of Parliament.

(2) In these regulations, unless the context otherwise requires—

"the Act of 1948" means the Local Government Act 1948 ;

"body" means any body to which Part VI of the Act of 1948 applies ;

"financial loss allowance" means a payment by way of financial loss allowance within the meaning of section 112 of the Act of 1948 ;

"travelling allowance" and "subsistence allowance" mean payments by way of travelling allowance and subsistence allowance, reprectively, within the meaning of section 113 of the Act of 1948 ;

"public transport" means any service provided for travel by the public by railway, ship, vessel, omnibus, trolley vehicle or tramway ; and

"the Minister" means the Minister of Housing and Local Government.

Maximum rates of allowances

3. The rates determined by bodies for travelling and subsistence allowances shall not exceed the rates prescribed, and shall be subject to the provisions contained, in schedules 1 and 2 to these regulations respectively.

(a) 1948 c. 26.   (b) 1889 c. 63.

Claims for allowances

4. A member of a body who desires to claim financial loss, travelling or subsistence allowance shall complete and submit to that body an application in the appropriate form set out in schedule 3 to these regulations or a form substantially to the like effect.

Issue of tickets and vouchers for travelling

5. Every body shall, so far as it considers it practicable, make arrangements for the issue to its members of tickets, or of vouchers, warrants or similar documents which can be exchanged for tickets, to cover journeys in respect of which travelling allowances would otherwise fall to be made.

Records of allowances paid

6.—(1) Every body shall keep records of all payments to members made by it under Part VI of the Act of 1948, indicating the amounts paid to each member and the heads under which they were paid, and such records shall be open to inspection at all reasonable hours by any local government elector for the area of the body.

(2) For the purposes of this regulation expenditure incurred in the issue to a member of any ticket or other document under the preceding regulation shall be deemed a payment made to that member.

Avoidance of duplication of allowances

7.—(1) Where a person necessarily suffers or incurs any loss or expense to which section 112 of the Act of 1948 applies, or necessarily incurs expenditure on travelling or subsistence, in respect of the performance in any one period of twenty-four hours of approved duties as a member of more than one body, he shall not be entitled to receive in respect of the performance of those duties payments which will exceed in the aggregate the amount to which he would have been entitled had all the said duties been performed by him as a member of one only of those bodies.

(2) Where a person becomes entitled to receive, in respect of the performance of any duties in any one period of twenty-four hours, financial loss, travelling or subsistence allowance under the Act of 1948 and any comparable allowance under any other enactment, the amount which he shall be entitled to receive in respect of the performance of those duties under either of those enactments shall be reduced by the amount of any payment so received by him under the other of those enactments, and any claim for any such allowance shall contain particulars of any amount received or claimed from any other authority or body.

Revocations

8. The following regulations are hereby revoked—

The Local Government (Allowances to Members) Regulations 1954(a)

The Local Government (Allowances to Members) Regulations 1962(b)

The Local Government (Allowances to Members) Regulations 1965(c)

(a) S.I. 1954/397 (1954 I, p. 1146).   (b) S.I. 1962/1782 (1962 II, p. 2139).
(c) S.I. 1965/194 (1965 I, p. 475).

SCHEDULE 1

RATES OF TRAVELLING ALLOWANCE, AND PROVISIONS RELATING THERETO

1.—(1) The rate for travel by public transport shall not exceed the amount of the ordinary fare or any available cheap fare, and where more than one class of fare is available the rate shall be determined, in the case of travel by ship by reference to first class fares, and in any other case by reference to second class fares unless the body determines, either generally or specially, that first class fares shall be substituted.

(2) The rate specified in the preceding sub-paragraph may be increased by supplementary allowances not exceeding expenditure actually incurred—

(a) on Pullman Car or similar supplements, reservation of seats and deposit or porterage of luggage, and

(b) on sleeping accommodation engaged by the member for an overnight journey, subject, however, to reduction by one-third of any subsistence allowance payable to him for that night.

2.—(1) The rate for travel by a member's own solo motor cycle of cylinder capacity not exceeding 500 c.c. shall not exceed—

(a) for the use of a solo motor cycle of cylinder capacity not exceeding 120 c.c., 2.75d. a mile ;

(b) for the use of a solo motor cycle of cylinder capacity exceeding 120 c.c. but not exceeding 150 c.c., 3.5d. a mile ;

(c) for the use of a solo motor cycle of cylinder capacity exceeding 150 c.c. but not exceeding 500 c.c., 4d. a mile.

(2) The rate for travel by a member's own private motor vehicle, or one belonging to a member of his family or otherwise provided for his use, other than a solo motor cycle of cylinder capacity not exceeding 500 c.c. shall not exceed 4d. a mile unless such travel—

(a) results in a substantial saving of the member's time ; or

(b) is in the interests of the body ; or

(c) is otherwise reasonable,

in which case the rate shall not exceed—

(i) for the use of a solo motor cycle of cylinder capacity exceeding 500 c.c., a motor cycle with side-car, or a motor or tri-car of cylinder capacity not exceeding 500 c.c., 5.75d. a mile ;

(ii) for the use of a motor car or tri-car of cylinder capacity—

(a) exceeding 500 c.c. but not exceeding 999 c.c., 11.25d. a mile ;

(b) exceeding 999 c.c. but not exceeding 1199 c.c., 12.75d. a mile ;

(c) exceeding 1199 c.c., 14.25d. a mile.

(3) The rates specified in sub-paragraphs (1) and (2) may be increased—

(a) in respect of the carriage of each passenger, not exceeding 4, to whom a travelling allowance would otherwise be payable under any enactment—

(i) where the rate payable does not exceed 4d. a mile, by not more than 1d. a mile, or

(ii) where any other rate is payable, by not more than ·5d. a mile ;

(b) by not more than the amount of any expenditure incurred on tolls, ferries or parking fees ;

(c) in the case of absence overnight from the usual place of residence, by not more than 2s. 6d. a night for garaging a car or tri-car, or 1s. 6d. a night for garaging a motor vehicle of any other type.

(4) For the purposes of this paragraph, cylinder capacity shall be calculated in the manner prescribed by regulation 46 of the Road Vehicles (Registration and Licensing) Regulations 1964(a).

3. The rate for travel by taxi-cab or cab shall not exceed—

(a) in cases of urgency or where no public transport is reasonably available, the amount of the actual fare and any reasonable gratuity paid, and

(b) in any other case, the amount of the fare for travel by appropriate public transport.

4. The rate for travel by a hired motor vehicle other than a taxi-cab or cab shall not exceed the rate which would have been applicable had the vehicle belonged to the member who hired it ;

Provided that where the body so approves the rate may be increased to an amount not exceeding the actual cost of the hiring.

5. The rate for travel by air shall not exceed the rate applicable to travel by appropriate alternative means of transport together with an allowance equivalent to the amount of any saving in financial loss allowance and subsistence allowance consequent on travel by air:

Provided that where the body resolves, either generally or specially, that the saving in time is so substantial as to justify payment of the fare for travel by air, there may be paid an amount not exceeding—

(a) the ordinary fare or any available cheap fare for travel by regular air service, or

(b) where no such service is available or in case of urgency, the fare actually paid by the member.

SCHEDULE 2

Rates of Subsistence Allowance, and Provisions Relating Thereto

1.—(1) The rate of subsistence allowance shall not exceed—

(a) in the case of an absence, not involving an absence overnight, from the usual place of residence—

    (i) of more than 4 but not more than 8 hours, 19s.;

    (ii) of more than 8 but not more than 12 hours, 35s.;

    (iii) of more than 12 but not more than 16 hours, 50s.;

    (iv) of more than 16 hours, 59s.;

(b) in the case of an absence overnight from the usual place of residence, 110s. :

Provided that for such an absence overnight in London, or for the purpose of attendance at an annual conference (including or not including an annual meeting) of the County Councils' Association, the Association of Municipal Corporations, the Urban District Councils' Association, the Rural District Councils' Association or such other association of bodies as the Minister may for the time being approve for the purpose, the rate may be increased by a supplementary allowance not exceeding 10s.;

(c) for the purposes of this sub-paragraph, London means the City of London and the London boroughs of Camden, Greenwich, Hackney, Hammersmith, Islington, Kensington and Chelsea, Lambeth, Lewisham, Southwark, Tower Hamlets, Wandsworth and Westminster.

(a) S.I. 1964/1178 (1964 II, p. 2722).

(2) Any rate determined under the preceding sub-paragraph shall be deemed to cover a continuous period of absence of 24 hours.

2. The rates specified in the preceding paragraph shall be reduced by an appropriate amount in respect of any meal provided free of charge by any authority or body during the period to which the allowance relates.

FORM OF APPLICATION FOR TRAVELLING AND SUBSISTENCE ALLOWANCES

1	2	3	4	5	6	7	8	9	10
Date	Place and time of departure	Place and time of return	Description of approved duties	Mode and class of travel	Fares and other authorised payments	Number of miles travelled by member's private motor vehicle, and rate per mile claimed	Toll, ferry and parking fees and garaging allowance	Travelling allowance claimed	Subsistence allowance claimed
					TOTALS			AMOUNTS NOW CLAIMED	

If the rate claimed is related to the type of vehicle and cylinder capacity, state what these are:—

If the rate claimed is more than 4d. a mile, state grounds on which higher rate is claimed:—

Particulars of amounts received or claimed by way of travelling or subsistence allowance from any other authority or body—

I declare that—
(a) I have necessarily incurred expenditure on travelling and subsistence for the purpose of enabling me to perform approved duties as a member of...;
(b) I have actually paid the fares and made the other payments shown in column 6 and paid the fees shown in column 8 above;
(c) The amounts claimed are strictly in accordance with the rates determined by...

I declare that the statements above are correct. Except as shown above I have not made, and will not make, any claim under any enactment for travelling or subsistence expenses or allowances in connection with the duties indicated above.

Date......................   Signature of member......................

SCHEDULE 3

FORM OF APPLICATION FOR FINANCIAL LOSS ALLOWANCE

1	2	3	4	5	6
Date	Place and time of departure	Place and time of return	Description of approved duties	Period of time over which earnings were lost or expense was incurred	Amount Claimed

Particulars of amounts received or claimed by way of financial loss allowance from any other authority or body—

I declare that I have actually and necessarily—

*(a) suffered loss of earnings which I would otherwise have made,

*(b) incurred additional expense, other than expense on account of travelling or subsistence, to which I would not otherwise have been subject,

for the purpose of enabling me to perform approved duties as a member of

.... and that the amount of such loss and expense is not less than the amount claimed in column 6 above. I declare that the statements above are correct. Except as shown above I have not made, and will not make, any claim under any enactment for financial loss allowance in connection with the duties indicated above.

Date.................... Signature of member....................

*Delete as appropriate

Given under the official seal of the Minister of Housing and Local Government on 22nd January 1970.

(L.S.)   *Anthony Greenwood,*
                    Minister of Housing and Local Government.

EXPLANATORY NOTE

(This Note is not part of the Regulations.)

The Regulations are primarily directed to the increase of the maximum rates of travelling and subsistence allowances to which members of local authorities, etc., are entitled under Part VI of the Local Government Act 1948. The opportunity is taken to consolidate, with minor amendments, the regulations prescribing maximum rates of subsistence and travelling allowances, the making of claims for these allowances and financial loss allowance, the keeping of records, the avoidance of duplicate payments, etc.

STATUTORY INSTRUMENTS

1970 No. 88

LONDON GOVERNMENT

The Greater London Council (Allowances to Members) Regulations 1970

Made - - -		*22nd January* 1970
Laid before Parliament		*30th January* 1970
Coming into Operation		*6th February* 1970

The Minister of Housing and Local Government, in exercise of his powers under section 117 of the Local Government Act 1948(a), as extended by section 23 of the Greater London Council (General Powers) Act 1966(b), and of all other powers enabling him in that behalf, hereby makes the following regulations:—

Title and commencement

1. These regulations may be cited as the Greater London Council (Allowances to Members) Regulations and shall come into operation on 6th February 1970.

Interpretation

2.—(1) In these regulations—

"the Act of 1966" means the Greater London Council (General Powers) Act 1966;

"the Council" means the Greater London Council; and

"day" means a period of 24 hours commencing at midnight;

and any reference to a period shall be read as referring to a period during which a member of the Council performs any approved duty as a member of the Council.

(2) For the purposes of these regulations a member of a committee or sub-committee of the Council shall be deemed to be a member of the Council.

(3) The Interpretation Act 1889(c) shall apply for the interpretation of these regulations as it applies for the interpretation of an Act of Parliament.

Maximum rates of allowance

3. For the purposes of section 23(3) of the Act of 1966, the rate at which a member of the Council shall be entitled to receive an allowance in respect of any period shall not exceed the rate prescribed in column (2) of the following table against the period in column (1) which is appropriate to the case.

(a) 1948 c. 26.   (b) 1966 c. xxviii.   (c) 1889 c. 63.

TABLE

(1) Period	(2) Rate
1. A morning (up to 1 p.m. in any day)	£2 19s. 0d.
2. An afternoon (from 1 p.m. onwards in any day)	£2 19s. 0d.
3. A period which starts before 1 p.m. and continues after 2 p.m in any day	£5 18s. 0d.
4. A period of absence overnight from the usual place of residence— (a) which does not exceed 24 hours .. .. (b) which does exceed 24 hours	£9 10s. 0d. £9 10s. 0d. for each complete 24 hours plus the rate appropriate to the remainder of the period.

Claims for allowances

4. A member of the Council who wishes to claim an allowance under these regulations shall make a declaration that he has not and will not make any claim for financial loss allowance or subsistence allowance from any other authority or body in respect of the approved duty to which the claim relates.

Record of allowances paid

5. The Council shall keep records of all payments to members made by the Council under the Act of 1966, and such records shall be open to inspection at all reasonable hours by any local government elector for the area of the Council.

Revocation

6. The Greater London Council (Allowances to Members) Regulations 1968**(a)** are hereby revoked.

Given under the official seal of the Minister of Housing and Local Government on 22nd January 1970.

(L.S.)

Anthony Greenwood,
Minister of Housing and
Local Government.

(a) S.I. 1968/1043.

EXPLANATORY NOTE

(This Note is not part of the Regulations.)

These regulations re-enact with amendments the Greater London Council (Allowances to Members) Regulations 1968. They prescribe the maximum rates of the payments which members of the Greater London Council and its committees and sub-committees, are entitled to receive instead of subsistence and financial loss allowances under Part VI of the Local Government Act 1948. The amendments are—

(1) the maximum rates are increased;

(2) rates are now prescribed for absences overnight;

(3) all rates are set out in a table.

STATUTORY INSTRUMENTS

1970 No. 89

LOCAL GOVERNMENT, ENGLAND AND WALES

The Local Government (Financial Loss Allowance) Regulations 1970

Made - - -	22nd January 1970
Laid before Parliament	30th January 1970
Coming into Operation	6th February 1970

The Minister of Housing and Local Government, in exercise of his powers under sections 112 and 117 of the Local Government Act 1948(a) as having effect by virtue of section 16 of the Local Government (Miscellaneous Provisions) Act 1953(b), and of all other powers enabling him in that behalf, hereby makes the following regulations:—

Citation and commencement

1. These regulations may be cited as the Local Government (Financial Loss Allowance) Regulations 1970 and shall come into operation on 6th February 1970.

Interpretation

2. The Interpretation Act 1889(c) applies for the interpretation of these regulations as it applies for the interpretation of an Act of Parliament.

Financial loss allowance

3. The amount which a member of a body to which Part VI of the Local Government Act 1948 applies shall be entitled to be paid by way of financial loss allowance within the meaning of section 112 of the said Act in respect of any one period of 24 hours shall not exceed—

(a) where the period of time over which earnings are lost or additional expense (other than expense on account of travelling or subsistence) is incurred is not more than 4 hours, the sum of £2; or

(b) where the said period of time is more than 4 hours, the sum of £4.

Revocation

4. The Local Government (Financial Loss Allowance) Regulations 1966(d) are hereby revoked.

Given under the official seal of the Minister of Housing and Local Government on 22nd January 1970.

(L.S.)

Anthony Greenwood,
Minister of Housing and Local Government.

(a) 1948 c. 26.   (b) 1953 c. 26.   (c) 1889 c. 63.   (d) S.I. 1966/870 (1966 II, p. 2057).

EXPLANATORY NOTE

(This Note is not part of the Regulations.)

The Regulations supersede the Local Government (Financial Loss Allowance) Regulations 1966 and prescribe new maximum amounts for the financial loss allowance to which members of local authorities, etc., are entitled in respect of the performance of their duties.

STATUTORY INSTRUMENTS

1970 No. 92

LONDON GOVERNMENT
REPRESENTATION OF THE PEOPLE
The Greater London Council Election Rules 1970

Made - - -	*22nd January* 1970
Laid before Parliament	*4th February* 1970
Coming into Operation	*16th February* 1970

In pursuance of the powers conferred upon me by paragraph 14 of Schedule 3 to the London Government Act 1963(**a**) and by section 61 of the Local Government Act 1933(**b**) (as it has effect in relation to elections to the Greater London Council by virtue of paragraphs 10 and 11(1) of Schedule 2 to the London Government Act 1963), I hereby make the following Rules for the conduct of an election of councillors of the Greater London Council and of the chairman of the Greater London Council, and the following Regulations prescribing the form of declaration of acceptance of office by the chairman of the Greater London Council, or by an alderman or a councillor of the Greater London Council :—

1.—(1) These Rules and Regulations may be cited as the Greater London Council Election Rules 1970 and shall come into operation on 16th February 1970 :

Provided that they shall not have effect in relation to an election notice of which has been published before that date.

(2) The Interpretation Act 1889(**c**) shall apply to the interpretation of these Rules and Regulations as it applies to the interpretation of an Act of Parliament.

(3) Any reference in any statutory instrument to a local elections rule shall, so far as it relates to the election of a councillor of the Greater London Council, be construed as a reference to the rule in Schedule 1 hereto (however numbered) dealing with the same subject.

2.—(1) The London Borough Council and Greater London Council Elections Rules 1963(**d**), the London Borough Council and Greater London Council Elections Rules 1964(**e**) and the London Borough Council and Greater London Council Election Forms Regulations 1964(**f**), so far as they relate to elections to the Greater London Council, are hereby revoked.

(2) Notwithstanding paragraph (1) of this Rule, the Rules therein mentioned (which apply to the election of councillors of the Greater London Council) shall apply to any election notice of which has been published before these Rules and Regulations come into operation.

(**a**) 1963 c. 33.   (**b**) 1933 c. 51.
(**c**) 1889 c. 63.
(**d**) S.I. 1963/1864 (1963 III, p. 3455).   (**e**) S.I. 1964/454 (1964 I, p. 725).
(**f**) S.I. 1964/222 (1964 I, p. 402).

3. In the application of the local elections rules contained in Schedule 2 to the Representation of the People Act 1949(a) to an election of councillors of the Greater London Council, adaptations, alterations and exceptions shall be made therein so that the said local elections rules shall read as set out in Schedule 1 hereto.

4. The declaration of acceptance of office by the chairman of the Greater London Council or by an alderman or councillor of the Greater London Council shall be in the form in Schedule 2 hereto, or a form to the like effect.

James Callaghan,
One of Her Majesty's Principal
Secretaries of State.

Home Office,
    Whitehall.
22nd January 1970.

SCHEDULE 1

ELECTION RULES

Arrangement of rules

PART I

PROVISIONS AS TO TIME

Rule
1. Timetable.
2. Computation of time.
3. Hours of poll.

PART II

STAGES COMMON TO CONTESTED AND UNCONTESTED ELECTIONS

4. Notice of election.
5. Nomination of candidates.
6. Subscription of nomination paper.
7. Consent to nomination.
8. Place for delivery of nomination papers.
9. Decisions as to validity of nomination papers.
10. Publication of nominations.
11. Withdrawal of candidates.
12. Nomination in more than one electoral area.
13. Method of election.

PART III

CONTESTED ELECTIONS

General provisions

14. Poll to be taken by ballot.
15. The ballot papers.
16. The official mark.
17. Prohibition of disclosure of vote.
18. Use of schools and public rooms.

(a) 1949 c. 68.

APPENDIX

FORMS

Notice of election.
Nomination paper.
Statement as to persons nominated.
Ballot paper.
Directions for the guidance of the voters in voting.
Certificate of employment.
Declaration to be made by the companion of a blind voter.

PART I

PROVISIONS AS TO TIME

Timetable

1. The proceedings at the election shall be conducted in accordance with the following Table.

TIMETABLE

Proceeding	*Time*
Publication of notice of election ...	Not later than the twentieth day before the day of election.
Delivery of nomination papers ...	Not later than noon on the fourteenth day before the day of election.
Despatch of notice of decisions on nominations and publication of statement as to persons nominated	Not later than noon on the thirteenth day before the day of election.
Delivery of notices of withdrawals of candidature	Not later than noon on the twelfth day before the day of election.
Notice of poll	Not later than the fifth day before the day of election.
Notice of appointment of polling or counting agents	Not later than the third day before the day of election.
Polling	On the day of election.

Computation of time

2.—(1) In computing any period of time for the purposes of the Timetable, a Sunday, day of the Christmas break, of the Easter break or of a bank holiday break or day appointed for public thanksgiving or mourning shall be disregarded and any such day shall not be treated as a day for the purpose of any proceedings up to the completion of the poll nor shall the returning officer be obliged to proceed with the counting of the votes thereon:

Provided that where under Part III of these rules a person ought to proceed with the preparation of special lists or the issue of postal ballot papers on the first or last days of the Christmas break, the Easter break or a bank holiday break, or on the Saturday in the Easter break, nothing in this rule shall absolve him from that duty.

(2) In this rule "the Christmas break" means the period beginning with the last week day before Christmas Day and ending with the first week day after Christmas Day which is not a bank holiday, "the Easter break" means the period beginning with the Thursday before and ending with the Tuesday after Easter Day, and "a bank holiday break" means any bank holiday not included in the Christmas break or the Easter break and the period beginning with the last week day before that bank holiday and ending with the next week day which is not a bank holiday.

Hours of poll

3. The poll shall commence at eight o'clock in the morning and be kept open till nine o'clock in the evening of the same day and no longer.

PART II

STAGES COMMON TO CONTESTED AND UNCONTESTED ELECTIONS

Notice of election

4.—(1) Notice of the election in the form in the Appendix, or a form to the like effect, shall be prepared, signed and published by the returning officer.

(2) The notice shall be published by causing it—

(a) to be affixed to the town hall of the borough which constitutes or includes the electoral area and, if the electoral area includes the City of London, at the Guildhall of the said City; and

(b) to be exhibited at such conspicuous places in the electoral area as the returning officer may determine.

(3) The notice of election shall state the date by which application to be treated as an absent voter and other applications and notices about postal or proxy voting must reach the registration officer in order that they may be effective for the election; and in addition the registration officer shall give notice of the date in the electoral area by such means as he thinks best calculated to bring the information to the notice of those concerned.

Nomination of candidates

5.—(1) Each candidate shall be nominated by a separate nomination paper in the form in the Appendix, or a form to the like effect, delivered at the place fixed for the purpose.

(2) The nomination paper shall state the full names, place of residence and (if desired) description of the candidate and the surname shall be placed first in the list of his names.

(3) The description (if any) shall not exceed six words in length, and need not refer to his rank, profession or calling so long as, with the other particulars of the candidate, it is sufficient to identify him.

Subscription of nomination paper

6.—(1) The nomination paper shall be subscribed by two electors for the electoral area as proposer and seconder, and by eight other electors for that area as assenting to the nomination.

(2) Where a nomination paper bears the signatures of more than the required number of persons as proposing, seconding or assenting to the nomination of a candidate, the signature or signatures (up to the required number) appearing first on the paper in each category shall be taken into account to the exclusion of any others in that category.

(3) The nomination paper shall give the electoral number of each person subscribing it.

(4) The returning officer shall provide nomination papers and shall supply any elector for the electoral area with as many nomination papers as may be required and shall, at the request of any such elector, prepare for signature a nomination paper.

(5) No person shall—

(a) subscribe more nomination papers than there are vacancies to be filled in the electoral area; or

(b) subscribe a nomination paper for more than one electoral area; or

(c) subscribe more than one nomination paper in respect of the same candidate:

Provided that a person shall not be prevented from subscribing a nomination paper by reason only of his having subscribed that of a candidate who has died or withdrawn before delivery of the first-mentioned paper.

(6) If any person subscribes nomination papers in contravention of the last foregoing paragraph, his signature shall be inoperative in all but those papers (up to the permitted number) which are first delivered.

(7) In this rule—

the expression "elector for the electoral area" means a person who is registered as a local government elector for the electoral area in the register to be used at the election or who, pending the publication of that register, appears from the electors lists therefor as corrected by the registration officer to be entitled to be so registered (and accordingly includes a person shown in the register or electors lists as below voting age if it appears therefrom that he will be of voting age on the day fixed for the poll, but not otherwise);

the expression "electoral number" means the distinctive letter or letters of the parliamentary polling district in which a person is registered together with his number in the said register, or pending the publication of the register, the distinctive letter or letters of the parliamentary polling district in which he is entitled to be registered together with his number (if any) in the electors lists therefor.

Consent to nomination

7.—(1) A person shall not be validly nominated unless his consent to nomination, given in writing on or within one month before the last day for the delivery of nomination papers, and attested by one witness, is delivered at the place and within the time appointed for the delivery of nomination papers:

Provided that, if the returning officer is satisfied that owing to the absence of a person from the United Kingdom it has not been reasonably practicable for his consent in writing to be given as aforesaid, a telegram consenting to his nomination and purporting to have been sent by him shall be deemed, for the purpose of this rule, to be consent in writing given by him on the day on which it purports to have been sent, and attestation of his consent shall not be required.

(2) A candidate's consent given under this rule shall contain a statement declaring, with reference to the date of his nomination, that to the best of his belief he will be or is qualified as required by law to be elected to and hold the office in question, and the statement shall give particulars of his qualification.

Place for delivery of nomination papers

8. Every nomination paper shall be delivered at the place fixed by the returning officer.

Decisions as to validity of nomination papers

9.—(1) Where a nomination paper and the candidate's consent thereto are delivered in accordance with these rules, the candidate shall be deemed to stand nominated unless and until the returning officer decides that the nomination paper is invalid, or proof is given to the satisfaction of the returning officer of the candidate's death, or the candidate withdraws.

(2) The returning officer shall be entitled to hold a nomination paper invalid only on one of the following grounds, that is to say,—

(a) that the particulars of the candidate or the persons subscribing the paper are not as required by law; and

(b) that the paper is not subscribed as so required.

(3) The returning officer shall examine the nomination papers, and decide whether the candidates have been validly nominated in accordance with these rules and shall do so as soon as practicable after each paper is delivered.

(4) Where he decides that a nomination paper is invalid, he shall endorse and sign on the paper the fact and the reasons for his decision.

(5) The returning officer shall send notice of his decision to each candidate at his place of residence as stated on his nomination paper.

(6) The decision of the returning officer that a nomination paper is valid shall be final and shall not be questioned in any proceeding whatsoever.

(7) Subject to the last foregoing paragraph, nothing in this rule shall prevent the validity of a nomination being questioned on an election petition.

Publication of nominations

10.—(1) The returning officer shall prepare and publish a statement in the form in the Appendix, or a form to the like effect, showing the persons who have been and stand nominated and any other persons who have been nominated, with the reason why they no longer stand nominated.

(2) The statement shall show the names, addresses and descriptions (if any) of the persons nominated as given in their nomination papers.

(3) The statement shall show the persons standing nominated arranged alphabetically in the order of their surnames, and, if there are two or more of them with the same surname, of their other names.

(4) In the case of a person nominated by more than one nomination paper, the returning officer shall take the particulars required by the foregoing provisions of this rule from such one of the papers as the candidate or the returning officer in default of the candidate may select.

(5) The statement as to persons nominated shall be published by causing it to be affixed to the place appointed for the delivery of nomination papers.

Withdrawal of candidates

11.—(1) A candidate may withdraw his candidature by notice of withdrawal signed by him and attested by one witness and delivered at the place appointed for the delivery of nomination papers.

(2) In the case of a candidate who is outside the United Kingdom, a notice of withdrawal signed by his proposer and accompanied by a written declaration also so signed of the candidate's absence from the United Kingdom shall be of the same effect as a notice of withdrawal signed by the candidate:

Provided that where the candidate stands nominated by more than one nomination paper a notice of withdrawal under this paragraph shall be effective if, but only if,—

(a) it and the accompanying declaration are signed by all the proposers except any who is, and is stated in the said declaration to be, outside the United Kingdom; or

(b) it is accompanied, in addition to the said declaration, by a written statement signed by the candidate that the proposer giving the notice is authorised to do so on the candidate's behalf during his absence from the United Kingdom.

Nomination in more than one electoral area

12. A candidate who is validly nominated for more than one electoral area must duly withdraw from his candidature in all those electoral areas except one, and if he does not so withdraw he shall be deemed to have withdrawn from his candidature in all those electoral areas.

Method of election

13.—(1) If the number of persons remaining validly nominated for the electoral area after any withdrawals under these rules exceeds the number of vacancies, the councillors shall be elected from among them at a poll under Part III of these rules.

(2) If the said number does not exceed the number of vacancies, the person or persons (if any) deemed to be elected under the following provisions of this rule shall be declared elected in accordance with Part IV of these rules.

(3) The person or persons (if any) remaining validly nominated for the electoral area after any withdrawals under these rules shall be deemed to be elected.

(4) If, at an ordinary election of councillors, no person remains validly nominated as aforesaid, or the number of persons so remaining validly nominated is less than the number of vacancies, the retiring councillors for the electoral area who, if duly nominated, would have been qualified for election or, if their number is more than that of the vacancies not filled under paragraph (3) of this rule, such of those councillors as were highest on the poll at the last ordinary election, or as filled the places of councillors who were highest on the poll at that election, or if the poll was equal or there was no poll, as may be determined by the drawing of lots conducted under the direction of the returning officer, shall be deemed to be elected to fill up the vacancies not filled under paragraph (3) of this rule.

PART III

CONTESTED ELECTIONS

GENERAL PROVISIONS

Poll to be taken by ballot

14. The votes at the poll shall be given by ballot, the result shall be ascertained by counting the votes given to each candidate, and the candidate or candidates to whom the majority of votes have been given shall be declared to have been elected.

The ballot papers

15.—(1) The ballot of every voter shall consist of a ballot paper, and the persons remaining validly nominated for the electoral area after any withdrawals under these rules, and no others, shall be entitled to have their names inserted in the ballot paper.

(2) Every ballot paper shall be in the form in the Appendix, and shall be printed in accordance with the directions therein, and—

(a) shall contain the names and other particulars of the candidates as shown in the statement of persons nominated;

(b) shall be capable of being folded up;

(c) shall have a number printed on the back;

(d) shall have attached a counterfoil with the same number printed on the face.

(3) The order of the names in the ballot paper shall be the same as in the statement of persons nominated.

The official mark

16.—(1) Every ballot paper shall be marked with an official mark, which shall be either embossed or perforated.

(2) The official mark shall be kept secret, and an interval of not less than seven years shall intervene between the use of the same official mark in the same electoral area at elections of a councillor of the Greater London Council.

Prohibition of disclosure of vote

17. No person who has voted at the election shall, in any legal proceeding to question the election, be required to state for whom he voted.

Use of schools and public rooms

18.—(1) The returning officer may use, free of charge, for the purpose of taking the poll or of counting the votes—

(a) a room in a school maintained or assisted by a local education authority or a school in respect of which grants are made out of moneys provided by Parliament to the person or body of persons responsible for the management of the school;

(b) a room the expense of maintaining which is payable out of any rate.

(2) The returning officer shall make good any damage done to, and defray any expense incurred by the persons having control over, any such room as aforesaid by reason of its being used for the purpose of taking the poll or of counting the votes.

(3) The use of a room in an unoccupied house for the purpose of taking the poll or of counting the votes shall not render a person liable to be rated or to pay any rate for that house.

ACTION TO BE TAKEN BEFORE THE POLL
Notice of poll

19.—(1) Notice of the poll shall be published by the returning officer at the places at which the notice of election is required to be published under rule 4 of these rules.

(2) Notice of the poll shall specify—

(*a*) the day and hours fixed for the poll;

(*b*) the number of councillors to be elected;

(*c*) the particulars of each candidate remaining validly nominated (the names and other particulars of the candidates, and the order of the names of the candidates, being the same as in the statement of persons nominated);

(*d*) the names of the proposer and seconder signing a candidate's nomination paper; and

(*e*) the situation of each polling station and the description of the persons entitled to vote thereat.

(3) In the case of a candidate nominated by more than one nomination paper, the nomination paper mentioned in sub-paragraph (*d*) of paragraph (2) of this rule shall be that from which the names and other particulars of the candidate shown in the statement of persons nominated are taken.

(4) The returning officer shall, as soon as practicable after publication of a notice of poll, give to each of the election agents a description in writing of the polling districts, if any.

Postal ballot papers

20. The returning officer shall as soon as practicable send to those entitled to vote by post, at the addresses furnished by them for the purpose, a ballot paper and a declaration of identity in the form set out in the Representation of the People Regulations 1969(**a**), or a form substantially to the like effect, together with an envelope for their return.

Provision of polling stations

21.—(1) The returning officer shall provide a sufficient number of polling stations and, subject to the following provisions of this rule, shall allot the electors to the polling stations in such manner as he thinks most convenient.

(2) One or more polling stations may be provided in the same room.

(3) The polling station allotted to electors from any parliamentary polling district wholly or partly within the electoral area shall, in the absence of special circumstances, be in the parliamentary polling place for that district, unless the polling place is outside the electoral area.

(4) The returning officer shall provide each polling station with such number of compartments as may be necessary in which the voters can mark their votes screened from observation.

Appointment of presiding officers and clerks

22.—(1) The returning officer shall appoint and pay a presiding officer to attend at each polling station and such clerks as may be necessary for the purposes of the election, but he shall not appoint any person who has been employed by or on behalf of a candidate in or about the election.

(2) The returning officer may, if he thinks fit, preside at a polling station and the provisions of these rules relating to a presiding officer shall apply to a returning officer so presiding with the necessary modifications as to things to be done by the returning officer to the presiding officer or by the presiding officer to the returning officer.

(**a**) S.I. 1969/904 (1969 II, p. 2602).

(3) A presiding officer may do, by the clerks appointed to assist him, any act (including the asking of questions) which he is required or authorised by these rules to do at a polling station except order the arrest, exclusion or removal of any person from the polling station.

Special lists

23. The registration officer shall as soon as practicable prepare the following special lists, namely—

(a) a list (in these rules referred to as "the absent voters list") giving the name and number on the register of every person entitled to vote at the election as an absent voter;

(b) a list (in these rules referred to as "the list of proxies") giving—

   (i) the names and numbers on the register of the electors for whom proxies have been appointed; and

   (ii) the names and addresses of the persons appointed;

(c) a list of any persons entitled to vote by post as proxy at the election.

Equipment of polling stations

24.—(1) The returning officer shall provide each presiding officer with such number of ballot boxes and ballot papers as in the opinion of the returning officer may be necessary.

(2) Every ballot box shall be so constructed that the ballot papers can be put therein, but cannot be withdrawn therefrom, without the box being unlocked.

(3) The returning officer shall provide each polling station with—

(a) materials to enable voters to mark the ballot papers;

(b) instruments for stamping thereon the official mark;

(c) copies of the register of electors for the electoral area or such part thereof as contains the names of the electors allotted to the station;

(d) the parts of any special lists prepared for the election corresponding to the register of electors for the electoral area or part thereof provided under the last foregoing sub-paragraph.

(4) A notice in the form in the Appendix, giving directions for the guidance of the voters in voting, shall be printed in conspicuous characters and exhibited inside and outside every polling station.

(5) In every compartment of every polling station there shall be exhibited a notice as follows:—"The voter may vote for not more than   candidate(s)".

Appointment of polling and counting agents

25.—(1) Each candidate may, before the commencement of the poll, appoint polling agents to attend at polling stations for the purpose of detecting personation and counting agents to attend at the counting of the votes:

Provided that—

(a) the returning officer may limit the number of counting agents, so however that the number shall be the same in the case of each candidate and the number allowed to a candidate shall not (except in special circumstances) be less than the number obtained by dividing the number of clerks employed on the counting by the number of candidates;

(b) the appointment of a polling agent may be on behalf of more than one candidate;

(c) not more than three or, if the number of candidates exceeds twenty, four polling agents shall be appointed to attend at any polling station.

(2) If the number of polling agents appointed to attend at a polling station exceeds the permitted number, only those polling agents, up to the permitted number, whose appointments are signed by or on behalf of the greater number of candidates, or, in the event of an equality in the number of signatures, only such of those polling agents

as may be determined by the returning officer, shall be deemed to have been duly appointed.

(3) Notice in writing of the appointment, stating the names and addresses of the persons appointed, shall be given by the candidate to the returning officer and shall be so given not later than the time appointed for that purpose in the Timetable.

(4) If an agent dies, or becomes incapable of acting, the candidate may appoint another agent in his place, and shall forthwith give to the returning officer notice in writing of the name and address of the agent appointed.

(5) The foregoing provisions of this rule shall be without prejudice to the requirements of section 60(1) of the Representation of the People Act 1949 as to the appointment of paid polling agents, and any appointment authorised by this rule may be made and the notice of appointment given to the returning officer by the candidate's election agent, instead of by the candidate.

(6) In the following provisions of these rules references to polling and counting agents shall be taken as references to agents whose appointments have been duly made and notified and, where the number of agents is restricted, who are within the permitted number.

(7) Any notice required to be given to a counting agent by the returning officer may be delivered at, or sent by post to, the address stated in the notice of appointment.

(8) A candidate may himself do any act or thing which any polling or counting agent of his, if appointed, would have been authorised to do, or may assist his agent in doing any such act or thing.

(9) A candidate's election agent may do or assist in doing anything which a polling or counting agent of his is authorised to do; and anything required or authorised by these rules to be done in the presence of the polling or counting agents may be done in the presence of a candidate's election agent instead of his polling agent or counting agents.

(10) Where by these rules any act or thing is required or authorised to be done in the presence of the polling or counting agents, the non-attendance of any agents or agent at the time and place appointed for the purpose, shall not, if the act or thing is otherwise duly done, invalidate the act or thing done.

Declaration of secrecy

26.—(1) Before the opening of the poll a declaration of secrecy in the form in paragraph (4) of this rule, or in a form as near thereto as circumstances admit, shall be made by—

(a) the returning officer and the presiding officers;

(b) every clerk authorised to attend at a polling station or the counting of the votes;

(c) every candidate attending at a polling station or at the counting of the votes and every election agent so attending;

(d) every candidate's wife or husband attending at the counting of the votes;

(e) every polling agent and counting agent;

(f) every person permitted by the returning officer to attend at the counting of the votes, though not entitled to do so.

(2) Notwithstanding anything in the foregoing paragraph, the following persons attending at the counting of the votes, that is to say:—

(a) any candidate;

(b) any election agent, or any candidate's wife or husband attending by virtue of the rule authorising election agents and candidate's wives or husbands to attend as such;

(c) any person permitted by the returning officer to attend, though not entitled to do so;

(*d*) any clerk making the declaration in order to attend at the counting of the votes;

need not make the declaration before the opening of the poll but shall make it before he or she is permitted to attend the counting, and a polling or counting agent appointed after the opening of the poll shall make the declaration before acting as such agent.

(3) The returning officer shall make the declaration in the presence of a Justice of the Peace, and any other person shall make the declaration in the presence either of a Justice of the Peace or of the returning officer, and subsections (1), (2), (3) and (6) of section 53 of the Representation of the People Act 1949 shall be read to the declarant by the person taking the declaration, or shall be read by the declarant in the presence of that person:

Provided that the declaration may be made by the returning officer or any other person before a person who is chairman of the Greater London Council, a county council or a district council or mayor of a borough or rural borough, and may be made by a person other than the returning officer before a person who is clerk of any such council or town clerk of a borough or rural borough.

(4) The declaration shall be as follows—

"I solemnly promise and declare that I will not do anything forbidden by subsections (1), (2), (3) and (6) of section 53 of the Representation of the People Act 1949, which have been read to [by] me.".

THE POLL

Admission to polling station

27.—(1) The presiding officer shall regulate the number of voters to be admitted to the polling station at the same time, and shall exclude all other persons except—

(*a*) the candidates and their election agents;

(*b*) the polling agents appointed to attend at the polling station;

(*c*) the clerks appointed to attend at the polling station;

(*d*) the constables on duty; and

(*e*) the companions of blind voters.

(2) Not more than one polling agent shall be admitted at the same time to a polling station on behalf of the same candidate.

(3) A constable or person employed by a returning officer shall not be admitted to vote in person elsewhere than at his own polling station under the provisions of the Representation of the People Act 1949 in that behalf, except on production and surrender of a certificate as to his employment, which shall be in the form in the Appendix, or a form to the like effect and signed by an officer of police of or above the rank of inspector or by the returning officer, as the case may be.

(4) Any certificate surrendered under this rule shall forthwith be cancelled.

Keeping of order in station

28.—(1) It shall be the duty of the presiding officer to keep order at his polling station.

(2) If a person misconducts himself in a polling station, or fails to obey the lawful orders of the presiding officer, he may immediately, by order of the presiding officer, be removed from the polling station by a constable in or near that station or by any other person authorised in writing by the returning officer to remove him, and the person so removed shall not, without the permission of the presiding officer, again enter the polling station during the day.

(3) Any person so removed may, if charged with the commission in the polling station of an offence, be dealt with as a person taken into custody by a constable for an offence without a warrant.

(4) The powers conferred by this rule shall not be exercised so as to prevent a voter who is otherwise entitled to vote at a polling station from having an opportunity of voting at that station.

Sealing of ballot boxes

29. Immediately before the commencement of the poll, the presiding officer shall show the ballot box empty to such persons, if any, as are present in the polling station, so that they may see that it is empty, and shall then lock it up and place his seal on it in such manner as to prevent its being opened without breaking the seal, and shall place it in his view for the receipt of ballot papers, and keep it so locked and sealed.

Questions to be put to voters

30.—(1) The presiding officer may, and if required by a candidate or his election or polling agent shall, put to any person applying for a ballot paper at the time of his application, but not afterwards, the following questions, or either of them, that is to say—

(a) in the case of a person applying as an elector—

(i) Are you the person registered in the register of local government electors now in force for this electoral area as follows [read the whole entry from the register]?

(ii) Have you already voted at the present election of a councillor [councillors] of the Greater London Council for this electoral area [adding in the case of an ordinary election or for any other electoral area] otherwise than as proxy for some other person?

(b) in the case of a person applying as proxy—

(i) Are you the person whose name appears as A.B. in the list of proxies for the present election of a councillor [councillors] of the Greater London Council as entitled to vote as proxy on behalf of C.D.?

(ii) Have you already voted here or elsewhere at the present election of a councillor [councillors] of the Greater London Council as proxy on behalf of C.D.?

(2) A ballot paper shall not be delivered to any person required to answer the above questions or any of them unless he has answered the questions or question satisfactorily.

(3) Save as by this rule authorised, no inquiry shall be permitted as to the right of any person to vote.

Challenge of voter

31.—(1) If at the time a person applies for a ballot paper for the purpose of voting in person, or after he has applied for a ballot paper for that purpose and before he has left the polling station, a candidate or his election or polling agent declares to the presiding officer that he has reasonable cause to believe that the applicant has committed an offence of personation and undertakes to substantiate the charge in a court of law, the presiding officer may order a constable to arrest the applicant, and the order of the presiding officer shall be sufficient authority for the constable so to do.

(2) A person against whom a declaration is made under this rule shall not by reason thereof be prevented from voting.

(3) A person arrested under the provisions of this rule shall be dealt with as a person taken into custody by a constable for an offence without a warrant.

Voting procedure

32.—(1) A ballot paper shall be delivered to a voter who applies therefor, and immediately before delivery—

(a) the ballot paper shall be stamped with the official mark, either embossed or perforated;

(b) the number, name and description of the elector as stated in the copy of the register of electors shall be called out;

(c) the number of the elector shall be marked on the counterfoil;

(d) a mark shall be placed in the register of electors against the number of the elector to denote that a ballot paper has been received but without showing the particular ballot paper which has been received; and

(e) in the case of a person applying for a ballot paper as proxy, a mark shall also be placed against his name in the list of proxies.

(2) The voter, on receiving the ballot paper, shall forthwith proceed into one of the compartments in the polling station and there secretly mark his paper and fold it up so as to conceal his vote, and shall then show to the presiding officer the back of the paper so as to disclose the official mark, and put the ballot paper so folded up into the ballot box in the presence of the presiding officer.

(3) The voter shall vote without undue delay, and shall leave the polling station as soon as he has put his ballot paper into the ballot box.

Votes marked by presiding officer

33.—(1) The presiding officer, on the application of—

(a) a voter who is incapacitated by blindness or other physical cause from voting in manner directed by these rules; or

(b) if the poll is taken on a Saturday, a voter who declares that he is a Jew, and objects on religious grounds to vote in manner directed by these rules; or

(c) a voter who declares orally that he is unable to read;

shall, in the presence of the polling agents, cause the vote of the voter to be marked on a ballot paper in manner directed by the voter, and the ballot paper to be placed in the ballot box.

(2) The name and number on the register of electors of every voter whose vote is marked in pursuance of this rule, and the reason why it is so marked, shall be entered on a list (in these rules called "the list of votes marked by the presiding officer").

In the case of a person voting as proxy for an elector, the number to be entered together with the name of the voter shall be the number of the elector.

Voting by blind persons

34.—(1) If a voter makes an application to the presiding officer to be allowed on the ground of blindness to vote with the assistance of another person by whom he is accompanied (in these rules referred to as "the companion"), the presiding officer shall require the voter to declare orally whether he is so incapacitated by his blindness as to be unable to vote without assistance.

(2) If the presiding officer is satisfied that the voter is so incapacitated and is also satisfied by a written declaration made by the companion (in these rules referred to as "the declaration made by the companion of a blind voter") that the companion is a qualified person within the meaning of this rule and has not previously assisted more than one blind person to vote at the election, the presiding officer shall grant the application, and thereupon anything which is by these rules required to be done to or by the said voter in connection with the giving of his vote may be done to, or with the assistance of, the companion.

(3) For the purposes of this rule, a person shall be qualified to assist a blind voter to vote, if that person is either—

(a) a person who is entitled to vote as an elector at the election; or

(b) the father, mother, brother, sister, husband, wife, son or daughter of the blind voter and has attained the age of eighteen years.

(4) The name and number in the register of electors of every voter whose vote is given in accordance with this rule and the name and address of the companion shall be entered on a list (in these rules referred to as "the list of blind voters assisted by companions").

In the case of a person voting as proxy for an elector, the number to be entered together with the name of the voter shall be the number of the elector.

(5) The declaration made by the companion—

(a) shall be in the form in the Appendix;

(b) shall be made before the presiding officer at the time when the voter applies to vote with the assistance of a companion and shall forthwith be given to the presiding officer who shall attest and retain it.

(6) No fee or other payment shall be charged in respect of the declaration.

Tendered ballot papers

35.—(1) If a person, representing himself to be—

(a) a particular elector named on the register and not named in the absent voters list; or

(b) a particular person named in the list of proxies as proxy for an elector and not named in the list of persons entitled to vote by post as proxy,

applies for a ballot paper after another person has voted in person either as the elector or his proxy, the applicant shall, on satisfactorily answering the questions permitted by law to be asked at the poll, be entitled, subject to the following provisions of this rule, to mark a ballot paper (in these rules referred to as "a tendered ballot paper") in the same manner as any other voter.

(2) A tendered ballot paper shall—

(a) be of a colour differing from the other ballot papers;

(b) instead of being put into the ballot box, be given to the presiding officer and endorsed by him with the name of the voter and his number in the register of electors, and set aside in a separate packet.

(3) The name of the voter and his number on the register of electors shall be entered on a list (in these rules referred to as the "tendered votes list").

(4) In the case of a person voting as proxy for an elector, the number to be endorsed or entered together with the name of the voter shall be the number of that elector.

Spoilt ballot papers

36. A voter who has inadvertently dealt with his ballot paper in such manner that it cannot be conveniently used as a ballot paper may, on delivering it to the presiding officer and proving to his satisfaction the fact of the inadvertence, obtain another ballot paper in the place of the ballot paper so delivered (in these rules referred to as "a spoilt ballot paper"), and the spoilt ballot paper shall be immediately cancelled.

Adjournment of poll in case of riot

37. For the purpose of the adjournment of the poll in the event of riot or open violence, a presiding officer shall have the power by law belonging to a presiding officer at a parliamentary election.

Procedure on close of poll

38.—(1) As soon as practicable after the close of the poll, the presiding officer shall, in the presence of the polling agents, make up into separate packets, sealed with his own seal and the seals of such polling agents as desire to affix their seals—

(a) each ballot box in use at the station, sealed so as to prevent the introduction of additional ballot papers and unopened, but with the key attached;

(b) the unused and spoilt ballot papers placed together;

(c) the tendered ballot papers;

(d) the marked copies of the register of electors and of the list of proxies;

(e) the counterfoils of the used ballot papers and the certificates as to employment on duty on the day of the poll;

(*f*) the tendered votes list, the list of blind voters assisted by companions, the list of votes marked by the presiding officer, a statement of the number of voters whose votes are so marked by the presiding officer under the heads "physical incapacity", "Jews", and "unable to read", and the declarations made by the companions of blind voters;

and shall deliver the packets or cause them to be delivered to the returning officer to be taken charge of by him:

Provided that if the packets are not delivered by the presiding officer personally to the returning officer, the arrangements for their delivery shall require the approval of the returning officer.

(2) The marked copies of the register of electors and of the list of proxies shall be in one packet but shall not be in the same packet as the counterfoils of the used ballot papers and the certificates as to employment on duty on the day of the poll.

(3) The packets shall be accompanied by a statement (in these rules referred to as "the ballot paper account") made by the presiding officer showing the number of ballot papers entrusted to him, and accounting for them under the heads of ballot papers issued and not otherwise accounted for, unused, spoilt and tendered ballot papers.

COUNTING OF VOTES

Attendance at counting of votes

39.—(1) The returning officer shall make arrangements for counting the votes in the presence of the counting agents as soon as practicable after the close of the poll, and shall give to the counting agents notice in writing of the time and place at which he will begin to count the votes.

(2) No person other than—

(*a*) the returning officer and his clerks;

(*b*) the candidates and their wives or husbands;

(*c*) the election agents;

(*d*) the counting agents;

may be present at the counting of the votes, unless permitted by the returning officer to attend.

(3) A person not entitled to attend at the counting of the votes shall not be permitted to do so by the returning officer unless the returning officer is satisfied that the efficient counting of the votes will not be impeded, and the returning officer has either consulted the election agents or thought it impracticable to consult them.

(4) The returning officer shall give the counting agents all such reasonable facilities for overseeing the proceedings, and all such information with respect thereto, as he can give them consistently with the orderly conduct of the proceedings and the discharge of his duties in connection therewith.

(5) In particular, where the votes are counted by sorting the ballot papers according to the candidate for whom the vote is given and then counting the number of ballot papers for each candidate, the counting agents shall be entitled to satisfy themselves that the ballot papers are correctly sorted.

The count

40.—(1) Before the returning officer proceeds to count the votes, he shall—

(*a*) in the presence of the counting agents open each ballot box and, taking out the ballot papers therein, count and record the number thereof and in the presence of the election agents who are present verify each ballot paper account;

(*b*) count such of the postal ballot papers as have been duly returned and record the number counted; and

(*c*) then mix together the whole of the ballot papers mentioned in the foregoing sub-paragraphs.

(2) A postal ballot paper shall not be deemed to be duly returned, unless it is returned in the proper envelope so as to reach the returning officer before the close of the poll and is accompanied by the declaration of identity duly signed and authenticated.

(3) The returning officer shall not count any tendered ballot paper.

(4) The returning officer, while counting and recording the number of ballot papers and counting the votes, shall keep the ballot papers with their faces upwards and take all proper precautions for preventing any person from seeing the numbers printed on the back of the papers.

(5) The returning officer shall verify each ballot paper account by comparing it with the number of ballot papers recorded by him, and the unused and spoilt ballot papers in his possession and the tendered votes list (opening and resealing the packets containing the unused and spoilt ballot papers and the tendered votes list) and shall draw up a statement as to the result of the verification, which any election agent may copy.

(6) The returning officer shall, so far as practicable, proceed continuously with counting the votes, allowing only time for refreshment:

Provided that he may, in so far as he and the agents agree, exclude the hours between nine o'clock in the evening and nine o'clock on the following morning.

For the purposes of this proviso the agreement of a candidate or his election agent shall be as effective as the agreement of his counting agents.

(7) During the excluded time the returning officer shall place the ballot papers and other documents relating to the election under his own seal and the seals of such of the counting agents as desire to affix their seals and shall otherwise take proper precautions for the security of the papers and documents.

Re-count

41.—(1) A candidate or his election agent may, if present when the counting or any re-count of the votes is completed, require the returning officer to have the votes re-counted or again re-counted but the returning officer may refuse to do so if in his opinion the request is unreasonable.

(2) No step shall be taken on the completion of the counting or any re-count of votes until the candidates and election agents present at the completion thereof have been given a reasonable opportunity to exercise the right conferred by this rule.

Rejected ballot papers

42.—(1) Any ballot paper—

    (a) which does not bear the official mark; or

    (b) on which votes are given for more candidates than the voter is entitled to vote for; or

    (c) on which anything is written or marked by which the voter can be identified except the printed number on the back; or

    (d) which is unmarked or void for uncertainty;

shall, subject to the provisions of this rule, be void and not counted.

(2) Where the voter is entitled to vote for more than one candidate, a ballot paper shall not be deemed to be void for uncertainty as respects any vote as to which no uncertainty arises and that vote shall be counted.

(3) A ballot paper on which a vote is marked—

    (a) elsewhere than in the proper place; or

    (b) otherwise than by means of a cross; or

    (c) by more than one mark;

shall not by reason thereof be deemed to be void (either wholly or as respects that vote), if an intention that the vote shall be for one or other of the candidates clearly appears, and the way the paper is marked does not of itself identify the voter and it is not shown that he can be identified thereby.

(4) The returning officer shall endorse—

　(a) the word "rejected" on any ballot paper which under this rule is not to be counted; and

　(b) in the case of a ballot paper on which any vote is counted under paragraph (2) of this rule, the words "rejected in part" and a memorandum specifying the votes counted;

and shall add to the endorsement the words "rejection objected to" if an objection is made by a counting agent to his decision.

(5) The returning officer shall draw up a statement showing the number of ballot papers rejected, including those rejected in part, under the several heads of—

　(a) want of official mark;

　(b) voting for more candidates than voter is entitled to;

　(c) writing or mark by which voter could be identified;

　(d) unmarked or wholly void for uncertainty;

　(e) rejected in part.

Decisions on ballot papers

43. The decision of the returning officer on any question arising in respect of a ballot paper shall be final, but shall be subject to review on an election petition.

Equality of votes

44. Where, after the counting of the votes (including any re-count) is completed, an equality of votes is found to exist between any candidates and the addition of a vote would entitle any of those candidates to be declared elected, the returning officer shall forthwith decide between those candidates by lot, and proceed as if the candidate on whom the lot falls had received an additional vote.

PART IV

FINAL PROCEEDINGS IN CONTESTED AND UNCONTESTED ELECTIONS

Declaration of result

45.—(1) In a contested election, when the result of the poll has been ascertained the returning officer shall forthwith declare to be elected the candidate or candidates to whom the majority of votes have been given, and shall as soon as possible publish the name or names of the candidate or candidates elected and the total number of votes given for each candidate, whether elected or not, together with the number of rejected ballot papers under each head shown in the statement of rejected ballot papers.

(2) In an uncontested election, the returning officer shall, not later than eleven o'clock in the morning on the day of election, publish the name or names of the person or persons elected.

The return

46. The returning officer shall forthwith upon declaration of the result of the election return the name of each person elected to the clerk to the Greater London Council.

PART V

DISPOSAL OF DOCUMENTS

Sealing of ballot papers

47.—(1) On the completion of the counting at a contested election the returning officer shall seal up in separate packets the counted and rejected ballot papers, including ballot papers rejected in part.

(2) The returning officer shall not open the sealed packets of tendered ballot papers or of counterfoils and certificates as to employment on duty on the day of the poll, or of marked copies of the register of electors and lists of proxies.

Delivery of documents to clerk to the Council

48. The returning officer shall then forward to the clerk to the Greater London Council the following documents, that is to say—

(a) the packets of ballot papers in his possession;

(b) the ballot paper accounts and the statements of rejected ballot papers and of the result of the verification of the ballot paper accounts;

(c) the tendered votes lists, the lists of blind voters assisted by companions, the lists of votes marked by the presiding officer and the statements relating thereto, and the declarations made by the companions of blind voters;

(d) the packets of counterfoils and certificates as to employment on duty on the day of the poll;

(e) the packets containing marked copies of registers and of lists of proxies,

endorsing on each packet a description of its contents, the date of the election to which they relate and the name of the electoral area for which the election was held.

Orders for production of documents

49.—(1) An order—

(a) for the inspection or production of any rejected ballot papers, including ballot papers rejected in part; or

(b) for the opening of a sealed packet of counterfoils and certificates as to employment on duty on the day of the poll or for the inspection of counted ballot papers,

may be made by either a county court having jurisdiction in Greater London or any part thereof or an election court, if the court is satisfied by evidence on oath that the order is required for the purpose of instituting or maintaining a prosecution for an offence in relation to ballot papers, or for the purpose of an election petition.

(2) The order may be made subject to such conditions as to persons, time, place and mode of inspection, production or opening as the court making the order may think expedient and may direct the clerk to the Greater London Council to retain the ballot papers and the sealed packets of counterfoils and certificates intact for such period as may be specified in the order:

Provided that in making and carrying into effect the order, care shall be taken that the way in which the vote of any particular elector has been given shall not be disclosed until it has been proved that his vote was given and the vote has been declared by a competent court to be invalid.

(3) An appeal shall lie to the High Court from any order of a county court made under this rule.

(4) Any power given under this rule to a county court may be exercised by any judge of the court otherwise than in open court.

(5) Where an order is made for the production by the clerk to the Greater London Council of any document in his possession relating to any specified election, the production by him or his agent of the document ordered, in such manner as may be directed by that order shall be conclusive evidence that the document relates to the specified election; and any endorsement on any packet of ballot papers so produced shall be prima facie evidence that the ballot papers are what they are stated to be by the endorsement.

(6) The production from proper custody of a ballot paper purporting to have been used at any election, and of a counterfoil marked with the same printed number and having a number marked thereon in writing, shall be prima facie evidence that the elector whose vote was given by that ballot paper was the person who at the time of the election had affixed to his name in the register of electors the same number as the number written on the counterfoil.

(7) Save as by this rule provided, no person shall be allowed to inspect any rejected or counted ballot papers in the possession of the clerk to the Greater London Council or to open any sealed packets of counterfoils and certificates.

Retention and public inspection of documents

50.—(1) The clerk to the Greater London Council shall retain for six months among the records of the Council all documents relating to an election which are, in pursuance of these rules, forwarded to him by a returning officer and then, unless otherwise directed by an order under the last foregoing rule, shall cause them to be destroyed.

(2) The said documents, except ballot papers, counterfoils and certificates as to employment on duty on the day of the poll, shall during a period of six months from the day of election be open to public inspection at such time and in such manner as may be determined by the Greater London Council with the consent of the Secretary of State.

(3) The clerk to the Greater London Council shall, on request, supply copies of or extracts from the documents open to public inspection on payment of such fees, and subject to such conditions, as may be determined by the Council with the consent of the Secretary of State.

Supplemental provisions as to documents

51. Subject to the provisions of these rules, the clerk to the Greater London Council shall, in respect of the custody and destruction of ballot papers and other documents coming into his possession in pursuance of these rules, be subject to the directions of the Council.

PART VI

SUPPLEMENTAL

Countermand or abandonment of poll on death of candidate

52.—(1) If at a contested election proof is given to the satisfaction of the returning officer before the result of the election is declared that one of the persons named or to be named as candidate in the ballot papers has died, then the returning officer shall countermand the poll or, if polling has begun, direct that the poll be abandoned, and the provisions of section 36(2) of the Representation of the People Act 1949 shall apply to any further election ordered under the Local Government Act 1933.

(2) Where the poll is abandoned by reason of the death of a candidate, the proceedings at or consequent on that poll shall be interrupted, and the presiding officer at any polling station shall take the like steps (so far as not already taken) for the delivery to the returning officer of ballot boxes and of ballot papers and other documents as he is required to take on the close of the poll in due course, and the returning officer shall dispose of ballot papers and other documents in his possession as he is required to do on the completion in due course of the counting of the votes; but—

(a) it shall not be necessary for any ballot paper account to be prepared or verified; and

(b) the returning officer, without taking any step or further step for the counting of the ballot papers or of the votes, shall seal up all the ballot papers, whether the votes on them have been counted or not, and it shall not be necessary to seal up counted and rejected ballot papers in separate packets.

(3) The foregoing provisions of these rules as to the inspection, production, retention and destruction of ballot papers and other documents relating to a poll at an election shall apply to any such documents relating to a poll abandoned by reason of the death of a candidate, with the following modifications:—

(a) ballot papers on which the votes were neither counted nor rejected shall be treated as counted ballot papers; and

(b) no order shall be made for the production or inspection of any ballot papers or for the opening of a sealed packet of counterfoils or certificates as to employment on duty on the day of the poll unless the order is made by a court with reference to a prosecution.

General duty of returning officer

53. It shall be the general duty of the returning officer to do any act or thing that may be necessary for effectually conducting the election under these rules.

Interpretation

54.—(1) The expression "electoral area" means a London borough other than the City of Westminster, and the City of Westminster together with the City of London, the Inner Temple and the Middle Temple.

(2) A reference in this Schedule to a rule shall be construed as a reference to a rule contained in this Schedule.

(3) Any reference in this Schedule to any enactment shall be taken as a reference to that enactment as amended or replaced by any other enactment.

APPENDIX

Note:—The forms contained in this Appendix may be adapted so far as circumstances require.

NOTICE OF ELECTION

GREATER LONDON

ELECTION OF A COUNCILLOR [COUNCILLORS] OF THE GREATER LONDON COUNCIL for the Electoral Area.

1. An election is to be held of a councillor [councillors] of the Greater London Council for the said electoral area.

2. Nomination papers must be delivered at   on any day after the date of this notice, but not later than noon on the   day of

3. Forms of nomination paper may be obtained from the returning officer at   . The returning officer will, at the request of any local government elector for the said electoral area, prepare for signature a nomination paper.

4. If the election is contested, the poll will take place on the day of   .

(Signed)..

Returning Officer.

day of   , 19   .

NOTE 1.—The attention of candidates and electors is drawn to the rules for filling up nomination papers and other provisions relating to nomination contained in the election rules in Schedule 1 to the Greater London Council Election Rules 1970.

NOTE 2.—Every person guilty of a corrupt or illegal practice will, on conviction, be liable to the penalties imposed by the Representation of the People Act 1949.

NOTE 3.—Electors and their proxies should take note that applications to be treated as an absent voter and other applications and notices about postal or proxy voting must reach the electoral registration officer at (insert address) by the   day of   next if they are to be effective for this election.

Rule 5.

NOMINATION PAPER

ELECTION OF A COUNCILLOR [COUNCILLORS] OF THE GREATER LONDON COUNCIL for the Electoral Area.

Date of publication of notice of election..

We, the undersigned, being local government electors for the said electoral area, do hereby nominate the undermentioned person as a candidate at the said election.

Candidate's surname	Other names in full	Description (if any)	Home address in full

Signatures	Electoral Number (*see* note 3)	
	Distinctive Letter(s)	Number
Proposer...	....	....
Seconder...	....	....
We, the undersigned, being local government electors for the said electoral area, do hereby assent to the foregoing nomination.		
1..	....	....
2..	....	....
3..	....	....
4..	....	....
5..	....	....
6..	....	....
7..	....	....
8..	....	....

NOTE 1.—The attention of candidates and electors is drawn to the rules for filling up nomination papers and other provisions relating to nomination contained in the election rules in Schedule 1 to the Greater London Council Election Rules 1970.

NOTE 2.—Where a candidate is commonly known by some title he may be described by his title as if it were his surname.

NOTE 3.—A person's electoral number consists of the distinctive letter or letters of the parliamentary polling district in which he is registered together with his number in the register to be used at the election except that before publication of the register the distinctive letter or letters of the parliamentary polling district in which he is entitled to be registered together with his number (if any) in the electors lists for that register shall be used instead.

NOTE 4.—An elector may not—

(a) subscribe more nomination papers than there are vacancies to be filled in the electoral area ; or

(b) subscribe a nomination paper for more than one electoral area ; or

(c) subscribe more than one nomination paper in respect of the same candidate.

NOTE 5.—A person whose name is entered in the register or electors lists may not subscribe a nomination paper if the entry gives as the date on which he will become of voting age a date later than the day fixed for the poll.

STATEMENT AS TO PERSONS NOMINATED   Rule 10.

GREATER LONDON

The following is a statement as to the persons nominated for election as Councillor [Councillors] of the Greater London Council for the
Electoral Area.

Persons nominated				Pro-poser's name	Decision of returning officer that nomination paper is invalid, or other reason why a person nominated no longer stands nominated
Surname	Other names in full	Home address in full	Description (if any)		
1.	2.	3.	4.	5.	6.

The persons opposite whose names no entry is made in column 6 have been and stand validly nominated.

Dated this   day of   , 19   .

....

Returning Officer.

Rule 15.

BALLOT PAPER

Form of Front of Ballot Paper

Counterfoil
No.

The counterfoil is to have a number to correspond with that on the back of the Ballot Paper.

1 | **BROWN**
(JOHN EDWARD Brown, of 2 The Cottages, Barlington, Labour.)

2 | **BROWN**
(THOMAS WILLIAM Brown, of 15 Barchester Road, Barlington, Liberal.)

3 | **JONES**
(William David Jones, of The Grange, Barlington, Conservative.)

4 | **MERTON**
(Hon. George Travis, commonly called Viscount Merton, of Barlington.)

5 | **SMITH**
(Mary Smith, of School House, Barlington, schoolteacher, Progressive.)

6 | **WILLIAMS**
(Elizabeth Williams, of 3 Ivy Lane, Barlington, housewife.)

Form of Back of Ballot Paper

No.

Election for the   electoral area of Greater London.

day of   , 19   .

Note.—The number on the ballot paper is to correspond with that on the counterfoil.

Directions as to printing the ballot paper

1. Nothing is to be printed on the ballot paper except in accordance with these directions.

2. So far as practicable, the following arrangements shall be observed in the printing of the ballot paper:—

(*a*) no word shall be printed on the face except the particulars of the candidates;

(*b*) no rule shall be printed on the face except the horizontal rules separating the particulars of the candidates from one another and the vertical rules separating those particulars from the numbers on the left-hand side and the spaces on the right where the vote is to be marked;

(*c*) the whole space between the top and bottom of the paper shall be equally divided between the candidates by the rules separating their particulars.

3. The surname of each candidate shall in all cases be printed by itself in large capitals, and his full particulars shall be set out below it and shall be printed in ordinary type except that small capitals shall be used—

(*a*) if his surname is the same as another candidate's, for his other names; and

(*b*) if his other names are also the same as the other candidate's, either for his residence or for his description unless each of them is the same as that of another candidate with the same surname and other names.

4. The number on the back of the ballot paper shall be printed in small characters.

DIRECTIONS FOR THE GUIDANCE OF THE VOTERS IN VOTING

Rule 24.

1. The voter should see that the ballot paper, before it is handed to him, is stamped with the official mark.

2. The voter will go into one of the compartments and, with the pencil provided in the compartment, place a cross on the right-hand side of the ballot paper, opposite the name of each candidate for whom he votes, thus X.

3. The voter will then fold up the ballot paper so as to show the official mark on the back, and leaving the compartment will, without showing the front of the paper to any person, show the official mark on the back to the presiding officer, and then, in the presence of the presiding officer, put the paper into the ballot box, and forthwith leave the polling station.

4. If the voter inadvertently spoils a ballot paper he can return it to the officer, who will, if satisfied of such inadvertence, give him another paper.

5. If the voter votes for more than   candidate(s) or places any mark on the paper by which he may afterwards be identified, his ballot paper will be void, and will not be counted.

6. If the voter fraudulently takes a ballot paper out of a polling station or fraudulently puts into the ballot box any paper other than the one given to him by the officer, he will be liable on conviction to imprisonment for a term not exceeding six months, or to a fine not exceeding twenty pounds or to both such imprisonment and such fine.

Rule 27.

CERTIFICATE OF EMPLOYMENT

Election in the   Electoral Area of Greater London.

I certify that (name).................... who is numbered..............
in the register of electors for the electoral area named above, is likely to be unable
to go in person to the polling station allotted to him at the election on (date of
poll)...................... by reason of the particular circumstances of his
employment on that date—

*(*a*) as a constable.

*(*b*) by me for a purpose connected with the election.

Signature ....

*Police rank ....
(Inspector or above)

*Returning Officer

Date......................

*Delete whichever is inapplicable.

NOTE.—The person named above is entitled to vote at any polling station of the
above electoral area on production and surrender of this certificate to the presiding
officer.

Rule 34.

DECLARATION TO BE MADE BY THE COMPANION OF A
BLIND VOTER

I, A.B., of   , having been requested to assist C.D. [*in the case
of a blind person voting as proxy add* voting as proxy for G.H.], who is numbered
on the register of local government electors for the   electoral
area of Greater London, to record his vote at the election now being held for the said
*State the   electoral area, do hereby declare that [I am entitled to vote as an elector at the said
relationship   election] [I am the*   of the said voter and have attained the
of the
companion   age of eighteen years] and that I have not previously assisted any blind person [except
to the voter.   E.F., of   ] to vote at the said election.

(Signed) A.B.

day of   , 19   .

I, the undersigned, being the presiding officer for the polling station for the
electoral area of Greater London, do hereby certify that the above
declaration, having been first read to the above-named declarant, was signed by the
declarant in my presence.

(Signed) X. Y.

day of   , 19   , at   minutes past
o'clock
[a.m.] [p.m.]

NOTE.—If the person making the above declaration knowingly and wilfully makes
therein a statement false in a material particular, he will be guilty of an offence.

SCHEDULE 2

DECLARATION OF ACCEPTANCE OF OFFICE BY THE CHAIRMAN OF THE GREATER LONDON COUNCIL OR BY AN ALDERMAN OR A COUNCILLOR OF THE GREATER LONDON COUNCIL

I, A.B., having been elected to the office of*   , hereby declare that I take the said office upon myself, and will duly and faithfully fulfil the duties thereof according to the best of my judgment and ability.

*Insert description of office.

Dated this   day of   , 19 .

Signature..

This declaration was made and subscribed before us

Members of the
Greater London
Council†.

{ ....

....

†If the declaration is made and subscribed before the clerk to the Greater London Council, or a justice of the peace or magistrate, or a commissioner for oaths, or a British consul, adapt form accordingly.

EXPLANATORY NOTE

(This Note is not part of the Rules.)

These Rules and Regulations revoke and replace the London Borough Council and Greater London Council Elections Rules 1963, the London Borough Council and Greater London Council Elections Rules 1964 and the London Borough Council and Greater London Council Election Forms Regulations 1964, so far as they relate to elections to the Greater London Council, with amendments consequential on the provisions of the Representation of the People Act 1969 (c.15). They also prescribe the form of declaration of acceptance of office by the chairman of the Greater London Council and by an alderman or a councillor of the Greater London Council.

STATUTORY INSTRUMENTS

1970 No. 94

FOOD AND DRUGS

COMPOSITION AND LABELLING

The Cheese Regulations 1970

Made - - -	23rd *January* 1970
Laid before Parliament	30th *January* 1970
Coming into Operation	31st *January* 1970

The Minister of Agriculture, Fisheries and Food and the Secretary of State for Social Services, acting jointly, in exercise of the powers conferred on them by sections 4, 7 and 123 of the Food and Drugs Act 1955(a), as read with the Secretary of State for Social Services Order 1968(b), and of all other powers enabling them in that behalf, hereby make the following regulations after consultation with such organisations as appear to them to be representative of interests substantially affected by the regulations and reference to the Food Hygiene Advisory Council under section 82 of the said Act (insofar as the regulations are made in exercise of the powers conferred by the said section 7) :—

PART I

PRELIMINARY

Citation and commencement

1. These regulations may be cited as the Cheese Regulations 1970, and shall come into operation on 31st January 1970.

Interpretation

2.—(1) In these regulations, unless the context otherwise requires—

"the Act" means the Food and Drugs Act 1955 ;

"cheese" means the fresh or matured product intended for sale for human consumption, which is obtained as follows—

    (*a*) in the case of any cheese other than whey cheese—

        (i) by coagulating any or a combination of any of the following substances, namely milk, cream, skimmed milk, partly skimmed milk, concentrated skimmed milk, reconstituted dried milk and butter milk, and

        (ii) partially draining the whey resulting from any such coagulation ;

(a) 4 & 5 Eliz. 2. c. 16.   (b) S.I. 1968/1699 (1968 III, p. 4585).

(*b*) in the case of whey cheese—

    (i) by concentrating whey with or without the addition of milk and milk fat, and moulding such concentrated whey, or

    (ii) by coagulating whey with or without the addition of milk and milk fat ;

"cheese spread" means cheese which has been subjected to a process of melting and mixing with milk products other than cheese, with or without the addition of emulsifying salts ;

"compound product" means food which consists of a combination of two or more foods and which does not contain less than 10 per cent. cheese, processed cheese or cheese spread or any mixture of two or more of them, as a percentage of the compound product, but does not include any pie, pudding, cake, confectionery, biscuit, Welsh rarebit or any product similar to Welsh rarebit ;

"container" includes any form of packaging of food for sale as a single item, whether by way of wholly or partly enclosing the food or by way of attaching the food to some other article, and in particular includes a wrapper or confining band ;

"emulsifying salts" means the sodium, potassium, calcium or ammonium salts of citric, phosphoric, polyphosphoric and tartaric acid ;

"food" means food intended for sale for human consumption and includes drink, chewing gum and other products of a like nature and use, and articles and substances used as ingredients in the preparation of food or drink or of such products, but does not include—

    (*a*) water, live animals or birds,

    (*b*) fodder or feeding stuffs for animals, birds or fish, or

    (*c*) articles or substances used only as drugs ;

"food and drugs authority" has the meaning assigned to it by section 83 of the Act ;

"hard cheese" means cheese other than soft cheese, whey cheese, processed cheese or cheese spread ;

"human consumption" includes use in the preparation of food for human consumption ;

"processed cheese" means cheese which has been subjected to a process of melting and mixing with or without the addition of emulsifying salts ;

"sell" includes offer or expose for sale or have in possession for sale, and "sale" and "sold" shall be construed accordingly ;

"sell by retail" means sell to a person buying otherwise than for the purpose of re-sale but does not include selling to a caterer for the purposes of his catering business, or selling to a manufacturer for the purposes of his manufacturing business ;

"soft cheese" means cheese which is readily deformed by moderate pressure, but does not include whey cheese, processed cheese or cheese spread, and any reference to soft cheese includes a reference to cream cheese or curd cheese ;

"starter" means a living culture in milk, cream, skimmed milk, partly skimmed milk, concentrated skimmed milk, reconstituted dried milk, or butter milk, of lactic-acid-producing bacteria ;

"whey cheese" means the product obtained by one or other of the processes referred to in paragraph (*b*) of the foregoing definition of "cheese" ; AND other expressions have the same meaning as in the Act.

(2) The Interpretation Act 1889(**a**) shall apply to the interpretation of these regulations as it applies to the interpretation of an Act of Parliament and as if these regulations and the regulations hereby revoked were Acts of Parliament.

(3) All percentages mentioned in these regulations are percentages calculated by weight, and unless a contrary intention is expressed, are calculated on the total weight of the cheese.

(4) Any reference in these regulations to a label borne on a container shall be construed as including a reference to any legible marking on the container however effected.

(5) For the purpose of these regulations, the supply of food, otherwise than by sale, at, in or from any place where food is supplied in the course of a business, shall be deemed to be a sale of that food, and references to purchasing and purchasers shall be construed accordingly.

(6) Any reference in these regulations to any other regulations shall be construed as a reference to such regulations as amended by any subsequent regulations.

(7) Any reference in these regulations to a numbered regulation shall unless the reference is to a regulation of specified regulations, be construed as a reference to the regulation bearing that number in these regulations.

Exemptions

3. The following provisions of these regulations shall not apply, except insofar as they relate to advertisements other than labels or wrappers, in relation to any cheese, processed cheese, cheese spread or compound product sold, consigned or delivered for—

 (*a*) exportation to any place outside the United Kingdom ; or

 (*b*) consumption by a visiting force within the meaning of any of the provisions of Part I of the Visiting Forces Act 1952(**b**) ; or

 (*c*) use by a manufacturer for the purposes of his manufacturing business.

PART II

COMPOSITION AND DESCRIPTION OF CHEESE, PROCESSED CHEESE AND CHEESE SPREAD

Composition and description of hard cheese

4.—(1) Any hard cheese sold, consigned or delivered under the name of a variety specified in column 1 of Schedule 1 to these regulations, whether or not such cheese was manufactured in the United Kingdom, shall comply with the percentages for milk fat and water set out respectively in columns 2 and 3 of the said Schedule opposite the name of such cheese.

(2) Any hard cheese sold, consigned or delivered, other than hard cheese to which the foregoing paragraph of this regulation applies, shall satisfy either the requirements of sub-paragraph (*a*) or the requirements of sub-paragraph (*b*)

(**a**) 1889 c. 63.   (**b**) 1952 c. 67.

following, except that the appropriate description or declaration need be borne by any hard cheese sold, consigned or delivered otherwise than in a container only when such cheese is sold by retail—

    (*a*) such cheese shall bear one of the following descriptions and comply with the following compositional requirements for cheese of such description, namely—

        (i) "full fat hard cheese", if the cheese contains not less than 48 per cent. milk fat in the dry matter and not more than 48 per cent. water ;

        (ii) "medium fat hard cheese", if the cheese contains less than 48 per cent. and not less than 10 per cent. milk fat in the dry matter, and not more than 48 per cent. water ;

        (iii) "skimmed milk hard cheese", if the cheese contains less than 10 per cent. milk fat in the dry matter, and not more than 48 per cent. water ; or

    (*b*) such cheese shall bear a true declaration of either—

        (i) the minimum percentage milk fat content in the dry matter, and the maximum percentage water content, or

        (ii) the minimum percentage milk fat content,

so however that as respects any sale, consignment or delivery on or after 1st January 1973 of any hard cheese bearing such a declaration, that declaration shall be in such of the following forms as is appropriate : —

        (*aa*) "x% fat in dry matter" and "y% moisture", and the declaration shall be completed by inserting at "x" and "y" respectively the percentages described in sub-paragraph (*b*)(i) of this paragraph ;

        (*ab*) "x% fat", and the declaration shall be completed by inserting at "x" the percentage described in sub-paragraph (*b*)(ii) of this paragraph.

(3) No person shall sell, consign or deliver, as the case may be, any hard cheese in contravention of this regulation.

Composition and description of soft cheese

5.—(1) Any soft cheese sold, consigned or delivered under the name of a variety specified in column 1 of Schedule 1 to these regulations whether or not such cheese was manufactured in the United Kingdom, shall comply with the percentages for milk fat and water set out respectively in columns 2 and 3 of the said Schedule opposite the name of such cheese.

(2) Any soft cheese sold, consigned or delivered, other than soft cheese to which the foregoing paragraph of this regulation applies and other than cheese which bears one of the descriptions specified in paragraph (3) of this regulation and complies with the compositional requirements so specified in relation to that description, shall bear one of the following descriptions, and comply with the following compositional requirements for cheese of such description except that the appropriate description need be borne by any soft cheese sold, consigned or delivered otherwise than in a container only when such cheese is sold by retail—

    (*a*) "full fat soft cheese", if the cheese contains not less than 20 per cent. milk fat, and not more than 60 per cent. water ;

(b) "medium fat soft cheese", if the cheese contains less than 20 per cent. but not less than 10 per cent. milk fat, and not more than 70 per cent. water ;

(c) "low fat soft cheese", if the cheese contains less than 10 per cent. but not less than 2 per cent. milk fat, and not more than 80 per cent. water ;

(d) "skimmed milk soft cheese", if the cheese contains less than 2 per cent. milk fat, and not more than 80 per cent. water.

(3) Any soft cheese sold, consigned or delivered, as "cream cheese" shall contain not less than 45 per cent. milk fat, and bear the description "cream cheese":

Provided that if such cheese contains not less than 65 per cent. milk fat, it may bear the description "double cream cheese".

(4) No person shall sell, consign or deliver, as the case may be, any soft cheese in contravention of this regulation.

Composition and description of whey cheese

6.—(1) Any whey cheese sold, consigned or delivered shall bear one of the following descriptions and comply with the following compositional requirements for cheese of such description, except that the appropriate description need be borne by any whey cheese sold, consigned or delivered otherwise than in a container only when such cheese is sold by retail—

(a) "full fat whey cheese", if the cheese contains not less than 33 per cent. milk fat in the dry matter;

(b) "whey cheese", if the cheese contains less than 33 per cent. and not less than 10 per cent. milk fat in the dry matter;

(c) "skimmed whey cheese", if the cheese contains less than 10 per cent. milk fat in the dry matter.

(2) No person shall sell, consign or deliver, as the case may be, any whey cheese in contravention of this regulation.

Composition and description of processed cheese

7.—(1) Any processed cheese sold, consigned or delivered under a description containing the word "processed" with the name of a variety of cheese specified in column 1 of Schedule 1 to these regulations, whether or not such processed cheese was manufactured in the United Kingdom, shall either—

(a) comply with the percentages for milk fat and water set out respectively in columns 2 and 3 of the said Schedule opposite the name of such cheese, except that processed Cheddar cheese shall contain not less than 48 per cent. milk fat in the dry matter, and not more than 43 per cent. water; or

(b) comply with the provisions of paragraph (2) of this regulation.

(2) Any processed cheese sold, consigned or delivered, other than any processed cheese to which the foregoing paragraph of this regulation applies, shall satisfy either the requirements of sub-paragraph (a) or the requirements of sub-paragraph (b) following, except that the appropriate description or declaration

need be borne by any processed cheese sold, consigned or delivered otherwise than in a container only when such processed cheese is sold by retail—

(a) such processed cheese shall bear one of the following descriptions, and comply with the following compositional requirements for processed cheese of such description, namely—

(i) "full fat processed cheese", if the processed cheese contains not less than 48 per cent. milk fat in the dry matter, and not more than 48 per cent. water;

(ii) "medium fat processed cheese", if the processed cheese contains less than 48 per cent. and not less than 10 per cent. milk fat in the dry matter, and not more than 48 per cent. water;

(iii) "skimmed milk processed cheese", if the processed cheese contains less than 10 per cent. milk fat in the dry matter, and not more than 48 per cent. water; or

(b) such processed cheese shall bear a true declaration of either—

(i) the minimum percentage milk fat content in the dry matter and the maximum percentage water content, or

(ii) the minimum percentage milk fat content,

so however that as respects any sale, consignment or delivery on or after 1st January 1973 of any processed cheese bearing such a declaration, that declaration shall be in such of the following forms as is appropriate:—

(aa) "x% fat in dry matter" and "y% moisture", and the declaration shall be completed by inserting at "x" and "y" respectively the percentages described in sub-paragraph (b)(i) of this paragraph;

(ab) "x% fat", and the declaration shall be completed by inserting at "x" the percentage described in sub-paragraph (b)(ii) of this paragraph.

(3) Any processed cheese sold, consigned or delivered which is a mixture of cheese of two or more varieties shall either conform to one of the compositional requirements of paragraph (2)(a) of this regulation and bear the appropriate description specified therein for such processed cheese or bear one of the declarations specified in paragraph (2)(b) of this regulation.

(4) The name of a variety of cheese, used in the preparation of a processed cheese, may be inserted between the words "processed" and "cheese" in the appropriate description required by paragraphs (2)(a) and (3) of this regulation.

(5) No person shall sell, consign or deliver, as the case may be, any processed cheese in contravention of this regulation.

Composition and description of cheese spread

8.—(1) Any cheese spread sold, consigned or delivered shall contain not less than 20 per cent. milk fat and not more than 60 per cent. water; and shall bear the description "cheese spread" or "cheese food", with or without the name of the variety or description of cheese used as a constituent of such cheese spread inserted immediately before the words "cheese spread" or "cheese food", except that such description need be borne by cheese spread sold, consigned or delivered otherwise than in a container only when such cheese spread is sold by retail.

(2) No person shall sell, consign or deliver, as the case may be, any cheese spread in contravention of this regulation.

Compound products

9.—(1) Any cheese, processed cheese or cheese spread for which compositional requirements are specified in these regulations and which is used as an ingredient of a compound product, shall comply with the compositional requirements so specified for such cheese, processed cheese or cheese spread.

(2) No person shall sell, consign or deliver, as the case may be, any compound product in contravention of this regulation.

General requirements as to composition and description

10.—(1) No person shall sell any food under such a description as to lead an intending purchaser to believe that he is purchasing any cheese, processed cheese, cheese spread or compound product respectively for which compositional requirements are specified in these regulations if the food does not comply with the appropriate requirements as to composition set out in these regulations in relation to that cheese, processed cheese, cheese spread or compound product.

(2) Where a person sells any food to a purchaser in response to a request for any kind of cheese, processed cheese, cheese spread or compound product for which compositional requirements are specified in these regulations, he shall be deemed to sell cheese, processed cheese, cheese spread or a compound product of that kind and under such a description as is specified in these regulations in relation to that kind of cheese, processed cheese, cheese spread or compound product unless he clearly notifies the purchaser at the time of sale that the cheese, processed cheese, cheese spread or compound product is not of that kind.

Permitted ingredients in cheese, processed cheese and cheese spread

11. No person shall sell, consign or deliver any cheese, processed cheese or cheese spread which contains any ingredient other than the substances mentioned in the definition of "cheese", "processed cheese" or "cheese spread" as the case may be, in regulation 2(1), water, such preservatives in such amounts as are permitted by the Preservatives in Food Regulations 1962(a), any mould characteristic of the variety of cheese concerned and any or all of the following ingredients where appropriate in relation to the kind of cheese specified, namely:—

(*a*) Hard cheese may contain common salt (sodium chloride), calcium chloride, calcium hydroxide, starter, rennet, carotene and annatto;

(*b*) The rind of hard cheese may contain any colouring matter permitted by the Colouring Matter in Food Regulations 1966(**b**);

(*c*) Soft cheese and whey cheese may contain the ingredients mentioned in paragraph (*a*) of this regulation, alginic acid, calcium alginate, sodium alginate, carrageen, edible gums, edible starches (whether modified or not), flavourings and lecithin;

(*d*) Processed cheese and cheese spread may contain—

　(i) the ingredients mentioned or referred to in paragraph (*c*) of this regulation;

　(ii) emulsifying salts;

(**a**) S.I. 1962/1532 (1962 II, p. 1655). (**b**) S.I. 1966/1203 (1966 III, p. 3203).

(iii) any colouring matter permitted by paragraphs 1 to 4 of Part III of Schedule 1 to the Colouring Matter in Food Regulations 1966; and

(iv) lactic acid and citric acid;

(e) Hard sage cheese may contain—

(i) the ingredients mentioned in paragraph (a) of this regulation;

(ii) sage; and

(iii) any green colouring matter permitted by paragraph 3 of Part III of Schedule 1 to the Colouring Matter in Food Regulations 1966;

(f) Soft sage cheese may contain—

(i) the ingredients mentioned or referred to in paragraph (c) of this regulation;

(ii) sage; and

(iii) any green colouring matter mentioned or referred to in paragraph 3 of Part III of Schedule 1 to the Colouring Matter in Food Regulations 1966;

(g) Sage cheese spread may contain the ingredients mentioned or referred to in paragraph (d) of this regulation and sage.

Part III
Labelling and Advertisement

Labelling and advertisement of cheese, processed cheese, cheese spread and compound products

12.—(1) No person shall sell, consign or deliver any cheese, processed cheese or cheese spread in a container unless such container bears a label on which there appears the appropriate description or declaration specified in regulation 4, 5, 6, 7 or 8 for such cheese, processed cheese or cheese spread:

Provided that in the case of hard cheese, soft cheese or processed cheese which complies with regulation 4(1), 5(1) or 7(1), as the case may be, the label may bear instead of such description or declaration—

(a) in the case of hard cheese or soft cheese, the name of the variety of such cheese, or

(b) in the case of processed cheese, the word "processed" with the name of the variety of such processed cheese.

(2) No person shall sell by retail any cheese, processed cheese or cheese spread otherwise than in a container unless there appears on a ticket placed on or in immediate proximity to such cheese, processed cheese or cheese spread so as to be clearly visible to an intending purchaser, the appropriate description or declaration specified in regulation 4, 5, 6, 7 or 8 for such cheese, processed cheese or cheese spread:

Provided that in the case of hard cheese, soft cheese or processed cheese which complies with regulation 4(1), 5(1) or 7(1), as the case may be, the ticket may bear instead of such description or declaration—

(a) in the case of hard cheese or soft cheese, the name of the variety of such cheese, or

(b) in the case of processed cheese, the word "processed" with the name of the variety of such processed cheese.

(3) No person shall sell, consign or deliver any compound product in a container unless such container bears a label on which there appears as part of the description of such product the appropriate description or declaration specified in regulation 4, 5, 6, 7 or 8 for the cheese, processed cheese or cheese spread present in such compound product together with a true description of any other food, except an ingredient permitted by regulation 11, present in such compound product:

Provided that in the case of any hard cheese, soft cheese or processed cheese which complies with regulation 4(1), 5(1) or 7(1), as the case may be, the label may bear instead of such description or declaration—

    (a) in the case of hard cheese or soft cheese, the name of the variety of such cheese, or

    (b) in the case of processed cheese, the word "processed" with the name of the variety of such processed cheese.

(4) No person shall sell by retail any compound product otherwise than in a container unless there appears on a ticket placed on or in immediate proximity to such compound product so as to be clearly visible to an intending purchaser, as the description of such compound product, the appropriate description or declaration specified in regulation 4, 5, 6, 7 or 8 for the cheese, processed cheese or cheese spread present in such compound product together with a true description of any other food, except an ingredient permitted by regulation 11, present in such compound product:

Provided that in the case of hard cheese, soft cheese or processed cheese which complies with regulation 4(1), 5(1) or 7(1), as the case may be, the ticket may bear instead of such description or declaration—

    (a) in the case of hard cheese or soft cheese, the name of the variety of such cheese, or

    (b) in the case of processed cheese, the word "processed" with the name of the variety of such processed cheese.

(5) Notwithstanding the provisions of regulations 4, 5, 6, 7 and 8 and the preceding paragraphs of this regulation, the appropriate description of any cheese, processed cheese or cheese spread may include, if penicillium moulds have produced blue-green veining in such cheese, processed cheese or cheese spread the word "blue-veined", or if such cheese, processed cheese or cheese spread contains sage, the word "sage".

13.—(1) Any advertisement for cheese, processed cheese or cheese spread shall include such one of the descriptions specified in regulation 4, 5, 6, 7 or 8 or such one of the declarations specified in regulation 4 or 7, as the case may be, as is appropriate to that cheese, processed cheese or cheese spread:

Provided that in the case of hard cheese, soft cheese or processed cheese which complies with regulation 4(1), 5(1) or 7(1), as the case may be, the advertisement may include instead of such description or declaration—

    (a) in the case of hard cheese or soft cheese, the name of the variety of such cheese, or

    (b) in the case of processed cheese, the word "processed" with the name of the variety of such processed cheese.

(2) Any cheese, processed cheese or cheese spread which is the subject of any description contained in any advertisement in accordance with the foregoing

paragraph of this regulation shall comply with the compositional requirements specified in regulation 4, 5, 6, 7 or 8 for cheese, processed cheese or cheese spread of such description.

(3) Any advertisement for any compound product shall include the description of such compound product specified in regulation 12(3) and (4) and the compound product so described shall comply with the compositional requirements specified in regulation 9.

(4) Notwithstanding the provisions of regulations 4, 5, 6, 7 and 8 and paragraph (1) of this regulation, the description of any cheese, processed cheese or cheese spread may include, if penicillium moulds have produced blue-green veining in such cheese, processed cheese or cheese spread the word "blue-veined", or if such cheese, processed cheese or cheese spread contains sage, the word "sage".

(5) No person shall publish or be a party to the publication of any advertisement which does not comply with this regulation.

Requirements as to marking on labels on containers and on tickets

14.—(1) As respects any sale, consignment or delivery on or before 31st December 1972, all letters, words or numerals required by virtue of regulation 12 to appear on a label on a container or on a ticket respectively shall conform to the requirements set out in paragraph 1 of Schedule 2 to these regulations.

(2) As respects any sale, consignment or delivery on or after 1st January 1973, all letters, words or numerals required by virtue of regulation 12 to appear on a label on a container or on a ticket respectively shall conform to the requirements set out in paragraph 2 of the said Schedule 2.

Labelling and advertisement of cream cheese

15. No person shall—

(a) give with any cheese sold by him, or display with any cheese offered or exposed by him for sale any label, whether attached to or printed on the container or not, which bears any words or pictorial device, or

(b) publish, or be a party to the publication of, any advertisement for cheese which includes any words or pictorial device, or

(c) use on, or in connection with, the sale of cheese any description,

being words, a device or a description which are or is calculated to indicate either directly or indirectly that such cheese contains cream or is made from cream, unless such cheese complies with the compositional requirement for cream cheese which is specified in regulation 5(3).

PART IV

ADMINISTRATION AND GENERAL

Penalties and enforcement

16.—(1) If any person contravenes or fails to comply with any of the foregoing provisions of these regulations he shall be guilty of an offence and shall be liable to a fine not exceeding one hundred pounds or to imprisonment for a term not exceeding three months, or to both, and, in the case of a continuing offence, to a further fine not exceeding five pounds for each day during which the offence continues after conviction.

(2) Each food and drugs authority shall enforce and execute such provisions in their area.

(3) The requirement of section 109(3) of the Act (which requires notice to be given to the Minister of Agriculture, Fisheries and Food of intention to institute proceedings for an offence against any provisions of these regulations relating to the labelling, advertising or description of food) shall not apply as respects any proceedings instituted by a council for an offence against any such provisions of these regulations.

Defences

17.—(1) In any proceedings for an offence against these regulations in relation to the publication of an advertisement, it shall be a defence for the defendant to prove that, being a person whose business it is to publish or arrange for the publication of advertisements, he received the advertisement for publication in the ordinary course of business.

(2) In any proceedings against the manufacturer or importer of cheese, processed cheese, cheese spread or of any compound product for an offence against these regulations in relation to the publication of an advertisement, it shall rest on the defendant to prove that he did not publish and was not a party to the publication of, the advertisement.

Applications of various sections of the Act

18.—(1) Sections 108(3) and (4) (which relate to prosecutions), 110(1), (2) and (3) (which relate to evidence of analysis), 112 (which relates to the power of a court to require analysis by the Government Chemist), 113 (which relates to a contravention due to some person other than the person charged), 115(2) (which relates to the conditions under which a warranty may be pleaded as a defence) and 116 (which relates to offences in relation to warranties and certificates of analysis) of the Act shall apply for the purposes of these regulations as if references therein to proceedings, or a prosecution, under or taken or brought under the Act included references to proceedings, or a prosecution as the case may be, taken or brought for an offence under these regulations and as if the reference in the said section 112 to subsection (4) of section 108 included a reference to that subsection as applied by these regulations.

(2) Paragraph (b) of the proviso to section 108(1) of the Act shall apply for the purposes of these regulations as if the reference therein to section 116 of the Act included a reference to that section as applied by these regulations.

Revocations

19. The Cheese Regulations 1965(a) and the Cheese (Amendment) Regulations 1966(b) are hereby revoked.

(a) S.I. 1965/2199 (1965 III, p. 6422).   (b) S.I. 1966/1640 (1966 III, p. 5097).

In Witness whereof the Official Seal of the Minister of Agriculture, Fisheries and Food is hereunto affixed on 22nd January 1970.

(L.S.)

Cledwyn Hughes,
Minister of Agriculture, Fisheries and Food.

R. H. S. Crossman,
Secretary of State for Social Services.

23rd January 1970.

Regulations 4, 5 and 7   **SCHEDULE 1**

Column 1	Column 2	Column 3
Variety of Cheese	Minimum Percentage of Milk Fat in the Dry Matter	Maximum Percentage of Water Calculated on the total Weight of the Cheese
Cheddar	48	39
Blue Stilton	48	42
Derby	48	42
Leicester	48	42
Cheshire	48	44
Dunlop	48	44
Gloucester	48	44
Double Gloucester	48	44
Caerphilly	48	46
Wensleydale	48	46
White Stilton	48	46
Lancashire	48	48
Edam	40	46
Loaf Edam	40	46
Baby Edam	40	47
Baby Loaf Edam	40	47
Gouda	48	43
Baby Gouda	48	45
Danablu	50	47
Danbo	45	46
Havarti	45	50
Samsoe	45	44
Emmental or Emmentaler	45	40
Gruyere or Greyerzer or Gruviera	45	38

Column 1	Column 2	Column 3
Variety of Cheese	Minimum Percentage of Milk Fat in the Dry Matter	Maximum Percentage of Water Calculated on the total Weight of the Cheese
Tilsiter or Tilsit or Tylzycki	45	47
Limburger	50	50
Saint Paulin	40	56
Svecia	45	41
Provolone	45	47

SCHEDULE 2

REQUIREMENTS AS TO MARKING ON LABELS

ON CONTAINERS AND ON TICKETS

1. As respects any sale, consignment or delivery on or before 31st December 1972, every letter, word or numeral appearing on a label on a container, or on a ticket, which is required so to appear by virtue of regulation 12 shall—

(*a*) be clearly legible;

(*b*) appear in a prominent position on the label or ticket;

(*c*) be printed in a dark colour upon a light coloured ground or in a light colour upon a dark coloured ground;

(*d*) be of uniform colour and size, except that the initial letter in any such word may be larger than the other letters in that word:

Provided that the requirements of this sub-paragraph shall not have effect in relation to the sale, consignment or delivery, as the case may be, of any compound product.

2. As respects any sale, consignment or delivery on or after 1st January 1973—

(*a*) every letter, word or numeral appearing on a label on a container, or on a ticket, which is required so to appear by virtue of regulation 12 shall be in characters of uniform colour and size, save that the initial letter of any word may be taller than any other letter in that word:

Provided that in the case of a compound product this requirement shall apply only in respect of such letters, words or numerals as describe the cheese, processed cheese or cheese spread, as the case may be, present in such compound product;

(*b*) any declaration required by regulation 4(2)(*b*) or 7(2)(*b*) shall be so situated as to be in immediate proximity to and simultaneously visible together with the name of the cheese, processed cheese or cheese spread to an intending purchaser under normal conditions of purchase and use.

EXPLANATORY NOTE

(This Note is not part of the Regulations.)

These regulations, which apply to England and Wales only, re-enact with amendments the Cheese Regulations 1965, as amended, and come into operation on 31st January 1970.

The regulations—

(*a*) specify requirements for the composition and description of cheese including hard cheese, soft cheese (including cream cheese), whey cheese, processed cheese and cheese spread (regulations 4, 5, 6, 7, 8 and Schedule 1) amended to prescribe compositional standards for additional varieties of cheese or processed cheese sold under varietal names (regulations 4, 5, 7 and Schedule 1);

(*b*) apply compositional requirements for cheese, processed cheese or cheese spread sold as part of a compound product (regulation 9);

(*c*) specify the permitted ingredients in cheese, processed cheese and cheese spread, amended to include calcium hydroxide as a permitted ingredient (regulation 11);

(*d*) specify requirements for the labelling and advertisement of cheese, processed cheese, cheese spread and compound products (regulations 12, 13, 14 and 15);

(*e*) provide for certain amendments to the requirements for the labelling of cheese, processed cheese, cheese spread and compound products to take effect on and after 1st January 1973 (regulations 4, 7, 14(2) and Schedule 2, paragraph 2).

The regulations do not apply, except insofar as they relate to advertisements, to cheese, processed cheese, cheese spread and compound products intended for export, for consumption by a visiting force or for use for manufacturing purposes (regulation 3).

STATUTORY INSTRUMENTS

1970 No. 95

CUSTOMS AND EXCISE

The Import Duty Drawbacks (No. 1) Order 1970

Made - - - -	*26th January* 1970
Laid before the	
House of Commons	*30th January* 1970
Coming into Operation	*5th February* 1970

The Lords Commissioners of Her Majesty's Treasury by virtue of the powers conferred on them by section 9 and 13 of, and Schedule 5 to, the Import Duties Act 1958(a) and section 2(5) of the Finance Act 1965(b), and of all other powers enabling them in that behalf, on the recommendation of the Board of Trade hereby make the following Order:—

1.—(1) This Order may be cited as the Import Duty Drawbacks (No. 1) Order 1970.

(2) The Interpretation Act 1889(c) shall apply for the interpretation of this Order as it applies for the interpretation of an Act of Parliament.

(3) This Order shall come into operation on 5th February 1970.

2. In Schedule 2 to the Import Duty Drawbacks (No. 10) Order 1968(d) (which relates to the drawbacks to be allowed on the exportation of goods produced or manufactured from imported articles), there shall be omitted the rate of drawback specified in column 3 against the entry for pigment produced or manufactured from combined cadmium.

Joseph Harper,
E. G. Perry,
Two of the Lords Commissioners
of Her Majesty's Treasury.

26th January 1970.

EXPLANATORY NOTE

(This Note is not part of the Order.)

This Order revokes the fixed rate of drawback of import duty in respect of exported pigment produced or manufactured from imported cadmium metal. The effect is that drawback will in future be related to the duty paid in respect of the quantity of imported cadmium metal used in the manufacture of the particular pigment exported.

(a) 1958 c. 6.   (b) 1965 c. 25.   (c) 1889 c. 63.
(d) S.I. 1968/1881 (1968 III, p. 4969).

STATUTORY INSTRUMENTS

1970 No. 96 (S.1.)

COURT OF SESSION, SCOTLAND
Act of Sederunt (Rules of Court Amendment No. 1) 1970

Made - - -	*23rd January* 1970
Coming into Operation	*3rd March* 1970

The Lords of Council and Session, under and by virtue of the powers conferred upon them by section 16 of the Administration of Justice (Scotland) Act 1933(**a**) and of all other powers competent to them in that behalf, considering that it has been agreed by the Civil Service Department that certain fees payable to short-hand writers should be increased, do hereby enact and declare as follows:—

1. Rule 347 of the Rules of the Court of Session(**b**) as substituted by the Act of Sederunt (Rules of Court Amendment No. 1) 1966(**c**) shall be amended as follows:—

(*a*) Paragraphs 1 and 2 of Chapter IV—Table of Fees to Shorthand Writers, shall be deleted and in place thereof there shall be substituted the following:—

	£	s.	d.
"1. Attending trials, proofs and commissions, per hour, with a minimum fee of £5 per day ...	1	14	0
The above fees will be paid by the Exchequer. No fee will be paid where intimation of post-ponement or settlement is made by 4 p.m. on the previous day.			
2. Extending Notes, except when these are trans-cribed daily, per sheet of 250 words	0	7	3
Extending Notes, when these are transcribed daily but not on stencils, per sheet of 250 words	0	9	3
Extending Notes, when these are transcribed daily on stencils, per sheet of 250 words ...	0	11	0"

2. This Act of Sederunt may be cited as the Act of Sederunt (Rules of Court Amendment No. 1) 1970 and shall come into operation on 3rd March 1970.

J. L. Clyde,
I.P.D.

Edinburgh,

23rd January 1970.

(**a**) 1933 c. 41.   (**b**) S.I. 1965/321 (1965 I, p. 803).   (**c**) S.I. 1966/335 (1966 I, p. 778).

EXPLANATORY NOTE

(This Note is not part of the Act of Sederunt.)

This Act of Sederunt prescribes a new table of fees payable to shorthand writers for attendance in the Court of Session and for extension of Notes.

STATUTORY INSTRUMENTS

1970 No. 98

CUSTOMS AND EXCISE

The Anti-Dumping Duty (Temporary Suspension) Order 1970

Made - - - -	*27th January* 1970
Laid before the	
House of Commons -	*30th January* 1970
Coming into Operation	*31st January* 1970

The Board of Trade in pursuance of the powers conferred upon them by sections 1, 10(3), 15(4) and 18(2) of the Customs Duties (Dumping and Subsidies) Act 1969(**a**) hereby make the following Order :—

1.—(1) This Order may be cited as the Anti-Dumping Duty (Temporary Suspension) Order 1970 and shall come into operation on 31st January 1970.

(2) The Interpretation Act 1889(**b**) shall apply to the interpretation of this Order as it applies to the interpretation of an Act of Parliament.

2. The duties imposed by the Anti-Dumping Duty Order 1967(**c**) on stearine originating in Australia or Belgium shall not be chargeable on any stearine imported into the United Kingdom during a period of twelve months beginning with the commencement of this Order.

Gwyneth Dunwoody,
Parliamentary Secretary to the
Board of Trade.

27th January 1970.

EXPLANATORY NOTE

(This Note is not part of the Order.)

This Order suspends for a period of twelve months the anti-dumping duties imposed by the Anti-Dumping Duty Order 1967 on stearine originating in Australia or Belgium.

(**a**) 1969 c. 16.   (**b**) 1889 c. 63.   (**c**) S.I. 1967/553 (1967 I, p. 1767).

1970 No. 102

FIRE SERVICES

The Fire Services (Appointments and Promotion) (Amendment) Regulations 1970

Made - - - -	*22nd January* 1970
Laid before Parliament	*3rd February* 1970
Coming into Operation	*16th February* 1970

In exercise of the powers conferred on me by section 18(1) of the Fire Services Act 1947(a), as amended by the Fire Services Act 1959(b), I hereby, after consultation with the Central Fire Brigades Advisory Council, make the following Regulations:—

1. These Regulations may be cited as the Fire Services (Appointments and Promotion) (Amendment) Regulations 1970 and shall come into operation on 16th February 1970.

2. In so far as the Fire Services (Appointments and Promotion) Regulations 1965(c), as amended(d), provide that a candidate for appointment to, or promotion in, a fire brigade shall be a British subject or a citizen of the Republic of Ireland they shall cease to have effect and, accordingly—

 (*a*) paragraph (*a*) shall be omitted from Regulation 2(1) thereof (which relates to the qualifications for appointment in the rank of junior fireman, in the case of a male person), and

 (*b*) paragraph (*a*) shall be omitted from Regulation 3(1) (which relates to the qualifications for promotion to, or appointment in, the rank of fireman, in the case of a male person who is to serve whole-time on terms under which he is or may be required to engage in fire-fighting).

James Callaghan,
One of Her Majesty's Principal
Secretaries of State.

Home Office,
 Whitehall.
22nd January 1970.

(a) 1947 c. 41.   (b) 1959 c. 44.
(c) S.I. 1965/577 (1965 I, p. 1817).
(d) The amending Regulations are not relevant to the subject matter of these Regulations.

EXPLANATORY NOTE

(This Note is not part of the Regulations.)

These Regulations amend the Fire Services (Appointments and Promotion) Regulations 1965.

They revoke those provisions of the Regulations of 1965 which require that a candidate for appointment to, or promotion in, a fire brigade shall be a British subject or a citizen of the Republic of Ireland. The provisions in question relate to male persons only and their appointment in the rank of junior fireman or appointment in, or promotion to, the rank of fireman for whole-time fire-fighting duties.

STATUTORY INSTRUMENTS

1970 No. 106 (S.2)

LOCAL GOVERNMENT, SCOTLAND

The Local Government (Financial Loss Allowance) (Scotland) Regulations 1970

Made - - -	*22nd January* 1970
Laid before Parliament	*4th February* 1970
Coming into Operation	*6th February* 1970

In exercise of the powers conferred on me by sections 112 and 117 as read with section 118 of the Local Government Act 1948(**a**) and as amended by section 16 of the Local Government (Miscellaneous Provisions) Act 1953(**b**), and of all other powers enabling me in that behalf, I hereby make the following regulations :—

1.—(1) These regulations may be cited as the Local Government (Financial Loss Allowance) (Scotland) Regulations 1970 and shall come into operation on 6th February 1970.

(2) The Local Government (Travelling Allowances, etc.) (Scotland) Regulations 1954(**c**), the Local Government (Travelling Allowances, etc.) (Scotland) Amendment Regulations 1957(**d**), 1962(**e**) and 1966(**f**) so far as they relate to the payment of financial loss allowance are hereby revoked.

2.—(1) In these regulations, unless the context otherwise requires :—

"the Act" means the Local Government Act 1948, as amended by section 16 of the Local Government (Miscellaneous Provisions) Act 1953 ;

"body" means any body to which Part VI of the Act applies for the time being.

(2) The Interpretation Act 1889(**g**) applies for the interpretation of these regulations as it applies for the interpretation of an Act of Parliament.

3. The rates to be determined by bodies for the payment of financial loss allowance shall not exceed the maximum rates mentioned, and shall be subject to the provisions contained, in Schedule 1 to these regulations.

4. Every member of a body who desires to claim any payment by way of financial loss allowance, shall complete and submit to that body an application in the form set out in Schedule 2 to these regulations or in a form substantially to the like effect.

(**a**) 1948 c. 26.	(**b**) 1953 c. 26.
(**c**) S.I. 1954/265 (1954 I, p. 1159).	(**d**) S.I. 1957/1089 (1957 I, p. 1336).
(**e**) S.I. 1962/935 (1962 II, p. 1077).	(**f**) S.I. 1966/899 (1966 II, p. 2152).
(**g**) 1889 c. 63.	

5.—(1) Where a person necessarily suffers or incurs any loss or expense to which section 112 of the Act applies, in respect of the performance by him in any one period of twenty-four hours of approved duties as a member of more than one body, he shall be entitled to receive and there shall be payable by the bodies concerned, in respect of the performance of those duties, such payments by way of financial loss allowance as will be equal in the aggregate to the payment to which he would have been entitled had all the said duties been performed by him as a member of one only of these bodies.

(2) Where in any one period of twenty-four hours a person becomes entitled in respect of the performance of any duties to receive payments by way of, or in the nature of, financial loss allowance, both under Part VI of the Act and under any other enactment, the amount which he shall be entitled to receive under either of those enactments in respect of financial loss allowance shall be reduced by any amount received by him in respect of financial loss allowance under the other of those enactments, and any claim for any such payment as aforesaid shall contain particulars of any amount so received.

William Ross,
One of Her Majesty's Principal
Secretaries of State.

St. Andrew's House,
Edinburgh.
22nd January 1970.

SCHEDULE 1

MAXIMUM RATES OF PAYMENTS BY WAY OF LOSS OF EARNINGS OR ADDITIONAL
EXPENSES, AND PROVISIONS RELATING 'THERETO

The payment which a member of a body shall be entitled to receive by way of financial loss allowance in respect of any one period of twenty-four hours shall not exceed—

    (i) where the period of time over which earnings are lost or additional expenses are incurred is not more than four hours, the sum of £2 ;

    (ii) where the said period of time is more than four hours, the sum of £4.

SCHEDULE 2

FORM OF APPLICATION FOR FINANCIAL LOSS ALLOWANCE

Date (1)	Place and time of departure (2)	Place and time of return (3)	Description of approved duties (4)	Amount Claimed (5)

Particulars of amounts received or claimed by way of financial loss allowance from other authorities or bodies.

Amount now claimed   ..   ..

I declare that I have actually and necessarily—

    (a) suffered loss of earnings which I should otherwise have made, or

    (b) incurred additional expense, other than expense on account of travelling or subsistence,

for the purpose of enabling me to perform approved duties as a member of ....and that the amount of such loss and expense is not less than the sum claimed.

I declare that the statements above are correct. Except as shown above I have not made, and will not make, any claim under any enactment for financial loss allowance in connection with the duties indicated above.

Date.................. Signature of Member.............................

EXPLANATORY NOTE

(This Note is not part of the Regulations.)

These Regulations replace the provisions of the Local Government (Travelling Allowances, etc.) (Scotland) Regulations which relate to the maximum rates of allowances payable by bodies specified in Part VI of the Local Government Act 1948 to their members who, in the performance of approved duty as defined by section 115 of that Act, suffer financial loss.

The Regulations prescribe, in pursuance of section 16 of the Local Government (Miscellaneous Provisions) Act 1953, the maximum amounts which may be paid to members of the bodies referred to by way of financial loss allowance for loss of earnings or additional expenses (other than travelling or subsistence) incurred in the performance of their duties as such members.

STATUTORY INSTRUMENTS

1970 No. 107 (S.3)

LOCAL GOVERNMENT, SCOTLAND

The Local Government (Travelling Allowances, etc.) (Scotland) Regulations 1970

Made - - -	*22nd January* 1970
Laid before Parliament	*4th February* 1970
Coming into Operation	*6th February* 1970

In exercise of the powers conferred on me by sections 113 and 117 as read with section 118 of the Local Government Act 1948(a), and of all other powers enabling me in that behalf, I hereby make the following regulations :—

1.—(1) These regulations may be cited as the Local Government (Travelling Allowances, etc.) (Scotland) Regulations 1970 and shall come into operation on 6th February 1970.

(2) The Local Government (Travelling Allowances, etc.) (Scotland) Regulations 1954(b), the Local Government (Travelling Allowances, etc.) (Scotland) Amendment Regulations 1954(c), 1959(d), 1965(e), and the Local Government (Travelling Allowances, etc.) (Scotland) Amendment (No. 2) Regulations 1962(f) are hereby revoked.

2.—(1) In these regulations, unless the context otherwise requires :—

"the Act" means the Local Government Act 1948 ;

"body" means any body to which Part VI of the Act applies for the time being ; and

"public service" means any service provided for travel by the public by railway, ship, vessel, omnibus, trolley vehicle or tramway.

(2) The Interpretation Act 1889(g) applies for the interpretation of these regulations as it applies for the interpretation of an Act of Parliament.

3. The rates to be determined by bodies for the payment of travelling allowances and subsistence allowances shall not exceed the maximum rates mentioned, and shall be subject to the provisions contained, in Schedules 1 and 2 to these regulations respectively.

4. Every member of a body who desires to claim any payment by way of travelling allowance and subsistence allowance shall complete and submit to that body an application in the form set out in Schedule 3 to these regulations or in a form substantially to the like effect.

(a) 1948 c. 26.
(b) S.I. 1954/265 (1954 I, p. 1159).
(c) S.I. 1954/400 (1954 I, p. 1165).
(d) S.I. 1959/1282 (1959 I, p. 1615).
(e) S.I. 1965/196 (1965 I, p. 501).
(f) S.I. 1962/1834 (1962 II, p. 2172).
(g) 1889 c. 63.

5. Every body shall, so far as is in its opinion practicable, make arrangements for the issue to its members of tickets, or of vouchers, warrants or similar documents for exchange by such members for tickets, to cover journeys in respect of which payments by way of travelling allowance would otherwise fall to be made.

6.—(1) Every body shall keep records of all payments to members made by it under Part VI of the Act, indicating the amounts paid to each member and the heads under which they were paid, and such records shall be open to inspection at all reasonable hours by any local government elector for the area of the body.

(2) For the purposes of this regulation expenditure incurred in the issue to a member of any ticket or other document under regulation 5 shall be deemed to have been paid to that member.

7.—(1) Where a person necessarily incurs expenditure on travelling or subsistence in respect of the performance by him in any one period of twenty-four hours of approved duties as a member of more than one body, he shall be entitled to receive and there shall be payable by the bodies concerned, in respect of the performance of those duties, such payments by way of travelling allowance and subsistence allowance as will, under either of those heads, be equal in the aggregate to the payment to which he would have been entitled under that head had all the said duties been performed by him as a member of one only of these bodies.

(2) Where in any one period of twenty-four hours a person becomes entitled in respect of the performance of any duties to receive payments by way of, or in the nature of, travelling allowance or subsistence allowance both under Part VI of the Act and under any other enactment, the amount which he shall be entitled to receive under either of those enactments in respect of either of the heads aforementioned shall be reduced by any amount received by him in respect of that head under the other of those enactments, and any claim for any such payment as aforesaid shall contain particulars of any amount so received.

> *William Ross,*
> One of Her Majesty's Principal
> Secretaries of State.

St. Andrew's House,
Edinburgh.

22nd January 1970.

SCHEDULE 1

Maximum Rates of Payments by way of Travelling Allowance, and Provisions Relating Thereto

1. The rate for travel by public service shall not exceed the amount of the ordinary, or any available cheap, fare, and where more than one class of fare is available the rate shall be determined, in the case of travel by ship, by reference to first class fares, and in any other case by reference to second class fares, unless the body determines, either generally or specially, that first class fares shall be substituted:

Provided that the said rate may be increased by supplementary allowances not exceeding expenditure actually incurred—

(a) on Pullman car or similar supplements, reservation of seats, and deposit or porterage of luggage, and

(b) on sleeping accommodation engaged by the member for an over-night journey, subject, however, to reduction by one-third of any subsistence allowance payable to him for that night.

2. The rate for travel by taxi-cab or cab—

(a) in cases of urgency or where no public service is reasonably available, shall not exceed the amount of the actual fare and any reasonable gratuity paid, and

(b) in any other case, shall not exceed the amount of the fare for travel by an appropriate public service.

3. The rate for travel by a member's own solo motor cycle, motor scooter, moped or any other vehicle of a similar type, not exceeding a cylinder capacity of 500 c.c., shall not exceed—

(a) for the use of a vehicle of cylinder capacity of 120 c.c. or less, 2¼d. a mile ;

(b) for the use of a vehicle of cylinder capacity from 121 c.c. to 150 c.c., 3¼d. a mile ;

(c) for the use of a vehicle of cylinder capacity from 151 c.c., to 500 c.c., 4d. a mile.

The rate for travel by a member's own vehicle shall not exceed 4d. a mile unless the vehicle used is of a category other than the above and, in the opinion of the body, it is reasonable that the member should so travel. For travel in these circumstances the rate shall not exceed—

(d) for the use of a solo motor cycle of cylinder capacity exceeding 500 c.c., a motor cycle with side-car, or a motor car or tri-car of cylinder capacity of 500 c.c. or less, 5¼d. a mile ;

(e) for the use of a motor car or tri-car of cylinder capacity of—

(i) 501 c.c. to 999 c.c., 11¼d. a mile,

(ii) 1000 c.c. to 1199 c.c., 1s. 0¼d. a mile,

(iii) Over 1199 c.c., 1s. 2¼d. a mile ;

Provided that the above rates may be increased by—

(i) not more than ¼d. a mile for the carriage of each additional person to whom an allowance for travelling would otherwise be payable, on journeys qualifying for the rates of allowances set out in sub-paragraphs (a) to (e) above ;

(ii) not more than 1d. a mile, subject to a limit of 4d. a mile for four or more passengers, for the carriage of each additional person to whom an allowance for travelling would otherwise be payable, on journeys not qualifying for the rates of allowances set out in sub-paragraphs (a) to (e) above ;

(iii) not more than the amount of any expenditure incurred on tolls, ferries or parking fees ;

(iv) in the case of absence overnight from the usual place of residence, not more than 2s. 6d. a night for garaging a car or tri-car, or 1s. 6d. a night for garaging a motor vehicle of any other type.

(f) for the purpose of this paragraph, cylinder capacity shall be calculated in the manner prescribed by regulation 46 of the Road Vehicles (Registration and Licensing) Regulations 1964(a).

(a) S.I. 1964/1178 (1964 II, p. 2722).

4. The rate for travel by a hired motor vehicle other than a taxi-cab or cab shall not exceed the rate which would have been applicable had the vehicle belonged to the member who hired it: provided that where the body so approves the rate may be increased to an amount not exceeding the actual cost of the hiring.

5. The rate for travel by air shall not exceed the rate applicable to travel by appropriate alternative means of transport together with an allowance equivalent to the amount of any saving in financial loss allowance and subsistence allowance consequent on travel by air:

Provided that, where the body resolves, either generally or specially, that the saving in time is so substantial as to justify payment of the fare for travel by air, there may be paid an amount not exceeding

(a) the ordinary, or any available cheap, fare for travel by regular air service, or

(b) where no such service is available or in case of urgency, the fare actually paid by the member.

SCHEDULE 2

MAXIMUM RATES OF PAYMENTS BY WAY OF SUBSISTENCE ALLOWANCE, AND PROVISIONS RELATING THERETO

1. For an absence, not involving an absence overnight, from the usual place of residence—

(a) of more than four hours but not more than eight hours, the rate shall not exceed 19s. ;

(b) of more than eight hours but not more than twelve hours, the rate shall not exceed 35s. ;

(c) of more than twelve hours but not more than sixteen hours, the rate shall not exceed 50s. ;

(d) of more than sixteen hours, the rate shall not exceed 59s.

2.—(1) The rate for an absence overnight from the usual place of residence shall not exceed the sum of 110s. ; provided that for such an absence in London or for the purpose of attendance at an annual conference of such associations of bodies to which Part VI of the Act applies as the Secretary of State may for the time being approve for the purpose, the rate may be increased by a supplementary allowance not exceeding 10s.

(2) The rate determined under this paragraph shall be deemed to cover a continuous period of absence of twenty-four hours.

(3) For the purposes of this paragraph London means the City of London and the London boroughs of Camden, Greenwich, Hackney, Hammersmith, Islington, Kensington and Chelsea, Lambeth, Lewisham, Southwark, Tower Hamlets, Wandsworth and Westminster.

SCHEDULE 3

FORM OF APPLICATION FOR TRAVELLING AND SUBSISTENCE ALLOWANCE

Date	Place and time of departure	Place and time of return	Description of approved duties	Mode and class of travel	No. of miles travelled by private motor vehicle, other than taxi-cab or cab, and rate applicable	Fares and other authorised payments	Travelling allowance claimed	Subsistence allowance claimed
(1)	(2)	(3)	(4)	(5)	(6)	(7)	(8)	(9)
					Totals ...	...	...	...
Particulars of amounts received or claimed by way of travelling or subsistence allowance from other authorities or bodies								
					Amounts now claimed	...		

I declare that I have actually and necessarily incurred expenditure on travelling and subsistence for the purpose of enabling me to perform approved duties as a member of................, that I have actually paid the fares and made the other payments, shown above, and that the amounts claimed are strictly in accordance with the rates determined by...................

I declare that the statements above are correct. Except as shown above I have not made, and will not make, any claim under any enactment for travelling or subsistence expenses or allowances in connection with the duties indicated above.

Date................   Signature of Member..................

EXPLANATORY NOTE

(This Note is not part of the Regulations.)

These Regulations replace the provisions of the Local Government (Travelling Allowances, etc.) (Scotland) Regulations which relate to the maximum rates of allowances payable by bodies specified in Part VI of the Local Government Act 1948 to their members who, in the performance of approved duty as defined by section 115 of that Act, incur expenditure on travel by public transport or private vehicle or by way of subsistence expenses.

New maximum rates are prescribed for day and night subsistence allowances for travel by public transport and for mileage allowances for travel by private motor vehicles.

STATUTORY INSTRUMENTS

1970 No. 108 (S.4)

FOOD AND DRUGS

COMPOSITION AND LABELLING

The Cheese (Scotland) Regulations 1970

Made - - -	*28th January* 1970
Laid before Parliament	*30th January* 1970
Coming into Operation	*31st January* 1970

In exercise of the powers conferred upon me by sections 4, 7 and 56 of the Food and Drugs (Scotland) Act 1956(a), and of all other powers enabling me in that behalf, and after consultation with such organisations as appear to me to be representative of interests substantially affected by these regulations and after reference to the Scottish Food Hygiene Council under section 25 of the said Act (in so far as the regulations are made in exercise of the powers conferred by the said section 7), I hereby make the following regulations :—

PART I

PRELIMINARY

Citation and commencement

1. These regulations may be cited as the Cheese (Scotland) Regulations 1970, and shall come into operation on 31st January 1970.

Interpretation

2.—(1) In these regulations, unless the context otherwise requires—

"the Act" means the Food and Drugs (Scotland) Act 1956 ;

"cheese" means the fresh or matured product intended for sale for human consumption, which is obtained as follows—

(*a*) in the case of any cheese other than whey cheese—

    (i) by coagulating any or a combination of any of the following substances, namely milk, cream, skimmed milk, partly skimmed milk, concentrated skimmed milk, reconstituted dried milk and butter milk, and

    (ii) partially draining the whey resulting from any such coagulation ;

(*b*) in the case of whey cheese—

    (i) by concentrating whey with or without the addition of milk and milk fat, and moulding such concentrated whey, or

    (ii) by coagulating whey with or without the addition of milk and milk fat ;

(a) 1956 c. 30.

"cheese spread" means cheese which has been subjected to a process of melting and mixing with milk products other than cheese, with or without the addition of emulsifying salts ;

"compound product" means food which consists of a combination of two or more foods and which does not contain less than 10 per cent. cheese, processed cheese or cheese spread or any mixture of two or more of them, as a percentage of the compound product, but does not include any pie, pudding, cake, confectionery, biscuit, Welsh rarebit or any product similar to Welsh rarebit ;

"container" includes any form of packaging of food for sale as a single item, whether by way of wholly or partly enclosing the food or by way of attaching the food to some other article, and in particular includes a wrapper or confining band ;

"emulsifying salts" means the sodium, potassium, calcium or ammonium salts of citric, phosphoric, polyphosphoric and tartaric acid ;

"food" means food intended for sale for human consumption and includes drink, chewing gum and other products of a like nature and use, and articles and substances used as ingredients in the preparation of food or drink or of such products, but does not include—

(a) water, live animals or birds,

(b) fodder or feeding stuffs for animals, birds or fish, or

(c) articles or substances used only as drugs ;

"hard cheese" means cheese other than soft cheese, whey cheese, processed cheese or cheese spread ;

"human consumption" includes use in the preparation of food for human consumption ;

"processed cheese" means cheese which has been subjected to a process of melting and mixing with or without the addition of emulsifying salts ;

"sell" includes offer or expose for sale or have in possession for sale, and "sale" and "sold" shall be construed accordingly ;

"sell by retail" means sell to a person buying otherwise than for the purpose of re-sale, but does not include selling to a caterer for the purposes of his catering business, or selling to a manufacturer for the purposes of his manufacturing business ;

"soft cheese" means cheese which is readily deformed by moderate pressure, but does not include whey cheese, processed cheese or cheese spread, and any reference to soft cheese includes a reference to cream cheese or curd cheese ;

"starter" means a living culture in milk, cream, skimmed milk, partly skimmed milk, concentrated skimmed milk, reconstituted dried milk, or butter milk, of lactic-acid-producing bacteria ;

"whey cheese" means the product obtained by one or other of the processes referred to in paragraph (b) of the foregoing definition of "cheese" ;

and other expressions have the same meaning as in the Act.

(2) The Interpretation Act 1889(a) shall apply for the interpretation of these regulations as it applies for the interpretation of an Act of Parliament.

(3) All percentages mentioned in these regulations are percentages calculated by weight, and unless a contrary intention is expressed, are calculated on the total weight of the cheese.

(a) 1889 c. 63.

(4) Any reference in these regulations to a label borne on a container shall be construed as including a reference to any legible marking on the container however effected.

(5) For the purpose of these regulations, the supply of food, otherwise than by sale, at, in or from any place where food is supplied in the course of a business, shall be deemed to be a sale of that food, and references to purchasing and purchasers shall be construed accordingly.

(6) Any reference in these regulations to any other regulations shall be construed as a reference to such regulations as amended by any subsequent regulations.

(7) Any reference in these regulations to a numbered regulation shall, unless the reference is to a regulation of specified regulations, be construed as a reference to the regulation bearing that number in these regulations.

Exemptions

3. The following provisions of these regulations shall not apply, except in so far as they relate to advertisements other than labels or wrappers, in relation to any cheese, processed cheese, cheese spread or compound product sold, consigned or delivered for—

(*a*) exportation to any place outside the United Kingdom ; or

(*b*) consumption by a visiting force within the meaning of any of the provisions of Part I of the Visiting Forces Act 1952(**a**) ; or

(*c*) use by a manufacturer for the purposes of his manufacturing business.

PART II

COMPOSITION AND DESCRIPTION OF CHEESE, PROCESSED CHEESE AND CHEESE SPREAD

Composition and description of hard cheese

4.—(1) Any hard cheese sold, consigned or delivered under the name of a variety specified in column 1 of Schedule 1 to these regulations, whether or not such cheese was manufactured in the United Kingdom, shall comply with the percentages for milk fat and water set out respectively in columns 2 and 3 of the said Schedule opposite the name of such cheese.

(2) Any hard cheese sold, consigned or delivered, other than hard cheese to which the foregoing paragraph of this regulation applies, shall satisfy either the requirements of sub-paragraph (*a*) or the requirements of sub-paragraph (*b*) following, except that the appropriate description or declaration need be borne by any hard cheese sold, consigned or delivered otherwise than in a container only when such cheese is sold by retail—

(*a*) such cheese shall bear one of the following descriptions and comply with the following compositional requirements for cheese of such description, namely—

    (i) "full fat hard cheese", if the cheese contains not less than 48 per cent. milk fat in the dry matter and not more than 48 per cent. water ;

    (ii) "medium fat hard cheese", if the cheese contains less than 48 per cent. and not less than 10 per cent. milk fat in the dry matter, and not more than 48 per cent. water ;

   (iii) "skimmed milk hard cheese", if the cheese contains less than 10 per cent. milk fat in the dry matter, and not more than 48 per cent. water ; or

 (b) such cheese shall bear a true declaration of either—

   (i) the minimum percentage milk fat content in the dry matter, and the maximum percentage water content, or

   (ii) the minimum percentage milk fat content,

so however that as respects any sale, consignment or delivery on or after 1st January 1973 of any hard cheese bearing such a declaration, that declaration shall be in such of the following forms as is appropriate :—

   (aa) "x% fat in dry matter" and "y% moisture", and the declaration shall be completed by inserting at "x" and "y" respectively the percentages described in sub-paragraph (b)(i) of this paragraph ;

   (ab) "x% fat", and the declaration shall be completed by inserting at "x" the percentage described in sub-paragraph (b)(ii) of this paragraph.

(3) No person shall sell, consign or deliver, as the case may be, any hard cheese in contravention of this regulation.

Composition and description of soft cheese

5.—(1) Any soft cheese sold, consigned or delivered under the name of a variety specified in column 1 of Schedule 1 to these regulations whether or not such cheese was manufactured in the United Kingdom, shall comply with the percentages for milk fat and water set out respectively in columns 2 and 3 of the said Schedule opposite the name of such cheese.

(2) Any soft cheese sold, consigned or delivered, other than soft cheese to which the foregoing paragraph of this regulation applies and other than cheese which bears one of the descriptions specified in paragraph (3) of this regulation and complies with the compositional requirements so specified in relation to that description, shall bear one of the following descriptions, and comply with the following compositional requirements for cheese of such description except that the appropriate description need be borne by any soft cheese sold, consigned or delivered otherwise than in a container only when such cheese is sold by retail—

   (a) "full fat soft cheese", if the cheese contains not less than 20 per cent. milk fat, and not more than 60 per cent. water ;

   (b) "medium fat soft cheese", if the cheese contains less than 20 per cent. but not less than 10 per cent. milk fat, and not more than 70 per cent. water ;

   (c) "low fat soft cheese", if the cheese contains less than 10 per cent. but not less than 2 per cent. milk fat, and not more than 80 per cent. water ;

   (d) "skimmed milk soft cheese", if the cheese contains less than 2 per cent. milk fat, and not more than 80 per cent. water.

(3) Any soft cheese sold, consigned or delivered, as "cream cheese" shall contain not less than 45 per cent. milk fat, and bear the description "cream cheese" :

Provided that if such cheese contains not less than 65 per cent. milk fat, it may bear the description "double cream cheese".

(4) No person shall sell, consign or deliver, as the case may be, any soft cheese in contravention of this regulation.

Composition and description of whey cheese

6.—(1) Any whey cheese sold, consigned or delivered shall bear one of the following descriptions and comply with the following compositional requirements for cheese of such description, except that the appropriate description need be borne by any whey cheese sold, consigned or delivered otherwise than in a container only when such cheese is sold by retail—

(a) "full fat whey cheese", if the cheese contains not less than 33 per cent. milk fat in the dry matter;

(b) "whey cheese", if the cheese contains less than 33 per cent. and not less than 10 per cent. milk fat in the dry matter;

(c) "skimmed whey cheese", if the cheese contains less than 10 per cent. milk fat in the dry matter.

(2) No person shall sell, consign or deliver, as the case may be, any whey cheese in contravention of this regulation.

Composition and description of processed cheese

7.—(1) Any processed cheese sold, consigned or delivered under a description containing the word "processed" with the name of a variety of cheese specified in column 1 of Schedule 1 to these regulations, whether or not such processed cheese was manufactured in the United Kingdom, shall either—

(a) comply with the percentages for milk fat and water set out respectively in columns 2 and 3 of the said Schedule opposite the name of such cheese, except that processed Cheddar cheese shall contain not less than 48 per cent. milk fat in the dry matter, and not more than 43 per cent. water; or

(b) comply with the provisions of paragraph (2) of this regulation.

(2) Any processed cheese sold, consigned or delivered, other than any processed cheese to which the foregoing paragraph of this regulation applies, shall satisfy either the requirements of sub-paragraph (a) or the requirements of sub-paragraph (b) following, except that the appropriate description or declaration need be borne by any processed cheese sold, consigned or delivered otherwise than in a container only when such processed cheese is sold by retail—

(a) such processed cheese shall bear one of the following descriptions, and comply with the following compositional requirements for processed cheese of such description, namely—

(i) "full fat processed cheese", if the processed cheese contains not less than 48 per cent. milk fat in the dry matter, and not more than 48 per cent. water;

(ii) "medium fat processed cheese", if the processed cheese contains less than 48 per cent. and not less than 10 per cent. milk fat in the dry matter, and not more than 48 per cent. water;

(iii) "skimmed milk processed cheese", if the processed cheese contains less than 10 per cent. milk fat in the dry matter, and not more than 48 per cent. water; or

(b) such processed cheese shall bear a true declaration of either—

(i) the minimum percentage milk fat content in the dry matter and the maximum percentage water content, or

(ii) the minimum percentage milk fat content,

so however that as respects any sale, consignment or delivery on or after 1st January 1973 of any processed cheese bearing such a declaration, that declaration shall be in such of the following forms as is appropriate:—

(*aa*) "x % fat in dry matter" and "y % moisture", and the declaration shall be completed by inserting at "x" and "y" respectively the percentages described in sub-paragraph (*b*)(i) of this paragraph;

(*ab*) "x % fat", and the declaration shall be completed by inserting at "x" the percentage described in sub-paragraph (*b*)(ii) of this paragraph.

(3) Any processed cheese sold, consigned or delivered which is a mixture of cheese of two or more varieties shall either conform to one of the compositional requirements of paragraph (2)(*a*) of this regulation and bear the appropriate description specified therein for such processed cheese or bear one of the declarations specified in paragraph (2)(*b*) of this regulation.

(4) The name of a variety of cheese, used in the preparation of a processed cheese, may be inserted between the words "processed" and "cheese" in the appropriate description required by paragraphs (2)(*a*) and (3) of this regulation.

(5) No person shall sell, consign or deliver, as the case may be, any processed cheese in contravention of this regulation.

Composition and description of cheese spread

8.—(1) Any cheese spread sold, consigned or delivered shall contain not less than 20 per cent. milk fat and not more than 60 per cent. water; and shall bear the description "cheese spread" or "cheese food", with or without the name of the variety or description of cheese used as a constituent of such cheese spread inserted immediately before the words "cheese spread" or "cheese food", except that such description need be borne by cheese spread sold, consigned or delivered otherwise than in a container only when such cheese spread is sold by retail.

(2) No person shall sell, consign or deliver, as the case may be, any cheese spread in contravention of this regulation.

Compound products

9.—(1) Any cheese, processed cheese or cheese spread for which compositional requirements are specified in these regulations and which is used as an ingredient of a compound product, shall comply with the compositional requirements so specified for such cheese, processed cheese or cheese spread.

(2) No person shall sell, consign or deliver, as the case may be, any compound product in contravention of this regulation.

General requirements as to composition and description

10.—(1) No person shall sell any food under such a description as to lead an intending purchaser to believe that he is purchasing any cheese, processed cheese, cheese spread or compound product respectively for which compositional requirements are specified in these regulations if the food does not comply with the appropriate requirements as to composition set out in these regulations in relation to that cheese, processed cheese, cheese spread or compound product.

(2) Where a person sells any food to a purchaser in response to a request for any kind of cheese, processed cheese, cheese spread or compound product for which compositional requirements are specified in these regulations, he shall be deemed to sell cheese, processed cheese, cheese spread or a compound product of that kind and under such a description as is specified in these regulations in relation to that kind of cheese, processed cheese, cheese spread or compound product unless he clearly notifies the purchaser at the time of sale that the cheese, processed cheese, cheese spread or compound product is not of that kind.

Permitted ingredients in cheese, processed cheese and cheese spread

11. No person shall sell, consign or deliver any cheese, processed cheese or cheese spread which contains any ingredient other than the substances mentioned in the definition of "cheese", "processed cheese" or "cheese spread" as the case may be, in regulation 2(1), water, such preservatives in such amounts as are permitted by the Preservatives in Food (Scotland) Regulations 1962**(a)**, any mould characteristic of the variety of cheese concerned and any or all of the following ingredients where appropriate in relation to the kind of cheese specified, namely:—

(*a*) Hard cheese may contain common salt (sodium chloride), calcium chloride, calcium hydroxide, starter, rennet, carotene and annatto;

(*b*) The rind of hard cheese may contain any colouring matter permitted by the Colouring Matter in Food (Scotland) Regulations 1966**(b)**;

(*c*) Soft cheese and whey cheese may contain the ingredients mentioned in paragraph (*a*) of this regulation, alginic acid, calcium alginate, sodium alginate, carrageen, edible gums, edible starches (whether modified or not), flavourings and lecithin;

(*d*) Processed cheese and cheese spread may contain—
  (i) the ingredients mentioned or referred to in paragraph (*c*) of this regulation;
  (ii) emulsifying salts;
  (iii) any colouring matter permitted by paragraphs 1 to 4 of Part III of Schedule 1 to the Colouring Matter in Food (Scotland) Regulations 1966; and
  (iv) lactic acid and citric acid;

(*e*) Hard sage cheese may contain—
  (i) the ingredients mentioned in paragraph (*a*) of this regulation;
  (ii) sage; and
  (iii) any green colouring matter permitted by paragraph 3 of Part III of Schedule 1 to the Colouring Matter in Food (Scotland) Regulations 1966;

(*f*) Soft sage cheese may contain—
  (i) the ingredients mentioned or referred to in paragraph (*c*) of this regulation;
  (ii) sage; and
  (iii) any green colouring matter mentioned or referred to in paragraph 3 of Part III of Schedule 1 to the Colouring Matter in Food (Scotland) Regulations 1966;

(*g*) Sage cheese spread may contain the ingredients mentioned or referred to in paragraph (*d*) of this regulation and sage.

(a) S.I. 1962/1926 (1962 II, p. 2371).   **(b)** S.I. 1966/1384 (1966 III, p.3715).

Part III

Labelling and Advertisement

Labelling and advertisement of cheese, processed cheese, cheese spread and compound products

12.—(1) No person shall sell, consign or deliver any cheese, processed cheese or cheese spread in a container unless such container bears a label on which there appears the appropriate description or declaration specified in regulation 4, 5, 6, 7 or 8 for such cheese, processed cheese or cheese spread:

Provided that in the case of hard cheese, soft cheese or processed cheese which complies with regulation 4(1), 5(1) or 7(1) as the case may be, the label may bear instead of such description or declaration—

(*a*) in the case of hard cheese or soft cheese, the name of the variety of such cheese, or

(*b*) in the case of processed cheese, the word "processed" with the name of the variety of such processed cheese.

(2) No person shall sell by retail any cheese, processed cheese or cheese spread otherwise than in a container unless there appears on a ticket placed on or in immediate proximity to such cheese, processed cheese or cheese spread so as to be clearly visible to an intending purchaser, the appropriate description or declaration specified in regulation 4, 5, 6, 7 or 8 for such cheese, processed cheese or cheese spread:

Provided that in the case of hard cheese, soft cheese or processed cheese which complies with regulation 4(1), 5(1) or 7(1), as the case may be, the ticket may bear instead of such description or declaration—

(*a*) in the case of hard cheese or soft cheese, the name of the variety of such cheese, or

(*b*) in the case of processed cheese, the word "processed" with the name of the variety of such processed cheese.

(3) No person shall sell, consign or deliver any compound product in a container unless such container bears a label on which there appears as part of the description of such product the appropriate description or declaration specified in regulation 4, 5, 6, 7 or 8 for the cheese, processed cheese or cheese spread present in such compound product together with a true description of any other food, except an ingredient permitted by regulation 11, present in such compound product:

Provided that in the case of any hard cheese, soft cheese or processed cheese which complies with regulation 4(1), 5(1) or 7(1), as the case may be, the label may bear instead of such description or declaration—

(*a*) in the case of hard cheese or soft cheese, the name of the variety of such cheese, or

(*b*) in the case of processed cheese, the word "processed" with the name of the variety of such processed cheese.

(4) No person shall sell by retail any compound product otherwise than in a container unless there appears on a ticket placed on or in immediate proximity to such compound product so as to be clearly visible to an intending purchaser as the description of such compound product, the appropriate description or declaration specified in regulation 4, 5, 6, 7 or 8 for the cheese, processed cheese or cheese spread present in such compound product together with a true des-

cription of any other food, except an ingredient permitted by regulation 11, present in such compound product:

Provided that in the case of hard cheese, soft cheese or processed cheese which complies with regulation 4(1), 5(1) or 7(1), as the case may be, the ticket may bear instead of such description or declaration—

    (a) in the case of hard cheese or soft cheese, the name of the variety of such cheese, or

    (b) in the case of processed cheese, the word "processed" with the name of the variety of such processed cheese.

(5) Notwithstanding the provisions of regulations 4, 5, 6, 7 and 8 and the preceding paragraphs of this regulation, the appropriate description of any cheese, processed cheese or cheese spread may include, if penicillium moulds have produced blue-green veining in such cheese, processed cheese or cheese spread the word "blue-veined", or if such cheese, processed cheese or cheese spread contains sage, the word "sage".

13.—(1) Any advertisement for cheese, processed cheese or cheese spread shall include such one of the descriptions specified in regulation 4, 5, 6, 7 or 8 or such one of the declarations specified in regulation 4 or 7, as the case may be, as is appropriate to that cheese, processed cheese or cheese spread:

Provided that in the case of hard cheese, soft cheese or processed cheese which complies with regulation 4(1), 5(1) or 7(1), as the case may be, the advertisement may include instead of such description or declaration—

    (a) in the case of hard cheese or soft cheese, the name of the variety of such cheese, or

    (b) in the case of processed cheese, the word "processed" with the name of the variety of such processed cheese.

(2) Any cheese, processed cheese or cheese spread which is the subject of any description contained in any advertisement in accordance with the foregoing paragraph of this regulation shall comply with the compositional requirements specified in regulation 4, 5, 6, 7 or 8 for cheese, processed cheese or cheese spread of such description.

(3) Any advertisement for any compound product shall include the description of such compound product specified in regulation 12(3) and (4) and the compound product so described shall comply with the compositional requirements specified in regulation 9.

(4) Notwithstanding the provisions of regulations 4, 5, 6, 7 and 8 and paragraph (1) of this regulation, the description of any cheese, processed cheese or cheese spread may include, if penicillium moulds have produced blue-green veining in such cheese, processed cheese or cheese spread the word "blue-veined", or if such cheese, processed cheese or cheese spread contains sage, the word "sage".

(5) No person shall publish or be a party to the publication of any advertisement which does not comply with this regulation.

Requirements as to marking on labels on containers and on tickets

14.—(1) As respects any sale, consignment or delivery on or before 31st December 1972, all letters, words or numerals required by virtue of regulation 12 to appear on a label on a container or on a ticket respectively shall conform to the requirements set out in paragraph 1 of Schedule 2 to these regulations.

(2) As respects any sale, consignment or delivery on or after 1st January 1973, all letters, words or numerals required by virtue of regulation 12 to appear on a label on a container or on a ticket respectively shall conform to the requirements set out in paragraph 2 of the said Schedule 2.

Labelling and advertisement of cream cheese

15. No person shall—

(*a*) give with any cheese sold by him, or display with any cheese offered or exposed by him for sale any label, whether attached to or printed on the container or not, which bears any words or pictorial device, or

(*b*) publish, or be a party to the publication of, any advertisement for cheese which includes any words or pictorial device, or

(*c*) use on, or in connection with, the sale of cheese any description, being words, a device or a description which are or is calculated to indicate either directly or indirectly that such cheese contains cream or is made from cream, unless such cheese complies with the compositional requirement for cream cheese which is specified in regulation 5(3).

PART IV

ADMINISTRATION AND GENERAL

Enforcement

16.—(1) The local authority of any area shall, subject to the provisions of the next following paragraph, enforce and execute the provisions of these regulations within their area.

(2) Where any part of the area of a local authority lies within the area of a port local authority such of the functions of the local authority under these regulations in relation to any food imported into that part shall, in so far as these functions fall to be exercised by the port local authority by virtue of any order made under section 172 of the Public Health (Scotland) Act 1897**(a)**, be exercised by that port local authority.

(3) In this regulation "local authority" means the council of a county or of a large burgh within the meaning of the Local Government (Scotland) Act 1947**(b)**; and any small burgh within the meaning of that Act shall, for the purposes of these regulations, be included in the county in which it is situated; and "port local authority" includes a joint port local authority.

Penalties

17.—(1) If any person contravenes or fails to comply with any of the foregoing provisions of these regulations he shall be guilty of an offence under these regulations.

(2) Any person who is guilty of an offence under these regulations shall be liable—

(*a*) on summary conviction to—

(i) a fine not exceeding £100 or to imprisonment for a term not exceeding 6 months or to both such fine and imprisonment; and

---

(a) 1897 c. 38. (b) 1947 c. 43.

(ii) in the case of a continuing offence, to a further fine not exceeding £10 for every day during which the offence is continued; or

(b) on conviction on indictment to—

(i) a fine not exceeding £500 or to imprisonment for a term not exceeding one year or to both such fine and imprisonment; and

(ii) in the case of a continuing offence, to a further fine not exceeding £50 for every day during which the offence is continued.

Defences

18.—(1) In any proceedings for an offence against these regulations in relation to the publication of an advertisement, it shall be a defence for the accused to prove that, being a person whose business it is to publish or arrange for the publication of advertisements, he received the advertisement for publication in the ordinary course of business and did not himself make, or cause to be made, any material alteration in the substance of that advertisement.

(2) In any proceedings against the manufacturer or importer of cheese, processed cheese, cheese spread or of any compound product for an offence against these regulations in relation to the publication of an advertisement, it shall rest on the accused to prove that he did not publish, and was not a party to the publication of, the advertisement.

Application of various sections of the Act

19.—(1) Sections 41(2) and (5) (which relates to proceedings), 42(1), (2) and (3) (which relates to evidence of certificates of analysis), 44 (which relates to the power of a court to require analysis by the Government Chemist), 46(2) (which relates to the conditions under which a warranty may be pleaded as a defence) and 47 (which relates to offences in relation to warranties and certificates of analysis) of the Act shall apply for the purposes of these regulations as if references therein to proceedings, or a prosecution, under or taken under the Act included references to proceedings, or a prosecution as the case may be, taken for an offence against these regulations and in addition as if—

(a) in the case of section 44(1) of the Act, the reference therein to section 41(5) of the Act included a reference to said section 41(5) as applied by these regulations; and

(b) in the case of section 47(1) and (2) of the Act, the references therein to an offence against the Act included references to an offence against these regulations.

(2) Section 41(4) of the Act shall apply for the purposes of these regulations as if the reference therein to section 47 of the Act included a reference to said section 47 as applied by these regulations.

Revocation

20.—(1) The Cheese (Scotland) Regulations 1966(a) and the Cheese (Scotland) (Amendment) Regulations 1967(b) are hereby revoked.

(2) Section 38 of the Interpretation Act 1889 shall apply as if these regulations

---

(a) S.I. 1966/98 (1966 I, p. 210). (b) S.I. 1967/93 (1967 I, p. 196).

were an Act of Parliament and as if the regulations revoked by these regulations were Acts of Parliament repealed by an Act of Parliament.

William Ross,
One of Her Majesty's Principal
Secretaries of State.

St. Andrew's House,
Edinburgh.
28th January 1970.

Regulations 4, 5 and 7   SCHEDULE 1

Column 1	Column 2	Column 3
Variety of Cheese	Minimum Percentage of Milk Fat in the Dry Matter	Maximum Percentage of Water Calculated on the total Weight of the Cheese
Cheddar	48	39
Blue Stilton	48	42
Derby	48	42
Leicester	48	42
Cheshire	48	44
Dunlop	48	44
Gloucester	48	44
Double Gloucester	48	44
Caerphilly	48	46
Wensleydale	48	46
White Stilton	48	46
Lancashire	48	48
Edam	40	46
Loaf Edam	40	46
Baby Edam	40	47
Baby Loaf Edam	40	47
Gouda	48	43
Baby Gouda	48	45
Danablu	50	47
Danbo	45	46
Havarti	45	50
Samsoe	45	44
Emmental or Emmentaler	45	40
Gruyère or Greyerzer or Gruviera	45	38

Column 1	Column 2	Column 3
Variety of Cheese	Minimum Percentage of Milk Fat in the Dry Matter	Maximum Percentage of Water Calculated on the total Weight of the Cheese
Tilsiter or Tilsit or Tylzycki	45	47
Limburger	50	50
Saint Paulin	40	56
Svecia	45	41
Provolone	45	47

Regulation 14   SCHEDULE 2

REQUIREMENTS AS TO MARKING ON LABELS
ON CONTAINERS AND ON TICKETS

1. As respects any sale, consignment or delivery on or before 31st December 1972, every letter, word or numeral appearing on a label on a container, or on a ticket, which is required so to appear by virtue of regulation 12 shall—

(*a*) be clearly legible;

(*b*) appear in a prominent position on the label or ticket;

(*c*) be printed in a dark colour upon a light-coloured ground or in a light colour upon a dark-coloured ground;

(*d*) be of uniform colour and size, except that the initial letter in any such word may be larger than the other letters in that word:

Provided that the requirements of this sub-paragraph shall not have effect in relation to the sale, consignment or delivery, as the case may be, of any compound product.

2. As respects any sale, consignment or delivery on or after 1st January 1973—

(*a*) every letter, word or numeral appearing on a label on a container, or on a ticket, which is required so to appear by virtue of regulation 12 shall be in characters of uniform colour and size, save that the initial letter of any word may be taller than any other letter in that word:

Provided that, in the case of a compound product this requirement shall apply only in respect of such letters, words or numerals as describe the cheese, processed cheese or cheese spread, as the case may be, present in such compound product;

(*b*) any declaration required by regulation 4(2)(*b*) or 7(2)(*b*) shall be so situated as to be in immediate proximity to and simultaneously visible together with the name of the cheese, processed cheese or cheese spread to an intending purchaser under normal conditions of purchase and use.

EXPLANATORY NOTE

(This Note is not part of the Regulations.)

These Regulations, which apply to Scotland only, re-enact with amendments the Cheese (Scotland) Regulations 1966, as amended, and come into operation on 31st January 1970.

The Regulations—

(a) specify requirements for the composition and description of cheese including hard cheese, soft cheese (including cream cheese), whey cheese, processed cheese and cheese spread (Regulations 4, 5, 6, 7, 8 and Schedule 1) amended to prescribe compositional standards for additional varieties of cheese or processed cheese sold under varietal names (Regulations 4, 5, 7 and Schedule 1);

(b) apply compositional requirements for cheese, processed cheese or cheese spread sold as part of a compound product (Regulation 9);

(c) specify the permitted ingredients in cheese, processed cheese and cheese spread, amended to include calcium hydroxide as a permitted ingredient (Regulation 11);

(d) specify requirements for the labelling and advertisement of cheese, processed cheese, cheese spread and compound products (Regulations 12, 13, 14 and 15);

(e) provide for certain amendments to the requirements for the labelling of cheese, processed cheese, cheese spread and compound products to take effect on and after 1st January 1973 (Regulations 4, 7, 14(2) and Schedule 2, paragraph 2).

The Regulations do not apply, except in so far as they relate to advertisements, to cheese, processed cheese, cheese spread and compound products intended for export, for consumption by a visiting force or for use for manufacturing purposes (Regulation 3).

STATUTORY INSTRUMENTS

1970 No. 109

BUILDING AND BUILDINGS

The Building (Fifth Amendment) Regulations 1970

Made - - - -	*28th January* 1970
Laid before Parliament	*5th February* 1970
Coming into Operation	*1st April* 1970

The Minister of Housing and Local Government, in exercise of the powers conferred on him under sections 61 and 62 of the Public Health Act 1936(**a**), as amended by section 11 of and Part III of Schedule 1 to the Public Health Act 1961(**b**) and section 4 of the Public Health Act 1961, and as read with the Transfer of Functions (Building Control) Order 1964(**c**) and the Transfer of Functions (Building Control and Historic Buildings) Order 1966(**d**), and of all other powers enabling him in that behalf, after consultation with the Building Regulations Advisory Committee and such other bodies as appear to him to be representative of the interests concerned, hereby makes the following regulations:—

Citation and Commencement

1. These regulations may be cited as the Building (Fifth Amendment) Regulations 1970 and shall come into operation on 1st April 1970.

Interpretation

2. The Interpretation Act 1889(**e**) shall apply for the interpretation of these regulations as it applies for the interpretation of an Act of Parliament.

Transitional Provisions

3. These regulations shall not apply to any work which was—

(*a*) completed before the date of the coming into operation of these regulations ; or

(*b*) completed after that date in accordance with plans deposited with the local authority before that date, with or without any departure or deviation from those plans ;

and for the purpose of this regulation " work " means the erection of a building, the alteration or extension of a building, the execution of any works or the installation of any fittings.

(**a**) 1936 c. 49.   (**b**) 1961 c. 64.   (**c**) S.I. 1964/263 (1964 I, p. 457).
(**d**) S.I. 1966/692 (1966 II, p. 1558).   (**e**) 1889 c. 63.

Amendment of Building Regulations 1965

4. The Building Regulations 1965(**a**), as amended(**b**), shall be further amended as follows—

(*a*) in regulation D2 there shall be substituted for the word " In " the words " Subject to the provisions of regulation D19, in " ; and

(*b*) after regulation D18 (as inserted in the Building Regulations 1965 by regulation 10 of the Building (Third Amendment) Regulations 1967) there shall be inserted the following:—

" Further requirements for the structure of certain buildings

D19.—(1) In addition to the requirements of regulation D8, the provisions of this regulation shall apply to a building having five or more storeys (including basement storeys, if any).

(2) In this regulation—

" portion ", in relation to a structural member, means that part of a member which is situated or spans between adjacent supports or between a support and the extremity of a member:

Provided that, in the case of a wall, a portion shall be taken to have a length which is the lesser of the following, namely. the length determined in accordance with the preceding provisions of this definition or 2.25 times the height of the portion (or, if its height varies, its greatest height) ;

" storey " means that part of a building which is situated between either—

(*a*) the top surfaces of two vertically adjacent floors of the building ; or

(*b*) the top surface of the uppermost floor and the roof covering of the building ;

" structural failure " means the failure of a structural member fully to perform its function in contributing to the structural stability of the building of which it forms part ;

" structural member " means a member essential to the structural stability of a building.

(3) In the application of this regulation—

(*a*) dead load shall be determined in accordance with the provisions of regulation D2(*a*) ;

(*b*) imposed load other than wind load shall be determined in accordance with the provisions of regulation D2(*a*) except that—

(i) paragraphs (1) and (3) of rule 3 of Schedule 5 shall have effect as if the Table to that rule permitted a reduction of not more than $66\frac{2}{3}$ per cent. irrespective of the number of floors supported ; and

(ii) for the purposes of paragraph (5) of this regulation, the maximum reductions permitted by rule 3 of Schedule 5 as modified by the preceding sub-paragraph shall be made ;

(*c*) wind load may be taken as not less than one third of the load determined in accordance with the provisions of regulation D2(*b*) ; and

---

(**a**) S.I. 1965/1373 (1965 II, p, 3890).
(**b**) S.I. 1966/1144, 1967/1645, 1969/639 (1966 III, p. 2750; 1967 III, p. 4494; 1969 II, p. 1762).

(*d*) the load which would cause structural collapse shall exceed the combined dead load and imposed load on the structure together with, for the purposes of paragraph (5) of this regulation, the loads specified in sub-paragraphs (*b*) and (*c*) of that paragraph, by at least 5 per cent.

(4) A building to which the provisions of this regulation apply shall be so constructed that if any portion of any one structural member (other than a portion which satisfies the conditions specified in paragraph (5) of this regulation) were to be removed—

(*a*) structural failure consequent on that removal would not occur within any storey other than the storey of which that portion forms part, the storey next above (if any) and the storey next below (if any) ; and

(*b*) any structural failure would be localised within each such storey.

(5) The conditions referred to in paragraph (4) of this regulation are that the portion should be capable of sustaining without structural failure the following loads applied simultaneously—

(*a*) the combined dead load and imposed load ;

(*b*) a load of 5 pounds per square inch applied to that portion from any direction ; and

(*c*) the load, if any, which would be directly transmitted to that portion by any immediately adjacent part of the building if that part were subjected to a load of 5 pounds per square inch applied in the same direction as the load specified in sub-paragraph (*b*).

Deemed-to-satisfy provision for localisation of structural failure

D20.—(*1*) *In this regulation "storey" and "structural failure" shall have the same respective meanings as in regulation D19(2).*

(2) *The requirements of regulation D19(4)(b) shall be deemed to be satisfied if the area within which structural failure would occur would not exceed 750 square feet or 15 per cent. of the area of the storey, measured in the horizontal plane, whichever is the less.".*

Given under the official seal of the Minister of Housing and Local Government on 28th January 1970.

(L.S.)   *Anthony Greenwood,*
                           Minister of Housing and Local Government.

EXPLANATORY NOTE

(This Note is not part of the Regulations.)

These Regulations amend the Building Regulations 1965 by imposing additional requirements as to the structural stability of buildings of five or more storeys (including any basement). Buildings must be constructed so that if any portion of any one essential structural member (other than a portion which satisfies certain specific conditions as to load) were to be removed, the consequent structural failure would be limited as specified in the Regulations. The Regulations also add a deemed-to-satisfy provision in relation to the same matters.

The Regulations come into force on 1st April 1970, but do not apply to work which has been completed or for which plans have been deposited with local authorities before that date.

STATUTORY INSTRUMENTS

1970 No. 110

WAGES COUNCILS

The Wages Regulation (Unlicensed Place of Refreshment) Order 1970

Made - - -	*28th January* 1970
Coming into Operation	*30th March* 1970

Whereas the Secretary of State has received from the Unlicensed Place of Refreshment Wages Council the wages regulation proposals set out in the Schedule hereto ;

Now, therefore, the Secretary of State in exercise of her powers under section 11 of the Wages Councils Act 1959(a), and of all other powers enabling her in that behalf, hereby makes the following Order :—

1. This Order may be cited as the Wages Regulation (Unlicensed Place of Refreshment) Order 1970.

2.—(1) In this Order the expression "the specified date" means the 30th March 1970, provided that where, as respects any worker who is paid wages at intervals not exceeding seven days, that date does not correspond with the beginning of the period for which the wages are paid, the expression "the specified date" means, as respects that worker, the beginning of the next such period following that date.

(2) The Interpretation Act 1889(b) shall apply to the interpretation of this Order as it applies to the interpretation of an Act of Parliament and as if this Order and the Order hereby revoked were Acts of Parliament.

3. The wages regulation proposals set out in the Schedule hereto shall have effect as from the specified date and as from that date the Wages Regulation (Unlicensed Place of Refreshment) Order 1967(c) shall cease to have effect.

Signed by order of the Secretary of State.

A. A. Jarratt,

Deputy Under Secretary of State,

Department of Employment and Productivity.

28th January 1970.

(a) 1959 c. 69.
(b) 1889 c. 63.
(c) S.I. 1967/1528 (1967 III, p. 4251).

ARRANGEMENT OF SCHEDULE
PART I—REMUNERATION FOR EMPLOYMENT

PART II—ANNUAL HOLIDAY AND HOLIDAY REMUNERATION

PART III—DEFINITIONS

PART IV—GENERAL

SCHEDULE

Article 3

The following minimum remuneration and provisions as to holidays and holiday remuneration shall be substituted for the statutory minimum remuneration and provisions as to holidays and holiday remuneration set out in the Wages Regulation (Unlicensed Place of Refreshment) Order 1967 (hereinafter referred to as "Order U.P.R.(36)").

PART I

REMUNERATION FOR EMPLOYMENT

WORKERS OTHER THAN OCCASIONAL WORKERS

1. Subject to the provisions of paragraphs 6, 8, 9, 10, 11, 12 and 13, the minimum remuneration for workers (other than occasional workers) to whom this Schedule applies shall be—

(1) for workers other than managers and manageresses, in accordance with the provisions of paragraph 2, 3 or 4;

(2) for managers and manageresses who normally work for the employer for not less than 36 hours in a week, in accordance with the provisions of paragraph 5:

Provided that, in calculating the remuneration for the purposes of this Schedule—

(*a*) recognised breaks for mealtimes shall be excluded;

(*b*) an employer shall be treated as supplying full board and lodging or meals to a worker if he makes them available to the worker.

WORKERS (OTHER THAN MANAGERS, MANAGERESSES AND OCCASIONAL WORKERS) SUPPLIED WITH MEALS LONDON AREA—MALE WORKERS

2.—(1) The HOURLY minimum remuneration for male workers employed in the London area (as defined in paragraph 27) who are supplied by the employer with meals whilst on duty but not with full board and lodging, is that set out in Columns 2 to 6 inclusive of the Table below with any additions payable under Columns 7, 8 and 9.

Grade or description of worker (see paragraph 25 for definitions)	For all time worked other than on Sunday or a rest day			For all time worked on a Sunday which is not the worker's rest day	For all time worked on a rest day	Additions to the hourly rates set out in Columns 2 to 6		
	between 7 a.m. and 7 p.m.	(*a*) between 5 a.m. and 7 a.m. (*b*) between 7 p.m. and 11 p.m.	between 11 p.m. and 5 a.m.			For all time worked in excess of 9 hours on any day other than Sunday or a rest day	For all time worked in excess of 44 hours in any week: For the first 6 hours	For all time worked in excess of 44 hours in any week: For all time after the first 6 hours
(Column 1)	(Column 2)	(Column 3)	(Column 4)	(Column 5)	(Column 6)	(Column 7)	(Column 8)	(Column 9)
	Per hour s. d.	Per hour s. d.	Per hour s. d.	Per hour s. d.	Per hour s. d.	Per hour s. d.	Per hour s. d.	Per hour s. d.
Assistant Manager—								
Aged 21 years or over	5 5¼	6 1½	6 9½	6 9½	10 10½	1 4¼	1 5¼	2 10½
" 20 and under 21 years ...	4 11¼	5 6¾	6 2	6 2	9 10½	1 2¾	1 3¾	2 7½
" 19 " " 20 " ...	4 7½	5 2¼	5 9½	5 9½	9 3	1 2	1 3	2 6
" under 19 years	4 4	4 10½	5 5	5 5	8 8	1 1	1 2	2 4

Assistant-in-Charge—								
Aged 21 years or over	5 3½	5 11½	6 7½	6 7½	10 7	1 4	1 5	2 10
„ 20 and under 21 years ...	4 9½	5 4¾	6 0	6 0	9 7	1 2½	1 3½	2 7
„ 19 „ „ 20 „ ...	4 5¾	5 0½	5 7¼	5 7¼	8 11½	1 1½	1 2½	2 5
„ under 19 years	4 2¼	4 8½	5 2¾	5 2¾	8 4½	1 0½	1 1½	2 3
Floor Supervisor—								
Aged 21 years or over	4 9¼	5 4½	5 11½	5 11½	9 6½	1 2¼	1 3¼	2 6½
„ 20 and under 21 years ...	4 3¾	4 10¼	5 4¾	5 4¾	8 7½	1 1	1 2	2 4
„ 19 „ „ 20 „ ...	4 0	4 6	5 0	5 0	8 0	1 0	1 1	2 2
„ under 19 years	3 8½	4 2	4 7¾	4 7¾	7 5	11¼	1 0¼	2 0½
Clerk—								
Aged 21 years or over	4 10	5 5¼	6 0½	6 0½	9 8	1 2½	1 3½	2 7
„ 20 and under 21 years ...	4 4½	4 11	5 5¾	5 5¾	8 9	1 1¼	1 2¼	2 4½
„ 19 „ „ 20 „ ...	4 0¾	4 6¾	5 1	5 1	8 1½	1 0¼	1 1¼	2 2½
„ 18 „ „ 19 „ ...	3 9¼	4 3	4 8½	4 8½	7 6½	11¼	1 0¼	2 0½
„ 17 „ „ 18 „ ...	3 3¼	3 8¼	4 1	4 1	6 6½	9¾	10¾	1 9½
„ 16 „ „ 17 „ ...	3 0¼	3 4¾	3 9¼	3 9¼	6 0½	9	10	1 8
„ 15 „ „ 16 „ ...	2 9½	3 1¾	3 6	3 6	5 7	8½	9½	1 7
Cashier or Clerical Assistant—								
Aged 21 years or over	4 8½	5 3½	5 10¾	5 10¾	9 5	1 2¼	1 3¼	2 6½
„ 20 and under 21 years ...	4 3	4 9½	5 3¾	5 3¾	8 6	1 0¾	1 1¾	2 3½
„ 19 „ „ 20 „ ...	3 11¼	4 5¼	4 11	4 11	7 10½	11¾	1 0¾	2 1½
„ 18 „ „ 19 „ ...	3 7¾	4 1¼	4 6¾	4 6¾	7 3½	11	1 0	2 0
„ 17 „ „ 18 „ ...	3 1¾	3 6½	3 11¼	3 11¼	6 3½	9½	10½	1 9
„ 16 „ „ 17 „ ...	2 10¾	3 3	3 7½	3 7½	5 9½	8¾	9¾	1 7½
„ 15 „ „ 16 „ ...	2 8	3 0	3 4	3 4	5 4	8	9	1 6
Refreshment Bar, Buffet or Service Attendant—								
Aged 21 years or over	4 8	5 3	5 10	5 10	9 4	1 2	1 3	2 6
„ 20 and under 21 years ...	4 2½	4 8¾	5 3¼	5 3¼	8 5	1 0¾	1 1¾	2 3½
„ 19 „ „ 20 „ ...	3 10¾	4 4½	4 10½	4 10½	7 9½	11¾	1 0¾	2 1½
„ 18 „ „ 19 „ ...	3 7¼	4 0¾	4 6	4 6	7 2½	10¾	11¾	1 11½
„ 17 „ „ 18 „ ...	3 1¼	3 6	3 10½	3 10½	6 2½	9¼	10¼	1 8½
„ 16 „ „ 17 „ ...	2 10¼	3 2½	3 6¾	3 6¾	5 8½	8½	9½	1 7
„ 15 „ „ 16 „ ...	2 7½	2 11½	3 3½	3 3½	5 3	8	9	1 6

LONDON AREA—MALE WORKERS—(*contd.*)

Grade or description of worker (see paragraph 25 for definitions)	For all time worked other than on Sunday or a rest day			For all time worked on a Sunday which is not the worker's rest day	For all time worked on a rest day	Additions to the hourly rates set out in Columns 2 to 6		
	between 7 a.m. and 7 p.m.	(*a*) between 5 a.m. and 7 a.m. (*b*) between 7 p.m. and 11 p.m.	between 11 p.m. and 5 a.m.			For all time worked in excess of 9 hours on any day other than Sunday or a rest day	For all time worked in excess of 44 hours in any week: For the first 6 hours	For all time worked in excess of 44 hours in any week: For all time after the first 6 hours
(Column 1)	(Column 2)	(Column 3)	(Column 4)	(Column 5)	(Column 6)	(Column 7)	(Column 8)	(Column 9)
	Per hour s. d.	Per hour s. d.	Per hour s. d.	Per hour s. d.	Per hour s. d.	Per hour s. d.	Per hour s. d.	Per hour s. d.
Waiter—								
Aged 21 years or over	4 4¼	4 10¾	5 5¼	5 5¼	8 8½	1 1	1 2	2 4
„ 20 and under 21 years ..	3 11¼	4 5¼	4 11	4 11	7 10½	11¾	1 0¾	2 1½
„ 19 „ „ 20 „ ...	3 7¼	4 0¾	4 6	4 6	7 2½	10¾	11¾	1 11½
„ 18 „ „ 19 „ ...	3 3½	3 8½	4 1½	4 1½	6 7	10	11	1 10
„ 17 „ „ 18 „ ...	2 10½	3 2¾	3 7¼	3 7¼	5 9	8¾	9¾	1 7½
„ 16 „ „ 17 „ ...	2 8¼	3 0¼	3 4¼	3 4¼	5 4½	8	9	1 6
„ 15 „ „ 16 „ ...	2 5¼	2 9	3 0½	3 0½	4 10½	7¼	8¼	1 4½
Chef	6 0½	6 9½	7 6¾	7 6¾	12 1	1 6¼	1 7¼	3 2½
Head Cook	5 8¾	6 5¼	7 2	7 2	11 5½	1 5¼	1 6¼	3 0½
Cook—								
Aged 21 years or over	5 5	6 1¼	6 9¼	6 9¼	10 10	1 4¼	1 5¼	2 10½
„ 20 and under 21 years ...	4 11	5 6½	6 1¾	6 1¾	9 10	1 2¾	1 3¾	2 7½
„ 19 „ „ 20 „ ...	4 7¼	5 2¼	5 9	5 9	9 2½	1 1¾	1 2¾	2 5½
„ under 19 years	4 3¾	4 10¼	5 4¾	5 4¾	8 7½	1 1	1 2	2 4

Assistant Cook—								
Aged 21 years or over	5 0	5 7½	6 3	6 3	10 0	1 3	1 4	2 8
" 20 and under 21 years ...	4 6½	5 1¼	5 8¼	5 8¼	9 1	1 1¾	1 2¾	2 5½
" 19 " " 20 " ...	4 2¾	4 9	5 3½	5 3½	8 5½	1 0¾	1 1¾	2 3½
" 18 " " 19 " ...	3 11¼	4 5¼	4 11	4 11	7 10½	11¾	1 0¾	2 1½
" 17 " " 18 " ...	3 5¼	3 10½	4 3½	4 3½	6 10½	10¼	11¼	1 10½
" 16 " " 17 " ...	3 2¼	3 7	3 11¾	3 11¾	6 4½	9½	10½	1 9
" 15 " " 16 " ...	2 11½	3 4	3 8½	3 8½	5 11	9	10	1 8
Service Cook—								
Aged 21 years or over	4 8¾	5 3¾	5 11	5 11	9 5½	1 2¼	1 3¼	2 6½
" 20 and under 21 years ...	4 3¼	4 9¾	5 4	5 4	8 6½	1 0¾	1 1¾	2 3½
" 19 " " 20 " ...	3 11½	4 5½	4 11½	4 11½	7 11	1 0	1 1	2 2
" 18 " " 19 " ...	3 8	4 1½	4 7	4 7	7 4	11	1 0	2 0
" 17 " " 18 " ...	3 2	3 6¾	3 11½	3 11½	6 4	9½	10½	1 9
" 16 " " 17 " ...	2 11	3 3½	3 7¾	3 7¾	5 10	8¾	9¾	1 7½
" 15 " " 16 " ...	2 8¼	3 0¼	3 4¼	3 4¼	5 4½	8	9	1 6
Any other worker except a Manager—								
Aged 21 years or over	4 7½	5 2½	5 9½	5 9½	9 3	1 2	1 3	2 6
" 20 and under 21 years ...	4 2	4 8¼	5 2½	5 2½	8 4	1 0½	1 1½	2 3
" 19 " " 20 " ...	3 10¼	4 4	4 9¾	4 9¾	7 8½	11½	1 0½	2 1
" 18 " " 19 " ...	3 6¾ ...	4 0	4 5½	4 5½	7 1½	10¾	11¾	1 11½
" 17 " " 18 " ...	3 0¾	3 5¼	3 10	3 10	6 1½	9¼	10¼	1 8½
" 16 " " 17 " ...	2 9¾	3 2	3 6¼	3 6¼	5 7½	8½	9½	1 7
" 15 " " 16 " ...	2 7	2 11	3 2¾	3 2¾	5 2	7¾	8¾	1 5½

LONDON AREA—FEMALE WORKERS

(2) The HOURLY minimum remuneration for female workers employed in the London area (as defined in paragraph 27) who are supplied by the employer with meals whilst on duty but not with full board and lodging, is that set out in Columns 2 to 6 inclusive of the Table below with any additions payable under Columns 7, 8 and 9.

Grade or description of worker (see paragraph 25 for definitions)	For all time worked other than on Sunday or a rest day			For all time worked on a Sunday which is not the worker's rest day	For all time worked on a rest day	Additions to the hourly rates set out in Columns 2 to 6		
	between 7 a.m. and 7 p.m.	(*a*) between 5 a.m. and 7 a.m. (*b*) between 7 p.m. and 11 p.m.	between 11 p.m. and 5 a.m.			For all time worked in excess of 9 hours on any day other than Sunday or a rest day	For all time worked in excess of 44 hours in any week: For the first 6 hours	For all time worked in excess of 44 hours in any week: For all time after the first 6 hours
(Column 1)	(Column 2)	(Column 3)	(Column 4)	(Column 5)	(Column 6)	(Column 7)	(Column 8)	(Column 9)
	Per hour s. d.	Per hour s. d.	Per hour s. d.	Per hour s. d.	Per hour s. d.	Per hour s. d.	Per hour s. d.	Per hour s. d.
Assistant Manageress—								
Aged 21 years or over	4 5¼	5 0	5 6½	5 6½	8 10½	1 1¼	1 2¼	2 4½
„ 20 and under 21 years ...	4 1½	4 7¾	5 2	5 2	8 3	1 0½	1 1½	2 3
„ 19 „ „ 20 „ ...	3 11¼	4 5¼	4 11	4 11	7 10½	11¾	1 0¾	2 1½
„ under 19 years	3 9¼	4 3	4 8½	4 8½	7 6½	11¼	1 0¼	2 0½
Assistant-in-Charge—								
Aged 21 years or over	4 3	4 9½	5 3¾	5 3¾	8 6	1 0¾	1 1¾	2 3½
„ 20 and under 21 years ...	3 11¼	4 5¼	4 11	4 11	7 10½	11¾	1 0¾	2 1½
„ 19 „ „ 20 „ ...	3 9	4 2¾	4 8¼	4 8¼	7 6	11¼	1 0¼	2 0½
„ under 19 years	3 7	4 0½	4 5¾	4 5¾	7 2	10¾	11¾	1 11½
Floor Supervisor—								
Aged 21 years or over	3 10½	4 4¼	4 10¼	4 10¼	7 9	11¾	1 0¾	2 1½
„ 20 and under 21 years ...	3 7¼	4 0¾	4 6	4 6	7 2½	10¾	11¾	1 11½
„ 19 „ „ 20 „ ...	3 5	3 10¼	4 3¼	4 3¼	6 10	10¼	11¼	1 10½
„ under 19 years	3 3	3 8	4 0¾	4 0¾	6 6	9¾	10¾	1 9½

Hostess, Receptionist or Seater—								
Aged 21 years or over	3 8¾	4 2¼	4 8	4 8	7 5½	11¼	1 0¼	2 0½
„ 20 and under 21 years ...	3 5½	3 10¾	4 4	4 4	6 11	10½	11½	1 11
„ 19 „ „ 20 „ ...	3 3¼	3 8¼	4 1	4 1	6 6½	9¾	10¾	1 9½
„ 18 „ „ 19 „ ...	3 1¼	3 6	3 10¼	3 10¼	6 2½	9¼	10¼	1 8½
„ 17 „ „ 18 „ ...	2 9	3 1¼	3 5¼	3 5¼	5 6	8¼	9¼	1 6½
„ 16 „ „ 17 „ ...	2 7½	2 11½	3 3½	3 3½	5 3	8	9	1 6
„ 15 „ „ 16 „ ...	2 6	2 9¾	3 1½	3 1½	5 0	7½	8½	1 5
Clerk—								
Aged 21 years or over	3 10¾	4 4½	4 10½	4 10½	7 9½	11¾	1 0¾	2 1½
„ 20 and under 21 years ...	3 7½	4 1	4 6½	4 6½	7 3	11	1 0	2 0
„ 19 „ „ 20 „ ...	3 5¼	3 10½	4 3½	4 3½	6 10½	10¼	11¼	1 10½
„ 18 „ „ 19 „ ...	3 3¼	3 8¼	4 1	4 1	6 6½	9¾	10¾	1 9½
„ 17 „ „ 18 „ ...	2 11	3 3½	3 7¾	3 7¾	5 10	8¾	9¾	1 7½
„ 16 „ „ 17 „ ...	2 9½	3 1¾	3 6	3 6	5 7	8½	9½	1 7
„ 15 „ „ 16 „ ...	2 8	3 0	3 4	3 4	5 4	8	9	1 6
Cashier or Clerical Assistant—								
Aged 21 years or over	3 8	4 1½	4 7	4 7	7 4	11	1 0	2 0
„ 20 and under 21 years ...	3 4¾	3 9¾	4 3	4 3	6 9½	10¼	11¼	1 10½
„ 19 „ „ 20 „ ...	3 2½	3 7¼	4 0¼	4 0¼	6 5	9¾	10¾	1 9½
„ 18 „ „ 19 „ ...	3 0½	3 5	3 9¾	3 9¾	6 1	9¼	10¼	1 8½
„ 17 „ „ 18 „ ...	2 8¼	3 0¼	3 4¼	3 4¼	5 4½	8	9	1 6
„ 16 „ „ 17 „ ...	2 6¾	2 10½	3 2½	3 2½	5 1½	7¾	8¾	1 5½
„ 15 „ „ 16 „ ...	2 5¼	2 9	3 0½	3 0½	4 10½	7¼	8¼	1 4½
Refreshment Bar, Buffet or Service Attendant—								
Aged 21 years or over	3 7½	4 1	4 6½	4 6½	7 3	11	1 0	2 0
„ 20 and under 21 years ...	3 4¼	3 9¼	4 2¼	4 2¼	6 8½	10	11	1 10
„ 19 „ „ 20 „ ...	3 2	3 6¾	3 11½	3 11½	6 4	9½	10½	1 9
„ 18 „ „ 19 „ ...	3 0	3 4½	3 9	3 9	6 0	9	10	1 8
„ 17 „ „ 18 „ ...	2 7¾	2 11¾	3 3¾	3 3¾	5 3½	8	9	1 6
„ 16 „ „ 17 „ ...	2 6¼	2 10	3 1¾	3 1¾	5 0½	7½	8½	1 5
„ 15 „ „ 16 „ ...	2 4¾	2 8¼	3 0	3 0	4 9½	7¼	8¼	1 4½

LONDON AREA—FEMALE WORKERS—(*contd.*)

Grade or description of worker **(see paragraph 25 for definitions)**	For all time worked other than on Sunday or a rest day			For all time worked on a Sunday which is not the worker's rest day	For all time worked on a rest day	Additions to the hourly rates set out in Columns 2 to 6		
	between 7 a.m. and 7 p.m.	(*a*) between 5 a.m. and 7 a.m. (*b*) between 7 p.m. and 11 p.m.	between 11 p.m. and 5 a.m.			For all time worked in excess of 9 hours on any day other than Sunday or a rest day	For all time worked in excess of 44 hours in any week: For the first 6 hours	For all time worked in excess of 44 hours in any week: For all time after the first 6 hours
(Column 1)	(Column 2)	(Column 3)	(Column 4)	(Column 5)	(Column 6)	(Column 7)	(Column 8)	(Column 9)
	Per hour s. d.	Per hour s. d.	Per hour s. d.	Per hour s. d.	Per hour s. d.	Per hour s. d.	Per hour s. d.	Per hour s. d.
Shop Assistant—								
Aged 21 years or over	*3 9*	*4 2¾*	*4 8¼*	*4 8¼*	*7 6*	*11¼*	*1 0¼*	*2 0½*
„ 20 and under 21 years ...	*3 5¾*	*3 11*	*4 4¼*	*4 4¼*	*6 11½*	*10½*	*11½*	*1 11*
„ 19 „ „ 20 „ ...	*3 3½*	*3 8½*	*4 1½*	*4 1½*	*6 7*	*10*	*11*	*1 10*
„ 18 „ „ 19 „ ...	*3 1½*	*3 6¼*	*3 11*	*3 11*	*6 3*	*9½*	*10½*	*1 9*
„ 17 „ „ 18 „ ...	*2 9¼*	*3 1½*	*3 5½*	*3 5½*	*5 6½*	*8¼*	*9¼*	*1 6½*
„ 16 „ „ 17 „ ...	*2 7¾*	*2 11¾*	*3 3¾*	*3 3¾*	*5 3½*	*8*	*9*	*1 6*
„ 15 „ „ 16 „ ...	*2 6¼*	*2 10*	*3 1¾*	*3 1¾*	*5 0½*	*7½*	*8½*	*1 5*
Waitress—								
Aged 21 years or over	*3 5*	*3 10¼*	*4 3¼*	*4 3¼*	*6 10*	*10¼*	*11¼*	*1 10½*
„ 20 and under 21 years ...	*3 2*	*3 6¾*	*3 11½*	*3 11½*	*6 4*	*9½*	*10½*	*1 9*
„ 19 „ „ 20 „ ...	*3 0*	*3 4½*	*3 9*	*3 9*	*6 0*	*9*	*10*	*1 8*
„ 18 „ „ 19 „ ...	*2 10¼*	*3 2½*	*3 6¾*	*3 6¾*	*5 8½*	*8½*	*9½*	*1 7*
„ 17 „ „ 18 „ ...	*2 6½*	*2 10¼*	*3 2¼*	*3 2¼*	*5 1*	*7¾*	*8¾*	*1 5½*
„ 16 „ „ 17 „ ...	*2 4¾*	*2 8¼*	*3 0*	*3 0*	*4 9½*	*7¼*	*8¼*	*1 4¼*
„ 15 „ „ 16 „ ...	*2 2¼*	*2 5½*	*2 8¾*	*2 8¾*	*4 4½*	*6½*	*7½*	*1 3*
Chef	*4 11½*	*5 7*	*6 2½*	*6 2½*	*9 11*	*1 3*	*1 4*	*2 8*
Head Cook	*4 8*	*5 3*	*5 10*	*5 10*	*9 4*	*1 2*	*1 3*	*2 6*

Cook—								
Aged 21 years or over	4 2¼	4 8½	5 2¾	5 2¾	8 4½	1 0½	1 1½	2 3
„ 20 and under 21 years ...	3 10½	4 4¼	4 10¼	4 10¼	7 9	11¾	1 0¾	2 1½
„ 19 „ „ 20 „ ...	3 8¼	4 1¾	4 7¼	4 7¼	7 4½	11	1 0	2 0
„ under 19 years	3 6¼	3 11½	4 4¾	4 4¾	7 0½	10½	11½	1 11
Assistant Cook—								
Aged 21 years or over	3 10¼	4 4	4 9¾	4 9¾	7 8½	11½	1 0½	2 1
„ 20 and under 21 years ...	3 7	4 0½	4 5¾	4 5¾	7 2	10¾	11¾	1 11½
„ 19 „ „ 20 „ ...	3 4¾	3 9¾	4 3	4 3	6 9½	10¼	11¼	1 10½
„ 18 „ „ 19 „ ...	3 2¾	3 7½	4 0½	4 0½	6 5½	9¾	10¾	1 9½
„ 17 „ „ 18 „ ...	2 10½	3 2¾	3 7¼	3 7¼	5 9	8¾	9¾	1 7½
„ 16 „ „ 17 „ ...	2 9	3 1¼	3 5¼	3 5¼	5 6	8¼	9¼	1 6½
„ 15 „ „ 16 „ ...	2 7½	2 11½	3 3½	3 3½	5 3	8	9	1 6
Service Cook—								
Aged 21 years or over	3 8¼	4 1¾	4 7¼	4 7¼	7 4½	11	1 0	2 0
„ 20 and under 21 years ...	3 5	3 10¼	4 3¼	4 3¼	6 10	10¼	11¼	1 10½
„ 19 „ „ 20 „ ...	3 2¾	3 7½	4 0½	4 0½	6 5½	9¾	10¾	1 9½
„ 18 „ „ 19 „ ...	3 0¾	3 5¼	3 10	3 10	6 1½	9¼	10¼	1 8½
„ 17 „ „ 18 „ ...	2 8½	3 0½	3 4¾	3 4¾	5 5	8¼	9¼	1 6½
„ 16 „ „ 17 „ ...	2 7	2 11	3 2¾	3 2¾	5 2	7¾	8¾	1 5½
„ 15 „ „ 16 „ ...	2 5½	2 9¼	3 1	3 1	4 11	7½	8½	1 5
Any other worker except a Manageress—								
Aged 21 years or over	3 7	4 0½	4 5¾	4 5¾	7 2	10¾	11¾	1 11½
„ 20 and under 21 years ...	3 3¾	3 8¾	4 1¾	4 1¾	6 7½	10	11	1 10
„ 19 „ „ 20 „ ...	3 1½	3 6¼	3 11	3 11	6 3	9½	10½	1 9
„ 18 „ „ 19 „ ...	2 11½	3 4	3 8½	3 8½	5 11	9	10	1 8
„ 17 „ „ 18 „ ...	2 7¼	2 11¼	3 3	3 3	5 2½	7¾	8¾	1 5½
„ 16 „ „ 17 „ ...	2 5¾	2 9½	3 1¼	3 1¼	4 11½	7½	8½	1 5
„ 15 „ „ 16 „ ...	2 4¼	2 7¾	2 11¼	2 11¼	4 8½	7	8	1 4

PROVINCIAL A AREA—MALE WORKERS

3.—(1) The HOURLY minimum remuneration for male workers employed in Provincial A area (as defined in paragraph 27) who are supplied by the employer with meals whilst on duty but not with full board and lodging, is that set out in Columns 2 to 6 inclusive of the Table below with any additions payable under Columns 7, 8 and 9.

Grade or description of worker **(see paragraph 25 for definitions)**	For all time worked other than on Sunday or a rest day			For all time worked on a Sunday which is not the worker's rest day	For all time worked on a rest day	Additions to the hourly rates set out in Columns 2 to 6		
	between 7 a.m. and 7 p.m.	(*a*) between 5 a.m. and 7 a.m. (*b*) between 7 p.m. and 11 p.m.	between 11 p.m. and 5 a.m.			For all time worked in excess of 9 hours on any day other than Sunday or a rest day	For all time worked in excess of 44 hours in any week: For the first 6 hours	For all time worked in excess of 44 hours in any week: For all time after the first 6 hours
(Column 1)	(Column 2)	(Column 3)	(Column 4)	(Column 5)	(Column 6)	(Column 7)	(Column 8)	(Column 9)
	Per hour s. d.	Per hour s. d.	Per hour s. d.	Per hour s. d.	Per hour s. d.	Per hour s. d.	Per hour s. d.	Per hour s. d.
Assistant Manager—								
Aged 21 years or over	5 3¾	5 11¾	6 7¾	6 7¾	10 7½	1 4	1 5	2 10
„ 20 and under 21 years ...	4 9¾	5 5	6 0¼	6 0¼	9 7½	1 2½	1 3½	2 7
„ 19 „ „ 20 „ ...	4 6	5 0¾	5 7½	5 7½	9 0	1 1½	1 2½	2 5
„ under 19 years	4 2½	4 8¾	5 3¼	5 3¼	8 5	1 0¾	1 1¾	2 3½
Assistant-in-Charge—								
Aged 21 years or over	5 2	5 9¾	6 5½	6 5½	10 4	1 3½	1 4½	2 9
„ 20 and under 21 years ...	4 8	5 3	5 10	5 10	9 4	1 2	1 3	2 6
„ 19 „ „ 20 „ ...	4 4¼	4 10¾	5 5¼	5 5¼	8 8½	1 1	1 2	2 4
„ under 19 years	4 0¾	4 6¾	5 1	5 1	8 1½	1 0¼	1 1¼	2 2½
Floor Supervisor—								
Aged 21 years or over	4 7¾	5 2¾	5 9¾	5 9¾	9 3½	1 2	1 3	2 6
„ 20 and under 21 years ...	4 2¼	4 8½	5 2¾	5 2¾	8 4½	1 0½	1 1½	2 3
„ 19 „ „ 20 „ ...	3 10½	4 4¼	4 10¼	4 10¼	7 9	11¾	1 0¾	2 1½
„ under 19 years	3 7	4 0½	4 5¾	4 5¾	7 2	10¾	11¾	1 11½

Clerk—								
Aged 21 years or over	4 8½	5 3½	5 10¾	5 10¾	9 5	1 2¼	1 3¼	2 6½
„ 20 and under 21 years ...	4 3	4 9½	5 3¾	5 3¾	8 6	1 0¾	1 1¾	2 3½
„ 19 „ „ 20 „ ...	3 11¼	4 5¼	4 11	4 11	7 10½	11¾	1 0¾	2 1½
„ 18 „ „ 19 „ ...	3 7¾	4 1¼	4 6¾	4 6¾	7 3½	11	1 0	2 0
„ 17 „ „ 18 „ ...	3 1¾	3 6½	3 11¼	3 11¼	6 3½	9½	10½	1 9
„ 16 „ „ 17 „ ...	2 10¾	3 3	3 7½	3 7½	5 9½	8¾	9¾	1 7½
„ 15 „ „ 16 „ ...	2 8	3 0	3 4	3 4	5 4	8	9	1 6
Cashier or Clerical Assistant—								
Aged 21 years or over	4 7	5 2	5 8¾	5 8¾	9 2	1 1¾	1 2¾	2 5½
„ 20 and under 21 years ...	4 1½	4 7¾	5 2	5 2	8 3	1 0½	1 1½	2 3
„ 19 „ „ 20 „ ...	3 9¾	4 3½	4 9¼	4 9¼	7 7½	11½	1 0½	2 1
„ 18 „ „ 19 „ ...	3 6¼	3 11½	4 4¾	4 4¾	7 0½	10½	11½	1 11
„ 17 „ „ 18 „ ...	3 0¼	3 4¾	3 9¼	3 9¼	6 0½	9	10	1 8
„ 16 „ „ 17 „ ...	2 9¼	3 1½	3 5½	3 5½	5 6½	8¼	9¼	1 6½
„ 15 „ „ 16 „ ...	2 6½	2 10¼	3 2¼	3 2¼	5 1	7¾	8¾	1 5½
Refreshment Bar, Buffet or Service Attendant—								
Aged 21 years or over	4 6½	5 1¼	5 8¼	5 8¼	9 1	1 1¾	1 2¾	2 5½
„ 20 and under 21 years ...	4 1	4 7¼	5 1¼	5 1¼	8 2	1 0¼	1 1¼	2 2½
„ 19 „ „ 20 „ ...	3 9¼	4 3	4 8½	4 8½	7 6½	11¼	1 0¼	2 0½
„ 18 „ „ 19 „ ...	3 5¾	3 11	4 4¼	4 4¼	6 11½	10½	11½	1 11
„ 17 „ „ 18 „ ...	2 11¾	3 4¼	3 8¾	3 8¾	5 11½	9	10	1 8
„ 16 „ „ 17 „ ...	2 8¾	3 0¾	3 5	3 5	5 5¼	8¼	9¼	1 6½
„ 15 „ „ 16 „ ...	2 6	2 9¾	3 1½	3 1½	5 0	7½	8½	1 5
Waiter—								
Aged 21 years or over	4 2¾	4 9	5 3½	5 3½	8 5½	1 0¾	1 1¾	2 3½
„ 20 and under 21 years ...	3 9¾	4 3½	4 9¼	4 9¼	7 7½	11½	1 0½	2 1
„ 19 „ „ 20 „ ...	3 5¾	3 11	4 4¼	4 4¼	6 11½	10½	11½	1 11
„ 18 „ „ 19 „ ...	3 2	3 6¾	3 11½	3 11½	6 4	9½	10½	1 9
„ 17 „ „ 18 „ ...	2 9	3 1¼	3 5¼	3 5¼	5 6	8¼	9¼	1 6½
„ 16 „ „ 17 „ ...	2 6¾	2 10½	3 2½	3 2½	5 1½	7¾	8¾	1 5½
„ 15 „ „ 16 „ ...	2 3¾	2 7¼	2 10¾	2 10¾	4 7½	7	8	1 4
Chef	5 11	6 8	7 4¾	7 4¾	11 10	1 5¾	1 6¾	3 1½
Head Cook	5 7¼	6 3¾	7 0	7 0	11 2½	1 4¾	1 5¾	2 11½

PROVINCIAL A AREA—MALE WORKERS—(contd.)

Grade or description of worker (see paragraph 25 for definitions)	For all time worked other than on Sunday or a rest day			For all time worked on a Sunday which is not the worker's rest day	For all time worked on a rest day	Additions to the hourly rates set out in Columns 2 to 6		
	between 7 a.m. and 7 p.m.	(a) between 5 a.m. and 7 a.m. (b) between 7 p.m. and 11 p.m.	between 11 p.m. and 5 a.m.			For all time worked in excess of 9 hours on any day other than Sunday or a rest day	For all time worked in excess of 44 hours in any week	
							For the first 6 hours	For all time after the first 6 hours
(Column 1)	(Column 2) Per hour s. d.	(Column 3) Per hour s. d.	(Column 4) Per hour s. d.	(Column 5) Per hour s. d.	(Column 6) Per hour s. d.	(Column 7) Per hour s. d.	(Column 8) Per hour s. d.	(Column 9) Per hour s. d.
Cook—								
Aged 21 years or over ...	5 3½	5 11½	6 7½	6 7½	10 7	1 4	1 5	2 10
„ 20 and under 21 years	4 9½	5 4½	6 0	6 0	9 7	1 2½	1 3½	2 7
„ 19 „ 20 „ ...	4 5¾	5 0½	5 7¼	5 7¼	8 11½	1 1½	1 2½	2 5
„ under 19 years ...	4 2¼	4 8½	5 2¾	5 2¾	8 4½	1 0½	1 1½	2 3
Assistant Cook—								
Aged 21 years or over ...	4 10½	5 5¼	6 1¼	6 1¼	9 9	1 2¾	1 3¾	2 7½
„ 20 and under 21 years	4 5	4 11¾	5 6¼	5 6¼	8 10	1 1½	1 2½	2 4½
„ 19 „ 20 „ ...	4 1½	4 7½	5 1½	5 1½	8 2½	1 0½	1 1½	2 2½
„ 18 „ 19 „ ...	3 9¾	4 3½	4 9¼	4 9¼	7 7½	11½	1 0½	2 1
„ 17 „ 18 „ ...	3 3½	3 8½	4 1½	4 1½	7 1½	10	11	1 10
„ 16 „ 17 „ ...	3 0¾	3 5¼	3 10	3 10	6 1½	9½	10½	1 8½
„ 15 „ 16 „ ...	2 10	3 2¼	3 6½	3 6½	5 8	8½	9½	1 7

Service Cook—								
Aged 21 years or over	4 7¼	5 2¼	5 9	5 9	9 2½	1 1¾	1 2¾	2 5½
„ 20 and under 21 years ...	4 1¾	4 8	5 2¼	5 2¼	8 3½	1 0½	1 1½	2 3
„ 19 „ „ 20 „ ...	3 10	4 3¾	4 9½	4 9½	7 8	11½	1 0½	2 1
„ 18 „ „ 19 „ ...	3 6½	3 11¾	4 5¼	4 5¼	7 1	10¾	11¾	1 11½
„ 17 „ „ 18 „ ...	3 0½	3 5	3 9¾	3 9¾	6 1	9¼	10¼	1 8½
„ 16 „ „ 17 „ ...	2 9½	3 1¾	3 6	3 6	5 7	8½	9½	1 7
„ 15 „ „ 16 „ ...	2 6¾	2 10½	3 2½	3 2½	5 1½	7¾	8¾	1 5½
Any other worker except a Manager—								
Aged 21 years or over	4 6	5 0¾	5 7½	5 7½	9 0	1 1½	1 2½	2 5
„ 20 and under 21 years ...	4 0½	4 6½	5 0¾	5 0¾	8 1	1 0¼	1 1¼	2 2½
„ 19 „ „ 20 „ ...	3 8¾	4 2¼	4 8	4 8	7 5½	11¼	1 0¼	2 0½
„ 18 „ „ 19 „ ...	3 5¼	3 10½	4 3½	4 3½	6 10½	10¼	11¼	1 10½
„ 17 „ „ 18 „ ...	2 11¼	3 3¾	3 8	3 8	5 10½	8¾	9¾	1 7½
„ 16 „ „ 17 „ ...	2 8¼	3 0¼	3 4¼	3 4¼	5 4½	8	9	1 6
„ 15 „ „ 16 „ ...	2 5½	2 9¼	3 1	3 1	4 11	7½	8½	1 5

PROVINCIAL A AREA—FEMALE WORKERS

(2) The HOURLY minimum remuneration for female workers employed in Provincial A area (as defined in paragraph 27) who are supplied by the employer with meals whilst on duty but not with full board and lodging, is that set out in Columns 2 to 6 inclusive of the Table below with any additions payable under Columns 7, 8 and 9.

Grade or description of worker **(see paragraph 25 for definitions)**	For all time worked other than on Sunday or a rest day			For all time worked on a Sunday which is not the worker's rest day	For all time worked on a rest day	Additions to the hourly rates set out in Columns 2 to 6		
	between 7 a.m. and 7 p.m.	(*a*) between 5 a.m. and 7 a.m. (*b*) between 7 p.m. and 11 p.m.	between 11 p.m. and 5 a.m.			For all time worked in excess of 9 hours on any day other than Sunday or a rest day	For all time worked in excess of 44 hours in any week: For the first 6 hours	For all time worked in excess of 44 hours in any week: For all time after the first 6 hours
(Column 1)	(Column 2)	(Column 3)	(Column 4)	(Column 5)	(Column 6)	(Column 7)	(Column 8)	(Column 9)
	Per hour s. d.	Per hour s. d.	Per hour s. d.	Per hour s. d.	Per hour s. d.	Per hour s. d.	Per hour s. d.	Per hour s. d.
Assistant Manageress—								
Aged 21 years or over	4 3¾	4 10¼	5 4¾	5 4¾	8 7½	1 1	1 2	2 4
„ 20 and under 21 years ...	4 0	4 6	5 0	5 0	8 0	1 0	1 1	2 2
„ 19 „ „ 20 „ ...	3 9¾	4 3½	4 9¼	4 9¼	7 7½	11½	1 0½	2 1
„ under 19 years	3 7¾	4 1¼	4 6¾	4 6¾	7 3½	11	1 0	2 0
Assistant-in-Charge—								
Aged 21 years or over	4 1½	4 7¾	5 2	5 2	8 3	1 0½	1 1½	2 3
„ 20 and under 21 years ...	3 9¾	4 3½	4 9¼	4 9¼	7 7½	11½	1 0½	2 1
„ 19 „ „ 20 „ ...	3 7½	4 1	4 6½	4 6½	7 3	11	1 0	2 0
„ under 19 years	3 5½	3 10¾	4 4	4 4	6 11	10½	11½	1 11
Floor Supervisor—								
Aged 21 years or over	3 9	4 2¾	4 8¼	4 8¼	7 6	11¼	1 0¼	2 0½
„ 20 and under 21 years ...	3 5¾	3 11	4 4¼	4 4¼	6 11½	10½	11½	1 11
„ 19 „ „ 20 „ ...	3 3½	3 8½	4 1½	4 1½	6 7	10	11	1 10
„ under 19 years	3 1½	3 6¼	3 11	3 11	6 3	9½	10½	1 9

Hostess, Receptionist or Seater—								
Aged 21 years or over	3 7¼	4 0¾	4 6	4 6	7 2½	10¾	11¾	1 11½
„ 20 and under 21 years ...	3 4	3 9	4 2	4 2	6 8	10	11	1 10
„ 19 „ „ 20 „ ...	3 1¾	3 6½	3 11¼	3 11¼	6 3½	9½	10½	1 9
„ 18 „ „ 19 „ ...	2 11¾	3 4¼	3 8¾	3 8¾	5 11½	9	10	1 8
„ 17 „ „ 18 „ ...	2 7½	2 11½	3 3½	3 3½	5 3	8	9	1 6
„ 16 „ „ 17 „ ...	2 6	2 9¾	3 1½	3 1½	5 0	7½	8½	1 5
„ 15 „ „ 16 „ ...	2 4½	2 8	2 11¾	2 11¾	4 9	7¼	8¼	1 4½
Clerk—								
Aged 21 years or over	3 9¼	4 3	4 8½	4 8½	7 6½	11¼	1 0¼	2 0½
„ 20 and under 21 years ...	3 6	3 11¼	4 4½	4 4½	7 0	10½	11½	1 11
„ 19 „ „ 20 „ ...	3 3¾	3 8¾	4 1¾	4 1¾	6 7½	10	11	1 10
„ 18 „ „ 19 „ ...	3 1¾	3 6½	3 11¼	3 11¼	6 3½	9½	10½	1 9
„ 17 „ „ 18 „ ...	2 9½	3 1¾	3 6	3 6	5 7	8½	9½	1 7
„ 16 „ „ 17 „ ...	2 8	3 0	3 4	3 4	5 4	8	9	1 6
„ 15 „ „ 16 „ ...	2 6½	2 10¼	3 2¼	3 2¼	5 1	7¾	8¾	1 5½
Cashier or Clerical Assistant—								
Aged 21 years or over	3 6½	3 11¾	4 5¼	4 5¼	7 1	10¾	11¾	1 11½
„ 20 and under 21 years ...	3 3¼	3 8¼	4 1	4 1	6 6½	9¾	10¾	1 9½
„ 19 „ „ 20 „ ...	3 1	3 5¾	3 10¼	3 10¼	6 2	9¼	10¼	1 8½
„ 18 „ „ 19 „ ...	2 11	3 3½	3 7¾	3 7¾	5 10	8¾	9¾	1 7½
„ 17 „ „ 18 „ ...	2 6¾	2 10½	3 2½	3 2½	5 1½	7¾	8¾	1 5½
„ 16 „ „ 17 „ ...	2 5¼	2 9	3 0½	3 0½	4 10½	7¼	8¼	1 4½
„ 15 „ „ 16 „ ...	2 3¾	2 7¼	2 10¾	2 10¾	4 7½	7	8	1 4
Refreshment Bar, Buffet or Service Attendant—								
Aged 21 years or over	3 6	3 11¼	4 4½	4 4½	7 0	10½	11½	1 11
„ 20 and under 21 years ...	3 2¾	3 7½	4 0½	4 0½	6 5½	9¾	10¾	1 9½
„ 19 „ „ 20 „ ...	3 0½	3 5	3 9¾	3 9¾	6 1	9¼	10¼	1 8½
„ 18 „ „ 19 „ ...	2 10½	3 2¾	3 7¼	3 7¼	5 9	8¾	9¾	1 7½
„ 17 „ „ 18 „ ...	2 6¼	2 10	3 1¾	3 1¾	5 0½	7½	8½	1 5
„ 16 „ „ 17 „ ...	2 4¾	2 8¼	3 0	3 0	4 9½	7¼	8¼	1 4½
„ 15 „ „ 16 „ ...	2 3¼	2 6¾	2 10	2 10	4 6½	6¾	7¾	1 3½

PROVINCIAL A AREA—FEMALE WORKERS—(contd.)

Grade or description of worker (see paragraph 25 for definitions) (Column 1)	For all time worked other than on Sunday or a rest day — between 7 a.m. and 7 p.m. (Column 2) Per hour s. d.	For all time worked other than on Sunday or a rest day — (a) between 5 a.m. and 7 a.m. (b) between 7 p.m. and 11 p.m. (Column 3) Per hour s. d.	For all time worked other than on Sunday or a rest day — between 11 p.m. and 5 a.m. (Column 4) Per hour s. d.	For all time worked on a Sunday which is not the worker's rest day (Column 5) Per hour s. d.	For all time worked on a rest day (Column 6) Per hour s. d.	Additions to the hourly rates set out in Columns 2 to 6 — For all time worked in excess of 9 hours on any day other than Sunday or a rest day (Column 7) Per hour s. d.	Additions … — For all time worked in excess of 44 hours in any week — For the first 6 hours (Column 8) Per hour s. d.	Additions … — For all time worked in excess of 44 hours in any week — For all time worked after the first 6 hours (Column 9) Per hour s. d.
Shop Assistant—								
Aged 21 years or over	3 7½	4 1	4 6½	4 6½	7 3	11	1 0	2 0
„ 20 and under 21 years	3 4½	3 9½	4 2½	4 2½	6 8½	10	11	1 10
„ 19 „	3 2	3 6½	3 11½	3 11½	6 4	9½	10½	1 9
„ 18 „	3 0	3 4½	3 9	3 9	6 0	9	10	1 8
„ 17 „	2 7½	2 11½	3 3¾	3 3¾	5 5	8	9	1 6
„ 16 „	2 6½	2 10	3 1½	3 1½	5 0½	7½	8½	1 5
„ 15 „	2 4½	2 8½	3 0	3 0	4 9¼	7½	8½	1 4½
Waitress—								
Aged 21 years or over	3 3½	3 8½	4 1½	4 1½	6 7	10	11	1 10
„ 20 and under 21 years	3 0½	3 5	3 9¾	3 9¾	6 1	9½	10½	1 8½
„ 19 „	2 10½	3 2¾	3 7½	3 7½	5 9	8½	9½	1 7½
„ 18 „	2 8¾	3 0¾	3 5	3 5	5 5½	8½	9½	1 6½
„ 17 „	2 5	2 8½	3 0¾	3 0¾	4 10	7½	8½	1 4½
„ 16 „	2 3½	2 6½	2 10	2 10	4 6½	6½	7½	1 3½
„ 15 „	2 0½	2 3½	2 7	2 7	4 1½	6½	7½	1 2½
Chef	4 10	5 5½	6 0½	6 0½	9 8	1 2½	1 3½	2 7
Head Cook	4 6½	5 1½	5 8½	5 8½	9 1	1 1½	1 2¾	2 5½

Cook—								
Aged 21 years or over	4 0¾	4 6¾	5 1	5 1	8 1½	1 0¼	1 1¼	2 2½
„ 20 and under 21 years ...	3 9	4 2¾	4 8¼	4 8¼	7 6	11¼	1 0¼	2 0½
„ 19 „ „ 20 „ ...	3 6¾	4 0	4 5½	4 5½	7 1½	10¾	11¾	1 11½
„ under 19 years	3 4¾	3 9¾	4 3	4 3	6 9½	10¼	11¼	1 10½
Assistant Cook—								
Aged 21 years or over	3 8¾	4 2¼	4 8	4 8	7 5½	11¼	1 0¼	2 0½
„ 20 and under 21 years ...	3 5½	3 10¾	4 4	4 4	6 11	10½	11½	1 11
„ 19 „ „ 20 „ ...	3 3¼	3 8¼	4 1	4 1	6 6½	9¾	10¾	1 9½
„ 18 „ „ 19 „ ...	3 1¼	3 6	3 10½	3 10½	6 2½	9¼	10¼	1 8½
„ 17 „ „ 18 „ ...	2 9	3 1¼	3 5¼	3 5¼	5 6	8¼	9¼	1 6½
„ 16 „ „ 17 „ ...	2 7½	2 11½	3 3½	3 3½	5 3	8	9	1 6
„ 15 „ „ 16 „ ...	2 6	2 9¾	3 1½	3 1½	5 0	7½	8½	1 5
Service Cook—								
Aged 21 years or over	3 6¾	4 0	4 5½	4 5½	7 1½	10¾	11¾	1 11½
„ 20 and under 21 years ...	3 3½	3 8½	4 1½	4 1½	6 7	10	11	1 10
„ 19 „ „ 20 „ ...	3 1¼	3 6	3 10½	3 10½	6 2½	9¼	10¼	1 8½
„ 18 „ „ 19 „ ...	2 11¼	3 3¾	3 8	3 8	5 10½	8¾	9¾	1 7½
„ 17 „ „ 18 „ ...	2 7	2 11	3 2¾	3 2¾	5 2	7¾	8¾	1 5½
„ 16 „ „ 17 „ ...	2 5½	2 9¼	3 1	3 1	4 11	7½	8½	1 5
„ 15 „ „ 16 „ ...	2 4	2 7½	2 11	2 11	4 8	7	8	1 4
Any other worker except a Manageress—								
Aged 21 years or over	3 5½	3 10¾	4 4	4 4	6 11	10½	11½	1 11
„ 20 and under 21 years ...	3 2¼	3 7	3 11¾	3 11¾	6 4½	9½	10½	1 9
„ 19 „ „ 20 „ ...	3 0	3 4½	3 9	3 9	6 0	9	10	1 8
„ 18 „ „ 19 „ ...	2 10	3 2¼	3 6½	3 6½	5 8	8½	9½	1 7
„ 17 „ „ 18 „ ...	2 5¾	2 9½	3 1¼	3 1¼	4 11½	7½	8½	1 5
„ 16 „ „ 17 „ ...	2 4¼	2 7¾	2 11¼	2 11¼	4 8½	7	8	1 4
„ 15 „ „ 16 „ ...	2 2¾	2 6	2 9½	2 9½	4 5½	6¾	7¾	1 3½

PROVINCIAL B AREA—MALE WORKERS

4.—(1) The HOURLY minimum remuneration for male workers employed in Provincial B area (as defined in paragraph 27) who are supplied by the employer with meals whilst on duty but not with full board and lodging, is that set out in Columns 2 to 6 inclusive of the Table below with any additions payable under Columns 7, 8 and 9.

Grade or description of worker **(see paragraph 25 for definitions)**	For all time worked other than on Sunday or a rest day			For all time worked on a Sunday which is not the worker's rest day	For all time worked on a rest day	Additions to the hourly rates set out in Columns 2 to 6		
	between 7 a.m. and 7 p.m.	(a) between 5 a.m. and 7 a.m. (b) between 7 p.m. and 11 p.m.	between 11 p.m. and 5 a.m.			For all time worked in excess of 9 hours on any day other than Sunday or a rest day	For all time worked in excess of 44 hours in any week: For the first 6 hours	For all time worked in excess of 44 hours in any week: For all time after the first 6 hours
(Column 1)	(Column 2)	(Column 3)	(Column 4)	(Column 5)	(Column 6)	(Column 7)	(Column 8)	(Column 9)
	Per hour s. d.	Per hour s. d.	Per hour s. d.	Per hour s. d.	Per hour s. d.	Per hour s. d.	Per hour s. d.	Per hour s. d.
Assistant Manager—								
Aged 21 years or over	5 2¼	5 10	6 5¾	6 5¾	10 4½	1 3½	1 4½	2 9
„ 20 and under 21 years ...	4 8¼	5 3¼	5 10¼	5 10¼	9 4½	1 2	1 3	2 6
„ 19 „ „ 20 „ ...	4 4½	4 11	5 5¾	5 5¾	8 9	1 1¼	1 2¼	2 4½
„ under 19 years	4 1	4 7¼	5 1¼	5 1¼	8 2	1 0¼	1 1¼	2 2½
Assistant-in-Charge—								
Aged 21 years or over	5 0½	5 8	6 3¾	6 3¾	10 1	1 3¼	1 4¼	2 8½
„ 20 and under 21 years ...	4 6½	5 1¼	5 8¼	5 8¼	9 1	1 1¾	1 2¾	2 5½
„ 19 „ „ 20 „ ...	4 2¾	4 9	5 3½	5 3½	8 5½	1 0¾	1 1¾	2 3½
„ under 19 years	3 11¼	4 5¼	4 11	4 11	7 10½	11¾	1 0¾	2 1½
Floor Supervisor—								
Aged 21 years or over	4 6¼	5 1	5 7¾	5 7¾	9 0½	1 1½	1 2½	2 5
„ 20 and under 21 years ...	4 0¾	4 6¾	5 1	5 1	8 1½	1 0¼	1 1¼	2 2½
„ 19 „ „ 20 „ ...	3 9	4 2¾	4 8¼	4 8¼	7 6	11¼	1 0¼	2 0½
„ under 19 years	3 5½	3 10¾	4 4	4 4	6 11	10½	11½	1 11

Clerk—								
Aged 21 years or over	4 7	5 2	5 8¾	5 8¾	9 2	1 1¾	1 2¾	2 5½
„ 20 and under 21 years ...	4 1½	4 7¾	5 2	5 2	8 3	1 0½	1 1½	2 3
„ 19 „ „ 20 „ ...	3 9¾	4 3½	4 9¼	4 9¼	7 7½	11½	1 0½	2 1
„ 18 „ „ 19 „ ...	3 6¼	3 11½	4 4¾	4 4¾	7 0½	10½	11½	1 11
„ 17 „ „ 18 „ ...	3 0¼	3 4¾	3 9¼	3 9¼	6 0½	9	10	1 8
„ 16 „ „ 17 „ ...	2 9¼	3 1½	3 5½	3 5½	5 6½	8¼	9¼	1 6½
„ 15 „ „ 16 „ ...	2 6½	2 10¼	3 2¼	3 2¼	5 1	7¾	8¾	1 5½
Cashier or Clerical Assistant—								
Aged 21 years or over	4 5½	5 0¼	5 7	5 7	8 11	1 1½	1 2½	2 5
„ 20 and under 21 years ...	4 0	4 6	5 0	5 0	8 0	1 0	1 1	2 2
„ 19 „ „ 20 „ ...	3 8¼	4 1¾	4 7¼	4 7¼	7 4½	11	1 0	2 0
„ 18 „ „ 19 „ ...	3 4¾	3 9¾	4 3	4 3	6 9½	10¼	11¼	1 10½
„ 17 „ „ 18 „ ...	2 10¾	3 3	3 7½	3 7½	5 9½	8¾	9¾	1 7½
„ 16 „ „ 17 „ ...	2 7¾	2 11¾	3 3¾	3 3¾	5 3½	8	9	1 6
„ 15 „ „ 16 „ ...	2 5	2 8¾	3 0¼	3 0¼	4 10	7¼	8¼	1 4½
Refreshment Bar, Buffet or Service Attendant—								
Aged 21 years or over	4 5	4 11¾	5 6¼	5 6¼	8 10	1 1¼	1 2¼	2 4½
„ 20 and under 21 years ...	3 11½	4 5½	4 11½	4 11½	7 11	1 0	1 1	2 2
„ 19 „ „ 20 „ ...	3 7¾	4 1¼	4 6¾	4 6¾	7 3½	11	1 0	2 0
„ 18 „ „ 19 „ ...	3 4¼	3 9¼	4 2¼	4 2¼	6 8½	10	11	1 10
„ 17 „ „ 18 „ ...	2 10¼	3 2½	3 6¾	3 6¾	5 8½	8½	9½	1 7
„ 16 „ „ 17 „ ...	2 7¼	2 11¼	3 3	3 3	5 2½	7¾	8¾	1 5½
„ 15 „ „ 16 „ ...	2 4½	2 8	2 11¾	2 11¾	4 9	7¼	8¼	1 4½
Waiter—								
Aged 21 years or over	4 1¼	4 7½	5 1½	5 1½	8 2½	1 0¼	1 1¼	2 2½
„ 20 and under 21 years ...	3 8¼	4 1¾	4 7¼	4 7¼	7 4½	11	1 0	2 0
„ 19 „ „ 20 „ ...	3 4¼	3 9¼	4 2¼	4 2¼	6 8½	10	11	1 10
„ 18 „ „ 19 „ ...	3 0½	3 5	3 9¾	3 9¾	6 1	9¼	10¼	1 8½
„ 17 „ „ 18 „ ...	2 7½	2 11½	3 3½	3 3½	5 3	8	9	1 6
„ 16 „ „ 17 „ ...	2 5¼	2 9	3 0½	3 0½	4 10½	7¼	8¼	1 4½
„ 15 „ „ 16 „ ...	2 2¼	2 5½	2 8¾	2 8¾	4 4½	6½	7½	1 3
Chef	5 9½	6 6¼	7 3	7 3	11 7	1 5½	1 6½	3 1
Head Cook	5 5¾	6 2	6 10¼	6 10¼	10 11½	1 4½	1 5½	2 11

PROVINCIAL B AREA—MALE WORKERS—(*contd.*)

Grade or description of worker **(see paragraph 25 for definitions)** (Column 1)	For all time worked other than on Sunday or a rest day: between 7 a.m. and 7 p.m. (Column 2)	For all time worked other than on Sunday or a rest day: (*a*) between 5 a.m. and 7 a.m. (*b*) between 7 p.m. and 11 p.m. (Column 3)	For all time worked other than on Sunday or a rest day: between 11 p.m. and 5 a.m. (Column 4)	For all time worked on a Sunday which is not the worker's rest day (Column 5)	For all time worked on a rest day (Column 6)	Additions to the hourly rates set out in Columns 2 to 6: For all time worked in excess of 9 hours on any day other than Sunday or a rest day (Column 7)	Additions to the hourly rates set out in Columns 2 to 6: For all time worked in excess of 44 hours in any week: For the first 6 hours (Column 8)	Additions to the hourly rates set out in Columns 2 to 6: For all time worked in excess of 44 hours in any week: For all time after the first 6 hours (Column 9)
	Per hour s. d.	Per hour s. d.	Per hour s. d.	Per hour s. d.	Per hour s. d.	Per hour s. d.	Per hour s. d.	Per hour s. d.
Cook—								
Aged 21 years or over	5 2	5 9¾	6 5½	6 5½	10 4	1 3½	1 4½	2 9
„ 20 and under 21 years ...	4 8	5 3	5 10	5 10	9 4	1 2	1 3	2 6
„ 19 „ „ 20 „ ...	4 4¼	4 10¾	5 5¼	5 5¼	8 8½	1 1	1 2	2 4
„ under 19 years	4 0¾	4 6¾	5 1	5 1	8 1½	1 0¼	1 1¼	2 2½
Assistant Cook—								
Aged 21 years or over	4 9	5 4¼	5 11¼	5 11¼	9 6	1 2¼	1 3¼	2 6½
„ 20 and under 21 years ...	4 3½	4 10	5 4½	5 4½	8 7	1 1	1 2	2 4
„ 19 „ „ 20 „ ...	3 11¾	4 5¾	4 11¾	4 11¾	7 11½	1 0	1 1	2 2
„ 18 „ „ 19 „ ...	3 8¼	4 1¾	4 7¼	4 7¼	7 4½	11	1 0	2 0
„ 17 „ „ 18 „ ...	3 2¼	3 7	3 11¾	3 11¾	6 4½	9½	10½	1 9
„ 16 „ „ 17 „ ...	2 11¼	3 3¾	3 8	3 8	5 10½	8¾	9¾	1 7½
„ 15 „ „ 16 „ ...	2 8½	3 0½	3 4¾	3 4¾	5 5	8¼	9¼	1 6½
Service Cook—								
Aged 21 years or over	4 5¾	5 0½	5 7¼	5 7¼	8 11½	1 1½	1 2½	2 5
„ 20 and under 21 years ...	4 0¼	4 6¼	5 0¼	5 0¼	8 0½	1 0	1 1	2 2
„ 19 „ „ 20 „ ...	3 8½	4 2	4 7¾	4 7¾	7 5	11¼	1 0¼	2 0½
„ 18 „ „ 19 „ ...	3 5	3 10¼	4 3¼	4 3¼	6 10	10¼	11¼	1 10½
„ 17 „ „...18 „ ...	2 11	3 3½	3 7¾	3 7¾	5 10	8¾	9¾	1 7½
„ 16 „ „ 17 „ ...	2 8	3 0	3 4	3 4	5 4	8	9	1 6
„ 15 „ „ 16 „ ...	2 5¼	2 9	3 0½	3 0½	4 10½	7¼	8¼	1 4½

Any other worker except a Manager—								
Aged 21 years or over	4 4½	4 11	5 5¾	5 5¾	8 9	1 1¼	1 2¼	2 4½
„ 20 and under 21 years ...	3 11	4 5	4 10¾	4 10¾	7 10	11¾	1 0¾	2 1½
„ 19 „ „ 20 „ ...	3 7¼	4 0¾	4 6	4 6	7 2½	10¾	11¾	1 11½
„ 18 „ „ 19 „ ...	3 3¾	3 8¾	4 1¾	4 1¾	6 7½	10	11	1 10
„ 17 „ „ 18 „ ...	2 9¾	3 2	3 6¼	3 6¼	5 7½	8½	9½	1 7
„ 16 „ „ 17 „ ...	2 6¾	2 10½	3 2½	3 2½	5 1½	7¾	8¾	1 5½
„ 15 „ „ 16 „ ...	2 4	2 7½	2 11	2 11	4 8	7	8	1 4

PROVINCIAL B AREA—FEMALE WORKERS

(2) The HOURLY minimum remuneration for female workers employed in Provincial B area (as defined in paragraph 27) who are supplied by the employer with meals whilst on duty but not with full board and lodging, is that set out in Columns 2 to 6 inclusive of the Table below with any additions payable under Columns 7, 8 and 9.

Grade or description of worker **(see paragraph 25 for definitions)**	For all time worked other than on Sunday or a rest day			For all time worked on a Sunday which is not the worker's rest day	For all time worked on a rest day	Additions to the hourly rates set out in Columns 2 to 6		
	between 7 a.m. and 7 p.m.	(*a*) between 5 a.m. and 7 a.m. (*b*) between 7 p.m. and 11 p.m.	between 11 p.m. and 5 a.m.			For all time worked in excess of 9 hours on any day other than Sunday or a rest day	For all time worked in excess of 44 hours in any week: For the first 6 hours	For all time worked in excess of 44 hours in any week: For all time after the first 6 hours
(Column 1)	(Column 2)	(Column 3)	(Column 4)	(Column 5)	(Column 6)	(Column 7)	(Column 8)	(Column 9)
	Per hour s. d.	Per hour s. d.	Per hour s. d.	Per hour s. d.	Per hour s. d.	Per hour s. d.	Per hour s. d.	Per hour s. d.
Assistant Manageress—								
Aged 21 years or over	4 2¼	4 8½	5 2¾	5 2¾	8 4½	1 0½	1 1½	2 3
" 20 and under 21 years ...	3 10½	4 4¼	4 10¼	4 10¼	7 9	11¾	1 0¾	2 1½
" 19 " " 20 " ...	3 8¼	4 1¾	4 7¼	4 7¼	7 4½	11	1 0	2 0
" under 19 years	3 6¼	3 11½	4 4¾	4 4¾	7 0½	10½	11½	1 11
Assistant -in-Charge—								
Aged 21 years or over	4 0	4 6	5 0	5 0	8 0	1 0	1 1	2 2
" 20 and under 21 years ...	3 8¼	4 1¾	4 7¼	4 7¼	7 4½	11	1 0	2 0
" 19 " " 20 " ...	3 6	3 11¼	4 4½	4 4½	7 0	10½	11½	1 11
" under 19 years	3 4	3 9	4 2	4 2	6 8	10	11	1 10
Floor Supervisor—								
Aged 21 years or over	3 7½	4 1	4 6½	4 6½	7 3	11	1 0	2 0
" 20 and under 21 years ...	3 4¼	3 9¼	4 2¼	4 2¼	6 8½	10	11	1 10
" 19 " " 20 " ...	3 2	3 6¾	3 11½	3 11½	6 4	9½	10½	1 9
" under 19 years	3 0	3 4½	3 9	3 9	6 0	9	10	1 8

Hostess, Receptionist or Seater—								
Aged 21 years or over	3 5¾	3 11	4 4¼	4 4¼	6 11½	10½	11½	1 11
„ 20 and under 21 years ...	3 2½	3 7¼	4 0¼	4 0¼	6 5	9¾	10¾	1 9½
„ 19 „ „ 20 „ ...	3 0¼	3 4¾	3 9¼	3 9¼	6 0½	9	10	1 8
„ 18 „ „ 19 „ ...	2 10¼	3 2½	3 6¾	3 6¾	5 8½	8½	9½	1 7
„ 17 „ „ 18 „ ...	2 6	2 9¾	3 1½	3 1½	5 0	7½	8½	1 5
„ 16 „ „ 17 „ ...	2 4½	2 8	2 11¾	2 11¾	4 9	7¼	8¼	1 4½
„ 15 „ „ 16 „ ...	2 3	2 6½	2 9¾	2 9¾	4 6	6¾	7¾	1 3½
Clerk—								
Aged 21 years or over	3 7¾	4 1¼	4 6¾	4 6¾	7 3½	11	1 0	2 0
„ 20 and under 21 years ...	3 4½	3 9½	4 2¾	4 2¾	6 9	10¼	11¼	1 10½
„ 19 „ „ 20 „ ...	3 2¼	3 7	3 11¾	3 11¾	6 4½	9½	10½	1 9
„ 18 „ „ 19 „ ...	3 0¼	3 4¾	3 9¼	3 9¼	6 0½	9	10	1 8
„ 17 „ „ 18 „ ...	2 8	3 0	3 4	3 4	5 4	8	9	1 6
„ 16 „ „ 17 „ ...	2 6½	2 10¼	3 2¼	3 2¼	5 1	7¾	8¾	1 5½
„ 15 „ „ 16 „ ...	2 5	2 8¾	3 0¼	3 0¼	4 10	7¼	8¼	1 4½
Cashier or Clerical Assistant—								
Aged 21 years or over	3 5	3 10¼	4 3¼	4 3¼	6 10	10¼	11¼	1 10½
„ 20 and under 21 years ...	3 1¾	3 6½	3 11¼	3 11¼	6 3½	9½	10½	1 9
„ 19 „ „ 20 „ ...	2 11½	3 4	3 8½	3 8½	5 11	9	10	1 8
„ 18 „ „ 19 „ ...	2 9½	3 1¾	3 6	3 6	5 7	8½	9½	1 7
„ 17 „ „ 18 „ ...	2 5¼	2 9	3 0½	3 0½	4 10½	7¼	8¼	1 4½
„ 16 „ „ 17 „ ...	2 3¾	2 7¼	2 10¾	2 10¾	4 7½	7	8	1 4
„ 15 „ „ 16 „ ...	2 2¼	2 5½	2 8¾	2 8¾	4 4½	6½	7½	1 3
Refreshment Bar, Buffet or Service Attendant—								
Aged 21 years or over	3 4½	3 9½	4 2¾	4 2¾	6 9	10¼	11¼	1 10½
„ 20 and under 21 years ...	3 1¼	3 6	3 10½	3 10½	6 2½	9¼	10¼	1 8½
„ 19 „ „ 20 „ ...	2 11	3 3½	3 7¾	3 7¾	5 10	8¾	9¾	1 7½
„ 18 „ „ 19 „ ...	2 9	3 1¼	3 5¼	3 5¼	5 6	8¼	9¼	1 6½
„ 17 „ „ 18 „ ...	2 4¾	2 8¼	3 0	3 0	4 9½	7¼	8¼	1 4½
„ 16 „ „ 17 „ ...	2 3¼	2 6¾	2 10	2 10	4 6½	6¾	7¾	1 3½
„ 15 „ „ 16 „ ...	2 1¾	2 5	2 8¼	2 8¼	4 3½	6½	7½	1 3

PROVINCIAL B AREA—FEMALE WORKERS—(*cont.*)

Grade or description of worker (see paragraph 25 for definitions) (Column 1)	For all time worked other than on Sunday or a rest day: between 7 a.m. and 7 p.m. (Column 2)	(*a*) between 5 a.m. and 7 a.m. (*b*) between 7 p.m. and 11 p.m. (Column 3)	between 11 p.m. and 5 a.m. (Column 4)	For all time worked on a Sunday which is not the worker's rest day (Column 5)	For all time worked on a rest day (Column 6)	Additions to the hourly rates set out in Columns 2 to 6: For all time worked in excess of 9 hours on any day other than Sunday or a rest day (Column 7)	For all time worked in excess of 44 hours in any week: For the first 6 hours (Column 8)	For all time after the first 6 hours (Column 9)
	Per hour s. d.	Per hour s. d.	Per hour s. d.	Per hour s. d.	Per hour s. d.	Per hour s. d.	Per hour s. d.	Per hour s. d.
Shop Assistant—								
Aged 21 years or over	3 6	3 11¼	4 4½	4 4½	7 0	10½	11½	1 11
„ 20 and under 21 years ...	3 2¾	3 7½	4 0½	4 0½	6 5½	9¾	10¾	1 9½
„ 19 „ „ 20 „ ...	3 0½	3 5	3 9¾	3 9¾	6 1	9¼	10¼	1 8½
„ 18 „ „ 19 „ ...	2 10½	3 2¾	3 7¼	3 7¼	5 9	8¾	9¾	1 7½
„ 17 „ „ 18 „ ...	2 6¼	2 10	3 1¾	3 1¾	5 0½	7½	8½	1 5
„ 16 „ „ 17 „ ...	2 4¾	2 8¼	3 0	3 0	4 9½	7¼	8¼	1 4½
„ 15 „ „ 16 „ ...	2 3¼	2 6¾	2 10	2 10	4 6½	6¾	7¾	1 3½
Waitress—								
Aged 21 years or over	3 2	3 6¾	3 11½	3 11½	6 4	9½	10½	1 9
„ 20 and under 21 years ...	2 11	3 3½	3 7¾	3 7¾	5 10	8¾	9¾	1 7½
„ 19 „ „ 20 „ ...	2 9	3 1¼	3 5¼	3 5¼	5 6	8¼	9¼	1 6½
„ 18 „ „ 19 „ ...	2 7¼	2 11¼	3 3	3 3	5 2½	7¾	8¾	1 5½
„ 17 „ „ 18 „ ...	2 3½	2 7	2 10½	2 10½	4 7	7	8	1 4
„ 16 „ „ 17 „ ...	2 1¾	2 5	2 8¼	2 8¼	4 3½	6½	7½	1 3
„ 15 „ „ 16 „ ...	1 11¼	2 2¼	2 5	2 5	3 10½	5¾	6¾	1 1½

Chef	4 8½	5 3½	5 10¾	5 10¾	9 5	1 2¼	1 3¼	2 6½
Head Cook	4 5	4 11¾	5 6¼	5 6¼	8 10	1 1¼	1 2¼	2 4½
Cook—								
Aged 21 years or over	3 11¼	4 5¼	4 11	4 11	7 10½	11¾	1 0¾	2 1½
„ 20 and under 21 years ...	3 7½	4 1	4 6½	4 6½	7 3	11	1 0	2 0
„ 19 „ „ 20 „ ...	3 5¼	3 10½	4 3½	4 3½	6 10½	10¼	11¼	1 10½
„ under 19 years	3 3¼	3 8¼	4 1	4 1	6 6½	9¾	10¾	1 9½
Assistant Cook—								
Aged 21 years or over	3 7¼	4 0¾	4 6	4 6	7 2½	10¾	11¾	1 11½
„ 20 and under 21 years ...	3 4	3 9	4 2	4 2	6 8	10	11	1 10
„ 19 „ „ 20 „ ...	3 1¾	3 6½	3 11¼	3 11¼	6 3½	9½	10½	1 9
„ 18 „ „ 19 „ ...	2 11¾	3 4¼	3 8¾	3 8¾	5 11½	9	10	1 8
„ 17 „ „ 18 „ ...	2 7½	2 11½	3 3½	3 3½	5 3	8	9	1 6
„ 16 „ „ 17 „ ...	2 6	2 9¾	3 1½	3 1½	5 0	7½	8½	1 5
„ 15 „ „ 16 „ ...	2 4½	2 8	2 11¾	2 11¾	4 9	7¼	8¼	1 4½
Service Cook—								
Aged 21 years or over	3 5¼	3 10½	4 3½	4 3½	6 10½	10¼	11¼	1 10½
„ 20 and under 21 years ...	3 2	3 6¾	3 11½	3 11½	6 4	9½	10½	1 9
„ 19 „ „ 20 „ ...	2 11¾	3 4¼	3 8¾	3 8¾	5 11½	9	10	1 8
„ 18 „ „ 19 „ ...	2 9¾	3 2	3 6¼	3 6¼	5 7½	8½	9½	1 7
„ 17 „ „ 18 „ ...	2 5½	2 9¼	3 1	3 1	4 11	7½	8½	1 5
„ 16 „ „ 17 „ ...	2 4	2 7½	2 11	2 11	4 8	7	8	1 4
„ 15 „ „ 16 „ ...	2 2½	2 5¾	2 9¼	2 9¼	4 5	6¾	7¾	1 3½

PROVINCIAL B AREA—FEMALE WORKERS—(*cont.*)

Grade or description of worker **(see paragraph 25 for definitions)**	For all time worked other than on Sunday or a rest day			For all time worked on a Sunday which is not the worker's rest day	For all time worked on a rest day	Additions to the hourly rates set out in Columns 2 to 6		
	between 7 a.m. and 7 p.m.	(*a*) between 5 a.m. and 7 a.m. (*b*) between 7 p.m. and 11 p.m.	between 11 p.m. and 5 a.m.			For all time worked in excess of 9 hours on any day other than Sunday or a rest day	For all time worked in excess of 44 hours in any week	
							For the first 6 hours	For all time after the first 6 hours
(Column 1)	(Column 2)	(Column 3)	(Column 4)	(Column 5)	(Column 6)	(Column 7)	(Column 8)	(Column 9)
	Per hour s. d.	Per hour s. d.	Per hour s. d.	Per hour s. d.	Per hour s. d.	Per hour s. d.	Per hour s. d.	Per hour s. d.
Any other worker except a Manageress—								
Aged 21 years or over	*3 4*	*3 9*	*4 2*	*4 2*	*6 8*	*10*	*11*	*1 10*
„ 20 and under 21 years ...	*3 0¾*	*3 5¼*	*3 10*	*3 10*	*6 1½*	*9¼*	*10¼*	*1 8½*
„ 19 „ „ 20 „ ...	*2 10½*	*3 2¾*	*3 7¼*	*3 7¼*	*5 9*	*8¾*	*9¾*	*1 7½*
„ 18 „ „ 19 „ ...	*2 8½*	*3 0½*	*3 4¾*	*3 4¾*	*5 5*	*8¼*	*9¼*	*1 6½*
„ 17 „ „ 18 „ ...	*2 4¼*	*2 7¾*	*2 11¼*	*2 11¼*	*4 8½*	*7*	*8*	*1 4*
„ 16 „ „ 17 „ ...	*2 2¾*	*2 6*	*2 9½*	*2 9½*	*4 5½*	*6¾*	*7¾*	*1 3½*
„ 15 „ „ 16 „ ...	*2 1¼*	*2 4½*	*2 7½*	*2 7½*	*4 2½*	*6¼*	*7¼*	*1 2½*

MANAGERS AND MANAGERESSES (OTHER THAN OCCASIONAL WORKERS) SUPPLIED WITH MEALS

5. The minimum remuneration for managers and manageresses (as defined in paragraph 25) who normally work for the employer for not less than 36 hours in a week in the London, Provincial A or Provincial B area (as defined in paragraph 27) and who are supplied by the employer with meals whilst on duty but not with full board and lodging, is as follows:—

(1)

	London area	Provincial A area	Provincial B area
	Per week	Per week	Per week
	s. d.	s. d.	s. d.
Manager	270 6	264 6	258 6
Manageress	221 6	215 6	209 6

(2) (a) IN ADDITION for all time worked other than on a Sunday or a rest day—

    (i) between 5 a.m. and 7 a.m.   ..   ..   at the rate of $\frac{1}{8}$th time ;

    (ii) between 7 p.m. and 11 p.m.   ..   ..   at the rate of $\frac{1}{8}$th time ;

    (iii) between 11 p.m. and 5 a.m.   ..   ..   at the rate of $\frac{1}{4}$ time ;

    (iv) in excess of 9 hours in a day   ..   ..   at the rate of $\frac{1}{4}$ time ;

(b) IN ADDITION for all time worked on a Sunday which is not the worker's rest day ..   ..   at the rate of $\frac{1}{4}$ time.

For the purposes of this sub-paragraph "$\frac{1}{8}$th time" and "$\frac{1}{4}$ time" mean respectively $\frac{1}{8}$th and $\frac{1}{4}$ of the hourly rate, and "hourly rate" means 1/44th of the remuneration payable under sub-paragraph (1) of this paragraph.

(3) IN ADDITION for work on a rest day, one-sixth of the remuneration payable under sub-paragraph (1) of this paragraph.

WORKERS SUPPLIED WITH FULL BOARD AND LODGING

6. Where a worker is supplied by the employer with full board and lodging for seven days a week, the minimum remuneration shall be that payable under the provisions of paragraph 2, 3, 4 or 5 to a worker of the same grade or description employed in the same area for the same hours REDUCED by the appropriate amount as follows:—

Age of worker	London area		Provincial A area		Provincial B area	
	Male	Female	Male	Female	Male	Female
	Per week		Per week		Per week	
	s. d.	s. d.	s. d.	s. d.	s. d.	s. d.
Aged 21 years or over ...	28 5	27 5	24 5	23 5	20 5	19 5
„ 20 and under 21 years	24 1	23 1	20 1	19 1	16 1	15 1
„ 19 „ „ 20 „	21 7	20 7	17 7	16 7	13 7	12 7
„ 18 „ „ 19 „	19 1	18 1	15 1	14 1	11 1	10 1
„ 17 „ „ 18 „	14 9	13 9	10 9	9 9	6 9	5 9
„ 16 „ „ 17 „	12 3	11 3	8 3	7 3	4 3	3 3
„ 15 „ „ 16 „	9 9	8 9	5 9	4 9	1 9	9

OCCASIONAL WORKERS SUPPLIED WITH MEALS

7. The HOURLY minimum remuneration for an occasional worker (not being a part-time worker) who is supplied by the employer with meals whilst on duty is, in the case of a worker other than a manager or manageress, the remuneration specified in Column 2 of the appropriate Table in paragraph 2, 3 or 4 for a worker of the same grade or description employed in the same area and, in the case of a manager or manageress, 1/44th of the appropriate weekly remuneration specified in paragraph 5 (1), INCREASED as follows:—

(1) in respect of hours of work other than on Sunday or a customary holiday—

    (*a*) between 5 a.m. and 11 p.m. .. .. by 12½ per cent.;

    (*b*) between 11 p.m. and 5 a.m. .. .. by 40 per cent.;

(2) for all time worked on Sunday .. .. by 25 per cent.;

(3) for all time worked on a customary holiday .. .. by 40 per cent.:

Provided that where an occasional worker works on Sunday or a customary holiday for less than four hours he shall for the purposes of this paragraph be treated as if he had worked for four hours on that day.

WORKERS (INCLUDING OCCASIONAL WORKERS) NOT SUPPLIED WITH FULL BOARD AND LODGING OR MEALS

8. Where a worker is not supplied by the employer with either full board and lodging or meals whilst on duty, the minimum remuneration shall be that payable under the provisions of paragraph 2, 3, 4, 5 or 7 to a worker of the same grade or description employed in the same area INCREASED as follows:—

(1) in the case of a worker other than a manager or manageress, by 5d. per hour for the first 44 hours worker by him in any week ;

(2) in the case of a manager or manageress, by 18s. 6d. per week.

WORKERS WHO ARE NOT REQUIRED TO WORK ON A CUSTOMARY HOLIDAY

9.—(1) Where a worker, other than an occasional worker, is not required to work on a customary holiday he shall be paid for the customary holiday—

    (*a*) not less than the amount to which he would have been entitled under the provisions of this Schedule had the day not been a customary holiday and had he worked for a number of hours ordinarily worked by him on that day of the week, and

    (*b*) in the case of a worker who is normally supplied by his employer with either full board or meals whilst on duty, IN ADDITION to the amount payable under (*a*) above, an amount of—

        3s. 4d. for a worker other than a part-time worker, or

        1s. 8d. for a part-time worker:

Provided that the above provision shall apply only if the worker has been in the employer's employment for the six days immediately preceding the holiday and (unless excused by the employer or absent by reason of proved sickness) worked for the employer the number of hours ordinarily worked by him on the last working day on which work was available for him prior to the holiday and the number of hours ordinarily worked by him on the next such working day following the holiday.

(2) Where a customary holiday falls on the worker's rest day, or half day, and no alternative rest day or half day is allowed in that week, then the worker shall in addition to the payment specified in sub-paragraph (1) of this paragraph be paid in respect of that rest day or half day at the hourly rate (as defined in paragraph 12) INCREASED by 5d. for the number of hours ordinarily worked by him on a full day or half day as the case may be.

WORKERS WHO WORK ON A CUSTOMARY HOLIDAY AND ARE ALLOWED A DAY OF HOLIDAY IN LIEU

10. Where a worker, other than an occasional worker, works on a customary holiday and is allowed by his employer a day of holiday in lieu of the customary holiday on a day other than a rest day or half day within the period of 42 days from the customary holiday, he shall be paid as follows:—

(1) for his work on the customary holiday .. .. the remuneration to which he is entitled under the other provisions of this Schedule and IN ADDITION hourly remuneration at one-quarter of the hourly rate (as defined in paragraph 12) for all time worked on that day:

Provided that where the worker works on a customary holiday for less than four hours, he shall be treated as if he had worked for four hours on that day; and

(2) for the day of holiday in lieu of the customary holiday .. .. .. the hourly rate (as defined in paragraph 12) INCREASED by 5d. and multiplied by 8 or, in the case of a part-time worker, by 4.

WORKERS WHO WORK ON A CUSTOMARY HOLIDAY AND ARE NOT ALLOWED A DAY OF HOLIDAY IN LIEU

11. Where a worker, other than an occasional worker, works on a customary holiday and is NOT allowed by his employer a day of holiday in lieu of the customary holiday on a day other than a rest day or half day within the period of 42 days from the customary holiday, he shall be paid as follows:—

(1) for his work on the customary holiday .. .. the remuneration to which he is entitled under the other provisions of this Schedule and IN ADDITION hourly remuneration at one-quarter of the hourly rate (as defined in paragraph 12) for all time worked on that day:

Provided that where the worker works on a customary holiday for less than four hours, he shall be treated as if he had worked for four hours on that day; and

(2) for the working day next following the 42nd day after the customary holiday or for the last day of his employment, whichever shall first occur .. (a) the remuneration to which he is entitled under the other provisions of this Schedule, and (b) the hourly rate (as defined in paragraph 12) INCREASED by 5d. and multiplied by 8 or, in the case of a part-time worker, by 4.

12. For the purposes of paragraphs 9, 10 and 11, "hourly rate" means—

(1) in the case of a worker other than a manager or manageress, the remuneration under Column 2 of the Table in paragraph 2, 3 or 4 for a worker of the same grade or description employed in the same area;

(2) in the case of a manager or manageress, 1/44th of the remuneration provided by paragraph 5 (1).

GUARANTEED WEEKLY REMUNERATION

13.—(1) Notwithstanding the other provisions of this Schedule, where in any week a worker to whom this paragraph applies performs some work to which this Schedule applies and the total remuneration (including any holiday remuneration payable under this Schedule but excluding any remuneration for work performed on a customary holiday or payable under the provisions of paragraph 11 (2) (*b*)) due to the worker in respect of that week under those provisions is less than the guaranteed weekly remuneration, the minimum remuneration payable to that worker for that week shall, in lieu of the minimum remuneration otherwise payable under those provisions be, subject to the provisions of this paragraph, the appropriate guaranteed weekly remuneration provided for by sub-paragraph (3) hereof.

(2) The provisions of this paragraph shall apply in any week to a worker who during the three months immediately preceding that week has been in the continuous employment of the employer and who normally works for the employer for not less than 36 hours a week on work to which this Schedule applies.

For the purposes of this sub-paragraph a worker shall be treated as having been in the continuous employment of the employer in any week in which he performs any work to which this Schedule applies or throughout which he is absent on holiday or otherwise with the permission of the employer, or on account of his proved sickness.

(3) Subject to the provisions of sub-paragraphs (5) to (8) of this paragraph, the guaranteed weekly remuneration payable in respect of a week to a worker is the remuneration to which the worker would have been entitled under this Schedule if he had worked the hours normally worked by him in a week, but excluding from such hours any time worked for which remuneration is payable under Columns 8 and 9 of the Tables in paragraphs 2, 3 and 4.

(4) For the purposes of this paragraph a worker shall be treated as though he had worked on work to which this Schedule applies on any holiday allowed to and taken by him in that week under this Schedule or on any customary holiday or day in lieu thereof on which he is not required to work : Provided that a worker shall not be treated as having so worked in any week throughout which he is on holiday.

(5) Guaranteed weekly remuneration is not payable in respect of any week unless during that week the worker, in respect of the hours normally worked by him in a week, is

    (*a*) capable of and available for work ; and

    (*b*) willing to perform such services outside his usual occupation as may reasonably be required by the employer when work is not available to him in his usual occupation in the undertaking:

Provided that a worker shall not cease to be capable of and available for work by reason of the fact that he has been allowed a holiday ; and provided further that guaranteed weekly remuneration shall not cease to be payable to a worker in respect of any week by reason only of the fact that the worker is absent for any part of that week because of proved sickness but shall be reduced in the case of a six-day worker, a five-day worker or a four-day worker by one-sixth, one-fifth or one-fourth, respectively, for each day on which he is so absent from work in that week.

(6) Guaranteed weekly remuneration is not payable in respect of any week if the worker's employment is terminated before the end of that week.

(7) If the employer is unable to provide the worker with work by reason of a strike or other circumstances outside the control of the employer and gives the worker four days' notice to that effect, guaranteed weekly remuneration shall not be payable after the expiry of such notice in respect of any week during which or part of which the employer continues to be unable to provide work as aforesaid:

Provided that in respect of the week in which the said notice expires there shall be paid to the worker, in addition to any remuneration payable in respect of time worked in that week, any remuneration that would have been payable if the worker had worked his normal hours of work on any days in the week prior to the expiry of the notice.

(8) The guaranteed weekly remuneration payable to a worker in any week shall be reduced in the case of a six-day worker, a five-day worker or a four-day worker by one-sixth, one-fifth or one-fourth, respectively, for each customary holiday falling in that week on which the worker has performed for the employer some work to which this Schedule applies:

Provided that the remuneration payable to the worker under this Schedule for such work shall be additional to the guaranteed weekly remuneration reduced as aforesaid.

JEWISH UNDERTAKINGS

14. Where it is the established practice in a Jewish undertaking for the employer to require attendance on Sunday instead of Saturday the provisions of this Schedule referring to Sunday shall apply in like manner as if in such provisions Sunday were treated as a week day and the word "Saturday" were substituted for "Sunday".

For the purposes of this paragraph "Jewish undertaking" means an undertaking carried on by a person or persons of the Jewish religion or a member or members of any religious body regularly observing the Jewish Sabbath and includes an undertaking carried on by a partnership or company if the majority of the partners or the directors of the company are persons of the Jewish religion or members of any religious body as aforesaid.

Part II
ANNUAL HOLIDAY AND HOLIDAY REMUNERATION
DURATION OF ANNUAL HOLIDAY

15.—(1) Subject to the provisions of sub-paragraph (2) of this paragraph and paragraphs 16, 17 and 18, an employer shall, between 1st April 1970 and 31st October 1970, and in each succeeding year between 1st April and 31st October, allow a holiday (hereinafter referred to as an "annual holiday") to every worker in his employment, other than an occasional worker, to whom this Schedule applies who was employed by him during the 12 months immediately preceding the commencement of the holiday season (hereinafter referred to as the "qualifying period") for any of the periods specified below, and the duration of the annual holiday shall be related to the period of the worker's employment during the qualifying period as follows:—

Period of employment during the qualifying period	Duration of annual holiday for a worker whose normal working week (as defined in paragraph 26) is				
	more than 5 days	5 days	4 days	3 days	2 days
(1)	(2)	(3)	(4)	(5)	(6)
At least 8 weeks	2 days	1 day	1 day	1 day	—
„ „ 12 „	3 „	2 days	2 days	1 „	1 day
„ „ 16 „	4 „	3 „	2 „	2 days	1 „
„ „ 20 „	5 „	4 „	3 „	2 „	1 „
„ „ 24 „	6 „	5 „	4 „	3 „	2 days
„ „ 28 „	7 „	6 „	4 „	3 „	2 „
„ „ 32 „	8 „	6 „	5 „	4 „	2 „
„ „ 36 „	9 „	7 „	5 „	4 „	3 „
„ „ 40 „	10 „	8 „	6 „	5 „	3 „
„ „ 44 „	11 „	9 „	7 „	5 „	3 „
„ „ 48 „	12 „	10 „	8 „	6 „	4 „

(2) Notwithstanding the provisions of sub-paragraph (1) of this paragraph, where a worker who is normally employed on not less than four days a week and who has not been in the continuous employment of his employer during the four years immediately preceding the commencement of the holiday season has qualified under the said sub-paragraph for more days of annual holiday than the number of days on which it is normal for the worker to work in a week, the employer may require that worker to take part of his annual holiday after the end of the holiday season and before the 31st March next following.

The number of days which an employer may so require a worker to take shall be related to the period of the worker's employment during the four years immediately preceding the commencement of the holiday season in accordance with the following Table and shall not exceed the number of days specified in Column 2, 3 or 4 of that Table appropriate to the worker:—

Period of continuous employment during the four years immediately preceding the commencement of the holiday season	Number of days of annual holiday which the employer may require the worker to take after the end of the holiday season for a worker whose normal working week (as defined in paragraph 26) is		
	more than 5 days	5 days	4 days
(1)	(2)	(3)	(4)
At least 28 weeks	1 day	1 day	—
„ „ 32 „	2 days	1 „	1 day
„ „ 36 „	3 „	2 days	1 „
„ „ 40 „	4 „	3 „	2 days
„ „ 44 „	5 „	4 „	3 „
„ „ 48 „	6 „	5 „	4 „
„ „ 18 months	5 „	5 „	4 „
„ „ 24 „	4 „	4 „	3 „
„ „ 30 „	3 „	3 „	2 „
„ „ 36 „	2 „	2 „	2 „
„ „ 42 „	1 day	1 day	1 day
„ „ 48 „	nil	nil	nil

Any days of annual holiday allowed to a worker after the end of a holiday season under the provisions of this sub-paragraph or of Order U.P.R. (36) shall be treated for the purposes of this Schedule as having been allowed during such holiday season.

(3) In this Schedule the expression "holiday season" means in relation to the year 1970 the period commencing on 1st April 1970 and ending on 31st October 1970 and in relation to each succeeding year the period commencing on 1st April and ending on 31st October in that year.

AGREEMENT TO ALLOW ANNUAL HOLIDAY OUTSIDE THE HOLIDAY SEASON

16. Notwithstanding the provisions of paragraph 15, where a worker elects to take his annual holiday, or part thereof, outside the holiday season and in pursuance of an agreement in writing with his employer that the employer will allow such holiday at a given date after the end of the holiday season and before the commencement of the next following holiday season, the days of holiday so allowed shall for the purposes of this Schedule be treated as having been allowed during the preceding holiday season.

APPLICATIONS TO VARY THE HOLIDAY SEASON

17. Notwithstanding the provisions of paragraph 15, the Wages Council may vary the holiday season as there set out in respect of any establishment if it receives an application for that purpose from an employer and is satisfied that it is reasonable to do so to meet special circumstances. Such variation may provide for the commencement of the holiday season earlier than 1st April or its extension beyond 31st October. An application relating to the commencement of the holiday season shall be made to the Wages Council not later than six weeks before the proposed operative date and an application to extend the duration of the holiday season, before 15th July. Any such alteration in the holiday season shall not become effective until notice of the decision of the Wages Council has been communicated to the employer concerned.

In the case of any variation of the commencement of the holiday season under this provision the duration of the holiday of the worker or workers concerned shall be related to the period immediately preceding the commencement of the holiday season as varied.

SPELLS OF ANNUAL HOLIDAY

18. Subject to the provisions of paragraphs 15 (2) and 16, an annual holiday shall be allowed on consecutive working days other than customary holidays and days of holiday shall be treated as consecutive notwithstanding that a rest day or a customary holiday or a day in lieu of a customary holiday intervenes:

Provided that where the duration of an annual holiday for which a worker has qualified and which he is to be allowed during the holiday season in any year exceeds the number of days constituting the worker's normal working week, the holiday may be allowed in two periods consisting in respect of each period of consecutive working days and in such a case one of those periods shall consist of days not less in number than the number of days constituting the worker's normal working week.

GENERAL

19. An employer shall give to a worker reasonable notice of the commencing date or dates and of the duration of his annual holiday. Such notice may be given individually to the worker or by the posting of a notice in the place where the worker is employed.

20. Where any day of annual holiday allowed to any worker under this Schedule falls upon a day of holiday or half holiday to which the worker may be entitled under any enactment other than the Wages Councils Act 1959, that holiday or half holiday may be treated as part of the annual holiday allowed under this schedule except that holidays required to be allowed under the Shops Act 1950(a) shall be treated as follows:—

(1) in the case of establishments in which section 17 of the Shops Act 1950 applies:—

    (a) where a worker's total annual holiday under this Schedule does not exceed the number of days constituting his normal working week, not more than one of the half holidays allowed under the said section of the Act may be treated as part of the worker's annual holiday;

    (b) where a worker's total annual holiday exceeds the number of days constituting his normal working week, not more than two of the half holidays allowed under the said section of the Act may be treated as part of the worker's annual holiday;

(2) in the case of establishments in which section 21 of the Shops Act 1950 applies:—

    (a) any of the six consecutive days of holiday on full pay allowed under the said section of the Act may be treated as a day of annual holiday; and (*b*) other holidays or half holidays allowed under the said section of the Act may be treated as part of the worker's annual holiday to the following extent:—

(i) where a worker's total annual holiday does not exceed the number of days constituting his normal working week—not more than one half holiday allowed under the said section of the Act ;

(ii) where a worker's total annual holiday exceeds the number of days constituting his normal working week—not more than two half holidays or one whole holiday on a weekday allowed under the said section of the Act.

REMUNERATION FOR ANNUAL HOLIDAY

21.—(1) Subject to the provisions of paragraph 22, a worker qualified to be allowed an annual holiday under this Schedule shall be paid by his employer in respect thereof, on the last pay day preceding such annual holiday, one day's holiday pay (as defined in paragraph 26) in respect of each day thereof.

(2) Where under the provisions of paragraph 15 (2), 16 or 18 an annual holiday is allowed in more than one period the holiday remuneration shall be apportioned accordingly.

22. Where under the provisions of paragraph 23 of this Schedule or of Order U.P.R. (36) accrued holiday remuneration has been paid by the employer to the worker, in respect of any period of employment in the 12 months immediately preceding the holiday season within which an annual holiday is allowed by the employer to the worker in accordance with the provisions of this Schedule, the amount of holiday remuneration payable by the employer in respect of the said annual holiday shall be reduced by the amount of the said accrued holiday remuneration, unless that remuneration has been deducted from a previous payment of holiday remuneration made under the provisions of this Schedule or of Order U.P.R. (36).

ACCRUED HOLIDAY REMUNERATION PAYABLE ON TERMINATION OF EMPLOYMENT

23. Subject to the provisions of this paragraph, where a worker, other than an occasional worker, ceases to be employed by an employer after the provisions of this Schedule became effective, the employer shall, immediately on the termination of the employment (hereinafter called "the termination date"), pay to the worker accrued holiday remuneration, that is to say:—

(1) in respect of employment in the 12 months up to the 1st April immediately preceding the termination date, a sum equal to the holiday remuneration for any days of annual holiday for which he has qualified, except days of annual holiday which he has been allowed or has become entitled to be allowed before leaving the employment ; and

(2) in respect of any employment since the 1st April immediately preceding the termination date, a sum equal to the holiday remuneration which would have been payable to him if he could have been allowed an annual holiday in respect of that employment at the time of leaving it:

Provided that—

(*a*) accrued holiday remuneration shall not be payable to a worker if he is dismissed on the grounds of gross misconduct and is so informed in writing by the employer at the time of dismissal ;

(*b*) where a worker is employed under a written contract of service and terminates his employment without having given to his employer the notice of that termination required under that contract, any accrued holiday remuneration payable by the employer to the worker shall be an amount equal to that payable under the foregoing provisions of this paragraph reduced by an amount equal to one day's holiday pay multiplied by the number of days of notice required under the written contract ;

(c) where, during the period or periods in respect of which the said accrued holiday remuneration is payable, the worker has been allowed any day or days of holiday for which he had not qualified under the provisions of this Schedule or of Order U.P.R. (36), any accrued holiday remuneration payable as aforesaid shall be reduced by the amount of any sum paid by the employer to the worker in respect of such day or days of holiday.

CALCULATION OF EMPLOYMENT

24. For the purposes of calculating any period of employment qualifying a worker for an annual holiday or for any accrued holiday remuneration under this Schedule the worker shall be treated as having been employed for a week in respect of any week in which he has worked for the employer on not less than two days and has performed some work which entitled him to statutory minimum remuneration.

For the purposes of this paragraph a worker shall be treated as having worked for the employer when absent from work in any of the following circumstances: —

(1) on days of annual holiday allowed under this Schedule, on customary holidays and days in lieu of customary holidays ;

(2) during proved sickness of or accident to the worker up to and not exceeding a maximum of 12 weeks in the aggregate during—

(a) the period of 12 months immediately preceding the commencement of the holiday season ; and

(b) any period commencing on the 1st April preceding the termination date and ending on the termination date:

Provided that for the purposes of paragraph 15 (2) all absences through proved sickness of or accident to the worker while in the employment of the employer, prior to the period of 12 months specified in sub-paragraph (2) (a) of this paragraph, shall be treated as employment ;

(3) by leave of the employer.

PART III

DEFINITIONS

DEFINITIONS OF GRADES OR DESCRIPTIONS OF WORKERS

25. In this Schedule the following expressions have the meanings hereby respectively assigned to them, that is to say: —

"ASSISTANT COOK" means a worker (not being a service cook) who is wholly or mainly engaged in cooking or in preparing and cooking food (not being the preparation for cooking of vegetables or the preparation of salads) and duties ancillary thereto where the cooking is performed under the immediate supervision of a cook or of a person who is required to perform the duties of a cook.

"ASSISTANT-IN-CHARGE" means a worker wholly or mainly engaged in catering work who is in direct control of a catering undertaking in which not more than four persons (exclusive of the assistant-in-charge) are employed and who is immediately responsible for its operation.

In computing the number of persons employed on the staff of the undertaking all workers shall be included except that in the case of workers who do not normally work for 36 hours in a week the number to be counted shall be the number disregarding fractions obtained by dividing by 36 the aggregate of the hours usually worked in the week by all such workers.

"ASSISTANT MANAGER" OR "ASSISTANT MANAGERESS" means a worker wholly or mainly engaged on catering work who assists the person who is in direct control of a catering undertaking in which not less than five persons, exclusive of the person who is in direct control, are employed (whether or not such person is a manager or manageress as defined in this Schedule) and who takes charge during the absence of such person.

"CASHIER" means a worker wholly or mainly engaged in taking cash or giving change and duties ancillary thereto.

"CHEF" means a worker experienced in all departments of the kitchen who performs or directs the duties of a head cook and in addition is responsible for the planning of menus and who may order supplies.

"CLERICAL ASSISTANT" means a worker (other than a clerk) wholly or mainly engaged at a place of refreshment on clerical or office work.

"CLERK" means a worker (not being a cashier) whose work is performed at a place of refreshment and who is wholly or mainly engaged in clerical or office work and who is wholly responsible to the proprietor, manager, manageress, assistant manager or assistant manageress for the control of records of goods or cash and/or correspondence, and work incidental thereto.

"COOK" means a worker (not being an assistant cook or service cook) wholly or mainly engaged in any of the following duties and duties ancillary thereto ; cooking or preparing and cooking food requiring the mixing of two or more ingredients and/or cooking or preparing and cooking meat, poultry, game or fish.

"FLOOR SUPERVISOR" means a worker in charge of the whole or part of a floor or room who is responsible for tables, the seating of customers and the control of staff and duties ancillary thereto.

"HEAD COOK" means a cook experienced in all departments of the kitchen whose duties mainly consist of preparing and cooking food and include the control of kitchen staff and who is employed in a kitchen in which not less than three cooks or assistant cooks are employed.

"HOSTESS, RECEPTIONIST OR SEATER" means a worker in charge of the whole or part of a floor or room who is responsible for tables and the seating of customers.

"MANAGER" OR "MANAGERESS" means a worker wholly or mainly engaged on catering work and in direct control of a catering undertaking in which not less than five persons (exclusive of the manager or manageress) are employed and who is immediately responsible for its operation.

In computing the number of persons employed on the staff of the undertaking all workers shall be included except that in the case of workers who do not normally work for 36 hours in a week the number to be counted shall be the number disregarding fractions obtained by dividing by 36 the aggregate of the hours usually worked in the week by all such workers.

"OCCASIONAL WORKER" means a worker who undertakes engagements on either an hourly or a day to day basis.

"PART-TIME WORKER" means a worker (other than an occasional worker) who normally works for the employer for less than 36 hours in a week.

"REFRESHMENT BAR, BUFFET OR SERVICE ATTENDANT" means a worker wholly or mainly engaged in serving customers or waiting staff from a bar, buffet, service or similar place and duties ancillary thereto and whose duties may include dispensing, sandwich making, toasting, the heating and preparation of food, the cleansing of utensils, glass, cutlery, etc., and the taking of cash.

"SERVICE COOK" means a worker (not being an assistant cook) who is wholly or mainly engaged in preparing light refreshments and duties ancillary thereto or re-heating completely cooked food and duties ancillary thereto.

For the purposes of this definition "preparing light refreshments" includes sandwich making, the re-heating of soups, the complete preparation of toast dishes, salads, meals consisting of cold meat, cold fish, canned or preserved foods (but not including the carving of cold meat or fish) and the complete preparation of beverages.

"SHOP ASSISTANT" means a worker who is wholly or mainly employed in connection with any retail sale of goods (other than food or drink for immediate consumption) on premises where the main activity is the supply of food or drink for immediate consumption.

"WAITER" OR "WAITRESS" means a worker wholly or mainly engaged in the serving of food or drink or food and drink at tables and duties ancillary thereto and who takes orders and gives bills.

OTHER DEFINITIONS

26. In this Schedule, except where the context otherwise requires, the following expressions have the meanings hereby respectively assigned to them, that is to say:—

AREAS—"London Area", "Provincial A Area", "Provincial B Area" have the meanings respectively assigned to them in paragraph 27.

"CATERING CONTRACTING BUSINESS" means a business or part of a business wholly or mainly engaged in supplying food or drink for immediate consumption—

(1) on premises not ordinarily occupied by the person or body of persons carrying on the business; or

(2) in a railway train where the business is carried on otherwise than by a railway company or any Board established by the Transport Act 1962(a) or any subsidiary thereof;

and any activities incidental or ancillary thereto.

"CATERING UNDERTAKING" means any undertaking or any part of an undertaking which consists wholly or mainly in the carrying on (whether for profit or not) of one or more of the following activities, that is to say, the supply of food or drink for immediate consumption, the provision of living accommodation for guests or lodgers or for persons employed in the undertaking and any other activity so far as it is incidental or ancillary to any such activity as aforesaid of the undertaking.

"CENTRAL CATERING ESTABLISHMENT" means an establishment wholly or mainly engaged in the preparation of food or drink for immediate consumption at two or more places of refreshment carried on by the person or body of persons carrying on the establishment but does not include an establishment wholly or mainly engaged in the preparation of food or drink for consumption on the same premises or in the same building as those on which or as that in which the establishment itself is carried on.

"CUSTOMARY HOLIDAY" means
(1) In England and Wales—Christmas Day (or, if Christmas Day falls on a Sunday, such weekday as may be prescribed by national proclamation or if no such day is prescribed the next following Tuesday), Boxing Day, Good Friday, Easter Monday, Whit Monday (or where another day is substituted therefor by national proclamation, that day), August Bank Holiday and any day proclaimed as an additional Bank Holiday or a general holiday;
(2) In Scotland—
  (a) New Year's Day (or the following day if New Year's Day falls on a Sunday), the local Spring holiday, the local Autumn holiday, and any day proclaimed as an additional Bank Holiday or a general holiday throughout Scotland;
  (b) three other weekdays in the course of a calendar year, to be fixed by the employer and notified to the worker not less than three weeks before the holiday, or any other day or days falling within the same calendar year which may be substituted for such day or days by agreement between the employer and the worker or his representative; or
(3) Where in any establishment it is not the custom or practice to observe such days as are specified in (1) or (2) (a) above as holidays, other days,

(a) 1962 c. 46.

not fewer in number, as may be substituted for such days by agreement between the employer and the worker or his representative.

"FULL BOARD" means not less than four meals a day of good and sufficient quality and quantity.

"LODGING" means clean and adequate accommodation and facilities for eating, sleeping, washing and leisure.

"MEAL" means a meal of good and sufficient quality and quantity.

"NORMAL WORKING WEEK" means the average number of days worked in a week by a worker during the first four of the last five weeks in which he worked for the employer prior to
- (1) the annual holiday ; or
- (2) where accrued holiday remuneration is payable, the termination date ; and for the purposes of this definition
  - (a) a worker shall be treated as having worked for the employer on any day on which he was absent from work owing to proved illness or accident to the worker, on annual holiday, on a customary holiday or a day in lieu of a customary holiday ;
  - (b) a fraction of a day shall be reckoned as a day.

"ONE DAY'S HOLIDAY PAY" means the amount obtained by dividing the total remuneration applicable to the worker for the first four of the last five weeks during which he worked for the employer prior to the holiday or the termination date, as the case may be, by the number of days on which the worker worked for the employer during the said four weeks.

In this definition the expression "remuneration applicable" means the statutory minimum remuneration to which the worker would be entitled under this Schedule if he were not supplied by the employer with either full board and lodging or meals on duty, but excluding all remuneration in respect of time worked for which remuneration is payable under Columns 8 and 9 of the Tables in paragraphs 2, 3 and 4.

"PLACE OF REFRESHMENT" means any place which is used either regularly or occasionally as or for the purposes of a restaurant, dining-room, café, tea shop, buffet or similar place, or a coffee stall, snack bar, or other similar stall or bar.

"RESIDENTIAL ESTABLISHMENT" means an establishment which either contains four or more rooms ordinarily available as sleeping accommodation for guests or lodgers or, if it contains less than four such rooms, which contains sleeping accommodation ordinarily available for not less than eight guests or lodgers.

"REST DAY" means one day in each week which has been notified to the worker before the commencement of that week as a rest day, or failing such notification, Sunday.

"STATUTORY MINIMUM REMUNERATION" means minimum remuneration (other than holiday remuneration) fixed by a wages regulation order made by the Secretary of State to give effect to proposals submitted to her by the Wages Council.

"UNLICENSED PLACE OF REFRESHMENT" means any place of refreshment where intoxicating liquor—
- (1) cannot legally be sold (or supplied in the case of a restaurant, dining-room, buffet or bar at a club) for consumption on the premises ; or
- (2) can legally be so sold or supplied by reason only of the fact that an occasional licence in relation to that place is for the time being in force, being a licence granted to some person other than the person carrying on, or a person in the employment of the person carrying on, the activities (other than the supply of intoxicating liquor) of a catering undertaking at that place.

"WAGES COUNCIL" means the Unlicensed Place of Refreshment Wages Council.

"WEEK" means pay week.

AREAS

27. In this Schedule:—

(1) "LONDON AREA" means the Metropolitan Police District, as defined in the London Government Act 1963(a), the City of London, the Inner Temple and the Middle Temple.

(2) "PROVINCIAL A AREA" means:—

(a) in Scotland,

(i) the following burghs:—

ABERDEEN
  COUNTY
  Aberdeen (including
  part in Kincardine
  County)
  Fraserburgh
  Peterhead
ANGUS COUNTY
  Arbroath
  Brechin
  Dundee
  Forfar
  Montrose
ARGYLL COUNTY
  Dunoon
AYR COUNTY
  Ardrossan
  Ayr
  Irvine
  Kilmarnock
  Largs
  Prestwick
  Saltcoats
  Stevenston
  Troon
BANFF COUNTY
  Buckie
BUTE COUNTY
  Rothesay
CLACKMANNAN
  COUNTY
  Alloa
DUMFRIES
  COUNTY
  Dumfries
DUNBARTON
  COUNTY
  Bearsden
  Clydebank
  Dumbarton
  Helensburgh
  Kirkintilloch
  Milngavie

EAST LOTHIAN
  COUNTY
  North Berwick

FIFE COUNTY
  Buckhaven and
  Methil
  Burntisland
  Cowdenbeath
  Dunfermline
  Kirkcaldy
  Leven
  Lochgelly
  St. Andrews

INVERNESS
  COUNTY
  Inverness

KINCARDINE
  COUNTY
  Stonehaven

LANARK COUNTY
  Airdrie
  Coatbridge
  Glasgow
  Hamilton
  Lanark
  Motherwell and
  Wishaw
  Rutherglen

MIDLOTHIAN
  COUNTY
  Dalkeith
  Edinburgh
  Musselburgh

MORAY COUNTY
  Elgin

ORKNEY COUNTY
  Kirkwall

PERTH COUNTY
  Perth

RENFREW COUNTY
  Barrhead
  Gourock
  Greenock
  Johnstone
  Paisley
  Port Glasgow
  Renfrew

ROSS AND
  CROMARTY
  COUNTY
  Stornoway

ROXBURGH
  COUNTY
  Hawick

SELKIRK COUNTY
  Galashiels

STIRLING COUNTY
  Denny and Dunipace
  Falkirk
  Grangemouth
  Kilsyth
  Stirling

WEST LOTHIAN
  COUNTY
  Armadale
  Bathgate
  Bo'ness

WIGTOWN
  COUNTY
  Stranraer

ZETLAND COUNTY
  Lerwick

(ii) the following Special Lighting Districts, the boundaries of which have been defined, namely, Vale of Leven and Renton in the County of Dunbarton, and Larbert and Airth in the County of Stirling, and

(iii) the following areas the boundaries of which were defined as Special Lighting Districts prior to 10th March 1943, namely,

(a) 1963 c. 33.

Bellshill and Mossend, Blantyre, Cambuslang, Larkhall and Holytown, New Stevenston and Carfin, all in the County of Lanark ;

(*b*) in England and Wales, the areas administered by County Borough, Municipal Borough or Urban District Councils, except where they are included in the London area or are listed in (3) (*b*) of this paragraph.

(3) "PROVINCIAL B AREA" means : —

(*a*) in Scotland, all areas other than those listed in (2) (*a*) of this paragraph ;

(*b*) in England and Wales, all areas not included in the London area administered by Rural District Councils, and the areas administered by the following Municipal Borough and Urban District Councils : —

ENGLAND (excluding Monmouthshire)

BEDFORDSHIRE
Ampthill
Sandy

BERKSHIRE
Wallingford
Wantage

**BUCKINGHAM-
SHIRE**
Buckingham
Linslade
Marlow
Newport Pagnell

CHESHIRE
Alsager
Longdendale

CORNWALL
Bodmin
Bude Stratton
Fowey
Helston
Launceston
Liskeard
Looe
Lostwithiel
Padstow
Penryn
St. Just
Torpoint

DERBYSHIRE
Bakewell
Whaley Bridge
Wirksworth

DEVON
Ashburton
Buckfastleigh
Budleigh Salterton
Crediton
Dartmouth
Great Torrington
Holsworthy
Honiton
Kingsbridge

DEVON—contd.
Lynton
Northam
Okehampton
Ottery St. Mary
Salcombe
Seaton
South Molton
Tavistock
Totnes

DORSET
Blandford Forum
Lyme Regis
Shaftesbury
Sherborne
Wareham
Wimborne Minster

DURHAM
Barnard Castle
Tow Law

ELY, ISLE OF
Chatteris

ESSEX
Brightlingsea
Burnham-on-Crouch
Saffron Walden
West Mersea
Wivenhoe

**GLOUCESTER-
SHIRE**
Nailsworth
Tewkesbury

HEREFORDSHIRE
Bromyard
Kington
Ledbury

HERTFORDSHIRE
Baldock
Chorleywood
Royston
Sawbridgeworth

**HUNTINGDON-
SHIRE**
Huntingdon and
Godmanchester
Ramsey
St. Ives
St. Neots

KENT
Lydd
New Romney
Queenborough
Sandwich
Tenterden

LANCASHIRE
Carnforth
Grange

LINCOLNSHIRE
Alford
Barton-upon-
Humber
Bourne
Brigg
Horncastle
Mablethorpe and
Sutton
Market Rasen
Woodhall Spa

NORFOLK
Cromer
Diss
Downham Market
Hunstanton
North Walsham
Sheringham
Swaffham
Thetford
Wells-next-the-Sea
Wymondham

ENGLAND (excluding Monmouthshire) —contd.

NORTHAMPTON-SHIRE
Brackley
Burton Latimer
Higham Ferrers
Oundle

NORTHUMBER-LAND
Alnwick
Amble

OXFORDSHIRE
Bicester
Chipping Norton
Thame
Woodstock

RUTLAND
Oakham

SHROPSHIRE
Bishop's Castle
Church Stretton
Ellesmere
Market Drayton
Newport
Wem

SOMERSET
Chard
Crewkerne
Glastonbury
Ilminster
Portishead
Shepton Mallet
Street
Watchet
Wellington

SUFFOLK
Aldeburgh
Beccles
Bungay
Eye
Hadleigh
Halesworth
Haverhill
Leiston-cum-Sizewell
Saxmundham
Southwold
Sudbury
Stowmarket
Woodbridge

SUSSEX
Arundel
Rye

WESTMORLAND
Appleby
Lakes

WILTSHIRE
Bradford-on-Avon
Calne
Malmesbury
Marlborough
Melksham
Westbury
Wilton

WORCESTERSHIRE
Bewdley
Droitwich

YORKSHIRE
Hedon
Hornsea
Malton
Norton
Pickering
Richmond
Tickhill
Withernsea

WALES AND MONMOUTHSHIRE

ANGLESEY
Amlwch
Beaumaris
Llangefni
Menai Bridge

BRECONSHIRE
Builth Wells
Hay
Llanwrtyd Wells

CAERNARVON-SHIRE
Bethseda
Betws-y-Coed
Criccieth
Llanfairfechan
Penmaenmawr
Portmadoc
Pwllheli

CARDIGANSHIRE
Aberayron
Cardigan
Lampeter
New Quay

CARMARTHEN-SHIRE
Cwmamman
Kidwelly
Llandeilo
Llandovery
Newcastle Emlyn

DENBIGHSHIRE
Llangollen
Llanrwst
Ruthin

FLINTSHIRE
Buckley
Mold

GLAMORGAN
Cowbridge

MERIONETHSHIRE
Bala
Barmouth
Dolgellau
Towyn

MONMOUTHSHIRE
Caerlon
Chepstow
Usk

MONTGOMERY-SHIRE
Llanfyllin
Llanidloes
Machynlleth
Montgomery
Newtown and Llanllwchaiarn
Welshpool

PEMBROKESHIRE
Fishguard and Goodwick
Narberth
Neyland
Tenby

RADNORSHIRE
Knighton
Llandrindod Wells
Presteigne

(4) Any reference to a local government area shall be construed as a reference to that area as it was on 23rd April 1961, unless otherwise stated.

Part IV

GENERAL

WORKERS TO WHOM THE SCHEDULE APPLIES

28. Subject to the provisions of paragraph 29, the workers to whom this Schedule applies are all workers employed in Great Britain in a catering undertaking who are employed by the person or body of persons carrying on that undertaking and who are so employed either

(1) for the purposes of such of the activities of the undertaking as are carried on at an unlicensed place of refreshment or in the course of a catering contracting business ; or

(2) in connection with the provision of food or drink or living accommodation provided wholly or mainly for workers employed for the purposes of any of the activities specified in sub-paragraph (1) of this paragraph ;

and who are engaged on any of the following work, that is to say : —

(a) the preparation of food or drink ;

(b) the service of food or drink ;

(c) work incidental to such preparation or service ;

(d) work connected with the provision of living accommodation for workers employed for the purposes of any of the activities specified in sub-paragraph (1) of this paragraph ;

(e) work in connection with any retail sale of goods on premises where the main activity is the supply of food or drink for immediate consumption ;

(f) transport work ;

(g) work performed at any office or at any store or warehouse or similar place or at any garage or stable or similar place ;

(h) any work other than that specified in sub-paragraphs (a) to (g) hereof performed on or about the premises or place where food or drink is prepared or served including work in connection with any service or amenity provided on or about such premises or place.

29. This Schedule does not apply to any of the following workers in respect of their employment in any of the following circumstances, that is to say : —

(1) workers who are employed in a central catering establishment in respect of their employment in that establishment ;

(2) workers who are employed by the same employer partly in a catering undertaking and partly in some other undertaking, if their employment in the catering undertaking is confined to work specified either in sub-paragraph (f) or sub-paragraph (g) of paragraph 28 or partly to work specified in the said sub-paragraph (f) and partly to work specified in the said sub-paragraph (g), and they are mainly employed on work in or in connection with that other undertaking ;

(3) workers who are employed for the purposes of any of the activities carried on at a hotel, inn, boarding-house, guest house, hostel, holiday camp, club or other similar establishment and who are so employed by the person or body of persons carrying on such establishment, unless the establishment is either

(a) an establishment which is not a residential establishment within the meaning of this Schedule and the worker is employed for the purposes of the activities carried on at a place of refreshment where food or drink is supplied mainly for persons who do not reside at the establishment ; or

(b) carried on by the person or persons carrying on a catering undertaking such as is referred to in paragraph 28 for the purpose of providing accommodation wholly or mainly for the workers mentioned in that paragraph ;

(4) workers who are employed for the purposes of any of the activities carried on at any of the following establishments, that is to say : —

    (*a*) any hospital, nursing home or convalescent home or similar establishment providing accommodation for the sick, infirm or mentally defective ;

    (*b*) any orphanage, children's home or similar establishment ;

    (*c*) any institution or home where living accommodation is provided for the aged or indigent ;

    (*d*) any university, college, school or similar establishment ;

and who are employed by the person or body of persons carrying on the establishment or, in the case of any of the establishments specified in sub-paragraph (*d*) hereof, by such person or body of persons aforesaid or by the person or body of persons carrying on any boarding-house which forms part of the establishment ;

(5) workers who are employed by—

    (*a*) a railway company or by the British Railways Board or London Transport Board for the purposes of any of the activities carried on at a railway station or in a railway train ;

    (*b*) the Pullman Car Company Limited ;

(6) workers who are employed for the purposes of any of the activities carried on at a theatre, music-hall or other similar place of entertainment ordinarily used for the public performance of stage plays or variety entertainments, unless the worker is so employed in the course of a catering contracting business ;

(7) workers who are employed for the purposes of any of the activities carried on at a travelling stall, barrow or other similar vehicle from which food or drink is sold by an itinerant salesman ;

(8) workers who are employed by the Crown or by a local authority ;

(9) workers in relation to whom the Industrial and Staff Canteen Undertakings Wages Council operates, in respect of any employment which is for the time being within the field of operation of that Wages Council ;

(10) workers who are employed wholly or mainly on work performed at any office, unless the office forms part of or is situated in the same premises as an unlicensed place of refreshment.

30. Nothing in the provisions of this Schedule shall be construed as authorising either : —

(1) the making of any deduction or the giving of any remuneration in any manner that is illegal by virtue of the Truck Acts 1831 to 1940(**a**), or of any other enactment ; or

(2) the giving of any remuneration to a worker in respect of any employment which is unlawful under the provisions of any enactment.

EXPLANATORY NOTE
(*This Note is not part of the Order.*)

This Order, which has effect from 30th March 1970, sets out the statutory minimum remuneration payable and the holidays to be allowed to workers in substitution for the statutory minimum remuneration fixed, and holidays provided for, in the Wages Regulation (Unlicensed Place of Refreshment) Order 1967 (Order U.P.R. (36)), which Order is revoked.

New provisions are printed in italics.

(**a**) 1831 c. 37; 1887 c. 46; 1896 c. 44; 1940 c. 38.

STATUTORY INSTRUMENTS

1970 No. 112

SUGAR

The Sugar (Rates of Surcharge and Surcharge Repayments) (No. 3) Order 1970

Made - - - -	28*th January* 1970
Laid before Parliament	2*nd February* 1970
Coming into Operation	3*rd February* 1970

The Minister of Agriculture, Fisheries and Food, in exercise of the powers conferred on him by sections 7(4), 8(6) and 33(4) of the Sugar Act 1956(a) having effect subject to the provisions of section 3 of, and Part II of Schedule 5 to, the Finance Act 1962(b), and section 58 of the Finance Act 1968(c) and of all other powers enabling him in that behalf, with the concurrence of the Treasury, on the advice of the Sugar Board, hereby makes the following order:—

1.—(1) This order may be cited as the Sugar (Rates of Surcharge and Surcharge Repayments) (No. 3) Order 1970; and shall come into operation on 3rd February 1970.

(2) The Interpretation Act 1889(d) shall apply for the interpretation of this order as it applies for the interpretation of an Act of Parliament.

2. Notwithstanding the provisions of Article 2 of the Sugar (Rates of Surcharge and Surcharge Repayments) (No. 2) Order 1970(e), the rates of surcharge payable under and in accordance with the provisions of section 7 of the Sugar Act 1956, having effect as aforesaid, in respect of sugar and invert sugar imported or home produced or used in the manufacture of imported composite sugar products shall on and after 3rd February 1970 be those rates specified in Schedule 1 to this order.

3. For the purpose of section 8(3)(*b*) of the Sugar Act 1956, having effect as aforesaid, the rates of surcharge repayments in respect of invert sugar produced in the United Kingdom from materials on which on or after 3rd February 1970 sugar duty has been paid or, by virtue of paragraph 1 of Part II of Schedule 5 to the Finance Act 1962, is treated as having been paid shall, notwithstanding the provisions of Article 3 of the Sugar (Rates of Surcharge and Surcharge Repayments) (No. 2) Order 1970 be those specified in Schedule 2 to this order.

(a) 1956 c. 48.   (b) 1962 c. 44.
(c) 1968 c. 44.   (d) 1889 c. 63.
(e) S.I. 1970/54 (1970 I, p.338).

In Witness whereof the Official Seal of the Minister of Agriculture, Fisheries and Food is hereunto affixed on 28th January 1970.

(L.S.)

                            R. P. Fraser,

                       Authorised by the Minister.

We concur.

28th January 1970.

                         Ernest Armstrong,

                           Neil McBride,

             Two of the Lords Commissioners of
                     Her Majesty's Treasury.

SCHEDULE 1

PART I

SURCHARGE RATES FOR SUGAR

Polarisation	Rate of Surcharge per cwt.	
	s.	d.
Exceeding—		
99°	16	4·0
98° but not exceeding 99° ..	15	4·8
97° ,, ,, ,, 98° ..	15	0·3
96° ,, ,, ,, 97° ..	14	7·6
95° ,, ,, ,, 96° ..	14	2·9
94° ,, ,, ,, 95° ..	13	10·2
93° ,, ,, ,, 94° ..	13	5·5
92° ,, ,, ,, 93° ..	13	0·8
91° ,, ,, ,, 92° ..	12	8·0
90° ,, ,, ,, 91° ..	12	3·3
89° ,, ,, ,, 90° ..	11	10·6
88° ,, ,, ,, 89° ..	11	5·9
87° ,, ,, ,, 88° ..	11	2·0
86° ,, ,, ,, 87° ..	10	10·1
85° ,, ,, ,, 86° ..	10	6·6
84° ,, ,, ,, 85° ..	10	3·0
83° ,, ,, ,, 84° ..	9	11·5
82° ,, ,, ,, 83° ..	9	8·0
81° ,, ,, ,, 82° ..	9	4·8
80° ,, ,, ,, 81° ..	9	1·7
79° ,, ,, ,, 80° ..	8	10·6
78° ,, ,, ,, 79° ..	8	7·4
77° ,, ,, ,, 78° ..	8	4·3
76° ,, ,, ,, 77° ..	8	1·2
Not exceeding 76°	7	10·5

Part II

Surcharge Rates for Invert Sugar

Sweetening matter content by weight	Rate of Surcharge per cwt.
	s. d.
70 per cent. or more	10 4
Less than 70 per cent. and more than 50 per cent.	7 5
Not more than 50 per cent.	3 8

SCHEDULE 2

Surcharge Repayment Rates for Invert Sugar

Sweetening matter content by weight	Rate of Surcharge Repayment per cwt.
	s. d.
More than 80 per cent.	12 3
More than 70 per cent. but not more than 80 per cent.	10 4
More than 60 per cent. but not more than 70 per cent.	7 5
More than 50 per cent. but not more than 60 per cent.	5 11
Not more than 50 per cent. and the invert sugar not being less in weight than 14 lb. per gallon	3 8

EXPLANATORY NOTE

(This Note is not part of the Order.)

This order prescribes—

(a) reductions equivalent to 2s. 4d. per cwt. of refined sugar in the rates of surcharge payable on sugar and invert sugar which become chargeable with surcharge on or after 3rd February 1970;

(b) correspondingly reduced rates of surcharge repayment in respect of invert sugar produced in the United Kingdom from materials on which surcharge has been paid.

STATUTORY INSTRUMENTS

1970 No. 113

SUGAR

The Composite Sugar Products (Surcharge and Surcharge Repayments—Average Rates) (No. 4) Order 1970

Made - - - -	28*th January* 1970
Laid before Parliament	2*nd February* 1970
Coming into Operation	3*rd February* 1970

Whereas the Minister of Agriculture, Fisheries and Food (hereinafter called " the Minister ") has on the recommendation of the Commissioners of Customs and Excise (hereinafter called " the Commissioners ") made an order(a) pursuant to the powers conferred upon him by sections 9(1) and 9(4) of the Sugar Act 1956(b), having effect subject to the provisions of section 3 of, and Part II of Schedule 5 to, the Finance Act 1962(c), to the provisions of section 52(2) of the Finance Act 1966(d), and to the provisions of Section 58 of the Finance Act 1968(e), providing that in the case of certain descriptions of composite sugar products surcharge shall be calculated on the basis of an average quantity of sugar or invert sugar taken to have been used in the manufacture of the products, and that certain other descriptions of composite sugar products shall be treated as not containing any sugar or invert sugar, and that in the case of certain descriptions of goods in the manufacture of which sugar or invert sugar is used, surcharge repayments shall be calculated on the basis of an average quantity of sugar or invert sugar taken to have been so used:

Now, therefore, the Minister, on the recommendation of the Commissioners and in exercise of the powers conferred upon him by sections 9(1), 9(4) and 33(4) of the Sugar Act 1956, having effect as aforesaid, and of all other powers enabling him in that behalf, hereby makes the following order:—

1.—(1) This order may be cited as the Composite Sugar Products (Surcharge and Surcharge Repayments—Average Rates) (No. 4) Order 1970, and shall come into operation on 3rd February 1970.

(2) The Interpretation Act 1889(f) shall apply for the interpretation of this order as it applies for the interpretation of an Act of Parliament.

2. Surcharge payable on or after 3rd February 1970 under and in accordance with the Sugar Act 1956, having effect as aforesaid, in respect of sugar and invert sugar used in the manufacture of the descriptions of imported composite sugar products specified in column 2 of Schedule 1 to this order shall, notwithstanding the provisions of the Sugar (Rates of Surcharge and Surcharge Repayments) (No. 3) Order 1970(g) and the Composite Sugar Products (Surcharge and Surcharge Repayments—Average Rates) (No. 3) Order 1970(a), be calculated by reference to the weight of the products at the rates specified in relation thereto in column 3 of the said Schedule.

(a) S.I. 1970/55 (1970 I, p. 341).	(b) 1956 c. 48.	(c) 1962 c. 44.
(d) 1966 c. 18.	(e) 1968 c. 44.	(f) 1889 c. 63.
(g) S.I. 1970/112 (1970 I, p. 528).		

3. Imported composite sugar products other than those of a description specified in Schedules 1 and 2 to this order shall be treated as not containing any sugar or invert sugar for the purposes of surcharge payable on or after 3rd February 1970.

4. Surcharge repayments payable on and after 3rd February 1970 under and in accordance with the provisions of section 8 of the Sugar Act 1956, having effect as aforesaid, in respect of sugar and invert sugar used in the manufacture of the descriptions of goods specified in column 1 of Schedule 3 to this order shall, notwithstanding the provisions of the Sugar (Rates of Surcharge and Surcharge Repayments) (No. 3) Order 1970(a) and the Composite Sugar Products (Surcharge and Surcharge Repayments—Average Rates) (No. 3) Order 1970(b), be calculated by reference to the quantity of the goods at the rates specified in relation thereto in column 2 of the said Schedule.

In Witness whereof the Official Seal of the Minister of Agriculture, Fisheries and Food is hereunto affixed on 28th January 1970.

(L.S.)   *R. P. Fraser,*
                                        Authorised by the Minister.

SCHEDULE 1

In this Schedule:—

" Tariff heading " means a heading or, where the context so requires, a subheading of the Customs Tariff 1959 (see paragraph (1) of Article 2 of the Import Duties (General) (No. 3) Order 1969(c)).

Tariff heading	Description of Imported Composite Sugar Products	Rate of Surcharge
		per cwt. s. d.
04.02	Milk and cream, preserved, concentrated or sweetened, containing more than 10 per cent. by weight of added sugar	7 3
17.02 (B) (2) and 17.05 (B)	Syrups containing sucrose sugar, whether or not flavoured or coloured, but not including fruit juices containing added sugar in any proportion:—	
	containing 70 per cent. or more by weight of sweetening matter	10 4
	containing less than 70 per cent., and more than 50 per cent., by weight of sweetening matter..	7 5
	containing not more than 50 per cent. by weight of sweetening matter	3 8

(a) S.I. 1970/112 (1970 I, p. 528).   (b) S.I. 1970/55 (1970 I, p. 341).
(c) S.I. 1969/1413 (1969 III, p. 4150).

Tariff heading	Description of Imported Composite Sugar Products	Rate of Surcharge
		Per cwt. s. d.
17.02 (F) ..	Caramel:—	
	Solid	16 4
	Liquid	11 5
17.04	Sugar confectionery, not containing cocoa ..	13 3
18.06	Chocolate and other food preparations containing cocoa and added sugar:—	
	Chocolate couverture not prepared for retail sale; chocolate milk crumb, liquid ..	7 3
	Chocolate milk crumb, solid	8 11
	Solid chocolate bars or blocks, milk or plain, with or without fruit or nuts; other chocolate confectionery consisting wholly of chocolate or of chocolate and other ingredients not containing added sugar, but not including such goods when packed together in retail packages with goods liable to surcharge at a higher rate	7 4
	Other	9 6
19.08	Pastry, biscuits, cakes and other fine bakers' wares containing added sugar:—	
	Biscuits, wafers and rusks containing more than 12½ per cent. by weight of added sugar, and other biscuits, wafers and rusks included in retail packages with such goods.. ..	4 1
	Cakes with covering or filling containing added sugar; meringues	5 5
	Other	2 0
20.01	Vegetables and fruit, prepared or preserved by vinegar or acetic acid, containing added sugar:—	
	Containing 10 per cent. or more by weight of added sugar	5 9
	Other	1 3
20.03	Fruit preserved by freezing, containing added sugar	2 0
20.04	Fruit, fruit-peel and parts of plants, preserved by sugar (drained, glacé or crystallised)	10 9
20.05	Jams, fruit jellies, marmalades, fruit purée and fruit pastes, being cooked preparations, containing added sugar	10 3
20.06	Fruit otherwise prepared or preserved, containing added sugar:—	
	Ginger	8 2
	Other	2 0

SCHEDULE 2

Tariff heading	Description of Imported Composite Sugar Products
17.05 (A) and (B)	Sugar and invert sugar, flavoured or coloured.

SCHEDULE 3

Description of goods	Rate of surcharge repayment per bulk barrel of 36 gallons
Lager	8·1d.
All beer other than lager	7·3d.

EXPLANATORY NOTE

(This Note is not part of the Order.)

This order provides for reductions on and after 3rd February 1970 in the average rates of surcharge payable on imported composite sugar products of the descriptions specified in Schedule 1 and in the average rates of surcharge repayment in respect of exported goods of the descriptions specified in Schedule 3. These correspond to the reductions in surcharge rates effected by the Sugar (Rates of Surcharge and Surcharge Repayments) (No. 3) Order 1970 (S.I. 1970/112). Provision is also made for certain imported composite sugar products to be treated as not containing any sugar or invert sugar.

STATUTORY INSTRUMENTS

1970 No. 117

SEA FISHERIES

WHITE FISH INDUSTRY

The White Fish Authority (General Levy) Regulations Confirmatory Order 1970

Made - - -	*28th January* 1970
Laid before Parliament	*5th February* 1970
Coming into Operation	*15th February* 1970

Whereas the White Fish Authority (hereinafter referred to as "the Authority"), in exercise of the powers conferred on them by sections 5, 11 and 15 of the Sea Fish Industry Act 1951(**a**), as amended and extended by section 4 of the Sea Fisheries Act 1968(**b**) and as extended to Northern Ireland by the Northern Ireland (Sea Fish Industry) Order 1951(**c**), and of all other powers enabling them in that behalf, have made the White Fish Authority (General Levy) Regulations 1969 (hereinafter referred to as "the Regulations") ;

And Whereas the Authority have transmitted to the Minister of Agriculture, Fisheries and Food, the Secretary of State for Scotland, being the Secretary of State concerned with the sea fishing industry in Scotland, and the Secretary of State for the Home Department, being the Secretary of State concerned with the sea fishing industry in Northern Ireland, (hereinafter referred to as "the Ministers") the objections to the Regulations which have been duly made to the Authority and have not been withdrawn and the Ministers have considered such objections ;

And Whereas the Ministers, after consultation with the Authority, have considered it desirable to make such modifications in the Regulations as hereinafter appear and have caused notice thereof to be published in such manner as they thought best adapted for informing persons affected ;

Now therefore the Ministers, in exercise of the powers conferred on them by section 5(6) of the Sea Fish Industry Act 1951, as extended to Northern Ireland, and of all other powers enabling them in that behalf, hereby make the following Order : —

1. This Order may be cited as the White Fish Authority (General Levy) Regulations Confirmatory Order 1970 and shall come into operation on 15th February 1970.

(**a**) 1951 c. 30.　　　　　　　　　　　　(**b**) 1968 c. 77.
(**c**) S.I. 1951/1797 (1951 I, p. 738).

2. The Regulations, having been modified in the following respects, that is to say,

(*a*) by adding at the end of the first paragraph of Regulation 1 the following paragraph:

"Provided that the said levy shall not be payable in respect of any molluscs (not being oysters, scallops or queen scallops) in shell or of any oysters purchased for cultivation or in respect of canned or bottled white fish or white fish products";

(*b*) by inserting after the word "Provided" in Regulation 1 the word "also";

(*c*) by substituting in Regulation 6 for the words and figures "thirtieth day of November 1969" the words and figures "fifteenth day of February 1970";

(*d*) by deleting from the Schedule to the Regulations, wherever they appear, the words "at firsthand";

(*e*) by deleting from the Schedule to the Regulations the item in Column 1 "Canned and bottled white fish" and the figures in Column 2 opposite such item;

(*f*) by substituting in the second column of the Schedule to the Regulations rates of levy in place of those first appearing therein;

are hereby confirmed and are set out in the Schedule to this Order.

In Witness whereof the official seal of the Minister of Agriculture, Fisheries and Food is hereunto affixed on 21st January 1970.

(L.S.)   *Cledwyn Hughes,*
Minister of Agriculture, Fisheries and Food.

Given under the seal of the Secretary of State for Scotland on 22nd January 1970.

(L.S.)   *William Ross,*
Secretary of State for Scotland.

Given under the hand of the Secretary of State for the Home Department on 28th January 1970.

James Callaghan,
Secretary of State for the Home Department.

SCHEDULE

THE WHITE FISH AUTHORITY (GENERAL LEVY) REGULATIONS 1969

1. There shall be paid to the Authority subject to and in accordance with the provisions of these regulations by every person who purchases any white fish or any white fish product on a firsthand sale thereof a levy (hereinafter referred to as "the said levy")

at the rate per stone set out in the second column of the Schedule hereto in respect of any white fish or white fish product specified opposite thereto in the first column of the said Schedule so purchased by him.

Provided that the said levy shall not be payable in respect of any molluscs (not being oysters, scallops or queen scallops) in shell or of any oysters purchased for cultivation or in respect of canned or bottled white fish or white fish products.

Provided also that if any white fish or any white fish product is purchased on a firsthand sale through or from a wholesale merchant who sells on commission the said levy shall be paid to the Authority by the said wholesale merchant, who shall be entitled to recover as a civil debt from the purchaser of such white fish or white fish product a sum equal to the amount of the said levy so paid.

2. The amount payable to the Authority by any person in respect of the said levy under the last foregoing regulation shall be paid to the Authority within seven days after the end of either the week during which there took place the firsthand sale of the white fish or white fish product in respect of which the said levy is payable or the week during which such white fish or white fish product was imported or brought into the United Kingdom, whichever is the later.

3.(a) Every person who sells white fish or white fish products otherwise than by retail shall keep or cause to be kept an accurate record of all his purchases and sales of white fish and white fish products (other than sales by retail), including in respect of each such purchase or sale the date thereof, the name and address of the seller or purchaser, the description of the white fish or white fish product purchased or sold, the net weight of each description thereof purchased or sold and the price paid or charged.

(b) Every person who sells white fish or white fish products by retail and every fish frier shall keep or cause to be kept an accurate record of all his purchases of white fish and white fish products, including in respect of each such purchase the date thereof, the name and address of the seller, the description of the white fish or white fish product, the net weight of each description thereof and the price paid.

(c) In respect of every sale or purchase of white fish or of a white fish product which it is customary or usual to sell or purchase by reference to a method of calculation of quantity other than a calculation by weight, the records which are required to be kept under the provisions of the two foregoing paragraphs of this regulation by the persons referred to therein, shall, in addition to and not in derogation of the requirements of the said paragraphs, include particulars of the white fish or white fish product so sold or purchased by reference to the said method of calculation of quantity.

(d) The retention by any person of an accurate invoice or a copy thereof shall, as respects any of the matters hereinbefore mentioned of which sufficient particulars are contained therein, be deemed to be to that extent a compliance by that person with the foregoing provisions of this regulation.

4.—(1) In these regulations, unless the context otherwise requires, the following expressions have the meanings hereby respectively assigned to them that is to say:—

"firsthand sale" means—

(a) in relation to any white fish or white fish product which has been landed outside the United Kingdom and to any white fish product manufactured outside the United Kingdom from such white fish or white fish product which in either case is purchased by a person carrying on business in the white fish industry and is imported or brought into the United Kingdom for the purposes of any such business, the first sale thereof (whether in the United Kingdom or elsewhere) to such a person as aforesaid;

(b) in relation to any other white fish or white fish product which is landed in the United Kingdom, the first sale thereof (other than a sale by retail) whether prior to or after it has been landed in the United Kingdom.

"sale by retail" means—

a sale to a person buying otherwise than for the purpose of re-sale or processing or use as bait, and includes a sale to a person for the purposes of a catering business (other than a fish frying business); and

"sell by retail" has a corresponding meaning.

"stone" means—

a weight of fourteen pounds avoirdupois.

"week" means—

a period of seven consecutive days ending at midnight on any Saturday.

"wholesale merchant" means—

any person selling or offering for sale white fish or white fish products otherwise than by retail.

(2) The Interpretation Act 1889 shall apply to the interpretation of these regulations as it applies to the interpretation of an Act of Parliament.

5. The White Fish Authority (General Levy) Regulations 1952, The White Fish Authority (General Levy) (Amendment) Regulations 1953, The White Fish Authority (General Levy) (Amendment) Regulations 1956 and The White Fish Authority (General Levy) (Amendment) Regulations 1962 are hereby revoked.

6. These regulations which may be cited as the White Fish Authority (General Levy) Regulations 1969 shall come into operation on the fifteenth day of February 1970.

The Common Seal of the ⎫
WHITE FISH AUTHORITY ⎬   (L.S.)
was hereunto affixed in the ⎪
presence of:— ⎭

Member: Charles Hardie

Secretary: L. W. Jackson

SCHEDULE

Column 1	Column 2 Rate per stone
White Fish	
White fish other than white fish sold for fishmeal production...	1.2d.
White fish sold for fishmeal production	0.12d.
White Fish Products	
Fresh, frozen and chilled white fish	
Gutted	1.2d.
Headless and gutted	1.6d.
Fillets, skin on	2.4d.
Fillets, skinless	3d.
Smoked white fish	
Headless and gutted	2d.
Fillets, skin on	3d.
Fillets, skinless	3.2d.
Salted and cured white fish	
Wet	2.4d.
Dried	3.6d.
White fish products sold for fishmeal production	0.12d.
White fishmeal	0.6d.
Any white fish product not referred to above	2.4d.

EXPLANATORY NOTE

(This Note is not part of the Order.)

This Order confirms, after modification, Regulations made by the White Fish Authority in place of the White Fish Authority (General Levy) Regulations 1952 (S.I. 1952/1077) (as amended by Regulations of 1953, 1956 and 1962) (S.I. 1953/887, 1956/1061, 1963/1169) which are revoked.

The Regulations impose a levy on firsthand sales of white fish and their products landed with certain exceptions. The levy, payable by the firsthand buyer, is based on a rate of 1.2d. per stone on whole white fish and their equivalents with variations up to 3.6d. for their products, 0.12d. for fish sold for reduction to meal and 0.6d. for fishmeal.

The Regulations apply to the United Kingdom.

STATUTORY INSTRUMENTS

1970 No. 118 (C.3)

ALIENS

The Immigration Appeals Act 1969 (Commencement No. 1) Order 1970

Made - - - - *28th January* 1970

In exercise of the powers conferred on me by section 24(5) of the Immigration Appeals Act 1969(a), I hereby make the following Order:—

1. This Order may be cited as the Immigration Appeals Act 1969 (Commencement No. 1) Order 1970.

2. Section 14 of the Immigration Appeals Act 1969 shall come into operation on 1st February 1970.

James Callaghan,
One of Her Majesty's Principal
Secretaries of State.

Home Office,
    Whitehall.
28th January 1970.

EXPLANATORY NOTE
(*This Note is not part of the Order.*)

This Order brings section 14 of the Immigration Appeals Act 1969 (which enables provision to be made by Order in Council for immigration appeals in respect of aliens corresponding to the provisions of Part I of that Act in respect of Commonwealth citizens) into operation on 1st February 1970.

(a) 1969 c. 21.

STATUTORY INSTRUMENTS

1970 No. 120

BRITISH NATIONALITY

The British Nationality (Amendment) Regulations 1970

Made - - -		*28th January* 1970
Coming into Operation		*16th February* 1970

In exercise of the powers conferred on me by section 29(1) of the British Nationality Act 1948(a) as amended and extended by section 1 of the South Africa Act 1962(b) and Schedule 1 thereto, section 3(2) of the British Nationality Act 1964(c), section 6(2) of the British Nationality (No. 2) Act 1964(d), section 5(2) of the British Nationality Act 1965(e) and section 12 of the West Indies Act 1967(f) and Schedule 3 thereto, I hereby make the following Regulations:—

1. These Regulations may be cited as the British Nationality (Amendment) Regulations 1970 and shall come into operation on 16th February 1970.

2. In paragraph (2) (*a*) of Regulation 27 of the British Nationality Regulations 1969(g) (which, in accordance with paragraph (1), provides that in relation to specified associated states references in the Regulations to the Governor shall be construed as references to the Secretary to the Cabinet) for the words "or of Saint Lucia" there shall be substituted the words ", of Saint Lucia or of Saint Vincent".

James Callaghan,
One of Her Majesty's Principal
Secretaries of State.

Home Office,
Whitehall.
28th January 1970.

EXPLANATORY NOTE

(This Note is not part of the Regulations.)

These Regulations amend the British Nationality Regulations 1969.

Regulation 27(1) of the 1969 Regulations provides that they shall apply in relation to an associated state in like manner as in relation to a colony subject, however, to adaptations of references to "the Governor". Where a direction has been given under paragraph 4 of Schedule 3 to the West Indies Act 1967, such references are to be construed as references to the officer specified in the direction. Regulation 27(2) sets out the effect of such directions given in the case of specified associated states.

The present Regulations amend Regulation 27(2) so as to take account of such a direction given in the case of St. Vincent (which became an associated state on 27th October 1969).

(a) 1948 c. 56.	(b) 1962 c. 23.	(c) 1964 c. 22.
(d) 1964 c. 54.	(e) 1965 c. 34.	
(f) 1967 c. 4.	(g) S.I. 1969/760 (1969 II, p. 2142).	

STATUTORY INSTRUMENTS

1970 No. 121 (L. 4)

SUPREME COURT OF JUDICATURE, ENGLAND

The Supreme Court Funds (Amendment) Rules 1970

Made - - - -	30*th January* 1970
Laid before Parliament	6*th February* 1970
Coming into Operation for all purposes except those of paragraph 6 in the Schedule	16*th February* 1970
for the purposes of paragraph 6 in the Schedule	1*st March* 1970

The Lord Chancellor, with the concurrence of the Treasury and in pursuance of the powers contained in section 7(1) of the Administration of Justice Act 1965(**a**), hereby makes the following Rules—

1. These Rules may be cited as the Supreme Court Funds (Amendment) Rules 1970 and shall come into operation—

(*a*) for all purposes except those of paragraph 6 in the Schedule on 16th February 1970, and

(*b*) for the purposes of paragraph 6 in the Schedule on 1st March 1970.

2. The amendments set out in the Schedule to these Rules shall be made to the Supreme Court Funds Rules 1927(**b**), as subsequently amended(**c**).

Dated 29th January 1970.

Gardiner, C.

We concur

Dated 30th January 1970.

Joseph Harper,
Walter Harrison,

Two of the Lords Commissioners
of Her Majesty's Treasury.

(a) 1965 c. 2.   (b) S.R. & O. 1927/1184 (1927, p. 1638).
(c) The relevant amending instruments are S.R. & O. 1933/61, 912, 1935/666, 1942/983, 1943/1331, 1947/2547; S.I. 1951/210, 1960/728, 1931, 1961/2299, 1962/554, 1965/1608, 1966/876, 1968/106, 1969/206 (1933, pp. 1826, 1827; 1935, p. 1649; 1942 I, p. 807; 1943 I, p. 939; 1947 I, p. 2089; 1951 II, p. 679; 1960 III, pp. 3122, 3125; 1961 III, p. 4053; 1962 I, p. 531; 1965 II, p. 4621; 1966 II, p. 2069; 1968 I, p. 302; 1969 I, p. 521).

SCHEDULE

AMENDMENTS TO THE SUPREME COURT FUNDS RULES 1927

1. In rule 32 (which relates to lodgments in the Queen's Bench Division), the words " a copy " shall be substituted for the words " an office copy " in both places where they occur and the following proviso shall be added at the end of the second paragraph: —

"Provided that the Accountant General may issue a direction for lodgment notwithstanding such party's failure to produce an order or copy thereof, if he is satisfied that an order has been made (whether drawn up or not) and the reasons for such failure are set out in Form No. 23 ".

2. In rule 44(1) (which relates to the payment of money lodged under Order 22 of the Rules of the Supreme Court), the words " on the written authority of the plaintiff " and " or 37 " shall be omitted.

3. The following amendments shall be made in the proviso to rule 45 (which relates to the authority for dealing with funds in court): —

(a) in paragraph (1), for the words " £200 " and " £100 ", there shall be substituted the words " £500 " and " £250 " respectively ; and

(b) in paragraph (2), for the words " £200 " in both places where they appear, there shall be substituted the words " £500 ".

4. Rule 51 (which relates to payments made on the authority of another person) shall be deleted.

5. In rule 67(2)(l) (which relates to the carrying over of accrued interest), for the words " rule 46(3) ", there shall be substituted the words " rule 43(2) ".

6. In rule 78(1) (which relates to the rate of interest accruing on money placed to a short-term investment account), for the words " $6\frac{1}{2}$ per cent." there shall be substituted the words " 7 per cent.".

7. The following amendments shall be made in the Appendix (which contains the Forms referred to in the Rules) :—

(1) in Form No. 11 (Payment Schedule), there shall be deleted the column headed " Name in full and address of the Person (if any) to give authority for payment " ;

(2) in Part I of Form No. 23 (form of request for a direction for lodgment in the Queen's Bench Division), for paragraphs (A), (B), (C) and (D) there ·shall be substituted the following paragraphs: —

" (A) On behalf of the defendant [state name] in satisfaction of claim of above named [state name of party], subject to Order 22, rule 1 of the Rules of the Supreme Court 1965 ; the hearing has/has not* begun.

(B) On behalf of defendant [state name] against claim of above named [state name of party] with defence setting up tender, subject to Order 22, rule 1 of the Rules of the Supreme Court 1965.

(C) Under Order dated   [If neither the Order nor a copy thereof is produced, state here the reasons for failure to produce it].

(D) In the following circumstances [here state the circumstances (not being circumstances falling within paragraphs (A), (B) or (C) above) in which the money is to be lodged]. " ;

(3) for Form No. 36 (Request for payment of money lodged), there shall be substituted the following Form :—

" FORM NO. 36

Rule 44(1)

In the High Court of Justice, ...Division

(1) Request for payment of money lodged or appropriated in satisfaction of claim under rule 1 or rule 8 of Order 22.

Ledger Credit .... v. ....19......

To the Accountant General, Royal Courts of Justice, W.C.2.

    I hereby notify that the sum of £   :   :   paid into Court and placed to the above ledger credit has been accepted by the plaintiff in satisfaction of the claim in respect of which it was paid in, and I request that payment of the said sum may be made to:

    *(1) the Plaintiff [*give full name*] ....

    of   ....

    (2) Messrs. ....

    of   ....
the solicitors for the plaintiff.

I declare that:—

    (i) due notice has been given of the acceptance within the time limited by Order 22, rule 3 ;

    (ii) the plaintiff is not a person in respect of whom a certificate under Part I of the Legal Aid and Advice Act 1949 is, or has been, in force in these proceedings ;

    †(iii) the payment is not to, or for the credit of, a person resident outside the scheduled territories, as defined by the Exchange Control Act 1947.

Witnessed by   (Signature) ....
  (Address)   a partner in the firm of
                                [delete if inappropriate]
  (Occupation)

Witnessed by   (Signature) ....
  (Address)

(Occupation)
                 Date .... 19......

    N.B. This request, which may be signed either by the plaintiff or by a partner in the firm of his solicitors, must be accompanied by the original receipt and notice of payment in and by a copy of the notice of acceptance.

    A request made by a plaintiff company must be completed under the company's seal.

    * Delete (1) or (2) as the case may be.

    † If this declaration (iii) cannot be made, it should be deleted and permission from the Exchange Control authorities must be obtained before payment can be made.

(2) Request for Remittance by Post

(If remittance by post is required, the person to whom payment is to be made, i.e. the plaintiff or his solicitor, as the case may be, should complete the following request.)

Date .... 19......

I request that the above sum of £   :   :   may be remitted to me by post at the above address by cheque to my/our account at ....
....Bank.

(Signature) ....

(In the case of a firm, one partner to sign as " A partner in the firm of .... " , and in the case of a company, the secretary may sign) " ;

(4) Forms Nos. 37, 56 and 57 shall be omitted.

EXPLANATORY NOTE
(This Note is not part of the Rules.)

These Rules amend the Supreme Court Funds Rules 1927. The amendment to rule 32 enables money to be paid into court in the Queen's Bench Division in pursuance of an order without the production of the order or an office copy. The amendments affecting rules 44 and 51 and Forms 11, 36, 37, 56 and 57 are consequential upon the amendment to Order 22, rule 10(2) of the Rules of the Supreme Court made by the Rules of the Supreme Court (Amendment No. 2) 1969 (S.I. 1969/1894) which abolish the need for a solicitor to have his client's express authority to receive money paid out of court. The amendments to rule 45 increase the amounts which can be paid out of court, or otherwise dealt with, without an order ; the amendment to rule 78(1) increases from 6½ per cent. to 7 per cent. per annum the rate of interest on money standing to the credit of a short-term investment account.

The Rules also make minor and consequential amendments to the Appendix of Forms.

STATUTORY INSTRUMENTS

1970 No. 123

ROAD TRAFFIC

The Drivers' Hours (Goods Vehicles) (Keeping of Records) Regulations 1970

Made - - -	*29th January* 1970
Laid before Parliament	*5th February* 1970
Coming into Operation	*1st March* 1970

The Minister of Transport, in exercise of his powers under section 98 of the Transport Act 1968(**a**) and of all other enabling powers, and after consultation with representative organisations in accordance with section 101(6) of the said Act of 1968, hereby makes the following Regulations :—

Commencement and citation

1. These Regulations shall come into operation on the 1st March 1970 and may be cited as the Drivers' Hours (Goods Vehicles) (Keeping of Records) Regulations 1970.

Interpretation

2.—(1) In these Regulations, unless the context otherwise requires—

"the Act" means the Transport Act 1968 ;

"driver's record book" means a book which is required to be kept by a driver by these Regulations and which, subject to Regulation 9 of these Regulations, complies with Regulation 4 of these Regulations ;

"record sheet" means any such sheet as is required to be contained in a driver's record book by Regulation 4(2) of these Regulations, whether that sheet relates to one, or to more than one, working day of the driver to whom the book relates ;

and any expression which is also used in Part V or Part VI of the Act has the same meaning as in the said Part V or Part VI respectively.

(2) Any reference in these Regulations to any enactment or instrument shall be construed, unless the context otherwise requires, as a reference to that enactment or instrument as amended by any subsequent enactment or instrument.

(3) The Interpretation Act 1889(**b**) shall apply for the interpretation of these Regulations as it applies for the interpretation of an Act of Parliament.

Record books for goods vehicle drivers

3.—(1) Subject to the following provisions of these Regulations—

(*a*) a driver of a goods vehicle shall enter, and the employer of an employee-driver of a goods vehicle shall cause any such driver of a goods vehicle to enter, in a driver's record book a current record which shall give in respect of each working day of that driver, the information prescribed in the sheets as set out in Schedule 1 to these Regulations as information which is required to be furnished by a driver, and

---

(**a**) 1968 c. 73.   (**b**) 1889 c. 63.

(*b*) any such employer as aforesaid shall make such entries in the said record book as are by those sheets required to be made therein by that employer.

(2) Subject as aforesaid, where an employee-driver is required by paragraph (1) of this Regulation to enter a current record in a driver's record book, his employer shall issue to him, and from time to time as may be necessary while that employee-driver remains in the employment of that employer keep him supplied with, a new driver's record book for use in accordance with these Regulations :

Provided that if on the date of the coming into operation of these Regulations or at any time thereafter an employee-driver has more than one employer in relation to whom he is an employee-driver of a goods vehicle, the employer who is to issue a new driver's record book to him shall be the employer for whom that employee-driver first acts in the course of his employment on or after the said date or time.

(3) Where during the currency of a driver's record book an employee-driver ceases to be employed by an employer who has issued that book to him he shall return that book, including all duplicate and unused record sheets, to that employer and, if he is at that time employed by some other person or persons in relation to whom he is an employee-driver of a goods vehicle, that other person, or if there is more than one such other person, that one of them for whom he first acts in the course of his employment after ceasing to be so employed as aforesaid, shall issue a new driver's record book to him for use in accordance with these Regulations.

(4) This Regulation applies to a driver who in any working week drives both goods and passenger vehicles as it applies to a driver who only drives a goods vehicle, and the information required to be furnished in the driver's record book by a driver of both goods and passenger vehicles shall be the required information in relation to his employments in connection with both goods and passenger vehicles, but if a driver of both goods and passenger vehicles has a different employer in relation to his employment in connection with goods vehicles from his employer in relation to his employment in connection with passenger vehicles, references in the foregoing paragraphs of this Regulation to his employer shall be construed as references to his employer in relation to his employment in connection with goods vehicles.

Form of drivers' record books

4. Subject to Regulation 9 of these Regulations, a driver's record book shall contain—

(1) a front sheet as set out in Part I of Schedule 1 to these Regulations, and

(2) record sheets as set out in Part II of the said Schedule 1, the number of sheets to be contained in the book being sufficient to provide entries relating to at least 14 working days, each sheet relating either to a single working day or to not more than 7 working days, and

(3) a duplicate of each of the record sheets which are contained therein, and

(4) one sheet of carbon paper or other means whereby an entry in a record sheet may be simultaneously reproduced on the duplicate of that sheet.

Manner of keeping drivers' record books

5. Subject to the following provisions of these Regulations, the following requirements shall be complied with as respects the making of entries in a driver's record book, the detachment and delivery of record sheets and the return of record books—

(1) an owner-driver or an employer of an employee-driver shall enter or secure that there is entered—

   (*a*) on the front sheet before the book is used—

      (i) the number of a current operator's licence held by the owner-driver or the employer of the employee-driver, and

      (ii) a book serial number, which differs from the serial numbers on any other books used by the owner-driver or issued by the employer, and

      (iii) the number of record sheets contained in the book, and

   (*b*) on each record sheet before it is used, its number in the book, the book serial number and the number of a current operator's licence required to be entered on the front sheet of the book by paragraph (1)(*a*)(i) of this Regulation,

(2) an employee-driver shall enter all the information required by these Regulations to be entered in the record book except where it is indicated in the book that the information is to be entered by his employer,

(3) a driver shall when making any entry in a record sheet contained in the book and when signing ensure by the use of carbon paper or otherwise that the entry or signature is simultaneously reproduced on the duplicate of that sheet,

(4) all times required to be entered in any record sheet shall be shown as times a.m. or p.m. unless they are entered in accordance with the 24-hour clock system,

(5) in making any entry in any record sheet which relates to driving periods at the wheel as required by column 4 of the form set out in Part II of Schedule 1 to these Regulations consecutive periods of driving during a working day which are interrupted by intervals not exceeding 15 minutes may be entered as if they were one driving period unless the result would be to enter a total driving time for that working day which would exceed the period for which the driver is permitted to drive on that day by or under the Act,

(6) in making an entry in any record sheet which relates to details of journeys as required by column 10 of the form set out in Part II of Schedule 1 to these Regulations a driver shall enter the place of departure and the place of arrival for each driving period entered in column 4 of the said form, but where a driver does not during a working day drive a goods or passenger vehicle outside a radius of 25 miles from the operating centre of the vehicle, the information to be entered in a record sheet relating to that day in the said column 10 may be limited to the area served by the journeys made by the driver during that day,

(7) when all the entries which are required to be made in any record sheet which is contained in a driver's record book have been made in respect of any working day the driver shall enter his signature in the place provided for that day and for that purpose,

(8) an employee-driver shall within 7 days of any record sheet being completed in his current driver's record book detach it from that book and forthwith deliver it to the employer who issued or should have issued that book to him, and that employer shall examine and sign such sheet within 7 days of receipt thereof, and an owner-driver shall within 7 days of such record sheet being completed detach such sheet and deliver it to the address required to be given on the front sheet of the book in Item I paragraph 4 :

Provided that a person shall not be guilty of an offence under this sub-paragraph if he shows that it was not reasonably practicable for such sheet to be so delivered or so examined and signed by the employer within the prescribed periods and that the sheet was so delivered, examined or signed as soon as reasonably practicable,

(9) when all the record sheets contained in a driver's record book issued to an employee-driver have been completed, that employee-driver shall return that book including all duplicate record sheets to the employer who issued it to him,

(10) no driver shall enter in any driver's record book any information which is required to be furnished by these Regulations if—

(a) in the case of an employee-driver, the book was not supplied to him by his employer, unless a driver's record book so supplied is not available to him, or

(b) he is in possession of another such book in which he has entered information which is required to be so furnished and which is not completed.

Supply of information and production of drivers' record books by employers and employee-drivers

6.—(1) Where an employee-driver has or has had during any period more than one employer in relation to whom he is an employee-driver—

(a) each employer, who is not an employer who is required by these Regulations to issue a driver's record book to that employee-driver, shall require that driver to produce his current driver's record book and shall enter in the front sheet contained therein the information he is required to enter therein by the form of that front sheet as set out in Part I of Schedule 1 to these Regulations, and

(b) each employer of that employee-driver shall, whenever he is requested to do so by any of the other employers of that employee-driver, supply to that other employer such information as is in his possession relating to the whole or any part of any working week of that driver as is specified in paragraph (4) of this Regulation.

(2) Where an employee-driver changes his employment the employer by whom the employee-driver has ceased to be so employed shall on being so requested by the employee-driver, or his new employer, supply the employee-driver or the new employer with such information as is in his possession relating to the whole or any part of a current working week of that employee-driver as is specified in paragraph (4) of this Regulation.

(3) Any information required to be supplied by the foregoing provisions of this Regulation shall, if so required by the person entitled to require it to be supplied, be supplied in writing.

(4) The information relating to the whole or any part of the current working week of an employee-driver which is to be supplied in accordance with the foregoing provisions of this Regulation is—

(a) any period during which that employee-driver has been off duty for a period of not less than 24 hours in respect of that week as required by section 96(6) of the Act or as so required by that provision as having effect in relation to that employee-driver by virtue of any exemption having effect under regulations made under section 96(10) of the Act, and

(b) the number of hours for the purpose of the weekly limit under section 96(5) of the Act for which that employee-driver has been on duty during that week.

(5) An employee-driver shall produce his current driver's record book for inspection by the employer who issued it to him, or by any other person in relation to whom he is at any time during the period of the currency of that book an employee-driver, whenever required to do so by that employer or that other person.

(6) An employee-driver shall return his current driver's record book to the employer who issued it to him at the end of any working week if required to do so by that employer.

Drivers' record books to be carried by drivers

7. A driver shall have his current driver's record book including all duplicate and unused record sheets in his possession at all times while he is driving a goods or passenger vehicle and he is on duty.

Preservation of drivers' record books

8.—(1) An owner-driver shall preserve his driver's record book intact when it has been completed or he has ceased to use it, and the employer of an employee-driver to whom any driver's record book relating to that employee-driver has been returned shall preserve that book intact, for the period specified in the next following paragraph, and any owner-driver who has detached record sheets from his driver's record book as required by Regulation 5(8) of these Regulations and any employer of an employee-driver to whom any record sheets have been delivered by his employee-driver as required by that provision shall also preserve those sheets for the same period.

(2) The period for which drivers' record books and record sheets must be preserved as required by this Regulation shall be six months reckoned in the case of an owner-driver from the day on which that book was completed or ceased to be used by him, or in the case of an employee-driver from the day on which that book was returned to his employer :

Provided that if so required by a licensing authority or a chief officer of police in any particular case, any such book or sheet as aforesaid as may be specified by any particular or general description shall be preserved for such further period or periods, not exceeding in the aggregate six months, as may be specified in any such requirement.

Authorised departures from form of drivers' record books

9. Notwithstanding anything in the foregoing provisions of these Regulations, drivers' record books may be issued containing sheets which differ from the sheets set out in Part I or II of Schedule 1 to these Regulations (whether in size, layout, sequence, numbering, content or otherwise) so long as any sheet contained in any such book contains the same wording as in the corresponding sheet in the said Part I or II and is so framed as to ensure that all the information required by such corresponding sheet is required to be entered in the sheet actually contained in the book and in such a manner as to be readily identifiable by any person entitled under any enactment or under these Regulations to inspect any such book.

Registers of drivers' record books

10.—(1) Subject to the following provisions of these Regulations every owner-driver of a goods vehicle shall maintain a register in the form specified in Schedule 2 to these Regulations of all drivers' record books used by him and every employer of an employee-driver of a goods vehicle shall maintain such a register or more than one such register as provided for by paragraph (2) of this Regulation of all drivers' record books known by him to have been issued to or to be used by any of his employee-drivers and every such owner-driver and employer as aforesaid shall make in that register or registers all such entries relating to the information to be recorded therein as is required by the form set out in the said Schedule 2 to be entered in that register or registers:

Provided that where a record book is not returned there shall be entered in the register, instead of the date of the return of the record book, the reason why the record book was not returned and the date when such entry was made.

(2) Where for the purpose of any trade, business or other activity carried on by him an employer of employee-drivers operates from more than one place goods vehicles which are driven by his employee-drivers, that employer may maintain for each such place a separate register of drivers' record books, each such register being a register complying with the requirements of paragraph (1) of this Regulation (subject to paragraph (4) of this Regulation) but relating only to the drivers' record books known by him to have been issued to or to be used by any of his employee-drivers in relation to the driving of vehicles operated from that place.

(3) An owner-driver and the employer of any employee-driver by whom any such register as aforesaid is required to be maintained shall preserve that register for a period of 12 months from whichever is the last to occur of the following dates, that is to say—

(a) the date on which he ceased to use a book or on which there was returned to him the last of the books issued by him to any employee-driver, the use or issue of which is recorded in that register, or

(b) if any book the issue of which by him is recorded in that register has not been returned to him as required by these Regulations the date when the reason why the record book was not returned was entered in that register.

(4) Notwithstanding anything in the foregoing provisions of these Regulations, registers may be maintained in a form which differs from that specified in Schedule 2 to these Regulations (whether in size, layout, sequence, numbering, content or otherwise) so long as the register contains the same wording as in the form in the said Schedule and such register is so framed as to ensure that all the information required by the form in the said Schedule is required to be entered in the actual register and in such manner as to be readily identifiable by any person entitled under any enactment to inspect any such register.

Miscellaneous provisions relating to drivers' record books and registers of such books

11.—(1) Subject to Regulations 5(1) and 12 of these Regulations each item of information which is required by these Regulations to be entered in a driver's record book or a register of drivers' record books shall be entered therein as soon as the required information is available.

(2) No person shall erase or obliterate any entry once made in a driver's record book or a register of such books, and if a correction is required it shall be made by striking the original entry through in such a way that it may still be read and by writing in the appropriate correction near to the entry so struck through, and any person making such a correction shall initial it.

(3) Any person making an entry in a driver's record book or in a register of such books shall make it in ink, indelible pencil or with a ball point pen.

Exemptions

12.—(1) Where a driver does not during any period of twenty-four hours commencing at midnight drive any goods vehicle other than a vehicle the use of which is exempted from any requirement to have an operator's licence or, in the case of a vehicle in the public service of the Crown, would be so exempted by virtue of section 60(2) of the Act, were it not such a vehicle, that driver and if he is an employee-driver, his employer, shall be exempted for that period from the specified requirements.

(2) Where in any period of 24 hours beginning at midnight a driver does not drive a vehicle to which these Regulations apply for more than four hours and does not drive any such vehicle outside a radius of twenty-five miles from the operating centre of the vehicle then he and, if he is an employee-driver, his employer shall be exempted for that period (hereinafter referred to as "the exempted period") from the specified requirements:

Provided that where the exempted period is followed by a period of twenty-four hours in respect of any part of which a driver is not exempted from all the specified requirements the driver shall be required to enter in his driver's record book the date and time when his last working day ended if such day ended during the exempted period.

For the purposes of computing the said four hours no account shall be taken of any time spent in driving a vehicle elsewhere than on a road if the vehicle is being so driven in the course of operations of agriculture or forestry or in the course of carrying out work in the construction, reconstruction, alteration or extension or maintenance of, or of a part of, a building, or of any other fixed works of construction or civil engineering (including works for the construction, improvement or maintenance of a road) and, for the purposes of this paragraph, where the vehicle is being driven on, or on a part of, a road in the course of the carrying out of any work for the improvement or maintenance of, or of that part of, that road, it shall be treated as being driven elsewhere than on a road.

(3) In this Regulation the expression "the specified requirements" means all the requirements of these Regulations as respects the entering of a current record in a driver's record book and, in the case of drivers, the having possession of such a book in accordance with Regulation 7 of these Regulations.

Given under the Official Seal of the Minister of Transport the 29th January 1970.

Fred Mulley,
Minister of Transport.

Front Sheet—Schedule 1 Part I

DRIVER'S RECORD BOOK
Transport Act 1968 Section 98

1. Operator's licence no.

2. Book serial no.

3. Number of sheets ......with duplicates

I. TO BE COMPLETED BY THE EMPLOYER OR OWNER DRIVER

4. Record book issued by (name address and signature on behalf of employer or owner driver)

5. Date of issue

6. Place of issue

II. TO BE COMPLETED BY ANY OTHER EMPLOYERS OF DRIVER DURING THE CURRENCY OF THIS BOOK

The person named below is also employed as a driver by (name, address and signature on behalf of employer)

III. TO BE COMPLETED BY THE DRIVER

Driver's full name and address

Record Sheet—Schedule 1 Part II

TRANSPORT ACT 1968 SECTION 98
RECORD OF HOURS OF DUTY, DRIVING AND REST

	Operator's licence no.	Book serial no.	Sheet no.

(1) FULL NAME OF DRIVER

(2) LAST WORKING DAY ENDED: DATE   TIME

(3) START OF WORKING DAY		(4) DRIVING PERIODS (AT THE WHEEL)				(5) STATUTORY BREAKS— ON DUTY		(6) STATUTORY OR OTHER BREAKS —OFF DUTY		(7) END OF WORKING DAY		(8) TOTAL DUTY DURING WORKING DAY		(9) VEHICLES DRIVEN	(10) DETAILS OF JOURNEYS (OR AREA SERVED)		(11) DRIVER'S SIGNATURE
		FROM	TO	TOTALS		FROM	TO	FROM	TO						FROM	TO	
Date	Time	Time	Time	Hrs.	Mins.	Time	Time	Time	Time	Date	Time	Hrs.	Mins.	Regn. marks	Place name	Place name	

(12) EMPLOYER'S CERTIFICATION

I have examined the entries in this sheet

Signature

Date

Position held (e.g. Transport Manager)

Schedule 2

Register No.   Page No.

Section 98 Transport Act 1968

Register of Drivers' Record Books

Name of employer or owner-driver

Operator's licence number

Place at which books issued

Driver's record book serial no.	Issued to (Driver's full name and address)	Date of issue and signature* of employer or owner-driver	Name and address of any other known employer of driver	Date of return of record book*

*Only to be entered by the employer if he issued the driver's record book.

EXPLANATORY NOTE

(This Note is not part of the Regulations.)

These Regulations relate to the keeping of records by drivers of goods vehicles of their hours of duty, driving time and rest periods. Drivers of goods vehicles are required to keep a current record of the prescribed information in their drivers' record books and the employers of such drivers are required to cause them to keep such a record (Regulation 3(1) and Schedule 1). Employers are required to keep drivers supplied with drivers' record books (Regulation 3(2)) and a record of books issued must be kept in a register in the prescribed form (Regulation 10 and Schedule 2). The Regulations prescribe the form of driver's record books (Regulations 4 and 9) and the manner of keeping them and require a completed driver's record book to be returned to the driver's employer (Regulations 5 and 11). Employers are required to enter certain information in record books (Regulations 3(1)(*b*), 5(1) and 6(1)) and to supply certain information on request to other employers of a driver (Regulations 5(1) and 6). Drivers are required to produce their drivers' record books for inspection or to return them when required to do so by their employers (Regulation 6(5) and (6)). Drivers who are driving and on duty must have their drivers' record books with them (Regulation 7). Completed drivers' record books and registers must be preserved for the prescribed periods (Regulations 8 and 10(3)). Drivers of certain vehicles are exempted from the requirements of the Regulations as to the keeping of a current record and having with them a driver's record book (Regulation 12).

STATUTORY INSTRUMENTS

1970 No. 124

SEEDS

The Plant Varieties (Index) (Amendment) Regulations 1970

Made - - -	*28th January* 1970
Coming into Operation	*9th February* 1970

The Minister of Agriculture, Fisheries and Food, the Secretary of State for Scotland and the Secretary of State for the Home Department (being the Secretary of State concerned with agriculture in Northern Ireland), acting jointly, in exercise of the powers vested in them by paragraph 5 of Schedule 5 to the Plant Varieties and Seeds Act 1964(**a**), as extended to Northern Ireland by the Plant Varieties and Seeds (Northern Ireland) Order 1964(**b**), and of all other powers enabling them in that behalf, after consultation with the representatives of such interests as appear to them to be concerned, with the approval of the Treasury, hereby make the following Regulations :—

Citation and commencement

1. These Regulations may be cited as the Plant Varieties (Index) (Amendment) Regulations 1970 and shall come into operation on 9th February 1970.

Amendment of principal Regulations

2. The Plant Varieties (Index) Regulations 1969(**c**) (hereinafter referred to as "the principal Regulations") are hereby amended—

(*a*) by adding at the end of Schedule 1 the two further Parts headed "Part VIII" and "Part IX" set out in the Schedule to these Regulations (being particulars of the reproductive and other plant material of broad and field beans and of runner beans and of the quantity, description and quality thereof to be delivered in accordance with Regulation 9 of the principal Regulations) and

(*b*) by adding in the second column of Schedule 2, after the item "(*g*) a lettuce variety", the items

"(*h*) a broad bean or field bean variety

(*i*) a runner bean variety"

and in the fourth column of the said Schedule, opposite each of the items added as aforesaid the figures "30 0 0".

(**a**) 1964 c. 14. (**b**) S.I. 1964/1574 (1964 III, p. 3543).
(**c**) S.I. 1969/1027 (1969 II, p. 3030).

In Witness whereof the official seal of the Minister of Agriculture, Fisheries and Food is hereunto affixed on 19th January 1970.

(L.S.)   *Cledwyn Hughes,*
                          Minister of Agriculture, Fisheries and Food.

Given under the seal of the Secretary of State for Scotland on 22nd January 1970.

(L.S.)   *William Ross,*
                              Secretary of State for Scotland.

Given under the hand of the Secretary of State for the Home Department on 26th January 1970.

                                    James Callaghan,
                          Secretary of State for the Home Department.

Approved on 28th January 1970.

                                    Ernest Armstrong,
                                    Neil McBride,
                          Two of the Lords Commissioners of
                                Her Majesty's Treasury.

SCHEDULE

PART VIII

BROAD AND FIELD BEANS

Quantity

1.—(1) During the year beginning with the making of the application 9 lb. of seed shall be delivered.

(2) During each of the immediately succeeding years until the completion of the tests and trials there shall be delivered such reproductive and other plant material in such quantity and of such description and quality as shall appear to the Ministers to be necessary or desirable for the proper completion of the tests and trials.

Packing

2. The seed shall be packed in a suitable container of sufficient strength to withstand mechanical damage during transit.

Quality

3.—(1) *Health*

The seed shall be free from serious seed-borne diseases.

(2) *Purity and germination*

The seed shall be accompanied by a report of a test made at an official seed testing station established under the Seeds Act 1920(a) or a seed testing station

---

(a) 1920 c. 54.

licensed under that Act and made within the 3 months immediately preceding the delivery of the seed stating that in a sample of 1 lb.: —

(a) the percentage of purity was not less than 98, and

(b) the percentage of germination was not less than 70.

Dressings and treatments

4. The seed shall not have been subjected to any fungicidal or insecticidal treatment.

Part IX
Runner Beans

Quantity

1.—(1) During the year beginning with the making of the application 9 lb. of seed shall be delivered.

(2) During each of the immediately succeeding years until the completion of the tests and trials there shall be delivered such reproductive and other plant material in such quantity and of such description and quality as shall appear to the Ministers to be necessary or desirable for the proper completion of the tests and trials.

Packing

2. The seed shall be packed in a suitable container of sufficient strength to withstand mechanical damage during transit.

Quality

3.—(1) *Health*

The seed shall be free from serious seed-borne diseases.

(2) *Purity and germination*

The seed shall be accompanied by a report of a test made at an official seed testing station established under the Seeds Act 1920 or a seed testing station licensed under that Act and made within the 3 months immediately preceding the delivery of the seed stating that in a sample of 1 lb.: —

(a) the percentage of purity was not less than 99, and

(b) the percentage of germination was not less than 60.

Dressings and treatments

4. The seed shall not have been subjected to any fungicidal or insecticidal treatment.

EXPLANATORY NOTE
(This Note is not part of the Regulations.)

These Regulations amend the Plant Varieties (Index) Regulations 1969 by adding particulars of the reproductive material of broad beans, field beans and runner beans to be delivered, and prescribing the fees to be paid in connection with applications for additions to the Index of Plant Varieties.

STATUTORY INSTRUMENTS

1970 No. 128 (S.5)

ANIMALS

PREVENTION OF CRUELTY

The Spring Traps Approval (Scotland) Amendment Order 1970

Made - - -	*29th January* 1970
Coming into Operation	*1st February* 1970

In exercise of the powers conferred upon him by sections 50(3) and 85(3) of the Agriculture (Scotland) Act 1948(a) as amended by section 10 of the Pests Act 1954(b) and of all other powers enabling him in that behalf, the Secretary of State hereby makes the following order:—

Citation, commencement and interpretation

1.—(1) This order may be cited as the Spring Traps Approval (Scotland) Amendment Order 1970 and shall come into operation on 1st February 1970.

(2) The Interpretation Act 1889(c) shall apply for the interpretation of this order as it applies for the interpretation of an Act of Parliament.

Amendment of Order

2. The Schedule to the Spring Traps Approval (Scotland) Order 1958(d) as amended by the Spring Traps Approval (Scotland) Amendment Order 1966(e) and the Spring Traps Approval (Scotland) Amendment Order 1968(f) (which sets out the types and makes of traps approved for the purposes of section 50 of the Agriculture (Scotland) Act 1948 as amended by section 10 of the Pests Act 1954 and the conditions as to the animals for which and the circumstances in which traps so approved may be used) shall be further amended by making the following addition thereto:—

"*Type and make of Trap*	*Conditions*
Fenn Vermin Trap Mark IV (Heavy Duty) manufactured by or under the authority of Mr. A. A. Fenn, of F.H.T. Works, High Street, Astwood Bank, Redditch, Worcestershire.	The trap shall be used only:— (*a*) for the purpose of killing or taking grey squirrels or stoats, weasels, or other small ground vermin, and for that purpose shall be set only in tunnels whether natural or constructed for the purpose, or (*b*) for the purpose of killing or taking rats or mice and for that purpose shall be set only in the open on their runs or in tunnels whether natural or constructed for the purpose."

(a) 1948 c. 45.	(b) 1954 c. 68.
(c) 1889 c. 63.	(d) S.I. 1958/1780 (1958 I, p. 160).
(e) S.I. 1966/844 (1966 II, p. 1983).	(f) S.I. 1968/676 (1968 I, p. 1513).

Given under the Seal of the Secretary of State for Scotland.

H. Whitby,
Secretary.

Department of Agriculture and Fisheries for Scotland,
St. Andrew's House,
Edinburgh.
29th January 1970.

EXPLANATORY NOTE
(This Note is not part of the Order.)

It is an offence under section 50 of the Agriculture (Scotland) Act 1948 as amended by section 10 of the Pests Act 1954, to use for the purpose of killing or taking animals any spring trap other than one of a type and kind approved by the Secretary of State. By the Spring Traps Approval (Scotland) Order 1958 as amended by the Spring Traps Approval (Scotland) Amendment Order 1966 and the Spring Traps Approval (Scotland) Amendment Order 1968 the Secretary of State specified certain traps as approved and the conditions under which such traps might be lawfully used. This Amendment Order has the effect of adding the Fenn Vermin Trap Mark IV (Heavy Duty) to those already specified.

STATUTORY INSTRUMENTS

1970 No. 131

REPRESENTATION OF THE PEOPLE

The London Borough Council Election Rules 1970

Made - - -	*30th January* 1970
Laid before Parliament	*12th February* 1970
Coming into Operation	*16th February* 1970

In pursuance of the powers conferred upon me by paragraph 13 of Schedule 3 to the London Government Act 1963(**a**) and by section 61 of the Local Government Act 1933(**b**) (as it has effect in relation to elections to a London borough council by virtue of section 1(6) of the London Government Act 1963), I hereby make the following Rules for the conduct of an election of London borough councillors and of the mayor of a London borough, and the following Regulations prescribing the form of declaration of acceptance of office by the mayor, an alderman or a councillor of a London borough :—

1.—(1) These Rules and Regulations may be cited as the London Borough Council Election Rules 1970 and shall come into operation on 16th February 1970 :

Provided that they shall not have effect in relation to an election notice of which has been published before that date.

(2) The Interpretation Act 1889(**c**) shall apply to the interpretation of these Rules and Regulations as it applies to the interpretation of an Act of Parliament.

(3) Any reference in any statutory instrument to a local elections rule shall, so far as it relates to the election of a councillor of a London borough, be construed as a reference to the rule in Schedule 1 hereto (however numbered) dealing with the same subject.

2.—(1) The London Borough Council and Greater London Council Election Forms Regulations 1964(**d**), so far as they relate to elections to the council of a London borough, and the London Borough Council Elections Rules 1968(**e**) are hereby revoked.

(2) Notwithstanding paragraph (1) of this Rule, the Rules and Regulations therein mentioned shall apply to any election notice of which has been published before these Rules and Regulations come into operation.

3. In the application of the local elections rules contained in Schedule 2 to the Representation of the People Act 1949(**f**) to an election of London borough councillors, adaptations, alterations and exceptions shall be made therein so that the said local elections rules shall read as set out in Schedule 1 hereto.

(**a**) 1963 c. 33.	(**b**) 1933 c. 51.
(**c**) 1889 c. 63.	(**d**) S.I. 1964/222 (1964 I, p. 402).
(**e**) S.I. 1968/497 (1968 I, p. 1208).	(**f**) 1949 c. 68.

4. The declaration of acceptance of office by the mayor, an alderman or a councillor of a London borough shall be in the form in Schedule 2 hereto, or a form to the like effect.

James Callaghan,
One of Her Majesty's Principal
Secretaries of State.

Home Office,
　Whitehall.
30th January 1970.

SCHEDULE 1

LOCAL ELECTIONS RULES

Arrangement of rules

PART I

PROVISIONS AS TO TIME

Rule
1. Timetable.
2. Computation of time.
3. Hours of poll.

PART II

STAGES COMMON TO CONTESTED AND UNCONTESTED ELECTIONS

4. Notice of election.
5. Nomination of candidates.
6. Subscription of nomination paper.
7. Consent to nomination.
8. Place for delivery of nomination papers.
9. Decisions as to validity of nomination papers.
10. Publication of nominations.
11. Withdrawal of candidates.
12. Nomination in more than one ward.
13. Method of election.

PART III

CONTESTED ELECTIONS

General provisions

14. Poll to be taken by ballot.
15. The ballot papers.
16. The official mark.
17. Prohibition of disclosure of vote.
18. Use of schools and public rooms.

Action to be taken before the poll

19. Notice of poll.
20. Postal ballot papers.
21. Provision of polling stations.
22. Appointment of presiding officers and clerks.

Part I

Provisions as to Time

Timetable

1. The proceedings at the election shall be conducted in accordance with the following Table.

Timetable

Proceeding	*Time*
Publication of notice of election ...	Not later than the twentieth day before the day of election.
Delivery of nomination papers ...	Not later than noon on the fourteenth day before the day of election.
Despatch of notice of decisions on nominations and publication of statement as to persons nominated	Not later than noon on the thirteenth day before the day of election.
Delivery of notices of withdrawals of candidature	Not later than noon on the twelfth day before the day of election.
Notice of poll	Not later than the fifth day before the day of election.
Notice of appointment of polling or counting agents	Not later than the third day before the day of election.
Polling	On the day of election.

Computation of time

2.—(1) In computing any period of time for the purposes of the Timetable, a Sunday, day of the Christmas break, of the Easter break or of a bank holiday break or day appointed for public thanksgiving or mourning shall be disregarded and any such day shall not be treated as a day for the purpose of any proceedings up to the completion of the poll nor shall the returning officer be obliged to proceed with the counting of the votes thereon:

Provided that where under Part III of these rules a person ought to proceed with the preparation of special lists or the issue of postal ballot papers on the first or last days of the Christmas break, the Easter break or a bank holiday break, or on the Saturday in the Easter break, nothing in this rule shall absolve him from that duty.

(2) In this rule "the Christmas break" means the period beginning with the last week day before Christmas Day and ending with the first week day after Christmas Day which is not a bank holiday, "the Easter break" means the period beginning with the Thursday before and ending with the Tuesday after Easter Day, and "a bank holiday break" means any bank holiday not included in the Christmas break or the Easter break and the period beginning with the last week day before that bank holiday and ending with the next week day which is not a bank holiday.

Hours of poll

3. The poll shall commence at eight o'clock in the morning and be kept open till nine o'clock in the evening of the same day and no longer.

PART II

STAGES COMMON TO CONTESTED AND UNCONTESTED ELECTIONS

Notice of election

4.—(1) Notice of the election in the form in the Appendix, or a form to the like effect, shall be prepared, signed and published by the returning officer.

(2) The notice shall be published by causing it to be affixed to the town hall and to be exhibited at such conspicuous places in the ward as the returning officer may determine.

(3) The notice of election shall state the date by which application to be treated as an absent voter and other applications and notices about postal or proxy voting must reach the registration officer in order that they may be effective for the election; and in addition the registration officer shall give notice of the date in the ward by such means as he thinks best calculated to bring the information to the notice of those concerned.

Nomination of candidates

5.—(1) Each candidate shall be nominated by a separate nomination paper in the form in the Appendix, or a form to the like effect, delivered at the place fixed for the purpose.

(2) The nomination paper shall state the full names, place of residence and (if desired) description of the candidate and the surname shall be placed first in the list of his names.

(3) The description (if any) shall not exceed six words in length, and need not refer to his rank, profession or calling so long as, with the other particulars of the candidate, it is sufficient to identify him.

Subscription of nomination paper

6.—(1) The nomination paper shall be subscribed by two electors for the ward as proposer and seconder, and by eight other electors for the ward as assenting to the nomination.

(2) Where a nomination paper bears the signatures of more than the required number of persons as proposing, seconding or assenting to the nomination of a candidate, the signature or signatures (up to the required number) appearing first on the paper in each category shall be taken into account to the exclusion of any others in that category.

(3) The nomination paper shall give the electoral number of each person subscribing it.

(4) The returning officer shall provide nomination papers and shall supply any elector for the ward with as many nomination papers as may be required and shall, at the request of any such elector, prepare for signature a nomination paper.

(5) No person shall—

(a) subscribe more nomination papers than there are vacancies to be filled in the ward; or

(b) subscribe a nomination paper for more than one ward; or

(c) subscribe more than one nomination paper in respect of the same candidate:

Provided that a person shall not be prevented from subscribing a nomination paper by reason only of his having subscribed that of a candidate who has died or withdrawn before delivery of the first-mentioned paper.

(6) If any person subscribes nomination papers in contravention of the last fore-going paragraph, his signature shall be inoperative in all but those papers (up to the permitted number) which are first delivered.

(7) In this rule—

the expression "elector for the ward" means a person who is registered as a local government elector for the ward in the register to be used at the election or who, pending the publication of that register, appears from the electors lists therefor as corrected by the registration officer to be entitled to be so registered (and accordingly includes a person shown in the register or electors lists as below voting age if it appears therefrom that he will be of voting age on the day fixed for the poll, but not otherwise);

the expression "electoral number" means the distinctive letter or letters of the parliamentary polling district in which a person is registered together with his number in the said register, or pending the publication of the register, the distinctive letter or letters of the parliamentary polling district in which he is entitled to be registered together with his number (if any) in the electors lists therefor.

Consent to nomination

7.—(1) A person shall not be validly nominated unless his consent to nomination, given in writing on or within one month before the last day for the delivery of nomination papers, and attested by one witness, is delivered at the place and within the time appointed for the delivery of nomination papers:

Provided that, if the returning officer is satisfied that owing to the absence of a person from the United Kingdom it has not been reasonably practicable for his consent in writing to be given as aforesaid, a telegram consenting to his nomination and purporting to have been sent by him shall be deemed, for the purpose of this rule, to be consent in writing given by him on the day on which it purports to have been sent, and attestation of his consent shall not be required.

(2) A candidate's consent given under this rule shall contain a statement declaring, with reference to the date of his nomination, that to the best of his belief he will be or is qualified as required by law to be elected to and hold the office in question, and the statement shall give particulars of his qualification.

Place for delivery of nomination papers

8. Every nomination paper shall be delivered at the place fixed by the returning officer.

Decisions as to validity of nomination papers

9.—(1) Where a nomination paper and the candidate's consent thereto are delivered in accordance with these rules, the candidate shall be deemed to stand nominated unless and until the returning officer decides that the nomination paper is invalid, or proof is given to the satisfaction of the returning officer of the candidate's death, or the candidate withdraws.

(2) The returning officer shall be entitled to hold a nomination paper invalid only on one of the following grounds, that is to say,—

(a) that the particulars of the candidate or the persons subscribing the paper are not as required by law; and

(b) that the paper is not subscribed as so required.

(3) The returning officer shall examine the nomination papers, and decide whether the candidates have been validly nominated in accordance with these rules and shall do so as soon as practicable after each paper is delivered.

(4) Where he decides that a nomination paper is invalid, he shall endorse and sign on the paper the fact and the reasons for his decision.

(5) The returning officer shall send notice of his decision to each candidate at his place of residence as stated on his nomination paper.

(6) The decision of the returning officer that a nomination paper is valid shall be final and shall not be questioned in any proceeding whatsoever.

(7) Subject to the last foregoing paragraph, nothing in this rule shall prevent the validity of a nomination being questioned on an election petition.

Publication of nominations

10.—(1) The returning officer shall prepare and publish a statement in the form in the Appendix, or a form to the like effect, showing the persons who have been and stand nominated and any other persons who have been nominated, with the reason why they no longer stand nominated.

(2) The statement shall show the names, addresses and descriptions (if any) of the persons nominated as given in their nomination papers.

(3) The statement shall show the persons standing nominated arranged alphabetically in the order of their surnames, and, if there are two or more of them with the same surname, of their other names.

(4) In the case of a person nominated by more than one nomination paper, the returning officer shall take the particulars required by the foregoing provisions of this rule from such one of the papers as the candidate or the returning officer in default of the candidate may select.

(5) The statement as to persons nominated shall be published by causing it to be affixed to the place appointed for the delivery of nomination papers.

Withdrawal of candidates

11.—(1) A candidate may withdraw his candidature by notice of withdrawal signed by him and attested by one witness and delivered at the place appointed for the delivery of nomination papers.

(2) In the case of a candidate who is outside the United Kingdom, a notice of withdrawal signed by his proposer and accompanied by a written declaration also so signed of the candidate's absence from the United Kingdom shall be of the same effect as a notice of withdrawal signed by the candidate:

Provided that where the candidate stands nominated by more than one nomination paper a notice of withdrawal under this paragraph shall be effective if, but only if,—

  (a) it and the accompanying declaration are signed by all the proposers except any who is, and is stated in the said declaration to be, outside the United Kingdom; or

  (b) it is accompanied, in addition to the said declaration, by a written statement signed by the candidate that the proposer giving the notice is authorised to do so on the candidate's behalf during his absence from the United Kingdom.

Nomination in more than one ward

12. A candidate who is validly nominated for more than one ward must duly withdraw from his candidature in all those wards except one, and if he does not so withdraw he shall be deemed to have withdrawn from his candidature in all those wards.

Method of election

13.—(1) If the number of persons remaining validly nominated for the ward after any withdrawals under these rules exceeds the number of vacancies, the councillors shall be elected from among them at a poll under Part III of these rules.

(2) If the said number does not exceed the number of vacancies, the person or persons (if any) deemed to be elected under the following provisions of this rule shall be declared elected in accordance with Part IV of these rules.

(3) The person or persons (if any) remaining validly nominated for the ward after any withdrawals under these rules shall be deemed to be elected.

(4) If, at an ordinary election of councillors, no person remains validly nominated as aforesaid, or the number of persons so remaining validly nominated is less than the number of vacancies, the retiring councillors for the ward who, if duly nominated, would have been qualified for election or, if their number is more than that of the vacancies not filled under paragraph (3) of this rule, such of those councillors as were highest on the poll at the last ordinary election, or as filled the places of councillors who were highest on the poll at that election, or if the poll was equal or there was no poll, as may be determined by the drawing of lots conducted under the direction of the returning officer, shall be deemed to be elected to fill up the vacancies not filled under paragraph (3) of this rule.

PART III

CONTESTED ELECTIONS

GENERAL PROVISIONS

Poll to be taken by ballot

14. The votes at the poll shall be given by ballot, the result shall be ascertained by counting the votes given to each candidate, and the candidate or candidates to whom the majority of votes have been given shall be declared to have been elected.

The ballot papers

15.—(1) The ballot of every voter shall consist of a ballot paper, and the persons remaining validly nominated for the ward after any withdrawals under these rules, and no others, shall be entitled to have their names inserted in the ballot paper.

(2) Every ballot paper shall be in the form in the Appendix, and shall be printed in accordance with the directions therein, and—

  (a) shall contain the names and other particulars of the candidates as shown in the statement of persons nominated;

  (b) shall be capable of being folded up;

  (c) shall have a number printed on the back;

  (d) shall have attached a counterfoil with the same number printed on the face.

(3) The order of the names in the ballot paper shall be the same as in the statement of persons nominated.

The official mark

16.—(1) Every ballot paper shall be marked with an official mark, which shall be either embossed or perforated.

(2) The official mark shall be kept secret, and an interval of not less than seven years shall intervene between the use of the same official mark at elections for the same London borough.

Prohibition of disclosure of vote

17. No person who has voted at the election shall, in any legal proceeding to question the election, be required to state for whom he voted.

Use of schools and public rooms

18.—(1) The returning officer may use, free of charge, for the purpose of taking the poll or of counting the votes—

  (a) a room in a school maintained or assisted by a local education authority or a school in respect of which grants are made out of moneys provided by Parliament to the person or body of persons responsible for the management of the school;

  (b) a room the expense of maintaining which is payable out of any rate.

(2) The returning officer shall make good any damage done to, and defray any expense incurred by the persons having control over, any such room as aforesaid by reason of its being used for the purpose of taking the poll or of counting the votes.

(3) The use of a room in an unoccupied house for the purpose of taking the poll or of counting the votes shall not render a person liable to be rated or to pay any rate for that house.

ACTION TO BE TAKEN BEFORE THE POLL

Notice of poll

19.—(1) Notice of the poll shall be published by the returning officer at the places at which the notice of election is required to be published under rule 4 of these rules.

(2) Notice of the poll shall specify—

(a) the day and hours fixed for the poll;

(b) the number of councillors to be elected;

(c) the particulars of each candidate remaining validly nominated (the names and other particulars of the candidates, and the order of the names of the candidates, being the same as in the statement of persons nominated);

(d) the names of the proposer and seconder signing a candidate's nomination paper; and

(e) the situation of each polling station and the description of the persons entitled to vote thereat.

(3) In the case of a candidate nominated by more than one nomination paper, the nomination paper mentioned in sub-paragraph (d) of paragraph (2) of this rule shall be that from which the names and other particulars of the candidate shown in the statement of persons nominated are taken.

(4) The returning officer shall, as soon as practicable after publication of a notice of poll, give to each of the election agents a description in writing of the polling districts, if any.

Postal ballot papers

20. The returning officer shall as soon as practicable send to those entitled to vote by post, at the addresses furnished by them for the purpose, a ballot paper and a declaration of identity in the form set out in the Representation of the People Regulations 1969(a), or a form substantially to the like effect, together with an envelope for their return.

Provision of polling stations

21.—(1) The returning officer shall provide a sufficient number of polling stations and, subject to the following provisions of this rule, shall allot the electors to the polling stations in such manner as he thinks most convenient.

(2) One or more polling stations may be provided in the same room.

(3) The polling station allotted to electors from any parliamentary polling district wholly or partly within the ward shall, in the absence of special circumstances, be in the parliamentary polling place for that district, unless the polling place is outside the ward.

(4) The returning officer shall provide each polling station with such number of compartments as may be necessary in which the voters can mark their votes screened from observation.

Appointment of presiding officers and clerks

22.—(1) The returning officer shall appoint and pay a presiding officer to attend at each polling station and such clerks as may be necessary for the purposes of the election, but he shall not appoint any person who has been employed by or on behalf of a candidate in or about the election.

(a) S.I. 1969/904 (1969 II, p. 2602).

(2) The returning officer may, if he thinks fit, preside at a polling station and the provisions of these rules relating to a presiding officer shall apply to a returning officer so presiding with the necessary modifications as to things to be done by the returning officer to the presiding officer or by the presiding officer to the returning officer.

(3) A presiding officer may do, by the clerks appointed to assist him, any act (including the asking of questions) which he is required or authorised by these rules to do at a polling station except order the arrest, exclusion or removal of any person from the polling station.

Special lists

23. The registration officer shall as soon as practicable prepare the following special lists, namely—

   (a) a list (in these rules referred to as "the absent voters list") giving the name and number on the register of every person entitled to vote at the election as an absent voter;

   (b) a list (in these rules referred to as "the list of proxies") giving—

      (i) the names and numbers on the register of the electors for whom proxies have been appointed; and

      (ii) the names and addresses of the persons appointed;

   (c) a list of any persons entitled to vote by post as proxy at the election.

Equipment of polling stations

24.—(1) The returning officer shall provide each presiding officer with such number of ballot boxes and ballot papers as in the opinion of the returning officer may be necessary.

(2) Every ballot box shall be so constructed that the ballot papers can be put therein, but cannot be withdrawn therefrom, without the box being unlocked.

(3) The returning officer shall provide each polling station with—

   (a) materials to enable voters to mark the ballot papers;

   (b) instruments for stamping thereon the official mark;

   (c) copies of the register of electors for the ward or such part thereof as contains the names of the electors allotted to the station;

   (d) the parts of any special lists prepared for the election corresponding to the register of electors for the ward or part thereof provided under the last fore-going sub-paragraph.

(4) A notice in the form in the Appendix, giving directions for the guidance of the voters in voting, shall be printed in conspicuous characters and exhibited inside and outside every polling station.

(5) In every compartment of every polling station there shall be exhibited a notice as follows:— "The voter may vote for not more than......candidate(s)".

Appointment of polling and counting agents

25.—(1) Each candidate may, before the commencement of the poll, appoint polling agents to attend at polling stations for the purpose of detecting personation and counting agents to attend at the counting of the votes:

Provided that—

   (a) the returning officer may limit the number of counting agents, so however that the number shall be the same in the case of each candidate and the number allowed to a candidate shall not (except in special circumstances) be less than the number obtained by dividing the number of clerks employed on the counting by the number of candidates;

(b) the appointment of a polling agent may be on behalf of more than one candidate;

(c) not more than three or, if the number of candidates exceeds twenty, four polling agents shall be appointed to attend at any polling station.

(2) If the number of polling agents appointed to attend at a polling station exceeds the permitted number, only those polling agents, up to the permitted number, whose appointments are signed by or on behalf of the greater number of candidates, or, in the event of an equality in the number of signatures, only such of those polling agents as may be determined by the returning officer, shall be deemed to have been duly appointed.

(3) Notice in writing of the appointment, stating the names and addresses of the persons appointed, shall be given by the candidate to the returning officer and shall be so given not later than the time appointed for that purpose in the Timetable.

(4) If an agent dies, or becomes incapable of acting, the candidate may appoint another agent in his place, and shall forthwith give to the returning officer notice in writing of the name and address of the agent appointed.

(5) The foregoing provisions of this rule shall be without prejudice to the requirements of section 60(1) of the Representation of the People Act 1949 as to the appointment of paid polling agents, and any appointment authorised by this rule may be made and the notice of appointment given to the returning officer by the candidate's election agent, instead of by the candidate.

(6) In the following provisions of these rules references to polling and counting agents shall be taken as references to agents whose appointments have been duly made and notified and, where the number of agents is restricted, who are within the permitted number.

(7) Any notice required to be given to a counting agent by the returning officer may be delivered at, or sent by post to, the address stated in the notice of appointment.

(8) A candidate may himself do any act or thing which any polling or counting agent of his, if appointed, would have been authorised to do, or may assist his agent in doing any such act or thing.

(9) A candidate's election agent may do or assist in doing anything which a polling or counting agent of his is authorised to do; and anything required or authorised by these rules to be done in the presence of the polling or counting agents may be done in the presence of a candidate's election agent instead of his polling agent or counting agents.

(10) Where by these rules any act or thing is required or authorised to be done in the presence of the polling or counting agents, the non-attendance of any agents or agent at the time and place appointed for the purpose, shall not, if the act or thing is otherwise duly done, invalidate the act or thing done.

Declaration of secrecy

26.—(1) Before the opening of the poll a declaration of secrecy in the form in paragraph (4) of this rule, or in a form as near thereto as circumstances admit, shall be made by—

(a) the returning officer and the presiding officers;

(b) every clerk authorised to attend at a polling station or the counting of the votes;

(c) every candidate attending at a polling station or at the counting of the votes and every election agent so attending;

(d) every candidate's wife or husband attending at the counting of the votes;

(e) every polling agent and counting agent;

(f) every person permitted by the returning officer to attend at the counting of the votes, though not entitled to do so.

(2) Notwithstanding anything in the foregoing paragraph, the following persons attending at the counting of the votes, that is to say:—

(*a*) any candidate;

(*b*) any election agent, or any candidate's wife or husband attending by virtue of the rule authorising election agents and candidates' wives or husbands to attend as such;

(*c*) any person permitted by the returning officer to attend, though not entitled to do so;

(*d*) any clerk making the declaration in order to attend at the counting of the votes;

need not make the declaration before the opening of the poll but shall make it before he or she is permitted to attend the counting, and a polling or counting agent appointed after the opening of the poll shall make the declaration before acting as such agent.

(3) The returning officer shall make the declaration in the presence of a Justice of the Peace, and any other person shall make the declaration in the presence either of a Justice of the Peace or of the returning officer, and subsections (1), (2), (3) and (6) of section 53 of the Representation of the People Act 1949 shall be read to the declarant by the person taking the declaration, or shall be read by the declarant in the presence of that person:

Provided that the declaration may be made by the returning officer or any other person before a person who is chairman of the Greater London Council, a county council or a district council or mayor of a borough or rural borough, and may be made by a person other than the returning officer before a person who is clerk of any such council or town clerk of a borough or rural borough.

(4) The declaration shall be as follows—

"I solemnly promise and declare that I will not do anything forbidden by sub-sections (1), (2), (3) and (6) of section 53 of the Representation of the People Act 1949, which have been read to [by] me.".

The Poll

Admission to polling station

27.—(1) The presiding officer shall regulate the number of voters to be admitted to the polling station at the same time, and shall exclude all other persons except—

(*a*) the candidates and their election agents;

(*b*) the polling agents appointed to attend at the polling station;

(*c*) the clerks appointed to attend at the polling station;

(*d*) the constables on duty; and

(*e*) the companions of blind voters.

(2) Not more than one polling agent shall be admitted at the same time to a polling station on behalf of the same candidate.

(3) A constable or person employed by a returning officer shall not be admitted to vote in person elsewhere than at his own polling station under the provisions of the Representation of the People Act 1949 in that behalf, except on production and surrender of a certificate as to his employment, which shall be in the form in the Appendix, or a form to the like effect, and signed by an officer of police of or above the rank of inspector or by the returning officer, as the case may be.

(4) Any certificate surrendered under this rule shall forthwith be cancelled.

Keeping of order in station

28.—(1) It shall be the duty of the presiding officer to keep order at his polling station.

(2) If a person misconducts himself in a polling station, or fails to obey the lawful orders of the presiding officer, he may immediately, by order of the presiding officer, be removed from the polling station by a constable in or near that station or by any

other person authorised in writing by the returning officer to remove him, and the person so removed shall not, without the permission of the presiding officer, again enter the polling station during the day.

(3) Any person so removed may, if charged with the commission in the polling station of an offence, be dealt with as a person taken into custody by a constable for an offence without a warrant.

(4) The powers conferred by this rule shall not be exercised so as to prevent a voter who is otherwise entitled to vote at a polling station from having an opportunity of voting at that station.

Sealing of ballot boxes

29. Immediately before the commencement of the poll, the presiding officer shall show the ballot box empty to such persons, if any, as are present in the polling station, so that they may see that it is empty, and shall then lock it up and place his seal on it in such manner as to prevent its being opened without breaking the seal, and shall place it in his view for the receipt of ballot papers, and keep it so locked and sealed.

Questions to be put to voters

30.—(1) The presiding officer may, and if required by a candidate or his election or polling agent shall, put to any person applying for a ballot paper at the time of his application, but not afterwards, the following questions, or either of them, that is to say—

(a) in the case of a person applying as an elector—

    (i) Are you the person registered in the register of local government electors now in force for this ward as follows [*read the whole entry from the register*]?

    (ii) Have you already voted at the present election [*adding in the case of an election for several wards* in this or any other ward] otherwise than as proxy for some other person?

(b) in the case of a person applying as proxy—

    (i) Are you the person whose name appears as A.B. in the list of proxies for this election as entitled to vote as proxy on behalf of C.D.?

    (ii) Have you already voted here or elsewhere at the present election as proxy on behalf of C.D.?

(2) A ballot paper shall not be delivered to any person required to answer the above questions or any of them unless he has answered the questions or question satisfactorily.

(3) Save as by this rule authorised, no inquiry shall be permitted as to the right of any person to vote.

Challenge of voter

31.—(1) If at the time a person applies for a ballot paper for the purpose of voting in person, or after he has applied for a ballot paper for that purpose and before he has left the polling station, a candidate or his election or polling agent declares to the presiding officer that he has reasonable cause to believe that the applicant has committed an offence of personation and undertakes to substantiate the charge in a court of law, the presiding officer may order a constable to arrest the applicant, and the order of the presiding officer shall be sufficient authority for the constable so to do.

(2) A person against whom a declaration is made under this rule shall not by reason thereof be prevented from voting.

(3) A person arrested under the provisions of this rule shall be dealt with as a person taken into custody by a constable for an offence without a warrant.

Voting procedure

32.—(1) A ballot paper shall be delivered to a voter who applies therefor, and immediately before delivery—

(a) the ballot paper shall be stamped with the official mark, either embossed or perforated;

(b) the number, name and description of the elector as stated in the copy of the register of electors shall be called out;

(c) the number of the elector shall be marked on the counterfoil;

(d) a mark shall be placed in the register of electors against the number of the elector to denote that a ballot paper has been received but without showing the particular ballot paper which has been received; and

(e) in the case of a person applying for a ballot paper as proxy, a mark shall also be placed against his name in the list of proxies.

(2) The voter, on receiving the ballot paper, shall forthwith proceed into one of the compartments in the polling station and there secretly mark his paper and fold it up so as to conceal his vote, and shall then show to the presiding officer the back of the paper so as to disclose the official mark, and put the ballot paper so folded up into the ballot box in the presence of the presiding officer.

(3) The voter shall vote without undue delay, and shall leave the polling station as soon as he has put his ballot paper into the ballot box.

Votes marked by presiding officer

33.—(1) The presiding officer, on the application of—

(a) a voter who is incapacitated by blindness or other physical cause from voting in manner directed by these rules; or

(b) if the poll is taken on a Saturday, a voter who declares that he is a Jew, and objects on religious grounds to vote in manner directed by these rules; or

(c) a voter who declares orally that he is unable to read;

shall, in the presence of the polling agents, cause the vote of the voter to be marked on a ballot paper in manner directed by the voter, and the ballot paper to be placed in the ballot box.

(2) The name and number on the register of electors of every voter whose vote is marked in pursuance of this rule, and the reason why it is so marked, shall be entered on a list (in these rules called "the list of votes marked by the presiding officer").

In the case of a person voting as proxy for an elector, the number to be entered together with the name of the voter shall be the number of the elector.

Voting by blind persons

34.—(1) If a voter makes an application to the presiding officer to be allowed on the ground of blindness to vote with the assistance of another person by whom he is accompanied (in these rules referred to as "the companion"), the presiding officer shall require the voter to declare orally whether he is so incapacitated by his blindness as to be unable to vote without assistance.

(2) If the presiding officer is satisfied that the voter is so incapacitated and is also satisfied by a written declaration made by the companion (in these rules referred to as "the declaration made by the companion of a blind voter") that the companion is a qualified person within the meaning of this rule and has not previously assisted more than one blind person to vote at the election, the presiding officer shall grant the application, and thereupon anything which is by these rules required to be done to or by the said voter in connection with the giving of his vote may be done to, or with the assistance of, the companion.

(3) For the purposes of this rule, a person shall be qualified to assist a blind voter to vote, if that person is either—

    (a) a person who is entitled to vote as an elector at the election; or

    (b) the father, mother, brother, sister, husband, wife, son or daughter of the blind voter and has attained the age of eighteen years.

(4) The name and number in the register of electors of every voter whose vote is given in accordance with this rule and the name and address of the companion shall be entered on a list (in these rules referred to as "the list of blind voters assisted by companions").

In the case of a person voting as proxy for an elector, the number to be entered together with the name of the voter shall be the number of the elector.

(5) The declaration made by the companion—

    (a) shall be in the form in the Appendix;

    (b) shall be made before the presiding officer at the time when the voter applies to vote with the assistance of a companion and shall forthwith be given to the presiding officer who shall attest and retain it.

(6) No fee or other payment shall be charged in respect of the declaration.

Tendered ballot papers

35.—(1) If a person, representing himself to be—

    (a) a particular elector named on the register and not named in the absent voters list; or

    (b) a particular person named in the list of proxies as proxy for an elector and not named in the list of persons entitled to vote by post as proxy,

applies for a ballot paper after another person has voted in person either as the elector or his proxy, the applicant shall, on satisfactorily answering the questions permitted by law to be asked at the poll, be entitled, subject to the following provisions of this rule, to mark a ballot paper (in these rules referred to as "a tendered ballot paper") in the same manner as any other voter.

(2) A tendered ballot paper shall—

    (a) be of a colour differing from the other ballot papers;

    (b) instead of being put into the ballot box, be given to the presiding officer and endorsed by him with the name of the voter and his number in the register of electors, and set aside in a separate packet.

(3) The name of the voter and his number on the register of electors shall be entered on a list (in these rules referred to as the "tendered votes list").

(4) In the case of a person voting as proxy for an elector, the number to be endorsed or entered together with the name of the voter shall be the number of that elector.

Spoilt ballot papers

36. A voter who has inadvertently dealt with his ballot paper in such manner that it cannot be conveniently used as a ballot paper may, on delivering it to the presiding officer and proving to his satisfaction the fact of the inadvertence, obtain another ballot paper in the place of the ballot paper so delivered (in these rules referred to as "a spoilt ballot paper"), and the spoilt ballot paper shall be immediately cancelled.

Adjournment of poll in case of riot

37. For the purpose of the adjournment of the poll in the event of riot or open violence, a presiding officer shall have the power by law belonging to a presiding officer at a parliamentary election.

It

Procedure on close of poll

38.—(1) As soon as practicable after the close of the poll, the presiding officer shall, in the presence of the polling agents, make up into separate packets, sealed with his own seal and the seals of such polling agents as desire to affix their seals—

(*a*) each ballot box in use at the station, sealed so as to prevent the introduction of additional ballot papers and unopened, but with the key attached;

(*b*) the unused and spoilt ballot papers placed together;

(*c*) the tendered ballot papers;

(*d*) the marked copies of the register of electors and of the list of proxies;

(*e*) the counterfoils of the used ballot papers and the certificates as to employment on duty on the day of the poll;

(*f*) the tendered votes list, the list of blind voters assisted by companions, the list of votes marked by the presiding officer, a statement of the number of voters whose votes are so marked by the presiding officer under the heads "physical incapacity", "Jews", and "unable to read", and the declarations made by the companions of blind voters;

and shall deliver the packets or cause them to be delivered to the returning officer to be taken charge of by him:

Provided that if the packets are not delivered by the presiding officer personally to the returning officer, the arrangements for their delivery shall require the approval of the returning officer.

(2) The marked copies of the register of electors and of the list of proxies shall be in one packet but shall not be in the same packet as the counterfoils of the used ballot papers and the certificates as to employment on duty on the day of the poll.

(3) The packets shall be accompanied by a statement (in these rules referred to as "the ballot paper account") made by the presiding officer showing the number of ballot papers entrusted to him, and accounting for them under the heads of ballot papers issued and not otherwise accounted for, unused, spoilt and tendered ballot papers.

COUNTING OF VOTES

Attendance at counting of votes

39.—(1) The returning officer shall make arrangements for counting the votes in the presence of the counting agents as soon as practicable after the close of the poll, and shall give to the counting agents notice in writing of the time and place at which he will begin to count the votes.

(2) No person other than—

(*a*) the returning officer and his clerks;

(*b*) the candidates and their wives or husbands;

(*c*) the election agents;

(*d*) the counting agents;

may be present at the counting of the votes, unless permitted by the returning officer to attend.

(3) A person not entitled to attend at the counting of the votes shall not be permitted to do so by the returning officer unless the returning officer is satisfied that the efficient counting of the votes will not be impeded, and the returning officer has either consulted the election agents or thought it impracticable to consult them.

(4) The returning officer shall give the counting agents all such reasonable facilities for overseeing the proceedings, and all such information with respect thereto, as he can give them consistently with the orderly conduct of the proceedings and the discharge of his duties in connection therewith.

(5) In particular, where the votes are counted by sorting the ballot papers according to the candidate for whom the vote is given and then counting the number of ballot papers for each candidate, the counting agents shall be entitled to satisfy themselves that the ballot papers are correctly sorted.

The count

40.—(1) Before the returning officer proceeds to count the votes, he shall—

(a) in the presence of the counting agents open each ballot box and, taking out the ballot papers therein, count and record the number thereof and in the presence of the election agents who are present verify each ballot paper account;

(b) count such of the postal ballot papers as have been duly returned and record the number counted; and

(c) then mix together the whole of the ballot papers mentioned in the foregoing sub-paragraphs.

(2) A postal ballot paper shall not be deemed to be duly returned, unless it is returned in the proper envelope so as to reach the returning officer before the close of the poll and is accompanied by the declaration of identity duly signed and authenticated.

(3) The returning officer shall not count any tendered ballot paper.

(4) The returning officer, while counting and recording the number of ballot papers and counting the votes, shall keep the ballot papers with their faces upwards and take all proper precautions for preventing any person from seeing the numbers printed on the back of the papers.

(5) The returning officer shall verify each ballot paper account by comparing it with the number of ballot papers recorded by him, and the unused and spoilt ballot papers in his possession and the tendered votes list (opening and resealing the packets containing the unused and spoilt ballot papers and the tendered votes list) and shall draw up a statement as to the result of the verification, which any election agent may copy.

(6) The returning officer shall, so far as practicable, proceed continuously with counting the votes, allowing only time for refreshment:

Provided that he may, in so far as he and the agents agree, exclude the hours between nine o'clock in the evening and nine o'clock on the following morning.

For the purposes of this proviso the agreement of a candidate or his election agent shall be as effective as the agreement of his counting agents.

(7) During the excluded time the returning officer shall place the ballot papers and other documents relating to the election under his own seal and the seals of such of the counting agents as desire to affix their seals and shall otherwise take proper precautions for the security of the papers and documents.

Re-count

41.—(1) A candidate or his election agent may, if present when the counting or any re-count of the votes is completed, require the returning officer to have the votes re-counted or again re-counted but the returning officer may refuse to do so if in his opinion the request is unreasonable.

(2) No step shall be taken on the completion of the counting or any re-count of votes until the candidates and election agents present at the completion thereof have been given a reasonable opportunity to exercise the right conferred by this rule.

Rejected ballot papers

42.—(1) Any ballot paper—

(a) which does not bear the official mark; or

(b) on which votes are given for more candidates than the voter is entitled to vote for; or

(c) on which anything is written or marked by which the voter can be identified except the printed number on the back; or

(d) which is unmarked or void for uncertainty;

shall, subject to the provisions of this rule, be void and not counted.

(2) Where the voter is entitled to vote for more than one candidate, a ballot paper shall not be deemed to be void for uncertainty as respects any vote as to which no uncertainty arises and that vote shall be counted.

(3) A ballot paper on which a vote is marked—

(a) elsewhere than in the proper place; or

(b) otherwise than by means of a cross; or

(c) by more than one mark;

shall not by reason thereof be deemed to be void (either wholly or as respects that vote), if an intention that the vote shall be for one or other of the candidates clearly appears, and the way the paper is marked does not of itself identify the voter and it is not shown that he can be identified thereby.

(4) The returning officer shall endorse—

(a) the word "rejected" on any ballot paper which under this rule is not to be counted; and

(b) in the case of a ballot paper on which any vote is counted under paragraph (2) of this rule, the words "rejected in part" and a memorandum specifying the votes counted;

and shall add to the endorsement the words "rejection objected to" if an objection is made by a counting agent to his decision.

(5) The returning officer shall draw up a statement showing the number of ballot papers rejected, including those rejected in part, under the several heads of—

(a) want of official mark;

(b) voting for more candidates than voter is entitled to;

(c) writing or mark by which voter could be identified;

(d) unmarked or wholly void for uncertainty;

(e) rejected in part.

Decisions on ballot papers

43. The decision of the returning officer on any question arising in respect of a ballot paper shall be final, but shall be subject to review on an election petition.

Equality of votes

44. Where, after the counting of the votes (including any re-count) is completed, an equality of votes is found to exist between any candidates and the addition of a vote would entitle any of those candidates to be declared elected, the returning officer shall forthwith decide between those candidates by lot, and proceed as if the candidate on whom the lot falls had received an additional vote.

PART IV

FINAL PROCEEDINGS IN CONTESTED AND UNCONTESTED ELECTIONS

Declaration of result

45.—(1) In a contested election, when the result of the poll has been ascertained the returning officer shall forthwith declare to be elected the candidate or candidates to whom the majority of votes have been given, and shall as soon as possible publish the name or names of the candidate or candidates elected and the total number of votes given for each candidate, whether elected or not, together with the number of rejected ballot papers under each head shown in the statement of rejected ballot papers.

(2) In an uncontested election, the returning officer shall, not later than eleven o'clock in the morning on the day of election, publish the name or names of the person or persons elected.

PART V

DISPOSAL OF DOCUMENTS

Sealing of ballot papers

46.—(1) On the completion of the counting at a contested election the returning officer shall seal up in separate packets the counted and rejected ballot papers, including ballot papers rejected in part.

(2) The returning officer shall not open the sealed packets of tendered ballot papers or of counterfoils and certificates as to employment on duty on the day of the poll, or of marked copies of the register of electors and lists of proxies.

Marking of packets

47. The returning officer shall endorse on each of the following packets, that is to say—

(a) the packets of ballot papers in his possession;

(b) the ballot paper accounts and the statements of rejected ballot papers and of the result of the verification of the ballot paper accounts;

(c) the tendered votes lists, the lists of blind voters assisted by companions, the lists of votes marked by the presiding officer and the statements relating thereto, and the declarations made by the companions of blind voters;

(d) the packets of counterfoils and certificates as to employment on duty on the day of the poll;

(e) the packets containing marked copies of registers and of lists of proxies, a description of its contents, the date of the election to which they relate and the name of the ward for which the election was held.

Orders for production of documents

48.—(1) An order—

(a) for the inspection or production of any rejected ballot papers, including ballot papers rejected in part; or

(b) for the opening of a sealed packet of counterfoils and certificates as to employment on duty on the day of the poll or for the inspection of counted ballot papers,

may be made by either a county court having jurisdiction in the London borough or any part thereof or an election court, if the court is satisfied by evidence on oath that the order is required for the purpose of instituting or maintaining a prosecution for an offence in relation to ballot papers, or for the purpose of an election petition.

(2) The order may be made subject to such conditions as to persons, time, place and mode of inspection, production or opening as the court making the order may think expedient and may direct the town clerk having custody of the ballot papers and the sealed packets of counterfoils and certificates to retain them intact for such period as may be specified in the order:

Provided that in making and carrying into effect the order, care shall be taken that the way in which the vote of any particular elector has been given shall not be disclosed until it has been proved that his vote was given and the vote has been declared by a competent court to be invalid.

(3) An appeal shall lie to the High Court from any order of a county court made under this rule.

(4) Any power given under this rule to a county court may be exercised by any judge of the court otherwise than in open court.

(5) Where an order is made for the production by the town clerk of any document in his possession relating to any specified election, the production by him or his agent of the document ordered, in such manner as may be directed by that order shall be conclusive evidence that the document relates to the specified election; and any endorsement on any packet of ballot papers so produced shall be prima facie evidence that the ballot papers are what they are stated to be by the endorsement.

(6) The production from proper custody of a ballot paper purporting to have been used at any election, and of a counterfoil marked with the same printed number and having a number marked thereon in writing, shall be prima facie evidence that the elector whose vote was given by that ballot paper was the person who at the time of the election has affixed to his name in the register of electors the same number as the number written on the counterfoil.

(7) Save as by this rule provided, no person shall be allowed to inspect any rejected or counted ballot papers in the possession of the town clerk or to open any sealed packets of counterfoils and certificates.

Retention and public inspection of documents

49.—(1) The town clerk shall retain for six months among the records of the London borough all documents relating to an election which were held by him as returning officer and then, unless otherwise directed by an order under the last foregoing rule, shall cause them to be destroyed.

(2) The said documents, except ballot papers, counterfoils and certificates as to employment on duty on the day of the poll, shall during a period of six months from the day of election be open to public inspection at such time and in such manner as may be determined by the council of the London borough with the consent of the Secretary of State.

(3) The town clerk shall, on request, supply copies of or extracts from the documents open to public inspection on payment of such fees, and subject to such conditions, as may be determined by the council of the London borough with the consent of the Secretary of State.

Supplemental provisions as to documents

50. Subject to the provisions of these rules, the town clerk shall, in respect of the custody and destruction of ballot papers and other documents coming into his possession in pursuance of these rules, be subject to the directions of the council of the London borough.

PART VI

SUPPLEMENTAL

Countermand or abandonment of poll on death of candidate

51.—(1) If at a contested election proof is given to the satisfaction of the returning officer before the result of the election is declared that one of the persons named or to be named as candidate in the ballot papers has died, then the returning officer shall countermand the poll or, if polling has begun, direct that the poll be abandoned, and the provisions of section 36(2) of the Representation of the People Act 1949 shall apply to any further election ordered under the Local Government Act 1933.

(2) Where the poll is abandoned by reason of the death of a candidate, the proceedings at or consequent on that poll shall be interrupted, and the presiding officer at any polling station shall take the like steps (so far as not already taken) for the delivery to the returning officer of ballot boxes and of ballot papers and other documents as he is required to take on the close of the poll in due course, and the returning

officer shall dispose of ballot papers and other documents in his possession as he is required to do on the completion in due course of the counting of the votes; but—

> (a) it shall not be necessary for any ballot paper account to be prepared or verified; and

> (b) the returning officer, without taking any step or further step for the counting of the ballot papers or of the votes, shall seal up all the ballot papers, whether the votes on them have been counted or not, and it shall not be necessary to seal up counted and rejected ballot papers in separate packets.

(3) The foregoing provisions of these rules as to the inspection, production, retention and destruction of ballot papers and other documents relating to a poll at an election shall apply to any such documents relating to a poll abandoned by reason of the death of a candidate, with the following modifications:—

> (a) ballot papers on which the votes were neither counted nor rejected shall be treated as counted ballot papers; and

> (b) no order shall be made for the production or inspection of any ballot papers or for the opening of a sealed packet of counterfoils or certificates as to employment on duty on the day of the poll unless the order is made by a court with reference to a prosecution.

General duty of returning officer

52. It shall be the general duty of the returning officer to do any act or thing that may be necessary for effectually conducting the election under these rules.

Interpretation

53.—(1) A reference in this Schedule to a rule shall be construed as a reference to a rule contained in this Schedule.

(2) Any reference in this Schedule to any enactment shall be taken as a reference to that enactment as amended or replaced by any other enactment.

APPENDIX

Note:—The forms contained in this Appendix may be adapted so far as circumstances require.

NOTICE OF ELECTION   Rule 4.

LONDON BOROUGH OF

ELECTION OF COUNCILLORS for the [Ward of the]
[Wards of the] London Borough.

1. An election is to be held of   councillors for If the notice
the said [ward] [wards] [London borough].   relates to two
                                                                             or more
2. Nomination papers must be delivered at   on any day after the wards, in-
date of this notice, but not later than noon on the   day of   dicate the
                                                                             number of
                                                                          · councillors
3. Forms of nomination paper may be obtained from the returning officer at for each
                    . The returning officer will at the request of any local ward.
government elector for the electoral area prepare for signature a nomination paper.

4. If the election is contested, the poll will take place on the
day of

                                        (Signed)..............................
                                        Returning Officer.

          day of   , 19 .

NOTE 1.—The attention of candidates and electors is drawn to the rules for filling up nomination papers and other provisions relating to nomination contained in the election rules in Schedule 1 to the London Borough Council Election Rules 1970.

NOTE 2.—Every person guilty of a corrupt or illegal practice will, on conviction, be liable to the penalties imposed by the Representation of the People Act 1949.

NOTE 3.—Electors and their proxies should take note that applications to be treated as an absent voter and other applications and notices about postal or proxy voting must reach the electoral registration officer at (*insert address*) by the day of   next if they are to be effective for this election.

Rule 5.

NOMINATION PAPER

ELECTION OF COUNCILLORS for the [Ward of the] London Borough of   .

Date of publication of notice of election...

We, the undersigned, being local government electors for the said [ward] [London borough], do hereby nominate the undermentioned person as a candidate at the said election.

Candidate's surname	Other names in full	Description (if any)	Home address in full

Signatures	Electoral Number (*see* note 3)	
	Distinctive Letter(s)	Number
Proposer...	....	....
Seconder...	....	....
We, the undersigned, being local government electors for the said [ward] [London borough], do hereby assent to the foregoing nomination.		
1.	....	....
2.	....	....
3.	....	....
4.	....	....
5.	....	....
6.	....	....
7.	....	....
8.	....	....

NOTE 1.—The attention of candidates and local government electors is drawn to the rules for filling up nomination papers and other provisions relating to nomination contained in the election rules in Schedule 1 to the London Borough Council Election Rules 1970.

Note 2.—Where a candidate is commonly known by some title he may be described by his title as if it were his surname.

NOTE 3.—A person's electoral number consists of the distinctive letter or letters of the parliamentary polling district in which he is registered together with his number in the register to be used at the election except that before publication of the register the distinctive letter or letters of the parliamentary polling district in which he is entitled to be registered together with his number (if any) in the electors lists for that register shall be used instead.

NOTE 4.—An elector may not—

(a) subscribe more nomination papers than there are vacancies to be filled in the electoral area; or

(b) subscribe a nomination paper for more than one ward of a London borough divided into wards; or

(c) subscribe more than one nomination paper in respect of the same candidate.

NOTE 5.—A person whose name is entered in the register or electors lists may not subscribe a nomination paper if the entry gives as the date on which he will become of voting age a date later than the day fixed for the poll.

STATEMENT AS TO PERSONS NOMINATED

Rule 10.

LONDON BOROUGH OF

The following is a statement as to the persons nominated for election as Councillors for the [Ward of the] [Wards of the] London Borough.

[Ward] [Wards] [London Borough]	Persons nominated				Proposer's name	Decision of returning officer that nomination paper is invalid, or other reason why a person nominated no longer stands nominated
	Surname	Other names in full	Home address in full	Description (if any)		
1.	2.	3.	4.	5.	6.	7.

The persons opposite whose names no entry is made in column 7 have been and stand validly nominated.

Dated this   day of   , 19 .

....
Returning Officer.

Rule 15.

BALLOT PAPER

Form of Front of Ballot Paper

Counterfoil
No.

The counterfoil is to have a number to correspond with that on the back of the Ballot Paper.

1	**BROWN** (JOHN EDWARD Brown, of 2 The Cottages, Barlington, Labour.)
2	**BROWN** (THOMAS WILLIAM Brown, of 15 Barchester Road, Barlington, Liberal.)
3	**JONES** (William David Jones, of The Grange, Barlington, Conservative.)
4	**MERTON** (Hon. George Travis, commonly called Viscount Merton, of Barlington.)
5	**SMITH** (Mary Smith, of School House, Barlington, schoolteacher, Progressive.)
6	**WILLIAMS** (Elizabeth Williams, of 3 Ivy Lane, Barlington, housewife.)

Form of Back of Ballot Paper

No.

Election for the .... ward of the London borough of ....

.... day of .... , 19 .

Note.—*The number on the ballot paper is to correspond with that on the counterfoil.*

Directions as to printing the ballot paper

1. Nothing is to be printed on the ballot paper except in accordance with these directions.

2. So far as practicable, the following arrangements shall be observed in the printing of the ballot paper:—

(*a*) no word shall be printed on the face except the particulars of the candidates;

(*b*) no rule shall be printed on the face except the horizontal rules separating the particulars of the candidates from one another and the vertical rules separating those particulars from the numbers on the left-hand side and the spaces on the right where the vote is to be marked;

(*c*) the whole space between the top and bottom of the paper shall be equally divided between the candidates by the rules separating their particulars.

3. The surname of each candidate shall in all cases be printed by itself in large capitals, and his full particulars shall be set out below it and shall be printed in ordinary type except that small capitals shall be used—

(*a*) if his surname is the same as another candidate's, for his other names; and

(*b*) if his other names are also the same as the other candidate's, either for his residence or for his description unless each of them is the same as that of another candidate with the same surname and other names.

4. The number on the back of the ballot paper shall be printed in small characters.

DIRECTIONS FOR THE GUIDANCE OF THE VOTERS IN VOTING

Rule 24.

1. The voter should see that the ballot paper, before it is handed to him, is stamped with the official mark.

2. The voter will go into one of the compartments and, with the pencil provided in the compartment, place a cross on the right-hand side of the ballot paper, opposite the name of each candidate for whom he votes, thus X.

3. The voter will then fold up the ballot paper so as to show the official mark on the back, and leaving the compartment will, without showing the front of the paper to any person, show the official mark on the back to the presiding officer, and then, in the presence of the presiding officer, put the paper into the ballot box, and forthwith leave the polling station.

4. If the voter inadvertently spoils a ballot paper he can return it to the officer, who will, if satisfied of such inadvertence, give him another paper.

5. If the voter votes for more than   candidate(s) or places any mark on the paper by which he may afterwards be identified, his ballot paper will be void, and will not be counted.

6. If the voter fraudulently takes a ballot paper out of a polling station or fraudulently puts into the ballot box any paper other than the one given to him by the officer, he will be liable on conviction to imprisonment for a term not exceeding six months, or to a fine not exceeding twenty pounds or to both such imprisonment and such fine.

Rule 27.

CERTIFICATE OF EMPLOYMENT

Election in the [Ward of the] London Borough of   .

I certify that (name)...................... who is numbered..............
in the register of electors for the electoral area named above, is likely to be unable
to go in person to the polling station allotted to him at the election on (date of
poll).........................by reason of the particular circumstances of his
employment on that date—

*(a) as a constable,

*(b) by me for a purpose connected with the election.

Signature ....

*Police rank ....
(Inspector or above)

*Returning Officer

Date......................

*Delete whichever is inapplicable.

NOTE.—The person named above is entitled to vote at any polling station of the
above electoral area on production and surrender of this certificate to the presiding
officer.

Rule 34.

DECLARATION TO BE MADE BY THE COMPANION OF A BLIND VOTER

I, A.B., of   , having been requested to assist C.D. [*in the case of a
blind person voting as proxy add* voting as proxy for G.H.], who is numbered
on the register of local government electors for the
ward of the London borough of   , to record his
vote at the election now being held for the said ward, do hereby declare that [I am
*State the
relationship
of the
companion
to the voter.* entitled to vote as an elector at the said election] [I am the*   of
the said voter and have attained the age of eighteen years] and that I have not previously
assisted any blind person [except E.F., of   ] to vote at the said election.

(Signed) A.B.

day of   , 19 .

I, the undersigned, being the presiding officer for the polling station for the
ward of the London borough of   do hereby
certify that the above declaration, having been first read to the above-named declarant
was signed by the declarant in my presence.

(Signed) X. Y.

day of   , 19 , at   minutes past   o'clock
[a.m.] [p.m.]

Note.—if the person making the above declaration knowingly and wilfully makes
therein a statement false in a material particular, he will be guilty of an offence.

SCHEDULE 2

*Insert
description
of office.

DECLARATION OF ACCEPTANCE OF OFFICE BY THE MAYOR OF A LONDON BOROUGH OR BY AN ALDERMAN OR A COUNCILLOR OF A LONDON BOROUGH

I, A.B., having been elected to the office of*   , hereby declare
†If the
declaration
is made and
subscribed
before the
town clerk,
or a justice of
the peace or
magistrate,
or a com-
missioner
for oaths, or
a British
consul, adapt
form
accordingly. that I take the said office upon myself, and will duly and faithfully fulfil the duties
thereof according to the best of my judgment and ability.

Dated this   day of   , 19 .

Signature.........................

This declaration was made and subscribed before us

Members of the London Borough
Council.†   { ....

....

EXPLANATORY NOTE

(This Note is not part of the Rules.)

These Rules and Regulations revoke and replace the London Borough Council and Greater London Council Election Forms Regulations 1964, so far as they relate to elections to the council of a London borough, and the London Borough Council Elections Rules 1968 with amendments consequential on the provisions of the Representation of the People Act 1969 (c.15). They also prescribe the form of declaration of acceptance of office by the mayor, an alderman or a councillor of a London borough.

STATUTORY INSTRUMENTS

1970 No. 134 (S.6)

COURT OF SESSION, SCOTLAND

Act of Sederunt (Rules of Court Amendment No. 2) 1970

Made - - -	*30th January* 1970
Coming into Operation	*31st January* 1970

The Lords of Council and Session, under and by virtue of the powers conferred upon them by section 16 of the Administration of Justice (Scotland) Act 1933(a) and of all other powers competent to them in that behalf, do hereby enact and declare as follows :—

1. The Rules of Court (b) shall be amended as follows :—

(1) In Rule 189(*a*) the words "Save as hereinafter provided, all petitions initiated in the Court of Session and not invoking the *nobile officium*" shall be deleted, and there shall be substituted the words "All petitions initiated in the Court of Session and not falling within any of the classes mentioned in Rule 190".

(2) In Rule 189(*a*) (xx) there shall be added after the words "any Act of Parliament", the words "or at common law".

(3) In Rule 190 the words "Save as provided in the immediately foregoing rule, all" shall be deleted, and there shall be substituted the word "All".

(4) In Rule 190 (vii) the words "falling under Rule 189(*a*) (iii)" shall be deleted, and there shall be substituted the words "mentioned in the examples contained in Rule 189(*a*)".

2. This Act of Sederunt may be cited as the Act of Sederunt (Rules of Court Amendment No. 2) 1970, and shall come into operation on 31st January 1970.

And the Lords appoint this Act of Sederunt to be inserted in the Books of Sederunt.

J. L. Clyde,
I.P.D.

Edinburgh,
30th January 1970.

EXPLANATORY NOTE

(This Note is not part of the Act of Sederunt.)

This Act of Sederunt amends the Rules of Court by providing that petitions for the custody of children at common law shall be presented to the Outer House.

(a) 1933 c. 41.   (b) S.I. 1965/321 (1965 I, p. 803).

STATUTORY INSTRUMENTS

1970 No. 136 (L.5.)

LAND CHARGES
The Land Charges Rules 1970

Made - - -	*2nd February* 1970	
Coming into Operation	*1st March* 1970	

The Lord Chancellor, in exercise of the powers conferred on him by section 19 of the Land Charges Act 1925**(a)** and section 25(7) of the Law of Property Act 1969**(b)**, hereby makes the following Rules:—

1. These Rules may be cited as the Land Charges Rules 1970 and shall come into operation on 1st March 1970.

2. The Interpretation Act 1889**(c)** shall apply to the interpretation of these Rules as it applies to the interpretation of an Act of Parliament.

3. Where compensation has been claimed under section 25 of the Law of Property Act 1969 in respect of a registered land charge, the Chief Land Registrar shall make such entries in or amendments and additions to the relevant registers and the alphabetical index kept under the Land Charges Act 1925 as he deems necessary in order to bring the charge to the notice of any person who makes, or requires to be made, a search of the said registers or index relating to the estate or interest affected by the charge.

Dated 2nd February 1970.

Gardiner, C.

EXPLANATORY NOTE
(*This Note is not part of the Rules.*)

These Rules empower the Chief Land Registrar to amend the register of land charges and its alphabetical index so as to facilitate the disclosure of land charges which, because they are not readily discoverable by purchasers of the land, have given rise to a claim for compensation under section 25 of the Law of Property Act 1969.

(a) 1925 c. 22.   **(b)** 1969 c. 59.   **(c)** 1889 c. 63.

STATUTORY INSTRUMENTS

1970 No. 138

PENSIONS

The Superannuation (Teaching and Public Boards) Interchange (Amendment) Rules 1970

Made - - - -	*3rd February* 1970
Laid before Parliament	*12th February* 1970
Coming into Operation	*13th February* 1970

The Secretary of State for Education and Science, with the consent of the Minister for the Civil Service, in exercise of the powers conferred on him by sections 2 and 15 of the Superannuation (Miscellaneous Provisions) Act 1948(a), as amended by section 11 of the Superannuation (Miscellaneous Provisions) Act 1967(b) and the Minister for the Civil Service Order 1968(c), hereby makes the following Rules :—

1. These Rules may be cited as the Superannuation (Teaching and Public Boards) Interchange (Amendment) Rules 1970 and shall come into operation on 13th February 1970.

2. The Interpretation Act 1889(d) shall apply for the interpretation of these Rules as it applies for the interpretation of an Act of Parliament.

3. Schedule 3 to the Superannuation (Teaching and Public Boards) Interchange Rules 1968(e) is hereby amended by the addition thereto of the following bodies and dates:—

The Consumer Council	...	...	...	15th March 1965.
The Post Office	...	...	...	1st October 1969.

4. In relation to a person becoming, or ceasing to be, employed by a body added to Schedule 3 to the Superannuation (Teaching and Public Boards) Interchange Rules 1968 by rule 2 the operative date for the purposes of those Rules shall be the date of the coming into operation of these Rules.

Given under the Official Seal of the Secretary of State for Education and Science on 29th January 1970.

(L.S.)   *Edward Short,*

Secretary of State for Education and Science.

Consent of the Minister for the Civil Service given under his Official Seal on 3rd February 1970.

(L.S.)   *K. H. McNeill,*

Authorised by the Minister for the Civil Service.

(a) 1948 c. 33. (b) 1967 c. 28. (c) S.I. 1968/1656 (1968 III, p. 4485).
(d) 1889 c. 63.   (e) S.I. 1968/1120 (1968 II, p. 3078).

EXPLANATORY NOTE

(This Note is not part of the Rules.)

These Rules extend to the Consumer Council and the Post Office the existing arrangements for the preservation of superannuation rights upon changes of employment between teaching and other public boards.

In accordance with section 2(5) of the Superannuation (Miscellaneous Provisions) Act 1948 the Rules may have retrospective effect in some instances.

STATUTORY INSTRUMENTS

1970 No. 139

WAGES COUNCILS

The Wages Regulation (Rubber Proofed Garment) Order 1970

Made - - -	*3rd February* 1970
Coming into Operation	*5th March* 1970

Whereas the Secretary of State has received from the Rubber Proofed Garment Making Industry Wages Council the wages regulation proposals set out in Schedules 1 and 2 hereof ;

Now, therefore, the Secretary of State in exercise of her powers under section 11 of the Wages Councils Act 1959(a), and of all other powers enabling her in that behalf, hereby makes the following Order :—

1. This Order may be cited as the Wages Regulation (Rubber Proofed Garment) Order 1970.

2.—(1) In this Order the expression "the specified date" means the 5th March 1970, provided that where, as respects any worker who is paid wages at intervals not exceeding seven days, that date does not correspond with the beginning of the period for which the wages are paid, the expression "the specified date" means, as respects that worker, the beginning of the next such period following that date.

(2) The Interpretation Act 1889(b) shall apply to the interpretation of this Order as it applies to the interpretation of an Act of Parliament and as if this Order and the Order hereby revoked were Acts of Parliament.

3. The wages regulation proposals set out in Schedules 1 and 2 hereof shall have effect as from the specified date and as from that date the Wages Regulation (Rubber Proofed Garment) Order 1969(c) shall cease to have effect.

Signed by order of the Secretary of State.
3rd February 1970.

A. A. Jarratt,
Deputy Under Secretary of State,
Department of Employment and Productivity.

(a) 1959 c. 69.   (b) 1889 c. 63.
(c) S.I. 1969/131 (1969 I, p. 357).

SCHEDULE 1

The following minimum remuneration shall be substituted for the statutory minimum remuneration fixed by the Wages Regulation (Rubber Proofed Garment) Order 1969 (Order R.P.G. (27)).

STATUTORY MINIMUM REMUNERATION

PART I

APPLICATION

1. Subject to the provisions of Part VI of this Schedule relating to guaranteed weekly remuneration, the minimum remuneration payable to all workers (including homeworkers) to whom this Schedule applies for all work except work to which a minimum overtime rate applies under Part V is:—

(1) in the case of a time worker, the hourly general minimum time rate payable to the worker under Part II, III or IV of this Schedule;

(2) in the case of a worker employed on piece work, piece rates each of which would yield, in the circumstances of the case, to an ordinary worker (that is to say, a worker of ordinary skill and experience in the class of work in question) at least the same amount of money as the hourly piece work basis time rate applicable to the worker under Part II or III of this Schedule or, where no piece work basis time rate applies, at least the same amount of money as the hourly general minimum time rate which would be payable to the worker if the worker were a time worker.

2.—(1) Subject to the provisions of sub-paragraph (2) of this paragraph, this Schedule applies to workers in relation to whom the Rubber Proofed Garment Making Industry Wages Council operates, being workers employed in Great Britain in the rubber proofed garment making industry, that is to say—

(a) in manufacturing, altering, repairing, renovating or re-making rubber proofed garments; or

(b) in warehousing or packing rubber proofed garments or in any other operation incidental to any of the activities included in (a) of this sub-paragraph, where the warehousing, packing or other operation is carried on in conjunction with any of the activities included as aforesaid.

(2) This Schedule does not apply to workers—

(a) in respect of employment in connection with headgear, unless the employment is in conjunction or association with manufacture, alteration, repair, renovation, or re-making of rubber proofed garments other than headgear; or

(b) in relation to whom any Wages Council (other than the Rubber Proofed Garment Making Industry Wages Council) operates in respect of any employment which is for the time being within the field of the operation of that Wages Council;

(c) employed as foremen or forewomen.

(3) In this Schedule the expression "rubber proofed garments" does not include any garment or headgear made from oil or chemically proofed fabrics or from plastic film or textiles processed with plastic, but, save as aforesaid, means all garments (including headgear) made from textiles processed with rubber or rubber substitute, or from any material if in the manufacture of the garment any of the processes of smearing, sticking, or cementing with a solution of rubber or rubber substitute either by hand or machine, is involved.

PART II

MALE WORKERS
GENERAL MINIMUM TIME RATES AND PIECE WORK BASIS
TIME RATES

3.—(1) Subject to the provisions of this Schedule, the general minimum time rates payable to male workers with the qualifications specified in Column 2 of the next following Table when employed on time work and the piece work basis time rates applicable to such workers when employed on piece work are those set out in Columns 3 and 4 respectively of the said Table:—

Column 1	Column 2	Column 3	Column 4
Class of worker	Qualifying period of employment or age of worker	General minimum time rates	Piece work basis time rates
		Per week s. d.	Per week s. d.
(a) MEASURE CUTTER, that is to say, a worker employed in any process of measure cutting who is capable of taking a complete set of measures and of cutting all garments from patterns, and with sufficient technical knowledge to draft and alter the balance and distribution of widths, lengths, etc., for any garment: Provided that where the worker is employed in the London District the said rate shall be	Not less than three years' employment after the age of 18 years as a measure cutter	258 0 267 0	284 0 293 7
(b) CUTTER OR TRIMMER, that is to say, a worker substantially employed in one or more of the following processes:— (i) marking-in, or marking-up cloth or linings or other materials; (ii) laying-up, hooking-up or folding cloth or linings or other materials; (iii) cutting cloth or linings or other materials or cutting out patterns of any description to be used afterwards for the cutting out of garments; and (iv) dividing (that is to say, the process ordinarily carried on by cutters or their assistants of dividing, parting or separating the parts of garments after being cut and of assembling them into suitable bundles for making up), other than a measure cutter to whom the minimum rates	Not less than three years' employment after the age of 18 years as a cutter of any of the classes specified in Column 1 or as a knifeman	248 2	272 10

Column 1	Column 2	Column 3	Column 4
Class of worker	Qualifying period of employment or age of worker	General minimum time rates	Piece work basis time rates
		Per week s. d.	Per week s. d.
specified in (a) of this Table apply or a knife cutter or knifeman: Provided that where the worker is employed in the London District the said rates shall be	... ...	257 0	282 8
(c) KNIFE CUTTER or KNIFE-MAN, that is to say, a worker wholly or mainly employed on band, electric or handknife processes:	Not less than three years' employment after the age of 18 years as a cutter of any of the classes specified in Column 1 or as a knifeman	248 2	272 10
Provided that where the worker is employed in the London District the said rates shall be	... ...	257 0	282 8
(d) MAKER, that is to say, a worker employed in assembling a garment, or part thereof, by any process other than stitching.	Not less than three years' employment as a maker, machinist or passer, or		
(e) MACHINIST, that is to say, a worker employed in machining and capable of machining any one garment or part thereof.	(i) having been a learner to whom paragraph 5 applied has completed 3 years as such or attained 21 years or		
(f) PASSER, that is to say, a worker employed in examining garments, either in the course of being made up or upon completion.	(ii) having been a learner to whom (j) of this paragraph applied has completed one year as such	263 6	289 10
(g) WAREHOUSEMAN, that is to say, a worker employed, wholly or mainly, upon one or more of the following operations:— assembling, keeping, storing and distributing stock, and cutting off lengths of cloth, linings or other materials, except where such operations are mainly connected with the sale of finished garments.	Not less than three years' employment as a warehouseman after the age of 18 years ...	239 3	263 2
(h) PACKER, that is to say, a worker employed, wholly or mainly, in packing goods and materials.	Not less than three years' employment as a packer after the age of 18 years	235 6	259 2
(i) PORTER, that is to say, a worker employed, wholly or mainly, upon one or more of the operations of unpacking, moving, loading or unloading goods or materials.	Aged 21 years or over	225 5	248 1

Column 1	Column 2	Column 3	Column 4
Class of worker	Qualifying period of employ-ment or age of worker	General minimum time rates	Piece work · basis time rates
		Per week s. d.	Per week s. d.
(j) LEARNER, as defined in paragraph 11.	Aged 21 years or over who was not employed in the industry before attaining the age of 21 years:—		
	During the first month of his employment in the industry	150 3	
	During the second and third months of such employment	166 0	
	During the next following nine months of such employment	198 0	
	Thereafter	263 6	
(k) ALL OTHER WORKERS (not being workers to whom paragraph 5 applies).	Aged 21 years or over	219 7	
	„ 20 and under 21 years ...	216 3	
	„ 19 „ „ 20 „ ...	197 5	
	„ 18 „ „ 19 „ ...	178 8	252 10
	„ 17 „ „ 18 „ ...	161 4	
	„ 16 „ „ 17 „ ...	139 9	
	„ 15 „ „ 16 „ ...	118 0	

(2) In this paragraph, "The London District" means the Metropolitan Police District, as defined in the London Government Act 1963(a), the City of London, the Inner Temple and the Middle Temple.

Part III

FEMALE WORKERS
GENERAL MINIMUM TIME RATES AND PIECE WORK BASIS TIME RATES

4. Subject to the provisions of this Schedule, the general minimum time rates payable to female workers with the qualifications specified in Column 2 of the next following Table when employed on time work and the piece work basis time rates applicable to such workers when employed on piece work are those set out in Columns 3 and 4 respectively of the said Table:—

Column 1	Column 2	Column 3	Column 4
Class of worker	Qualifying period of employment or age of worker	General minimum time rates	Piece work basis time rates
		Per week s. d.	Per week s. d.
(a) MAKER, that is to say, a worker employed in assembling a garment, or part thereof, by any process other than stitching. (b) MACHINIST, other than a machinist referred to in (e). (c) PASSER, that is to say, a worker employed in examining garments, either in the course of being made up or upon completion. (d) FINISHER, that is to say, a worker employed in sewing by hand a part or parts of a garment.	Not less than three years' employment as a maker, machinist, passer or finisher, or (i) having been a learner to whom paragraph 5 applied has completed 3 years as such or attained 21 years, or (ii) having been a learner to whom (f) of this paragraph applied has completed one year as such	192 10	221 9
(e) BUTTONHOLE MACHINIST, BUTTON MACHINIST, BAR TACKER, MARKER, FOLDER, EYELETTER AND STUDDER.	(i) Workers aged 21 years or over (or on the completion of three years' experience in the industry, whichever is the earlier)	192 10	221 9
	(ii) Workers (other than those mentioned in (i) above) aged:—		
	20 and under 21 years ...	168 11	
	19 „ „ 20 „ ...	161 4	
	18 „ „ 19 „ ...	154 1	
	17 „ „ 18 „ ...	130 5	
	16 „ „ 17 „ ...	106 6	
	15 „ „ 16 „ ...	91 9	

Column 1	Column 2	Column 3	Column 4
Class of worker	Qualifying period of employ-ment or age of worker	General minimum time rates	Piece work basis time rates
		Per week s. d.	Per week s. d.
(f) LEARNER, as defined in paragraph 11.	Aged 21 years or over:— (i) who was not employed in the industry before attain-ing the age of 21 years:— During the first month of her employment in the industry	143 3	
	During the second and third months of such em-ployment	154 1	
	During the next follow-ing nine months of such employment	176 1	
	Thereafter	192 10	
	(ii) with six months' experience on power-operated mac-hinery, other than in the industry:— During the first two months of her employ-ment in the industry ...	154 1	
	During the next follow-ing ten months of such employment	176 1	
	Thereafter	192 10	
(g) ALL OTHER WORKERS (not being workers to whom paragraph 5 applies).	Aged 21 years or over	188 2	⎫
	„ 20 and under 21 years ...	164 2	⎪
	„ 19 „ „ 20 „ ...	156 8	⎪
	„ 18 „ „ 19 „ ...	149 3	⎬ 216 1
	„ 17 „ „ 18 „ ...	125 5	⎪
	„ 16 „ „ 17 „ ...	101 10	⎪
	„ 15 „ „ 16 „ ...	87 0	⎭

PART IV

MALE OR FEMALE WORKERS AGED UNDER 21 EMPLOYED AS LEARNERS
GENERAL MINIMUM TIME RATES

5. The following general minimum time rates are payable to male or female workers aged under 21 years who are employed as learners:—

Period of service with employer	Age of worker on first entering the trade		
	Under 17 years	17 and under 18 years	18 years or over
	Per week s. d.	Per week s. d.	Per week s. d.
First six months	91 9	110 3	128 6
Second „ „	110 3	128 6	147 0
Third „ „	128 6	147 0	165 2
Fourth „ „	147 0	165 2	183 7
Fifth „ „	165 2	183 7	183 7
Sixth „ „	183 7	183 7	183 7

Provided that, where such a worker completes three years' service or attains the age of 21 years, whichever is the earlier, the worker shall be paid the appropriate adult time rate.

PART V

OVERTIME AND WAITING TIME
NORMAL NUMBER OF HOURS

6. Subject to the provisions of this Part of this Schedule, the minimum overtime rates set out in paragraph 7 are payable to a worker in respect of any time worked:—

(1) in excess of the hours following, that is to say,

    (a) in any week   ...   .   40 hours

    (b) on any day other than a Saturday, Sunday or customary holiday—

        where the normal working hours exceed 8...   ...   ... $8\frac{1}{2}$ hours

or   where the normal working hours are not more than 8   ...   8 hours

(2) on a Saturday, Sunday or customary holiday.

MINIMUM OVERTIME RATES

7.—(1) Minimum overtime rates are payable to any worker (other than a home-worker) as follows:—

    (a) on any day other than a Saturday, Sunday or customary holiday—

        (i) for the first 2 hours of overtime worked   ...   ...   time-and-a-quarter

        (ii) for the next 2 hours ...   .   time-and-a-half

        (iii) thereafter   ...   .   double time

    (b) on a Saturday, not being a customary holiday—

        (i) for the first 4 hours worked...   ...   .   time-and-a-half

        (ii) thereafter   ...   .   double time

    (c) on a Sunday or customary holiday—

        for all time worked   ...   .   double time (*d*) in any week, exclusive of any time in respect of which any minimum overtime rate is payable under the foregoing provisions of this sub-paragraph—

for all time worked in excess of 40 hours ... ... time-and-a-quarter

(2) Where the employer normally requires the worker's attendance on Sunday and not on Saturday, for the purposes of this Part of this Schedule (except where in the case of a woman or young person such attendance on Sunday is unlawful) Saturday shall be treated as a Sunday and, subject to the provisions of sub-paragraph (3) of this paragraph, Sunday shall be treated as a Saturday.

(3) Where another weekday is substituted for Saturday, or, in a case where the provisions of sub-paragraph (2) of this paragraph apply, for Sunday, as the worker's weekly short day, for the purposes of this Part of this Schedule (except where in the case of a woman or young person such substitution is unlawful) that other weekday shall be treated as a Saturday, and Saturday or Sunday, as the case may be, shall be treated as a weekday other than the worker's weekly short day.

8. In this Part of this Schedule—

(1) the expression "customary holiday" means—

    (*a*) (i) in England and Wales—

Christmas Day (or, if Christmas Day falls on a Sunday, such weekday as may be appointed by national proclamation, or, if none is so appointed, the next following Tuesday), Boxing Day, Good Friday, Easter Monday, Whit Monday (or where another day is substituted therefor by national proclamation, that day), August Bank Holiday and one other day (being a day on which the worker normally works for the employer) in the course of a calendar year, to be fixed by the employer and notified to the worker not less than three weeks before the holiday:

Provided that in the case of a worker who normally works on each weekday except Saturday—

    (*a*) if Christmas Day falls on a Saturday, the Friday immediately preceding or the next following Tuesday shall be a customary holiday;

    (*b*) if Boxing Day falls on a Saturday, the Thursday immediately preceding or the next following Monday shall be a customary holiday;

    (ii) in Scotland—

New Year's Day (or, if New Year's Day falls on a Sunday, the following Monday);
the local Spring holiday;
the local Autumn holiday; and

four other days (being days on which the worker normally works for the employer) in the course of a calendar year, to be fixed by the employer and notified to the worker not less than three weeks before the holiday;

or (*b*) in the case of each of the said days a day substituted by the employer therefor, being a day recognised by local custom as a day of holiday in substitution for the said day;

(2) the expressions "time-and-a-quarter", "time-and-a-half" and "double time" mean respectively—

    (*a*) in the case of a time worker, one and a quarter times, one and a half times and twice the hourly general minimum time rate otherwise payable to the worker;

    (*b*) in the case of a worker who is employed on piece work,

        (i) a time rate equal respectively to one quarter, one half and the whole of the hourly piece work basis time rate applicable to the worker or, where no hourly piece work basis time rate applies, the hourly general minimum time rate which would be payable to the worker if he were a time worker and a minimum overtime rate did not apply and, in addition thereto,

        (ii) the piece rates otherwise payable to the worker under paragraph 1(2).

WAITING TIME

9.—(1) A worker is entitled to payment of the minimum remuneration specified in this Schedule for all time during which he is present on the premises of his employer unless he is present thereon in any of the following circumstances:—

(a) without the employer's consent, express or implied;

(b) for some purpose unconnected with his work and other than that of waiting for work to be given to him to perform;

(c) by reason only of the fact that he is resident thereon;

(d) during normal meal times in a room or place in which no work is being done and he is not waiting for work to be given to him to perform.

(2) The minimum remuneration payable under sub-paragraph (1) of this paragraph to a piece worker not engaged on piece work is a time rate equal to the piece work basis time rate otherwise applicable to the worker or where no piece work basis time rate would be applicable, the appropriate general minimum time rate.

PART VI

GUARANTEED WEEKLY REMUNERATION

10.—(1) Subject to the provisions of this paragraph, a worker, other than a home-worker, who has been in the employment of the employer for not less than four weeks and who ordinarily works for the employer at least 33 hours weekly on work to which this Schedule applies shall be paid not less than the guaranteed weekly remuneration in respect of any week in which he is in the employment of the employer, and either performs no work to which this Schedule applies or works for less than 33 hours on such work.

(2) The guaranteed weekly remuneration is 33 hours' pay calculated at the hourly general minimum time rate ordinarily applicable to the worker or which would be applicable if he were a time worker.

(3) The guaranteed weekly remuneration in any week shall be reduced by the amount of any holiday remuneration paid, or payable, by the employer to the worker in respect of any holiday allowed to, and taken by, the worker in that week under the provisions of the Wages Councils Act 1959.

(4) In calculating the number of hours worked in any week for the purposes of this paragraph, the worker shall be treated as though he had worked on any holiday allowed to, and taken by, him in that week under the provisions of the Wages Councils Act 1959, for the number of hours ordinarily worked by him on that day of the week, provided that the worker shall not be treated as having worked in any week throughout which he is on holiday.

(5) Payment of the guaranteed weekly remuneration in any week is subject to the condition that the worker throughout the period of his ordinary employment in that week, excluding any day allowed to him as a holiday as aforesaid, is—

(a) capable of and available for work; and

(b) willing to perform such duties outside his normal occupation as the employer may reasonably require if his normal work is not available to him in the establishment in which he is employed.

(6) The guaranteed weekly remuneration shall not be payable to a worker for any week—

(a) in which work is not available for him by reason of a strike or lockout; or

(b) in which the worker has been dismissed on the grounds of serious misconduct; or

(c) in which the amount of remuneration payable to the worker, calculated in accordance with the preceding paragraphs of this Schedule, exceeds the amount of the remuneration which would be payable to him under the provisions of this paragraph.

(7) If the employer is unable to provide the worker with work by reason of shortage of supplies or orders or other circumstances beyond his control and gives the worker not less than one week's notice to that effect, guaranteed weekly remuneration shall not be payable after the expiry of such notice in respect of any week during the whole of which the employer is unable to provide work as aforesaid:

Provided that the period of such suspension of guaranteed weekly remuneration shall not exceed four consecutive weeks on any one occasion and shall not exceed eight weeks in the aggregate in any six consecutive calendar months.

(8) In this paragraph "week" means pay week.

PART VII

INTERPRETATION

11. In this Schedule—

"HOMEWORKER" means a worker who works in his own home or in any other place which is not under the control or management of the employer.

"HOURLY GENERAL MINIMUM TIME RATE" means the general minimum time rate applicable to the worker under Part II, III or IV of this Schedule divided by 40.

"HOURLY PIECE WORK BASIS TIME RATE" means the piece work basis time rate applicable to the worker under Part II or III of this Schedule divided by 40.

"LEARNER" means a worker (other than a worker to whom paragraph 4(e) applies) who is employed during the whole or a substantial part of his time in learning the processes of making, machining, passing or finishing, by an employer who provides the worker with reasonable facilities for such learning.

"THE INDUSTRY" means the rubber proofed garment making industry as defined in paragraph 2.

Article 3.

SCHEDULE 2

HOLIDAYS AND HOLIDAY REMUNERATION

The Wages Regulation (Rubber Proofed Garment) (Holidays) Order 1967(a) (Order R.P.G. (23)) shall have effect as if in the Schedule thereto for sub-paragraph (2) of paragraph 2 (which relates to customary holidays) there were substituted the following:—

"(2) The said customary holidays are:—

(a) (i) In England and Wales—

Christmas Day (or, if Christmas Day falls on a Sunday, such weekday as may be appointed by national proclamation, or, if none is so appointed, the next following Tuesday), Boxing Day, Good Friday, Easter Monday, Whit Monday (or where another day is substituted therefor by national proclamation, that day), August Bank Holiday and one other day (being a day on which the worker normally works for the employer) in the course of a calendar year, to be fixed by the employer and notified to the worker not less than three weeks before the holiday:

Provided that in the case of a worker who normally works on each weekday except Saturday—

(a) if Christmas Day falls on a Saturday, the Friday immediately preceding or the next following Tuesday shall be a customary holiday;

(b) if Boxing Day falls on a Saturday, the Thursday immediately preceding or the next following Monday shall be a customary holiday.

(ii) In Scotland—

New Year's Day (or, if New Year's Day falls on a Sunday, the following Monday);

(a) S.I. 1967/628 (1967 I, p. 1881).

the local Spring holiday;

the local Autumn holiday; and

four other days (being days on which the worker normally works for the employer) in the course of a calendar year, to be fixed by the employer and notified to the worker not less than three weeks before the holiday;

or (b) in the case of each of the said days a day substituted by the employer therefor, being a day recognised by local custom as a day of holiday in substitution for the said day."

EXPLANATORY NOTE

(This Note is not part of the Order.)

This Order has effect from 5th March 1970.   Schedule 1 sets out the statutory minimum remuneration payable in substitution for that fixed by the Wages Regulation (Rubber Proofed Garment) Order 1969 (Order R.P.G. (27)), which Order is revoked.   Schedule 2 repeats without alteration the amendment to the Wages Regulation (Rubber Proofed Garment) (Holidays) Order 1967 (Order R.P.G. (23)), which was contained in Order R.P.G. (27).

New provisions are printed in italics.

STATUTORY INSTRUMENTS

1970 No. 140 (S.7)

NURSES AND MIDWIVES

The Nurses (Scotland) (Amendment) Rules 1970
Approval Instrument 1970

Made - - - -	*29th January* 1970
Laid before Parliament	*12th February* 1970
Coming into Operation	*13th February* 1970

Whereas the General Nursing Council for Scotland, in exercise of the powers conferred on them by section 6 of the Nurses (Scotland) Act 1951(a), on 13th January, 1970, made the Nurses (Scotland) Amendment Rules 1970 and have submitted the said Rules to the Secretary of State for approval;

Now, therefore, in exercise of the powers conferred on me by section 33 of the Nurses (Scotland) Act, 1951, and of all other powers enabling me in that behalf, I hereby approve the said Rules in the form set out in the Schedule hereto. This Instrument may be cited as the Nurses (Scotland) (Amendment) Rules 1970 Approval Instrument 1970, and shall come into operation on 13th February 1970.

William Ross,
One of Her Majesty's Principal
Secretaries of State.

St. Andrew's House,
  Edinburgh.

29th January 1970.

SCHEDULE

The Nurses (Scotland) (Amendment) Rules 1970, dated 13th January, 1970
made by the General Nursing Council for Scotland
The General Nursing Council for Scotland, in exercise of the powers conferred on them by section 6 of the Nurses (Scotland) Act 1951, hereby make the following Rules:—

(a) 1951 c. 55.

1. These Rules may be cited as the Nurses (Scotland) (Amendment) Rules 1970, and shall be read as one with the Nurses (Scotland) Rules 1954 **(a)**, as amended **(b)**, hereinafter referred to as "the principal Rules".

2. The Interpretation Act 1889**(c)** applies for the interpretation of these Rules as it applies for the interpretation of an Act of Parliament.

3. The Nurses (Scotland) Rules 1954, as amended, shall be further amended as follows:—

(1) For paragraph (2) of Rule 21 of the principal Rules there shall be substituted the following paragraph:—

"(2) Any person who makes application under the previous sub-section of this Rule shall pay a fee of £3 to the Council at the time of making such application for registration in the appropriate part or parts of the Register. There shall be payable at the time of registration a registration fee of such amount as the Council may from time to time determine in respect of each Part of the Register to which she desires to be admitted."

(2) After paragraph (6) of Rule 25 of the principal Rules there shall be added the following paragraph:—

"(7) (i) The senior nurse of an approved Training Institution, or such other officer as the Council may authorise in that behalf, shall within 30 days of the admission of a student nurse to an introductory training course notify the Council in writing of the full name of the student nurse, her age, her educational qualifications and the date on which she commenced her training and such other particulars as the Council may reasonably require, and shall send to the Council with the notification any evidence of the age and educational qualifications of the student nurse that the Council may require.

(ii) The Council shall keep an Index of Student Nurses and shall, on being satisfied that a student nurse has been admitted to an introductory training course in accordance with the provisions of paragraph (7)(i) of this Rule and on receipt of the fee due under Section 6(1) of the Nurses (Scotland) Act 1951 as read with Section 7(1) of the Nurses Act 1969 which fee the Council may, with the approval of the Secretary of State, from time to time determine and which shall be paid within 30 days after admission to the introductory training course, include her name in the index, provided that a registered nurse who subsequently enters training for admission to another part of the Register shall not be required to pay any further fee.

(iii) The senior nurse of an approved Training Institution, or such other officer as the Council may authorise on her behalf, shall, if a student nurse being trained in that Institution discontinues her training notify the Council of the fact and of the reason for the discontinuation and if the student has completed not less than 26 weeks' training shall at the same time send to the Council a statement giving particulars of the training completed. No person shall be able to enter an introductory training course more than three times for training for admission for any one part of the Register."

(3) For Rule 44 of the principal Rules there shall be substituted the following Rule:—

"44. The Council shall grant a Certificate of Registration as a Nurse Tutor (hereinafter in this part of the Rules referred to as "the Council's Certificate") in the form set out in the Fourth Schedule to these Rules to any nurse registered in the General Part of the Register who makes application in writing to the Registrar for such Certificate and who satisfies the following requirements:—

(1)(*a*) The applicant must have undergone at least four years' experience in nursing since registration on any Part of the Register, including at least two years experience as Sister or Male Charge Nurse in charge of a ward in an approved training school.

(a) S.I, 1954/493 (1954 I, p. 1478).
(b) The relevant amending instruments are S.I. 1956/133, 1961/670, 1962/252, 2195, 1963/1543, 1965/1197 (1956 II, p. 1719; 1961 I, p. 1417; 1962 I, p. 256; III, p. 2988; 1963 III, p. 2919; 1965 II, p. 3408). (c) 1889 c. 63.

(*b*) The applicant must have completed a whole time Nurse Tutor course of two years duration in an Institution approved by the Council in that behalf.

(*c*) The applicant must hold a Nurse Tutor Certificate granted by a university approved by the Council in that behalf.

or (2) The applicant must have successfully completed a course of training which is for the time being recognised by the Secretary of State as entitling her to be a qualified teacher for the purposes of regulations made, or having effect as if made, under the Teaching Council (Scotland) Act 1965 and the Education (Scotland) Acts 1962, and 1969, and has had since registration not less than three years experience in nursing of which

> (i) not less than 1 year has been spent as a person in charge of a ward or department of an approved training institution in which pupil or student nurses are regularly training, and

> (ii) not less than 1 year has been spent in other clinical nursing acceptable to the Council for the purposes of this paragraph, and

> (iii) not less than 1 year has been spent in the teaching of nursing at an approved training institution under the supervision of a person holding the Council's Certificate.

or (3) The applicant's name is included on any roll of teachers for the time being maintained by the Council for the Training of Health Visitors and she has had not less than two years experience in nursing since registration, of which

> (i) at least one year shall have been as a health visitor, and

> (ii) at least one year shall have been as a person in charge of a ward or department of an approved training institution in which pupil or student nurses are regularly trained.

or (4) In any particular case the applicant appears to the Council and the Secretary of State to be qualified in the teaching of nursing otherwise than as mentioned in the preceding provision of this Rule.

Notwithstanding what is hereinbefore provided in paragraphs (1), (2) and (3) of this Rule, the Council may at their discretion waive compliance with any of the requirements specified in these paragraphs to such extent as they think fit in any particular case."

(4) In paragraph (1) of Rule 50 of the principal Rules, for "Rule 44(3)" there shall be substituted "Rules 44(1), (2) and (3)".

Made by the General Nursing Council for Scotland on this 13th day of January, 1970.

Jessie G. M. Main,
Registrar
General Nursing Council for Scotland.

5 Darnaway Street
Edinburgh.

EXPLANATORY NOTE
(*This Note is not part of this Instrument.*)

The Amendment Rules make provision for fees to be paid by student nurses on entering training and by nurses trained abroad on applying for registration by the General Nursing Council; and for the introduction of alternative qualifications for the granting of a certificate of registration as a Nurse Tutor.

STATUTORY INSTRUMENTS

1970 No. 141 (S.8)

NURSES AND MIDWIVES

The Enrolled Nurses (Scotland) (Amendment) Rules 1970 Approval Instrument 1970

Made - - -	29*th January* 1970
Laid before Parliament	12*th February* 1970
Coming into Operation	13*th February* 1970

Whereas the General Nursing Council for Scotland, in exercise of the powers conferred on them by section 6 of the Nurses (Scotland) Act 1951(a) on 13th January 1970 made the Enrolled Nurses (Scotland) (Amendment) Rules 1970, and have submitted the said Rules to the Secretary of State for approval;

Now, therefore, in exercise of the powers conferred on me by section 33 of the Nurses (Scotland) Act 1951, and of all other powers enabling me in that behalf, I hereby approve the said Rules in the form set out in the Schedule hereto.

This Instrument may be cited as the Enrolled Nurses (Scotland) Rules 1970, Approval Instrument 1970 and shall come into operation on the 13th day February 1970.

William Ross,
One of Her Majesty's Principal
Secretaries of State.

St. Andrew's House,
Edinburgh.
29th January 1970.

SCHEDULE

The Enrolled Nurses (Scotland) (Amendment) Rules 1970, dated 13th January 1970 made by the General Nursing Council for Scotland.

The General Nursing Council for Scotland, in exercise of the powers conferred by them by section 6 of the Nurses (Scotland) Act 1951 hereby make the following Rules:—

1. These Rules may be cited as the Enrolled Nurses (Scotland) (Amendment) Rules 1970, and shall be read as one with the Enrolled Nurses (Scotland) Rules 1961(b) as amended (c), hereinafter referred to as "the principal Rules".

(a) 1951 c. 55.   (b) S.I. 1962/780 (1962 I, p. 774).   (c) S.I. 1962/2569 (1962 III, p. 3456).

2. The Enrolled Nurses (Scotland) Rules 1961, as amended, shall be further amended as follows:—

For Rule 23 of the principal Rules there shall be substituted the following Rule:—

"23. An Index of Pupil Nurses (in these Rules referred to as "the Index of Pupils") shall be kept by the Council and when an applicant has been accepted by a Complete School or a Component School as a pupil, the Matron, Superintendent Nurse or other person occupying a similar position in the Training School, shall report to the Council, within 30 days of the commencement of the pupil's training, her full name, evidence of age, educational qualifications and any other particulars the Council may reasonably require, and in the case of a Candidate who under Rule 29 of these Rules is entitled to enter for the examination after a reduced period of training particulars of her previous training as a Student Nurse, and on receipt of the fee due under Section 6(1) of the Nurses (Scotland) Act 1951 as read with Section 7(1) of the Nurses Act 1969 which fee the Council may, with the approval of the Secretary of State from time to time determine and which shall be paid within 30 days after commencement of the pupil's training, the name of the pupil shall be included in the Index of Pupils."

Made by the General Nursing Council for Scotland on this 13th day of January 1970.

Jessie G. M. Main,
Registrar,
General Nursing Council for Scotland.

5 Darnaway Street,
Edinburgh.

EXPLANATORY NOTE

(This Note is not part of this Instrument.)

The Amendment Rules make provision for fees to be paid by pupil nurses on entering training.

STATUTORY INSTRUMENTS

1970 No. 142 (S.9)

NURSES AND MIDWIVES

The General Nursing Council for Scotland (Election Scheme) Rules 1969 Approval Instrument 1970

Made	- - -	*29th January* 1970
Laid before Parliament		*12th February* 1970
Coming into Operation		*13th February* 1970

Whereas the General Nursing Council for Scotland have, in exercise of their powers under section 33 and paragraph 4 of the Schedule 1 of the Nurses (Scotland) Act 1951(a) made the General Nursing Council for Scotland (Election Scheme) Rules 1969 and have submitted the said rules to the Secretary of State for his approval :

Now, therefore, in exercise of the powers conferred on me by section 33(3) of the Nurses (Scotland) Act 1951 and of all other powers enabling me in that behalf, I hereby approve the said rules in the form set out in the Schedule hereto.

This instrument may be cited as the General Nursing Council for Scotland (Election Scheme) Rules 1969, Approval Instrument 1970 and shall come into operation on the 13th day of February 1970.

William Ross,
One of Her Majesty's Principal
Secretaries of State.

St Andrew's House,
Edinburgh.
29th January 1970.

SCHEDULE

The General Nursing Council for Scotland (Election Scheme) Rules
1969, dated 28th November 1969, made by the General Nursing
Council for Scotland

The General Nursing Council for Scotland in exercise of the powers conferred on them by Section 33 and paragraph 4 of Schedule 1 of the Nurses (Scotland) Act 1951, and all other powers enabling them in that behalf, hereby make the following rules : —

1. These rules may be cited as the General Nursing Council for Scotland (Election Scheme) Rules 1969.

2. The Interpretation Act 1889(b) applies to the interpretation of these rules as it applies to the interpretation of an Act of Parliament.

(a) 1951 c.55. (b) 1889 c.63.

3. The Sixth and Seventh Schedules of the Nurses (Scotland) Rules 1954 approved by the Nurses (Scotland) Rules 1954 Approval Instrument 1954(**a**) and Part VIII and the Sixth and Seventh Schedules of the Enrolled Nurses (Scotland) Rules 1961 approved by the Enrolled Nurses (Scotland) Rules 1961 Approval Instrument 1962(**b**) are hereby revoked:

Provided that such revocation shall not affect any right, privilege, obligation or liability acquired, accrued or incurred, or anything duly done or suffered, under those rules.

4. The members of the General Nursing Council for Scotland who are required by the provisions of paragraph 1(*a*) of Schedule I of the Nurses (Scotland) Act 1951 as amended by section 3(1) of the Nurses Act 1969 to be elected in accordance with the provisions of paragraph 2 of that Schedule as substituted by subsection (2) of section 3 of the Nurses Act 1969, shall be elected in accordance with the Scheme set out in the Schedule to these rules.

SCHEDULE TO THE RULES

Interpretation

1. Unless the context otherwise requires, expressions used in this Scheme have the same meanings as in the Nurses (Scotland) Rules 1954 and the Enrolled Nurses (Scotland) Rules 1961 made by the Council under section 6 of the Nurses (Scotland) Act 1951.

Returning Officer

2.—(1) The Council shall at least six months before the date on which their elected members cease to hold office appoint a person, not being a member or an officer of the Council, to be the Returning Officer for the ensuing election.

(2) The Council shall appoint a Deputy Returning Officer, not being a member or an officer of the Council, to act for the Returning Officer in the event of his absence or inability to act, and the expression "Returning Officer" in this Scheme includes the Deputy Returning Officer so acting.

(3) The Returning Officer shall have power, subject to the approval of the Council, to employ and pay out of the monies provided to him by the Council the staff necessary for the conduct of the election.

(4) Subject to the provisions of this Scheme, the Returning Officer shall be responsible for the conduct of the election.

Qualification of Candidates and Electors

3.—(1) The numbers and qualifications of the several classes of persons to be elected are specified in the first and second columns of the following table, and the qualifications of the persons entitled to nominate and to take part in the election of candidates of each of these classes are specified in the third column of the table. Each of the nurses to be elected shall on the last date fixed for the receipt of nomination papers be engaged in Scotland in work for which the employment of a registered nurse or an enrolled nurse, as the case may be, is requisite or for which a registered nurse or an enrolled nurse, as the case may be, is commonly employed.

(**a**) S.I. 1954/493 (1954 I, p. 1478).   (**b**) S.I. 1962/780 (1962 I. p. 774).

TABLE

Number of persons to be elected	Qualifications of persons to be elected	Qualifications of persons entitled to nominate and take part in election
6	Registered general nurses	{ Registered general nurses { Registered fever nurses
1	Registered mental nurse being a man	Registered mental nurses
1	Registered mental nurse being a women	
1	Registered nurse for mental defectives	Registered nurses for mental defectives
1	Registered sick children's nurse	Registered sick children's nurses
2	Registered nurse tutors	Registered nurse tutors
2	Enrolled nurses	Enrolled nurses

(2) In order to be eligible for election under this Scheme, a person must have the requisite qualifications on the date of nomination and on the date of the election. In order to be entitled to nominate for the election, a person must have the requisite qualifications on the date of nomination and in order to be entitled to take part in the election a person must have the requisite qualifications on the date of the election.

Publication of Notice of Election

4. The Returning Officer shall fix the last day on which nomination papers are to be received, and at least twenty-eight clear days before the day so fixed shall cause a notice of the election to be published, specifying the number and description of persons to be elected, the place to which the nomination papers are to be sent, and the last day on which they are to be received. The notice shall be, as nearly as may be, in the form marked A in the Appendix to this Scheme, and shall be published once in at least two recognised journals circulating among nurses, and in a daily newspaper published in each of the following places, namely: Edinburgh, Glasgow, Aberdeen and Dundee.

Nomination

5.—(1) Each candidate for election shall be nominated by a separate nomination paper signed by not fewer than two persons having the requisite qualifications for nominating the candidate. Nomination papers shall be obtainable from the Registrar on demand.

(2) A nurse shall not nominate a candidate for election by nurses holding a particular qualification unless she herself holds the requisite qualification specified in Rule 3.

(3) Each nomination paper shall state the name, address and requisite qualifications of the person nominated and also the addresses and requisite qualifications of the persons signing such paper, and shall be, as nearly as may be, in the appropriate form marked B in the Appendix to this Scheme.

(4) Any person having the requisite qualifications for nominating a candidate may nominate any number of candidates not exceeding the number to be elected.

(5) Every nomination paper shall, before twelve noon of the last day fixed for the receipt of nomination papers, be delivered by post or otherwise to the Returning Officer, General Nursing Council for Scotland, 5 Darnaway Street, Edinburgh EH3 6DP and shall be accompanied by a declaration in writing signed by the person nominated, in the form marked C in the Appendix to this Scheme or to the like effect, acknowledging that such person consents to be nominated and that the particulars are correct. Every nomination paper in respect of which any requirement of this Scheme has not been complied with, or which is not received by the Returning Officer before twelve noon of the last day fixed for the receipt of nomination papers, shall be invalid: provided that no misnomer or inaccurate or incomplete description of any person or place named in any nomination paper shall invalidate that paper if, in the opinion of the Returning Officer, the description of the person or place is such as to be commonly understood.

Conduct of Election

6. The election of the six persons to represent registered general nurses shall be conducted in the following manner:—
    (1) If the number of duly nominated candidates does not exceed six, the Returning Officer shall forthwith declare such candidates to be elected.

    (2) If the number of duly nominated candidates exceeds the number to be elected, the Returning Officer shall cause ballot papers and identification envelopes to be prepared. Ballot papers shall contain the names, addresses and professional status of all the persons nominated, and state the last day on which ballot papers may be received, and the place to which they are to be returned, and the identification envelope shall bear a declaration of identity.

    Ballot papers and identification envelopes shall be, as nearly as may be, in the forms marked D and E in the Appendix to this Scheme.

    (3) The Returning Officer shall, twenty-one clear days at least before the last day fixed for the receipt of ballot papers, cause a ballot paper to be forwarded by post to each person qualified to take part in the election at her registered address, together with an identification envelope. Each elector shall be entitled to receive one ballot paper and one identification envelope, and no more, and votes shall not be given except upon the ballot papers provided by the Returning Officer.

    (4) Each elector shall vote by marking the ballot paper delivered to her with a X against the name or names of the person or persons (not exceeding the number of persons to be elected), for whom she votes, and shall place her ballot paper folded face inwards in the appropriate identification envelope, and securely fasten the same. The elector shall sign the declaration printed on the said envelope, place it inside a covering sealed envelope bearing the address of the Returning Officer, and send it by post or otherwise to the Returning Officer. Every ballot paper in respect of which any requirement of this Scheme has not been complied with, or on which the elector has placed any mark whereby she may be afterwards identified, or which is not received by the Returning Officer before twelve noon on the last day fixed for the receipt of ballot papers, shall be invalid.

    (5) The Returning Officer, immediately after the last day fixed for the receipt of ballot papers, shall cause the validity of the votes to be ascertained by an examination of the identification envelopes and by such other evidence, if any, as he may think necessary, and shall cause such of the identification envelopes as are found to be valid to be opened, and the ballot papers withdrawn, kept folded face inwards, and placed in a ballot box. When all the ballot papers have been transferred to the ballot box they shall be examined and counted, and the number of valid votes given for each candidate shall be ascertained. Any candidate, or agent appointed by her to represent her, may be present during the examination of the identification envelopes and the counting of the ballot papers.

(6) The six candidates having the greatest number of votes shall be declared elected by the Returning Officer. If an equality of votes is found to exist between any of the candidates, and the addition of a vote would entitle any of such candidates to be declared elected, the Returning Officer shall determine by lot which of the candidates whose votes are equal shall be declared elected.

(7) The foregoing provisions with regard to the conduct of the election of registered general nurses shall apply with the necessary modifications to the election of persons representing respectively registered mental nurses, registered nurses for mental defectives, registered sick children's nurses, registered nurse tutors and enrolled nurses.

Powers of Returning Officers

7.—(1) Any question arising with regard to the validity of a nomination or ballot paper, or otherwise in connection with any election held under this Scheme, shall be determined by the Returning Officer whose decision shall be final.

(2) No election held under this Scheme shall be invalidated by reason of mis-description or non-compliance with the provisions of this Scheme, or by reason of any mis-count or of the non-delivery, loss, or miscarriage in the course of post of any document required under this Scheme to be despatched by post, if the Returning Officer certifies in writing that the election was conducted substantially in accordance with the provisions of the Scheme, and that the result of such misdescription, non-compliance, mis-count, non-delivery, loss or miscarriage did not affect the result of the election; provided that any unsuccessful candidate or her agent may, within fourteen days after the declaration by the Returning Officer of the result of the election, appeal to the Secretary of State for Scotland against a Certificate given by the Returning Officer under this sub-paragraph, and the decision of the Secretary of State for Scotland shall be final.

(3) The Identification Envelopes and Ballot Papers shall be destroyed by the Returning Officer on the expiry of one calendar month from the date of the declaration of the result of the election, unless there shall have been an appeal as provided for under the immediately preceding sub-paragraph of this Scheme, in which event the Secretary of State for Scotland shall order the destruction of the said Envelopes and Ballot Papers, on the determination of the appeal.

Notice and Publication of Result of Election

8. The Returning Officer shall forthwith give to every person elected written notice of her election, and shall furnish the Council with a list of the persons certified by him to have been duly elected, showing the number of votes cast for each of such persons. The Returning Officer shall also publish the names and addresses of the elected candidates in the journals and newspapers specified in paragraph 4 of this Scheme.

Secrecy of Ballot

9. The Returning Officer, and every officer, clerk, or servant employed in connection with the election shall maintain, and aid in maintaining, the secrecy of the ballot, and shall not communicate to any person any information as to the manner in which any elector has recorded her vote.

APPENDIX

Rule 4

Form A (Notice of Election)
Nurses (Scotland) Acts 1951 to 1969

Notice is hereby given that pursuant to the Nurses (Scotland) Acts 1951 to 1969 an election of 14 members of the General Nursing Council for Scotland, 12 to represent the nurses registered on the Register of that Council and 2 to represent the nurses enrolled upon the Roll of that Council, is about to be held.

The following table shows the numbers and qualifications of the persons to be elected and the qualifications of the persons entitled to nominate and take part in the election of each class of candidate. Each person to be elected shall, on the last date fixed for the receipt of nomination papers, be engaged in Scotland in work for which the employment of a registered nurse or an enrolled nurse, as the case may be, is requisite or for which a registered nurse or an enrolled nurse, as the case may be, is commonly employed.

TABLE

Qualifications of Candidates and Electors

Number of persons to be elected	Qualifications of persons to be elected	Qualifications of persons entitled to nominate and take part in election
6	Registered general nurses	{ Registered general nurses { Registered fever nurses
1	Registered mental nurse being a man	Registered mental nurses
1	Registered mental nurse being a women	
1	Registered nurse for mental defectives	Registered nurses for mental defectives
1	Registered sick children's nurse	Registered sick children's nurses
2	Registered nurse tutors	Registered nurse tutors
2	Enrolled nurses	Enrolled nurses

In order to be eligible for election under this Scheme a person must have the requisite qualifications on the date of nomination and on the date of the election. In order to be entitled to nominate for election a person must have the requisite qualifications on the date of nomination, and in order to be entitled to take part in the election a person must have the requisite qualifications on the date of the election.

Each candidate must be nominated by a separate nomination paper. Any person having the requisite qualifications for nominating a candidate may nominate any number of candidates not exceeding the number to be elected.

Every nomination paper must state the name, address and requisite qualifications of the candidate nominated ; it must be signed by not fewer than two persons having the requisite qualifications for nominating the candidate ; and the address and requisite qualifications of each one so signing must be appended to his or her signature.

The nomination paper must be accompanied by a declaration in writing signed by the person nominated, acknowledging that he or she consents to be nominated and that the particulars are correct, and must be delivered by post or otherwise before the hour of twelve noon on the day of   19 , addressed to the Returning Officer, The General Nursing Council for Scotland, 5 Darnaway

Street, Edinburgh EH3 6DP. Every nomination paper which is not received at the address given above before the hour of twelve noon on the   day of   will be invalid.

Nomination papers may be obtained on application to the Registrar, The General Nursing Council for Scotland, 5 Darnaway Street, Edinburgh EH3 6DP.

Returning Officer.

(Date)

Rule 5

FORM B (Form of Nomination Paper)

We, the undersigned, being nurses

(1)

hereby nominate   (2)

of   (3)

who is   (4)

and whose registration/enrolment number is   (5)

and who is employed in Scotland at   (6)

where he/she is engaged in (a) nursing

(7)

or (b) other work for which the employment of a registered/enrolled nurse is requisite or for which a registered/enrolled nurse is commonly employed, that is to say   (8)

as a proper person to be elected to the General Nursing Council for Scotland

by   (9)

Signatures of Nominators	Addresses	Registered/Enrolled Qualification and Number

(Date)

(1) Here insert the words "registered general *or* fever nurses", or "registered mental nurses", or "registered nurse for mental defectives", or "registered sick children's nurses", or "registered general nurses who hold the Certificate of Registration as "nurse tutors" or "enrolled nurses" as the case may be.

(2) Here insert full name, including fore names of candidate.

(3) Here insert candidate's address.

(4) Here insert the words "a registered general nurse", or "a registered mental nurse", or "a registered nurse for mental defectives", or "a registered sick children's nurse", or "a registered general nurse who holds the Certificate of Registration as a Nurse Tutor", or "an enrolled nurse" as the case may be.

(5) Here insert candidate's registration/enrolment number.

(6) Here insert candidate's place and postal address of employment.

(7) Here insert candidate's present post.

(8) If the candidate is not actually employed in nursing, then state briefly the nature of the work in which he or she is employed.

(9) Here insert the words "registered general *and* fever nurses", or "registered mental nurses", or "registered nurses for mental defectives", or "registered sick children's nurses", or "registered general nurses who hold the Certificate of Registration as nurse tutors" or "enrolled nurses" as the case may be.

N.B. A nurse shall not nominate a candidate for election by nurses registered in a particular part of the Register unless he or she is himself or herself registered in that particular part except that a registered fever nurse may nominate a registered general nurse for election. In the case of Nurse Tutors, the nurses making the nomination must hold Certificates of Registration as Nurse Tutors. And in the case of Enrolled Nurses, the nurses making the nomination must be enrolled in the Roll of Nurses. Each nomination paper must be signed by not fewer than two persons having the requisite qualifications.

All nomination papers must be accompanied by a written declaration of consent by the person nominated.
Nomination papers, should, except for the signatures of nominators, be completed in block capitals.

Rule 5

FORM C (Form of Declaration to be issued with the nomination papers for return by the Candidate nominated)

ELECTION OF DIRECT REPRESENTATIVES TO THE GENERAL NURSING COUNCIL
FOR SCOTLAND

(Date)

I consent to be nominated as a candidate for election as a representative of the nurses (1)

to serve on the General Nursing Council for Scotland. I declare that the statements in the nomination paper with regard to my qualifications are correct.

Name

Address

Registration/Enrolment Number

(1) Here insert the words "registered in the General part of the Register and the part of the Register for fever nurses", or "registered in the Supplementary part of the Register for mental nurses", or "registered in the Supplementary part of the Register for nurses for mental defectives", or "registered in the Supplementary part of the Register for sick children's nurses", or "registered in the General part of the Register and who hold(s) Certificate(s) of Registration as Nurse Tutor(s)", or "enrolled on the Roll of Nurses" as the case may be.

Form D

Election to the General Nursing Council for Scotland by nurses (including male nurses) registered in the general part or the fever part of the Register.

BALLOT PAPER I

Election of SIX Registered Nurses

Elector's Mark X	Name of Candidate Nominated	Address	Professional Status

N.B. Only registered general nurses or registered fever nurses are entitled to vote for candidates in this ballot paper.

The elector must put a mark thus, X, against the name or names of the candidates for whom he or she votes.

The elector must not vote for more than six candidates.

The elector may vote for fewer candidates than are to be elected.

If the elector places any mark on this ballot paper by which such elector may be afterwards identified, the ballot paper will be null and void.

This paper must be folded face inwards and placed in the identification envelope which must be signed by the elector in the place marked for that purpose, securely fastened, and placed in a covering envelope bearing the address of the Returning Office which must then be sent by post or otherwise to the Returning Officer and must be received there before the hour of twelve noon on the   day of   19 .

Election to the General Nursing Council for Scotland by nurses registered
in the part of the Register for mental nurses.

BALLOT PAPER II

Election of ONE male and ONE female nurse registered in the part
of the register for mental nurses.

	Elector's Mark X	Name of Candidate	Address	Professional Status
Part I— Female Nurses				
Part II— Male Nurses				

N.B. Only registered mental nurses are entitled to vote for candidates on this ballot paper.

The elector must put a mark thus, X, against the name or names of the candidate or candidates for whom he or she votes.

Two only of the above-named candidates are to be elected ; one of these must be a female mental nurse and the other a male mental nurse, and the elections will be determined accordingly.

The elector must not vote for more than one female mental nurse, or for more than one male mental nurse.

The elector may vote for fewer candidates than are to be elected.

If the elector places any mark on this ballot paper by which such elector may be afterwards identified, the ballot paper will be null and void.

This paper must be folded face inwards and placed in the identification envelope which must be signed by the elector in the place marked for that purpose, securely fastened, and placed in a covering envelope bearing the address of the Returning Officer which must then be sent by post or otherwise to the Returning Officer and must be received there before the hour of twelve noon on the   day of
19 .

Election to the General Nursing Council for Scotland by nurses registered in the
part of the Register of nurses for mental defectives.

BALLOT PAPER III

Election of ONE nurse registered in the part of the Register of
nurses for mental defectives

Electors Mark X	Name of Candidate Nominated	Address	Professional Status

N.B. Only registered nurses for mental defectives are entitled to vote for candidates in this ballot paper.

The elector must put a mark thus, X, against the name of the candidate for whom he or she votes.

One only of the above-named candidates is to be elected. If the elector votes for more than one candidate or places any mark on the ballot paper by which such elector may be afterwards identified, the ballot paper will be null and void.

This paper must be folded face inwards and placed in the identification envelope which must be signed by the elector in the place marked for that purpose, securely fastened, and placed in a covering envelope bearing the address of the Returning Officer which must then be sent by post or otherwise to the Returning Officer and must be received there before the hour of twelve noon on the   day of
19 .

Election to the General Nursing Council for Scotland by nurses on the part of the Register for sick children's nurses.

BALLOT PAPER IV

Election of ONE nurse registered in the part of the
Register for sick children's nurses

Elector's Mark X	Name of Candidate Nominated	Address	Professional Status

N.B. Only registered sick children's nurses are entitled to vote for candidates in this ballot paper.

The elector must put a mark thus, X, against the name of the candidate for whom she votes.

One only of the above-named candidates is to be elected. If the elector votes for more than one candidate or places any mark on this ballot paper by which such elector may afterwards be identified, the ballot paper will be null and void.

This paper must be folded face inwards and placed in the identification envelope which must be signed by the elector in the place marked for that purpose, securely fastened, and placed in a covering envelope bearing the address of the Returning Officer which must then be sent by post or otherwise to the Returning Officer and must be received there before the hour of twelve noon on the   day of
19 .

Election to the General Nursing Council for Scotland by nurses who hold Certificates of Registration as Nurse Tutors.

BALLOT PAPER V
Election of TWO Nurse Tutors

Elector's Mark X	Name of Candidate Nominated	Address	Professional Status

N.B.—Only Nurses who hold Certificates of Registration as Nurse Tutors are entitled to vote for candidates in this ballot paper.

The elector must put a mark thus, X, against the name or names of the candidates for whom he or she votes.

The elector must not vote for more than two candidates.

The elector may vote for fewer candidates than are to be elected.

If the elector places any mark on this ballot paper by which such elector may be afterwards identified, the ballot paper will be null and void.

This paper must be folded face inwards and placed in the identification envelope which must be signed by the elector in the place marked for that purpose, securely fastened, and placed in a covering envelope bearing the address of the Returning Officer which must then be sent by post or otherwise to the Returning Officer and must be received there before the hour of twelve noon on the   day of
      19 .

Election to the General Nursing Council for Scotland by nurses enrolled in the Roll of Nurses.

BALLOT PAPER VI
Election of TWO enrolled nurses

Elector's Mark X	Name of Candidate	Address	Professional Status

N.B. Only nurses enrolled in the Roll of Nurses are entitled to vote for candidates in this ballot paper.

The elector must put a mark thus, X, against the name or names of the candidates for whom he or she votes.

The elector must not vote for more than two candidates.

The elector may vote for fewer candidates than are to be elected.

If the elector places any mark on this ballot paper by which such elector may be afterwards identified, the ballot paper will be null and void.

This paper must be folded face inwards and placed in the identification envelope which must be signed by the elector in the place marked for that purpose, securely fastened, and placed in a covering envelope bearing the address of the Returning Officer which must then be sent by post or otherwise to the Returning Officer and must be received there before the hour of twelve noon on the   day of

     19 .

Rule 6

Form E (Form of identification envelope)
Identification envelope I

General Nursing Council for Scotland

(Identification Envelope)

TO

I, the undersigned, hereby declare that I am the person to whom the enclosed ballot paper is addressed as above, that I am a nurse registered in the   part of the Register and that I have not marked any other ballot paper in this part of the election.

(Signature)

Identification envelope II

General Nursing Council for Scotland

(Identification Envelope)

TO
I, the undersigned, hereby declare that I am the person to whom the enclosed ballot paper is addressed as above, that I am a nurse enrolled in the Roll of Nurses, and that I have not marked any other ballot paper in this part of the election.

(Signature)

Made by the General Nursing Council for Scotland on the 28th day of November 1969.

(Sgd.) *Jessie G. M. Main,*
Registrar,
General Nursing Council for Scotland.

5, Darnaway Street,
Edinburgh.

EXPLANATORY NOTE

(This Note is not part of this Instrument.)

These Rules supersede those which formed part of the Nurses (Scotland) Rules 1954 (in the Sixth and Seventh Schedules) and the Enrolled Nurses (Scotland) Rules 1961 (in Part VIII and the Sixth and Seventh Schedules).

The changes made take into account the alteration of the constitution of the General Nursing Council in the Nurses Act 1969.

STATUTORY INSTRUMENTS

1970 No. 143

PENSIONS

The Personal Injuries (Civilians) (Amendment) Scheme 1970

Made - - -	*3rd February* 1970
Laid before Parliament	*11th February* 1970
Coming into Operation	*12th February* 1970

The Secretary of State for Social Services, with the consent of the Treasury, in exercise of the powers conferred upon him by section 2 of the Personal Injuries (Emergency Provisions) Act 1939(a), and of all other powers enabling him in that behalf, hereby makes the following Scheme :—

Citation, interpretation and commencement

1. This Scheme, which may be cited as the Personal Injuries (Civilians) (Amendment) Scheme 1970, amends the Personal Injuries (Civilians) Scheme 1964(b), as amended (c), (hereinafter referred to as "the principal Scheme"), and the Personal Injuries (Civilians) (Amendment) Scheme 1969(d) (hereinafter referred to as "the 1969 Scheme"), and shall come into operation on 12th February 1970.

Definitions

2. In this Scheme—

    (1) "the appointed day" means 15th February 1971 (the day appointed under section 1 of the Decimal Currency Act 1967(e)) ;

    (2) "the new currency" means the new currency of the United Kingdom provided for by the Decimal Currency Act 1967.

Higher maximum rate of allowance for part-time treatment

3.—(1) In Schedule 3 to the principal Scheme, for paragraph 11 (part-time treatment allowance under Article 23) there shall be substituted the paragraph set out in Part I of the Schedule hereto.

(2) In Part II of the Schedule to the 1969 Scheme (Schedules in the new currency to be substituted in the principal Scheme on the appointed day) for paragraph 11 of Schedule 3 (part-time treatment allowance under Article 23) there shall be substituted the paragraph set out in Part II of the Schedule hereto.

(a) 2 & 3 Geo. 6. c. 82.   (b) S.I. 1964/2077 (1964 III, p. 5187).
(c) The relevant amending Scheme is S.I. 1969/1035 (1969 II, p. 3055).
(d) S.I. 1969/1035 (1969 II, p. 3055).   (e) 1967 c. 47.

Signed by authority of the Secretary of State for Social Services.

David Ennals,
Minister of State,
Department of Health and Social Security.

30th January 1970.
We consent.

E. G. Perry,
Neil McBride,
Two of the Lords Commissioners of
Her Majesty's Treasury.

3rd February 1970.

SCHEDULE

PART I

Paragraph to be substituted in Schedule 3 to the principal Scheme

"11. Part-time treatment allowance under Article 23 .. .. 80s. per day (maximum)"

PART II

Paragraph to be substituted in Schedule 3 in Part II of the Schedule to the 1969 Scheme

"11. Part-time treatment allowance under Article 23 .. .. £4 per day (maximum)"

EXPLANATORY NOTE
(This Note is not part of the Scheme.)

This Scheme increases the maximum rate of the allowance payable under the Personal Injuries (Civilians) Scheme 1964 to certain persons having regard to any remunerative time lost as a result of receiving part-time treatment for their pensioned disablement.

STATUTORY INSTRUMENTS

1970 No. 144

ROAD TRAFFIC

The Drivers' Hours (Goods Vehicles) (Exemptions) Regulations 1970

Made - - -	*2nd February* 1970
Laid before Parliament	*9th February* 1970
Coming into Operation	*1st March* 1970

The Minister of Transport, in exercise of his powers under section 96(10) of the Transport Act 1968(a) and of all other enabling powers, and after consultation with representative organisations in accordance with section 101(6) of the said Act of 1968, hereby makes the following Regulations :—

Commencement and citation

1. These Regulations shall come into operation on the 1st March 1970, and may be cited as the Drivers' Hours (Goods Vehicles) (Exemptions) Regulations 1970.

Interpretation

2.—(1) In these Regulations, unless the context otherwise requires, "the Act" means the Transport Act 1968 and any other expression which is also used in Part VI of the Act has the same meaning as in that Part of that Act.

(2) Any reference in the Schedule to these Regulations to a numbered section is a reference to the section bearing that number in the Act except where otherwise expressly provided.

(3) Any reference in an entry in column 1 of Parts I or II of the Schedule to these Regulations to an emergency or to a special need is a reference to such a case of emergency or to such a special need as is specified in column 2 in relation to that entry.

(4) Any reference in these Regulations to an enactment or instrument shall be construed, unless the context otherwise requires, as a reference to that enactment or instrument as amended by any subsequent enactment or instrument.

(5) The Interpretation Act 1889(b) shall apply for the interpretation of these Regulations as it applies for the interpretation of an Act of Parliament.

(a) 1968 c. 73.   (b) 1889 c. 63.

Exemptions from requirements as to drivers' hours

3. For the purpose of enabling drivers of goods vehicles to deal with the cases of emergency and to meet the special needs specified in Parts I and II of the Schedule hereto such drivers are hereby exempted from the requirements of subsections (1) to (6) of section 96 to the extent specified in column 1 of the said Parts I and II in relation to them, subject, however, to the conditions therein specified or referred to in relation to them.

Given under the Official Seal of the Minister of Transport the 2nd February 1970.

(L.S.)

Fred Mulley,
Minister of Transport.

SCHEDULE
(See Regulation 3)

PART I
CASES OF EMERGENCY

Column 1	Column 2
Drivers exempted, requirements exempted from and conditions of exemption	Emergencies

1. A driver who spends time on duty to deal with an emergency—

(1) is exempted from the requirements of section 96(1), (2) and (3) in respect of any working day during which he spends such time on duty, subject to the condition that after spending time on duty (whether to deal with an emergency or for other purposes) during a working day for a period of 11 hours, or for periods which in the aggregate amount to 11 hours, he does not during that day spend any further time on duty except to deal with an emergency:

Provided that where a driver spends time on duty to deal with an emergency which interrupts what would otherwise have been an interval for rest between two successive working days, this condition shall not preclude him from subsequently spending not more than 11 hours on duty (of which not more than 10 hours shall be spent in driving vehicles to which Part VI of the Act applies) for other purposes, if he has had, since he was last on duty for such other purposes, two or more intervals for rest which amount in the aggregate to a period of not less than 11 hours;

(2) is exempted from the requirement of section 96(5) in respect of any working week during which he spends such time on duty subject to the condition that after spending 60 hours on duty during that week (whether to deal with an emergency or for other purposes) he does not spend any further time on duty in that week except to deal with an emergency.

1. Events which—
  (a) cause or are likely to cause such—
    (i) danger to the life or health of one or more individuals or animals, or
    (ii) a serious interruption in the maintenance of public services for the supply of water, gas, electricity or drainage or of telecommunication or postal services, or
    (iii) a serious interruption in the use of roads or airports, or
  (b) are likely to cause such serious damage to property,
as to necessitate the taking of immediate action to prevent the occurrence or continuance of such danger or interruption or the occurrence of such damage.

Column 1	Column 2
Drivers exempted, requirements exempted from and conditions of exemption	Emergencies
2. A driver who in the course of the last 24 hours forming part of a working week spends time on duty to deal with an emergency is exempted from the requirement of section 96(6) in relation to that week, subject to the condition that he does not, during that period of 24 hours, after spending time on duty to deal with an emergency spend time on duty for any other purpose.	2. As in entry 1 of this column.

PART II

CASES OF SPECIAL NEED

Column 1	Column 2
Drivers exempted, requirements exempted from and conditions of exemption	Special Needs

Post Office
1. A driver of a goods vehicle which is used for the purposes of the Post Office is exempted from the requirements of—
    (*a*) section 96(3) in respect of any working day falling wholly or partly in the month of December of any year during which he spends time on duty to meet a special need, subject to the condition that no such day shall exceed 14 hours,
    (*b*) subsections (5) and (6) of section 96 in respect of any working week falling wholly or partly in the month of December in any year, subject, in the case of the exemption from the requirements of—
        (i) section 96(5), to the condition that he is not on duty in any such working week for periods amounting in the aggregate to more than 66 hours, and
        (ii) section 96(6), to the conditions specified in Part III of this Schedule.

1. Work done solely in connection with the handling of the large volume of mail which arises in the Christmas and New Year season.

Carriage of fish or agricultural produce
2. A driver—
    (1) is exempted from the requirement of section 96(3) in relation to any working day during which the time spent by him on duty is spent only in meet-

2. Work done solely in connection with the removal direct to another place—
    (*a*) of fish from the place where it is landed, when such removal

Column 1	Column 2
Drivers exempted, requirements exempted from and conditions of exemption	Special Needs

ing a special need, subject to the condition that that working day does not exceed 14 hours,

(2) is exempted from the requirements of section 96(5) and section 96(6) in respect of any working week during which he spends such time on duty, subject in the case of the exemption from the requirement of—

   (a) section 96(5), to the condition that he is not on duty in that week for periods amounting in the aggregate to more than 66 hours, and

   (b) section 96(6), to the conditions specified in Part III of this Schedule.

is effected immediately after it is landed, or

(b) from agricultural premises of anything produced at those premises in the course of agriculture, when such removal is effected immediately after the harvesting of that produce.

In this paragraph "agriculture" has the same meaning as in Part VI of the Act, except that it does not include dairy farming or live-stock breeding and keeping, and "agricultural" shall be construed accordingly.

Carriage of animals

3. A driver who spends time on duty to meet a special need during a working day is exempted from the requirement of section 96(3) in relation to that working day, subject to the conditions that—

(1) during that day he is off duty for a period which is, or for periods which taken together are, not less than the time by which that working day exceeds 10 hours, and

(2) that working day does not exceed 14 hours.

3. Work done solely in connection with the carriage of animals.

Carriage of bread

4. A driver who spends time on duty to meet a special need—

(1) during a working day falling wholly or partly on a Friday or during any two working days each of which falls wholly or partly within a period of 7 days immediately preceding a bank holiday is exempted from the requirement of section 96(3) in relation to such a working day or days, subject to the condition that no such day shall exceed 14 hours,

(2) during each working day forming part of a working week is exempted from the requirement of section 96(6) in relation to that working week, subject to the conditions specified in Part III of this Schedule.

In this paragraph the expression "bank holiday" means a holiday which is, or is to be

4. Work done wholly or mainly in connection with the carriage of bread.

Column 1	Column 2
Drivers exempted, requirements exempted from and conditions of exemption	Special Needs

observed as, a bank holiday, or a holiday, under the Bank Holidays Act 1871(a) or the Holidays Extension Act 1875(b), either generally or in the particular locality where the journey or part of the journey takes place.

Carriage of milk
5. A driver who, during each working day forming part of a working week, spends time on duty to meet a special need is exempted from the requirement of section 96(6) in relation to that working week, subject to the conditions specified in Part III of this Schedule.

5. Work done wholly or mainly in connection with the carriage of milk.

Blood transfusion service
6. A driver who, during a working day, spends time on duty to meet a special need is exempted from the requirement of section 96(3) in relation to that day, subject to the conditions that—
  (a) he is able to obtain rest and refreshment during that day for a period which is, or for periods which taken together are, not less than the time by which the working day exceeds 10 hours,
  (b) that day does not exceed 14 hours, and
  (c) he has not taken advantage of this exemption from the requirement of section 96(3) on more than one previous working day which forms part of the working week of which that day forms part.

6. Work done solely in connection with the collection and delivery of blood for the purposes of transfusion.

Distribution of newspapers, magazines and periodicals
7. A driver who, during any working day, spends time firstly between 3 a.m. and 7 a.m. and then between 2 p.m. and 6 p.m. on duty to meet a special need is exempted from the requirements of—
  (1) section 96(3) in relation to that working day, subject to the conditions that—
    (a) the working day does not exceed 14 hours, and
    (b) he is off duty during the working day for a period which is, or periods which in the aggregate are, not less than 4 hours,

7. Work done solely in connection with the distribution of newspapers, magazines or periodicals to wholesalers or to persons or premises for the purposes of their sale by retail by those persons or at those premises.

(a) 1871 c. 17.　　　　　　　　　(b) 1875 c. 13.

Column 1	Column 2
Drivers exempted, requirements exempted from and conditions of exemption	Special Needs

(2) section 96(4) in respect of the interval for rest between that and any succeeding working day, subject to the condition that he has between those two successive working days an interval for rest which is not less than 10 hours.

In any case where a driver is exempt by virtue of this paragraph from the requirement of section 96(4), he shall be exempted from the requirements of subsections (1) to (3) of section 96 in respect of the second of the two succeeding days mentioned in sub-paragraph (2) of this paragraph to the following extent, that is to say for the purposes of the expression "working day" in those subsections he shall be deemed to have had an interval for rest between the said successive working days of not less then eleven hours.

Part III

Conditions applicable to exemptions from section 96(6)

Where any entry in column 1 in Part II of this Schedule provides for an exemption from the requirement of section 96(6) in relation to any such working week of a driver as is mentioned in that entry to enable that driver to spend time on duty to meet a special need subject to the conditions specified in this Part of this Schedule, the conditions so referred to are the following—

  (i) that the driver has, in respect of each working week in the course of which he has not had such a period off duty as is required by section 96(6), a period of not less than 24 hours for which he is off duty,

  (ii) that any such period is taken within a period of 28 days starting from the beginning of the working week in respect of which he is required to have that period and is taken by him in addition to any other period for which the driver is required by these conditions or by section 96(6) to be off duty in the case of any other working week.

EXPLANATORY NOTE

(This Note is not part of the Regulations.)

These Regulations provide exemptions subject to conditions from the requirements of section 96(1) to (6) of the Transport Act 1968 (which relates to permitted driving times and periods of duty) to enable drivers of goods vehicles to deal with certain cases of emergency and to meet certain special needs (Regulation 3 and the Schedule).

STATUTORY INSTRUMENTS

1970 No. 145

ROAD TRAFFIC

The Drivers' Hours (Passenger Vehicles) (Exemptions) Regulations 1970

Made - - -	*3rd February* 1970
Laid before Parliament	*9th February* 1970
Coming into Operation	*1st March* 1970

The Minister of Transport, in exercise of his powers under section 96(10) of the Transport Act 1968(a) and of all other enabling powers, and after consultation with representative organisations in accordance with section 101(6) of the said Act of 1968, hereby makes the following Regulations :—

Commencement and citation

1. These Regulations shall come into operation on the 1st March 1970, and may be cited as the Drivers' Hours (Passenger Vehicles) (Exemptions) Regulations 1970.

Interpretation

2.—(1) In these Regulations, unless the context otherwise requires,—
"the Act" means the Transport Act 1968,
"emergency" means an event which—
(*a*) causes or is likely to cause such—
  (i) danger to the life or health of one or more individuals, or
  (ii) a serious interruption in the maintenance of public services for the supply of water, gas, electricity or drainage or of telecommunication or postal services, or
  (iii) a serious interruption in the use of roads, or
  (iv) a serious interruption in private transport or in public transport (not being an interruption caused by a trade dispute (within the meaning of the Trade Disputes Act 1906(**b**)) involving persons who carry passengers for hire or reward), or
(*b*) is likely to cause such serious damage to property,

as to necessitate the taking of immediate action to prevent the occurrence or continuance of such danger or interruption or the occurrence of such damage ;

and any other expression which is also used in Part VI of the Act has the same meaning as in that Part of that Act.

(a) 1968 c. 73.   (b) 1906 c. 47.

(2) Any reference in these Regulations to an enactment or instrument shall be construed, unless the context otherwise requires, as a reference to that enactment or instrument as amended by any subsequent enactment or instrument.

(3) The Interpretation Act 1889(a) shall apply for the interpretation of these Regulations as it applies for the interpretation of an Act of Parliament.

Exemptions from requirements as to drivers' hours

3.—(1) Any driver of a passenger vehicle who spends time on duty to deal with an emergency is, in accordance with paragraphs (2) and (3) of this Regulation, hereby exempted from the requirements of subsections (1) to (6) of section 96 of the Act in respect of the time so spent.

(2) Any time so spent by such a driver shall for the purposes of—

(*a*) subsection (1) of the said section 96 be deemed not to have been spent in driving vehicles to which Part VI of the Act applies, and

(*b*) subsections (1) to (6) of the said section 96 (including the expression "working day" used therein)—

(i) be deemed to have been spent by him off duty, and

(ii) if it would apart from the emergency have been spent in taking an interval for rest or an interval for rest and refreshment be deemed to have been so spent by him.

(3) The requirements of subsection (6) of the said section 96 shall, in relation to such a driver, be deemed to be satisfied in respect of a working week in which he spends time on such duty if he is off duty for a period of twenty-four hours in accordance with that subsection less a period equal to the total time which he spends on such duty in that week.

4. Any driver of a passenger vehicle who spends time on duty during a working day to meet a special need, that is to say work done solely in connection with the collection and delivery of blood for the purposes of transfusion, is hereby exempted from the requirements of section 96(3) in relation to that day, subject to the conditions that—

(*a*) he is able to obtain rest and refreshment during that day for a period which is, or for periods which taken together are, not less than the time by which the working day exceeds 10 hours,

(*b*) that day does not exceed 14 hours, and

(*c*) he has not taken advantage of this exemption from the requirements of section 96(3) on more than one previous working day which forms part of the working week of which that day forms part.

Given under the Official Seal of the Minister of Transport the 3rd February 1970.

(L.S.)

Fred Mulley,
Minister of Transport.

(a) 1889 c. 63.

EXPLANATORY NOTE

(This Note is not part of the Regulations.)

These Regulations provide exemptions from the requirements of section 96(1) to (6) of the Transport Act 1968 (which relates to permitted driving times and periods of duty) to enable drivers of passenger vehicles to deal with certain cases of emergency (Regulation 3) and to meet a special need (Regulation 4).

STATUTORY INSTRUMENTS

1970 No. 146

GENOCIDE

The Genocide Act 1969 (Overseas Territories) Order 1970

Made - - - -	4th February 1970
Coming into Operation	30th April 1970

At the Court at Buckingham Palace, the 4th day of February 1970

Present,

The Queen's Most Excellent Majesty in Council

Her Majesty, in exercise of the powers conferred upon Her by section 3(2) of the Genocide Act 1969(a), is pleased, by and with the advice of Her Privy Council, to order, and it is hereby ordered, as follows :—

1. This Order may be cited as the Genocide Act 1969 (Overseas Territories) Order 1970 and shall come into operation on 30th April 1970.

2. The Interpretation Act 1889(b) shall apply, with the necessary adaptations, for the purpose of interpreting this Order and otherwise in relation thereto as it applies for the purpose of interpreting, and in relation to, Acts of Parliament.

3. Section 1 of the Genocide Act 1969, adapted and modified as in Schedule 1 to this Order, and section 4 of, and the Schedule to, that Act shall extend to the territories specified in Schedule 2 to this Order.

W. G. Agnew.

SCHEDULE 1

SECTION 1 OF THE GENOCIDE ACT 1969 AS EXTENDED TO THE TERRITORIES
SPECIFIED IN SCHEDULE 2

1.—(1) A person commits an offence of genocide if he commits any act falling within the definition of "genocide" in Article II of the Genocide Convention as set out in the Schedule to this Act.

(2) A person guilty of an offence of genocide shall on conviction in Seychelles or the Turks and Caicos Islands and on conviction on indictment in Bermuda, the British Virgin Islands or the Falkland Islands and Dependencies—

(a) if the offence consists of the killing of any person, be sentenced to imprisonment for life ;

(b) in any other case, be liable to imprisonment for a term not exceeding fourteen years.

(3) Proceedings for an offence of genocide shall not be instituted in a territory specified in Schedule 2 to the Genocide Act 1969 (Overseas Territories) Order 1970 except by or with the consent of—

(a) in Bermuda, the British Virgin Islands or Seychelles, the person for the time being performing the functions of Attorney-General of the territory concerned;

(a) 1969 c. 12.   (b) 1889 c. 63.

(b) in the Falkland Islands and Dependencies, the officer for the time being administering the Government ;

(c) in the Turks and Caicos Islands, the person for the time being performing the functions of Administrator.

SCHEDULE 2

TERRITORIES TO WHICH PROVISIONS OF THE GENOCIDE ACT 1969 ARE EXTENDED

Bermuda
British Virgin Islands
Falkland Islands and Dependencies
Seychelles
Turks and Caicos Islands.

EXPLANATORY NOTE

(This Note is not part of the Order.)

This Order extends, with adaptations and modifications, certain provisions of the Genocide Act 1969 to the overseas territories specified in Schedule 2. The Genocide Act 1969 gave effect to the Genocide Convention.

STATUTORY INSTRUMENTS

1970 No. 147

FUGITIVE CRIMINAL

The Extradition (Genocide) Order 1970

Made - - - -	*4th February* 1970
Laid before Parliament	*10th February* 1970
Coming into Operation	*30th April* 1970

At the Court at Buckingham Palace, the 4th day of February 1970

Present,

The Queen's Most Excellent Majesty in Council

Whereas a Convention on the Prevention and Punishment of the Crime of Genocide (hereinafter referred to as " the Genocide Convention ") was approved by the General Assembly of the United Nations on 9th December 1948, the terms of which are set out in Schedule 1 to this Order:

And whereas the states mentioned in Schedule 2 to this Order are states with which extradition treaties are in force and which are Contracting Parties to the Genocide Convention:

And whereas the Genocide Act 1969(a) has been enacted to give effect to the Genocide Convention:

And whereas an instrument of accession to the Genocide Convention was deposited on behalf of the United Kingdom of Great Britain and Northern Ireland with the Secretary-General of the United Nations on 30th January 1970 and the Genocide Convention will enter into force for the United Kingdom on 30th April 1970:

And whereas the application of the Genocide Convention is extended by notification in accordance with Article XII of the Convention to the Channel Islands, the Isle of Man and the British possessions mentioned in Schedule 3 to this Order:

Now, therefore, Her Majesty, in exercise of the powers conferred upon Her by section 2 of the Extradition Act 1870(b), is pleased, by and with the advice of Her Privy Council, to order, and it is hereby ordered, as follows:—

1. This Order may be cited as the Extradition (Genocide) Order 1970 and shall come into operation on 30th April 1970.

2. The Interpretation Act 1889(c) shall apply, with the necessary adaptations, for the purpose of interpreting this Order and otherwise in relation thereto as it applies for the purpose of interpreting, and in relation to, Acts of Parliament.

3. The Extradition Acts 1870 to 1935 as amended by the Genocide Act 1969 shall apply in the case of the states mentioned in Schedule 2 to this Order under and in accordance with the extradition treaties therein described as supplemented by the Genocide Convention.

4. The operation of this Order is limited to the United Kingdom, the Channel Islands, the Isle of Man and the British possessions mentioned in Schedule 3 to this Order, being British possessions to which the application of the Genocide Convention is extended.

W. G. Agnew.

(a) 1969 c. 12.   (b) 1870 c. 52.   (c) 1889 c. 63.

SCHEDULE 1

ENGLISH TEXT OF THE GENOCIDE CONVENTION

THE CONTRACTING PARTIES,

HAVING CONSIDERED the declaration made by the General Assembly of the United Nations in its resolution 96 (I) dated 11 December 1946 that genocide is a crime under international law, contrary to the spirit and aims of the United Nations and condemned by the civilized world ;

RECOGNIZING that at all periods of history genocide has inflicted great losses on humanity ; and

BEING CONVINCED that, in order to liberate mankind from such an odious scourge, international co-operation is required,

HEREBY AGREE AS HEREINAFTER PROVIDED:

ARTICLE I

The Contracting Parties confirm that genocide, whether committed in time of peace or in time of war, is a crime under international law which they undertake to prevent and to punish.

ARTICLE II

In the present Convention, genocide means any of the following acts committed with intent to destroy, in whole or in part, a national, ethnical, racial or religious group, as such:

(a) Killing members of the group ;

(b) Causing serious bodily or mental harm to members of the group ;

(c) Deliberately inflicting on the group conditions of life calculated to bring about its physical destruction in whole or in part ;

(d) Imposing measures intended to prevent births within the group ;

(e) Forcibly transferring children of the group to another group.

ARTICLE III

The following acts shall be punishable:

(a) Genocide ;

(b) Conspiracy to commit genocide ;

(c) Direct and public incitement to commit genocide ;

(d) Attempt to commit genocide ;

(e) Complicity in genocide.

ARTICLE IV

Persons committing genocide or any of the other acts enumerated in article III shall be punished, whether they are constitutionally responsible rulers, public officials or private individuals.

ARTICLE V

The Contracting Parties undertake to enact, in accordance with their respective Constitutions, the necessary legislation to give effect to the provisions of the present Convention and, in particular, to provide effective penalties for persons guilty of genocide or of any of the other acts enumerated in article III.

ARTICLE VI

Persons charged with genocide or any of the other acts enumerated in article III shall be tried by a competent tribunal of the State in the territory of which the act was committed, or by such international penal tribunal as may have jurisdiction with respect to those Contracting Parties which shall have accepted its jurisdiction.

ARTICLE VII

Genocide and the other acts enumerated in article III shall not be considered as political crimes for the purpose of extradition.

The Contracting Parties pledge themselves in such cases to grant extradition in accordance with their laws and treaties in force.

ARTICLE VIII

Any Contracting Party may call upon the competent organs of the United Nations to take such action under the Charter of the United Nations as they consider appropriate for the prevention and suppression of acts of genocide or any of the other acts enumerated in article III.

ARTICLE IX

Disputes between the Contracting Parties relating to the interpretation, application or fulfilment of the present Convention, including those relating to the responsibility of a State for genocide or for any of the other acts enumerated in article III, shall be submitted to the International Court of Justice at the request of any of the parties to the dispute.

ARTICLE X

The present Convention, of which the Chinese, English, French, Russian and Spanish texts are equally authentic, shall bear the date of 9 December 1948.

ARTICLE XI

The present Convention shall be open until 31 December 1949 for signature on behalf of any Member of the United Nations and of any non-member State to which an invitation to sign has been addressed by the General Assembly.

The present Convention shall be ratified, and the instruments of ratification shall be deposited with the Secretary-General of the United Nations.

After 1 January 1950 the present Convention may be acceded to on behalf of any Member of the United Nations and of any non-member State which has received an invitation as aforesaid.

Instruments of accession shall be deposited with the Secretary-General of the United Nations.

ARTICLE XII

Any Contracting Party may at any time, by notification addressed to the Secretary-General of the United Nations, extend the application of the present Convention to all or any of the territories for the conduct of whose foreign relations that Contracting Party is responsible.

ARTICLE XIII

On the day when the first twenty instruments of ratification or accession have been deposited, the Secretary-General shall draw up a *procès-verbal* and transmit a copy thereof to each Member of the United Nations and to each of the non-member States contemplated in article XI.

The present Convention shall come into force on the ninetieth day following the date of deposit of the twentieth instrument of ratification or accession.

Any ratification or accession effected subsequent to the latter date shall become effective on the ninetieth day following the deposit of the instrument of ratification or accession.

Article XIV

The present Convention shall remain in effect for a period of ten years as from the date of its coming into force.

It shall thereafter remain in force for successive periods of five years for such Contracting Parties as have not denounced it at least six months before the expiration of the current period.

Denunciation shall be effected by a written notification addressed to the Secretary-General of the United Nations.

Article XV

If, as a result of denunciations, the number of Parties to the present Convention should become less than sixteen, the Convention shall cease to be in force as from the date on which the last of these denunciations shall become effective.

Article XVI

A request for the revision of the present Convention may be made at any time by any Contracting Party by means of a notification in writing addressed to the Secretary-General.

The General Assembly shall decide upon the steps, if any, to be taken in respect of such request.

Article XVII

The Secretary-General of the United Nations shall notify all Members of the United Nations and the non-member States contemplated in article XI of the following:

(a) Signatures, ratifications and accessions received in accordance with article XI;

(b) Notifications received in accordance with article XII;

(c) The date upon which the present Convention comes into force in accordance with article XIII;

(d) Denunciations received in accordance with article XIV;

(e) The abrogation of the Convention in accordance with article XV;

(f) Notifications received in accordance with article XVI.

Article XVIII

The original of the present Convention shall be deposited in the archives of the United Nations.

A certified copy of the Convention shall be transmitted to each Member of the United Nations and to each of the non-member States contemplated in article XI.

Article XIX

The present Convention shall be registered by the Secretary-General of the United Nations on the date of its coming into force.

SCHEDULE 2

STATES WITH WHICH THE UNITED KINGDOM HAS EXTRADITION TREATIES AND
WHICH ARE CONTRACTING PARTIES TO THE GENOCIDE CONVENTION

State	Date of Treaty
Albania	22nd July 1926
Argentina	22nd May 1889
Belgium	29th October 1901/5th March 1907/ 3rd March 1911/8th August 1923/ 2nd July 1928
Chile	26th January 1897
Colombia	27th October 1888
Cuba	3rd October 1904
Czechoslovakia	11th November 1924/4th June 1926
Denmark	31st March 1873/15th October 1935
Ecuador	20th September 1880
El Salvador	23rd June 1881
Finland	30th May 1924
France	14th August 1876/13th February 1896/ 17th October 1908
Federal Republic of Germany	14th May 1872/23rd February 1960
Greece	11th/24th September 1910
Guatemala	4th July 1885/30th May 1914
Haiti	7th December 1874
Hungary	3rd December 1873/ 18th September 1936
Iceland	31st March 1873/25th October 1938
Iraq	2nd May 1932
Israel	4th April 1960
Italy	5th February 1873
Liberia	16th December 1892
Mexico	7th September 1886
Monaco	17th December 1891
Netherlands	26th September 1898
Nicaragua	19th April 1905
Norway	26th June 1873/18th February 1907
Panama	25th August 1906
Peru	26th January 1904
Poland	11th January 1932
Rumania	21st March 1893
Spain	4th June 1878/19th February 1889
Sweden	26th April 1963/6th December 1965/ 6th June 1966
Uruguay	26th March 1884/20th March 1891
Yugoslavia	6th December 1900

SCHEDULE 3

BRITISH POSSESSIONS TO WHICH THE APPLICATION OF THE GENOCIDE CONVENTION
IS EXTENDED

Bahama Islands
Bermuda
British Virgin Islands
Dominica
Falkland Islands and Dependencies
Fiji
Gibraltar
Grenada

Hong Kong
Pitcairn
St. Helena
St. Lucia
St. Vincent
Seychelles
Turks and Caicos Islands

EXPLANATORY NOTE

(*This Note is not part of the Order.*)

This Order applies the Extradition Acts 1870 to 1935 as amended by the Genocide Act 1969 to the offence of genocide in the case of those states with which the United Kingdom has extradition treaties and which are also parties to the Genocide Convention.

STATUTORY INSTRUMENTS

1970 No. 148

FUGITIVE CRIMINAL

The Fugitive Offenders (Genocide) Order 1970

Made - - - -	*4th February* 1970
Laid before Parliament	*10th February* 1970
Coming into Operation	*30th April* 1970

At the Court at Buckingham Palace, the 4th day of February 1970

Present,

The Queen's Most Excellent Majesty in Council

Her Majesty, in exercise of the powers conferred upon Her by section 17 of the Fugitive Offenders Act 1967(a), as extended by section 3(1) of the Genocide Act 1969(b), is pleased, by and with the advice of Her Privy Council, to order, and it is hereby ordered, as follows:—

1. This Order may be cited as the Fugitive Offenders (Genocide) Order 1970 and shall come into operation on 30th April 1970.

2. The Interpretation Act 1889(c) shall apply, with the necessary adaptations, for the purpose of interpreting this Order and otherwise in relation thereto as it applies for the purpose of interpreting, and in relation to, Acts of Parliament.

3.—(1) There shall be deemed to be included among the descriptions of offences set out in Schedule 1 to the Fugitive Offenders Act 1967 as extended to the countries mentioned in the Schedule to this Order any offence of genocide and (so far as not so included by virtue of the foregoing) any attempt or conspiracy to commit such an offence and any direct and public incitement to commit such an offence.

(2) For the purposes of the Fugitive Offenders Act 1967 as extended to any country mentioned in the Schedule to this Order, no offence which, if committed in that country, would be punishable as an offence of genocide or as an attempt, conspiracy or incitement to commit such an offence shall be regarded as an offence of a political character.

(3) It shall not be an objection to any proceedings taken against a person by virtue of the preceding paragraphs of this Article that under the law in force at the time when and in the place where he is alleged to have committed the act of which he is accused or of which he was convicted he could not have been punished therefor.

W. G. Agnew.

(a) 1967 c. 68.　　(b) 1969 c. 12.　　(c) 1889 c. 63.

SCHEDULE

COUNTRIES REFERRED TO IN ARTICLE 3 OF THE ORDER

Bahama Islands
Bermuda
British Virgin Islands
Falkland Islands and Dependencies
Fiji
Gibraltar
Hong Kong
Pitcairn
Seychelles
Turks and Caicos Islands

EXPLANATORY NOTE

(This Note is not part of the Order.)

The Genocide Act 1969 (which gave effect to the Genocide Convention) amends the Fugitive Offenders Act 1967 by adding genocide to the offences for which a person may be returned to a Commonwealth country and by providing that it shall not be treated as an offence of a political character. This Order provides that those amendments shall apply to the 1967 Act as extended to the countries mentioned in the Schedule, being countries to which the Genocide Convention extends.

STATUTORY INSTRUMENTS

1970 No. 149

FUGITIVE CRIMINAL

The Fugitive Offenders (Designated Commonwealth Countries) Order 1970

Made - - -	*4th February* 1970
Laid before Parliament	*10th February* 1970
Coming into Operation	*16th February* 1970

At the Court at Buckingham Palace, the 4th day of February 1970

Present,

The Queen's Most Excellent Majesty in Council

Her Majesty, in exercise of the powers conferred on Her by sections 2(1) and (4) and 20(2) of the Fugitive Offenders Act 1967(a), is pleased, by and with the advice of Her Privy Council, to order, and it is hereby ordered, as follows:—

1. This Order may be cited as the Fugitive Offenders (Designated Commonwealth Countries) Order 1970 and shall come into operation on 16th February 1970.

2. The Cook Islands (being a territory for the external relations of which New Zealand is responsible) are hereby designated for the purposes of section 1 of the Fugitive Offenders Act 1967 as a separate country at the request of the Government of New Zealand.

3. The territory of Papua and New Guinea, Norfolk Island, Australian Antarctic territory, the territory of Cocos (Keeling) Islands, the territory of Christmas Island, the territory of Heard and McDonald Islands and the territory of Ashmore and Cartier Islands (being territories for the external relations of which Australia is responsible) shall be treated as part of Australia for the purposes of the Fugitive Offenders (Designated Commonwealth Countries) Order 1967(b) (which designates certain Commonwealth countries for the purposes of the Fugitive Offenders Act 1967) and the reference to Australia in the Schedule to that Order shall be construed accordingly.

4. Niue and the Tokelau Islands (being territories for the external relations of which New Zealand is responsible) shall be treated as part of New Zealand for the purposes of the Fugitive Offenders (Designated Commonwealth Countries) Order 1967 and the reference to New Zealand in the Schedule to that Order shall be construed accordingly.

W. G. Agnew.

(a) 1967 c. 68.   (b) S.I. 1967/1302 (1967 II, p. 3770).

EXPLANATORY NOTE

(This Note is not part of the Order.)

Section 2(1) of the Fugitive Offenders Act 1967 enables any country within the Commonwealth to be designated by Order in Council for the purposes of the Act (so that the provisions of the Act relating to the return of offenders to the independent Commonwealth countries and not those relating to United Kingdom dependencies will apply). Section 2(4) enables any territory for the external relations of which a Commonwealth country is responsible to be treated as part of that country, or (at the request of that country) as a separate country, for the purposes of such an Order in Council. Australia and New Zealand have already been designated and this Order designates the Cook Islands (for whose external relations New Zealand is responsible) as a separate country and provides that the dependencies set out in Articles 3 and 4 shall be treated as part of Australia or New Zealand, as the case may be.

STATUTORY INSTRUMENTS

1970 No. 150

SOCIAL SECURITY

The Family Allowances and National Insurance (New Zealand) Order 1970

Made - - - - *4th February* 1970

At the Court at Buckingham Palace, the 4th day of February 1970

Present,

The Queen's Most Excellent Majesty in Council

Whereas at Wellington on 19th June 1969 an Agreement between the Government of the United Kingdom of Great Britain and Northern Ireland and the Government of New Zealand on social security (which Agreement is set out in the Schedule hereto) was signed on behalf of those Governments:

And Whereas by Article 36 of the said Agreement it was provided that the Agreement should enter into force on a date to be agreed by Exchange of Letters between the Contracting Parties:

And Whereas by an Exchange of Letters on 11th December 1969 between the Contracting Parties it was agreed that the Agreement should enter into force on 1st January 1970:

And Whereas by section 105(1) of the National Insurance Act 1965(a), as extended by section 22(1) of the Family Allowances Act 1965(b), it is provided that Her Majesty may, by Order in Council, make provision for modifying or adapting the said Acts of 1965 in their application to cases affected by agreements with other governments providing for reciprocity in matters specified in those sections:

Now, therefore, Her Majesty, in pursuance of the said section 105(1), as so extended, and of all other powers enabling Her in that behalf, is pleased, by and with the advice of Her Privy Council, to order, and it is hereby ordered, as follows:—

Citation and interpretation

1.—(1) This Order may be cited as the Family Allowances and National Insurance (New Zealand) Order 1970.

(2) Reference in this Order to any enactment, order or regulations shall include references to such enactment, order or regulations as amended by any subsequent enactment, order or regulations.

(3) The rules for the construction of Acts of Parliament contained in the Interpretation Act 1889(c) shall apply in relation to this Order and in relation to the Regulations and Order revoked by it as if this Order and the Regulations and Order revoked by it were Acts of Parliament, and as if the revocation were a repeal.

(a) 1965 c. 51.   (b) 1965 c. 53.   (c) 1889 c. 63.

Modification of Acts

2.—(1) Subject to the provisions of sub-paragraph (2) of this paragraph, the provisions contained in the Agreement set out in the Schedule to this Order shall have full force and effect, so far as the same relate to England, Wales and Scotland and provide by way of agreement with the Government of New Zealand for reciprocity with the said Government in any matters specified in section 105(1) of the National Insurance Act 1965, as extended by section 22(1) of the Family Allowances Act 1965; and the Family Allowances Acts 1965 to 1969 and the National Insurance Acts 1965 to 1969 shall have effect subject to such modifications as may be required therein for the purpose of giving effect to any such provisions.

(2) Article 36 of the said Agreement shall be construed as if for the words "on a date to be agreed by Exchange of Letters between the Contracting Parties" there were substituted the words "on 1 January 1970".

Revocation of Regulations and Order

3. The Family Allowances (New Zealand Reciprocal Arrangements) Regulations 1948**(a)** and the National Insurance (New Zealand) Order 1956**(b)** are hereby revoked.

W. G. Agnew.

SCHEDULE

AGREEMENT ON SOCIAL SECURITY BETWEEN THE GOVERNMENT OF NEW ZEALAND AND THE GOVERNMENT OF THE UNITED KINGDOM OF GREAT BRITAIN AND NORTHERN IRELAND

THE Government of New Zealand and the Government of the United Kingdom of Great Britain and Northern Ireland,

Having established reciprocity in the field of social security by means of the reciproca arrangements on family benefits which they made in 1948 and the Agreement on Social Security which they made in 1955,

Desiring to extend and modify the scope of that reciprocity and to take account of changes in their legislation,

Have agreed as follows:

PART I—DEFINITIONS AND GENERAL PROVISIONS

Article 1

For the purposes of this Agreement, unless the context otherwise requires—

(a) "age benefit", "invalid's benefit", "mother's allowance", "orphan's benefit" and "superannuation benefit" have the same meaning as in the legislation of New Zealand;

(b) "benefit" means pension, allowance or benefit payable under the legislation of one (or the other) country and includes any increase payable for a dependant;

(c) "child" means, in relation to any person, a child, as defined in the legislation which is being applied, who would be treated under that legislation as being a child of that person or included in his family;

(d) "competent authority" means, in relation to the United Kingdom, the Secretary of State for Social Services, the Ministry of Health and Social Services for Northern Ireland, or the Isle of Man Board of Social Services, as the case may require, and, in relation to New Zealand, the Social Security Commission;

(a) S.I. 1948/2600 (Rev. VII, p. 634: 1948 I, p. 1029).   **(b)** S.I. 1956/88 (1956 I, p. 1671).

(e) "contribution" means a flat-rate contribution;

(f) "country" means, according to the context, the United Kingdom or New Zealand;

(g) "family benefit" means, in relation to the United Kingdom, family allowances payable under the legislation of the United Kingdom and, in relation to New Zealand, family benefit payable under the legislation of New Zealand;

(h) "the former Agreement" means the Agreement on Social Security signed in Wellington on 20 December 1955 on behalf of the Contracting Parties;

(i) "full standard rate", in relation to any benefit payable under the legislation of the United Kingdom, means the rate at which the benefit would be paid to the person concerned, subject to any earnings rule which may be appropriate, if the relevant contribution conditions were fully satisfied in his case;

(j) "guardian's allowance", "retirement pension", "widow's allowance", "widowed mother's allowance" and "widow's basic pension" have the same meaning as in the legislation of the United Kingdom;

(k) "legislation" means, according to the context, the laws, orders and regulations specified in Article 2 which are or have been or may hereafter be in force in any part of one (or the other) country;

(l) "New Zealand" does not include the Cook Islands, Niue or the Tokelau Islands;

(m) "parent" includes a person who is treated as a parent under the legislation which is being applied;

(n) "pension age" means, in relation to any person, the age at which that person is treated as reaching pensionable age under the legislation of the United Kingdom;

(o) "qualified to receive" means entitled to receive subject to any condition about giving notice or making a claim and to any earnings rule, means test or disqualification which may be appropriate;

(p) "the reciprocal arrangements on family benefits" means the reciprocal arrangements on family benefits made in 1948 by the Minister of Social Security in New Zealand with the Minister of National Insurance in Great Britain and the Ministry of Labour and National Insurance for Northern Ireland;

(q) "sickness benefit" and "unemployment benefit", in relation to one (or the other) country, have the same meaning as in the legislation of that country;

(r) "United Kingdom" means England, Scotland, Wales, Northern Ireland and the Isle of Man;

(s) "widow's benefit", in relation to the United Kingdom, means a widow's allowance, widowed mother's allowance or widow's pension, payable under the legislation of that country or a widow's basic pension so payable to a woman who became a widow before 5 July 1948 and, in relation to New Zealand, has the same meaning as in the legislation of that country, and includes a mother's allowance payable under that legislation;

(t) "widow's pension" means widow's pension payable under the legislation of the United Kingdom other than a widow's basic pension.

Article 2

Legislation

(1) The provisions of this Agreement shall apply—

    (a) in relation to the United Kingdom—

        (i) to the National Insurance Act 1965, the National Insurance Act (Northern Ireland) 1966, the National Insurance (Isle of Man) Act 1948 and any enactments repealed or consolidated by, or repealed by enactments consolidated by, those Acts; and

        (ii) to the Family Allowances Act 1965, the Family Allowances Act (Northern Ireland) 1966 and the Family Allowances (Isle of Man) Act, 1946; and

    (b) in relation to New Zealand, to the Social Security Act 1964.

(2) Subject to the provisions of paragraph (3) of this Article, the Agreement shall apply also to any law, order or regulation which carries into effect, amends, supplements or consolidates the legislation specified in paragraph (1) of this Article.

(3) The Agreement shall apply, only if the Contracting Parties so agree, to laws, orders or regulations which amend or supplement the legislation specified in paragraph (1) of this Article for the purpose of giving effect to any reciprocal agreement on social security which one (or the other) Party has made with the government of a third country.

PART II—BENEFIT FOR OLD AGE

UNITED KINGDOM RETIREMENT PENSIONS BY VIRTUE OF RESIDENCE IN NEW ZEALAND

Article 3

(1) Where a person who is in the United Kingdom or resident there claims a retirement pension, the provisions of the following paragraphs of this Article shall apply for the purpose of his claim.

(2) The claimant shall be treated as if he, or, in the case of a claim made ·by a married woman or widow by virtue of her husband's insurance, her husband, had paid contributions under the legislation of the United Kingdom for any period during which he was resident in New Zealand and for any other period (not exceeding thirteen weeks in the case of any one journey) during which he was travelling from either country to the other.

(3) Where the claimant is a married woman claiming by virtue of her own insurance, the provisions of paragraph (2) of this Article shall not apply to her in respect of any period during which she was a married woman unless—

(a) at the time when she was last in New Zealand, she was qualified to receive age benefit or superannuation benefit otherwise than by virtue of this Agreement or the former Agreement and was, or could have been, treated as an unmarried woman for the purpose of that benefit; or

(b) she has paid one hundred and fifty six contributions under the legislation of the United Kingdom (other than contributions which would not be taken into account for the purpose of any claim to receive benefit under that legislation) for any period after her marriage and before the time when she reached pension age.

(4) Where the claimant is a woman claiming by virtue of her own insurance, her marriage having been terminated by the death of her husband or otherwise, and her husband's contributions are taken into account for the purpose of her claim, she shall be treated as if he had paid contributions under the legislation of the United Kingdom for any period during which he was resident in New Zealand and for any other period (not exceeding thirteen weeks in the case of any one journey) during which he was travelling from either country to the other.

(5) Where the claimant is a woman who—

(a) would have been qualified to receive widow's benefit (other than a widow's basic pension) for any period, by virtue of Article 8 of this Agreement, if this Agreement had been in force during that period; or

(b) would have been entitled, under the arrangements made for crediting contributions to widows who claim retirement pensions under the legislation of the United Kingdom, to have contributions credited to her for any period, if this Agreement had been in force during that period;

she shall be treated as if contributions had been credited to her for that period.

(6) Where the claimant was receiving age benefit or superannuation benefit (otherwise than by virtue of this Agreement or the former Agreement) at the time when he was last in New Zealand and was over pension age at that time, he shall be treated as if he satisfied the contribution conditions for a retirement pension at the full standard rate.

Provided that, if the claimant is a married woman who does not satisfy either of the conditions specified in paragraph (3) of this Article, she shall be treated as if her husband and not she satisfied the said contribution conditions.

(7) This Article shall have effect subject to the provisions of Article 26.

Article 4

For the purpose of any claim to receive a retirement pension, a person who is in the United Kingdom or resident there shall be deemed to have retired from regular employment on the date when he reaches pension age if, within four months before that date or at any time thereafter, he has received age benefit or superannuation benefit.

Article 5

For the purpose of those provisions of the legislation of the United Kingdom which concern the payment of contributions for any period after the insured person has reached pension age and the increase of the weekly rate of retirement pension by virtue of those contributions, a person who was resident in New Zealand for any period shall be treated as if he had been insured under that legislation since the beginning of that period.

United Kingdom Retirement Pensions in New Zealand

Article 6

(1) Where a person would be qualified to receive a retirement pension (otherwise than by virtue of Article 3 of this Agreement or Article 3 of the former Agreement) if he were in the United Kingdom, he shall be qualified to receive that pension while he is in New Zealand.

(2) This Article shall have effect subject to the provisions of Article 28.

New Zealand Age Benefit and Superannuation Benefit by Virtue of Residence in the United Kingdom

Article 7

(1) For the purpose of any claim to receive age benefit or superannuation benefit, a person who is permanently resident in New Zealand shall be treated as if he had been resident there during any period during which he was resident in the United Kingdom. Provided that—

    (a) this Article shall not apply, for the purpose of any claim to receive age benefit, to any man who has not reached the age of 65 or to any woman who has not reached the age of 60;

    (b) nothing in this Article shall be construed as meaning that any person who claims age benefit or superannuation benefit by virtue of this Agreement shall be qualified to receive such benefit under the conditions specified in the legislation of New Zealand for persons who were resident in that country on 15 March 1938.

(2) This Article shall have effect subject to the provisions of Articles 29 and 30.

PART III—BENEFIT FOR WIDOWHOOD

United Kingdom Widow's Benefit by Virtue of Residence in New Zealand

Article 8

(1) Where a woman who is in the United Kingdom or resident there claims widow's benefit under the legislation of the United Kingdom, the provisions of the following paragraphs of this Article shall apply for the purpose of her claim.

(2) The claimant shall be treated as if her husband had paid contributions under the legislation of the United Kingdom for any period during which he was resident in New Zealand and for any other period (not exceeding thirteen weeks in the case of any one journey) during which he was travelling from either country to the other.

(3) Where the claimant was receiving widow's benefit under the legislation of New Zealand (otherwise than by virtue of this Agreement or the former Agreement) at the time when she was last in that country, she shall be qualified to receive, under the legislation of the United Kingdom, at the full standard rate—

(a) a widowed mother's allowance, if she has a child in her family, or has residing with her a person under the age of nineteen years and the widow's benefit which she was receiving at the time when she was last in New Zealand included a mother's allowance in respect of that child or person;

(b) a widow's pension or retirement pension, as the case may require, if she is not qualified to receive a widowed mother's allowance but had reached the age of fifty years either before she last left New Zealand or when she ceased to be qualified to receive a widowed mother's allowance.

(4) The claimant shall not be qualified to receive for the same period more than one widow's benefit under the legislation of the United Kingdom.

(5) Any pension or allowance which has been granted to the claimant in respect of the death of her husband under the War Pensions Act 1954 of New Zealand shall be treated as if it were a benefit awarded to her in respect of his death under a Service Pensions Instrument as defined in the National Insurance (Overlapping Benefits) Regulations.

(6) This Article shall have effect subject to the provisions of Article 26.

UNITED KINGDOM WIDOW OR WIDOW'S CHILD IN NEW ZEALAND
Article 9

(1) Where a woman would be qualified to receive widow's benefit under the legislation of the United Kingdom (otherwise than by virtue of Article 8 of this Agreement or Article 7 of the former Agreement) if she were in the United Kingdom, she shall be qualified to receive that benefit while she is in New Zealand.

(2) Where a woman would be qualified to receive a widowed mother's allowance under the legislation of the United Kingdom if her child or a person under the age of nineteen who is residing with her were in the United Kingdom, she shall be qualified to receive that allowance while that child or person is in New Zealand.

(3) This Article shall have effect subject to the provisions of Article 28.

NEW ZEALAND WIDOW'S BENEFIT BY VIRTUE OF RESIDENCE IN THE UNITED KINGDOM
Article 10

(1) For the purpose of any claim to receive widow's benefit under the legislation of New Zealand, a woman who is permanently resident in that country shall be treated as if—

(a) her husband or herself had been ordinarily resident in New Zealand during any period during which he or she, as the case may be, was ordinarily resident in the United Kingdom;

(b) any child whose place of birth is in the United Kingdom had been born in New Zealand; and

(c) her husband had died in New Zealand if he died in the United Kingdom.

(2) This Article shall have effect subject to the provisions of Articles 29 and 30.

PART IV—BENEFIT FOR ORPHANHOOD
UNITED KINGDOM GUARDIAN'S ALLOWANCE BY VIRTUE OF RESIDENCE IN NEW ZEALAND
Article 11

(1) If at any time a parent of a child was resident in New Zealand, then, for the purpose of any claim to receive a guardian's allowance in respect of that child under the legislation of the United Kingdom, the child shall be treated as if that parent had been insured under that legislation.

(2) This Article shall have effect subject to the provisions of Article 26.

NEW ZEALAND ORPHAN'S BENEFIT BY VIRTUE OF RESIDENCE IN THE UNITED KINGDOM

Article 12

For the purpose of any claim to receive orphan's benefit under the legislation of New Zealand in respect of a child who is permanently resident in that country—

(*a*) a child whose place of birth is in the United Kingdom shall be treated as a child born in New Zealand; and

(*b*) any period during which the child's last surviving parent was ordinarily resident in the United Kingdom shall be treated as a period during which that parent was ordinarily resident in New Zealand.

PART V—FAMILY BENEFIT

Article 13

(1) If a person who claims family benefit under the legislation of the United Kingdom or a child for whom family benefit is so claimed is ordinarily resident in the United Kingdom, that person or child shall be treated for the purpose of the claim—

(*a*) as if his place of birth were in the United Kingdom if it is in New Zealand; and

(*b*) as if he had been resident or present in the United Kingdom during any period during which he was respectively resident or present in New Zealand.

(2) This Article shall have effect subject to the provisions of Article 17.

Article 14

(1) The following provisions shall apply only to any child who is ordinarily resident in the United Kingdom and is in New Zealand during any part of a period of absence from the United Kingdom and only in relation to any family benefit which would have been payable for the child under the legislation of the United Kingdom if he had remained in that country—

(*a*) where the period does not exceed six months, benefit shall be payable for the whole period;

(*b*) where the period exceeds six months, benefit may be payable at the discretion of the competent authority of the United Kingdom.

(2) The following provisions shall apply only to any child born to a woman at a time when she is ordinarily resident in the United Kingdom and absent from that country for a period during any part of which she is in New Zealand and only in relation to any family benefit which would have been payable for the child under the legislation of the United Kingdom if the child had been born in that country and had remained there—

(*a*) where the period does not exceed six months, arrears of benefit shall be payable when she returns with the child to the United Kingdom;

(*b*) where the period exceeds six months, arrears of benefit may, at the discretion of the competent authority of the United Kingdom, be payable when she returns with the child to that country.

(3) The provisions of paragraphs (1) and (2) of this Article shall not apply where the benefit is not claimed within six months after the child or the woman, as the case may be, returns to the United Kingdom.

(4) This Article shall have effect subject to the provisions of Article 17.

Article 15

(1) If a person who has been entitled to receive family benefit for a child under the legislation of the United Kingdom is in New Zealand and is not qualified to receive family benefit for that child under the legislation of New Zealand, he shall be treated for the purpose of maintaining entitlement as if he were in the United Kingdom.

(2) The provisions of paragraph (1) of this Article, as well as the provisions of paragraphs (1), (3) and (4) of Article 14, shall apply, subject to the conditions set out in those paragraphs, in any case where a person who has been entitled to receive family benefit under the legislation of the United Kingdom and the child for whom he has been so entitled are both absent from the United Kingdom.

Article 16

(1) For the purpose of any claim to receive family benefit under the legislation of New Zealand for a child who is considered by the competent authority of New Zealand likely to remain in that country for at least three years, that child shall be deemed to have been born in New Zealand if one of the following conditions is satisfied—

(a) the child was born in the United Kingdom;

(b) the mother gave birth to the child while only temporarily absent from the United Kingdom;

(c) the child has at any time resided continuously in the United Kingdom for not less than twelve months.

(2) This Article shall have effect subject to the provisions of Article 17.

Article 17

Subject to the provisions of Article 18, where family benefit has been paid for a child under the legislation of one country for any period, no family benefit shall be paid for that child under the legislation of the other country for that period.

Article 18

Nothing in this Agreement shall be construed as preventing the competent authority of New Zealand from authorising arrears of family benefit in respect of the whole or any part of a period of temporary absence from New Zealand as provided for in the legislation of that country provided that any amount received under the legislation of the United Kingdom during the period of absence shall be deducted from any arrears so authorised.

PART VI—BENEFIT FOR SICKNESS, INVALIDITY AND UNEMPLOYMENT

Article 19

(1) Where a person claims, under the legislation of the United Kingdom, sickness benefit at a time when he is ordinarily gainfully occupied in that country, or would but for his incapacity for work be so occupied, or unemployment benefit at a time when he is ordinarily gainfully occupied under a contract of service in that country, he shall be treated under that legislation—

(a) as if he had paid contributions—

(i) as an employed person for any period during which he was gainfully occupied in New Zealand under a contract of service;

(ii) as a self-employed person for any other period during which he was gainfully occupied in New Zealand; and

(iii) as a non-employed person for any period (not exceeding thirteen weeks in the case of any one journey) during which he was travelling from either country to the other;

(b) as if he had had contributions credited to him—

(i) as an employed person for any period during which he was resident in New Zealand and was unemployed and available for work or was incapable of work at a time when he was ordinarily gainfully occupied under a contract of service; and

(ii) as a self-employed person for any other period during which he was resident in New Zealand and was incapable of work at a time when he was, or would but for his incapacity for work be, ordinarily gainfully occupied; and

(c) as if he had been resident in the United Kingdom during any period during which he was resident in New Zealand.

(2) Nothing in paragraph (1) of this Article shall diminish any right which a person has, apart from this Agreement, to draw sickness benefit or unemployment benefit under the legislation of the United Kingdom.

(3) Where a person was receiving sickness benefit or invalid's benefit under the legislation of New Zealand when he was last in that country and is incapable of work at the time when he arrives in the United Kingdom, he shall be treated under the legislation of the United Kingdom as if, at that time, he satisfied the contribution conditions under which sickness benefit is payable for an indefinite period.

Article 20

(1) Where a person claims sickness benefit under the legislation of New Zealand at a time when he is ordinarily gainfully occupied in that country ,or would but for his incapacity for work be so occupied, or unemployment benefit at a time when he would ordinarily be gainfully occupied in that country, any period during which he was resident in the United Kingdom shall be treated as a period during which he was resident in New Zealand.

(2) Where a person who is permanently resident in New Zealand claims invalid's benefit under the legislation of that country, he shall be treated for the purpose of that claim as if—

(a) he had been resident in New Zealand during any period during which he was resident in the United Kingdom;

(b) any blindness or permanent incapacity for work originating in the United Kingdom had originated in New Zealand.

(3) Nothing in this Article shall be construed as meaning that any person who claims invalid's benefit by virtue of this Agreement shall be qualified to receive that benefit under the conditions specified in the legislation of New Zealand for persons who were resident in that country on 4 September 1936.

PART VII—OTHER PROVISIONS ABOUT BENEFIT

New Zealand Benefit by Virtue of Residence in New Zealand
Article 21

For the purpose of any claim to receive any benefit under the legislation of New Zealand otherwise than by virtue of this Agreement, any period for which the claimant has received age benefit, superannuation benefit, widow's benefit or invalid's benefit under that legislation by virtue of this Agreement or the former Agreement shall be ignored in determining whether he satisfies any condition requiring him to have resided continuously in New Zealand for a prescribed number of years.

Meaning of "Resident in New Zealand"
Article 22

(1) For the purposes of Articles 3, 8, 11, 13 and 19 of this Agreement, a person shall be treated as having been resident in New Zealand during any period of absence from that country if he was employed outside New Zealand during that period and was liable to pay income tax under the legislation of that country for that period on his earnings arising from that employment.

(2) For the purposes of Articles 3, 8 and 11 of this Agreement, no account shall be taken of any period during which a person was resident in New Zealand before he reached the age of 16 or after he reached pension age.

Meaning of "Resident in the United Kingdom"
Article 23

(1) For the purposes of Articles 7, 10, 12 and 20 of this Agreement, a person shall be treated as having been resident in the United Kingdom or ordinarily resident there, as the case may be, during any period of absence from that country for which he, or, if the person is a woman who is or has been married, her husband, has paid contributions voluntarily or compulsorily under the legislation of that country, or for which he had contributions credited to him under that legislation; and any other period during which he was absent from that country in any circumstances may, at the discretion of the competent authority of New Zealand, be treated as if it were a period during which he was absent in similar circumstances from New Zealand.

(2) For the purpose of Article 7 of this Agreement, no account shall be taken of any period during which a person was resident in the United Kingdom before he reached the age of 16.

UNITED KINGDOM BENEFICIARY WITH DEPENDANT IN NEW ZEALAND
Article 24

(1) Where a woman who is qualified to receive a widowed mother's allowance under the legislation of the United Kingdom otherwise than by virtue of Article 8 of this Agreement or Article 7 of the former Agreement would be qualified to receive also an increase of that benefit for an only, elder or eldest child if the child were in the United Kingdom, she shall be qualified to receive that increase while the child is in New Zealand.

(2) Where a person who is qualified to receive any benefit under the legislation of the United Kingdom, otherwise than by virtue of Article 3 or Article 8 of this Agreement or Article 3 or Article 7 of the former Agreement, would be qualified to receive also an increase of that benefit for a dependant if the dependant were in the United Kingdom, he shall be qualified to receive that increase while the dependant is in New Zealand provided that he shall not be qualified to receive any increase of benefit for children who are permanently resident in New Zealand (other than an increase to which paragraph (1) of this Article refers).

ARREARS OF BENEFIT
Article 25

Where any person makes a claim—

(a) for retirement pension, widow's benefit or guardian's allowance under the legislation of the United Kingdom within three months after his last arrival in that country; or

(b) for age benefit, superannuation benefit, widow's benefit, invalid's benefit or orphan's benefit under the legislation of New Zealand within three months after his last arrival in that country;

and shows that, apart from satisfying the condition of making a claim, he was entitled to receive the benefit in question, by virtue of the provisions of this Agreement, for any period between the date of his arrival and the date of his claim, arrears of benefit shall be payable for that period.

ABSENCE FROM THE UNITED KINGDOM
Article 26

(1) A person shall not be qualified, by virtue of the provisions of Articles 3, 8 and 11 of this Agreement, to receive benefit for any period of absence from the United Kingdom, unless he is resident in the United Kingdom and had been so resident before that period began.

(2) A person shall not be qualified, by virtue of the provisions of Article 11 of this Agreement, to receive a guardian's allowance in respect of a child for any period of that child's absence from the United Kingdom, unless the child is resident in the United Kingdom and had been so resident before that period began.

NEW ZEALAND BENEFICIARY TEMPORARILY IN THE UNITED KINGDOM
Article 27

(1) The provisions of this Article shall apply only to any person who is ordinarily resident in New Zealand and absent from New Zealand wholly or mainly for the purpose of a visit to the United Kingdom, and only in relation to any age benefit, superannuation benefit, widow's benefit, invalid's benefit or orphan's benefit which he would have been qualified to receive (otherwise than by virtue of this Agreement or the former Agreement) if he had remained in New Zealand.

(2) Where the period of absence from New Zealand does not exceed one year, the beneficiary shall be qualified to receive arrears of benefit for the whole period of his absence.

(3) Where the period of absence from New Zealand exceeds one year but does not exceed two years, the beneficiary may, at the discretion of the competent authority of New Zealand, be qualified, on his return to New Zealand, to receive arrears of benefit for the first six months of his absence.

(4) For the purpose of determining the sum due to any beneficiary under paragraph (2) or paragraph (3) of this Article, the amount of any retirement pension, widow's benefit, guardian's allowance, sickness benefit or unemployment benefit, which he has received under the legislation of the United Kingdom for the period of his absence from New Zealand shall be disregarded in the computation of his income but shall be deducted from the amount which would otherwise have been payable under that paragraph.

(5) For the purpose of applying the provisions of paragraph (4) of this Article in any case where the beneficiary is a man whose wife is not qualified to receive any age benefit, superannuation benefit or invalid's benefit under the legislation of New Zealand, the amount of any retirement pension, sickness benefit or unemployment benefit which she has received under the legislation of the United Kingdom during the period of his absence from New Zealand shall be treated as if it were such an amount which he had received under that legislation during that period.

Rate of United Kingdom Benefit in New Zealand

Article 28

Where a person, who is not ordinarily resident in the United Kingdom and is in New Zealand, is qualified to receive benefit under the legislation of the United Kingdom, the rate of that benefit shall be determined in accordance with those provisions of that legislation which concern the payment of benefit to persons who are not ordinarily resident in the United Kingdom.

New Zealand Benefit by Virtue of Residence in the United Kingdom

Article 29

None of the provisions of Articles 7, 10 and 20 of this Agreement shall apply to any person who has failed to apply for any benefit which may be payable to him under the legislation of the United Kingdom.

Duplicate Rights in New Zealand

Article 30

(1) For the purpose of any claim to receive benefit under the legislation of New Zealand, whether by virtue of this Agreement or otherwise (other than benefit payable by virtue of Article 27 of this Agreement), the amount of any benefit which the claimant is entitled to receive under the legislation of the United Kingdom shall be disregarded in the computation of his income and shall be deducted from the amount of benefit which would otherwise have been payable to him under the legislation of New Zealand.

Provided that, in the case of a married claimant, the amount to be deducted shall be the aggregate amount of any benefit which the claimant and the claimant's wife or husband are entitled to receive under the legislation of the United Kingdom, or such part of that aggregate amount as may be determined by the competent authority of New Zealand.

(2) For the purpose of applying the provisions of paragraph (1) of this Article to any claim to receive benefit by virtue of this Agreement, the amount of any benefit which the claimant is entitled to receive under the legislation of the United Kingdom shall be deemed to include the amount of any pension which has been required, under the legislation of the United Kingdom, to be assured because the claimant was contracted out of the graduated pension scheme established under that legislation.

Overpayments

Article 31

Where a person has received any sum by way of benefit under the legislation of one country and it is found that he was not entitled to receive that sum but was entitled to receive benefit for the same period under the legislation of the other country, the sum so received shall be treated as having been paid on account of the benefit due under the legislation of the latter country.

PART VIII—ADMINISTRATION

Article 32

The competent authorities—

(*a*) shall make such administrative arrangements as may be required for the purpose of giving effect to the present Agreement and shall determine all matters of an incidental and supplementary nature which in their opinion are relevant for that purpose;

(*b*) shall communicate to each other information regarding any measure taken by them to give effect to the Agreement;

(*c*) shall supply to each other, on request, information regarding the circumstances of any persons who claim benefit in accordance with the provisions of the Agreement or regarding the circumstances of the dependants of such persons; and

(*d*) shall communicate to each other as soon as possible information regarding any changes made in their legislation which affect the application of the Agreement.

Article 33

Where any benefit is payable under the legislation of one country to a person in the other country, the payment may, at the request of the competent authority of the former country, be made by the competent authority of the latter country as agent for the competent authority of the former country.

PART IX—TRANSITIONAL AND FINAL PROVISIONS

Article 34

(1) No provision of this Agreement shall confer any right to receive any benefit for a period before the date of entry into force of the Agreement.

(2) Any contribution which a person has paid or had credited to him under the legislation of the United Kingdom before the date of entry into force of the Agreement and any period during which a person has been resident in either country before that date or gainfully occupied, unemployed or incapable of work before that date, shall be taken into account for the purpose of determining the right to receive any benefit, in accordance with the provisions of the Agreement.

(3) No provision of this Agreement shall diminish any rights which a person has acquired under the legislation of either country before the date of entry into force of this Agreement, whether by virtue of the former Agreement or otherwise.

Article 35

In the event of the termination of this Agreement, any rights acquired by a person in accordance with its provisions shall be maintained, and the Contracting Parties shall negotiate for the settlement of any rights then in course of acquisition by virtue of its provisions.

Article 36

(1) This Agreement shall enter into force on a date to be agreed by Exchange of Letters between the Contracting Parties and shall remain in force for a period of one year from that date. Thereafter it shall continue in force from year to year unless notice of termination is given in writing by either Party at least six months before the expiry of any such yearly period.

(2) Subject to the provisions of Article 34 of this Agreement, the former Agreement and the reciprocal arrangements on family benefits shall be terminated on the date of entry into force of this Agreement.

IN WITNESS WHEREOF the undersigned, being duly authorised thereto by their respective Governments, have signed this Agreement.

DONE at Wellington this 19th day of June 1969.

For the Government of New Zealand:	For the Government of the United Kingdom of Great Britain and Northern Ireland:
D. N. McKay	Ian Maclennan

EXPLANATORY NOTE
(This Note is not part of the Order.)

This Order gives effect in England, Wales and Scotland to the Agreement (set out in the Schedule) made between the Governments of the United Kingdom and of New Zealand in so far as it relates to the matters for which provision is made by the Family Allowances Acts 1965 to 1969 and the National Insurance Acts 1965 to 1969, and provides that the Agreement shall enter into force on 1st January 1970.

STATUTORY INSTRUMENTS

1970 No. 151

ALIENS

The Aliens (Appeals) Order 1970

Made - - - - 4*th February* 1970
Laid before Parliament 10*th February* 1970
Coming into Operation—
Articles 1, 6(2) *and* 12(1) 11*th February* 1970
*Remaining provisions: in accordance with
Article* 1 *of this Order.*

ARRANGEMENT OF ARTICLES

PART I
PRELIMINARY

At the Court at Buckingham Palace, the 4th day of February 1970

Present,

The Queen's Most Excellent Majesty in Council

Her Majesty, in pursuance of section 1 of the Aliens Restriction Act 1914(a), as amended by the Aliens Restriction (Amendment) Act 1919(b), of section 14 of the Immigration Appeals Act 1969(c), and of all other powers enabling Her in that behalf, is pleased, by and with the advice of Her Privy Council, to order, and it is hereby ordered, as follows—

PART I

PRELIMINARY

Citation, meaning of " the principal Order " and commencement

1.—(1) This Order may be cited as the Aliens (Appeals) Order 1970.

(2) In this Order " the principal Order " means the Aliens Order 1953(d) as amended by the Aliens Order 1957(e), the Aliens Order 1960(f), the Aliens Order 1964(g), the Aliens Order 1967(h), the Aliens Order 1968(i) and, except where the context otherwise requires, Part III of this Order.

(3) This Article and Articles 6(2) and 12(1) of this Order shall come into operation on 11th February 1970 ; and the remaining provisions of this Order shall come into operation on such date as the Secretary of State may by order appoint, and different dates may be appointed for different purposes of those provisions.

PART II

APPEALS

Appeal against exclusion from United Kingdom

2.—(1) Subject to the provisions of this Part of this Order, a person may appeal to an adjudicator against—

(*a*) a refusal at an approved port to grant him leave to land ;

(*b*) a prohibition imposed under Article 2(2)(*a*) of the principal Order at an approved port on his landing from a ship ;

(*c*) a refusal of an application for the grant to him of a visa, being an application duly made to a person having authority to grant a visa on behalf of the Government of the United Kingdom ;

(*d*) a refusal by the Secretary of State to revoke an instruction issued by him to immigration officers which names the appellant as a person who is to be refused leave to land.

(2) The adjudicator shall dismiss any appeal under this Article if it appears to him that, at the time of the refusal or prohibition, a deportation order was in force in the case of the appellant.

(3) The Schedule to this Order shall have effect for suspending the enforcement of any such refusal as is mentioned in paragraph (1)(*a*) of this Article while an appeal against it is pending under this Part of this Order.

(a) 1914 c. 12.   (b) 1919 c. 92.   (c) 1969 c. 21.
(d) S.I. 1953/1671 (1953 I, p. 94).
(e) S.I. 1957/597 (1957 I, p. 142).
(f) S.I. 1960/2214 (1960 I, p. 291).
(g) S.I. 1964/2034 (1964 III, p. 5116).
(h) S.I. 1967/1282 (1967 II, p. 3712).
(i) S.I. 1968/1649 (1968 III, p. 4471).

Appeal against landing conditions, etc.

3.—(1) Subject to the provisions of this Part of this Order, a person may appeal to an adjudicator against—

(*a*) the imposition in his case at an approved port of any landing condition limiting the period during which he may remain in the United Kingdom to less than seven days ;

(*b*) the variation by a notice under Article 5(3) of the principal Order of any landing condition which has been imposed in his case ;

(*c*) a refusal to revoke or vary, by such a notice as aforesaid, any landing condition which has been imposed in his case ;

(*d*) the imposition on him by an order under Article 22 of the principal Order of any special restriction (not being a restriction imposed on him as a member of a class) or a refusal to revoke or vary any such restriction ;

(*e*) a refusal in the case of the appellant of permission under paragraph 2 or 3 of Schedule 1 to the principal Order, or a refusal of such permission in the terms applied for, or the imposition of any condition as a term of such permission.

(2) Where an appeal is duly brought under paragraph (1)(*a*), (*c*) or (*e*) of this Article the appellant shall not, so long as the appeal is pending, be required to leave the United Kingdom by reason of any condition limiting the period during which he may remain there or by reason of paragraph 2 of Schedule 1 to the principal Order ; and where an appeal is duly brought under paragraph (1)(*b*) of this Article the variation which is the subject of the appeal shall not take effect so long as the appeal is pending.

(3) In paragraph (1)(*b*) and (*c*) of this Article " landing condition " includes any condition so far as it has effect in the United Kingdom by virtue of Article 6 of the principal Order (conditions imposed in the Channel Islands or Isle of Man).

Appeal against deportation orders

4.—(1) Subject to paragraph (2) of this Article and to the other provisions of this Part of this Order, a person may appeal—

(*a*) to an adjudicator against—

(i) a decision of the Secretary of State to make a deportation order in his case by virtue of paragraph (*c*) of Article 20(2) of the principal Order ;

(ii) a refusal by the Secretary of State to revoke a deportation order made in his case by virtue of paragraph (*a*), (*b*) or (*c*) of the said Article 20(2) ;

(*b*) to the Tribunal, against a decision of the Secretary of State to make a deportation order in his case by virtue of paragraph (*b*) of the said Article 20(2).

(2) A person shall not be entitled to appeal under paragraph (1)(*a*)(ii) of this Article until he has complied with the requirement in the order in question that he should leave the United Kingdom or while he is in breach of the requirement in it that he should remain out of the United Kingdom.

(3) A deportation order shall not be made so long as an appeal may be brought against the decision to make that order and, if such an appeal is duly brought, so long as the appeal is pending.

Appeal against directions for removal from United Kingdom

5.—(1) Subject to paragraph (4) of this Article and to the other provisions of this Part of this Order, a person may appeal to an adjudicator against the giving of directions for his removal from the United Kingdom in any case where the directions are given—

(a) by virtue of Article 9 of the principal Order on the ground that he is to be treated by virtue of that Article as having been refused leave to land in the United Kingdom (alien landing without leave or member of ship's crew failing to leave as required etc.) ; or

(b) by virtue of Article 21 of the principal Order on the ground that he has returned to the United Kingdom in breach of a deportation order.

(2) In any appeal under paragraph (1) of this Article against the giving of any directions, the only question for the determination of the adjudicator shall be whether the facts of the case are such that there was in law power to give the directions on the ground on which they were given or, in the case of an appeal under sub-paragraph (a) of that paragraph, either on that ground or on the ground that a deportation order was in force in the case of the appellant ; and if the adjudicator determines that question in the affirmative he shall dismiss the appeal.

(3) Subject to paragraphs (4) and (5) of this Article and to the other provisions of this Part of this Order, where directions are given for the removal of a person from the United Kingdom he may appeal to an adjudicator on the ground that he ought not to be removed to the country to which he would be removed if the directions were carried out.

(4) A person shall not be entitled to appeal under paragraph (1) or (3) of this Article against directions which are given by virtue of Article 9(1)(b) or (c) of the principal Order in a case where he has landed from the ship in question elsewhere than at an approved port ; and a person shall not be entitled to appeal under paragraph (3) of this Article against directions which are given by virtue of a refusal elsewhere than at an approved port to grant him leave to land.

(5) Where a person appeals against the giving of any directions both under paragraph (1) and under paragraph (3) of this Article the appeals shall be heard together ; and where a person appeals under Article 2(1)(a) or Article 4 of this Order, then, if the Secretary of State or an immigration officer has served on him (whether before or after the appeal is brought) a notice stating that any directions for his removal from the United Kingdom which may be given by virtue of the refusal or deportation order which is the subject of the appeal will be such as to effect his removal to a country, or one of several countries, specified in the notice—

(a) the appellant shall be entitled in that appeal to object that he ought not to be removed to the country, or to any of the countries, specified in the notice ; and

(b) no appeal shall lie under paragraph (3) of this Article against any directions which are subsequently given by virtue of the refusal or deportation order in question if their effect would be his removal to a country to which he has not objected as aforesaid or as respects which his objection has not been sustained.

(6) Where before a person appeals under Article 2(1)(a) of this Order directions have been given for his removal and those directions cease to have effect in consequence of the bringing of the appeal, the appellant

shall be treated as having been served with a notice under paragraph (5) of this Article specifying the country to which he would have been removed if those directions had been carried out.

(7) The Schedule to this Order shall have effect as respects the suspension of any directions while an appeal in respect of them is pending under this Part of this Order.

Further appeal from adjudicator to Tribunal

6.—(1) Subject to paragraph (2) of this Article, any party to an appeal to an adjudicator may, if dissatisfied with his determination thereon, appeal to the Tribunal.

(2) Rules of procedure may provide that, in such cases as may be specified in the rules, an appeal shall lie under this Article only with the leave of the adjudicator or the Tribunal, or only with the leave of the Tribunal ; but—

(*a*) an appeal shall lie under this Article without leave where the adjudicator has allowed an appeal under Article 2(1)(*a*) of this Order and the Secretary of State certifies that he considers it desirable in the public interest that the case should be decided by the Tribunal ; and

(*b*) if leave to appeal under this Article is by virtue of the rules required in a case where the adjudicator has dismissed an appeal under the said Article 2(1)(*a*), the authority having power under the rules to grant leave shall grant it if satisfied that the person who was the appellant before the adjudicator held, at the time of the refusal which is the subject of the appeal, a valid visa for his journey issued to him on behalf of the Government of the United Kingdom.

Determination of appeals

7.—(1) Subject to Articles 2(2) and 5(2) of this Order, an adjudicator who hears an appeal under this Part of this Order—

(*a*) shall allow the appeal if he considers—

   (i) that the decision or action against which the appeal is brought was not in accordance with the law or with any immigration rules applicable to the case ; or

   (ii) where the decision or action involved the exercise of a discretion by the Secretary of State or an officer, that the discretion should have been exercised differently ; and

(*b*) in any other case, shall dismiss the appeal.

(2) For the purposes of paragraph (1)(*a*) of this Article the adjudicator may review any determination of a question of fact on which the decision or action was based ; and for the purposes of paragraph (1)(*a*)(ii) of this Article no decision or action which is in accordance with the immigration rules shall be treated as having involved the exercise of a discretion by the Secretary of State by reason only of the fact that he has been requested by or on behalf of the appellant to depart, or to authorise an officer to depart, from the rules and has refused to do so.

(3) In relation to an appeal which under this Part of this Order is heard at first instance by the Tribunal, the foregoing provisions of this Article shall apply to the Tribunal as they apply to an adjudicator.

(4) On an appeal under this Part of this Order to the Tribunal from the determination of an adjudicator, the Tribunal may affirm the determination

or make any other determination which could have been made by the adjudicator.

(5) Where an adjudicator or the Tribunal allows an appeal, the adjudicator or Tribunal shall give such directions for giving effect to the determination as the adjudicator or Tribunal thinks requisite, and may also make recommendations with respect to any other action which the adjudicator or Tribunal considers should be taken in the case under the principal Order.

(6) Subject to Article 8(2) of this Order, it shall be the duty of the Secretary of State and of any officer to whom directions are given under paragraph (5) of this Article to comply therewith, except that directions given by an adjudicator need not be complied with so long as an appeal can be brought against his determination and, if such an appeal is duly brought, so long as the appeal is pending.

Special procedure in cases involving national security, etc., or forgery of documents

8.—(1) Where a person appeals against any decision or action to an adjudicator, or by virtue of Article 4(1)(b) of this Order to the Tribunal, and it appears to the Secretary of State that the decision or action was taken wholly or mainly in the interests of national security or of the relations between the United Kingdom and any other country or otherwise on grounds of a political nature, the Secretary of State may direct that the appeal—

    (a) if it would otherwise be heard by an adjudicator, shall be referred to and heard by the Tribunal as constituted for the purpose of hearing appeals referred to it under section 9(1) of the Immigration Appeals Act 1969(**a**) ;

    (b) if it comes before the Tribunal by virtue of the said Article 4(1)(b), shall be heard by the Tribunal as so constituted.

(2) Article 7(6) of this Order shall not apply to a case which is dealt with in accordance with directions given under paragraph (1) of this Article.

(3) If—

    (a) in the case of an appeal which is dealt with in accordance with directions given under paragraph (1) of this Article, the Secretary of State certifies that the disclosure to the appellant of any matters relevant to the case would be contrary to the interests of national security ; or

    (b) in the case of any appeal under this Part of this Order in which it is alleged that a passport, visa or employment permit (or any part thereof or entry therein) on which a party relies is a forgery, the adjudicator or Tribunal hearing the appeal determines that the disclosure to that party of any matters relating to the method of detection would be contrary to the public interest,

those matters shall be presented to the adjudicator or Tribunal without being disclosed as aforesaid ; and for the purposes of this paragraph any part of the proceedings may take place in the absence of the appellant or that party, as the case may be, and of his representatives.

Reference of cases for further consideration

9.—(1) Where in any case—

    (a) an appeal to an adjudicator (or an appeal which is heard at first instance by the Tribunal) has been dismissed ; or

_____

(a) 1969 c. 21.

(*b*) the Tribunal has affirmed the determination of an adjudicator dismissing an appeal,

the Secretary of State may at any time refer for consideration under this Article any matter relating to the case which was not before the adjudicator or Tribunal.

(2) Any reference under this Article shall be to an adjudicator or to the Tribunal, and the adjudicator or Tribunal shall consider the matter which is the subject of the reference and report to the Secretary of State the opinion of the adjudicator or Tribunal thereon.

Release of appellants pending hearing

10. Schedule 3 to the Immigration Appeals Act 1969(a) (release of appellants pending appeal) shall apply to any person who has an appeal pending under this Part of this Order and is for the time being detained under Article 8(4), 11 or 21(5) of the principal Order as it applies to any such person as is specified in paragraph 1 of that Schedule ; and in paragraph 5(1)(*b*) of that Schedule the reference to section 7(2)(*a*) of that Act shall include a reference to Article 6(2)(*a*) of this Order.

Members of ships' crews

11.—(1) A person who has appealed under Article 2(1)(*b*) of this Order may be brought ashore under the authority of an immigration officer for the purpose of prosecuting his appeal and may, while on shore for that purpose, be detained under the authority of an immigration officer or constable ; and Article 28 of the principal Order (arrest and detention) shall have effect as if this paragraph were contained in that Order.

(2) If while an appeal under the said Article 2(1)(*b*) is pending the appellant's ship leaves the port in question but the appellant remains on shore with the authority of an immigration officer, the appellant shall thereafter be treated for the purposes of the principal Order as if he had been refused leave to land and the appeal shall thereafter be treated for the purposes of this Order as if it were an appeal under Article 2(1)(*a*) of this Order.

Supplementary provisions

12.—(1) In section 6 of the Immigration Appeals Act 1969(a) (regulations about notices) and section 11 of that Act (rules of procedure) references to Part I of that Act shall include references to this Part of this Order, and in subsection (2) of the said section 11 references to sections 5(3), 5(4), 7 and 9 of that Act shall respectively include references to Articles 5(3), 5(5), 6 and 8 of this Order.

(2) In Schedule 1 to the said Act of 1969, in paragraph 11 the reference to Part I of that Act shall include a reference to this Part of this Order, and in paragraph 12 the reference to section 9 of that Act shall include a reference to Article 8 of this Order.

(3) In paragraph (1) of Article 27 of the principal Order (proof of instruments) the reference to the principal Order shall include a reference to this Part of this Order, and in paragraph (2) of that Article the reference to legal proceedings shall include a reference to proceedings under this Part of this Order.

(a) 1969 c. 21.

Interpretation of Part II

13.—(1) In this Part of this Order—

" adjudicator " and " the Tribunal " mean respectively an adjudicator and the Tribunal appointed for the purposes of Part I of the Immigration Appeals Act 1969(**a**) ;

" employment permit " means a permit of the kind mentioned in Article 4(1)(*b*) of the principal Order ;

" immigration rules " means rules made by the Secretary of State for the administration of—

(*a*) the control of entry into the United Kingdom of aliens ; and

(*b*) the control of aliens after entry,

being rules which have been published and laid before Parliament ;

" rules of procedure " means rules made under section 11 of the said Act of 1969 as applied by this Order ;

and any expression not defined above which is also used in the principal Order has the same meaning as in that Order.

(2) For the purpose of this Order an appeal under this Part of this Order shall be treated as pending during the period beginning when notice of appeal is duly given and ending when the appeal is finally determined or withdrawn ; and, in the case of an appeal to an adjudicator, the appeal shall not be treated as finally determined so long as a further appeal can be brought by virtue of Article 6 of this Order and, if such an appeal is duly brought, until it is determined or withdrawn.

(3) The Interpretation Act 1889(**b**) shall apply for the interpretation of this Part of this Order as it applies for the interpretation of an Act of Parliament.

(4) No provision of this Part of this Order shall be construed as conferring a right of appeal against any decision or action which was taken before the coming into operation of that provision.

PART III

AMENDMENTS OF PRINCIPAL ORDER

Continued application of previous landing conditions to aliens returning after visits abroad

14.—(1) At the beginning of paragraph (4) of Article 5 of the principal Order (which provides that landing conditions imposed in the case of an alien who lands in the United Kingdom shall cease to apply to him if he subsequently enters any country outside the common travel area) there shall be inserted the words " Subject to paragraph (4A) of this Article ".

(2) After the said paragraph (4) there shall be inserted the following paragraph—

" (4A) Paragraph (4) of this Article shall not apply—

(*a*) to any landing conditions imposed under paragraph (1) of this Article if a notice in writing disapplying the said paragraph (4) is given to the alien by the immigration officer at the time when the conditions are imposed ; or

---

(a) 1969 c. 21.   (b) 1889 c. 63.

(*b*) to any landing conditions varied under paragraph (3) of this Article if such a notice as aforesaid is given to the alien by the Secretary of State at the time when the conditions are varied ;

but the giving of such a notice as aforesaid shall not be construed as entitling the alien to leave to land on his seeking to re-enter the United Kingdom, and any landing conditions subject to which leave to land is then granted shall (so far as inconsistent) prevail over the conditions to which the notice relates."

(3) In paragraph (5) of the said Article 5 for the words " by paragraph (4) of this Article " there shall be substituted the words " by paragraphs (4) and (4A) of this Article ", for the words " any such landing conditions as aforesaid " there shall be substituted the words " any landing conditions imposed by virtue of this Article " and for the words " the said paragraph (4) " there shall be substituted the words " the said paragraph (4) or (4A) ".

Detention of aliens for examination

15. In paragraph (3) of Article 7 of the principal Order (which provides, among other things, for the detention of an alien pending and during his examination under that Article) for the words " pending and during the examination " there shall be substituted the words " until the examination is completed ".

Removal of aliens refused leave to land

16.—(1) In paragraph (1) of Article 8 of the principal Order (which enables directions to be given for the removal from the United Kingdom of an alien who is refused leave to land) for paragraphs (i) and (ii) of sub-paragraph (*c*) (which specify the countries to which an alien may be removed under that sub-paragraph) there shall be substituted the following paragraphs—

" (i) a country of which the alien is a national ; or

(ii) a country in which he has obtained a passport or other document of identity ; or

(iii) a country in which he embarked for the United Kingdom ; or

(iv) a country to which there is reason to believe that the alien will be admitted ".

(2) In paragraph (2) of the said Article 8 (which precludes the giving of directions under that Article after the expiration of two months from the date on which the alien arrived) for the words " under this Article " there shall be substituted the words " under paragraph (1) of this Article ".

(3) After the said paragraph (2) there shall be inserted the following paragraph—

" (2A) If it appears to the Secretary of State—

(*a*) that in the circumstances it is not practicable for directions to be given under paragraph (1) of this Article in respect of an alien ; or

(*b*) that directions so given would be ineffective ; or

(*c*) that directions can no longer be so given because of paragraph (2) of this Article,

the Secretary of State, or any person acting under his authority, may give to the owners or agents of any ship or aircraft the like directions as could be, or could have been, given under paragraph (1)(c) of this Article to the owners or agents of the ship or aircraft in which the alien arrived in the United Kingdom ; but in any such case the costs of complying with the directions shall be defrayed by the Secretary of State."

(4) In paragraphs (3) and (4) of the said Article 8 (supplementary provisions as to directions under paragraph (1) of that Article) for the words " under paragraph (1) of this Article " there shall be substituted the words " under this Article ".

Deportation for breach of landing conditions, etc.

17.—(1) In paragraph (2) of Article 20 of the principal Order (which specifies the circumstances in which a deportation order may be made in the case of an alien) after sub-paragraph (b) there shall be inserted the words " or

(c) if the Secretary of State is satisfied that the alien has failed to comply with a landing condition or with any requirement which applies to him by virtue of the First Schedule to this Order."

(2) In paragraph (3) of the said Article 20 for the words " paragraph (2)(b) " there shall be substituted the words " paragraph (2)(b) or (c) ".

Detention on notification of decision to make deportation order

18. After paragraph (4) of Article 21 of the principal Order (under which an alien is liable to be detained if a deportation order has been made in his case or if a recommendation for his deportation is in force) there shall be added the following paragraph—

" (5) An alien who—

(a) in accordance with regulations under section 6 of the Immigration Appeals Act 1969 as applied by Part II of the Aliens (Appeals) Order 1970, has been given notice of a decision to make a deportation order in his case under Article 20(2)(b) or (c) of this Order ; and

(b) is neither detained in pursuance of the sentence or order of any court nor for the time being released on bail by any court having power so to release him,

may be detained under the authority of the Secretary of State until the deportation order is made or, by reason of the final determination of an appeal under Part II of the Aliens (Appeals) Order 1970 in favour of the alien, cannot be made."

Enforcement of deportation orders

19. At the end of Article 21 of the principal Order, as amended by Article 18 of this Order, there shall be added the following paragraph—

" (6) It is hereby declared that the powers conferred by this Article in respect of an alien in whose case a deportation order has been made continue to be exercisable so long as the order remains in force and, in particular, can be exercised in respect of an alien who has returned to the United Kingdom in breach of a deportation order whether or not he was granted leave to land on the occasion when he returned."

Power of entry to effect arrest

20.—(1) After paragraph (1) of Article 28 of the principal Order (under which a person liable to be detained under the Order may be arrested without warrant by an immigration officer or a constable) there shall be inserted the following paragraph—

"(1A) If a justice of the peace is satisfied by written information substantiated on oath that there is reasonable ground for suspecting that a person who is liable to be arrested under this Article is to be found on any premises, he may grant a warrant authorising any constable acting for the police area in which the premises are situated, at any time or times within one month from the date of the warrant, to enter, if need be by force, the premises named in the warrant for the purpose of searching for and arresting that person."

(2) In Article 32 of the principal Order (application to Scotland) after paragraph (*a*) there shall be inserted the following paragraph—

"(*aa*) in paragraph (1A) of Article 28—

(i) for the reference to a justice of the peace there shall be substituted a reference to a sheriff, or a magistrate or justice of the peace, having jurisdiction in the place where the premises are situated ;

(ii) for the reference to written information substantiated on oath there shall be substituted a reference to evidence on oath."

(3) In Article 33 of the principal Order (application to Northern Ireland) after paragraph (*d*) there shall be inserted the following paragraph—

"(*dd*) in paragraph (1A) of Article 28 the words 'acting for the police area in which the premises are situated' shall be omitted."

W. G. Agnew.

SCHEDULE

Articles 2 and 5.

SUSPENSION OF DIRECTIONS FOR REMOVAL PENDING APPEAL

Directions following a refusal of leave to land which is under appeal

1. Subject to the provisions of this Schedule, where an appeal is duly brought under Article 2(1)(*a*) of this Order—

(*a*) no directions for the removal of the appellant from the United Kingdom shall, so long as the appeal is pending, be given by virtue of the refusal which is the subject of the appeal ; and

(*b*) except so far as already carried out, any directions which have been so given before the appeal was brought shall cease to have effect.

Directions which are under appeal

2. Subject to the provisions of this Schedule, where an appeal is duly brought under Article 5 of this Order against the giving of any directions, those directions, except so far as already carried out, shall be of no effect so long as the appeal is pending.

Members of ship's crews and stowaways

3. The foregoing provisions of this Schedule shall not prevent—

(*a*) the giving of directions for the removal of an appellant who has arrived in the United Kingdom as a member of the crew of a ship or as a stowaway ; or

(*b*) the continuance in force of directions for the removal of any such person which have already been given.

Removal where adjudicator dismisses appeal

4.—(1) Where an appeal under Article 2(1)(*a*) or 5 of this Order has been dismissed by an adjudicator, then, unless forthwith after the appeal has been dismissed—

(*a*) the appellant duly gives notice of appeal against the determination of the adjudicator ; or

(*b*) in a case in which leave to appeal against that determination is required and the adjudicator has power to grant leave, the appellant duly applies for and obtains the leave of the adjudicator,

paragraph 1 of this Schedule shall not prevent the giving of directions for the removal of the appellant, and for the purposes of paragraph 2 of this Schedule the appeal shall be treated as if it were no longer pending.

(2) Where a person who has been removed from the United Kingdom under directions given or in force by virtue of sub-paragraph (1) of this paragraph subsequently appeals successfully to the Tribunal against the determination of the adjudicator, the Tribunal may order the Secretary of State to pay to that person such sum as the Tribunal may direct in respect of any expenses incurred by that person in consequence of his having been removed as aforesaid.

Detention

5. The foregoing provisions of this Schedule shall not affect the powers of detention conferred by Article 8(4) or 11 of the principal Order except that a person shall not be detained on board a ship or aircraft so as to compel him to leave the United Kingdom in it at a time when by virtue of those provisions no directions for his removal can be given or any such directions have ceased to have effect or are for the time being of no effect.

Time limit for giving of directions

6. In calculating the period of two months referred to in paragraph (2) of Article 8 of the principal Order (being the time limit for giving directions for the removal of a person from the United Kingdom under paragraph (1) of that Article) there shall be disregarded, in the case of a person who duly brings an appeal under Part II of this Order, the period during which the appeal is pending.

EXPLANATORY NOTE

(*This Note is not part of the Order.*)

Part II of this Order provides for appeals against decisions taken in respect of the immigration and deportation of aliens on the general lines of Part I of the Immigration Appeals Act 1969 in respect of Commonwealth citizens.

Part III makes the following miscellaneous amendments to the Aliens Order 1953 : —

(*a*) Under Article 5(4) of the 1953 Order landing conditions imposed on an alien cease to apply where he goes abroad. Article 14 of the present Order provides that they will continue to apply if notice is given to him at the time of imposition.

(*b*) Article 7 of the 1953 Order provides that an alien seeking to land may be detained pending and during his examination. Article 15 of the present Order makes it clear that detention may continue during any interruptions of the examination.

(*c*) Article 16 of the present Order provides that the countries to which an alien refused leave to land may be removed under Article 8 of the 1953 Order shall include any country in which he has obtained a passport or other document of identity, and that in certain circumstances the owners of a ship or aircraft other than that in which he arrived may be directed to remove him.

(*d*) Article 17 of the present Order makes failure to comply with a landing condition an additional ground for deportation.

(*e*) Article 18 of the present Order provides that an alien given notice of an intention to make a deportation order may be detained pending the making of the order or any appeal against it.

(*f*) Article 19 of the present Order makes it clear that the powers of detention and removal for the purpose of deportation apply to an alien who has returned to the United Kingdom in breach of a deportation order.

(*g*) Article 20 of the present Order enables a search warrant to be issued in respect of a person liable to arrest under the 1953 Order.

The substantive provisions of this Order will come into operation on dates to be appointed by the Secretary of State.

STATUTORY INSTRUMENTS

1970 No. 153

INCOME TAX

The Double Taxation Relief (Taxes on Income) (Finland) Order 1970

Laid before the House of Commons in draft

Made - - - *4th February* 1970

At the Court at Buckingham Palace, the 4th day of February 1970

Present,

The Queen's Most Excellent Majesty in Council

Whereas a draft of this Order was laid before the Commons House of Parliament in accordance with the provisions of section 347(6) of the Income Tax Act 1952(**a**), and an Address has been presented to Her Majesty by that House praying that an Order may be made in the terms of this Order :

Now, therefore, Her Majesty, in exercise of the powers conferred upon Her by section 347(1) of the said Income Tax Act 1952, as amended by section 39 and section 64 of the Finance Act 1965(**b**), and of all other powers enabling Her in that behalf, is pleased, by and with the advice of Her Privy Council, to order, and it is hereby ordered, as follows :—

1. This Order may be cited as the Double Taxation Relief (Taxes on Income) (Finland) Order 1970.

2. It is hereby declared—

    (*a*) that the arrangements specified in the Convention set out in the Schedule to this Order have been made with the Government of the Republic of Finland with a view to affording relief from double taxation in relation to income tax, corporation tax or capital gains tax and taxes of a similar character imposed by the laws of Finland ; and

    (*b*) that it is expedient that those arrangements should have effect.

W. G. Agnew.

(a) 15 & 16 Geo. 6 & 1 Eliz. 2. c. 10.   (b) 1965 c. 25.

SCHEDULE

CONVENTION BETWEEN THE GOVERNMENT OF THE UNITED KINGDOM OF GREAT BRITAIN AND NORTHERN IRELAND AND THE GOVERNMENT OF THE REPUBLIC OF FINLAND FOR THE AVOIDANCE OF DOUBLE TAXATION AND THE PREVENTION OF FISCAL EVASION WITH RESPECT TO TAXES ON INCOME AND CAPITAL

The Government of the United Kingdom of Great Britain and Northern Ireland and the Government of the Republic of Finland;

Desiring to conclude a new Convention for the avoidance of double taxation and the prevention of fiscal evasion with respect to taxes on income and capital;

Have agreed as follows:—

ARTICLE 1

Personal scope

This Convention shall apply to persons who are residents of one or both of the Contracting States.

ARTICLE 2

Taxes covered

(1) The taxes which are the subject of this Convention are:

(*a*) in the United Kingdom of Great Britain and Northern Ireland:
   (i) the income tax (including surtax);
   (ii) the corporation tax; and
   (iii) the capital gains tax;

(*b*) in Finland:
   (i) the State income and capital tax;
   (ii) the communal tax;
   (iii) the church tax; and
   (iv) the sailors' tax.

(2) This Convention shall also apply to any identical or substantially similar taxes which are imposed in either Contracting State after the date of signature of this Convention in addition to, or in place of, the existing taxes. The competent authorities of the Contracting States shall notify to each other any changes which are made in their respective taxation laws.

ARTICLE 3

General definitions

(1) In this Convention, unless the context otherwise requires:

(*a*) the term "United Kingdom" means Great Britain and Northern Ireland, including any area outside the territorial sea of the United Kingdom which in accordance with international law has been or may hereafter be designated, under the laws of the United Kingdom concerning the Continental Shelf, as an area within which the rights of the United Kingdom with respect to the sea bed and sub-soil and their natural resources may be exercised;

(*b*) the term "Finland" means the Republic of Finland, including any area outside the territorial sea of Finland within which in accordance with international law and under the laws of Finland concerning the Continental Shelf the rights of Finland with respect to the sea bed and sub-soil and their natural resources may be exercised;

(*c*) the term "nationals" means:

   (i) in relation to the United Kingdom, all citizens of the United Kingdom and Colonies who derive their status as such from their connection with the United Kingdom and all legal persons, partnerships and associations deriving their status as such from the law in force in the United Kingdom;

   (ii) in relation to Finland, all individuals possessing the nationality of Finland and all legal persons, partnerships, associations and other entities deriving their status as such from the law in force in Finland;

(d) the term "United Kingdom tax" means tax imposed in the United Kingdom being tax to which this Convention applies by virtue of the provisions of Article 2; the term "Finnish tax" means tax imposed in Finland being tax to which this Convention applies by virtue of the provisions of Article 2;

(e) the term "tax" means United Kingdom tax or Finnish tax, as the context requires;

(f) the terms "a Contracting State" and "the other Contracting State" mean the United Kingdom or Finland, as the context requires;

(g) the term "person" comprises an individual, a company and any other body of persons;

(h) the term "company" means any body corporate or any entity which is treated as a body corporate for tax purposes;

(i) the terms "enterprise of a Contracting State" and "enterprise of the other Contracting State" mean respectively an enterprise carried on by a resident of a Contracting State and an enterprise carried on by a resident of the other Contracting State;

(j) the term "competent authority" means, in the case of the United Kingdom, the Commissioners of Inland Revenue or their authorised representative, and in the case of Finland, the Ministry of Finance or its authorised representative.

(2) As regards the application of this Convention by a Contracting State any term not otherwise defined shall, unless the context otherwise requires, have the meaning which it has under the laws of that Contracting State relating to the taxes which are the subject of this Convention.

ARTICLE 4
Fiscal domicile

(1) For the purposes of this Convention, the term "resident of a Contracting State" means, subject to the provisions of paragraphs (2) and (3) of this Article, any person who, under the law of that State, is liable to taxation therein by reason of his domicile, residence, place of management or any other criterion of a similar nature; the term does not include any individual who is liable to tax in that Contracting State only if he derives income from sources therein. The terms "resident of the United Kingdom" and "resident of Finland" shall be construed accordingly.

(2) Where by reason of the provisions of paragraph (1) of this Article an individual is a resident of both Contracting States, then his status shall be determined in accordance with the following rules:

(a) he shall be deemed to be a resident of the Contracting State in which he has a permanent home available to him. If he has a permanent home available to him in both Contracting States, he shall be deemed to be a resident of the Contracting State with which his personal and economic relations are closest (centre of vital interests);

(b) if the Contracting State in which he has his centre of vital interests cannot be determined, or if he has not a permanent home available to him in either Contracting State, he shall be deemed to be a resident of the Contracting State in which he has an habitual abode;

(c) if he has an habitual abode in both Contracting States or in neither of them, he shall be deemed to be a resident of the Contracting State of which he is a national;

(d) if he is a national of both Contracting States or of neither of them, the competent authorities of the Contracting States shall settle the question by mutual agreement.

(3) Where by reason of the provisions of paragraph (1) of this Article a person other than an individual is a resident of both Contracting States, then it shall be deemed to be a resident of the Contracting State in which its place of effective management is situated.

ARTICLE 5

Permanent establishment

(1) For the purposes of this Convention, the term "permanent establishment" means a fixed place of business in which the business of the enterprise is wholly or partly carried on.

(2) The term "permanent establishment" shall include especially:

(*a*) a place of management;

(*b*) a branch;

(*c*) an office;

(*d*) a factory;

(*e*) a workshop;

(*f*) a mine, quarry or other place of extraction of natural resources;

(*g*) a building site or construction or assembly project which exists for more than twelve months.

(3) The term "permanent establishment" shall not be deemed to include:

(*a*) the use of facilities solely for the purpose of storage, display or delivery of goods or merchandise belonging to the enterprise;

(*b*) the maintenance of a stock of goods or merchandise belonging to the enterprise solely for the purpose of storage, display or delivery;

(*c*) the maintenance of a stock of goods or merchandise belonging to the enterprise solely for the purpose of processing by another enterprise;

(*d*) the maintenance of a fixed place of business solely for the purpose of purchasing goods or merchandise, or for collecting information, for the enterprise;

(*e*) the maintenance of a fixed place of business solely for the purpose of advertising, for the supply of information, for scientific research or for similar activities which have a preparatory or auxiliary character, for the enterprise.

(4) An enterprise of a Contracting State shall be deemed to have a permanent establishment in the other Contracting State if it carries on the activity of providing the services within that other Contracting State of public entertainers or athletes referred to in Article 18.

(5) A person acting in a Contracting State on behalf of an enterprise of the other Contracting State—other than an agent of an independent status to whom the provisions of paragraph (6) of this Article apply—shall be deemed to be a permanent establishment in the first-mentioned State if he has, and habitually exercises in that State, an authority to conclude contracts in the name of the enterprise, unless his activities are limited to the purchase of goods or merchandise for the enterprise.

(6) An enterprise of a Contracting State shall not be deemed to have a permanent establishment in the other Contracting State merely because it carries on business in that other State through a broker, general commission agent or any other agent of an independent status, where such persons are acting in the ordinary course of their business.

(7) The fact that a company which is a resident of a Contracting State controls or is controlled by a company which is a resident of the other Contracting State, or which carries on business in that other State (whether through a permanent establishment or otherwise), shall not of itself constitute either company a permanent establishment of the other.

ARTICLE 6

Limitation of relief

Where under any provision of this Convention income is relieved from ı ˙ nish tax and, under the law in force in the United Kingdom, an individual in respect of the said income is subject to tax by reference to the amount thereof which is remitted to or received in the United Kingdom and not by reference to the full amount thereof, then the relief to be allowed under this Convention in Finland shall apply only to so much of the income as is remitted to or received in the United Kingdom.

ARTICLE 7

Income from immovable property

(1) Income from immovable property may be taxed in the Contracting State in which such property is situated.

(2) (a) The term "immovable property" shall, subject to the provisions of sub-paragraph (b) below, be defined in accordance with the law of the Contracting State in which the property in question is situated.

(b) The term "immovable property" shall in any case include property accessory to immovable property, livestock and equipment used in agriculture and forestry, rights to which the provisions of general law respecting landed property apply, usufruct of immovable property and rights to variable or fixed payments as consideration for the working of, or the right to work, mineral deposits, sources and other natural resources; ships, boats and aircraft shall not be regarded as immovable property.

(3) The provisions of paragraph (1) of this Article shall apply to income derived from the direct use, letting, or use in any other form of immovable property. They shall also apply to income derived as consideration for the occupation of or the right to occupy immovable property.

(4) The provisions of paragraphs (1) and (3) of this Article shall also apply to the income from immovable property of an enterprise and to income from immovable property used for the performance of professional services.

ARTICLE 8

Business profits

(1) The profits of an enterprise of a Contracting State shall be taxable only in that State unless the enterprise carries on business in the other Contracting State through a permanent establishment situated therein. If the enterprise carries on business as aforesaid, the profits of the enterprise may be taxed in the other State but only so much of them as is attributable to that permanent establishment.

(2) Where an enterprise of a Contracting State carries on business in the other Contracting State through a permanent establishment situated therein, there shall in each Contracting State be attributed to that permanent establishment the profits which it might be expected to make if it were a distinct and separate enterprise engaged in the same or similar activities under the same or similar conditions and dealing at arm's length with the enterprise of which it is a permanent establishment.

(3) In the determination of the profits of a permanent establishment, there shall be allowed as deductions expenses of the enterprise (other than expenses which would not be deductible if the permanent establishment were a separate enterprise) which are incurred for the purposes of the permanent establishment, including executive and general administration expenses so incurred, whether in the State in which the permanent establishment is situated or elsewhere.

(4) In so far as it has been customary in a Contracting State, according to its law, to determine the profits to be attributed to a permanent establishment on the basis of an apportionment of the total income of the enterprise to its various parts, nothing in paragraph (2) of this Article shall preclude that Contracting State from determining the profits to be taxed by such an apportionment as may be customary; the method of apportionment adopted shall, however, be such that the result shall be in accordance with the principles of this Article.

(5) No profits shall be attributed to a permanent establishment by reason of the mere purchase by that permanent establishment of goods or merchandise for the enterprise.

(6) For the purposes of the preceding paragraphs, the profits to be attributed to the permanent establishment shall be determined by the same method year by year unless there is good and sufficient reason to the contrary.

(7) Where profits include items which are dealt with separately in other Articles of this Convention, then the provisions of those Articles shall not be affected by the provisions of this Article.

ARTICLE 9

Shipping and air transport

A resident of a Contracting State shall be taxable only in that Contracting State on profits from the operation of ships or aircraft other than profits from voyages of ships or aircraft confined solely to places in the other Contracting State.

ARTICLE 10

Associated enterprises

Where

    (a) an enterprise of a Contracting State participates directly or indirectly in the management, control or capital of an enterprise of the other Contracting State; or

    (b) the same persons participate directly or indirectly in the management, control or capital of an enterprise of a Contracting State and an enterprise of the other Contracting State;

and in either case conditions are made or imposed between the two enterprises in their commercial or financial relations which differ from those which would be made between independent enterprises, then any profits which would, but for those conditions, have accrued to one of the enterprises, but, by reason of those conditions, have not so accrued, may be included in the profits of that enterprise and taxed accordingly.

ARTICLE 11

Dividends

(1) Dividends paid by a company being a resident of a Contracting State which are beneficially owned by a resident of the other Contracting State may be taxed in that other State.

(2) However, such dividends may also be taxed in the Contracting State of which the company paying the dividends is a resident, and according to the law of that State, but the tax so charged shall not exceed:

    (a) 5 per cent of the gross amount of the dividends if the beneficial owner is a company (excluding a partnership) which controls directly or indirectly at least 25 per cent of the voting power of the company paying the dividends;

    (b) in all other cases, 15 per cent of the gross amount of the dividends.

This paragraph shall not affect the taxation of the company in respect of the profits out of which the dividends are paid.

(3) The term "dividends" as used in this Article means income from shares or other rights, not being debt-claims, participating in profits, as well as income from other corporate rights assimilated to income from shares by the taxation law of the State of which the company making the distribution is a resident and also includes any other item (other than interest or royalties relieved from tax under the provisions of Article 12 or Article 13 of this Convention) which, under the law of the Contracting State of which the company paying the dividend is a resident, is treated as a dividend or distribution of a company.

(4) The provisions of paragraphs (1) and (2) of this Article shall not apply if the beneficial owner of the dividends, being a resident of a Contracting State, has in the other Contracting State, of which the Company paying the dividends is a resident, a permanent establishment and the holding by virtue of which the dividends are paid is effectively connected with a business carried on through that permanent establishment. In such a case, the provisions of Article 8 shall apply.

(5) If the beneficial owner of a dividend being a resident of a Contracting State owns 10 per cent or more of the class of shares in respect of which the dividend is paid then the relief from tax provided for in paragraph (2) of this Article shall not apply to the dividend to the extent that it can have been paid only out of profits which the company paying the dividend earned or other income which it received in a period ending twelve months or more before the relevant date. For the purposes of this paragraph the term "relevant date" means the date on which the beneficial owner of the dividend became the owner of 10 per cent or more of the class of shares in question.

Provided that this paragraph shall not apply if the beneficial owner of the dividend shows that the shares were acquired for bona fide commercial reasons and not primarily for the purpose of securing the benefit of this Article.

(6) Where a company which is a resident of a Contracting State derives profits or income from the other Contracting State, that other State may not impose any tax on the dividends paid by the company and beneficially owned by persons who are not residents of that other State, or subject the company's undistributed profits to a tax on undistributed profits, even if the dividends paid or the undistributed profits consist wholly or partly of profits or income arising in that other State.

ARTICLE 12

Interest

(1) Interest derived and beneficially owned by a resident of a Contracting State shall be taxable only in that State.

(2) The term "interest" as used in this Article means income from Government securities, bonds or debentures, whether or not secured by mortgage and whether or not carrying a right to participate in profits, and other debt-claims of every kind as well as all other income assimilated to income from money lent by the taxation law of the State in which the income arises.

(3) The provisions of paragraph (1) of this Article shall not apply if the beneficial owner of the interest, being a resident of a Contracting State, has in the other Contracting State a permanent establishment and the debt-claim from which the interest arises is effectively connected with a business carried on through that permanent establishment. In such a case, the provisions of Article 8 shall apply.

(4) Without prejudice to the provisions of paragraph (6) of this Article, any provision of the law of one of the Contracting States which, with or without any further requirement, relates only to interest paid to a non-resident company, or which relates only to interest payments between inter-connected companies with or without any further requirement, shall not operate so as to require such interest paid to a company which is a resident of the other Contracting State to be left out of account as a deduction in computing the taxable profits of the company paying the interest.

(5) The exemption from tax provided for in paragraph (1) of this Article shall not apply to interest on any form of debt-claim dealt in on a stock exchange where the beneficial owner of the interest:

(a) does not bear tax in respect thereof in the Contracting State of which it is a resident; and

(b) sells (or makes a contract to sell) the debt-claim from which such interest is derived within three months of the date on which such beneficial owner acquired such debt-claim.

(6) Where, owing to a special relationship between the payer and the beneficial owner or between both of them and some other person, the amount of the interest paid, having regard to the debt-claim for which it is paid, exceeds the amount which would have been agreed upon by the payer and the beneficial owner in the absence of such relationship, the provisions of this Article shall apply only to the last-mentioned amount. In that case, the excess part of the payments shall remain taxable according to the law of each Contracting State, due regard being had to the other provisions of this Convention.

(7) The provisions of this Article shall not apply if the debt-claim in respect of which the interest is paid was created or assigned mainly for the purpose of taking advantage of this Article and not for bona fide commercial reasons.

ARTICLE 13

Royalties

(1) Royalties derived and beneficially owned by a resident of a Contracting State shall be taxable only in that State.

(2) The term "royalties" as used in this Article means payments of any kind received as a consideration for the use of, or the right to use, any copyright of literary, artistic or scientific work (including cinematograph films, and films or tapes for radio or television broadcasting), any patent, trade mark, design or model, plan, secret formula or process, or for the use of, or the right to use, industrial, commercial or scientific equipment, or for information concerning industrial, commercial or scientific experience.

(3) The provisions of paragraph (1) of this Article shall not apply if the beneficial owner of the royalties, being a resident of a Contracting State, has in the other Contracting State a permanent establishment and the right or property giving rise to the royalties is effectively connected with a business carried on through that permanent establishment. In such a case, the provisions of Article 8 shall apply.

(4) Without prejudice to the provisions of paragraph (5) of this Article, any provision of the law of a Contracting State which requires royalties paid by a company to be left out of account as a deduction in computing the company's taxable profits as being a distribution shall not operate in relation to royalties paid to a resident of the other Contracting State. The preceding sentence shall not however apply to royalties derived and beneficially owned by a company which is a resident of that other Contracting State where:

  (a) the same persons participate directly or indirectly in the management or control of the company paying the royalties and the company beneficially owning the royalties; and

  (b) more than 50 per cent of the voting power in the company beneficially owning the royalties is controlled directly or indirectly by a person or persons resident in the Contracting State in which the company paying the royalties is resident.

(5) Where, owing to a special relationship between the payer and the beneficial owner or between both of them and some other person, the amount of the royalties paid, having regard to the use, right or information for which they are paid, exceeds the amount which would have been agreed upon by the payer and the beneficial owner in the absence of such relationship, the provisions of this Article shall apply only to the last-mentioned amount. In that case, the excess part of the payments shall remain taxable according to the law of each Contracting State, due regard being had to the other provisions of this Convention.

ARTICLE 14

Capital gains

(1) Capital gains from the alienation of immovable property, as defined in paragraph (2) of Article 7, may be taxed in the Contracting State in which such property is situated.

(2) Capital gains from the alienation of movable property forming part of the business property of a permanent establishment which an enterprise of a Contracting State has in the other Contracting State or of movable property pertaining to a fixed base available to a resident of a Contracting State in the other Contracting State for the purpose of performing professional services, including such gains from the alienation of such a permanent establishment (alone or together with the whole enterprise) or of such a fixed base, may be taxed in the other State.

(3) Notwithstanding the provisions of paragraph (2) of this Article, capital gains derived by a resident of a Contracting State from the alienation of ships and aircraft operated in international traffic and movable property pertaining to the operation of such ships and aircraft shall be taxable only in that Contracting State.

(4) Capital gains from the alienation of any property other than those mentioned in paragraphs (1), (2) and (3) of this Article shall be taxable only in the Contracting State of which the alienator is a resident.

(5) The provisions of paragraph (4) of this Article shall not affect the right of a Contracting State to levy according to its own law a tax on capital gains from the alienation of any property derived by an individual who is a resident of the other Contracting State and has been a resident of the first-mentioned Contracting State at any time during the five years immediately preceding the alienation of the property.

ARTICLE 15

Independent personal services

(1) Income derived by a resident of a Contracting State in respect of professional services or other independent activities of a similar character shall be taxable only in that State unless he has a fixed base regularly available to him in the other Contracting State for the purpose of performing his activities. If he has such a fixed base, the income may be taxed in the other Contracting State but only so much of it as is attributable to that fixed base.

(2) The term "professional services" includes especially independent scientific, literary, artistic, educational or teaching activities as well as the independent activities of physicians, lawyers, engineers, architects, dentists and accountants.

ARTICLE 16

Employments

(1) Subject to the provisions of Articles 17, 19, 20, 21 and 22, salaries, wages and other similar remuneration derived by a resident of a Contracting State in respect of an employment shall be taxable only in that State unless the employment is exercised in the other Contracting State. If the employment is so exercised, such remuneration as is derived therefrom may be taxed in that other State.

(2) Notwithstanding the provisions of paragraph (1) of this Article, remuneration derived by a resident of a Contracting State in respect of an employment exercised in the other Contracting State shall be taxable only in the first-mentioned State if:

(a) the recipient is present in the other State for a period or periods not exceeding in the aggregate 183 days in the fiscal year concerned; and

(b) the remuneration is paid by, or on behalf of, an employer who is not a resident of the other State; and

(c) the remuneration is not borne by a permanent establishment or a fixed base which the employer has in the other State.

(3) Notwithstanding the preceding provisions of this Article, remuneration in respect of an employment exercised aboard a ship or aircraft in international traffic may be taxed in the Contracting State of which the person deriving the profits from the operation of the ship or aircraft is a resident.

ARTICLE 17

Directors' fees

Directors' fees and similar payments derived by a resident of a Contracting State in his capacity as a member of the board of directors of a company which is a resident of the other Contracting State may be taxed in that other State.

ARTICLE 18

Artistes and athletes

Notwithstanding the provisions of Articles 15 and 16, income derived by public entertainers, such as theatre, motion picture, radio or television artistes, and musicians, and by athletes, from their personal activities as such may be taxed in the Contracting State in which those activities are exercised.

ARTICLE 19

Pensions

(1) Subject to the provisions of paragraphs (1) and (2) of Article 20, pensions and other similar remuneration paid in consideration of past employment to a resident of a Contracting State and any annuity paid to such a resident shall be taxable only in that State.

(2) The term "annuity" means a stated sum payable periodically at stated times during life or during a specified or ascertainable period of time under an obligation to make the payments in return for adequate and full consideration in money or money's worth.

ARTICLE 20

Governmental functions

(1) Remuneration or pensions paid out of public funds of the United Kingdom or Northern Ireland or of the funds of any local authority in the United Kingdom to any individual in respect of services rendered to the Government of the United Kingdom or Northern Ireland or a local authority in the United Kingdom in the discharge of functions of a governmental nature, shall be taxable only in the United Kingdom unless the individual is a Finnish national without also being a United Kingdom national.

(2) Remuneration or pensions paid by, or out of funds created by Finland or a local authority or public community thereof to any individual in respect of services rendered to the Government of Finland or a local authority or public community thereof, in the discharge of functions of a governmental nature, shall be taxable only in Finland unless the individual is a national of the United Kingdom without also being a Finnish national.

(3) The provisions of paragraphs (1) and (2) of this Article shall not apply to remuneration or pensions in respect of services rendered in connection with any trade or business.

ARTICLE 21

Students

(1) An individual who is a resident of a Contracting State immediately before his visit to the other Contracting State and who is temporarily present in that other Contracting State solely:

(*a*) as a student at a university, college, school or other educational institution; or

(*b*) as a business, technical, agricultural or forestry apprentice; or

(*c*) as the recipient of a grant, allowance or award from a religious, charitable, scientific or educational organisation made for the primary purpose of study;

shall not be taxed in that other Contracting State in respect of:

(i) remittances from abroad for the purpose of his maintenance, education or training;

(ii) the grant, allowance or award; and

(iii) remuneration for services rendered in that other Contracting State, provided that the services are in connection with his studies or training or the remuneration constitutes earnings reasonably necessary for his maintenance or education.

(2) The benefits under the provisions of paragraph (1) of this Article shall extend only for such period of time as may be reasonably or customarily required to effectuate the purpose of the visit, but in no event shall any individual have the benefits of the provisions of that paragraph for more than five years.

(3) An individual who is, or was immediately before visiting a Contracting State, a resident of the other Contracting State, and who is present in the first-mentioned Contracting State as a recipient of a grant, allowance or award from a religious, charitable, scientific or educational organisation made for the primary purpose of research to be carried out in a period which does not exceed two years, shall not be taxed in that first-mentioned Contracting State in respect of the grant, allowance or award.

ARTICLE 22

Teachers

A professor or teacher who visits a Contracting State for a period not exceeding two years for the purpose of teaching at a university, college, school or other educational institution in that Contracting State and who is, or was immediately before that visit, a resident of the other Contracting State shall be exempt from tax in the first-mentioned Contracting State on any remuneration for such teaching in respect of which he is subject to tax in the other Contracting State.

ARTICLE 23

Income not expressly mentioned

Items of income of a resident of a Contracting State being income of a class or from sources not expressly mentioned in the foregoing Articles of this Convention shall be taxable only in that State.

ARTICLE 24

Capital

(1) Capital represented by immovable property, as defined in paragraph (2) of Article 7, may be taxed in the Contracting State in which such property is situated.

(2) Capital represented by movable property forming part of the business property of a permanent establishment of an enterprise, or by movable property pertaining to a fixed base used for the performance of professional services, may be taxed in the Contracting State in which the permanent establishment or fixed base is situated.

(3) Notwithstanding the provisions of paragraph (2) of this Article, ships and aircraft operated in international traffic and movable property pertaining to the operation of such ships and aircraft shall be taxable only in the Contracting State of which the operator is a resident.

(4) All other elements of capital of a resident of a Contracting State shall be taxable only in that State.

ARTICLE 25

Elimination of double taxation

(1) Subject to the provisions of the law of the United Kingdom regarding the allowance as a credit against United Kingdom tax of tax payable in a territory outside the United Kingdom (which shall not affect the general principle hereof):

(a) Finnish tax payable under the laws of Finland and in accordance with this Convention, whether directly or by deduction, on profits, income or chargeable gains from sources within Finland (excluding in the case of a dividend, tax payable in respect of the profits out of which the dividend is paid) shall be allowed as a credit against any United Kingdom tax computed by reference to the same profits, income or chargeable gains by reference to which the Finnish tax is computed;

(b) in the case of a dividend paid by a company which is a resident of Finland to a company which is a resident of the United Kingdom and which controls directly or indirectly at least 10 per cent of the voting power in the company paying the dividend, the credit shall take into account (in addition to any Finnish tax creditable under the provisions of sub-paragraph (*a*) of this paragraph) the Finnish tax payable by the company in respect of the profits out of which such dividend is paid, if at the time when the dividend is paid a company which is a resident of Finland is exempt from Finnish tax in respect of dividends received from a company which is a resident of Finland.

(2) (*a*) Where a resident of Finland derives income or owns capital which, in accordance with the provisions of this Convention, may be taxed in the United Kingdom, Finland shall, subject to the provisions of sub-paragraph (*b*) of this paragraph, allow as a deduction from the income or capital tax that part of the income tax or capital tax, respectively, which is appropriate, as the case may be, to the income derived from or the capital owned in the United Kingdom.

(*b*) Where a resident of Finland derives income or chargeable gains which, in accordance with the provisions of paragraph (2) of Article 11 and paragraph (5) of Article 14 may be taxed in the United Kingdom, Finland shall allow as a deduction from the tax on the income of that person an amount equal to the tax paid in the United Kingdom. Such deduction shall not, however, exceed that part of the tax, as computed before the deduction is given, which is appropriate to the income or chargeable gains derived from the United Kingdom.

(*c*) Notwithstanding the provisions of sub-paragraph (*b*) of this paragraph, dividends paid by a company which is a resident of the United Kingdom to a company which is a resident of Finland shall be exempt from Finnish tax. This exemption shall not apply unless in accordance with the laws of Finland the dividends would have been exempt from Finnish tax if the first-mentioned company had been a resident of Finland and not a resident of the United Kingdom.

(*d*) Where a resident of Finland derives income which in accordance with the provisions of paragraph (1) of Article 20 shall be taxable only in the United Kingdom, such income shall be exempt from Finnish tax; however, the graduated rates of Finnish tax may be calculated as though income thus exempted were included in the amount of the total income.

(3) For the purposes of paragraph (1) of this Article income, profits and capital gains owned by a resident of the United Kingdom which may be taxed in Finland in accordance with this Convention shall be deemed to arise from sources in Finland.

ARTICLE 26

Personal allowances

(1) Subject to the provisions of paragraph (3) of this Article, individuals who are residents of Finland shall be entitled to the same personal allowances, reliefs and reductions for the purposes of United Kingdom tax as British subjects not resident in the United Kingdom.

(2) Subject to the provisions of paragraph (3) of this Article, individuals who are residents of the United Kingdom shall be entitled to the same personal allowances, reliefs and reductions for the purposes of Finnish tax as Finnish nationals not resident in Finland.

(3) Nothing in this Convention shall entitle an individual who is a resident of a Contracting State and whose income from the other Contracting State consists solely of dividends, interest or royalties (or solely of any combination thereof) to the personal allowances, reliefs and reductions of the kind referred to in this Article for the purposes of taxation in that other Contracting State.

ARTICLE 27

Non-discrimination

(1) The nationals of a Contracting State shall not be subjected in the other Contracting State to any taxation or any requirement connected therewith which is other or more burdensome than the taxation and connected requirements to which nationals of that other State in the same circumstances are or may be subjected.

(2) The taxation on a permanent establishment which an enterprise of a Contracting State has in the other Contracting State shall not be less favourably levied in that other State than the taxation levied on enterprises of that other State carrying on the same activities.

(3) Enterprises of a Contracting State, the capital of which is wholly or partly owned or controlled, directly or indirectly by one or more residents of the other Contracting State, shall not be subjected in the first-mentioned Contracting State to any taxation or any requirement connected therewith which is other or more burdensome than the taxation and connected requirements to which other similar enterprises of that first-mentioned State are or may be subjected.

(4) In determining for the purpose of United Kingdom tax whether a company is a close company, the term "recognised stock exchange" shall include the Helsinki Stock Exchange.

(5) Nothing contained in this Article shall be construed as obliging either Contracting State to grant to individuals not resident in that State any of the personal allowances, reliefs and reductions for tax purposes which are granted to individuals so resident, nor as obliging the United Kingdom to grant to a company which is a resident of Finland a greater relief from United Kingdom income tax chargeable upon dividends received from a company which is a resident of the United Kingdom than the relief to which the first-mentioned company may be entitled under the provisions of Article 11 of this Convention.

(6) In this Article the term "taxation" means taxes of every kind and description.

ARTICLE 28

Mutual agreement procedure

(1) Where a resident of a Contracting State considers that the actions of one or both of the Contracting States result or will result for him in taxation not in accordance with this Convention, he may, notwithstanding the remedies provided by the national laws of those States, present his case to the competent authority of the Contracting State of which he is a resident.

(2) The competent authority shall endeavour, if the objection appears to it to be justified and if it is not itself able to arrive at an appropriate solution, to resolve the case by mutual agreement with the competent authority of the other Contracting State, with a view to the avoidance of taxation not in accordance with the Convention.

(3) The competent authorities of the Contracting States shall endeavour to resolve by mutual agreement any difficulties or doubts arising as to the interpretation or application of the Convention.

(4) The competent authorities of the Contracting States may communicate with each other directly for the purpose of reaching an agreement in the sense of the preceding paragraphs.

ARTICLE 29

Exchange of information

The competent authorities of the Contracting States shall exchange such information (being information which is at their disposal under their respective taxation laws in the normal course of administration) as is necessary for carrying out the provisions of this Convention or for the prevention of fraud or the administration of statutory provisions against legal avoidance in relation to the taxes which are the subject of this Convention. Any information so exchanged shall be treated as secret but may be disclosed to persons (including a court or administrative body) concerned with assessment, collection, enforcement or prosecution in respect of taxes which are the subject of this Convention. No information shall be exchanged which would disclose any trade, business, industrial or professional secret or any trade process.

ARTICLE 30

Territorial extension

(1) This Convention may be extended, either in its entirety or with modifications, to any territory for whose international relations either Contracting Party is responsible and which imposes taxes substantially similar in character to those to which this Convention applies. Any such extension shall take effect from such date and subject to such modifications and conditions, including conditions as to termination, as may be specified and agreed between the Contracting States in notes to be exchanged through diplomatic channels.

(2) Unless otherwise agreed by both Contracting States, the termination of this Convention shall terminate the application of this Convention to any territory to which it has been extended under the provisions of this Article.

ARTICLE 31

Entry into force

(1) This Convention shall be ratified and the instruments of ratification shall be exchanged at Helsinki as soon as possible.

(2) The Convention shall enter into force after the expiration of thirty days following the date on which the instruments of ratification are exchanged(a) and shall thereupon have effect:

(a) in the United Kingdom:

    (i) as respects income tax (including surtax) and capital gains tax, for any year of assessment beginning on or after 6th April, 1968; and

    (ii) as respects corporation tax, for any financial year beginning on or after 1st April, 1968;

(b) in Finland:

as respects Finnish taxes for any year of assessment beginning on or after 1st January, 1969, and chargeable on the income or capital of the tax year 1968 or thereafter.

(3) Subject to the provisions of paragraph (4) of this Article the Convention between the Government of the United Kingdom and the Government of Finland for the Avoidance of Double Taxation and the Prevention of Fiscal Evasion with respect to Taxes on Income signed at London on 12th December, 1951(b), as amended by the Protocol signed at London on 16th June, 1966(c) (hereinafter referred to as "the 1951 Convention"), shall cease to have effect as respects taxes to which this Convention in accordance with the provisions of paragraph (2) of this Article applies.

(4) Subject to the provisions of paragraph (5) of this Article where any provision of the 1951 Convention would have afforded any greater relief from tax any such provision as aforesaid shall continue to have effect for any year of assessment or financial year or tax year beginning before the entry into force of this Convention.

(5) The provisions of sub-paragraphs (a) and (b) of paragraph (2) of this Article, of paragraph (3) of this Article and of paragraph (4) of this Article shall not apply in relation to dividends but the provisions of this Convention shall have effect, and the provisions of the 1951 Convention shall cease to be effective, in relation to dividends payable on or after the date of entry into force of this Convention.

(6) The following Agreements between the Contracting Parties shall not have effect in relation to any tax for any period for which this Convention has effect, as respects that tax:

(a) the Agreement between the Government of the United Kingdom and the Government of Finland for the Reciprocal Exemption from Income Tax in certain cases of Profits from the Business of Shipping signed at London on 18th November, 1925(d);

(a) Instruments of ratification were exchanged on 5th January 1970.
(b) S.I. 1953/191 (1953 I, p. 852).   (c) S.I. 1967/164 (1967 I, p. 277).
(d) S.R. & O. 1925/1353 (Rev. X, p. 388; 1925, p. 597).

(b) the Agreement between the Government of the United Kingdom and the Government of Finland for the Reciprocal Exemption from Income Tax in certain cases of Profits or Gains arising through an Agency signed at London on 21st February, 1935(a).

(7) The 1951 Convention shall terminate on the last date on which it has effect in accordance with the foregoing provisions of this Article.

ARTICLE 32

Termination

This Convention shall remain in force until denounced by one of the Contracting States. Either Contracting State may denounce the Convention, through diplomatic channels, by giving notice of termination at least six months before the end of any calendar year after the year 1972. In such event, the Convention shall cease to have effect:

(a) in the United Kingdom:
  (i) as respects income tax (including surtax) and capital gains tax, for any year of assessment beginning on or after 6th April in the calendar year next following that in which the notice is given;
  (ii) as respects corporation tax, for any financial year beginning on or after 1st April in the calendar year next following that in which the notice is given;

(b) in Finland:
  as respects Finnish tax for any tax year beginning on or after 1st January in the calendar year next following that in which the notice is given.

In witness whereof the undersigned, duly authorised thereto by their respective Governments, have signed this Convention.

Done in duplicate at London this 17th day of July, 1969, in the English and Finnish languages, both texts being equally authoritative.

For the Government of the United Kingdom of Great Britain and Northern Ireland:

MICHAEL STEWART

For the Government of the Republic of Finland:

AHTI KARJALAINEN

(a) S.R. & O. 1935/304 (Rev. X, p. 385; 1935, p. 663).

EXPLANATORY NOTE

(This Note is not part of the Order.)

Under the Convention with Finland scheduled to this Order (which is to replace the Convention signed in London on 12th December 1951 as amended by the Protocol signed in London on 16th June 1966), shipping and air transport profits, certain trading profits not arising through a permanent establishment, interest, royalties, pensions (other than Government pensions) and the earnings of temporary business visitors are (subject to certain conditions) to be taxed only in the country of the taxpayer's residence. Government salaries and pensions are normally to be taxed by the paying government only. The remuneration of visiting teachers and professors, and certain payments to visiting students are (subject to certain conditions) to be exempt in the country visited. Capital gains arising from the disposal of movable property are normally to be taxed only in the country of the taxpayer's residence unless they arise from the disposal of assets of a permanent establishment which the taxpayer has in the other country.

The rate of tax in the source country on dividends paid to residents of the other country is, in general, not to exceed 5 per cent if the recipient is a company which controls at least 25 per cent of the voting power in the paying company, or 15 per cent in other cases.

Where income continues to be taxable in both countries, relief from double taxation is to be given by the country of the taxpayer's residence. In the case of a dividend paid by a Finnish company, credit for the tax on the profits out of which the dividend is paid is, while certain provisions of Finnish law are in force, to be given for United Kingdom tax purposes where the recipient of the dividend is a United Kingdom company which controls at least 10 per cent of the voting power in the paying company.

There are provisions safeguarding nationals and enterprises of one country against discriminatory taxation in the other country, and for the exchange of information and consultation between the taxation authorities of the two countries.

The Convention is in general to take effect in the United Kingdom for 1968-69 and subsequent years.

STATUTORY INSTRUMENTS

1970 No. 154

INCOME TAX

The Double Taxation Relief (Taxes on Income) (Norway) Order 1970

Laid before the House of Commons in draft

Made - - - *4th February* 1970

At the Court at Buckingham Palace, the 4th day of February 1970

Present,

The Queen's Most Excellent Majesty in Council

Whereas a draft of this Order was laid before the Commons House of Parliament in accordance with the provisions of section 347(6) of the Income Tax Act 1952(a), and an Address has been presented to Her Majesty by that House praying that an Order may be made in the terms of this Order:

Now, therefore, Her Majesty, in exercise of the powers conferred upon Her by section 347(1) of the said Income Tax Act 1952, as amended by section 39 and section 64 of the Finance Act 1965(b), and of all other powers enabling Her in that behalf, is pleased, by and with the advice of Her Privy Council, to order, and it is hereby ordered, as follows:—

1. This Order may be cited as the Double Taxation Relief (Taxes on Income) (Norway) Order 1970.

2. It is hereby declared—

(*a*) that the arrangements specified in the Convention set out in the Schedule to this Order have been made with the Government of the Kingdom of Norway with a view to affording relief from double taxation in relation to income tax, corporation tax or capital gains tax and taxes of a similar character imposed by the laws of Norway; and

(*b*) that it is expedient that those arrangements should have effect.

W. G. Agnew.

(**a**) 15 & 16 Geo. 6 & 1 Eliz. 2. c. 10.　　　(**b**) 1965 c. 25.

SCHEDULE

CONVENTION BETWEEN THE GOVERNMENT OF THE UNITED KINGDOM OF GREAT BRITAIN AND NORTHERN IRELAND AND THE GOVERNMENT OF THE KINGDOM OF NORWAY FOR THE AVOIDANCE OF DOUBLE TAXATION AND THE PREVENTION OF FISCAL EVASION WITH RESPECT TO TAXES ON INCOME AND CAPITAL

The Government of the United Kingdom of Great Britain and Northern Ireland and the Government of the Kingdom of Norway;

Desiring to conclude a new Convention for the avoidance of double taxation and the prevention of fiscal evasion with respect to taxes on income and capital;

Have agreed as follows:—

ARTICLE 1

Personal scope

This Convention shall apply to persons who are residents of one or both of the Contracting States.

ARTICLE 2

Taxes covered

(1) The taxes which are the subject of this Convention are:

(a) in the United Kingdom of Great Britain and Northern Ireland:

(i) the income tax (including surtax);

(ii) the corporation tax; and

(iii) the capital gains tax;

(b) in Norway:

(i) national capital tax;

(ii) national income tax;

(iii) national contributions to the tax equalisation fund;

(iv) national dues on the profits of non-resident artistes;

(v) special tax in aid of developing countries;

(vi) municipal capital tax;

(vii) municipal property tax;

(viii) municipal income tax;

(ix) tax on dependent children's earnings; and

(x) seamen's tax.

(2) This Convention shall also apply to any identical or substantially similar taxes which are imposed by either Contracting State after the date of signature of this Convention in addition to, or in place of, the existing taxes.

(3) The competent authorities of the Contracting States shall notify to each other any changes which are made in their respective taxation laws.

ARTICLE 3

General definitions

(1) In this Convention, unless the context otherwise requires:

(a) the term "United Kingdom" means Great Britain and Northern Ireland, including any area outside the territorial sea of the United Kingdom which in accordance with international law has been or may hereafter be designated, under the laws of the United Kingdom concerning the Continental Shelf, as an area within which the rights of the United Kingdom with respect to the sea bed and sub-soil and their natural resources may be exercised;

(b) the term "Norway" means the Kingdom of Norway, including any area adjacent to the territorial waters of Norway which by Norwegian legislation, and in accordance with international law, has been or may hereafter be designated as an area within which the rights of Norway with respect to the sea bed and sub-soil and their natural resources may be exercised; the term does not comprise Spitsbergen (including Bear Island), Jan Mayen and the Norwegian dependencies outside Europe;

(c) the term "nationals" means:

(i) in relation to the United Kingdom, all citizens of the United Kingdom and Colonies who derive their status as such from their connection with the United Kingdom and all legal persons, partnerships and associations deriving their status as such from the law in force in the United Kingdom;

(ii) in relation to Norway, all citizens of Norway and all legal persons, partnerships and associations deriving their status as such from the law in force in Norway;

(d) the term "United Kingdom tax" means tax imposed by the United Kingdom being tax to which this Convention applies by virtue of the provisions of Article 2; the term "Norwegian tax" means tax imposed by Norway being tax to which this Convention applies by virtue of the provisions of Article 2;

(e) the term "tax" means United Kingdom tax or Norwegian tax, as the context requires;

(f) the terms "a Contracting State" and "the other Contracting State" mean the United Kingdom or Norway, as the context requires;

(g) the term "person" comprises an individual, a company and any other body of persons;

(h) the term "company" means any body corporate or any entity which is treated as a body corporate for tax purposes;

(i) the terms "enterprise of a Contracting State" and "enterprise of the other Contracting State" mean respectively an enterprise carried on by a resident of a Contracting State and an enterprise carried on by a resident of the other Contracting State;

(j) the term "international traffic" includes any voyage of a ship or aircraft operated by a resident of a Contracting State other than a voyage confined solely to the other Contracting State;

(k) the term "competent authority" means, in the case of the United Kingdom the Commissioners of Inland Revenue or their authorised representative, and in the case of Norway the Ministry of Finance and Customs or its authorised representative.

(2) As regards the application of this Convention by a Contracting State any term not otherwise defined shall, unless the context otherwise requires, have the meaning which it has under the laws of that Contracting State relating to the taxes which are the subject of this Convention.

ARTICLE 4

Fiscal domicile

(1) For the purposes of this Convention, the term "resident of a Contracting State" means, subject to the provisions of paragraphs (2) and (3) of this Article, any person who, under the law of that State, is liable to taxation therein by reason of his domicile, residence, place of management or any other criterion of a similar nature; the term does not include any individual who is liable to tax in that Contracting State only if he derives income from sources therein. The terms "resident of the United Kingdom" and "resident of Norway" shall be construed accordingly.

(2) Where by reason of the provisions of paragraph (1) of this Article an individual is a resident of both Contracting States, then his status shall be determined in accordance with the following rules:

(a) he shall be deemed to be a resident of the Contracting State in which he has a permanent home available to him. If he has a permanent home available to him in both Contracting States, he shall be deemed to be a resident of the Contracting State with which his personal and economic relations are closest (centre of vital interests);

(b) if the Contracting State in which he has his centre of vital interests cannot be determined, or if he has not a permanent home available to him in either Contracting State, he shall be deemed to be a resident of the Contracting State in which he has an habitual abode;

(c) if he has an habitual abode in both Contracting States or in neither of them, he shall be deemed to be a resident of the Contracting State of which he is a national;

(d) if he is a national of both Contracting States or of neither of them, the competent authorities of the Contracting States shall settle the question by mutual agreement.

(3) Where by reason of the provisions of paragraph (1) of this Article a person other than an individual is a resident of both Contracting States, then it shall be deemed to be a resident of the Contracting State in which its place of effective management is situated.

ARTICLE 5

Permanent establishment

(1) For the purposes of this Convention, the term "permanent establishment" means a fixed place of business in which the business of the enterprise is wholly or partly carried on.

(2) The term "permanent establishment" shall include especially:

(a) a place of management;

(b) a branch;

(c) an office;

(d) a factory;

(e) a workshop;

(f) a mine, quarry or other place of extraction of natural resources;

(g) a building site or construction or assembly project which exists for more than twelve months.

(3) The term "permanent establishment" shall not be deemed to include:

(a) the use of facilities solely for the purpose of storage, display or delivery of goods or merchandise belonging to the enterprise;

(b) the maintenance of a stock of goods or merchandise belonging to the enterprise solely for the purpose of storage, display or delivery;

(c) the maintenance of a stock of goods or merchandise belonging to the enterprise solely for the purpose of processing by another enterprise;

(d) the maintenance of a fixed place of business solely for the purpose of purchasing goods or merchandise, or for collecting information, for the enterprise;

(e) the maintenance of a fixed place of business solely for the purpose of advertising, for the supply of information, for scientific research or for similar activities which have a preparatory or auxiliary character, for the enterprise.

(4) An enterprise of a Contracting State shall be deemed to have a permanent establishment in the other Contracting State if it carries on the activity of providing the services within that other Contracting State of public entertainers or athletes referred to in Article 18.

(5) A person acting in a Contracting State on behalf of an enterprise of the other Contracting State—other than an agent of an independent status to whom the provisions of paragraph (6) of this Article apply—shall be deemed to be a permanent establishment in the first-mentioned State if he has, and habitually exercises in that State, an authority to conclude contracts in the name of the enterprise, unless his activities are limited to the purchase of goods or merchandise for the enterprise.

(6) An enterprise of a Contracting State shall not be deemed to have a permanent establishment in the other Contracting State merely because it carries on business in that other State through a broker, general commission agent or any other agent of an independent status, where such persons are acting in the ordinary course of their business.

(7) The fact that a company which is a resident of a Contracting State controls or is controlled by a company which is a resident of the other Contracting State, or which carries on business in that other State (whether through a permanent establishment or otherwise), shall not of itself constitute either company a permanent establishment of the other.

ARTICLE 6

Limitation of relief

Where under any provision of this Convention income is relieved from Norwegian tax and, under the law in force in the United Kingdom, an individual, in respect of the said income, is subject to tax by reference to the amount thereof which is remitted to or received in the United Kingdom and not by reference to the full amount thereof, then the relief to be allowed under this Convention in Norway shall apply only to so much of the income as is remitted to or received in the United Kingdom.

ARTICLE 7

Income from immovable property

(1) Income from immovable property may be taxed in the Contracting State in which such property is situated.

(2) (a) The term "immovable property" shall, subject to the provisions of subparagraph (b) below, be defined in accordance with the law of the Contracting State in which the property in question is situated.

(b) The term "immovable property" shall in any case include property accessory to immovable property, livestock and equipment used in agriculture and forestry, rights to which the provisions of general law respecting landed property apply, usufruct of immovable property and rights to variable or fixed payments as consideration for the working of, or the right to work, mineral deposits, sources and other natural resources; ships, boats and aircraft shall not be regarded as immovable property.

(3) The provisions of paragraph (1) of this Article shall apply to income derived from the direct use, letting, or use in any other form of immovable property.

(4) In the determination of the income from immovable property which a resident of a Contracting State has in the other Contracting State expenses (including interest on debt-claims) which are incurred for the purposes of such property shall be allowed as deductions on the same conditions as are provided for residents of that other State.

(5) The provisions of paragraphs (1), (3) and (4) of this Article shall also apply to the income from immovable property of an enterprise and to income from immovable property used for the performance of professional services.

ARTICLE 8

Business profits

(1) The profits of an enterprise of a Contracting State shall be taxable only in that State unless the enterprise carries on business in the other Contracting State through a permanent establishment situated therein. If the enterprise carries on business as aforesaid, the profits of the enterprise may be taxed in the other State but only so much of them as is attributable to that permanent establishment.

(2) Where an enterprise of a Contracting State carries on business in the other Contracting State through a permanent establishment situated therein, there shall in each Contracting State be attributed to that permanent establishment the profits which it might be expected to make if it were a distinct and separate enterprise engaged in the same or similar activities under the same or similar conditions and dealing at arm's length with the enterprise of which it is a permanent establishment.

(3) In the determination of the profits of a permanent establishment, there shall be allowed as deductions expenses of the enterprise (other than expenses which would not be deductible if the permanent establishment were a separate enterprise) which are incurred for the purposes of the permanent establishment, including executive and general administrative expenses so incurred, whether in the State in which the permanent establishment is situated or elsewhere.

(4) In so far as it has been customary in a Contracting State, according to its law, to determine the profits to be attributed to a permanent establishment on the basis of an apportionment of the total income of the enterprise to its various parts, nothing in paragraph (2) of this Article shall preclude that Contracting State from determining the profits to be taxed by such an apportionment as may be customary; the method of apportionment adopted shall, however, be such that the result shall be in accordance with the principles of this Article.

(5) No profits shall be attributed to a permanent establishment by reason of the mere purchase by that permanent establishment of goods or merchandise for the enterprise.

(6) For the purposes of the preceding paragraphs, the profits to be attributed to the permanent establishment shall be determined by the same method year by year unless there is good and sufficient reason to the contrary.

(7) Where profits include items which are dealt with separately in other Articles of this Convention, then the provisions of those Articles shall not be affected by the provisions of this Article.

ARTICLE 9

Shipping and air transport

A resident of a Contracting State shall be exempt from tax in the other Contracting State on profits from the operation of ships or aircraft in international traffic.

ARTICLE 10

Associated enterprises

Where

(a) an enterprise of a Contracting State participates directly or indirectly in the management, control or capital of an enterprise of the other Contracting State; or

(b) the same persons participate directly or indirectly in the management, control or capital of an enterprise of a Contracting State and an enterprise of the other Contracting State;

and in either case conditions are made or imposed between the two enterprises in their commercial or financial relations which differ from those which would be made between independent enterprises, then any profits which would, but for those conditions, have accrued to one of the enterprises, but, by reason of those conditions, have not so accrued, may be included in the profits of that enterprise and taxed accordingly.

ARTICLE 11

Dividends

(1) Dividends paid by a company being a resident of a Contracting State which are beneficially owned by a resident of the other Contracting State may be taxed in that other State.

(2) However, such dividends may also be taxed in the Contracting State of which the company paying the dividends is a resident, and according to the law of that State, but the tax so charged shall not exceed:

(*a*) 5 per cent of the gross amount of the dividends if the beneficial owner is a company which controls directly or indirectly at least 25 per cent of the voting power of the company paying the dividends;

(*b*) in all other cases, 15 per cent of the gross amount of the dividends.

The provisions of this paragraph shall not affect the taxation of the company in respect of the profits out of which the dividends are paid.

(3) The term "dividends" as used in this Article means income from shares, or other rights, not being debt-claims, participating in profits, as well as income from other corporate rights assimilated to income from shares by the taxation law of the State of which the company making the distribution is a resident and also includes any other item (other than interest or royalties relieved from tax under the provisions of Article 12 or Article 13 of this Convention) which, under the law of the Contracting State of which the company paying the dividend is a resident, is treated as a dividend or distribution of a company.

(4) The provisions of paragraphs (1) and (2) of this Article shall not apply if the beneficial owner of the dividends, being a resident of a Contracting State, has in the other Contracting State, of which the company paying the dividends is a resident, a permanent establishment and the holding by virtue of which the dividends are paid is effectively connected with a business carried on through that permanent establishment. In such a case, the provisions of Article 8 shall apply.

(5) If the beneficial owner of a dividend being a resident of a Contracting State owns 10 per cent or more of the class of shares in respect of which the dividend is paid then the relief from tax provided for in paragraph (2) of this Article shall not apply to the dividend to the extent that it can have been paid only out of profits which the company paying the dividend earned or other income which it received in a period ending twelve months or more before the relevant date. For the purposes of this paragraph the term "relevant date" means the date on which the beneficial owner of the dividend became the owner of 10 per cent or more of the class of shares in question.

Provided that this paragraph shall not apply if the beneficial owner of the dividend shows that the shares were acquired for bona fide commercial reasons and not primarily for the purpose of securing the benefit of this Article.

(6) Where a company which is a resident of a Contracting State derives profits or income from the other Contracting State, that other State may not impose any tax on the dividends paid by the company and beneficially owned by persons who are not residents of that other State, or subject the company's undistributed profits to a tax on undistributed profits, even if the dividends paid or the undistributed profits consist wholly or partly of profits or income arising in that other State.

(7) If the system of taxation applicable in either of the Contracting States to the profits and dividends of companies is altered after the date of signature of this Convention the competent authorities may consult each other in order to determine whether it is necessary for this reason to amend the provisions of this Convention relating to dividends.

ARTICLE 12

Interest

(1) Interest derived and beneficially owned by a resident of a Contracting State shall be taxable only in that State.

(2) The term "interest" as used in this Article means income from Government securities, bonds or debentures, whether or not secured by mortgage and whether or not carrying a right to participate in profits, and other debt-claims of every kind as well as all other income assimilated to income from money lent by the taxation law of the State in which the income arises.

(3) The provisions of paragraph (1) of this Article shall not apply if the beneficial owner of the interest, being a resident of a Contracting State, has in the other Contracting State a permanent establishment and the debt-claim from which the interest arises is effectively connected with a business carried on through that permanent establishment. In such a case, the provisions of Article 8 shall apply.

(4) Any provision of the law of one of the Contracting States which relates only to interest paid to a non-resident company with or without any further requirement, or which relates only to interest payments between inter-connected companies with or without any further requirement, shall not operate so as to require such interest paid to a company which is a resident of the other Contracting State to be left out of account as a deduction in computing the taxable profits of the company paying the interest as being a dividend or distribution.

(5) The exemption from tax provided for in paragraph (1) of this Article shall not apply to interest on any form of debt-claim dealt in on a stock exchange where the beneficial owner of the interest:

(a) does not bear tax in respect thereof in the Contracting State of which it is a resident; and

(b) sells (or makes a contract to sell) the debt-claim from which such interest is derived within three months of the date on which such beneficial owner acquired such debt-claim.

(6) Where, owing to a special relationship between the payer and the beneficial owner or between both of them and some other person, the amount of the interest paid, having regard to the debt-claim for which it is paid, exceeds the amount which would have been agreed upon by the payer and the beneficial owner in the absence of such relationship, the provisions of this Article shall apply only to the last-mentioned amount. In that case, the excess part of the payments shall remain taxable according to the law of each Contracting State, due regard being had to the other provisions of this Convention.

(7) The provisions of this Article shall not apply if the debt-claim in respect of which the interest is paid was created or assigned mainly for the purpose of taking advantage of this Article and not for bona fide commercial reasons.

ARTICLE 13

Royalties

(1) Royalties derived and beneficially owned by a resident of a Contracting State shall be taxable only in that State.

(2) The term "royalties" as used in this Article means payments of any kind received as a consideration for the use of, or the right to use, any copyright of literary, artistic or scientific work (including cinematograph films, and films or tapes for radio or television broadcasting), any patent, trade mark, design or model, plan, secret formula or process, or for the use of, or the right to use, industrial, commercial or scientific equipment, or for information concerning industrial, commercial or scientific experience.

(3) The provisions of paragraph (1) of this Article shall not apply if the beneficial owner of the royalties, being a resident of a Contracting State, has in the other Contracting State a permanent establishment and the right or property giving rise to the royalties is effectively connected with a business carried on through that permanent establishment. In such a case, the provisions of Article 8 shall apply.

(4) Any provision of the law of a Contracting State which requires royalties paid by a company to be left out of account as a deduction in computing the company's taxable profits as being a dividend or distribution shall not operate in relation to royalties paid to a resident of the other Contracting State. The preceding sentence shall not however apply to royalties derived and beneficially owned by a company which is a resident of that other Contracting State where:

(a) the same persons participate directly or indirectly in the management or control of the company paying the royalties and the company beneficially owning the royalties; and

(b) more than 50 per cent of the voting power in the company beneficially owning the royalties is controlled directly or indirectly by a person or persons resident in the Contracting State in which the company paying the royalties is resident.

(5) Where, owing to a special relationship between the payer and the beneficial owner or between both of them and some other person, the amount of the royalties paid, having regard to the use, right or information for which they are paid, exceeds the amount which would have been agreed upon by the payer and the beneficial owner in the absence of such relationship, the provisions of this Article shall apply only to the last-mentioned amount. In that case, the excess part of the payments shall remain taxable according to the law of each Contracting State, due regard being had to the other provisions of this Convention.

ARTICLE 14

Capital gains

(1) Capital gains from the alienation of immovable property, as defined in paragraph (2) of Article 7, may be taxed in the Contracting State in which such property is situated.

(2) Capital gains from the alienation of movable property forming part of the business property of a permanent establishment which an enterprise of a Contracting State has in the other Contracting State or of movable property pertaining to a fixed base available to a resident of a Contracting State in the other Contracting State for the purpose of performing professional services, including such gains from the alienation of such a permanent establishment (alone or together with the whole enterprise) or of such a fixed base, may be taxed in the other State.

(3) Notwithstanding the provisions of paragraph (2) of this Article, capital gains derived by a resident of a Contracting State from the alienation of ships and aircraft operated in international traffic and movable property pertaining to the operation of such ships and aircraft shall be taxable only in that Contracting State.

(4) Capital gains from the alienation of any property other than those mentioned in paragraphs (1), (2) and (3) of this Article shall be taxable only in the Contracting State of which the alienator is a resident.

(5) The provisions of paragraph (4) of this Article shall not affect the right of a Contracting State to levy according to its own law a tax on capital gains from the alienation of any property derived by an individual who is a resident of the other Contracting State and has been a resident of the first-mentioned Contracting State at any time during the five years immediately preceding the alienation of the property.

ARTICLE 15

Independent personal services

(1) Income derived by a resident of a Contracting State in respect of professional services or other independent activities of a similar character shall be taxable only in that State unless he has a fixed base regularly available to him in the other Contracting State for the purpose of performing his activities. If he has such a fixed base, the income may be taxed in the other Contracting State but only so much of it as is attributable to that fixed base.

(2) The term "professional services" includes especially independent scientific, literary, artistic, educational or teaching activities as well as the independent activities of physicians, lawyers, engineers, architects, dentists and accountants.

ARTICLE 16

Employments

(1) Subject to the provisions of Articles 17, 19, 20, 21 and 22, salaries, wages and other similar remuneration derived by a resident of a Contracting State in respect of an employment shall be taxable only in that State unless the employment is exercised in the other Contracting State. If the employment is so exercised, such remuneration as is derived therefrom may be taxed in that other State.

(2) Notwithstanding the provisions of paragraph (1) of this Article, remuneration derived by a resident of a Contracting State in respect of an employment exercised in the other Contracting State shall be taxable only in the first-mentioned State if:

(a) the recipient is present in the other State for a period or periods not exceeding in the aggregate 183 days in the fiscal year concerned; and

(b) the remuneration is paid by, or on behalf of, an employer who is not a resident of the other State; and

(c) the remuneration is not borne by a permanent establishment or a fixed base which the employer has in the other State.

(3) Notwithstanding the preceding provisions of this Article, remuneration in respect of an employment exercised aboard a ship or aircraft in international traffic may be taxed in the Contracting State of which the person deriving the profits from the operation of the ship or aircraft is a resident.

ARTICLE 17

Directors' fees, etc.

Directors' fees and similar payments derived by a resident of a Contracting State in his capacity as a member of the board of directors or of the committee of the shareholders' representatives (*representantskapet*) of a company which is a resident of the other Contracting State may be taxed in that other State.

ARTICLE 18

Artistes and athletes

Notwithstanding the provisions of Articles 15 and 16, income derived by public entertainers, such as theatre, motion picture, radio or television artistes, and musicians, and by athletes, from their personal activities as such may be taxed in the Contracting State in which those activities are exercised.

ARTICLE 19

Pensions and annuities

(1) Subject to the provisions of paragraphs (1) and (2) of Article 20, pensions and other similar remuneration paid in consideration of past employment to a resident of a Contracting State and any annuity paid to such a resident shall be taxable only in that State.

(2) The term "annuity" means a stated sum payable periodically at stated times during life or during a specified or ascertainable period of time under an obligation to make the payments in return for adequate and full consideration in money or money's worth.

ARTICLE 20

Governmental functions

(1) Remuneration or pensions paid out of public funds of the United Kingdom or Northern Ireland or of the funds of any local authority in the United Kingdom to any individual in respect of services rendered to the Government of the United Kingdom or Northern Ireland or a local authority in the United Kingdom in the discharge of functions of a governmental nature, shall be taxable only in the United Kingdom unless the individual is a Norwegian national.

(2) Remuneration or pensions paid by, or out of funds created by, Norway or a local authority thereof to any individual in respect of services rendered to the Government of Norway or a local authority thereof, in the discharge of functions of a governmental nature, shall be taxable only in Norway unless the individual is a national of the United Kingdom.

(3) The provisions of paragraphs (1) and (2) of this Article shall not apply to remuneration or pensions in respect of services rendered in connection with any trade or business.

ARTICLE 21

Students

(1) Payments which a student or business apprentice who is or was immediately before visiting a Contracting State a resident of the other Contracting State and who is present in the first-mentioned Contracting State solely for the purpose of his education or training receives for the purpose of his maintenance, education or training shall not be taxed in the first-mentioned State, provided that such payments are made to him from sources outside that State.

(2) An individual who,while a student at a university or other recognised educational institution in a Contracting State, is employed either in that Contracting State or in the other Contracting State for a period or periods not exceeding a total of 100 days during the fiscal year concerned shall not be taxed in the Contracting State where the employment is exercised in respect of his remuneration therefrom if:

(a) the employment is directly related to his studies or educational training; and

(b) he was not, immediately before the commencement of his studies at the university or institution in the first-mentioned Contracting State, a resident of the Contracting State where the employment is exercised.

ARTICLE 22

Teachers

A professor or teacher who visits a Contracting State for the purpose of teaching at a university, college, school or other educational institution in that Contracting State, whose visit does not exceed two years and who is, or was immediately before that visit, a resident of the other Contracting State shall be exempt from tax in the first-mentioned Contracting State on any remuneration for such teaching in respect of which he is subject to tax in the other Contracting State.

ARTICLE 23

Income not expressly mentioned

Items of income of a resident of a Contracting State being income of a class or from sources not expressly mentioned in the foregoing Articles of this Convention shall be taxable only in that State.

ARTICLE 24

Capital

(1) Capital represented by immovable property, as defined in paragraph (2) of Article 7, may be taxed in the Contracting State in which such property is situated.

(2) Capital represented by movable property forming part of the business property of a permanent establishment of an enterprise, or by movable property pertaining to a fixed base used for the performance of professional services, may be taxed in the Contracting State in which the permanent establishment or fixed base is situated.

(3) Notwithstanding the provisions of paragraph (2) of this Article, ships and aircraft operated in international traffic and movable property pertaining to the operation of such ships and aircraft shall be taxable only in the Contracting State of which the operator is a resident.

(4) All other elements of capital of a resident of a Contracting State shall be taxable only in that State.

ARTICLE 25

Partnerships concerned with shipping or air transport

Notwithstanding the preceding provisions of this Convention, where ships or aircraft are operated in international traffic by a partnership which includes one or more partners resident in a Contracting State and one or more partners resident in the other Contracting State profits referred to in Article 9, capital gains referred to in paragraph (3) of Article 14 and capital referred to in paragraph (3) of Article 24, shall be taxable, in proportion to the share of the said partners, only in the Contracting State of which each such partner is a resident.

ARTICLE 26

Elimination of double taxation

(1) *Credit method—United Kingdom*

Subject to the provisions of the law of the United Kingdom regarding the allowance as a credit against United Kingdom tax of tax payable in a territory outside the United Kingdom (which shall not affect the general principle hereof):

(a) Norwegian tax payable under the laws of Norway and in accordance with this Convention, whether directly or by deduction, on profits, income or chargeable gains from sources within Norway (excluding in the case of a dividend, tax payable in respect of the profits out of which the dividend is paid) shall be allowed as a credit against any United Kingdom tax computed by reference to the same profits, income or chargeable gains by reference to which the Norwegian tax is computed;

(b) in the case of a dividend paid by a company which is a resident of Norway to a company which is a resident of the United Kingdom and which controls directly or indirectly at least 10 per cent of the voting power in the company paying the dividend, the credit shall take into account (in addition to any Norwegian tax creditable under the provisions of sub-paragraph (a) of this paragraph) the Norwegain tax payable by the company in respect of the profits out of which such dividend is paid.

(2) *Exemption method—Norway*

(a) Where a resident of Norway derives income or owns capital which, in accordance with the provisions of this Convention, may be taxed in the United Kingdom, Norway shall, subject to the provisions of sub-paragraph (b) of this paragraph, exempt such income or capital from tax but may, in calculating tax on the remaining income or capital of that person, apply the rate of tax which would have been applicable if the exempted income or capital had not been so exempted.

(*b*) Where a resident of Norway derives income which, in accordance with the provisions of Article 11 may be taxed in the United Kingdom, Norway shall allow as a deduction from the tax of the income of that person an amount equal to the tax paid in the United Kingdom. Such deduction shall not, however, exceed that part of the tax, as computed before the deduction is given, which is appropriate to the income derived from the United Kingdom.

(*c*) Notwithstanding the provisions of sub-paragraph (*b*) of this paragraph dividends paid by a company which is a resident of the United Kingdom to a company being a resident of Norway which controls directly or indirectly at leas t 10 per cent of the voting power in the company paying the dividends shall be exempt from Norwegian tax.

(3) For the purposes of paragraph (1) of this Article income, profits and capital gains owned by a resident of the United Kingdom which may be taxed in Norway in accordance with this Convention shall be deemed to arise from sources in Norway.

(4) Where profits on which an enterprise of a Contracting State has been charged to tax in that State are also included in the profits of an enterprise of the other State and the profits so included are profits which would have accrued to that enterprise of the other State if the conditions made between the enterprises had been those which would have been made between independent enterprises dealing at arm's length, the amount included in the profits of both enterprises shall be treated for the purposes of this Article as income from a source in the other State of the enterprise of the first-mentioned State and relief shall be given accordingly under the provisions of paragraph (1) or paragraph (2) of this Article.

ARTICLE 27

Personal allowances

(1) Subject to the provisions of paragraph (3) of this Article, individuals who are residents of Norway shall be entitled to the same personal allowances, reliefs and reductions for the purposes of United Kingdom tax as British subjects not resident in the United Kingdom.

(2) Subject to the provisions of paragraph (3) of this Article, individuals who are residents of the United Kingdom shall be entitled to the same personal allowances, reliefs and reductions for the purposes of Norwegian tax as Norwegian nationals not resident in Norway.

(3) Nothing in this Convention shall entitle an individual who is a resident of a Contracting State and whose income from the other Contracting State consists solely of dividends, interest or royalties (or solely of any combination thereof) to the personal allowances, reliefs and reductions of the kind referred to in this Article for the purposes of taxation in that other Contracting State.

ARTICLE 28

Non-discrimination

(1) The nationals of a Contracting State shall not be subjected in the other Contracting State to any taxation or any requirement connected therewith which is other or more burdensome than the taxation and connected requirements to which nationals of that other State in the same circumstances are or may be subjected.

(2) The taxation on a permanent establishment which an enterprise of a Contracting State has in the other Contracting State shall not be less favourably levied in that other State than the taxation levied on enterprises of that other State carrying on the same activities.

(3) Enterprises of a Contracting State, the capital of which is wholly or partly owned or controlled, directly or indirectly, by one or more residents of the other Contracting State, shall not be subjected in the first-mentioned Contracting State to any taxation or any requirement connected therewith which is other or more burdensome than the taxation and connected requirements to which other similar enterprises of that first-mentioned State are or may be subjected.

(4) In determining for the purpose of United Kingdom tax whether a company is a close company, the term "recognised stock exchange" shall include any stock exchange in Norway which is a stock exchange within the meaning of the Norwegian law relating to stock exchanges.

(5) Nothing contained in this Article shall be construed as obliging either Contracting State to grant to individuals not resident in that State any of the personal allowances, reliefs and reductions for tax purposes which are granted to individuals so resident, nor as conferring any exemption from tax in a Contracting State in respect of dividends paid to a company which is a resident of the other Contracting State.

(6) The provisions of this Article shall not be construed as obliging Norway to grant to nationals of the United Kingdom, not being nationals of Norway, the exceptional tax relief which is accorded to Norwegian nationals and individuals born of parents having Norwegian nationality pursuant to Section 22 of the Norwegian Taxation Act for the Rural Districts and Section 17 of the Norwegian Taxation Act for the Urban Districts.

(7) In this Article the term "taxation" means taxes of every kind and description.

ARTICLE 29

Mutual agreement procedure

(1) Where a resident of a Contracting State considers that the actions of one or both of the Contracting States result or will result for him in taxation not in accordance with this Convention, he may, notwithstanding the remedies provided by the national laws of those States, present his case to the competent authority of the Contracting State of which he is a resident.

(2) The competent authority shall endeavour, if the objection appears to it to be justified and if it is not itself able to arrive at an appropriate solution, to resolve the case by mutual agreement with the competent authority of the other Contracting State, with a view to the avoidance of taxation not in accordance with the Convention.

(3) The competent authorities of the Contracting States shall endeavour to resolve by mutual agreement any difficulties or doubts arising as to the interpretation or application of the Convention.

(4) The competent authorities of the Contracting States may communicate with each other directly for the purpose of reaching an agreement in the sense of the preceding paragraphs.

ARTICLE 30

Exchange of information

The competent authorities of the Contracting States shall exchange such information (being information which is at their disposal under their respective taxation laws in the normal course of administration) as is necessary for carrying out the provisions of this Convention or for the prevention of fraud or the administration of statutory provisions against legal avoidance in relation to the taxes which are the subject of this Convention. Any information so exchanged shall be treated as secret but may be disclosed to persons (including a court or administrative body) concerned with assessment, collection, enforcement or prosecution in respect of taxes which are the subject of this Convention. No information shall be exchanged which would disclose any trade, business, industrial or professional secret or any trade process.

ARTICLE 31

Territorial extension

(1) This Convention may be extended, either in its entirety or with modifications, to:

   (a) any territory for whose international relations the United Kingdom is responsible and which imposes taxes substantially similar in character to those to which this Convention applies;

(b) any territory of Norway which is specifically excluded from the application of this Convention under the provisions of paragraph 1 (b) of Article 3, or other areas for which Norwegian tax legislation may apply, in which taxes are imposed which are substantially similar in character to those to which this Convention applies.

Any such extension shall take effect from such date and subject to such modifications and conditions, including conditions as to termination, as may be specified and agreed between the Contracting States in notes to be exchanged through diplomatic channels.

(2) Unless otherwise agreed by both Contracting States, the termination of this Convention shall terminate the application of this Convention to any territory to which it has been extended under the provisons of this Article.

ARTICLE 32

Entry into force

(1) This Convention shall be ratified and the instruments of ratification shall be exchanged at Oslo as soon as possible.

(2) This Convention shall enter into force after the expiration of thirty days following the date on which the instruments of ratification are exchanged(a) and shall thereupon have effect:

(a) in the United Kingdom:

(i) as respects income tax (including surtax) and capital gains tax, for any year of assessment beginning on or after 6th April, 1968; and

(ii) as respects corporation tax, for any financial year beginning on or after 1st April, 1968;

(b) in Norway:

as respects taxes for any year of assessment beginning on or after 1st January, 1969 and chargeable on capital or income of the calendar year 1968 or thereafter (including accounting periods closed in any such year).

(3) Subject to the provisions of paragraph (4) of this Article the Convention between the Government of the United Kingdom and the Government of Norway for the Avoidance of Double Taxation and the Prevention of Fiscal Evasion with respect to Taxes on Income signed at London on 2nd May, 1951(b), as amended by the Protocol signed at London on 29th June, 1966(c) (hereinafter referred to as "the 1951 Convention"), shall cease to have effect as respects taxes to which this Convention in accordance with the provisions of paragraph (2) of this Article applies.

(4) Subject to the provisions of paragraph (5) of this Article where any provision of the 1951 Convention would have afforded any greater relief from tax any such provision as aforesaid shall continue to have effect:

(a) in the United Kingdom, for any year of assessment or financial year, and

(b) in Norway, for any income year (including an accounting period)

beginning, in either case, before the entry into force of this Convention.

(5) The provisions of sub-paragraphs (a) and (b) of paragraph (2) of this Article, of paragraph (3) of this Article and of paragraph (4) of this Article shall not apply in relation to dividends but the provisions of this Convention shall have effect, and the provisions of the 1951 Convention shall cease to be effective, in relation to dividends payable on or after the expiration of sixty days following the date of entry into force of this Convention.

(a) Instruments of ratification were exchanged on 17th December 1969.
(b) S.I. 1951/1798 (1951 I, p.1112).   (c) S.I. 1967/1488 (1967 III, p.4195).

(6) The Agreement between the Government of the United Kingdom and the Government of Norway for the Reciprocal Exemption from Income Tax in certain cases of Profits accruing from the Business of Shipping, signed at London on 18th December, 1924(a), and the Agreement between the Government of the United Kingdom and the Government of Norway for the Reciprocal Exemption from Taxes in certain cases of Profits or Gains arising through an Agency, signed at London on 21st December, 1938(b), shall not have effect:

(a) in Norway, for the period for which this Convention has effect in that country;

(b) in the United Kingdom, in relation to any tax for any period for which this Convention has effect as respects that tax.

(7) The 1951 Convention shall terminate on the last date on which it has effect in accordance with the foregoing provisions of this Article.

(8) This Convention shall not affect any Agreement in force extending the 1951 Convention in accordance with Article XX thereof.

ARTICLE 33

Termination

This Convention shall remain in force until denounced by one of the Contracting States. Either Contracting State may denounce the Convention, through diplomatic channels, by giving notice of termination at least six months before the end of any calendar year after the year 1972. In such event, the Convention shall cease to have effect:

(a) in the United Kingdom:

(i) as respects income tax (including surtax) and capital gains tax, for any year of assessment beginning on or after 6th April in the calendar year next following that in which the notice is given:

(ii) as respects corporation tax, for any financial year beginning on or after 1st April in the calendar year next following that in which the notice is given;

(b) in Norway:

as respects taxes for any year of assessment chargeable on capital or income of the calendar year (including accounting periods closed in any such year) next following that year in which the notice is given.

In witness whereof the undersigned, duly authorised thereto by their respective Governments, have signed this Convention.

Done in duplicate at London this 22nd day of January 1969, in the English and Norwegian languages, both texts being equally authoritative.

For the Government of the United Kingdom of Great Britain and Northern Ireland:

CHALFONT

For the Government of the Kingdom of Norway:

PAUL KOHT

(a) S.R. & O. 1925/103 (Rev. X, p.472: 1925 p.600).
(b) S.R. & O. 1939/1319 (Rev. X, p. 469: 1939 II, p.1734).

EXPLANATORY NOTE
(This Note is not part of the Order.)

Under the Convention with Norway scheduled to this Order (which is to replace the Convention signed in London on 2nd May 1951 as amended by the Protocol signed in London on 29th June 1966), shipping and air transport profits, certain trading profits not arising through a permanent establishment, interest, royalties, pensions (other than Government pensions) and the earnings of temporary business visitors are (subject to certain conditions) to be taxed only in the country of the taxpayer's residence. Government salaries and pensions are normally to be taxed by the paying government only. The remuneration of visiting teachers and professors, and payments made for the maintenance of visiting students are (subject to certain conditions) to be exempt in the country visited. Capital gains arising from the disposal of movable property are normally to be taxed only in the country of the taxpayer's residence unless they arise from the disposal of assets of a permanent establishment which the taxpayer has in the other country.

The rate of tax in the source country on dividends paid to residents of the other country is, in general, not to exceed 5 per cent if the recipient is a company which controls at least 25 per cent of the voting power in the paying company, or 15 per cent in other cases.

Where income continues to be taxable in both countries, relief from double taxation is to be given by the country of the taxpayer's residence. In the case of a dividend paid by a Norwegian company, credit for the tax on the profits out of which the dividend is paid is to be given for United Kingdom tax purposes where the recipient of the dividend is a United Kingdom company which controls at least 10 per cent of the voting power in the paying company.

There are provisions safeguarding nationals and enterprises of one country against discriminatory taxation in the other country, and for the exchange of information and consultation between the taxation authorities of the two countries.

The Convention is in general to take effect in the United Kingdom for 1968-69 and subsequent years.

STATUTORY INSTRUMENTS

1970 No. 156

CIVIL AVIATION

The Air Navigation (Fifth Amendment) Order 1970

Made - - - -	*4th February* 1970
Laid before Parliament	*10th February* 1970
Coming into Operation	
(*a*) *for the purposes of Article* 3(1)(3)(4) *and* (8) - -	*1st May* 1970
(*b*) *for all other purposes*	*16th February* 1970

At the Court at Buckingham Palace, the 4th day of February 1970

Present,

The Queen's Most Excellent Majesty in Council

Her Majesty, in exercise of the powers conferred upon Her by sections 8, 57 and 59 of the Civil Aviation Act 1949(**a**), and of all other powers enabling Her in that behalf, is pleased, by and with the advice of Her Privy Council, to order, and it is hereby ordered, as follows:

Citation and Operation

1. This Order may be cited as the Air Navigation (Fifth Amendment) Order 1970 and shall come into operation on 1st May 1970 for the purposes of Article 3(1)(3)(4) and (8), and on 16th February 1970 for all other purposes.

Interpretation

2.—(1) In this Order, " the Principal Order " means the Air Navigation Order 1966(**b**), as amended (**c**).

(2) The Interpretation Act 1889(**d**) applies for the purpose of the interpretation of this Order as it applies for the purpose of the interpretation of an Act of Parliament.

Amendment of Air Navigation Order 1966

3. The Principal Order shall be further amended as follows:

(1) In Article 7(3)(*a*) " or aircraft radio maintenance engineer " shall be deleted ;

(2) In Article 8(3) after " which identifies " the words " the aircraft and " shall be deleted ;

(3) In Article 8(4)(*a*) " or aircraft radio maintenance engineer " shall be deleted ;

(4) In Article 9(1) " or an aircraft radio maintenance engineer " shall be deleted ;

(**a**) 1949 c. 67. (**b**) S.I. 1966/1184 (1966 III, p. 3073).
(**c**) S.I. 1968/1857 (1968 III, p. 4883). (**d**) 1889 c. 63.

(5) In Article 19(*a*) " time " shall be deleted ;

(6) In Article 83(1):

(*a*) after the definition of " Aerodrome " there shall be inserted the following definition:

" " Aerodrome traffic zone " in relation to any aerodrome means the airspace extending from the aerodrome to a height of 2,000 feet above the level of the aerodrome and within a distance of 3,000 yards of its boundaries except any part of that airspace which is within the aerodrome traffic zone of another aerodrome which is notified for the purposes of this Order as being the controlling aerodrome " ;

(*b*) after the definition of " Flight level " there shall be inserted the following definition:

" " Flight visibility " means the visibility forward from the flight deck of an aircraft in flight " ;

(*c*) after the definition of " Lifejacket " there shall be inserted the following definition:

" " Log Book " in the case of an aircraft log book, engine log book or variable pitch propeller log book, includes a record kept either in a book, or by any other means approved by the Board in the particular case " ;

(*d*) after the definition of " Visual Flight Rules " there shall be inserted the following definition:

" " Visual Meteorological Conditions " means weather permitting flight in accordance with the Visual Flight Rules " ;

(7) In Schedule 1 Part A Column 4 after " Aeroplane (Amphibian) " there shall be inserted " Aeroplane (Self-launching Motor Glider) " ;

(8) In Schedule 4:

(*a*) for the sub-heading " *Aircraft Maintenance Engineers—* " there shall be substituted " *Aircraft Maintenance Engineers—Category X* " ;

(*b*) for the sub-heading " *Aircraft Radio Maintenance Engineers —Category A (Radio)* " there shall be substituted " *Aircraft Maintenance Engineers—Category R (Radio)* ", and immediately after sub-paragraph (*b*) there shall be inserted:

" The privileges of the licence shall also include the issue of certificates of compliance in respect of inspections, overhauls, repairs, replacements and modifications of any aircraft radio apparatus approved under this Order, if the licence bears an endorsement to that effect." ;

(*c*) the sub-heading " *Aircraft Radio Maintenance Engineers— Category B (Radio)* " and the description of the privileges of the licence shall be deleted ;

(9) In Schedule 9 Part A—Licences, in the privileges of a Private Pilot's Licence (Aeroplanes):

(*a*) in sub-paragraph (*b*) for " in respect of the flight " there shall be substituted " for his services as pilot on the flight " ;

(*b*) in sub-paragraphs (*c*)(i)(*aa*) and (*bb*) " flight " shall be inserted immediately before " visibility " ;

(*c*) for sub-paragraph (*c*)(ii) the following sub-paragraph shall be substituted:

"(ii) on a special VFR flight in a control zone in a flight visibility of less than 5 nautical miles, except on a route or in an aerodrome traffic zone notified for the purposes of this sub-paragraph;";

(10) In Schedule 9 Part B—Ratings, in the Instrument Meteorological Conditions Rating (Aeroplanes):

(*a*) for sub-paragraph (*a*) there shall be substituted the following sub-paragraph:

"(*a*) on a flight outside controlled airspace, with or without passengers, in either Visual Meteorological Conditions or Instrument Meteorological Conditions; or";

(*b*) for sub-paragraph (*b*) there shall be substituted the following sub-paragraph:

"(*b*) on a special VFR flight in a control zone in a flight visibility of not less than $1\frac{1}{2}$ nautical miles.".

W. G. Agnew.

EXPLANATORY NOTE

(This Note is not part of the Order.)

This Order amends the Air Navigation Order 1966, as previously amended.

In addition to some minor and drafting amendments the following changes are made in the Articles mentioned below:

(1) The Aircraft Radio Maintenance Engineer's Licence—Category B (Radio) is abolished, and changes are made in the titles of other Aircraft Maintenance Engineers' Licences. The privileges of the licence abolished may now be exercised by the holder of an Aircraft Maintenance Engineers—Category R (Radio) Licence, if the licence bears an endorsement to that effect (Articles 7(3)(*a*), 8(4)(*a*), 9(1) and Schedule 4).

(2) The certificate of compliance no longer needs to identify the aircraft to which the overhaul, repair, replacement or modification relates (Article 8(3)).

(3) Particulars to be recorded in the personal flying log books of flight crew need no longer include the time of arrival and departure of each flight (Article 19(*a*)).

(4) Aircraft, engine and variable pitch propeller records can be kept either in a book or by any other means approved by the Board in the particular case (Article 83(1)).

(5) Self-launching motor gliders are added to the aeroplane class of aircraft in the Table of general classification of aircraft (Schedule 1).

(6) In the privileges of a Private Pilot's Licence (Aeroplanes) "flight visibility", defined as meaning visibility forward from the flight deck of an aircraft in flight, is substituted for "visibility" (Schedule 9 Part A(*c*)(i)(*aa*) and (*bb*)). The holder of such a licence, not including an Instrument Meteorological Conditions rating, will now be permitted to

fly on a special VFR flight in a control zone in a flight visibility of less than 5 nautical miles if he flies on a route or in an aerodrome traffic zone notified for that purpose in a " Notam-United Kingdom " or in the " United Kingdom Air Pilot " (Schedule 9 Part A(c)(ii)).

(7) The holder of the IMC Rating (Aeroplanes) will be entitled to fly:
  (a) outside controlled airspace whatever the meteorological conditions and whether or not passengers are carried ;
  (b) on a special VFR flight in a control zone in a flight visibility of not less than 1½ nautical miles, instead of in a visibility of less than 5 nautical miles, as heretofore.

(Schedule 9 Part B(a) and (b)).

STATUTORY INSTRUMENTS

1970 No. 157

CUSTOMS AND EXCISE

The European Free Trade Association (Iceland) Order 1970

Made - - - *4th February* 1970

Coming into Operation *1st March* 1970

At the Court at Buckingham Palace, the 4th day of February 1970

Present,

The Queen's Most Excellent Majesty in Council

Her Majesty, in exercise of the powers conferred upon Her by section 10 of the European Free Trade Association Act 1960(a) and of all other powers enabling Her in that behalf, is pleased, by and with the advice of Her Privy Council, to order, and it is hereby ordered, as follows:—

1. This Order may be cited as the European Free Trade Association (Iceland) Order 1970, and shall come into operation on 1st March 1970.

2. Iceland is declared to be a country which is included in the area of the European Free Trade Association.

W. G. Agnew.

(a) 1960 c. 19.

STATUTORY INSTRUMENTS

1970 No. 158

MERCHANT SHIPPING

The Merchant Shipping (Load Lines Convention) (Various Countries) Order 1970

Made - - -	*4th February* 1970
Laid before Parliament	*10th February* 1970
Coming into Operation	*17th February* 1970

At the Court at Buckingham Palace, the 4th day of February 1970

Present,

The Queen's Most Excellent Majesty in Council

Whereas by section 31(1) of the Merchant Shipping (Load Lines) Act 1967(**a**) it is enacted that Her Majesty may, if satisfied that the Government of any country has accepted or acceded to the International Convention on Load Lines 1966, by Order in Council make a declaration to that effect:

And whereas Her Majesty is satisfied that the Governments of the countries specified in the Schedule hereto have accepted or acceded to the said Convention:

Now, therefore, Her Majesty in pursuance of the powers conferred upon Her by the said section 31(1) and of all other powers enabling Her in that behalf is pleased, by and with the advice of Her Privy Council, to order, and it is hereby ordered, as follows:—

1. This Order may be cited as the Merchant Shipping (Load Lines Convention) (Various Countries) Order 1970, and shall come into operation on 17th February 1970.

2. It is hereby declared that the Governments of the countries specified in the Schedule to this Order have accepted or acceded to the International Convention on Load Lines 1966.

W. G. Agnew.

SCHEDULE

Federative Republic of Brazil
Republic of Cyprus
Czechoslovak Socialist Republic
Republic of Korea
Polish People's Republic
People's Republic of Southern Yemen

(**a**) 1967 c. 27.

1970 No. 159

MERCHANT SHIPPING

The Merchant Shipping (Safety Convention) (Various Countries) Order 1970

Made - - -	*4th February* 1970
Laid before Parliament	*10th February* 1970
Coming into Operation	*17th February* 1970

At the Court at Buckingham Palace, the 4th day of February 1970

Present,

The Queen's Most Excellent Majesty in Council

Whereas by section 31 of the Merchant Shipping (Safety Convention) Act 1949(a) as amended by section 1 of the Merchant Shipping Act 1964(b) it is enacted that Her Majesty, if satisfied that the Government of any country has accepted the International Convention for the Safety of Life at Sea 1960 (hereinafter referred to as "the 1960 Convention"), may by Order in Council make a declaration to that effect:

And whereas Her Majesty is satisfied that the Governments of the countries specified in the Schedule to this Order have accepted the 1960 Convention:

Now, therefore, Her Majesty, in pursuance of the powers conferred upon Her by the aforesaid sections and of all other powers enabling Her in that behalf is pleased, by and with the advice of Her Privy Council, to order, and it is hereby ordered, as follows:—

1. This Order may be cited as the Merchant Shipping (Safety Convention) (Various Countries) Order 1970, and shall come into operation on 17th February 1970.

2. It is hereby declared that the Governments of the countries specified in the Schedule to this Order have accepted the 1960 Convention.

W. G. Agnew.

SCHEDULE

Republic of Honduras.
Republic of Singapore.
People's Republic of Southern Yemen.
Syrian Arab Republic.
Republic of Venezuela.

(a) 1949 c. 43.   (b) 1964 c. 47.

STATUTORY INSTRUMENTS

1970 No. 161

NATIONAL HEALTH SERVICE, ENGLAND AND WALES

The National Health Service (University Hospital of South Manchester Designation) Order 1970

Made - - -	*4th February* 1970
Laid before Parliament	*11th February* 1970
Coming into Operation	*1st April* 1970

The Secretary of State for Social Services, being satisfied that the group of hospitals specified in Schedule 1 to this order and vested in him provides for the University of Manchester facilities for undergraduate and post-graduate clinical teaching and after consultation with that University, in exercise of his powers under section 5 of the Health Services and Public Health Act 1968(a) and of all other powers enabling him in that behalf, hereby makes the following order:—

1.—(1) This order may be cited as the National Health Service (University Hospital of South Manchester Designation) Order 1970 and shall come into operation on 1st April 1970.

(2) The Interpretation Act 1889(b) applies to the interpretation of this order as it applies to the interpretation of an Act of Parliament.

2. The group of hospitals specified in Schedule 1 to this order (hereinafter in this order referred to as "the group") is hereby designated as a university hospital.

3. Part II of Schedule 3 to the National Health Service Act 1946(c) (Constitution of Hospital Management Committees) shall have effect in relation to the Committee appointed to exercise functions with respect to the management and control of the group, as modified and set out in Schedule 2 to this order.

SCHEDULE 1
LIST OF HOSPITALS
1. Withington Hospital (including Burton House and Newholme).
2. Christie Hospital and Holt Radium Institute.
3. Manchester Ear Hospital.
4. Duchess of York Hospital for Babies.
5. Manchester Audiology Clinic.

SCHEDULE 2
CONSTITUTION OF THE UNIVERSITY HOSPITAL MANAGEMENT COMMITTEE OF SOUTH MANCHESTER

The provisions of Part II of Schedule 3 to the National Health Service Act 1946 shall have effect as modified and set out below:—

(1) subject to the following provisions of this schedule, the Hospital Management Committee shall consist of a Chairman, appointed by the Manchester Regional Hospital Board after consultation with the University of Manchester, and 15 other members appointed by the Board;

(a) 1968 c. 46.　　(b) 1889 c. 63.　　(c) 1946 c. 81.

(2) of the 15 other members 3 shall be nominated by the University of Manchester, but of these 3 not more than 2 shall be medical practitioners or dental practitioners, and 3 shall be nominated by the medical and dental staff of the group after consultation with the Manchester Regional Hospital Board and the University of Manchester;

(3) other members shall include persons appointed after consultation with:—

  (i) any local health authority whose area comprises the area or any part of the area served by the group; and

  (ii) any Executive Council whose area comprises the area or any part of the area served by the group; and

  (iii) such other organisations as appear to the Board to be concerned;

(4) not more than 6 members shall be medical practitioners or dental practitioners;

(5) before making appointments to fill vacancies the Board shall consult the Committee.

R. H. S. Crossman,
Secretary of State for Social Services.

4th February 1970.

EXPLANATORY NOTE

(This Note is not part of the Order.)

This Order designates the group of hospitals set out in Schedule 1 as a university hospital, associated with the University of Manchester, and provides for a modified form of Hospital Management Committee (as set out in Schedule 2) to manage and control it.

STATUTORY INSTRUMENTS

1970 No. 163 (L.6)

PENSIONS

The Pensions Appeal Tribunals (England and Wales) (Amendment) Rules 1970

Made - - -	*3rd February* 1970
Laid before Parliament	*11th February* 1970
Coming into Operation	*16th February* 1970

The Lord Chancellor, in exercise of the powers conferred on him by paragraph 5(4) of the Schedule to the Pensions Appeal Tribunals Act 1943(**a**) and after consultation with the Council on Tribunals in accordance with section 8 of the Tribunals and Inquiries Act 1958(**b**), hereby makes the following Rules :—

1. These Rules may be cited as the Pensions Appeal Tribunals (England and Wales) (Amendment) Rules 1970 and shall come into operation on 16th February 1970.

2. The Pensions Appeal Tribunals (England and Wales) Rules 1946(**c**) as amended (**d**) shall be further amended as follows :—

In Rule 27(3) (which relates to the expenses allowable to appellants and their attendants), for the words "65s. 0d." there shall be substituted "80s. 0d."

Dated 3rd February 1970.

Gardiner, C.

EXPLANATORY NOTE

(This Note is not part of the Rules.)

These Rules further amend the Pensions Appeal Tribunals (England and Wales) Rules 1946, by increasing from 65s. to 80s. the maximum allowance payable to an appellant or his representative or attendant for loss of time.

(**a**) 1943 c. 39.   (**b**) 1958 c. 66.
(**c**) S.R. & O. 1946/1708 (Rev. XVII, p. 733; 1946 I, p. 1313).
(**d**) The relevant amending instruments are: S.I. 1949/2105, 1957/1827, 1962/1614, 1966/1421 (1949 I, p. 3008; 1957 II, p. 1833; 1962 II, p. 1886; 1966 III, p. 3787).

STATUTORY INSTRUMENTS

1970 No. 165

CUSTOMS AND EXCISE

The Export of Goods (Control) (Amendment) Order 1970

Made - - - - *4th February* 1970
Coming into Operation *18th February* 1970

The Board of Trade, in exercise of the powers conferred on them by section 1 of the Import, Export and Customs Powers (Defence) Act 1939(**a**), hereby order as follows:—

1.—(1) This Order may be cited as the Export of Goods (Control) (Amendment) Order 1970 and shall come into operation on 18th February 1970.

(2) The Interpretation Act 1889(**b**) shall apply to the interpretation of this Order as it applies to the interpretation of an Act of Parliament.

2. The Export of Goods (Control) Order 1967(**c**), as amended(**d**), shall have effect as if—

(i) there were added as paragraph (l) of Article 2(1) the following:—

" (l) pork to any port or destination in the Republic of Ireland " ; and

(ii) the following entry were included in Schedule 1, Part I, Group 8, namely—

"Pork, fresh, chilled or frozen (excluding offals) ...   ...   A".

R. L. Davies,
An Assistant Secretary of the
Board of Trade.

4th February 1970.

EXPLANATORY NOTE

(This Note is not part of the Order.)

This Order further amends the Export of Goods (Control) Order 1967 by including pork among the goods of which the export is controlled. An exception is made in relation to export to the Republic of Ireland.

(**a**) 1939 c. 69.   (**b**) 1889 c. 63.   (**c**) S.I. 1967/675 (1967 I, p. 2080).
(**d**) The relevant amending order is S.I. 1968/132 (1968 I, p. 353).

STATUTORY INSTRUMENTS

1970 No. 168

MINES AND QUARRIES

The Quarry Vehicles Regulations 1970

Made - - - -	*3rd February* 1970
Laid before Parliament	*13th February* 1970
Coming into Operation	*29th April* 1970

Whereas in pursuance of Part I of Schedule 2 to the Mines and Quarries Act 1954(a) the Minister of Technology has published notice of his intention to make the following regulations and has not received any objection to the draft thereof in respect to which he is required to refer the draft regulations for inquiry and report:

Now, therefore, the Minister of Technology in exercise of his powers under section 141 of the Mines and Quarries Act 1954 and of all other powers him enabling hereby makes the following regulations:—

Commencement and citation

1. These regulations shall come into operation on 29th April 1970 and may be cited as the Quarry Vehicles Regulations 1970.

Interpretation

2.—(1) In these regulations, unless the context otherwise requires, the following expressions have the meanings hereby respectively assigned to them, that is to say—

"the Act" means the Mines and Quarries Act 1954;

"appropriate person" in relation to a quarry means—

(*a*) with regard to any matter the responsibility for which is for the time being duly reserved to the owner in accordance with section 100 of the Act, the owner of the quarry;

(*b*) with regard to any other matter, the manager of the quarry or where there are two or more managers, the manager having jurisdiction over the relevant part of the quarry;

"hours of darkness" means the time between half-an-hour after sunset and half-an-hour before sunrise;

(a) 1954 c. 70.

"quarry vehicle" in relation to a quarry means a mechanically propelled vehicle (including mechanically propelled plant) which forms part of the equipment of the quarry and is not—

(a) a vehicle intended or adapted for use on rails or a ropeway; or

(b) a vehicle constructed or adapted for use only under the control of a pedestrian; or

(c) a motor cycle;

"traffic sign" means any object or device (whether fixed or portable) for conveying to users of vehicles warnings, information, requirements, restrictions or prohibitions of any description;

"trailer" means any vehicle drawn by a quarry vehicle.

(2) Expressions to which meanings are assigned by the Act, Part 1 of the Mines and Quarries (Tips) Act 1969 or by these regulations shall (unless the contrary intention appears) have the same meanings in any document issued under the provisions of these regulations.

(3) The Interpretation Act 1889(a) shall apply to the interpretation of these regulations as it applies to the interpretation of an Act of Parliament.

Provision of audible warning instruments and lighting

3.—(1) No quarry vehicle shall be used at a quarry unless it is provided with an instrument capable of giving adequate audible warning of its approach or position.

(2) No quarry vehicle or trailer other than a mechanically propelled drilling machine shall be used at a quarry during the hours of darkness unless there is provided (whether as part of the vehicle's equipment or otherwise) sufficient and suitable artificial lighting to enable the vehicle to be safely used, having regard to the particular purpose for which and the circumstances in which it is then to be used.

Safety provisions in respect of Tipping Vehicles

4.—(1) No quarry vehicle or trailer equipped with a tipping body shall be used at a quarry unless there are provided (whether as part of the equipment of the vehicle or trailer or otherwise) one or more sufficient devices for keeping the tipping body from collapsing from the raised position, being devices whose mode of operation is independent of the tipping mechanism.

(2) The appropriate person at a quarry shall take such steps, including provision where appropriate of stop blocks, anchor chains or other suitable devices, as are necessary to prevent the occurrence at every place at which any quarry vehicle or trailer equipped with a tipping body or tipping gear is unloaded of accidents likely to cause bodily injury to persons being accidents caused by vehicles so used running away, falling or overturning.

Precautions by users of Tipping Vehicles

5. A person who uses at a quarry a quarry vehicle or trailer equipped with a tipping body or tipping gear shall take precautions, including where necessary using any safety devices provided by the appropriate person at a quarry, at every place at which any such vehicle is unloaded, to prevent the vehicle from running away, falling or overturning.

(a) 1889 c. 63.

Leaving Vehicles Secure

6. No person employed at a quarry in charge of a quarry vehicle thereat shall alight from the vehicle unless he has ensured that it is so placed or is so secured that it cannot accidentally move or be set in motion.

Careless Driving

7. A person who drives a quarry vehicle at a quarry without due care and attention, having regard to all the circumstances of the case including the nature, condition and use of the road or other place over which the vehicle is being driven and the visibility at the time, shall be guilty of an offence.

Rules

8.—(1) The manager of a quarry at which quarry vehicles are used, or where there are two or more managers, the manager having jurisdiction over the relevant part of the quarry shall make rules for regulating the conduct of persons employed thereat, or any class of persons so employed, being rules for the purpose of securing compliance with these regulations and in particular rules as to—

> (*a*) the occasions upon which, and the manner in which devices provided pursuant to regulation 4(1) of these regulations are to be used by the said persons for preventing the tipping body of the quarry vehicle or trailer from collapsing from the raised position;

> (*b*) the precautions to be taken by the said persons at places at which such a vehicle as is mentioned in regulation 5 of these regulations is unloaded, including the use of such devices as are necessary to prevent the occurrence therein mentioned.

(2) The appropriate person at a quarry shall erect such traffic signs as may be requisite for giving effect to these regulations and the rules regulating the conduct of persons employed thereat made for the purpose of securing compliance with these regulations for the time being in force.

(3) If an inspector is of opinion that rules made for the purposes of paragraph (1) of this regulation do not in some respect make sufficient provision for securing compliance with these regulations he may serve on the manager who made the rules a notice stating that he is of that opinion, specifying the matter for which in his opinion provision, or as the case may be different provision, ought to be made as aforesaid and the nature of that provision that, in his opinion, ought to be made, and requiring the said manager, before the expiration of such period beginning with the day on which the notice becomes operative as may be specified therein, to amend the rules accordingly.

(4) The provisions of Part XV of the Act with respect to references upon notices served by inspectors shall apply to a notice served under the last preceding paragraph, and the relevant ground of objection shall be that adequate provision is already made by the said rules made for the purpose of securing compliance with these regulations for ensuring the safety of persons employed at the quarry.

(5) Without prejudice to the generality of section 135 of the Act a copy of any of the said rules made for the purpose of securing compliance with these regulations for the time being in force shall be kept in the covered accommodation at the quarry or near thereto provided in pursuance of that section.

(6) It shall be the duty of the appropriate person at any quarry with respect to which the said rules made for the purpose of securing compliance with these regulations are for the time being in force to supply to any person whose duties consist of or include the driving of quarry vehicles, signalling or supervision of the use of quarry vehicles, a copy of the rules or a document setting out the effect of the rules so far as they concern him.

Drivers of quarry vehicles

9.—(1) No person employed at a quarry shall drive thereat any quarry vehicle—

> (*a*) unless he is a person appointed by the appropriate person at a quarry as the driver of that vehicle or of vehicles of a class to which that vehicle belongs and he has attained the age of seventeen years; or

> (*b*) unless he is a person authorised by the appropriate person at a quarry to receive training as a driver of that vehicle or vehicles of a class to which that vehicle belongs and he drives the vehicle only under the close personal supervision of a competent person appointed by the appropriate person.

(2) The appropriate person at a quarry shall secure that no person authorised to receive training pursuant to paragraph (1)(*b*) of this regulation drives any quarry vehicle thereat while receiving such training unless there are at the front and rear of the vehicle prominent signs indicating that the driver of the vehicle is under instruction.

Overhead obstructions

10. At every quarry at which there is any place at which there is any overhead structure or cable which could obstruct the passage of any quarry vehicle or trailer or any load which may be carried thereby or any extending part thereof in its highest position, one or more prominent signs indicating the clearance beneath that structure or cable shall be so exhibited at that place as to be easily seen and read by any driver of any vehicle which may approach that place.

Exemptions

11. An inspector may by notice served on the appropriate person exempt any quarry or any part thereof or any vehicle or class of vehicles thereat from the application of any provision of these regulations if he is satisfied that the safety of persons employed at the quarry will not be prejudiced in consequence of the granting of the exemption.

Dated 3rd February 1970.

Anthony Wedgwood Benn,
Minister of Technology

EXPLANATORY NOTE

(This Note is not part of the Regulations.)

These regulations made by the Minister of Technology under the Mines and Quarries Act 1954 set out the conditions which must be observed when quarry vehicles and trailers are used at quarries and make provision with regard to the driving of quarry vehicles and for leaving them secure.

The regulations provide for the manager making rules for regulating the conduct of persons employed at the quarry, being rules for the purpose of securing compliance with the regulations, and set out particular matters for inclusion in the rules. The regulations further provide that an inspector may by notice served on the manager require an addition or amendment to be made to the rules as he considers necessary. Provision is also made with regard to the erection of such traffic signs as may be requisite for giving effect to the regulations and the rules and for signs indicating the clearance beneath overhead obstructions.

STATUTORY INSTRUMENTS

1970 No. 169 (C.4)

ROAD TRAFFIC

The Vehicle and Driving Licences Act 1969
(Commencement No. 5) Order 1970

Made - - -	*3rd February* 1970
Laid before Parliament	*16th February* 1970
Coming into Operation	*1st April* 1970

The Minister of Transport hereby makes this Order in exercise of his powers under section 38(2) of the Vehicle and Driving Licences Act 1969(a) and of all other enabling powers.

1. This Order may be cited as the Vehicle and Driving Licences Act 1969 (Commencement No. 5) Order 1970.

2. Section 27 of the Vehicle and Driving Licences Act 1969 shall come into operation on 1st April 1970.

3. Sections 13, 14, 15, 16(1), 16(2) (in so far as it relates to paragraphs 1, 2, 3, 5 and 7 of Schedule 2), 16(3), 16(4), 23(1)(a), (b), (c), (d) and (e), 23(2), 35 (in so far as it relates to notices authorised to be served on any person by section 100 or 102(2) of the Road Traffic Act 1960(b)) and 37 (in so far as it relates to sections 99(4), 109(3), 110(a), 113(g), 115, 225 and 226(2) of the Road Traffic Act 1960) of the Vehicle and Driving Licences Act 1969 shall come into operation on 1st June 1970.

Given under the Official Seal of the Minister of Transport the 3rd February 1970.

(L.S.)

Fred Mulley,
Minister of Transport.

EXPLANATORY NOTE

(*This Note is not part of the Order.*)

This Order brings into operation the following provisions of the Vehicle and Driving Licences Act 1969 on the 1st June 1970 except for section 27 which it brings into operation on the 1st April 1970:—

Section 13, which substitutes a new section for section 100 of the Road Traffic Act 1960 relating to the requirements as to the physical fitness of drivers.

Section 14, which substitutes new sections for sections 101 and 102 of the Act of 1960 relating to the grant and duration of driving licences and makes provision for the transitional operation of driving licences current at the time of the substitution.

(a) 1969 c. 27.   (b) 1960 c. 16.

Section 15, which substitutes a new section for section 103 of the Act of 1960 relating to appeals in respect of driving licences.

Section 16(1), which adds two subsections to section 98 of the Act of 1960. The first creates a defence against the offence of driving or employing a person to drive without a driving licence and the second enables regulations to provide that new residents in Great Britain shall be treated as holders of driving licences for the purposes of that offence.

Section 16(2), which amends the Act of 1960 in accordance with Schedule 2 to the Act of 1969. The relevant amendments in the Schedule are—

paragraph 1, which repeals section 99(4) removing the power to provide by regulation for dispensing with tests of competence for persons not resident in Great Britain,

paragraph 2, which amends section 99(5) and relates to the effect on a person's entitlement to a driving licence when the requirements of the tests of competence or groups of vehicles for driving licences' purposes are changed,

paragraph 3, which amends section 110 making it no longer an offence to apply for a licence whilst disqualified,

paragraph 5, which makes a drafting amendment to section 115,

paragraph 7, which makes a number of minor changes to section 225(2) (seizure of driving licences by police constables upon revocation by licensing authorities).

Section 16(3), which amends section 7(4) of the Road Traffic Act 1962 providing a defence to the offence of not producing a driving licence to a court when convicted of certain road traffic offences in a case where a person has applied for a new licence.

Section 16(4), which makes drafting amendments to section 7(7) of the Road Traffic Act 1962 relating to the grant of a driving licence free of time-expired endorsements.

Section 23(1)(a), (b), (c), (d) and (e) and (2), which relate to fees for driving tests, driving licences, replacement vehicle licences, replacement registration documents and the furnishing of information.

Section 27, which provides for certain records maintained by the Minister or a local authority to be admissible in evidence.

Section 35 (in so far as it relates to notices authorised to be served on any person by section 100 or 102(2) of the Act of 1960), which relates to the method of service of notices relating to driving licences.

Section 37 (in so far as it relates to the specified provisions of the Act of 1960), which repeals a number of provisions of the Act of 1960. These repeals are consequential on amendments made to that Act by provisions mentioned above.

STATUTORY INSTRUMENTS

1970 No. 170

ROAD TRAFFIC

The Motor Vehicles (Driving Licences) Regulations 1970

Made - - -	*3rd February* 1970
Laid before Parliament	*16th February* 1970
Coming into Operation	*1st June* 1970

ARRANGEMENT OF REGULATIONS

SCHEDULES

The Minister of Transport hereby makes these Regulations in exercise of his powers under section 98 of the Road Traffic Act 1960(**a**), as amended by section 16 of the Vehicle and Driving Licences Act 1969(**b**), section 99 of the said Act of 1960, as extended by section 25 of the Road Traffic Act 1962(**c**) and as amended by section 51 of and Schedule 4 to that Act and section 16(2) of and Schedule 2 to the said Act of 1969, sections 100 and 101 of the said Act of 1960, as amended by sections 13 and 14 of the said Act of 1969, section 113 of the said Act of 1960, as amended by section 23 of the said Act of 1969, section 114 of the said Act of 1960, section 225 of the said Act of 1960, as amended by section 22(5) of the said Act of 1969 and section 253 of the said Act of 1960, and of all other enabling powers, and after consultation with representative organisations in accordance with section 260(2) of the said Act of 1960, and, in the case of Regulations 5 and 17, with the approval of the Treasury.

Part I—Preliminary

Commencement and citation

1. These Regulations shall come into operation on the 1st June 1970, and may be cited as the Motor Vehicles (Driving Licences) Regulations 1970.

Revocation, savings and transitional provisions

2.—(1) The Regulations specified in Schedule 1 to these Regulations are hereby revoked but, subject as hereinafter provided,—

(*a*) in so far as any application or appointment made, notice or approval given, licence, certificate or other document granted or issued or other thing done, under the said Regulations could have been made, given, granted, issued or done under a corresponding provision of these Regulations, it shall not be invalidated by the said revocation but shall have effect as if made, given, granted, issued or done under that corresponding provision, and

(*b*) any reference in any such application, appointment, notice, approval, licence, certificate or other document to any provision of the Regulations revoked by these Regulations, whether specifically or by means of a general description, shall, unless the context otherwise requires, be construed as a reference to the corresponding provision of these Regulations.

(2) The provisions of Regulation 6 of these Regulations shall apply in relation to a provisional licence granted before the date of the coming into operation of these Regulations and in force on that date, as they apply in relation to a provisional licence granted on or after that date.

(**a**) 1960 c. 16.   (**b**) 1969 c. 27.
(**c**) 1962 c. 59.

Interpretation

3.—(1) In these Regulations, unless the context otherwise requires, the following expressions have the meanings hereby respectively assigned to them, that is to say :—

"Act of 1960" means the Road Traffic Act 1960 ;

"agricultural tractor" means a motor tractor used primarily for work on land in connection with agriculture ;

"clerk to the traffic commissioners" means the clerk to the traffic commissioner for the Metropolitan Traffic Area or the clerk to the traffic commissioners for any other traffic area ;

"disability" includes disease ;

"full licence" means a licence other than a provisional licence ;

"group" in relation to a class or description of motor vehicles means a group of motor vehicles of the classes or descriptions specified in the second column of Schedule 3 to these Regulations, and a group identified by a letter means the group corresponding to the letter in the first column of that Schedule ;

"licence" means a licence to drive a motor vehicle granted under Part II of the Act of 1960 ;

"licensing authority" means—

    (*a*) in relation to England and Wales, the council of a county or of a county borough ; and

    (*b*) in relation to Scotland, the council of a county or of a burgh containing within its boundaries as ascertained, fixed or determined for police purposes, a population according to the census for the time being last taken of or exceeding 50,000 ;

"moped" means a motor cycle whereof the cylinder capacity of the engine does not exceed 50 cubic centimetres, being a cycle equipped with pedals by means whereof it is capable of being propelled ;

"provisional licence" means a licence granted by virtue of section 101(2) of the Act of 1960 ;

"the Minister" means the Minister of Transport ;

"test" means a test of competence to drive conducted under section 99 of the Act of 1960 ;

"vehicle propelled by electrical power" means a vehicle of which the motive power is solely derived from any electrical storage battery carried on the vehicle and not connected to any source of power when the vehicle is in motion ;

"vehicle with automatic transmission" means a vehicle in which the driver is not provided with any means whereby he may, independently of the use of the accelerator or the brakes, vary gradually the proportion of the power being produced by the engine which is transmitted to the road wheels of the vehicle.

(2) In these Regulations references to any enactment shall be construed as references to that enactment as amended by or under any subsequent enactment.

(3) The Interpretation Act 1889(a) shall apply for the interpretation of these Regulations as it applies for the interpretation of an Act of Parliament, and as if for the purposes of section 38 of that Act these Regulations were an Act of Parliament and the Regulations revoked by Regulation 2 of these Regulations were Acts of Parliament thereby repealed.

PART II—LICENCES

Applications for the grant of licences

4. Applications for the grant of a licence may be received and dealt with at any time within two months before the date on which the grant of the licence is to take effect.

Fees for licences

5. The fee payable for a licence shall be :—

(a) £1, in the case of a full or provisional licence,

(b) 5s.0d . in the case of a duplicate licence or a licence granted in exchange for a subsisting licence, except where the licence is granted free of charge pursuant to section 102(4) of the Act of 1960.

Conditions attached to provisional licences

6.—(1) Subject to the provisions of paragraphs (2), (3) and (4) of this Regulation the holder of a provisional licence shall comply with the following conditions in relation to motor vehicles of a class or description which he is authorised to drive by virtue of the provisional licence, that is to say he shall not drive or ride such a motor vehicle—

(a) otherwise than under the supervision of a qualified driver who is present with him in or on the vehicle ;

(b) unless there is clearly displayed in a conspicuous manner on the front and on the back of the vehicle a distinguishing mark in the form set out in Schedule 2 to these Regulations ;

(c) while it is being used to draw a trailer ;

(d) in the case of a motor cycle not having attached thereto a side-car, while carrying on it a person who is not a qualified driver :

Provided that where the holder of a provisional licence has passed a test which authorises him to be granted a full licence comprising a particular class or description of vehicles the above-mentioned conditions shall cease to apply in relation to the driving or riding (as the case may be) by him of motor vehicles of that class or description.

(2) The condition specified in paragraph (1)(a) of this Regulation shall not apply when the holder of the provisional licence—

(a) is undergoing a test or a test of competence to drive heavy goods vehicles under Part V of the Act of 1960 ; or

(b) is driving a vehicle (not being a motor car) constructed to carry only one person and not adapted to carry more than one person ; or

(c) is driving a vehicle the unladen weight of which does not exceed 16 hundredweight, being a vehicle propelled by electrical power, constructed or adapted to carry only one person and constructed or adapted for the carriage of goods or burden of any description ; or

---

(a) 1889 c. 63.

(*d*) is driving a road roller the unladen weight of which does not exceed 3 tons, being a vehicle constructed or adapted for the carriage of goods or burden of any description ; or

(*e*) is riding a motor bicycle, whether or not having attached thereto a side-car.

(3) The condition specified in paragraph (1)(*c*) of this Regulation shall not apply when the holder of the provisional licence is driving an agricultural tractor, nor shall it prevent the holder of a provisional licence driving an articulated vehicle.

(4) The condition specified in paragraph (1)(*d*) of this Regulation shall not apply when the holder of the provisional licence is riding a pedal cycle of the tandem type to which additional means of propulsion by mechanical power are attached.

(5) In this Regulation "qualified driver" means a person who holds a full licence authorising him to drive as a full licence holder a motor vehicle of the same class or description as the vehicle being driven by the holder of the provisional licence.

Restricted provisional licences

7. A provisional licence shall be restricted so as to authorise only the driving of motor vehicles of a class or description comprised in group K in any case where the applicant is unable to read in good daylight (with the aid of glasses if worn) a registration mark fixed to a motor vehicle at a distance of 75 feet in the case of a registration mark containing letters and figures $3\frac{1}{2}$ inches high or at a distance of 67 feet in the case of a registration mark containing letters and figures $3\frac{1}{8}$ inches high.

Full licences not carrying provisional entitlement

8. A full licence which authorises its holder to drive certain classes and descriptions of motor vehicles shall not authorise its holder to drive motor vehicles of all other classes and descriptions subject to the same conditions as if he were authorised by a provisional licence to drive the last-mentioned vehicles if it is a licence which :—

(*a*) is limited to vehicles of a particular construction or design pursuant to section 100(4)(ii) of the Act of 1960 or section 100(4) of the Act of 1960 before it was amended by section 13 of the Vehicle and Driving Licences Act 1969 ; or

(*b*) authorises its holder to drive vehicles in group K only.

Signature of licences

9. Every person to whom a licence is granted shall forthwith sign it in ink with his usual signature.

Lost or defaced licences

10.—(1) If the holder of a licence satisfies the licensing authority by whom it was granted that the licence has been lost or defaced the licensing authority shall, on payment of the fee prescribed in Regulation 5, issue to him a duplicate licence and shall endorse thereon any particulars endorsed upon the original licence and the duplicate so issued shall have the same effect as the original.

(2) If at any time while a duplicate licence is in force the original licence is found, the person to whom the original licence was issued, if it is in his possession, shall return it to the licensing authority by whom it was issued, or if it is not in his possession but he becomes aware that it is found, shall take all reasonable steps to obtain possession of it and if successful shall return it as soon as may be to the said licensing authority.

Records of licences and endorsements

11. Every licensing authority shall establish and keep a record of all licences granted by them and a record of all endorsements from time to time duly made on such licences.

Production from records of particulars relating to licences

12. A licensing authority shall, upon application being made to them by or on behalf of any other licensing authority, by or on behalf of the traffic commissioners within the meaning of section 120 of the Act of 1960 or a licensing authority within the meaning of section 193 of that Act, by any officer of police not below the rank of inspector, or by a constable authorised by such officer, forthwith provide, without fee, a copy of the particulars recorded by them relating to any licence granted by them.

PART III—TESTS OF COMPETENCE TO DRIVE

Persons by whom tests may be conducted

13. Tests may be conducted :—

(a) by examiners appointed by the Minister ;

(b) by the Secretary of State for Defence, in so far as concerns the testing of persons in the service of the Crown under his department ;

(c) in England and Wales, by the chief officer of any fire brigade maintained in pursuance of the Fire Services Act 1947(a) or, in Scotland, by the firemaster of such a brigade, in so far as concerns the testing of members of any such brigade or of persons employed in the driving of motor vehicles for the purposes of any such brigade ;

(d) by any chief officer of police in so far as concerns the testing :—

(i) of members of a police force ; or

(ii) of persons employed in the driving of vehicles for police purposes by a police authority or by the Receiver for the Metropolitan Police District ;

(e) by the Commissioner of Police of the Metropolis in so far as concerns the testing of any person who is the holder of or is an applicant for a licence to drive a motor cab by virtue of the Metropolitan Public Carriage Act 1869(b) and of any person residing in the Metropolitan Traffic Area who is the holder of, or an applicant for, a licence to drive a public service vehicle ; and

(f) by any person appointed for the purpose by the Minister under the provisions of the following Regulation.

(a) 1947 c. 41. (b) 1869 c. 115.

14.—(1) Any person may apply to the Minister to be appointed to conduct tests of persons employed or proposed to be employed by him as drivers, and the Minister may, if he is satisfied that :—

> (*a*) the number of drivers of motor vehicles ordinarily employed by the applicant exceeds 250 ;
>
> (*b*) proper arrangements will be made by the applicant for the conduct of such tests in accordance with these Regulations ; and
>
> (*c*) proper records of such tests and the results thereof will be kept by the applicant,

grant the application subject to any special conditions which he may think fit to impose.

(2) The Minister may at any time revoke an appointment made by him under this Regulation and the authority to conduct tests shall thereupon cease.

15. Any person authorised by virtue of paragraph (*b*), (*c*), (*d*), (*e*) or (*f*) of Regulation 13 of these Regulations to conduct tests may, subject to the approval of the Minister, authorise suitable persons to act as examiners of those who submit themselves for a test.

Appointments for tests and notice of cancellation thereof

16.—(1) A person who desires to take a test to be conducted by an examiner appointed under paragraph (*a*) of Regulation 13 of these Regulations shall apply for an appointment for such a test to the clerk to the traffic commissioners.

(2) An applicant for such an appointment as aforesaid shall, when making the application, pay to the said clerk such fee in respect of the test as is specified in paragraph (3) of the following Regulation and the clerk shall make any arrangements necessary for the taking of the test.

(3) For the purposes of paragraph (*b*) of subsection (2) of section 25 of the Road Traffic Act 1962 (which subsection specifies the only circumstances in which a fee paid on application for an appointment for a test may be repaid) notice cancelling an appointment for such a test as is mentioned in paragraph (1) of this Regulation shall be given to the clerk to the traffic commissioners by whom the appointment was made not less than three clear days (excluding Saturdays, Sundays, any bank holiday, Christmas Day or Good Friday) before the date of the appointment.

For the purposes of this paragraph "bank holiday" means a day which is, or is to be observed as a bank holiday or a holiday under the Bank Holidays Act 1871(**a**) or the Holidays Extension Act 1875(**b**), either generally or in the locality in which is situated the office of the clerk to the traffic commissioners to whom notice cancelling an appointment for a test falls to be given.

Fees in respect of tests

17.—(1) The following provisions of this Regulation shall apply as respects the fees payable in respect of tests.

(2) No fee shall be payable in respect of a test conducted by a person authorised by virtue of paragraph (*b*), (*c*), (*d*) or (*f*) of Regulation 13 of these Regulations.

(**a**) 1871 c. 17.   (**b**) 1875 c. 13.

(3) The fee payable in respect of a test to be conducted by an examiner appointed under paragraph (*a*) of the said Regulation 13 or by a person authorised by virtue of paragraph (*e*) of that Regulation : —

(*a*) in the case of a test to be taken on a vehicle of a class or description in Group J shall be 2s. 6d.; and

(*b*) in the case of a test to be taken on any other vehicle, shall be £1 15s. 0d.

(4) The fee payable in respect of a test to be conducted by a person authorised by virtue of paragraph (*e*) of the said Regulation 13 shall be paid to that person to be retained by him as remuneration.

Nature of tests

18.—(1) Subject to the following provisions of this Regulation, the test which a person is required to pass before a licence can be granted to him authorising him to drive a motor vehicle of a class or description comprised in any particular group shall be a test carried out on a vehicle of that class or description which satisfies the person conducting the test :—

(*a*) that the person taking the test is fully conversant with the contents of the Highway Code ;

(*b*) generally that the person taking the test is competent to drive, without danger to and with due consideration for other users of the road, the vehicle on which he is tested ; and

(*c*) that the person taking the test is able to comply with such of the additional requirements specified in Schedule 4 to these Regulations as are referred to in the third column of Schedule 3 to these Regulations in relation to the group which comprises the class or description of vehicle on which he is tested ;

Provided that the person conducting the test may be satisfied as to the matters specified in this paragraph where he concludes that the person being tested should only be passed in relation to vehicles of a particular construction or design despite the fact that the test was not conducted on a vehicle of that construction or design.

(2) A person who has passed a test to drive vehicles of a class or description comprised in any particular group shall be deemed for the purposes of the Act of 1960 and of these Regulations competent to drive, in addition to vehicles of a class or description comprised in that particular group, also vehicles of a class or description comprised in any other group which is referred to in the fourth column of the said Schedule 3 as being an additional group in relation to that particular group.

Production of vehicle for test etc.

19.—(1) A person submitting himself for a test shall—

(*a*) provide for the purposes of the test a motor vehicle, which—

(i) is suitable for the purposes of the test,

(ii) is not fitted with a device designed to permit a person other than the driver to operate the accelerator, unless any pedal or lever by which the device is operated and any other parts which it may be necessary to remove to make the device inoperable by such a person during the test have been removed ;

(*b*) produce to the examiner who is to conduct his test his licence or other driving permit by virtue of which he is entitled to drive in Great Britain and shall sign the examiner's attendance record.

(2) Where a person submitting himself for a test fails to produce a vehicle or a vehicle which complies with the foregoing paragraph or fails to produce his licence as aforesaid or fails to sign the examiner's attendance record the examiner may refuse to conduct the test.

Evidence of results of tests

20.—(1) A person who passes a test shall be furnished with a certificate to that effect in the form (adapted as the case may require) set out in Part I of Schedule 5 to these Regulations.

(2) A person who fails to pass a test shall be furnished with a statement to that effect in the form (adapted as the case may require) set out in Part II of the said Schedule 5.

(3) An applicant for a licence who before the licence is granted is required to satisfy the licensing authority that he has passed a test shall at the time when the licence is granted to him deliver the certificate furnished to him under paragraph (1) of this Regulation to the licensing authority for their retention.

Period of ineligibility for a subsequent test

21. Subject to the provisions of section 99(3) of the Act of 1960 the period during which a person who has submitted himself for a test and failed to pass that test shall be ineligible to submit himself to another test on a vehicle of a class or description comprised in the same group shall be one month.

PART IV—SUPPLEMENTARY

Disabilities

22.—(1) The following disabilities are prescribed for the purposes of section 100(1) of the Act of 1960 :—

(*a*) epilepsy ;

(*b*) mental disorder for which the applicant for the licence or, as the case may be, the holder of the licence is liable to be detained under the Mental Health Act 1959(**a**) or is receiving treatment as an in-patient in a hospital or mental nursing home within the meaning of that Act ;

(*c*) mental disorder for which the applicant for the licence or, as the case may be, the holder of the licence is liable to be detained under the Mental Health (Scotland) Act 1960(**b**) or is receiving treatment as an in-patient in a hospital within the meaning of that Act ;

(*d*) severe subnormality as a result of which the applicant for the licence or, as the case may be, the holder of the licence is subject to guardianship under the Mental Health Act 1959 or is either resident in accommodation provided by, or by arrangement with, a local health authority under section 28 of the National Health Service Act 1946(**c**) or otherwise receiving care from a local health authority under that section ;

(**a**) 1959 c. 72. (**b**) 1960 c. 61.
(**c**) 1946 c. 81.

(e) mental deficiency such that he is incapable of living an independent life or of guarding himself against serious exploitation as a result of which the applicant for the licence or, as the case may be, the holder of the licence is subject to guardianship under the Mental Health (Scotland) Act 1960 or is either resident in accommodation provided by, or by arrangement with, a local health authority under section 27 of the National Health Service (Scotland) Act 1947(a) or otherwise receiving care from a local health authority under that section ;

(f) any form of mental disorder or mental defect as a result of which the estate of the said applicant or, as the case may be, of the said holder is in the hands of a receiver, curator bonis or judicial factor ;

(g) liability to sudden attacks of disabling giddiness or fainting ;

(h) inability to read in good daylight (with the aid of glasses if worn) a registration mark fixed to a motor vehicle at a distance of 75 feet in the case of a registration mark containing letters and figures $3\frac{1}{2}$ inches high or at a distance of 67 feet in the case of a registration mark containing letters and figures $3\frac{1}{8}$ inches high:

Provided that in the case of an applicant for a licence authorising the driving of vehicles of a class or description comprised in group K only the reading distance shall be 45 feet in the case of a registration mark containing letters and figures $3\frac{1}{2}$ inches high and 40 feet in the case of letters and figures $3\frac{1}{8}$ inches high.

(2) Epilepsy is prescribed for the purpose of section 100(3)(b) of the Act of 1960 and an applicant for a licence suffering from epilepsy shall satisfy the conditions that—

(a) he shall have been free from any epileptic attack whilst awake for at least three years from the date when the licence is to have effect,

(b) in the case of an applicant who has had such attacks whilst asleep during that period he shall have been subject to such attacks since before the beginning of that period,

(c) the driving of a vehicle by him in pursuance of the licence is not likely to be a source of danger to the public.

(3) The disabilities prescribed for the purposes of section 100(3)(c) of the Act of 1960 shall be those prescribed in paragraphs (a) to (h) inclusive of paragraph (1) of this Regulation.

Persons who become resident in Great Britain

23.—(1) A person who becomes resident in Great Britain shall during the period of 3 months after he becomes so resident be treated for the purposes of subsections (1) and (2) of section 98 of the Act of 1960 as the holder of a licence authorising him to drive motor vehicles of the classes and descriptions which he is authorised to drive by any permit of which he is a holder, if he satisfies the conditions specified in paragraph (2) of this Regulation.

(2) The conditions mentioned in the last preceding paragraph are that :—

(a) the person who becomes resident shall be the holder of a permit which is for the time being valid,

(b) he is not disqualified by an order of a Court for holding or obtaining a licence in Great Britain.

<hr>

(a) 1947 c. 27.

(3) The following enactments relating to licences or licence holders shall apply in relation to permits or the holders of permits (as the case may be) subject to modifications, in accordance with the following provisions:—

(a) subsections (1) and (2) of section 112 of the Act of 1960 (which relate to the duties of a court when they order a disqualification or an endorsement or allow an appeal against such an order) shall apply as if the references to a licence included a reference to a permit, except for the first two references in subsection (1), but in subsection (1) with the omission of the words "for the purpose of endorsement" and as if for the words "may dispose of it as the authority think fit" onwards there were substituted the words "shall keep the licence until the disqualification has expired or been removed or the person entitled to the licence leaves Great Britain and in either case has made a demand in writing for its return to him";

(b) subsection (4) of section 7 of the Road Traffic Act 1962 (which relates to the duty of a licence holder to produce it to a court) shall apply as if the references to a licence included a reference to a permit, but with the omission of the words "for endorsement" and "then, unless he satisfies the court that he has applied for a new licence and has not received it";

(c) subsection (4) of section 106 of the Act of 1960 (which relates to the duty of a court when they order a disqualification to be removed) shall apply in relation to the holder of a permit as if for the words "endorsed on the licence" onwards there were substituted the words "notified to the Minister";

(d) subsections (1) and (4) of section 225 of the Act of 1960 (which authorise a police constable to require the production of a licence) shall apply as if the references to a licence included a reference to a permit;

(e) subsection (2) of section 228 of the Act of 1960 (which authorises a police constable to arrest a driver committing certain offences unless the driver gives his name and address or produces his driving licence) shall apply as if the references to a licence included a reference to a permit;

(f) section 233 of the Act of 1960 (which relates to the forgery and misuse of licences) shall apply as if the reference in paragraph (1)(a) to a licence included a reference to a permit.

(4) In this Regulation "permit" means a "domestic driving permit", a "Convention driving permit" or a "British Forces (B.F.G.) driving licence" as defined in Article 2(6) of the Motor Vehicles (International Circulation) Order 1957(a), as amended by Article 4 of the Motor Vehicles (International Circulation) (Amendment) Order 1962(b), not being a domestic driving permit or a British Forces (B.F.G.) driving licence in the case of which the Minister has made any order which is for the time being in force under Article 2(5) of the said Order of 1957, as so amended.

Statement of date of birth

24. The circumstances in which a person specified in subsection (1) of section 225 of the Road Traffic Act 1960 shall, on being required by a police constable, state his date of birth are as follows:—

(a) where that person fails to produce forthwith for examination his licence on being required to do so by a police constable under the said subsection, or

---

(a) S.I. 1957/1074 (1957 II, p. 2154).   (b) S.I. 1962/1344 (1962 II, p. 1483).

(*b*) where on being so required produces a licence which was granted by a local authority, whether or not on behalf of the Minister, or which the police constable has reason to suspect was not granted to that person, was granted to that person in error or contains an alteration in the particulars made with intent to deceive.

Invalid carriages

25. For the purposes of Part II of the Act of 1960 and all regulations made thereunder (which relate to the minimum age for driving motor vehicles and the licensing of drivers thereof) the maximum weight specified in subsection (5) of section 253 (which subsection defines the expression "invalid carriage" for the purposes of the Act) shall be varied from five hundredweight to eight hundredweight.

Entitlement to groups

26. The groups of vehicles specified in column 2 of the table in Schedule 3 to these Regulations are hereby designated as groups for the purposes of paragraphs (*a*) and (*b*) of section 99(1) of the Act of 1960.

Given under the Official Seal of the Minister of Transport the 3rd February 1970.

(L.S.)

Fred Mulley,
Minister of Transport.

SCHEDULE 1

(See Regulation 2(1))

REGULATIONS REVOKED

Title	Year and Number
The Motor Vehicles (Driving Licences) Regulations 1963	S.I. 1963/1026 (1963 II, p. 1730)
The Motor Vehicles (Driving Licences) (Amendment) Regulations 1963	S.I. 1963/1552 (1963 III, p. 2928)
The Motor Vehicles (Invalid Carriages) Regulations 1963	S.I. 1963/1553 (1963 III, p. 2930)
The Motor Vehicles (Driving Licences) (Amendment) Regulations 1965	S.I. 1965/278 (1965 I, p. 691)
The Motor Vehicles (Driving Licences) (Amendment) Regulations 1968	S.I. 1968/947 (1968 II, p. 2453)
The Motor Vehicles (Driving Licences) (Amendment) Regulations 1969	S.I. 1969/252 (1969 I, p. 640)
The Motor Vehicles (Driving Licences) (Amendment) (No. 2) Regulations 1969	S.I. 1969/1614 (1969 III, p. 5107)

SCHEDULE 2 (See Regulation 6)

DIAGRAM OF DISTINGUISHING MARK TO BE DISPLAYED ON A
MOTOR VEHICLE BEING DRIVEN UNDER A
PROVISIONAL LICENCE

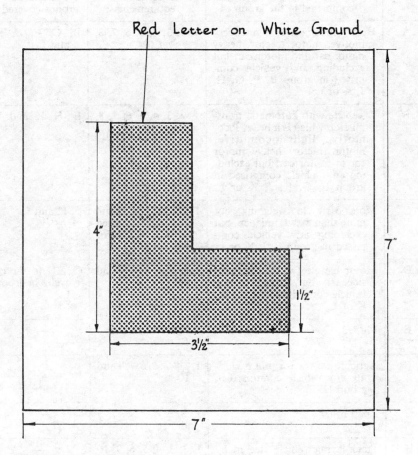

Red Letter on White Ground

The corners of the white ground may be
rounded off.

SCHEDULE 3 (See Regulation 18)

GROUPS OF MOTOR VEHICLES FOR DRIVING TEST PURPOSES

Group	Class or description of vehicle comprised in the group	Additional requirements	Additional groups covered
A	Heavy locomotive, light loco-motive, motor tractor, heavy motor car and motor car, but excluding any vehicle comprised in group B, F, G, H, J, K or L.	1, 2, 3, 4, 5, 6, 7, 8, 9 and 10	B, C, E, F, K and L
B	A vehicle with automatic trans-mission which is a heavy loco-motive, light locomotive, motor tractor, heavy motor car or motor car, but exclud-ing any vehicle comprised in group F, G, H, J, K or L.	1, 2, 3, 4, 5, 6, 7, 8, 9 and 10	E, F, K and L
C	Motor tricycle weighing not more than 8 cwt. unladen, but excluding any vehicle com-prised in group E, J, K or L.	1, 2, 3, 4, 5, 6, 9 and 10 and if fitted with a means for reversing 7 and 8	E, K and L
D	Motor bicycle (with or without sidecar), but excluding any vehicle comprised in group E, K or L.	1, 2, 3, 4, 5, 6, 9 and 10	C, E and motor cycles in group L
E	Moped.	1, 2, 3, 4, 5, 6, 9 and 10	—
F	Agricultural tractor, but exclud-ing any vehicle comprised in group H.	1, 2, 3, 4, 5, 6, 7, 9 and 10	K
G	Road roller.	1, 2, 3, 4, 5, 6, 7, 9 and 10	—
H	Track-laying vehicle steered by its tracks.	1, 2, 3, 4, 5, 6, 9, 10 and 12	—
J	Invalid carriage.	1, 2, 3, 4, 5, 6 and 10	—
K	Mowing machine or vehicle con-trolled by a pedestrian.	1, 2, 3, 4, 5 and 6	—
L	Vehicle propelled by electrical power, but excluding any vehicle comprised in group J or K.	1, 2, 3, 4, 5, 6, 9 and 10 and if fitted with a means for re-versing 7 and 8	K
M	Trolley vehicle.	1, 2, 3, 4, 5, 6, 9, 10 and 11	—

Group	Class or description of vehicle comprised in the group	Additional requirements	Additional groups covered
N	Vehicle exempted from duty under section 6(6) of the Vehicles (Excise) Act 1962(a).	1, 2, 3, 4, 5 and 6	—

SCHEDULE 4 (See Regulation 18)

ADDITIONAL REQUIREMENTS FOR DRIVING TESTS

The additional requirements as to certain of which a candidate for a test must satisfy the person conducting the test in accordance with Regulation 18 of these Regulations and the preceding Schedule are his ability to do the following:—

1. Read in good daylight (with the aid of glasses if worn) a registration mark fixed to a motor vehicle at a distance of 75 feet in the case of a registration mark containing letters and figures $3\frac{1}{2}$ inches high or at a distance of 67 feet in the case of a registration mark containing letters and figures $3\frac{1}{8}$ inches high:

   Provided that in the case of a driving test carried out on a vehicle of a class or description comprised in group K the reading distance shall be 45 feet in the case of letters and figures $3\frac{1}{2}$ inches high and 40 feet in the case of letters and figures $3\frac{1}{8}$ inches high;

2. Start the engine of the vehicle;

3. Move away straight ahead or at an angle;

4. Overtake, meet or cross the path of other vehicles and take an appropriate course;

5. Turn right-hand and left-hand corners correctly;

6. Stop the vehicle in an emergency and normally, and in the latter case bring it to rest at an appropriate part of the road;

7. Drive the vehicle backwards and whilst so doing enter a limited opening either to the right or to the left;

8. Cause the vehicle to face in the opposite direction by the use of forward and reverse gears;

9. Give by mechanical means, if fitted to the vehicle, and by arm, except in the case of a vehicle with a left hand drive or a disabled driver for whom it is impracticable or undesirable to give signals by arm, appropriate signals in a clear and unmistakable manner at appropriate times to indicate his intended actions;

10. Act correctly and promptly on all signals given by traffic signs and traffic controllers and take appropriate action on signs given by other road users;

11. Turn right-hand and left-hand corners without de-wiring;

12. Drive the vehicle backwards and cause it to face in the opposite direction by means of its tracks.

(a) 1962 c. 13.

SCHEDULE 5 (See Regulation 20)

FORM OF CERTIFICATE AND STATEMENT OF DRIVING TEST RESULT

PART I

ROAD TRAFFIC ACT 1960

Form of certificate of passing of a test of competence to drive

....

has been examined and has passed the test of competence to drive........................

....prescribed for the

purposes of section 99 of the Road Traffic Act 1960.

PART II

ROAD TRAFFIC ACT 1960

Form of statement of failure to pass test of competence to drive

....

has this day been examined and has failed to pass the test of competence to drive prescribed for the purposes of section 99 of the Road Traffic Act 1960.

EXPLANATORY NOTE

(This Note is not part of the Regulations.)

These Regulations consolidate with amendment the Motor Vehicles (Invalid Carriages) Regulations 1963, the Motor Vehicles (Driving Licences) Regulations 1963 and the amending Regulations specified in Schedule 1 to these Regulations.

The provisions which are re-enacted deal with applications for the grant of licences, conditions attached to provisional licences, the requirement to sign licences, lost or defaced licences, records of licences and endorsements and the production of particulars from the records, persons who may conduct tests of competence to drive, appointments for tests and cancellation thereof, fees in respect of tests, nature of tests, production of vehicles for tests, evidence of the results of tests, period of ineligibility for a subsequent test and disabilities.

The following are the principal changes:—

(1) No provision is made about the form of application for or of licences.

(2) (*a*) The fee for a full driving licence is increased from 15/- to £1 and for a provisional licence from 10/- for a period of 6 months to £1 for a period of 12 months.

(*b*) The fee for duplicate and exchange licences is 5/- (except when a free licence is issued under section 102(4) of the Road Traffic Act 1960). The fee for duplicate and some exchange licences was previously 2/6 (Regulation 5).

(3)   The kinds of full licences which do not confer a provisional entitlement in addition to a full entitlement are prescribed. These are full licences which authorise the holder to drive only mowing machines and pedestrian controlled vehicles (Group K) and full licences which authorise the holder to drive only vehicles of a particular construction or design on the ground of a disability (Regulation 8).

(4)   The licensing authority is required to give particulars relating to any licence granted by them to licensing authorities responsible for the granting of public service vehicle driver licences and heavy goods vehicle driver licences when requested to do so by such an authority (Regulation 12).

(5)   The Postmaster General, the Royal Automobile Club, the Automobile Association and the Royal Scottish Automobile Club will no longer be authorised by the Regulations to conduct tests (Regulation 13).

(6)   No provision is made for a separate test of fitness.

(7)   Epilepsy is prescribed as a disease in the case of which a licensing authority may grant a licence if the prescribed conditions are satisfied (Regulation 22(2)).

(8)   Provision is made allowing a person who has recently become resident in Great Britain to drive for 3 months after becoming resident if he holds a valid foreign domestic driving licence, an international driving permit or a British Forces (Germany) driving licence. The holder must also satisfy the condition that he is not disqualified for holding or obtaining a licence in Great Britain and enactments relating to licences and licence holders are applied appropriately. No provision is made about the entitlement to drive of persons not resident in Great Britain (Regulation 23).

(9)   The circumstances in which the police may, under the provisions of section 22(5) of the Vehicle and Driving Licences Act 1969, obtain the date of birth of a person who is required to produce to them his driving licence under section 225 of the Road Traffic Act 1960 are prescribed (Regulation 24).

(10)   The maximum unladen weight of an invalid carriage is increased from 6 cwt. to 8 cwt. for driving licence and driving test purposes (Regulation 25).

(11)   The groups into which vehicles are divided for the purposes of driving tests are varied as follows:—

     (a) tracked agricultural tractors and other tracked vehicles are placed in a single group (Group H),

     (b) electrically propelled motor bicycles are placed in the same group as other electrically propelled vehicles (Group L), instead of being grouped with other motor bicycles (Group D),

     (c) three wheeled mopeds are placed in the moped group (Group E), instead of being grouped with other motor tricycles (Group C) (Schedule 3).

STATUTORY INSTRUMENTS

1970 No. 171

LONDON GOVERNMENT

The London Authorities (Transfer of Housing Estates etc.) Order 1970

Made - - -	*5th February* 1970
Laid before Parliament	*18th February* 1970
Coming into Operation	*25th March* 1970

Whereas the Greater London Council and the councils of certain London boroughs have requested the Minister of Housing and Local Government to provide by an order under section 23(3) of the London Government Act 1963(a) for the transfer of certain housing accommodation for the time being vested in the Greater London Council;

And whereas the said councils have agreed the terms of such transfer;

And whereas the said Minister is required by the said section 23(3) to give effect to those terms;

And whereas certain further matters appear to the Minister necessary and proper for the purposes of or in consequence of that transfer:

Now therefore the Minister of Housing and Local Government, in exercise of his powers under sections 23(3), 84 and 85 of the London Government Act 1963 and all other powers enabling him in that behalf, hereby makes the following order:—

Title, commencement and interpretation

1. This order may be cited as the London Authorities (Transfer of Housing Estates etc.) Order 1970, and shall come into operation on 25th March 1970.

2.—(1) The Interpretation Act 1889(b) applies to the interpretation of this order as it applies to the interpretation of an Act of Parliament.

(2) In this order—

"the deposited Schedule" means the Schedule "Properties transferred by article 3 of the London Authorities (Transfer of Housing Estates etc.) Order 1970" prepared in duplicate and sealed with the official seal of the Minister and as to which further provision is made in article 3(2);

"officer" includes the holder of any place, situation or employment;

"the Minister" means the Minister of Housing and Local Government; and

"transferee authority", in relation to housing accommodation transferred by article 3, means the London borough council to whom that accommodation is so transferred.

(a) 1963 c. 33.   (b) 1889 c. 63.

(3) In the articles of this order, unless the context otherwise requires, any reference to housing accommodation shall include—

(a) a reference to garages, parking spaces and estate amenities ; and

(b) a reference to shops where any such shop gives such access to a dwelling transferred by article 3 as to render the said shop and dwelling suitable for occupation by a single occupier ;

and references to an area of housing accommodation shall be construed accordingly.

(4) In this order, unless the context otherwise requires, references to any enactment shall be construed as references to that enactment as amended, extended or applied by or under any other enactment or by this order.

(5) Any reference in this order to a numbered article shall, unless the reference is to an article of a specified order, be construed as a reference to the article bearing that number in this order.

(6) Any reference in any article of this order to a numbered paragraph shall, unless the reference is to a paragraph of a specified article, be construed as a reference to the paragraph bearing that number in the first-mentioned article.

Transfer of property

3.—(1) Subject to the provisions of article 13(3) and of Part III of the Schedule to this order, on 1st April 1970 any property described in any Part of the deposited Schedule and all liabilities (other than liabilities in respect of money borrowed) attaching to the Greater London Council in respect of any such property shall by virtue of this order be transferred to and vest in or attach to the authority named in the description of such Part, and—

(a) all contracts, deeds, bonds, agreements and other instruments subsisting in favour of, or against, and all notices in force which were given (or having effect as if they had been given) by, or to, the Greater London Council in respect of such property and liabilities shall be of full force and effect in favour of, or against, the authority named as aforesaid ; and

(b) any action or proceeding or any cause of action or proceeding, pending or existing at 1st April 1970, by, or against, the Greater London Council in respect of such property and liabilities shall not be prejudicially affected by reason of this order, and may be continued, prosecuted and enforced by, or against, the authority named as aforesaid.

(2) One duplicate of the deposited Schedule is deposited in the offices of the Minister and the other in the offices of the Greater London Council. Copies of the deposited Schedule have been deposited with the transferee authorities and shall be open to inspection at all reasonable times.

(3) Nothing in paragraph (1) shall affect any grant or subsidy receivable by the Greater London Council in respect of housing accommodation transferred by that paragraph.

4. Any property or liability transferred by article 3 to the authority for any area shall be held or discharged by them in respect of the area.

5. Any byelaws in force for the regulation of any property transferred by the said article shall have effect as if they had been made by the authority to whom such property is transferred.

6. Any legal proceedings pending at 1st April 1970 may be amended in such manner as may be necessary or proper in consequence of this order.

7. Where under this order or any adjustment made in consequence hereof any liability or part of a liability charged indifferently on all the revenues of a public body or on any particular revenues or fund of such body is transferred to another public body, the liability or part of the liability shall be charged indifferently on all the revenues of the public body to whom it is transferred and shall cease to be a charge on any revenues or fund of the public body from whom it is transferred.

In this article, 'public body' and 'revenues' have the same meanings as in the Local Government Act 1933(**a**).

8. Where by virtue of this order any matter in respect of which, if this order had not been made, sums would have become due and owing to a consolidated loans fund is transferred to an authority other than the authority by whom such fund is maintained on and after 1st April 1970, such sums shall be paid by the first-mentioned authority to the authority by whom the fund is maintained.

Covenants affecting property

9. Unless the Greater London Council and the transferee authority otherwise agree, section 62 of the Law of Property Act 1925(**b**) (which implies certain words in conveyances of land, subject to the terms of the conveyance and the provisions therein contained) shall have effect—

(*a*) in respect of any property transferred by article 3 ; and

(*b*) in respect of any property, being property vested in the Greater London Council, which is affected by the said transfer,

as if the property described in (*a*) and (*b*) respectively had been the subject of a conveyance on 1st April 1970.

10.—(1) This article applies to any land within the extent of an area of housing accommodation transferred by article 3, being land in respect of which the Greater London Council have powers under section 151 of the Housing Act 1957(**c**) to enforce covenants entered into on the sale or exchange of land.

(2) In respect of any land to which this article applies—

(*a*) the Greater London Council shall consult with the transferee authority before exercising their powers under the said section 151 ;

(*b*) the transferee authority may require the Greater London Council to exercise the said powers in any case where such exercise is requisite in the interests of the area of housing accommodation within the extent of which the land is situated.

(3) The Greater London Council shall notify the transferee authority of any land to which this article applies and provide sufficient particulars of the covenants to which the said section 151 relates.

11. Any covenant (not being a covenant affected by article 10) which would be enforceable by the Greater London Council immediately before 1st April 1970 in respect of land within the extent of an area of housing accommodation transferred by article 3, being land which was sold or exchanged by the Greater London Council or by the London County Council and, immediately before such sale or exchange, was held by them for the purposes of the Housing Act 1957 or of any Act re-enacted by that Act, shall be of full force and effect in favour of the transferee authority.

(a) 1933 c. 51.　　　　(b) 1925 c. 20.　　　　(c) 1957 c. 56.

Rent books

12. Until a new rent book is issued by a transferee authority in respect of any housing accommodation transferred by article 3, notification to the tenant of the said accommodation of that transfer shall be deemed to be a compliance by the said authority as landlord with the requirements of section 2(1)(*a*) of the Landlord and Tenant Act 1962(**a**).

Terms of transfer of housing accommodation

13.—(1) A transferee authority shall make payments to the Greater London Council in accordance with the provisions of Part I of the Schedule to this order.

(2) The Greater London Council shall pay to a transferee authority sums calculated in accordance with the provisions of Part II of the said Schedule.

(3) The Greater London Council may exercise the rights and shall discharge the liabilities described in Part III of the said Schedule.

Housing Revenue Account

14. Notwithstanding the provisions of paragraphs 1 and 2 of Schedule 5 to the Housing (Financial Provisions) Act 1958(**b**), the Greater London Council and each transferee authority shall enter in their Housing Revenue Account any sums receivable or payable under or by virtue of this order, being sums which relate to matters which would have been so entered if this order had not been made.

Nomination rights

15.—(1) Until 1st April 1982 the Greater London Council may, without payment, nominate tenants to such proportion of the vacancies in the dwellings transferred by article 3 to a transferee authority, not exceeding 65 per centum of such vacancies, as they may determine from time to time.

(2) Without prejudice to paragraph (1), the Greater London Council may agree with a transferee authority, before 1st April 1982 in respect of nominations in excess of the said 65 per centum, or after that date as to any nominations, and any such agreement may include such terms (whether as to payment or otherwise) as may be agreed between the parties or, in default of agreement, as may be determined by the Minister or by an arbitrator appointed by him.

(3) Nothing in this article shall affect any agreement as to nominations subsisting between the Greater London Council and a London borough council at the coming into operation of this order.

Notices to be given

16. To enable the Greater London Council to provide the Minister with such information as he may require from time to time in order to determine any question relating to a grant or subsidy or the amount thereof, a transferee authority shall notify the Greater London Council of any action taken in respect of any housing accommodation transferred by article 3, being such action as may affect the payment of such a grant or subsidy or the amount thereof.

17.—(1) This article applies to each financial year until 1st April 1973.

(2) Where the Greater London Council—

(**a**) 1962 c. 50. (**b**) 1958 c. 42.

(a) have, as from 1st April or any later date in any year, applied a general increase to the rents payable on housing accommodation provided by them ; or

(b) have resolved to apply (whether or not they have authority to apply) any such general increase as from 31st March next following, or any earlier date,

they shall give notice to that effect to each transferee authority not later than 31st December in the said year.

(3) A notice given under paragraph (2) shall include sufficient details of how the increase would have applied to the housing accommodation transferred under article 3 to the transferee authority concerned if the transfer had not been effected.

(4) The Greater London Council shall provide to each transferee authority sufficient information from time to time of the cost and functioning of the rent rebate scheme operated by them under section 113 of the Housing Act 1957.

(5) The Greater London Council shall notify each transferee authority by 30th September in each year of their estimate of the average cost of maintenance and management of each dwelling owned by them in the year concerned, such notice including separate particulars as to flats and other housing accommodation so owned.

Transfer of staff

18.—(1) The Greater London Council shall make a scheme for the transfer to transferee authorities of any officers employed by them at or in connection with any area of housing accommodation transferred by article 3.

(2) The scheme mentioned in paragraph (1) shall specify—

(a) the officers or categories of officers liable to be transferred ;

(b) the method of determining the number of officers in each category to be transferred ;

(c) the means of selecting officers in any category for transfer ; and

(d) the date of transfer,

and different provision may be made for different circumstances.

(3) The scheme mentioned in paragraph (1) may require the payment by a transferee authority to the Greater London Council until 1st April 1972 of sums equal to not more than one-half of the basic remuneration of any officer who, with the agreement of the transferee authority, is not transferred under the said scheme although he falls within a category specified therein for such transfer.

Protection of staff

19.—(1) This article applies—

(a) where an officer is transferred under the scheme mentioned in article 18 ; and

(b) where an officer (not being an officer within item (a)) is transferred in consequence of any transfer of housing accommodation by the Greater London Council in circumstances approved by the Minister for the purposes of this article on the application of the said Council.

(2) Every officer entering (or having entered) the employment of a transferee

authority shall, so long as he continues in that employment by virtue of the transfer, enjoy terms and conditions of employment not less favourable than those he enjoyed immediately before such transfer:

Provided that this paragraph shall apply to the scale of the salary or remuneration of the officer only so long as he is engaged in duties reasonably comparable to those in which he was engaged immediately before his transfer.

Any question whether duties are reasonably comparable as aforesaid shall be determined by a tribunal established under section 12 of the Industrial Training Act 1964(**a**).

Superannuation

20.—(1) Where an officer who, immediately before his transfer to a transferee authority under the scheme mentioned in article 18 or as mentioned in article 19(1)(*b*)—

(*a*) was subject to an election not to participate in the benefits of the superannuation fund maintained by the Greater London Council under Part I of the Local Government Superannuation Act 1937(**b**) ; and

(*b*) had an expectation of a gratuity payable according to years of service,

that election shall remain in effect and such a gratuity shall, subject to terms and conditions which are not less beneficial, be payable in respect of his previous service and of any service rendered to the transferee authority.

(2) Section 35 of the Local Government Superannuation Act 1937 shall apply to an expectation under this article as it applies to a right under that Act.

Arbitration

21. Subject to any provision of this order, any dispute arising under this order or in consequence thereof shall be determined by an arbitrator appointed by agreement between the parties in dispute or, in default of agreement, by the Minister and, subject as aforesaid, the provisions of the Arbitration Act 1950(**c**) shall apply to any arbitration under this article.

SCHEDULE   *Article* 13

TERMS OF TRANSFER OF HOUSING ACCOMMODATION

PART I—PAYMENTS TO THE GREATER LONDON COUNCIL

1. In the year ending on 31st March 1971, a transferee authority shall pay to the Greater London Council by quarterly instalments in arrears a sum being the amount of the rents which were receivable by the latter authority on 31st March 1970 less the amount of—

(*a*) the estimated value of rent rebates in the said year based on the said rents calculated as if the housing accommodation had not been transferred; and

(*b*) the costs of management and costs of maintenance which were met in the year ending on 31st March 1970.

2. In each of the years ending on 31st March 1972, 31st March 1973 and 31st March 1974, a transferee authority shall pay to the Greater London Council by quarterly instalments in arrears a sum being the amount of the rents which would have been

(**a**) 1964 c. 16.   (**b**) 1937 c. 68.   (**c**) 1950 c. 27.

receivable by the latter authority on 31st March 1971, 31st March 1972 or 31st March 1973, as the case may be, if the housing accommodation had not been transferred, less the amount of—

(a) the estimated value of rent rebates in the said year on the basis of the said rents; and

(b) the costs of management and costs of maintenance which would have been met in the year ending on 31st March 1971, 31st March 1972 or 31st March 1973 as the case may be if the housing accommodation had not been transferred.

3. In each subsequent year until 31st March 1982, a transferee authority shall make the like payments to the Greater London Council as those mentioned in the last preceding paragraph with reference to the year ending on 31st March 1974.

4. In this Schedule, references to rents receivable on 31st March in a year are references to the amount of those rents on that basis for the year immediately after the said date.

5. In this Schedule, references to rents, rent rebates, costs of management and costs of maintenance are references to the rents, rebates or costs in respect of the housing accommodation transferred by article 3 to the transferee authority.

6. In the calculation of the amount of payments for the purposes of this Schedule, no regard shall be taken of any improvement carried out wholly or partly at the expense of a transferee authority or of any disposal or demolition of housing accommodation transferred.

7. In the calculation of rent rebates for the purposes of this Schedule, no regard shall be had to any change of tenancy after 31st March 1970.

8.—(1) In the calculation of the costs of management and costs of maintenance for the purposes of this Schedule, the Greater London Council shall assess such costs in respect of separate classes, namely flats and other housing accommodation transferred by article 3, and, in the calculation of costs of maintenance, each such class shall be divided into housing accommodation first occupied before 1st January 1940 and on or after the said date.

(2) The Treasurer of the Greater London Council shall certify—

(a) the average cost of management and the average cost of maintenance of each class and division of housing accommodation assessed under this paragraph; and

(b) the number of units transferred in each such class and division;

and the costs of management and the costs of maintenance shall be the total sum of the average costs in (a) multiplied by the relevant number in (b).

9. Where a transferee authority takes any action in respect of housing accommodation transferred by article 3 which results in the reduction or withdrawal of any grant or subsidy payable, that authority shall pay to the Greater London Council such sum (whether annually or as a single amount) as may be agreed to represent the value of the grant or subsidy which would have been paid.

10. After 31st March 1982, a transferee authority shall pay to the Greater London Council such sum as may be agreed to meet the liabilities of the latter authority with respect to the housing accommodation transferred by article 3 to the transferee authority, and any such agreement may include terms as to payment over a period and as to the allocation of any grant or subsidy receivable by the Greater London Council.

Part II—Sums Payable by the Greater London Council

1. By 30th September 1970 the Greater London Council shall pay to each transferee authority the two sums calculated under this Part of this Schedule.

2. The first sum is $\frac{x}{y}$ of the amount of the total balance of the Housing Repairs Account of the Greater London Council on 31st March 1970, where—

    x is that number of dwellings to which the said account relates which are transferred by article 3 to the transferee authority; and

    y is the total number of dwellings to which the said account relates on 31st March 1970.

3. The second sum is $\frac{p}{q}$ of the amount of the total balance of the Key Deposit Account of the Greater London Council on 31st March 1970, where—

    p is that number of dwellings to which the said account relates which are transferred by article 3 to the transferee authority; and

    q is the total number of dwellings to which the Housing Revenue Account of the Greater London Council relates on 31st March 1970.

PART III—RIGHTS AND LIABILITIES OF THE GREATER LONDON COUNCIL

1. The Greater London Council shall be entitled, on giving due notice, to use any equipment, plant, stores or materials transferred by article 3 for the purpose of the maintenance of any part of the area of housing accommodation concerned which is retained by them.

2. The Greater London Council shall meet the costs of works of modernisation or major improvement, being costs incurred in respect of a period before 1st April 1970.

3. The Greater London Council shall meet all costs of repair and minor improvement started or contracted for before 1st April 1970.

Given under the official seal of the Minister of Housing and Local Government on 5th February 1970.

(L.S.)   *Anthony Greenwood,*
Minister of Housing and Local Government.

EXPLANATORY NOTE

(This Note is not part of the Order.)

This Order gives effect to the terms agreed between the Greater London Council and the councils of certain London boroughs for the transfer of housing accommodation to the latter councils, and makes consequential provision as to the transfer and protection of staff and other matters.

STATUTORY INSTRUMENTS

1970 No. 172

IRON AND STEEL

The British Steel Corporation (Financial Year) Order 1970

Made - - -	*5th February* 1970
Laid before Parliament	*12th February* 1970
Coming into Operation	*13th February* 1970

The Minister of Technology, in exercise of his powers under section 13 of the Iron and Steel Act 1969(a) and of all other powers him enabling, hereby makes the following order:—

1. This Order may be cited as the British Steel Corporation (Financial Year) Order 1970 and shall come into operation on 13th February 1970.

2. The day on which the third financial year of the British Steel Corporation ends shall be 28th March 1970.

3. Each of the British Steel Corporation's financial years after the third shall be a period beginning with the end of the preceding financial year and ending

    (a) if the last day of March next following is a Saturday, with that day; or

    (b) if not, with the Saturday which (whether falling in March or April) falls nearest to the last day of March next following.

Dated 5th February 1970

Anthony Wedgwood Benn,
Minister of Technology

(a) 1969 c. 45.

STATUTORY INSTRUMENTS

1970 No. 173

TAXES

The Capital Gains Tax (Exempt Gilt-edged Securities) Order 1970

Made - - - *4th February* 1970

The Treasury, in exercise of the powers conferred on them by section 41(2) of the Finance Act 1969(**a**), hereby make the following Order:—

1. This Order may be cited as the Capital Gains Tax (Exempt Gilt-edged Securities) Order 1970.

2. The Interpretation Act 1889(**b**) shall apply for the interpretation of this Order as it applies for the interpretation of an Act of Parliament.

3. The following securities, being stocks denominated in sterling and issued after 15th April 1969 under section 12 of the National Loans Act 1968(**c**), are hereby specified for the purposes of section 41 of the Finance Act 1969 (gilt-edged securities exempt from tax on capital gains):—

> 9 per cent. Treasury Loan 1994.
> 8¾ per cent. Treasury Loan 1997.
> 8½ per cent. Treasury Loan 1980-1982.

> *Ernest Armstrong,*
> *Neil McBride,*
> Two of the Lords Commissioners
> of Her Majesty's Treasury.

4th February 1970.

EXPLANATORY NOTE
(This Note is not part of the Order.)

This Order adds, to the list of stocks and registered bonds which are exempt from tax on capital gains, and which are specified in Part I of Schedule 18 to the Finance Act 1969, the following gilt-edged securities:—

> 9 per cent. Treasury Loan 1994;
> 8¾ per cent. Treasury Loan 1997; and
> 8½ per cent. Treasury Loan 1980-1982.

(a) 1969 c. 32.	(b) 1889 c. 63.	(c) 1968 c. 13.

STATUTORY INSTRUMENTS

1970 No. 174
CORONERS
EXPENSES
The Coroners (Fees and Allowances) (Amendment) Rules 1970

Made - - -	*2nd February* 1970
Coming into Operation	*2nd March* 1970

In pursuance of the power conferred upon me by section 1(1) of the Coroners Act 1954(a), I hereby make the following Rules:—

1. These Rules may be cited as the Coroners (Fees and Allowances) (Amendment) Rules 1970 and shall come into operation on 2nd March 1970.

2. In Rule 4 of the Coroners (Fees and Allowances) Rules 1966(b), as amended (c) (which relates to the payment of a loss allowance in respect of a witness attending at an inquest to give evidence other than professional or expert evidence), for the words "sixty-five shillings" there shall be substituted the words "four pounds" and for the words "thirty-two shillings and sixpence", in both places where those words occur, there shall be substituted the words "two pounds".

James Callaghan,
One of Her Majesty's Principal
Secretaries of State.

Home Office,
 Whitehall.
2nd February 1970.

EXPLANATORY NOTE
(This Note is not part of the Rules.)

These Rules provide for an increase in the maximum amount payable as loss allowance to witnesses at inquests, other than professional or expert witnesses.

(a) 1954 c. 31.   (b) S.I. 1966/11 (1966 I, p. 9).
 (c) The relevant amending instrument is S.I. 1967/38 (1967 I, p. 107).

STATUTORY INSTRUMENTS

1970 No. 175

JURIES

The Jurors' Allowances (Amendment) Regulations 1970

Made - - -	*4th February* 1970
Coming into Operation	*2nd March* 1970

In exercise of the power conferred upon me by section 1 of the Juries Act 1949(a), as amended by the Juries Act 1954(b), I hereby, with the consent of the Treasury, make the following Regulations:—

1. These Regulations may be cited as the Jurors' Allowances (Amendment) Regulations 1970 and shall come into operation on 2nd March 1970.

2. In Regulation 3 of the Jurors' Allowances Regulations 1967(c) (which relates to the compensation of jurors for loss of earnings and expense), for the words "thirty-two shillings and sixpence", "sixty-five shillings" and "one hundred and thirty shillings", there shall be substituted the words "two pounds", "four pounds" and "eight pounds" respectively.

James Callaghan,

One of Her Majesty's Principal
Secretaries of State.

2nd February 1970.

We consent,

Walter Harrison,

Joseph Harper,

Two of the Lords Commissioners
of Her Majesty's Treasury.

4th February 1970.

(a) 1949 c. 27. (b) 1954 c. 41. (c) S.I. 1967/72 (1967 I, p. 154).

EXPLANATORY NOTE

(This Note is not part of the Regulations.)

These Regulations provide for an increase in the maximum amount payable to jurors as compensation for loss of earnings or additional expense (other than expense on account of travelling or subsistence).

STATUTORY INSTRUMENTS

1970 No. 176

CRIMINAL PROCEDURE, ENGLAND AND WALES
COSTS AND EXPENSES
The Witnesses' Allowances (Amendment) Regulations 1970

Made - - -	*2nd February* 1970
Coming into Operation	*2nd March* 1970

In pursuance of the power conferred upon me by section 12 of the Costs in Criminal Cases Act 1952(**a**), I hereby make the following Regulations:—

1. These Regulations may be cited as the Witnesses' Allowances (Amendment) Regulations 1970 and shall come into operation on 2nd March 1970.

2.—(1) In Regulations 4 and 7 of the Witnesses' Allowances Regulations 1966(**b**), as amended (**c**) (which relate respectively to the payment of a loss allowance in respect of a witness attending to give evidence other than professional or expert evidence and to the payment of an allowance in respect of loss of wages of a seaman who is detained on shore for the purpose of attending to give evidence and thereby misses his ship), for the words "sixty-five shillings" there shall be substituted the words "four pounds".

(2) In the said Regulation 4 for the words "thirty-two shillings and sixpence" in both places where they occur there shall be substituted the words "two pounds".

James Callaghan,
One of Her Majesty's Principal
Secretaries of State.

Home Office,
   Whitehall.
2nd February 1970.

EXPLANATORY NOTE
(This Note is not part of the Regulations.)

These Regulations increase the maximum amounts payable as loss allowance to witnesses other than professional or expert witnesses in criminal cases and as allowance to seamen who miss their ships as a result of being required to attend court to give evidence.

(**a**) 1952 c. 48.   (**b**) S.I. 1966/10 (1966 I, p. 5).
(**c**) The relevant amending instument is S.I. 1967/39 (1967 I, p. 109).

STATUTORY INSTRUMENTS

1970 No. 177 (S.11)

SHERIFF COURT, SCOTLAND

Act of Sederunt (Increase of Fees of Shorthand Writers in the Sheriff Courts) 1970

Made - · - -	*5th February* 1970
Laid before Parliament	*17th February* 1970
Coming into Operation	*3rd March* 1970

The Lords of Council and Session, under and by virtue of the powers conferred upon them by section 40 of the Sheriff Courts (Scotland) Act 1907(a) and of all other powers competent to them in that behalf, considering that it has been agreed by the Civil Service Department that certain fees payable to shorthand writers should be increased, do hereby enact and declare as follows:—

1. The schedule annexed to the Act of Sederunt of 7th May 1935(b) as amended by the Act of Sederunt (Increase of Fees of Shorthand Writers in the Sheriff Courts) 1965(c) shall be further amended by deleting Chapter II thereof, being the chapter relating to Shorthand Writers' Fees, and by substituting therefor the following:—

"Chapter II—Shorthand Writers' Fees

		£	s.	d.
1.	Attending trials, proofs and commissions per hour ...	1	14	0
	With a minimum fee of £5 per day if the Court is at a town where the shorthand writer carries on business or has a branch office, or £6 13s. per day if the shorthand writer's place of business is at a distance exceeding 5 miles from the Court, and subsistence allowance appropriate to Civil Servants entitled to Class B rates.			
	No fee will be paid where intimation of postponement or settlement is made by 4 p.m. on the previous day.			
2.	Extending Notes, per sheet of 250 words	0	6	6
	Note—An extra allowance will be payable when notes are extended overnight.			
3.	Carbon Copies, per sheet (1st copy)	0	1	3
	Other copies	0	1	0"

2. This Act of Sederunt may be cited as the Act of Sederunt (Increase of Fees of Shorthand Writers in the Sheriff Courts) 1970, and shall come into operation on 3rd March 1970.

And the Lords appoint this Act of Sederunt to be inserted in the Books of Sederunt.

Edinburgh,   *J. L. Clyde,*
5th February 1970.   *I.P.D.*

(a) 1907 c. 51.   (b) S.R. & O. 1935/488 (Rev. XX, p. 880; 1935, p. 1588).
(c) S.I. 1965/1468 (1965 II, p. 4309).

EXPLANATORY NOTE

(This Note is not part of the Act of Sederunt.)

This Act of Sederunt prescribes a new table of fees payable to shorthand writers for attendance in the Sheriff Court and for extension of Notes.

STATUTORY INSTRUMENTS

1970 No. 179

WEIGHTS AND MEASURES

The Measuring Instruments (Liquid Fuel and Lubricants) (Amendment) Regulations 1970

Made - - -		*10th February* 1970
Laid before Parliament		*17th February* 1970
Coming into Operation		*18th February* 1970

The Board of Trade, in pursuance of the powers conferred upon them by sections 11, 14(1), 54(1) and 58(1) of the Weights and Measures Act 1963(a) and all other powers enabling them in that behalf, hereby make the following Regulations :—

1.—(1) These Regulations may be cited as the Measuring Instruments (Liquid Fuel and Lubricants) (Amendment) Regulations 1970 and shall come into operation on 18th February 1970.

(2) In these Regulations—

"the principal Regulations" means the Measuring Instruments (Liquid Fuel and Lubricants) Regulations 1963(b), as amended (c) ; and

references to fuel include references to a mixture of fuel and lubricant.

(3) The Interpretation Act 1889(d) shall apply to the interpretation of these Regulations as it applies to the interpretation of an Act of Parliament.

2. The principal Regulations shall have effect as if there were substituted for Regulation 11 (positioning of instruments) the following :—

"**11.**—(1) Subject to paragraph (2) hereof, a measuring instrument which forms part of a fixed installation shall be so positioned that a purchaser may readily obtain a clear and unobstructed view—

(*a*) of all the operations carried out by any other person using the instrument to measure the fuel or lubricant being supplied to the purchaser ; and

(*b*) of any device on the instrument which indicates the quantity supplied or the amount payable or that delivery is being effected.

(2) Paragraph (1) of this Regulation shall not apply to any instrument for use only for measuring kerosene except where the instrument is—

(*a*) situated on premises where petroleum is sold, or

(*b*) used for measuring kerosene in the course of delivery into the fuel tanks of vehicles, vessels or aircraft".

(a) 1963 c. 31.
(c) S.I. 1968/1541 (1968 III, p. 4326).
(b) S.I. 1963/1709 (1963 III, p. 3278).
(d) 1889 c. 63.

3.—(1) The principal Regulations shall have effect—

(*a*) in relation to the adapting of instruments fitted with a price computing mechanism to compute prices in decimal currency, and

(*b*) in relation to the use of instruments which have been so adapted, subject to the following provisions of this Regulation.

(2) Until 15th February 1971, Regulation 23(*a*) (instruments to be of an approved pattern) shall not apply to any instrument which fails to comply with any such pattern as is mentioned in that Regulation as a consequence of its having been adapted as aforesaid.

(3) For the purposes of Regulation 27 (limits of error) any alteration or adjustment of an instrument connected with its adaptation to compute prices in decimal currency shall be treated as occasioned by a change in price, and shall be so treated even though it is not occasioned by any immediate change in price or that the only change is to a decimal price which is the exact equivalent of the previous price.

(4) Nothing in the principal Regulations shall make it unlawful to use any instrument for trade during a relevant period (as hereinafter defined) solely because a stamp upon it has been obliterated or destroyed by, or by the duly authorised agent of, a person who is a manufacturer of, or is regularly engaged in the repair of, instruments for measuring fuel or lubricants if such obliteration or destruction was to facilitate or permit the adaptation of the instrument to compute prices in decimal currency.

In this paragraph "relevant period" means—

(i) where the stamp protecting the calibration of the meter remains intact and notice of the fact that some other stamp has been obliterated or destroyed has been sent or given to the chief inspector of weights and measures for the area in which the instrument is situated, a period beginning when notice is so sent or given and expiring at the end of the twenty eighth following day ; and

(ii) where the stamp protecting the calibration of the meter has been obliterated or destroyed and the person responsible has attached to the instrument some seal or other device which must be defaced or removed before the calibration can be adjusted and notice of the obliteration or destruction of that stamp has been sent or given as aforesaid, a period beginning when notice is so sent or given and expiring at the end of the fifth following day.

(5) The principal Regulations shall require that any measuring instrument fitted with a price computing mechanism which is adapted as aforesaid before 15th February 1971 shall until that date—

(i) if used to measure only a single grade of fuel, bear a clear and legible indication in characters not less than $\frac{1}{4}$ inch high of the price in shillings and pence per gallon of that fuel, or

(ii) if used to measure fuel of different grades, bear such an indication of the price in shillings and pence per gallon of each of the available grades, being an indication which clearly relates the price to the appropriate grade.

(6) The principal Regulations shall require in the case of any instrument which is so adapted before 1st June 1970 that it no longer computes prices by reference to the shilling—

(*a*) that the part of the mechanism which shows the computed prices of deliveries shall until the transitional date be constantly set to zero or temporarily obscured or set to show such prices entirely in pence of the present currency ; and

(b) where it is set to show prices as aforesaid, that the instrument bears a printed table indicating in characters not less than $\frac{1}{4}$ inch high the number of shillings represented by every multiple of 12 pence not exceeding 492 pence and the amount in pounds, shillings and pence represented by 500 pence and every greater multiple of 100 pence not exceeding 1000.

In this paragraph and the next following paragraph, "transitional date" means that day not earlier than 1st June 1970 on which the instrument is further adapted to comply with paragraph (7) of this Regulation.

(7) The principal Regulations shall require—

    (i) in the case of any instrument adapted not later than 31st May 1970, that from the transitional date or 7th June (whichever is the earlier) until 15th February 1971, and

    (ii) in the case of any instrument first adapted on or after 1st June 1970, that from the time it is first used for trade after being adapted until 15th February 1971,

the instrument in question—

(a) shows in relation to any delivery a sum computed by reference to an appropriate price per gallon in decimal currency as the sum which would be payable in decimal currency for that delivery ;

(b) bears a clear and legible notice in the form set out in the Schedule hereto printed in characters not less than one-quarter of an inch high ; and

(c) bears in addition to the indication of price or prices required by paragraph (5) of this Regulation, a like indication of the decimal price or prices by reference to which the price computing mechanism is set to operate.

In this paragraph "an appropriate price per gallon in decimal currency" means a price which is, or which if varied by not more than 1/10th of a decimal penny would be, the exact equivalent of the actual price of the relevant fuel in shillings and pence per gallon.

Gwyneth Dunwoody,
**Parliamentary Secretary
to the Board of Trade.**

10th February 1970.

SCHEDULE

NOTICE

This pump has been converted to operate in decimal currency. Until D Day prices may be checked by reference to the table below.

Decimal Indication	Price in shillings and pence		Decimal Indication	Price in shillings and pence	
p.	s.	d.	p.	s.	d.
½		1	10	2	0
1		2	20	4	0
1½		4	30	6	0
2		5	40	8	0
2½		6	50	10	0
3		7	60	12	0
3½		8	70	14	0
4		10	80	16	0
4½		11	90	18	0
5	1	0			
5½	1	1			
6	1	2			
6½	1	4			
7	1	5			
7½	1	6			
8	1	7			
8½	1	8			
9	1	10			
9½	1	11			

EXPLANATORY NOTE
(This Note is not part of the Regulations.)

These Regulations further amend the Measuring Instruments (Liquid Fuel and Lubricants) Regulations 1963.

Regulation 2 provides that instruments for measuring kerosene need no longer be so situated that customers can see them in use unless they are situated at petrol stations or used for refuelling vehicles, vessels or aircraft.

Regulation 3 makes modifications (essentially of a temporary nature) to the 1963 Regulations in their application to price computing instruments adapted for use with decimal currency. Instruments converted after 1st June 1970 must compute in decimal currency by reference to a decimal price shown on the instrument. Prices must also be shown in existing currency and a printed conversion table put on the instrument.

Instruments converted before that date must have their price computing mechanism blanked off or set to zero or set to compute prices entirely in pennies of the present currency until they are further converted (between 1st and 7th June 1970) to conform with the requirements applicable to instruments converted after 1st June 1970.

The operation of the 1963 Regulations is also qualified so as to allow instruments on which the stamps applied by inspectors of weights and measures have been obliterated or destroyed in the course of conversion to be used for trade for limited periods before being retested.

STATUTORY INSTRUMENTS

1970 No. 181

NATIONAL HEALTH SERVICE, ENGLAND AND WALES

The National Health Service (General Dental Services— Seniority Payments) Regulations 1970

Made - - -	10*th February* 1970
Laid before Parliament	18*th February* 1970
Coming into Operation	26*th February* 1970

The Secretary of State for Social Services, in exercise of his powers under section 40 of the National Health Service Act 1946(a) and of all other powers enabling him in that behalf, hereby makes the following regulations:—

1. These regulations may be cited as the National Health Service (General Dental Services—Seniority Payments) Regulations 1970 and shall come into operation on 26th February 1970.

2.—(1) In these regulations, unless the context otherwise requires—

"the principal regulations" means the National Health Service (General Dental Services) Regulations 1967(b) as amended (c);

"quarter" means a period of 3 months ending on 31st March, 30th June, 30th September or 31st December;

"reckonable remuneration" means superannuable remuneration less any seniority payments paid under these regulations, and in assessing such reckonable remuneration any provision in proviso (d) to regulation 64(2) of the National Health Service (Superannuation) Regulations 1961(d) as amended by regulation 50(*b*) of the National Health Service (Superannuation) (Amendment) Regulations 1966(e) that no account shall be taken of any remuneration in excess of a specified amount shall be disregarded;

"seniority payment" has the meaning assigned to it in regulation 3 of these regulations;

"superannuable remuneration" means remuneration in respect of general dental services as defined in regulation 64(2) of the National Health Service (Superannuation) Regulations 1961 as amended by regulation 50 of the National Health Service (Superannuation) (Amendment) Regulations 1966 less any earnings from a salaried appointment at a health centre, whether or not the practitioner is entitled to participate in the benefits provided under those regulations.

(2) Unless the context otherwise requires, words and expressions used in these regulations have the same meanings as they have in the principal regulations.

(a) 1946 c. 81.   (b) S.I. 1967/937 (1967 II, p. 2816).
(c) The amending Regulations are not relevant to the subject matter of these Regulations.
(d) S.I. 1961/1441 (1961 II, p. 2824).
(e) S.I. 1966/1523 (1966 III, p. 4309).

(3) Unless the context otherwise requires, references in these regulations to any enactment or statutory instrument are references to that enactment or statutory instrument as amended or re-enacted by any subsequent enactment or statutory instrument.

(4) The Interpretation Act 1889(a) applies to the interpretation of these regulations as it applies to the interpretation of an Act of Parliament.

3.—(1) Subject to these regulations, a practitioner providing general dental services who duly makes application on a form provided for the purpose—

    (a) if he is on the dental list of only one Council, to that Council; or

    (b) if he is on the dental list of more than one Council, to only one of those Councils;

shall, if he has complied with the conditions of eligibility set out in paragraph 2(a) and (b) of this regulation, be entitled, so long as he complies with the conditions of eligibility set out in paragraph (2)(c), (d) and (e) of this regulation to receive from that Council a payment (hereinafter referred to as a "seniority payment") calculated in accordance with paragraph (4) of this regulation in respect of any quarter (hereinafter referred to as a "relevant quarter") beginning on or after the beginning of the financial year ending on 31st March 1970.

(2) A practitioner shall be eligible for payment of a seniority payment if—

    (a) on the first day of the first quarter to which his application relates he is a person—

        (i) who has provided general dental services, otherwise than as a salaried practitioner at a health centre or as an assistant, in England, Wales, Scotland, Northern Ireland or the Isle of Man for a period of 10 years since 5th July 1948, of which not less than a period of 5 years (whether or not either of such periods has been continuous) has been within the period of 10 years ending on the first day of that quarter; and

        (ii) who has during the period of 10 years ending on 31st March last preceding the first day of that quarter received superannuable remuneration totalling £5,000 or more; and

        (iii) who has attained the age of 55 years; and

    (b) he has duly made application for payment of a seniority payment—

        (i) in the case of an application in respect of a relevant quarter ending on or before 31st December 1969, not later than 31st March 1970, or such later date as the Secretary of State may, in any particular case, specify, or

        (ii) in the case of an application in respect of any other relevant quarter, not later than the end of the quarter next following that relevant quarter; and

    (c) he has not before the first day of any relevant quarter been awarded a superannuation benefit, other than a return of contributions, in respect of the provision of general dental services in England, Wales, Scotland, Northern Ireland or the Isle of Man; and

    (d) he has at any time during any relevant quarter been included in the dental list of a Council in England or Wales as a practitioner undertaking to provide general dental services, otherwise than as a salaried practitioner at a health centre or as an assistant, whether or not he has also been such a salaried practitioner or assistant; and

---

(a) 1889 c. 63.

(e) on the last day of any relevant quarter he has not attained the age of 70 years.

(3) If a practitioner who has been entitled to receive seniority payments ceases to be included in the dental list of the Council to whom he has duly made application under this regulation, but subsequently makes application not later than the date specified in paragraph 2(b) (ii) of this regulation on a form provided for the purpose to a Council, whether or not it is a Council from whom he has been entitled to receive seniority payments, in whose dental list he is included at the time of such application, he shall, subject to paragraph (2)(c), (d) and (e) of this regulation, be entitled to receive seniority payments from that Council calculated in accordance with paragraph (4) of this regulation.

(4) The payment in respect of any quarter which a practitioner shall be entitled to receive under these regulations shall, if his reckonable remuneration in that quarter was an amount specified in column (1) of the Schedule to these regulations, be the amount specified opposite to that amount in column (2) of that Schedule.

(5) Any seniority payments shall be in addition to any payments payable under the principal regulations and paragraph 6 of Part I of Schedule 1 to the principal regulations (Fees and remuneration) shall not apply to any seniority payments.

4. Regulation 33 (Recovery of overpayments) of the principal regulations shall apply to any payment made to a practitioner under these regulations.

SCHEDULE

Regulation 3(4) SCALE OF SENIORITY PAYMENTS

Column (1) Amount of Reckonable Remuneration in the quarter	Column (2) Amount of Seniority Payment for the quarter
£200 or more	£50
£197 or more but less than £200	£49
£194 „ „ „ „ „ £197	£48
£191 „ „ „ „ „ £194	£47
£188 „ „ „ „ „ £191	£46
£185 „ „ „ „ „ £188	£45
£182 „ „ „ „ „ £185	£44
£179 „ „ „ „ „ £182	£43
£176 „ „ „ „ „ £179	£42
£173 „ „ „ „ „ £176	£41
£170 „ „ „ „ „ £173	£40
£167 „ „ „ „ „ £170	£39
£164 „ „ „ „ „ £167	£38
£161 „ „ „ „ „ £164	£37
£158 „ „ „ „ „ £161	£36
£155 „ „ „ „ „ £158	£35
£152 „ „ „ „ „ £155	£34
£149 „ „ „ „ „ £152	£33
£146 „ „ „ „ „ £149	£32
£143 „ „ „ „ „ £146	£31
£140 „ „ „ „ „ £143	£30
£137 „ „ „ „ „ £140	£29
£134 „ „ „ „ „ £137	£28
£131 „ „ „ „ „ £134	£27
£128 „ „ „ „ „ £131	£26
£125 „ „ „ „ „ £128	£25
£122 „ „ „ „ „ £125	£24
£119 „ „ „ „ „ £122	£23
£116 „ „ „ „ „ £119	£22
£113 „ „ „ „ „ £116	£21
£110 „ „ „ „ „ £113	£20
£107 „ „ „ „ „ £110	£19
£104 „ „ „ „ „ £107	£18
£101 „ „ „ „ „ £104	£17
£98 „ „ „ „ „ £101	£16
£95 „ „ „ „ „ £98	£15
£92 „ „ „ „ „ £95	£14
£89 „ „ „ „ „ £92	£13
£86 „ „ „ „ „ £89	£12
£83 „ „ „ „ „ £86	£11
£80 „ „ „ „ „ £83	£10
£77 „ „ „ „ „ £80	£9
£74 „ „ „ „ „ £77	£8
£71 „ „ „ „ „ £74	£7
£68 „ „ „ „ „ £71	£6
£65 „ „ „ „ „ £68	£5
£62 „ „ „ „ „ £65	£4
£59 „ „ „ „ „ £62	£3
£56 „ „ „ „ „ £59	£2
£53 „ „ „ „ „ £56	£1
Less than £53	Nil

R. H. S. Crossman,
Secretary of State for Social
Services.

10th February 1970.

EXPLANATORY NOTE

(This Note is not part of the Regulations.)

These Regulations provide for the payment of "seniority payments" to dentists providing general dental services, other than as salaried practitioners providing those services at a health centre or as assistants. These payments are payable to a dentist aged between 55 and 70 who has not been awarded a super-annuation benefit and are calculated by reference to his earnings during a preceding quarter.

STATUTORY INSTRUMENTS

1970 No. 187

TRANSPORT

PENSIONS AND COMPENSATION

The British Transport (Compensation to Employees) Regulations 1970

Laid before Parliament in draft

Made - - -	*9th February* 1970
Coming into Operation	*19th February* 1970

ARRANGEMENT OF REGULATIONS

PART I

PRELIMINARY

PART II

ENTITLEMENT TO COMPENSATION

PART III

RESETTLEMENT COMPENSATION

PART IV

LONG-TERM COMPENSATION FOR LOSS OF EMPLOYMENT OR LOSS OR DIMINUTION OF EMOLUMENTS OR WORSENING OF POSITION

SCHEDULE 1

Table showing relevant events, first material dates and compensating authorities.

SCHEDULE 2

Tables mentioned in regulation 2(2).

The Minister of Transport in exercise of his powers under section 135(1) of the Transport Act 1968(a), and that Minister and the Secretary of State acting jointly where the said section 135(1) is to be construed in accordance with the provisions of section 135(7) of that Act, in exercise of their joint powers under the said section 135(1) and of all other enabling powers, hereby make the following regulations a draft of which has been laid before Parliament and has been approved by resolution of each House of Parliament in accordance with section 135(5) of the said Act:—

PART I

PRELIMINARY

Citation and commencement

1.—(1) These regulations may be cited as the British Transport (Compensation to Employees) Regulations 1970.

(2) These regulations shall come into operation 14 days after a draft thereof has been approved by a resolution of each House of Parliament and shall have effect from the 18th November 1968.

Interpretation

2.—(1) In these regulations, unless the context otherwise requires, the following expressions have the meanings hereby respectively assigned to them, that is to say :—

"accrued pension", in relation to a pensionable officer who has suffered loss or diminution of pension rights, means—

(a) if his last relevant pension scheme provided benefits in which he had a right to participate, the pension to which he would have become entitled in respect of his pensionable service according to the method of calculation, modified where necessary for the purpose of giving effect to these regulations, prescribed by that scheme if, at the date on which he suffered the said loss or diminution, he had attained normal retiring age and complied with any requirement of that scheme as to a minimum period of qualifying service or contribution and completed any additional contributory payments or payments in respect of added years which he was in the course of making ; and

(b) in any other case, such portion of the pension (if any) of which he had reasonable expectations as the compensating authority consider equitable, having regard to his age, the length of his employment at the date of loss or diminution and all the other circumstances of the case ;

"accrued retiring allowance", in relation to a pensionable officer who has suffered loss or diminution of pension rights, means—

(a) if his last relevant pension scheme provided benefits in which he had a right to participate, any lump sum payment to which he would have become entitled in respect of his pensionable service according to the method of calculation, modified where necessary for the purpose of

(a) 1968 c. 73.

giving effect to these regulations, prescribed by that scheme if, at the date on which he suffered the said loss or diminution, he had attained normal retiring age and complied with any requirement of that scheme as to a minimum period of qualifying service or contribution and completed any additional contributory payments or payments in respect of added years which he was in the course of making ; and

(b) in any other case, such portion of the lump sum payment (if any) of which he had reasonable expectations as the compensating authority consider equitable, having regard to his age, the length of his employment at the date of loss or diminution and all the other circumstances of the case ;

"accrued incapacity pension" and "accrued incapacity retiring allowance" have the same respective meanings as "accrued pension" and "accrued retiring allowance" except that the reference to a person's attaining normal retiring age shall be construed as a reference to his becoming incapable of discharging efficiently the duties of his employment by reason of permanent ill-health or infirmity of mind or body ;

"the Act" means the Transport Act 1968 ;

"added years" means years purchased under the provisions of the last relevant pension scheme for the purpose of being reckoned as pensionable service and includes any additional years of service which, having been granted under any enactment or scheme, have subsequently become and are so reckonable under or by virtue of rules made under section 2 of the Superannuation (Miscellaneous Provisions) Act 1948(a), or any other enactment ;

"additional contributory payments" means—

(a) any additional contributory payments made under a pension scheme as a condition of reckoning any period of employment as service or as a period of contribution for the purposes of the scheme, or, where the scheme provides for the reckoning of non-contributing service, as contributing service for the purposes of the scheme ; or

(b) any payments made for the purpose of increasing the length at which any period of service or of contribution would be reckonable for the purpose of calculating a benefit under a pension scheme ; or

(c) any payments similar to any of those mentioned in the foregoing sub-paragraphs made in pursuance of rules under section 2 of the Superannuation (Miscellaneous Provisions) Act 1948 ;

"attributable loss", in relation to a person who suffers loss of employment, or loss or diminution of emoluments or pension rights, or worsening of his position, means any such loss, diminution or worsening as aforesaid which is properly attributable to the happening of the relevant event ;

"the Boards" has the same meaning as in section 159(1) of the Act, and "a Board" means any of the Boards ;

"the Bus Company" means the National Bus Company established under section 24 of the Act ;

"the Commission" means the British Transport Commission ;

"compensating authority" has the meaning assigned to that expression in regulation 4 ;

"compensation question" means a question arising in relation to these regulations—

(a) as to a person's entitlement to compensation for loss of employment,

---

(a) 11 & 12 Geo. 6. c. 33.

or for loss or diminution of emoluments or pension rights, or worsening of his position, or

(b) as to the manner of a person's employment or the comparability of his duties ;

"emoluments" means any of the following payments or other benefits made to or enjoyed by an officer in respect of services rendered by him as such : —

(a) all salary, wages, fees and other payments of a similar nature for his own use,

(b) all bonuses, allowances, commission, gratuities and special duty and over-time pay, which are of a recurring nature, whether seasonal or otherwise and whether obtaining by law or customary practice,

(c) the money value of all travel privileges, free accommodation, and other allowances in kind, privileges or benefits, whether obtaining by law or customary practice,

but does not include payments for travelling, subsistence, accommodation, engagement of assistance or other expenses in the course of employment or over-time or other payments of a temporary nature ; and

"net emoluments", in relation to any employment, means the annual rate (modified where necessary in accordance with regulation 40) of the emoluments of that employment less such part of those emoluments as the officer was liable to contribute under a pension scheme, and in relation to any employment which has been lost, the emoluments of which have been diminished or in which the officer has suffered loss or diminution of pension rights or a worsening of his position, the expression means the annual rate of emoluments aforesaid immediately before the loss, diminution or worsening, as the case may be :

Provided that where fees or other variable payments were paid to an officer as part of his emoluments during any period immediately preceding the loss, diminution or worsening the amount in respect of fees or other variable payments to be included in the annual rate of emoluments shall be the annual average of the fees or other payments paid to him during the period of 5 years immediately preceding the loss, diminution or worsening or such other period as the compensating authority may think reasonable in the circumstances ;

"enactment" means any Act or instrument made under an Act ;

"Executive" means a Passenger Transport Executive for the establishment of which provision has been made by an order under section 9(1) of the Act ;

"existing operator" means an existing operator within the meaning of Schedule 6 to the Act ;

"the Freight Corporation" means the National Freight Corporation established under section 1 of the Act ;

"full-time basis", in relation to the employment of a person on such a basis, means a basis on which that person is required to devote on the average not less than 30 hours per week to that employment during which he is not at liberty to undertake other work in consideration of a fee or remuneration ;

"the Holding Company" means the Transport Holding Company ;

"long-term compensation" means compensation payable in accordance with the provisions of Part IV of these regulations for loss of employment or loss or diminution of emoluments or worsening of a person's position ;

"first material date", in relation to any person who suffers attributable loss, means the appropriate date specified in column (2) of Schedule 1 to these regulations opposite to the relevant event which is specified in column (1) of that Schedule and to the happening of which that loss is properly attributable ;

"second material date", in relation to any person who suffers attributable loss, means the date on which he suffers that loss or on which the relevant event happens, whichever date is the earlier ;

"minimum pensionable age" means, in relation to a pensionable officer, the earliest age at which, under his last relevant pension scheme, he could have become entitled to a pension, other than a pension payable in consequence of his redundancy or his incapacity to discharge efficiently the duties of his employment by reason of permanent ill-health or infirmity of mind or body ;

"the Minister" means the Minister of Transport, and, in relation to a transfer such as is mentioned in section 135(1)(a) of the Act to or from the Scottish Group or a subsidiary of theirs, means the Minister and the Secretary of State acting jointly ;

"nationalised transport body" means any of the following :—

(a) a Board ;
(b) the Holding Company ;
(c) the Freight Corporation ;
(d) the Bus Company ;
(e) the Scottish Group ;

"national service" means service which is relevant service within the meaning of the Reserve and Auxiliary Forces (Protection of Civil Interests) Act 1951(a), and includes service immediately following such service as aforesaid, being service in any of Her Majesty's naval, military or air forces pursuant to a voluntary engagement entered into with the consent of the person or body under whom an officer held his last relevant employment ;

"normal retiring age" means, in the case of a pensionable officer to whom an age of compulsory retirement applied by virtue of his last relevant pension scheme or of the conditions of the employment in which he suffered the attributable loss, that age, and in any other case, the age of 65 years if the officer is a male, or 60 years if the officer is a female ;

"officer" in relation to the Commission or a nationalised transport body does not include a member of the Commission or of such a body, but subject as aforesaid, includes the holder of any employment whether by virtue of an agreement for the rendering by him of personal services, by appointment, or otherwise ; and the expression "office" shall be construed accordingly ;

"pensionable emoluments", in relation to a person who has or had pension rights, means those emoluments which are required in accordance with the provisions of the pension scheme relating to those rights to be taken into account for the purpose of calculating the pension payable to or in respect of him under that scheme ;

"pensionable officer", in relation to a person who has suffered attributable loss, means an officer who immediately before such loss had pension rights under a pension scheme ;

"pension scheme", in relation to a pensionable officer, means any form of arrangement associated with his employment for the payment of pensions, whether subsisting by virtue of Act of Parliament, trust, contract or otherwise ; and "last relevant pension scheme", in relation to a pensionable officer

---

(a) 14 & 15 Geo. 6. c. 65.

means a pension scheme under which that officer had or has pension rights which were the subject of a loss or diminution properly attributable to the happening of the relevant event;

"the Railways Board" means the British Railways Board;

"reckonable service", in relation to a person, means any period of employment on a full-time basis in any relevant employment and includes any period of war service or national service undertaken on his ceasing to hold any such employment but does not include employment of which account has been taken, or is required to be taken, in calculating the amount of any pension to which he has become entitled;

"relevant employment", in relation to a person who suffers attributable loss, means—

(a) employment under the Crown, or
(b) employment in the service of the Commission, a nationalised transport body, an Executive or a subsidiary of any of the foregoing bodies, or
(c) employment in the service of a person whose business consists of, or includes, the provision of bus services, being employment in connection with such provision, or
(d) employment such as is mentioned in regulation 3(4)(b) or (c) of the British Transport Reorganisation (Compensation to Employees) Regulations 1962(a), or
(e) employment preceding any of the foregoing employments, being employment which is reckonable for the purposes of his last relevant pension scheme,

but, except as provided in regulations 7(1)(c), 13(1)(c) and 19(2)(c), does not include service in the armed forces of the Crown;

"relevant event", in relation to a person who suffers attributable loss, means whichever of the events specified in column (1) of Schedule 1 to these regulations is the event to the happening of which that loss is properly attributable;

"resettlement compensation" means compensation payable in accordance with Part III of these regulations for loss of employment;

"retirement compensation" means compensation payable in accordance with the provisions of regulation 21, 22, 23 or 24;

"the Scottish Group" means the Scottish Transport Group established under section 24 of the Act;

"subsidiary", in relation to the Commission or a nationalised transport body, has the same meaning as in the Transport Act 1962(b), and in this connection no account shall be taken of the provisions of section 51(5) of the Act;

"tribunal" means a tribunal established under section 12 of the Industrial Training Act 1964(c);

"war service" means war service within the meaning of the Local Government Staffs (War Service) Act 1939(d), the Teachers Superannuation (War Service) Act 1939(e) (or, in Scotland, the Education (Scotland) (War Service Superannuation) Act 1939(f)), the Police and Firemen (War Service) Act 1939(g) or employment for war purposes within the meaning of the Superannuation Schemes (War Service) Act 1940(h) and includes any period of

(a) S.I. 1962/2834 (1962 III, p. 4051).
(b) 10 & 11 Eliz. 2. c. 46.
(c) 1964 c. 16.
(d) 2 & 3 Geo. 6. c. 94.
(e) 2 & 3 Geo. 6. c. 95.
(f) 2 & 3 Geo. 6. c. 96.
(g) 2 & 3 Geo. 6. c. 103.
(h) 3 & 4 Geo. 6. c. 26.

service in the First World War in the armed forces of the Crown or in the forces of the Allied or Associated Powers if such service immediately followed a period of relevant employment and was undertaken either compulsorily or with the permission of the employer in that employment.

(2) (*a*) Where under any provision of these regulations an annual value is to be assigned to a capital sum or a capital value to an annual amount, the annual or capital value shall be ascertained in accordance with the tables set out in Schedule 2 to these regulations in so far as they provide for the particular case.

(*b*) For the purpose of determining the application of the said tables the headings and the note to each table shall be treated as a part of the table.

(*c*) Where the said tables do not provide for a case in which an annual value is to be assigned to a capital sum or a capital value to an annual amount, the annual or capital value shall be such as may be agreed between the compensating authority and the person to whom the capital sum or annual amount is payable.

(3) Unless the context otherwise requires, references in these regulations to the provisions of any enactment shall be construed as references to those provisions as amended, re-enacted or modified by or under any subsequent enactment.

(4) References in these regulations to a numbered regulation shall, unless the reference is to a regulation of specified regulations, be construed as references to the regulation bearing that number in these regulations.

(5) References in any of these regulations to a numbered paragraph shall, unless the reference is to a paragraph of a specified regulation, be construed as references to the paragraph bearing that number in the first mentioned regulation.

(6) The Interpretation Act 1889(**a**) shall apply for the interpretation of these regulations as it applies for the interpretation of an Act of Parliament.

PART II

ENTITLEMENT TO COMPENSATION

Persons to whom the regulations apply

3. These regulations shall apply to any person who suffers attributable loss and who—

    (*a*) was employed immediately before the first material date on a full-time basis, as an officer of a nationalised transport body or a subsidiary of such a body or as an officer of an existing operator, or

    (*b*) would have been so employed at that time but for any national service on which he was then engaged.

Grounds of entitlement to compensation–Compensating authorities

4.—(1) Subject to the provisions of these regulations, any person to whom these regulations apply shall be entitled to have his case considered for the payment of compensation under these regulations, and such compensation shall be determined in accordance with these regulations.

(2) Compensation for attributable loss suffered by a person to whom these regulations apply shall be payable by the appropriate authority specified in

---

(**a**) 52 & 53 Vict. c. 63.

column (3) of Schedule 1 to these regulations opposite to the relevant event which is specified in column (1) of that Schedule and to the happening of which that loss is properly attributable, and the said authority is referred to in these regulations, in relation to the person suffering that loss, as "the compensating authority".

(3) Where the same loss of employment or loss or diminution of emoluments or pension rights or worsening of position is properly attributable to the happening of more than one relevant event:—

(a) not more than one claim shall be made or satisfied under these regulations in respect of that loss, diminution or worsening, as the case may be, and

(b) for the purpose of ascertaining the first material date, the second material date and the compensating authority in relation to the person who suffers that loss, diminution or worsening, regard shall be had only to the last of those relevant events to happen.

National service

5.—(1) Where any person to whom these regulations apply would have been employed immediately before the first material date as an officer of a nationalised transport body or of a subsidiary of such a body, or as an officer of an existing operator, but for any national service on which he was then engaged, then if before the expiry of two months after ceasing to be so engaged, or, if prevented by sickness or other reasonable cause, as soon as practicable thereafter, he gives notice to the compensating authority that he is available for employment, that person shall be entitled—

(a) in a case where, in consequence of an event specified in any of paragraphs (a) to (d) of section 135(1) of the Act, he is not given or offered re-employment in his former office or in any reasonably comparable office (whether in the same or in a different service), to have his case considered for payment of compensation for loss of employment, and (if appropriate) for loss or diminution of pension rights, and

(b) in a case where, in consequence of any such event, he is so re-employed with diminished emoluments, or with loss or diminution of pension rights or worsening of his position as compared with the emoluments, pension rights or position which he would have enjoyed had he continued in his former employment, to have his case considered for payment of compensation for diminution of emoluments, or for loss or diminution of pension rights, or for worsening of his position (as the case may warrant).

(2) The loss of employment which is the cause of a claim for compensation under paragraph (1)(a) shall be treated as having occurred on the earlier of the two following dates, that is to say, the date of the refusal of re-employment or a date one month after the date on which the person gave notice that he was available for employment, and the person shall be deemed to have been entitled to the emoluments which he would have enjoyed at such earlier date had he continued in his former employment.

PART III

RESETTLEMENT COMPENSATION

Resettlement compensation for loss of employment

6. The compensating authority shall, subject to the provisions of these regulations, pay resettlement compensation to any person to whom these regulations apply and who satisfies the conditions set out in regulation 7.

Conditions for payment of resettlement compensation

7.—(1) Without prejudice to any other requirement of these regulations, the conditions for the payment of resettlement compensation to any person are that—

(a) he has, before, on, or not later than 10 years after the date of the relevant event, suffered loss of employment which is properly attributable to the happening of the relevant event ;

(b) he has not at the date of the loss attained normal retiring age ;

(c) he has, for a period beginning 3 years immediately before the second material date and ending on the date of the loss, been continuously engaged (disregarding breaks not exceeding in the aggregate 6 months) on a full-time basis in relevant employment ; and for this purpose the expression "relevant employment" includes any period of national service immediately following such employment ;

(d) he has made a claim for such compensation in accordance with the provisions of Part VII of these regulations not later than—

(i) the end of the period in respect of which resettlement compensation can be payable in his case under the provisions of regulation 9, or

(ii) 13 weeks after the coming into operation of these regulations, whichever is the later ;

(e) the loss of employment which is the cause of his claim has occurred for some reason other than misconduct or incapacity to perform such duties as, immediately before the loss, he was performing or might reasonably have been required to perform ; and

(f) he has not, subject to paragraph (3), been offered any reasonably comparable employment under the Crown or in the service of a nationalised transport body, an Executive or a subsidiary of either of those bodies.

(2) In ascertaining for the purpose of this regulation whether a person has been offered employment which is reasonably comparable with the employment which he has lost, the following facts shall be disregarded—

(a) the fact that the employment so offered is employment by a body such as is mentioned in paragraph (1)(f) other than the person or body in whose employment he suffered the attributable loss ;

(b) the fact that the duties of the employment so offered are duties in connection with activities which did not form part of the activities of that section of the undertaking of the nationalised transport body, subsidiary thereof or existing operator in which he was employed ;

(c) the fact that the duties of the employment so offered involve a transfer of his employment from one place to another in Great Britain.

(3) No account shall be taken for the purposes of this regulation of an offer of employment where the compensating authority are satisfied—

(a) that acceptance would have involved undue hardship to the person, or

(b) that he was prevented from accepting the offer by reason of ill-health or other circumstances beyond his control.

Amount of resettlement compensation

8.—(1) The amount of resettlement compensation which may be paid to a person shall, for each week for which such compensation is payable, be a sum ascertained by taking two thirds of the weekly rate of the net emoluments which that person has lost and deducting therefrom, in addition to the items mentioned in regulation 32(3) and (4), such of the following items as may be applicable—

(*a*) unemployment, sickness or injury benefit under any Act relating to National Insurance claimable by him in respect of such week (excluding any amount claimable by him in respect of a dependant) ; and

(*b*) two thirds of the net emoluments received by him in respect of such week from work or employment undertaken as a result of the loss of employment.

(2) For the purposes of this regulation the weekly rate of a person's net emoluments shall be deemed to be seven three hundred and sixty-fifths of those emoluments.

Period for payment of resettlement compensation

9. Subject to the provisions of these regulations, resettlement compensation shall be payable to a person only in respect of the period of 13 weeks next succeeding the week in which he lost the employment in connection with which his claim has been made or, in the case of a person who has then attained the age of 45 years, the said 13 weeks and one additional week for every year of his age between the date of his attaining the age of 45 years and the date of the loss of employment, subject to a maximum addition of 13 such weeks.

Additional provisions relating to resettlement compensation

10.—(1) Resettlement compensation shall be payable to a person at intervals equivalent to those at which the emoluments of his employment were previously paid or at such other intervals as may be agreed between the person and the compensating authority.

(2) Resettlement compensation shall be terminated by the compensating authority—

(*a*) if without reasonable cause the recipient fails to comply with any of the provisions of regulation 11, or

(*b*) if on being requested to do so, he fails to satisfy the compensating authority that, so far as he is able, he is seeking suitable employment.

Claimant for resettlement compensation to furnish particulars of employment

11. Every person claiming or in receipt of resettlement compensation shall (after as well as before the compensation begins to be paid)—

(*a*) forthwith supply the compensating authority in writing with particulars of any employment which he obtains or of any change in his earnings from any such employment, and

(*b*) if the compensating authority so require, so long as he is out of employment and is not receiving sickness or injury benefit, register with the Department of Employment and Productivity.

Part IV

Long-term Compensation for Loss of Employment or Loss or Diminution of Emoluments or Worsening of Position

Long-term compensation

12. The compensating authority shall, subject to the provisions of these regulations, pay long-term compensation to any person to whom these regulations apply and who satisfies the conditions set out in regulation 13 and this Part of these regulations shall apply to that person.

Conditions for payment of long-term compensation

13.—(1) Without prejudice to any other requirement of these regulations, the conditions for the payment of long-term compensation to any person are that—

(a) he has, before, on, or not later than 10 years after the date of the relevant event, suffered loss of employment or loss or diminution of emoluments or worsening of his position, being loss, diminution or worsening (as the case may be) which is properly attributable to the happening of the relevant event ;

(b) he has not, save as is provided in regulation 17, at the date of such loss, diminution or worsening attained normal retiring age ;

(c) he has, for a period beginning 8 years immediately before the second material date and ending on the date of the attributable loss, been continuously engaged (without a break of more than 12 months at any one time) on a full-time basis in relevant employment ; and for this purpose the expression "relevant employment" includes any period of national service immediately following such employment ;

(d) he has made a claim for such compensation in accordance with the provisions of Part VII of these regulations not later than—
   (i) 2 years after the date on which the loss, diminution or worsening which is the cause of his claim was suffered, or
   (ii) 2 years after the coming into operation of these regulations, or
   (iii) in a case where the claimant could not reasonably have known of the existence of the cause of his claim for compensation at the time when it in fact occurred, 2 years after the first date on which he could reasonably have known of its existence,
   whichever is the latest ; and

(e) if the cause of the claim for compensation is loss of employment—
   (i) the loss has occurred for some reason other than misconduct or incapacity to perform such duties as, immediately before the loss, he was performing or might reasonably have been required to perform ; and
   (ii) he has not been offered any reasonably comparable employment under the Crown or in the service of a nationalised transport body, an Executive or a subsidiary of either of those bodies.

(2) If the cause of the claim for compensation is loss of employment paragraphs (2) and (3) of regulation 7 (which relate to offers of employment) shall apply for the purposes of this regulation as they apply for the purposes of regulation 7.

(3) Claims for long-term compensation for loss of employment shall in all respects be treated as claims for such compensation for the loss of emoluments occasioned thereby and the provisions of these regulations shall apply to all such claims accordingly.

(4) Any person to whom this Part of these regulations applies and who, by reason of his position as an officer being worsened, has suffered any loss or injury attributable to the happening of the relevant event, not being a pecuniary loss in respect of which he is entitled to any other compensation or payments under Part IV or V of these regulations, shall, subject to the provisions of these regulations, be entitled to receive in respect of that loss or injury, long-term compensation for the worsening of his position calculated in the following manner, that is to say—

(a) the pecuniary value of the loss or injury shall be expressed in terms of his net emoluments immediately before his position was worsened,

(b) such person shall be treated for the purposes of these regulations as a person who has suffered a diminution of emoluments the amount of which is equal to the pecuniary value so expressed, and

(c) where that person has been awarded any other long-term compensation, as well as compensation for the worsening of his position, the sums payable in respect of that other compensation shall, for the purposes of adjusting, suspending or withholding any long-term compensation under regulation 31 or 32 or both, be aggregated with any sums payable in respect of the compensation for worsening of his position and the payments of the sums so aggregated shall be regarded for those purposes as combined payments under the award of that other long-term compensation and not as separate payments under each of the awards of long-term compensation.

Factors to be considered in determining payment of long-term compensation

14.—(1) For the purpose of determining the amount (subject to the limits set out in these regulations) of long-term compensation (if any) payable under these regulations to any person for loss or diminution of emoluments, the compensating authority shall have regard to such of the following factors as may be relevant, that is to say—

(a) the conditions upon which the person held the employment which he has lost, or the emoluments of which have been lost or diminished, including in particular its security of tenure, whether by law or practice ;

(b) the emoluments and other conditions, including security of tenure, whether by law or practice, of any work or employment undertaken by the person as a result of the loss of employment ;

(c) the extent to which he has sought suitable employment and the emoluments which he might have acquired by accepting other suitable employment offered to him ;

(d) all the other circumstances of his case:

Provided that if the claimant entered the employment which he has lost or in which he has suffered the diminution of emoluments, after the first material date, no account shall be taken of that fact for the purpose of this regulation.

(2) In ascertaining for the purposes of paragraph (1)(c) whether a person has been offered suitable employment in a case where the cause of the claim for compensation is loss of employment, regulation 7(3) shall apply as it applies for the purpose of ascertaining whether employment is reasonably comparable with employment which has been lost.

Amount of long-term compensation payable for loss of emoluments

15.—(1) Long-term compensation for loss of emoluments shall, subject to the provisions of these regulations, be payable until the normal retiring age or death of a person to whom it is payable, whichever first occurs, and shall not exceed a maximum annual sum calculated in accordance with the provisions of paragraphs (2) to (4).

(2) The said maximum annual sum shall, subject as hereinafter provided, be the aggregate of the following sums, namely—

(*a*) for every year of the person's reckonable service, one sixtieth of the net emoluments which he has lost ; and

(*b*) in the case of a person who has attained the age of 40 years at the date of the loss, a sum calculated in accordance with the provisions of paragraph (3) appropriate to his age at that date ;

but the said maximum annual sum shall in no case exceed two thirds of the net emoluments which the person has lost.

(3) The sum referred to in paragraph (2)(*b*) shall be—

(*a*) in the case of a person who has attained the age of 40 years but has not attained the age of 50 years at the date of the loss, the following fraction of the net emoluments which he has lost—

(i) where his reckonable service is less than 10 years, one sixtieth for each year of such service after attaining the age of 40 years ; or

(ii) where his reckonable service amounts to 10 years but is less than 15 years, one sixtieth for each year of such service after attaining the age of 40 years and one additional sixtieth ; or

(iii) where his reckonable service amounts to 15 years but is less than 20 years, one sixtieth for each year of such service after attaining the age of 40 years and two additional sixtieths ; or

(iv) where his reckonable service amounts to 20 years or more, one sixtieth for each year of such service after attaining the age of 40 years and three additional sixtieths ;

but the sum so calculated shall not in any case exceed one sixth of the said net emoluments ;

(*b*) in the case of a person who has attained the age of 50 years but has not attained the age of 60 years at the date of the loss, one sixtieth of the said net emoluments for each year of his reckonable service after attaining the age of 40 years, up to a maximum of 15 years ; and

(*c*) in the case of a person who has attained the age of 60 years at the date of the loss, one sixtieth of the said net emoluments for each year of his reckonable service after attaining the age of 45 years.

(4) Where a person has become entitled (whether immediately or prospectively on attaining some greater age) to a pension by way of annual amounts under his last relevant pension scheme, the maximum annual sum referred to in paragraph (1) shall be the maximum sum calculated under paragraphs (2) and (3) as if he had not become so entitled.

(5) Where long-term compensation is payable in respect of any period and resettlement compensation has also been paid in respect of that period, the long-term compensation for that period shall be limited to the amount (if any) by which it exceeds the resettlement compensation paid as aforesaid.

(6) Long-term compensation shall be payable to a person at intervals equivalent to those at which the emoluments of his employment were previously paid or at such other intervals as may be agreed between the person and the compensating authority.

Long-term compensation for diminution of emoluments

16. Long-term compensation for diminution of emoluments in respect of any employment shall, subject to the provisions of these regulations, be awarded and paid in accordance with the following provisions :—

> (*a*) the compensation shall consist of an annual sum which shall be payable to a person at intervals equivalent to those at which the emoluments of his employment are or were previously paid or at such other intervals as may be agreed between the person and the compensating authority, and shall, subject to the provisions of these regulations, be payable until normal retiring age or death, whichever first occurs ; and

> (*b*) the said annual sum shall not exceed the maximum annual sum which could have been awarded under regulation 15 if the person had suffered loss of employment and the loss of emoluments occasioned thereby had been equivalent to the amount of the diminution :

Provided that no compensation shall be payable if the emoluments have been diminished by less than $2\frac{1}{2}$ per cent.

Compensation payable to non-pensionable officer on reaching normal retiring age

17.—(1) Where a person to whom this Part of these regulations applies and who is not a pensionable officer is receiving long-term compensation for loss or diminution of emoluments or worsening of his position and attains normal retiring age, the compensating authority may, if satisfied that the person would have continued to work as an officer for a substantial period beyond normal retiring age, continue to pay compensation to him for the remainder of his life at half its former rate.

(2) Where a person to whom this Part of these regulations applies and who is not a pensionable officer suffers loss or diminution of emoluments, or worsening of his position, on or after attaining normal retiring age, the compensating authority may, if satisfied that the person had he not so suffered would have continued in the normal course of events to work for a substantial period as an officer, pay compensation to him for the remainder of his life at a rate not exceeding one half of that to which he would have been entitled under regulation 15 had he not attained normal retiring age at the date on which he suffered the loss, diminution or worsening, as the case may be.

Date from which long-term compensation is to be payable

18.—(1) Long-term compensation shall be payable with effect from the date of the claim or from any earlier date permitted by the succeeding provisions of this regulation.

(2) Where a claim for long-term compensation is duly made within 13 weeks of the occurrence of the loss or diminution which is the cause of the claim, or within 13 weeks of the coming into operation of these regulations whichever is the later, the award shall be made retrospective to the date on which the loss or diminution occurred.

(3) Where a claim for long-term compensation is made after the expiry of the period mentioned in paragraph (2), the award may, at the discretion of the compensating authority, be made retrospective to a date not earlier than 13 weeks prior to the date on which the claim was made :

Provided that if the compensating authority are satisfied that the failure to make the claim within the period mentioned in paragraph (2) was due to ill-health or other circumstances beyond the claimant's control, the award may be made retrospective to a date not earlier than that on which the loss or diminution occurred.

PART V

RETIREMENT COMPENSATION AND PAYMENTS ON DEATH

Entitlement to retirement compensation and other payments

19.—(1) The compensating authority shall, subject to the provisions of these regulations, pay retirement compensation to any person to whom this Part of these regulations applies, and shall make the other payments for which provision is made in regulations 27 to 29.

(2) This Part of these regulations applies to a pensionable officer who, before, on, or not later than 10 years after the date of the relevant event, has suffered loss or diminution of pension rights which is properly attributable to the happening of the relevant event and who—

(*a*) is a person to whom these regulations apply ;

(*b*) has not at the date on which the loss or diminution was suffered reached normal retiring age ;

(*c*) has been continuously engaged (without a break of more than 12 months at any one time) on a full-time basis in relevant employment during the period beginning 8 years immediately before the second material date and ending on the date of the loss or diminution; and for this purpose the expression "relevant employment" includes any period of national service immediately following such employment.

(3) (*a*) Any claim for retirement compensation or other compensation under this Part of these regulations shall be made in accordance with the provisions of Part VII of these regulations not later than—

(i) 2 years after the date on which the loss or diminution of pension rights which is the cause of the claim was suffered, on

(ii) 2 years after the coming into operation of these regulations, or

(iii) in a case where the claimant could not reasonably have known of the existence of the cause of his claim for compensation at the time when it in fact occurred, 2 years after the first date on which he could reasonably have known of its existence,

whichever is the latest, and

(*b*) no such compensation as aforesaid shall be payable to or in respect of any claimant before he has reached normal retiring age unless either he has elected to take retirement compensation earlier in accordance with the following provisions of this Part of these regulations or the compensation is compensation payable under regulation 27 or 28.

(4) Retirement compensation and any other such payments as are mentioned in paragraph (1) shall not, however, be paid or made—

(*a*) to or in respect of a person who has suffered loss or diminution of pension rights which has been occasioned by loss of employment in consequence of a relevant event, if his employment could have been terminated by reason of misconduct or incapacity to perform such duties as, immediately before that loss of employment, he was performing or might reasonably have been required to perform ; or

(*b*) to or in respect of a person who has been offered reasonably comparable employment under the Crown or in the service of a nationalised transport body, an Executive or a subsidiary of either of those bodies and who would not have suffered a loss or diminution of pension rights had he accepted that employment ; or

(c) to or in respect of a person who has suffered a diminution of pension rights which has been occasioned by a diminution in his pensionable emoluments of less than $2\frac{1}{2}$ per cent.

(5) If the claim results from loss of employment, paragraphs (2) and (3) of regulation 7 (which relate to offers of employment) shall apply for the purposes of this regulation as they apply for the purposes of regulation 7.

(6) References in this Part of these regulations to the date of loss or diminution of pension rights or to the date on which a loss or diminution of pension rights was suffered shall, subject to regulation 5, be interpreted as references to the date on which the loss of employment or emoluments took place or the diminution of emoluments began or the change in the terms of service occurred which occasioned the loss or diminution of pension rights.

Factors governing payment of retirement compensation

20.—(1) Where retirement compensation is payable under any one of regulations 21, 22, 23 and 24, such compensation shall not be payable under any other of those regulations.

(2) For the purpose of determining the amount of any retirement compensation which may, subject to the limits set out in these regulations, be payable thereunder, regard shall be had to the extent of the loss or the diminution of pension rights suffered and also to such of the factors set out in regulation 14(1) as may be relevant, and in addition the following further factors shall be taken into consideration—

(a) the terms of any pension scheme associated with any new employment undertaken ; and

(b) the extent to which the person in question has sought pensionable employment, and the terms of any pension scheme which would have applied if he had accepted other suitable employment offered to him.

(3) If a person has attained the age of 40 years at the date on which he suffered loss or diminution of pension rights, the compensating authority, in calculating the amount of the retirement compensation payable to him, shall credit him with additional years of service or an additional period of contribution on the following basis, namely—

(a) 2 years, whether or not he has completed any years of service after attaining the age of 40 years, and

(b) 2 years for each of the first 4 completed years of his reckonable service between the date when he attained the age of 40 years and the date of the loss or diminution, and

(c) one year for each such year of service after the fourth ;

but the additional years of service or period of contribution so credited shall not exceed the shortest of the following periods, namely—

(i) such number of years as, when added to his pensionable service, would amount to the maximum period of such service which would have been reckonable by him had he continued in his employment until attaining normal retiring age, or

(ii) the number of years of his reckonable service, or

(iii) 15 years ;

and in calculating the amount of any retirement compensation payable to him any period so added shall be aggregated with any years of service or period of contribution entailing reduction of the relevant pension or retiring allowance because of a retirement pension payable under section 30 of the National Insurance Act 1965(a).

(4) When retirement compensation is awarded, or when an award is reviewed under regulation 34, the additional compensation payable in consequence of any years of service or period of contribution credited to a person under paragraph (3) may be reduced or withheld to such extent as the compensating authority may think reasonable having regard to the pension scheme (if any) associated with any further employment obtained by him.

(5) If under his last relevant pension scheme the amount of any benefit to which a person might have become entitled could have been increased at the discretion of the body, trustees or other persons administering the pension scheme or of any other body or person, the compensating authority may increase, to an extent not exceeding that to which his accrued pension, accrued retiring allowance, accrued incapacity pension or accrued incapacity retiring allowance might have been increased or supplemented, the corresponding component of any retirement compensation payable to him ; and in this connection the compensating authority shall have regard to the terms of any relevant resolutions of such body, trustees or other persons with regard to the increase of benefits and to the provisions of any enactment protecting the interests of that person.

(6) If under his last relevant pension scheme a person would have been entitled to surrender a proportion of any pension which might have become payable to him in favour of his spouse or any dependant, then, if he so desires and informs the compensating authority by notice in writing accordingly within one month after becoming entitled to retirement compensation under these regulations, he may surrender a proportion of so much of the said compensation as is payable by way of an annual sum on the like terms and conditions and in consideration of the like payments by the compensating authority as if the said annual sum were a pension to which he had become entitled under the said pension scheme.

(7) In calculating for the purposes of regulation 21, 22, 23 or 24 the amount of the annual sum which is equal to a person's accrued pension, no account shall be taken of any reduction falling to be made in that pension by reason of the provisions of any Act relating to National Insurance until the person reaches the age at which under his last relevant pension scheme the pension would have been so reduced.

(8) In paragraph (3) the expression "reckonable service" includes any period of employment of which account has been taken or is required to be taken in calculating the amount of any pension to which a person has become entitled under the last relevant pension scheme.

Retirement compensation for loss of a pension payable to pensionable officer on attainment of normal retiring age

21. Subject to the provisions of these regulations, when a person to whom this Part of these regulations applies reaches normal retiring age, the retirement compensation payable to him for loss of pension rights shall be—

(*a*) an annual sum equal to the amount of his accrued pension, and

(*b*) a lump sum equal to the amount of his accrued retiring allowance (if any).

(a) 1965 c. 51.

Retirement compensation payable to pensionable officer on his becoming incapacitated or reaching minimum pensionable age

22.—(1) Where a person to whom this Part of these regulations applies and who has suffered loss of his pension rights before attaining what would have been his normal retiring age—

(*a*) becomes incapacitated in circumstances in which, if he had not suffered such loss as aforesaid, he would have become entitled to a pension under his last relevant pension scheme, or

(*b*) attains the age which, if he had not suffered the said loss, would have been his minimum pensionable age,

he shall be entitled on the happening of either of those events to claim, in lieu of any compensation to which he would otherwise be entitled under these regulations—

(i) in a case where sub-paragraph (*a*) of this paragraph applies, an annual sum equal to the amount of his accrued incapacity pension and a lump sum equal to the amount of his accrued incapacity retiring allowance (if any), and

(ii) in a case where sub-paragraph (*b*) of this paragraph applies, an annual sum equal to the amount of his accrued pension and a lump sum equal to the amount of his accrued retiring allowance (if any),

subject however to the conditions specified in paragraph (5).

(2) On receipt of a claim under paragraph (1) the compensating authority shall consider whether the claimant is a person to whom that paragraph applies, and within 13 weeks after the date of the receipt of the claim—

(*a*) if they are satisfied that he is not such a person, they shall notify him in writing accordingly; or

(*b*) if they are satisfied that he is such a person, they shall assess the amount of compensation payable to him and notify him in writing accordingly;

and any such notification shall, for the purposes of these regulations, be deemed to be a notification by the authority of a decision on a claim for compensation.

(3) A compensating authority may require any person who makes a claim under paragraph (1)(*a*) to submit himself to a medical examination by a registered medical practitioner selected by that authority, and if they do so, they shall also afford the person an opportunity of submitting a report from his own medical adviser as a result of an examination by him, and the authority shall take that report into consideration together with the report of the medical practitioner selected by them.

(4) If a person wishes to receive compensation under this regulation, he shall so inform the compensating authority in writing within one month from the receipt of a notification under paragraph (2) or, where the claim has been the subject of an appeal, from the decision of the tribunal thereon; and the compensation shall be payable as from the date on which the compensating authority received the claim.

(5) The calculation of compensation under this regulation shall be subject to the following conditions—

(*a*) where the compensating authority, by virtue of regulation 20, have credited the person with additional years of service or an additional period of contribution, no account shall be taken of any additional years or period beyond the number of years which he could have served, had he not lost his employment (in a case where the loss of pension rights was the result of a loss of employment), before the date on which the claim was received by the compensating authority; and

(b) if, by reason of any provision of the last relevant pension scheme for a minimum pension or benefit, the amount of any such pension or retiring allowance is in excess of that attributable to the person's actual service, no account shall be taken of any such additional years or period except to the extent (if any) by which they exceed the number of years represented by the difference between his actual service and the period by reference to which the minimum pension or benefit has been calculated; and

(c) if the number of years by reference to which an accrued incapacity pension or accrued incapacity retiring allowance is to be calculated is less than any minimum number of years of qualifying service prescribed by the relevant pension scheme, the amount of such pension or retiring allowance shall, notwithstanding any minimum pension or benefit prescribed by the pension scheme, not exceed such proportion of such minimum pension or benefit as the number of years of pensionable service bears to the minimum number of years of qualifying service.

Option to take retirement compensation prematurely

23.—(1) If a person to whom this Part of these regulations applies has suffered a loss of pension rights and loss of employment after attaining the age of 50 years both losses being attributable to the happening of the relevant event and so requests the compensating authority by notice in writing, he shall be entitled, as from the date on which the compensating authority receives such notice, to an annual sum equal to the amount of his accrued pension and a lump sum equal to the amount of his accrued retiring allowance (if any), and in that event he shall not be entitled to receive any further payment of long-term compensation after the date on which compensation under this regulation becomes payable: Provided that—

(i) in calculating the amount of the compensation payable to a person who has given such notice as aforesaid no account shall be taken of any additional years of service or period of contribution credited to him under regulation 20; and

(ii) where the person has claimed long-term compensation the said notice shall be given not later than 2 years after a decision on the claim has been notified or, where the decision has been reviewed under regulation 34(3), not later than 2 years after the review, or if there has been more than one such review, after the latest.

(2) Regulation 22(2) and (4) shall apply in relation to a notice given under the last foregoing paragraph as it applies to a claim made under paragraph (1) of that regulation.

(3) Where an annual sum is payable under this regulation in respect of any period and resettlement compensation is also payable in respect of that period, the said annual sum shall be limited to the amount (if any) by which it exceeds the resettlement compensation payable as aforesaid.

(4) If a person to whom this Part of these regulations applies has suffered a diminution of pension rights otherwise than by reason of a diminution of his pensionable emoluments and has also suffered a loss of employment after attaining the age of 50 years, such diminution and loss being both attributable to the happening of the relevant event, the provisions of this regulation shall apply and have effect in relation to him in like manner as if he were such a person as is mentioned in paragraph (1) except that the lump sum (if any) referred to in that paragraph shall be reduced by the amount of any pension paid or

payable by way of a lump sum under his last relevant pension scheme and except that the annual sum so referred to shall be such annual sum as is therein provided but reduced, on and after the date on which he is first entitled under the said scheme to be paid any instalment of his pension by way of annual amounts, by the amount of each such instalment and paragraph (2) of regulation 24 shall have the like effect in the application of this paragraph as it does in the application of paragraph (1)(*b*) of that regulation.

Retirement compensation for diminution of pension rights

24.—(1) Regulations 21 and 22 shall apply and have effect in relation to a person to whom this Part of these regulations applies and who has suffered a diminution of pension rights as if—

(*a*) where that person has suffered such diminution by reason of a diminution of his pensionable emoluments, the annual sum and the lump sum (if any) payable to him as retirement compensation under those regulations were equal to such an annual sum and such a lump sum (if any) as respectively bear the same ratio to the sums which would be payable under those regulations, had he suffered a loss (instead of a diminution) of pension rights, as the ratio which the amount of the diminution of his pensionable emoluments bears to those emoluments before their diminution, and

(*b*) where that person has suffered diminution of pension rights for any other reason, the annual sum and the lump sum (if any) payable to him as retirement compensation under those regulations were equal to the annual sum and lump sum (if any) which would be payable under those regulations, had he suffered a loss (instead of a diminution) of pension rights, respectively reduced by the amount of any sums payable under his last relevant pension scheme in each year after retirement compensation becomes payable and by the amount of any lump sum paid or payable under that scheme.

(2) In the application of paragraph (1)(*b*) to an officer to or in respect of whom the provisions of any order made under section 74 of the Transport Act 1962 as read with section 136 of the Act have effect so as to secure the payment or payments comprised in his accrued pension rights, the references in that paragraph to his last relevant pension scheme shall include a reference to any arrangements made under that scheme pursuant to such an order and to any arrangements made under that order for the purpose of discharging any liability of a body to make payments prescribed thereby.

Pension contributions

25.—(1) A person entitled to retirement compensation under these regulations for loss of pension rights shall pay to the compensating authority an amount equal to any sum which was paid to him by way of return of pension contributions, including any interest, after ceasing to be employed, and the compensating authority may at his request repay that amount to him at any time before he becomes entitled as aforesaid, but if that amount is not paid to the compensating authority, or is repaid by them to the person, the compensation shall be reduced by an annual amount the capital value of which is equal to the amount of the said contributions.

(2) For the purposes of this regulation the expression "pension contributions" shall include payments made to the pension fund by the person in respect of added years and any additional contributory payments so made by him.

Retirement compensation of a person who obtains further pensionable employment

26. Where a person to whom this Part of these regulations applies, after suffering loss or diminution of pension rights, enters new employment in which he is subject to any pension scheme and thereafter becomes entitled to reckon for the purposes of that scheme any service or period of contribution which falls to be taken into account for the purpose of assessing the amount of any retirement compensation payable to him, his entitlement to retirement compensation shall be reviewed and no retirement compensation shall be payable in respect of such service or period unless the annual rate of the pensionable emoluments to which he was entitled immediately before such loss or diminution exceeds the annual rate on entry of the pensionable emoluments of the new employment by more than $2\frac{1}{2}$ per cent. of such first-mentioned emoluments, and any retirement compensation so payable to him shall, in so far as it is calculated by reference to remuneration, be calculated by reference to the difference between the said annual rates:

Provided that this regulation shall not operate to increase the amount of any retirement compensation payable in respect of loss or diminution of pension rights beyond the amount which would have been payable if the person had attained normal retiring age immediately before he suffered the loss or diminution of pension rights.

Compensation payable to widow or dependants of a claimant

27.—(1) Payments in accordance with this regulation and regulations 28 and 29 shall be made to or for the benefit of the widow, child or other dependant or to the personal representatives of a person to whom this Part of these regulations applies.

(2) If the widow, child or other dependant of that person might, but for the loss or diminution of his pension rights have become entitled to a pension or, as the case may be, to a larger pension under his last relevant pension scheme, the widow, child or other dependant concerned shall be entitled to receive an annual sum equal to the prescribed proportion of any retirement compensation by way of annual amounts payable to the person under regulation 21, 22, 23 or 24 immediately before his death or, if he dies before becoming entitled to receive compensation under any of those regulations, the prescribed proportion of the compensation by way of annual amounts which he would have received under regulation 22 or, as the case may be, under that regulation as applied by regulation 24, had he become entitled thereto immediately before his death:
Provided that—

    (i) where any retirement compensation has been surrendered under regulation 20(6) or compounded under regulation 35, any sum payable under this regulation shall be calculated as if such surrender or compounding had not taken place;

    (ii) where the pension scheme provides for payment of the pension to any person on behalf of a child or other dependant, any annual sum payable as aforesaid to a child or other dependant shall be paid to that person on behalf of the child or dependant in the like manner and for the like period as is provided in the pension scheme;

    (iii) in calculating the sum payable as aforesaid, it shall be assumed that the retirement compensation payable, or which would have been payable, to a person under regulation 21, 22, 23 or 24 had been such sum as would have been payable if the accrued pension or accrued incapacity pension had not been reduced by reason of the provisions of any Act relating to National Insurance;

(iv) where by virtue of a provision of the pension scheme, the annual pension which would have been paid to the widow, child or other dependant but for the loss or diminution of pension rights would not have exceeded, or would not have been less than, or would have been a specified amount, or an amount ascertainable when calculated in like manner as is provided in paragraph (5)(*b*), the aggregate of the annual sum payable under this regulation and any annual pension payable under the pension scheme to the widow, child or other dependant shall correspondingly not exceed, not be less than or shall be equal to that specified amount or, as the case may be, the amount ascertained when so calculated as aforesaid.

(3) Any annual sum payable to or for the benefit of a widow, child or other dependant under this regulation shall cease to be payable in any circumstances in which a corresponding pension under the pension scheme referred to in paragraph (2) would have ceased to be payable.

(4) Except where the compensation has been reduced under regulation 25, compensation payable under this regulation and regulation 28 shall in the aggregate be reduced by an amount the capital value whereof is equal to the amount of any pension contributions as defined in regulation 25(2) returned to the person in respect of whom the compensation is payable and either not paid to the compensating authority or repaid by the compensating authority to him, the compensation under each such regulation being reduced in proportion to the capital value of each amount.

(5) In this regulation "prescribed proportion" means—

(*a*) where provision is made in any last relevant pension scheme of a person to whom this Part of these regulations applies for the pension payable to his widow, child or other dependant to be of such annual amounts as will bear a certain proportion to that person's pension (whether that person's pension is payable to him under that same pension scheme or under another such scheme dealing exclusively with his pension), that certain proportion, and

(*b*) where no such provision is made, the proportion which the annual amounts of the pension to which the widow, child or other dependant of the person in question would have become entitled, in the circumstances mentioned in paragraph (6), (such amounts being calculated in the manner specified in paragraph (7)), bears to the amount of that person's accrued pension or, as the case may be, accrued incapacity pension as assessed for the purpose of calculating his retirement compensation except that any reduction in the amount of such pension made by reason of the provisions of any Act relating to National Insurance shall, for the purpose of this sub-paragraph, be disregarded.

(6) The circumstances referred to in paragraph (5)(*b*) are that the person to whom this Part of these regulations applies had died immediately before the date on which he suffered the loss or diminution of the pension rights concerned, having then complied with any requirements of the pension scheme as to a minimum period of qualifying service or contribution and completed any additional contributory payments or payments in respect of added years which he was then in the course of making.

(7) The calculation referred to in paragraph (5)(*b*) shall be made on the basis of the method prescribed by the last relevant pension scheme of the person in question for the calculation of benefits for a widow, child or other dependant, but in making that calculation in a case where that person has attained the age

of 40 years at the date when he suffered the loss or diminution of pension rights he shall be credited, unless he is a person who is entitled to retirement compensation under regulation 23, with such number of additional years of service or such period of contribution as was or may be properly credited to him under regulation 20(3) (subject to the provisions of paragraph (5) of regulation 22 if the person in question is entitled to compensation under that regulation) for the purpose of calculating the amount of his retirement compensation:

Provided always that in so crediting him as aforesaid, any number of years of service or period of contribution prescribed by the scheme to be taken into account as a limit in calculating any pension payable to the widow, child or other dependant shall not as a result be exceeded.

Compensation where death grant would have been payable

28.—(1) If the widow or the personal representatives of a person to whom this Part of these regulations applies (in this regulation called "the deceased person") might, but for that person having suffered a loss or diminution of pension rights, have become entitled to a death grant under his last relevant pension scheme, she or they, as the case may be, shall be entitled to receive a sum calculated in accordance with the provisions of this regulation and of regulation 27(4) which sum shall hereafter in this regulation be referred to as "the said sum".

(2) The amount of the said sum shall be ascertained in accordance with the method of calculation of the death grant prescribed by the deceased person's last relevant pension scheme, as modified for the purpose of this regulation by paragraph (3), but in making this calculation in any particular case such of the following assumptions as may be applicable shall be made—

(*a*) where the deceased person had not been in receipt of retirement compensation, it shall be assumed that he had died immediately before the date on which he suffered the loss or diminution of pension rights;

(*b*) where the deceased person had been in receipt of retirement compensation, it shall be assumed that he had retired on that date; and

(*c*) except where the deceased person had been in receipt of retirement compensation under regulation 23, it shall be assumed that on the date on which he suffered the loss or diminution of pension rights he had served for a further period of pensionable service equivalent to the aggregate of any additional years of service or period of contribution credited to him under regulation 20(3), but so however that—

(i) in a case where the deceased person had been in receipt of retirement compensation under regulation 22, such further period shall not exceed the period between the date on which the said loss or diminution was suffered and the date of the claim under that regulation, and

(ii) in any other case such further period shall not exceed the period between the date on which the said loss or diminution was suffered and the actual date of the death of the deceased person.

(3) For the purpose of applying the method of calculation specified in paragraph (2) in a case where the last relevant pension scheme contains a provision to the effect that payment of death grant is to be related to the period which has elapsed from retirement to death, the reference in that provision to such a period shall be treated as a reference to the period which has elapsed from the first accrual of retirement compensation to the actual death of the deceased person.

(4) If the number of years of the deceased person's service or period of contribution is less than the minimum number of years of qualifying service or period prescribed by the pension scheme for the receipt of a death grant, the said sum shall not exceed such proportion of the death grant calculated as aforesaid as the number of years of the person's pensionable service or period of contribution bears to the minimum number of years of qualifying service or period prescribed by the pension scheme.

(5) There shall be deducted from the said sum the amount of any retirement compensation paid to or in respect of the deceased person or where any part of that compensation has been surrendered under regulation 20(6), the amount which would have been paid but for any such surrender.

(6) Where payment of more than one such sum under this regulation is made in relation to one death, the part of the total amount of retirement compensation to be deducted from each such sum under paragraph (5) shall bear the same proportion to such total amount as the said sum in question bears to the aggregate of such sums paid under this regulation in relation to that death.

(7) For the purpose of calculating any death grant which might be payable under the last relevant pension scheme, an annual sum payable to, or for the benefit of, a widow, child or other dependant under regulation 27 shall be deemed to be a pension payable to, or for the benefit of, the widow, child or dependant, as the case may be.

(8) If the widow or the personal representatives of the deceased person became entitled under his last relevant pension scheme to a smaller death grant than would have been payable had he not suffered a diminution of pension rights attributable to the happening of the relevant event, she or they, as the case may be, shall be entitled to receive a sum calculated in accordance with the foregoing provisions of this regulation modified as follows:—

(a) in a case where the reduction of the death grant has occurred because the diminution of pension rights has been occasioned by the diminution of the deceased person's pensionable emoluments, the amount of the pensionable emoluments to be taken into account for ascertaining the said sum in accordance with paragraph (2) shall be the amount of that diminution, and

(b) in all other cases, the sum payable to the widow or the personal representatives shall be the said sum calculated in accordance with the foregoing provisions of this regulation but reduced by the amount of the death grant to which the widow or the personal representatives became entitled as aforesaid.

Balances payable to claimant's widow or personal representatives

29.—(1) If no annual sum is payable to the widow, child or other dependant of any person under regulation 27 and no sum is payable under regulation 28 and the person dies before he has received in the aggregate by way of retirement compensation a sum equivalent to the amount of any contributions repaid by him under regulation 25, together with compound interest thereon calculated at the rate of 3 per cent. per annum with half-yearly rests up to the date of his death as from the 1st April or 1st October following the half year in which the amount was paid, there shall be paid to his personal representatives the difference between the aggregate amount received by way of retirement compensation as aforesaid and the said equivalent sum.

(2) If an annual sum becomes payable to a widow under regulation 27 and on her re-marriage or death the sum ceases to be payable, and any sum payable to a child or other dependant under that regulation has ceased to be payable, and if the aggregate amount of the payments which were made as aforesaid to her husband by way of retirement compensation and to the widow or personal representatives under regulation 28 is less than a sum equivalent to the amount which would have been payable to the personal representatives under that regulation if no annual sum had been payable under regulation 27, there shall be paid to her or her personal representatives the difference between such aggregate amount and the said equivalent sum.

(3) For the purposes of this regulation a person who has surrendered any part of his retirement compensation under regulation 20(6) shall be deemed to have received during any period the amount of compensation for that period which he would have received but for any such surrender.

Intervals for payment of compensatio.. under Part V

30. Any compensation awarded as an annual sum under this Part of these regulations to or in respect of any person shall be payable at intervals equivalent to those at which the corresponding benefit would have been payable under the person's last relevant pension scheme or at such other intervals as may be agreed between the person entitled to receive the compensation and the compensating authority.

PART VI

ADJUSTMENT, REVIEW AND COMPOUNDING OF COMPENSATION

Adjustment of compensation where pension is also payable

31.—(1) Where any period of service of which account was taken in calculating the amount of any compensation payable under Part IV or V of these regulations is subsequently taken into account for the purpose of calculating the amount of any pension payable to or in respect of any person in accordance with a pension scheme associated with any employment undertaken subsequent to the date on which the attributable loss was suffered which gave rise to the claim for compensation (in this regulation called "the said scheme"), the compensating authority may in accordance with this regulation withhold or reduce the compensation payable in respect of any period for which such pension is being received.

(2) If the part of any pension by way of annual amounts which is attributable to a period of service mentioned in paragraph (1) equals or exceeds the part of any compensation by way of annual amounts which is attributable to the same period, that part of the compensation may be withheld, or if such part of the pension is less than such part of the compensation, the compensation may be reduced by an amount not exceeding such part of the pension.

(3) Where a death benefit is or becomes payable under the said scheme in respect of any person who is for the purposes of regulation 28 called therein the deceased person, any sum payable under that regulation in respect of such a person may be reduced by an amount not greater than the proportion of the death benefit which the period of service mentioned in paragraph (1) bears to the total period of service of which account was taken in the calculation of the death benefit.

(4) In addition to any reduction authorised by paragraph (2) or (3), if, in the circumstances mentioned in paragraph (1), compensation by way of annual amounts is attributable in part to any provision of the said scheme for a minimum

benefit or pension, the compensation may be reduced by an amount not exceeding that part.

(5) Where any additional years of service or period of contribution have been credited to a person under regulation 20(3), if the number of such years or such period is equal to or less than the period spent in the subsequent employment mentioned in paragraph (1), the compensation by way of annual amounts may be reduced (in addition to any other reduction authorised by this regulation) by an amount not exceeding that attributable to the additional years or period so credited or, if the number of such years or such period is greater than the period spent in the subsequent employment, by such proportion of that amount as the period spent in the subsequent employment bears to the number of additional years or the period so credited.

(6) Where compensation has been calculated in accordance with regulation 26, the provisions of this regulation shall apply only in relation to such part (if any) of the pension mentioned in paragraph (1) as is attributable to pensionable emoluments in excess of those to which the person was entitled on entering the new employment referred to in regulation 26.

(7) Where long-term compensation is payable to a person in respect of diminution of emoluments or worsening of his position or of both, the provisions of this regulation shall apply only in relation to such part (if any) of the pension as is under the said scheme attributable to his emoluments in the said subsequent employment, being emoluments in excess of those emoluments to which that person was entitled immediately before he suffered the diminution of emoluments or worsening of his position, or if he suffered both, before he suffered whichever was the earlier.

(8) Where retirement compensation is payable to a pensionable officer in respect of diminution of pension rights occasioned by a diminution of pensionable emoluments, the provisions of this regulation shall apply only in relation to such part (if any) of the pension as is attributable to pensionable emoluments in excess of those to which that officer was entitled immediately prior to the diminution of his pension rights.

Reduction of compensation in certain cases

32.—(1) If under a person's last relevant pension scheme any benefit or pension for which the scheme provided would have been subject to reduction or suspension on his taking up other employment specified in that behalf in the scheme, any retirement compensation to which he is entitled for loss or diminution of pension rights shall, where such employment is taken up, be reduced or suspended in the like manner and to the like extent:

Provided that in calculating the amount of the reduction of the compensation in a case where by the provisions of the scheme the amount of the reduction of the benefit or pension is to be related to the emoluments of the employment taken up, the amount of any pension by way of annual amounts payable to the person under his last relevant pension scheme shall be treated as emoluments which shall for the purpose of the calculation be aggregated with the actual emoluments of the said employment.

(2) There shall be deducted from the retirement compensation payable to any person any additional contributory payments remaining unpaid at the date when he suffered loss or diminution of pension rights; and any such payments not recovered at the date of his death shall be deducted from any compensation payable in respect of that person under regulation 27, 28 or 29.

(3) Where a person is entitled to compensation under these regulations and the circumstances are such that he is also entitled to—

(*a*) a redundancy payment under the Redundancy Payments Act 1965(**a**), or

(*b*) any similar payment in consequence of the loss of his employment under any contract or arrangement with the body or person by whom he was employed (other than payments by way of a return of contributions under a pension scheme), or

(*c*) any payment under or by virtue of the provisions of any enactment relating to the reinstatement in civil employment of persons who have been in the service of the Crown,

the compensation which would, apart from this paragraph, become due to the person, whether by instalments or lump sum or both, shall in the aggregate be reduced by the amount of the payments referred to in this paragraph.

(4) Where any resettlement or long-term compensation is payable to or in respect of any person, and that person or his widow, child or other dependant or his personal representatives is or are also entitled (whether immediately or on the person's attaining some greater age) to a pension under that person's last relevant pension scheme, any instalment of such compensation which is payable in respect of any period shall be reduced by the amount of the instalment of such pension which is payable in respect of the same period.

(5) For the purposes of paragraph (4) no account shall be taken of any sum payable in consequence of the surrender by any person of part of his pension under any provision in that behalf in his last relevant pension scheme with a view to obtaining or increasing allowances for his widow, child or other dependant; and the person shall be deemed to have received during any period the amount of pension which he would have received but for any such surrender.

(6) Where in any week a person is entitled to long-term compensation and is also entitled to unemployment, sickness or injury benefit under any Act relating to National Insurance, other than a benefit claimable by him in respect of a dependant, there shall be deducted from the long-term compensation payable for that week a sum equal to the amount by which the aggregate of such National Insurance benefit claimable in respect of that week and the weekly rate at which the long-term compensation would be payable but for this regulation exceeds two thirds of the weekly rate of the net emoluments of the employment which he has lost or in which the emoluments have been diminished:

Provided that this paragraph shall not apply in relation to any such sickness or injury benefit in so far as—

(*i*) an equivalent sum is deducted from the emoluments of his current employment, and

(*ii*) such deduction from those emoluments has not occasioned an increase in his long-term compensation.

(7) In paragraph (6) the expression "weekly rate" means seven three hundred and sixty-fifths of the relevant annual rate.

Notification of change of circumstances
33. Where—

(*a*) a pensionable officer after suffering any attributable loss enters any new

---

(**a**) 1965 c. 62.

employment referred to in regulation 26 or becomes entitled to any pension on ceasing to hold any such employment, or

(*b*) a person entitled to long-term compensation enters employment the remuneration whereof is payable out of public funds or by any national-ised transport body or subsidiary thereof, or ceases to hold such employ-ment, or receives any increase in his remuneration in such employment, or

(*c*) a person entitled to retirement compensation enters employment in which the compensation is subject to reduction or suspension under regulation 32, or ceases to hold such employment, or receives any increase in his remuneration in such employment, or

(*d*) a person entitled to long-term compensation starts to receive any benefit, any increase in benefit or any further benefit under any Act relating to National Insurance,

he shall forthwith inform the compensating authority in writing of that fact.

Review of awards of long-term or retirement compensation

34.—(1) The compensating authority shall, within a period of 2 years after the date on which any decision on a claim for long-term or retirement compen-sation (other than compensation payable under regulation 23) is notified to a claimant under regulation 36 and at intervals of not more than 6 months, review their decision or, where the claim has been the subject of an appeal, the decision of the tribunal, and these regulations shall apply in relation to any such review as they apply in relation to the initial determination of the claim; and on such review, in the light of any material change in the circumstances of the case, compen-sation may be awarded, or compensation previously awarded may be increased, reduced or discontinued, subject to the limits set out in these regulations:

Provided that where the person to whom the decision relates ceases to hold the employment in which his emoluments were diminished, a review shall be held within 3 months after the date on which he ceases to hold that employment.

(2) After the expiration of the period of 2 years mentioned in paragraph (1), the compensating authority may, at their discretion, carry out reviews in accordance with that paragraph at intervals of not less than 12 months.

(3) The person to whom the decision relates may at any time require the compensating authority to carry out a review in accordance with paragraph (1) if he considers that there has been a change in the circumstances of his case which is material for the purposes of these regulations.

(4) Notwithstanding anything contained in the foregoing provisions of this regulation, the compensating authority shall review a decision (whether of the authority or the tribunal) on a claim for long-term compensation for loss of employment, diminution of emoluments or worsening of a person's position after the expiration of the said period of 2 years if at any time—

(*a*) the person to whom the decision relates becomes engaged in employ-ment (hereinafter referred to as his "current employment") the remuner-ation whereof is payable out of public funds, or by any nationalised transport body or subsidiary thereof, and which he has undertaken subsequent to the date on which he suffered the loss, diminution or worsening, and

(*b*) the aggregate of the net emoluments of his current employment, any pension or benefit by way of annual amounts payable to him in respect of the employment which he has lost or in which he suffered the diminution or worsening and the long-term compensation payable to him exceeds the net emoluments of the employment which he has lost or, as the case may be, in which he so suffered.

(5) The compensating authority shall further review any decision reviewed under paragraph (4) whenever the net emoluments of the person's current employment are increased.

(6) If on any review under paragraph (4) or (5) the compensation is reduced, it shall not be reduced below the amount by which the net emoluments of the person's current employment, together with any pension or benefit by way of annual amounts payable to him in respect of the employment in which he has suffered the attributable loss, falls short of the net emoluments of the employment in which he suffered that loss.

(7) The compensating authority shall give to a person to whom a decision relates not less than 14 days' notice of any review of that decision to be carried out under this regulation unless the review is carried out at his request.

(8) Nothing in this regulation shall preclude the making of any adjustment of compensation required by regulation 31 or 32.

Compounding of awards

35.—(1) In a case where an annual sum which has been or might be awarded under these regulations does not exceed £26, the compensating authority may, at their discretion, compound their liability in respect thereof by paying a lump sum equivalent to the capital value of the annual sum and, if any lump sum payment has been or might be awarded in addition to such annual sum under regulation 21, 22, 23 or 24, the compensating authority may likewise discharge their liability in respect thereof by an immediate payment.

(2) In any other case, if the person who has been awarded long-term or retirement compensation requests them to do so, the compensating authority may, after having regard to the state of health of that person and the other circumstances of the case, compound up to one quarter of their liability to make payments under the award (other than payments to a widow, child or other dependant under regulation 27) by the payment of an equivalent amount as a lump sum or, where any compensation has been awarded as a lump sum, by increasing that compensation to such equivalent amount; and in calculating for this purpose the liability of the authority to make such payments, account shall be taken of the annual value of lump sum payments of compensation.

(3) The making of a composition under paragraph (2) in relation to an award of long-term or retirement compensation shall not prevent the subsequent making of a composition under paragraph (1) in relation to that award, but, subject as aforesaid, not more than one composition may be made in relation to any award.

Part VII

Procedure and Miscellaneous

Procedure on making claims

36.—(1) Every claim for compensation under these regulations and every request for a review of an award of long-term or retirement compensation shall be made in accordance with this regulation.

(2) Every such claim and request shall be made to the compensating authority in writing, shall set out the grounds on which the claim or request is made and shall state whether any other claim for compensation has been made by the claimant under these regulations.

(3) Resettlement compensation shall be claimed separately from any other form of compensation claimable under these regulations.

(4) The compensating authority shall consider any such claim or request in accordance with the relevant provisions of these regulations and shall notify the person making the claim or request in writing of their decision—

 (*a*) in the case of a claim for resettlement compensation, not later than one month after the receipt of the claim, and

 (*b*) in the case of a claim for, or request for the review of an award of, compensation under Part IV or V of these regulations, not later than 13 weeks after the receipt of the claim or request, and

 (*c*) in any other case, as soon as possible after the decision;

but the decision of a compensating authority shall not be invalidated by reason of the fact that notice of the decision is given after the expiry of the period mentioned in this paragraph.

(5) Every notification of a decision by the compensating authority (whether granting or refusing compensation or reviewing an award, or otherwise affecting any compensation under these regulations) shall contain a statement—

 (*a*) giving reasons for the decision;

 (*b*) showing how any compensation has been calculated and, in particular, if the amount is less than the maximum which could have been awarded under these regulations, showing the factors taken into account in awarding that amount; and

 (*c*) directing the attention of the claimant to his right under regulation 42, if he is aggrieved by the decision, to institute proceedings before a tribunal and giving him the address to which the application instituting such proceedings should be sent.

Claimants to furnish information

37.—(1) Any person claiming or receiving compensation or whose award of compensation is being reviewed shall furnish all such information as the compensating authority may at any time reasonably require; and he shall verify the same in such manner, including the production of books or original documents in his possession or control, as may be reasonably so required.

(2) Any such person shall, on receipt of reasonable notice, present himself for interview at such place as the compensating authority may reasonably require; and any person who attends for interview may, if he so desires, be represented by his adviser.

Procedure on death of claimant

38.—(1) In the event of the death of a claimant or of a person who, if he had survived, could have been a claimant, a claim for compensation under these regulations may be continued or made, as the case may be, by his personal representatives.

(2) Where any such claim is continued or made as aforesaid by personal representatives, the personal representatives shall, as respects any steps to be taken or thing to be done by them in order to continue or make the claim, be deemed for the purposes of these regulations to be the person entitled to claim, but, save as aforesaid, the person in whose right they continue or make the claim shall be deemed for the purposes of these regulations to be such person, and the relevant provisions of these regulations shall be construed accordingly:

Provided that the compensating authority may in any such case extend the period within which a claim is required to be made by regulation 7, 13 or 19.

Calculation of service

39. For the purpose of making any calculation under these regulations in respect of a person's reckonable service, all periods of such service shall be aggregated and, except where reference is made to completed years of service, if the aggregated service includes a fraction of a year, that fraction shall, if it equals or exceeds 6 months, be treated as a year, and shall, in any other case be disregarded.

Temporary variation of emoluments

40. In calculating for the purposes of these regulations the amount of any emoluments lost, or the amount by which any emoluments have been diminished, and in determining the net emoluments, the accrued pension or the accrued retiring allowance of any person who has suffered attributable loss, no account shall be taken of any increase in the amount of the person's emoluments which is due to any temporary allowance made in consequence of the happening of the relevant event and otherwise than in the ordinary course of his employment.

Compensation not assignable

41. Subject to any statutory provision in that behalf, any compensation to which a person becomes entitled under these regulations shall be paid by the compensating authority and shall be payable to, or in trust for, the person who is entitled to receive it, and shall not be assignable:

Provided that, without prejudice to any other right of recovery, any compensation paid in error to a person may be recovered by the compensating authority from him by deduction from any compensation payable to him under these regulations.

Right of appeal from decision of compensating authority

42.—(1) Every person who is aggrieved by any decision of the compensating authority with respect to a compensation question or by any failure on the part of the compensating authority to notify him of any such decision within the appropriate time prescribed by these regulations, may within 13 weeks of the notification to him of the decision or the expiry of the prescribed time, as the case may be, institute proceedings for the determination of the question by a tribunal in accordance with the Industrial Tribunals (Employment and Compensation) Regulations 1967(a), or in Scotland, the Industrial Tribunals (Employment and Compensation) (Scotland) Regulations 1967(b) and these regulations; and the tribunal shall determine the question accordingly.

(2) For the purpose of any such proceedings a person or persons may be appointed to sit with the tribunal as assessor or assessors.

(3) The compensating authority shall give effect to the decision of the tribunal subject to any modifications that may be required in consequence of any appeal from that decision on a point of law.

Given under the Official Seal of the Minister of Transport the 9th February 1970

(L.S.)

Fred Mulley,
Minister of Transport.

Given under the Seal of the Secretary of State for Scotland on 9th February 1970

(L.S.)

William Ross,
Secretary of State for Scotland.

(a) S.I. 1967/361 (1967 I, p. 1205).   (b) S.I. 1967/362 (1967 I, p. 1220).

Regulation 4

SCHEDULE 1

Table showing the events which can occasion a claim for compensation under these regulations and the first material dates and compensating authorities in connection therewith

Relevant Event (1)	First Material Date (2)	Compensating Authority (3)
1. Transfer of property, rights or liabilities under section 4 or 5 of the Act.	The date of the passing of the Act.	The nationalised transport body by whom, or by whose subsidiary, the person suffering the attributable loss was employed immediately before the occurrence of that loss.
2. Transfer of property, rights or liabilities under section 7 or 8 of the Act.	The date of the confirmation of the scheme under section 7 or of the making of the order under section 8.	The nationalised transport body by whom, or by whose subsidiary, the person suffering the attributable loss was employed immediately before the occurrence of that loss.
3. Transfer of property, rights or liabilities under section 28 of the Act.	The date of the passing of the Act.	The Bus Company, where the transfer is to that Company, or the Scottish Group, where the transfer is to that Group.
4. Transfer of property, rights or liabilities under section 29(2) of the Act.	The date of the passing of the Act.	The Bus Company, where the transfer is to that Company, or the Scottish Group, where the transfer is to that Group.
5. Transfer of property, rights or liabilities under section 29(5) of the Act.	The date of the confirmation of the scheme or the making of the order under section 29(5).	The nationalised transport body by whom, or by whose subsidiary, the person suffering the attributable loss was employed immediately before the occurrence of that loss.
6. Transfer of property, rights or liabilities under section 53 of the Act.	The date of the making of the order under section 53.	The nationalised transport body, publicly owned body or Minister of the Crown by whom, or by whose subsidiary, the person suffering the attributable loss was employed immediately before the occurrence of that loss.
7. Transfer of property, rights or liabilities under section 144 of the Act.	The date of the passing of the Act.	The Railways Board.

Relevant Event (1)	First Material Date (2)	Compensating Authority (3)
8. Change in the manner in which the carrying on of the activities of the Railways Board or the Freight Corporation is organised made either in pursuance of a direction under section 6(1) or 45(5) of the Act, or with the consent of the Minister in order to give effect to conclusions reported under the said section 45.	The date of the giving of the direction, where a direction is given, or the date of the report of the conclusions where the change is made with the Minister's consent and without a direction.	The Railways Board, where the change affects that Board, or the Freight Corporation, where the change affects that Corporation.
9. Making of adaptations such as are mentioned in paragraph 5(4) of Schedule 16 to the Act.	The date of the making of the order under paragraph 5(4) of Schedule 16.	The nationalised transport body, by whom, or by whose subsidiary, the person suffering the attributable loss was employed immediately before the occurrence of that loss.
10. Revocation under paragraph 10(1) of Schedule 6 to the Act of a consent granted under that Schedule.	The date of the service on the operator under paragraph 10 of Schedule 6 of the notice revoking the consent.	The Executive who have revoked the consent.

NOTE:—In determining for the purpose of this Schedule whether a subsidiary is a subsidiary of a particular nationalised transport body, no account shall be taken of the provisions of section 51(5) of the Act.

Regulation 2(2)   **SCHEDULE 2**

TABLE I

Table showing the capital value of an annual amount of £1 payable for life

Age	Capital value of £1 per annum payable for life	
	Female	Male
	£ s. d.	£ s. d.
Under 35	15 11 0	15 3 0
35 and under 40	15 2 0	14 12 0
40 and under 45	14 11 0	13 19 0
45 and under 50	13 18 0	13 2 0
50	13 9 0	12 11 0
51	13 5 0	12 7 0
52	13 2 0	12 3 0
53	12 18 0	11 18 0
54	12 14 0	11 14 0
55	12 10 0	11 9 0
56	12 6 0	11 5 0
57	12 2 0	11 0 0
58	11 18 0	10 15 0
59	11 13 0	10 10 0
60	11 8 0	10 5 0
61	11 4 0	10 0 0
62	10 19 0	9 14 0
63	10 14 0	9 9 0
64	10 8 0	9 3 0
65	10 3 0	8 18 0
66	9 18 0	8 12 0
67	9 12 0	8 7 0
68	9 7 0	8 1 0
69	9 1 0	7 16 0
70	8 15 0	7 10 0

NOTE:—This table is for use in connection with regulation 35(1) and (2) for the compounding of annual retirement compensation which a person is currently entitled to receive under regulation 21, 22, 23 or 24. Where the compensation is payable before age 60 (females), 65 (males) but will be reduced on the attainment of that age (in connection with National Insurance pension) the table should be used in conjunction with Table II, i.e. Table II should be used for valuing that part of the compensation which ceases to be payable at age 60 or 65 as the case may be and this table should be used for valuing the remainder.

TABLE II

Table showing the capital value of an amount of £1 per annum ceasing
at age 60 (females), 65 (males)

Age	Capital Value					
	Female			Male		
	£	s.	d.	£	s.	d.
Under 35	13	8	0	14	2	0
35 and under 40	12	5	0	13	3	0
40 and under 45	10	14	0	11	19	0
45 and under 50	8	13	0	10	8	0
50	7	3	0	9	6	0
51	6	12	0	8	18	0
52	6	0	0	8	9	0
53	5	7	0	7	19	0
54	4	13	0	7	10	0
55	3	18	0	6	19	0
56	3	3	0	6	8	0
57	2	6	0	5	17	0
58	1	9	0	5	4	0
59		10	0	4	11	0
60	—			3	17	0
61	—			3	2	0
62	—			2	6	0
63	—			1	8	0
64	—				10	0

NOTE:—This table is for use in connection with regulation 35(1) and (2) for the compounding
of any part of annual retirement compensation which will cease to be payable on the attainment
of age 60 (females), 65 (males).   Table I should be used in relation to the remainder of such
compensation, i.e. the part which is payable for life—see note on that table.

TABLE III

Table showing the capital value of an annual amount of £1 payable to a
widow until death or remarriage

Age of widow at date of widowhood	Capital value of £1 per annum as at date of widow-hood	Age of widow at date of widowhood	Capital value of £1 per annum as at date of widow-hood
	£ s. d.		£ s. d.
20	6 0 0	45	11 18 0
21	6 0 0	46	12 1 0
22	6 0 0	47	12 3 0
23	6 0 0	48	12 5 0
24	6 0 0	49	12 6 0
25	6 5 0	50	12 6 0
26	6 12 0	51	12 6 0
27	6 19 0	52	12 5 0
28	7 6 0	53	12 4 0
29	7 13 0	54	12 3 0
30	8 0 0	55	12 1 0
31	8 8 0	56	11 19 0
32	8 15 0	57	11 16 0
33	9 2 0	58	11 13 0
34	9 8 0	59	11 10 0
35	9 15 0	60	11 6 0
36	10 1 0	61	11 3 0
37	10 6 0	62	10 19 0
38	10 11 0	63	10 14 0
39	10 16 0	64	10 8 0
40	11 1 0	65	10 3 0
41	11 5 0	66	9 18 0
42	11 9 0	67	9 12 .0
43	11 12 0	68	9 7 0
44	11 15 0	69	9 1 0
		70	8 15 0

NOTE:—This table is for use in connection with regulation 35(1) for compounding annual compensation payable to a widow under regulation 27. It should also be used, where a reduction of compensation under regulation 27(4) falls to be apportioned between the compensation payable under that regulation and under regulation 28, for ascertaining the capital value of annual compensation to a widow.

TABLE IV

Table showing the annual amount payable for life equivalent in value
to a lump sum of £100

Age	Annual sum, payable for life, equal in value to a lump sum of £100	
	Female	Male
	£ s. d.	£ s. d.
Under 35	6 8 7	6 12 0
35 and under 40	6 12 5	6 17 0
40 and under 45	6 17 5	7 3 4
45 and under 50	7 3 11	7 12 8
50	7 8 8	7 19 4
51	7 10 11	8 1 11
52	7 12 8	8 4 7
53	7 15 0	8 8 1
54	7 17 6	8 10 11
55	8 0 0	8 14 8
56	8 2 7	8 17 9
57	8 5 3	9 1 10
58	8 8 1	9 6 0
59	8 11 8	9 10 6
60	8 15 5	9 15 1
61	8 18 7	10 0 0
62	9 2 8	10 6 2
63	9 6 11	10 11 8
64	9 12 4	10 18 7
65	9 17 0	11 4 9
66	10 2 0	11 12 7
67	10 8 4	11 19 6
68	10 13 11	12 8 5
69	11 1 0	12 16 5
70	11 8 7	13 6 8

NOTE:—This table is for use in connection with regulation 25(1) for ascertaining the annual amount by which retirement compensation under regulation 21, 22 or 23 is to be reduced where a claimant has not paid to the compensating authority an amount equal to any sum paid to him by way of pension contributions or that amount has been repaid to him by the compensating authority at his request. It should also be used in connection with regulation 35(2) for calculating for the purposes of that paragraph the annual value of retirement compensation awarded as a lump sum.

TABLE V

Table showing the annual amount payable to a widow until death or
remarriage equivalent in value to a lump sum of £100

Age of widow at date of widowhood	Annual amount equal in value to a lump sum of £100	Age of widow at date of widowhood	Annual amount equal in value to a lump sum of £100
	£ s. d.		£ s. d.
20	16 13 4	45	8 8 1
21	16 13 4	46	8 6 0
22	16 13 4	47	8 4 7
23	16 13 4	48	8 3 3
24	16 13 4	49	8 2 7
25	16 0 0	50	8 2 7
26	15 3 0	51	8 2 7
27	14 7 9	52	8 3 3
28	13 14 0	53	8 3 11
29	13 1 5	54	8 4 7
30	12 10 0	55	8 6 0
31	11 18 1	56	8 7 4
32	11 8 7	57	8 9 6
33	10 19 9	58	8 11 8
34	10 12 9	59	8 13 11
35	10 5 2	60	8 17 0
36	9 19 0	61	8 19 5
37	9 14 2	62	9 2 8
38	9 9 7	63	9 6 11
39	9 5 2	64	9 12 4
40	9 1 0	65	9 17 0
41	8 17 9	66	10 2 0
42	8 14 8	67	10 8 4
43	8 12 5	68	10 13 11
44	8 10 3	69	11 1 0
		70	11 8 7

NOTE:—This table is for use in connection with regulation 27(4) for ascertaining the annual
amount by which compensation to a widow is to be reduced in the circumstances described
in that paragraph.   If a reduction is required to be apportioned between compensation payable
under regulations 27 and 28, the capital value of annual compensation to a widow should be
ascertained by reference to Table III.

TABLE VI

Table showing, according to the outstanding period of long-term compensation, the capital value of each £100 of the total amount of long-term compensation compounded

Outstanding number of complete years of long-term compensation	Capital value of each £100 of the total amount of long-term compensation					
	Female			Male		
	£	s.	d.	£	s.	d.
0	98	8	0	98	4	0
1	95	4	0	94	16	0
2	92	2	0	91	10	0
3	89	4	0	88	6	0
4	86	8	0	85	8	0
5	83	16	0	82	14	0
6	81	6	0	80	2	0
7	78	18	0	77	14	0
8	76	14	0	75	8	0
9	74	12	0	73	4	0
10	72	12	0	71	4	0
11	70	12	0	69	6	0
12	68	16	0	67	10	0
13	67	0	0	65	14	0
14	65	6	0	64	2	0
15	63	14	0	62	10	0
16	62	2	0	61	0	0
17	60	12	0	59	12	0
18	59	4	0	58	4	0
19	57	16	0	56	18	0
20	56	10	0	55	12	0
21	55	4	0	54	8	0
22	54	0	0	53	4	0
23	52	16	0	52	0	0
24	51	12	0	50	18	0
25	50	10	0	49	18	0
26	49	8	0	48	18	0
27	48	8	0	47	18	0
28	47	8	0	46	18	0
29	46	8	0	45	18	0
30	45	10	0	45	0	0

NOTE:—This table is for use in connection with regulation 35(1) and (2) for compounding awards of long-term compensation under Part IV of these regulations. The total amount of the annual long-term compensation which is to be compounded must first be calculated, i.e. the amount which the person would receive on account of that compensation or the part of it which is to be compounded, if it were paid until "normal retiring age" (as defined in these regulations). For each £100 so calculated, the lump sum payment will be the amount shown in the table according to the number of complete years in the period between the date of compounding and "normal retiring age".

EXPLANATORY NOTE

(This Note is not part of the Regulations.)

1. These regulations, made under section 135 of the Transport Act 1968 (the Act), have, by virtue of paragraph 3 of that section, retrospective effect from 18th November 1968. They provide for the payment of compensation by the appropriate compensating authority (listed in Schedule 1 to the regulations) to or in respect of any person who suffers loss of employment, or loss or diminution of emoluments or pension rights, or worsening of his position, which is properly attributable to the happening of the relevant event specified in the Act. The relevant events are also set out in Schedule 1 to the regulations.

2. Part I of the regulations contains definitions. Part II specifies the persons to whom the regulations apply and the grounds of entitlement to compensation. The regulations apply to persons employed full-time by a nationalised transport body or a subsidiary thereof or by an existing bus operator as defined in Schedule 6 to the Act.

3. The compensation payable is—

(*a*) resettlement compensation for loss of employment (Part III of the regulations);

(*b*) long-term compensation for loss of employment or loss or diminution of emoluments or worsening of position (Part IV);

(*c*) retirement compensation for loss or diminution of pension rights (Part V);

(*d*) payments in respect of a deceased pensionable officer to his widow, child or other dependant or to his personal representatives in circumstances specified in the regulations (Part V).

4. Resettlement compensation is payable for a period not exceeding 26 weeks to officers continuously engaged for at least 3 years (disregarding breaks not exceeding in the aggregate 6 months) in relevant employment before the prescribed date. The qualifying conditions and factors to be considered are set out in regulation 7. The method of calculating the amount of compensation is contained in regulation 8.

5. Long-term and retirement compensation are payable to officers continuously engaged for at least 8 years (without a break of more than 12 months at any one time) in relevant employment before the prescribed date. The qualifying and other conditions are set out for the former in regulations 13 and 14 and for the latter in regulations 19 and 20.

6. The method of calculating the maximum amount of long-term compensation is laid down in regulations 15 (loss of emoluments) and 16 (diminution of emoluments). This amount is a proportion, not exceeding two thirds of the net emoluments lost or of the amount by which emoluments have been diminished, as the case may be. This compensation is payable from a date determined under regulation 18 and can be payable up to normal retiring age. In the case of a non-pensionable officer, compensation not exceeding one half of the rate of long-term compensation may be paid beyond normal retiring age (regulation 17).

7. Retirement compensation payable to a pensionable officer for loss of pension rights is based upon his accrued pension rights (regulation 21) supplemented in the case of persons aged 40 or over at the date of the loss by the addition of notional years of service (regulation 20). Provision for retirement compensation (including the concept of additional years) in the case of a pensionable officer who suffers diminution of pension rights instead of a loss is

provided by regulation 24 which also lays down the method of calculating the retirement compensation payable in such cases. Retirement compensation is ordinarily payable from normal retiring age but in certain circumstances is payable earlier (regulations 22 and 23).

8. Provision is made for payments to the widow, child or other dependant or to the personal representatives of a claimant who dies where such persons would have derived benefit under the relevant pension scheme (regulations 27 to 29).

9. Part VI of the regulations provides for long-term and retirement compensation to be reviewed and for awards to be varied in the light of changing circumstances (regulation 34). It also contains provisions for the adjustment, suspension and compounding of compensation in certain circumstances.

10. Part VII contains provisions relating to the procedure for making claims and notifying decisions and confers upon a claimant who is aggrieved by a decision on a compensation question or the failure of a compensating authority to notify their decision, a right to refer the question for determination by a tribunal established under section 12 of the Industrial Training Act 1964.

STATUTORY INSTRUMENTS

1970 No. 188 (C.5)

TRANSPORT

The Transport Act 1968 (Commencement No. 5) Order 1970

Made - - - *10th February* 1970

The Secretary of State and the Minister of Transport make this Order acting in exercise of their respective powers under section 166 of the Transport Act 1968(a), as shown in the Schedule to this Order:—

1. This Order may be cited as the Transport Act 1968 (Commencement No. 5) Order 1970.

2. The provisions of the Transport Act 1968 (hereinafter referred to as "the Act") specified in Schedules 1 and 2 to this Order shall come into force on the 1st March 1970 and the 1st September 1970 respectively.

James Callaghan,
One of Her Majesty's Principal
Secretaries of State.

Home Office,
Whitehall.

6th February 1970.

Sealed with the Official Seal of the Minister of Transport the 10th February 1970.

(L.S.)

Fred Mulley,
Minister of Transport.

SCHEDULE 1
PROVISIONS COMING INTO FORCE ON THE 1ST MARCH 1970

Provisions brought into force by the Secretary of State
In Part IX of the Act
Section 131 (other than subsection (1) thereof).

SCHEDULE 2
PROVISIONS COMING INTO FORCE ON THE 1ST SEPTEMBER 1970

A. *Provisions brought into force by the Secretary of State*
In Part IX of the Act
Section 131(1).

B. *Provisions brought into force by the Minister of Transport*
In Part X of the Act
Section 165 so far as it relates to the provision in Schedule 18 specified below.
In Schedule 18 to the Act
In Part II of that Schedule (Repeals in Road Traffic Regulation Act 1967 (1967 c. 76))—the repeal of the words "left or parked" in section 80(1)(a) of that Act.

(a) 1968 c. 73.

EXPLANATORY NOTE

(This Note is not part of the Order.)

This Order brings into force section 131 of the Transport Act 1968 (which relates to fixed penalty procedure and traffic wardens) and a consequential repeal in Schedule 18 to that Act. When this Order takes effect, the whole of Part IX of the Transport Act 1968 and the whole of Part II to Schedule 18 to that Act will have come into force.

STATUTORY INSTRUMENTS

1970 No. 189

LOCAL GOVERNMENT, ENGLAND AND WALES
The Parish Meetings (Polls) Rules 1970

Made - - -	*10th February* 1970
Laid before Parliament	*19th February* 1970
Coming into Operation	*1st March* 1970

In pursuance of the powers conferred upon me by paragraph 5(5) of Part VI of Schedule 3 to the Local Government Act 1933(**a**) (as substituted by section 5(1) of the Local Government Elections Act 1956(**b**)), and by section 165(1) of the Representation of the People Act 1949(**c**), I hereby make the following Rules for the conduct of the election of the chairman of a parish meeting at a parish meeting and for the conduct of a poll consequent on a parish meeting :—

1.—(1) These Rules may be cited as the Parish Meetings (Polls) Rules 1970 and shall come into operation on 1st March 1970:

Provided that they shall not have effect in relation to a poll which has been demanded before that date.

(2) The Interpretation Act 1889(**d**) shall apply to the interpretation of these Rules as it applies to the interpretation of an Act of Parliament.

2.—(1) The Parish Meetings (Polls) Rules 1950(**e**) and the Parish Meetings (Polls) (No. 2) Rules 1950(**f**) are hereby revoked.

(2) Notwithstanding paragraph (1) of this Rule, the Rules therein mentioned shall apply to any poll which has been demanded before these Rules come into operation.

3.—(1) At a poll consequent on a parish meeting the chairman of that parish meeting shall be the returning officer unless he is unwilling or unable to act or the poll concerns the appointment to any office and he is a candidate therefor.

(2) If the chairman does not act as returning officer, he shall forthwith appoint another person to be the returning officer for that poll and shall send him such particulars as will enable him to give notice of the poll.

(3) If the chairman dies before appointing another person to act as returning officer, the chairman of the rural district council in which the parish is situate shall forthwith appoint another person to be the returning officer for that poll.

(4) The returning officer shall appoint an office for the purpose of the poll.

(**a**) 1933 c. 51.
(**c**) 1949 c. 68.
(**e**) S.I. 1950/984 (1950 II, p. 164).
(**b**) 1956 c. 43.
(**d**) 1889 c. 63.
(**f**) S.I. 1950/1272 (1950 II, p. 185).

4. In the application of those provisions of the Representation of the People Act 1949 referred to in section 165(1) of that Act, other than section 53 thereof, to the election of the chairman of a parish meeting at a parish meeting or to a poll consequent on a parish meeting the following adaptations, modifications and exceptions shall have effect :—

(*a*) where the poll is to be taken on any question other than that of the election of the chairman of the parish meeting or of an appointment to any other office only the following of the aforesaid provisions shall apply, namely, section 47, section 99, section 100, section 101, section 140(3) so far as it is applied by section 151, section 146, section 150, section 151, section 154, section 156, section 157, section 158, section 159 and section 163 ;

(*b*) references to the clerk of the authority for which the election was held shall be taken as references to the chairman of the parish council or, in a rural parish not having a separate parish council, to the chairman of the parish meeting ;

(*c*) references to the authority for which the election was held shall be taken as references to the parish and references to the area thereof shall be construed accordingly except in section 115(7) of the said Act where the expression "the area of the authority for which the election was held" means the rural district in which the parish is situate or a borough or urban district adjacent to that rural district ;

(*d*) in section 47(2), section 86(1) and section 87(1) of the said Act for the expression "local government election" there shall be substituted the expression "election under the Local Government Act" ;

(*e*) in section 119(2)(*b*) of the said Act for the words "such amount not exceeding five hundred pounds" there shall be substituted the words "an amount of fifty pounds or such smaller amount or such larger amount not exceeding three hundred pounds" ;

(*f*) references to an election under the Local Government Act shall be deemed to include a reference to the election of the chairman of the parish meeting at a parish meeting and to a poll consequent on a parish meeting.

5. In the application of section 53 of, and the local elections rules contained in Schedule 2 to, the Representation of the People Act 1949 to a poll consequent on a parish meeting, adaptions, alterations and exceptions shall be made therein so that they shall read as set out in the Schedule hereto.

James Callaghan,
One of Her Majesty's Principal
Secretaries of State.

Home Office,
Whitehall.
10th February 1970.

SCHEDULE

Arrangement of rules

APPENDIX

Forms

Notice of abandonment of poll.

Notice of poll.

Ballot paper on a question other than a question of appointment to an office.

Ballot paper on a question of appointment to an office.

Directions for the guidance of the voters in voting where the poll is on a question other than a question of appointment to an office.

Directions for the guidance of the voters in voting where the poll is on a question of appointment to an office.

Declaration to be made by the companion of a blind voter.

Declaration of result of poll on a question other than a question of appointment to an office.

Declaration of result of poll on a question of appointment to an office.

Timetable

1. The proceedings at the poll shall be conducted in accordance with the following Table.

TIMETABLE

Proceeding	*Time*
Delivery of notices of withdrawals of candidature.	Not later than noon on the fourth day after the day on which the poll was demanded.
Notice of poll	Not later than the fifth day before the day of the poll.
Notice of appointment of polling or counting agents.	Not later than the third day before the day of the poll.
Polling	On the day of the poll which shall be such day as shall be fixed by the returning officer not earlier than the fourteenth day nor, unless for special reasons the Secretary of State otherwise directs, later than the twenty-first day after the day on which the poll was demanded.

Computation of time

2.—(1) In computing any period of time for the purposes of the Timetable, a Sunday, day of the Christmas break, of the Easter break or of a bank holiday break or day appointed for public thanksgiving or mourning shall be disregarded and any such day shall not be treated as a day for the purpose of any proceedings up to the completion of the poll nor shall the returning officer be obliged to proceed with the counting of the votes thereon.

(2) In this rule "the Christmas break" means the period beginning with the last week day before Christmas Day and ending with the first week day after Christmas Day which is not a bank holiday, "the Easter break" means the period beginning with the Thursday before and ending with the Tuesday after Easter Day, and "a bank holiday break" means any bank holiday not included in the Christmas break or the Easter break and the period beginning with the last week day before that bank holiday and ending with the next week day which is not a bank holiday.

Hours of poll

3.—(1) The poll shall commence at the hour fixed for the parish by the county council by any general or special order or, if no such order has been made, at four o'clock in the afternoon and be kept open till eight o'clock in the evening of the same day and no longer:

Provided that in the case of a poll taken on a question of appointment to any office the poll shall be kept open till nine o'clock in the evening if candidates who have not withdrawn to a number not less than the number of persons to be elected have, by written notices signed by them and delivered at the place and within the time for delivery of notices of withdrawals of candidature, so requested.

(2)) A notice under this rule shall not have effect as respects any candidate if revoked by a further written notice signed by him and delivered as aforesaid.

Withdrawal of candidates

4.—(1) A candidate may not later than the time appointed for that purpose in the Timetable withdraw his candidature by a notice of withdrawal signed by him and attested by one witness and delivered at the office appointed by the returning officer.

(2) If by reason of any withdrawal under this rule the number of remaining candidates becomes equal to or less than the number of persons to be elected, a poll shall not be taken and those candidates shall be deemed to be elected and the returning officer shall as soon as possible publish notice of the abandonment of the poll in the form in the Appendix, or in a form to the like effect, stating that no poll will be taken and giving a list of the persons elected and shall send a copy to each of those candidates and, if he was not the chairman of the meeting at which the poll was demanded, to that chairman.

Poll to be taken by ballot

5. The votes at the poll shall be given by ballot, and the poll shall be conducted in accordance with these rules.

The ballot papers

6.—(1) The ballot of every voter shall consist of a ballot paper.

(2) Every ballot paper shall be in the appropriate form in the Appendix, and shall be printed in accordance with the appropriate directions therein and—

    (a) (i) if the poll is taken on a question of appointment to any office, shall contain the full names, places of residence and descriptions of the candidates arranged alphabetically in the order of their surnames and, if there are two or more of them with the same surname, of their other names;

      (ii) if the poll is taken on any other question, shall state the question or questions on which the poll is to be taken;

    (b) shall be capable of being folded up;

    (c) shall have a number printed on the back;

    (d) shall have attached a counterfoil with the same number printed on the face or the back.

(3) Where a poll on a question of appointment to any office and a poll on any other question are taken together, ballot papers of a different colour shall be used for each poll.

The official mark

7.—(1) Every ballot paper shall be marked with an official mark, which shall be either embossed or perforated.

(2) The official mark shall be kept secret.

Prohibition of disclosure of vote

8. No person who has voted at the poll shall, in any legal proceeding to question the poll, be required to state how or for whom he voted.

Use of schools and public rooms

9.—(1) The returning officer may use, free of charge, for the purpose of taking the poll or counting the votes—

 (*a*) a room in a school maintained or assisted by a local education authority or a school in respect of which grants are made out of moneys provided by Parliament to the person or body of persons responsible for the management of the school;

 (*b*) a room the expense of maintaining which is payable out of any rate.

(2) The returning officer shall make good any damage done to, and defray any expense incurred by the persons having control over, any such room as aforesaid by reason of its being used for the purpose of taking the poll or of counting the votes.

(3) The use of a room in an unoccupied house for the purpose of taking the poll or of counting the votes shall not render a person liable to be rated or to pay any rate for that house.

Notice of poll

10.—(1) Notice of the poll in the form in the Appendix shall be published by the returning officer and the manner of publication shall be the same as in the case of notice of a parish meeting.

(2) Notice of the poll shall specify—

 (*a*) the day and hours fixed for the poll;

 (*b*) (i) if the poll is taken on a question of appointment to any office, the name of the office, the number of vacancies and the particulars of each candidate who has not withdrawn (the order of the names of the candidates and the particulars being the same as in the ballot paper);

  (ii) if the poll is taken on any other question, the particulars of the question;

 (*c*) the name of the proposer of each candidate or of the proposer of the resolution in respect of which the poll is taken as the case may be; and

 (*d*) the situation of each polling station and the description of the persons entitled to vote thereat.

Provision of polling stations

11.—(1) The returning officer shall provide one polling station or such other number of polling stations as the county council may by any general or special order direct and shall, if more than one polling station is provided, allot the voters to the polling stations in such manner as he thinks most convenient.

(2) One or more polling stations may be provided in the same room.

(3) The returning officer shall provide each polling station with such number of compartments as may be necessary in which the voters can mark their votes screened from observation.

Appointment of presiding officers and clerks

12.—(1) The returning officer shall appoint and may pay a presiding officer to attend at each polling station and such clerks as may be necessary for taking the poll and counting the votes.

(2) The returning officer may, if he thinks fit, preside at a polling station and the provisions of these rules relating to a presiding officer shall apply to a returning officer so presiding with the necessary modifications as to things to be done by the returning officer to the presiding officer or by the presiding officer to the returning officer.

(3) A presiding officer may do, by the clerks appointed to assist him, any act (including the asking of questions) which he is required or authorised by these rules to do at a polling station except order the arrest, exclusion or removal of any person from the polling station.

Equipment of polling stations

13.—(1) The returning officer shall provide each presiding officer with such number of ballot boxes and ballot papers as in the opinion of the returning officer may be necessary.

(2) Every ballot box shall be so constructed that the ballot papers can be put therein, but cannot be withdrawn therefrom, without the box being unlocked.

(3) The returning officer shall provide each polling station with—

(a) materials to enable voters to mark the ballot papers;

(b) instruments for stamping thereon the official mark;

(c) copies of the register of electors for the parish or such part thereof as contains the names of the voters allotted to the station.

(4) A notice in the appropriate form in the Appendix, giving directions for the guidance of the voters in voting, shall be printed in conspicuous characters and exhibited inside and outside every polling station.

(5) Where the poll is taken on a question of appointment to any office there shall be exhibited in every compartment of every polling station a notice as follows:—"The voter may vote for not more than   candidate(s) as [insert name of office]"; so however that if the poll is taken on questions of appointment to two or more offices, the notice may be adapted accordingly.

Appointment of polling and counting agents

14.—(1) Each candidate may appoint one polling agent to attend at each polling station for the purpose of detecting personation and one counting agent to attend at the counting of the votes.

(2) Notice in writing of the appointment, stating the names and addresses of the persons appointed, shall be given by the candidate to the returning officer and shall be so given not later than the time appointed for that purpose in the Timetable.

(3) If an agent dies, or becomes incapable of acting, the candidate may appoint another agent in his place, and shall forthwith give to the returning officer notice in writing of the name and address of the agent appointed.

(4) In the following provisions of these rules references to polling and counting agents shall be taken as references to agents whose appointments have been duly made and notified and who are within the permitted number.

(5) Any notice required to be given to a counting agent by the returning officer may be delivered at, or sent by post to, the address stated in the notice of appointment.

(6) A candidate may himself do any act or thing which any polling or counting agent of his, if appointed, would have been authorised to do, or may assist his agent in doing any such act or thing.

(7) Where by these rules any act or thing is required or authorised to be done in the presence of the polling or counting agents, the non-attendance of any agents or agent at the time and place appointed for the purpose, shall not, if the act or thing is otherwise duly done, invalidate the act or thing done.

Declaration of secrecy

15.—(1) Before the opening of the poll a declaration of secrecy in the form in paragraph (4) of this rule, or in a form as near thereto as circumstances admit, shall be made by—

(a) the returning officer and the presiding officers;

(b) every clerk authorised to attend at a polling station or at the counting of the votes;

(c) every candidate attending at a polling station or at the counting of the votes;

(d) every candidate's wife or husband attending at the counting of the votes;

(e) every polling agent and counting agent;

(f) where the poll is taken on a question other than a question of appointment to any office, the proposer of the resolution in respect of which the poll is taken who attends at the counting of the votes;

(g) every person permitted by the returning officer to attend at the counting of the votes, though not entitled to do so.

(2) Notwithstanding anything in the foregoing paragraph, the following persons attending at the counting of the votes, that is to say:—

(a) any candidate or, where the poll is taken on a question other than a question of appointment to any office, the proposer of the resolution in respect of which the poll is taken;

(b) any candidate's wife or husband attending by virtue of rule 28 of these rules, authorising candidates' wives or husbands to attend as such;

(c) any person permitted by the returning officer to attend, though not entitled to do so;

(d) any clerk making the declaration in order to attend at the counting of the votes;

need not make the declaration before the opening of the poll but shall make it before he or she is permitted to attend the counting, and a person becoming obliged to make a declaration by reason of his appointment after the opening of the poll shall make the declaration before acting under the appointment.

(3) The returning officer shall make the declaration in the presence of a Justice of the Peace, and any other person shall make the declaration in the presence either of a Justice of the Peace or of the returning officer, and paragraphs (5), (6), (7) and (9) of this rule shall be read to the declarant by the person taking the declaration, or shall be read by the declarant in the presence of that person:

Provided that the declaration may be made by the returning officer or any other person before a person who is chairman of the Greater London Council, a county council or a district council or mayor of a borough or rural borough, and may be made by a person other than the returning officer before a person who is clerk of any such council or town clerk of a borough or rural borough.

(4) The declaration shall be as follows:—

"I solemnly promise and declare that I will not do anything forbidden by paragraphs (5), (6), (7) and (9) of rule 15 of the Schedule to the Parish Meetings (Polls) Rules 1970 which have been read to [by] me."

(5) The following persons, that is to say:—

(a) the returning officer and every presiding officer or clerk attending at a polling station;

(b) every candidate or polling agent so attending,

shall maintain and aid in maintaining the secrecy of voting and shall not, except for some purpose authorised by law, communicate to any person before the poll is closed any information as to—

(i) the name of any voter who has or has not applied for a ballot paper or voted at a polling station;

(ii) the number in the register of electors of any voter who has or has not applied for a ballot paper or voted at a polling station; or

(iii) the official mark.

(6) Every person attending at the counting of the votes shall maintain and aid in maintaining the secrecy of voting and shall not—

(a) ascertain or attempt to ascertain at the counting of the votes the number on the back of any ballot paper;

(b) communicate any information obtained at the counting of the votes as to the candidate for whom or the manner in which any vote is given on any particular ballot paper.

(7) No person whatsoever shall—

(a) interfere with or attempt to interfere with a voter when recording his vote;

(b) otherwise obtain or attempt to obtain in a polling station information as to the candidate for whom or the manner in which a voter in that station is about to vote or has voted;

(c) communicate at any time to any person any information obtained in a polling station as to the candidate for whom or the manner in which a voter in that station is about to vote or has voted, or as to the number on the back of the ballot paper given to a voter at that station;

(d) directly or indirectly induce a voter to display his ballot paper after he has marked it so as to make known to any person the name of the candidate for whom or the manner in which he has or has not voted.

(8) No person having undertaken to assist a blind voter to vote shall communicate at any time to any person any information as to the candidate for whom or the manner in which that voter intends to vote or has voted, or as to the number on the back of the ballot paper given for the use of that voter.

(9) If any person acts in contravention of paragraph (5), (6), (7) or (8) of this rule, he shall be liable on summary conviction to imprisonment for a term not exceeding six months.

Admission to polling station

16. The presiding officer shall regulate the number of voters to be admitted to the polling station at the same time, and shall exclude all other persons except—

(a) the candidates;

(b) the polling agents appointed to attend at the polling station;

(c) the clerks appointed to attend at the polling station;

(d) the constables on duty; and

(e) the companions of blind voters.

Keeping of order in station

17.—(1) It shall be the duty of the presiding officer to keep order at his polling station.

(2) If a person misconducts himself in a polling station, or fails to obey the lawful orders of the presiding officer, he may immediately, by order of the presiding officer, be removed from the polling station by a constable in or near that station or by any other person authorised in writing by the returning officer to remove him, and the person so removed shall not, without the permission of the presiding officer, again enter the polling station during the day.

(3) Any person so removed may, if charged with the commission in the polling station of an offence, be dealt with as a person taken into custody by a constable for an offence without a warrant.

(4) The powers conferred by this rule shall not be exercised so as to prevent a voter who is otherwise entitled to vote at a polling station from having an opportunity of voting at that station.

Sealing of ballot boxes

18. Immediately before the commencement of the poll, the presiding officer shall show the ballot box empty to such persons, if any, as are present in the polling station, so that they may see that it is empty, and shall then lock it up and place his seal on it in such manner as to prevent its being opened without breaking the seal, and shall place it in his view for the receipt of ballot papers, and keep it so locked and sealed.

Questions to be put to voters

19.—(1) The presiding officer may, and if required by a candidate or his polling agent shall, put to any person applying for a ballot paper at the time of his application, but not afterwards, the following questions, or either of them that is to say:—

    (i) Are you the person registered in the register of local government electors now in force for this parish as follows (*read the whole entry from the register*)?

    (ii) Have you already voted at the present poll?

(2) A ballot paper shall not be delivered to any person required to answer the above questions or either of them unless he has answered the questions or question satisfactorily.

(3) Save as by this rule authorised, no inquiry shall be permitted as to the right of any person to vote.

Challenge of voter

20.—(1) If at the time a person applies for a ballot paper, or after he has applied for a ballot paper and before he has left the polling station, a candidate or his polling agent declares to the presiding officer that he has reasonable cause to believe that the applicant has committed an offence of personation and undertakes to substantiate the charge in a court of law, the presiding officer may order a constable to arrest the applicant, and the order of the presiding officer shall be sufficient authority for the constable so to do.

(2) A person against whom a declaration is made under this rule shall not by reason thereof be prevented from voting.

(3) A person arrested under the provisions of this rule shall be dealt with as a person taken into custody by a constable for an offence without a warrant.

Voting procedure

21.—(1) A ballot paper shall be delivered to a voter who applies therefor, and immediately before delivery—

    (*a*) the ballot paper shall be stamped with the official mark, either embossed or perforated;

    (*b*) the number, name and description of the voter as stated in the copy of the register of electors shall be called out;

    (*c*) the number of the voter shall be marked on the counterfoil; and

    (*d*) a mark shall be placed in the register of electors against the number of the voter to denote that a ballot paper has been received but without showing the particular ballot paper which has been received.

(2) The voter, on receiving the ballot paper, shall forthwith proceed into one of the compartments in the polling station and there secretly mark his paper and fold it up so as to conceal his vote, and shall then show to the presiding officer the back of the paper, so as to disclose the official mark and put the ballot paper so folded up into the ballot box in the presence of the presiding officer.

(3) The voter shall vote without undue delay, and shall leave the polling station as soon as he has put his ballot paper into the ballot box.

Votes marked by presiding officer

22.—(1) The presiding officer, on the application of—

    (*a*) a voter who is incapacitated by blindness or other physical cause from voting in manner directed by these rules; or

    (*b*) if the poll is taken on a Saturday, a voter who declares that he is a Jew, and objects on religious grounds to vote in manner directed by these rules; or

(c) a voter who declares orally that is he unable to read,

shall, in the presence of the polling agents, cause the vote of the voter to be marked on a ballot paper in manner directed by the voter, and the ballot paper to be placed in the ballot box.

(2) The name and number in the register of electors of every voter whose vote is marked in pursuance of this rule, and the reason why it is so marked, shall be entered on a list (in these rules called "the list of votes marked by the presiding officer").

Voting by blind persons

23.—(1) If a voter makes an application to the presiding officer to be allowed on the ground of blindness to vote with the assistance of another person by whom he is accompanied (in these rules referred to as "the companion"), the presiding officer shall require the voter to declare orally whether he is so incapacitated by his blindness as to be unable to vote without assistance.

(2) If the presiding officer is satisfied that the voter is so incapacitated and is also satisfied by a written declaration made by the companion (in these rules referred to as "the declaration made by the companion of a blind voter") that the companion is a qualified person within the meaning of this rule and has not previously assisted more than one blind person to vote at the poll, the presiding officer shall grant the application, and thereupon anything which is by these rules required to be done to or by the said voter in connection with the giving of his vote may be done to, or with the assistance of, the companion.

(3) For the purposes of this rule, a person shall be qualified to assist a blind voter to vote, if that person is either—

    (a) a person who is entitled to vote at the poll; or

    (b) the father, mother, brother, sister, husband, wife, son or daughter of the blind voter and has attained the age of eighteen years.

(4) The name and number in the register of electors of every voter whose vote is given in accordance with this rule and the name and address of the companion shall be entered on a list (in these rules referred to as "the list of blind voters assisted by companions").

(5) The declaration made by the companion—

    (a) shall be in the form in the Appendix;

    (b) shall be made before the presiding officer at the time when the voter applies to vote with the assistance of a companion and shall forthwith be given to the presiding officer who shall attest and retain it.

(6) No fee or other payment shall be charged in respect of the declaration.

Tendered ballot papers

24.—(1) If a person, representing himself to be a particular voter named in the register, applies for a ballot paper after another person has voted as the voter, the applicant shall, on satisfactorily answering the questions permitted by law to be asked at the poll, be entitled, subject to the following provisions of this rule, to mark a ballot paper (in these rules referred to as "a tendered ballot paper") in the same manner as any other voter.

(2) A tendered ballot paper shall—

    (a) be of a colour differing from the other ballot papers;

    (b) instead of being put into the ballot box, be given to the presiding officer and endorsed by him with the name of the voter and his number in the register of electors, and set aside in a separate packet.

(3) The name of the voter and his number in the register of electors shall be entered on a list (in these rules referred to as the "tendered votes list").

Spoilt ballot papers

25. A voter who has inadvertently dealt with his ballot paper in such manner that it cannot be conveniently used as a ballot paper may, on delivering it to the presiding officer and proving to his satisfaction the fact of the inadvertence, obtain another ballot paper in the place of the ballot paper so delivered (in these rules referred to as "a spoilt ballot paper"), and the spoilt ballot paper shall be immediately cancelled.

Adjournment of poll in case of riot

26.—(1) Where the proceedings at any polling station are interrupted or obstructed by riot or open violence, the presiding officer shall adjourn the proceedings till the following day and shall forthwith give notice to the returning officer.

(2) Where the poll is adjourned at any polling station—

(a) the hours of polling on the day to which it is adjourned shall be the same as for the original day; and

(b) references in these rules to the close of the poll shall be construed accordingly.

Procedure on close of poll

27.—(1) As soon as practicable after the close of the poll, the presiding officer shall, in the presence of the polling agents, make up into separate packets, sealed with his own seal and the seals of such polling agents as desire to affix their seals—

(a) each ballot box in use at the station, sealed so as to prevent the introduction of additional ballot papers and unopened, but with the key attached;

(b) the unused and spoilt ballot papers placed together;

(c) the tendered ballot papers;

(d) the marked copy of the register of electors;

(e) the counterfoils of the used ballot papers;

(f) the tendered votes list, the list of blind voters assisted by companions, the list of votes marked by the presiding officer, a statement of the number of voters whose votes are so marked by the presiding officer under the heads "physical incapacity", "Jews", and "unable to read", and the declarations made by the companions of blind voters;

and shall deliver the packets or cause them to be delivered to the returning officer to be taken charge of by him:

Provided that if the packets are not delivered by the presiding officer personally to the returning officer, the arrangements for their delivery shall require the approval of the returning officer.

(2) The marked copy of the register of electors shall not be in the same packet as the counterfoils of the used ballot papers.

(3) The packets shall be accompanied by a statement (in these rules referred to as "the ballot paper account") made by the presiding officer showing the number of ballot papers entrusted to him, and accounting for them under the heads of ballot papers issued and not otherwise accounted for, and unused, spoilt and tendered ballot papers.

Attendance at counting of votes

28.—(1) The returning officer shall make arrangements for counting the votes in the presence of the counting agents as soon as practicable after the close of the poll, and shall give to the counting agents notice in writing of the time and place at which he will begin to count the votes.

(2) No person other than—

(a) the returning officer and his clerks;

(b) the candidates and their wives or husbands;

(c) where the poll is taken on a question other than a question of appointment to any office, the proposer of the resolution in respect of which the poll is taken;

(*d*) the counting agents,

may be present at the counting of the votes, unless permitted by the returning officer to attend.

(3) A person not entitled to attend at the counting of the votes shall not be permitted to do so by the returning officer unless the returning officer is satisfied that the efficient counting of the votes will not be impeded.

(4) The returning officer shall give the counting agents all such reasonable facilities for overseeing the proceedings, and all such information with reference thereto, as he can give them consistently with the orderly conduct of the proceedings and the discharge of his duties in connection therewith.

(5) In particular, where the votes are counted by sorting the ballot papers according to the candidate for whom the vote is given and then counting the number of ballot papers for each candidate, the counting agents shall be entitled to satisfy themselves that the ballot papers are correctly sorted.

The count

29.—(1) Before the returning officer proceeds to count the votes, he shall—

(*a*) in the presence of the counting agents open each ballot box and, taking out the ballot papers therein, count and record the number thereof and verify each ballot paper account;

(*b*) where a poll on a question of appointment to any office and a poll on any other question have been taken together, separate the ballot papers relating to each poll and count and record the numbers relating to each poll; and

(*c*) then mix together the whole of the ballot papers relating to the poll or each poll, as the case may be, contained in the ballot boxes.

(2) The returning officer shall not count any tendered ballot paper.

(3) The returning officer, while separating, counting and recording the number of ballot papers and counting the votes, shall keep the ballot papers with their faces upwards and take all proper precautions for preventing any person from seeing the numbers printed on the back of the papers.

(4) The returning officer shall verify each ballot paper account by comparing it with the number of ballot papers recorded by him, and the unused and spoilt ballot papers in his possession and the tendered votes list (opening and resealing the packets containing the unused and spoilt ballot papers and the tendered votes list) and shall draw up a statement as to the result of the verification which any counting agent may copy.

(5) The returning officer shall, so far as practicable, proceed continuously with counting the votes, allowing only time for refreshment:

Provided that he may, in so far as he thinks necessary, exclude the hours between eight o'clock in the evening and nine o'clock on the following morning.

(6) During the excluded time the returning officer shall place the ballot papers and other documents relating to the poll under his own seal and the seals of such of the counting agents as desire to affix their seals and shall otherwise take proper precautions for the security of the papers and documents.

Re-count

30.—(1) A candidate may, if present when the counting or any re-count of the votes is completed, require the returning officer to have the votes re-counted or again re-counted but the returning officer may refuse to do so if in his opinion the request is unreasonable.

(2) No steps shall be taken on the completion of the counting or any re-count of votes until the candidates present at the completion thereof have been given a reasonable opportunity to exercise the right conferred by this rule.

Rejected ballot papers

31.—(1) Any ballot paper—

(*a*) which does not bear the official mark; or

(*b*) on which votes are given for more candidates than the voter is entitled to vote for; or

(*c*) on which anything is written or marked by which the voter can be identified except the printed number on the back; or

(*d*) which is unmarked or void for uncertainty,

shall, subject to the provisions of this rule, be void and not counted.

(2) Where the voter is entitled to vote for more than one candidate or on more than one question, as the case may be, a ballot paper shall not be deemed to be void for uncertainty as respects any vote as to which no uncertainty arises and that vote shall be counted.

(3) A ballot paper on which a vote is marked—

(*a*) elsewhere than in the proper place; or

(*b*) otherwise than by means of a cross; or

(*c*) by more than one mark,

shall not by reason thereof be deemed to be void (either wholly or as respects that vote), if an intention that the vote shall be for one or other of the candidates or for or against any question clearly appears, and the way the paper is marked does not of itself identify the voter and it is not shown that he can be identified thereby.

(4) The returning officer shall endorse—

(*a*) the word "rejected" on any ballot paper which under this rule is not to be counted; and

(*b*) in the case of a ballot paper on which any vote is counted under paragraph (2) of this rule, the words "rejected in part" and a memorandum specifying the votes counted;

and shall add to the endorsement the words "rejection objected to" if an objection is made by a counting agent to his decision.

(5) The returning officer shall draw up a statement showing the number of ballot papers rejected, including those rejected in part, under the several heads of—

(*a*) want of official mark;

(*b*) voting for more candidates than voter is entitled to;

(*c*) writing or mark by which voter could be identified;

(*d*) unmarked or wholly void for uncertainty;

(*e*) rejected in part.

Decisions on ballot papers

32. The decision of the returning officer on any question arising in respect of a ballot paper shall be final, but shall be subject to review on an election petition.

Equality of votes

33. Where, after the counting of the votes (including any re-count) is completed, an equality of votes is found to exist between any candidates or for and against any question and the addition of a vote would entitle any of those candidates to be declared elected or would decide the question, the returning officer shall forthwith decide either between those candidates or that question by lot, and proceed as if the candidate or the answer in favour of or against the question on whom or on which the lot falls had received an additional vote.

Declaration of result

34. When the result of the poll has been ascertained the returning officer shall forthwith—

(a) in the case of a poll on a question of appointment to any office, declare to be elected the candidate or candidates for whom the majority of votes have been given and shall as soon as possible publish a notice in the appropriate form in the Appendix, or a form to the like effect, showing the name or names of the candidate or candidates elected, the total number of votes given for each candidate whether elected or not and the number of rejected ballot papers under each head shown in the statement of rejected ballot papers;

(b) in the case of a poll on any other question, declare the number of votes given for and against the question and whether the proposal to which the question relates has been carried or lost and shall as soon as possible publish a notice in the appropriate form in the Appendix, or a form to the like effect, of the result as declared and showing the number of rejected ballot papers under each head shown in the statement of rejected ballot papers.

The return

35. The returning officer, if he is not the chairman of the meeting at which the poll was demanded, shall forthwith upon declaration of the result of the poll return the name of each person elected or the result of the poll, as the case may be, to that chairman.

Sealing of ballot papers

36.—(1) On the completion of the counting the returning officer shall seal up in separate packets the counted and rejected ballot papers, including ballot papers rejected in part.

(2) The returning officer shall not open the sealed packets of tendered ballot papers or of counterfoils or of marked copies of the register of electors.

Delivery of documents to clerk of the council

37. The returning officer shall then forward to the clerk of the council of the rural district in which the parish is situate the following documents, that is to say:—

(a) the packets of ballot papers in his possession;

(b) the ballot paper accounts and the statements of rejected ballot papers and of the result of the verification of the ballot paper accounts;

(c) the tendered votes lists, the lists of blind voters assisted by companions, the lists of votes marked by the presiding officer and the statements relating thereto, and the declarations made by the companions of blind voters;

(d) the packets of counterfoils;

(e) the packets containing marked copies of the register of electors,

endorsing on each packet a description of its contents, the date of the poll to which they relate and the name of the parish for which the poll was held.

Orders for production of documents

38.—(1) An order—

(a) for the inspection or production of any rejected ballot papers, including ballot papers rejected in part; or

(b) for the opening of a sealed packet of counterfoils or for the inspection of counted ballot papers,

may be made by either a county court having jurisdiction in the parish or an election court if the court is satisfied by evidence on oath that the order is required for the purpose of instituting or maintaining a prosecution for an offence in relation to ballot papers, or for the purpose of an election petition.

(2) The order may be made subject to such conditions as to persons, time, place and mode of inspection, production or opening as the court making the order may think expedient and may direct the clerk of the rural district council having custody of the ballot papers and the sealed packets of counterfoils to retain them intact for such period as may be specified in the order:

Provided that in making and carrying into effect the order, care shall be taken that the way in which the vote of any particular voter has been given shall not be disclosed until it has been proved that his vote was given and the vote has been declared by a competent court to be invalid.

(3) An appeal shall lie to the High Court from any order of a county court made under this rule.

(4) Any power given under this rule to a county court may be exercised by any judge of the court otherwise than in open court.

(5) Where an order is made for the production by the clerk of the rural district council of any document in his possession relating to any specified poll, the production by him or his agent of the document ordered in such manner as may be directed by that order shall be conclusive evidence that the document relates to the specified poll; and any endorsement on any packet of ballot papers so produced shall be prima facie evidence that the ballot papers are what they are stated to be by the endorsement.

(6) The production from proper custody of a ballot paper purporting to have been used at any poll, and of a counterfoil marked with the same printed number and having a number marked thereon in writing shall be prima facie evidence that the voter whose vote was given by that ballot paper was the person who at the time of the poll had affixed to his name in the register of electors the same number as the number written on the counterfoil.

(7) Save as by this rule provided, no person shall be allowed to inspect any rejected or counted ballot papers in the possession of the clerk of the rural district council or to open any sealed packets of counterfoils.

Retention and public inspection of documents

39.—(1) The clerk of the rural district council shall retain for six months among the records of the rural district all documents relating to a poll which are, in pursuance of these rules, forwarded to him by a returning officer or held by him and then, unless otherwise directed by an order under the last foregoing rule, shall cause them to be destroyed.

(2) The said documents, except ballot papers and counterfoils, shall during a period of six months from the day of the poll be open to public inspection at such time and in such manner as may be determined by the county council.

(3) The clerk of the rural district council shall, on request, supply copies of or extracts from the documents open to public inspection on payment of such fees, and subject to such conditions, as may be determined by the county council.

Supplemental provisions as to documents

40. Subject to the provisions of these rules, the clerk of the rural district council shall, in respect of the custody and destruction of ballot papers and other documents coming into his possession in pursuance of these rules, be subject to the directions of the rural district council.

Countermand or abandonment of poll on death of candidate

41.—(1) If before the result of the poll is declared proof is given to the satisfaction of the returning officer that a candidate who has not withdrawn has died, then the returning officer shall countermand the poll or, if polling has begun, direct that the poll be abandoned.

(2) Where the poll is abandoned by reason of the death of a candidate, the proceedings at or consequent on that poll shall be interrupted, and the presiding officer at any polling station shall take the like steps (so far as not already taken) for the delivery to the returning officer of ballot boxes and of ballot papers and other documents as he is required to take on the close of the poll in due course, and the returning officer shall dispose of ballot papers and other documents in his possession as he is required to do on the completion in due course of the counting of the votes; but—

    (*a*) it shall not be necessary for any ballot paper account to be prepared or verified; and

    (*b*) the returning officer, without taking any step or further step for the counting of the ballot papers or of the votes, shall seal up all the ballot papers, whether the votes on them have been counted or not, and it shall not be necessary to seal up counted and rejected ballot papers in separate packets.

(3) The foregoing provisions of these rules as to the inspection, production, retention and destruction of ballot papers and other documents relating to a poll shall apply to any such documents relating to a poll abandoned by reason of the death of a candidate, with the following modifications:—

    (*a*) ballot papers on which the votes were neither counted nor rejected shall be treated as counted ballot papers; and

    (*b*) no order shall be made for the production or inspection of any ballot papers or for the opening of a sealed packet of counterfoils unless the order is made by a court with reference to a prosecution.

(4) Where a poll is countermanded or abandoned by reason of the death of a candidate, the county council may by order make any appointment or make provision for the holding of a parish meeting or do such other thing as appears to them to be expedient in the circumstances.

General duty of returning officer

42. It shall be the general duty of the returning officer to do any act or thing that may be necessary for effectually conducting the poll under these rules.

Interpretation

43.—(1) In these rules unless the context otherwise requires—

the expression "appointment to any office" includes the election of the chairman of the parish meeting;

the expression "question" means a question other than a question of appointment to any office in respect of which the poll is taken.

(2) For any reference in these rules to a parish there shall, if the poll is held for part of a parish, be substituted a reference to part of a parish.

(3) A reference in this Schedule to a rule shall be construed as a reference to a rule contained in this Schedule.

(4) Any person before whom a declaration is authorised to be made under these rules may take the declaration.

APPENDIX

Note.—The forms contained in this Appendix may be adapted as far as circumstances require.

Notice of Abandonment of Poll

Parish of   .   Rule 4.

Whereas at a Parish Meeting for the Parish of
held on the   day of   , 19   , a
demand was made for a poll as to which of the following candidates should be appointed as [*insert name of office*] for the said parish, and such demand was not withdrawn:—

[*insert names, place of residence, and description of each candidate.*]

And whereas the said [*insert name*] has since withdrawn his candidature and the number of the remaining candidates does not exceed the number of persons to be appointed to the said office, I hereby give notice that the poll demanded will not take place, and I hereby declare that the said [*insert names*] are appointed to the said office.

Dated this   day of   , 19   .

....
                                     Returning Officer.

Rule 10.

NOTICE OF POLL

Parish of .

Whereas at a Parish Meeting for the Parish of ,
held on the day of , 19 , a poll was demanded
on [the appointment to the following office] [the following question].

NOTICE IS HEREBY GIVEN THAT—

1. A poll on the said question[s] will be taken on the day of
, 19 , between the hours of and .

*If the poll does not relate to a question of appointment to any office, omit this paragraph. If it relates to questions of appointment to two or more offices, adapt form accordingly.
†Insert particulars as to each candidate with respect to whom the poll is to be taken, in the alphabetical order of the candidates' surnames, or if their surnames are the same as their other names.

*2. The number of persons to be appointed as [*insert name of office*] is

*3. The names, places of residence, and descriptions of the candidates for election and the names of their respective proposers are as follows:—

Names of Candidate (Surname first)†	Description	Home address in full	Names of Proposer (Surname first)

‡4. The names and address of the proposer of the resolution in respect of which the poll is taken are as follows:—

‡If the poll relates to a question of appointment to any office, omit this paragraph.

§If there is only one polling station, adapt form accordingly.

§5. The situation of the polling stations and the description of the persons entitled to vote at each are as follows:—

Polling Station	Persons entitled to vote thereat

Dated this day of , 19 .

....
Returning Officer.
[*State office for purpose of poll.*]

BALLOT PAPER ON A QUESTION OTHER THAN A QUESTION OF APPOINTMENT TO AN OFFICE   Rule 6.

Form of Front of Ballot Paper

POLL ON THE FOLLOWING QUESTIONS

Counterfoil No.	Questions	Answers	
		Yes	No
NOTE: *The counterfoil is to have a number to correspond with that on the back of the Ballot Paper.*	1. That the Parish Meeting consent to the Parish being grouped with the Parish of Blackacre under a common Parish Council.		
	2. That section 3(1) of the Parish Councils Act 1957 (which empowers the Parish Meeting to light roads and public places in the Parish) be adopted for the Parish.		

Form of Back of Ballot Paper

No.

Poll consequent on Parish Meeting for the Parish of

Note.—The number on the ballot paper is to correspond with that on the counterfoil.

Directions as to printing ballot paper

Nothing is to be printed on the ballot paper except in accordance with the preceding form of ballot paper on a question other than a question of appointment to an office.

Rule 6.

BALLOT PAPER ON A QUESTION OF APPOINTMENT TO AN OFFICE

Form of Front of Ballot Paper

Counterfoil
No.

NOTE:
The counterfoil is
to have a number to
correspond with
that on the back
of the Ballot Paper.

1

BROWN

(JOHN EDWARD Brown, of 2 The Cottages, Barlington, Grayshire, Labour.)

2

BROWN

(THOMAS WILLIAM Brown, of 15 Barchester Road, Barlington, Grayshire, Liberal.)

3

JONES

(William David Jones, of The Grange, Barlington, Grayshire, Conservative.)

4

MERTON

(Hon. George Travis, commonly called Viscount Merton, of Barlington, Grayshire.)

5

SMITH

(Mary Smith, of School House, Barlington, Grayshire, schoolteacher, Progressive.)

6

WILLIAMS

(Elizabeth Williams, of 3 Ivy Lane, Barlington, Grayshire, housewife.)

Form of Back of Ballot Paper

No.

Poll on appointment of [*insert name of office*] for the Parish of

Note.—The number on the ballot paper is to correspond with that on the counterfoil.

Directions as to printing the ballot paper

1. Nothing is to be printed on the ballot paper except in accordance with these directions.

2. So far as practicable, the following arrangements shall be observed in the printing of the ballot paper:—

   (*a*) no word shall be printed on the face except the particulars of the candidates;

   (*b*) no rule shall be printed on the face except the horizontal rules separating the particulars of the candidates from one another and the vertical rules separating those particulars from the numbers on the left-hand side and the spaces on the right where the vote is to be marked;

   (*c*) the whole space between the top and bottom of the paper shall be equally divided between the candidates by the rules separating their particulars.

3. The surname of each candidate shall in all cases be printed by itself in large capitals, and his full particulars shall be set out below it and shall be printed in ordinary type except that small capitals shall be used—

   (*a*) if his surname is the same as another candidate's for his other names; and

   (*b*) if his other names are also the same as the other candidate's either for his residence or for his description unless each of them is the same as that of another candidate with the same surname and other names.

4. The number on the back of the ballot paper shall be printed in ordinary type.

DIRECTIONS FOR THE GUIDANCE OF THE VOTERS IN VOTING WHERE THE POLL IS ON A QUESTION OTHER THAN A QUESTION OF APPOINTMENT TO AN OFFICE   Rule 13.

1. The voter should see that the ballot paper, before it is handed to him, is stamped with the official mark.

2. The voter will go into one of the compartments and, with the pencil provided in the compartment, place a cross thus X in the column of the ballot paper headed "Yes" or in that headed "No" according to whether he wishes to vote in favour of or against the question opposite to which he places the cross.

Where the ballot paper refers to more than one question the voter may vote in the manner described on each question in the ballot paper.

3. The voter will then fold up the ballot paper so as to show the official mark on the back, and leaving the compartment will, without showing the front of the paper to any person, show the official mark on the back to the presiding officer, and then, in the presence of the presiding officer, put the paper into the ballot box, and forthwith leave the polling station.

4. If the voter inadvertently spoils a ballot paper, he can return it to the officer, who will, if satisfied of such inadvertence, give him another paper.

5. If the voter places any mark on the paper by which he may afterwards be identified, his ballot paper will be void, and will not be counted.

Rule 13. DIRECTIONS FOR THE GUIDANCE OF THE VOTERS IN VOTING WHERE THE POLL IS ON A QUESTION OF APPOINTMENT TO AN OFFICE

1. The voter should see that the ballot paper, before it is handed to him, is stamped with the official mark.

2. The voter will go into one of the compartments and, with the pencil provided in the compartment, place a cross on the right-hand side of the ballot paper, opposite the name of each candidate for whom he votes, thus X.

3. The voter will then fold up the ballot paper so as to show the official mark on the back, and leaving the compartment will, without showing the front of the paper to any person, show the official mark on the back to the presiding officer, and then, in the presence of the presiding officer, put the paper into the ballot box, and forthwith leave the polling station.

4. If the voter inadvertently spoils a ballot paper he can return it to the officer, who will, if satisfied of such inadvertence, give him another paper.

5. If the voter votes for more than   candidate(s), or places any mark on the paper by which he may be afterwards identified, his ballot paper will be void, and will not be counted.

———

Rule 23. DECLARATION TO BE MADE BY THE COMPANION OF A BLIND VOTER

I, A.B., of   , having been requested to assist C.D., who is numbered   on the register of local government electors for the Parish of   to record his vote at the poll now being held for the said parish
State the do hereby declare that [I am entitled to vote at the said poll] [I am the
relationship of the said voter and have attained the age of eighteen years], and that I have not
of the previously assisted any blind person [except E.F., of   ],
companion to vote at the said poll.
to the voter.

(Signed) A.B.

day of   , 19   .

I, the undersigned, being the presiding officer for the
polling station for the Parish of   , do hereby certify that the above declaration, having been first read to the above-named declarant, was signed by the declarant in my presence.

(Signed) G.H.

day of   , 19   , at   minutes past o'clock [a.m.] [p.m.].

Note.—If the person making the above declaration knowingly and wilfully makes therein a statement false in a material particular, he will be guilty of an offence.

DECLARATION OF RESULT OF POLL ON A QUESTION OTHER THAN A QUESTION OF   Rule 34.
APPOINTMENT TO AN OFFICE

Parish of   .

Whereas a poll of the local government electors of the Parish of
was taken on the   day of   , 19   , on the following
question[s], namely [*state the question or questions upon which the poll was taken*].

I, the undersigned, being the returning officer at the said poll, hereby give notice
that the number of votes given thereat was as follows:—

     For the question   ...   .   votes.

     Against the question   ...   .   votes.

...

     Majority for [*or* against]   ...   .

‡REJECTED BALLOT PAPERS

‡If no ballot papers rejected omit this part of form.

.........ballot papers were rejected for the following reason(s):—

§(*a*) want of official mark............[*insert number*]

§(*b*) writing or mark by which voter could be identified............[*insert number*]

§(*c*) unmarked or wholly void for uncertainty............[*insert number*]

§............ballot papers were rejected in part.

§Delete if inapplicable.

And I hereby declare that the said question was carried [*or* lost].

     Dated this   day of   , 19   .

                         ....

                         Returning Officer.

Rule 34.

If the poll has been taken on questions of appointment to two or more offices, adapt form accordingly.

DECLARATION OF RESULT OF POLL ON A QUESTION OF APPOINTMENT TO AN OFFICE

Parish of   .

Whereas a poll of the local government electors of the Parish of was taken on the   day of   , 19 , as to the person[s] to be appointed as [*insert name of office*] for the parish.

I, the undersigned, being the returning officer at the said poll, hereby give notice that the number of votes given for each candidate at the poll was as follows:—

Names of Candidate		Home address in full	Number of Votes given
Surname	Other Names		

‡If no ballot papers rejected omit this part of form.

§Delete if inapplicable.

‡REJECTED BALLOT PAPERS

............ballot papers were rejected for the following reason(s):—

§(*a*) want of official mark............[*insert number*]

§(*b*) voting for more candidates than voter is entitled to............[*insert number*]

§(*c*) writing or mark by which voter could be identified............[*insert number*]

§(*d*) unmarked or wholly void for uncertainty............[*insert number*]

§............ballot papers were rejected in part.

And I hereby declare that the said   are duly appointed to the said office.

Dated this   day of   , 19 .

....
Returning Officer.

EXPLANATORY NOTE
(This Note is not part of the Rules.)

These Rules revoke and replace the Parish Meetings (Polls) Rules 1950, as amended, with amendments consequential on the provisions of the Representation of the People Act 1969 (c. 15).

1970 No. 194

WEIGHTS AND MEASURES
ADMINISTRATION

The Weights and Measures (Testing and Adjustment Fees) (Amendment) Regulations 1970

Made - - -	*12th February* 1970
Laid before Parliament	*17th February* 1970
Coming into Operation	*18th February* 1970

The Board of Trade, in pursuance of the powers conferred upon them by sections 11(3) and 58 of the Weights and Measures Act 1963(**a**) and of all other powers enabling them in that behalf, hereby make the following Regulations :—

1.—(1) These Regulations may be cited as the Weights and Measures (Testing and Adjustment Fees) (Amendment) Regulations 1970, and shall come into operation on 18th February 1970.

(2) The Interpretation Act 1889(**b**) shall apply to the interpretation of these Regulations as it applies to the interpretation of an Act of Parliament.

2. The Weights and Measures (Testing and Adjustment Fees) Regulations 1967(**c**) shall have effect as if for paragraph D of the Schedule there were substituted the following :—

"D—*Measuring instruments for liquid fuel or lubricants, or for mixtures of such fuel and lubricants*

	£	s.	d.
Container types, unsubdivided, each instrument	1	11	6
Blending types (with price computer mechanism), for first retesting after adaptation to compute prices in decimal currency, each instrument	4	0	0
Blending types, for retesting consequent solely on alteration of setting of price computer mechanism (other than on the occasion mentioned above), each instrument	1	11	6
Blending types, on any other occasion, each instrument ..	5	5	0
Other types, single (with price computer mechanism), for first retesting after adaptation to compute prices in decimal currency, each instrument	2	0	0
Other types, single, on any other occasion, each instrument ..	3	3	0".

Gwyneth Dunwoody,
Parliamentary Secretary
to the Board of Trade.

12th February 1970.

(**a**) 1963 c. 31.   (**b**) 1889 c. 63.   (**c**) S.I. 1967/788 (1967 II, p. 2310).

EXPLANATORY NOTE

(This Note is not part of the Regulations.)

These Regulations amend the Weights and Measures (Testing and Adjustment Fees) Regulations 1967.

Special fees are prescribed for the first retesting of price computing instruments for measuring fuel or lubricants after they have been adapted to compute prices in decimal currency. The new fees are £4 for instruments of the blending type and £2 for other instruments.

STATUTORY INSTRUMENTS

1970 No. 195 (S. 12)

PROBATION AND AFTER CARE

Termination of Probation Grant (Scotland) Order 1970

Made - - - - 6th February 1970

In exercise of the powers conferred on me by paragraph 8 of Schedule 7 to the Social Work (Scotland) Act 1968(**a**), and of all other powers enabling me in that behalf, I hereby make the following order :—

1. This order may be cited as the Termination of Probation Grant (Scotland) Order 1970.

2. The provisions of subsection 3(*a*) and (*b*) and of subsections (4) and (5) of section 75 of the Criminal Justice (Scotland) Act 1949(**b**) (which subsections make provision with respect to the payment out of moneys provided by Parliament of grants towards expenditure relating to the probation service in Scotland) shall cease to have effect except insofar as these provisions relate to the payment of grant towards expenditure which was incurred before the making of this order.

> *William Ross,*
> One of Her Majesty's Principal
> Secretaries of State.

St. Andrew's House,
  Edinburgh.
6th February 1970.

EXPLANATORY NOTE

(This Note is not part of the Order.)

This Order provides formally for the cessation of probation grants following the abolition of probation committees and the transfer of their functions to local authority social work committees from 17th November 1969.

(**a**) 1968 c. 49.   (**b**) 1949 c. 94.

STATUTORY INSTRUMENTS

1970 No. 196 (C. 6) (S. 13)

SOCIAL WORK, SCOTLAND

The Social Work (Scotland) Act 1968 (Commencement No. 3) Order 1970

Made -   -   -   -   6th February 1970

In exercise of the powers conferred on me by section 98 of the Social Work (Scotland) Act 1968(**a**), I hereby make the following order: —

1. This order may be cited as the Social Work (Scotland) Act 1968 (Commencement No. 3) Order 1970.

2. Section 92 (effect of Act on rate support grant) of the Social Work (Scotland) Act 1968 shall come into operation on 9th February 1970.

William Ross,
One of Her Majesty's Principal
Secretaries of State.

St. Andrew's House,
   Edinburgh.
6th February 1970.

EXPLANATORY NOTE

(*This Note is not part of the Order.*)

This Order brings into operation section 92 of the Social Work (Scotland) Act 1968 on 9th February 1970.

(**a**) 1968 c. 49.

STATUTORY INSTRUMENTS

1970 No. 197

REPRESENTATION OF THE PEOPLE

The Rural Borough Council Election Rules 1970

Made - - -	11*th February* 1970
Laid before Parliament	20*th February* 1970
Coming into Operation	1*st March* 1970

In pursuance of the powers conferred upon me by sections 29, 78 and 165(1) of the Representation of the People Act 1949(**a**) and by section 61 of the Local Government Act 1933(**b**) (as extended by paragraphs 1 and 7 of Schedule 7 to the Local Government Act 1958(**c**)), I hereby make the following Rules for the conduct of an election of rural borough councillors and of the mayor of a rural borough, and the following Regulations prescribing the form of declaration of acceptance of office by the mayor of a rural borough and by a rural borough councillor :—

1.—(1) These Rules and Regulations may be cited as the Rural Borough Council Election Rules 1970 and shall come into operation on 1st March 1970.

(2) The Interpretation Act 1889(**d**) shall apply to the interpretation of these Rules and Regulations as it applies to the interpretation of an Act of Parliament.

2. The Rural Borough Council Election Rules 1965(**e**) are hereby revoked.

3.—(1) For an election of rural borough councillors the clerk of the council of the rural district in which the rural borough is situate shall be the returning officer, and if at such election the office of clerk of the rural district council is vacant or the clerk is for any reason unable to act, the chairman of the rural district council shall forthwith appoint another person to be the returning officer for that election :

Provided that where the rural borough councillors and any rural district councillors are to be elected on the same date and for the same area, the returning officer for the election of the rural district councillors shall be the returning officer for the election of the rural borough councillors.

(2) The returning officer may by writing under his hand appoint a fit person to be his deputy for all or any of the purposes of an election, but

---

(**a**) 1949 c. 68.   (**b**) 1933 c. 51.

(**c**) 1958 c. 55.   (**d**) 1889 c. 63.

(**e**) S.I. 1965/2122 (1965 III, p. 6240).

where the rural borough councillors and any rural district councillors are to be elected on the same date and for the same area and a person is appointed deputy for any of the purposes of the election of the rural district councillors, that person shall be deemed to be appointed the returning officer's deputy for the corresponding purposes of the election of the rural borough councillors ; and any functions which a returning officer is authorised or required to discharge in relation to the election may be discharged by a deputy so appointed.

(3) A deputy acting as returning officer under the provisions of this Rule shall, as respects the election for which he is so acting, follow the instructions of the returning officer.

4. Where the poll at an election of rural district councillors is taken together with the poll at an election of rural borough councillors, one ballot box may, if the returning officer thinks fit, be used for the two elections ; but, if separate ballot boxes are used, no vote for any rural borough councillor shall be rendered invalid by the ballot paper being placed in the box intended for the reception of ballot papers for rural district councillors.

5. In the application of those provisions of the Representation of the People Act 1949 referred to in section 165(1) of that Act to an election of the mayor of a rural borough and of rural borough councillors the following adaptation and modification shall have effect :—

For any reference to the clerk of the authority for which the election is held there shall be substituted a reference to the clerk of the council of the rural district in which the rural borough is situate.

In section 119(2)(*b*) of the said Act for the words "such amount not exceeding five hundred pounds" there shall be substituted the words "an amount of fifty pounds or such smaller amount or such larger amount not exceeding three hundred pounds".

6. In the application of the local elections rules contained in Schedule 2 to the Representation of the People Act 1949 to an election of rural borough councillors, adaptations, alterations and exceptions shall be made therein so that the said local elections rules shall read as set out in Schedule 1 hereto.

7.—(1) The declaration of acceptance of office by the mayor of a rural borough or by a rural borough councillor shall be in the form in Schedule 2 hereto, or a form to the like effect.

(2) The declaration as to election expenses shall be in the form in Schedule 2 hereto, or a form to the like effect.

James Callaghan,
One of Her Majesty's Principal
Secretaries of State.

Home Office,
  Whitehall.
11th February 1970.

SCHEDULE 1

Election Rules

Arrangement of rules

Part I

Provisions as to Time

Part II

Stages Common to Contested and Uncontested Elections

Part III

Contested Elections

General provisions

Action to be taken before the poll

The poll

PART I

PROVISIONS AS TO TIME

Timetable

1. The proceedings at the election shall be conducted in accordance with the following Table.

TIMETABLE

Proceeding	Time
Publication of notice of election	Not later than the twenty-fifth day before the day of election.
Delivery of nomination papers	Not later than noon on the nineteenth day before the day of election.
Despatch of notices of decisions on nominations and publication of statement as to persons nominated	Not later than noon on the seventeenth day before the day of election.
Delivery of notices of withdrawals of candidature	Not later than noon on the sixteenth day before the day of election.
Notice of poll	Not later than the fifth day before the day of election.
Notice of appointment of polling or counting agents	Not later than the third day before the day of election.
Polling	On the day of election.

Computation of time

2.—(1) In computing any period of time for the purposes of the Timetable, a Sunday, day of the Christmas break, of the Easter break or of a bank holiday break or day appointed for public thanksgiving or mourning shall be disregarded and any such day shall not be treated as a day for the purpose of any proceedings up to the completion of the poll nor shall the returning officer be obliged to proceed with the counting of the votes thereon.

(2) In this rule "the Christmas break" means the period beginning with the last week day before Christmas Day and ending with the first week day after Christmas Day which is not a bank holiday, "the Easter break" means the period beginning with the Thursday before and ending with the Tuesday after Easter Day, and "a bank holiday break" means any bank holiday not included in the Christmas break or the Easter break and the period beginning with the last week day before that bank holiday and ending with the next week day which is not a bank holiday.

Hours of poll

3.—(1) The poll shall commence—

(a) where the poll is taken together with the poll at an election of rural district councillors, at the hour at which the last-mentioned poll commences;

(b) in any other case, at the hour fixed for the rural borough by the county council by any general or special order or, if no such order has been made, at noon,

and be kept open till eight o'clock in the evening of the same day and no longer:

Provided that the poll shall be kept open till nine o'clock in the evening—

(i) where the poll is taken together with the poll at an election of rural district councillors, if the poll at the last-mentioned election is kept open till nine o'clock in the evening; or

(ii) whether or not the poll is so taken, if candidates remaining validly nominated at the election of rural borough councillors to a number not less than the number of vacancies at that election have, by written notices signed by them and delivered at the place and within the time for delivery of notices of withdrawals of candidature at that election, so requested.

(2) A notice under this rule shall not have effect as respects any candidate if revoked by a further written notice signed by him and delivered as aforesaid.

PART II

STAGES COMMON TO CONTESTED AND UNCONTESTED ELECTIONS

Notice of election

4.—(1) Notice of the election in the form in the Appendix, or a form to the like effect, shall be prepared, signed and published by the returning officer.

(2) The notice shall be published by causing it to be affixed to the offices of the rural borough council and, in the case of a ward election, to be exhibited at such conspicuous places in the ward as the returning officer may determine.

Nomination of candidates

5.—(1) Each candidate shall be nominated by a separate nomination paper in the form in the Appendix, or a form to the like effect, delivered at the place fixed for the purpose.

(2) The nomination paper shall state the full names, place of residence and (if desired) description of the candidate and the surname shall be placed first in the list of his names.

(3) The description (if any) shall not exceed six words in length, and need not refer to his rank, profession or calling so long as, with the other particulars of the candidate, it is sufficient to identify him.

Subscription of nomination paper

6.—(1) The nomination paper shall be subscribed by two electors for the electoral area as proposer and seconder.

(2) Where a nomination paper bears the signatures of more than the required number of persons as proposing or seconding the nomination of a candidate, the signature appearing first on the paper in each category shall be taken into account to the exclusion of any others in that category.

(3) The nomination paper shall give the electoral number of each person subscribing it.

(4) The returning officer shall provide nomination papers and he and any other person whom he may appoint for the purpose shall supply any elector for the electoral area with as many nomination papers as may be required and shall, at the request of any such elector, prepare for signature a nomination paper.

(5) No person shall—
(*a*) subscribe more nomination papers than there are vacancies to be filled in the electoral area; or
(*b*) subscribe a nomination paper for more than one ward of a rural borough divided into wards; or
(*c*) subscribe more than one nomination paper in respect of the same candidate:

Provided that a person shall not be prevented from subscribing a nomination paper by reason only of his having subscribed that of a candidate who has died or withdrawn before delivery of the first-mentioned paper.

(6) If any person subscribes nomination papers in contravention of the last foregoing paragraph, his signature shall be inoperative in all but those papers (up to the permitted number) which are first delivered.

(7) In this rule—

the expression "elector for the electoral area" means a person who is registered as a local government elector for the electoral area in the register to be used at the election or who, pending the publication of that register, appears from the electors lists therefor as corrected by the registration officer to be entitled to be so registered (and accordingly includes a person shown in the register or electors lists as below voting age if it appears therefrom that he will be of voting age on the day fixed for the poll, but not otherwise);

the expression "electoral number" means the distinctive letter or letters of the parliamentary polling district in which a person is registered together with his number in the said register, or pending the publication of the register, the distinctive letter or letters of the parliamentary polling district in which he is entitled to be registered together with his number (if any) in the electors lists therefor.

Consent to nomination

7.—(1) A person shall not be validly nominated unless his consent to nomination, given in writing on or within one month before the last day for the delivery of nomination papers, and attested by one witness, is delivered at the place and within the time appointed for the delivery of nomination papers:

Provided that if the returning officer is satisfied that owing to the absence of a person from the United Kingdom it has not been reasonably practicable for his consent in writing to be given as aforesaid, a telegram consenting to his nomination and purporting to have been sent by him shall be deemed, for the purpose of this rule, to be consent in writing given by him on the day on which it purports to have been sent, and attestation of his consent shall not be required.

(2) A candidate's consent given under this rule shall contain a statement declaring, with reference to the date of his nomination, that to the best of his belief he will be or is qualified as required by law to be elected to and hold the office in question, and the statement shall give particulars of his qualification.

Place for delivery of nomination papers

8. Every nomination paper shall be delivered at the place fixed by the returning officer.

Decisions as to validity of nomination papers

9.—(1) Where a nomination paper and the candidate's consent thereto are delivered in accordance with these rules, the candidate shall be deemed to stand nominated unless and until the returning officer decides that the nomination paper is invalid, or proof is given to the satisfaction of the returning officer of the candidate's death, or the candidate withdraws.

(2) The returning officer shall be entitled to hold a nomination paper invalid only on one of the following grounds, that is to say:—

(a) that the particulars of the candidate or the persons subscribing the paper are not as required by law; or

(b) that the paper is not subscribed as so required.

(3) The returning officer shall examine the nomination papers, and decide whether the candidates have been validly nominated in accordance with these rules and shall do so as soon as practicable after each paper is delivered.

(4) Where he decides that a nomination paper is invalid, he shall endorse and sign on the paper the fact and the reasons for his decision.

(5) The returning officer shall send notice of his decision to each candidate at his place of residence as stated on his nomination paper.

(6) The decision of the returning officer that a nomination paper is valid shall be final and shall not be questioned in any proceeding whatsoever.

(7) Subject to the last foregoing paragraph, nothing in this rule shall prevent the validity of a nomination being questioned on an election petition.

Publication of nominations

10.—(1) The returning officer shall prepare and publish a statement in the form in the Appendix, or a form to the like effect, showing the persons who have been and stand nominated and any other persons who have been nominated, with the reason why they no longer stand nominated.

(2) The statement shall show the names, addresses and descriptions (if any) of the persons nominated as given in their nomination papers.

(3) The statement shall show the persons standing nominated arranged alphabetically in the order of their surnames, and, if there are two or more of them with the same surname, of their other names.

(4) In the case of a person nominated by more than one nomination paper, the returning officer shall take the particulars required by the foregoing provisions of this rule from such one of the papers as the candidate or the returning officer in default of the candidate may select.

(5) The statement as to persons nominated shall be published by causing it to be affixed to the place appointed for the delivery of nomination papers.

Withdrawal of candidates

11.—(1) A candidate may withdraw from his candidature by notice of withdrawal signed by him and attested by one witness and delivered at the place appointed for the delivery of nomination papers.

(2) In the case of a candidate who is outside the United Kingdom, a notice of withdrawal signed by his proposer and accompanied by a written declaration also so signed of the candidate's absence from the United Kingdom shall be of the same effect as a notice of withdrawal signed by the candidate:

Provided that where the candidate stands nominated by more than one nomination paper a notice of withdrawal under this paragraph shall be effective if, but only if—

(a) it and the accompanying declaration are signed by all the proposers, except any who is, and is stated in the said declaration to be, outside the United Kingdom; or

(b) it is accompanied, in addition to the said declaration, by a written statement signed by the candidate that the proposer giving the notice is authorised to do so on the candidate's behalf during his absence from the United Kingdom.

Nomination in more than one ward

12. A candidate who is validly nominated for more than one ward of a rural borough must duly withdraw from his candidature in all those wards except one, and if he does not so withdraw he shall be deemed to have withdrawn from his candidature in all those wards.

Method of election

13.—(1) If the number of persons remaining validly nominated for the electoral area after any withdrawals under these rules exceeds the number of vacancies, the councillors shall be elected from among them at a poll under Part III of these rules.

(2) If the said number does not exceed the number of vacancies, the person or persons (if any) deemed to be elected under the following provisions of this rule shall be declared elected in accordance with Part IV of these rules.

(3) The person or persons (if any) remaining validly nominated for the electoral area after any withdrawals under these rules shall be deemed to be elected.

(4) If, at an ordinary election of rural borough councillors, no person remains validly nominated as aforesaid, or the number of persons so remaining validly nominated is less than the number of vacancies, the retiring councillors for the electoral area who, if duly nominated, would have been qualified for election or, if their number is more than that of the vacancies not filled under paragraph (3) of this rule, such of those councillors as were highest on the poll at the last ordinary election, or as filled the places of councillors who were highest on the poll at that election, or if the poll was equal or there was no poll, as may be determined by the drawing of lots conducted under the direction of the returning officer, shall be deemed to be elected to fill up the vacancies not filled under paragraph (3) of this rule.

PART III

CONTESTED ELECTIONS

GENERAL PROVISIONS

Poll to be taken by ballot

14. The votes at the poll shall be given by ballot, the result shall be ascertained by counting the votes given to each candidate, and the candidate or candidates to whom the majority of votes have been given shall be declared to have been elected.

The ballot papers

15.—(1) The ballot of every voter shall consist of a ballot paper and the persons remaining validly nominated for the electoral area after any withdrawals under these rules, and no others, shall be entitled to have their names inserted in the ballot paper.

(2) Every ballot paper shall be in the form in the Appendix, and shall be printed in accordance with the directions therein, and—

(a) shall contain the names and other particulars of the candidates as shown in the statement of persons nominated;

(b) shall be capable of being folded up;

(c) shall have a number printed on the back;

(d) shall have attached a counterfoil with the same number printed on the face or the back;

(e) shall be of a different colour from that of any ballot papers used in an election of rural district councillors held on the same date and for the same area.

(3) The order of the names in the ballot paper shall be the same as in the statement of persons nominated.

The official mark

16.—(1) Every ballot paper shall be marked with an official mark, which shall be either embossed or perforated.

(2) The official mark shall be kept secret.

Prohibition of disclosure of vote

17. No person who has voted at the election shall, in any legal proceeding to question the election, be required to state for whom he voted.

Use of schools and public rooms

18.—(1) The returning officer may use, free of charge, for the purpose of taking the poll or of counting the votes—

(a) a room in a school maintained or assisted by a local education authority or a school in respect of which grants are made out of moneys provided by Parliament to the person or body of persons responsible for the management of the school;

(b) a room the expense of maintaining which is payable out of any rate.

(2) The returning officer shall make good any damage done to, and defray any expense incurred by the persons having control over, any such room as aforesaid by reason of its being used for the purpose of taking the poll or of counting the votes.

(3) The use of a room in an unoccupied house for the purpose of taking the poll or of counting the votes shall not render a person liable to be rated or to pay any rate for that house.

ACTION TO BE TAKEN BEFORE THE POLL

Notice of poll

19.—(1) Notice of the poll shall be published by the returning officer, and the manner of publication shall be the same as in the case of the notice of election.

(2) Notice of the poll shall specify—

(a) the day and hours fixed for the poll;

(b) the number of councillors to be elected;

(c) the particulars of each candidate remaining validly nominated (the names and other particulars of the candidates, and the order of the names of the candidates, being the same as in the statement of persons nominated);

(d) the names of the proposer and seconder signing a candidate's nomination paper; and

(e) the situation of each polling station and the description of the persons entitled to vote thereat.

(3) In the case of a candidate nominated by more than one nomination paper, the nomination paper mentioned in sub-paragraph (d) of paragraph (2) of this rule shall be that from which the names and other particulars of the candidate shown in the statement of persons nominated are taken.

Provision of polling stations

20.—(1) The returning officer shall provide a sufficient number of polling stations and, subject to the following provisions of this rule, shall allot the electors to the polling stations in such manner as he thinks most convenient.

(2) One or more polling stations may be provided in the same room.

(3) The polling station allotted to electors from any parliamentary polling district wholly or partly within the electoral area shall, in the absence of special circumstances, be in the parliamentary polling place for that district, unless the polling place is outside the electoral area.

(4) The returning officer shall provide each polling station with such number of compartments as may be necessary in which the voters can mark their votes screened from observation.

Appointment of presiding officers and clerks

21.—(1) The returning officer shall appoint and may pay a presiding officer to attend at each polling station and such clerks as may be necessary for the purposes of the election, but he shall not appoint any person who has been employed by or on behalf of a candidate in or about the election.

(2) The returning officer may, if he thinks fit, preside at a polling station and the provisions of these rules relating to a presiding officer shall apply to a returning officer so presiding with the necessary modifications as to things to be done by the returning officer to the presiding officer or by the presiding officer to the returning officer.

(3) A presiding officer may do, by the clerks appointed to assist him, any act (including the asking of questions) which he is required or authorised by these rules to do at a polling station except order the arrest, exclusion or removal of any person from the polling station.

List of proxies

22. The registration officer shall as soon as practicable prepare a special list (in these rules referred to as "the list of proxies") giving—

(a) the names and numbers on the register of the electors for whom proxies have been appointed;

(b) the names and addresses of the persons appointed.

Equipment of polling stations

23.—(1) The returning officer shall provide each presiding officer with such number of ballot boxes and ballot papers as in the opinion of the returning officer may be necessary.

(2) Every ballot box shall be so constructed that the ballot papers can be put therein, but cannot be withdrawn therefrom, without the box being unlocked.

(3) The returning officer shall provide each polling station with—

(a) materials to enable voters to mark the ballot papers;

(b) instruments for stamping thereon the official mark;

(c) copies of the register of electors for the electoral area or such part thereof as contains the names of the electors allotted to the station;

(d) the parts of the list of proxies prepared for the election corresponding to the register of electors for the electoral area or part thereof provided under the last foregoing paragraph.

(4) A notice in the form in the Appendix, giving directions for the guidance of the voters in voting, shall be printed in conspicuous characters and exhibited inside and outside every polling station.

(5) In every compartment of every polling station there shall be exhibited a notice as follows:— "The voter may vote for not more than   candidate(s)"; so however that the notice may be adapted so far as circumstances require.

Appointment of polling and counting agents

24.—(1) Each candidate may, before the commencement of the poll, appoint polling agents to attend at polling stations for the purpose of detecting personation and one or more counting agents up to the number he may be authorised by the returning officer to appoint to attend at the counting of the votes:
Provided that—

    (a) the number of counting agents authorised by the returning officer shall be the same in the case of each candidate;

    (b) the appointment of an agent may be on behalf of more than one candidate;

    (c) not more than three or, if the number of candidates exceeds twenty, four polling agents shall be appointed to attend at any polling station.

(2) If the number of polling agents appointed to attend at a polling station exceeds the permitted number, only those agents, up to the permitted number, whose appointments are signed by or on behalf of the greater number of candidates, or, in the event of an equality in the number of signatures, only such of those agents as may be determined by the returning officer, shall be deemed to have been duly appointed.

(3) Notice in writing of the appointment, stating the names and addresses of the persons appointed, shall be given by the candidate to the returning officer and shall be so given not later than the time appointed for that purpose in the Timetable.

(4) If an agent dies, or becomes incapable of acting, the candidate may appoint another agent in his place, and shall forthwith give to the returning officer notice in writing of the name and address of the agent appointed.

(5) In the following provisions of these rules references to polling and counting agents shall be taken as references to agents whose appointments have been duly made and notified and who are within the permitted number.

(6) Any notice required to be given to a counting agent by the returning officer may be delivered at, or sent by post to, the address stated in the notice of appointment.

(7) A candidate may himself do any act or thing which any polling or counting agent of his, if appointed, would have been authorised to do, or may assist his agent in doing any such act or thing.

(8) Where by these rules any act or thing is required or authorised to be done in the presence of the polling or counting agents, the non-attendance of any agents or agent at the time and place appointed for the purpose, shall not, if the act or thing is otherwise duly done, invalidate the act or thing done.

Declaration of secrecy

25.—(1) Before the opening of the poll a declaration of secrecy in the form in paragraph (4) of this rule, or in a form as near thereto as circumstances admit, shall be made by—

    (a) the returning officer and the presiding officers;

    (b) every clerk authorised to attend at a polling station or the counting of the votes;

    (c) every candidate attending at a polling station or at the counting of the votes;

    (d) every candidate's wife or husband attending at the counting of the votes;

    (e) every polling agent and counting agent;

    (f) every person permitted by the returning officer to attend at the counting of the votes, though not entitled to do so.

(2) Notwithstanding anything in the foregoing paragraph, the following persons attending at the counting of the votes, that is to say:—

    (a) any candidate;

(*b*) any candidate's wife or husband attending by virtue of the rule authorising candidates' wives or husbands to attend as such;

(*c*) any person permitted by the returning officer to attend, though not entitled to do so;

(*d*) any clerk making the declaration in order to attend at the counting of the votes;

need not make the declaration before the opening of the poll but shall make it before he or she is permitted to attend the counting, and a person becoming obliged to make a declaration by reason of his appointment after the opening of the poll shall make the declaration before acting under the appointment.

(3) The returning officer shall make the declaration in the presence of a Justice of the Peace, and any other person shall make the declaration in the presence either of a Justice of the Peace or of the returning officer, and subsections (1), (2), (3) and (6) of section 53 of the Representation of the People Act 1949 shall be read to the declarant by the person taking the declaration, or shall be read by the declarant in the presence of that person:

Provided that the declaration may be made by the returning officer or any other person before a person who is chairman of the Greater London Council, a county Council or a district council or mayor of a borough or rural borough, and may be made by a person other than the returning officer before a person who is clerk of any such council or town clerk of a borough or rural borough.

(4) The declaration shall be as follows:—

"I solemnly promise and declare that I will not at this election for the [Ward of the] Rural Borough of   do anything forbidden by subsections (1), (2), (3) and (6) of section 53 of the Representation of the People Act 1949, which have been read to [by] me."

THE POLL

Admission to polling station

26.—(1) The presiding officer shall regulate the number of voters to be admitted to the polling station at the same time, and shall exclude all other persons except—

(*a*) the candidates;

(*b*) the polling agents appointed to attend at the polling station;

(*c*) the clerks appointed to attend at the polling station;

(*d*) the constables on duty; and

(*e*) the companions of blind voters.

(2) Not more than one polling agent shall be admitted at the same time to a polling station on behalf of the same candidate.

(3) A constable or person employed by a returning officer shall not be admitted to vote in person elsewhere than at his own polling station under the provisions of the Representation of the People Act 1949 in that behalf, except on production and surrender of a certificate as to his employment which shall be in the form in the Appendix, or a form to the like effect, and signed by an officer of police of or above the rank of inspector or by the returning officer, as the case may be.

(4) Any certificate surrendered under this rule shall forthwith be cancelled.

Keeping of order in station

27.—(1) It shall be the duty of the presiding officer to keep order at his polling station.

(2) If a person misconducts himself in a polling station, or fails to obey the lawful orders of the presiding officer, he may immediately, by order of the presiding officer, be removed from the polling station by a constable in or near that station or by any other person authorised in writing by the returning officer to remove him, and the person so removed shall not, without the permission of the presiding officer, again enter the polling station during the day.

(3) Any person so removed may, if charged with the commission in the polling station of an offence, be dealt with as a person taken into custody by a constable for an offence without a warrant.

(4) The powers conferred by this rule shall not be exercised so as to prevent a voter who is otherwise entitled to vote at a polling station from having an opportunity of voting at that station.

Sealing of ballot boxes

28. Immediately before the commencement of the poll, the presiding officer shall show the ballot box empty to such persons, if any, as are present in the polling station, so that they may see that it is empty, and shall then lock it up and place his seal on it in such manner as to prevent it being opened without breaking the seal, and shall place it in his view for the receipt of ballot papers, and keep it so locked and sealed.

Questions to be put to voters

29.—(1) The presiding officer may, and if required by a candidate or his polling agent shall, put to any person applying for a ballot paper at the time of his application, but not afterwards, the following questions, or either of them, that is to say:—

(a) in the case of a person applying as an elector—

(i) Are you the person registered in the register of local government electors now in force for this rural borough [ward] as follows [read the whole entry from the register]?

(ii) Have you already voted at the present election [adding in the case of an election for several wards, in this or any other ward] otherwise than as proxy for some other person?

(b) in the case of a person applying as proxy—

(i) Are you the person whose name appears as A.B. in the list of proxies for this election as entitled to vote as proxy on behalf of C.D.?

(ii) Have you already voted here or elsewhere at the present election as proxy on behalf of C.D.?

(2) A ballot paper shall not be delivered to any person required to answer the above questions or any of them unless he has answered the questions or question satisfactorily.

(3) Save as by this rule authorised, no inquiry shall be permitted as to the right of any person to vote.

Challenge of voter

30.—(1) If at the time a person applies for a ballot paper for the purpose of voting in person, or after he has applied for a ballot paper for that purpose and before he has left the polling station, a candidate or his polling agent declares to the presiding officer that he has reasonable cause to believe that the applicant has committed an offence of personation and undertakes to substantiate the charge in a court of law, the presiding officer may order a constable to arrest the applicant, and the order of the presiding officer shall be sufficient authority for the constable so to do.

(2) A person against whom a declaration is made under this rule shall not by reason thereof be prevented from voting.

(3) A person arrested under the provisions of this rule shall be dealt with as a person taken into custody by a constable for an offence without a warrant.

Voting procedure

31.—(1) A ballot paper shall be delivered to a voter who applies therefor, and immediately before delivery—

(a) the ballot paper shall be stamped with the official mark, either embossed or perforated;

(*b*) the number, name and description of the elector as stated in the copy of the register of electors shall be called out;

(*c*) the number of the elector shall be marked on the counterfoil;

(*d*) a mark shall be placed in the register of electors against the number of the elector to denote that a ballot paper has been received but without showing the particular ballot paper which has been received; and

(*e*) in the case of a person applying for a ballot paper as proxy, a mark shall also be placed against his name in the list of proxies.

(2) The voter, on receiving the ballot paper, shall forthwith proceed into one of the compartments in the polling station and there secretly mark his paper and fold it up so as to conceal his vote, and shall then show to the presiding officer the back of the paper, so as to disclose the official mark and put the ballot paper so folded up into the ballot box in the presence of the presiding officer.

(3) The voter shall vote without undue delay, and shall leave the polling station as soon as he has put his ballot paper into the ballot box.

Votes marked by presiding officer

32.—(1) The presiding officer, on the application of—

(*a*) a voter who is incapacitated by blindness or other physical cause from voting in manner directed by these rules; or

(*b*) if the poll is taken on a Saturday, a voter who declares that he is a Jew, and objects on religious grounds to vote in manner directed by these rules; or

(*c*) a voter who declares orally that he is unable to read;

shall, in the presence of the polling agents, cause the vote of the voter to be marked on a ballot paper in manner directed by the voter, and the ballot paper to be placed in the ballot box.

(2) The name and number in the register of electors of every voter whose vote is marked in pursuance of this rule, and the reason why it is so marked, shall be entered on a list (in these rules called "the list of votes marked by the presiding officer").

In the case of a person voting as proxy for an elector, the number to be entered together with the name of the voter shall be the number of the elector.

Voting by blind persons

33.—(1) If a voter makes an application to the presiding officer to be allowed on the ground of blindness to vote with the assistance of another person by whom he is accompanied (in these rules referred to as "the companion"), the presiding officer shall require the voter to declare orally whether he is so incapacitated by his blindness as to be unable to vote without assistance.

(2) If the presiding officer is satisfied that the voter is so incapacitated and is also satisfied by a written declaration made by the companion (in these rules referred to as "the declaration made by the companion of a blind voter") that the companion is a qualified person within the meaning of this rule and has not previously assisted more than one blind person to vote at the election, the presiding officer shall grant the application, and thereupon anything which is by these rules required to be done to or by the said voter in connection with the giving of his vote may be done to, or with the assistance of, the companion.

(3) For the purposes of this rule, a person shall be qualified to assist a blind voter to vote, if that person is either—

(*a*) a person who is entitled to vote as an elector at the election; or

(*b*) the father, mother, brother, sister, husband, wife, son or daughter of the blind voter and has attained the age of eighteen years.

(4) The name and number in the register of electors of every voter whose vote is given in accordance with this rule and the name and address of the companion shall be entered on a list (in these rules referred to as "the list of blind voters assisted by companions").

In the case of a person voting as proxy for an elector, the number to be entered together with the name of the voter shall be the number of the elector.

(5) The declaration made by the companion—

(a) shall be in the form in the Appendix;

(b) shall be made before the presiding officer at the time when the voter applies to vote with the assistance of a companion and shall forthwith be given to the presiding officer who shall attest and retain it.

(6) No fee or other payment shall be charged in respect of the declaration.

Tendered ballot papers

34.—(1) If a person, representing himself to be—

(a) a particular elector named in the register; or

(b) a particular person named in the list of proxies as proxy for an elector,

applies for a ballot paper after another person has voted in person either as the elector or his proxy, the applicant shall, on satisfactorily answering the questions permitted by law to be asked at the poll, be entitled, subject to the following provisions of this rule, to mark a ballot paper (in these rules referred to as "a tendered ballot paper") in the same manner as any other voter.

(2) A tendered ballot paper shall—

(a) be of a colour differing from the other ballot papers;

(b) instead of being put into the ballot box, be given to the presiding officer and endorsed by him with the name of the voter and his number in the register of electors, and set aside in a separate packet.

(3) The name of the voter and his number in the register of electors shall be entered on a list (in these rules referred to as the "tendered votes list").

(4) In the case of a person voting as proxy for an elector, the number to be endorsed or entered together with the name of the voter shall be the number of that elector.

Spoilt ballot papers

35. A voter who has inadvertently dealt with his ballot paper in such manner that it cannot be conveniently used as a ballot paper may, on delivering it to the presiding officer and proving to his satisfaction the fact of the inadvertence, obtain another ballot paper in the place of the ballot paper so delivered (in these rules referred to as "a spoilt ballot paper"), and the spoilt ballot paper shall be immediately cancelled.

Adjournment of poll in case of riot

36. For the purpose of the adjournment of the poll in the event of riot or open violence, a presiding officer shall have the power by law belonging to a presiding officer at a parliamentary election.

Procedure on close of poll

37.—(1) As soon as practicable after the close of the poll, the presiding officer shall, in the presence of the polling agents, make up into separate packets, sealed with his own seal and the seals of such polling agents as desire to affix their seals—

(a) each ballot box in use at the station, sealed so as to prevent the introduction of additional ballot papers and unopened, but with the key attached;

(b) the unused and spoilt ballot papers placed together;

(c) the tendered ballot papers;

(d) the marked copies of the register of electors and of the list of proxies;

(e) the counterfoils of the used ballot papers and the certificates as to employment on duty on the day of the poll;

(f) the tendered votes list, the list of blind voters assisted by companions, the list of votes marked by the presiding officer, a statement of the number of voters whose votes are so marked by the presiding officer under the heads "physical incapacity", "Jews", and "unable to read" and the declarations made by the companions of blind voters;

and shall deliver the packets or cause them to be delivered to the returning officer to be taken charge of by him:

Provided that if the packets are not delivered by the presiding officer personally to the returning officer, the arrangements for their delivery shall require the approval of the returning officer.

(2) The marked copies of the register of electors and of the list of proxies shall be in one packet but shall not be in the same packet as the counterfoils of the used ballot papers and the certificates as to employment on duty on the day of the poll.

(3) The packets shall be accompanied by a statement (in these rules referred to as "the ballot paper account") made by the presiding officer showing the number of ballot papers entrusted to him, and accounting for them under the heads of ballot papers issued and not otherwise accounted for, unused, spoilt and tendered ballot papers.

COUNTING OF VOTES

Attendance at counting of votes

38.—(1) The returning officer shall make arrangements for counting the votes in the presence of the counting agents as soon as practicable after the close of the poll, and shall give to the counting agents notice in writing of the time and place at which he will begin to count the votes.

(2) No person other than—

(a) the returning officer and his clerks;

(b) the candidates and their wives or husbands;

(c) the counting agents;

may be present at the counting of the votes, unless permitted by the returning officer to attend.

(3) A person not entitled to attend at the counting of the votes shall not be permitted to do so by the returning officer unless the returning officer is satisfied that the efficient counting of the votes will not be impeded, and the returning officer has either consulted the candidates or thought it impracticable to consult them.

(4) The returning officer shall give the counting agents all such reasonable facilities for overseeing the proceedings, and all such information with reference thereto, as he can give them consistently with the orderly conduct of the proceedings and the discharge of his duties in connection therewith.

(5) In particular, where the votes are counted by sorting the ballot papers according to the candidate for whom the vote is given and then counting the number of ballot papers for each candidate, the counting agents shall be entitled to satisfy themselves that the ballot papers are correctly sorted.

The count

39.—(1) Before the returning officer proceeds to count the votes, he shall—

(a) in the presence of the counting agents open each ballot box and, taking out the ballot papers therein, count and record the number thereof and verify each ballot paper account;

(b) if polls have been taken together for the election of rural borough councillors and rural district councillors, separate the ballot papers relating to the election of rural borough councillors from those relating to rural district councillors and count and record the numbers relating to each election; and

(c) then mix together the whole of the ballot papers relating to the election of rural borough councillors contained in the ballot boxes.

(2) The returning officer shall not count any tendered ballot paper.

(3) The returning officer, while separating, counting and recording the number of ballot papers and counting the votes, shall keep the ballot papers with their faces upwards and take all proper precautions for preventing any person from seeing the numbers printed on the back of the papers.

(4) The returning officer shall verify each ballot paper account by comparing it with the number of ballot papers recorded by him, and the unused and spoilt ballot papers in his possession and the tendered votes list (opening and resealing the packets containing the unused and spoilt ballot papers and the tendered votes list) and shall draw up a statement as to the result of the verification which any counting agent may copy.

(5) The returning officer shall, so far as practicable, proceed continuously with counting the votes, allowing only time for refreshment:

Provided that he may, in so far as he thinks necessary, exclude the hours between eight o'clock in the evening and nine o'clock on the following morning.

(6) During the excluded time the returning officer shall place the ballot papers and other documents relating to the election under his own seal and the seals of such of the counting agents as desire to affix their seals and shall otherwise take proper precautions for the security of the papers and documents.

Re-count

40.—(1) A candidate may, if present when the counting or any re-count of the votes is completed, require the returning officer to have the votes re-counted or again re-counted but the returning officer may refuse to do so if in his opinion the request is unreasonable.

(2) No step shall be taken on the completion of the counting or any re-count of votes until the candidates present at the completion thereof have been given a reasonable opportunity to exercise the right conferred by this rule.

Rejected ballot papers

41.—(1) Any ballot paper—

 (a) which does not bear the official mark; or

 (b) on which votes are given for more candidates than the voter is entitled to vote for; or

 (c) on which anything is written or marked by which the voter can be identified except the printed number on the back; or

 (d) which is unmarked or void for uncertainty;

shall, subject to the provisions of this rule, be void and not counted.

(2) Where the voter is entitled to vote for more than one candidate, a ballot paper shall not be deemed to be void for uncertainty as respects any vote as to which no uncertainty arises and that vote shall be counted.

(3) A ballot paper on which a vote is marked—

 (a) elsewhere than in the proper place; or

 (b) otherwise than by means of a cross; or

 (c) by more than one mark;

shall not by reason thereof be deemed to be void (either wholly or as respects that vote), if an intention that the vote shall be for one or other of the candidates clearly appears and the way the paper is marked does not of itself identify the voter and it is not shown that he can be identified thereby.

(4) The returning officer shall endorse—

 (a) the word "rejected" on any ballot paper which under this rule is not to be counted; and

 (b) in the case of a ballot paper on which any vote is counted under paragraph (2) of this rule, the words "rejected in part" and a memorandum specifying the votes counted;

and shall add to the endorsement the words "rejection objected to" if an objection is made by a counting agent to his decision.

(5) The returning officer shall draw up a statement showing the number of ballot papers rejected, including those rejected in part, under the several heads of—

(a) want of official mark;

(b) voting for more candidates than voter is entitled to;

(c) writing or mark by which voter could be identified;

(d) unmarked or wholly void for uncertainty;

(e) rejected in part.

Decisions on ballot papers

42. The decision of the returning officer on any question arising in respect of a ballot paper shall be final, but shall be subject to review on an election petition.

Equality of votes

43. Where, after the counting of the votes (including any re-count) is completed, an equality of votes is found to exist between any candidates and the addition of a vote would entitle any of those candidates to be declared elected, the returning officer shall forthwith decide between those candidates by lot, and proceed as if the candidate on whom the lot falls had received an additional vote.

PART IV

FINAL PROCEEDINGS IN CONTESTED AND UNCONTESTED ELECTIONS

Declaration of result

44.—(1) In a contested election, when the result of the poll has been ascertained the returning officer shall forthwith declare to be elected the candidate or candidates for whom the majority of votes have been given, and shall as soon as possible publish the name or names of the candidate or candidates elected and the total number of votes given for each candidate, whether elected or not, together with the number of rejected ballot papers under each head shown in the statement of rejected ballot papers.

(2) In an uncontested election, the returning officer shall, not later than eleven o'clock in the morning on the day of election, publish the name or names of the person or persons elected.

The return

45. The returning officer shall forthwith upon declaration of the result of the election return the name of each person elected to the town clerk of the rural borough.

PART V

DISPOSAL OF DOCUMENTS

Sealing of ballot papers

46.—(1) On the completion of the counting at a contested election the returning officer shall seal up in separate packets the counted and rejected ballot papers, including ballot papers rejected in part.

(2) The returning officer shall not open the sealed packets of tendered ballot papers or of counterfoils and certificates as to employment on duty on the day of the poll, or of marked copies of the register of electors and lists of proxies.

Delivery of documents to clerk of the council

47. The returning officer shall then forward to the clerk of the council of the rural district in which the rural borough is situate the following documents, that is to say:—

(a) the packets of ballot papers in his possession;

(b) the ballot paper accounts and the statements of rejected ballot papers and of the result of the verification of the ballot paper accounts;

(*c*) the tendered votes lists, the lists of blind voters assisted by companions, the lists of votes marked by the presiding officer and the statements relating thereto, and the declarations made by the companions of blind voters;

(*d*) the packets of counterfoils and certificates as to employment on duty on the day of the poll;

(*e*) the packets containing marked copies of registers and of lists of proxies,

endorsing on each packet a description of its contents, the date of the election to which they relate and the name of the electoral area for which the election was held.

Orders for production of documents

48.—(1) An order—

(*a*) for the inspection or production of any rejected ballot papers, including ballot papers rejected in part; or

(*b*) for the opening of a sealed packet of counterfoils and certificates as to employment on duty on the day of the poll or for the inspection of counted ballot papers,

may be made by either a county court having jurisdiction in the rural borough or an election court if the court is satisfied by evidence on oath that the order is required for the purpose of instituting or maintaining a prosecution for an offence in relation to ballot papers, or for the purpose of an election petition.

(2) The order may be made subject to such conditions as to persons, time, place and mode of inspection, production or opening as the court making the order may think expedient and may direct the clerk of the rural district council having custody of the ballot papers and the sealed packets of counterfoils and certificates to retain them intact for such period as may be specified in the order:

Provided that in making and carrying into effect the order, care shall be taken that the way in which the vote of any particular elector has been given shall not be disclosed until it has been proved that his vote was given and the vote has been declared by a competent court to be invalid.

(3) An appeal shall lie to the High Court from any order of a county court made under this rule.

(4) Any power given under this rule to a county court may be exercised by any judge of the court otherwise than in open court.

(5) Where an order is made for the production by the clerk of the rural district council of any document in his possession relating to any specified election, the production by him or his agent of the document ordered in such manner as may be directed by that order shall be conclusive evidence that the document relates to the specified election; and any endorsement on any packet of ballot papers so produced shall be prima facie evidence that the ballot papers are what they are stated to be by the endorsement.

(6) The production from proper custody of a ballot paper purporting to have been used at any election, and of a counterfoil marked with the same printed number and having a number marked thereon in writing shall be prima facie evidence that the elector whose vote was given by that ballot paper was the person who at the time of the election had affixed to his name in the register of electors the same number as the number written on the counterfoil.

(7) Save as by this rule provided, no person shall be allowed to inspect any rejected or counted ballot papers in the possession of the clerk of the rural district council or to open any sealed packets of counterfoils and certificates.

Retention and public inspection of documents

49.—(1) The clerk of the rural district council shall retain for six months among the records of the rural district all documents relating to an election which are, in pursuance of these rules, forwarded to him by a returning officer or held by him and then, unless otherwise directed by an order under the last foregoing rule, shall cause them to be destroyed.

(2) The said documents, except ballot papers, counterfoils and certificates as to employment on duty on the day of the poll, shall during a period of six months from the day of election be open to public inspection at such time and in such manner as may be determined by the county council.

(3) The clerk of the rural district council shall, on request, supply copies of or extracts from the documents open to public inspection on payment of such fees, and subject to such conditions, as may be determined by the county council.

Supplemental provisions as to documents

50. Subject to the provisions of these rules, the clerk of the rural district council shall, in respect of the custody and destruction of ballot papers and other documents coming into his possession in pursuance of these rules, be subject to the directions of the rural district council.

PART VI

SUPPLEMENTAL

Countermand or abandonment of poll on death of candidate

51.—(1) If at a contested election proof is given to the satisfaction of the returning officer before the result of the election is declared that one of the persons named or to be named as candidate in the ballot papers has died, then the returning officer shall countermand the poll for the election of rural borough councillors or, if polling has begun, direct that the poll be abandoned.

(2) Where the poll is abandoned by reason of the death of a candidate, the proceedings at or consequent on that poll shall be interrupted, and the presiding officer at any polling station shall take the like steps (so far as not already taken) for the delivery to the returning officer of ballot boxes and of ballot papers and other documents as he is required to take on the close of the poll in due course, and the returning officer shall dispose of ballot papers and other documents in his possession as he is required to do on the completion in due course of the counting of the votes; but—

    (a) it shall not be necessary for any ballot paper account to be prepared or verified; and

    (b) the returning officer, without taking any step or further step for the counting of the ballot papers or of the votes, shall seal up all the ballot papers, whether the votes on them have been counted or not, and it shall not be necessary to seal up counted and rejected ballot papers in separate packets.

(3) The foregoing provisions of these rules as to the inspection, production, retention and destruction of ballot papers and other documents relating to a poll at an election shall apply to any such documents relating to a poll abandoned by reason of the death of a candidate, with the following modifications:—

    (a) ballot papers on which the votes were neither counted nor rejected shall be treated as counted ballot papers; and

    (b) no order shall be made for the production or inspection of any ballot papers or for the opening of a sealed packet of counterfoils or certificates as to employment on duty on the day of the poll unless the order is made by a court with reference to a prosecution.

General duty of returning officer

52. It shall be the general duty of the returning officer to do any act or thing that may be necessary for effectually conducting the election under these rules.

Interpretation

53.—(1) The expression "electoral area" means the rural borough or, if the rural borough is divided into wards, a ward.

(2) A reference in this Schedule to a rule shall be construed as a reference to a rule contained in this Schedule.

(3) Any reference in this Schedule to any enactment shall be taken as a reference to that enactment as amended or replaced by any other enactment.

APPENDIX

Note.—The forms contained in this Appendix may be adapted so far as circumstances require.

NOTICE OF ELECTION

Rule 4.

RURAL BOROUGH OF

ELECTION OF RURAL BOROUGH COUNCILLORS for the [
Ward of the] [Wards of the] Rural Borough.

1. An election is to be held of   Rural Borough Councillors If the notice
for the said [ward] [wards] [rural borough]. relates to more than

2. Nomination papers must be delivered at   on any day after the one election,
date of this notice, but not later than noon on the   day of   . adapt form accordingly.

3. Forms of nomination paper may be obtained from the returning officer at
       or from   at   . Either will at the
request of any local government elector for the electoral area prepare for signature a nomination paper.

4. If the election is contested, the poll will take place on the
day of   .

                        (Signed).....................................
                                       Returning Officer.

       day of   , 19 .

NOTE 1.—The attention of candidates and electors is drawn to the rules for filling up nomination papers and other provisions relating to nomination contained in the election rules in Schedule 1 to the Rural Borough Council Election Rules 1970.

NOTE 2.—Every person guilty of a corrupt or illegal practice will, on conviction, be liable to the penalties imposed by the Representation of the People Act 1949.

NOMINATION PAPER

Rule 5.

ELECTION OF RURAL BOROUGH COUNCILLORS for the [Ward of the]
Rural Borough of

Date of publication of notice of election...

We, the undersigned, being local government electors for the said [ward] [rural borough], do hereby nominate the undermentioned person as a candidate at the said election.

Candidate's surname	Other names in full	Description (if any)	Home address in full

| Signatures | Electoral Number (*see* note 3) | |
	Distinctive Letter(s)	Number
Proposer..	....	....
Seconder...	....	....

NOTE 1.—The attention of candidates and local government electors is drawn to the rules for filling up nomination papers and other provisions relating to nomination contained in the election rules in Schedule 1 to the Rural Borough Council Election Rules 1970.

NOTE 2.—Where a candidate is commonly known by some title he may be described by his title as if it where his surname.

NOTE 3.—A person's electoral number consists of the distinctive letter or letters of the parliamentary polling district in which he is registered together with his number in the register to be used at the election except that before publication of the register the distinctive letter or letters of the parliamentary polling district in which he is entitled to be registered together with his number (if any) in the electors lists for that register shall be used instead.

NOTE 4.—An elector may not—

(a) subscribe more nomination papers than there are vacancies to be filled in the electoral area; or

(b) subscribe a nomination paper for more than one ward of a rural borough divided into wards; or

(c) subscribe more than one nomination paper in respect of the same candidate.

NOTE 5.—A person whose name is entered in the register or electors lists may not subscribe a nomination paper if the entry gives as the date on which he will become of voting age a date later than the day fixed for the poll.

Rule 10.

STATEMENT AS TO PERSONS NOMINATED

RURAL BOROUGH OF

The following is a statement as to the persons nominated for election as Rural Borough Councillors for the [Ward of the] [Wards of the] Rural Borough.

[Ward] [Wards] [Rural Borough] 1.	Persons nominated				Decision of returning officer that nomination paper is invalid, or other reason why a person nominated no longer stands nominated 6.
	Surname 2.	Other names in full 3.	Home address in full 4.	Description (if any) 5.	

The persons opposite whose names no entry is made in column 6 have been and stand validly nominated.

Dated this   day of   , 19 .

....
Returning Officer.

BALLOT PAPER

Form of Front of Ballot Paper

ELECTION OF RURAL BOROUGH COUNCILLORS

Rule 15.

Counterfoil No. *The counterfoil is to have a number to correspond with that on the back of the Ballot Paper.*		
	1	**BROWN** (JOHN EDWARD Brown, of 2 The Cottages, Barlington, Grayshire, Labour.)
	2	**BROWN** (THOMAS WILLIAM Brown, of 15 Barchester Road, Barlington, Grayshire, Liberal.)
	3	**JONES** (William David Jones, of The Grange, Barlington, Grayshire, Conservative.)
	4	**MERTON** (Hon. George Travis, commonly called Viscount Merton, of Barlington, Grayshire.)
	5	**SMITH** (Mary Smith, of School House, Barlington, Grayshire, schoolteacher, Progressive.)
	6	**WILLIAMS** (Elizabeth Williams, of 3 Ivy Lane, Barlington, Grayshire, housewife.)

Form of Back of Ballot Paper

No.

Election for the [Rural Borough of   ] [Ward
of the Rural Borough of   ]   day of   ,
19 .

Note.—The number on the ballot paper is to correspond with that on the counterfoil.

Directions as to printing the ballot paper

1. Nothing is to be printed on the ballot paper except in accordance with these directions.

2. So far as practicable, the following arrangements shall be observed in the printing of the ballot paper:—

    (*a*) no word shall be printed on the face except the particulars of the candidates and a heading "ELECTION OF RURAL BOROUGH COUNCILLORS";

    (*b*) no rule shall be printed on the face except the horizontal rules separating the particulars of the candidates from one another and the vertical rules separating those particulars from the numbers on the left-hand side and the spaces on the right where the vote is to be marked;

    (*c*) the whole space beneath the heading shall be equally divided between the candidates by the rules separating their particulars.

3. The surname of each candidate shall in all cases be printed by itself in large capitals, and his full particulars shall be set out below it and shall be printed in ordinary type except that small capitals shall be used—

    (*a*) if his surname is the same as another candidate's, for his other names; and

    (*b*) if his other names are also the same as the other candidate's, either for his residence or for his description unless each of them is the same as that of another candidate with the same surname and other names.

4. The number on the back of the ballot paper shall be printed in ordinary type.

Rule 23. DIRECTIONS FOR THE GUIDANCE OF THE VOTERS IN VOTING

1. The voter should see that the ballot paper, before it is handed to him, is stamped with the official mark.

2. The voter will go into one of the compartments and, with the pencil provided in the compartment, place a cross on the right-hand side of the ballot paper, opposite the name of each candidate for whom he votes, thus X.

3. The voter will then fold up the ballot paper so as to show the official mark on the back, and leaving the compartment will, without showing the front of the paper to any person, show the official mark on the back to the presiding officer, and then, in the presence of the presiding officer, put the paper into the ballot box, and forthwith leave the polling station.

4. If the voter inadvertently spoils a ballot paper he can return it to the officer, who will, if satisfied of such inadvertence, give him another paper.

5. If the voter votes for more than   candidate(s) or places any mark on the paper by which he may afterwards be identified, his ballot paper will be void, and will not be counted.

6. If the voter fraudulently takes a ballot paper out of a polling station or fraudulently puts into the ballot box any paper other than the one given to him by the officer, he will be liable on conviction to imprisonment for a term not exceeding six months, or to a fine not exceeding twenty pounds or to both such imprisonment and such fine.

Rule 26. CERTIFICATE OF EMPLOYMENT

Election in the [Ward of the] Rural Borough of

I certify that (name)............................ who is numbered............................
in the register of electors for the electoral area named above, is likely to be unable to go in person to the polling station allotted to him at the election on (date of poll).........
......................by reason of the particular circumstances of his employment on that date—

    (a) as a constable,

    (b) by me for a purpose connected with the election.

Signature ....

*Police rank...

(Inspector or above)

*Returning Officer

Date.....................................

*Delete whichever is inapplicable.

NOTE.—The person named above is entitled to vote at any polling station of the above electoral area on production and surrender of this certificate to the presiding officer.

DECLARATION TO BE MADE BY THE COMPANION OF A BLIND VOTER

Rule 33.

I, A.B., of   , having been requested to assist C.D. [*in the case of a blind person voting as proxy add* voting as proxy for G. H.], who is numbered   on the register of local government electors for the [Rural Borough of   ] [Ward of the Rural Borough of   ], to record his vote at the election now being held for the said [rural borough] [ward], do hereby declare that [I am entitled to vote as an elector at the said election] [I am the*   of the said voter and have attained the age of eighteen years], and that I have not previously assisted any blind person [except E. F., of   ], to vote at the said election.

*State the relationship of the companion to the voter.

(Signed) A. B.

day of   , 19 .

I, the undersigned, being the presiding officer for the   polling station for the [Rural Borough of   ] [Ward of the Rural Borough of   ], do hereby certify that the above declaration, having been first read to the above-named declarant, was signed by the declarant in my presence.

(Signed) X. Y.

day of   , 19 , at   minutes past   o'clock [a.m.] [p.m.].

NOTE.—If the person making the above declaration knowingly and wilfully makes therein a statement false in a material particular, he will be guilty of an offence.

SCHEDULE 2

DECLARATION OF ACCEPTANCE OF OFFICE BY THE MAYOR OF A RURAL BOROUGH COUNCIL OR BY A RURAL BOROUGH COUNCILLOR

I, A. B., having been elected to the office of *   , hereby declare that I take the said office upon myself, and will duly and faithfully fulfil the duties thereof according to the best of my judgment and ability.

*Insert description of office.

Dated this   day of   , 19 .

Signature..................................

This declaration was made and subscribed before me
A member of the Rural Borough Council....................................

DECLARATION AS TO EXPENSES

Election for the [Ward of the] Rural Borough of

Date of publication of notice of election...

Full name of candidate...

I declare as follows:—

1. The amount paid by me or on my behalf for my election expenses at the above election was £

2. To the best of my knowledge and belief no other election expenses have been paid or incurred by me or by any other person or organization in connection with my candidature.

3. To the best of my knowledge and belief the accompanying return of election expenses is complete and correct as required by law.

4. I understand that the law does not allow any election expenses not mentioned in the return to be defrayed except in pursuance of a court order.

Signature of candidate..

EXPLANATORY NOTE

(This Note is not part of the Rules.)

These Rules revoke and replace the Rural Borough Council Election Rules 1965 with amendments consequential on the provisions of the Representation of the People Act 1969 (c.15).

STATUTORY INSTRUMENTS

1970 No. 198

CRIMINAL PROCEDURE, ENGLAND AND WALES

The Fixed Penalty (Procedure) Regulations 1970

Made - - - -	11*th February* 1970
Laid before Parliament	19*th February* 1970
Coming into Operation	1*st March* 1970

In pursuance of the powers conferred upon me by section 80(11) of the Road Traffic Regulation Act 1967(a), I hereby make the following Regulations:—

1.—(1) These Regulations may be cited as the Fixed Penalty (Procedure) Regulations 1970.

(2) (*a*) The Interpretation Act 1889(b) shall apply to the interpretation of these Regulations as it applies to the interpretation of an Act of Parliament. ·

(*b*) In these Regulations the expression "local authority" has the meaning assigned to it by section 35(4) of the Road Traffic Regulation Act 1967.

(3) These Regulations shall not extend to Scotland.

(4) These Regulations shall come into operation on 1st March 1970.

(5) The Regulations contained in Schedule 2 to these Regulations are hereby revoked.

2. A notice under section 80(2) of the Road Traffic Regulation Act 1967 offering the opportunity of the discharge of any liability to conviction of an offence to which that section applies by payment of a fixed penalty (hereafter in these Regulations referred to as "a notice") shall be in the form in Schedule 1 to these Regulations or a form to the like effect.

3. A copy of any notice given or affixed under the said section 80 shall, as soon as practicable, be forwarded by or on behalf of the constable or traffic warden giving or affixing the notice—

(*a*) to the justices' clerk to whom the fixed penalty is payable, unless the justices' clerk has notified the chief officer of police that he does not wish to receive a copy of any such notice ; and

(*b*) to the local authority for the area in which the offence alleged was committed, if that local authority has notified the chief officer of police that it wishes to receive a copy of any such notice.

4.—(1) Payment of a fixed penalty shall be made—

(*a*) if the offence alleged was committed in the inner London area, to the chief clerk at the Marylebone magistrates' court;

(*b*) if the offence alleged was committed in the south-west London area, to the clerk to the justices for the Kingston-upon-Thames petty sessional division;

(*c*) if the offence alleged was committed in the south-east London area, to the clerk to the justices for the Croydon petty sessional division;

(*d*) if the offence alleged was committed in the north-east London area, to the clerk to the justices for the Beacontree petty sessional division;

(*e*) if the offence alleged was committed in the Middlesex area, to the clerk to the justices for the Brentford petty sessional division;

(a) 1967 c. 76.   (b) 1889 c. 63.

(f) if the offence alleged was committed in the petty sessional division of Campden, Cheltenham, Newent, Northleach, Stow-on-the-Wold, Tewkesbury or Winchcombe, to the clerk to the justices for the Cheltenham petty sessional division;

(g) if the offence alleged was committed elsewhere, to the clerk to the justices for the petty sessions area in which the offence alleged was committed.

(2) In this Regulation the expressions "inner London area", "south-west London area", "south-east London area", "north-east London area" and "Middlesex area" have the meanings respectively assigned to them by section 2 of the Administration of Justice Act 1964(a).

5.—(1) The person paying a fixed penalty shall either forward with the remittance Part 2 of the relevant notice or identify the notice by specifying its serial number.

(2) If, owing to the failure of the person paying a fixed penalty to comply with the provisions of paragraph (1) of this Regulation, the justices' clerk is unable to identify the relevant notice, the clerk shall, as soon as practicable, return the remittance to that person.

6.—(1) When any payment is made in accordance with these Regulations, it shall be of the amount specified in the notice or, where payment is made in respect of more than one notice, of the total of the amounts specified in the notices.

(2) Any such amount or amounts as aforesaid shall be paid to the justices' clerk specified in the relevant notice or notices.

(3) Where any amount is paid otherwise than in accordance with the foregoing paragraphs of this Regulation, the justices' clerk may return it to the payer.

7.—(1) Where criminal proceedings in respect of the act or omission constituting the offence specified in a notice are taken by a constable, traffic warden or local authority, notification thereof shall, as soon as practicable, be given by or on behalf of the constable, traffic warden or local authority to the justices' clerk specified in the notice.

(2) The justices' clerk shall not, after receiving the said notification, accept payment of the fixed penalty to which the notice relates.

8. Subject to the foregoing provisions of these Regulations, a justices' clerk shall, as soon as practicable after payment of a fixed penalty has been made to him—

(a) send to the payer a receipt for the payment ; and

(b) notify the chief officer of police and the local authority for the area in which the offence was committed that such payment has been made, except where the chief officer of police or the local authority, as the case may be, has informed the clerk that he, or it, does not wish to be notified.

James Callaghan,
One of Her Majesty's Principal
Secretaries of State.

Home Office,
        Whitehall.
11th February 1970.

(a) 1964 c. 42.

SCHEDULE 1 Regulation 2

Serial No. (of notice)............

*NOTE: *It is an offence for anyone, other than the person liable for the under-*   *Delete if*
mentioned offence or the driver or the person in charge of the vehicle or   notice not
any person authorised by any such person, to remove or interfere with   affixed to a
this notice.   vehicle.

SECTION 80: ROAD TRAFFIC REGULATION ACT 1967

NOTICE OF OPPORTUNITY TO PAY FIXED PENALTY

PART 1

Motor vehicle, index No...was seen
in (*insert name of road*)..
[from.....................to.....................] [at..]
on the.................day of.................19 , in circumstances giving me
reasonable cause to believe that the offence described at [( )] below, was being
or had been committed.

(*here insert statement of the offence alleged as in the following examples*):—   *The use of
box numbers

*[(1)] The vehicle was waiting in a restricted street. (Section 6(9) of the Road   to indicate
Traffic Regulation Act 1967).   the different
offences is

*[(2)] The vehicle was left in a street parking place without the initial charge   optional.
being paid. (Section 42(1) of the Road Traffic Regulation Act 1967).

*[(3)] The vehicle was left in a street parking place for more than two hours
after the excess charge was incurred. (Section 42(1) of the Road
Traffic Regulation Act 1967).

Police Constable/Traffic Warden Signature ....

Number ....

If before the end of days from the above date, the sum of £
(being the fixed penalty for the offence) is paid to the clerk to the justices,
(*insert address of clerk to the justices*), the police will not take proceedings for
the offence, and any liability to conviction of the offence will be discharged.
Cash should be sent only by registered post; cheques, postal orders or money
orders should be made payable to

A receipt for the payment will be given. Payments must be of the exact
amount shown on the notice or the exact total of the various amounts, if payment
is made in respect of more than one notice. Payment must be made to the
justices' clerk specified in the notice relating to that payment. A justices' clerk
will not accept amounts which are, or include, amounts required to be paid to
another justices' clerk.

The person paying the fixed penalty must forward with the remittance Part 2
of this notice or identify this notice by quoting its serial number.

If the fixed penalty is not paid, the offender is liable to prosecution.

PART 2

Serial No. (of notice)............

To clerk to the justices (*insert address of clerk to the justices*)

I enclose the sum of £   as payment of the fixed penalty for the offence mentioned in Part 1 of this notice.

Name (in block capitals)...

Address (in block capitals)..

Regulation 1   **SCHEDULE 2**

REGULATIONS REVOKED

Regulations	References
The Fixed Penalty (Procedure) Regulations 1960	S.I. 1960/1600 (1960 I, p. 857).
The Fixed Penalty (Procedure) Regulations 1967	S.I. 1967/71 (1967 I, p. 152).
The Fixed Penalty (Procedure) (No. 2) Regulations 1967	S.I. 1967/184 (1967 I, p. 331).
The Fixed Penalty (Procedure) (No. 3) Regulations 1967	S.I. 1967/1025 (1967 II, p.3110).

EXPLANATORY NOTE

(This Note is not part of the Regulations.)

These Regulations prescribe the procedure to be followed in the enforcement of fixed penalties for certain road traffic offences under section 80 of the Road Traffic Regulation Act 1967. They consolidate with minor amendments the Fixed Penalty (Procedure) Regulations 1960 and subsequent amending regulations, which are revoked.

STATUTORY INSTRUMENTS

1970 No. 199 (C.7)

PUBLIC HEALTH, ENGLAND AND WALES

The Caravan Sites Act 1968 (Part II) (Commencement)
Order 1970

Made - - - 11*th February* 1970

The Minister of Housing and Local Government and the Secretary of State, in exercise of the power conferred on each of them by section 17(2) of the Caravan Sites Act 1968(a) in relation to England and Wales respectively, hereby make the following order :—

1. Part II of the Caravan Sites Act 1968 shall come into force in England and Wales on 1st April 1970.

2. This Order may be cited as the Caravan Sites Act 1968 (Part II) (Commencement) Order 1970.

Given under the official seal of the Minister of Housing and Local Government on 11th February 1970.

(L.S.) *Anthony Greenwood,*
Minister of Housing and Local Government.

George Thomas,
One of Her Majesty's Principal Secretaries of State.

11th February 1970.

(a) 1968 c. 52.

STATUTORY INSTRUMENTS

1970 No. 201

REPRESENTATION OF THE PEOPLE
The Parish Council Election Rules 1970

Made	- - -	11*th February* 1970
Laid before Parliament		23*rd February* 1970
Coming into Operation		1*st March* 1970

In pursuance of the powers conferred upon me by sections 29, 78 and 165(1) of the Representation of the People Act 1949(**a**) and paragraph 31(1) of Schedule 8 to the Local Government Act 1958(**b**), and by section 61 of the Local Government Act 1933(**c**), I hereby make the following Rules for the conduct of an election of parish councillors and of the chairman of a parish council, and the following Regulations prescribing the form of declaration of acceptance of office by the chairman of a parish council and by a parish councillor :—

1.—(1) These Rules and Regulations may be cited as the Parish Council Election Rules 1970 and shall come into operation on 1st March 1970.

(2) The Interpretation Act 1889(**d**) shall apply to the interpretation of these Rules and Regulations as it applies to the interpretation of an Act of Parliament.

2. The Parish Council Election Rules 1952(**e**), the Parish Council Election (No. 2) Rules 1952(**f**), the Parish Council Election Rules 1954(**g**), the Parish Council Election Rules 1959(**h**) and the Parish Council Election Rules 1962(**i**) are hereby revoked.

3.—(1) For an election of parish councillors the clerk of the council of the rural district in which the parish is situate shall be the returning officer, and if at such election the office of clerk of the rural district council is vacant or the clerk is for any reason unable to act, the chairman of the rural district council shall forthwith appoint another person to be the returning officer for that election :

Provided that where the parish councillors and any rural district councillors are to be elected on the same date and for the same area, the returning officer for the election of the rural district councillors shall be the returning officer for the election of the parish councillors.

(2) The returning officer may by writing under his hand appoint a fit person to be his deputy for all or any of the purposes of an election, but where the parish councillors and any rural district councillors are to be elected on the same date and for the same area and a person is appointed deputy for any of the purposes of the election of the rural district councillors, that person shall be deemed to be appointed the returning officer's deputy for the corresponding

---

(**a**) 1949 c. 68.
(**c**) 1933 c. 51.
(**e**) S.I. 1952/91 (1952 III, p. 2795).
(**g**) S.I. 1954/1483 (1954 II, p. 1918).
(**i**) S.I. 1962/1267 (1962 II, p. 1369).

(**b**) 1958 c. 55.
(**d**) 1889 c. 63.
(**f**) S.I. 1952/368 (1952 III, p. 2820).
(**h**) S.I. 1959/431 (1959 II, p. 2309).

purposes of the election of the parish councillors ; and any functions which a returning officer is authorised or required to discharge in relation to the election may be discharged by a deputy so appointed.

(3) A deputy acting as returning officer under the provisions of this Rule shall, as respects the election for which he is so acting, follow the instructions of the returning officer.

4. Where the poll at an election of rural district councillors is taken together with the poll at an election of parish councillors, one ballot box may, if the returning officer thinks fit, be used for the two elections ; but, if separate ballot boxes are used, no vote for any parish councillor shall be rendered invalid by the ballot paper being placed in the box intended for the reception of ballot papers for rural district councillors.

5. In the application of those provisions of the Representation of the People Act 1949 referred to in section 165(1) of that Act to an election of the chairman of a parish council and of parish councillors the following adaptation and modification shall have effect :—

For any reference to the clerk of the authority for which the election is held there shall be substituted a reference to the clerk of the council of the rural district in which the parish is situate.

In section 119(2)(*b*) of the said Act for the words "such amount not exceeding five hundred pounds" there shall be substituted the words "an amount of fifty pounds or such smaller amount or such larger amount not exceeding three hundred pounds".

6. In the application of the local elections rules contained in Schedule 2 to the Representation of the People Act 1949 to an election of parish councillors, adaptations, alterations and exceptions shall be made therein so that the said local elections rules shall read as set out in Schedule 1 hereto.

7.—(1) The declaration of acceptance of office by the chairman of a parish council or by a parish councillor shall be in the form in Schedule 2 hereto, or a form to the like effect.

(2) The declaration as to election expenses shall be in the form in Schedule 2 hereto, or a form to the like effect.

James Callaghan,
One of Her Majesty's Principal
Secretaries of State.

Home Office,
Whitehall
11th February 1970.

SCHEDULE 1

ELECTION RULES

Arrangement of rules

PART I

PROVISIONS AS TO TIME

Rule
1. Timetable.
2. Computation of time.
3. Hours of poll.

PART II

STAGES COMMON TO CONTESTED AND UNCONTESTED ELECTIONS

4. Notice of election.
5. Nomination of candidates.
6. Subscription of nomination paper.
7. Consent to nomination.
8. Place for delivery of nomination papers.
9. Decisions as to validity of nomination papers.
10. Publication of nominations.
11. Withdrawal of candidates.
12. Nomination in more than one ward.
13. Method of election.

PART III

CONTESTED ELECTIONS

General provisions

14. Poll to be taken by ballot.
15. The ballot papers.
16. The official mark.
17. Prohibition of disclosure of vote.
18. Use of schools and public rooms.

Action to be taken before the poll

19. Notice of poll.
20. Provision of polling stations.
21. Appointment of presiding officers and clerks.
22. List of proxies.
23. Equipment of polling stations.
24. Appointment of polling and counting agents.
25. Declaration of secrecy.

The poll

Counting of votes

PART. IV
FINAL PROCEEDINGS IN CONTESTED AND UNCONTESTED ELECTIONS

PART V
DISPOSAL OF DOCUMENTS

PART VI
SUPPLEMENTAL

APPENDIX
FORMS

Part I

Provisions as to Time

Timetable

1. The proceedings at the election shall be conducted in accordance with the following Table.

Timetable

Proceeding	Time
Publication of notice of election ...	Not later than the twenty-fifth day before the day of election.
Delivery of nomination papers ...	Not later than noon on the nineteenth day before the day of election.
Despatch of notices of decisions on nominations and publication of statement as to persons nominated	Not later than noon on the seventeenth day before the day of election.
Delivery of notices of withdrawals of candidature	Not later than noon on the sixteenth day before the day of election.
Notice of poll	Not later than the fifth day before the day of election.
Notice of appointment of polling or counting agents	Not later than the third day before the day of election.
Polling	On the day of election.

Computation of time

2.—(1) In computing any period of time for the purposes of the Timetable, a Sunday, day of the Christmas break, of the Easter break or of a bank holiday break or day appointed for public thanksgiving or mourning shall be disregarded and any such day shall not be treated as a day for the purpose of any proceedings up to the completion of the poll nor shall the returning officer be obliged to proceed with the counting of the votes thereon.

(2) In this rule "the Christmas break" means the period beginning with the last week day before Christmas Day and ending with the first week day after Christmas Day which is not a bank holiday, "the Easter break" means the period beginning with the Thursday before and ending with the Tuesday after Easter Day, and "a bank holiday break" means any bank holiday not included in the Christmas break or the Easter break and the period beginning with the last week day before that bank holiday and ending with the next week day which is not a bank holiday.

Hours of poll

3.—(1) The poll shall commence—

(a) where the poll is taken together with the poll at an election of rural district councillors, at the hour at which the last-mentioned poll commences ;

(b) in any other case, at the hour fixed for the parish by the county council by any general or special order or, if no such order has been made, at noon,

and be kept open till eight o'clock in the evening of the same day and no longer :

Provided that the poll shall be kept open till nine o'clock in the evening—

(i) where the poll is taken together with the poll at an election of rural district councillors, if the poll at the last-mentioned election is kept open till nine o'clock in the evening ; or

(ii) whether or not the poll is so taken, if candidates remaining validly nominated at the election of parish councillors to a number not less than the number of vacancies at that election have, by written notices signed by them and delivered at the place and within the time for delivery of notices of withdrawals of candidature at that election, so requested.

(2) A notice under this rule shall not have effect as respects any candidate if revoked by a further written notice signed by him and delivered as aforesaid.

PART II

STAGES COMMON TO CONTESTED AND UNCONTESTED ELECTIONS

Notice of election

4.—(1) Notice of the election in the form in the Appendix, or a form to the like effect, shall be prepared, signed and published by the returning officer.

(2) The notice shall be published—

(a) by causing it to be exhibited in some conspicuous place on or near the principal door of each church or chapel in the electoral area ; and

(b) by causing it to be exhibited in some other conspicuous place or places in the electoral area ; and

(c) in such other manner, if any, as the returning officer thinks desirable for giving publicity to the notice.

Nomination of candidates

5.—(1) Each candidate shall be nominated by a separate nomination paper in the form in the Appendix, or a form to the like effect, delivered at the place fixed for the purpose.

(2) The nomination paper shall state the full names, place of residence and (if desired) description of the candidate and the surname shall be placed first in the list of his names.

(3) The description (if any) shall not exceed six words in length, and need not refer to his rank, profession or calling so long as, with the other particulars of the candidate, it is sufficient to identify him.

Subscription of nomination paper

6.—(1) The nomination paper shall be subscribed by two electors for the electoral area as proposer and seconder.

(2) Where a nomination paper bears the signatures of more than the required number of persons as proposing or seconding the nomination of a candidate, the signature appearing first on the paper in each category shall be taken into account to the exclusion of any others in that category.

(3) The nomination paper shall give the electoral number of each person subscribing it.

(4) The returning officer shall provide nomination papers and he and any other person whom he may appoint for the purpose shall supply any elector for the electoral area with as many nomination papers as may be required and shall, at the request of any such elector, prepare for signature a nomination paper.

(5) No person shall—

(a) subscribe more nomination papers than there are vacancies to be filled in the electoral area ; or

(b) subscribe a nomination paper for more than one ward of a parish divided into wards ; or

(c) subscribe more than one nomination paper in respect of the same candidate :

Provided that a person shall not be prevented from subscribing a nomination paper by reason only of his having subscribed that of a candidate who has died or withdrawn before delivery of the first-mentioned paper.

(6) If any person subscribes nomination papers in contravention of the last foregoing paragraph, his signature shall be inoperative in all but those papers (up to the permitted number) which are first delivered.

(7) In this rule—

the expression "elector for the electoral area" means a person who is registered as a local government elector for the electoral area in the register to be used at the election or who, pending the publication of that register, appears from the electors lists therefor as corrected by the registration officer to be entitled to be so registered (and accordingly includes a person shown in the register or electors lists as below voting age if it appears therefrom that he will be of voting age on the day fixed for the poll, but not otherwise) ;

the expression "electoral number" means the distinctive letter or letters of the parliamentary polling district in which a person is registered together with his number in the said register, or pending the publication of the register, the distinctive letter or letters of the parliamentary polling district in which he is entitled to be registered together with his number (if any) in the electors lists therefor.

Consent to nomination

7.—(1) A person shall not be validly nominated unless his consent to nomination, giving in writing on or within one month before the last day for the delivery of nomination papers, and attested by one witness, is delivered at the place and within the time appointed for the delivery of nomination papers:

Provided that if the returning officer is satisfied that owing to the absence of a person from the United Kingdom it has not been reasonably practicable for his consent in writing to be given as aforesaid, a telegram consenting to his nomination and purporting to have been sent by him shall be deemed, for the purpose of this rule, to be consent in writing given by him on the day on which it purports to have been sent, and attestation of his consent shall not be required.

(2) A candidate's consent given under this rule shall contain a statement declaring, with reference to the date of his nomination, that to the best of his belief he will be or is qualified as required by law to be elected to and hold the office in question, and the statement shall give particulars of his qualification.

Place for delivery of nomination papers

8. Every nomination paper shall be delivered at the place fixed by the returning officer.

Decisions as to validity of nomination papers

9.—(1) Where a nomination paper and the candidate's consent thereto are delivered in accordance with these rules, the candidate shall be deemed to stand nominated unless and until the returning officer decides that the nomination paper is invalid, or proof is given to the satisfaction of the returning officer of the candidate's death, or the candidate withdraws.

(2) The returning officer shall be entitled to hold a nomination paper invalid only on one of the following grounds, that is to say:—

(a) that the particulars of the candidate or the persons subscribing the paper are not as required by law ; or

(b) that the paper is not subscribed as so required.

(3) The returning officer shall examine the nomination papers, and decide whether the candidates have been validly nominated in accordance with these rules and shall do so as soon as practicable after each paper is delivered.

(4) Where he decides that a nomination paper is invalid, he shall endorse and sign on the paper the fact and the reasons for his decision.

(5) The returning officer shall send notice of his decision to each candidate at his place of residence as stated on his nomination paper.

(6) The decision of the returning officer that a nomination paper is valid shall be final and shall not be questioned in any proceeding whatsoever.

(7) Subject to the last foregoing paragraph, nothing in this rule shall prevent the validity of a nomination being questioned on an election petition.

Publication of nominations

10.—(1) The returning officer shall prepare and publish a statement in the form in the Appendix, or a form to the like effect, showing the persons who have been and stand nominated and any other persons who have been nominated, with the reason why they no longer stand nominated.

(2) The statement shall show the names, addresses and descriptions (if any) of the persons nominated as given in their nomination papers.

(3) The statement shall show the persons standing nominated arranged alphabetically in the order of their surnames, and, if there are two or more of them with the same surname, of their other names.

(4) In the case of a person nominated by more than one nomination paper, the returning officer shall take the particulars required by the foregoing provisions of this rule from such one of the papers as the candidate or the returning officer in default of the candidate may select.

(5) The statement as to persons nominated shall be published by causing it to be affixed to the place appointed for the delivery of nomination papers.

Withdrawal of candidates

11.—(1) A candidate may withdraw from his candidature by notice of withdrawal signed by him and attested by one witness and delivered at the place appointed for the delivery of nomination papers.

(2) In the case of a candidate who is outside the United Kingdom, a notice of withdrawal signed by his proposer and accompanied by a written declaration also so signed of the candidate's absence from the United Kingdom shall be of the same effect as a notice of withdrawal signed by the candidate:

Provided that where the candidate stands nominated by more than one nomination paper a notice of withdrawal under this paragraph shall be effective if, but only if—

(a) it and the accompanying declaration are signed by all the proposers, except any who is, and is stated in the said declaration to be, outside the United Kingdom ; or

(b) it is accompanied, in addition to the said declaration, by a written statement signed by the candidate that the proposer giving the notice is authorised to do so on the candidate's behalf during his absence from the United Kingdom.

Nomination in more than one ward

12. A candidate who is validly nominated for more than one ward of a parish must duly withdraw from his candidature in all those wards except one, and if he does not so withdraw he shall be deemed to have withdrawn from his candidature in all those wards.

Method of election

13.—(1) If the number of persons remaining validly nominated for the electoral area after any withdrawals under these rules exceeds the number of vacancies, the councillors shall be elected from among them at a poll under Part III of these rules.

(2) If the said number does not exceed the number of vacancies, the person or persons (if any) deemed to be elected under the following provisions of this rule shall be declared elected in accordance with Part IV of these rules.

(3) The person or persons (if any) remaining validly nominated for the electoral area after any withdrawals under these rules shall be deemed to be elected.

(4) If, at an ordinary election of parish councillors, no person remains validly nominated as aforesaid, or the number of persons so remaining validly nominated is less than the number of vacancies, the retiring councillors for the electoral area who, if duly nominated, would have been qualified for election or, if their number is more than that of the vacancies not filled under paragraph (3) of this rule, such of those councillors as were highest on the poll at the last ordinary election, or as filled the places of councillors who were highest on the poll at that election, or if the poll was equal or there was no poll, as may be determined by the drawing of lots conducted under the direction of the returning officer, shall be deemed to be elected to fill up the vacancies not filled under paragraph (3) of this rule.

PART III

CONTESTED ELECTIONS

GENERAL PROVISIONS

Poll to be taken by ballot

14. The votes at the poll shall be given by ballot, the result shall be ascertained by counting the votes given to each candidate, and the candidate or candidates to whom the majority of votes have been given shall be declared to have been elected.

The ballot papers

15.—(1) The ballot of every voter shall consist of a ballot paper and the persons remaining validly nominated for the electoral area after any withdrawals under these rules, and no others, shall be entitled to have their names inserted in the ballot paper.

(2) Every ballot paper shall be in the form in the Appendix, and shall be printed in accordance with the directions therein, and—

    (a) shall contain the names and other particulars of the candidates as shown in the statement of persons nominated ;

    (b) shall be capable of being folded up ;

    (c) shall have a number printed on the back ;

    (d) shall have attached a counterfoil with the same number printed on the face or the back ;

    (e) shall be of a different colour from that of any ballot papers used in an election of rural district councillors held on the same date and for the same area.

(3) The order of the names in the ballot paper shall be the same as in the statement of persons nominated.

The official mark

16.—(1) Every ballot paper shall be marked with an official mark, which shall be either embossed or perforated.

(2) The official mark shall be kept secret.

Prohibition of disclosure of vote

17. No person who has voted at the election shall, in any legal proceeding to question the election, be required to state for whom he voted.

Use of schools and public rooms

18.—(1) The returning officer may use, free of charge, for the purpose of taking the poll or of counting the votes—

    (a) a room in a school maintained or assisted by a local education authority or a school in respect of which grants are made out of moneys provided by Parliament to the person or body of persons responsible for the management of the school ;

(b) a room the expense of maintaining which is payable out of any rate.

(2) The returning officer shall make good any damage done to, and defray any expense incurred by the persons having control over, any such room as aforesaid by reason of its being used for the purpose of taking the poll or of counting the votes.

(3) The use of a room in an unoccupied house for the purpose of taking the poll or of counting the votes shall not render a person liable to be rated or to pay any rate for that house.

ACTION TO BE TAKEN BEFORE THE POLL

Notice of poll

19.—(1) Notice of the poll shall be published by the returning officer, and the manner of publication shall be the same as in the case of the notice of election.

(2) Notice of the poll shall specify—

(a) the day and hours fixed for the poll ;

(b) the number of councillors to be elected ;

(c) the particulars of each candidate remaining validly nominated (the names and other particulars of the candidates, and the order of the names of the candidates, being the same as in the statement of persons nominated) ;

(d) the names of the proposer and seconder signing a candidate's nomination paper ; and

(e) the situation of each polling station and the description of the persons entitled to vote thereat.

(3) In the case of a candidate nominated by more than one nomination paper, the nomination paper mentioned in sub-paragraph (d) of paragraph (2) of this rule shall be that from which the names and other particulars of the candidate shown in the statement of persons nominated are taken.

Provision of polling stations

20.—(1) The returning officer shall provide a sufficient number of polling stations and, subject to the following provisions of this rule, shall allot the electors to the polling stations in such manner as he thinks most convenient.

(2) One or more polling stations may be provided in the same room.

(3) The polling station allotted to electors from any parliamentary polling district wholly or partly within the electoral area shall, in the absence of special circumstances, be in the parliamentary polling place for that district, unless the polling place is outside the electoral area.

(4) The returning officer shall provide each polling station with such number of compartments as may be necessary in which the voters can mark their votes screened from observation.

Appointment of presiding officers and clerks

21.—(1) The returning officer shall appoint and may pay a presiding officer to attend at each polling station and such clerks as may be necessary for the purposes of the election, but he shall not appoint any person who has been employed by or on behalf of a candidate in or about the election.

(2) The returning officer may, if he thinks fit, preside at a polling station and the provisions of these rules relating to a presiding officer shall apply to a returning officer so presiding with the necessary modifications as to things to be done by the returning officer to the presiding officer or by the presiding officer to the returning officer.

(3) A presiding officer may do, by the clerks appointed to assist him, any act (including the asking of questions) which he is required or authorised by these rules to do at a polling station except order the arrest, exclusion or removal of any person from the polling station.

List of proxies

22. The registration officer shall as soon as practicable prepare a special list (in these rules referred to as "the list of proxies") giving—

(a) the names and numbers on the register of the electors for whom proxies have been appointed ;

(b) the names and addresses of the persons appointed.

Equipment of polling stations

23.—(1) The returning officer shall provide each presiding officer with such number of ballot boxes and ballot papers as in the opinion of the returning officer may be necessary.

(2) Every ballot box shall be so constructed that the ballot papers can be put therein, but cannot be withdrawn therefrom, without the box being unlocked.

(3) The returning officer shall provide each polling station with—

(a) materials to enable voters to mark the ballot papers ;

(b) instruments for stamping thereon the official mark ;

(c) copies of the register of electors for the electoral area or such part thereof as contains the names of the electors allotted to the station ;

(d) the parts of the list of proxies prepared for the election corresponding to the register of electors for the electoral area or part thereof provided under the last foregoing paragraph.

(4) A notice in the form in the Appendix, giving directions for the guidance of the voters in voting, shall be printed in conspicuous characters and exhibited inside and outside every polling station.

(5) In every compartment of every polling station there shall be exhibited a notice as follows:— "The voter may vote for not more than   candidate(s)" ; so however that the notice may be adapted so far as circumstances require.

Appointment of polling and counting agents

24.—(1) Each candidate may, before the commencement of the poll, appoint polling agents to attend at polling stations for the purpose of detecting personation and one or more counting agents up to the number he may be authorised by the returning officer to appoint to attend at the counting of the votes:

Provided that—

(a) the number of counting agents authorised by the returning officer shall be the same in the case of each candidate ;

(b) the appointment of an agent may be on behalf of more than one candidate ;

(c) not more than three or, if the number of candidates exceeds twenty, four polling agents shall be appointed to attend at any polling station.

(2) If the number of polling agents appointed to attend at a polling station exceeds the permitted number, only those agents, up to the permitted number, whose appointments are signed by or on behalf of the greater number of candidates, or, in the event of an equality in the number of signatures, only such of those agents as may be determined by the returning officer, shall be deemed to have been duly appointed.

(3) Notice in writing of the appointment, stating the names and addresses of the persons appointed, shall be given by the candidate to the returning officer and shall be so given not later than the time appointed for that purpose in the Time-table.

(4) If an agent dies, or becomes incapable of acting, the candidate may appoint another agent in his place, and shall forthwith give to the returning officer notice in writing of the name and address of the agent appointed.

(5) In the following provisions of these rules references to polling and counting agents shall be taken as references to agents whose appointments have been duly made and notified and who are within the permitted number.

(6) Any notice required to be given to a counting agent by the returning officer may be delivered at, or sent by post to, the address stated in the notice of appointment.

(7) A candidate may himself do any act or thing which any polling or counting agent of his, if appointed, would have been authorised to do, or may assist his agent in doing any such act or thing.

(8) Where by these rules any act or thing is required or authorised to be done in the presence of the polling or counting agents, the non-attendance of any agents or agent at the time and place appointed for the purpose, shall not, if the act or thing is otherwise duly done, invalidate the act or thing done.

Declaration of secrecy

25.—(1) Before the opening of the poll a declaration of secrecy in the form in paragraph (4) of this rule, or in a form as near thereto as circumstances admit, shall be made by—

(a) the returning officer and the presiding officers ;

(b) every clerk authorised to attend at a polling station or the counting of the votes ;

(c) every candidate attending at a polling station or at the counting of the votes ;

(d) every candidate's wife or husband attending at the counting of the votes ;

(e) every polling agent and counting agent ;

(f) every person permitted by the returning officer to attend at the counting of the votes, though not entitled to do so.

(2) Notwithstanding anything in the foregoing paragraph, the following persons attending at the counting of the votes, that is to say :—

(a) any candidate ;

(b) any candidate's wife or husband attending by virtue of the rule authorising candidates' wives or husbands to attend as such ;

(c) any person permitted by the returning officer to attend, though not entitled to do so ;

(d) any clerk making the declaration in order to attend at the counting of the votes ;

need not make the declaration before the opening of the poll but shall make it before he or she is permitted to attend the counting, and a person becoming obliged to make a declaration by reason of his appointment after the opening of the poll shall make the declaration before acting under the appointment.

(3) The returning officer shall make the declaration in the presence of a Justice of the Peace, and any other person shall make the declaration in the presence either of a Justice of the Peace or of the returning officer, and subsections (1), (2), (3) and (6) of section 53 of the Representation of the People Act 1949 shall be read to the declarant by the person taking the declaration, or shall be read by the declarant in the presence of that person:

Provided that the declaration may be made by the returning officer or any other person before a person who is chairman of the Greater London Council, a county council or a district council or mayor of a borough or rural borough, and may be made by a person other than the returning officer before a person who is clerk of any such council or town clerk of a borough or rural borough.

(4) The declaration shall be as follows:—

"I solemnly promise and declare that I will not at this election for the [Ward of the] Parish of   do anything forbidden by subsections (1), (2), (3) and (6) of section 53 of the Representation of the People Act 1949, which have been read to [by] me."

THE POLL

Admission to polling station

26.—(1) The presiding officer shall regulate the number of voters to be admitted to the polling station at the same time, and shall exclude all other persons except—

(a) the candidates ;

(b) the polling agents appointed to attend at the polling station ;

(c) the clerks appointed to attend at the polling station ;

(d) the constables on duty ; and

(e) the companions of blind voters.

(2) Not more than one polling agent shall be admitted at the same time to a polling station on behalf of the same candidate.

(3) A constable or person employed by a returning officer shall not be admitted to vote in person elsewhere than at his own polling station under the provisions of the Representation of the People Act 1949 in that behalf, except on production and surrender of a certificate as to his employment which shall be in the form in the Appendix, or a form to the like effect, and signed by an officer of police of or above the rank of inspector or by the returning officer, as the case may be.

(4) Any certificate surrendered under this rule shall forthwith be cancelled.

Keeping of order in station

27.—(1) It shall be the duty of the presiding officer to keep order at his polling station.

(2) If a person misconducts himself in a polling station, or fails to obey the lawful orders of the presiding officer, he may immediately, by order of the presiding officer, be removed from the polling station by a constable in or near that station or by any other person authorised in writing by the returning officer to remove him, and the person so removed shall not, without the permission of the presiding officer, again enter the polling station during the day.

(3) Any person so removed may, if charged with the commission in the polling station of an offence, be dealt with as a person taken into custody by a constable for an offence without a warrant.

(4) The powers conferred by this rule shall not be exercised so as to prevent a voter who is otherwise entitled to vote at a polling station from having an opportunity of voting at that station.

Sealing of ballot boxes

28. Immediately before the commencement of the poll, the presiding officer shall show the ballot box empty to such persons, if any, as are present in the polling station, so that they may see that it is empty, and shall then lock it up and place his seal on it in such manner as to prevent it being opened without breaking the seal, and shall place it in his view for the receipt of ballot papers, and keep it so locked and sealed.

Questions to be put to voters

29.—(1) The presiding officer may, and if required by a candidate or his polling agent shall, put to any person applying for a ballot paper at the time of his application, but not afterwards, the following questions, or either of them, that is to say: —

(a) in the case of a person applying as an elector—

    (i) Are you the person registered in the register of local government electors now in force for this parish [ward] as follows [read the whole entry from the register]?

    (ii) Have you already voted at the present election [adding in the case of an election for several wards, in this or any other ward] otherwise than as proxy for some other person?

(b) in the case of a person applying as proxy—

    (i) Are you the person whose name appears as A.B. in the list of proxies for this election as entitled to vote as proxy on behalf of C.D.?

    (ii) Have you already voted here or elsewhere at the present election as proxy on behalf of C.D.?

(2) A ballot paper shall not be delivered to any person required to answer the above questions or any of them unless he has answered the questions or question satisfactorily.

(3) Save as by this rule authorised, no inquiry shall be permitted as to the right of any person to vote.

Challenge of voter

30.—(1) If at the time a person applies for a ballot paper for the purpose of voting in person, or after he has applied for a ballot paper for that purpose and before he has left the polling station, a candidate or his polling agent declares to the presiding officer that he has reasonable cause to believe that the applicant has committed an offence of personation and undertakes to substantiate the charge in a court of law, the presiding officer may order a constable to arrest the applicant, and the order of the presiding officer shall be sufficient authority for the constable so to do.

(2) A person against whom a declaration is made under this rule shall not by reason thereof be prevented from voting.

(3) A person arrested under the provisions of this rule shall be dealt with as a person taken into custody by a constable for an offence without a warrant.

Voting procedure

31.—(1) A ballot paper shall be delivered to a voter who applies therefor, and immediately before delivery—

(a) the ballot paper shall be stamped with the official mark, either embossed or perforated ;

(b) the number, name and description of the elector as stated in the copy of the register of electors shall be called out ;

(c) the number of the elector shall be marked on the counterfoil ;

(d) a mark shall be placed in the register of electors against the number of the elector to denote that a ballot paper has been received but without showing the particular ballot paper which has been received ; and

(e) in the case of a person applying for a ballot paper as proxy, a mark shall also be placed against his name in the list of proxies.

(2) The voter, on receiving the ballot paper, shall forthwith proceed into one of the compartments in the polling station and there secretly mark his paper and fold it up so as to conceal his vote, and shall then show to the presiding officer the back of the paper, so as to disclose the official mark and put the ballot paper so folded up into the ballot box in the presence of the presiding officer.

(3) The voter shall vote without undue delay, and shall leave the polling station as soon as he has put his ballot paper into the ballot box.

Votes marked by presiding officer

32.—(1) The presiding officer, on the application of—

    (*a*) a voter who is incapacitated by blindness or other physical cause from voting in manner directed by these rules ; or

    (*b*) if the poll is taken on a Saturday, a voter who declares that he is a Jew, and objects on religious grounds to vote in manner directed by these rules ; or

    (*c*) a voter who declares orally that he is unable to read ;

shall, in the presence of the polling agents, cause the vote of the voter to be marked on a ballot paper in manner directed by the voter, and the ballot paper to be placed in the ballot box.

(2) The name and number in the register of electors of every voter whose vote is marked in pursuance of this rule, and the reason why it is so marked, shall be entered on a list (in these rules called "the list of votes marked by the presiding officer").

In the case of a person voting as proxy for an elector, the number to be entered together with the name of the voter shall be the number of the elector.

Voting by blind persons

33.—(1) If a voter makes an application to the presiding officer to be allowed on the ground of blindness to vote with the assistance of another person by whom he is accompanied (in these rules referred to as "the companion"), the presiding officer shall require the voter to declare orally whether he is so incapacitated by his blindness as to be unable to vote without assistance.

(2) If the presiding officer is satisfied that the voter is so incapacitated and is also satisfied by a written declaration made by the companion (in these rules referred to as "the declaration made by the companion of a blind voter") that the companion is a qualified person within the meaning of this rule and has not previously assisted more than one blind person to vote at the election, the presiding officer shall grant the application, and thereupon anything which is by these rules required to be done to or by the said voter in connection with the giving of his vote may be done to, or with the assistance of, the companion.

(3) For the purposes of this rule, a person shall be qualified to assist a blind voter to vote, if that person is either—

    (*a*) a person who is entitled to vote as an elector at the election ; or

    (*b*) the father, mother, brother, sister, husband, wife, son or daughter of the blind voter and has attained the age of eighteen years.

(4) The name and number in the register of electors of every voter whose vote is given in accordance with this rule and the name and address of the companion shall be entered on a list (in these rules referred to as "the list of blind voters assisted by companions").

In the case of a person voting as proxy for an elector, the number to be entered together with the name of the voter shall be the number of the elector.

(5) The declaration made by the companion—

    (*a*) shall be in the form in the Appendix ;

    (*b*) shall be made before the presiding officer at the time when the voter applies to vote with the assistance of a companion and shall forthwith be given to the presiding officer who shall attest and retain it.

(6) No fee or other payment shall be charged in respect of the declaration.

Tendered ballot papers

34.—(1) If a person, representing himself to be—

(a) a particular elector named in the register ; or

(b) a particular person named in the list of proxies as proxy for an elector,

applies for a ballot paper after another person has voted in person either as the elector or his proxy, the applicant shall, on satisfactorily answering the questions permitted by law to be asked at the poll, be entitled, subject to the following provisions of this rule, to mark a ballot paper (in these rules referred to as "a tendered ballot paper") in the same manner as any other voter.

(2) A tendered ballot paper shall—

(a) be of a colour differing from the other ballot papers;

(b) instead of being put into the ballot box, be given to the presiding officer and endorsed by him with the name of the voter and his number in the register of electors, and set aside in a separate packet.

(3) The name of the voter and his number in the register of electors shall be entered on a list (in these rules referred to as the "tendered votes list").

(4) In the case of a person voting as proxy for an elector, the number to be endorsed or entered together with the name of the voter shall be the number of that elector.

Spoilt ballot papers

35. A voter who has inadvertently dealt with his ballot paper in such manner that it cannot be conveniently used as a ballot paper may, on delivering it to the presiding officer and proving to his satisfaction the fact of the inadvertence, obtain another ballot paper in the place of the ballot paper so delivered (in these rules referred to as "a spoilt ballot paper"), and the spoilt ballot paper shall be immediately cancelled.

Adjournment of poll in case of riot

36. For the purpose of the adjournment of the poll in the event of riot or open violence, a presiding officer shall have the power by law belonging to a presiding officer at a parliamentary election.

Procedure on close of poll

37.—(1) As soon as practicable after the close of the poll, the presiding officer shall, in the presence of the polling agents, make up into separate packets, sealed with his own seal and the seals of such polling agents as desire to affix their seals—

(a) each ballot box in use at the station, sealed so as to prevent the introduction of additional ballot papers and unopened, but with the key attached;

(b) the unused and spoilt ballot papers placed together;

(c) the tendered ballot papers;

(d) the marked copies of the register of electors and of the list of proxies;

(e) the counterfoils of the used ballot papers and the certificates as to employment on duty on the day of the poll;

(f) the tendered votes list, the list of blind voters assisted by companions, the list of votes marked by the presiding officer, a statement of the number of voters whose votes are so marked by the presiding officer under the heads "physical incapacity", "Jews", and "unable to read" and the declarations made by the companions of blind voters;

and shall deliver the packets or cause them to be delivered to the returning officer to be taken charge of by him:

Provided that if the packets are not delivered by the presiding officer personally to the returning officer, the arrangements for their delivery shall require the approval of the returning officer.

(2) The marked copies of the register of electors and of the list of proxies shall be in one packet but shall not be in the same packet as the counterfoils of the used ballot papers and the certificates as to employment on duty on the day of the poll.

(3) The packets shall be accompanied by a statement (in these rules referred to as "the ballot paper account") made by the presiding officer showing the number of ballot papers entrusted to him, and accounting for them under the heads of ballot papers issued and not otherwise accounted for, unused, spoilt and tendered ballot papers.

COUNTING OF VOTES

Attendance at counting of votes

38.—(1) The returning officer shall make arrangements for counting the votes in the presence of the counting agents as soon as practicable after the close of the poll, and shall give to the counting agents notice in writing of the time and place at which he will begin to count the votes.

(2) No person other than—

    (*a*) the returning officer and his clerks;

    (*b*) the candidates and their wives or husbands;

    (*c*) the counting agents;

may be present at the counting of the votes, unless permitted by the returning officer to attend.

(3) A person not entitled to attend at the counting of the votes shall not be permitted to do so by the returning officer unless the returning officer is satisfied that the efficient counting of the votes will not be impeded and the returning officer has either consulted the candidates or thought it impracticable to consult them.

(4) The returning officer shall give the counting agents all such reasonable facilities for overseeing the proceedings, and all such information with reference thereto, as he can give them consistently with the orderly conduct of the proceedings and the discharge of his duties in connection therewith.

(5) In particular, where the votes are counted by sorting the ballot papers according to the candidate for whom the vote is given and then counting the number of ballot papers for each candidate, the counting agents shall be entitled to satisfy themselves that the ballot papers are correctly sorted.

The count

39.—(1) Before the returning officer proceeds to count the votes, he shall—

    (*a*) in the presence of the counting agents open each ballot box and, taking out the ballot papers therein, count and record the number thereof and verify each ballot paper account;

    (*b*) if polls have been taken together for the election of parish councillors and rural district councillors, separate the ballot papers relating to the election of parish councillors from those relating to rural district councillors and count and record the numbers relating to each election; and

    (*c*) then mix together the whole of the ballot papers relating to the election of parish councillors contained in the ballot boxes.

(2) The returning officer shall not count any tendered ballot paper.

(3) The returning officer, while separating, counting and recording the number of ballot papers and counting the votes, shall keep the ballot papers with their faces upwards and take all proper precautions for preventing any person from seeing the numbers printed on the back of the papers.

(4) The returning officer shall verify each ballot paper account by comparing it with the number of ballot papers recorded by him, and the unused and spoilt ballot papers in his possession and the tendered votes list (opening and resealing the packets containing the unused and spoilt ballot papers and the tendered votes list) and shall draw up a statement as to the result of the verification which any counting agent may copy.

(5) The returning officer shall, so far as practicable, proceed continuously with counting the votes, allowing only time for refreshment:

Provided that he may, in so far as he thinks necessary, exclude the hours between eight o'clock in the evening and nine o'clock on the following morning.

(6) During the excluded time the returning officer shall place the ballot papers and other documents relating to the election under his own seal and the seals of such of the counting agents as desire to affix their seals and shall otherwise take proper precautions for the security of the papers and documents.

Re-count

40.—(1) A candidate may, if present when the counting or any re-count of the votes is completed, require the returning officer to have the votes re-counted or again re-counted but the returning officer may refuse to do so if in his opinion the request is unreasonable.

(2) No step shall be taken on the completion of the counting or any re-count of votes until the candidates present at the completion thereof have been given a reasonable opportunity to exercise the right conferred by this rule.

Rejected ballot papers

41.—(1) Any ballot paper—

    (a) which does not bear the official mark; or

    (b) on which votes are given for more candidates than the voter is entitled to vote for; or

    (c) on which anything is written or marked by which the voter can be identified except the printed number on the back; or

    (d) which is unmarked or void for uncertainty;

shall, subject to the provisions of this rule, be void and not counted.

(2) Where the voter is entitled to vote for more than one candidate, a ballot paper shall not be deemed to be void for uncertainty as respects any vote as to which no uncertainty arises and that vote shall be counted.

(3) A ballot paper on which a vote is marked—

    (a) elsewhere than in the proper place; or

    (b) otherwise than by means of a cross; or

    (c) by more than one mark;

shall not by reason thereof be deemed to be void (either wholly or as respects that vote), if an intention that the vote shall be for one or other of the candidates clearly appears and the way the paper is marked does not of itself identify the voter and it is not shown that he can be identified thereby.

(4) The returning officer shall endorse—

    (a) the word "rejected" on any ballot paper which under this rule is not to be counted; and

    (b) in the case of a ballot paper on which any vote is counted under paragraph (2) of this rule, the words "rejected in part" and a memorandum specifying the votes counted;

and shall add to the endorsement the words "rejection objected to" if an objection is made by a counting agent to his decision.

(5) The returning officer shall draw up a statement showing the number of ballot papers rejected, including those rejected in part, under the several heads of—

    (a) want of official mark;

    (b) voting for more candidates than voter is entitled to;

    (c) writing or mark by which voter could be identified;

    (d) unmarked or wholly void for uncertainty;

    (e) rejected in part.

Decisions on ballot papers

42. The decision of the returning officer on any question arising in respect of a ballot paper shall be final, but shall be subject to review on an election petition.

Equality of votes

43. Where, after the counting of the votes (including any re-count) is completed, an equality of votes is found to exist between any candidates and the addition of a vote would entitle any of those candidates to be declared elected, the returning officer shall forthwith decide between those candidates by lot, and proceed as if the candidate on whom the lot falls had received an additional vote.

PART IV

FINAL PROCEEDINGS IN CONTESTED AND UNCONTESTED ELECTIONS

Declaration of result

44.—(1) In a contested election, when the result of the poll has been ascertained the returning officer shall forthwith declare to be elected the candidate or candidates for whom the majority of votes have been given, and shall as soon as possible publish the name or names of the candidate or candidates elected and the total number of votes given for each candidate, whether elected or not, together with the number of rejected ballot papers under each head shown in the statement of rejected ballot papers.

(2) In an uncontested election, the returning officer shall, not later than eleven o'clock in the morning on the day of election, publish the name or names of the person or persons elected.

The return

45. The returning officer shall forthwith upon declaration of the result of the election return the name of each person elected to the clerk of the parish council or, if there is no such clerk, to the chairman of the parish council or, if there is no such chairman, to the chairman of the parish meeting for the parish.

PART V

DISPOSAL OF DOCUMENTS

Sealing of ballot papers

46.—(1) On the completion of the counting at a contested election the returning officer shall seal up in separate packets the counted and rejected ballot papers, including ballot papers rejected in part.

(2) The returning officer shall not open the sealed packets of tendered ballot papers or of counterfoils and certificates as to employment on duty on the day of the poll, or of marked copies of the register of electors and lists of proxies.

Delivery of documents to clerk of the council

47. The returning officer shall then forward to the clerk of the council of the rural district in which the parish is situate the following documents, that is to say:—

(a) the packets of ballot papers in his possession;

(b) the ballot paper accounts and the statements of rejected ballot papers and of the result of the verification of the ballot paper accounts;

(c) the tendered votes lists, the lists of blind voters assisted by companions, the lists of votes marked by the presiding officer and the statements relating thereto, and the declarations made by the companions of blind voters;

(d) the packets of counterfoils and certificates as to employment on duty on the day of the poll;

(e) the packets containing marked copies of registers and of lists of proxies, endorsing on each packet a description of its contents, the date of the election to which they relate and the name of the electoral area for which the election was held.

Orders for production of documents

48.—(1) An order—

(*a*) for the inspection or production of any rejected ballot papers, including ballot papers rejected in part; or

(*b*) for the opening of a sealed packet of counterfoils and certificates as to employment on duty on the day of the poll or for the inspection of counted ballot papers,

may be made by either a county court having jurisdiction in the parish or an election court if the court is satisfied by evidence on oath that the order is required for the purpose of instituting or maintaining a prosecution for an offence in relation to ballot papers, or for the purpose of an election petition.

(2) The order may be made subject to such conditions as to persons, time, place and mode of inspection, production or opening as the court making the order may think expedient and may direct the clerk of the rural district council having custody of the ballot papers and the sealed packets of counterfoils and certificates to retain them intact for such period as may be specified in the order:

Provided that in making and carrying into effect the order, care shall be taken that the way in which the vote of any particular elector has been given shall not be disclosed until it has been proved that his vote was given and the vote has been declared by a competent court to be invalid.

(3) An appeal shall lie to the High Court from any order of a county court made under this rule.

(4) Any power given under this rule to a county court may be exercised by any judge of the court otherwise than in open court.

(5) Where an order is made for the production by the clerk of the rural district council of any document in his possession relating to any specified election, the production by him or his agent of the document ordered in such manner as may be directed by that order shall be conclusive evidence that the document relates to the specified election; and any endorsement on any packet of ballot papers so produced shall be prima facie evidence that the ballot papers are what they are stated to be by the endorsement.

(6) The production from proper custody of a ballot paper purporting to have been used at any election, and of a counterfoil marked with the same printed number and having a number marked thereon in writing, shall be prima facie evidence that the elector whose vote was given by that ballot paper was the person who at the time of the election had affixed to his name in the register of electors the same number as the number written on the counterfoil.

(7) Save as by this rule provided, no person shall be allowed to inspect any rejected or counted ballot papers in the possession of the clerk of the rural district council or to open any sealed packets of counterfoils and certificates.

Retention and public inspection of documents

49.—(1) The clerk of the rural district council shall retain for six months among the records of the rural district all documents relating to an election which are, in pursuance of these rules, forwarded to him by a returning officer or held by him and then, unless otherwise directed by an order under the last foregoing rule, shall cause them to be destroyed.

(2) The said documents, except ballot papers, counterfoils and certificates as to employment on duty on the day of the poll, shall during a period of six months from the day of election be open to public inspection at such time and in such manner as may be determined by the county council.

(3) The clerk of the rural district council shall, on request, supply copies of or extracts from the documents open to public inspection on payment of such fees, and subject to such conditions, as may be determined by the county council.

Supplemental provisions as to documents

50. Subject to the provisions of these rules, the clerk of the rural district council shall, in respect of the custody and destruction of ballot papers and other documents coming into his possession in pursuance of these rules, be subject to the directions of the rural district council.

PART VI

SUPPLEMENTAL

Countermand or abandonment of poll on death of candidate

51.—(1) If at a contested election proof is given to the satisfaction of the returning officer before the result of the election is declared that one of the persons named or to be named as candidate in the ballot papers has died, then the returning officer shall countermand the poll for the election of parish councillors or, if polling has begun, direct that the poll be abandoned.

(2) Where the poll is abandoned by reason of the death of a candidate, the proceedings at or consequent on that poll shall be interrupted, and the presiding officer at any polling station shall take the like steps (so far as not already taken) for the delivery to the returning officer of ballot boxes and of ballot papers and other documents as he is required to take on the close of the poll in due course, and the returning officer shall dispose of ballot papers and other documents in his possession as he is required to do on the completion in due course of the counting of the votes; but—

    (a) it shall not be necessary for any ballot paper account to be prepared or verified; and

    (b) the returning officer, without taking any step or further step for the counting of the ballot papers or of the votes, shall seal up all the ballot papers, whether the votes on them have been counted or not, and it shall not be necessary to seal up counted and rejected ballot papers in separate packets.

(3) The foregoing provisions of these rules as to the inspection, production, retention and destruction of ballot papers and other documents relating to a poll at an election shall apply to any such documents relating to a poll abandoned by reason of the death of a candidate, with the following modifications:—

    (a) ballot papers on which the votes were neither counted nor rejected shall be treated as counted ballot papers; and

    (b) no order shall be made for the production or inspection of any ballot papers or for the opening of a sealed packet of counterfoils or certificates as to employment on duty on the day of the poll unless the order is made by a court with reference to a prosecution.

General duty of returning officer

52. It shall be the general duty of the returning officer to do any act or thing that may be necessary for effectually conducting the election under these rules.

Interpretation

53.—(1) The expression "electoral area" means the parish or, if the parish is divided into wards, a ward.

(2) A reference in this Schedule to a rule shall be construed as a reference to a rule contained in this Schedule.

(3) Any reference in this Schedule to any enactment shall be taken as a reference to that enactment as amended or replaced by any other enactment.

APPENDIX

Note.—The forms contained in this Appendix may be adapted so far as circumstances require.

NOTICE OF ELECTION

Rule 4.

PARISH OF

ELECTION OF PARISH COUNCILLORS for the [Ward of the]
[Wards of the] Parish.

1. An election is to be held of   Parish Councillors for the said [ward] [wards] [parish].

2. Nomination papers must be delivered at   on any day after the date of this notice, but not later than noon on the   day of   .

3. Forms of nomination paper may be obtained from the returning officer at   or from   at   . Either will at the request of any local government elector for the electoral area prepare for signature a nomination paper.

4. If the election is contested, the poll will take place on the   day of   .

(Signed)...

Returning Officer.

                    day of   , 19   .

NOTE 1.—The attention of candidates and electors is drawn to the rules for filling up nomination papers and other provisions relating to nomination contained in the election rules in Schedule 1 to the Parish Council Election Rules 1970.

NOTE 2.—Every person guilty of a corrupt or illegal practice will, on conviction, be liable to the penalties imposed by the Representation of the People Act 1949.

If the notice relates to more than one election, adapt form accordingly.

NOMINATION PAPER

Rule 5.

ELECTION OF PARISH COUNCILLORS for the [Ward of the] Parish of

Date of publication of notice of election...

We, the undersigned, being local government electors for the said [ward] [parish], do hereby nominate the undermentioned person as a candidate at the said election.

Candidate's surname	Other names in full	Description (if any)	Home address in full

Signatures	Electoral Number (*see* note 3)	
	Distinctive Letter(s)	Number
Proposer...............		
Seconder...............		

NOTE 1.—The attention of candidates and local government electors is drawn to the rules for filling up nomination papers and other provisions relating to nomination contained in the election rules in Schedule 1 to the Parish Council Election Rules 1970.

NOTE 2.—Where a candidate is commonly known by some title he may be described by his title as if it were his surname.

NOTE 3.—A person's electoral number consists of the distinctive letter or letters of the parliamentary polling district in which he is registered together with his number in the register to be used at the election except that before publication of the register the distinctive letter or letters of the parliamentary polling district in which he is entitled to be registered together with his number (if any) in the electors lists for that register shall be used instead.

NOTE 4.—An elector may not—

(a) subscribe more nomination papers than there are vacancies to be filled in the electoral area; or

(b) subscribe a nomination paper for more than one ward of a parish divided into wards; or

(c) subscribe more than one nomination paper in respect of the same candidate.

NOTE 5.—A person whose name is entered in the register or electors lists may not subscribe a nomination paper if the entry gives as the date on which he will become of voting age a date later than the day fixed for the poll.

Rule 10.   STATEMENT AS TO PERSONS NOMINATED

PARISH OF

The following is a statement as to the persons nominated for election as Parish Councillors for the [Ward of the] [Wards of the] Parish.

[Ward] [Wards] [Parish]	Persons nominated				Decision of returning officer that nomination paper is invalid, or other reason why a person nominated no longer stands nominated
	Surname	Other names in full	Home address in full	Description (if any)	
1.	2.	3.	4.	5.	6.

The persons opposite whose names no entry is made in column 6 have been and stand validly nominated.

Dated this   day of   , 19 .

....
Returning Officer.

BALLOT PAPER   Rule 15.

Form of Front of Ballot Paper

ELECTION OF PARISH COUNCILLORS

Counterfoil No.		
The counterfoil is to have a number to correspond with that on the back of the Ballot Paper.	**1** **BROWN** (JOHN EDWARD Brown, of 2 The Cottages, Barlington, Grayshire, Labour.)	
	2 **BROWN** (THOMAS WILLIAM Brown, of 15 Barchester Road, Barlington, Grayshire, Liberal.)	
	3 **JONES** (William David Jones, of The Grange, Barlington, Grayshire, Conservative.)	
	4 **MERTON** (Hon. George Travis, commonly called Viscount Merton, of Barlington, Grayshire.)	
	5 **SMITH** (Mary Smith, of School House, Barlington, Grayshire, schoolteacher, Progressive.)	
	6 **WILLIAMS** (Elizabeth Williams, of 3 Ivy Lane, Barlington, Grayshire, housewife.)	

Form of Back of Ballot Paper

No.

Election for the [Parish of   ] [Ward of the

Parish of   ]   day of   , 19 .

Note.—The number on the ballot paper is to correspond with that on the counterfoil.

Directions as to printing the ballot paper

1. Nothing is to be printed on the ballot paper except in accordance with these directions.

2. So far as practicable, the following arrangements shall be observed in the printing of the ballot paper:—

(*a*) no word shall be printed on the face except the particulars of the candidates and a heading "ELECTION OF PARISH COUNCILLORS";

(*b*) no rule shall be printed on the face except the horizontal rules separating the particulars of the candidates from one another and the vertical rules separating those particulars from the numbers on the left-hand side and the spaces on the right where the vote is to be marked;

(*c*) the whole space beneath the heading shall be equally divided between the candidates by the rules separating their particulars.

3. The surname of each candidate shall in all cases be printed by itself in large capitals, and his full particulars shall be set out below it and shall be printed in ordinary type except that small capitals shall be used—

(*a*) if his surname is the same as another candidate's, for his other names; and

(*b*) if his other names are also the same as the other candidate's, either for his residence or for his description unless each of them is the same as that of another candidate with the same surname and other names.

4. The number on the back of the ballot paper shall be printed in ordinary type.

DIRECTIONS FOR THE GUIDANCE OF THE VOTERS IN VOTING

Rule 23.

1. The voter should see that the ballot paper, before it is handed to him, is stamped with the official mark.

2. The voter will go into one of the compartments and, with the pencil provided in the compartment, place a cross on the right-hand side of the ballot paper, opposite the name of each candidate for whom he votes, thus X.

3. The voter will then fold up the ballot paper so as to show the official mark on the back, and leaving the compartment will, without showing the front of the paper to any person, show the official mark on the back to the presiding officer, and then, in the presence of the presiding officer, put the paper into the ballot box, and forthwith leave the polling station.

4. If the voter inadvertently spoils a ballot paper he can return it to the officer, who will, if satisfied of such inadvertence, give him another paper.

5. If the voter votes for more than   candidate(s) or places any mark on the paper by which he may afterwards be identified, his ballot paper will be void, and will not be counted.

6. If the voter fraudulently takes a ballot paper out of a polling station or fraudulently puts into the ballot box any paper other than the one given to him by the officer, he will be liable on conviction to imprisonment for a term not exceeding six months, or to a fine not exceeding twenty pounds or to both such imprisonment and such fine.

Rule 26.

CERTIFICATE OF EMPLOYMENT

Election in the [Ward of the] Parish of

I certify that (name)................................. who is numbered.......................
in the register of electors for the electoral area named above, is likely to be unable to
go in person to the polling station allotted to him at the election on (date of poll)......
.......................by reason of the particular circumstances of his employment on that
date—

    *(a) as a constable,

    *(b) by me for a purpose connected with the election.

Signature ....

*Police rank...
(Inspector or above)

*Returning Officer

Date...........................

*Delete whichever is inapplicable.

NOTE.—The person named above is entitled to vote at any polling station of the
above electoral area on production and surrender of this certificate to the presiding
officer.

Rule 33.

DECLARATION TO BE MADE BY THE COMPANION OF A BLIND VOTER

I, A. B., of   , having been requested to assist
C. D. [in the case of a blind person voting as proxy add voting as proxy for G. H.], who
is numbered   on the register of local government electors for
the [Parish of   ] [Ward of the Parish
of   ], to record his vote at the election now being held
for the said [parish] [ward], do hereby declare that [I am entitled to vote as an elector
at the said election] [I am the*   of the said voter and have attained the age
of eighteen years], and that I have not previously assisted any blind person [except
E. F., of   ], to vote at the said election.

*State the
relationship
of the
companion
to the voter.

(Signed) A. B.

day of   , 19 .

I, the undersigned, being the presiding officer for the   polling
station for the [Parish of   ] [Ward of the Parish
of   ], do hereby certify that the above declaration, having been first
read to the above-named declarant, was signed by the declarant in my presence.

(Signed) X. Y.

day of   , 19 , at   minutes past   o'clock
[a.m.] [p.m.].

NOTE.—If the person making the above declaration knowingly and wilfully makes
therein a statement false in a material particular, he will be guilty of an offence.

SCHEDULE 2

DECLARATION OF ACCEPTANCE OF OFFICE BY THE CHAIRMAN OF A PARISH COUNCIL OR BY A PARISH COUNCILLOR

*Insert
description
of office,

I, A. B., having been elected to the office of*   , hereby declare
that I take the said office upon myself, and will duly and faithfully fulfil the duties
thereof according to the best of my judgment and ability.

Dated this   day of   , 19 .

Signature................................

This declaration was made and subscribed before me

A member of the Parish Council...

DECLARATION AS TO EXPENSES

Election for the [Ward of the] Parish of

Date of publication of notice of election...

Full name of candidate...

I declare as follows:—

1. The amount paid by me or on my behalf for my election expenses at the above
election was £   .

2. To the best of my knowledge and belief no other election expenses have been
paid or incurred by me or by any other person or organization in connection with my
candidature.

3. To the best of my knowledge and belief the accompanying return of election
expenses is complete and correct as required by law.

4. I understand that the law does not allow any election expenses not mentioned in
the return to be defrayed except in pursuance of a court order.

Signature of candidate..

EXPLANATORY NOTE

(This Note is not part of the Rules.)

These Rules revoke and replace the Parish Council Election Rules 1952, as
amended, with amendments consequential on the provisions of the Representation of the People Act 1969 (c. 15).

STATUTORY INSTRUMENTS

1970 No. 202

ROAD TRAFFIC

The Goods Vehicles (Operators' Licences) (Temporary Use in Great Britain) Regulations 1970

Made - - -	11*th February* 1970	
Laid before Parliament	26*th February* 1970	
Coming into Operation	1*st March* 1970	

The Minister of Transport, in exercise of his powers under sections 89(1) and 91(1), (4) and (5) of the Transport Act 1968(**a**), and of all other enabling powers, and after consultation with representative organisations in accordance with section 91(8) of the said Act of 1968, and with the Council on Tribunals in relation to Regulation 12 of, and Schedule 2 to, these Regulations in accordance with the requirements of section 8 of the Tribunals and Inquiries Act 1958(**b**), hereby makes the following Regulations :—

Citation and commencement

1. These Regulations may be cited as the Goods Vehicles (Operators' Licences) (Temporary Use in Great Britain) Regulations 1970, and shall come into operation on the 1st March 1970.

Interpretation

2.—(1) In these Regulations, unless the context otherwise requires, the following expressions have the meanings hereby respectively assigned to them, that is to say :—

"the Act" means the Transport Act 1968 ;

"foreign goods vehicle" means a goods vehicle—

(*a*) which has been brought temporarily into Great Britain and does not remain in Great Britain for more than 90 days ; and

(*b*) which is engaged in carrying goods by road on a journey, and has used on that journey, or will use before the end of that journey, roads outside the United Kingdom ; and

(*c*) which is not used at any time during the said journey for the carriage of goods loaded at one place in the United Kingdom and delivered at another place in the United Kingdom ; and

"Northern Ireland goods vehicle" means a goods vehicle—

(*a*) which has been brought temporarily into Great Britain and does not remain in Great Britain for more than 90 days ; and

(*b*) which is engaged in carrying goods by road on a journey, and has used on that journey, or will use before the end of that journey, roads outside Great Britain ; and

---

(**a**) 1968 c. 73.   (**b**) 1958 c. 66.

(c) which is not used at any time during the said journey for the carriage of goods loaded at one place in Great Britain and delivered at another place in Great Britain ; and

(d) which, in the case of a motor vehicle, is registered in Northern Ireland ; and

(e) which, in the case of a trailer, is only drawn in Great Britain by a motor vehicle which is a Northern Ireland goods vehicle.

(2) In these Regulations, unless the context otherwise requires, any reference to the use of a goods vehicle for the carriage of goods shall be construed as a reference to the use of that vehicle on roads for the carriage of those goods for hire or reward or for or in connection with any trade or business carried on by the user of the vehicle.

(3) The Interpretation Act 1889(a) shall apply for the interpretation of these Regulations as it applies for the interpretation of an Act of Parliament.

Exemption for Northern Ireland and foreign goods vehicles used for certain purposes

3. Section 60(1) of the Act (users of certain goods vehicles to hold operators' licences) shall not apply to the use in Great Britain of a Northern Ireland or foreign goods vehicle for the carriage only of such goods as are specified in Schedule 1 to these Regulations.

Exemption for Austrian goods vehicles in certain cases

4.—(1) In this Regulation "Austrian goods vehicle" means a foreign goods vehicle—

(a) which is owned by or operated by or on behalf of a person—

(i) who is authorised under Austrian law to use that vehicle for the carriage of goods in the Republic of Austria ; or

(ii) who, if Austrian law permits him so to use that vehicle without being so authorised, uses that vehicle primarily or substantially for that purpose in that country ; and

(b) which, in the case of a trailer, is only drawn in Great Britain by a motor vehicle which is an Austrian goods vehicle.

(2) Section 60(1) of the Act shall not apply to the use in Great Britain of an Austrian goods vehicle for the carriage of such goods as are specified in the next following paragraph of this Regulation.

(3) The goods referred to in the last preceding paragraph of this Regulation are :—

(a) any such goods as are specified in Schedule 1 to these Regulations ;

(b) any goods, being—

(i) luggage being carried to or from an airport ;

(ii) works of art ;

(iii) carried exclusively for publicity or educational purposes ;

(iv) properties, equipment or animals being carried to or from theatrical, musical, cinematographic or circus performances or sporting events, exhibitions or fairs, or to or from the making of radio or television broadcasts or films ;

(a) 1889 c. 63.

(v) carried for fairs and exhibitions ;

(vi) carried in connection with household removals by undertakings using specialised personnel and equipment for that purpose ;

(c) any goods being carried for or in connection with any trade or business carried on by a user of the vehicle if there is carried on the vehicle a document containing particulars of the user, his trade or business, the goods, their loading and unloading points, the vehicle and the route ;

(d) any goods if there is carried on the vehicle a permit valid for the journey on which the goods are being carried issued by the Minister of Transport.

Exemption for French goods vehicles in certain cases

5.—(1) In this Regulation "French goods vehicle" means a foreign goods vehicle which is owned by or operated by or on behalf of a person—

(a) who is authorised under French law to use that vehicle for the carriage of goods in the French Republic ; or

(b) who, if French law permits him so to use that vehicle without being so authorised, uses that vehicle primarily or substantially for that purpose in that country.

(2) Section 60(1) of the Act shall not apply to the use in Great Britain of a French goods vehicle for the carriage of such goods as are specified in the next following paragraph of this Regulation.

(3) The goods referred to in the last preceding paragraph of this Regulation are :—

(a) any such goods as are specified in Schedule 1 to these Regulations ;

(b) luggage being carried to or from an airport ;

(c) refuse and sewage ;

(d) any goods if there is carried on the vehicle a permit valid for the journey on which the goods are being carried issued by the Minister of Transport.

Exemption for German goods vehicles in certain cases

6.—(1) In this Regulation "German goods vehicle" means a foreign goods vehicle—

(a) which is owned by or operated by or on behalf of a person—

(i) who is authorised under the law of the Federal Republic of Germany to use that vehicle for the carriage of goods in the Federal Republic of Germany ; or

(ii) who, if the law of the Federal Republic of Germany permits him so to use that vehicle without being so authorised, uses that vehicle primarily or substantially for that purpose in that country ; and

(b) which, in the case of a trailer, is only drawn in Great Britain by a motor vehicle which is a German goods vehicle.

(2) Section 60(1) of the Act shall not apply to the use in Great Britain of a German goods vehicle for the carriage of such goods as are specified in the next following paragraph of this Regulation which is engaged on a journey between any two countries and has used on that journey, or will use before the end of that journey, roads in the Federal Republic of Germany.

(3) The goods referred to in the last preceding paragraph of this Regulation are :—

(a) any such goods as are specified in Schedule 1 to these Regulations ;

(b) any goods, being—

(i) luggage being carried to or from an airport ;

(ii) works of art ;

(iii) carried exclusively for publicity or educational purposes ;

(iv) properties or equipment being carried to or from theatrical, musical, film or sporting events, circuses, exhibitions or fairs, or to or from the making of radio or television broadcasts or films ;

(v) carried for fairs and exhibitions ;

(vi) live animals, other than animals intended for slaughter ;

(c) any goods being carried for or in connection with any trade or business carried on by the user of the vehicle, if there is carried on the vehicle a document containing the following particulars, that is to say : —

(i) the place at which and the date on which the document was made out ;

(ii) the name and address of the user and an accurate description of the nature of his business ;

(iii) if the goods are to be accepted from, or delivered to, any other person, the name and address of that other person and an accurate description of the nature of his business ;

(iv) the loading point or points ;

(v) the unloading point or points ;

(vi) the nature of the load ;

(vii) the gross weight, or other indication of quantity, of the load ;

(viii) the carrying capacity of the vehicle, by weight ;

(ix) the index mark and registration number of the vehicle, or if those do not exist, the number of the chassis ;

(x) the distance of the loaded journey in Great Britain, in kilometres ;

(xi) the point or points at which the vehicle will enter and leave Great Britain ; and

(xii) the signature of the user or his authorised representative ;

(d) any goods if there is carried on the vehicle a permit valid for the journey on which the goods are being carried issued by the Minister of Transport.

Exemption for Italian goods vehicles in certain cases

7.—(1) In this Regulation "Italian goods vehicle" means a foreign goods vehicle which is owned by or operated by or on behalf of a person who is authorised under Italian law to use that vehicle for the carriage of goods in the Italian Republic.

(2) Section 60(1) of the Act shall not apply to the use in Great Britain of an Italian goods vehicle for the carriage of such goods as are specified in the next following paragraph of this Regulation—

(a) between the Italian Republic and the United Kingdom ; or

(b) in transit through the United Kingdom, between any two other countries.

(3) The goods referred to in the last preceding paragraph of this Regulation are any goods if there is carried on the vehicle a permit valid for the journey on which the goods are being carried issued by the Minister of Transport.

Exemption for Netherlands goods vehicles in certain cases

8.—(1) In this Regulation—

"Netherlands goods vehicle" means a foreign goods vehicle—

   (a) which is owned by or operated by or on behalf of a person—

   (i) who is authorised under the law of the Kingdom of the Netherlands to use that vehicle for the carriage of goods in that Kingdom; on

   (ii) who, if such law permits him so to use that vehicle without being so authorised, uses that vehicle primarily or substantially for that purpose in that Kingdom ; and

   (b) which, in the case of a trailer, is only drawn in Great Britain by a motor vehicle which is a Netherlands goods vehicle ; and

"relevant date" means the date on which the Agreement between the Government of the United Kingdom of Great Britain and Northern Ireland and the Government of the Kingdom of the Netherlands on the International Carriage of Goods by Road signed on the 19th September 1969 enters into force for the United Kingdom, which date will be notified in the London Gazette.

(2) On and after the relevant date section 60(1) of the Act shall not apply to the use in Great Britain of a Netherlands goods vehicle for the carriage of any goods.

Exemption for Rumanian goods vehicles in certain cases

9.—(1) In this Regulation—

"relevant date" means the date on which the Agreement between the Government of the United Kingdom of Great Britain and Northern Ireland and the Government of the Socialist Republic of Rumania on International Road Transport signed on the 12th June 1969 enters into force for the United Kingdom, which date will be notified in the London Gazette ; and

"Rumanian goods vehicle" means a foreign goods vehicle—

   (a) which, in the case of a motor vehicle, is registered in the Socialist Republic of Rumania ; and

   (b) which, in the case of a trailer, is only drawn in Great Britain by a motor vehicle which is a Rumanian goods vehicle.

(2) On and after the relevant date section 60(1) of the Act shall not apply to the use in Great Britain of a Rumanian goods vehicle for the carriage of any goods—

   (a) between the Socialist Republic of Rumania and the United Kingdom ; or

   (b) in transit through the United Kingdom, between any two other countries ; or

   (c) if the Minister has authorised such use, between the United Kingdom and any other country except the Socialist Republic of Rumania.

Exemption for Swedish goods vehicles in certain cases

10.—(1) In this Regulation "Swedish goods vehicle" means a foreign goods vehicle—

  (*a*) which is owned by or operated by or on behalf of a person—
    (i) who is authorised under Swedish law to use that vehicle for the carriage of goods in the Kingdom of Sweden ; or
    (ii) who, if Swedish law permits him so to use that vehicle without being so authorised, uses that vehicle primarily or substantially for that purpose in that country ; and

  (*b*) which, in the case of a trailer, is only drawn in Great Britain by a motor vehicle which is a Swedish goods vehicle.

(2) Section 60(1) of the Act shall not apply to the use in Great Britain of a Swedish goods vehicle for the carriage of any goods.

Exemption for Yugoslav goods vehicles in certain cases

11.—(1) In this Regulation "Yugoslav goods vehicle" means a foreign goods vehicle—

  (*a*) which is owned by or operated by or on behalf of a person—
    (i) who is authorised under Yugoslav law to use that vehicle for the carriage of goods in the Socialist Federal Republic of Yugoslavia ; or
    (ii) who, if Yugoslav law permits him so to use that vehicle without being so authorised, uses that vehicle primarily or substantially for that purpose in that country ; and

  (*b*) which, in the case of a trailer, is only drawn in Great Britain by a motor vehicle which is a Yugoslav goods vehicle.

(2) Section 60(1) of the Act shall not apply to the use in Great Britain of a Yugoslav goods vehicle for the carriage of such goods as are specified in the next following paragraph of this Regulation—

  (*a*) between the Socialist Federal Republic of Yugoslavia and the United Kingdom ; or

  (*b*) in transit through the United Kingdom, between any two other countries ; or

  (*c*) if the Minister of Transport has authorised such use, between the United Kingdom and any other country except the Socialist Federal Republic of Yugoslavia.

(3) The goods referred to in the last preceding paragraph of this Regulation are :—

  (*a*) any such goods as are specified in Schedule 1 to these Regulations ;

  (*b*) any goods, being—
    (i) works of art ;
    (ii) carried exclusively for publicity or educational purposes ;
    (iii) properties, equipment or animals being carried to or from theatrical, musical, cinematographic or circus performances or sporting events, exhibitions or fairs, or to or from the making of radio or television broadcasts or films ;
    (iv) carried for fairs or exhibitions ;
    (v) carried in connection with household removals by undertakings using specialised personnel and equipment for that purpose ;

(vi) carried in circumstances such that the total laden weight of the motor vehicle and any trailer drawn thereby does not exceed 6,000 kilograms ;

(c) any goods if there is carried on the vehicle a permit valid for the journey on which the goods are being carried issued by the Minister of Transport.

Simplified procedure for the grant, etc. of operators' licences
12.—(1) Subject to paragraph (3) of this Regulation Part V of the Act shall have effect subject to the modifications specified in Part I of Schedule 2 to these Regulations in relation to Northern Ireland and foreign goods vehicles.

(2) The Goods Vehicles (Operators' Licences) Regulations 1969**(a)** and the Goods Vehicles (Carriers' and Operators' Licences) (Fees) Regulations 1969**(b)** shall have effect subject to the amendments specified in Part II of the said Schedule in relation to Northern Ireland and foreign goods vehicles.

(3) Part V of the Act shall not have effect subject to the modifications specified in Part I of the said Schedule 2 in relation to the use of Northern Ireland and foreign goods vehicles in a case where by virtue of these Regulations Section 60(1) of the Act does not apply to the use of such a vehicle in Great Britain or would not apply if the necessary permits, authorisations or documents were issued, given or carried.

Given under the Official Seal of the Minister of Transport the 11th February 1970.

(L.S.)

Fred Mulley,
Minister of Transport.

SCHEDULE 1 (see Regulations 3, 4, 5, 6 and 11)

GOODS WHICH MAY BE CARRIED IN GREAT BRITAIN BY A NORTHERN IRELAND OR FOREIGN GOODS VEHICLE WITHOUT AN OPERATOR'S LICENCE

1. Goods or luggage being carried to or from an airport in a case where an air service has been diverted.

2. Postal packets (as defined by section 87 of the Post Office Act 1953**(c)**).
3. Damaged vehicles.

4. Animal corpses (other than those intended for human consumption) for the purpose of disposal.

5. Bees or fish stock.

6. The body of a deceased person.

SCHEDULE 2 (see Regulation 12)

PART I

MODIFICATIONS TO PART V OF THE TRANSPORT ACT 1968 IN RELATION TO NORTHERN IRELAND AND FOREIGN GOODS VEHICLES

Part V of the Act shall have effect:—

(a) as if in Section 61(1) the words "Subject to subsection (2) of this section" and

---

(a) S.I. 1969/1636 (1969 III, p. 5141).   **(b)** S.I. 1969/1799 (1969 III, p. 5612).
(c) 1953 c. 36.

paragraph (*c*) were omitted, and as if for the last paragraph of the subsection there were substituted the following paragraph:—

"For the purposes of paragraph (*b*) of this subsection different types of trailers may be distinguished in a licence and a maximum number may be specified in the licence for trailers of each type.";

(*b*) as if section 61(2), (3) and (4) were omitted;

(*c*) as if for section 62(1) there were substituted the following subsection:—

"(1) A person applying for an operator's licence with a view to enabling goods vehicles brought temporarily into Great Britain to be used shall apply to such licensing authority as the Minister may from time to time direct and shall not at any time hold more than one such licence.";

(*d*) as if in section 62(2) paragraph (*c*) were omitted;

(*e*) as if section 62(3) were omitted;

(*f*) as if at the end of section 63(2) there were added the words "or notice of any application in respect of a vehicle brought temporarily into Great Britain.";

(*g*) as if in section 64(1) for the words from "whether the requirements" to the end of the subsection, there were substituted the words "whether the applicant satisfies the requirement that he is a fit and proper person to hold an operator's licence, having regard in particular to his previous known conduct.";

(*h*) as if section 64(2), (4)(*b*) and (5) were omitted;

(*i*) as if section 65 were omitted;

(*j*) as if for section 67(2) there were substituted the following subsection:—

"(2) With a view to enabling goods vehicles brought temporarily into Great Britain to be used, an operator's licence may be granted for any period not exceeding three months.";

(*k*) as if section 67(3) were omitted;

(*l*) as if in section 67(4) for the words "(*a*) the application; and (*b*) any appeal under section 70 of this Act arising out of the application, are" there were substituted the words "the application is";

(*m*) as if section 67(5) were omitted;

(*n*) as if in section 68(1) for paragraph (*a*) there were substituted the following paragraph:—

"(*a*) that additional vehicles be specified therein, or that the maximum number of trailers specified therein under paragraph (*b*) of section 61(1) of this Act be increased; or";

and as if paragraph (*c*) were omitted;

(*o*) as if in section 68(4) after sub-paragraph (*c*) there were added the following sub-paragraph:—

"or (*d*) where the application is in respect of a vehicle brought temporarily into Great Britain,";

(*p*) as if section 68(5) were omitted;

(*q*) as if in section 69 subsection (1)(*a*) and the last paragraph of subsection (5) were omitted;

(*r*) as if at the end of section 70(2) there were added the words "or from the refusal of an application to grant or vary an operator's licence in respect of a vehicle brought temporarily into Great Britain,"; and

(*s*) as if at the end of section 89(1) there were added the following proviso:—

"Provided that in the case of vehicles brought temporarily into Great Britain the licensing authority may waive the payment of such fees either wholly or in part."

Part II

Amendments to Regulations in Relation to Northern Ireland and Foreign Goods Vehicles

1. The Goods Vehicles (Operators' Licences) Regulations 1969 shall have effect as if:—

 (*a*) in Regulation 4 paragraphs (1) and (2) were omitted;

 (*b*) in Regulation 14(1), for the words "and may elect" onwards, there were substituted the words:—

 "at a place specified by the person requiring its production.".

2. The Goods Vehicles (Carriers' and Operators' Licences) (Fees) Regulations 1969 shall have effect as if in Regulation 5:—

 (*a*) for paragraph (1) there were substituted the following paragraph:—

 "(1) Whenever a motor vehicle is specified in an operator's licence the holder of the licence shall pay a fee at the rate of £1 in respect of each motor vehicle so specified."; and

 (*b*) paragraph (3)(*a*) were omitted.

EXPLANATORY NOTE

(This Note is not part of the Regulations.)

These Regulations exempt operators of Northern Ireland and foreign goods vehicles brought temporarily into Great Britain from the requirement to obtain an operator's licence under Part V of the Transport Act 1968 when the vehicles are used only for the carriage of certain kinds of goods (Regulation 3 and Schedule 1).

In Regulations 4—11 further provision is made for exempting from this requirement the operators of goods vehicles of certain specified foreign countries when used temporarily in Great Britain for the carriage of wider ranges of goods.

Regulation 12 and Schedule 2 make certain other amendments to Part V of the Transport Act 1968, and make certain amendments to the Goods Vehicles (Operators' Licences) Regulations 1969 and the Goods Vehicles (Carriers' and Operators' Licences) (Fees) Regulations 1969, in relation to Northern Ireland and foreign goods vehicles when temporarily in Great Britain. These amendments simplify the procedure for the issue of short-term operator's licences for such vehicles and also relate to the authorisation of such vehicles under the licences, to the variation, revocation and production of such licences, to the fees for, and the duration of, such licences and to appeals from decisions of licensing authorities in connection therewith.

Except for Regulations 8 and 9, the Regulations take effect on the 1st March 1970. Regulation 8 (which relates to Netherlands goods vehicles) and Regulation 9 (which relates to Rumanian goods vehicles) will take effect when the relevant international Agreement referred to therein (in Regulation 8 this is the Agreement with the Government of the Kingdom of the Netherlands which was signed on the 19th September 1969 and which has been issued as Cmnd. 4202 and in Regulation 9 this is the Agreement with the Government of the Socialist Republic of Rumania which was signed on the 12th June 1969 and which has been issued as Cmnd. 4129) enters into force.

STATUTORY INSTRUMENTS

1970 No. 204 (L. 8)
COUNTY COURTS
PROCEDURE
The County Court (Amendment No. 2) Rules 1970

Made - - - - 9th February 1970
Coming into Operation 9th March 1970

1.—(1) These Rules may be cited as the County Court (Amendment No. 2) Rules 1970.

(2) In these Rules an Order and Rule referred to by number means the Order and Rule so numbered in the County Court Rules 1936(**a**), as amended(**b**), and Appendices B, C, D and E mean respectively Appendices B, C, D and E to those Rules.

(3) The Interpretation Act 1889(**c**) shall apply for the interpretation of these Rules as it applies for the interpretation of an Act of Parliament.

2. Order 47 shall be amended as follows:—

(1) Rule 2 shall be revoked.

(2) The following Rule shall be substituted for Rule 5:—

Scales of costs
" 5.—(1) For the regulation of solicitors' charges and disbursements otherwise than under Rule 37 of this Order there shall be a Lower Scale and three Higher Scales, namely Scale 1, Scale 2 and Scale 3.

(2) The Higher Scales, which shall be those set out in Appendix B, shall have effect subject to and in accordance with the Rules of this Order and the directions contained in the Scales.

(3) The Scale of Costs applicable to a sum of money only shall be as follows:—

Sum of money	Scale Applicable
Exceeding £5 and not exceeding £20	Lower Scale
Exceeding £20 and not exceeding £50	Scale 1
Exceeding £50 and not exceeding £200	Scale 2
Exceeding £200	Scale 3

(4) Where the sum of money does not exceed £5, no solicitors' charges shall be allowed, unless a certificate is granted under Rule 13 of this Order.

(5) In addition to the disbursements shown in the Higher Scales the appropriate court fees shall be allowable."

(**a**) S.R. & O. 1936/626 (1936 I, p. 282).
(**b**) The relevant amending instruments are S.R. & O. 1936/1312, 1938/18, 731, 1475, 1939/815, S.I. 1950/1231, 1993, 1951/1354, 1953/1728, 1954/1675, 1955/1799, 1957/174, 1136, 1959/1251, 1960/1275, 1961/1526, 1964/353, 1965/2147, 1969/585 (1936 I, p. 655; 1938 I, pp. 977, 986, 990; 1939 I, p. 469; 1950 I, pp. 400, 440; 1951 I, p. 357; 1953 I, p. 404; 1954 I, p. 541; 1955 I, p. 530; 1957 I, pp. 512, 517; 1959 I, p. 795; 1960 I, p. 809 1961 II, p. 3177; 1964 I, p. 543; 1965 III, p. 6292; 1969 I, p. 1551).
(**c**) 1889 c. 63.

(3) In Rule 12 for the words " Rule 13 " there shall be substituted the words " Rules 13 and 36 ".

(4) In Rule 15(1) for the words " and 14 " there shall be substituted the words " 14 and 36 ".

(5) The following Rule shall be substituted for Rule 17:—

Allowance or disallowance of items by judge

" 17. Where the costs of any action or matter are on one of the Higher Scales, the judge may direct the registrar to allow or disallow on taxation any item in the Scale."

(6) Rule 18 shall be revoked.

(7) In Rule 19 for the words " Scale 2, 3 or 4 " there shall be substituted the words " one of the Higher Scales ".

(8) Rule 21 shall be amended as follows:—

(*a*) In paragraph (1) for the words " Scale 3 or 4 " there shall be substituted the words " Scale 2 or 3 ".

(*b*) In paragraph (2) for the words " Scale 2, 3 or 4 " there shall be substituted the words " one of the Higher Scales ".

(*c*) In paragraph (3) the words " or the scale of costs falls to be determined by a sum of money exceeding £400 " shall be omitted and for the list of items following the word " namely " there shall be substituted the following list:—

" items 1, 2, 5, 6, 7, 8, 18, 26, 29 and 30 ".

(*d*) At the end of the Rule there shall be added the following paragraph:—

" (5) Where the costs of any proceedings are on scale 3 and no direction has been given by the judge that this paragraph shall not apply, the registrar may, if satisfied as to the matters mentioned in paragraph (2), exercise the powers conferred on him by paragraph (3) notwithstanding that no direction has been given by the judge under paragraph (2) ".

(9) In Rule 23 for the words " Scale 2, 3 or 4 " there shall be substituted the words " one of the Higher Scales ".

(10) Rule 29 shall be amended as follows:—

(*a*) At the beginning there shall be inserted the words " (1) Subject to paragraph (2) ".

(*b*) At the end there shall be added the following paragraph:—

" (2) Where the costs are on Scale 3, the registrar on taxing or fixing and allowing the costs may, if satisfied that the sum specified in Appendix C may be inadequate in the circumstances, allow such larger sum as he thinks reasonable, notwithstanding that, in the case of a sum prescribed in column 1, no order has been made under the proviso to paragraph (1) ".

(11) Rule 30 shall be amended as follows:—

(*a*) In paragraphs (2) and (4), for the words " 5 guineas " there shall be substituted the words " £8 ".

(*b*) In paragraph (2), for the words " 10 guineas " there shall be substituted the words " £15 ".

(12) Rule 37 shall be amended as follows:—

(a) The following paragraph shall be substituted for paragraph (1):—

" (1) Where costs are on the Lower Scale, they shall be fixed and allowed without taxation and any reference in these Rules to taxation shall, in relation to such costs, be treated as a reference to fixing and allowing them under this paragraph."

(b) In paragraph (2) for the words " Scale 2, 3 or 4 " there shall be substituted the words " one of the Higher Scales ".

(c) In paragraph (3) for the words " the last foregoing paragraph " there shall be substituted the words " paragraph (1) or (2) ".

3. The following Appendix shall be substituted for Appendix B:—

" APPENDIX B

Order 47,
Rule 5(2)

HIGHER SCALES OF COSTS

Item No.		Scale 1	Scale 2	Scale 3
	Solicitors' Charges			
	Particulars of claim, &c.	£ s.	£ s.	£ s.
1	Preparing particulars of claim or originating application, petition, or request for entry of appeal to a county court, or particulars of counterclaim, or third-party notice; preparing defence (to claim or counterclaim), answer, or reply if ordered; preparing preliminary act or pleading in admiralty action ...	– 10 to 2 0	– 10 to 3 0	1 0 to 6 0
	Note 1.—This item includes copies and is only to be allowed where the document is signed by the solicitor or his clerk duly authorised in that behalf.			
	Note 2.—Where the document is settled by counsel, items 2(a) and 3 are allowable and not this item.			
2	*Preparation of documents* (a) Preparing instructions to counsel to settle any pleading or other document or to advise on evidence or to advise on merits where counsel's fee is allowed under item 30	– 10 to 1 0	– 10 to 2 0	1 10 to 3 0
	(b) Preparing any necessary document not otherwise provided for and all necessary copies thereof	– 10	– 10	– 10
	And for every folio or part thereof beyond 5	– 2	– 2	– 2
	Note.—Item 2(b) is not to be allowed for preparing a praecipe or a notice of acceptance or non-acceptance of an admission and proposal as to time of payment.			

lee

Item No.		Scale 1	Scale 2	Scale 3
	Solicitors' Charges			
		£ s.	£ s.	£ s.
	Copies			
3	For copies of documents (including brief) not otherwise provided for, which the registrar considers necessary—			
	(*a*) for photographic copies, such sum as the registrar thinks reasonable	– –	– –	– –
	(*b*) for carbon copies, per 2 folios ...	– 1	– 1	– 1
	(*c*) in any other case, per folio ...	– 1	– 1	– 1
	Perusing			
4	Any document not otherwise provided for, which the registrar is satisfied justifies a charge for perusal	– 5	– 5	– 5
	And per folio beyond 5	– 1	– 1	– 1
	Preparing for trial			
5	Preparing for trial or hearing of action or matter	3 0 to 16 0	5 0 to 45 0	Such sum as is fair and reasonable in all the circumstances *not exceeding* £80.

Note.—This item is intended to cover any work, not otherwise provided for, done in preparing for a trial or hearing, including—

(*a*) taking instructions to sue, defend, counterclaim or appeal, or for preliminary act, pleading or bail in admiralty action;

(*b*) taking instructions for preparing any document to which item 2(*b*) applies;

(*c*) considering the facts, evidence and law;

(*d*) preparing notes of facts or argument;

(*e*) attending on and corresponding with client;

(*f*) interviewing and corresponding with witnesses and potential witnesses and taking proofs of their evidence;

(*g*) preparing and serving notices to produce and admit documents and to admit facts;

(*h*) perusing pleadings, affidavits and other relevant documents;

(*i*) making necessary searches;

(*j*) inspecting any property or place material to the proceedings;

(*k*) where counsel is instructed, instructions for and drawing brief;

(*l*) where the action or matter does not proceed to trial or hearing, work done in connection with the negotiation of a settlement;

(*m*) the general care and conduct of the proceedings; and

Item No.		Scale 1	Scale 2	Scale 3
	Solicitors' Charges			
		£ s.	£ s.	£ s.
	(*n*) the exceptional cost, if any, of conducting county court business in the area in which the solicitor practises, due to the small volume of such business in that area.			
	Attendances			
6	At court on trial of action or matter for each day or part of a day—			
	(*a*) without counsel	2 0 to 10 0	3 0 to 20 0	5 0 to 35 0
	(*b*) with counsel	1 0 to 4 0	2 0 to 6 0	3 0 to 8 0
	Note.—An attendance on the examination of a witness under Order 20, Rule 18(1), is to be treated as an attendance to which this item relates.			
7	At court where trial is adjourned for want of time or upon payment of the costs of the day—			
	(*a*) without counsel	2 0 to 4 0	2 0 to 6 0	3 0 to 10 0
	(*b*) with counsel	1 0 to 2 0	1 10 to 4 0	1 10 to 6 0
8	At court or in chambers on any application to judge or registrar in the course of or relating to the proceedings, including instructions, notice and service, and brief where counsel is instructed—			
	(*a*) without counsel	1 0 to 3 0	1 0 to 8 0	1 10 to 12 0
	(*b*) with counsel	1 0 to 2 0	1 0 to 3 0	2 0 to 6 0
	Note.—Interpleader and garnishee proceedings are to be treated as an application to which this item refers.			
	Note to items 5, 6, 7 and 8.—These items apply to an arbitration, inquiry or reference, but item 5 may only be allowed once in the same proceedings. If the reference or inquiry was directed at the trial and the reference or inquiry began on the same day, item 6 may only be allowed once in respect of that day.			
9	To lodge papers, when proceedings transferred to county court, including preparation of all necessary documents	2 0	2 0	2 0

Item No.	Solicitors' Charges	Scale 1 £ s.	Scale 2 £ s.	Scale 3 £ s.
10	On examination of witness under Order 14, Rule 1(10), or Order 25, Rule 2, for each hour or part thereof—			
	(a) without counsel	1 10	2 0	3 0
	(b) with counsel	1 0	1 10	2 0
11	Where in consequence of anything done by the opposite party during the proceedings, attendance on the client is necessary to advise or receive instructions, for each attendance not otherwise provided for	1 0	1 0	1 0 to 2 0
12	(a) To obtain or give any necessary and proper consent or admission	1 0	1 0	1 0
	(b) Upon the opposite party, for each attendance not otherwise provided for	1 0	1 0	1 0
	(c) To arrange for attendance of a witness without subpoena	– 10	– 10	– 10
	(d) On counsel in conference where counsel's fee allowed under item 28 (to include appointing conference), for each half hour or part thereof ...	1 0	1 10	1 10
	Note to items 11 and 12(a) and (b).—If the attendance is by telephone half of the charge is to be allowed.			
	Note to item 12(c).—Only one charge is to be allowed where only one attendance is necessary to arrange for more than one witness.			
13	At court to hear a deferred judgment or on further consideration pursuant to Order 29, Rules 18 and 19, or on entry of judgment on an award or report—			
	(a) without counsel	1 0 to 3 0	1 0 to 6 0	2 0 to 8 0
	(b) with counsel	1 0 to 2 0	1 0 to 3 0	2 0 to 4 0
14	At court, on hearing of judgment summons if costs allowed under Order 25, Rule 66(1), and for each attendance where the hearing is not concluded on the day on which it is commenced—			
	(a) without counsel	2 0	2 0	2 0
	(b) with counsel	1 0	1 0	1 0
	Note.—This item includes attending to enter and service (unless allowed under Order 25, Rule 66(2)).			

Item No.		Scale 1	Scale 2	Scale 3
	Solicitors' Charges			
		£ s.	£ s.	£ s.
15	On deponent being sworn to an affidavit	– 10	– 10	– 10
	Note 1.—This charge may be allowed where the solicitor or his clerk is the deponent.			
	Note 2.—This charge is not to be allowed in respect of an affidavit of service or an affidavit under Order 20, Rule 5(2).			
16	To deliver any document pursuant to any County Court Rule	– 10	– 10	– 10
17	Any attendance at the court office not otherwise provided for, which the registrar is satisfied justifies a charge ...	– 10	– 10	– 10
	Service			
18	Of any document required to be served personally, other than a judgment summons unless allowed under Order 25, Rule 66(2), including copy ...	– 10 to 1 0	– 10 to 1 0	1 0 to 2 0
19	(*a*) Of any document authorised to be served by post, including copy ...			
	(*b*) For preparing a certificate resulting in postal service of an ordinary summons	– 5	– 5	– 5
	Notes to items 18 *and* 19.			
	Note 1.—Where any two or more documents to be served on the same party have been or could have been served together, one charge only for service is to be allowed.			
	Note 2.—Where two or more parties have been or could have been served together, one charge only for service is to be allowed.			
	Note 3.—Where two or more defendants were served at the same address, only one charge is to be allowed under item 19(*b*).			
	Note 4.—These items are not to be allowed where item 20(*a*) is applicable.			
20	Substituted service—			
	(*a*) if service by solicitor, to include attendances, making appointments to serve summons, preparing and attending to swear and file affidavits and to obtain order, and the fees paid for oaths	2 0	2 0 to 3 0	2 0 to 5 0
	(*b*) if service by bailiff, for attendances to request steps to be taken and to obtain order	1 0	1 0	1 0

Item No.		Scale 1	Scale 2	Scale 3

Solicitors' Charges

		£ s.	£ s.	£ s.
21	Of process out of England and Wales, to include drawing, copying, attending to swear and file all affidavits and to obtain order, and the fees paid for oaths, such sum as the registrar thinks reasonable	– –	– –	– –

Letters, &c.

22	Letter before action	– 10	– 10	– 10
23	Letters in lieu of attendances which could properly be allowed under items 11, 12, 16 and 17	– 10	– 10	– 10
24	Circular letters	– 5	– 5	– 5

Taxation of costs

25	(a) For taxation of the costs of the action or matter, to include preparing bill, all necessary copies and notice, service, obtaining appointment to tax and attending taxation	2 0	3 0 to 6 0	3 0 to 10 0
	(b) For any other taxation, to include preparing bill, all necessary copies and notice, service, obtaining appointment to tax and attending taxation... ...	1 0	1 0 to 2 0	2 0 to 3 0

Disbursements

Fees to Counsel

26	With brief on trial or hearing	3 0 to 10 0	4 0 to 25 0	9 0 to 35 0
27	Where there is no local bar in the court town or within 25 miles thereof, if in the opinion of the registrar the maximum fee allowable with the brief is insufficient, a further fee may be allowed, not exceeding for each day on which the trial or hearing takes place	3 0	3 0	4 0
	Note 1.—For the purpose of this item there shall be deemed to be a local bar only in such places as may from time to time be specified in a certificate of the General Council of the Bar published in their Annual Statement.			
	Note 2.—This item is not to be allowed in any court within 25 miles of Charing Cross.			

Item No.		Scale 1	Scale 2	Scale 3
	Disbursements			
		£ s.	£ s.	£ s.
28	On conference in chambers or elsewhere, if the fee was marked on the brief when delivered, or in the opinion of the registrar the conference was necessary, for each half hour or part thereof ...	2 10	2 10	2 10
	and for leading counsel if case certified fit for more counsel than one	– –	3 10	3 10
29	(*a*) Where trial or hearing of action is not concluded on day on which it is commenced or is adjourned for want of time or on payment of the costs of the day, for each day or part of day on which it is continued	3 0 to 5 0	3 0 to 10 0	3 0 to 18 0
	(*b*) With brief on examination of witness under Order 20, Rule 18(1), for each day or part of day			
	(*c*) With brief on further consideration pursuant to Order 29, Rules 18 and 19, or to hear a deferred judgment; with brief on application in the course of or relating to proceedings; with brief on examination of witness under Order 14, Rule 1(10), or Order 25, Rule 2; with brief on hearing of judgment summons	3 0 to 5 0	3 0 to 10 0	3 0 to 14 0
30	(*a*) For settling any document which in the opinion of the registrar is proper to be settled by counsel	3 0	3 0 to 5 0	3 0 to 6 0
	(*b*) For advising in writing on any question in the proceedings on which in the opinion of the registrar it was proper to obtain counsel's advice, including advising on evidence, advising on merits before action brought or defence filed and advising on quantum or on proposal and terms of settlement	3 0	3 0 to 5 0	3 0 to 6 0

Notes to items 26, 27, 28, 29 and 30.
Note 1.—The note to items 5, 6, 7 and 8 applies to fees to counsel as it applies to preparing for trial, attending court or attending in chambers.
Note 2.—Fees to counsel are not to be allowed unless the payment of them is vouched by the signature of counsel.

Plans, Photographs, &c.

Item No.		Scale 1	Scale 2	Scale 3
31	For plans, drawings, charts, photographs or models for use at the trial, which in the opinion of the registrar it was reasonable to obtain, the sum actually and reasonably paid	– –	– –	– –

Item No.		Scale 1	Scale 2	Scale 3
	Disbursements			
		£ s.	£ s.	£ s.
	Miscellaneous			
32	(a) For obtaining any documentary evidence or police reports or statements from the police which in the opinion of the registrar it was reasonably necessary to obtain for the purpose of the action or matter,			
	(b) for an advertisement in pursuance of an order for substituted service by advertisement, and			
	(c) for making any search in the companies register, the business names register or any other public register which in the opinion of the registrar it was reasonably necessary to make for the purpose of the action or matter, the sum actually and reasonably paid	– –	– –	– –
33	For oaths, sum paid, unless included in another item	– –	– –	– –
34	(a) For postages, carriage and transmission of documents a sum *not exceeding*	2 0	3 0	4 0
	(b) For telegrams and telephone calls, the sum actually and reasonably paid	– –	– –	– –
35	Where solicitor does not carry on business within two miles of place of trial of action or matter or place of hearing of application to which item 8 relates—			
	(a) the travelling and out of pocket expenses reasonably incurred by him in attending the place of trial or hearing; or	– –	– –	– –
	(b) if agent employed, for correspondence with agent	1 0	2 0	3 0
36	Where solicitor does not carry on business within two miles of the place of inspection of documents—			
	(a) the travelling and out of pocket expenses reasonably incurred by him in attending the place of inspection; or			
	(b) if agent employed, for correspondence with agent	1 0	2 0	3 0
37	In addition to item 26 (taxation) where solicitor does not carry on business within two miles of the court office—			
	(a) the travelling and out of pocket expenses reasonably incurred by him in attending the taxation; or	– –	– –	– –

Item No.	Scale 1	Scale 2	Scale 3
Disbursements			
	£ s.	£ s.	£ s.
(b) if agent reasonably employed, for correspondence with agent ...	1 0	2 0	3 0
Note to items 35(a), 36(a) and 37(a). Where in the opinion of the registrar it would have been reasonable to employ a solicitor carrying on business nearer to the court, the place of inspection of documents or the court office, as the case may be, he shall not allow more than he would have allowed to such a solicitor."			

4. The following Appendix shall be substituted for Appendix C:—

"APPENDIX C

COMPENSATION FOR LOSS OF TIME

Order 20, Rule 8(5)(a); Order 47, Rules 29 and 30

Class of Person	Column 1 Sum to be paid or tendered at time of service of witness summons	Column 2 Maximum sum per day allowable on taxation (including any sum paid under column 1)
	£ s.	£ s.
(a) Professional persons, and owners, directors or managers of businesses	4 0	10 0
(b) Police officers	3 0	3 0
(c) Clerks, artisans, labourers and all other persons	1 10	4 0 "

5. The following Appendix shall be substituted for Appendix D:—

"APPENDIX D

FIXED COSTS

PART I

ORDINARY, DEFAULT AND GARNISHEE SUMMONSES

Directions

Order 47, Rule 36

1. The Tables in this Part of this Appendix show the amount to be entered on the summons in respect of solicitor's charges—

    (a) in an action for the recovery of a sum of money, for the purpose only of Order 11, Rule 7, and Part II of this Appendix; or

    (b) in garnishee proceedings, for the purpose only of Order 27, Rule 7; or (*c*) in an action for the recovery of property, including land, with or without a claim for a sum of money, for the purpose of Part II of this Appendix or of fixing the amount which the plaintiff may receive in respect of solicitor's charges without taxation in the event of the defendant giving up possession and paying the amount claimed, if any, and costs.

2. In addition to the amount entered in accordance with the relevant Table the appropriate court fees shall be entered on the summons.

3. In the Tables the expression " claim " means—

(*a*) the sum of money claimed, or

(*b*) in relation to an action for the recovery of land (with or without a claim for a sum of money), a sum exceeding £100, or

(*c*) in relation to an action for the recovery of property other than money or land, the value of the property claimed or, in the case of goods supplied under a hire-purchase agreement, the unpaid balance of the hire-purchase price.

4. Where the solicitor has prepared a certificate for postal service of an ordinary summons, the amount of charges specified in paragraph (*a*) of the relevant Table shall be increased by 3*s*.

5. The Tables do not apply where the summons is to be served out of England and Wales or where substituted service is ordered.

TABLES OF FIXED COSTS

TABLE I

Where claim exceeds £5 but does not exceed £20

	Amount of Charges £ s.
(*a*) Where service is not by solicitor	1 10
(*b*) Where service is by solicitor	2 0

TABLE II

Where claim exceeds £20 but does not exceed £100

	Amount of Charges £ s.
(*a*) Where service is not by solicitor	3 0
(*b*) Where service is by solicitor	4 0

TABLE III

Where claim exceeds £100

	Amount of Charges £ s.
(*a*) Where service is not by solicitor	6 0
(*b*) Where service is by solicitor	7 0

Part II

Judgments

Directions

Where an amount in respect of solicitor's charges has been entered on the summons under Part I of this Appendix and judgment is entered or given in the circumstances mentioned in one of the paragraphs in column 1 of the following Table, the amount to be included in the judgment in respect of the plaintiff's solicitor's charges shall be the amount entered on the summons together with the amount shown in column 2 of the Table under the sum of money by reference to which the amount entered on the summons was fixed.

Where judgment is entered or given for a sum less than the amount claimed or for the delivery of goods of which the value or the balance of the hire purchase price is a sum less than the amount claimed, the foregoing paragraph shall, unless the court otherwise directs, have effect as if the amount entered on the summons had been fixed by reference to that sum.

Table

Fixed Costs on Judgments

Column 1	Column 2 Sum of money		
	A Exceeding £5 but not exceeding £20	B Exceeding £20 but not exceeding £100	C Exceeding £100
	£ s.	£ s.	£ s.
(a) Where judgment is entered in a default action in default of defence	– 10	1 0	1 10
(b) Where judgment is entered on the defendant's admission and the plaintiff's acceptance of his proposal as to mode of payment ...			
(c) Where judgment is entered on an admission delivered by the defendant and the court's decision is given as to the date of payment or instalments by which payment is to be made			
(d) Where judgment is given in an ordinary action for— (i) recovery of a liquidated sum of money; or (ii) delivery of goods; or (iii) possession of land suspended on payment of arrears of rent, whether claimed or not, in addition to current rent, and the defendant has neither delivered a defence, admission or counterclaim, nor otherwise denied liability	1 0	2 0	4 0 "

6. The following Appendix shall be substituted for Appendix E:—

" APPENDIX E

Order 47,
Rule 37(3)

ASSESSMENT OF COSTS

Directions

1. This Table shows the amount which, pursuant to Order 47, Rule 37(3), may be allowed where costs are to be assessed without taxation. The amount includes the fee for counsel where applicable.

2. In addition to the amount shown in the Table there may be allowed, where appropriate—

(i) court fees,

(ii) allowances to witnesses,

(iii) in a case on one of the Higher Scales, a charge on that scale in respect of service of process by the solicitor or substituted service or the preparation of a certificate resulting in postal service, and

(iv) in a case on the Lower Scale, a charge of 10s. in respect of service of process by the solicitor.

Column 1 Scale	*Column* 2 Amount of Charges
Lower Scale	£3 to £8
Scale 1	£5 to £10
Scale 2	£10 to £15
Scale 3	£15 to £25 "

7.—(1) Where costs fall to be taxed, fixed or assessed under Appendix B, D or E by virtue of a judgment or order given, entered or made after the date of the coming into operation of these Rules, or fall to be taxed by virtue of Order 11, Rule 7(3A)(*b*) or 8(*d*), or Order 18, Rule 2, in consequence of a payment into court or a notice of discontinuance made or given after that date, the costs may be taxed, fixed or assessed, as the case may be, as if all the work to which they relate had been done after that date.

(2) Except as provided in paragraph (1), nothing in these Rules shall apply in relation to anything done before the date of the coming into operation of these Rules.

We, the undersigned members of the Rule Committee appointed by the Lord Chancellor under section 102 of the County Courts Act 1959(a), having by virtue of the powers vested in us in this behalf made the foregoing Rules, do hereby certify the same under our hand and submit them to the Lord Chancellor accordingly.

D. O. McKee.
Connolly H. Gage.
Hugh Mais.
H. S. Ruttle.
David Pennant.
W. Ralph Davies.
E. A. Everett.
Arthur Figgis.
K. W. Mellor.
A. F. Stapleton Cotton.
D. A. Marshall.

I allow these Rules, which shall come into operation on 9th March 1970.

Dated 9th February 1970.

Gardiner, C.

EXPLANATORY NOTE

(*This Note is not part of the Rules.*)

These Rules increase the costs allowable in county court proceedings by substituting new scales of costs and new tables of fixed and assessed costs for those set out in Appendices B, D and E to the County Court Rules. The new scales consist of a Lower Scale, to apply where the claim exceeds £5 but not £20, and three Higher Scales, of which Scale 1 is to apply between £20 and £50, Scale 2 between £50 and £200 and Scale 3 over £200. Only the Higher Scales are set out in the new Appendix B, since costs on the Lower Scale, unless fixed under Appendix D, will be assessed under Appendix E. Consequential amendments are made in Order 47 and the registrar on taxation is given a discretion to allow increased costs, without a certificate of the judge, in all cases on Scale 3.

The Rules also increase the amounts which, under Appendix C to the County Court Rules, may be allowed to witnesses as compensation for loss of time, and give the registrar a discretion to exceed the prescribed amount in cases on Scale 3. The fees allowable in respect of expert witnesses are also raised.

(a) 1959 c. 22.

STATUTORY INSTRUMENTS

1970 No. 205

INDUSTRIAL TRAINING

The Industrial Training (Petroleum Board) Order 1970

Made - - - -	*12th February* 1970
Laid before Parliament	*23rd February* 1970
Coming into Operation	*4th March* 1970

The Secretary of State after consultation with the Petroleum Industry Training Board and with organisations and associations of organisations appearing to be representative respectively of substantial numbers of employers engaging in the activities hereinafter mentioned and of substantial numbers of persons employed in those activities and with the bodies established for the purpose of carrying on under national ownership industries in which the said activities are carried on to a substantial extent and in exercise of her powers under section 9 of the Industrial Training Act 1964(a) and of all other powers enabling her in that behalf hereby makes the following Order:—

Citation, commencement and interpretation

1.—(1) This Order may be cited as the Industrial Training (Petroleum Board) Order 1970 and shall come into operation on 4th March 1970.

(2) In this Order—

(a) "the Act" means the Industrial Training Act 1964;

(b) "the Board" means the Petroleum Industry Training Board;

(c) "the levy Order" means the Industrial Training Levy (Petroleum) Order 1968(b);

(d) "the principal Order" means the Industrial Training (Petroleum Board) Order 1967(c).

(3) The Interpretation Act 1889(d) shall apply to the interpretation of this Order as it applies to the interpretation of an Act of Parliament and as if this Order and the principal Order were Acts of Parliament.

Activities of the Board

2. The activities in relation to which the Board exercises the functions conferred by the Act upon industrial training boards shall, in lieu of the activities specified in Schedule 1 to the principal Order, be the activities specified in the Schedule to this Order, and accordingly in the principal Order the latter Schedule shall be substituted for the former Schedule.

Transitional provisions

3.—(1) The chairman and other members of the Board on the day upon which this Order comes into operation shall continue to be members of the Board and

---

(a) 1964 c. 16.   (b) 1968/1453 (1968 III, p. 4193).
(c) S.I. 1967/648 (1967 I, p. 2032).   (d) 1889 c. 63.

to hold and vacate their offices in accordance with the terms of the instruments appointing them to be members.

(2) The provisions of this Order shall not—

(*a*) extend the operation of the levy Order;

(*b*) affect the operation of the levy Order in relation to the assessment of an employer within the meaning of that Order in respect of an establishment that was engaged in the first levy period wholly or mainly in activities included in the Schedule to this Order;

(*c*) affect the operation of any assessment notice served by the Board under the provisions of the levy Order before the date upon which this Order comes into operation or any appeal or other proceedings arising out of any such notice.

12th February 1970.

Barbara Castle,
First Secretary of State and Secretary of State
for Employment and Productivity.

SCHEDULE Article 2

The Petroleum Industry

1. Subject to the provisions of this Schedule, the activities of the petroleum industry are the following activities in so far as they are exercised within Great Britain:—

(*a*) the searching or boring for or getting of petroleum;

(*b*) the distillation, conversion, extraction, refining or blending of petroleum or any petroleum product;

(*c*) the production or blending of petroleum jelly, solid lubricants, grease or wax;

(*d*) the collection or recovery of any waste petroleum product;

(*e*) the public warehousing of petroleum or any petroleum product;

(*f*) dealing in petroleum or any petroleum product;

(*g*) the administration, control, co-ordination or direction of one or more establishments engaged outside Great Britain wholly or mainly in any of the activities above-mentioned, or the provision of an advisory or information service for any such establishment;

(*h*) any activities (other than those above-mentioned) being—

(i) related activities incidental or ancillary to principal activities of the petroleum industry; or

(ii) activities undertaken in the administration, control or direction of one or more establishments, being establishments engaged wholly or mainly in principal activities of that industry, in related activities incidental or ancillary thereto, or in the administration, control or direction of one or more other establishments engaged in such principal or related activities;

and carried out, in either case, by the employer engaged in those principal activities or, where that employer is a company, by the company or by an associated company of the company;

(*i*) any activities of industry or commerce (other than petroleum activities) carried out at or from an establishment mainly engaged—

(i) in petroleum activities; or

(ii) in petroleum activities and in activities described in the Appendix to this Schedule, but to a greater extent in petroleum activities than in activities described in that Appendix in relation to any one industry.

2. Notwithstanding anything contained in this Schedule, there shall not be included in the activities of the petroleum industry:—

(a) the activities of any establishment engaged—

(i) mainly in activities not being petroleum activities or activities described in the Appendix to this Schedule; or

(ii) to a less extent in petroleum activities than in activities described in that Appendix in relation to any one industry;

(b) the activities of any establishment engaged wholly or mainly in related activities, being activities—

(i) incidental or ancillary to the activities of one or more establishments (in this sub-paragraph hereafter referred to as "the principal establishment") engaged wholly or mainly in any activities not being principal activities of the petroleum industry; and

(ii) carried out by the employer carrying on the principal establishment or, where that employer is a company, by the company or by an associated company of the company;

(c) the activities of any establishment engaged wholly or mainly in the activities following or any of them, that is to say—

(i) the lifting or extracting of mineral deposits (not being petroleum) or products of minerals from the earth or of such mineral deposits from the bed of any lake or river or of the sea;

(ii) selling, by retail, motor spirit, diesel fuel or lubricating or other oils for use in motor vehicles;

(iii) the manufacture of any chemical from a feedstock derived from petroleum or research or development connected with such manufacture;

(iv) the manufacture of acids, bases, alkalis, salts, esters or their intermediates or derivatives;

(v) the manufacture of organo-silicon, organo-phosphorus, organo-sulphur or organo-metallic compounds; or

(vi) the management and operation of ships;

(d) the activities of—

(i) the Electricity Council, the Central Electricity Generating Board or an Area Electricity Board;

(ii) the North of Scotland Hydro-Electric Board or the South of Scotland Electricity Board; or

(iii) the Gas Council or an Area Gas Board;

(e) any operations when carried out by the master or a member of the crew of a ship, or by a person ordinarily employed as a seaman who is employed in or about a ship in port by the owner or charterer thereof on work of a kind ordinarily done by a seaman on a ship while it is in port; or

(f) the supply of food or drink for immediate consumption.

3. In this Schedule unless the context otherwise requires:—

(a) "company" includes any body corporate, and "subsidiary" has the same meaning as by virtue of section 154 of the Companies Act 1948(a) it has for the purposes of that Act;

(b) "dealing" means by way of business and in the capacity of principal, agent or broker—

(a) 1948 c. 38.

(i) in relation to petroleum or petroleum products situate in Great Britain, buying or selling the same;

(ii) in relation to petroleum or petroleum products situate elsewhere, importing the same into Great Britain;

(*c*) "office premises" has the same meaning as in section 1(2) of the Offices, Shops and Railway Premises Act 1963(a);

(*d*) "petroleum" includes any mineral oil or relative hydrocarbon and natural gas existing in its natural condition in strata, but does not include coal or bituminous shales or other stratified deposits from which oil can be extracted by destructive distillation;

(*e*) "petroleum activities" means any one or more of the principal activities of the petroleum industry and the activities included in that industry by virtue of paragraph 1(*h*) of this Schedule;

(*f*) "petroleum product" means crude oil, bitumen obtained therefrom, liquefied petroleum gas, aviation fuel, motor spirit, kerosene, white spirit, diesel fuel, fuel oil, gas oil, lubricating oil or any similar product;

(*g*) "principal activities of the petroleum industry" means activities which, subject to the provisions of paragraph 2 of this Schedule, are specified in paragraph 1, other than sub-paragraphs (*h*) and (*i*) thereof, as activities of the petroleum industry;

(*h*) "public warehousing" means keeping any premises (not being a public garage or parking place) wholly or mainly for the storage of petroleum or any petroleum product for reward for persons other than the occupier or, where the occupier is a company, for persons other than the company or an associated company of the company;

(*i*) "recovery" includes any of the operations of cleaning, dehydration, distillation or re-blending;

(*j*) "related activities" means any of the following activities, that is to say—

(i) research, development, design or drawing;

(ii) buying, selling, testing, advertising, packing, distribution, transport or any similar operations;

(iii) operations of a kind performed at office premises or laboratories, or at stores, warehouses or similar places;

(iv) cleaning, washing or garaging vehicles, or carrying out running repairs or minor adjustments thereto; or

(v) training of employees or apprentices.

4. For the purposes of this Schedule, two companies shall be taken to be associated companies if one is a subsidiary of the other or both are subsidiaries of a third company, and "associated company" shall be construed accordingly.

(a) 1963 c. 41.

APPENDIX

The activities that would be included in an industry specified in Column 1 hereof by virtue of the industrial training order specified in the corresponding entry in Column 2, if the provisions specified in Column 3 were omitted from that order.

Column 1	Column 2	Column 3
The wool, jute and flax industry	The Industrial Training (Wool Industry Board) Order 1964 as amended by the Industrial Training (Wool, Jute and Flax Board) Order 1968(a)	Schedule 1 Paragraph 1(s)
The iron and steel industry	The Industrial Training (Iron and Steel Board) Order 1964 as amended by the Industrial Training (Iron and Steel Board) Order 1969(b)	Schedule 1 Paragraph 1(k)
The construction industry	The Industrial Training (Construction Board) Order 1964 as amended by the Industrial Training (Construction Board) Order 1967(c)	Schedule 1 Paragraph 1(l)
The engineering industry	The Industrial Training (Engineering Board) Order 1964 as amended by the Industrial Training (Engineering Board) Order 1968 and the Industrial Training (Engineering Board) Order 1968 (Amendment) Order 1969(d)	Schedule 1 Paragraph 1(m)
The shipbuilding industry	The Industrial Training (Shipbuilding Board) Order 1964 as amended by the Industrial Training (Shipbuilding Board) Order 1968(e)	Schedule 1 Paragraph 1(g)
The ceramics, glass and mineral products industry	The Industrial Training (Ceramics, Glass and Mineral Products Board) Order 1965 as amended by the Industrial Training (Ceramics, Glass and Mineral Products Board) Order 1969(f)	Schedule 1 Paragraph 1(p)
The furniture and timber industry	The Industrial Training (Furniture and Timber Industry Board) Order 1965 as amended by the Industrial Training (Furniture and Timber Industry Board) Order 1969(g)	Schedule 1 Paragraph 1(x)
The man-made fibres producing industry	The Industrial Training (Man-made Fibres Producing Industry Board) Order 1966 as amended by the Industrial Training (Man-made Fibres Producing Industry Board) Order 1969(h)	Schedule 1 Paragraph 1(e)

(a) S.I. 1964/907, 1968/898 (1964 II, p. 1928; 1968 II, p. 2376).
(b) S.I. 1964/949, 1969/884 (1964 II, p. 2127; 1969 II, p. 2517).
(c) S.I. 1964/1079, 1967/924 (1964 II, p. 2384; 1967 II, p. 2757).
(d) S.I. 1964/1086, 1968/1333, 1969/1376 (1964 II, p. 2402; 1968 II, p. 3694; 1969 III, p. 4103).
(e) S.I. 1964/1782, 1968/1614 (1964 III, p. 3928; 1968 III, p. 4432).
(f) S.I. 1965/1391, 1969/689 (1965 II, p. 4062; 1969 II, p. 1860).
(g) S.I. 1965/2028, 1969/1290 (1965 III, p. 5998; 1969 III, p. 3820).
(h) S.I. 1966/143, 1969/1210 (1966 I, p. 257; 1969 II, p. 3545).

Column 1	Column 2	Column 3
The carpet industry	The Industrial Training (Carpet Board) Order 1966 as amended by the Industrial Training (Carpet Board) Order 1968**(a)**	Schedule 1 Paragraph 1(*f*)
The knitting, lace and net industry	The Industrial Training (Knitting, Lace and Net Industry Board) Order 1966**(b)**	Schedule 1 Paragraph 1(*j*)
The cotton and allied textiles industry	The Industrial Training (Cotton and Allied Textiles Board) Order 1966**(c)**	Schedule 1 Paragraph 1(*p*)
The agricultural, horti-cultural and forestry in-dustry	The Industrial Training (Agricultural, Horti-cultural and Forestry Board) Order 1966**(d)**	Schedule 1 Paragraph 1(*m*)
The road transport industry	The Industrial Training (Road Transport Board) Order 1966 as amended by the Industrial Training (Road Transport Board) Order 1969 and the Industrial Training (Road Transport Board) Order 1969 (Amendment) Order 1969**(e)**	Schedule 1 Paragraph 1(*p*)
The hotel and catering in-dustry	The Industrial Training (Hotel and Catering Board) Order 1966 as amended by the Industrial Training (Hotel and Catering Board) Order 1969**(f)**	Schedule 1 Paragraph 1(*e*)
The civil air transport in-dustry	The Industrial Training (Civil Air Trans-port Board) Order 1967**(g)**	Schedule 1 Paragraph 1(*h*)
The rubber and plastics processing industry	The Industrial Training (Rubber and Plastics Processing Board) Order 1967**(h)**	Schedule 1 Paragraph 1(*k*)
The chemical and allied products industry	The Industrial Training (Chemical and Allied Products Board) Order 1967**(i)**	Schedule 1 Paragraph 1(*s*)
The paper and paper pro-ducts industry	The Industrial Training (Paper and Paper Products Board) Order 1968**(j)**	Schedule 1 Paragraph 1(*j*)
The printing and publishing industry	The Industrial Training (Printing and Publishing Board) Order 1968**(k)**	Schedule 1 Paragraph 1(*n*)
The distributive industry	The Industrial Training (Distributive Board) Order 1968**(l)**	Schedule 1 Paragraph 1(*h*)
The food, drink and tobacco industry	The Industrial Training (Food, Drink and Tobacco Board) Order 1968**(m)**	Schedule 1 Paragraph 1(*q*)
The footwear, leather and fur skin industry	The Industrial Training (Footwear, Leather and Fur Skin Board) Order 1968**(n)**	Schedule 1 Paragraph 1(*v*)
The clothing and allied products industry	The Industrial Training (Clothing and Allied Products Board) Order 1969**(o)**	Schedule 1 Paragraph 1(*j*)
The hairdressing and allied services industry	The Industrial Training (Hairdressing and Allied Services Board) Order 1969**(p)**	Schedule 1 Paragraph 1(*g*)

(a) S.I. 1966/245, 1968/1882 (1966 I, p. 499; 1968 III, p. 5017).
(b) S.I. 1966/246 (1966 I, p. 506).   **(c)** S.I. 1966/823 (1966 II, p. 1907).
(d) S.I. 1966/969 (1966 II, p. 2333).
(e) S.I. 1966/1112, 1969/879, 1871 (1966 III, p. 2712; 1969 II, p. 2495; 1969 III, p. 5815).
(f) S.I. 1966/1347, 1969/1405 (1966 III, p. 3669; 1969 III, p. 4132).
(g) S.I. 1967/263 (1967 I, p. 968).   **(h)** S.I. 1967/1062 (1967 II, p. 3151).
(i) S.I. 1967/1386 (1967 III, p. 4049).   **(j)** S.I. 1968/787 (1968 II, p. 2194).
(k) S.I. 1968/786 (1968 II, p. 2185).   **(l)** S.I. 1968/1032 (1968 II, p. 2709).
(m) S.I. 1968/1033 (1968 II, p. 2721).   **(n)** S.I. 1968/1763 (1968 III, p. 4785).
(o) S.I. 1969/1375 (1969 III, p. 4094).   **(p)** S.I. 1969/1634 (1969 III, p. 5133).

EXPLANATORY NOTE

(This Note is not part of the Order.)

This Order re-defines the activities in relation to which the Petroleum Industry Training Board exercises its functions. The Board was established on 18th May 1967 by the Industrial Training (Petroleum Board) Order 1967.

Amongst the activities henceforth to be included in the petroleum industry are—

    (*a*) the production or blending of solid lubricants;

    (*b*) the collection or recovery of waste petroleum products;

    (*c*) the public warehousing of petroleum or petroleum products.

STATUTORY INSTRUMENTS

1970 No. 211

LONDON GOVERNMENT

The London Government Order 1970

Made - - -	*12th February* 1970
Laid before Parliament	*20th February* 1970
Coming into Operation	*1st March* 1970

The Minister of Housing and Local Government, in exercise of his powers under section 84 of the London Government Act 1963(**a**) and as regards article 9 of this order under that section as extended by section 35 of the Administration of Justice Act 1964(**b**), and of all other powers enabling him in that behalf, hereby makes the following order—

Title and commencement

1. This order may be cited as the London Government Order 1970, and shall come into operation on 1st March 1970.

Interpretation

2.—(1) The Interpretation Act 1889(**c**) applies to the interpretation of this order as it applies to the interpretation of an Act of Parliament.

(2) In this order—

"the Act" means the London Government Act 1963 ;

"the City" means the City of London ; and

"the Common Council" means the Common Council of the City of London.

(3) In this order, unless the context otherwise requires, references to any enactment shall be construed as references to that enactment as amended, extended or applied by or under any other enactment.

Miscellaneous provision as to public general and other Acts

3.—(1) In the Electricity (Supply) Act 1919(**d**), in section 21, the reference to the local planning authority within the meaning of the Town and Country Planning Act 1947(**e**) shall be construed, in relation to land in a London borough or in the City, as including a reference to the Greater London Council but not to the borough council or to the Common Council.

(2) In the Children and Young Persons Act 1933(**f**), in section 12(5), after "county borough" where first occurring there shall be inserted "or the Greater London Council".

(3) In the Crown Lands Act 1936(**g**), in section 2(4), for "the London County Council" there shall be substituted "the Greater London Council".

(**a**) 1963 c.33.	(**b**) 1964 c. 42.
(**c**) 1889 c.63.	(**d**) 1919 c.100.
(**e**) 1947 c.51.	(**f**) 1933 c.12.
(**g**) 1936 c.47.	

(4) In the Water Act 1945(**a**), in Schedule 3, in paragraph 94(1), there shall be added "or where they supply, or propose to supply, water, or have, or propose to construct, any waterworks, in Greater London, with the clerk to the Greater London Council".

(5) In the Marriage Act 1949(**b**), in section 57(4), for the words following "the certified copy" there shall be substituted—

"and that sum shall be reimbursed to the superintendent registrar—

(*a*) in the case of a registration district in the City of London, the Inner Temple and the Middle Temple, by the Common Council of the City of London ;

(*b*) in any other case, by the council of the county, county borough or London borough in which his registration district is situated".

(6) In section 42 of the London County Council (General Powers) Act 1953(**c**) (which makes provision as to the proof of resolutions passed, orders made and reports received by the Greater London Council and the councils of the inner London boroughs and of appointments of officers made and authorities to officers given by such councils)—

(*a*) in subsections (1) and (2)—

for "the council or a committee thereof" there shall be substituted "the council, or a predecessor, or a committee of any such body" ;

for "the council or committee" there shall be substituted "the council, or predecessor, or committee" ;

(*b*) in subsection (3), there shall be added—

"and "predecessor" means, in the case of any council named in column (1) of the following table, a council specified in respect of such council in column (2).

TABLE

(1)	(2)
The Greater London Council	The London County Council The county council of Middlesex
The council of the London borough of Camden	The council of the metropolitan borough of Hampstead, Holborn or St. Pancras
The council of the London borough of Greenwich	The council of the metropolitan borough of Greenwich or Woolwich
The council of the London borough of Hackney	The council of the metropolitan borough of Hackney, Shoreditch or Stoke Newington
The council of the London borough of Hammersmith	The council of the metropolitan borough of Fulham or Hammersmith
The council of the London borough of Islington	The council of the metropolitan borough of Finsbury or Islington

(**a**) 1945 c.42.   (**b**) 1949 c.76.
(**c**) Section substituted by S.I. 1965/540 (1965 I, p. 1597).

TABLE—continued

(1)	(2)
The council of the Royal borough of Kensington and Chelsea	The council of the metropolitan borough of Chelsea or Kensington
The council of the London borough of Lambeth	The council of the metropolitan borough of Lambeth
The council of the London borough of Lewisham	The council of the metropolitan borough of Deptford or Lewisham
The council of the London borough of Southwark	The council of the metropolitan borough of Bermondsey, Camberwell or Southwark
The council of the London borough of Tower Hamlets	The council of the metropolitan borough of Bethnal Green, Poplar or Stepney
The council of the London borough of Wandsworth	The council of the metropolitan borough of Battersea or Wandsworth
The council of the City of Westminster	The council of the metropolitan borough of Westminster, Paddington or St. Marylebone".

(7) In the Forestry Act 1967(a), in section 40(2)(c), after "parish", there shall be inserted "the Greater London Council,".

(8) The enactments specified in the Schedule to this order are hereby repealed to the extent mentioned in column (3) thereof.

Construction of references to superseded provisions

4. Where by or under the Act—

    (a) a provision of an enactment or instrument has been repealed or revoked ; and

    (b) a corresponding provision has been applied to the relevant area or to any part thereof

any reference in any local Act or in any instrument made under any Act to the provision mentioned in (a) shall, in the application of such Act or instrument to the relevant area or to such part, as the case may be, unless the contrary intention appears, be construed as a reference to the provision mentioned in (b).

In this article—

    "the relevant area" has the meaning assigned to it by section 87(9) of the Act ; and

    "local Act" includes an Act confirming a provisional order.

Deposit of plans and documents

5. All enactments or statutory orders relating to the deposit of plans or documents, other than those relating to judicial business, shall, in their application to Greater London, be construed as if the clerk to the Greater London Council were therein substituted for the clerk of the peace.

(a) 1967 c.10.

When acting under any such enactment or statutory order, the said clerk shall act under the direction of the Greater London Council.

In this article. "enactment" and "statutory order" have the same meanings as in the Local Government Act 1933(**a**).

Drainage of contiguous premises

6.—(1) In paragraph 14(5) of Part III of Schedule 9 to the Act (which as extended to the City by the London Government (No. 2) Order 1965(**b**) enables the drainage in common of certain houses to be required by the council of an inner London borough or the Common Council), there shall be added—

"In this sub-paragraph, "house" includes a school and also a factory or other building in which persons are employed and, in relation to a house as hereinbefore defined, includes the curtilage thereof.".

(2) Paragraph 14(6) of the said Part III shall apply to the City and in such application the reference to a borough council shall be read as a reference to the Common Council.

Compensation for injury to or the death of officers of the London County Council

7. Section 75 of the Act (which makes provision for compensation for injury to or the death of officers), in its application to the Greater London Council, shall, in so far as it empowers the increase of compensation paid by periodical payments, extend to any officer of the London County Council, or to any widow or widower or child of any such officer, to whom compensation was being paid immediately before 1st April 1965 under section 44 of the London County Council (General Powers) Act 1895(**c**) or section 92 of the London Government Act 1939(**d**).

The said section shall also extend to the payment of compensation to the widow or widower or child of any such officer.

Common Council—Legal proceedings in relation to certain functions

8. In relation to—

  (*a*) any functions of the Greater London Council delegated to the Common Council under section 5(1) of the Act ;

  (*b*) any administrative, clerical, professional, scientific or technical services undertaken by the Common Council for the Greater London Council under section 5(3)(*a*) of the Act,

but subject in the case of item (*a*) to any restrictions or conditions imposed by the Greater London Council under the said section 5(1), sections 276 (Power of local authority to prosecute or defend legal proceedings) and 277 (Appearance of local authority in legal proceedings) of the Local Government Act 1933 shall apply to the Common Council as if it were a local authority within the meaning of that Act.

(**a**) 1933 c.51. (**b**) S.I. 1965/1444 (1965 II, p. 4267).
(**c**) 1895 c.cxxvii. (**d**) 1939 c. 40.

Appointment of auditors of accounts of certain conservators of commons

9. In any provision specified in column (1) of the following table, for the words specified in respect of such provision in column (2) there shall be substituted the words so specified in column (3).

TABLE

(1)	(2)	(3)
Section 30(5) of the Wimbledon and Putney Commons Act 1871(a)	"the chairman of the Court of Quarter Sessions for the county of Surrey"	"the chairman of the court of quarter sessions for the south-west London area"
Clause 27 of the scheme approved by the Metropolitan Commons (Mitcham) Supplemental Act 1891(b)	"the chairman of quarter sessions for the county of Surrey"	do.
Clause 20 of the scheme approved by the Metropolitan Commons (Harrow Weald) Supplemental Act 1899(c)	"the Chairman of Quarter Sessions for the county of Middlesex"	"the chairman of the court of quarter sessions for the Middlesex area"

Corporation of wardens of the parish of St. Saviour, Southwark

10. The power of electing five wardens, namely the Warden of the Great Account, the Renter Warden, the College Warden, the Bell Warden and the Newcomen's Warden, of the corporation of wardens of the parish of St. Saviour, Southwark, shall be exercisable by the council of the London borough of Southwark.

An appointment of a person to be such a warden shall not be made except on the nomination of councillors for the ward or wards consisting of or comprising the area of the parish of St. Saviour, Southwark, as existing in the metropolitan borough of Southwark until 31st March 1930 :

Provided that if in any case such councillors fail to make a nomination within one calendar month from the time for which a meeting of the councillors was first summoned for the purpose, the council may make the appointment without any such nomination.

A nomination under this article shall be made in accordance with rules made or approved by the Charity Commissioners.

Southwark Borough Market

11.—(1) In the Southwark (Borough Market) Scheme 1907(d)—

(*a*) in the sixth recital, "(which council is in this Scheme referred to as the Borough Council)" shall be omitted ;

(*b*) in section 2(1), for "the said St. Saviour's Ward" there shall be substituted "the ward or wards consisting of or comprising the specified area" ;

(*c*) in section 2(3), for "a ratepayer of the parish of St. Saviour" there shall be substituted "a ratepayer of the specified area" ;

(a) 1871 c.cciv.
(c) 1899 c.xxxvii.
(b) 1891 c.xxvi.
(d) Confirmed by 7 Edw. 7. c. xlvi.

(*d*) in section 6—

    (i) for "in relief of the rates of the parish of St. Saviour" there shall be substituted "in relief of the rates chargeable on hereditaments in the specified area" ; and

    (ii) for "over the parish of St. Saviour" there shall be substituted "over the specified area" ;

(*e*) in section 10 the following paragraph shall be inserted—

"(2A) In the foregoing sections of this Scheme—

"Borough Council" means the council of the London borough of Southwark ; and

"the specified area" means the area of the parish of St. Saviour, Southwark, as existing in the metropolitan borough of Southwark until 31st March 1930." ;

(*f*) in rule 1 in the Schedule, for "councillors of St. Saviour's ward" there shall be substituted "councillors of the ward or wards described in section 2(1)" ;

(*g*) in rule 2 in the Schedule, for "of the St. Saviour's Ward" there shall be substituted "of the said ward or wards", and

(*h*) in rule 3 in the Schedule, for "four" there shall be substituted "two".

(2) The trustees appointed by the council of the London borough of Southwark in office at the coming into operation of this order shall remain in office as if they had been appointed in accordance with the Southwark (Borough Market) Scheme 1907 as amended by paragraph (1) of this article.

(3) Article 13(*a*) of the Metropolitan Borough of Southwark (Union of Parishes) Order 1930 shall cease to have effect.

Victoria Embankment and the Thames adjoining

12. The embankment southward of the gardens of the Societies of the Inner and Middle Temples, respectively, referred to in section 29 of the Thames Embankment Act 1862(**a**), the road thereon, and the river Thames adjoining, to the middle of the river, shall form part of the City.

The boundaries established by this article shall be mered by Ordnance Survey.

Festival Pleasure Gardens and Pier

13.—(1) In section 3 of the Festival of Britain (Supplementary Provisions) Act 1949(**b**), any reference to the London County Council shall be construed as a reference to the Greater London Council.

(2) In relation to the Festival Pleasure Gardens Pier (being a landing stage constructed by the London County Council under section 1 of the Public Works (Festival of Britain) Act 1949(**c**) as extended by section 7 of the Festival of Britain (Supplementary Provisions) Act 1949), any reference in section 1 or 11(9) of the first-mentioned Act or in section 7 of the Act secondly mentioned to the London County Council shall be construed as a reference to the Greater London Council.

(**a**) 1862 c. 93.   (**b**) 1949 c.102.
(**c**) 1949 c.26.

Contributions in respect of Knockholt sewerage scheme

14. The liability of the Kent County Council under the agreement made under section 2 of the Rural Water Supplies and Sewerage Act 1944(a) with the Orpington Urban District Council in respect of the Knockholt sewerage scheme shall cease in respect of any contributions payable between 31st March 1965 and 1st April 1969.

Contribution by the Greater London Council to the London borough council of Enfield

15. The Greater London Council may contribute to the London borough council of Enfield, in respect of expenses incurred by that council in the re-location of Sumex Paints Ltd. following the acquisition of their premises (such acquisition and relocation having been approved by the county council of Middlesex), such sum as may be agreed between the two councils.

SCHEDULE
REPEALS

(1) Chapter	(2) Short Title	(3) Extent of Repeal
1894 c.60	The Merchant Shipping Act 1894	In section 214(7), the words "in the administrative county of London the county council, and else-where"
1906 c.33	The Local Authorities (Treasury Powers) Act 1906	In section 1(1), the words "except the London County Council"
1907 c.40	The Notification of Births Act 1907	In any application to Greater London, the whole Act In section 2(4) the words "(other than the county of London)"
1908 c.36	The Small Holdings and Allotments Act 1908	In any application to Greater London, section 52(1) Section 53(1) In section 53(4), paragraphs (a) and (b)
1913 c.19	The Local Government (Adjustments) Act 1913	The whole Act
1926 c.52	The Small Holdings and Allotments Act 1926	In any application to Greater London, the words "under section fifty-two of the principal Act" in s.14(4)
1939 c.73	The Housing (Emergency Powers) Act 1939	In section 3(1A), the words "the London County Council"

Given under the official seal of the Minister of Housing and Local Government on 12th February 1970.

(L.S.)

Anthony Greenwood,
Minister of Housing and Local Government.

(a) 1944 c.26.

EXPLANATORY NOTE

(This Note is not part of the Order.)

This order makes further incidental, consequential, transitional and supplementary provision in relation to Greater London, relating to—

(*a*) the amendment of certain Acts ;

(*b*) the construction of references to superseded provisions ;

(*c*) the deposit of plans and documents ;

(*d*) the drainage of contiguous premises ;

(*e*) the increase of compensation paid by periodical payments to, or in respect of, certain officers of the London County Council ;

(*f*) the taking of proceedings by the Common Council in relation to delegated functions ;

(*g*) a number of matters of local significance.

STATUTORY INSTRUMENTS

1970 No. 212

TRADE MARKS
The Trade Marks (Customs) Regulations 1970

Made - - -		13*th February* 1970
Laid before Parliament		20*th February* 1970
Coming into Operation		3*rd March* 1970

The Commissioners of Customs and Excise, in exercise of the powers conferred on them by section 64A(3) of the Trade Marks Act 1938(a), as amended by section 17 of the Trade Descriptions Act 1968(b), and of all other powers enabling them in that behalf, hereby make the following Regulations :—

1.—(1) These Regulations may be cited as the Trade Marks (Customs) Regulations 1970.

(2) The Interpretation Act 1889(c) shall apply for the interpretation of these Regulations as it applies for the interpretation of an Act of Parliament.

(3) These Regulations shall come into force on the 3rd day of March 1970.

2. If notice (hereinafter called "the notice") is given under section 64A(1) of the said Act of 1938 as so amended by a person who is registered as the proprietor or registered user of a trade mark in respect of certain goods, it shall be in the form set out in the Schedule to these Regulations ; and separate notices shall be given in respect of each consignment of such goods bearing the said trade mark.

3. A fee of five pounds in respect of each notice shall be paid to the Commissioners immediately after the notice has been given.

4. The person who gives the notice, or a notice purporting to be the notice, shall, if so required, give to the Commissioners such security or further security by deposit of money or bond as the Commissioners shall think fit in respect of any liability or expense which they may incur in consequence of the detention of any goods to which the notice relates or in consequence of anything done in relation to goods so detained ; and if such security or further security is not given within the time specified by the Commissioners, then (but without prejudice to the operation of the next following Regulation) the notice shall have no effect.

5. In every case, whether any security or further security is given or not, the person who has given the notice or purported notice shall keep the Commissioners indemnified against all such liability and expense as is mentioned in the preceding Regulation and in particular shall repay to them all expense which may be incurred by them in consequence of the detention of, or anything done in relation to, any goods to which the notice relates.

(a) 1938 c. 22.   (b) 1968 c. 29.
(c) 1889 c. 63.

6.—(1) The person who gives the notice shall, within seven days of giving it, or within such further time as the Commissioners may allow, furnish them with a Certificate of the Registrar of Trade Marks as to the matters covered by paragraph 1 of the notice in relation to the trade mark specified therein.

(2) If such a certificate is not so furnished within such time then the goods shall not be detained, or, if detained, shall be released, and (but without prejudice to the operation of the preceding Regulation) any notice given in respect of them shall have no effect.

Dorothy Johnstone,
Commissioner of Customs and Excise.

13th February 1970.
King's Beam House,
Mark Lane,
London, E.C.3.

SCHEDULE

TRADE MARKS ACT, 1938, SECTION 64A

To the Commissioners of Customs and Excise,
King's Beam House, London, E.C.3.

(1) Insert full name and address of person giving the notice. This notice should be completed by the proprietor or registered user of the trade mark, or an authorised agent. A registered user can give notice in relation only to goods in respect of which he is re-registered as a registered user.

1. I/We(1)...
    (name of person/firm/company/authorised agent)

of..

hereby give you notice that(2)......................................

(2) Insert full name and address of proprietor as registered at the Patent Office.

of..is/are the

(3) Here place a copy or give an exact description of the mark as registered at the Patent Office.

proprietor of the following trade mark namely(3)...........

....

....

....

....

which is registered at the Patent Office under No...............

for the period ending..

(4) Here state the specification of the goods in respect of which the trade mark has been registered at the Patent Office.

in respect of (4)..

..........................being goods of Class(5)...............

(5) Insert the number of the Class in which the specified goods are registered at the Patent Office.

(6) Insert full name and address of registered user. Delete the words in brackets where notice is given by the proprietor of the trade mark.

[and that(6)...

of...is registered as registered user of the said trade mark in respect of all the goods in respect of
the following

(7) Insert particulars where the permitted use of the trade mark by the registered user is not in respect of all the goods in respect of which it is registered.

which it is registered(7)..................................
goods

....

....]
2. Goods covered by this specification and bearing this trade mark are expected to arrive in the United Kingdom:—

(8) Insert date and time of expected arrival of goods.

(a) on(8)   (b) at(9)
The consignment particulars are:—
    (i) name of ship, or flight number of aircraft:

(9) Insert place where goods are expected to arrive.

    (ii) name and address of importer:

    (iii) description of goods (including Customs Tariff classification):

    (iv) number of, and marks on, packages:

3. The use within the United Kingdom of this trade mark in relation to those goods will infringe the proprietor's exclusive right to that use.

4. I/We request the Commissioners to treat the said goods as prohibited.

Dated this   of   19 .

Signature..
    *Proprietor/partner/director/secretary/duly authorised person

*Delete as necessary.

Witness ....

Address ....

....

....

Occupation..

EXPLANATORY NOTE
(This Note is not part of the Regulations.)

These Regulations prescribe the manner in which the proprietor or registered user of a trade mark may give the Commissioners of Customs and Excise notice of the expected arrival in the United Kingdom of goods which infringe the proprietor's exclusive right and which he wishes to be treated as prohibited goods. They also specify the conditions to be observed by the person giving such a notice.

H.M.S.O
£10/10/-
12 section